Cases on Copyright

Unfair Competition, and Related Topics Bearing on the Protection of Literary, Musical, and Artistic Works

SEVENTH EDITION

by

RALPH S. BROWN
Late Simeon E. Baldwin Professor of Law
Yale University

ROBERT C. DENICOLA
Margaret Larson Professor of Intellectual Property
University of Nebraska

NEW YORK, NEW YORK
FOUNDATION PRESS
1998

COPYRIGHT © 1958, 1960, 1974, 1978, 1985, 1990, 1995 FOUNDATION PRESS
COPYRIGHT © 1998 By FOUNDATION PRESS.

11 Penn Plaza, Tenth Floor
New York, NY 10001
Phone (212) 760–8700
Fax (212) 760–8705

Library of Congress Cataloging-in-Publication Data

Brown, Ralph S. (Ralph Sharp), 1913–1998
    Cases on copyright, unfair competition, and related topics bearing
on the protection of literary, musical, and artistic works / by
Ralph S. Brown and Robert C. Denicola. — 7th ed.
    p.   cm. — (University casebook series)
    Includes bibliographical references and index.
    ISBN 1–56662–607–2 (hardcover)
    1. Copyright—United States—Cases. 2. Competition, Unfair—
United States—Cases. I. Denicola, Robert C., 1949–   .
II. Title. III. Series.
KF2993.B76 1998
346.7304'8—dc21   98–14119

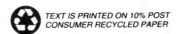 TEXT IS PRINTED ON 10% POST
CONSUMER RECYCLED PAPER

To E.M.B.

R.S.B.

To Christine

R.C.D.

Ralph Brown died just prior to the publication of this Seventh Edition. He had been a co-author of this casebook since its first publication in 1960. He was a generous collaborator, a patient teacher, and a good friend.

R.C.D.

*

PREFACE

The First Edition of this casebook in 1960, whose senior collaborator was Harvard Professor (later Justice) Benjamin Kaplan, was, we believe, the first of its kind. It was also—and remains—distinctive in giving substantial attention to topics related to copyright, notably unfair competition. Copyright and its cousins—unfair competition, publicity rights, moral rights, and corners of contract—continue to expand and ramify. Frequent amendments to the Copyright Act require interpretation, and the growth of unfair competition appears relentless. The immediate consequence is that, despite our best efforts, this Seventh Edition is somewhat longer than its predecessor, which had already stretched the limits of coverage in a three-credit course. We doubt that anyone can get through all of it. To help in planning assignments, we have made modest alterations in organization—virtually all the materials on federal copyright law appear now in Part I. Most of that can be covered even in a two-credit course.

Copyright law continues to undergo important transformations as new technologies spawn new questions. Copyright has swallowed but not yet digested the programs that energize computers. The "broadcast" media continue to change shape with new forms of transmission and new means of reception. The technology of photocopying still eludes control even as it is supplanted by electronic storage and transmission. The "information superhighway" will have a very high speed limit. Can the creators of works protect themselves and still keep up with the traffic? In the face of emerging technologies, can either Congress or the courts effectively secure to authors the exclusive right to their writings without undermining the ultimate purpose of the constitutional grant?

In spite of all these matters, we are not inclined to skimp on the fundamentals. In his Preface to the First Edition, Professor Kaplan recalled Justice Story's now familiar observation that copyrights, in company with patents, "approach, nearer than any other class of cases belonging to forensic discussions, to what may be called the metaphysics of the law, where the distinctions are, or at least may be, very subtle and refined, and, sometimes, almost evanescent." [a] Who is an "author"? What is a "writing"? What are the exclusive rights of authors in their writings and when are those rights infringed? The courts continue to instruct us on all these questions.

---

a. Folsom v. Marsh, 9 Fed.Cas. 342, 344 (C.C.D.Mass.1841) (No. 4901).

We remain too timid to predict what may come next, except to mark the obvious and portentous acceleration of the technologies that disseminate works of the mind. Meanwhile, there is a plethora of issues to tantalize and entertain both students and teachers.

R.S.B.
R.C.D.

SUMMARY OF CONTENTS

TABLE OF CONTENTS

CHAPTER 9.   Moral Rights and Publicity Rights ----------------- 717

TABLE OF CASES

Principal cases are in bold type. Non-principal cases are in roman type. References are to Pages.

CASES ON COPYRIGHT

UNFAIR COMPETITION, AND RELATED TOPICS BEARING ON THE PROTECTION OF LITERARY, MUSICAL, AND ARTISTIC WORKS

*

PART ONE

COPYRIGHT

CHAPTER 1

THE BOUNDARIES OF COPYRIGHT

SECTION 1. A FIRST LOOK AT COPYRIGHT

Sony Corp. of America v. Universal City Studios, Inc.

Supreme Court of the United States, 1984.
464 U.S. 417, 104 S.Ct. 774.

■ JUSTICE STEVENS delivered the opinion of the Court.

Petitioners manufacture and sell home video tape recorders. Respondents own the copyrights on some of the television programs that are broadcast on the public airwaves. Some members of the general public use video tape recorders sold by petitioners to record some of these broadcasts, as well as a large number of other broadcasts. The question presented is whether the sale of petitioners' copying equipment to the general public violates any of the rights conferred upon respondents by the Copyright Act.

Respondents commenced this copyright infringement action against petitioners in the United States District Court for the Central District of California in 1976. Respondents alleged that some individuals had used Betamax video tape recorders (VTR's) to record some of respondents' copyrighted works which had been exhibited on commercially sponsored television and contended that these individuals had thereby infringed respondents' copyrights. Respondents further maintained that petitioners were liable for the copyright infringement allegedly committed by Betamax consumers because of petitioners' marketing of the Betamax VTR's. Respondents sought no relief against any Betamax consumer. Instead, they sought money damages and an equitable accounting of profits from petitioners, as well as an injunction against the manufacture and marketing of Betamax VTR's.

After a lengthy trial, the District Court denied respondents all the relief they sought and entered judgment for petitioners. 480 F.Supp. 429 (1979). The United States Court of Appeals for the Ninth Circuit reversed the District Court's judgment on respondent's copyright claim, holding petitioners liable for contributory infringement and ordering the District

1

Court to fashion appropriate relief. 659 F.2d 963 (1981). We granted certiorari, 457 U.S. 1116 (1982); since we had not completed our study of the case last Term, we ordered reargument, 463 U.S. 1226 (1983). We now reverse. * * *

The lengthy trial of the case in the District Court concerned the private, home use of VTR's for recording programs broadcast on the public airwaves without charge to the viewer. No issue concerning the transfer of tapes to other persons, the use of home-recorded tapes for public performances, or the copying of programs transmitted on pay or cable television systems was raised. See 480 F.Supp. 429, 432–433, 442 (1979). * * *

II

Article I, Sec. 8 of the Constitution provides that:

"The Congress shall have Power ... to Promote the Progress of Science and useful Arts, by securing for limited Times to Authors and Inventors the exclusive Right to their respective Writings and Discoveries."

The monopoly privileges that Congress may authorize are neither unlimited nor primarily designed to provide a special private benefit. Rather, the limited grant is a means by which an important public purpose may be achieved. It is intended to motivate the creative activity of authors and inventors by the provision of a special reward, and to allow the public access to the products of their genius after the limited period of exclusive control has expired.

"The copyright law, like the patent statute, makes reward to the owner a secondary consideration. In Fox Film Corp. v. Doyal, 286 U.S. 123, 127, Chief Justice Hughes spoke as follows respecting the copyright monopoly granted by Congress, 'The sole interest of the United States and the primary object in conferring the monopoly lie in the general benefits derived by the public from the labors of authors.' It is said that reward to the author or artist serves to induce release to the public of the products of his creative genius." United States v. Paramount Pictures, 334 U.S. 131, 158.

As the text of the Constitution makes plain, it is Congress that has been assigned the task of defining the scope of the limited monopoly that should be granted to authors or to inventors in order to give the public appropriate access to their work product. Because this task involves a difficult balance between the interests of authors and inventors in the control and exploitation of their writings and discoveries on the one hand, and society's competing interest in the free flow of ideas, information, and commerce on the other hand, our patent and copyright statutes have been amended repeatedly.[10]

---

10. In its Report accompanying the comprehensive revision of the Copyright Act in 1909, the Judiciary Committee of the House of Representatives explained this balance:

From its beginning, the law of copyright has developed in response to significant changes in technology. Indeed, it was the invention of a new form of copying equipment—the printing press—that gave rise to the original need for copyright protection.[12] Repeatedly, as new developments have occurred in this country, it has been the Congress that has fashioned the new rules that new technology made necessary. Thus, long before the enactment of the Copyright Act of 1909, 35 Stat. 1075, it was settled that the protection given to copyrights is wholly statutory. Wheaton v. Peters, 33 U.S. (8 Peters) 591, 661–662 (1834). The remedies for infringement "are only those prescribed by Congress." Thompson v. Hubbard, 131 U.S. 123, 151 (1889). * * *

In a case like this, in which Congress has not plainly marked our course, we must be circumspect in construing the scope of rights created by a legislative enactment which never contemplated such a calculus of interests. In doing so, we are guided by Justice Stewart's exposition of the correct approach to ambiguities in the law of copyright:

> "The limited scope of the copyright holder's statutory monopoly, like the limited copyright duration required by the Constitution, reflects a balance of competing claims upon the public interest: Creative work is to be encouraged and rewarded, but private motivation must ultimately serve the cause of promoting broad public availability of literature, music, and the other arts. The immediate effect of our copyright law is to secure a fair return for an 'author's' creative labor. But the ultimate aim is, by this incentive, to stimulate artistic creativity for the general public good. 'The sole interest of the United States and the primary object in conferring the monopoly,' this Court has said, 'lie in the general benefits derived by the public from the labors of authors.' Fox Film Corp. v. Doyal, 286 U.S. 123, 127. See Kendall v. Winsor, 21 How. 322, 327–328; Grant v. Raymond, 6 Pet. 218, 241–242. When technological change has rendered its literal terms ambiguous, the Copyright Act must be construed in light of this basic purpose."

"The enactment of copyright legislation by Congress under the terms of the Constitution is not based upon any natural right that the author has in his writings, ... but upon the ground that the welfare of the public will be served and progress of science and useful arts will be promoted by securing to authors for limited periods the exclusive rights to their writings.

"In enacting a copyright law Congress must consider ... two questions: First, how much will the legislation stimulate the producer and so benefit the public, and, second, how much will the monopoly granted be detrimental to the public? The granting of such exclusive rights, under the proper terms and conditions, confers a benefit upon the public that outweighs the evils of the temporary monopoly." H.R.Rep. No. 2222, 60th Cong., 2d Sess. 7 (1909).

12. "Copyright protection became necessary with the invention of the printing press and had its early beginnings in the British censorship laws. The fortunes of the law of copyright have always been closely connected with freedom of expression, on the one hand, and with technological improvements in means of dissemination, on the other. Successive ages have drawn different balances among the interest of the writer in the control and exploitation of his intellectual property, the related interest of the publisher, and the competing interest of society in the untrammeled dissemination of ideas." Foreword to B. Kaplan, An Unhurried View of Copyright vii–viii (1967).

Twentieth Century Music Corp. v. Aiken, 422 U.S. 151, 156 (footnotes omitted).

Copyright protection "subsists ... in original works of authorship fixed in any tangible medium of expression." 17 U.S.C. § 102(a). This protection has never accorded the copyright owner complete control over all possible uses of his work. Rather, the Copyright Act grants the copyright holder "exclusive" rights to use and to authorize the use of his work in five qualified ways, including reproduction of the copyrighted work in copies. Id., § 106. All reproductions of the work, however, are not within the exclusive domain of the copyright owner; some are in the public domain. Any individual may reproduce a copyrighted work for a "fair use;" the copyright owner does not possess the exclusive right to such a use. Compare id., § 106 with id., § 107.

"Anyone who violates any of the exclusive rights of the copyright owner," that is, anyone who trespasses into his exclusive domain by using or authorizing the use of the copyrighted work in one of the five ways set forth in the statute, "is an infringer of the copyright." Id., § 501(a). Conversely, anyone who is authorized by the copyright owner to use the copyrighted work in a way specified in the statute or who makes a fair use of the work is not an infringer of the copyright with respect to such use.

The Copyright Act provides the owner of a copyright with a potent arsenal of remedies against an infringer of his work, including an injunction to restrain the infringer from violating his rights, the impoundment and destruction of all reproductions of his work made in violation of his rights, a recovery of his actual damages and any additional profits realized by the infringer or a recovery of statutory damages, and attorneys fees. Id., §§ 502–505.

The two respondents in this case do not seek relief against the Betamax users who have allegedly infringed their copyrights. Moreover, this is not a class action on behalf of all copyright owners who license their works for television broadcast, and respondents have no right to invoke whatever rights other copyright holders may have to bring infringement actions based on Betamax copying of their works. As was made clear by their own evidence, the copying of the respondents' programs represents a small portion of the total use of VTR's. It is, however, the taping of respondents own copyrighted programs that provides them with standing to charge Sony with contributory infringement. To prevail, they have the burden of proving that users of the Betamax have infringed their copyrights and that Sony should be held responsible for that infringement.

[The Court next considered the issue of contributory infringement and concluded that Sony could be liable only if the Betamax had no substantial noninfringing uses. That portion of the Court's opinion is reprinted at p. 453 infra.]

IV

The question is thus whether the Betamax is capable of commercially significant noninfringing uses. In order to resolve that question, we need not explore *all* the different potential uses of the machine and determine whether or not they would constitute infringement. Rather, we need only consider whether on the basis of the facts as found by the District Court a significant number of them would be noninfringing. Moreover, in order to resolve this case we need not give precise content to the question of how much use is commercially significant. For one potential use of the Beta-max plainly satisfies this standard, however it is understood: private, noncommercial time–shifting in the home. It does so both (A) because respondents have no right to prevent other copyright holders from autho-rizing it for their programs, and (B) because the District Court's factual findings reveal that even the unauthorized home time–shifting of respon-dents' programs is legitimate fair use.

A. *Authorized Time–Shifting*

Each of the respondents owns a large inventory of valuable copyrights, but in the total spectrum of television programming their combined market share is small. The exact percentage is not specified, but it is well below 10%. If they were to prevail, the outcome of this litigation would have a significant impact on both the producers and the viewers of the remaining 90% of the programming in the Nation. No doubt, many other producers share respondents' concern about the possible consequences of unrestricted copying. Nevertheless the findings of the District Court make it clear that time–shifting may enlarge the total viewing audience and that many producers are willing to allow private time–shifting to continue, at least for an experimental time period. * * *

If there are millions of owners of VTR's who make copies of televised sports events, religious broadcasts, and educational programs such as *Mister Rogers' Neighborhood,* and if the proprietors of those programs welcome the practice, the business of supplying the equipment that makes such copying feasible should not be stifled simply because the equipment is used by some individuals to make unauthorized reproductions of respon-dents' works. The respondents do not represent a class composed of all copyright holders. Yet a finding of contributory infringement would inevi-tably frustrate the interests of broadcasters in reaching the portion of their audience that is available only through time–shifting. * * *

B. *Unauthorized Time–Shifting*

Even unauthorized uses of a copyrighted work are not necessarily infringing. An unlicensed use of the copyright is not an infringement unless it conflicts with one of the specific exclusive rights conferred by the copyright statute. Twentieth Century Music Corp. v. Aiken, 422 U.S. 151, 154–155. Moreover, the definition of exclusive rights in § 106 of the present Act is prefaced by the words "subject to sections 107 through 118." Those sections describe a variety of uses of copyrighted material that "are not infringements of copyright notwithstanding the provisions of § 106." The most pertinent in this case is § 107, the legislative endorsement of the doctrine of "fair use."

[The Court concluded that "home time-shifting" is a fair use under § 107 and thus does not infringe the copyright owner's exclusive rights. "[T]ime-shifting merely enables a viewer to see such a work which he had been invited to witness in its entirety free of charge * * *." The portion of the Court's opinion dealing with fair use is reprinted at p. 389 infra.]

V

"The direction of Art. I is that *Congress* shall have the power to promote the progress of science and the useful arts. When, as here, the Constitution is permissive, the sign of how far Congress has chosen to go can come only from Congress." Deepsouth Packing Co. v. Laitram Corp., 406 U.S. 518, 530 (1972).

One may search the Copyright Act in vain for any sign that the elected representatives of the millions of people who watch television every day have made it unlawful to copy a program for later viewing at home, or have enacted a flat prohibition against the sale of machines that make such copying possible.

It may well be that Congress will take a fresh look at this new technology, just as it so often has examined other innovations in the past. But it is not our job to apply laws that have not yet been written. Applying the copyright statute, as it now reads, to the facts as they have been developed in this case, the judgment of the Court of Appeals must be reversed.

It is so ordered.

[Justice Blackmun's dissent, in which Justices Marshall, Powell and Rehnquist joined, is reprinted in part at p. 392 infra.]

NOTES AND QUESTIONS

(1) Sections 102 and 106 are the bedrock provisions of the Copyright Act of 1976. Section 102 describes the subject matter of copyright. According to the 1976 House Report [a], the list of works is "illustrative and not limitative." Some of the works listed in § 102 are defined in § 101; the general category of "original works of authorship" is not. The subject matter of copyright is further amplified in §§ 103–105.

Section 106 enumerates the exclusive rights given to the owner of a copyright. These rights are subject to the complicated set of limitations and qualifications in §§ 107–121. Almost all of these sections will be taken up in the course of these materials.

Given the basic structure of the Copyright Act—broadly defined rights followed by a series of specific limitations—is Part V of the Court's opinion

---

a. H.R.Rep. No. 94–1476, 94th Cong., 2d Sess. 53 (1976). This authoritative Report, cited here simply as the House Report (H.R.Rep.), will be quoted frequently in these materials.

[Editors' footnotes throughout this casebook are lettered. Footnotes from judicial opinions and other materials, when reprinted, retain their original numbering; footnotes are omitted without indication.]

in *Sony* a sensible approach to the statute?   The Court of Appeals had taken a different view of the structure of the Copyright Act:

> The statutory framework is unambiguous; the grant of exclusive rights is only limited by the statutory exceptions. * * * The issue is not whether Congress exhibited an intent to protect a copyright holder from certain reproduction of his works.   It had already expressed its intent to do so by extending the "bundle of rights" set forth in § 106 to copyright owners, *subject to specific sections,* to-wit: §§ 107–118.   Consequently, our concern must be whether Congress has exhibited the intent to limit the rights of copyright owners in ways not specified in §§ 107–118. (659 F.2d 963, 966)

(2) Looking ahead, what facts would be relevant in deciding whether the unauthorized reproduction in *Sony* is a "fair use"?

(3) What interests might prompt recognition of exclusive rights in "works of authorship"?   The incentive rationale offered by the Court in *Sony* is a traditional response. Since works of authorship are intangible, without copyright protection it would be difficult for creators to capture the economic value of their creations. (Would the creator's headstart in the market provide sufficient reward?)   In a case to be considered later the Supreme Court had said:

> The economic philosophy behind the clause empowering Congress to grant patents and copyrights is the conviction that encouragement of individual effort by personal gain is the best way to advance public welfare through the talents of authors and inventors in "Science and useful Arts."   Sacrificial days devoted to such creative activities deserve rewards commensurate with the services rendered.

Mazer v. Stein, p. 138 infra.   Does the last sentence appeal to interests beyond incentive?   A former United States Register of Copyrights has said that "the fundamental claim of copyright is one of justice."   Ladd, The Harm of the Concept of Harm in Copyright, 30 J.Copyr.Soc. 421, 425 (1983). See also Yen, Restoring the Natural Law: Copyright as Labor and Possession, 51 Ohio St.L.J. 517 (1990).

What costs are incurred by recognizing exclusive rights in works of authorship? Legal restrictions on dissemination and use seem particularly wasteful since, unlike tangible goods, works of authorship can be enjoyed by an unlimited number of users without depriving anyone else of the work. Exclusive rights not only interfere with the public's enjoyment of the work, but also with the creation of new works derived from the original. But all this assumes that the original work has been created in the first place, which returns us to the incentive rationale. Copyright law is in part a trade-off between the benefits derived from encouraging the creation of works and the costs of restricting access. (Could the need for incentive be met without restricting dissemination and use? Would a system of direct government subsidy be preferable to copyright?) Since the United States has become a major exporter of works of authorship, our copyright law also reflects concern over foreign revenues and international trade.

The economic and moral arguments underlying the recognition of exclusive rights in works of authorship are discussed in R. Brown, Eligibility for Copyright Protection: A Search for Principled Standards, 70 Minn. L.Rev. 579 (1985). For an expansive treatment of similar themes, see Gordon, An Inquiry into the Merits of Copyright: The Challenges of Consistency, Consent, and Encouragement Theory, 41 Stan.L.Rev. 1343 (1989).[b]

The incentive rationale for copyright is challenged in Breyer, The Uneasy Case for Copyright: A Study of Copyright in Books, Photocopies, and Computer Programs, 84 Harv.L.Rev. 281 (1970), and defended in Tyerman, The Economic Rationale for Copyright Protection for Published Books: A Reply to Professor Breyer, 18 U.C.L.A. L.Rev. 1100 (1971). See generally Landes & Posner, An Economic Analysis of Copyright Law, 18 J.Leg.Stud. 325 (1989).[c]

COPYRIGHT AND THE PUBLIC DOMAIN

Prior to January 1, 1978, the effective date of the 1976 Copyright Act, many works of authorship were protected, if at all, under state rather than federal law. As we will see, the 1976 Act dramatically reduced (but did not quite eliminate) the role of state copyright law. See § 301. State protection of artistic and intellectual works had come to be called "common law copyright." Much of it did in fact spring from the process of judicial decision-making we know as the common law, but the states sometimes enacted copyright statutes too. So it is not quite correct to refer to state copyright as "common law copyright," or to say "statutory copyright" when we mean "federal copyright"—but it is familiar usage to talk that way, counterposing "common law" and "statutory" when we really mean "state-created" and "Congress-created."

Then and now, however, a work might fall beyond the protection of both state and federal copyright law. It is then in the public domain,

---

b. Other recent investigations of the foundations of copyright include Netanel, Copyright and a Democratic Civil Society, 106 Yale L.J. 283 (1996) (emphasizing copyright's role in support of democratic culture); Sterk, Rhetoric and Reality in Copyright Law, 94 Mich.L.Rev. 1197 (1996) (attributing the contours of copyright law to the political power of the copyright industries); Lacey, Of Bread and Roses and Copyrights, 1989 Duke L.J. 1532 (since authors write for a variety of reasons, "the basic assumption of copyright is seriously flawed"). But recall, too, Samuel Johnson's famous remark: "No man but a blockhead ever wrote, except for money." Boswell, *Life of Johnson.*

c. See also Lunney, Reexamining Copyright's Incentives–Access Paradigm, 49 Vand. L.Rev. 483 (1996) (balance of incentive and access must take account of alternative uses for creative resources). Economists as well as lawyers disagree about the impact of modern copying technologies such as photocopiers and audio and video recorders. Compare Johnson, The Economics of Copying, 93 J.Pol.Econ. 158 (1985), arguing for restrictions on copying, with Liebowitz, Copying and Indirect Appropriability: Photocopying of Journals, id. at 945, arguing that copyright owners can indirectly extract payment for unauthorized copies through price discrimination.

meaning approximately that anyone may copy it. But note that the constitutional clause quoted in *Sony* also authorizes rights for inventors in their discoveries. Inventors may obtain patents, and what is claimed in a patent will not be free for public use. The states do not have patent laws as such and there are no "common law" patents, but state trade secret law also creates rights in intellectual property. Finally, in Part Two of these materials we will see other legal doctrines that have the effect of creating exclusive rights in intellectual property and that thus may be said to limit the public domain.

These materials will be concerned largely with creating and maintaining exclusive rights. Relegation to the public domain will sometimes appear to be an inferior kind of thing that happens to deserving authors and inventors when for some reason they lose control of their creations. Viewed in another way, the public domain is the accumulated wisdom of the ages. Justice Brandeis' dissent in International News Service v. Associated Press, p. 587 infra, reminds us that "The general rule of law is, that the noblest of human productions—knowledge, truths ascertained, conceptions, and ideas—become, after voluntary communication to others, free as the air to common use."

Thomas Jefferson was even more eloquent:

> If nature has made any one thing less susceptible than all others of exclusive property, it is the action of the thinking power called an idea, which an individual may exclusively possess as long as he keeps it to himself; but the moment it is divulged, it forces itself into the possession of every one, and the receiver cannot dispossess himself of it. Its peculiar character, too, is that no one possesses the less, because every other possess the whole of it. He who receives an idea from me, receives instructions himself without lessening mine; as he who lights his taper at mine, receives light without darkening me. That ideas should freely spread from one to another over the globe, for the moral and mutual instruction of man, and improvement of his condition, seems to have been peculiarly and benevolently designed by nature, when she made them, like fire, expansible over all space, without lessening their density in any point, and like the air in which we breathe, move and have our physical being, incapable of confinement or exclusive appropriation.[d]

d. 13 Writings of Thomas Jefferson, 333–34 (Lipscomb ed., 1904) (letter to I. McPherson, Aug. 13, 1813). The function of the public domain in preserving access to the raw material of future authorship is emphasized in Litman, The Public Domain, 39 Emory L.J. 965 (1990). For a similar argument drawn from the concept of "progress" as embodied in the Patent and Copyright clause, see Chon, Postmodern "Progress": Reconsidering the Copyright and Patent Power, 34 DePaul L.Rev. 97 (1993). Cf. Samuels, The Public Domain in Copyright Law, 41 J.Copyr.Soc. 137 (1993), recounting the various ways in which material may enter the public domain and questioning the utility of any unified public domain theory.

A NOTE ON REFERENCE WORKS

The leading treatises on copyright law are M. and D. Nimmer, Nimmer on Copyright (Matthew Bender) and P. Goldstein, Copyright (Aspen). Shorter texts include Abrams, The Law of Copyright (Clark Boardman Callaghan); Leaffer, Understanding Copyright Law (Matthew Bender); Patry, Copyright Law and Practice (BNA). The best contemplative works remain B. Kaplan, An Unhurried View of Copyright (Columbia Univ. Press 1967) and Chafee, Reflections on the Law of Copyright, 45 Colum.L.Rev. 503, 719 (1945).

The voluminous legislative history of the 1976 Copyright Act is compiled in The Kaminstein Legislative History Project: A Compendium and Analytical Index of Materials Leading to the Copyright Act of 1976 (A. Latman & J. Lightstone eds., Fred Rothman 1981). As part of the revision process leading to the 1976 Act, a series of valuable studies was prepared for the Copyright Office. They are reprinted in Copyright Society of the U.S.A., Studies on Copyright (Arthur Fisher Memorial Ed.1963).

Articles and other useful materials on copyright law appear regularly in the Journal of the Copyright Society. The Copyright Law Reporter (CCH) provides a convenient collection of legislative, judicial, and administrative materials. The United States Patent Quarterly (BNA) reports copyright cases, along with cases on patents, trademarks, and unfair competition. Current developments can be followed in the weekly Patent, Trademark & Copyright Journal (BNA).

SECTION 2. COPYRIGHT DISTINCT FROM PROPERTY RIGHTS IN OBJECTS

Pushman v. New York Graphic Society, Inc.

Court of Appeals of New York, 1942.
287 N.Y. 302, 39 N.E.2d 249.

■ DESMOND, JUDGE. Plaintiff, who is an artist, brought this suit in 1940 for an injunction to enjoin the defendants from making reproductions of a painting executed by plaintiff and which he had sold outright to the University of Illinois in 1930, for $3,600. This painting was not copyrighted under the copyright laws of the United States. Special Term denied the injunction and dismissed the complaint on the merits, writing an opinion and decision, 25 N.Y.S.2d 32, in which it is said that the only question in the case is as to whether an artist after giving an absolute and unconditional bill of sale of his painting, still retains such a common law copyright in it as to be able to prevent commercial reproduction. Appellate Division, First Department, one of the justices dissenting, affirmed without opinion. 262 A.D. 729, 28 N.Y.S.2d 711.

Plaintiff, Pushman, has an international reputation as an artist, for his execution of still life subjects in color. He has been painting for fifty years;

his original works command substantial prices and many of them are held by museums and collectors. In 1930 he completed the painting, entitled "When Autumn is Here," which is the subject of this action. He turned the painting over for sale to Grand Central Art Galleries which seems to be a mutual organization of artists for sale of their works, as agent for them. All the evidence is that the plaintiff did not state that he was seeking to reserve reproduction rights in his painting and that he made no such reservation at any time up to and including the sale to the University. There is evidence here of a general practice of this gallery whereby whenever it sold a painting to a purchaser who was in the reproduction business, which of course would not include the University, the Gallery negotiated a separate written agreement between the artist and the purchaser covering reproduction rights. Pushman never expressly authorized the Gallery to sell the rights to reproduce this painting, nor did he forbid it. Shortly after this painting was sent to the Gallery for sale, the manager of the Gallery took it and a number of others to the University of Illinois where he exhibited them publicly for sale. The University chose seven of these paintings, including the one by plaintiff here in suit. The University would not pay plaintiff's asking price of $5,000 and so the Gallery sold it to the University for $3,600. All this took place in 1930. The painting remained at the University until 1940 when the University sold to the defendant, New York Graphic Society, Inc., the right to make reproductions. The trial proofs had been made by defendants and the reproductions were about to be put on the market when plaintiff learned of the project and brought this suit. * * *

We are, of course, concerned here with the so-called common law copyright, not statutory copyright. This common law copyright is sometimes called the right of first publication. There is no question but that it is a different and independent right from the usual right of ownership of an article of personal property. Stephens v. Cady, 14 How. 528, 530. The Stephens case quotes Lord Mansfield as saying it is "a property in notion, and has no corporeal tangible substance." There is no doubt that in New York State the separate common law copyright or control of the right to reproduce belongs to the artist or author until disposed of by him and will be protected by the courts. Oertel v. Wood, 40 How.Prac. 10; Howitt v. Street & Smith Publications, Inc., 276 N.Y. 345, 350, 12 N.E.2d 435. Such is the holding of the case of Werckmeister v. Springer Lithographing Co., C.C., 63 F. 808, at page 811, which says that the painting itself may be transferred without a transfer of the common law rights of publishing or restricting publication, and that the ownership of the painting itself does not necessarily carry with it the common law copyright. The same thing is held in Caliga v. Inter–Ocean Newspaper Co., 7 Cir., 157 F. 186, 188, affirmed 215 U.S. 182. Palmer v. DeWitt, 47 N.Y. 532, 7 Am.Rep. 480, is not direct authority either way on the case before us.

We are not helped here by the cases which say that an artist's separate common law copyright does not necessarily pass with the sale of the painting. The question is whether it did pass with the sale of this painting. We think it follows from the authorities above cited that it did so pass and that an artist must, if he wishes to retain or protect the reproduction right, make some reservation of that right when he sells the painting. The Parton case [Parton v. Prang, 18 F.Cas. 1273 (C.C.D.Mass.1872) (No. 10,784)] has always been considered as so holding. There are seemingly contrary expressions in some cases, such as the dictum in Stephens v. Cady, 14 How. at page 531, that the right to reproduce "will not pass with the manuscript unless included by express words in the transfer." Appellant cites also other authorities which say that the sale of a work of art does not carry with it the right of reproduction "unless such was the evident intent of the parties." But this begs the question. What was the intent of the parties? The whole tenor of the Prang case, as we read it, is that an ordinary, straight out bill of sale shows an intention to convey the artist's whole property in his picture. Here there is no substantial proof of a contrary intent.

We are not entering into a separate discussion as to whether by this sale *and* the public exhibition the artist is to be held to have "published" the work so that his common law right is lost. Special Term so held. See Keene v. Kimball, 16 Gray, Mass., 545, 77 Am.Dec. 426; Baker v. Taylor, Fed.Cas. No. 782. Nor need we examine into the equities, as did Special Term. Our conclusion is that under the cases and the texts, this unconditional sale carried with it the transfer of the common law copyright and right to reproduce. Plaintiff took no steps to withhold or control that right. "The courts cannot read words of limitation into a transfer which the parties do not choose to use." Dam v. Kirk La Shelle Co., 2 Cir., 175 F. 902, 904, 20 Ann.Cas. 1173.

The judgment of the Appellate Division should be affirmed, with costs.

■ LEHMAN, C.J., and LOUGHRAN, FINCH, RIPPEY, LEWIS, and CONWAY, JJ., concur.

Judgment affirmed.

———————

CHAMBERLAIN v. FELDMAN, 300 N.Y. 135, 89 N.E.2d 863 (1949). Judge Desmond, again writing for a unanimous court, reached a different conclusion on these facts. "In 1876, Samuel L. Clemens, under his pen name of 'Mark Twain', wrote a story entitled 'A Murder, A Mystery and A Marriage', and in the same year offered the manuscript to William Dean Howells, editor of the Atlantic Monthly, for publication. There followed, during the same year, some correspondence between Twain and Howells, in which was discussed an unusual project which the author had in mind: he proposed that a number of other famous writers of the period (such as Bret Harte and Howells himself) be enlisted, each to write his own final chapter for the work, so that for the mystery set up in the first few chapters, each author would compose a solution, in addition to, or in competition with Twain's own denouement. In other words, as planned by Twain, there was to be a common plot for the story, with a number of different endings. For one reason or another, including the reluctance of famous writers to dance to a rival's music, Twain's pet scheme came to nothing. Twenty years later, an entry in Twain's diary dated March 18, 1897, records a rather vague hope of the author to 'make a skeleton novelette plot and write all the stories myself' or use it as the basis for a prize story competition. Whether that entry referred to 'A Murder, A Mystery and A Marriage' we do not know, but there is undisputed proof, credited by both courts below, that when Mark Twain died in 1910, the manuscript of 'A Murder, A Mystery and A Marriage' was not found among his effects and had never been published anywhere, by anyone.

"In 1945, defendant Feldman bought the original manuscript (holographic and signed) at an auction sale, in New York City, of the rare books and manuscripts that had been in the possession, during his life, of Dr. James Brentano Clemens (no kin of Mark Twain) and had passed by inheritance to Dr. Clemens' wife. How Dr. Clemens came to have the writing is unknown. Mr. Feldman sought permission from plaintiffs, who are the present owners of all literary property formerly belonging to Mark Twain and not otherwise disposed of, to publish the work, but permission was refused. Defendant Feldman went ahead with the publication, however, and this suit was brought to enjoin him from reproducing or publishing the story, in any way. The complaint prays also for a direction to defendant to cancel a purported statutory copyright entered by defendant in the office of the Federal Register of Copyrights. It is not claimed that this statutory copyrighting, or attempt at such, was with the permission of plaintiffs, or any of them."

On these bare facts, the trial court found that Mark Twain had transferred the manuscript without reserving the literary property, but the Appellate Division "found no basis for presuming or inferring such a grant by Twain." The Court of Appeals agreed with the Appellate Division.

"With the facts in that posture, little problem remains. The common-law copyright, or right of first publication, is a right different from that of ownership of the physical paper; the first of those rights does not necessarily pass with the second; and 'the separate common law copyright or control of the right to reproduce belongs to the artist or author until disposed of by him and will be protected by the courts' (see Pushman v. New York Graphic Soc., 287 N.Y. 302, 307, 39 N.E.2d 249, 250, supra, and cases cited thereat; see similarly, as to statutory copyright, U.S. Code, tit. 17, § 27, 17 U.S.C.A. § 27). Since it has here been found to be the fact that, however the manuscript left the possession of the author, he never intended that it be published, it follows that defendant could not have bought the publication rights.

"A recent commentary on this case, 62 Harv.L.Rev. 1406–1407, suggests that it may be contrary to sound policy to keep meritorious literary achievement out of the public domain for so long a time as is here involved. Without expressing any views of our own as to the advisability of permitting literary flowers so to blush unseen, we state our agreement with the last sentence of that Law Review article, in which it is pointed out that any such change of public policy must be the doing of the Legislature."

The judgment of the Appellate Division perpetually restraining the defendant from publishing or reproducing the story was affirmed.

NOTES AND QUESTIONS

(1) Can *Chamberlain* be distinguished from *Pushman?* See also Forward v. Thorogood, 985 F.2d 604 (1st Cir.1993), involving a band that had given the organizer of a 1976 recording session the resulting demo tapes "for his own enjoyment." The court said that the transfer of the tapes did not carry with it the common law copyright in the unpublished recordings.

(2) The presumption invoked in *Pushman* that an unrestricted transfer of a work of fine art also conveys the common law right of reproduction was altered by statute in New York in 1966. See N.Y. Arts & Cult.Aff.L. § 14.01. Several other states have similar statutes. See, e.g., Cal.Civ.Code § 982; Or.Rev.Stat. § 359.355. All reserve reproduction rights to the artist unless expressly transferred in writing. Can these statutes have any effect as to transfers after Jan. 1, 1978, the effective date of the 1976 Copyright Act? See Ronald Litoff, Ltd. v. American Express Co., 621 F.Supp. 981 (S.D.N.Y.1985), holding that a claim for unauthorized reproduction brought under the New York statute is preempted by § 301(a) of the Copyright Act.

Suppose Pushman had sold his painting in 1998. Who would own the reproduction rights? See § 202 and § 204(a).

(3) Notice the reference at the conclusion of the *Pushman* case to the possibility that the artist might have lost his common law rights through "publication." We will hear more of "publication" in the sections that follow.

RIGHTS IN LETTERS

Another vivid instance of the separation of copyright from the material object occurs with letters. In his famous Digest of the Law of Copyright (annexed to the Report of the Royal Commission on Copyright, 1878, Cmd. 2036, p. lxv), Sir James Stephens summarizes the law of letters in the familiar way as follows: "A person who writes and sends a letter to another retains his copyright in such letter, except in so far as the particular circumstances of the case may give a right to publish such letter to the person addressed, or to his representatives, but the property in the material on which the letter is written passes to the person to whom it is sent, so as to entitle him to destroy or transfer it."[a] Warren and Brandeis relate the sender's right to prevent publication of the letter—and, indeed, all rights to prevent publication of "thoughts, sentiments, and emotions, expressed through the medium of writings or of the arts"—to "the more

---

a. For celebrated earlier precedents on letters, see Pope v. Curl, 2 Atk. 342, 26 Eng.Rep. 608 (Ch.1741); Thompson v. Stan-   hope, Amb. 737, 27 Eng.Rep. 476 (Ch.1774); Gee v. Pritchard, 2 Swans. 403, 36 Eng.Rep. 670 (Ch.1818) (Eldon, L.C.).

general right of the individual to be let alone." The Right to Privacy, 4 Harv.L.Rev. 193, 205 (1890).

The proposition that the receiver of a letter owns the physical paper seems traceable at least in part to the idea that if the rule were otherwise an unreasonable burden would be cast on the receiver to preserve the letter for the benefit of the sender. See Baker v. Libbie, 210 Mass. 599, 97 N.E. 109 (1912) (executor of the will of Mary Baker G. Eddy, founder of the Christian Science religion, failed in an effort to restrain an auctioneer of manuscripts from selling letters by Mrs. Eddy written to a relative on household matters).

NOTES AND QUESTIONS

(1) What circumstances might entitle the recipient of a letter to publish it without the sender's permission? Cf. Diamond v. Am–Law Pub. Corp., 745 F.2d 142 (2d Cir.1984), upholding a defense of "fair use" raised by The American Lawyer magazine in connection with its publication of a letter criticizing a story that the magazine had written about the sender. The letter said in part, "You are authorized to publish this letter but only in its entirety"; the magazine published only excerpts, omitting a portion attacking the magazine and its editor.

Letters sent by reclusive author J.D. Salinger to neighbors and friends (including his New Hampshire neighbor Learned Hand) were at the center of another recent dispute. The letters had been donated by the recipients to various libraries. The defendant Hamilton, in preparing a biography of Salinger, gained access to the letters, but only after signing library forms restricting reproduction. Quoted and paraphrased portions of the letters appeared in the biography. Should Salinger's copyright interest prevail? The Second Circuit's analysis of Hamilton's "fair use" defense is considered at p. 386 infra. See also Lish v. Harper's Magazine Foundation, 807 F.Supp. 1090 (S.D.N.Y.1992), rejecting Harper's claims of fair use and free speech in connection with its publication of a letter written by a well-known editor to the students in his creative writing class.

(2) How can the receiver's property right in the physical paper be accommodated to the sender's right of publication? Does the receiver have an unlimited privilege to destroy the paper? Does it really matter in an era of photocopies and computer files?

SECTION 3.   SEPARATING STATUTORY COPYRIGHT, COMMON LAW COPYRIGHT, AND THE PUBLIC DOMAIN

The materials in this section probe the boundaries between statutory copyright, common law copyright, and the public domain. The 1976 Act dramatically altered the old landscape, in which the concept of "publication" had been the dominant feature. The emphasis now is on fixation, so that an eligible work proceeds directly into federal copyright when it is "fixed in any tangible medium of expression."   But "publication" remains important too.

At the end of the preceding section we looked at the rather odd rules that have grown up around rights in letters.   Perhaps letters as a medium of communication are obsolete anyway.   Consider what property rights the parties to a conversation have in the content of what they say or hear.

Estate of Hemingway v. Random House

Court of Appeals of New York, 1968.
23 N.Y.2d 341, 296 N.Y.S.2d 771, 244 N.E.2d 250.

■ CHIEF JUDGE FULD.   On this appeal—involving an action brought by the estate of the late Ernest Hemingway and his widow against the publisher and author of a book, entitled "Papa Hemingway"—we are called upon to decide, primarily, whether conversations of a gifted and highly regarded writer may become the subject of common-law copyright, even though the speaker himself has not reduced his words to writing.

Hemingway died in 1961.   During the last 13 years of his life, a close friendship existed between him and A.E. Hotchner, a younger and far less well-known writer.   Hotchner, who met Hemingway in the course of writing articles about him, became a favored drinking and traveling companion of the famous author, a frequent visitor to his home and the adapter of some of his works for motion pictures and television.   During these years, Hemingway's conversation with Hotchner, in which others sometimes took part, was filled with anecdote, reminiscence, literary opinion and revealing comment about actual persons on whom some of Hemingway's fictional characters were based.   Hotchner made careful notes of these conversations soon after they occurred, occasionally recording them on a portable tape recorder.

During Hemingway's lifetime, Hotchner wrote and published several articles about his friend in which he quoted some of this talk at length. Hemingway, far from objecting to this practice, approved of it.   Indeed, the record reveals that other writers also quoted Hemingway's conversation without any objection from him, even when he was displeased with the articles themselves.

After Hemingway's death, Hotchner wrote "Papa Hemingway," drawing upon his notes and his recollections, and in 1966 it was published by the defendant Random House.   Subtitled "a personal memoir", it is a serious and revealing biographical portrait of the world-renowned writer. Woven through the narrative, and giving the book much of its interest and character, are lengthy quotations from Hemingway's talk, as noted or remembered by Hotchner.   Included also are two chapters on Hemingway's final illness and suicide in which Hotchner, writing of his friend with obvious feeling and sympathy, refers to events, and even to medical information, to which he was privy as an intimate of the family.   Hemingway's widow, Mary, is mentioned frequently in the book, and is sometimes quoted, but only incidentally.

The complaint, which seeks an injunction and damages, alleges four causes of action. The first three, in which the Estate of Hemingway and his widow join as plaintiffs, are, briefly stated, (1) that "Papa Hemingway" consists, in the main, of literary matter composed by Hemingway in which he had a common-law copyright; (2) that publication would constitute an unauthorized appropriation of Hemingway's work and would compete unfairly with his other literary creations; and (3) that Hotchner wrongfully used material which was imparted to him in the course of a confidential and fiduciary relationship with Hemingway. In the fourth cause of action, Mary Hemingway asserts that the book invades the right to privacy to which she herself is entitled under section 51 of the Civil Rights Law, Consol.Laws, c. 6.

The plaintiffs moved for a preliminary injunction. The motion was denied (49 Misc.2d 726, 268 N.Y.S.2d 531, affd. 25 A.D.2d 719, 269 N.Y.S.2d 366), and the book was thereafter published. After its publication, the defendants sought and were granted summary judgment dismissing all four causes of action. The Appellate Division unanimously affirmed the resulting orders and granted the plaintiffs leave to appeal to this court.

Turning to the first cause of action, we agree with the disposition made below but on a ground more narrow than that articulated by the court at Special Term. It is the position of the plaintiffs (under this count) that Hemingway was entitled to a common-law copyright on the theory that his directly quoted comment, anecdote and opinion were his "literary creations", his "literary property", and that the defendant Hotchner's note-taking only performed the mechanics of recordation. And, in a somewhat different vein, the plaintiffs argue that "[w]hat for Hemingway was oral one day would be or could become his written manuscript the next day", that his speech, constituting not just a statement of his ideas but the very form in which he conceived and expressed them, was as much the subject of common-law copyright as what he might himself have committed to paper.

Common-law copyright is the term applied to an author's proprietary interest in his literary or artistic creations before they have been made generally available to the public. It enables the author to exercise control over the first publication of his work or to prevent publication entirely—hence, its other name, the "right of first publication". (Chamberlain v. Feldman, 300 N.Y. 135, 139, 89 N.E.2d 863, 864.) No cases deal directly with the question whether it extends to conversational speech and we begin, therefore, with a brief review of some relevant concepts in this area of law.

It must be acknowledged—as the defendants point out—that nearly a century ago our court stated that common-law copyright extended to " '[e]very new and innocent product of mental labor which has been *embodied in writing, or some other material form*' ". (Palmer v. De Witt, 47 N.Y. 532, 537; emphasis supplied.) And, more recently, it has been said that "an author has no property right in his ideas unless * * * given embodiment in a tangible form." (O'Brien v. RKO Radio Pictures, D.C., 68 F.Supp. 13, 14.) However, as a noted scholar in the field has observed, "the underlying rationale for common law copyright (i.e., the recognition that a property status should attach to the fruits of intellectual labor) is applicable regardless of whether such labor assumes tangible form" (Nimmer, Copyright, § 11.1, p. 40). The principle that it is not the tangible embodiment of the author's work but the creation of the work itself which is protected finds recognition in a number of ways in copyright law.

One example, with some relevance to the problem before us, is the treatment which the law has accorded to personal letters—a kind of half-conversation in written form. * * *

Letters, however—like plays and public addresses, written or not—have distinct, identifiable boundaries and they are, in most cases, only occasional products. Whatever difficulties attend the formulation of suitable rules for the enforcement of rights in such works (see, e.g., Note, Personal Letters: In Need of a Law of Their Own, 44 Iowa L.Rev. 705), they are relatively manageable. However, conversational speech, the distinctive behavior of man, is quite another matter, and subjecting any part of it to the restraints of common-law copyright presents unique problems.

One such problem—and it was stressed by the court at Special Term (Schweitzer, J.)[2]—is that of avoiding undue restraints on the freedoms of speech and press and, in particular, on the writers of history and of biographical works of the genre of Boswell's "Life of Johnson". The safeguarding of essential freedoms in this area is, though, not without its complications. The indispensable right of the press to report on what people have *done,* or on what has *happened* to them or on what they have *said in public* (see Time, Inc. v. Hill, 385 U.S. 374; Curtis Pub. Co. v. Butts, 388 U.S. 130; Associated Press v. Walker, 388 U.S. 130) does not necessarily imply an unbounded freedom to publish whatever they may have *said in private conversation,* any more than it implies a freedom to copy and publish what people may have put down in *private writings.*

Copyright, both common-law and statutory, rests on the assumption that there are forms of expression, limited in kind, to be sure, which should not be divulged to the public without the consent of their author. The purpose, far from being restrictive, is to encourage and protect intellectual labor. (See Note, Copyright: Right to Common Law Copyright in Conversation of a Decedent, 67 Col.L.Rev. 366, 367, commenting on the decision denying the plaintiffs before us a preliminary injunction, 49 Misc.2d 726, 268 N.Y.S.2d 531.) The essential thrust of the First Amendment is to prohibit improper restraints on the *voluntary* public expression of ideas; it shields the man who wants to speak or publish when others wish him to be quiet. There is necessarily, and within suitably defined areas, a concomi-

---

2. Another problem—also remarked by the court—is the difficulty of measuring the relative self-sufficiency of any one party's contributions to a conversation, although it may be, in the case of some kinds of dialogue or interview, that the difficulty would not be greater than in deciding other questions of degree, such as plagiarism. (See, e.g., Nichols v. Universal Pictures Corp., C.C., 45 F.2d 119.)

tant freedom *not* to speak publicly, one which serves the same ultimate end as freedom of speech in its affirmative aspect.

The rules of common-law copyright assure this freedom in the case of written material.   However, speech is now easily captured by electronic devices and, consequently, we should be wary about excluding all possibility of protecting a speaker's right to decide when his words, uttered in private dialogue, may or may not be published at large.   Conceivably, there may be limited and special situations in which an interlocutor brings forth oral statements from another party which both understand to be the unique intellectual product of the principal speaker, a product which would qualify for common-law copyright if such statements were in writing.   Concerning such problems, we express no opinion;   we do no more than raise the questions, leaving them open for future consideration in cases which may present them more sharply than this one does.

On the appeal before us, the plaintiffs' claim to common-law copyright may be disposed of more simply and on a more narrow ground.

The defendant Hotchner asserts—without contradiction in the papers before us—that Hemingway never suggested to him or to anyone else that he regarded his conversational remarks to be "literary creations" or that he was of a mind to restrict Hotchner's use of the notes and recordings which Hemingway knew him to be accumulating.   On the contrary, as we have already observed, it had become a continuing practice, during Hemingway's lifetime, for Hotchner to write articles about Hemingway, consisting largely of quotations from the latter's conversation—and of all of this Hemingway approved.   In these circumstances, authority to publish must be implied, thus negativing the reservation of any common-law copyright.

Assuming, without deciding, that in a proper case a common-law copyright in certain limited kinds of spoken dialogue might be recognized, it would, at the very least, be required that the speaker indicate that he intended to mark off the utterance in question from the ordinary stream of speech, that he meant to adopt it as a unique statement and that he wished to exercise control over its publication.   In the conventional common-law copyright situation, this indication is afforded by the creation of the manuscript itself.   It would have to be evidenced in some other way if protection were ever to be accorded to some forms of conversational dialogue.

Such an indication is, of course, possible in the case of speech.   It might, for example, be found in prefatory words or inferred from the circumstances in which the dialogue takes place.[3]   Another way of formulating such a rule might to be to say that, although, in the case of most

---

3. This was the situation in Jenkins v. News Syndicate Co., 128 Misc. 284, 219 N.Y.S. 196. The plaintiff alleged that she had had a conference with a newspaper editor in which she described in detail the proposed content of some articles she was requested to write. Later, she decided not to write them and the newspaper thereupon published an "interview" with her, precisely quoting much of her conversation with the editor. The court held that she had stated a cause of action for damages on the theory of common-law copyright.

intellectual products, the courts are reluctant to find that an author has "published," so as to lose his common-law copyright (see Nimmer, Copyright, § 58.2, pp. 226–228), in the case of conversational speech—because of its unique nature—there should be a presumption that the speaker has not reserved any common-law rights unless the contrary strongly appears. However, we need not carry such speculation further in the present case since the requisite conditions are plainly absent here.

For present purposes, it is enough to observe that Hemingway's words and conduct, far from making any such reservation, left no doubt of his willingness to permit Hotchner to draw freely on their conversation in writing about him and to publish such material. What we have said disposes of the plaintiffs' claim both to exclusive and to joint copyright and we need not consider this aspect of the case any further. It follows, therefore, that the courts below were eminently correct in dismissing the first cause of action.

[The court also held that plaintiffs were not entitled to relief on their claims for unfair competition, breach of a confidential relationship, and invasion of privacy.]

In brief, then, it is our conclusion that, since no triable issues have been raised, the courts below very properly dismissed the complaint.

The orders appealed from should be affirmed, with costs.

■ JUDGES BURKE, SCILEPPI, BERGAN, KEATING, BREITEL, and JASEN concur.

Orders affirmed.

NOTES AND QUESTIONS

(1) How could a speaker desiring common law protection "indicate that he intended to mark off the utterance in question from the ordinary stream of speech"? Would the requirement be equally applicable to more formal "talk" such as an extemporaneous lecture? *Should* state law protect such works, or should some form of fixation be required? A claim of common law copyright in an interview was rejected in Falwell v. Penthouse Int'l, Ltd., 521 F.Supp. 1204 (W.D.Va.1981).

A California statute (Cal.Civ.C. §§ 980–85) states that an "author of any original work of authorship that is not fixed in any tangible medium of expression has an exclusive ownership in the representation or expression thereof * * *." It also states that such "ownership" may be transferred. Would the statute alter the outcome or reasoning in *Hemingway?*

(2) Federal copyright protection is available only to works "fixed in any tangible medium of expression." § 102. Section 301(b) expressly permits state common law copyright in works that remain unfixed. The 1976 House Report offers some examples: "choreography that has never been filmed or notated, an extemporaneous speech, 'original works of authorship' communicated solely through conversations or live broadcasts, and a dramatic sketch or musical composition improvised or developed from memory and without being recorded or written down." H.R.Rep. p. 131. A number of states have enacted statutes that make it a crime to record a live performance for commercial sale without the consent of the "owner"— a practice often described as "bootlegging". See, e.g., S.C. Code § 16–11–915; Tex.Bus. & Com.C. § 35.93. In 1994, Congress extended federal protection to live musical performances. 17 U.S.C.A. § 1101. Although § 1101 incorporates the civil remedies available under the Copyright Act, it does not grant a "copyright"; the performances are not "fixed" and thus are ineligible for copyright protection. Congress also imposed substantial criminal penalties for bootlegging. See 18 U.S.C.A. § 2319A. Protection of live performances under state law is not preempted. § 1101(d).

A lecture or speech that has been recorded on tape or written down on paper prior to its delivery is "fixed", thus triggering federal copyright protection (see § 302(a) and the § 101 definition of "created") and preempting state common law copyright (see § 301). Suppose the speaker has merely prepared notes. Is that a fixation? Of what? The entire speech? The portion the speaker could reconstruct using the notes? Only the portion actually written down? See the definition of "fixed" in § 101. And what if a completely extemporaneous speech is recorded by the speaker at the time it is delivered? Note the special provision in the statutory definition of "fixed" for live transmissions that are being simultaneously recorded.[a] Doesn't that imply that there is no claim under the 1976 Act against someone who copies material from a live performance that is being simultaneously fixed but *not* transmitted? At the conclusion of such a recorded performance, however, the work would be "fixed" and thus protected against subsequent copiers.

In Phillips v. Inc. Magazine, 1987 WL 8047 (E.D.Pa.1987), the court dismissed a claim for infringement of statutory copyright in statements made by the plaintiff, an attorney, during a telephone interview, subsequently quoted without attribution in defendant's magazine. The court held that the plaintiff's work was not "fixed." In a footnote, however, the court implied that the statements were now "fixed" through their appearance in the magazine, and thus subsequent use by the defendant might be an infringement. That isn't correct—is it? Is the plaintiff's work now "fixed" under the statutory definition in § 101? Even if it is, would a user who relies on access gained *prior* to fixation infringe the § 106 exclusive right "to reproduce the copyrighted work"?

(3) Suppose A's conversation is recreated by B in a copyrighted book. C then copies those portions of the book that purport accurately to represent A's words. In an action by B, is C liable for copyright infringement? Has C taken an "original" work of *B's* authorship? If A's words were part of a conversation with B, could the conversation as a whole be considered a "joint work" of A and B? See § 201(a) and the definition of "joint work"

---

a. The exception for simultaneously recorded transmissions was applied in Pacific and Southern Co. v. Duncan, 744 F.2d 1490 (11th Cir.1984), to uphold copyright in television news broadcasts despite the fact that the station typically erased the tapes after seven days.

in § 101. See also Urantia Foundation v. Maaherra, 114 F.3d 955 (9th Cir.1997) (questions put by humans to "celestial beings" contributed to the structure and arrangement of the "revelations," providing sufficient human authorship for copyright); Harris v. Miller, 50 U.S.P.Q. 306 (S.D.N.Y. 1941) (interviewer's portion of a conversation is a copyrightable contribution). Compare Quinto v. Legal Times, Inc., 506 F.Supp. 554 (D.D.C.1981) (arrangement and selection of quotations is copyrightable) with Suid v. Newsweek Magazine, 503 F.Supp. 146 (D.D.C.1980) (no infringement where selection and arrangement were not copied). See generally Dunlap, Copyright Protection for Oral Works—Expansion of the Copyright Law Into the Area of Conversations, 20 Bull.Copyr.Soc. 285 (1973).

A NOTE ON FIXATION

Why does federal copyright law insist on fixation in a tangible form? The requirement is obviously a convenient way to avoid the difficulties posed by ephemeral works, but does it also have a constitutional dimension? Recall the reference in Article I, Sec. 8 to "Authors" and their "Writings." The latter has been interpreted by the Supreme Court "to include any *physical rendering* of the fruits of creative intellectual or aesthetic labor." Goldstein v. California, p. 609 infra (emphasis added). If "Writings" entail tangibility, unfixed works are beyond the reach of Congress, at least with respect to its authority under the copyright clause. Thus, works must be fixed in a tangible form in order to qualify for federal copyright. The Copyright Act calls these tangible forms—the material objects in which works are embodied—"copies" and "phonorecords." Both are defined in § 101. "Phonorecords" are material objects in which sounds (other than sounds that are part of an audiovisual work) are fixed. A compact disc containing musical works is a "phonorecord"; so is a cassette tape. "Copies" are everything else in which works of authorship can be embodied. A book is a "copy," as are a photograph and a videotape. Some of this is summed up in the House Report:

> "[C]opies" and "phonorecords" together will comprise all of the material objects in which copyrightable works are capable of being fixed. The definitions of these terms in section 101, together with their usage in section 102 and throughout the bill, reflect a fundamental distinction between the "original work" which is the product of "authorship" and the multitude of material objects in which it can be embodied. Thus, in the sense of the bill, a "book" is not a work of authorship, but is a particular kind of "copy." Instead, the author may write a "literary work," which in turn can be embodied in a wide range of "copies" and "phonorecords," including books, periodicals, computer punch cards, microfilm, tape recordings, and so forth. It is possible to have an "original work of authorship" without having a "copy" or "phonorecord" embodying it, and it is also possible to have a "copy" or "phonorecord" embodying something that does not qualify as an "original work of authorship." The two essential elements—original work

and tangible object—must merge through fixation in order to produce subject matter copyrightable under the statute. (H.R.Rep. p. 53.)

The distinction between phonorecords and copies was intended to do more than harass the uninitiated. Rights and duties under the 1976 Act sometimes turn on the kind of material object in which the work is embodied.

As Note (2) following the *Hemingway* case illustrates, the seemingly clear-cut event of fixation can have its ambiguities. A series of cases involving claims of copyright in the sights and sounds produced by video games focused attention on the fixation requirement. Stern Electronics v. Kaufman, 669 F.2d 852 (2d Cir.1982), is typical. Plaintiff marketed a video game called "Scramble" and sought a preliminary injunction against a defendant who sold a game "virtually identical in both sight and sound." The plaintiff claimed infringement of its copyright on the audiovisual display produced during the play of its game. Defendant contended that the work was not "fixed" since "the sequence of some of the images appearing on the screen during each play of the game will vary depending upon the actions taken by the player." The court disagreed:

> We agree with the District Court that the player's participation does not withdraw the audiovisual work from copyright eligibility. No doubt the entire sequence of all the sights and sounds of the game are different each time the game is played, depending upon the route and speed the player selects for his spaceship and the timing and accuracy of his release of his craft's bombs and lasers. Nevertheless, many aspects of the sights and the sequence of their appearance remain constant during each play of the game. * * * It is true, as appellants contend, that some of these sights and sounds will not be seen and heard during each play of the game in the event that the player's spaceship is destroyed before the entire course is traversed. But the images remain fixed, capable of being seen and heard each time a player succeeds in keeping his spaceship aloft long enough to permit the appearances of all the images and sounds of a complete play of the game. The repetitive sequence of a substantial portion of the sights and sounds of the game qualifies for copyright protection as an audiovisual work.

"PUBLICATION" BEFORE AND AFTER THE 1976 ACT

Section 302(a) of the 1976 Act provides that "copyright in a work created on or after January 1, 1978, subsists from its creation * * *." "A work is 'created' when it is fixed in a copy or phonorecord for the first time." § 101. Since state copyright protection for works within the subject matter of the federal statute is preempted by § 301, *fixation* is the dividing-line between state common law and federal statutory protection.

Before the 1976 Copyright Act took effect on January 1, 1978, the reach of common law copyright was much more extensive. The dividing-line between common law and federal copyright was ordinarily defined by the act of *publication*. Unpublished works belonged to state law. Once a work was published, it was protected, if at all, by the federal copyright statutes passed beginning in 1790 under the authority of the constitutional clause.

The apparently bright line between unpublished and published works was first drawn by history. A great eighteenth-century English case raised questions about the nature of literary property—did it exist at all at common law? Did it exist after publication? Did the Statute of Anne (1710), the first copyright statute (reprinted in the Statutory Supplement), displace common law rights? In Donaldson v. Becket [b], the House of Lords, while affirming the existence of a common law copyright of unlimited duration, held that a *published* work could be protected only for the term of years provided by the statute (and, less clearly, that during that term the only remedies were those provided in the statute). The English statute and cases clearly influenced the shape and development of copyright law in this country. When similar issues came before the Supreme Court in Wheaton v. Peters, 33 U.S. 591 (1834), p. 33 infra, a similar result was reached within the framework of the Constitution and the supremacy clause.[c] Thus, once a work had been published, its author was entitled only to the protection offered by the federal copyright statute. If the statutory formalities (chiefly the requirement of a copyright notice) had not been met, the work fell into the public domain.

For English and American legislators of the eighteenth and early nineteenth century, the subject matter of copyright was, almost entirely, books. Books were something printed and published; before that they were manuscripts, which remained under common law protection. Indeed, the Statute of Anne spoke only of books; the first American statute (reprinted in the Statutory Supplement), appropriately for a new-found land, covered maps and charts as well as books. These could be effectively disseminated only by "printing, reprinting, publishing and vending" (these were the exclusive rights secured by the 1790 statute), so there were no gaps of any significance in the statutory scheme.

Meanwhile, beyond the paradigm of the book and its manuscript, the range of works that sought and got statutory copyright protection was expanding: in 1802, to "any historical or other print"; in 1831, to musical compositions; in 1865, to photographs; and in 1870, to paintings, drawings

b. 2 Bro.P.C. 129, 1 Eng.Rep. 837, 4 Burr. 2408, 98 Eng.Rep. 257 (H.L.1774). Consult B. Kaplan, An Unhurried View of Copyright (1967), ch. 1. The history of copyright in England and America is explored at length in L. Patterson, Copyright in Historical Perspective (1968).

c. These historic cases are re-examined in Abrams, The Historic Foundation of American Copyright Law: Exploding the Myth of Common Law Copyright, 29 Wayne L.Rev. 1119 (1983).

and other productions "intended as works of fine arts." All these, while unpublished, doubtless had common law protection.

The thorough-going revision of federal copyright law in 1909 made a brave try at delimiting the spheres of common law and statutory copyright. (The 1909 Act is reproduced in the Statutory Supplement.) Section 2 was a flat affirmation that

> Nothing in this title shall be construed to annul or limit the right of the author or proprietor of an unpublished work, at common law or in equity, to prevent the copying, publication, or use of such unpublished work without his consent, and to obtain damages therefor.

Yet at the same time, § 12 of the 1909 Act created a route to statutory copyright for some works "of which copies are not reproduced for sale," that is, for some unpublished works. Simple deposit requirements provided statutory protection for unpublished dramatic works, lectures, musical compositions, motion pictures, photographs, and other artistic works— everything indeed except books, periodicals, maps, prints, and reproductions of works of art (if one can take the classes for registration set out in § 5 as a fair representation of the scope of the 1909 Act). Section 12, however, was not viewed as preemptive of common law rights. Rather, it was construed as affording an option. But if one registered an unpublished work under § 12, it came to be agreed that this choice amounted to a displacement of common law rights.

Despite the alternative offered to some unpublished works by § 12, the primary means of acquiring federal copyright under the 1909 Act was through the mechanism provided in § 10: "Any person entitled thereto by this title may secure copyright for his work by publication thereof with the notice of copyright required by this title."

Since it was "publication" that divested the author of common law rights and, if accompanied by the appropriate formalities, initiated protection under the 1909 Act, courts were regularly called upon to determine what sorts of activities amounted to "publication." Some situations seemed easy enough. If the author of a literary work sold or otherwise distributed copies to the general public, publication had occurred. Other works presented greater difficulties. With respect to works of art like paintings and sculpture, for example, would common law protection be jeopardized if the artist publicly exhibited the work but did not distribute reproductions? The answer was never quite clear.

In the case of dramatic and musical works, the issue of public performance created particular concern. The influential decision of the Supreme Court in Ferris v. Frohman, 223 U.S. 424 (1912), held that the public performance of a dramatic work was not a publication. Whether the Court read history correctly is debatable,[d] but this did not much matter since it was now settled that performance did not constitute publication. A play

---

d. See Selvin, Should Performance Dedicate?, 42 Calif.L.Rev. 40 (1954).

could be exploited forever on the stage with perpetual common law copyright protection.

The position that public performance was not a publication that divested common law rights extended equally and easily to musical compositions. But the defense of common law rights in musical compositions had a harder time resisting the argument that widespread dissemination of the work on phonograph records amounted to publication. The issues here were shaped—or rather distorted—by another famous Supreme Court decision.

In White–Smith Music Publishing Co. v. Apollo Co., 209 U.S. 1 (1908), the Court rejected an attempt to enjoin the infringement of statutory copyright in two songs, "Little Cotton Dolly" and "Kentucky Babe," published in the form of sheet music. The acts of alleged infringement were the manufacture and sale by the defendant of perforated music rolls which, used in connection with player pianos, produced plaintiff's melodies in sound.

The Court concluded that the copyrights had not been infringed since the piano rolls could not be considered "copies" of the musical works within the meaning of the copyright act. "What is meant by a copy? * * * The [definition] which most commends itself to our judgment * * * defines a copy of a musical composition to be 'a written or printed record of it in intelligible notation.'" Piano rolls were not "copies" since "even those skilled in the making of these rolls are unable to read them as musical compositions."

Mr. Justice Holmes, concurring, wrote:

"In view of the facts and opinions in this country and abroad to which my brother Day has called attention I do not feel justified in dissenting from the judgment of the court, but the result is to give to copyright less scope than its rational significance and the ground on which it is granted seem to me to demand. Therefore I desire to add a few words to what he has said.

"The notion of property starts, I suppose, from confirmed possession of a tangible object and consists in the right to exclude others from interference with the more or less free doing with it as one wills. But in copyright property has reached a more abstract expression. The right to exclude is not directed to an object in possession or owned, but is *in vacuo*, so to speak. It restrains the spontaneity of men where but for it there would be nothing of any kind to hinder their doing as they saw fit. It is a prohibition of conduct remote from the persons or tangibles of the party having the right. It may be infringed a thousand miles from the owner and without his ever becoming aware of the wrong. It is a right which could not be recognized or endured for more than a limited time, and therefore, I may remark in passing, it is one which hardly can be conceived except as a product of statute, as the authorities now agree.

"The ground of this extraordinary right is that the person to whom it is given has invented some new collocation of visible or audible points,—of lines, colors, sounds, or words. The restraint is directed against reproducing this collocation, although but for the invention and the statute any one would be free to combine the contents of the dictionary, the elements of the spectrum, or the notes of the gamut in any way that he had the wit to devise. The restriction is confined to the specific form, to the collocation devised, of course, but one would expect that, if it was to be protected at all, that collocation would be protected according to what was its essence. One would expect the protection to be coextensive not only with the invention, which, though free to all, only one had the ability to achieve, but with the possibility of reproducing the result which gives to the invention its meaning and worth. A musical composition is a rational collocation of sounds apart from concepts, reduced to a tangible expression from which the collocation can be reproduced either with or without continuous human intervention. On principle anything that mechanically reproduces that collocation of sounds ought to be held a copy, or if the statute is too narrow ought to be made so by a further act, except so far as some extraneous consideration of policy may oppose. What license may be implied from a sale of the copyrighted article is a different and harder question, but I leave it untouched, as license is not relied upon as a ground for the judgment of the court.''

The specific holding in *White–Smith* that copyright owners could not control the mechanical reproduction of their works in piano rolls (or more significantly, in phonograph records) was soon modified by § 1(e) of the 1909 Act. That section established a compulsory licensing scheme that remains to this day (see § 115 and p. 538 infra), but the 1909 Act accomplished this without specifically overruling the Supreme Court's narrow interpretation of "copy."

Although *White–Smith* dealt only with the question of what constituted an infringing "copy" of a copyrighted work, many saw in it wider implications. If phonograph records and other "unintelligible" embodiments were not copies of the work for purposes of infringement, perhaps they were also not copies for purposes of determining whether their distribution by the copyright owner was a publication of the work. Although the case law did not consistently support such a view, many practitioners took the position that the sale and distribution of phonograph records was not a publication of the underlying musical composition, leaving common law protection intact, and this view seems to have been acted on in the conduct of business.[e]

The combined thrust of *White–Smith* and *Ferris* had considerable impact on the burgeoning broadcast industry. Broadcasts were perfor-

e. See McDonald, The Law of Broadcasting, in Seven Copyright Problems Analyzed 31, 45–56 (1952); Burton, Business Practices in the Copyright Field, id. at 87, 102–04. But cf. Kaplan, Publication in Copyright Law: The Question of Phonograph Records, 103 U.Pa.L.Rev. 469 (1955). The Second Circuit in Rosette v. Rainbo Record Mfg. Corp., 546 F.2d 461 (2d Cir.1976), adhered to the proposition that the distribution of phonorecords was not a publication of the musical work under the 1909 Act, but the Ninth Circuit disagreed in La Cienega Music Co. v. ZZ Top, 53 F.3d 950 (9th Cir.), cert. denied, 516 U.S. 927 (1995). A 1997 amendment adding § 303(b) to the 1976 Act overruled *La Cienega Music* and confirmed the prior understanding.

mances, and so under *Ferris* neither divested common law rights in the works they embodied nor provided entree to the federal statutory protection available for published works. And even when the broadcasts were recorded on tape, *White–Smith's* emphasis on intelligibility impeded access to federal copyright.[f]

By the middle of the twentieth century, almost everyone agreed that the federal copyright statute was outmoded, cumbersome, and at times, virtually unworkable. Although there was talk of revision, the 1909 Act survived for another quarter-century while a multitude of industries and interest groups struggled to construct the compromises ultimately embodied in the Copyright Act of 1976.[g]

Those who first encounter copyright law long after the passage of the 1976 Act may be tempted to dismiss all this as ancient history. The 1976 Act installs fixation in "copies" or "phonorecords" as the threshold of federal protection, and the definitions of these terms sweep away the arcane distinctions that emanated from *White–Smith*. But the past cannot be discarded so easily. For the millions of works created under the prior law, their status on January 1, 1978, the effective date of the 1976 Act, is crucial. Protection of works then under statutory copyright was continued, indeed extended, by the 1976 Act, and existing works then under common law protection were automatically brought within the scope of the federal statute. §§ 303, 304. But the 1976 Act did not provide protection for works that had already entered the public domain.[h] As to this, the old rules about publication remain decisive.

The old law of publication also remains important in another way. Although no longer marking the boundary between common law and federal copyright, publication retains significance under the 1976 Act. For some works, the duration of copyright is measured from the year of first publication. § 302(c). The rights of foreign authors under § 104 may turn on whether publication has occurred. Remedies under the Act may also depend upon whether the work has been published. See § 412. Reproduction rights of libraries, § 108, and the availability of the public broadcasting compulsory license, § 118, turn on publication, as do other rights. Publication also triggers the obligation to deposit copies of the work with the Copyright Office, § 407, and, prior to 1989, it determined whether a notice of copyright was necessary to insure continued protection for the work. §§ 401, 402. For all these purposes the 1976 Act created its own definition of publication in § 101. This statutory law of publication is in part a codification of what had gone before, and the prior law continues to influence interpretation of the 1976 Act. See generally Brylawski,

---

f. The Copyright Office did not accept videotapes until 1961.

g. See generally R. Brown, Unification: A Cheerful Requiem for Common–Law Copyright, 24 UCLA L.Rev. 1070 (1977). For a less enthusiastic appraisal of the 1976 Act see Henn, Cassandra Considers Copyright, 25

Bull.Copyr.Soc. 453 (1978). The contentious negotiations among the interest groups who in effect drafted the revision bill are detailed in Litman, Copyright, Compromise, and Legislative History, 72 Cornell L.Rev. 857 (1987).

h. 17 U.S.C.A.Trans. and Supp.Provisions § 103.

Publication: Its Role in Copyright Matters, Both Past and Present, 31 J.Copyr.Soc. 507 (1984).

King v. Mister Maestro, Inc.

United States District Court, Southern District of New York, 1963.
224 F.Supp. 101.

■ WYATT, DISTRICT JUDGE. Plaintiff moves for a preliminary injunction restraining defendants from selling phonograph records of a speech by him or from otherwise infringing the copyright claimed for the speech. The action is for a permanent injunction, damages and an accounting. * * *

Plaintiff, a highly educated Negro clergyman, has been also for some time a distinguished and effective leader in the movement to secure equal civil rights for Negro citizens. As such he has developed a unique literary and oratorical style and has delivered lectures, sermons and addresses to large crowds in many parts of the nation.

On June 23, 1963 in an auditorium at Detroit, Dr. King made a speech to which he gave no title but in the course of which he used the words "I have a dream".

Thereafter an assembly or "march" for civil rights was planned for Washington on August 28, 1963. Dr. King was one of the organizers and was invited to deliver a speech. He wrote his speech from time to time between August 24 and August 28, 1963; it was finished about 4 o'clock in the morning of August 28. The speech contains some of the ideas and words of the Detroit speech, but is much longer and has a great deal not contained in the Detroit speech. * * *

Dr. King did deliver a copy of his speech to the press representatives of the organizing committee and apparently did not forbid its reproduction for the press. While he may not have known of such reproduction or have expressly consented to it, the use made of it seems natural and reasonable. The significant and important fact is that the copies of the speech were distributed *only to the press* and that this distribution took place only in the "press tent". * * *

In the afternoon of August 28, some 200,000 people gathered before the Lincoln Memorial in Washington for a "freedom" demonstration in behalf of civil rights for Negro citizens. Among the speeches delivered was that by Dr. King.

Apparently it was Dr. King's speech which most stirred and impressed the crowd, especially his repetition of the words "I have a dream". * * *

Dr. King's speech (along with the speeches of others made at the same time) was broadcast by television and radio, recorded (sound and pictures) for newsreels, was later shown in movie houses, and of course was widely reported in the press. Excerpts from Dr. King's speech were published in many newspapers. The New York Post in its issue of September 1, 1963 published the complete text of the speech under the title "I Have A Dream

* * *". The Post thereafter offered for sale reprints of the speech. Dr. King says that he has not consented in any way to such reprinting and sale of the speech and did not give to the Post any copy of his speech.

Defendant 20th Century–Fox Record Corporation and Movietonews, Inc. are subsidiaries of Twentieth Century Fox Film Corporation. Movietonews, Inc. produces a newsreel for movie theaters called "Fox Movietone News" and took pictures of and made a sound record of Dr. King's speech on August 28, 1963 and of the speeches made on the same occasion by five other speakers.

Defendant 20th Century–Fox Record Corporation made a phonograph record from the newsreel sound track of the speeches including that of Dr. King, and about September 18, 1963 began selling these records in a cover, with a picture from the newsreel film of the crowd in front of the Lincoln Memorial. The cover is entitled "Freedom March on Washington August 28, 1963" and states that the record is of the speeches made that day (including that of Dr. King) which were "recorded live by Fox Movietone News". The record has both the voice and the words of Dr. King. Sales of the record have continued.

Defendant Mister Maestro, Inc. made and is selling a somewhat similar record entitled "The March on Washington", which record does not on its cover or elsewhere refer to Dr. King. The record does contain, however, part or all of the speech of Dr. King as delivered by him in Washington; it has both the voice and the words of Dr. King.

Defendants are selling their records without the consent of Dr. King and of course without paying anything to him. * * *

On September 30, 1963 Dr. King sent a copy of his speech to the Copyright Office for deposit and at the same time sent an application form for a certificate of registration of his claim to copyright. 17 U.S.C.A. §§ 11, 12, 207. The class to which the work was claimed to belong was Class C— "[l]ectures, sermons, addresses (prepared for oral delivery)". 17 U.S.C.A. § 5(c); 37 C.F.R. § 202.1. The "title of the work" was said to be "I Have A Dream". The claim to copyright was under 17 U.S.C.A. § 12, "works not reproduced for sale"—unpublished works. * * *

Subsequently a Class C certificate was duly issued, showing receipt of the application therefor on October 2, 1963. * * *

There seems to be no real dispute as to the facts set forth. The application raises only questions of law and if these are decided for plaintiff, a preliminary injunction is appropriate and necessary.

As an original proposition, it seems unfair and unjust for defendants to use the voice and the words of Dr. King without his consent and for their own financial profit. Of course, decision cannot be made simply because of such a feeling. This is a Court of law which must look to legal principles established by the Congress and by higher Courts. But under the circumstances here present it does seem that defendants should demonstrate that their use of the voice and words of plaintiff is permitted by legal principles so established.

The general principles of law here involved are relatively simple; their application in some cases is difficult.

At common law there was a property right in an unpublished work but after publication there was no copyright protection.

Congress has provided copyright protection after publication on certain conditions and also on conditions has given such protection before publication, somewhat parallel to the common law property right which the legislation specifically recognizes. * * *

Defendants stress the public nature of the delivery of the speech by Dr. King—the enormous crowd, the radio and television broadcasts, the movie newsreel pictures. The question is: was this a general publication of the speech so as to place it in the public domain?

The word "general" with respect to publication in this sense is of greatest significance. There can be a limited publication, which is a communication of the work to others under circumstances showing no dedication of the work to the public. A general publication is one which shows a dedication to the public so as to lose copyright. * * *

The public performance of a play is not a general publication. Ferris v. Frohman, 223 U.S. 424 (1912).

The public delivery of lectures on a memory system is not a general publication. Nutt v. National Institute Incorporated for the Improvement of Memory, 31 F.2d 236 (2d Cir.1929).

The playing of a song in public is not a general publication of the work. Heim v. Universal Pictures Co., 154 F.2d 480 (2d Cir.1946).

The broadcast by radio of a script is not a general publication thereof. Uproar Co. v. National Broadcasting Co., 8 F.Supp. 358, 362 (D.Mass.1934). * * *

The "oral delivery" of his speech by Dr. King, no matter how vast his audience, did not amount to a general publication of his literary work.

Defendants stress the delivery without copyright notice of an advance text of his speech and the distribution of it to the press. But within the concept of publication just examined, it is clear that this was a *limited,* as opposed to a general, publication. There is nothing to suggest that copies of the speech were ever offered to the *public;* the fact is clear that the "advance text" was given to the press only. * * *

The conclusion seems plain that there was no general publication by Dr. King in making his speech available to the press. * * *

* * * His right to a preliminary injunction is established. * * *

NOTES AND QUESTIONS ON PUBLICATION

(1) Was the distribution of Dr. King's speech, in any real sense, "limited"? The decision is criticized in Krasnow, Copyrights, Performers' Rights, and the March on Civil Rights, 53 Geo.L.J. 403 (1965), for distorting the idea of limited publication. Does the result nevertheless seem equitable?

In Academy of Motion Picture Arts & Sciences v. Creative House Promotions, Inc., 944 F.2d 1446 (9th Cir.1991), the court found that the restricted distribution of the Oscar statuette was a limited publication and thus protection had not been lost for lack of a copyright notice.

(2) What was the rationale for the proposition that a "general" publication divested common law rights in works of authorship? Some decisions saw the rule as a necessary corollary of the "limited times" restriction in the constitutional clause. See Letter Edged in Black Press, Inc. v. Public Building Comm. of Chicago, 320 F.Supp. 1303 (N.D.Ill.1970). Is this rationale consistent with the rule that a public performance is not a publication? In what sense does a general publication show, in the words of the court in *King,* "a dedication of the work to the public"?

In connection with publication under the 1909 Act, consider the following quotation from American Vitagraph v. Levy, 659 F.2d 1023 (9th Cir.1981): "[P]ublication may be more readily found if the issue is whether the copyright statute has been complied with than if forfeiture of common law rights is involved." This notion that the distribution necessary to cause the loss of common law rights (divestive publication) was greater than that required to bring a work within the protection of the 1909 Act through publication with copyright notice (investive publication) may help explain much of the case law on publication. Although protection under the 1976 Act commences upon fixation, prior to the 1988 amendments (see p. 36 infra) compliance with the copyright notice provisions upon publication of the work was a prerequisite to continued copyright protection. Which of the former concepts of publication corresponds more closely to its role in this statutory scheme?

(3) The rule that public performance is not publication is continued under the 1976 Act. (See the § 101 definition of "publication".) As for the public display of a work, the House Report offers this comment:

> It should be noted that, under the definition of "publication" in section 101, there would no longer be any basis for holding, as a few court decisions have done in the past, that the public display of a work of art under some conditions (e.g., without restriction against its reproduction) would constitute publication of the work. (H.R.Rep. p. 144.)

(4) Assume that Dr. King had delivered his speech in 1988. Would the speech have been protected by federal copyright at the time of his address? Would the events of the day have threatened the continuation of that protection? A similar case arose at the 1988 Democratic National Convention. Jesse Jackson gave a speech to the convention carried live by the major television networks. Copies of the speech had been provided to the press prior to its delivery; Jackson's national campaign office distributed additional copies in the weeks that followed. None apparently bore a notice of copyright. When the defendant began marketing a video tape of the convention address, Jackson brought an infringement action. Although § 401 at the time made copyright notice mandatory on published copies, the court granted a preliminary injunction, finding that the omission of notice was probably excused under the exceptions in § 405. Jackson v. MPI Home Video, 694 F.Supp. 483 (N.D.Ill.1988).

Would there be any risk of forfeiture if Dr. King's speech and its distribution to the press occurred today? Copyright notice and the other statutory formalities are the subject of the following section.

(5) Martin Luther King's "I Have a Dream" speech continues to generate litigation. In 1993, King's estate sued *USA Today* after the newspaper published the text of the speech on the 30th anniversary of its delivery; the newspaper settled, paying a licensing fee and legal costs. In 1996, the estate sued CBS over sales of a videotape narrated by Mike Wallace containing CBS news footage of King's speech. Blackmon, Estate of Dr. King Says in Suit, CBS Can't 'Have a Dream', Wall St.J., Nov. 20, 1996, p. B11. A King biographer worries that the estate's aggressive control over Dr. King's work raises the specter of censorship and undermines the substance of his legacy. Garrow, Are They Stifling the Work of Martin Luther King Jr.?, Wash. Post, Jan. 28, 1997, p. A13.

SECTION 4.   THE STATUTORY FORMALITIES

FORMALITIES AND COPYRIGHT

Procedural formalities have played a central role in American copyright law. They have often tripped up an incautious author or publisher. This is in part a legacy of the great case of Wheaton v. Peters, 33 U.S. (8 Pet.) 591 (1834). The contestants were Wheaton, the reporter of decisions for the Supreme Court from 1816 to 1827, and his successor, Peters, who published a series of Condensed Reports that included his predecessor's headnotes and commentary.[a] (The Court in this case declared that no reporter could have copyright in the opinions themselves.) The defense was that Wheaton and his publishers had not met all the statutory requirements for obtaining a federal copyright. This apparent flaw in his copyrights led Wheaton (represented by Daniel Webster) to assert the persistence of a common law right after publication, to which the copyright statute was only complementary and remedial. He thus recreated in this country the controversy over the nature of literary property that had come to a climax in England in Donaldson v. Becket, p. 24 supra, where the House of Lords had ruled that the Statute of Anne supplanted common law rights after publication. The Supreme Court took a parallel view with

a. An informative history of the early Supreme Court reporters and the controversy between Wheaton and Peters appears in Joyce, The Rise of the Supreme Court Reporter: An Institutional Perspective on the Marshall Court Ascendancy, 83 Mich.L.Rev. 1291 (1985).

respect to our statute.   It superseded the author's common law rights in published works, which the Court doubted had ever existed in the colonies anyway.   Rights in published works were therefore subject to the statutory formalities:

"This right, as has been shown, does not exist at common law—it originated, if at all, under the acts of Congress.   No one can deny that when the legislature are about to vest an exclusive right in an author or an inventor, they have the power to prescribe the conditions on which such right shall be enjoyed; and that no one can avail himself of such right who does not substantially comply with the requisitions of the law.   * * *

"The Act of Congress under which Mr. Wheaton, one of the complainants, in his capacity of reporter, was required to deliver eighty copies of each volume of his reports to the department of state, and which were, probably, faithfully delivered, does not exonerate him from the deposite of a copy under the act of 1790.   The eighty volumes were delivered for a different purpose; and cannot excuse the deposite of the one volume as specially required."

So, despite the fact that as the reporter for the Supreme Court Wheaton apparently delivered eighty copies to the Department of State, he was not excused from depositing in the same office "the one volume as specially required" by the copyright statute.   The case was remanded to ascertain the facts.   For every volume of the reports not in compliance, the complaint as to it was to be dismissed.[b]

The statutory formalities were modified from time to time, and indeed, the 1909 Act was supposed to represent a considerable relaxation.   It made acquisition of copyright on publication seemingly easy—all that was necessary was a notice of copyright on the published copies.   Both deposit and registration of the work were required, but they were not considered preconditions for securing copyright, and they could be accomplished after publication—"promptly."   In Washington Pub. Co. v. Pearson, 306 U.S. 30 (1939), it was decided that delay in deposit and registration did not cause a forfeiture of copyright, and further, that those requirements were merely a prerequisite to maintaining an infringement action.   But the statutory scheme was still cumbersome.   At least a half-dozen sections of the 1909 Act held implications for the notice requirement, and it continued to trap the unwary.[c]   A few examples will suffice.

b. Future Supreme Court Justice Oliver Wendell Holmes was defeated by the statutory formalities when he sought as executor of his father's estate to enjoin an infringement of *The Autocrat of the Breakfast Table*, published by the senior Holmes in twelve successive issues of the *Atlantic Monthly*. Since the issues of the magazine were not copyrighted, a later attempt to secure copyright on the complete work was ineffective. Holmes v. Hurst, 174 U.S. 82 (1899).

c. As with publication, the old rules retain significance. The notice requirements of the 1909 Act determine whether a work published prior to 1978 is in the public domain. Also, in the few instances in which the notice requirements of the 1976 Act may be more demanding than those of the prior law (see, e.g., the abbreviated notice permitted for some works under § 19 of the 1909 Act), works published before 1978 may continue to rely, in subsequent publications, on

In Group Publishers, Inc. v. Winchell, 86 F.Supp. 573 (S.D.N.Y.1949), copyright was lost because an assignee substituted its own name in the copyright notice before recording the assignment with the Copyright Office: "Strict compliance with the statutory requirements is essential to the perfection of the copyright itself and failure fully to conform to the form of notice prescribed by the act results in abandonment of the right and a dedication of one's work to the public." One case dismissed an infringement action because plaintiff's notice appeared on the back cover rather than on the "title page or the page immediately following" as required by § 20 of the 1909 Act. J.A. Richards, Inc. v. New York Post, Inc., 23 F.Supp. 619 (S.D.N.Y.1938). Another case withheld protection from a series of cartoons because the notice did not contain the name of the copyright proprietor, despite the appearance of his name in the title legend. Moger v. WHDH, Inc., 194 F.Supp. 605 (D.Mass.1961). Some judges, however, worked hard to avoid declaring a forfeiture against a deserving claimant who had failed to clear all the statutory hurdles. Thus, phrases such as "substantial compliance" and "adequate" notice sometimes appeared in the case law.

During the lengthy revision process that culminated in the 1976 Act, some urged that the requirement of a copyright notice be eliminated.[d] The structure of the 1976 Act offered some support for this view, since it was now fixation rather than publication that marked the beginning of federal protection. The case for elimination also drew upon international copyright law. Most of the nations of the world that are at all concerned with copyright have no notice requirements and their systems are predominantly free of other formalities. This was one of the differences that had long prevented our adherence to the Berne Convention, one of the two primary multinational copyright agreements. (See p. 810 infra.) The drafters of the 1976 Act attempted an elaborate compromise. The philosophy of the Act as initially adopted is described in the legislative history:

> A requirement that the public be given formal notice of every work in which copyright is claimed was a part of the first U.S. copyright statute enacted in 1790, and since 1802 our copyright laws have always provided that the published copies of copyrighted works must bear a specified notice as a condition of protection. Under the present law the copyright notice serves four principal functions:
>
>> (1) It has the effect of placing in the public domain a substantial body of published material that no one is interested in copyrighting;
>>
>> (2) It informs the public as to whether a particular work is copyrighted;

their original form of notice. 17 U.S.C.A. Trans. and Supp. Provisions § 108.

d. See generally Doyal *et al.*, Notice of Copyright, Copyr. Law Revision Study No. 7 (1957), in 1 Studies on Copyr. 229 (1963); Blaisdell, Commercial Use of the Copyright Notice, Copyr. Law Revision Study No. 8 (1959), id. p. 275.

(3) It identifies the copyright owner; and

(4) It shows the date of publication.

Ranged against these values of a notice requirement are its burdens and unfairness to copyright owners. One of the strongest arguments for revision of the present statute has been the need to avoid the arbitrary and unjust forfeitures now resulting from unintentional or relatively unimportant omissions or errors in the copyright notice. It has been contended that the disadvantages of the notice requirement outweigh its values and that it should therefore be eliminated or substantially liberalized.

The fundamental principle underlying the notice provisions of the bill is that the copyright notice has real values which should be preserved, and that this should be done by inducing use of notice without causing outright forfeiture for errors or omissions. Subject to certain safeguards for innocent infringers, protection would not be lost by the complete omission of copyright notice from large numbers of copies or from a whole edition, if registration for the work is made before or within 5 years after publication. Errors in the name or date in the notice could be corrected without forfeiture of copyright. (H.R.Rep. p. 143.)

This compromise survived for barely a decade. With the coming into effect on March 1, 1989 of the Berne Convention Implementation Act of 1988, P.L. 100–569, 102 Stat. 2853, notice of copyright became optional, ending the notice requirement that had endured in various forms for only a year short of two centuries.

NOTES AND QUESTIONS ON COPYRIGHT NOTICE

(1) The principal notice provisions are § 401 and § 402. As enacted in 1976, both sections required notice of copyright on all published works. The 1988 amendments replaced "shall" with "may", thus ending mandatory copyright notice. Habit, together with the remedial advantages offered in § 401(d) and § 402(d), will doubtless insure its continued presence on most works. (An exception may be works of fine art, where the appearance of a copyright notice sometimes has been decried as a defacement or mutilation.) Are there also non-legal benefits to continued use of the copyright notice?

The legislative history of the Berne Implementation Act indicates an apparent intent to eliminate the requirement of notice only for works first published after March 1, 1989. "The proposed legislation abolishes mandatory notice of copyright for works first published after the law comes into effect." H.R.Rep. No. 100–609, 100th Cong., 2d Sess. 45 (1988). But consider the introductory language to § 405—doesn't it imply that an omission of notice from copies distributed after the effective date of the amendment will not invalidate the copyright regardless of the date of first publication? The Copyright Office in Circular 1, Copyright Basics (1996), "does not take a position on whether copies of works first published with notice before March 1, 1989, which are distributed on and after March 1, 1989, must bear the copyright notice."   In Encore Shoe Corp. v. Bennett Industries, Inc., 18 U.S.P.Q.2d 1874 (D.Mass.1991), the court said in dictum that if a satisfactory copyright notice had appeared on pre–1989 publications, an omission of notice on post-amendment publications would not threaten the copyright.

The form and placement of notice sufficient to provide the remedial advantages offered in § 401(d) (and, for pre–1989 distributions, to preserve the validity of the copyright) are prescribed in § 401(b) and (c).   As indicated in § 401(c), Copyright Office regulations offer specific examples of satisfactory affixation.[e]   See 37 C.F.R. § 201.20.   Hopefully, the copyright notice following the title page of this casebook is a further example of compliance.   (Is it necessary to include the dates of earlier editions?   See § 401(b)(2).)

Consider the form of notice specified in § 401(b).   What is the purpose of including "the year of first publication"?   How often will that date be useful in determining when copyright expires?   See § 302.   Will the date reflect the age of the material contained in the work?   See § 401(b)(2).

Will the notice necessarily identify the owner of the copyright?   Recall that copyrights can be transferred.   The name appearing in the notice on existing copies does not magically change to reflect subsequent assignments.

(2) Examine the label on a cassette tape or compact disc.   Why is there typically no § 401 notice of copyright for the musical works recorded on the tape or disc?   What is the function of the notice that *does* appear?   See §§ 401 and 402, together with the § 101 definitions of "copies", "phonorecords", and "sound recordings."

(3) A copyright notice reminds users that the work is protected by copyright law, but the notice can also be misleading.   Consider a work that incorporates substantial material from the public domain.   The copyright notice will not reflect the fact that only a portion of the work is protected, and indeed may create the opposite impression.   Only when the public domain material consists of works of the United States Government (which are excluded from copyright under § 105) is the public likely to be protected by a more informative notice.[f]   See § 403.   (Should this casebook have a

---

e. The general prescription in § 401(c) that notice be affixed so as to "give reasonable notice of the claim of copyright" was found satisfied in Forry, Inc. v. Neundorfer, Inc., 837 F.2d 259 (6th Cir.1988), by a notice that appeared on the underside of a microchip attached to a circuit board.   The court noted that the copyrighted computer program could not be duplicated unless the chip was first removed from the board.

f. In Matthew Bender & Co. v. West Pub. Co., 42 U.S.P.Q.2d 1930 (S.D.N.Y.1997), the court suggested in dictum that the failure by West to identify in its federal case reports the specific editorial additions in which it claimed copyright would count against it in any fair use analysis.

§ 403 notice in view of its extensive use of federal judicial opinions?   What would such a notice say?)

As we have seen, for works published before Jan. 1, 1978, the effective date of the 1976 Act, the notice requirements of the 1909 Act determine whether the work has entered the public domain.   For publications occurring after March 1, 1989, copyright notice is no longer required.   For publications between Jan. 1, 1978 and March 1, 1989, the absence of notice can cause a forfeiture of copyright, but as the following case illustrates, the omission might be excused or cured under a complicated set of provisions that survive now as §§ 404–06.

Hasbro Bradley, Inc. v. Sparkle Toys, Inc.

United States Court of Appeals, Second Circuit, 1985.
780 F.2d 189.

Before FRIENDLY, MANSFIELD and WINTER, CIRCUIT JUDGES.

■ FRIENDLY, CIRCUIT JUDGE:

The companies involved in this copyright case in the District Court for the Southern District of New York are Takara Co., Ltd. ("Takara"), a Japanese company that designed the toys here in question;   plaintiff Hasbro Bradley, Inc. ("Hasbro"), a large American toy manufacturer and seller that acquired Takara's rights to United States copyrights for the toys;   and defendant Sparkle Toys, Inc. ("Sparkle"), a smaller American toy manufacturer and seller that copied the toys in Asia from models manufactured by Takara which did not carry the copyright notice required by § 401 of the Copyright Act of 1976 (the "Act"), 17 U.S.C. § 101 et seq., and by Article III(1) of the Revised Universal Copyright Convention (U.C.C.), 25 U.S.T. 1341 (1971), to which the United States and Japan are parties.   The appeal, by Sparkle, is from an order of Judge Broderick entered April 29, 1985, granting Hasbro a preliminary injunction prohibiting Sparkle from "distributing, selling, marketing, promoting, advertising, imitating or exploiting, in this country, its toys, formerly denoted 'Trans Robot,' which are in violation of plaintiff's registered copyrights in the sculptural embodiments of its 'Topspin' and 'Twin Twist' toys."

"Topspin" and "Twin Twist" (the "toys") are part of Hasbro's "The Transformers" series of changeable robotic action figures.   The sculptural expressions of the toys are original designs of Takara, which manufactures "The Transformers" for Hasbro.   Takara authored the designs in the summer of 1983 and by the end of November had completed molds for manufacturing the toys.   These molds did not contain a copyright notice. Takara avers that the omission was due to the facts that Japanese law does not recognize copyright in toy products and that Takara was unaware that American law does recognize copyright in such works but requires notice, even on copies of the work distributed outside the United States, for copyright protection to be claimed inside the United States. Production of the unmarked toys began in December 1983 and ended in February 1984. Between January and March, approximately 213,000 of the unmarked toys were sold; thereafter, sales were minor and were made only to remove inventory. Whether the unmarked toys were sold only in Asia or some of them were sold as well in the United States is in dispute. * * *

As previously stated, there is also no dispute that before the assignment of Takara's copyrights to Hasbro approximately 213,000 of the toys were sold, mostly in Japan, without copyright notice. This omission of notice from toys sold by Takara or with its authority outside the United States violated § 401(a) of the Act, which requires:

> Whenever a work protected under this title is published in the United States *or elsewhere* by authority of the copyright owner, a notice of copyright as provided by this section shall be placed on all publicly distributed copies from which the work can be visually perceived, either directly or with the aid of a machine or device.

(Emphasis added.) * * *

It is not contended that the omission of notice from the toys could have been excused under either subsections (1) or (3) of § 405(a); rather, reliance is placed on subsection (2). In effect, § 405(a)(2) allows a person who publishes a copyrightable work without notice to hold a kind of incipient copyright in the work for five years thereafter: if the omission is cured in that time through registration and the exercise of "a reasonable effort . . . to add notice to all copies . . . that are distributed to the public in the United States after the omission has been discovered," the copyright is perfected and valid retroactively for the entire period after cure; if the omission is not cured in that time, the incipient copyright never achieves enforceability. The *quid pro quo* in the Act for persons who have been misled by the omission of copyright notice before the cure is the more liberal provision of § 405(b), as compared with § 21 of the 1909 Act, regarding innocent infringers, of which more hereafter. * * *

The issue thus becomes whether Hasbro has cured Takara's omission of notice under § 405(a)(2). There is no question that Hasbro, as Takara's assignee, is permitted to effect cure through its own efforts. The "copyright claimant" entitled under the Act to register a copyright in the United States may be either the author of the work or his assignee, and any registration is of the work *per se* and redounds to the benefit of the assignor as well as the assignee. 3 *Nimmer,* supra, § 10.02[C][2], at 10–33. Not disputing this, Sparkle argues that Hasbro cannot effect cure under § 405(a)(2) because Takara's omission of notice was deliberate.

On its face, § 405(a)(2) is not restricted to unintentional omissions. Its language permits cure if registration is made "within five years after *the publication without notice*"—not, as Sparkle would read it, "the [unintentional] publication without notice." The difference between the broad language of § 405(a) and the more limited language of § 21 of the 1909 Act * * * shows that Congress no longer wished to deal only with omissions of notice due to accident or mistake. Moreover, the legislative history of the 1976 Act affords ample demonstration that Congress intended to bring deliberate omissions within the ambit of § 405(a)(2). The House Report comments with respect to § 405(a) that "[u]nder the proposed law a work published without any copyright notice will still be subject to statutory protection for at least 5 years, whether the omission was partial or total, *unintentional or deliberate.*" *House Report,* supra, at 147 (emphasis added), reprinted in 1976 U.S.Code Cong. & Ad.News at 5763. * * *

Against this, Sparkle relies on Judge Sand's opinion in Beacon Looms, Inc. v. S. Lichtenberg & Co., 552 F.Supp. 1305 (S.D.N.Y.1982), and on Professor Nimmer's approval of the reasoning of that opinion, see 2 *Nimmer,* supra, § 7.13[B][3].

The result in *Beacon Looms* depended almost entirely on the language in § 405(a)(2) that reasonable efforts to affix notice need begin only "after the omission has been discovered." Judge Sand reasoned that since "one cannot 'discover' an omission that has been deliberate," 552 F.Supp. at 1310, to permit the cure of deliberate omissions would do violence to the unambiguous "plain meaning" of the statute. * * *

With due respect, we cannot agree with *Beacon Looms.* The operative language of the statute in this context comes at the beginning of § 405(a), covers all three methods of cure, and is not restricted in any way. The language relied on by Judge Sand, which comes at the end of § 405(a)(2), is relevant only with respect to unmarked copies that have been publicly distributed in the United States. More important, the premise of the argument—namely, that a deliberate omission cannot be "discovered"—is unsound. As discussed above, an assignee or licensee may effect cure under § 405(a)(2) on behalf of itself and its assignor or licensor. In such a situation—the very one presented in this case—no violence is done to the statutory language by saying that the omission, though deliberate on the part of the assignor or licensor, was "discovered" by the person later attempting to cure it. Similarly, a deliberate omission at a lower level of a corporate hierarchy might well be "discovered," in realistic terms, by someone at a higher level. Instances like these at least indicate that the "discovered" language does not reveal a plain intent to exclude all deliberate omissions. * * *

* * * We therefore conclude that the omission of notice from the toys, even if deliberate on Takara's part, was subject to cure under § 405(a)(2), and we pass on to the question whether Hasbro in fact effectuated cure.

Apart from Sparkle's contention that Hasbro committed fraud on the Copyright Office [the court's discussion of this issue is omitted], there is no dispute that Hasbro validly registered its copyrights in the Takara designs within five years of publication of the unmarked toys, thus satisfying one of the two requirements for cure under § 405(a)(2). Sparkle admits also that Hasbro has affixed notice to all of the toys since sold under its authority in the United States and elsewhere. It argues, however, that Hasbro did not make "a reasonable effort" to affix notice to toys from the unmarked batch initially produced by Takara and thus failed to satisfy the second requirement of § 405(a)(2).   * * *

We are content, however, to leave undecided the question whether Hasbro would be obligated under § 405(a)(2) to make a reasonable effort to affix notice even with respect to unmarked toys distributed in the United States by persons other than itself or Takara.   At this juncture, Sparkle has yet to produce credible evidence that any of the unmarked toys have been publicly distributed in the United States *at all*, let alone evidence of who distributed them.   Whether any unmarked toys were introduced into the United States and, if so, who introduced them and what efforts to mark them would be reasonable are questions that can be resolved at trial when Hasbro seeks a permanent injunction.   * * *

Turning finally to Sparkle's claim that it should have been recognized as an innocent infringer under § 405(b), we think the record did not contain sufficient information for the district judge to have decided this issue, and he properly declined to do so.   However, it should be promptly dealt with, either on an application by Hasbro for a permanent injunction or on one by Sparkle for a declaration of its rights.

Affirmed.

NOTES AND QUESTIONS ON OMISSION OF NOTICE

(1) For publications subject to the mandatory notice provisions, the "reasonable effort" to add notice after the omission has been discovered[g] that is required to effect cure under § 405(a)(2) does not extend to copies already distributed to the public.   It does extend, however, to copies in the hands of distributors and retailers, in addition to those still in the possession of the copyright owner.   See Lifshitz v. Walter Drake & Sons, Inc., 806 F.2d 1426 (9th Cir.1986) (lack of effort to remedy omission on copies held by an independent distributor prevented cure); Shapiro & Son Bedspread Corp. v. Royal Mills Associates, 764 F.2d 69 (2d Cir.1985) (reversing summary judgment against the copyright owner since the rapid turnover of retailers' inventory made efforts to add notice useless).

(2) According to § 405(a)(1), if notice was omitted from only a "relatively small number of copies," copyright protection is not endangered.   Is "relatively small number" to be taken in an absolute sense ("a few") or in a relative sense ("a small proportion of the total")?   Is an omission of notice from four hundred copies too many?   From four hundred out of a total of forty thousand?   Compare Original Appalachian Artworks, Inc. v.

---

g. When is an omission of copyright notice "discovered"? Compare Hardwick Airmasters, Inc. v. Lennox Indus., Inc., 78 F.3d 1332 (8th Cir.1996) (claimant discovers the omission when he learns that his rights have been infringed, even if unaware of the legal significance of the omission) with Charles Garnier, Paris v. Andin Int'l, Inc., 36 F.3d 1214 (1st Cir.1994) (focusing on when the claimant learned of the legal consequences of the omission). The latter case also held that the § 405(a)(2) requirement of notice on subsequently distributed copies applies even as to copies distributed after March 1, 1989, when mandatory notice was abolished.

Toy Loft, Inc., 684 F.2d 821 (11th Cir.1982) with Donald Frederick Evans & Associates, Inc. v. Continental Homes, Inc., 785 F.2d 897 (11th Cir.1986).

(3) Section 405(a)(3) states that an omission of notice by a third party will not invalidate the copyright if the owner had in writing conditioned the authorization to publish on use of the notice. Does this imply that omissions in violation of oral or implied conditions *are* divestive? If so, the rule is more restrictive than prior law. See Judge Learned Hand's resolution of a dispute between Superman and Captain Marvel in National Comics Pub., Inc. v. Fawcett Pub., Inc., 191 F.2d 594 (2d Cir.1951), supplemented, 198 F.2d 927 (1952).

(4) The notice requirement has been especially troublesome for authors who contribute to a "collective work," another term defined in § 101. The 1909 Act in § 19 required notice in the name of the "copyright proprietor." This created difficulties in light of the judicial tendency to view copyright as an indivisible bundle of rights. Since a partial assignment was impossible, anything less than a complete transfer of copyright created a mere license. Licensees were not "proprietors," and thus a notice in their name technically did not comply with the 1909 Act. The 1976 Act in § 404 specifically authorizes copyright notice in the name of the publisher of a collective work regardless of copyright ownership in the individual contributions. This solution was anticipated in Goodis v. United Artists Television, Inc., 425 F.2d 397 (2d Cir.1970), involving rights in the television series "The Fugitive." Even if the author of an article gives a journal or magazine a mere license to publish, notice in the name of the publisher is thus sufficient to secure the remedial advantage of § 401(d), and in the case of a pre–1989 publication, to preserve the validity of the author's copyright.[h] (Why are advertisements excepted under § 404(a)? See Canfield v. The Ponchatoula Times, 759 F.2d 493 (5th Cir.1985).) With respect to pre–1989 publications, a contributor who has not transferred the copyright is subject to the rather slight risk that an infringer who deals with the person named in the notice may successfully invoke the good faith use defense in § 406(a). How can the risk be avoided? What sort of showing is necessary to establish good faith under § 406(a)? Does good faith reliance on a license from the person named in the notice require some measure of reasonableness in an objective sense, or will a pure heart suffice? See Quinto v. Legal Times of Washington, Inc., 506 F.Supp. 554 (D.D.C.1981), involving a contribution to a law school newspaper.

(5) The 1976 Act in § 201(d)(2) rejects the concept of indivisibility. The rights comprising copyright may now be separately owned. What consequences does this have for the copyright notice as specified in § 401 and § 402? Both refer to "the name of the owner of copyright." Note the definitions of "copyright owner" and "transfer of copyright ownership" in § 101. Does all this imply that assignees and exclusive licensees of specific

---

h. What rights does the publisher of a collective work have with respect to material contributed by others? If a student contributes a case note to the law review, for example, who owns the movie rights? Section 201(c) provides an initial presumption. Authors may of course transfer greater rights. But cf. § 204(a).

rights should use their own names in the notice? An incorrect name will not threaten the validity of the copyright, even on pre–1989 publications. See § 406(a). Will it threaten loss of the remedial benefits of notice under § 401(d)?

(6) If, as in *Hasbro*, even deliberate omissions of notice on pre–1989 publications could be cured under § 405(a)(2), the usefulness of the notice requirement was substantially reduced. Users relying on the absence of notice receive a measure of protection in § 405(b), but even these "inno-cent" infringers may be forced to disgorge profits and discontinue use. The House Report could offer only this advice: "Persons who undertake major enterprises * * * should check the Copyright Office registration records before starting even where copies have been published without notice." H.R.Rep. p. 148.

With its tolerance of defective notice and its liberal opportunities for cure, the 1976 Act effectively emasculated the requirement of copyright notice. It was thus a short step to the 1988 amendments that formally eliminated the notice requirement.

(7) As *Hasbro* indicates, the notice requirements under § 401 of the 1976 Act are applicable to works published both "in the United States or elsewhere." Prior to the elimination of the notice requirement in 1989, publication abroad without notice of copyright could inject the work into the public domain, at least with respect to protection here.[i] As part of the 1994 legislation implementing the Uruguay Round Trade Agreement that created the World Trade Organization, Congress in § 104A of the Copy-right Act automatically restored copyright, as of Jan. 1, 1996, in foreign works that had fallen into the public domain in the United States because of non-compliance with statutory formalities such as notice or renewal of copyright. A restored copyright lasts for the remainder of the copyright term that the work would have enjoyed if it had not entered the public domain. To be eligible for restoration, the foreign work must not be in the public domain in its source country, it must not have been published in the United States within 30 days of its first publication abroad, and the author must be a national or domiciliary of a country other than the United States that belongs to the World Trade Organization or the Berne Convention or is covered by a Presidential proclamation. (Thus, copyright restoration does not apply to works by U.S. authors that entered the public domain because of non-compliance with the applicable formalities.)

Section 104A provides a measure of protection to users who have been exploiting a work in which copyright is restored in reliance on its former public domain status. Upon notice as described in the statute, such a

---

i. The status of works published abroad without notice of copyright prior to the effec-tive date of the 1976 Act is less certain. Compare Twin Books Corp. v. Walt Disney Co., 83 F.3d 1162 (9th Cir.1996) (adhering to Heim v. Universal Pictures Co., 154 F.2d 480 (2d Cir.1946), in holding that under the 1909 Act copyright in *Bambi, A Life in the Woods* was not lost due to its 1923 publication with-out notice in Germany) with 37 C.F.R. § 202.2(a)(3) (works first published abroad before Jan. 1, 1978, must have borne an adequate copyright notice).

"reliance party" must stop reproducing the work, but can continue to sell off existing stock for twelve months. They can also continue to exploit existing derivative works upon payment of "reasonable compensation."

DEPOSIT AND REGISTRATION

Section 407(a) of the Copyright Act requires the copyright owner to deposit in the Copyright Office "two complete copies of the best edition" of the work within three months after publication. (Note the singularly unhelpful definition of "best edition" in § 101. See 37 C.F.R. § 202.19.) Copyright Office regulations exempt some works and require only one copy of others. The deposits enrich the collections of the Library of Congress. (The Library, located in Washington just beyond the U.S. Supreme Court Building, is an architectural wonder too often overlooked.) A failure to make the required deposit has no immediate legal consequences; it may elicit, however, a demand from the Acquisitions Division of the Copyright Office. A refusal to comply with a demand for deposit leaves the copyright owner subject to the prescribed penalties. § 407(d). Note that forfeiture of copyright is *not* among them.[j]

A system of copyright registration has long been a feature of American copyright law. The Copyright Office once offered these justifications for the registration system:

a. *Value to copyright owners*

Registration provides, for authors and other copyright owners, a permanent and official record of their copyright claims. It furnishes them with proof of the existence of their works at a particular time and the facts supporting their copyright claims. Particularly important to them is the certificate of registration, which constitutes prima facie evidence of the stated facts and is generally accepted in trade circles as proof of copyright.

b. *Value to users*

Registration serves other purposes, perhaps even more important, for persons who wish to use copyright materials. It provides accessible official records from which they can obtain information regarding the existence and basis of a copyright claim, the extent of the claim (e.g., in a new version of a preexisting work), its

---

j. The constitutionality of the deposit requirement was sustained against fifth and first amendment challenges in Ladd v. Law & Technology Press, 762 F.2d 809 (9th Cir. 1985), cert. denied, 475 U.S. 1045 (1986). At the time, § 407 required deposit only upon publication with notice of copyright; the deposit thus could be seen as a kind of fee imposed on those who voluntarily sought the protection of the Act. Under the 1988 amendments, deposit is triggered by the mere fact of publication. Does this alter the constitutional arguments?

duration, and its initial ownership.   In conjunction with the records of assignments and other transfers of ownership, it enables
users to trace title to the copyright.[k]

Registration is now governed by §§ 408–410. Both published and unpublished works may be registered. Since registration is intended in part to
inaugurate an official record of the copyright so that ownership may be
determined, the registration provisions should be viewed together with
§ 205 on recordation of transfers and other documents. Copyright Office
records can be accessed through Westlaw and over the Internet at the
Copyright Office's website.[l]

Despite the benefits ascribed to registration, the Copyright Act eschews
the most obvious means of insuring a comprehensive public record. Section 408(a) is explicit that "registration is not a condition of copyright
protection." This is in keeping with the Act's general abhorrence of
forfeiture.[m] Since registration is not compulsory, Congress determined
that it "should therefore be induced in some practical way." H.R.Rep. p.
158. This effort is carried forward in §§ 410–412.

Section 410(c) offers an inducement to registration by providing that a
certificate of registration obtained within five years of first publication is
prima facie evidence of the validity of the copyright and of the facts stated
in the certificate, thus shifting to an alleged infringer the burden of
contesting ownership and copyrightability. (Why the five-year limitation?
Are more tardy registrations less likely to be reliable?) Commencement of
an infringement action is itself barred "until registration of the copyright
claim has been made." § 411(a). (The exception to the registration requirement for "Berne Convention works" was added in 1988 to accommodate our treaty obligations; the Berne Convention does not require the
elimination of formalities with respect to domestic works.) The limitation
of remedies in § 412 for infringements of unregistered works provides a
particularly compelling incentive to register. The speculative nature of
actual damages and profits often precludes their recovery in copyright
litigation—preserving the ability to recover statutory damages, § 504(c),
and attorney's fees, § 505, is thus of particular importance. Finally, the
practical effect of registration in enhancing the marketability of the work is
itself a significant inducement.

Registration of copyright is a straight-forward process. It must be
done on a form prescribed by the Copyright Office.[n] The current registra-

---

k. Report of the Register of Copyrights
on the General Revision of the U.S. Copyright Law, House Comm. on the Judiciary,
87th Cong., 1st Sess. 72 (Comm.Print 1961),
in 2 Studies on Copyr. 1199, 1272 (1963).
See generally Kaplan, The Registration of
Copyright, Copyr.Law Revision Study No. 17
(1958), in 1 Studies on Copyr. 325 (1963).

Most countries have no official system
for registration of copyright or recordation of

transfers. How can users of works carry out
business transactions under such a regime?
See id.

l. http://lcweb.loc.gov/copyright

m. But recall § 405(a)(2), which requires registration within five years in order
to cure an omission of notice on pre–1989
publications.

n. The Copyright Office has created
several classes of works, each with its own

tion fee is $20, but the Register is authorized to adjust the fee periodically for inflation. § 708(b). The form and fee must be accompanied by the deposit specified in § 408(b). In general, deposit of one copy of unpublished and two copies of published works is required. For some published works, the regulations provide that deposit of a single copy will suffice. For others, "identifying material" such as a photograph is sufficient. See 37 C.F.R. §§ 202.20, 202.21. A modern Michelangelo, for example, is not required to ship a copy of his *David* to the Copyright Office. The same deposit will satisfy both the mandatory deposit requirement of § 407 and the registration requirements of § 408 if accompanied by the appropriate form and fee. See generally Hawes, Copyright Registration Practice (Clark Boardman Callaghan).

The Examining Division of the Copyright Office determines whether "the material deposited constitutes copyrightable subject matter and that the other legal and formal requirements of this title have been met." § 410(a). The scope of the Examining Division's inquiry is limited. It will of course take note of obvious discrepancies between the application and the deposited copies, but it does not undertake to verify the information supplied by the applicant; in particular, it does not attempt to verify the applicant's claim to be the author of the work.

The Copyright Office operates under a "rule of doubt"—a work will be registered as long as there is at least a reasonable doubt as to whether the work is copyrightable. Only a small percentage of the applications for registration are ultimately rejected.° The registration process can take

registration form. 37 C.F.R. § 202.3. Form TX (reproduced in the Statutory Supplement) is used for "nondramatic literary works"; Form PA—"works of the performing arts"; Form VA—"works of the visual arts"; Form SR—"sound recordings; Form SE—"serials." Short versions of the first three forms are available if the applicant is the sole author and copyright owner and if the work does not contain substantial preexisting material and is not a work made for hire. There is a twenty-four hour automated "hotline" for those desiring registration forms: (202) 707–9100. The Copyright Public Information Office ((202) 707–3000) provides more personal attention. Application forms can also be downloaded from the Copyright Office website, and photocopies are acceptable. The Copyright Office is also experimenting with an on-line registration system.

o. Appeal from an adverse decision of the Examining Division can be taken to the Copyright Office Board of Appeals. Section 701(d) subjects the actions of the Copyright Office to judicial review under the Administrative Procedure Act (5 U.S.C.A. § 551 et seq.). In reflecting on the appropriate scope of judicial review, consider the comments of Judge Silberman, concurring in Atari Games Corp. v. Oman, 888 F.2d 878 (D.C.Cir.1989): "We must bear in mind that when we review the Register's determination to accept or reject an application for registration, we do not make a final decision on the copyrightability of the item. In fact, as the majority opinion recognizes, the Copyright Office's imprimatur is worth only a rebuttable presumption as to copyrightability in an infringement action. * * * Every time the Register denies registration for too little creativity it cannot be expected to issue an opinion that compares with the learned offerings of my colleagues. I think that is why the courts have generally thought abuse of discretion to be the appropriate standard to review the Office's denial of a registration. Since the applicant can gain full judicial review of copyrightability in an infringement action, the costs of forcing too fine an analysis and too extensive an from one to four months, but "special handling" to reduce the processing time is available for an enhanced fee.

The volume of registrations is impressive. The Copyright Office processes over 600,000 registrations per year. Unpublished works account for more than one-third of the total.

explanation of a denial of registration are not worth the benefits—particularly when reviewing a question which has unavoidably subjective aspects such as how much creativity is sufficient to force the Copyright Office to register a proffered work."

CHAPTER 2

THE SUBJECT MATTER OF COPYRIGHT

SECTION 1. ORIGINAL WORKS OF AUTHORSHIP

Burrow–Giles Lithographic Co. v. Sarony

Supreme Court of the United States, 1884.
111 U.S. 53, 4 S.Ct. 279.

■ MILLER, J. This is a writ of error to the Circuit Court for the Southern District of New York. Plaintiff [in error] is a lithographer, and defendant a photographer, with large business in those lines in the city of New York. The suit was commenced by an action at law in which Sarony was plaintiff and the lithographic company was defendant, the plaintiff charging the defendant with violating his copyright in regard to a photograph, the title of which is "Oscar Wilde, No. 18." A jury being waived, the court made a finding of facts on which a judgment in favor of the plaintiff was rendered for the sum of $600 for the plates and 85,000 copies sold and exposed to sale, and $10 for copies found in his possession, as penalties under section 4965 of the Revised Statutes. * * *

The constitutional question is not free from difficulty. The eighth section of the first article of the Constitution is the great repository of the powers of Congress, and by the eighth clause of that section Congress is authorized "to promote the progress of science and useful arts, by securing, for limited times to authors and inventors, the exclusive right to their respective writings and discoveries." The argument here is that a photograph is not a writing nor the production of an author. * * *

It is insisted in argument, that a photograph being a reproduction on paper of the exact features of some natural object or of some person, is not a writing of which the producer is the author.

Section 4952 of the Revised Statutes places photographs in the same class as things which may be copyrighted with "books, maps, charts, dramatic or musical compositions, engravings, cuts, prints, paintings, drawings, statues, statuary, and models or designs intended to be perfected as works of the fine arts." * * *

The first Congress of the United States, sitting immediately after the formation of the Constitution, enacted that the "author or authors of any map, chart, book, or books, being a citizen or resident of the United States, shall have the sole right and liberty of printing, reprinting, publishing, and

Oscar Wilde—the Sarony photograph

vending the same for the period of fourteen years from the recording of the title thereof in the clerk's office, as afterwards directed." 1 Stat. p. 124, § 1.

This statute not only makes maps and charts subjects of copyright, but mentions them before books in the order of designation. The second section of an act to amend this act, approved April 29, 1802, 2 Stat. 171, enacts that from the first day of January thereafter he who shall invent and design, engrave, etch or work, or from his own works shall cause to be designed and engraved, etched or worked, any historical or other print or prints shall have the same exclusive right for the term of 14 years from recording the title thereof as prescribed by law.

By the first section of the act of February 3, 1831, 4 Stat. 436, entitled "An act to amend the several acts respecting copyright," musical compositions and cuts, in connection with prints and engravings, are added, and the period of protection is extended to 28 years. The caption or title of this act uses the word "copyright" for the first time in the legislation of Congress.

The construction placed upon the Constitution by the first act of 1790, and the act of 1802, by the men who were contemporary with its formation, many of whom were members of the convention which framed it, is of itself entitled to very great weight, and when it is remembered that the rights thus established have not been disputed during a period of nearly a century, it is almost conclusive.

Unless, therefore, photographs can be distinguished in the classification on this point from the maps, charts, designs, engravings, etchings, cuts, and other prints, it is difficult to see why Congress cannot make them the subject of copyright as well as the others.

These statutes certainly answer the objection that books only, or writing in the limited sense of a book and its author, are within the constitutional provision. Both these words are susceptible of a more enlarged definition than this. An author in that sense is "he to whom anything owes its origin; originator; maker; one who completes a work of science or literature." Worcester. So, also, no one would now claim that the word "writing" in this clause of the Constitution, though the only word used as to subjects in regard to which authors are to be secured, is limited to the actual script of the author, and excludes books and all other printed matter. By writings in that clause is meant the literary productions of those authors, and Congress very properly has declared these to include all forms of writing, printing, engraving, etching, etc., by which the ideas in the mind of the author are given visible expression. The only reason why photographs were not included in the extended list in the act of 1802 is probably that they did not exist, as photography as an art was then unknown, and the scientific principle on which it rests, and the chemicals and machinery by which it is operated, have all been discovered long since that statute was enacted.

Nor is it to be supposed that the framers of the Constitution did not understand the nature of copyright and the objects to which it was commonly applied, for copyright, as the exclusive right of a man to the production of his own genius or intellect, existed in England at that time, and the contest in the English courts, finally decided by a very close vote in the House of Lords, whether the statute of 8 Anne, c. 19, which authorized copyright for a limited time, was a restraint to that extent on the common law or not, was then recent.   * * *

We entertain no doubt that the Constitution is broad enough to cover an act authorizing copyright of photographs, so far as they are representatives of original intellectual conceptions of the author.

But it is said that an engraving, a painting, a print, does embody the intellectual conception of its author, in which there is novelty, invention, originality, and therefore comes within the purpose of the Constitution in securing its exclusive use or sale to its author, while the photograph is the mere mechanical reproduction of the physical features or outlines of some object, animate or inanimate, and involves no originality of thought or any novelty in the intellectual operation connected with its visible reproduction in shape of a picture.   That while the effect of light on the prepared plate may have been a discovery in the production of these pictures, and patents could properly be obtained for the combination of the chemicals, for their application to the paper or other surface, for all the machinery by which the light reflected from the object was thrown on the prepared plate, and for all the improvements in this machinery, and in the materials, the remainder of the process is merely mechanical, with no place for novelty, invention, or originality.   It is simply the manual operation, by the use of these instruments and preparations, of transferring to the plate the visible representation of some existing object, the accuracy of this representation being its highest merit.

This may be true in regard to the ordinary production of a photograph, and, further, that in such case a copyright is no protection.   On the question as thus stated we decide nothing.

In regard, however, to the kindred subject of patents for invention, they cannot by law be issued to the inventor until the novelty, the utility, and the actual discovery or invention by the claimant have been established by proof before the Commissioner of Patents;   and when he has secured such a patent, and undertakes to obtain redress for a violation of his right in a court of law, the question of invention, of novelty, of originality, is always open to examination.   Our copyright system has no such provision for previous examination by a proper tribunal as to the originality of the book, map, or other matter offered for copyright.   A deposit of two copies of the article or work with the Librarian of Congress, with the name of the author and its title page, is all that is necessary to secure a copyright.   It is, therefore, much more important that when the supposed author sues for a violation of his copyright, the existence of those facts of originality, of intellectual production, of thought, and conception on the part of the author should be proved, than in the case of a patent right.   In the case before us we think this has been done.

The third finding of facts says, in regard to the photograph in question, that it is a "useful, new, harmonious, characteristic, and graceful picture, and that plaintiff made the same . . . entirely from his own original mental conception, to which he gave visible form by posing the said Oscar Wilde in front of the camera, selecting and arranging the costume, draperies, and other various accessories in said photograph, arranging the subject so as to present graceful outlines, arranging and disposing the light and shade, suggesting and evoking the desired expression, and from such disposition, arrangement, or representation, made entirely by plaintiff, he produced the picture in suit."

These findings, we think, show this photograph to be an original work of art, the product of plaintiff's intellectual invention, of which plaintiff is the author, and of a class of inventions for which the Constitution intended that Congress should secure to him the exclusive right to use, publish and sell, as it has done by section 4952 of the Revised Statutes.   * * *

The judgment of the Circuit Court is accordingly affirmed.[a]

NOTES AND QUESTIONS

(1) The subject matter of copyright as described in § 102(a) consists of "original works of authorship."   What does this encompass?   Recall that the grant of constitutional authority speaks of "Authors" and their "Writings."   The 1909 Act in § 4 had addressed "all the writings of an author." This phrase raised the issue of whether the scope of the 1909 Act was intended to be coextensive with the constitutional grant, in effect making decisions on copyrightability a matter of constitutional interpretation.   To avoid this result, courts interpreted § 4 more narrowly than the constitutional clause.   In explaining the change in phraseology in the 1976 Act, the House Report offers these comments: "In using the phrase 'original works of authorship,' rather than 'all the writings of an author' now in section 4 of the statute, the committee's purpose is to avoid exhausting the constitutional power of Congress to legislate in this field, and to eliminate the uncertainties arising from the latter phrase."   (H.R.Rep. p. 51.)

a. In the Trade–Mark Cases, 100 U.S. 82 (1879), the question was whether federal power to enact trademark registration laws could be supported under Article I, Section 8. Congress had not attempted to invoke the commerce power, and the trademark statute of 1870, 16 Stat. 198, was part of a revision of the copyright and patent laws.   Justice Miller, writing for a unanimous Court, said that a trademark could not be considered the discovery of an inventor nor the writing of an author.   "While the word *writings* may be liberally construed, as it has been, to include original designs for engravings, prints, &c., it is only such as are *original,* and are founded in the creative powers of the mind.   The writings which are to be protected are the fruits of intellectual labor, embodied in the form of books, prints, engravings, and the like.   The trade-mark may be, and generally is, the adoption of something already in existence as the distinctive symbol of the party using it."

"Original works of authorship" takes its meaning from the more general concepts of "Authors" and "Writings." But what, in turn, do these latter terms mean? Note the definitions offered by Justice Miller in *Sarony*. Recall also the Court's description of "writings" in Goldstein v. California, quoted at p. 22 supra.

(2) Are all photographs "writings"? Is Sarony's photograph a "writing"? Are you comfortable with the manner in which the Court resolved the latter question?

What about "the ordinary production of a photograph," the question that the Court reserves? French law took a narrow view of what photographs qualify for copyright, protecting only those of an "artistic or documentary character." (The limitation was dropped in 1985.) So did English law until the 1956 statute declared that copyright would subsist in photographs "irrespective of artistic quality." See Gorman, Copyright Protection for the Collection and Representation of Facts, 76 Harv.L.Rev. 1569, 1596 (1963) (a valuable survey of many of the matters considered in this section), supplemented in his Fact or Fancy? The Implications for Copyright, 29 J.Copyr.Soc. 560 (1982).[b]

Bleistein v. Donaldson Lithographing Co.

Supreme Court of the United States, 1903.
188 U.S. 239, 23 S.Ct. 298.

MR. JUSTICE HOLMES delivered the opinion of the court:

This case comes here from the United States Circuit Court of Appeals for the Sixth Circuit by writ of error. * * * It is an action brought by the plaintiffs in error to recover the penalties prescribed for infringements of copyrights. Rev.Stat. §§ 4952, 4956, 4965 (U.S.Comp.Stat.1901, pp. 3406, 3407, 3414), amended by act of March 3, 1891 (26 Stat. at L. 1109, chap. 565), and act of March 2, 1895 (28 Stat. at L. 965, chap. 194). The alleged infringements consisted in the copying in reduced form of three chromolithographs prepared by employees of the plaintiffs for advertisements of a circus owned by one Wallace. Each of the three contained a portrait of Wallace in the corner and lettering bearing some slight relation to the scheme of decoration, indicating the subject of the design and the fact that the reality was to be seen at the circus. One of the designs was of an ordinary ballet, one of a number of men and women, described as the Stirk family, performing on bicycles, and one of groups of men and women whitened to represent statues. The Circuit Court directed a verdict for the defendant on the ground that the chromolithographs were not within the protection of the copyright law, and this ruling was sustained by the Circuit Court of Appeals. Courier Lithographing Co. v. Donaldson Lithographing Co., 104 F. 993.

b. For a valuable cultural and historical exploration of photography and copyright, including material on Wilde and Sarony, see J. Gaines, Contested Culture: The Image, the Voice, and the Law (1991), which also examines other famous copyright cases.

There was evidence warranting the inference that the designs belonged to the plaintiffs, they having been produced by persons employed and paid by the plaintiffs in their establishment to make those very things. Gill v. United States, 160 U.S. 426, 435; Colliery Engineer Co. v. United Correspondence Schools Co., 94 F. 152; Carte v. Evans, 27 F. 861. It fairly might be found also that the copyrights were taken out in the proper names. One of them was taken out in the name of the Courier Company and the other two in the name of the Courier Lithographing Company. The former was the name of an unincorporated joint-stock association formed under the laws of New York (Laws of 1894, chap. 235), and made up of the plaintiffs, the other a trade variant on that name. * * *

We shall do no more than mention the suggestion that painting and engraving unless for a mechanical end are not among the useful arts, the progress of which Congress is empowered by the Constitution to promote. The Constitution does not limit the useful to that which satisfies immediate bodily needs. Burrow–Giles Lithographing Co. v. Sarony, 111 U.S. 53. It is obvious also that the plaintiff's case is not affected by the fact, if it be one, that the pictures represent actual groups—visible things. They seem from the testimony to have been composed from hints or description, not from sight of a performance. But even if they had been drawn from the life, that fact would not deprive them of protection. The opposite proposition would mean that a portrait by Velasquez or Whistler was common property because others might try their hand on the same face. Others are free to copy the original. They are not free to copy the copy. Blunt v. Patten, 400 Fed.Cas. No. 1,580. See Kelly v. Morris, L.R. 1 Eq. 697; Morris v. Wright, L.R. 5 Ch. 279. The copy is the personal reaction of an individual upon nature. Personality always contains something unique. It expresses its singularity even in handwriting, and a very modest grade of art has in it something irreducible, which is one man's alone. That something he may copyright unless there is a restriction in the words of the act.

If there is a restriction it is not to be found in the limited pretensions of these particular works. The least pretentious picture has more originality in it than directories and the like, which may be copyrighted. Drone, Copyright, 153. See Henderson v. Tompkins, 60 F. 758, 765. The amount of training required for humbler efforts than those before us is well indicated by Ruskin. "If any young person, after being taught what is, in polite circles, called 'drawing,' will try to copy the commonest piece of real *work*,—suppose a lithograph on the title page of a new opera air, or a woodcut in the cheapest illustrated newspaper of the day—they will find themselves entirely beaten." Elements of Drawing, first ed. 3. There is no reason to doubt that these prints in their *ensemble* and in all their details, in their design and particular combinations of figures, lines and colors, are the original work of the plaintiffs' designer. If it be necessary, there is express testimony to that effect. It would be pressing the defendant's right to the verge, if not beyond, to leave the question of originality to the jury upon the evidence in this case, as was done in Hegeman v. Springer, 110 F. 374.

The Stirk Family

* * * Certainly works are not the less connected with the fine arts because their pictorial quality attracts the crowd and therefore gives them a real use—if use means to increase trade and to help to make money. A picture is none the less a picture and none the less a subject of copyright that it is used for an advertisement. And if pictures may be used to advertise soap, or the theatre, or monthly magazines, as they are, they may be used to advertise a circus. Of course, the ballet is as legitimate a subject for illustration as any other. A rule cannot be laid down that would excommunicate the paintings of Degas. * * *

It would be a dangerous undertaking for persons trained only to the law to constitute themselves final judges of the worth of pictorial illustrations, outside of the narrowest and most obvious limits. At the one extreme some works of genius would be sure to miss appreciation. Their very novelty would make them repulsive until the public had learned the new language in which their author spoke. It may be more than doubted, for instance, whether the etchings of Goya or the paintings of Manet would have been sure of protection when seen for the first time. At the other end, copyright would be denied to pictures which appealed to a public less educated than the judge. Yet if they command the interest of any public, they have a commercial value—it would be bold to say that they have not an aesthetic and educational value—and the taste of any public is not to be treated with contempt. It is an ultimate fact for the moment, whatever may be our hopes for a change. That these pictures had their worth and their success is sufficiently shown by the desire to reproduce them without regard to the plaintiffs' rights. See Henderson v. Tompkins, 60 F. 758, 765. We are of opinion that there was evidence that the plaintiffs have rights entitled to the protection of the law.

The judgment of the Circuit Court of Appeals is reversed; the judgment of the Circuit Court is also reversed and the cause remanded to that court with directions to set aside the verdict and grant a new trial.

■ MR. JUSTICE HARLAN, with whom concurred MR. JUSTICE MCKENNA, dissenting:

Judges Lurton, Day and Severens, of the Circuit Court of Appeals, concurred in affirming the judgment of the District Court. Their views were thus expressed in an opinion delivered by Judge Lurton: "What we hold is this: That if a chromo, lithograph, or other print, engraving, or picture has no other use than that of a mere advertisement, and no value aside from this function, it would not be promotive of the useful arts, within the meaning of the constitutional provision, to protect the 'author' in the exclusive use thereof, and the copyright statute should not be construed as including such a publication, if any other construction is admissible. If a mere label simply designating or describing an article to which it is attached, and which has no value separated from the article, does not come within the constitutional clause upon the subject of copyright, it must follow that a pictorial illustration designed and useful only as an advertisement, and having no intrinsic value other than its function as an advertisement, must be equally without the obvious meaning of the Constitution. It must have some connection with the fine arts to give it intrinsic value, and that it shall have is the meaning which we attach to the act of June 18, 1874 (18 Stat. at L. 78, chap. 301, U.S.Comp.Stat.1901, p. 3411), amending the provisions of the copyright law. We are unable to discover anything useful or meritorious in the design copyrighted by the plaintiffs in error other than as an advertisement of acts to be done or exhibited to the public in Wallace's show. No evidence, aside from the deductions which are to be drawn from the prints themselves, was offered to show that these designs had any original artistic qualities. The jury could not reasonably have found merit or value aside from the purely business object of advertising a show, and the instruction to find for the defendant was not error. Many other points have been urged as justifying the result reached in the court below. We find it unnecessary to express any opinion upon them, in view of the conclusion already announced. The judgment must be affirmed." Courier Lithographing Co. v. Donaldson Lithographing Co., 104 F. 993, 996.

I entirely concur in these views, and therefore dissent from the opinion and judgment of this court. The clause of the Constitution giving Congress power to promote the progress of science and useful arts, by securing for limited terms to authors and inventors the exclusive right to their respective works and discoveries, does not, as I think, embrace a mere advertisement of a circus.

■ MR. JUSTICE McKENNA authorizes me to say that he also dissents.

NOTES AND QUESTIONS

(1) Justice Holmes' famous opinion for the Court barely responds to the dissenting view that the posters were disqualified from copyright because they were advertisements. Yet, "there can be no question that Judge Lurton [in the opinion for the Court of Appeals] * * * correctly and fairly stated what was then generally thought to be the law with reference to advertising matter being the subject of copyright." Sanborn, J., in Ansehl v. Puritan Pharmaceutical Co., 61 F.2d 131, 134 (8th Cir.), cert. denied, 287 U.S. 666 (1932). *Ansehl* reviews the decisions that *Bleistein* effectively overruled and describes the subsequent acceptance of advertising material as a subject of copyright. *Should* materials such as magazine advertisements and television commercials be considered works of authorship eligible for copyright protection? What of labels and other packaging materials? See p. 578 infra. For an attempt to revive the older view, see Linder and Howard, Why Copyright Law Should Not Protect Advertising, 62 Ore.L.Rev. 231 (1983).

(2) Would Justice Holmes agree with the approach pursued by Justice Miller in upholding the copyrightability of Sarony's photograph of Oscar Wilde? Can judgments of aesthetic merit be avoided in determining eligibility for copyright? Consider also whether the standard of copyrightability should differ as applied to the various kinds of works listed in § 102.

At the beginning of the revision process leading to the 1976 Act, the 1961 Report of the Register of Copyrights recommended that in the new statute a copyrightable work "must represent an appreciable amount of creative authorship." House Comm. on the Judiciary, 87th Cong., 1st Sess., Copyright Law Revision 9 (1961). This standard was later abandoned. See the Register's Supplemental Report 3 (Comm. Print 1965). The House Report, commenting on the phrase "original works of authorship" in § 102, says that it is "intended to incorporate without change the standard of originality established by the courts under the present copyright statute. This standard does not include requirements of novelty, ingenuity, or esthetic merit, and there is no intention to enlarge the standard of copyright to require them." H.R.Rep. p. 51.[c]

Congress apparently has determined that works falling within the eight illustrative categories in § 102 are "works of authorship." But there remains the problem of determining whether a particular work fits within one of these categories of authorship. Is a single sentence a "literary work"? Is a drawing that consists of a few lines on paper a "graphic work"? Should the amount of "creativity" matter?

ATARI GAMES CORP. V. OMAN, 979 F.2d 242 (D.C.Cir.1992). This was the second appeal by an applicant seeking copyright registration for a video game called BREAKOUT, claimed as an "audiovisual work". "BREAKOUT is a relatively early video game of comparative simplicity. The sound accompaniment is four basic tones. The screen shows the two players' scores at the top. The players move a 'paddle' to hit a 'ball' against a 'wall.' The wall is built of eight rows of rectangles arranged in four monochromatic stripes (red, amber, green, yellow). When the square blue ball hits a rectangle, the rectangle vanishes. When the ball breaks through the wall of rectangles to the empty space beyond, it ricochets at greatly increased speed until it reemerges. Both the ball's speed and the size of the rectangular paddle change during play. The ball's movement does not follow the laws of physics; instead, the angle of the ball's rebound depends solely on where it impacts the paddle." In Judge Ginsburg's prior opinion at 888 F.2d 878 (D.C.Cir.1989), the court had reversed the District Court's summary judgment in favor of the Register, saying that it could not determine what standard the Copyright Office had used in denying registration. On remand the Register again refused registration and the District Court again affirmed on a summary judgment. The Court of Appeals again reversed. "[W]e hold that the rejection of BREAKOUT was unreasonable when measured against the Supreme Court's instruction that 'the requisite level of creativity [for copyrightability] is extremely low.'

c. The legislative history of the 1976 Act as it relates to the creativity requirement is reviewed in VerSteeg, Sparks in the Tinderbox: *Feist*, "Creativity," and the Legislative History of the 1976 Copyright Act, 56 U.Pitt.L.Rev. 549 (1995).

Feist Publications v. Rural Tel. Serv. Co., 499 U.S. 340, 345 (1991) [p. 79 infra]."

"Viewing BREAKOUT 'as a whole,' the Register found 'no original authorship in either the selection or arrangement of the images or their components.' " Judge Ginsburg found this conclusion difficult to reconcile with the standard of copyrightability announced in *Feist*. "To be copyrightable, a work must be fixed, original (i.e., not copied), and a 'work of authorship.' 17 U.S.C. § 102; see Feist, 499 U.S. at 345–46 (requirements for copyrightability). The only dispute now presented concerns BREAKOUT's qualification as a 'work of authorship,' which on statutory and constitutional grounds necessitates a modicum of creativity. See Feist, 499 U.S. 345–46, 362–64. * * * In *Feist,* decided eleven months after the Register reconsidered BREAKOUT, the Supreme Court extensively discussed and elucidated the creativity standard; the Court left no doubt that the requirement is indeed modest:

> [T]he requisite level of creativity is extremely low; even a slight amount will suffice. The vast majority of works make the grade quite easily, as they possess some creative spark, 'no matter how crude, humble or obvious' it might be.

Id., 499 U.S. at 345 (quoting M. Nimmer & D. Nimmer, Copyright § 1.08[C][1]). * * * We can accept the Register's assertion that the individual graphic elements of each screen are not copyrightable. Even so, BREAKOUT would be copyrightable if the requisite level of creativity is met by either the individual screens or the relationship of each screen to the others and/or the accompanying sound effects. * * * We are left with the impression that the Register may have so trained his observation on the details of the individual screens that he neglected genuinely to consider the sequential aspect of the work."

The case was remanded to the District Court with instructions to return it again to the Register for renewed consideration.

NOTES AND QUESTIONS

(1) John Muller & Co. v. New York Arrows Soccer Team, 802 F.2d 989 (8th Cir.1986), concerned an attempt to obtain copyright registration for the insignia of a soccer team. The insignia looked something like this:

[F2708]

A "work of authorship"? The Eighth Circuit upheld a denial of registration. A similar result was reached in another case involving a fabric design consisting of "two inch stripes, with small grid squares superimposed." The Register's finding that the work did not meet the "minimal amount of creative authorship" necessary for copyright was affirmed. Jon Woods Fashions, Inc. v. Curran, 8 U.S.P.Q. 1870 (S.D.N.Y.1988). Compare Prince Group, Inc. v. MTS Products, 967 F.Supp. 121 (S.D.N.Y.1997), agreeing with the Copyright Office that the plaintiff's polka dot fabric design was copyrightable; the dots were not perfect circles nor uniformly colored and were arranged in imperfect diagonal lines.

(2) According to a Copyright Office regulation, the following are not subject to copyright: "Words and short phrases such as names, titles, and slogans; familiar symbols or designs; mere variations of typographic ornamentation, lettering or coloring; mere listing of ingredients or contents." 37 C.F.R. § 202.1(a). What is the justification for this exclusion? In Magic Marketing, Inc. v. Mailing Services, Inc., 634 F.Supp. 769 (W.D.Pa. 1986), the regulation was invoked to reject a claim of infringement relating to phrases such as "Priority Message: Contents Require Immediate Attention" and "Gift Check Enclosed" printed on envelopes. The regulation was also cited in Publications Int'l Ltd. v. Meredith Corp., 88 F.3d 473 (7th Cir.1996), which rejected plaintiff's claim of copyright in recipes for delicacies such as Swiss 'n Cheddar Cheeseball appearing in *Discover Dannon— 50 Fabulous Recipes with Yogurt*; the listings of ingredients and instructions were mere facts and processes, with no creative expression. But in Applied Innovations Inc. v. Regents of Univ. of Minnesota, 876 F.2d 626 (8th Cir.1989), the Eighth Circuit held the regulation inapplicable to "short, simple, declarative sentences" such as "No one seems to understand me" and "I am a good mixer" used in a personality test.

Is the requirement of sufficient "authorship" best understood as a qualitative or a quantitative standard?

(3) An increasing number of judicial opinions draw an explicit distinction between the requirements of "originality" and "work of authorship." The opinion in *Atari* is one example.[d] The Copyright Office takes a similar approach. See Compendium II of Copyright Office Practices § 202. Does § 102(a) encourage such usage? (Compare the terminology in the first and second sentences.) Other decisions subsume both requirements under a more expansive concept of "originality." See, e.g., Feist Publications, Inc. v. Rural Telephone Service Co., p. 79 infra: "Original, as the term is used in copyright, means only that the work was independently created by the author (as opposed to copied from other works), and that it possesses at least some minimal degree of creativity."

(4) Is the determination of copyrightability an issue for the jury in an infringement action? In denying a motion for summary judgment in Lotus Development Corp. v. Borland Int'l, Inc., 788 F.Supp. 78 (D.Mass.1992), Judge Keeton offered the following comments on the copyrightability of elements of the user interface of the Lotus 1–2–3 spreadsheet program that were allegedly copied by defendant Borland in its Quattro spreadsheet program:

"The legal test for determining copyrightability * * * is a standard requiring an evaluative mixed law-fact determination, as distinguished from a bright-line rule calling for a finding about disputed historical facts such as who did what, where, and when. Moreover, this standard is far more heavily loaded with public policy implications than most other standards more commonly used in law, of which the negligence standard is an example. Juries applying the copyrightability standard would not be required or even permitted to explain their reasoning. They would be free as a practical matter to reach decisions inconsistent with the balance struck by Congress, as interpreted by the courts. * * *

"No provision of the Copyright Act declares explicitly that issues of fact bearing on copyrightability shall be submitted to juries, or instead shall be decided nonjury. Nor does the Constitution, including the Seventh Amendment. * * * A determination that issues of copyrightability are to be resolved by juries would have such severe adverse effects on the aim of assuring that like cases are treated alike and on the complexity and cost of litigation in computer software copyright cases that in practical effect the scope of copyright protection Congress manifestly intended could not be achieved. * * *

"For all these reasons, I reach the tentative conclusion * * * that at least in the circumstances of this case (and probably more generally, though I need not so determine here), the issue or issues of copyrightability, including any fact questions bearing upon them, must be determined by the court, not the jury."

---

d. For another example, see Baltimore Orioles, Inc. v. Major League Baseball Players Ass'n, 805 F.2d 663, 668 n. 6 (7th Cir. 1986), cert. denied, 480 U.S. 941 (1987). "Although the requirements of independent creation and intellectual labor both flow from the constitutional prerequisite of authorship and the statutory reference to original works of authorship, courts often engender confusion by referring to both concepts by the term 'originality.' For the sake of clarity, we shall use 'originality' to mean independent authorship and 'creativity' to denote intellectual labor."

Does the force of Judge Keeton's reasoning carry beyond computer software litigation?[e]

Alfred Bell & Co., Limited v. Catalda Fine Arts, Inc.

United States Court of Appeals, Second Circuit, 1951.
191 F.2d 99.

■ Before CHASE, CLARK and FRANK, CIRCUIT JUDGES.

The facts are reported in the opinions of the district judge. See 74 F.Supp. 973, and 86 F.Supp. 399.

[The facts as stated by Judge Smith in the District Court were these:

"The plaintiff, a British print producer and dealer, member of the Fine Arts Trade Guild, copyrighted in the United States eight mezzotint engravings of old masters produced at its order by three mezzotint engravers.

"The defendants, a color lithographer, a dealer in lithographs and the dealer's president, produced and sold color lithographs of the eight mezzotints. * * *

"* * * The mezzotint method lends itself to a fairly realistic reproduction of oil paintings. It is a tedious process requiring skill and patience and is, therefore, rather expensive compared with modern color photographic processes.

"The artists employed to produce these mezzotint engravings in suit attempted faithfully to reproduce paintings in the mezzotint medium so that the basic idea, arrangement, and color scheme of each painting are those of the original artist. The mezzotint engraving process is performed by first rocking a copper plate, that is, drawing across the plate under pressure a hand tool having many fine and closely spaced teeth. The tool is drawn across the plate many times in various directions so that the plate is roughened by the process. The outlines of the engraving are then placed upon the plate either by tracing with carbon paper from a photograph of the original work which it is desired to reproduce in this medium or by a tracing taken from such a photograph on gelatine sheets transferred to the copper plate by rubbing carbon black or some similar substance in the lines of the tracing on the gelatine sheet and transferring of them by pressing the sheet upon the copper plate. With the image on the roughened plate the engraver then scrapes with a hand tool the picture upon the plate, obtaining light and shade effects by the depth of the scraping of the roughened plate or ground. When the plate is completed, trial prints are taken from it and it may be altered to make the final result to the satisfaction of the engraver. When it is completed and a satisfactory proof

---

e. See also Judge Easterbrook's comment in Pivot Point Int'l Inc. v. Charlene Prod., Inc., 932 F.Supp. 220 (N.D.Ill.1996), that whether plaintiff's mannequin heads were copyrightable "is a question of law, which the court will decide." But cf. North Coast Indus. v. Jason Maxwell, Inc., 972 F.2d 1031 (9th Cir.1992), p. 79 infra (whether plaintiff's design was sufficiently different from earlier works to be copyrightable must be left to the trier of fact).

drawn from the plate, a thin steel coating is applied to it to preserve it during the printing of the final article, of which several hundred may be drawn from such a steel-faced plate before noticeable wearing of the plate. The final product is a print in color called in the trade a proof. The color is applied to the plate by hand before each print or proof is drawn from the plate. The color may be applied to the plate by the artist, but usually is done by one or more printers who follow a sample print or color guide in applying the colored ink in the depressions made by the engraver on the plate. It is possible by this process to make quite a satisfactory reproduction of the original painting in whatever size desired (the size of the photograph governing the size of the engraving), preserving the softness of line which is characteristic of the oil painting. It is not, however, possible to make a photographic copy of the painting by this method exact in all its details. The work of the engraver upon the plate requires the individual conception, judgment and execution by the engraver on the depth and shape of the depressions in the plate to be made by the scraping process in order to produce in this other medium the engraver's concept of the effect of the oil painting. No two engravers can produce identical interpretations of the same oil painting. * * *

"Concededly the defendants used proofs taken from the plaintiff's plates and sold by the plaintiff, carrying notice of plaintiff's copyright, as the subjects of their colored photoengravings."]

FRANK, CIRCUIT JUDGE. 1. Congressional power to authorize both patents and copyrights is contained in Article 1, § 8 of the Constitution. In passing on the validity of patents, the Supreme Court recurrently insists that this constitutional provision governs. On this basis, pointing to the Supreme Court's consequent requirement that, to be valid, a patent must disclose a high degree of uniqueness, ingenuity and inventiveness, the defendants assert that the same requirement constitutionally governs copyrights. As several sections of the Copyright Act—e.g., those authorizing copyrights of "reproductions of works of art," maps, and compilations— plainly dispense with any such high standard, defendants are, in effect, attacking the constitutionality of those sections. But the very language of the Constitution differentiates (a) "authors" and their "writings" from (b) "inventors" and their "discoveries." Those who penned the Constitution, of course, knew the difference. The pre-revolutionary English statutes had made the distinction. In 1783, the Continental Congress had passed a resolution recommending that the several states enact legislation to "secure" to authors the "copyright" of their books. Twelve of the thirteen states (in 1783–1786) enacted such statutes. Those of Connecticut and North Carolina covered books, pamphlets, maps, and charts.

Moreover, in 1790, in the year after the adoption of the Constitution, the first Congress enacted two statutes, separately dealing with patents and copyrights. The patent statute, enacted April 10, 1790, 1 Stat. 109, provided that patents should issue only if the Secretary of State, Secretary of War and the Attorney General, or any two of them "shall deem the invention or discovery sufficiently useful and important"; the applicant for a patent was obliged to file a specification "so particular" as "to distinguish the invention or discovery from other things before known and used * * * "; the patent was to constitute *prima facie* evidence that the patentee was "the first and true inventor or * * * discoverer * * * of the thing so specified." The Copyright Act, enacted May 31, 1790, 1 Stat. 124, covered "maps, charts, and books". A printed copy of the title of any map, chart or book was to be recorded in the Clerk's office of the District Court, and a copy of the map, chart or book was to be delivered to the Secretary of State within six months after publication. Twelve years later, Congress in 1802, 2 Stat. 171, added, to matters that might be copyrighted, engravings, etchings and prints.

Thus legislators peculiarly familiar with the purpose of the Constitutional grant, by statute, imposed far less exacting standards in the case of copyrights. They authorized the copyrighting of a mere map which, patently, calls for no considerable uniqueness. They exacted far more from an inventor. And, while they demanded that an official should be satisfied as to the character of an invention before a patent issued, they made no such demand in respect of a copyright. In 1884, in Burrow–Giles Lithographic Co. v. Sarony, 111 U.S. 53, 57, the Supreme Court, adverting to these facts said: "The construction placed upon the Constitution by the first act of 1790 and the act of 1802, by the men who were contemporary with its formation, many of whom were members of the convention which framed it, is of itself entitled to very great weight, and when it is remembered that the rights thus established have not been disputed during a period of nearly a century, it is almost conclusive." Accordingly, the Constitution, as so interpreted, recognizes that the standards for patents and copyrights are basically different.

The defendants' contention apparently results from the ambiguity of the word "original." It may mean startling, novel or unusual, a marked departure from the past. Obviously this is not what is meant when one speaks of "the original package," or the "original bill," or (in connection with the "best evidence" rule) an "original" document; none of those things is highly unusual in creativeness. "Original" in reference to a copyrighted work means that the particular work "owes its origin" to the "author." [8] No large measure of novelty is necessary. Said the Supreme Court in Baker v. Selden, 101 U.S. 99, 102–103: "The copyright of the book, if not pirated from other works, would be valid without regard to the novelty, or want of novelty, of its subject-matter. The novelty of the art or thing described or explained has nothing to do with the validity of the copyright. * * *."

In Bleistein v. Donaldson Lithographing Co., 188 U.S. 239, 250, 252, the Supreme Court cited with approval Henderson v. Tompkins, C.C., 60 F. 758, where it was said, 60 F. at page 764: "There is a *very broad distinction between what is implied in the word 'author,' found in the constitution, and the word 'inventor.' The latter carries an implication*

---

8. Burrow–Giles Lithographic Co. v. Sarony, 111 U.S. 53, 57–58.

*which excludes the results of only ordinary skill, while nothing of this is
necessarily involved in the former.* Indeed, the statutes themselves make
broad distinctions on this point. So much as relates to copyrights * * * is
expressed, so far as this particular is concerned, by the mere words,
'author, inventor, designer or proprietor,' with such aid as may be derived
from the words 'written, composed or made,' * * *. But *a multitude of
books rest safely under copyright, which show only ordinary skill and
diligence in their preparation.* Compilations are noticeable examples of
this fact. With reference to this subject, the courts have not undertaken to
assume the functions of critics, or to measure carefully the degree of
originality, or literary skill or training involved."

It is clear, then, that nothing in the Constitution commands that
copyrighted matter be strikingly unique or novel. Accordingly, we were
not ignoring the Constitution when we stated that a "copy of something in
the public domain" will support a copyright if it is a "distinguishable
variation"; [10] or when we rejected the contention that "like a patent, a
copyrighted work must be not only original, but new", adding, "That is not
* * * the law as is obvious in the case of maps or compendia, where later
works will necessarily be anticipated." [11] All that is needed to satisfy both
the Constitution and the statute is that the "author" contributed something more than a "merely trivial" variation, something recognizably "his
own." [12] Originality in this context "means little more than a prohibition
of actual copying." [13] No matter how poor artistically the "author's"
addition, it is enough if it be his own. Bleistein v. Donaldson Lithographing Co., 188 U.S. 239, 250.

On that account, we have often distinguished between the limited
protection accorded a copyright owner and the extensive protection granted
a patent owner. So we have held that "independent reproduction of a
copyrighted * * * work is not infringement", [14] whereas it is *vis a vis* a
patent. Correlative with the greater immunity of a patentee is the doctrine
of anticipation which does not apply to copyrights: The alleged inventor is
chargeable with full knowledge of all the prior art, although in fact he may
be utterly ignorant of it. The "author" is entitled to a copyright if he
independently contrived a work completely identical with what went before; similarly, although he obtains a valid copyright, he has no right to
prevent another from publishing a work identical with his, if not copied
from his. A patentee, unlike a copyrightee, must not merely produce

10. Gerlach–Barklow Co. v. Morris &
Bendien, 2 Cir., 23 F.2d 159, 161.

11. Sheldon v. Metro–Goldwyn Pictures
Corp., 2 Cir., 81 F.2d 49, 53. See also Ricker
v. General Electric Co., 2 Cir., 162 F.2d 141,
142.

12. Chamberlin v. Uris Sales Corp., 2
Cir., 150 F.2d 512; cf. Gross v. Seligman, 2
Cir., 212 F. 930.

13. Hoague–Sprague Corp. v. Frank C.
Meyer, Inc., D.C.N.Y., 31 F.2d 583, 586. See
also as to photographs Judge Learned Hand
in Jewelers Circular Publishing Co. v. Keystone Pub. Co., D.C.N.Y., 274 F. 932, 934.
* * *

14. Arnstein v. Edward B. Marks Music
Corp., 2 Cir., 82 F.2d 275; Ricker v. General
Electric Co., 2 Cir., 162 F.2d 141, 142.

something "original"; he must also be "the first inventor or discoverer." [15] "Hence it is possible to have a plurality of valid copyrights directed to closely identical or even identical works. Moreover, none of them, if independently arrived at without copying, will constitute an infringement of the copyright of the others." [16] * * *

2. We consider untenable defendants' suggestion that plaintiff's mezzotints could not validly be copyrighted because they are reproductions of works in the public domain. Not only does the Act include "Reproductions of a work of art", [19] but—while prohibiting a copyright of "the original text of any work * * * in the public domain" [20]—it explicitly provides for the copyrighting of "translations, or other versions of works in the public domain". [21] The mezzotints were such "versions." They "originated" with those who made them, and—on the trial judge's findings well supported by the evidence—amply met the standards imposed by the Constitution and the statute. There is evidence that they were not intended to, and did not, imitate the paintings they reproduced. But even if their substantial departures from the paintings were inadvertent, the copyrights would be valid. A copyist's bad eyesight or defective musculature, or a shock caused by a clap of thunder, may yield sufficiently distinguishable variations. [24] Having hit upon such a variation unintentionally, the "author" may adopt it as his and copyright it. [25]

Accordingly, defendants' arguments about the public domain become irrelevant. They could be relevant only in their bearing on the issue of infringement, i.e., whether the defendants copied the mezzotints. [26] But on the findings, again well grounded in the evidence, we see no possible doubt that defendants, who did deliberately copy the mezzotints, are infringers. For a copyright confers the exclusive right to copy the copyrighted work—a right not to have others copy it. Nor were the copyrights lost because of the reproduction of the mezzotints in catalogues. [27] * * *

---

15. See Amdur, Copyright Law and Practice (1936) 70.

16. Id. * * *

19. 17 U.S.C.A. § 5.

20. 17 U.S.C.A. § 8 (formerly § 7).

21. 17 U.S.C.A. § 7 (formerly § 6). * * *

24. Cf. Chamberlin v. Uris Sales Corp., 2 Cir., 150 F.2d 512 note 4.

25. Consider inadvertent errors in a translation. Compare cases holding that a patentable invention may stem from an accidental discovery. See, e.g., Radiator Specialty Co. v. Buhot, 3 Cir., 39 F.2d 373, 376; Nichols v. Minnesota Mining & Mfg. Co., 4 Cir., 109 F.2d 162, 165; New Wrinkle v. Fritz, D.C.W.D.N.Y., 45 F.Supp. 108, 117; Byerley v. Sun Co., 3 Cir., 184 F. 455, 456–457.

Many great scientific discoveries have resulted from accidents, e.g., the galvanic circuit and the x-ray.

26. Sheldon v. Metro–Goldwyn Pictures Corp., 2 Cir., 81 F.2d 49, 54; Detective Comics, Inc. v. Bruns Publications, 2 Cir., 111 F.2d 432, 433.

27. Gerlach–Barklow Co. v. Morris & Bendien, 2 Cir., 23 F.2d 159, 163; Basevi v. Edward O'Toole Co., D.C., 26 F.Supp. 41, 49.

QUESTIONS: In the terminology of the 1976 Act, the plaintiff's mezzotints are "derivative works." See § 101. Section 103(a) of the Act brings derivative works within the subject matter of copyright. Note the fundamental limitation in § 103(b). What do the plaintiff's copyrights protect? What difficulties does this create in determining infringement?

NOTE ON STANDARDS FOR COPYRIGHTS AND PATENTS

Judge Frank in Alfred Bell v. Catalda ably expressed the conventional understanding that Congress has power to cast one balance sheet for copyright, another for patents, and that both history and policy explain most of the differences. See also Schulman, Patents, Trademark and Copyright: An Informal Comparative Analysis, 10 N.Y.L.F. 174 (1964), and, as a curiosity, C.C. Langdell, Patent Rights and Copy Rights, 12 Harv.L.Rev. 553 (1899).

Does it assist the case for differing treatment of copyright and patent to read Art. I, § 8, cl. 8, as though it contained two separable grants? Thus: The Congress shall have power:

To promote the progress of science, by securing for limited times to authors the exclusive right to their writings.

To promote the progress of useful arts, by securing for limited times to inventors the exclusive right to their discoveries.

This reading, often bruited (see 1 Lipscomb's Walker on Patents § 2:1), acquired a casual endorsement by the Supreme Court in Graham v. John Deere Co., 383 U.S. 1, 5 (1966). Within this structure, how does one define "science" and "useful arts"? What did "science" and "art" mean in 1787? The term "useful art" appeared in the patent statute until 1952. But this dual reading does nothing to describe the gap between the modest requirement of original authorship and the demanding statutory and judicial standards for invention.

In 1952 Congress overhauled the patent statute, which comprises Title 35 of the United States Code. Section 101 states the fundamentals of patentability:

Whoever invents or discovers any new and useful process, machine, manufacture, or composition of matter, or any new and useful improvement thereof, may obtain a patent therefor, subject to the conditions and requirements of this title.

Section 103 adds a further requirement. Its negative form exemplifies the observation that it is easier to say what is not patentable than what is:

A patent may not be obtained * * * if the differences between the subject matter sought to be patented and the prior art are such that the subject matter as a whole would have been obvious at the time the invention was made to a person having ordinary skill in the art to which said subject matter pertains.

The main burden of § 103, the "non-obvious" requirement, came before the Supreme Court in 1966 in Graham v. John Deere Co., 383 U.S. 1 (1966). Justice Clark began by observing that,

> After a lapse of 15 years, the Court again focuses its attention on the patentability of inventions under the standard of Art. 1, § 8, cl. 8 of the Constitution and under the conditions prescribed by the laws of the United States. Since our last expression on patent validity, Great A. & P. Tea Co. v. Supermarket Equipment Corp., 340 U.S. 147 (1950), the Congress has for the first time expressly added a third statutory dimension to the two requirements of novelty and utility that had been the sole statutory test since the Patent Act of 1793. This is the test of obviousness * * *.

However, the Court comfortably

> concluded that the 1952 Act was intended to codify judicial precedents embracing the principle long ago announced by this Court in Hotchkiss v. Greenwood, 11 How. 248 (1851), and that, while the clear language of § 103 places emphasis on an inquiry into obviousness, the general level of innovation necessary to sustain patentability remains the same.

Indeed, the Court found the language of § 103 "strongly reminiscent of the language in *Hotchkiss*." There "[t]he patent involved a mere substitution of materials—porcelain or clay for wood or metal in doorknobs—and the Court condemned it, holding:

> "Unless more ingenuity and skill . . . were required . . . than were possessed by an ordinary mechanic acquainted with the business, there was an absence of that degree of skill and ingenuity which constitute essential elements of every invention. In other words, the improvement is the work of the skillful mechanic, not that of the inventor." [11 How.] at p. 267.

> *Hotchkiss,* by positing the condition that a patentable invention evidence more ingenuity and skill than that possessed by an ordinary mechanic acquainted with the business, merely distinguished between new and useful innovations that were capable of sustaining a patent and those that were not.

The Court then offered this guidance to the lower courts and the Patent and Trademark Office:

> Under § 103, the scope and content of the prior art are to be determined; differences between the prior art and the claims at issue are to be ascertained; and the level of ordinary skill in the pertinent art resolved. Against this background, the obviousness or nonobviousness of the subject matter is determined. Such secondary considerations as commercial success, long felt but unsolved needs, failure of others, etc., might be utilized to give light to the circumstances surrounding the origin of the subject

matter sought to be patented. As indicia of obviousness or nonobviousness, these inquiries may have relevancy.[f]

On the same day a companion case, United States v. Adams, 383 U.S. 39 (1966), contained a further application of the non-obviousness test and a consideration of the novelty requirement as well. The remaining test, that of utility, had a rare exposition by the Court a little later in the term in Brenner v. Manson, 383 U.S. 519 (1966). One view of the utility requirement has been to say that the market will determine whether an invention is useful. There was accordingly little need to frame and apply a legal restriction, except for the limiting cases characterized long ago by Justice Story as "injurious to the morals, the health, or the good order of society." Bedford v. Hunt, 3 Fed.Cas. 37 (C.C.D.Mass.1817) (No. 1,217). But the Court of Customs and Patent Appeals had decided in 1950 that a new compound for which there was no known use was not patentable, Application of Bremner, 182 F.2d 216 (C.C.P.A.1950), and now the Supreme Court pushed a step beyond this position by directing the Patent and Trademark Office to refuse a patent for the *process* of producing a compound of no practical utility. Consult Kitch, Graham v. John Deere Co.: New Standards for Patents, 1966 Sup.Ct.Rev. 293 (1967).

The content of "invention" is, at bottom, a constitutional question, like the essentials of an author's "writings." Within the Constitution's bounds, the statutes can and do limit the categories of inventions and writings that Congress deems eligible for patent or copyright protection, but the separation of constitutional and statutory imperatives is not a sharp one. For patents, as for copyrights, there are problems of what is "statutory subject matter" within the deceptively simple language of § 101. See, e.g., Diamond v. Chakrabarty, 447 U.S. 303 (1980), finding a genetically engineered bacterium to be patentable subject matter. Some of these problems—the patentability of computer programs notably—are relevant for us and will be taken up later.

Finally, we should note that concern with "originality" is more acute in patent than in copyright. The Patent Act requires the applicant to "make oath that he believes himself to be the *original* and *first* inventor of the process, machine, manufacture, or composition of matter, or improvement thereof, for which he solicits a patent." § 115 (emphasis added); see also § 102. Questions of priority of invention can become complicated. For copyright, as Judge Frank reminds us in *Alfred Bell*, independent creation is sufficient.

The leading treatises on patent law are D. Chisum, Chisum on Patents (Matthew Bender), and Lipscomb's Walker on Patents (Clark Boardman Callaghan).

---

f. See Merges, Commercial Success and Patent Standards: Economic Perspectives on Innovation, 76 Calif.L.Rev. 803 (1988), which criticizes a supposed trend in the Federal Circuit to overemphasize the "secondary considerations" mentioned by the Court.

ORIGINALITY IN WORKS DERIVED FROM PREEXISTING SOURCES

Italian Book Co., Inc. v. Rossi

United States District Court, Southern District of New York, 1928.
27 F.2d 1014.

■ THACHER, DISTRICT JUDGE. When Paolo Citorello, a Sicilian sailor, sang and played his guitar on a long ocean voyage, Sicilian folk songs he had heard and forgotten came back to his memory. He did not know how to read music, and such parts of the words and music as he could remember he sang and played by ear. What he could not remember he improvised. In this way he learned a song which he claimed as his own composition. At the end of the voyage he sang and played it to the representative of a company manufacturing phonograph records. The score was arranged for him by another, and upon his application a copyright was obtained, which he assigned to the plaintiff. The defendants have copied the copyrighted song, claiming that it is an old Sicilian folk song, the words of which were published as early as 1871.

How much of Citorello's composition was subconscious repetition of this old song, as he had heard it sung, and how much of it was original with him, no one can say. No doubt he had heard some variation of the old song and was trying to remember it, but the product differed in words and music from any version of it that has been proved, although the theme was the same and the music quite similar. To the extent of such differences he was the author of the new arrangement of the words and music of an old song. That these differences were of some importance may be inferred from the plaintiff's commercial success in selling it and the defendants' desire to appropriate it. There must have been something which Citorello added which brought the old song back into popularity with his own people in this country, and sufficient, I think, to support his claim of copyright. Gerlach–Barklow Co. v. Morris & Bendien, 23 F.2d 159 (C.C.A.2d). Of course, the defendants could make their own improvisation of the old song, or could copy it without change. They were free to copy the original, but not to copy Citorello's variation. I am satisfied that they did not go back to the original, but simply appropriated the Citorello song, making colorable changes in a clumsy effort to conceal their infringement.

Decree for plaintiff in usual form.

NOTES AND QUESTIONS

(1) Wihtol v. Wells, 231 F.2d 550 (7th Cir.1956), was about a hymn, with words and music copyrighted by Wihtol, who testified that he recalled the tune from his childhood in Latvia. When challenged by Wells, a defendant who claimed to have written a similar work, Wihtol's copyright was upheld. The Seventh Circuit said that the tune was old, "But it was original work on plaintiff's part when, some thirty years later, he devised a calculated melody score thus putting it in shape for all to read." (See also, involving the same hymn, Wihtol v. Crow, 309 F.2d 777 (8th Cir.1962), one of the

first "photocopying" cases, brought against a choirmaster who had run off 48 copies for his high school choir.)

In Tempo Music, Inc. v. Famous Music Corp., 838 F.Supp. 162 (S.D.N.Y.1993), the court said that a one note variation in Duke Ellington's jazz standard *Satin Doll*, which may have arisen from a typographical error, did not result in a copyrightable derivative work; but the court refused to hold as a matter of law that a harmony created to accompany the original tune could not be sufficiently creative to support a claim to copyright. See also Woods v. Bourne Co., 60 F.3d 978 (2d Cir.1995), excluding from copyright "stylized version[s]" and "cocktail pianist variations" of existing songs.

(2) The creator of an arrangement or adaptation of an old melody in reality may get substantial control over the underlying work, as illustrated by the cases above. This may be viewed as the reward for rescuing a song from oblivion; it may also be a racket, when performers are led to believe that they must pay to use collections of works that are old or of unknown authorship. Should disclaimers of copyright in public domain material be required as a condition of protection for the new material? What form would the disclaimers take? How could a composer disclose and disclaim the public domain song used to create a derivative work? Heald, Reviving the Rhetoric of the Public Interest: Choir Directors, Copy Machines, and New Arrangements of Public Domain Music, 46 Duke L.J. 241 (1996), concludes that many claims of copyright in new variations of musical works fail even the loosest interpretation of originality, but still generate royalties because users frequently cannot make comparisons with the original works.

(3) The various recordings of a popular musical work made possible by the compulsory license in § 115 (see p. 538 infra) often differ from the original composition. How far may a compulsory licensee deviate from the original? Can the licensee claim copyright in the new version as a derivative work? See § 115(a)(2).

(4) Suppose a folk song is known only through one or more versions under copyright. Is it permissible to reconstruct the public domain original from the copyrighted adaptations? Similar questions also arise in connection with other derivative works. Recall Justice Holmes' statement in *Bleistein*, p. 53 supra: "Others are free to copy the original. They are not free to copy the copy." Is this always true? Whether the "original" is a scene or a face, as in *Bleistein*, or an earlier work in the public domain, portions of the original become embodied in the copyrighted derivative work. Must a second author always seek out the original, or is there a privilege to extract it, if possible, from the first author's "copy"? It has been suggested that "[i]t might have been better * * * had Holmes resisted the temptation to turn a phrase," because it has sometimes led courts to forget that "[i]f a portion of the work has been copied from other sources and thus lacks originality, that portion is not a work of authorship. Since this renders unprotectable that component of the work, absent a copyright on the source, others are free to use it as they will, without returning to the original." [g]

L. BATLIN & SON, INC. V. SNYDER, 536 F.2d 486 (2d Cir.), cert. denied, 429 U.S. 857 (1976). "Uncle Sam mechanical banks have been on the American scene at least since June 8, 1886, when Design Patent No. 16,728, issued on a toy savings bank of its type. The basic delightful design has long since been in the public domain. The banks are well documented in collectors' books and known to the average person interested in Americana. A description of the bank is that Uncle Sam, dressed in his usual stove pipe hat, blue full dress coat, starred vest and red and white striped trousers, and leaning on his umbrella, stands on a four- or five-inch wide base, on which sits his carpetbag. A coin may be placed in Uncle Sam's extended hand. When a lever is pressed, the arm lowers, and the coin falls into the bag, while Uncle Sam's whiskers move up and down. The base has an embossed American eagle on it with the words 'Uncle Sam' on streamers above it, as well as the word 'Bank' on each side. Such a bank is listed in a number of collectors' books, the most recent of which may be F.H. Griffith, Mechanical Banks (1972 ed.) where it was listed as No. 280, and is said to be not particularly rare."

Snyder took an antique Uncle Sam bank to Hong Kong and had a reduced plastic version of it designed and manufactured there, in which he claimed copyright. Batlin bought cast iron Uncle Sam banks from Taiwan, and he ordered plastic models from Hong Kong that may well have come from the same mold as Snyder's. Both were refused entry by U.S. Customs because of Snyder's copyright.

Batlin brought an action for a declaration that Snyder's copyright was invalid. He won a preliminary injunction restraining enforcement of the copyright in the District Court, but it was set aside by a panel of the Court of Appeals. The propriety of the preliminary injunction restraining enforcement of Snyder's copyright was sustained on reconsideration en banc.

Judge Oakes, for a 6–3 majority, accepted the findings of Judge Metzner, 394 F.Supp. 1389, 1394 (S.D.N.Y.1975), that the differences between the public domain prototype and Snyder's plastic replica lay only in the direction of making it simpler and cheaper. He also agreed that the copyright test of originality has a "low threshold," and that Mazer v. Stein, p. 138 infra, "established that mass-produced commercial objects with a minimal element of artistic craftsmanship may satisfy the statutory requirement of [a work of art]." But, with respect to a reproduction of a work of art, he endorsed Nimmer's view that "the mere reproduction of a work of art in a different medium should not constitute the required originality." Referring to Sunset House District Corp. v. Doran, 304 F.2d

g. Denicola, Copyright in Collections of Facts: A Theory for the Protection of Nonfic-   tion Literary Works, 81 Colum.L.Rev. 516, 523 (1981).

251 (9th Cir.1962), where copyright validity and infringement were found in connection with a figure of Santa Claus, of which the defendant had made a "lazy copy," Judge Oakes said, "We do not follow the *Doran* case. We do follow the school of cases in this circuit and elsewhere supporting the proposition that to support a copyright there must be at least some substantial variation, not merely a trivial variation such as might occur in the translation to a different medium."

Both the court's opinion and the dissent by Judge Meskill (who wrote for the majority in the vacated panel decision) dwell on Alva Studios, Inc. v. Winninger, 177 F.Supp. 265 (S.D.N.Y.1959), where the work in which copyright was upheld was a reduced scale reproduction, for museum sales, of Rodin's "Hand of God." The majority emphasized the creativity, uniqueness, and inaccessibility of the original, and that "a significant public benefit accrues from its precise, artistic reproduction."

Judge Oakes, realizing that the dissenters were drawing different conclusions from the majority on the same facts and authorities, remarked in conclusion, "To be sure, the test of 'originality' may leave a lot to be desired, although it is the only one we have * * *. Here as elsewhere in the copyright law there are lines that must be drawn even though reasonable men may differ where."

DURHAM INDUSTRIES, INC. v. TOMY CORP., 630 F.2d 905 (2d Cir.1980). Durham, harried by Tomy, brought a declaratory judgment action. Both parties held licenses from Walt Disney Productions. "Tomy claims to hold copyrights on three wind-up plastic figures, each about three inches in height and each capable of locomotion, which are instantly recognizable as the Disney characters Mickey Mouse, Donald Duck and Pluto Dog. Durham has manufactured and distributed virtually indistinguishable versions of these three Disney figures, and Durham concedes that in making these toys it used Tomy's Disney figures as models. Tomy asserts that Durham has thereby infringed upon Tomy's exclusive right to copy its own creations."

" * * * One look at Tomy's figures reveals that, in each, the element of originality that is necessary to support a valid copyright is totally lacking. For half a century or so Disney's characters have peered at us from movie screens, comic books, television sets, posters, clothing, watches, dolls, and a variety of other media, and it would be safe to say that they have a recognition factor that any politician or celebrity would envy. * * * The three Tomy figures are instantly identifiable as embodiments of the Disney characters in yet another form: Mickey, Donald and Pluto are now represented as small, plastic, wind-up toys."

That the Tomy figures are derivative works, Judge Meskill wrote, does not impair their copyrightability, but "to support a copyright the original aspects of a derivative work must be more than trivial"; he applied the standard invoked in *Batlin*. Judge Meskill pointed out that any recognition of copyright in Tomy's figures would require other Disney licensees like Durham to depart from the originals to avoid infringement, so that "Disney's right to copy (or to permit others to copy) its own creations would, in effect, be circumscribed. Thus it is clear that the originality requirement imposed by the Constitution and the Copyright Act has particular significance in the case of derivative works based on copyrighted preexisting works."

The opinion noted that while *Batlin* arose under the 1909 Act and *Durham* in part under the 1976 Act, there was no difference in the standard of originality.

GRACEN V. BRADFORD EXCHANGE, 698 F.2d 300 (7th Cir.1983). This was an intramural quarrel. Bradford makes "collectors' plates." It had a license from MGM to make a set of plates illustrated with characters from the well-known film *The Wizard of Oz,* notably portraying Judy Garland as Dorothy. In a competition for paintings (based on photographs from the movie) that would "evoke all the warm feeling the people have for the film and its actors," Jorie Gracen, a clerical employee of Bradford and an amateur painter, won. But there was a falling-out about terms, and Bradford commissioned Auckland, an artist, to redo the portrait of Garland/Dorothy. Gracen obtained a copyright and joined MGM as a defendant when she sued Bradford and Auckland. This led to a counterclaim that Gracen had no authority to copy and display the MGM image of Dorothy, and in the trial court Gracen wound up on the wrong end of a $1500 summary judgment.

Judge Posner for the Court of Appeals found that the counterclaim raised questions of implied authority and of a possible oral license to Gracen that made summary judgment inappropriate. He then moved to the validity of her copyright:

"Miss Gracen reminds us that judges can make fools of themselves pronouncing on aesthetic matters. But artistic originality is not the same thing as the legal concept of originality in the Copyright Act. Artistic originality indeed might inhere in a detail, a nuance, a shading too small to be apprehended by a judge. * * * A portrait is not unoriginal for being a good likeness.

"But especially as applied to derivative works, the concept of originality in copyright law has as one would expect a legal rather than aesthetic function—to prevent overlapping claims."

He then discussed the problems of proof that would arise as Auckland tried to establish that he copied from the MGM photographs and not from Gracen's derivative painting. As for originality, "the purpose of the term in copyright law is not to guide aesthetic judgments but to assure a sufficiently gross difference between the underlying and the derivative

The Gracen Painting

A Photograph From *The Wizard of Oz*

work to avoid entangling subsequent artists depicting the underlying work in copyright problems.

"We are speaking, however, only of the requirement of originality in derivative works. If a painter paints from life, no court is going to hold that his painting is not copyrightable because it is an exact photographic likeness. * * *

" * * * If Miss Gracen had painted Judy Garland from life, her painting would be copyrightable even if we thought it *kitsch;* but a derivative work must be substantially different from the underlying work to be copyrightable. This is the test of L. Batlin & Son, Inc. v. Snyder, 536 F.2d at 491, a decision of the Second Circuit—the nation's premier copyright court—sitting en banc. * * *

"We agree with the district court that under the test of *Batlin* Miss Gracen's painting, whatever its artistic merit, is not an original derivative work within the meaning of the Copyright Act."

NOTES AND QUESTIONS ON ORIGINALITY IN DERIVATIVE WORKS

(1) What is the rationale for a requirement of substantial variation? Is Judge Posner's argument convincing? The Ninth Circuit, invoking both *Gracen* and *Durham*, argued that a requirement of adequate distinction between derivative and underlying works was mandated by the affirmation in § 103(b) that copyright in a derivative works does not affect the scope of copyright in preexisting material; granting plaintiff a copyright on its inflatable costumes based on copyrighted characters "would have the practical effect of providing [plaintiff] with a de facto monopoly on all inflatable costumes depicting the copyrighted characters." Entertainment Research Group, Inc. v. Genesis Creative Group, Inc., 122 F.3d 1211 (9th Cir.1997), cert. denied, 118 S.Ct. 1302 (1998).

Did Jorie Gracen's painting evince less "originality" than the mezzotints described in *Alfred Bell?* Olson, Copyright Originality, 48 Mo.L.Rev. 29, 55 (1983), declares that the "implications" of the *Batlin* decision "are awesome." How so? Consider the suggestion made in Page, The Works: Distinguishing Derivative Creations Under Copyright, 5 Cardozo Art. & Ent.L.J. 415 (1986), that "[w]hat the author adds to the work of his predecessors should be judged as though it were placed on a blank canvas or other naked medium." Is that possible? See also Wiley, Copyright at the School of Patent, 58 U.Chi.L.Rev. 119 (1991), arguing for a pragmatic approach to originality that emphasizes the need to maintain incentives; and VerSteeg, Rethinking Originality, 34 Wm. & Mary L.Rev. 801 (1993), an ambitious attempt to define the requisite creativity necessary for "authorship."

(2) The majority in *Batlin* accepted the copyrightability of a precise small-scale reproduction of Rodin's "Hand of God." Can you frame an acceptable rationale for that result—or for rejecting it?

(3) Consider the two works reproduced below, used by the plaintiff on beach towels with sufficient success to inspire imitation. The original design on the left, marketed in the 1960s, was allowed to enter the public domain. In 1976 the plaintiff created the "new" design on the right in which it now asserts a copyright against a competitor selling an exact copy. What result? See Sherry Manufacturing Co. v. Towel King of Florida, Inc., 753 F.2d 1565 (11th Cir.1985).

SHERRY'S ORIGINAL DESIGN

SHERRY'S NEW DESIGN

Yves St. Laurent's rendition of a Mondrian painting

Style 7114

(4) The Dutch painter Piet Mondrian was renowned for his use of bounded geometric shapes in a uniquely characteristic style. French designer Yves St. Laurent was the first to adapt Mondrian's designs to woman's clothing in the 1960s. A designer for North Coast Industries, undeniably influenced by Mondrian and St. Laurent, created "Style 7114." When a competitor began selling clothing with a similar design, North Coast sued for infringement. The district court gave summary judgment to the defendant, finding that the variations between the St. Laurent design and Style 7114 (see above) were too trivial to support a copyright.

The Ninth Circuit disagreed in North Coast Industries v. Jason Maxwell, Inc., 972 F.2d 1031 (9th Cir.1992), holding that the plaintiff was entitled to a trial on the issue of copyrightability. "If we were to accept the view that, as a matter of law the differences in the placement of geometric shapes should be regarded as trivial, we would be forced to conclude that Mondrian's creativity with geometric shapes ended with his first painting, and that he went on to paint the same painting a thousand times. This is not the judgment of art history, and it cannot be the correct judgment of a court as a matter of law." Is this consistent with the distinction between a legal and aesthetic conception of originality drawn by Judge Posner in *Gracen?*

(5) Modern computer technology permits the creation of "colorized" versions of classic black and white motion pictures. Is the new version a copyrightable derivative work? The Copyright Office announced in 1987 that it would accept such works for registration.[h] See Duggan & Pennella, The Case for Copyrights in "Colorized" Versions of Public Domain Feature Films, 34 J.Copyr.Soc. 333 (1987). The specter of a colorized *Citizen Kane,* however, stirs emotions, and the "right" to make such works has been hotly debated. That question raises the issue of "moral rights," a topic to be considered later. See p. 736 infra.

COMPILATIONS

Feist Publications, Inc. v. Rural Telephone Service Co.

Supreme Court of the United States, 1991.
499 U.S. 340, 111 S.Ct. 1282.

■ JUSTICE O'CONNOR delivered the opinion of the Court.

This case requires us to clarify the extent of copyright protection available to telephone directory white pages.

I

Rural Telephone Service Company is a certified public utility that provides telephone service to several communities in northwest Kansas. It is subject to a state regulation that requires all telephone companies operating in Kansas to issue annually an updated telephone directory.

h. In Maljack Prod., Inc. v. UAV Corp., 964 F.Supp. 1416 (C.D.Cal.1997), the court agreed with the Copyright Office that the "panning and scanning" done to a public domain movie to fit the images onto television screens resulted in a copyrightable derivative work.

Accordingly, as a condition of its monopoly franchise, Rural publishes a typical telephone directory, consisting of white pages and yellow pages. The white pages list in alphabetical order the names of Rural's subscribers, together with their towns and telephone numbers. The yellow pages list Rural's business subscribers alphabetically by category and feature classified advertisements of various sizes. Rural distributes its directory free of charge to its subscribers, but earns revenue by selling yellow pages advertisements.

Feist Publications, Inc., is a publishing company that specializes in area-wide telephone directories. Unlike a typical directory, which covers only a particular calling area, Feist's area-wide directories cover a much larger geographical range, reducing the need to call directory assistance or consult multiple directories. The Feist directory that is the subject of this litigation covers 11 different telephone service areas in 15 counties and contains 46,878 white pages listings—compared to Rural's approximately 7,700 listings. Like Rural's directory, Feist's is distributed free of charge and includes both white pages and yellow pages. Feist and Rural compete vigorously for yellow pages advertising.

* * * To obtain white pages listings for its area-wide directory, Feist approached each of the 11 telephone companies operating in northwest Kansas and offered to pay for the right to use its white pages listings.

Of the 11 telephone companies, only Rural refused to license its listings to Feist. Rural's refusal created a problem for Feist, as omitting these listings would have left a gaping hole in its area-wide directory, rendering it less attractive to potential yellow pages advertisers. In a decision subsequent to that which we review here, the District Court determined that this was precisely the reason Rural refused to license its listings. The refusal was motivated by an unlawful purpose "to extend its monopoly in telephone service to a monopoly in yellow pages advertising." Rural Telephone Service Co. v. Feist Publications, Inc., 737 F.Supp. 610, 622 (D.Kan. 1990).

Unable to license Rural's white pages listings, Feist used them without Rural's consent. Feist began by removing several thousand listings that fell outside the geographic range of its area-wide directory, then hired personnel to investigate the 4,935 that remained. These employees verified the data reported by Rural and sought to obtain additional information. As a result, a typical Feist listing includes the individual's street address; most of Rural's listings do not. Notwithstanding these additions, however, 1,309 of the 46,878 listings in Feist's 1983 directory were identical to listings in Rural's 1982–1983 white pages. Four of these were fictitious listings that Rural had inserted into its directory to detect copying.

Rural sued for copyright infringement in the District Court for the District of Kansas taking the position that Feist, in compiling its own directory, could not use the information contained in Rural's white pages. * * * The District Court granted summary judgment to Rural, explaining that "[c]ourts have consistently held that telephone directories are copyrightable" and citing a string of lower court decisions. 663 F.Supp. 214, 218 (1987). In an unpublished opinion, the Court of Appeals for the Tenth Circuit affirmed "for substantially the reasons given by the district court." * * *

II

A

This case concerns the interaction of two well-established propositions. The first is that facts are not copyrightable; the other, that compilations of facts generally are. Each of these propositions possesses an impeccable pedigree. That there can be no valid copyright in facts is universally understood. The most fundamental axiom of copyright law is that "[n]o author may copyright his ideas or the facts he narrates." Harper & Row, Publishers, Inc. v. Nation Enterprises, 471 U.S. 539, 556. Rural wisely concedes this point, noting in its brief that "[f]acts and discoveries, of course, are not themselves subject to copyright protection." At the same time, however, it is beyond dispute that compilations of facts are within the subject matter of copyright. Compilations were expressly mentioned in the Copyright Act of 1909, and again in the Copyright Act of 1976.

There is an undeniable tension between these two propositions. Many compilations consist of nothing but raw data—*i.e.*, wholly factual information not accompanied by any original written expression. On what basis may one claim a copyright in such a work? Common sense tells us that 100 uncopyrightable facts do not magically change their status when gathered together in one place. Yet copyright law seems to contemplate that compilations that consist exclusively of facts are potentially within its scope.

The key to resolving the tension lies in understanding why facts are not copyrightable. The *sine qua non* of copyright is originality. To qualify for copyright protection, a work must be original to the author. See *Harper & Row, supra*, at 547–549. Original, as the term is used in copyright, means only that the work was independently created by the author (as opposed to copied from other works), and that it possesses at least some minimal degree of creativity. 1 M. Nimmer & D. Nimmer, Copyright §§ 2.01[A], [B] (1990) (hereinafter Nimmer). To be sure, the requisite level of creativity is extremely low; even a slight amount will suffice. The vast majority of works make the grade quite easily, as they possess some creative spark, "no matter how crude, humble or obvious" it might be. *Id.*, § 1.08[C][1]. Originality does not signify novelty; a work may be original even though it closely resembles other works so long as the similarity is fortuitous, not the result of copying. To illustrate, assume that two poets, each ignorant of the other, compose identical poems. Neither work is novel, yet both are original and, hence, copyrightable. See Sheldon v. Metro–Goldwyn Pictures Corp., 81 F.2d 49, 54 (2d Cir.1936).

Originality is a constitutional requirement. The source of Congress' power to enact copyright laws is Article I, § 8, cl. 8, of the Constitution, which authorizes Congress to "secur[e] for limited Times to Authors ...

the exclusive Right to their respective Writings." In two decisions from the late 19th Century—The Trade–Mark Cases, 100 U.S. (10 Otto) 82 (1879); and Burrow–Giles Lithographic Co. v. Sarony, 111 U.S. 53 (1884)—this Court defined the crucial terms "authors" and "writings." In so doing, the Court made it unmistakably clear that these terms presuppose a degree of originality.

In *The Trade–Mark Cases,* the Court addressed the constitutional scope of "writings." For a particular work to be classified "under the head of writings of authors," the Court determined, "originality is required." 100 U.S., at 94. The Court explained that originality requires independent creation plus a modicum of creativity: "[W]hile the word *writings* may be liberally construed, as it has been, to include original designs for engraving, prints, &c., it is only such as are *original,* and are founded in the creative powers of the mind. The writings which are to be protected are *the fruits of intellectual labor,* embodied in the form of books, prints, engravings, and the like." *Ibid.* (emphasis in original).

In *Burrow–Giles,* the Court distilled the same requirement from the Constitution's use of the word "authors." The Court defined "author," in a constitutional sense, to mean "he to whom anything owes its origin; originator; maker." 111 U.S., at 58 (internal quotations omitted). As in *The Trade–Mark Cases,* the Court emphasized the creative component of originality. It described copyright as being limited to "original intellectual conceptions of the author," *ibid.,* and stressed the importance of requiring an author who accuses another of infringement to prove "the existence of those facts of originality, of intellectual production, of thought, and conception." *Id.,* at 59–60.

The originality requirement articulated in *The Trade–Mark Cases* and *Burrow–Giles* remains the touchstone of copyright protection today. * * *

It is this bedrock principle of copyright that mandates the law's seemingly disparate treatment of facts and factual compilations. "No one may claim originality as to facts." [Nimmer] § 2.11[A], p. 2–157. This is because facts do not owe their origin to an act of authorship. The distinction is one between creation and discovery: the first person to find and report a particular fact has not created the fact; he or she has merely discovered its existence. To borrow from *Burrow–Giles,* one who discovers a fact is not its "maker" or "originator." 111 U.S., at 58. "The discoverer merely finds and records." Nimmer § 2.03[E]. Census takers, for example, do not "create" the population figures that emerge from their efforts; in a sense, they copy these figures from the world around them. Denicola, Copyright in Collections of Facts: A Theory for the Protection of Nonfiction Literary Works, 81 Colum.L.Rev. 516, 525 (1981) (hereinafter Denicola). * * *

Factual compilations, on the other hand, may possess the requisite originality. The compilation author typically chooses which facts to include, in what order to place them, and how to arrange the collected data so that they may be used effectively by readers. These choices as to selection and arrangement, so long as they are made independently by the compiler and entail a minimal degree of creativity, are sufficiently original that Congress may protect such compilations through the copyright laws. Nimmer §§ 2.11[D], 3.03; Denicola 523, n. 38. * * *

This protection is subject to an important limitation. The mere fact that a work is copyrighted does not mean that every element of the work may be protected. Originality remains the *sine qua non* of copyright; accordingly, copyright protection may extend only to those components of a work that are original to the author. * * * In *Harper & Row,* for example, we explained that President Ford could not prevent others from copying bare historical facts from his autobiography, see 471 U.S., at 556–557, but that he could prevent others from copying his "subjective descriptions and portraits of public figures." *Id.,* at 563. Where the compilation author adds no written expression but rather lets the facts speak for themselves, the expressive element is more elusive. The only conceivable expression is the manner in which the compiler has selected and arranged the facts. * * *

This inevitably means that the copyright in a factual compilation is thin. Notwithstanding a valid copyright, a subsequent compiler remains free to use the facts contained in another's publication to aid in preparing a competing work, so long as the competing work does not feature the same selection and arrangement. * * *

It may seem unfair that much of the fruit of the compiler's labor may be used by others without compensation. As Justice Brennan has correctly observed, however, this is not "some unforeseen byproduct of a statutory scheme." *Harper & Row,* 471 U.S., at 589 (dissenting opinion). It is, rather, "the essence of copyright," *ibid.,* and a constitutional requirement. The primary objective of copyright is not to reward the labor of authors, but "[t]o promote the Progress of Science and useful Arts." Art. I, § 8, cl. 8. Accord Twentieth Century Music Corp. v. Aiken, 422 U.S. 151, 156 (1975). To this end, copyright assures authors the right to their original expression, but encourages others to build freely upon the ideas and information conveyed by a work. *Harper & Row, supra,* at 556–557. This principle, known as the idea/expression or fact/expression dichotomy, applies to all works of authorship. As applied to a factual compilation, assuming the absence of original written expression, only the compiler's selection and arrangement may be protected; the raw facts may be copied at will. This result is neither unfair nor unfortunate. It is the means by which copyright advances the progress of science and art.

   * * *

This, then, resolves the doctrinal tension: Copyright treats facts and factual compilations in a wholly consistent manner. Facts, whether alone or as part of a compilation, are not original and therefore may not be copyrighted. A factual compilation is eligible for copyright if it features an original selection or arrangement of facts, but the copyright is limited to the particular selection or arrangement. In no event may copyright extend to the facts themselves.

B

[The Court explains that a misreading of the 1909 statute "caused some lower courts temporarily to lose sight of [the originality] requirement." The statute only implicitly called for original authorship, and its catalog of registrable categories included without qualification "directories, gazetteers, and other compilations". § 5(a). This led some courts, including Jeweler's Circular Pub. Co. v. Keystone Pub. Co., 281 Fed. 83 (2d Cir.1922), "to infer erroneously that directories and the like were copyrightable *per se.*"]

Making matters worse, these courts developed a new theory to justify the protection of factual compilations. Known alternatively as "sweat of the brow" or "industrious collection," the underlying notion was that copyright was a reward for the hard work that went into compiling facts. The classic formulation of the doctrine appeared in *Jeweler's Circular Publishing Co.*, 281 Fed., at 88:

> "The right to copyright a book upon which one has expended labor in its preparation does not depend upon whether the materials which he has collected consist or not of matters which are publici juris, or whether such materials show literary skill *or originality,* either in thought or in language, or anything more than industrious collection. The man who goes through the streets of a town and puts down the names of each of the inhabitants, with their occupations and their street number, acquires material of which he is the author" (emphasis added).

The "sweat of the brow" doctrine had numerous flaws, the most glaring being that it extended copyright protection in a compilation beyond selection and arrangement—the compiler's original contributions—to the facts themselves. Under the doctrine, the only defense to infringement was independent creation. A subsequent compiler was "not entitled to take one word of information previously published," but rather had to "independently wor[k] out the matter for himself, so as to arrive at the same result from the same common sources of information." *Id.,* at 88–89 (internal quotations omitted). "Sweat of the brow" courts thereby eschewed the most fundamental axiom of copyright law—that no one may copyright facts or ideas. * * *

* * * [T]hey handed out proprietary interests in facts and declared that authors are absolutely precluded from saving time and effort by relying upon the facts contained in prior works. In truth, "[i]t is just such wasted effort that the proscription against the copyright of ideas and facts ... [is] designed to prevent." Rosemont Enterprises, Inc. v. Random House, Inc., 366 F.2d 303, 310 (2d Cir.1966), cert. denied, 385 U.S. 1009 (1967). "Protection for the fruits of such research ... may in certain circumstances be available under a theory of unfair competition. But to accord copyright protection on this basis alone distorts basic copyright principles in that it creates a monopoly in public domain materials without the necessary justification of protecting and encouraging the creation of 'writings' by 'authors.'" Nimmer § 3.04, p. 3–23 (footnote omitted).

C

* * *

Congress [in the 1976 Act] took another step to minimize confusion by deleting the specific mention of "directories ... and other compilations" in § 5 of the 1909 Act. As mentioned, this section had led some courts to conclude that directories were copyrightable *per se* and that every element of a directory was protected. In its place, Congress enacted two new provisions. First, to make clear that compilations were not copyrightable *per se*, Congress provided a definition of the term "compilation." Second, to make clear that the copyright in a compilation did not extend to the facts themselves, Congress enacted 17 U.S.C. § 103.

The definition of "compilation" is found in § 101 of the 1976 Act. It defines a "compilation" in the copyright sense as "a work formed by the collection and assembly of preexisting materials or of data *that* are selected, coordinated, or arranged *in such a way that* the resulting work as a whole constitutes an original work of authorship" (emphasis added).

The purpose of the statutory definition is to emphasize that collections of facts are not copyrightable *per se*. It conveys this message through its tripartite structure, as emphasized above by the italics. The statute identifies three distinct elements and requires each to be met for a work to qualify as a copyrightable compilation: (1) the collection and assembly of pre-existing material, facts, or data; (2) the selection, coordination, or arrangement of those materials; and (3) the creation, by virtue of the particular selection, coordination, or arrangement, of an "original" work of authorship. * * *

At first glance, the first requirement does not seem to tell us much. It merely describes what one normally thinks of as a compilation—a collection of pre-existing material, facts, or data. What makes it significant is that it is not the *sole* requirement. It is not enough for copyright purposes that an author collects and assembles facts. To satisfy the statutory definition, the work must get over two additional hurdles. In this way, the plain language indicates that not every collection of facts receives copyright protection. Otherwise, there would be a period after "data."

The third requirement is also illuminating. It emphasizes that a compilation, like any other work, is copyrightable only if it satisfies the originality requirement ("an *original* work of authorship"). Although § 102 states plainly that the originality requirement applies to all works, the point was emphasized with regard to compilations to ensure that courts would not repeat the mistake of the "sweat of the brow" courts by concluding that fact-based works are treated differently and measured by some other standard. As Congress explained it, the goal was to "make plain that the criteria of copyrightable subject matter stated in section 102 apply with full force to works ... containing preexisting material." H.R.Rep. [No. 94–1476], at 57; S.Rep. [No. 94–473], at 55.

The key to the statutory definition is the second requirement. It instructs courts that, in determining whether a fact-based work is an original work of authorship, they should focus on the manner in which the collected facts have been selected, coordinated, and arranged. This is a straight-forward application of the originality requirement. Facts are never original, so the compilation author can claim originality, if at all, only in the way the facts are presented. To that end, the statute dictates that the principal focus should be on whether the selection, coordination, and arrangement are sufficiently original to merit protection.

Not every selection, coordination, or arrangement will pass muster. This is plain from the statute. It states that, to merit protection, the facts must be selected, coordinated, or arranged "in such a way" as to render the work as a whole original. This implies that some "ways" will trigger copyright, but that others will not. * * * Otherwise, the phrase "in such a way" is meaningless and Congress should have defined "compilation" simply as "a work formed by the collection and assembly of preexisting materials or data that are selected, coordinated, or arranged." That Congress did not do so is dispositive. In accordance with "the established principle that a court should give effect, if possible, to every clause and word of a statute," Moskal v. United States, 498 U.S. 103, 109–110 (1990) (internal quotations omitted), we conclude that the statute envisions that there will be some fact-based works in which the selection, coordination, and arrangement are not sufficiently original to trigger copyright protection.

As discussed earlier, however, the originality requirement is not particularly stringent. A compiler may settle upon a selection or arrangement that others have used; novelty is not required. Originality requires only that the author make the selection or arrangement independently (*i.e.,* without copying that selection or arrangement from another work), and that it display some minimal level of creativity. Presumably, the vast majority of compilations will pass this test, but not all will. There remains a narrow category of works in which the creative spark is utterly lacking or so trivial as to be virtually nonexistent. See generally Bleistein v. Donaldson Lithographing Co., 188 U.S. 239, 251 (1903) (referring to "the narrowest and most obvious limits"). Such works are incapable of sustaining a valid copyright. Nimmer § 2.01[B].

Even if a work qualifies as a copyrightable compilation, it receives only limited protection. This is the point of § 103 of the Act. * * *

As § 103 makes clear, copyright is not a tool by which a compilation author may keep others from using the facts or data he or she has collected. "The most important point here is one that is commonly misunderstood today: copyright ... has no effect one way or the other on the copyright or public domain status of the preexisting material." H.R.Rep., at 57; S.Rep., at 55. The 1909 Act did not require, as "sweat of the brow" courts mistakenly assumed, that each subsequent compiler must start from scratch and is precluded from relying on research undertaken by another. See, *e.g., Jeweler's Circular Publishing Co.,* 281 Fed., at 88–89. Rather, the facts contained in existing works may be freely copied because copyright protects only the elements that owe their origin to the compiler—the selection, coordination, and arrangement of facts. * * *

The 1976 revisions have proven largely successful in steering courts in the right direction. A good example is Miller v. Universal City Studios, Inc., 650 F.2d, at 1369–1370: "A copyright in a directory . . . is properly viewed as resting on the originality of the selection and arrangement of the factual material, rather than on the industriousness of the efforts to develop the information. Copyright protection does not extend to the facts themselves, and the mere use of information contained in a directory without a substantial copying of the format does not constitute infringement" (citation omitted). Additionally, the Second Circuit, which almost 70 years ago issued the classic formulation of the "sweat of the brow" doctrine in *Jeweler's Circular Publishing Co.*, has now fully repudiated the reasoning of that decision. See, *e.g.*, Financial Information, Inc. v. Moody's Investors Service, Inc., 808 F.2d 204, 207 (2d Cir.1986), cert. denied, 484 U.S. 820 (1987); Financial Information, Inc. v. Moody's Investors Service, Inc., 751 F.2d 501, 510 (2d Cir.1984) (Newman, J., concurring); Hoehling v. Universal City Studios, Inc., 618 F.2d 972, 979 (2d Cir.1980). Even those scholars who believe that "industrious collection" should be rewarded seem to recognize that this is beyond the scope of existing copyright law. Denicola 516 ("the very vocabulary of copyright is ill suited to analyzing property rights in works of nonfiction"); id., at 520–521, 525; Ginsburg [Creation and Commercial Value: Copyright Protection of Works of Information, 90 Colum.L.Rev. 1865 (1990)] 1876, 1870.

III

There is no doubt that Feist took from the white pages of Rural's directory a substantial amount of factual information. At a minimum, Feist copied the names, towns, and telephone numbers of 1,309 of Rural's subscribers. Not all copying, however, is copyright infringement. To establish infringement, two elements must be proven: (1) ownership of a valid copyright, and (2) copying of constituent elements of the work that are original. *See Harper & Row,* 471 U.S., at 548. The first element is not at issue here; Feist appears to concede that Rural's directory, considered as a whole, is subject to a valid copyright because it contains some foreword text, as well as original material in its yellow pages advertisements.

The question is whether Rural has proved the second element. In other words, did Feist, by taking 1,309 names, towns, and telephone numbers from Rural's white pages, copy anything that was "original" to Rural? Certainly, the raw data does not satisfy the originality requirement. Rural may have been the first to discover and report the names, towns, and telephone numbers of its subscribers, but this data does not " 'ow[e] its origin' " to Rural. *Burrow–Giles,* 111 U.S., at 58. * * *

Rural essentially concedes the point by referring to the names, towns, and telephone numbers as "preexisting material." Section 103(b) states explicitly that the copyright in a compilation does not extend to "the preexisting material employed in the work."

The question that remains is whether Rural selected, coordinated, or arranged these uncopyrightable facts in an original way. As mentioned, originality is not a stringent standard; it does not require that facts be presented in an innovative or surprising way. It is equally true, however, that the selection and arrangement of facts cannot be so mechanical or routine as to require no creativity whatsoever. The standard of originality is low, but it does exist. * * *

The selection, coordination, and arrangement of Rural's white pages do not satisfy the minimum constitutional standards for copyright protection. As mentioned at the outset, Rural's white pages are entirely typical. Persons desiring telephone service in Rural's service area fill out an application and Rural issues them a telephone number. In preparing its white pages, Rural simply takes the data provided by its subscribers and lists it alphabetically by surname. The end product is a garden-variety white pages directory, devoid of even the slightest trace of creativity.

Rural's selection of listings could not be more obvious: it publishes the most basic information—name, town, and telephone number—about each person who applies to it for telephone service. This is "selection" of a sort, but it lacks the modicum of creativity necessary to transform mere selection into copyrightable expression. Rural expended sufficient effort to make the white pages directory useful, but insufficient creativity to make it original.

We note in passing that the selection featured in Rural's white pages may also fail the originality requirement for another reason. Feist points out that Rural did not truly "select" to publish the names and telephone numbers of its subscribers; rather, it was required to do so by the Kansas Corporation Commission as part of its monopoly franchise. See 737 F.Supp., at 612. Accordingly, one could plausibly conclude that this selection was dictated by state law, not by Rural.

Nor can Rural claim originality in its coordination and arrangement of facts. The white pages do nothing more than list Rural's subscribers in alphabetical order. This arrangement may, technically speaking, owe its origin to Rural; no one disputes that Rural undertook the task of alphabetizing the names itself. But there is nothing remotely creative about arranging names alphabetically in a white pages directory. It is an age-old practice, firmly rooted in tradition and so commonplace that it has come to be expected as a matter of course. * * * It is not only unoriginal, it is practically inevitable. This time-honored tradition does not possess the minimal creative spark required by the Copyright Act and the Constitution.

We conclude that the names, towns, and telephone numbers copied by Feist were not original to Rural and therefore were not protected by the copyright in Rural's combined white and yellow pages directory. As a constitutional matter, copyright protects only those constituent elements of a work that possess more than a *de minimis* quantum of creativity. Rural's white pages, limited to basic subscriber information and arranged alphabetically, fall short of the mark. As a statutory matter, 17 U.S.C. § 101 does not afford protection from copying to a collection of facts that are selected, coordinated, and arranged in a way that utterly lacks originality. Given that some works must fail, we cannot imagine a more likely candidate. Indeed, were we to hold that Rural's white pages pass muster, it is hard to believe that any collection of facts could fail.

Because Rural's white pages lack the requisite originality, Feist's use of the listings cannot constitute infringement. This decision should not be construed as demeaning Rural's efforts in compiling its directory, but rather as making clear that copyright rewards originality, not effort. As this Court noted more than a century ago, " 'great praise may be due to the plaintiffs for their industry and enterprise in publishing this paper, yet the law does not contemplate their being rewarded in this way.' " Baker v. Selden, 101 U.S., at 105.

The judgment of the Court of Appeals is

Reversed.

■ JUSTICE BLACKMUN concurs in the judgment.

BELLSOUTH ADVERTISING & PUB. CORP. v. DONNELLEY INFORMATION PUB., INC., 999 F.2d 1436 (11th Cir.1993), cert. denied, 510 U.S. 1101 (1994). "[W]e are called upon to apply *Feist Publications* * * *, which addressed copyright protection for a 'white pages' telephone directory, to resolve the infringement claims presented to us concerning a directory of a different color. * * * The pivotal issue in this case is whether that which was copied by the alleged infringer was protected by the registered claim of compilation copyright. * * *

"BellSouth Advertising & Publishing Corporation ('BAPCO') is a wholly owned subsidiary of BellSouth Corporation ('BellSouth') created for the purpose of preparing, publishing and distributing telephone directories. Using telephone listing information supplied by Southern Bell Telephone and Telegraph Company ('Southern Bell'), another wholly owned subsidiary of BellSouth, BAPCO publishes a classified, 'yellow pages,' advertising directory for the Greater Miami area. The BAPCO directory is organized into an alphabetical list of business classifications. Each business-rate telephone service subscriber is listed in alphabetical order under one appropriate heading without charge. A subscriber may purchase cross listings under different business classifications or advertisements to appear along with its business listing.

"After BAPCO published its 1984 directory for the Greater Miami area, Donnelley Information Publishing, Inc. and Reuben H. Donnelley Corp. (collectively 'Donnelley') began promoting and selling classified advertisements to be placed in a competitive classified directory for the Greater Miami area. To generate a list of business telephone subscribers to be solicited for placement in its directory, Donnelley gave copies of BAPCO's directory to Appalachian Computer Services, Inc. ('ACS'), a data entry company. Donnelley first marked each listing in the BAPCO directory with one alphanumeric code indicating the size and type of advertisement purchased by the subscriber and a similar code indicating the type of business represented by the BAPCO heading under which the listing appeared. For each listing appearing in the BAPCO directory, ACS created a computer data base containing the name, address, and telephone number of the subscriber, as well as the codes corresponding to business type and unit of advertising. From this data base, Donnelley printed sales lead sheets, listing this information for each subscriber, to be used to contact business telephone subscribers to sell advertisements and listings in the Donnelley directory. Relying on this information copied from the BAPCO directory, Donnelley ultimately prepared its own competitive directory for the Greater Miami area.''

The district court had granted summary judgment in favor of BAPCO, and the judgment was affirmed by a panel of the Eleventh Circuit, 933 F.2d 952 (11th Cir.1991). However, the panel decision was vacated and a rehearing en banc ordered at 977 F.2d 1435 (11th Cir.1992).

"[T]he district court found that BAPCO engaged in feats of coordination and arrangement to generate its yellow pages directory. The court explains that BAPCO arranged its directory in an alphabetized list of business types, with individual businesses listed in alphabetical order under the applicable headings. The Copyright Act protects 'original works of authorship.' 17 U.S.C. § 102(a). BAPCO's arrangement and coordination is 'entirely typical' for a business directory. *Feist*, 111 S.Ct. at 1296.'' (In a footnote, Judge Birch said, "While the listings in BAPCO's yellow pages required somewhat more organization and arrangement than the white pages directory considered in *Feist*, BAPCO's claim of 'originality' must be resolved by comparison to other business telephone directories. * * * '')

"The district court also identified acts of coordination and arrangement in the particular system of headings used in the BAPCO directory. * * *

" * * * BAPCO failed to present evidence that, even if copied, its heading structure constitutes original expression warranting copyright protection. Initially, many of the selected headings, for example 'Attorneys' or 'Banks,' represent such an obvious label for the entities appearing under these headings as to lack the requisite originality for copyright protection. BAPCO can claim no copyright in the idea of dividing churches by denomination or attorneys by area of specialty. Further, any expressive act in including a category such as 'Banks' or in dividing 'Attorneys' into categories such as 'Bankruptcy' or 'Criminal Law' would lose copyright protection because it would merge with the idea of listing such entities as a class of businesses in a business directory. The evidence submitted by Donnelley also establishes that many of BAPCO's headings result from certain standard industry practices, such as the recommendations of the National Yellow Pages Sales Association, with regard to the selection and phrasing of headings in business directories. Finally, as established by the testimony of BAPCO's representatives, the ultimate appearance of a particular subscriber under a certain heading is determined by the subscriber's willingness to purchase those listings in the BAPCO directory. While BAPCO may select the headings that are offered to the subscriber, it is the subscriber who selects from those alternatives the headings under which the subscriber will appear in the copyrighted directory. The headings that actually appear in the directory thus, do not owe their origin to BAPCO and BAPCO has claimed no copyright in the larger universe of headings that are offered to subscribers. Thus, the elements of selection, coordination and arrangement identified by the district court, and purportedly copied by Donnelley, as a matter of law, do not display the originality required to merit copyright protection. * * *.

"We reverse the judgment of the district court granting summary judgment to BAPCO on its claim of copyright infringement and enter judgment in favor of Donnelley on this claim."

Judge Hatchett in dissent remained unconvinced. "The majority's holding establishes a rule of law that transforms the multi-billion dollar classified publishing industry from a business requiring the production of a useful directory based on multiple layers of creative decision-making, into a business requiring no more than a successful race to a data processing agency to copy another publisher's copyrighted work-product. * * *

"The clearest example of BAPCO's original selection is its choice of the classified headings that would be included in the 1984 Yellow Pages. * * * BAPCO selected the approximate 7,000 classified heading in the 1984 Yellow Pages from the 4,700 primary headings and approximately 34,000 related headings in the BAPCO headings book. BAPCO presented the undisputed testimony of Gerald Brown that the BAPCO headings book is not standardized to coincide with the menu of classified headings used in National Yellow Page Sales Association (NYPSA) publications. Moreover, even if BAPCO's selection of classified headings is similar to other NYPSA publications, it would still be copyrightable under *Feist* so long as BAPCO selected independently. See *Feist,* 499 U.S. at 345, (holding that 'originality does not signify novelty; a work may be original even though it closely resembles other works so long as the similarity is fortuitous, not the result of copying')." (In a footnote Judge Hatchett argued, "In reasoning that BAPCO's selection of headings lack originality because many resemble NYPSA headings, the majority completely ignores the *Feist* Court's holding that an independent selection of data need not be 'novel' in order to be deemed original.")

"The originality of BAPCO's arrangement of business listings under a particular classified heading is also clear under the standard definition of 'arrangement' in the copyright laws. * * * Because most business subscribers offer multiple product lines, goods, and services, Johnson testified that BAPCO sales representatives were responsible for itemizing the products or services of a business subscriber, determining the degree of importance or profitability to the business, and recommending an appropriate classified heading for listing the business in the 1984 Yellow Pages." Judge Hatchett also noted that BAPCO's "Heading Committee" had final responsibility for deciding whether a classified heading selected by a customer was appropriate. "Accordingly, the evidence is clear that BAP-CO's arrangement was in no sense mechanical. On the contrary, the 1984 Yellow Pages reflects several layers of BAPCO choices on grouping 106,398 business listings under approximately 7,000 classified headings, which BAPCO selected from a heading book containing 4,700 primary entries and 34,000 related headings."

———————

KEY PUB., INC. V. CHINATOWN TODAY PUB. ENTERPRISES, 945 F.2d 509 (2d Cir.1991). "This appeal concerns the scope of copyright protection provid-ed a classified telephone directory published by appellee Key Publications, Inc. ('Key'). Appellants Galore Enterprises, Inc. and Ma Kam Yee ('Galore' and 'Ma'), appeal from Judge Ward's holding that their publication, the 1990 Chinese American–Life Guide ('Galore Directory'), infringed Key's copyright in the 1989–90 Chinese Business Guide & Directory ('1989–90 Key Directory'). We hold that the 1989–90 Key Directory is subject to copyright protection, but that the Galore Directory does not infringe Key's copyright. We therefore reverse. * * *

"This appeal specifically concerns the yellow pages listings contained in the 1989–90 Key Directory. Key's president, Lynn Wang, is responsible for assembling the Key directories. Beginning in 1983, Ms. Wang collected business cards from doctors and lawyers associated with the Chinese–American community, banks that did business in the Chinese–American community, and other establishments she thought ought to be included in the yellow pages section of the Directory. Additionally, a 'modest percent-age,' in the words of the district court, of the listings in the 1984 Key Directory were copied from another compilation, the 1981 Chinese Ameri-can Restaurant Directory ('Restaurant Directory'). Some of the copied listings were presumably included in later directories, including the 1989–90 Key Directory. The information collected in the 1989–90 Key Directory was sorted by type of business; each listing is placed in one of over 260 different categories; and each of the approximately 9000 listings consists of an English and a Chinese name, an address, and a telephone number. * * * The yellow pages of the Galore Directory contain approximately 2000 listings divided among twenty-eight different categories. Like the 1989–90 Key Directory, business establishments of interest to the New York Chi-nese–American community are listed in the Galore Directory. About seventy-five percent, or 1500, of the businesses listed in the Galore Directo-ry are also listed in the 1989–90 Key Directory. * * *

"[O]nly if the selection, coordination, or arrangement of listings in the directory is sufficiently original or creative will the directory be entitled to a copyright. Selection implies the exercise of judgment in choosing which facts from a given body of data to include in a compilation. * * * In assembling the directory, Ms. Wang had to select from a multitude of businesses in New York and elsewhere those of greatest interest to her audience—the New York City Chinese–American community. * * * Ms.

Wang testified that she excluded from the directory those businesses she did not think would remain open for very long, such as certain insurance brokers, take-out restaurants, and traditional Chinese medical practitioners. This testimony alone indicates thought and creativity in the selection of businesses included in the 1989–90 Key Directory. * * *

"In addition, the arrangement of the Key Directory is original within the meaning of the copyright laws. Arrangement 'refers to the ordering or grouping of data into lists or categories that go beyond the mere mechanical grouping of data as such, for example, the alphabetical, chronological, or sequential listings of data.' Copyright Office, Guidelines for Registration of Fact–Based Compilations 1 (Rev.Oct. 11, 1989), * * *. The 1989–90 Key Directory contains over 9000 listings divided among approximately 260 different categories. The format of the Key Directory is common to most classified directories, and particular categories have, of course, been used in other classified directories, e.g., 'ACCOUNTANTS,' 'BRIDAL SHOPS,' and 'SHOE STORES.' Nevertheless, some of the categories are of particular interest to the Chinese–American community and not common to yellow pages, e.g., 'BEAN CURD & BEAN SPROUT SHOPS.' And there is no evidence that the arrangement and designation of categories was copied from, or is substantially similar to, another directory. The lack of novelty is, as noted, not a bar to copyright protection."

Although Key's copyright was upheld, the court concluded that the Galore Directory was not an infringement. "What must be shown is substantial similarity between those elements, and only those elements, that provide copyrightability to the allegedly infringed compilation. * * * With regard to the arrangement of listings in the Galore Directory, it can hardly be described as even remotely similar to the arrangement utilized by the 1989–90 Key Directory. The Galore Directory contains only twenty-eight different categories, set out in APPENDIX A. The 1989–90 Key Directory contains over 260 different categories, set out in APPENDIX B. Not only is the magnitude of the difference in the number of categories enormous, but only three of the twenty-eight categories in the Galore Directory duplicate categories in the 1989–90 Key Directory. A facial examination thus readily reveals great dissimilarity. * * *

"Of course, as noted supra, infringement may also be found if there is a substantial similarity in the selection of businesses listed in the two publications. The district court found that seventy-five percent of the 2000 listings, 1500 listings, included in the Galore Directory duplicated listings contained in the 1989–90 Key Directory. The district court also found that the 1500 duplicate listings resulted from deliberate copying by Galore and Ma.

"However, the 1989–90 Key Directory contains over 9000 listings. Thus, just seventeen percent (1500/9000) of the listings in the 1989–90 Key Directory were also printed in the Galore Directory. Moreover, the listings copied do not come primarily from any particular portion of the 1989–90 Key Directory; no category of the 1989–90 Key Directory containing more than a few entries is duplicated in total in the Galore Directory. For example, of the 124 accountants listed in the 1989–90 Key Directory, only forty-two are also listed in the Galore Directory. Finally, at least twenty-five percent of the listings in the Galore Directory are not in the 1989–90 Key Directory.

"We conclude that, as a matter of law, the Galore Directory does not infringe the 1989–90 Key Directory."

NOTES AND QUESTIONS

(1) Does the *BellSouth* case move beyond *Feist* in limiting protection for compilations of facts? Is it inconsistent with *Key Publications?* Are the cases moving, as Judge Hatchett suggests in his dissent, toward a novelty requirement for compilations?

Examples of compilations that have survived the *Feist* analysis include a "pitching form" in Kregos v. Associated Press, 937 F.2d 700 (2d Cir. 1991), that combined nine statistics relating to the past performances of opposing pitchers in upcoming baseball games. Judge Newman noted that "there are at least scores of available statistics about pitching performances available to be calculated from the underlying data and therefore thousands of combinations of data that a selector can chose to include in a pitching form." But the plaintiff lost a subsequent appeal on the issue of infringement; plaintiff's copyright was "limited to the particular selections he made," and defendant AP's pitching form had 10 statistics, only six of which were the same as the plaintiff's. 3 F.3d 656 (2d Cir.1993), cert. denied, 510 U.S. 1112 (1994). In Lipton v. Nature Co., 71 F.3d 464 (2d Cir.1995), plaintiff's selection and "aesthetic" arrangement of so-called "terms of venery" (a pride of lions, a murder of crows, a parliament of owls), culled from fifteenth century manuscripts and published under the title *An Exaltation of Larks* was found sufficiently original to sustain an infringement claim against a defendant who sold posters bearing a strikingly similar compilation. Many of the post-*Feist* compilation cases are discussed in Strong, Database Protection After *Feist v. Rural Telephone Co.*, 42 J.Copyr.Soc. 39 (1994).

(2) Consider the following pre-*Feist* cases. Would the outcomes remain the same if the cases were litigated today? In light of *Feist,* would additional fact-finding be required?

(a) "Plaintiff Marion S. Schroeder was the compiler of *The Green Thumbook,* for which a concededly valid copyright was issued. Defendants are the publisher and the printer of the accused book, *The Gardener's Catalogue.* * * * Plaintiffs' book consists of listings of the names and addresses of suppliers of seeds, plants, publications, and other items useful to gardeners, with information about each supplier listed; and a similar list of plant societies. Defendants' book is much more voluminous. It includes gardening advice and information, illustrations, and miscellaneous similar material, in addition to listings of plant societies and suppliers of seeds, plants, etc. Without independent checking or verification, the compilers of defendants' book copied the names and addresses, but not the other information, appearing on 27 of the 63 pages of plaintiffs' book. The copied names and addresses, which amount to about one per cent of defendants' book, were publicly available, but plaintiff Marion S. Schroeder had collected and categorized them by her own individual effort." On this statement of facts, infringement was found. Schroeder v. William Morrow & Co., 566 F.2d 3 (7th Cir.1977).

(b) Plaintiffs published *Sport Americana Baseball Card Price Guide.* "The Guide lists some 18,000 different baseball cards and in each case furnishes the going market price. * * * The Guide also gives the prices for each card according to its condition: mint, very good/excellent and fair/good. In addition, the cards are placed into two groups; premium or star cards, and common cards. There are approximately 5,000 of the former, and they are considered particularly valuable because of the player featured on the card, e.g., a hall of famer, a rookie of the year, or because of the team on which he plays, or because of some characteristic of the card itself, such as an imperfection or the scarcity of the card. Common cards consist of the remaining cards listed in the series covered." Three months after publication of the *Guide,* the defendants began to publish *Card Price Update,* a monthly listing of baseball card prices. "CPU was published in a newspaper form, indicated the trends in prices by a plus or minus and listed separately only premium cards; however, its listing contained substantially the same 5,000 cards that the Guide had listed as premium cards. * * * [M]any of the prices and pictures in CPU are the same as those in the Guide, and a number of inadvertent errors in the Guide, including misspellings, inconsistent use of abbreviations and obvious omissions, are repeated in CPU." The court concluded that the *Guide* was copyrightable, and that the defendants had infringed. Eckes v. Card Prices Update, 736 F.2d 859 (2d Cir.1984).

(c) Plaintiff Worth published two books of trivia, *Super Trivia I* and *Super Trivia II,* each containing some 6,000 entries arranged alphabetically under various headings. "Worth alleges that Horn Abbot, Ltd., and its principals, the designers of the game *Trivial Pursuit,* and Selchow & Righter Company ('Selchow'), the marketer of the game, infringed the copyright in his books in their 'Genus,' 'Baby Boomer,' and 'Silver Screen,' editions of the game. *Trivial Pursuit* is a board game utilizing question and answer cards, in which the object of the game is to answer correctly 'trivia questions' in various subject areas in order to roll the dice, advance around the board, and collect color-coded wedges. Each edition of the game contains 6000 questions and answers arranged on 1000 cards. * * * Worth contends that 1,675 questions (27.9%) in the Genus edition were taken from *Super Trivia I,* 1,293 questions (21.6%) in the Silver Screen edition were taken from *Super Trivia I* and/or *II,* and 828 questions (13.8%) in the Baby Boomer edition were taken from *Super Trivia I* and/or *II.*" The court first rejected a claim of infringement in the expression of the individual questions: "The verbatim repetition of certain words in order to use the nonprotectible facts is also noninfringing; the game cards' repetition of words used by Worth to describe places, persons, and events constitute 'mere *indispensable* expression' of particular facts or ideas." It then concluded that there had been no infringement of Worth's compilation of factual entries. Worth v. Selchow & Richter Co., 827 F.2d 569 (9th Cir.1987), cert. denied, 485 U.S. 977 (1988).

(3) As the *Eckes* case, supra, illustrates, the presence of common errors can be compelling evidence of copying. See, e.g., Lakedale Tel. Co. v. Fronteer Directory Co., 230 U.S.P.Q. 694 (D.Minn.1986); but see J.R. O'Dwyer Co. v. Media Marketing Int'l, Inc., 755 F.Supp. 599 (S.D.N.Y. 1991), where the defendant offered sufficiently credible explanations for common errors to avoid a preliminary injunction. The "errors" in the copyrighted work are not always inadvert. See, e.g., Rockford Map Pub., Inc. v. Directory Service Co., 768 F.2d 145 (7th Cir.1985), cert. denied, 474 U.S. 1061 (1986), in which bogus middle initials of landowners on a plat map, spelling out the name of the copyright owner, also appeared on defendant's map. (Do publishers of casebooks employ similar strata-gems?) Proof of copying through common errors, however, does not necessarily establish infringement. See Cooling Systems and Flexibles, Inc. v. Stuart Radiator, Inc., 777 F.2d 485 (9th Cir.1985) (copied errors were part of uncopyrightable factual material).

(4) Commentary on *Feist* has been profuse. See, e.g., Karjala, Copyright and Misappropriation, 17 U.Dayton L.Rev. 885 (1992) and Yen, The Legacy of *Feist:* Consequences of the Weak Connection Between Copyright and the Economics of Public Goods, 52 Ohio St.L.J. 1343 (1991), both arguing that the failure to recognize authorship in the skill and effort of compiling raises the prospect of underprotection. Dreyfuss, A *Wiseguy's* Approach to Infor-mation Products: Muscling Copyright and Patent Into a Unitary Theory of Intellectual Property, 1992 Sup.Ct.Rev. 195, also worries about incentive and argues for greater flexibility in defining rights and remedies in prefer-ence to an all or nothing approach. Lange, Sensing the Constitution in *Feist*, 17 U.Dayton L.Rev. 367 (1992), takes a different view, hoping that *Feist* is the start of an effort to constrain intellectual property rights in the face of new technologies.

(5) A notable feature of the *Feist* opinion is its repetitive invocation of the Constitution (at least 13 times) as the source of the requirement of original authorship. This constitutional emphasis is decried in Heald, The Vices of Originality, 1991 Sup.Ct.Rev. 143 (1992), but applauded for its steadying influence in Abrams, Originality and Creativity in Copyright Law, 55 L. & Contemp.Prob. (No. 2) 3 (1992). Hamilton, Justice O'Connor's Opinion in *Feist Publications, Inc. v. Rural Telephone Service Co.,* An Uncommon Though Characteristic Approach, 38 J.Copyr.Soc. 83 (1990), notes that the breadth of the opinion is in contrast to Justice O'Connor's other intellectu-al property opinions. It is a recurring theme among the commentators that the Court did little to clarify the concept of "authorship"—the apparently modest requirement of some minimal creativity.   See, e.g., Raskind, Assessing the Impact of *Feist,* 17 U.Dayton L.Rev. 331 (1992).

———————

PROBLEM: West Publishing Company publishes judicial opinions in the familiar series of books known as the National Reporter System.   After receiving an opinion from a court, West checks the accuracy of citations and adds headnotes and a synopsis.   West then separates state and federal opinions.   State opinions then are divided by geographic region and assigned to the appropriate regional reporter.   Federal decisions are separated according to the level of the issuing court.   District court decisions are further divided by separating bankruptcy decisions and federal rules decisions from other district court decisions.

After the decisions are designated for a particular reporter series, they are assigned to the current volume of the series and arranged within the volume.   Decisions in F.2d, for example, are arranged by circuit, although typically there are more than one group of each circuit's opinions in each volume.   The volumes and pages are numbered sequentially.

Mead Data Central operates LEXIS, the computer-assisted legal research service.   Mead Data announced its intention to add "star pagination" to the decisions in its data base.   This feature would consist of "page breaks" inserted into the text of opinions in LEXIS.   The "page breaks" are brackets containing the page numbers from the West report of the case, inserted into the text of the LEXIS opinion at the point where one West page ends and the next begins.   The feature would permit LEXIS users to cite to the specific page of the West reporter on which a relevant quotation or point of law appears without ever consulting the West reporter volume.

West responded to Mead Data's announcement with a complaint alleging infringement of the copyright in its selection and arrangement of cases and moved for a preliminary injunction.   Does the "star pagination" feature infringe West's copyrights on its reporter volumes?   See West Publishing Co. v. Mead Data Central, Inc., 799 F.2d 1219 (8th Cir.1986), cert. denied, 479 U.S. 1070 (1987).   After the decision on the preliminary injunction, the case proceeded to trial, but the suit was settled when the parties agreed to a license.   The decision and settlement are both criticized in Patterson & Joyce, Monopolizing the Law: The Scope of Copyright Protection for Law Reports and Statutory Codes, 36 UCLA L.Rev. 719 (1989).

Litigation over West's copyrights continues. A district court in Minnesota held that the Eighth Circuit's decision upholding West's compilation copyright survived the Supreme Court's subsequent opinion in *Feist,* Oasis Pub. Co. v. West Pub. Co., 924 F.Supp. 918 (D.Minn.1996), but a few months later a district judge in New York ruled from the bench that publisher Matthew Bender's use of star pagination in a CD–ROM containing New York federal cases did not infringe West's copyright. Matthew

Bender & Co. v. West Pub. Co., 41 U.S.P.Q.2d 1321 (S.D.N.Y.1996).[i] Meanwhile, when Thomson Corp. announced that it intended to buy West, the Justice Department raised antitrust objections. A consent decree permitting the sale was approved when West agreed to provide a license for star pagination to any publisher that requested it; for small publishers, the royalties are deferred until 2001 or until a "final judicial determination" of West's copyright claim.

NOTES ON DATABASES

(1) A computer database is in essence an automated compilation—a collection of information capable of being manipulated and retrieved by an appropriate search program. WESTLAW and LEXIS are computer databases. So is the computerized listing of names and numbers used by telephone operators. The House Report states that the term "literary work * * * includes computer data bases." H.R.Rep. p. 54.

The issue of copyright in computer databases was among those examined by the National Commission on New Technological Uses of Copyrighted Works. The Commission, which happily eschewed the acronym NCONTUOCW in favor of CONTU, was established by Congress in 1974 to consider the copyright issues raised by photocopying and computer technologies.

The CONTU Report, submitted in 1978, concludes that computer databases are eligible for protection as "compilations" under the 1976 Act. It is often difficult, however, to think in terms of an arrangement or ordering of information in a computer database. The format in which the information is stored depends primarily on the nature of the particular storage technology, and the form in which the information is retrieved often is controlled by the user. The CONTU Report concludes that an "unauthorized taking of substantial segments of a copyrighted data base should be considered infringing." CONTU Rep. p. 42. Is this consistent with *Feist*?

In a 1986 report entitled Intellectual Property Rights in an Age of Electronics and Information, the Office of Technology Assessment examined the impact on intellectual property law of existing and anticipated advances in information technologies. On the issue of copyright in computer databases the report concluded that the "unique characteristics of computer database technology may severely curtail the usefulness of copyright protection for works of fact that are distributed on-line, since copyright protection extends only to the work's expression." Id. p. 75. The report noted both the ease with which the format of information can be altered and the difficulty of detecting infringement.

---

i. In a later decision in the same litigation, the court held that editorial changes made by West, such as the addition of attorneys' names and parallel citations and the correction of spelling errors, were not sufficient to support a derivative copyright claim. A competitor was thus free to electronically scan opinions from West reporters onto a CD–ROM. (West's headnotes and key numbers had not been copied.) Matthew Bender & Co. v. West Pub. Co., 42 U.S.P.Q.2d 1930 (S.D.N.Y.1997). (Would anything prevent another copier from simply duplicating and selling the first copier's CD–ROM?)

(2) Are compilations sufficiently distinctive to justify a separate statutory regime more precisely attuned than copyright to the nature and value of such works? An early case for separate treatment was made in Keating, Copyright Protection and the Information Explosion, 88 Dick.L.Rev. 268 (1984). In 1996 the European Union adopted a Directive on Legal Protection of Databases that requires member nations to grant protection against unauthorized "extraction" and "reutilization" of a "substantial part" of a database, irrespective of the work's eligibility for copyright. Protection for foreign databases is available only on the basis of reciprocal protection in the foreign country. A proposal for an international system of sui generis database protection was on the agenda at a World Intellectual Property Organization conference held in Geneva in December, 1996, but the proposal was tabled amid widespread opposition by scientific and educational interests.[j] WIPO has announced that it will continue to pursue an international database treaty.

Attempts to enact sui generis database protection in the United States began in 1996. In light of *Feist*'s emphasis on the constitutional basis of originality, does Congress have the power to protect unoriginal compilations? Could it rely on its authority under the commerce clause? See Ginsburg, No "Sweat"? Copyright and Other Protection of Works of Information after *Feist v. Rural Telephone*, 92 Colum.L.Rev. 338 (1992). A 1997 Copyright Office report on database protection prepared at the request of the Senate Judiciary Committee declined to offer a recommendation on sui generis legislation; it did, however, address the constitutional issue: "To the extent that the legislation promotes different policies from copyright, and does so in a different manner, it is similar to trademark law, and therefore seems likely to survive a constitutional challenge." The report also raised first amendment concerns, although it concluded that a legislative pronouncement confirming that individual facts remain in the public domain might be sufficient. Proposed legislation would protect databases against substantial extractions of information that harm the market for the work.

(3) Looking ahead, could *state* law prohibit the reproduction of factual information contained in a compilation? A number of cases indicate that § 301 of the Copyright Act preempts such state protection. See, e.g., Financial Information, Inc. v. Moody's Investors Service, Inc., 808 F.2d 204 (2d Cir.1986), cert. denied, 484 U.S. 820 (1987).

(4) Consider also works that owe their existence to the application of computer technology. Computer-generated graphics and music are now common in the broadcast and film industries. Musical works can be sampled and digitally manipulated to produce new works. Photographs and other graphic works can be digitally mapped and sampled to create new images. (Do such works infringe their source material? See p. 241 infra.)

---

j. The impact of proprietary claims in compilations of data on a science such as archaeology is described in Carson, Laser Technology in Archaeology, 10 Harv.J.L. & Tech. 281 (1997). Reichman and Samuelson, Intellectual Property Rights in Data?, 50 Vand.L.Rev. 51 (1997), argue that the approach taken by the European Union and the proposed WIPO treaty results in overprotection; they favor protection limited to unfair competition or a system of short-term rights and compulsory licenses.

More mundane illustrations are a mailing list created through the electronic manipulation of a database and a computer-generated list of random numbers useful to statisticians. A more unusual example was presented to the Copyright Office for registration in 1993. A computer was programmed to "think" like author Jacqueline Susann by inputting thousands of "rules" based on a detailed analysis of two of her steamier novels. (There was apparently an agreement of some sort with the author's estate). The computer then asked a series of questions, the programmer answered, and the machine produced a novel entitled *Just This Once*. The originator of the program says he wrote about one-quarter of the prose, the computer wrote a quarter, and half was a "collaboration of man and machine." A reviewer, comparing the book to a work in the same genre by author Jackie Collins, said that "if you like this stuff, you'd be much better off with the one written by the computer." See 46 Pat.,Tm. & Copyr.J. (BNA) 397 (1993). Are such computer–generated works copyrightable? Who is the author?

The issue of computer-generated works is discussed in the CONTU Report. The Commission concludes that "the author is the one who employs the computer," and that such works present "no special problem." As for copyrightability, the Report said, "The eligibility of any work for protection by copyright depends not upon the device or devices used in its creation, but rather upon the presence of at least minimal human creative effort at the time the work is produced." CONTU Rep. p. 45.

Is there sufficient creative effort on the part of a user who merely enters the command "compose" into a music composing program and awaits the result? Is there a case for authorship of the resulting work in the creator of the computer program? A case for joint authorship with the user of the program? These and other possibilities are considered in Samuelson, Allocating Ownership Rights in Computer–Generated Works, 47 U.Pitt.L.Rev. 1185 (1986), which reluctantly acquiesces in the CONTU position. The Office of Technology Assessment, however, distinguishing computers from cameras, typewriters, and other "inert" tools, concluded that "[i]f machines are in any sense co-creators, the rights of programmers and users of programs may not be easily determined within the present copyright system." O.T.A. Rep. p. 72. Clifford, Intellectual Property in the Era of the Creative Computer Program: Will the True Creator Please Stand Up?, 71 Tul.L.Rev. 1675 (1997), argues that the output of an autonomously creative computer program isn't (and shouldn't be) copyrightable.

MAPS

United States v. Hamilton

United States Court of Appeals, Ninth Circuit, 1978.
583 F.2d 448.

■ Before KILKENNY, SNEED, and KENNEDY, CIRCUIT JUDGES.

■ KENNEDY, CIRCUIT JUDGE:

The defendant in this criminal case admitted making and selling precise reproductions of a map bearing a copyright. The sole issue on appeal is whether the map that the defendant copied was of such originality that its copyright was valid. That inquiry requires us to decide a question of copyright law not addressed by previous decisions in this circuit.

The defendant, Edward S. Hamilton, was charged with two counts of knowing and willful infringement of a copyright in violation of 17 U.S.C. § 104.[1] The district court, sitting without a jury, found the defendant guilty and imposed a $700 fine. We find, as did the district court, that the copyright is valid; and the conviction is affirmed.

The maps involved in this case show the boundaries, roads, terrain, features, and improved areas of Ada County, Idaho. KDB Enterprises, a company which specializes in making maps of the Pacific Northwest and which holds about ninety copyrights for various maps, produced a map of Ada County, Idaho in 1970 and obtained copyright for it. KDB then produced a second map of Ada County in 1973 and received a certificate of copyright covering the new matter included on that map. The defendant here was charged with infringing the 1973 copyright by reproducing this second map, and all that is before us is the validity of the copyright for the map of later date.

Hamilton's principal contention, both here and in the trial court, has been that KDB's 1973 map lacks the quality of originality requisite for obtaining a copyright because it was merely a synthesis of information already depicted on maps in the public domain. The 1973 map did show terrain features which had been physically located by a KDB employee and which did not appear on any preexisting map. But a contribution which is more than merely trivial is required in order to satisfy the originality requirement of the Constitution and the copyright statutes, Alfred Bell & Co. v. Catalda Fine Arts, Inc., 191 F.2d 99, 102–03 (2d Cir.1951), and the defendant claims KDB's terrain investigations were so minimal that the 1973 map is not an original work. On the record before us it is a close question whether the extent of the geographic investigation done by KDB was so substantial that, considered alone, it can support the map copyright. We therefore find it necessary to decide whether the map maker's selection, arrangement, and presentation of terrain features which were already either in the public domain or subject to separate copyright (that KDB had a right to use) may be considered as part of the efforts and skill which constitute a cartographer's authorship.

The Third Circuit has held that a map which represents a new combination of information already in the public domain lacks any element worthy of copyright protection. Amsterdam v. Triangle Publications, 93 F.Supp. 79 (E.D.Pa.1950), aff'd on opinion below, 189 F.2d 104 (3rd

---

1. The alleged copyright infringement took place prior to the January 1, 1978 effective date of the 1976 General Revision of Copyright Law. 17 U.S.C. § 101 et seq. (1976).

Cir.1951). The *Amsterdam* court stated that a map may not be put under copyright unless "the publisher of the map in question obtains originally some of that information by the sweat of his own brow." 93 F.Supp. at 82. Thus, under the *Amsterdam* rule, as applied to this case, only those portions of the map recorded as a result of direct observation of terrain features would support the copyright. * * *

Amsterdam and perhaps the copyright cases from this circuit cited above suggest that we should insist upon a standard of originality that is more demanding in cases respecting maps than with other works subject to copyright. If this approach reflects a concern that cartographers might be excluded entirely from using valuable maps in the public domain because a private party has a previous copyright on a map which utilizes the public domain information, the fear, of course, is a false one; for the fact that one person studies other works so as to produce from those elements a new work with sufficient originality to obtain a copyright does not prevent a different author from making independent use of his own skills and efforts to do precisely the same thing. In this respect, the danger of removing a whole subject area from the public realm of experimentation and design does not exist, as it does under the patent laws, which permit the owner of a valid patent to exclude others from infringement even if they created the object or device solely by efforts of their own.

Amsterdam appears to rest on the judgment that the only facet of cartography that can result in an original product, the only feature of the art worth protecting, results from direct observation. However, we are unable to find a persuasive reason for adopting this premise, and we therefore decline to rule that maps present considerations that are distinct from all other copyright cases. Expression in cartography is not so different from other artistic forms seeking to touch upon external realities that unique rules are needed to judge whether the authorship is original. Recording by direct observation is only one measure of a cartographer's skill and talent, and originality should not be made synonymous with a requirement that features of a copyrighted map be observed and recorded directly before they will be entitled to copyright protection. For this reason, we think the *Amsterdam* rule is theoretically unsound. We are aware that under the conventional standards for determining originality a cartographer occasionally may have some difficulty proving that his map is an original compilation rather than a mere imitation. But this problem of proof does not justify failing to protect the many cartographers whose claims of original work can be established. Not protecting the product of creative compilation or synthesis would discourage progress in the field of cartography much more than the difficulty in a few cases of proving originality under the conventional standards. * * *

    * * * Trivial elements of compilation and arrangement, of course, are not copyrightable since they fall below the threshold of originality. For example, it is well-settled that copyright of a map does not give the author an exclusive right to the coloring, symbols, and key used in delineating boundaries of and locations within the territory depicted. Perris v. Hexam-

er, 99 U.S. (9 Otto) 674, 675–76 (1878); Christianson v. West Publishing Co., 149 F.2d 202, 203–04 (9th Cir.1945).

That maps have sufficient originality to support a copyright has been recognized since the first copyright statute, enacted in 1790, provided coverage for "maps, charts, and books." 1 Stat. 124 (1790). The early cases recognized that "[t]he elements of the copyright [in a map] consist in the selection, arrangement, and presentation of the component parts." General Drafting Co. v. Andrews, 37 F.2d 54, 55 (2d Cir.1930). See Emerson v. Davies, 8 Fed.Cas. 615, 619 (Cir.Ct.D.Mass.1845) (Story, J.). We rule that elements of compilation which amount to more than a matter of trivial selection may, either alone or when taken into consideration with direct observation, support a finding that a map is sufficiently original to merit copyright protection. Beginning with the Supreme Court's decision in Burrow–Giles Lithographic Co. v. Sarony, 111 U.S. 53 (1884), the courts have carefully delineated selection of subject, posture, background, lighting, and perhaps even perspective alone as protectible elements of a photographer's work. See, e.g., Time, Inc. v. Bernard Geis Associates, 293 F.Supp. 130, 141–43 (S.D.N.Y.1968). Similar attention to rewarding the cartographer's art requires us to recognize that the elements of authorship embodied in a map consist not only of the depiction of a previously undiscovered landmark or the correction or improvement of scale or placement, but also in selection, design, and synthesis.[5]

The record below establishes that there are elements both of synthesis from public sources and independent observation in the efforts used to create the 1973 map, and we find that, taken together, they support the validity of the 1973 copyright.

KDB used an Idaho Department of Highways map as the principal base in preparing the 1973 map. It relied upon the 1970 KDB map for some data added to the base. Substantial portions of the roads, landmarks, and features depicted on the 1973 KDB map also appear on maps published by United States Geological Survey, United States Forest Service, and the Bureau of Land Management. We think that the compilation that produced the 1973 map was a result of substantial creative efforts, and we weigh it heavily in support of the finding that the 1973 map was an original work.

In addition to the compilation and synthesis from the other maps, which were put in evidence, the court also found that "a significant portion" of the information on the 1973 KDB map, including rifle ranges,

---

5. We emphasize that compilations or new arrangements of material which represent merely trivial additions to or omissions from a preexisting map will not support a copyright absent some additional original work. For example, copying the outline of the United States and the boundaries of each state cannot be said to involve any element of original choice or arrangement. Christianson v. West Publishing Co., 149 F.2d 202 (9th Cir.1945). Similarly, the selection of principal cities of North America partly from memory and partly from census reports is "far from constituting such originality as to form a basis for copyright." Andrews v. Guenther Publishing Co., 60 F.2d 555, 557 (S.D.N.Y. 1932).

landing strips, motorcycle and jeep trails, landmarks, and names of subdivisions came from other sources. It is clear from the record that at least some of this information was derived from personal observations of a KDB employee who checked the motorcycle trails and other landmarks by ground and aerial observations. The parties differ as to whether the sources of the added information were in the public domain or were from direct observations of the KDB employees, but in our view of the matter that is irrelevant since synthesis can be an element of originality. The new information, when taken into account with the compilation and synthesis from the maps that were introduced in evidence, makes the 1973 map an original one that is subject to copyright. We conclude that the 1973 KDB map was an original product of significant efforts expended by those skilled in the cartographer's art. The copyright was valid. This being the only issue raised by Hamilton on appeal, his conviction must be affirmed.

MASON V. MONTGOMERY DATA, INC.,. 967 F.2d 135 (5th Cir.1992). Mason claimed copyright in a series of maps showing the ownership of real estate in Montgomery County, Texas. The information depicted on Mason's maps came from several sources, including tax and survey records, title abstracts, and existing city and county maps. He claimed infringement when title companies began to make unauthorized copies. The defendants argued that the maps were not copyrightable, relying on Feist Publications, Inc. v. Rural Tel. Service Co., p. 79 supra. The defendants did not dispute that Mason independently created his maps; the issue was whether the maps possessed the "minimal degree of creativity" required under *Feist*.

"Mason's maps pass muster under *Feist* because Mason's selection, coordination, and arrangement of the information that he depicted are sufficiently creative to qualify his maps as original 'compilations' of facts. * * * In his deposition and affidavit, Mason explained the choices that he independently made to select information from numerous and sometimes conflicting sources, and to depict that information on his maps.

"Mason's maps also possess sufficient creativity to merit copyright protection as pictorial and graphic works of authorship. Historically, most courts have treated maps solely as compilations of facts. * * * The Copyright Act, however, categorizes maps not as factual compilations but as 'pictorial, graphic, and sculptural works'—a category that includes photographs and architectural plans. * * *

"Because Mason's maps possess sufficient creativity in both the selection, coordination, and arrangement of the facts that they depict, and as in the pictorial, graphic nature of the way that they do so, we find no error in the district court's determination that Mason's maps are original."

NOTES AND QUESTIONS

(1) Both KDB's and Mason's maps were necessarily derivative works. What leeway to copy might this give the defendants? See § 103. Cf. C.S.

Hammond & Co. v. International College Globe, Inc., 210 F.Supp. 206 (S.D.N.Y.1962) (defendant used plaintiff's globe and other sources; no infringement found). On the "thin" protection available to maps under the *Feist* rationale, see Alexandria Drafting Co. v. Amsterdam, 43 U.S.P.Q.2d 1247 (E.D.Pa.1997) (no infringement despite significant copying). *Mason* and the issue of copyright protection for maps in the post-*Feist* era are reviewed in Karjala, Copyright in Electronic Maps, 35 Jurimetrics J. 395 (1995), sensing a return to "sweat of the brow" protection.

(2) The defendants in *Mason* also challenged the copyrightability of the maps under the "merger" doctrine, which holds, roughly, that when there is only one way to express an idea, copying will be permitted in order to avoid giving the first author a monopoly over the idea itself. See p. 120 infra. The court rejected the defense, holding that protection for Mason's maps "will not grant Mason a monopoly over the idea [of an effective pictorial expression of land ownership], because other mapmakers can express the same idea differently." The court distinguished its earlier decision in Kern River Gas Transmission Co. v. Coastal Corp., 899 F.2d 1458 (5th Cir.), cert. denied, 498 U.S. 952 (1990), in which the court applied the merger doctrine to deny copyright to a map depicting the proposed location of a gas pipeline.

SECTION 2. THE LIMITS OF STATUTORY SUBJECT MATTER

Baker v. Selden

Supreme Court of the United States, 1880.
101 U.S. 99.

■ MR. JUSTICE BRADLEY delivered the opinion of the court.

Charles Selden, the testator of the complainant in this case, in the year 1859 took the requisite steps for obtaining the copyright of a book, entitled "Selden's Condensed Ledger, or Bookkeeping Simplified," the object of which was to exhibit and explain a peculiar system of book-keeping. In 1860 and 1861, he took the copyright of several other books, containing additions to and improvements upon the said system. The bill of complaint was filed against the defendant, Baker, for an alleged infringement of these copyrights. The latter, in his answer, denied that Selden was the author or designer of the books, and denied the infringement charged, and contends on the argument that the matter alleged to be infringed is not a lawful subject of copyright.

The parties went into proofs, and the various books of the complainant, as well as those sold and used by the defendant, were exhibited before the examiner, and witnesses were examined on both sides. A decree was rendered for the complainant, and the defendant appealed.

The book or series of books of which the complainant claims the copyright consists of an introductory essay explaining the system of book-

ONE OF SELDEN'S BOOKKEEPING FORMS

[F2709]

keeping referred to, to which are annexed certain forms or blanks, consisting of ruled lines, and headings, illustrating the system and showing how it is to be used and carried out in practice. This system effects the same results as book-keeping by double entry; but, by a peculiar arrangement of columns and headings, presents the entire operation, of a day, a week, or a month, on a single page, or on two pages facing each other, in an account-book. The defendant uses a similar plan so far as results are concerned; but makes a different arrangement of the columns, and uses different headings. If the complainant's testator had the exclusive right to the use of the system explained in his book, it would be difficult to contend that the defendant does not infringe it, notwithstanding the difference in his form of arrangement; but if it be assumed that the system is open to public use, it seems to be equally difficult to contend that the books made and sold by the defendant are a violation of the copyright of the complainant's book considered merely as a book explanatory of the system. Where the truths of a science or the methods of an art are the common property of the whole world, any author has the right to express the one, or explain and use the other, in his own way. As an author, Selden explained the system in a particular way. It may be conceded that Baker makes and uses account-books arranged on substantially the same system; but the proof fails to show that he has violated the copyright of Selden's book, regarding the latter merely as an explanatory work; or that he has infringed Selden's right in any way, unless the latter became entitled to an exclusive right in the system.

The evidence of the complainant is principally directed to the object of showing that Baker uses the same system as that which is explained and illustrated in Selden's books. It becomes important, therefore, to determine whether, in obtaining the copyright of his books, he secured the exclusive right to the use of the system or method of book-keeping which the said books are intended to illustrate and explain. It is contended that he has secured such exclusive right, because no one can use the system without using substantially the same ruled lines and headings which he has appended to his books in illustration of it. In other words, it is contended that the ruled lines and headings, given to illustrate the system, are a part of the book, and, as such, are secured by the copyright; and that no one can make or use similar ruled lines and headings, or ruled lines and headings made and arranged on substantially the same system, without violating the copyright. And this is really the question to be decided in this case. Stated in another form, the question is, whether the exclusive property in a system of book-keeping can be claimed, under the law of copyright, by means of a book in which that system is explained? The complainant's bill, and the case made under it, are based on the hypothesis that it can be.

It cannot be pretended, and indeed it is not seriously urged, that the ruled lines of the complainant's account-book can be claimed under any special class of objects, other than books, named in the law of copyright existing in 1859. The law then in force was that of 1831, and specified only books, maps, charts, musical compositions, prints, and engravings. An account-book, consisting of ruled lines and blank columns, cannot be called by any of these names unless by that of a book.

There is no doubt that a work on the subject of book-keeping, though only explanatory of well-known systems, may be the subject of a copyright; but, then, it is claimed only as a book. Such a book may be explanatory either of old systems, or of an entirely new system; and, considered as a book, as the work of an author, conveying information on the subject of book-keeping, and containing detailed explanations of the art, it may be a very valuable acquisition to the practical knowledge of the community. But there is a clear distinction between the book, as such, and the art which it is intended to illustrate. The mere statement of the proposition is so evident, that it requires hardly any argument to support it. The same distinction may be predicated of every other art as well as that of book-keeping. A treatise on the composition and use of medicines, be they old or new; on the construction and use of ploughs, or watches, or churns; or on the mixture and application of colors for painting or dyeing; or on the mode of drawing lines to produce the effect of perspective,—would be the subject of copyright; but no one would contend that the copyright of the treatise would give the exclusive right to the art or manufacture described therein. The copyright of the book, if not pirated from other works, would be valid without regard to the novelty, or want of novelty, of its subject-matter. The novelty of the art or thing described or explained has nothing to do with the validity of the copyright. To give to the author of the book an exclusive property in the art described therein, when no examination of its novelty has ever been officially made, would be a surprise and a fraud upon the public. That is the province of letters-patent, not of copyright. The claim to an invention or discovery of an art or manufacture must be subjected to the examination of the Patent Office before an exclusive right therein can be obtained; and it can only be secured by a patent from the government.

The difference between the two things, letters-patent and copyright, may be illustrated by reference to the subjects just enumerated. Take the case of medicines. Certain mixtures are found to be of great value in the healing art. If the discoverer writes and publishes a book on the subject (as regular physicians generally do), he gains no exclusive right to the manufacture and sale of the medicine; he gives that to the public. If he desires to acquire such exclusive right, he must obtain a patent for the mixture as a new art, manufacture, or composition of matter. He may copyright his book, if he pleases; but that only secures to him the exclusive right of printing and publishing his book. So of all other inventions or discoveries.

The copyright of a book on perspective, no matter how many drawings and illustrations it may contain, gives no exclusive right to the modes of drawing described, though they may never have been known or used before. By publishing the book, without getting a patent for the art, the latter is given to the public.   The fact that the art described in the book by illustrations of lines and figures which are reproduced in practice in the application of the art, makes no difference.   Those illustrations are the mere language employed by the author to convey his ideas more clearly. Had he used words of description instead of diagrams (which merely stand in the place of words), there could not be the slightest doubt that others, applying the art to practical use, might lawfully draw the lines and diagrams which were in the author's mind, and which he thus described by words in his book.

The copyright of a work on mathematical science cannot give to the author an exclusive right to the methods of operation which he propounds, or to the diagrams which he employs to explain them, so as to prevent an engineer from using them whenever occasion requires.   The very object of publishing a book on science or the useful arts is to communicate to the world the useful knowledge which it contains.   But this object would be frustrated if the knowledge could not be used without incurring the guilt of piracy of the book.   And where the art it teaches cannot be used without employing the methods and diagrams used to illustrate the book, or such as are similar to them, such methods and diagrams are to be considered as necessary incidents to the art, and given therewith to the public; not given for the purpose of publication in other works explanatory of the art, but for the purpose of practical application.

Of course, these observations are not intended to apply to ornamental designs, or pictorial illustrations addressed to the taste.   Of these it may be said, that their form is their essence, and their object, the production of pleasure in their contemplation.   This is their final end.   They are as much the product of genius and the result of composition, as are the lines of the poet or the historian's periods.   On the other hand, the teachings of science and the rules and methods of useful art have their final end in application and use;   and this application and use are what the public derive from the publication of a book which teaches them.   But as embodied and taught in a literary composition or book, their essence consists only in their statement.   This alone is what is secured by the copyright.   The use by another of the same methods of statement, whether in words or illustrations, in a book published for teaching the art, would undoubtedly be an infringement of the copyright.

Recurring to the case before us, we observe that Charles Selden, by his books, explained and described a peculiar system of book-keeping, and illustrated his method by means of ruled lines and blank columns, with proper headings on a page, or on successive pages.   Now, whilst no one has a right to print or publish his book, or any material part thereof, as a book intended to convey instruction in the art, any person may practice and use the art itself which he has described and illustrated therein.   The use of the art is a totally different thing from a publication of the book explaining it.   The copyright of a book on book-keeping cannot secure the exclusive right to make, sell, and use account-books prepared upon the plan set forth in such book.   Whether the art might or might not have been patented, is a question which is not before us. It was not patented, and is open and free to the use of the public. And, of course, in using the art, the ruled lines and headings of accounts must necessarily be used as incident to it.

The plausibility of the claim put forward by the complainant in this case arises from a confusion of ideas produced by the peculiar nature of the art described in the books which have been made the subject of copyright. In describing the art, the illustrations and diagrams employed happen to correspond more closely than usual with the actual work performed by the operator who uses the art. Those illustrations and diagrams consist of ruled lines and headings of accounts; and it is similar ruled lines and headings of accounts which, in the application of the art, the book-keeper makes with his pen, or the stationer with his press; whilst in most other cases the diagrams and illustrations can only be represented in concrete forms of wood, metal, stone, or some other physical embodiment. But the principle is the same in all. The description of the art in a book, though entitled to the benefit of copyright, lays no foundation for an exclusive claim to the art itself. The object of the one is explanation; the object of the other is use. The former may be secured by copyright. The latter can only be secured, if it can be secured at all, by letters-patent. * * *

The conclusion to which we have come is, that blank account-books are not the subject of copyright; and that the mere copyright of Selden's book did not confer upon him the exclusive right to make and use account-books, ruled and arranged as designated by him and described and illustrated in said book.

The decree of the Circuit Court must be reversed, and the cause remanded with instructions to dismiss the complainant's bill; and it is

So ordered.

QUESTIONS: **(1)** Is the ''art'' vs. ''description of the art'' distinction raised in Baker v. Selden merely an alternative form of the ''idea'' vs. ''expression'' distinction put forward in other cases and codified in § 102(b)?

(2) Does the Court assume that plaintiff's ''art'' can be practiced only by means of similar forms? Is this consistent with the Court's description of the defendant's account books? If similar forms are necessary to the system, is the Court's distinction between copying for use and copying for explanation appropriate? Can the distinction be maintained in view of the Court's holding, as stated at the conclusion of its opinion, ''that blank account-books are not the subject of copyright''?

NOTES ON THE DENIAL OF COPYRIGHT IN ''SYSTEMS'' AND ''BLANK FORMS''

(1) In Brief English Systems v. Owen, 48 F.2d 555 (2d Cir.1931), plaintiff's assignor had devised a system of shorthand called Speedwriting that used regular English letters and punctuation marks. Infringement of copyright in pamphlets describing the system was charged against a defendant who, having been a teacher of Speedwriting, published a rival text. "A comparison of the two systems discloses that they are much alike," but, "[i]n so far as the plaintiff claims to have the exclusive right to the use of a published system of shorthand, this suit must fail. There is no literary merit in a mere system of condensing written words into less than the number of letters usually used to spell them out. Copyrightable material is found, if at all, in the explanation of how to do it." Defendant's explanation was found to be "substantially dissimilar and original." A decree for plaintiff was reversed.

Seltzer v. Sunbrock, 22 F.Supp. 621 (S.D.Cal.1938), concerned a plaintiff who was the originator and promoter of a type of protracted roller-skating race. He wrote and copyrighted two brief narrative accounts of such races, asserted that they were dramatic compositions, and claimed that the defendant's conduct of similar races was an infringement. In holding for the defendant, the court observed that "What Seltzer really composed was a description of a system for conducting races on roller skates. A system, as such, can never be copyrighted." A declaratory judgment in Seltzer's favor against another alleged infringer, Seltzer v. Corem, 26 F.Supp. 892 (N.D.Ind.), was reversed by the Seventh Circuit, following and approving the Sunbrock decision. 107 F.2d 75 (1939). Cf. Seltzer v. Flannagan, 99 N.Y.S.2d 649 (Sup.Ct.1950) (competitor enjoined from imitating plaintiff's name "Roller Derby").[a]

Business systems, generally speaking, are also ineligible for patents. See Loew's Drive–In Theatres v. Park–In Theatres, 174 F.2d 547 (1st Cir.), cert. denied, 338 U.S. 822 (1949) (method of operating a drive-in theater); State Street Bank and Trust Co. v. Signature Financial Group, Inc., 927 F.Supp. 502 (D.Mass.1996) (computerized accounting system for managing a mutual fund). But cf. Paine, Webber, Jackson & Curtis, Inc. v. Merrill Lynch, Pierce, Fenner & Smith, Inc., 564 F.Supp. 1358 (D.Del.1983). Merrill Lynch successfully defended a patent on the computer program for administering its Cash Management Account, which combines numerous financial services. Against the contention that the result of the computerized process was simply a combination of familiar business systems, the court said that "the claims allegedly teach a method of operation on a computer to effectuate a business activity," and satisfy 35 U.S.C.A. § 101, p. 67 supra.

(2) The Copyright Office has a regulation, 37 C.F.R. § 202(1)(c), denying copyright to "[b]lank forms, such as time cards, graph paper, account books, diaries, bank checks, scorecards, address books, report forms, order forms and the like, which are designed for recording information and do not in themselves convey information." Is this proposition required by

---

a. See also Cash Dividend Check Corp. v. Davis, 247 F.2d 458 (9th Cir.1957) (redeemable stamps); Nutt v. National Institute, Inc., 31 F.2d 236 (2d Cir.1929) (memory improvement system); Kepner–Tregoe, Inc. v. Carabio, 203 U.S.P.Q. 124 (E.D.Mich.1979) (problem-solving technique).

Baker v. Selden? Or is it merely an application of the general criteria of "authorship"? Is the Copyright Office justified in requiring some level of expository content as a condition of copyright?

In Harcourt, Brace & World, Inc. v. Graphic Controls Corp., 329 F.Supp. 517 (S.D.N.Y.1971), the question posed, said Judge Lasker, was "a novel and difficult question of law: Are printed answer sheets, created for use in conjunction with student achievement and intelligence tests and designed to be corrected by optical scanning machines, the proper subject of copyright?" The plaintiff had published a large number of standardized educational and psychological tests; the answer sheets had been accepted for registration by the Copyright Office. In the transaction at issue, the Buffalo Board of Education had invited bids for 130,000 answer sheets. Plaintiff's price was $8,805; defendant's was $2,487. Plaintiff claimed that its sheets had been copied. Judge Lasker held that the answer sheets were copyrightable, although the opportunity for creativity was limited because of the physical limitations of the machines that "read" the answers. Still, the answer sheet was not "merely a form upon which information is recorded (as, for example, in the case of the form on which a machine automatically records temperatures, Taylor v. Fawley–Brost [noted below]). The answer sheets here contain a mix of inherent meaning, of information conveyed, and the utility for the recording of responses. There is no clear division between the 'explanation' of a system (how to use the answer sheet in taking the examination) and its 'use' (using the answer sheet as a form upon which responses are recorded) as appeared to the court in Baker v. Selden, supra." Should the plaintiff's dominant position in the market for widely used tests invite a more stringent application of Baker v. Selden?

The Copyright Office in 1979 announced a rulemaking inquiry "regarding blank forms," but concluded the study in 1980 with a detailed statement in 45 Fed.Reg. 63297 reviewing the case law and affirming its regulation as firmly based on both Baker v. Selden and the general requirement of "original, creative expression." See also Bibbero Systems, Inc. v. Colwell Systems, Inc., 893 F.2d 1104 (9th Cir.1990), denying copyright in a medical claims form despite the inclusion of instructions, checklists, and assignment of claims provisions, but noting that "cases interpreting the blank forms rule do not yield a consistent line of reasoning"; John H. Harland Co. v. Clarke Checks, Inc., 711 F.2d 966 (11th Cir.1983), denying copyright to a checkbook format featuring a duplicate stub designed to record the details of checks written after being detached from the checkbook. (The plaintiff did win relief on trademark and trade dress infringement claims.)

(3) Taylor Instrument Co. v. Fawley–Brost Co., 139 F.2d 98 (7th Cir.1943), cert. denied, 321 U.S. 785 (1944), distinguished by Judge Lasker in *Harcourt, Brace,* supra, was a suit for infringement of copyrighted charts used in connection with plaintiff's recording thermometers. Defendant's charts were copied from plaintiff's and in some instances bore symbols indicating that they fit plaintiff's instruments. The court found plaintiff's charts uncopyrightable.   In Brown Instrument Co. v. Warner, 161 F.2d 910 (D.C.Cir.), cert. denied, 332 U.S. 801 (1947), where the Copyright Office was upheld in refusing registration for a similar recording chart, the court said that *Taylor Instrument* was correctly decided and "moreover, that the case is controlled by Baker v. Selden."   Judge Edgerton wrote:

> Articles intended for practical use in cooperation with a machine are not copyrightable.   White–Smith Music Pub. Co. v. Apollo Co., 209 U.S. 1.   Both law and policy forbid monopolizing a machine except within the comparatively narrow limits of the patent system.   In several patents on recording machines, the necessary printed chart is rightly claimed as one of the operative elements.   Since the machines which cooperate with the charts in suit are useless without them, to copyright the charts would in effect continue appellant's monopoly of its machines beyond the time authorized by the patent law.

Continental Casualty Co. v. Beardsley

United States Court of Appeals, Second Circuit, 1958.
253 F.2d 702.
Certiorari denied 358 U.S. 816, 79 S.Ct. 25.

■ Before HINCKS and LUMBARD, CIRCUIT JUDGES, and DIMOCK, DISTRICT JUDGE.

■ HINCKS, CIRCUIT JUDGE.   These are cross-appeals arising out of a suit brought by Continental Casualty Company (Continental) which sought a declaratory judgment that defendants' copyrights were invalid together with an injunction, an accounting, and counsel fees.   Continental also demanded damages for unfair competition and violation of the antitrust laws.   The defendant, Beardsley, counterclaimed alleging infringement by Continental of his valid copyrights and that Continental was liable for unfair competition.   The District Court held that the material in question was not properly copyrightable; that, even if it were, the copyright had been lost; and, further, that there was no infringement.   The District Court granted the declaratory relief sought by Continental and an injunction.   It rejected the unfair competition claims of both parties and Continental's antitrust claim and its request for an accounting and counsel fees.   Each party has appealed from every adverse ruling below.   In addition, Beardsley contends that in any event the injunction is too broad.

Copyrightability

This controversy had its inception in the late 1930's.   Defendant Beardsley was an insurance broker (also a member of the bar) who allegedly developed a blanket bond to cover replacement of lost securities which would operate *in futuro*.   In September 1939, he published his "plan" in a six-page pamphlet.   The entire pamphlet carried a copyright notice and Continental admits that the introductory three pages of narrative are validly copyrighted.   As to these three pages, however, there is no claim of infringement.   Continental contended below, and the court agreed, that the remaining three pages of forms to carry out the "plan" were not copyrightable. The forms included a proposed bond, an affidavit of loss and indemnity agreement, and drafts of an instruction letter and board resolutions. Beardsley had also devised various insurance instruments, some but not all of which he had copyrighted.

We find nothing which, as a matter of law, prevents the copyrighting of forms and insurance instruments such as those now before us. * * *

Notwithstanding this general authority in support of the copyrightability of forms, Continental relies upon Baker v. Selden, 101 U.S. 99. * * *

In Baker v. Selden, supra, the subject-matter was such that the explanation of the system could be treated as separable from account books prepared and arranged for the practice of the system. But not so here. For inseparably included in Beardsley's bonds and affidavits, which constitute the means for the practice of his Plan, is language explanatory of the Plan. Consequently, the holding of Baker v. Selden is not applicable here. See also Taylor Instrument Companies v. Fawley–Brost Co., 7 Cir., 139 F.2d 98, certiorari denied 321 U.S. 785, chart for recording temperatures; Aldrich v. Remington–Rand, D.C.N.D.Texas, 52 F.Supp. 732, sheets for keeping tax records; Page v. Wisden, 20 L.T.R. (n.s.) 435, cricket scoring sheet. And since the Constitution and Copyright Act read directly upon all the forms here involved, we hold them to be copyrightable.

This resolution of the question of copyrightability raises several very serious questions as to the scope of the protection granted which we now come to consider.

Infringement

We agree completely with the conclusion of the trial court that Beardsley did not succeed in proving infringement. * * *

There have been several cases dealing with the copyrighting of insurance and similar forms. Significantly, they uniformly are decided by holdings of non-infringement and leave undecided the copyrightability point.[3] These cases have set a stiff standard for proof of infringement.

In Dorsey v. Old Surety Life Ins. Co., 10 Cir., 98 F.2d 872, 874, the court found non-infringement declaring, "To constitute infringement in such cases a showing of appropriation in the exact form or substantially so of the copyrighted material should be required."

In Crume v. Pacific Mut. Life Ins. Co., 7 Cir., 140 F.2d 182, certiorari denied 322 U.S. 755, the court found non-infringement of plaintiff's pamphlet describing a method for reorganizing insurance companies. As in all of these cases, the court was keenly aware that to prohibit similarity of language would have the effect of giving the copyright owner a monopoly on his idea—which the cases uniformly deny to copyright owners. Thus, the court stated, 140 F.2d at pages 184–185:

---

3. We have had to decide the copyright question here because one portion of the judgment appealed from enjoined Beardsley from claiming a copyright on any of his forms.

" * * * In the instant situation there is no room for the skill of the mechanic or artisan in utilizing the plan or the method disclosed. Its use, to which the public is entitled, can be effected solely by the employment of words descriptive thereof. In our view, where the use can be effected only in such manner, there can be no infringement even though the plan or method be copied. We realize that such a view leaves little, if any, protection to the copyright owners; in fact, it comes near to invalidating the copyright. This situation, however, results from the fact that the practical use of the art explained by the copyright and lodged in the public domain can be attained solely by the employment of language which gives expression to that which is disclosed." Further, "We also observe that such comparison [of the documents] adds strength to the view heretofore expressed that defendant's rightful use of the art disclosed could only be accomplished by the employment of words which describe plaintiff's method. To hold that an idea, plan, method or art described in a copyright is open to the public but that it can be used only by the employment of different words and phrases which mean the same thing, borders on the preposterous. It is to exalt the accomplishment of a result by indirect means which could not be done directly. It places a premium upon evasion and makes this the test of infringement. Notwithstanding some authorities which support a theory permitting such a result, we think it is wrong and disapprove it." * * *

These cases indicate that in the fields of insurance and commerce the use of specific language in forms and documents may be so essential to accomplish a desired result and so integrated with the use of a legal or commercial conception that the proper standard of infringement is one which will protect as far as possible the copyrighted language and yet allow free use of the thought beneath the language. The evidence here shows that Continental in so far as it has used the language of Beardsley's forms has done so only as incidental to its use of the underlying idea. Chautauqua School of Nursing v. National School of Nursing, 2 Cir., 238 F. 151. In so doing it has not infringed.

[Judge Hincks concluded that Beardsley's copyright had in any event been forfeited by general publication of the forms without notice of copyright. Beardsley's claim for unfair competition was also rejected since Continental had done nothing to suggest that its plan had anything to do with Beardsley.]

Modified and affirmed.[b]

Morrissey v. Procter & Gamble Company

United States Court of Appeals, First Circuit, 1967.
379 F.2d 675.

■ Before ALDRICH, CHIEF JUDGE, McENTEE and COFFIN, CIRCUIT JUDGES.

■ ALDRICH, CHIEF JUDGE. This is an appeal from a summary judgment for the defendant. The plaintiff, Morrissey, is the copyright owner of a set of

---

b. Judge Palmieri's decision below, Continental Cas. Co. v. Beardsley, 151 F.Supp. 28 (S.D.N.Y.1957), is worth reading.

There is a note on the *Continental Casualty* case in 47 Calif.L.Rev. 174 (1959).

rules for a sales promotional contest of the "sweepstakes" type involving the social security numbers of the participants. Plaintiff alleges that the defendant, Procter & Gamble Company, infringed, by copying, almost precisely, Rule 1. In its motion for summary judgment, based upon affidavits and depositions, defendant denies that plaintiff's Rule 1 is copyrightable material, and denies access. The district court held for the defendant on both grounds.

Taking the second ground first, the defendant offered affidavits or depositions of all of its allegedly pertinent employees, all of whom denied having seen plaintiff's rules. Although the plaintiff, by deposition, flatly testified that prior to the time the defendant conducted its contest he had mailed to the defendant his copyrighted rules with an offer to sell, the court ruled that the defendant had "proved" nonaccess, and stated that it was "satisfied that no material issue as to access * * * lurks * * * [in the record.]"

The court did not explain whether it considered defendant's showing to have constituted proof overcoming the presumption of receipt arising from plaintiff's testimony of mailing, or whether it felt there was an unsatisfied burden on the plaintiff to show that the particularly responsible employees of the defendant had received his communication. Either view would have been error. A notice to the defendant at its principal office, as this one assertedly was, is proper notice. There is at least an inference that the letter reached its proper destination. Even if we assume that if, at the trial of the case, it should be found that the particular employees of the defendant responsible for the contest were in fact without knowledge of plaintiff's rules, defendant would be free of a charge of copying, cf. Pinci v. Twentieth Century–Fox Film Corp., S.D.N.Y., 1951, 95 F.Supp. 884; Dezendorf v. Twentieth Century–Fox Film Corp., S.D.Cal., 1940, 32 F.Supp. 359, aff'd, 9 Cir., 118 F.2d 561, on a motion for summary judgment a plaintiff should not have to go to the point of showing that every employee of a corporate defendant received his notification. Nor can it be said that no issue of fact as to access "lurks" merely because it seems to the court that plaintiff's own proof has been satisfactorily contradicted. Nothing is clearer than this on a motion for summary judgment; if a party has made an evidentiary showing warranting a favorable inference, contradiction cannot eliminate it. Summary judgment may not be granted where there is the "slightest doubt as to the facts." Peckham v. Ronrico Corp., 1 Cir., 1948, 171 F.2d 653, 657; Arnstein v. Porter, 2 Cir., 1946, 154 F.2d 464, 468. Defendant's argument misreads Dressler v. MV Sandpiper, 2 Cir., 1964, 331 F.2d 130. The presumption arising from mailing remained in the case.[1] * * *

---

1. The court did not discuss, nor need we, the additional fact that the almost exact following of plaintiff's wording and format in an area in which there is at least some room for maneuverability, might be found of itself to contradict defendants' denial of access. Cf. Arnstein v. Porter, supra.

The second aspect of the case raises a more difficult question. Before discussing it we recite plaintiff's Rule 1, and defendant's Rule 1, the italicizing in the latter being ours to note the defendant's variations or changes.

"1. Entrants should print name, address and social security number on a boxtop, or a plain paper. Entries must be accompanied by * * * boxtop or by plain paper on which the name * * * is copied from any source. Official rules are explained on * * * packages or leaflets obtained from dealer. If you do not have a social security number you may use the name and number of any member of your immediate family living with you. Only the person named on the entry will be deemed an entrant and may qualify for prize.

"Use the correct social security number belonging to the person named on entry * * * wrong number will be disqualified." (Plaintiff's Rule)

"1. Entrants should print name, address and *Social Security* number on a *Tide* boxtop, or *on* [a] plain paper. Entries must be accompanied by *Tide* boxtop *(any size)* or by plain paper on which the name 'Tide' is copied from any source. Official rules are *available* on *Tide Sweepstakes* packages, or *on* leaflets *at Tide* dealers, *or you can send a stamped, self-addressed envelope to* : *Tide* 'Shopping Fling' Sweepstakes, P.O. Box 4459, Chicago 77, Illinois.

"If you do not have a *Social Security* number, you may use the name and number of any member of your immediate family living with you. Only the person named on the entry will be deemed an entrant and may qualify for a prize.

"Use the correct *Social Security* number, belonging to the person named on *the* entry—wrong numbers will be disqualified." (Defendant's Rule)

The district court, following an earlier decision, Gaye v. Gillis, D.Mass., 1958, 167 F.Supp. 416, took the position that since the substance of the contest was not copyrightable, which is unquestionably correct, Baker v. Selden, 1879, 101 U.S. 99; Affiliated Enterprises v. Gruber, 1 Cir., 1936, 86 F.2d 958; Chamberlin v. Uris Sales Corp., 2 Cir., 1945, 150 F.2d 512, and the substance was relatively simple, it must follow that plaintiff's rule sprung directly from the substance and "contains no original creative authorship." 262 F.Supp. at 738. This does not follow. Copyright attaches to form of expression, and defendant's own proof, introduced to deluge the court on the issue of access, itself established that there was more than one way of expressing even this simple substance. Nor, in view of the almost precise similarity of the two rules, could defendant successfully invoke the principle of a stringent standard for showing infringement which some courts apply when the subject matter involved admits of little variation in form of expression. E.g., Dorsey v. Old Surety Life Ins. Co., 10 Cir., 1938, 98 F.2d 872, 874 ("a showing of appropriation in the exact form or substantially so."); Continental Casualty Co. v. Beardsley, 2 Cir., 1958,

253 F.2d 702, 705, cert. denied, 358 U.S. 816 ("a stiff standard for proof of infringement.").

Nonetheless, we must hold for the defendant. When the uncopyrightable subject matter is very narrow, so that "the topic necessarily requires," Sampson & Murdock Co. v. Seaver–Radford Co., 1 Cir., 1905, 140 F. 539, 541; cf. Kaplan, An Unhurried View of Copyright, 64–65 (1967), if not only one form of expression, at best only a limited number, to permit copyrighting would mean that a party or parties, by copyrighting a mere handful of forms, could exhaust all possibilities of future use of the substance. In such circumstances it does not seem accurate to say that any particular form of expression comes from the subject matter. However, it is necessary to say that the subject matter would be appropriated by permitting the copyrighting of its expression. We cannot recognize copyright as a game of chess in which the public can be checkmated. Cf. Baker v. Selden, supra.

Upon examination the matters embraced in Rule 1 are so straightforward and simple that we find this limiting principle to be applicable. Furthermore, its operation need not await an attempt to copyright all possible forms. It cannot be only the last form of expression which is to be condemned, as completing defendant's exclusion from the substance. Rather, in these circumstances, we hold that copyright does not extend to the subject matter at all, and plaintiff cannot complain even if his particular expression was deliberately adopted.

Affirmed.

HERBERT ROSENTHAL JEWELRY CORP. v. KALPAKIAN, 446 F.2d 738 (9th Cir.1971). Plaintiff charged defendants with infringing its copyright in a pin in the shape of a bee formed of gold and encrusted with jewels. After discussing the distinction between idea and expression, the court affirmed a judgment for defendants: "We think the production of jeweled bee pins is a larger private preserve than Congress intended to be set aside in the public market without a patent. A jeweled bee pin is therefore an 'idea' that defendants were free to copy. * * * The difficulty, as we have noted, is that on this record the 'idea' and its 'expression' appear to be indistinguishable. There is no greater similarity between the pins of plaintiff and defendants than is inevitable from the use of jewel-encrusted bee forms in both.

"When the 'idea' and its 'expression' are thus inseparable, copying the 'expression' will not be barred, since protecting the 'expression' in such circumstances would confer a monopoly of the 'idea' upon the copyright owner free of the conditions and limitations imposed by the patent law." The court cited *Baker* and *Morrissey,* with a "see also" to *Continental Casualty.*

Can the court be correct on the facts? Judge Friendly for the Second Circuit had earlier upheld an injunction apparently directed at the same pin, with no mention of *Baker*. See Herbert Rosenthal Jewelry Corp. v. Grossbardt, 436 F.2d 315 (2d Cir.1970).

NOTES AND QUESTIONS

(1) Courts have sometimes found legal forms uncopyrightable on the ground that they lacked originality; an unspoken assumption may be that judges feel on surer ground here than with works of art. See Donald v. Zack Meyer's T.V. Sales & Service, 426 F.2d 1027 (5th Cir.1970), cert. denied, 400 U.S. 992 (1971), in which a "common legal form" was held uncopyrightable. "The plaintiff did no original legal research which resulted in a significant addition to the standard conditional sales contract or chattel mortgage forms; he merely made trivial word changes by combining various forms and servilely imitating the already stereotyped language found therein." The same plaintiff lost again in Donald v. Uarco Business Forms, 344 F.Supp. 338 (W.D.Ark.1972), aff'd, 478 F.2d 764 (8th Cir.1973). Accord, M.M. Business Forms Corp. v. Uarco, Inc., 472 F.2d 1137 (6th Cir.1973). These outcomes have been sharply criticized. See Gorman, Fact or Fancy? The Implications for Copyright, 29 J.Copyr.Soc. 560, 584 (1982); Olson, The Legal Protection of Printed Systems, 81 W.Va.L.Rev. 45 (1979). Other cases have been more generous, especially with elaborate "forms." In Edwin K. Williams & Co. v. Edwin K. Williams & Co.–East, 542 F.2d 1053 (9th Cir.1976), cert. denied, 433 U.S. 908 (1977), the court found that a book of accounting forms, with several pages of instructions, "constituted an integrated work entitled to copyright protection." See also Baldwin Cooke Co. v. Keith Clark, Inc., 383 F.Supp. 650 (N.D.Ill.), aff'd, 505 F.2d 1250 (7th Cir.1974), extending copyright protection to an "Executive Planner"—a combination calendar, diary, information, and appointment book. The court found the Planner copyrightable as a compilation, distinguishing *Morrissey* and *M.M. Business Forms,* supra, because "[n]one of the works involved in those cases approach the sophistication and complexity of format and arrangement involved here."

(2) Think of a new game, played with some combination of cards, dice, and a board. How far can one protect it by copyright? By patent? Looking ahead, by trademark? As an illustration, see Selchow & Righter Co. v. Goldex Corp., 612 F.Supp. 19 (S.D.Fla.1985). The exclusive U.S. distributor of "Trivial Pursuit" invoked trademark rights (in the name), design patent (in the board), and copyright (in the board, rules, and cards) to block unauthorized imports from Canada. On patents, see also In re Cornish, 277 F.2d 185 (C.C.P.A.1960) (three-dimensional tic-tac-toe treated as patentable subject matter, but prior art precluded a patent); Marvin Glass & Associates v. De Luxe Topper Corp., 284 F.Supp. 558 (S.D.N.Y.1967) (finding no infringement of patent on an elaborate board game, but with insufficient attention to the issue of validity). On copyright, cf. Gelles–Widmer Co. v. Milton Bradley Co., 313 F.2d 143 (7th Cir.), cert. denied, 373 U.S. 913 (1963), upholding copyright on arithmetic and spelling "flash cards."

(3) Consider, as to forms, rules of games, and other instances where exposition and the matter expounded are closely entwined, which approach is preferable: copyright, but with a high standard for infringement, as in *Continental Casualty,* or no copyright, as in *Morrissey?* Or should one or both claimants have prevailed? See also, following *Morrissey,* Affiliated Hospital Products, Inc. v. Merdel Game Mfg. Co., 513 F.2d 1183 (2d Cir.1975).

(4) *Baker* and *Morrissey* have become parents to the doctrine of "merger." A subsequent case, describing the concept as "a close cousin to the idea/expression dichotomy," said that under the doctrine of merger "copyright protection will be denied to even some *expressions* of ideas if the idea behind the expression is such that it can be expressed only in a very limited number of ways. The doctrine is designed to prevent an author from monopolizing an idea merely by copyrighting a few expressions of it." Toro Co. v. R & R Products Co., 787 F.2d 1208, 1212 (8th Cir.1986). The court there declined to invoke the doctrine in connection with a parts numbering system. The doctrine also was held inapplicable to the expression of questions on the SAT test. Educational Testing Services v. Katzman, 793 F.2d 533 (3d Cir.1986). (We will see another rejection of the doctrine in connection with characters on a children's television program in *Sid & Marty Krofft,* p. 248 infra.) A combination of the merger doctrine and the "blank form" rule, however, was successfully invoked in Matthew Bender & Co. v. Kluwer Law Book Pub., Inc., 672 F.Supp. 107 (S.D.N.Y. 1987), to deny copyright to charts presenting information on damage awards in a legal textbook. See also Professor Nimmer's criticism of the merger doctrine in Nimmer on Copyright § 2.18.

Appeals to the doctrine of merger recur in cases involving computer programs. A broad application of the doctrine is rejected in the following case on copyrightability. The merger doctrine also appears in the materials on infringement of copyright in computer programs, p. 277 infra.

COPYRIGHT IN COMPUTER PROGRAMS

Apple Computer, Inc. v. Franklin Computer Corp.

United States Court of Appeals, Third Circuit, 1983.
714 F.2d 1240.
Certiorari dismissed, 464 U.S. 1033 (1984).

■ Before HUNTER, HIGGINBOTHAM and SLOVITER, CIRCUIT JUDGES.

■ SLOVITER, CIRCUIT JUDGE.

I.

INTRODUCTION

Apple Computer, Inc. appeals from the district court's denial of a motion to preliminarily enjoin Franklin Computer Corp. from infringing the copyrights Apple holds on fourteen computer programs. * * *

In this case the district court denied the preliminary injunction, *inter alia*, because it had "some doubt as to the copyrightability of the programs." Apple Computer, Inc. v. Franklin Computer Corp., 545 F.Supp. 812, 812 (E.D.Pa.1982). This legal ruling is fundamental to all future proceedings in this action and, as the parties and amici curiae seem to agree, has considerable significance to the computer services industry. Because we conclude that the district court proceeded under an erroneous view of the applicable law, we reverse the denial of the preliminary injunction and remand.

II.

FACTS AND PROCEDURAL HISTORY

Apple, one of the computer industry leaders, manufactures and markets personal computers (microcomputers), related peripheral equipment such as disk drives (peripherals), and computer programs (software). It presently manufactures Apple II computers and distributes over 150 programs. Apple has sold over 400,000 Apple II computers, employs approximately 3,000 people, and had annual sales of $335,000,000 for fiscal year 1981. One of the byproducts of Apple's success is the independent development by third parties of numerous computer programs which are designed to run on the Apple II computer.

Franklin, the defendant below, manufactures and sells the ACE 100 personal computer and at the time of the hearing employed about 75 people and had sold fewer than 1,000 computers. The ACE 100 was designed to be "Apple compatible," so that peripheral equipment and software developed for use with the Apple II computer could be used in conjunction with the ACE 100. Franklin's copying of Apple's operating system computer programs in an effort to achieve such compatibility precipitated this suit.

Like all computers both the Apple II and ACE 100 have a central processing unit (CPU) which is the integrated circuit that executes programs. In lay terms, the CPU does the work it is instructed to do. Those instructions are contained on computer programs.

There are three levels of computer language in which computer programs may be written. High level language, such as the commonly used BASIC or FORTRAN, uses English words and symbols, and is relatively easy to learn and understand (e.g., "GO TO 40" tells the computer to skip intervening steps and go to the step at line 40). A somewhat lower level language is assembly language, which consists of alphanumeric labels (e.g., "ADC" means "add with carry"). Statements in high level language, and apparently also statements in assembly language, are referred to as written in "source code." The third, or lowest level computer language, is machine language, a binary language using two symbols, 0 and 1, to indicate an open or closed switch (e.g., "01101001" means, to the Apple, add two numbers and save the result). Statements in machine language are referred to as written in "object code."

The CPU can only follow instructions written in object code. However, programs are usually written in source code which is more intelligible to humans. Programs written in source code can be converted or translated by a "compiler" program into object code for use by the computer. Programs are generally distributed only in their object code version stored on a memory device.

A computer program can be stored or fixed on a variety of memory devices, two of which are of particular relevance for this case. The ROM (Read Only Memory) is an internal permanent memory device consisting of a semi-conductor "chip" which is incorporated into the circuitry of the computer. A program in object code is embedded on a ROM before it is incorporated in the computer. Information stored on a ROM can only be read, not erased or rewritten.[3] The ACE 100 apparently contains EPROMs (Erasable Programmable Read Only Memory) on which the stored information can be erased and the chip reprogrammed, but the district court found that for purposes of this proceeding, the difference between ROMs and EPROMs is inconsequential. 545 F.Supp. at 813 n. 3. The other device used for storing the programs at issue is a diskette or "floppy disk", an auxiliary memory device consisting of a flexible magnetic disk resembling a phonograph record, which can be inserted into the computer and from which data or instructions can be read.

Computer programs can be categorized by function as either application programs or operating system programs. Application programs usually perform a specific task for the computer user, such as word processing, checkbook balancing, or playing a game. In contrast, operating system programs generally manage the internal functions of the computer or facilitate use of application programs. The parties agree that the fourteen computer programs at issue in this suit are operating system programs.[4]

Apple filed suit in the United States District Court for the Eastern District of Pennsylvania pursuant to 28 U.S.C. § 1338 on May 12, 1982, alleging that Franklin was liable for copyright infringement of the fourteen

---

3. In contrast to the permanent memory devices a RAM (Random Access Memory) is a chip on which volatile internal memory is stored which is erased when the computer's power is turned off.

4. [Three of the] fourteen programs at issue, briefly described, are:

(1) *Autostart ROM* is sold as part of the Apple Computer and is embedded on a ROM chip. The program has also been published in source code as part of a copyrighted book, the Apple II manual. When the computer's power is turned on, Autostart ROM performs internal routines that turn on the circuits in the computer and make its physical parts (e.g. input/output devices, screen, and memory) ready for use.

(2) *Applesoft* is Apple's version of the Beginner's All-purpose Symbolic Instruction Code (BASIC) language. The program is stored in ROM and is sold as part of the computer. Applesoft translates instructions written in the higher-level BASIC language into the lower-level machine code that the computer understands. * * *

(5) *DOS 3.3*, the disk operating system program, provides the instructions necessary to control the operation between the disk system (disk drive) and the computer itself. It controls the reading and writing functions of the disks and includes other routines which put all the data transfers in sequence. * * *

computer programs, patent infringement, unfair competition, and misappropriation. Franklin's answer in respect to the copyright counts included the affirmative defense that the programs contained no copyrightable subject matter. * * *

After expedited discovery, Apple moved for a preliminary injunction to restrain Franklin from using, copying, selling, or infringing Apple's copyrights. The district court held a three day evidentiary hearing limited to the copyright infringement claims. Apple produced evidence at the hearing in the form of affidavits and testimony that programs sold by Franklin in conjunction with its ACE 100 computer were virtually identical with those covered by the fourteen Apple copyrights. The variations that did exist were minor, consisting merely of such things as deletion of reference to Apple or its copyright notice. * * * Apple estimated the "works in suit" took 46 man-months to produce at a cost of over $740,000, not including the time or cost of creating or acquiring earlier versions of the programs or the expense of marketing the programs.

Franklin did not dispute that it copied the Apple programs. Its witness admitted copying each of the works in suit from the Apple programs. Its factual defense was directed to its contention that it was not feasible for Franklin to write its own operating system programs. David McWherter, now Franklin's vice-president of engineering, testified he spent 30–40 hours in November 1981 making a study to determine if it was feasible for Franklin to write its own Autostart ROM program and concluded it was not because "there were just too many entry points in relationship to the number of instructions in the program." Entry points at specific locations in the program can be used by programmers to mesh their application programs with the operating system program. McWherter concluded that use of the identical signals was necessary in order to ensure 100% compatibility with application programs created to run on the Apple computer. * * * Apple introduced evidence that Franklin could have rewritten programs, including the Autostart ROM program, and that there are in existence operating programs written by third parties which are compatible with Apple II.

Franklin's principal defense at the preliminary injunction hearing and before us is primarily a legal one, directed to its contention that the Apple operating system programs are not capable of copyright protection.

The district court denied the motion for preliminary injunction by order and opinion dated July 30, 1982. Apple moved for reconsideration in light of this court's decision in Williams Electronics, Inc. v. Artic International, Inc., 685 F.2d 870 (3d Cir.1982), which was decided August 2, 1982, three days after the district court decision. The district court denied the motion for reconsideration. We have jurisdiction of Apple's appeal pursuant to 28 U.S.C. § 1292(a)(1).

III.

THE DISTRICT COURT OPINION

* * *

We read the district court opinion as presenting the following legal issues: (1) whether copyright can exist in a computer program expressed in object code, (2) whether copyright can exist in a computer program embedded on a ROM, (3) whether copyright can exist in an operating system program, and (4) whether independent irreparable harm must be shown for a preliminary injunction in copyright infringement actions.

IV.

DISCUSSION

A.

Copyrightability of a Computer Program Expressed in Object Code

Certain statements by the district court suggest that programs expressed in object code, as distinguished from source code, may not be the proper subject of copyright. We find no basis in the statute for any such concern. Furthermore, our decision in Williams Electronics, Inc. v. Artic International, Inc., supra, laid to rest many of the doubts expressed by the district court.

In 1976, after considerable study, Congress enacted a new copyright law to replace that which had governed since 1909. Act of October 19, 1976, Pub.L. No. 94–553, 90 Stat. 2541 (codified at 17 U.S.C. §§ 101 *et seq.*). Under the law, two primary requirements must be satisfied in order for a work to constitute copyrightable subject matter—it must be an "original wor[k] of authorship" and must be "fixed in [a] tangible medium of expression." * * *

Although section 102(a) does not expressly list computer programs as works of authorship, the legislative history suggests that programs were considered copyrightable as literary works. See H.R.Rep. No. 1476, 94th Cong., 2d Sess. 54, reprinted in 1976 U.S.Code Cong. & Ad.News 5659, 5667 ("'literary works' ... includes ... computer programs"). Because a Commission on New Technological Uses ("CONTU") had been created by Congress to study, *inter alia,* computer uses of copyrighted works, Pub.L. No. 93–573, § 201, 88 Stat. 1873 (1974), Congress enacted a status quo provision, section 117, in the 1976 Act concerning such computer uses pending the CONTU report and recommendations.[6]

The CONTU Final Report recommended that the copyright law be amended, *inter alia,* "to make it explicit that computer programs, to the extent that they embody an author's original creation, are proper subject matter of copyright." National Commission on New Technological Uses of Copyrighted Works, *Final Report* 1 (1979) [hereinafter CONTU Report]. CONTU recommended two changes relevant here: that section 117, the status quo provision, be repealed and replaced with a section limiting exclusive rights in computer programs so as "to ensure that rightful

---

6. Section 117 applied only to the scope of protection to be accorded copyrighted works when used in conjunction with a computer and not to the copyrightability of programs. H.R.Rep. No. 1476, at 116, reprinted in 1976 U.S.Code Cong. & Ad.News at 5731.

possessors of copies of computer programs may use or adapt these copies for their use," id.; and that a definition of computer program be added to section 101.   Id. at 12.   Congress adopted both changes.   Act of Dec. 12, 1980, Pub.L. No. 96–517, § 10, 94 Stat. 3015, 3028.   The revisions embodied CONTU's recommendations to clarify the law of copyright of computer software.   H.R.Rep. No. 1307, 96th Cong., 2d Sess. 23, reprinted in 1980 U.S.Code Cong. & Ad.News 6460, 6482.

The 1980 amendments added a definition of a computer program:

> A "computer program" is a set of statements or instructions to be used directly or indirectly in a computer in order to bring about a certain result.

17 U.S.C. § 101.   The amendments also substituted a new section 117 which provides that "it is not an infringement for the owner of a copy of a computer program to make or authorize the making of another copy or adaptation of that computer program" when necessary to "the utilization of the computer program" or "for archival purposes only."   17 U.S.C. § 117.   The parties agree that this section is not implicated in the instant lawsuit.   The language of the provision, however, by carving out an exception to the normal proscriptions against copying, clearly indicates that programs are copyrightable and are otherwise afforded copyright protection.

We considered the issue of copyright protection for a computer program in Williams Electronics, Inc. v. Artic International, Inc., and concluded that "the copyrightability of computer programs is firmly established after the 1980 amendment to the Copyright Act."   685 F.2d at 875.   At issue in *Williams* were not only two audiovisual copyrights to the "attract" and "play" modes of a video game, but also the computer program which was expressed in object code embodied in ROM and which controlled the sights and sounds of the game.   Defendant there had argued "that when the issue is the copyright on a computer program, a distinction must be drawn between the 'source code' version of a computer program, which . . . can be afforded copyright protection, and the 'object code' stage, which . . . cannot be so protected," an argument we rejected.   Id. at 876.

The district court here questioned whether copyright was to be limited to works "designed to be 'read' by a human reader [as distinguished from] read by an expert with a microscope and patience", 545 F.Supp. at 821. The suggestion that copyrightability depends on a communicative function to individuals stems from the early decision of White–Smith Music Publishing Co. v. Apollo Co., 209 U.S. 1 (1908), which held a piano roll was not a copy of the musical composition because it was not in a form others, except perhaps for a very expert few, could perceive.   See 1 Nimmer on Copyright § 2.03[B][1] (1983).   However, it is clear from the language of the 1976 Act and its legislative history that it was intended to obliterate distinctions engendered by *White–Smith*.   H.R.Rep. No. 1476, supra, at 52, reprinted in 1976 U.S.Code Cong. & Ad.News at 5665.

Under the statute, copyright extends to works in any tangible means of expression *"from which they can be perceived,* reproduced, or otherwise communicated, either directly or *with the aid of machine or device.* " 17 U.S.C. § 102(a) (emphasis added). Further, the definition of "computer program" adopted by Congress in the 1980 amendments is "sets of statements or instructions to be used *directly or indirectly* in a computer in order to bring about a certain result." 17 U.S.C. § 101 (emphasis added). As source code instructions must be translated into object code before the computer can act upon them, only instructions expressed in object code can be used "directly" by the computer. See Midway Manufacturing Co. v. Strohon, 564 F.Supp. 741 at 750–751 (N.D.Ill.1983). This definition was adopted following the CONTU Report in which the majority clearly took the position that object codes are proper subjects of copyright. See CONTU Report at 21. The majority's conclusion was reached although confronted by a dissent based upon the theory that the "machine-control phase" of a program is not directed at a human audience. See CONTU Report at 28–30 (dissent of Commissioner Hersey).

The defendant in *Williams* had also argued that a copyrightable work "must be intelligible to human beings and must be intended as a medium of communication to human beings," id. at 876–77. We reiterate the statement we made in *Williams* when we rejected that argument: "[t]he answer to defendant's contention is in the words of the statute itself." 685 F.2d at 877.

The district court also expressed uncertainty as to whether a computer program in object code could be classified as a "literary work." However, the category of "literary work", one of the seven copyrightable categories, is not confined to literature in the nature of Hemingway's *For Whom the Bell Tolls.* The definition of "literary works" in section 101 includes expression not only in words but also "numbers, or other ... numerical symbols or indicia", thereby expanding the common usage of "literary works." Cf. Harcourt, Brace & World, Inc. v. Graphic Controls Corp., 329 F.Supp. 517, 523–24 (S.D.N.Y.1971) (the symbols designating questions or response spaces on exam answer sheets held to be copyrightable "writings" under 1909 Act); Reiss v. National Quotation Bureau, Inc., 276 F. 717 (S.D.N.Y.1921) (code book of coined words designed for cable use copyrightable). Thus a computer program, whether in object code or source code, is a "literary work" and is protected from unauthorized copying, whether from its object or source code version. Accord Midway Mfg. Co. v. Strohon, 564 F.Supp. at 750–751; see also GCA Corp. v. Chance, [217 U.S.P.Q. 718, 719–20 (N.D.Cal.1982).]

B.

Copyrightability of a Computer Program Embedded on a ROM

Just as the district court's suggestion of a distinction between source code and object code was rejected by our opinion in *Williams* issued three days after the district court opinion, so also was its suggestion that embodiment of a computer program on a ROM, as distinguished from in a traditional writing, detracts from its copyrightability.   In *Williams* we rejected the argument that "a computer program is not infringed when the program is loaded into electronic memory devices (ROMs) and used to control the activity of machines."   685 F.2d at 876.   Defendant there had argued that there can be no copyright protection for the ROMs because they are utilitarian objects or machine parts.   We held that the statutory requirement of "fixation", the manner in which the issue arises, is satisfied through the embodiment of the expression in the ROM devices.   * * *

C.

Copyrightability of Computer Operating System Programs

We turn to the heart of Franklin's position on appeal which is that computer operating system programs, as distinguished from application programs, are not the proper subject of copyright "regardless of the language or medium in which they are fixed."   Brief of Appellee at 15 (emphasis deleted).   Apple suggests that this issue too is foreclosed by our *Williams* decision because some portion of the program at issue there was in effect an operating system program.   Franklin is correct that this was not an issue raised by the parties in *Williams* and it was not considered by the court.   Thus we consider it as a matter of first impression.

Franklin contends that operating system programs are *per se* excluded from copyright protection under the express terms of section 102(b) of the Copyright Act, and under the precedent and underlying principles of Baker v. Selden, 101 U.S. 99 (1879).   These separate grounds have substantial analytic overlap.   * * *

Franklin reads Baker v. Selden as "stand[ing] for several fundamental principles, each presenting ... an insuperable obstacle to the copyrightability of Apple's operating systems."   It states:

> *First, Baker* teaches that use of a system itself does not infringe a copyright on the description of the system.   *Second, Baker* enunciates the rule that copyright does not extend to purely utilitarian works. *Finally, Baker* emphasizes that the copyright laws may not be used to obtain and hold a monopoly over an idea.   In so doing, *Baker* highlights the principal difference between the copyright and patent laws— a difference that is highly pertinent in this case.

Brief of Appellee at 22.

Section 102(b) of the Copyright Act, the other ground on which Franklin relies, appeared first in the 1976 version, long after the decision in Baker v. Selden.   * * * It is apparent that section 102(b) codifies a substantial part of the holding and dictum of Baker v. Selden.   See 1 Nimmer on Copyright § 2.18[D], at 2–207.

We turn to consider the two principal points of Franklin's argument.

1.   *"Process", "System" or "Method of Operation"*

Franklin argues that an operating system program is either a "process", "system", or "method of operation" and hence uncopyrightable.

Franklin correctly notes that underlying section 102(b) and many of the statements for which Baker v. Selden is cited is the distinction which must be made between property subject to the patent law, which protects discoveries, and that subject to copyright law, which protects the writings describing such discoveries. However, Franklin's argument misapplies that distinction in this case. Apple does not seek to copyright the method which instructs the computer to perform its operating functions but only the instructions themselves. The method would be protected, if at all, by the patent law, an issue as yet unresolved. See Diamond v. Diehr, 450 U.S. 175 (1981).

Franklin's attack on operating system programs as "methods" or "processes" seems inconsistent with its concession that application programs are an appropriate subject of copyright. Both types of programs instruct the computer to do something. Therefore, it should make no difference for purposes of section 102(b) whether these instructions tell the computer to help prepare an income tax return (the task of an application program) or to translate a high level language program from source code into its binary language object code form (the task of an operating system program such as "Applesoft", see note 4 supra). Since it is only the instructions which are protected, a "process" is no more involved because the instructions in an operating system program may be used to activate the operation of the computer than it would be if instructions were written in ordinary English in a manual which described the necessary steps to activate an intricate complicated machine. There is, therefore, no reason to afford any less copyright protection to the instructions in an operating system program than to the instructions in an application program. * * *

Franklin also argues that the operating systems cannot be copyrighted because they are "purely utilitarian works" and that Apple is seeking to block the use of the art embodied in its operating systems. This argument stems from the following dictum in Baker v. Selden:

> The very object of publishing a book on science or the useful arts is to communicate to the world the useful knowledge which it contains. But this object would be frustrated if the knowledge could not be used without incurring the guilt of piracy of the book. And where the art it teaches cannot be used without employing the methods and diagrams used to illustrate the book, or such as are similar to them, such methods and diagrams are to be considered as necessary incidents to the art, and given therewith to the public; not given for the purpose of publication in other works explanatory of the art, but for the purpose of practical application.

101 U.S. at 103. We cannot accept the expansive reading given to this language by some courts, see, e.g., Taylor Instrument Companies v. Fawley–Brost Co., 139 F.2d 98 (7th Cir.1943), cert. denied, 321 U.S. 785 (1944). In this respect we agree with the views expressed by Professor Nimmer in his treatise. See 1 Nimmer on Copyright § 2.18[C].

Although a literal construction of this language could support Franklin's reading that precludes copyrightability if the copyright work is put to a utilitarian use, that interpretation has been rejected by a later Supreme Court decision.   In Mazer v. Stein, 347 U.S. 201, 218 (1954), the Court stated: "We find nothing in the copyright statute to support the argument that the intended use or use in industry of an article eligible for copyright bars or invalidates its registration.   We do not read such a limitation into the copyright law."   Id. at 218.   The CONTU majority also rejected the expansive view some courts have given Baker v. Selden, and stated, "That the words of a program are used ultimately in the implementation of a process should in no way affect their copyrightability."   Id. at 21.   It referred to "copyright practice past and present, which recognizes copyright protection for a work of authorship regardless of the uses to which it may be put."   Id.   The Commission continued: "The copyright status of the written rules for a game *or a system for the operation of a machine* is unaffected by the fact that those rules direct the actions of those who play the game or *carry out the process*."   Id. (emphasis added).   * * *

Perhaps the most convincing item leading us to reject Franklin's argument is that the statutory definition of a computer program as a set of instructions to be used in a computer in order to bring about a certain result, 17 U.S.C. § 101, makes no distinction between application programs and operating programs.   Franklin can point to no decision which adopts the distinction it seeks to make.   In the one other reported case to have considered it, Apple Computer, Inc. v. Formula International, Inc., 562 F.Supp. 775 (C.D.Cal.1983), the court reached the same conclusion which we do, *i.e.* that an operating system program is not *per se* precluded from copyright.   * * *

2.   *Idea/Expression Dichotomy*

Franklin's other challenge to copyright of operating system programs relies on the line which is drawn between ideas and their expression. Baker v. Selden remains a benchmark in the law of copyright for the reading given it in Mazer v. Stein, supra, where the Court stated, "Unlike a patent, a copyright gives no exclusive right to the art disclosed; protection is given only to the expression of the idea—not the idea itself."   347 U.S. at 217 (footnote omitted).   * * *

* * * We believe that in the context before us, a program for an operating system, the line must be a pragmatic one, which also keeps in consideration "the preservation of the balance between competition and protection reflected in the patent and copyright laws".   Herbert Rosenthal Jewelry Corp. v. Kalpakian, 446 F.2d 738, 742 (9th Cir.1971).   As we stated in Franklin Mint Corp. v. National Wildlife Art Exchange, Inc., 575 F.2d 62, 64 (3d Cir.), cert. denied, 439 U.S. 880 (1978), "Unlike a patent, a copyright protects originality rather than novelty or invention."   In that opinion, we quoted approvingly the following passage from Dymow v. Bolton, 11 F.2d 690, 691 (2d Cir.1926):

> Just as a patent affords protection only to the means of reducing an inventive idea to practice, so the copyright law protects the means of expressing an idea; and it is as near the whole truth as generaliza-

tion can usually reach that, *if the same idea can be expressed in a plurality of totally different manners, a plurality of copyrights may result,* and no infringement will exist.

(emphasis added).

We adopt the suggestion in the above language and thus focus on whether the idea is capable of various modes of expression. If other programs can be written or created which perform the same function as an Apple's operating system program, then that program is an expression of the idea and hence copyrightable. In essence, this inquiry is no different than that made to determine whether the expression and idea have merged, which has been stated to occur where there are no or few other ways of expressing a particular idea. See, e.g., Morrissey v. Procter & Gamble Co., 379 F.2d 675, 678–79 (1st Cir.1967); Freedman v. Grolier Enterprises, Inc., 179 U.S.P.Q. 476, 478 (S.D.N.Y.1973) ("[c]opyright protection will not be given to a form of expression necessarily dictated by the underlying subject matter"); CONTU Report at 20.

The district court made no findings as to whether some or all of Apple's operating programs represent the only means of expression of the idea underlying them. Although there seems to be a concession by Franklin that at least some of the programs can be rewritten, we do not believe that the record on that issue is so clear that it can be decided at the appellate level. Therefore, if the issue is pressed on remand, the necessary finding can be made at that time.

Franklin claims that whether or not the programs can be rewritten, there are a limited "number of ways to arrange operating systems to enable a computer to run the vast body of Apple-compatible software", Brief of Appellee at 20. This claim has no pertinence to either the idea/expression dichotomy or merger. The idea which may merge with the expression, thus making the copyright unavailable, is the idea which is the subject of the expression. The idea of one of the operating system programs is, for example, how to translate source code into object code. If other methods of expressing that idea are not foreclosed as a practical matter, then there is no merger. Franklin may wish to achieve total compatibility with independently developed application programs written for the Apple II, but that is a commercial and competitive objective which does not enter into the somewhat metaphysical issue of whether particular ideas and expressions have merged. * * *

V.

For the reasons set forth in this opinion, we will reverse the denial of the preliminary injunction and remand to the district court for further proceedings in accordance herewith.

NOTES AND QUESTIONS ON COPYRIGHT IN COMPUTER PROGRAMS

(1) The *Apple* decision drew mixed reviews. Compare Samuelson, CONTU Revisited: The Case Against Copyright Protection for Computer Programs in Machine Readable Form, 1984 Duke L.J. 663 (1984), with Rodau, Protecting Computer Software: After *Apple* * * * Does Copyright Provide the Best Protection?, 57 Temp.L.Q. 527 (1984).

Did the court give adequate attention to the public interest in compatibility? Menell, Tailoring Legal Protection for Computer Software, 39 Stan.L.Rev. 1329 (1987), argues that the economics of the software market justifies a distinction between operating systems and application programs.

(2) Registration of copyright in computer software does not necessarily require disclosure of the entire program; only the first and last twenty-five pages of the program, in source code, are required. Even less will suffice if the program contains trade secrets. See 37 C.F.R. § 202.20(c)(2)(vii). Is there a policy of public access to works claiming the benefits of federal copyright? When "publication" was the crucial event, the answer was clearly yes. Now copyright subsists from creation, but registration is still a prerequisite to enforcement.[c]

(3) In the early years of the computer age trade secret law was the most common means of preventing the unauthorized copying of software. Trade secret law is well-suited to the protection of programs developed for internal use by the creator. For programs sold or licensed to others, the requisite secrecy can be maintained through the use of confidentiality agreements. Although contracts prohibiting disclosure by purchasers or licensees remain in use for programs of limited distribution, trade secret law is virtually useless for widely-marketed software. Even when the program is distributed only in object code form on disks or similar media, the ability to reconstruct the source code through "reverse engineering" limits the effectiveness of trade secret protection. (As to whether such reverse engineering may be actionable as copyright infringement, see p. 294 infra.) The possibility of preemption of a trade secret claim also must be taken into account. See p. 633 infra. The trade secret option is examined in Bender, Protection of Computer Programs: The Copyright/Trade Secret Interface, 47 U.Pitt.L.Rev. 907 (1986).

Self-help in the form of "copy protection" also has been employed by program creators. "Copy protection" is the use of mechanical or programming devices designed to impede reproduction. The development of "unlocking" programs aimed at defeating copy protection has produced a sequence of moves and countermoves between the participants that ultimately affords little security against duplication. Since copy protection

---

c. A Copyright Office regulation designed to maintain secrecy for registrations of "secure tests" was upheld in National Conference of Bar Examiners v. Multistate Legal Studies, Inc., 692 F.2d 478 (7th Cir.1982), cert. denied, 464 U.S. 814 (1983). The court said, "In sum, the statutory scheme of the Copyright Act demonstrates that the deposit provisions are not for the purpose of disclo-sure." What *is* the purpose? Kriess, Accessibility and Commercialization in Copyright Theory, 43 U.C.L.A. L.Rev. 1 (1995), argues broadly that public access (assured through fair use, withholding of injunctions, etc.) is part of the quid pro quo for protecting works that have been commercially exploited by their owners, even if technically unpublished.

also can cause problems for legitimate users, in many situations it is not seen as a viable means of protection.

The stakes in the software industry are huge. Estimates by the International Intellectual Property Alliance put 1995 losses from piracy of U.S.-owned business and entertainment software at more than $10 billion. China is said to be the biggest market for pirated software, surpassing $2 billion; many countries have piracy levels greater than 90 per cent. The Financial Times, Feb. 10, 1997, p. 6.

(4) The 1980 amendments to the Copyright Act sponsored by CONTU consisted of the definition of "computer program" added to § 101 and the exemption for utilization and backup copies in § 117. The amendments are interpreted in Maggs, Computer Programs as the Object of Intellectual Property in the United States of America, 30 Am.J.Comp.L. 251 (1982 Supp.). The original § 117 was a standstill provision dealing with the *use* of copyrighted works in conjunction with computers; it referred to the applicable (and non-existent) law as of the effective date of the 1976 Act.

The current version of § 117 is not without its ambiguities. Are its exemptions, for example, applicable to licensees as well as purchasers of programs? In MAI Systems Corp. v. Peak Computer, Inc., 991 F.2d 511 (9th Cir.1993), cert. dism'd, 510 U.S. 1033 (1994), the Ninth Circuit said no, and went on to hold that a computer service company that caused a copy of the plaintiff's operating system program to be created in RAM memory when it turned on the licensee's machine during a diagnostic procedure was an infringer.[d] But as Judge Hilton in DSC Communications Corp. v. Pulse Communications, Inc., 976 F.Supp. 359 (E.D.Va.1997), points out, § 117 protects a user who is "the owner of a copy of a computer program"; "It is necessary to determine ownership of the copy, not whether the transaction with [the copyright owner] involved a license to use the program." (The court concluded that since the transaction involved a single payment entitling the buyer to an unlimited period of possession, § 117 applied.)

Section 117(1) recognizes an owner's right to create a "copy" of the program by loading it into a computer. But when is the creation of such a copy an "essential step in the utilization of the computer program"? Suppose, for example, the input is for the purpose of analyzing rather than "running" the program? The Fifth Circuit in Vault Corp. v. Quaid Software Ltd., 847 F.2d 255 (5th Cir.1988), held that the exemption still applied. What is the scope of the "adaptation" right recognized in § 117(1)? Would the modification of a computer program by a user be an infringement in any event? See Aymes v. Bonelli, 47 F.3d 23 (2d Cir.1995) (§ 117 adaptation right successfully invoked to avoid infringement of the copyright owner's exclusive right to prepare derivative works). The significance of the adaptation right is emphasized in Samuelson, Modifying

---

d. McJohn, Fair Use of Copyrighted Software, 28 Rutgers L.J. 593 (1997), argues that "copying" by a computer service company is in any event a fair use. Legislation has been proposed to exempt copies created for purposes of machine maintenance or repair. See also Tapp and Wanat, Computer Software Copyright Issues: Section 117 and Fair Use, 22 Memphis St.U.L.Rev. 197 (1992).

Computer Software: Adjusting Copyright Doctrine to Accommodate a Technology, 28 Jurimetrics 179 (1988). See also R. Nimmer and Krauthaus, Copyright and Software Technology Infringement: Defining Third Party Development Rights, 62 Ind.L.J. 13 (1986).

Consider also § 117(2) and the right to make "archival" copies. Does this exemption apply when the purchased copy is not subject to the mechanical or electrical failures capable of destroying programs embodied in disks? See Atari, Inc. v. JS & A Group, Inc., 597 F.Supp. 5 (N.D.Ill. 1983) (exemption not applicable to program for PAC–MAN video game embodied in ROM chips). The court in *Vault,* supra, in an expansive reading of § 117(2), said that the owner of a program is entitled to make an archival copy in order to guard against *any* risk of destruction. The § 117 exemptions are analyzed in Kreiss, Section 117 of the Copyright Act, 1991 B.Y.U.L.Rev. 1497 (1991); Kelso & Rebay, Problems of Interpretation under the 1980 Computer Amendment, 23 Santa Clara L.Rev. 1001 (1983).

(5) Many software companies use "shrink-wrap" licenses in connection with their mass-marketed programs. These "licenses" are printed documents inserted within the transparent "shrink-wrap" plastic enclosing the product; they can be seen, and in theory read, before the package is opened. The documents say that by tearing open the package, the consumer consents to the terms of the agreement. The "license" often purports to retain title to the product in the seller, the buyer being characterized as a "licensee." They typically contain provisions limiting rental, modification, disassembly, and copying. Several examples of such licenses appear in Stern, Shrink–Wrap Licenses of Mass Marketed Software: Enforceable Contracts or Whistling in the Dark?, 11 Rutgers Computer & Tech.L.J. 51 (1985). Are these "licenses" enforceable under basic contract principles of offer and acceptance? Are they "unconscionable" or in violation of recognized public policy as evidenced, perhaps, by the rights of users recognized in § 117? Louisiana has a statute validating certain restrictions imposed through shrink-wrap licenses. See La.Rev.Stat. §§ 51:1961–66. Is the statute preempted by federal copyright law? The Fifth Circuit in *Vault,* supra, held that to the extent the statute conflicts with the rights granted to users under § 117, it is preempted by the Copyright Act. Rice, Public Goods, Private Contract and Public Policy: Federal Preemption of Software License Prohibitions Against Reverse Engineering, 53 U.Pitt.L.Rev. 543 (1992), argues more generally that any attempt to prevent the reverse engineering of computer programs through licensing restrictions is preempted. See also Hazen, Contract Principles as a Guide for Protecting Intellectual Property Rights in Computer Software, 20 U.C.Davis L.Rev. 105 (1986).

Shrink-wrap licenses survived a major challenge in ProCD, Inc. v. Zeidenberg, 86 F.3d 1447 (7th Cir.1996), when the Seventh Circuit overturned a district court decision that had found the license accompanying plaintiff's CD–ROM telephone directory unenforceable as a matter of contract law and preempted under § 301 of the Copyright Act. Plaintiff's product, compiled from over 3,000 telephone directories, was sold in a box that indicated the sale was subject to restrictions contained in the enclosed license agreement. The license, which was printed in the manual and encoded on the CD–ROM, permitted only noncommercial use and provided for a refund if the buyer found the terms unacceptable. Defendant put the database on the Internet, available to users for a fee. The district court had found the license unenforceable because the terms were not available to the buyer prior to purchase. Judge Easterbrook, citing purchases of insurance, airline tickets, and other transactions in which payment precedes the communication of detailed terms, held that "[n]otice on the outside, terms on the inside, and a right to return the software for a refund if the terms are unacceptable," followed by buyer's use of the product, were sufficient to establish an enforceable contract. (He also disagreed with the lower court's conclusion that the contractual restriction on reproduction and distribution of the uncopyrightable contents was preempted by federal copyright law. See p. 634 infra.) The approach taken by the district court is strongly supported in Lemley, Intellectual Property and Shrinkwrap Licenses, 68 S.Cal.L.Rev. 1239 (1995). Proposed Uniform Commercial Code Article 2B— Licenses, would generally confirm the contractual enforceability of shrink-wrap and similar mass-market licenses.

PATENT PROTECTION FOR COMPUTER PROGRAMS

Although the Copyright Office began accepting computer programs in 1964, the Patent and Trademark Office was more reluctant to enter the field. The PTO did not believe that computer programs were patentable subject matter, and it did not have the resources to search the prior art in this mushrooming industry. Inventors tried to describe computer applications as processes, or to claim a computer following a particular program as a novel machine. They found support in the Court of Customs and Patent Appeals, which first directed the PTO to issue a patent essentially for a program in Application of Prater, 415 F.2d 1393 (C.C.P.A.1969). A further obstacle to patentability was the doctrine that a process performable by "mental steps" (or "pencil and paper") is not patentable. The C.C.P.A. practically abandoned this rule in Application of Benson, 441 F.2d 682 (C.C.P.A.1971). When *Benson* reached the Supreme Court as Gottschalk v. Benson, 409 U.S. 63 (1972), Justice Douglas reversed, arguing that a "method of programming a general purpose digital computer to convert signals from binary coded decimal form into pure binary form" described a process so broad that "the patent would wholly pre-empt the mathematical formula and in practical effect would be a patent on the algorithm itself." Before such patents should issue, "considered action by the Congress is needed."

The Court of Customs and Patent Appeals continued to press for patentability, doing battle with both the Patent and Trademark Office and the Supreme Court. In the next computer-related case to reach the Supreme Court, Dann v. Johnston, 425 U.S. 219 (1976), the claimed invention was disposed of as obvious. In Parker v. Flook, 437 U.S. 584 (1978), Justice Stevens for the Court said that the only novel element in the invention was an equation or algorithm for computing "alarm limits" in chemical processes; this was unpatentable. But three justices dissented. The Court of Customs and Patent Appeals persisted. Finally, two more Justices were won over and in the following case a patent survived, 5–4.

DIAMOND V. DIEHR, 450 U.S. 175 (1981). The patent at issue involved a process for curing rubber. During the curing process sensors inside a mold continually take temperature readings and send them to a computer. When the rubber is cured to the desired specifications, the program sends a message that causes the mold to open. Justice Rehnquist, writing for the majority, said:

"[W]e think that a physical and chemical process for molding precision synthetic rubber products falls within the § 101 categories of possibly patentable subject matter. * * *

"Our conclusion regarding respondents' claims is not altered by the fact that in several steps of the process a mathematical equation and a programmed digital computer are used. This Court has undoubtedly recognized limits to § 101 and every discovery is not embraced within the statutory terms. Excluded from such patent protection are laws of nature, physical phenomena and abstract ideas. * * *

"Our recent holdings in Gottschalk v. Benson, supra, and Parker v. Flook, supra, both of which are computer-related, stand for nothing more than these long-established principles. * * *

"In contrast, the respondents here do not seek to patent a mathematical formula. Instead, they seek patent protection for a process of curing synthetic rubber. Their process admittedly employs a well-known mathematical equation [i.e., the Arrhenius equation, a standard calculation named for its inventor], but they do not seek to pre-empt the use of that equation. Rather, they seek only to foreclose from others the use of that equation in conjunction with all of the other steps in their claimed process. * * * Obviously, one does not need a 'computer' to cure natural or synthetic rubber, but if the computer use incorporated in the process patent significantly lessens the possibility of 'overcuring' or 'undercuring,' the process as a whole does not thereby become unpatentable subject matter. * * *

"In this case, it may later be determined that the respondents' process is not deserving of patent protection because it fails to satisfy the statutory conditions of novelty under § 102 or nonobviousness under § 103. A rejection on either of these grounds does not affect the determination that respondents' claims recited subject matter which was eligible for patent protection under § 101. * * *

" * * * We recognize, of course, that when a claim recites a mathematical formula (or scientific principle or phenomenon of nature), an inquiry must be made into whether the claim is seeking patent protection for that formula in the abstract. * * * [I]nsignificant postsolution activity will not transform an unpatentable principle into a patentable process. * * * On the other hand, when a claim containing a mathematical formula implements or applies that formula in a structure or process which, when considered as a whole, is performing a function which the patent laws were designed to protect (e.g., transforming or reducing an article to a different state or thing), then the claim satisfies the requirements of § 101."

Justice Stevens' dissent, joined by Brennan, Marshall, and Blackmun, maintained that since the only new element of the process was an unpatentable algorithm, the process as a whole was unpatentable. The Court's decision in Parker v. Flook, he said, was controlling; the postsolution activity that distinguished respondents' process from the *Flook* alarm limit was not itself novel, so *Flook,* he argued, dictated that the entire process was unpatentable.

NOTES AND QUESTIONS

(1) The cases since *Diehr* generally have continued to expand the availability of patent protection for computer programs. The Court of Customs and Patent Appeals (absorbed in 1982 into the Court of Appeals for the Federal Circuit) became adept at finding sufficient integration with a claimed process or apparatus to validate the patent. See In re Abele, 684 F.2d 902 (C.C.P.A.1982), and In re Pardo, 684 F.2d 912 (C.C.P.A.1982). More recent examples include In re Iwahashi, 888 F.2d 1370 (Fed.Cir.1989), and In re Alappat, 33 F.3d 1526 (Fed.Cir.1994).

The "mental steps" bar, however, has not disappeared. In re Meyer, 688 F.2d 789, 796 (C.C.P.A.1982), upheld the PTO in refusing a patent for a program that recorded the results of as many as fifty diagnostic tests (knee-tapping, etc.) performed by an examining neurologist. It appeared "that these standard tests have been employed for many years and that the more experienced the doctor and the better his memory, the less would be the need (if any) for this invention." The "claims are to a mathematical algorithm representing a mental process that has *not* been applied to physical elements or process steps and is, therefore, not limited to any otherwise statutory process, machine, manufacture, or composition of matter." *Meyer* was followed and another diagnostic system was held unpatentable as a mathematical algorithm in In re Grams, 888 F.2d 835 (Fed.Cir. 1989). Both *Meyer* and *Grams* were cited in a later case that upheld the denial of a patent for a novel way of conducting auctions. In re Schrader, 22 F.3d 290 (Fed.Cir.1994).[e]

e. In 1996 the PTO issued Examination Guidelines for Computer–Related Inventions. They are reproduced in 51 Pat.,Tm. & Copyr.J. (BNA) 422 (1996). The PTO has also issued guidelines for the examination of design patent applications relating to computer icons used in screen displays. Id. at 616. For a review of the precedents on patent protection for computer programs, see State Street Bank and Trust Co. v. Signature Financial Group, Inc., 927 F.Supp. 502 (D.Mass.1996), invalidating a patent on a computerized accounting system for managing mutual fund investments. "Quite simply, it involves no

(2) Greater use of patent law for the protection of software is advocated in Chisum, The Patentability of Algorithms, 47 U.Pitt.L.Rev. 959 (1986) (with an appendix of patents relating to computer programs). See also Oddi, An Uneasier Case for Copyright Than for Patent Protection of Computer Programs, 72 Neb.L.Rev. 351 (1993), concluding that the case for patent is more convincing than copyright, and that a sui generis alternative offers only speculative advantages at best. But see Samuelson, *Benson* Revisited: The Case Against Patent Protection for Algorithms and Other Computer–Related Inventions, 39 Emory L.Rev. 1025 (1990).

The patent alternative, however, continues to suffer from legal uncertainties and practical drawbacks. The time (patent applications may be pending for years) and the expense can be prohibitive, particularly in light of the rate at which software becomes obsolete. The scope of protection for the "program" aspects of a patented invention remains uncertain, and there is always the risk of a subsequent judicial determination of invalidity. But the rewards can be substantial. In 1994 a jury assessed $120 million in damages against Microsoft Corp. for including programming as part of its MS–DOS 6.0 software that infringed a patent in a method of compressing data to increase storage capacity. See New York Times, Feb. 24, 1994, p. D1. The case was eventually settled.

(3) Is the patchwork of copyright, trade secret, and patent law adequate for the protection of software? Is it more than adequate? Does it overprotect, for example, in the long duration of copyright or patent? (The patent law, in 35 U.S.C.A. § 41, provides for "maintenance fees" at three points during the life of the patent. They are substantial, and if not paid the invention falls into the public domain.)

(4) Is the computer industry of such importance, and are its characteristics sufficiently distinctive, that a separate body of law should be considered, tailored to those special characteristics? This was the route followed in connection with the protection of "mask works"—the patterns for semiconductor chips. See p. 176 infra.

On the wisdom of a sui generis approach to software, compare Samuelson, Creating a New Kind of Intellectual Property: Applying the Lessons of the Chip Law to Computer Programs, 70 Minn.L.Rev. 471 (1985), enthusiastically supporting separate software legislation, with Raskind, The Uncertain Case for Special Legislation Protecting Computer Software, 47 U.Pitt.L.Rev. 1131 (1986), advocating the judicious application of existing principles together with incremental changes in the Copyright Act. See also Miller, Copyright Protection for Computer Programs, Databases, and Computer–Generated Works: Is Anything New Since CONTU?, 106 Harv. L.Rev. 977 (1993), defending the assimilation of software into copyright as

further physical transformation or reduction than inputting numbers, calculating numbers, outputting numbers, and storing numbers. The same functions could be performed, albeit less efficiently, by an accountant armed with pencil, paper, calculator, and a filing system." The court also invoked the "business methods exception" to patentability. (But see Paine, Webber v. Merrill Lynch, 564 F.Supp. 1358 (D.Del.1983), upholding a patent on a business system.)

advocated in the CONTU Report.[f] Reliance on sui generis legislation might also impede international protection under the aegis of the major copyright and patent conventions.

(5) Apparently there are no limits on the attempts to expand the reach of copyright in new technologies. See, e.g., Kayton, Copyright in Living Genetically Engineered Works, 50 Geo.Wash.L.Rev. 191 (1982)!

COPYRIGHT IN COMMERCIAL DESIGN

Mazer v. Stein

Supreme Court of the United States, 1954.
347 U.S. 201, 74 S.Ct. 460.

■ MR. JUSTICE REED delivered the opinion of the Court.

This case involves the validity of copyrights obtained by respondents for statuettes of male and female dancing figures made of semi-vitreous china. The controversy centers around the fact that although copyrighted as "works of art," the statuettes were intended for use and used as bases for table lamps, with electric wiring, sockets and lamp shades attached.

Respondents are partners in the manufacture and sale of electric lamps. One of the respondents created original works of sculpture in the form of human figures by traditional clay-model technique. From this model, a production mold for casting copies was made. The resulting statuettes, without any lamp components added, were submitted by the respondents to the Copyright Office for registration as "works of art" or reproductions thereof under § 5(g) or § 5(h) of the copyright law, and certificates of registration issued. Sales (publication in accordance with the statute) as fully equipped lamps preceded the applications for copyright registration of the statuettes. 17 U.S.C. (Supp. V, 1952) §§ 10, 11, 13, 209; Rules and Regulations, 37 CFR, 1949, §§ 202.8 and 202.9. Thereafter, the statuettes were sold in quantity throughout the country both as lamp bases and as statuettes. The sales in lamp form accounted for all but an insignificant portion of respondents' sales.

Petitioners are partners and, like respondents, make and sell lamps. Without authorization, they copied the statuettes, embodied them in lamps and sold them.

The instant case is one in a series of reported suits brought by respondents against various alleged infringers of the copyrights, all presenting the same or a similar question. Because of conflicting decisions, we granted certiorari. * * *

----

f. A major effort to resurrect the sui generis alternative for software protection is made in Samuelson, Davis, Kapor, and Reichman, A Manifesto Concerning the Legal Protection of Computer Programs, 94 Colum.L.Rev. 2308 (1994). For an economic perspective on the choice of appropriate regime, see Dam, Some Economic Considerations in the Intellectual Property Protection of Software, 24 J.Leg.Stud. 321 (1995), concluding that copyright can offer an efficient system of protection.

THE PRINCIPAL STATUETTE IN MAZER v. STEIN.

Petitioners, charged by the present complaint with infringement of respondents' copyrights of reproductions of their works of art, seek here a reversal of the Court of Appeals decree upholding the copyrights. Petitioners in their petition for certiorari present a single question:

"Can statuettes be protected in the United States by copyright when the copyright applicant intended primarily to use the statuettes in the form of lamp bases to be made and sold in quantity and carried the intentions into effect?

"Stripped down to its essentials, the question presented is: Can a lamp manufacturer copyright his lamp bases?"

The first paragraph accurately summarizes the issue. The last gives it a quirk that unjustifiably, we think, broadens the controversy. The case requires an answer, not as to a manufacturer's right to register a lamp base but as to an artist's right to copyright a work of art intended to be reproduced for lamp bases. As petitioners say in their brief, their contention "questions the validity of the copyright based upon the actions of respondents." Petitioners question the validity of a copyright of a work of art for "mass" production. "Reproduction of a work of art" does not mean to them unlimited reproduction. Their position is that a copyright does not cover industrial reproduction of the protected article. Thus their reply brief states: "When an artist becomes a manufacturer or a designer for a manufacturer he is subject to the limitations of design patents and deserves no more consideration than any other manufacturer or designer." It is not the right to copyright an article that could have utility under § 5(g) and (h), * * * that petitioners oppose. Their brief accepts the copyrightability of the great carved golden salt cellar of Cellini but adds: "If, however, Cellini designed and manufactured this item in quantity so that the general public could have salt cellars, then an entirely different conclusion would be reached. In such case, the salt cellar becomes an article of manufacture having utility in addition to its ornamental value and would therefore have to be protected by design patent." It is publication as a lamp and registration as a statue to gain a monopoly in manufacture that they assert is such a misuse of copyright as to make the registration invalid.

No unfair competition question is presented. The constitutional power of Congress to confer copyright protection on works of art or their reproductions is not questioned.[5] Petitioners assume, as Congress has in its enactments and as do we, that the constitutional clause empowering legislation "To promote the Progress of Science and useful Arts, by securing for limited Times to Authors and Inventors the exclusive Right to their respective Writings and Discoveries", Art. I, § 8, cl. 8, includes within the term "Authors" the creator of a picture or a statue. The Court's consideration will be limited to the question presented by the petition for the writ of certiorari. In recent years the question as to utilitarian use of copyrighted articles has been much discussed.

---

5. We do not reach for constitutional questions not raised by the parties. * * *

In answering that issue, a review of the development of copyright coverage will make clear the purpose of the Congress in its copyright legislation. In 1790 the First Congress conferred a copyright on "authors of any map, chart, book or books already printed." Later, designing, engraving and etching were included; in 1831 musical compositions; dramatic compositions in 1856; and photographs and negatives thereof in 1865.

The Act of 1870 defined copyrightable subject matter as: "... any book, map, chart, dramatic or musical composition, engraving, cut, print, or photograph or negative thereof, or of a painting, drawing, chromo, *statue, statuary, and of models or designs intended to be perfected as works of the fine arts*." (Emphasis supplied.) The italicized part added three-dimensional work of art to what had been protected previously. In 1909 Congress again enlarged the scope of the copyright statute. The new Act provided in § 4: "That the works for which copyright may be secured under this Act shall include all the writings of an author." Some writers interpret this section as being coextensive with the constitutional grant, but the House Report, while inconclusive, indicates that it was "declaratory of existing law" only. Section 5 relating to classes of writings in 1909 read as shown in the margin with subsequent additions not material to this decision.[19] Significant for our purposes was the deletion of the fine-arts clause of the 1870 Act. Verbal distinctions between purely aesthetic articles and useful works of art ended insofar as the statutory copyright language is concerned.

The practice of the Copyright Office, under the 1870 and 1874 Acts and before the 1909 Act, was to allow registration "as works of the fine arts" of articles of the same character as those of respondents now under challenge. Seven examples appear in the Government's brief *amicus curiae*.[22] In 1910, interpreting the 1909 Act, the pertinent Copyright Regulations read as shown in the margin.[23] Because, as explained by the Government, this regulation "made no reference to articles which might fairly be considered works of art although they might also serve a useful purpose," it was reworded in 1917 as shown below.[24] The *amicus* brief gives sixty examples

---

19. [The Court's footnote sets out § 5 of the Act of 1909.]

22. E.g., "A female figure bearing an urn in front partly supported by drapery around the head. The figure nude from the waist up and below this the form concealed by conventionalized skirt draperies which flow down and forward forming a tray at the base. Sides and back of skirt in fluted form. The whole being designed as a candlestick with match tray. The figure standing and bent forward from hips and waist."

23. "Works of art.—This term includes all works belonging fairly to the so-called fine arts. (Paintings, drawings, and sculpture.)

"Productions of the industrial arts utilitarian in purpose and character are not subject to copyright registration, even if artistically made or ornamented." Rules and Regulations for the Registration of Claims to Copyright, Bulletin No. 15 (1910), 8.

[The rest of this 1910 regulation, which the Court's footnote omits, was as follows:

["No copyright exists in toys, games, dolls, advertising novelties, instruments or tools of any kind, glassware, embroideries, garments, laces, woven fabrics, or any similar articles."]

24. "Works of art and models or designs for works of art.—This term includes selected at five-year intervals, 1912–1952, said to be typical of registrations of works of art possessing utilitarian aspects.[25] The current pertinent regulation, published in 37 CFR, 1949, § 202.8, reads thus: "Works of art (Class G)—(a)—In General. This class includes works of artistic craftsmanship, in so far as their form but not their mechanical or utilitarian aspects are concerned, such as artistic jewelry, enamels, glassware, and tapestries, as well as all works belonging to the fine arts, such as paintings, drawings and sculpture. . . ." So we have a contemporaneous and long-continued construction of the statutes by the agency charged to administer them that would allow the registration of such a statuette as is in question here.

This Court once essayed to fix the limits of the fine arts.[27] That effort need not be appraised in relation to this copyright issue. It is clear Congress intended the scope of the copyright statute to include more than the traditional fine arts. Herbert Putnam, Esq., then Librarian of Congress and active in the movement to amend the copyright laws, told the joint meeting of the House and Senate Committees:

> "The term 'works of art' is deliberately intended as a broader specification than 'works of the fine arts' in the present statute with the idea that there is subject-matter (for instance, of applied design, not yet within the province of design patents), which may properly be entitled to protection under the copyright law." [28]

The successive acts, the legislative history of the 1909 Act and the practice of the Copyright Office unite to show that "works of art" and "reproductions of works of art" are terms that were intended by Congress to include the authority to copyright these statuettes. Individual perception of the beautiful is too varied a power to permit a narrow or rigid concept of art. As a standard we can hardly do better than the words of the present Regulation, § 202.8, supra, naming the things that appertain to the arts. They must be original, that is, the author's tangible expression of his ideas. Compare Burrow–Giles Lithographic Co. v. Sarony, 111 U.S. 53, 59–60. Such expression, whether meticulously delineating the model or mental image or conveying the meaning by modernistic form or color, is copyrightable. What cases there are confirm this coverage of the statute.[30]

all works belonging fairly to the so-called fine arts. (Paintings, drawings, and sculpture.)

"The protection of productions of the industrial arts, utilitarian in purpose and character, even if artistically made or ornamented depends upon action under the patent law; but registration in the Copyright Office has been made to protect artistic drawings notwithstanding they may afterwards be utilized for articles of manufacture." 37 CFR, 1939, § 201.4(7).

25. E.g., "Lighting fixture design. By F.E. Guitini. [Bowl-shaped bracket embellished with figure of half-nude woman standing in bunch of flowers.] Copyright December 28, 1912. Registration number G 42645. Copyright claimant: Kathodion Bronze Works, New York."

27. United States v. Perry, 146 U.S. 71.

28. Arguments before the Committees on Patents of the Senate and House of Representatives, conjointly, on S. 6330 and H.R. 19853, To Amend and Consolidate the Acts Respecting Copyright, 59th Cong., 1st Sess., June 6–9, 1906, p. 11. * * *

30. Burrow–Giles Lithographic Co. v. Sarony, 111 U.S. 53; Bleistein v. Donaldson Lithographing Co., 188 U.S. 239, 250; Louis

The conclusion that the statues here in issue may be copyrighted goes far to solve the question whether their intended reproduction as lamp stands bars or invalidates their registration. This depends solely on statutory interpretation. Congress may after publication protect by copyright any writing of an author. Its statute creates the copyright. It did not exist at common law even though he had a property right in his unpublished work.

But petitioners assert that congressional enactment of the design patent laws should be interpreted as denying protection to artistic articles embodied or reproduced in manufactured articles.[33] They say: "Fundamentally and historically, the Copyright Office is the repository of what each claimant considers to be a cultural treasure, whereas the Patent Office is the repository of what each applicant considers to be evidence of the advance in industrial and technological fields." Their argument is that design patents require the critical examination given patents to protect the public against monopoly. Attention is called to Gorham Mfg. Co. v. White, 14 Wall. 511, interpreting the design patent law of 1842, 5 Stat. 544, granting a patent to anyone who by "their own industry, genius, efforts, and expense, may have invented or produced any new and original design for a manufacture. ..." A pattern for flat silver was there upheld. The intermediate and present law differs little. "Whoever invents any new, original and ornamental design for an article of manufacture may obtain a patent therefor, ..." subject generally to the provisions concerning patents for invention. § 171, 66 Stat. 805, 35 U.S.C.A. § 171. As petitioner sees the effect of the design patent law: "If an industrial designer can not satisfy the novelty requirements of the design patent laws, then his design as used on articles of manufacture can be copied by anyone." Petitioner has furnished the Court a booklet of numerous design patents for statuettes, bases for table lamps and similar articles for manufacture, quite indistinguishable in type from the copyrighted statuettes here in issue.[35] Petitioner urges that overlapping of patent and copyright legislation so as to give an author or inventor a choice between patents and copyrights should not be permitted. We assume petitioner takes the position that protection for a statuette for industrial use can only be obtained by patent, if any protection can be given.

De Jonge & Co. v. Breuker & Kessler Co., C.C., 182 F. 150, 152; F.W. Woolworth Co. v. Contemporary Arts, 1 Cir., 193 F.2d 162, 164; see same case, 344 U.S. 228; Yuengling v. Schile, C.C., 12 F. 97, 100; Schumacher v. Schwencke, C.C., 25 F. 466; Pellegrini v. Allegrini, D.C., 2 F.2d 610.

33. Two cases are relied upon to support the position of the petitioners. Taylor Instrument Companies v. Fawley–Brost Co., 7 Cir., 139 F.2d 98, and Brown Instrument Co. v. Warner, 82 U.S.App.D.C. 232, 161 F.2d 910. These cases hold that the Mechanical Patent Law and Copyright Laws are mutually exclusive. As to overlapping of Design Patent and Copyright Laws, however, a different answer has been given by the courts. Louis De Jonge & Co. v. Breuker & Kessler Co., C.C., 182 F. 150, affirmed on other grounds in 3 Cir., 191 F. 35, and 235 U.S. 33; see also cases cited in note 37, infra.

35. E.g., Design Patent 170.445 Base for table lamps, a fanciful statuette of a girl standing in front of a high rock in bathing costume.

As we have held the statuettes here involved copyrightable, we need not decide the question of their patentability. Though other courts have passed upon the issue as to whether allowance by the election of the author or patentee of one bars a grant of the other, we do not.[37] We do hold that the patentability of the statuettes, fitted as lamps or unfitted, does not bar copyright as works of art. Neither the Copyright Statute nor any other says that because a thing is patentable it may not be copyrighted. We should not so hold.

Unlike a patent, a copyright gives no exclusive right to the art disclosed; protection is given only to the expression of the idea—not the idea itself. Thus, in Baker v. Selden, 101 U.S. 99, the Court held that a copyrighted book on a peculiar system of bookkeeping was not infringed by a similar book using a similar plan which achieved similar results where the alleged infringer made a different arrangement of the columns and used different headings. The distinction is illustrated in Fred Fisher, Inc. v. Dillingham, D.C., 298 F. 145, 151, when the court speaks of two men, each a perfectionist, independently making maps of the same territory. Though the maps are identical each may obtain the exclusive right to make copies of his own particular map, and yet neither will infringe the other's copyright. Likewise a copyrighted directory is not infringed by a similar directory which is the product of independent work.[40] The copyright protects originality rather than novelty or invention—conferring only "the sole right of multiplying copies." [41] Absent copying there can be no infringement of copyright. Thus, respondents may not exclude others from using statuettes of human figures in table lamps; they may only prevent use of copies of their statuettes as such or as incorporated in some other article. Regulation § 202.8, supra, makes clear that artistic articles are protected in "form but not their mechanical or utilitarian aspects." See Stein v. Rosenthal, D.C., 103 F.Supp. 227, 231. The dichotomy of protection for the aesthetic is not beauty and utility but art for the copyright and the invention of original and ornamental design for design patents. We find nothing in the copyright statute to support the argument that the intended use or use in industry of an article eligible for copyright bars or invalidates its registration. We do not read such a limitation into the copyright law.

Nor do we think the subsequent registration of a work of art published as an element in a manufactured article, is a misuse of the copyright. This is not different from the registration of a statuette and its later embodiment in an industrial article.

---

37. See Rosenthal v. Stein, note 3, supra; In re Blood, 57 App.D.C. 351, 23 F.2d 772; Korzybski v. Underwood & Underwood, Inc., 2 Cir., 36 F.2d 727; William A. Meier Glass Co. v. Anchor Hocking Glass Corp., D.C., 95 F.Supp. 264, 267; Jones Bros. Co. v. Underkoffler, D.C., 16 F.Supp. 729; Louis De Jonge & Co. v. Breuker & Kessler Co., C.C., 182 F. 150; 66 Harv.L.Rev. 884; 52 Mich. L.Rev. 33; cf. Taylor Instrument Companies v. Fawley–Brost Co., 7 Cir., 139 F.2d 98.

40. Sampson & Murdock Co. v. Seaver–Radford Co., 1 Cir., 140 F. 539. See, Annotation 26 A.L.R. 585.

41. Jeweler's Circular Pub. Co. v. Keystone Publishing, 2 Cir., 281 F. 83, 94, 26 A.L.R. 571.

"The copyright law, like the patent statutes, makes reward to the owner a secondary consideration." United States v. Paramount Pictures, 334 U.S. 131, 158. However, it is "intended definitely to grant valuable enforceable rights to authors, publishers, etc., without burdensome requirements; 'to afford greater encouragement to the production of literary [or artistic] works of lasting benefit to the world.'" Washingtonian Pub. Co. v. Pearson, 306 U.S. 30, 36.

The economic philosophy behind the clause empowering Congress to grant patents and copyrights is the conviction that encouragement of individual effort by personal gain is the best way to advance public welfare through the talents of authors and inventors in "Science and useful Arts." Sacrificial days devoted to such creative activities deserve rewards commensurate with the services rendered.

Affirmed.

■ Opinion of MR. JUSTICE DOUGLAS, in which MR. JUSTICE BLACK concurs.

An important constitutional question underlies this case—a question which was stirred on oral argument but not treated in the briefs. It is whether these statuettes of dancing figures may be copyrighted. Congress has provided that "works of art," "models or designs for works of art," and "reproductions of a work of art" may be copyrighted, 17 U.S.C. § 5; and the Court holds that these statuettes are included in the words "works of art." But may statuettes be granted the monopoly of the copyright?

Article I, § 8 of the Constitution grants Congress the power "To promote the Progress of Science and useful Arts, by securing for limited Times to Authors ... the exclusive Right to their respective Writings...." The power is thus circumscribed: it allows a monopoly to be granted only to "authors" for their "writings." Is a sculptor an "author" and is his statue a "writing" within the meaning of the Constitution? We have never decided the question. * * *

The interests involved in the category of "works of art," as used in the copyright law, are considerable. The Copyright Office has supplied us with a long list of such articles which have been copyrighted—statuettes, book ends, clocks, lamps, door knockers, candlesticks, inkstands, chandeliers, piggy banks, sundials, salt and pepper shakers, fish bowls, casseroles, and ash trays. Perhaps these are all "writings" in the constitutional sense. But to me, at least, they are not obviously so. It is time that we came to the problem full face. I would accordingly put the case down for reargument.

NOTES AND QUESTIONS

(1) What is the holding of *Mazer*? That all utilitarian objects are copyrightable as "sculptural works"? That an otherwise copyrightable "work of art" will not forfeit protection if reproduced as part of a useful article? (*Should* a light bulb protruding from the head of Rodin's *The Thinker* render the work uncopyrightable?)

(2) On the questions raised in the dissenting opinion, see Charlow, Descent into the Market Place, 8 Hastings L.J. 146 (1957); Derenberg, The Meaning of "Writings" in the Copyright Clause of the Constitution, Copyr. Law Revision Study No. 3 (1956), in 1 Studies on Copyr. 43 (1963).

————————

DESIGN PATENT

One argument urged upon the Court in Mazer v. Stein was that protection for the design of a useful article is the exclusive province of federal design patent law. Since 1842, design patent protection has been available for the appearance of an "article of manufacture." 5 Stat. 544 (1842). The current Patent Act at 35 U.S.C.A. § 171 provides:

> § 171.   Patents for designs
>
> Whoever invents any new, original and ornamental design for an article of manufacture may obtain a patent therefor, subject to the conditions and requirements of this title.
>
> The provisions of this title relating to patents for inventions shall apply to patents for designs, except as otherwise provided.

The second sentence of § 171 subjects design patents to the demanding standards applied to other patents, including the "non-obvious" requirement of § 103. The next case grapples with the consequences.

In re Nalbandian

United States Court of Customs and Patent Appeals, 1981.
661 F.2d 1214.

■ Before MARKEY, CHIEF JUDGE, and RICH, BALDWIN, MILLER and NIES, JUDGES.

■ NIES, JUDGE.

This appeal is from the decision of the Patent and Trademark Office (PTO) Board of Appeals (board) affirming the rejection under 35 U.S.C. § 103 by the examiner of appellant's application, serial No. 792,482, filed April 29, 1977, for "Combined Tweezer and Spotlight." We affirm.

The claimed ornamental design is for an implement referred to as an illuminable tweezer. The primary reference on which the examiner and the board relied is U.S. Patent Des. 175,259, issued to Johnson et al. (Johnson) on August 2, 1955, also for an illuminable tweezer. The respective designs are reproduced below:

Appellant's

Johnson's

* * *

The sole issue on appeal is whether appellant's design would have been obvious within the meaning of 35 U.S.C. § 103.   In the words of the statute, are

> ... the differences between the subject matter sought to be patented and the prior art ... such that the subject matter as a whole would have been obvious at the time the invention was made to a person having ordinary skill in the art to which said subject matter pertains[?]

In In re Laverne, 356 F.2d 1003 (1966), this court specifically rejected the interpretation generally given to the statutory language "one of ordinary skill in the art" as referring to a designer.   The court concluded that this interpretation would not effectuate the intent of Congress to promote progress in designs since it would result in the denial of patent protection for the work of competent designers.   Accordingly, it was held that the obviousness of designs over the prior art must be tested by the eyes of the "ordinary intelligent man," who was also referred to as the "ordinary observer."

Since the *Laverne* decision, the Second, Third, Tenth and District of Columbia circuits have specifically considered the "ordinary observer" test set forth therein and rejected it.   These circuits continue to interpret "one of ordinary skill" as requiring obviousness to be tested from the viewpoint of the "ordinary designer."   Since board decisions may be reviewed by the District of Columbia Circuit as well as this court, the PTO has been faced with two standards in design cases.

We believe it is appropriate to close this schism.   Accordingly, with this case we hold that the test of *Laverne* will no longer be followed.   In design cases we will consider the fictitious person identified in § 103 as "one of ordinary skill in the art" to be the designer of ordinary capability who designs articles of the type presented in the application.   This approach is consistent with Graham v. John Deere Co., 383 U.S. 1 (1966), which requires that the level of ordinary skill *in the pertinent art be determined.*
* * *

Rejection of the "ordinary observer" test under 35 U.S.C. § 103 does not preclude its application in other contexts. The "ordinary observer" test was applied in determining whether a claim to a design had been infringed as long ago as Gorham Co. v. White, 81 U.S. (14 Wall.) 511 (1871). Further, the "ordinary observer" test has been applied when determining anticipation under § 102 by courts which apply the "ordinary designer" test under § 103.

Applying the "ordinary designer" test of § 103 to the case at bar, the question is whether the changes made by appellant in the Johnson design for an illuminated tweezer would have been obvious to an ordinary designer of such implements. As noted, the claimed design is substantially identical in overall configuration to the design shown in Johnson for the same type of article. The differences in the finger grips of a slightly different shape and the straight, rather than slightly curved pincers, are de minimis. We also agree that it is well within the skill of an ordinary designer in the art to make the modification of the fluting and that it would have been obvious to do so. Such changes do not achieve a patentably distinct design. In re Lamb, 286 F.2d 610 (1961). We agree, therefore, that the PTO has shown a prima facie case of obviousness. * * *

Affirmed.

■ RICH, JUDGE, concurring.

A majority of my colleagues choose to swing the court into alignment with the three circuits which have affirmatively rejected the reasoning of our fifteen-year old *In re Laverne* opinion which, until now, this court has always unanimously accepted without question.

Laverne thus being dead, I deem it appropriate, as the father of the so-called "ordinary observer" test (as applied to 35 U.S.C. § 103), to say a few kind words over the corpse.

From the passages quoted from my opinion by the majority, it will be seen that what was written in 1966 was a response to the examiner's reliance on what would be produced by "the expected skill of a competent designer," perhaps an imaginary person of somewhat greater skill than the imaginary "ordinary designer" now enthroned by the majority. I was interested in retaining within the ambit of the patent system the made-for-hire products of "competent designers" so businessmen or corporations would find it economically advantageous to employ them, thus carrying out the objective of 35 U.S.C. § 171, to promote the ornamental design of articles of manufacture.

The majority is not now talking of "competent designers" but of "ordinary designers" from which it follows that there may be extraordinary designers who will produce unobvious designs which ordinary designers will not routinely produce. It is probably true, as the majority says, that all this is just semantics and courts will, with phraseology of their own choosing, continue to find designs patentable or unpatentable according to their judicial "hunches."

The real problem, however, is not whether the § 103 fictitious "person" is an ordinary observer or an ordinary designer but with the necessity under Title 35 of finding unobviousness in a design. The problem long antedates 1952 and its Patent Act and existed from the beginning, the pre-1952 test being the presence of "invention" in a design. The problem was well known to the drafters of the 1952 Act (of which I was one) and it was also known that many prior legislative efforts had been made to solve it.[1] When work on revision of the patent statutes began in 1950, a deliberate decision was made not to attempt any solution of the "controversial design problem" but simply to retain the substance of the existing design patent statute and attack the design problem at a later date, after the new Title 35 had been enacted.

Thus it was that the patentability of designs came to be subject to the new § 103 which was written with an eye to the kinds of inventions encompassed by § 101 with no thought at all of how it might affect designs. Therefore, the design protection problem was in no way made better; perhaps it was made worse.   * * *

The point of this review is to call attention to the resulting presently pending legislation, H.R. 20, 97th Congress, 1st Session, introduced January 5, 1981, by Mr. Railsback, a bill "To amend the copyright law, title 17 of the United States Code, to provide for protection of ornamental designs of useful articles." The present case and its companion, In re Spreter, 661 F.2d 1220 (Cust. & Pat.App.), concurrently decided, are but the latest examples of the need for a law tailored to the problems of designers, of their employers and clients in the business world, and of the government agencies now concerned. The now-pending legislation is substantially the same bill introduced in 1957, after the refining process of *24 years of legislative consideration. It is time to pass it* and get the impossible issue of obviousness in design patentability cases off the backs of the courts and the Patent and Trademark Office, giving some sense of certainty to the business world of what designs can be protected and how.   * * *

NOTES ON DESIGN PATENTS

(1) Design patents have issued for the ornamental designs of objects ranging from hosiery reinforcements to cement mixer trucks.[g] Some cases

1. Records I made in the mid 50's show that, beginning in 1914, some 45 bills were introduced in the House and Senate directed to some improved form of protection for designs. Many of these bills were, of course, duplicates, substantially the same bill being introduced in each house or reintroduced in successive years. Those interested in the history can examine Barbara A. Ringer's 70–page *Bibliography on Design Protection* published for Copyright Office use June 1, 1955, and an enlarged 160–page version or "supple-ment" compiled by W. Strauss, Varmer, Caruthers, and Berger on June 1, 1959, bearing the same title. Fabulous amounts of time and effort have been poured into solving the design protection problem with, to date, no legislative solution. See also Kelsey M. Mott's two-installment article The Standard of Ornamentality in the United States Design Patent Law, 48 ABA J. 548, 643 (June, July 1962).

g. See Glen Raven Knitting Mills, Inc. v. Sanson Hosiery Mills, Inc., 189 F.2d 845 reflect persistent attempts to capture the *function* of an article indirectly by means of a design claim, but courts resist this backdoor approach when they detect it. See Best Lock Corp. v. Ilco Unican Corp., 94 F.3d 1563 (Fed.Cir.1996) (design patent on the shape of key blanks was invalid; the shape was dictated by function because of the necessary compatibility with the corresponding lock); Power Controls Corp. v. Hybrinetics, Inc., 806 F.2d 234 (Fed.Cir.1986).

(2) The overlap between the subject matters of design patent and copyright raises the possibility of dual protection. Early cases put the creator to an election. The Court in *Mazer* noted the prior case law, but found it unnecessary to consider the election doctrine since the plaintiff had not sought a design patent.

In 1974, the Court of Customs and Patent Appeals repudiated the election doctrine. It reversed a Patent and Trademark Office decision rejecting a design patent application for a previously copyrighted watch bearing a caricature of Spiro Agnew (Spiro who?). In re Yardley, 493 F.2d 1389 (C.C.P.A.1974). The Copyright Office, however, continued to refuse registration to patented designs until 1995, when it finally abandoned the election doctrine. See 60 Fed.Reg. 15605 (Mar. 24, 1995).

(3) Does a "non-obvious" standard for ornamental designs under patent law require the kinds of artistic judgments generally eschewed by copyright law? Lindgren, The Sanctity of Design Patent: Illusion or Reality?, 10 Okla.City U.L.Rev. 195 (1985), reports that about 70% of the design patents challenged in federal courts between 1964 and 1983 were held *invalid*. The sample produced by cases attacking validity may be biased toward questionable patents; weak patents are attacked while strong patents collect royalties. The statistics nevertheless appear to vindicate the prevailing mistrust of design patent protection. But the tide may have turned as the Federal Circuit increasingly exercises its exclusive appellate jurisdiction over patents to uphold validity. See, e.g., Avia Group Int'l, Inc. v. L.A. Gear California, Inc., 853 F.2d 1557 (Fed.Cir.1988).

In contrast to the relative ease with which a copyright registration may be secured, obtaining a design patent is, as with other patents, a difficult business. The applicant (realistically, the applicant's attorney, who must be licensed to practice before the Patent and Trademark Office) is required to file an elaborate application detailing the claim. The PTO then conducts a search to determine novelty and nonobviousness. This may take considerable time—in some cases several years. Only after the patent issues can the patentee maintain suit for infringement, and then only as to acts committed after the grant. See Gayler v. Wilder, 51 U.S. 477, 493 (1850). Costs (including filing fees, issuance fees, and attorney's fees) mount quickly, particularly when protection is sought for a number of new designs.

(4th Cir.1951); In re Koehring, 37 F.2d 421 (C.C.P.A.1930). The appearance of a stadium grandstand, In re Hadden, 20 F.2d 275 (D.C.Cir.1927), and even the design produced by jets of water in a fountain, In re Hruby, 373 F.2d 997 (C.C.P.A.1967), have been found to lie within the statutory subject matter.

The design patent, if issued, has a term of fourteen years. 35 U.S.C.A. § 173. The degree of similarity that will constitute infringement of a patented design is measured with reference to the reaction of an "ordinary observer". See Gorham Manufacturing Co. v. White, 81 U.S. 511 (1872). There is also a modest $250 minimum damage award for infringement of a design patent. 35 U.S.C.A. § 289.

On design patents, see generally D. Chisum, Chisum on Patents § 1.04.

USEFUL ARTICLES AFTER *MAZER*

Soon after Mazer v. Stein, the regulations of the Copyright Office were amended to reflect the Court's carefully circumscribed holding. Registration of copyright in a "work of art" would not be affected by "the use of the work, the number of copies reproduced, or the fact that it appears on a textile material or textile product." 37 C.F.R. § 202.01(b) (current version at 37 C.F.R. § 202.10(a)). As this language suggests, textile designers were a major beneficiary of the new rule.

Before *Mazer,* manufacturers seeking protection for textile designs had hard going. See Cheney Brothers v. Doris Silk Corp., p. 638 infra; Verney Corp. v. Rose Fabric Converters Corp., 87 F.Supp. 802 (S.D.N.Y.1949). Design patents theoretically were available, but the delays and expense associated with the application process and the requirements of novelty and nonobviousness made them an unattractive alternative. Copyright was far better suited to the protection of such evanescent creations, and they were now securely within its scope. See Peter Pan Fabrics, Inc. v. Martin Weiner Corp., p. 236 infra. Indeed, graphic designs on utilitarian articles ranging from shoe soles to dinnerware were now within the subject matter of copyright. See SCOA Industries, Inc. v. Famolare, Inc., 192 U.S.P.Q. 216 (S.D.N.Y.1976); Syracuse China Corp. v. Stanley Roberts, Inc., 180 F.Supp. 527 (S.D.N.Y.1960).

Copyright claims embracing three-dimensional aspects of utilitarian objects presented greater difficulties. As the Copyright Office regulation quoted by the Court in *Mazer* indicates, jewelry had already found a place within the statutory scheme, but perhaps jewelry is not really utilitarian. Cf. § 101 (definition of "useful article").[h] A dancing figure used as a lamp base was now within the subject matter of copyright, but what of the design of a dress, the shape of an automobile, or the appearance of a silver tea service?

The Copyright Office, determined to preclude protection for industrial design, promulgated a regulation limiting copyright in utilitarian articles. The regulation inspired the formulation ultimately adopted in the 1976 Act. The Act includes a narrow codification of *Mazer* in § 113(a); the distinctions between works of art and industrial design pursued in the former

---

h. See Donald Bruce & Co. v. B.H. Multi Com Corp., 964 F.Supp. 265 (N.D.Ill.1997), holding that a ring is not a "useful article" under the § 101 definition, since it "is purely ornamental, its sole purpose is to portray its appearance."

regulation now appear in the § 101 definitions of "useful article" and "pictorial, graphic, and sculptural works." The regulation and its statutory offspring are discussed in the following case.

Kieselstein–Cord v. Accessories by Pearl, Inc.

United States Court of Appeals, Second Circuit, 1980.
632 F.2d 989.

■ Before OAKES and VAN GRAAFEILAND, CIRCUIT JUDGES, and WEINSTEIN, DISTRICT JUDGE.

■ OAKES, CIRCUIT JUDGE:

This case is on a razor's edge of copyright law. It involves belt buckles, utilitarian objects which as such are not copyrightable. But these are not ordinary buckles; they are sculptured designs cast in precious metals—decorative in nature and used as jewelry is, principally for ornamentation. We say "on a razor's edge" because the case requires us to draw a fine line under applicable copyright law and regulations. Drawing the line in favor of the appellant designer, we uphold the copyrights granted to him by the Copyright Office and reverse the district court's grant of summary judgment, 489 F.Supp. 732, in favor of the appellee, the copier of appellant's designs.

Appellant Barry Kieselstein–Cord designs, manufactures exclusively by handcraftsmanship, and sells fashion accessories. To produce the two buckles in issue here, the "Winchester" and the "Vaquero," he worked from original renderings which he had conceived and sketched.   * * *

* * * Sales of both buckles were made primarily in high fashion stores and jewelry stores, bringing recognition to appellant as a "designer." This recognition included a 1979 Coty American Fashion Critics' Award for his work in jewelry design as well as election in 1978 to the Council of Fashion Designers of America. Both the Winchester and the Vaquero buckles, donated by appellant after this lawsuit was commenced, have been accepted by the Metropolitan Museum of Art for its permanent collection.

As the court below found, appellee's buckles "appear to be line-for-line copies but are made of common metal rather than" precious metal. Appellee admitted to copying the Vaquero and selling its imitations, and to selling copies of the Winchester. Indeed some of the order blanks of appellee's customers specifically referred to "Barry K Copy," "BK copy," and even "Barry Kieselstein Knock-off." Thus the only legal questions for the court below were whether the articles may be protected under the copyright statutes and, if so, whether the copyrights were adequate under the laws.   * * *

* * * The thrust of appellee's argument, as well as of the court's decision below, is that appellant's buckles are not copyrightable because they are "useful articles" with no "pictorial, graphic, or sculptural features that can be identified separately from, and are capable of existing independently of, the utilitarian aspects" of the buckles. The 1976 copyright

statute does not provide for the copyrighting of useful articles except to the extent that their designs incorporate artistic features that can be identified separately from the functional elements of the articles.   See 17 U.S.C. §§ 101, 102. With respect to this question, the law adopts the language of the longstanding Copyright Office regulations, 37 C.F.R. § 202.10(c) (1977) [3] (revoked Jan. 5, 1978, 43 Fed.Reg. 965, 966 (1978)). The regulations in turn were adopted in the mid–1950's, under the 1909 Act, in an effort to implement the Supreme Court's decision in Mazer v. Stein, 347 U.S. 201 (1954). See H.R.Rep. No. 1476, 94th Cong., 2d Sess. 54–55 (1976), reprinted in [1976] U.S.Code Cong. & Admin.News, pp. 5659, 5668 [hereinafter cited as *House Report*]. The Court in *Mazer,* it will be recalled, upheld the validity of copyrights obtained for statuettes of male and female dancing figures despite the fact that they were intended for use and used as bases for table lamps, with electric wiring, sockets, and lampshades attached. *Mazer* itself followed a "contemporaneous and long-continued construction" by the Copyright Office of the 1870 and 1874 Acts as well as of the 1909 Act, under which the case was decided. 347 U.S. at 211–13. As Professor Nimmer points out, however, the Copyright Office's regulations in the mid–1950's that purported to "implement" this decision actually limited the Court's apparent open-ended extension of copyright protection to all aesthetically pleasing useful articles. See 1 Nimmer, supra, § 2.08[B], at 2–88 to 2–89. * * *

We are left nevertheless with the problem of determining when a pictorial, graphic, or sculptural feature "can be identified separately from, and [is] capable of existing independently of, the utilitarian aspects of the article," 17 U.S.C. § 101. This problem is particularly difficult because, according to the legislative history explored by the court below, such separability may occur either "physically or conceptually," House Report at 55, [1976] U.S.Code Cong. & Admin.News at 5668. As the late Judge

---

3. 37 C.F.R. § 202.10, reprinted in 4 Nimmer on Copyright, App. 11, at 11–13 to 11–14 (1980), provided as follows:

Works of Art (Class G)

(a) General[.] This class includes published or unpublished works of artistic craftsmanship, insofar as their form but not their mechanical or utilitarian aspects are concerned, such as artistic jewelry, enamels, glassware, and tapestries, as well as works belonging to the fine arts, such as paintings, drawings and sculpture. [Revoked Jan. 1, 1978, 43 Fed.Reg. 965, 966 (1978).]

(b) In order to be acceptable as a work of art, the work must embody some creative authorship in its delineation or form. The registrability of a work of art is not affected by the intention of the author as to the use of the work, the number of copies reproduced, or the fact that it appears on a textile material or textile product. The potential availability of protection under the design patent law will not affect the registrability of a work of art, but a copyright claim in a patented design or in the drawings or photographs in a patent application will not be registered after the patent has been issued. [Current version at 37 C.F.R. § 202.10(b) (1979).]

(c) If the sole intrinsic function of an article is its utility, the fact that the article is unique and attractively shaped will not qualify it as a work of art. However, if the shape of a utilitarian article incorporates features, such as artistic sculpture, carving, or pictorial representation, which can be identified separately and are capable of existing independently as a work of art, such features will be eligible for registration. [Revoked Jan. 1, 1978, 43 Fed.Reg. 965, 966 (1978).]

Winchester   Vaquero

Harold Leventhal observed in his concurrence in Esquire, Inc. v. Ringer, 591 F.2d 796, 807 (D.C.Cir.1978), cert. denied, 440 U.S. 908 (1979), legislative policy supports the Copyright Office's "effort to distinguish between the instances where the aesthetic element is conceptually severable and the instances where the aesthetic element is inextricably interwoven with the utilitarian aspect of the article."   Examples of conceptual separateness as an artistic notion may be found in many museums today and even in the great outdoors.   Professor Nimmer cites Christo's "Running Fence" as an example of today's "conceptual art": it "did not contain sculptural features that were physically separable from the utilitarian aspects of the fence, but the whole point of the work was that the artistic aspects of the work were conceptually separable."   1 Nimmer, supra, § 2.08[B] at 2–94.   * * *

   We see in appellant's belt buckles conceptually separable sculptural elements, as apparently have the buckles' wearers who have used them as ornamentation for parts of the body other than the waist.   The primary ornamental aspect of the Vaquero and Winchester buckles is conceptually separable from their subsidiary utilitarian function.   This conclusion is not at variance with the expressed congressional intent to distinguish copyrightable applied art and uncopyrightable industrial design, House Report at 55, [1976] U.S.Code Cong. & Admin.News at 5668.   Pieces of applied art, these buckles may be considered jewelry, the form of which is subject to copyright protection, * * *.

We reverse the grant of summary judgment to the appellee and remand the case for consideration of whether appellant has satisfied the copyright notice requirements.

■ WEINSTEIN, DISTRICT JUDGE (dissenting):

The trial judge was correct on both the law and the facts for the reasons given in his excellent opinion holding that plaintiff was not entitled to copyright protection.   Kieselstein–Cord v. Accessories By Pearl, Inc., 489 F.Supp. 732 (S.D.N.Y.1980).   The works sued on are, while admirable aesthetically pleasing examples of modern design, indubitably belt buckles and nothing else; their innovations of form are inseparable from the important function they serve—helping to keep the tops of trousers at waist level.

The conclusion that affirmance is required is reached reluctantly.   The result does deny protection to designers who use modern three-dimensional abstract works artfully incorporated into a functional object as an inseparable aspect of the article while granting it to those who attach their independent representational art, or even their trite gimmickry, to a useful object for purposes of enhancement.   Moreover, this result enables the commercial pirates of the marketplace to appropriate for their own profit, without any cost to themselves, the works of talented designers who enrich our lives with their intuition and skill.   The crass are rewarded, the artist who creates beauty is not.   All of us are offended by the flagrant copying of another's work.   This is regrettable, but it is not for this court to twist the law in order to achieve a result Congress has denied.   * * *

Interpretation and application of the copyright statute is facilitated by House Report No. 94–1476, U.S.Code Cong. & Admin.News 1976, p. 5658, by the Committee on the Judiciary.   It explicitly indicated that the rule of *Mazer* was incorporated.

> In accordance with the Supreme Court's decision in Mazer v. Stein, 347 U.S. 201 (1954), works of "applied art" encompass all original pictorial, graphic, and sculptural works that are intended to be or have been embodied in useful articles, regardless of factors such as mass production, commercial exploitation, and the potential availability of design patent protection . . .

> The Committee has added language to the definition of "pictorial, graphic, and sculptural works" in an effort to make clearer the distinction between works of applied art protectable under the bill and industrial designs not subject to copyright protection.   * * *

* * *

> In adopting this amendatory language [the separability test in § 101], the Committee is seeking to draw as clear a line as possible between copyrightable works of applied art and uncopyrighted works of industrial design.   A two-dimensional painting, drawing, or graphic work is

still capable of being identified as such when it is printed on or applied to utilitarian articles such as textile fabrics, wallpaper, containers, and the like. The same is true when a statue or carving is used to embellish an industrial product or, as in the *Mazer* case, is incorporated into a product without losing its ability to exist independently as a work of art. On the other hand, *although the shape of an industrial product may be aesthetically satisfying and valuable, the Committee's intention is not to offer it copyright protection under the bill.* Unless the shape of an automobile, airplane, ladies' dress, food processor, television set, or any other industrial product contains some element that, physically or conceptually, can be identified as separable from the utilitarian aspects of that article, the design would not be copyrighted under the bill. The test of separability and independence from "the utilitarian aspects of the article" does not depend upon the nature of the design—that is, even if the appearance of an article is determined by aesthetic (as opposed to functional) considerations, only elements, if any, which can be identified separately from the useful article as such are copyrightable. *And, even if the three-dimensional design contains some such element (for example, a carving on the back of a chair or a floral relief design on silver flatware), copyright protection would extend only to that element, and would not cover the overall configuration of the utilitarian article as such.*

1976 U.S.Code Cong. & Admin.News, pp. 5667–5668. (Emphasis supplied.)

Congress considered and declined to enact legislation that would have extended copyright protection to "[t]he 'design of a useful article' ... including its two-dimensional or three-dimensional features of shape and surface, which make up the appearance of the article." H.R. 2223, Title II, § 201(b)(2), 94th Cong., 1st Sess. (January 28, 1975). * * *

The distinctions between copyrightable "pictorial, graphic and sculptural works" and noncopyrightable industrial "designs" reflect serious concerns about the promotion of competition, the widespread availability of quality products and the advancement of technology through copying and modification. * * *

Important policies are obviously at stake. Should we encourage the artist and increase the compensation to the creative? Or should we allow cheap reproductions which will permit our less affluent to afford beautiful artifacts? Appellant sold the original for $600.00 and up. Defendant's version went for one-fiftieth of that sum.

Thus far Congress and the Supreme Court have answered in favor of commerce and the masses rather than the artists, designers and the well-to-do. Any change must be left to those higher authorities. The choices are legislative not judicial.

ESQUIRE, INC. V. RINGER, 591 F.2d 796 (D.C.Cir.1978), cert. denied, 440 U.S. 908 (1979). "This case," Judge Bazelon said, "presents the question whether the overall shape of certain outdoor lighting fixtures is eligible for copyright as a 'work of art.' The Register of Copyrights determined that the overall shape or configuration of such articles is not copyrightable. The district court disagreed, and issued a writ of mandamus directing the Register to enter the claim to copyright. Esquire, Inc. v. Ringer, 414 F.Supp. 939 (D.D.C.1976). For the reasons expressed below, we reverse."

Esquire had filed applications for copyright registration in connection with the designs of several outdoor lights. The Copyright Office, relying on § 202.10(c) of its regulations (quoted in footnote 3 in *Kieselstein–Cord*), found the designs uncopyrightable. "The Register interprets § 202.10(c) to bar copyright registration of the overall shape or configuration of a utilitarian article, no matter how aesthetically pleasing that shape or configuration may be." The court found the Register's interpretation "reasonable and well-supported." "In the Register's view, registration of

ONE OF THE ESQUIRE LIGHTING FIXTURES

the overall shape or configuration of utilitarian articles would lead to widespread copyright protection for industrial design. The Register reasons that aesthetic considerations enter into the design of most useful articles. Thus, if overall shape or configuration can qualify as a 'work of art,' 'the whole realm of consumer products—garments, toasters, refrigerators, furniture, bathtubs, automobiles, etc.—and industrial products designed to have aesthetic appeal—subway cars, computers, photocopying machines, typewriters, adding machines, etc.—must also qualify as works of art.' " That, the court believed, was beyond the intent of Congress, based in part on the legislative history of the 1976 Act, not yet then in effect.

Judge Bazelon expressed some sympathy for the district court's conclusion that the Register's interpretation of § 202.10(c) "amounted to impermissible discrimination" against modern abstract sculpture in favor of "the realistic or the ornate." He concluded, however, that the nondiscrimination principle espoused in *Bleistein,* p. 53 supra, should not be allowed to "undermine other plainly legitimate goals of copyright law—in this case the congressional directive that copyright protection should not be afforded to industrial designs."

NOTES AND QUESTIONS ON SEPARABILITY

(1) In *Esquire* the Copyright Office maintained that the "overall shape or configuration of a utilitarian article" is not copyrightable. The Court of Appeals apparently agreed. Is that a sensible rule? Is it consistent with *Kieselstein–Cord?* The automatic exclusion of overall shape is difficult to reconcile with a number of decisions recognizing copyright in the shapes of a variety of useful articles.[i] Would the *Esquire* rationale preclude copyright in the overall shape of a Mickey Mouse radio if the electronics were hidden in Mickey's tummy? Suppose Esquire's outdoor lighting fixtures had consisted of giant dancing figures clutching halogen flood lights in uplifted hands. Would the Register or the court have reached a different conclusion?

(2) The House Report's reference to "conceptually * * * separable" elements was dismissed by Judge Bazelon in *Esquire* as an "isolated reference." *Kieselstein–Cord* obviously disagrees. Should *physical* separability be required? Some recognition of conceptual separability seems necessary to avoid confining *Mazer* to only the most obvious of tacked-on decorations. The Compendium II of Copyright Office Practices § 505.03 (quoted in R.

---

i. E.g., Animal Fair, Inc. v. AMFESCO Industries, Inc., 620 F.Supp. 175 (D.Minn. 1985), aff'd, 794 F.2d 678 (8th Cir.1986) (bear paw design of slippers); R. Dakin & Co. v. A & L Novelty Co., 444 F.Supp. 1080 (E.D.N.Y.1978) (animal-shaped pajama bags). Consider also Ted Arnold Ltd. v. Silvercraft, 259 F.Supp. 733 (S.D.N.Y.1966), involving a copyright registration issued for a "simulation of an antique telephone" used to house a pencil sharpener. The court found the work copyrightable, arguing that the telephone casing could be physically separated from the utilitarian pencil sharpener. Judge MacMahon also responded to the argument that the work had been created specifically for a utilitarian use. "There was still room here for considerable artistic expression. * * * Customers are paying fifteen dollars for it, not because it sharpens pencils uncommonly well, but because it is also a decorative conversation piece."

Brown, Design Protection: An Overview, 34 UCLA L.Rev. 1341, 1353–54 (1987)) pays substantial attention to conceptual separability.

(3) The separability standard embodied in the § 101 definition of "pictorial, graphic, and sculptural works" applies only to the design of a "useful article." This term too is defined in § 101. What does the definition comprehend? An automobile presumably is a useful article; a portrait is not. What of a model airplane? A sheet of wrapping paper depicting a Christmas scene? A bust of Beethoven, useful in holding down papers or holding up books? (See Poe v. Missing Persons, 745 F.2d 1238 (9th Cir.1984), where the issue was whether "Aquatint No. 5" was a "swimsuit" or a "work of art which portrayed an article of clothing." The "work" as depicted in the court's opinion resembles a partially transparent bikini. A "useful article"?)

Carol Barnhart Inc. v. Economy Cover Corp.

United States Court of Appeals, Second Circuit, 1985.
773 F.2d 411.

■ Before MANSFIELD, MESKILL and NEWMAN, CIRCUIT JUDGES.

■ MANSFIELD, CIRCUIT JUDGE:

Carol Barnhart Inc. ("Barnhart"), which sells display forms to department stores, distributors, and small retail stores, appeals from a judgment of the Eastern District of New York, Leonard D. Wexler, Judge, granting a motion for summary judgment made by defendant Economy Cover Corporation ("Economy"), which sells a wide variety of display products primarily to jobbers and distributors. Barnhart's complaint alleges that Economy has infringed its copyright and engaged in unfair competition by offering for sale display forms copied from four original "sculptural forms" to which Barnhart holds the copyright. Judge Wexler granted Economy's motion for summary judgment on the ground that plaintiff's mannequins of partial human torsos used to display articles of clothing are utilitarian articles not containing separable works of art, and thus are not copyrightable. We affirm.

The bones of contention are four human torso forms designed by Barnhart, each of which is life-size, without neck, arms, or a back, and made of expandable white styrene. Plaintiff's president created the forms in 1982 by using clay, buttons, and fabric to develop an initial mold, which she then used to build an aluminum mold into which the poly-styrene is poured to manufacture the sculptural display form. There are two male and two female upper torsos. One each of the male and female torsos is unclad for the purpose of displaying shirts and sweaters, while the other two are sculpted with shirts for displaying sweaters and jackets. * * *

Economy, which sells its wide range of products primarily to jobbers, distributors, and national chain stores, not to retail stores, first learned in early 1983 that Barnhart was selling its display forms directly to retailers. After observing that no copyright notice appeared either on Barnhart's

Figure 1   Figure 2

Figure 3   Figure 4

forms or in its promotional literature, Economy contracted to have produced for it four forms which it has conceded, for purposes of its summary judgment motion, were "copied from Barnhart's display forms" and are "substantially similar to Barnhart's display forms." Economy began marketing its product, "Easy Pin Shell Forms," in September 1983. * * *

[The court held that the lack of copyright notice was not fatal to the plaintiff's claim in light of the potential application of § 405(a)(2), and then reviewed the treatment of utilitarian articles under the 1909 Act, together with the legislative history of the 1976 Act. Judge Mansfield quoted Reichman, Design Protection in Domestic and Foreign Copyright Law: From the Berne Revision of 1948 to the Copyright Act of 1976, 1983 Duke L.J. 1143, 1261, which notes that the addition by the House of the separability requirement "could then authorize the denial of copyrightability to modern, functional designs."]

Applying these principles, we are persuaded that since the aesthetic and artistic features of the Barnhart forms are inseparable from the forms' use as utilitarian articles the forms are not copyrightable. Appellant emphasizes that clay sculpting, often used in traditional sculpture, was used in making the molds for the forms. It also stresses that the forms have been responded to as sculptural forms, and have been used for purposes other than modeling clothes, e.g., as decorating props and signs without any clothing or accessories. While this may indicate that the forms are "aesthetically satisfying and valuable," it is insufficient to show that the forms possess aesthetic or artistic features that are physically or conceptually separable from the forms' use as utilitarian objects to display clothes. On the contrary, to the extent the forms possess aesthetically pleasing features, even when these features are considered in the aggregate, they cannot be conceptualized as existing independently of their utilitarian function.

Appellant seeks to rebut this conclusion by arguing that the four forms represent a concrete expression of a particular idea, e.g., the idea of a woman's blouse, and that the form involved, a human torso, is traditionally copyrightable. Appellant suggests that since the Barnhart forms fall within the traditional category of sculpture of the human body, they should be subjected to a lower level of scrutiny in determining its copyrightability. We disagree. We find no support in the statutory language or legislative history for the claim that merely because a utilitarian article falls within a traditional art form it is entitled to a lower level of scrutiny in determining its copyrightability. Recognition of such a claim would in any event conflict with the anti-discrimination principle Justice Holmes enunciated in Bleistein v. Donaldson Lithographing Co., supra, 188 U.S. at 251–52.

Nor do we agree that copyrightability here is dictated by our decision in Kieselstein–Cord v. Accessories by Pearl, Inc., 632 F.2d 989 (2d Cir. 1980), a case we described as being "on a razor's edge of copyright law." * * *

In concluding that the two buckles were copyrightable we relied on the fact that "[t]he primary ornamental aspect of the Vaquero and Winchester buckles is conceptually separable from their subsidiary utilitarian function." Id. at 993. A glance at the pictures of the two buckles, reproduced at id. 995, coupled with the description in the text, confirms their highly ornamental dimensions and separability. What distinguishes those buckles from the Barnhart forms is that the ornamented surfaces of the buckles were not in any respect required by their utilitarian functions; the artistic and aesthetic features could thus be conceived of as having been added to, or superimposed upon, an otherwise utilitarian article. The unique artistic design was wholly unnecessary to performance of the utilitarian function. In the case of the Barnhart forms, on the other hand, the features claimed to be aesthetic or artistic, e.g., the life-size configuration of the breasts and the width of the shoulders, are inextricably intertwined with the utilitarian feature, the display of clothes. Whereas a model of a human torso, in order to serve its utilitarian function, must have some configuration of the chest and some width of shoulders, a belt buckle can serve its function satisfactorily without any ornamentation of the type that renders the *Kieselstein–Cord* buckles distinctive.[5]

The judgment of the district court is affirmed.

■ JON O. NEWMAN, CIRCUIT JUDGE, dissenting:

This case concerns the interesting though esoteric issue of "conceptual separability" under the Copyright Act of 1976. Because I believe the majority has either misunderstood the nature of this issue or applied an incorrect standard in resolving the issue in this case, I respectfully dissent from the judgment affirming the District Court's grant of summary judgment for the defendant. * * *

---

5. Our learned colleague, Judge Newman, would have copyrightability of a utilitarian article turn on "whether visual inspection of the article and consideration of all pertinent evidence would engender in the [ordinary] observer's mind a separate non-utilitarian concept that can displace, at least temporarily, the utilitarian aspect." (Dissenting Op. p. 423). The difficulty with this proposal is that it uses as its yardstick a standard so ethereal as to amount to a "nontest" that would be extremely difficult, if not impossible, to administer or apply. * * *

Almost any utilitarian article may be viewed by some separately as art, depending on how it is displayed (e.g., a can of Campbell Soup or a pair of ornate scissors affixed to the wall of a museum of modern art). But it is the object, not the form of display, for which copyright protection is sought. Congress has made it reasonably clear that copyrightability of the object should turn on its ordinary use as viewed by the average observer, not by a temporary flight of fancy that could attach to any utilitarian object, including an automobile engine, depending on how it is displayed.

* * * However, regardless of which standard is applied we disagree with the proposition that the mannequins here, when viewed as hollowed-out three dimensional forms (as presented for copyright) as distinguished from two-dimensional photographs, could be viewed by the ordinary observer as anything other than objects having a utilitarian function as mannequins. It would only be by concealing the open, hollowed-out rear half of the object, which is obviously designed to facilitate pinning or tucking in of garments, that an illusion of a sculpture can be created. In that case (as with the photos relied on by the dissent) the subject would not be the same as that presented for copyright.

Some might suggest that "conceptual separability" exists whenever the design of a form has sufficient aesthetic appeal to be appreciated for its artistic qualities. That approach has plainly been rejected by Congress. The House Report makes clear that, if the artistic features cannot be identified separately, the work is not copyrightable even though such features are "aesthetically satisfying and valuable." H.R.Rep. No. 1476, supra, at 55, 1976 U.S.Code Cong. & Ad.News at 5668. A chair may be so artistically designed as to merit display in a museum, but that fact alone cannot satisfy the test of "conceptual separateness." The viewer in the museum sees and apprehends a well-designed chair, not a work of art with a design that is conceptually separate from the functional purposes of an object on which people sit.

How, then, is "conceptual separateness" to be determined? In my view, the answer derives from the word "conceptual." For the design features to be "conceptually separate" from the utilitarian aspects of the useful article that embodies the design, the article must stimulate in the mind of the beholder a concept that is separate from the concept evoked by its utilitarian function. * * *

The "separateness" of the utilitarian and non-utilitarian concepts engendered by an article's design is itself a perplexing concept. I think the requisite "separateness" exists whenever the design creates in the mind of the ordinary observer two different concepts that are not inevitably entertained simultaneously. Again, the example of the artistically designed chair displayed in a museum may be helpful. The ordinary observer can be expected to apprehend the design of a chair whenever the object is viewed. He may, in addition, entertain the concept of a work of art, but, if this second concept is engendered in the observer's mind simultaneously with the concept of the article's utilitarian function, the requisite "separateness" does not exist. The test is not whether the observer fails to recognize the object as a chair but only whether the concept of the utilitarian function can be displaced in the mind by some other concept. * * *

* * * Thus, the fact that an object has been displayed or used apart from its utilitarian function, the extent of such display or use, and whether such display or use resulted from purchases would all be relevant in determining whether the design of the object engenders a separable concept of a work of art. In addition, expert opinion and survey evidence ought generally to be received. The issue need not turn on the immediate reaction of the ordinary observer but on whether visual inspection of the article and consideration of all pertinent evidence would engender in the observer's mind a separate non-utilitarian concept that can displace, at least temporarily, the utilitarian concept. * * *

Our case involving the four styrene chest forms seems to me a much easier case than *Kieselstein–Cord*. An ordinary observer, indeed, an ordinary reader of this opinion who views the two unclothed forms depicted in figures 1 and 2 below, would be most unlikely even to entertain, from visual inspection alone, the concept of a mannequin with the utilitarian function of displaying a shirt or a blouse. The initial concept in the observer's mind, I believe, would be of an art object, an entirely understandable mental impression based on previous viewing of unclad torsos displayed as artistic sculptures. Even after learning that these two forms are used to display clothing in retail stores, the only reasonable conclusion that an ordinary viewer would reach is that the forms have both a utilitarian function and an entirely separate function of serving as a work of art. I am confident that the ordinary observer could reasonably conclude only that these two forms are not simply mannequins that happen to have sufficient aesthetic appeal to qualify as works of art, but that the conception in the mind is that of a work of art *in addition to and capable of being entertained separately from* the concept of a mannequin, if the latter concept is entertained at all. As appellant contends, with pardonable hyperbole, the design of Michelangelo's "David" would not cease to be copyrightable simply because cheap copies of it were used by a retail store to display clothing.   * * *

As for the two forms, depicted in figures 3 and 4 below, of chests clothed with a shirt or a blouse, I am uncertain what concept or concepts would be engendered in the mind of an ordinary observer. I think it is likely that these forms too would engender the separately entertained concept of an art object whether or not they also engendered the concept of a mannequin. But this is not the only conclusion a reasonable trier could reach as to the perception of an ordinary observer.   * * *

I would grant summary judgment to the copyright proprietor as to the design of the two nude forms and remand for trial with respect to the two clothed forms.

Brandir International, Inc. v. Cascade Pacific Lumber Co.

United States Court of Appeals, Second Circuit, 1987.
834 F.2d 1142.

■ Before OAKES and WINTER, CIRCUIT JUDGES, and ZAMPANO, DISTRICT JUDGE.

■ OAKES, CIRCUIT JUDGE:

In passing the Copyright Act of 1976 Congress attempted to distinguish between protectable "works of applied art" and "industrial designs not subject to copyright protection." See H.R.Rep. No. 1476, 94th Cong., 2d Sess. 54, reprinted in 1976 U.S.Code Cong. & Admin.News 5659, 5667 (hereinafter H.R.Rep. No. 1476). The courts, however, have had difficulty framing tests by which the fine line establishing what is and what is not copyrightable can be drawn. Once again we are called upon to draw such a line, this time in a case involving the "RIBBON Rack," a bicycle rack made of bent tubing that is said to have originated from a wire sculpture. (A photograph of the rack is contained in the appendix to this opinion.) We are also called upon to determine whether there is any trademark protection available to the manufacturer of the bicycle rack, appellant Brandir

International, Inc.   The Register of Copyright, named as a third-party defendant under the statute, 17 U.S.C. § 411, but electing not to appear, denied copyrightability.   In the subsequent suit brought in the United States District Court for the Southern District of New York, Charles S. Haight, Jr., Judge, the district court granted summary judgment on both the copyright and trademark claims to defendant Cascade Pacific Lumber Co., d/b/a Columbia Cascade Co., manufacturer of a similar bicycle rack. We affirm as to the copyright claim, but reverse and remand as to the trademark claim.

Against the history of copyright protection well set out in the majority opinion in Carol Barnhart Inc. v. Economy Cover Corp., 773 F.2d 411, 415–18 (2d Cir.1985), and in Denicola, Applied Art and Industrial Design: A Suggested Approach to Copyright in Useful Articles, 67 Minn.L.Rev. 707, 709–17 (1983), Congress adopted the Copyright Act of 1976.   The "works of art" classification of the Copyright Act of 1909 was omitted and replaced by reference to "pictorial, graphic, and sculptural works," 17 U.S.C. § 102(a)(5).   According to the House Report, the new category was intended to supply "as clear a line as possible between copyrightable works of applied art and uncopyrighted works of industrial design."   H.R.Rep. No. 1476, at 55, U.S.Code Cong. & Admin.News 1976, p. 5668.   * * *

LEVINE'S WIRE SCULPTURES AND THE RIBBON
BICYCLE RACK

In Carol Barnhart Inc. v. Economy Cover Corp., 773 F.2d 411 (2d Cir.1985), a divided panel of this circuit affirmed a district court grant of summary judgment of noncopyrightability of four life-sized, anatomically correct human torso forms.   *Carol Barnhart* distinguished *Kieselstein–Cord*, but it surely did not overrule it.   The distinction made was that the ornamented surfaces of the *Kieselstein–Cord* belt buckles "were not in any respect required by their utilitarian functions," but the features claimed to be aesthetic or artistic in the *Carol Barnhart* forms were "inextricably intertwined with the utilitarian feature, the display of clothes."   773 F.2d at 419. But cf. Animal Fair, Inc. v. Amfesco Indus., Inc., 620 F.Supp. 175, 186–88 (D.Minn.1985) (holding bear-paw design conceptually separable from the utilitarian features of a slipper), aff'd mem., 794 F.2d 678 (8th Cir.1986). As Judge Newman's dissent made clear, the *Carol Barnhart* majority did not dispute "that 'conceptual separability' is distinct from 'physical separability' and, when present, entitles the creator of a useful article to a copyright on its design." 773 F.2d at 420.

"Conceptual separability" is thus alive and well, at least in this circuit. The problem, however, is determining exactly what it is and how it is to be applied. Judge Newman's illuminating discussion in dissent in *Carol Barnhart,* see 773 F.2d at 419–24, proposed a test that aesthetic features are conceptually separable if "the article . . . stimulate[s] in the mind of the beholder a concept that is separate from the concept evoked by its utilitarian function." Id. at 422. This approach has received favorable endorsement by at least one commentator, W. Patry, Latman's The Copyright Law 43–45 (6th ed. 1986), who calls Judge Newman's test the "temporal displacement" test. It is to be distinguished from other possible ways in which conceptual separability can be tested, including whether the primary use is as a utilitarian article as opposed to an artistic work, whether the aesthetic aspects of the work can be said to be "primary," and whether the article is marketable as art, none of which is very satisfactory. But Judge Newman's test was rejected outright by the majority as "a standard so ethereal as to amount to a 'nontest' that would be extremely difficult, if not impossible, to administer or apply." 773 F.2d at 419 n. 5.

Perhaps the differences between the majority and the dissent in *Carol Barnhart* might have been resolved had they had before them the Denicola article on Applied Art and Industrial Design: A Suggested Approach to Copyright in Useful Articles, supra. There, Professor Denicola points out that although the Copyright Act of 1976 was an effort " 'to draw as clear a line as possible,' " in truth "there is no line, but merely a spectrum of forms and shapes responsive in varying degrees to utilitarian concerns." 67 Minn.L.Rev. at 741. Denicola argues that "the statutory directive requires a distinction between works of industrial design and works whose origins lie outside the design process, despite the utilitarian environment in which they appear." He views the statutory limitation of copyrightability as "an attempt to identify elements whose form and appearance reflect the unconstrained perspective of the artist," such features not being the product of industrial design. Id. at 742. "Copyrightability, therefore, should turn on the relationship between the proffered work and the process of industrial design." Id. at 741. He suggests that "the dominant characteristic of industrial design is the influence of nonaesthetic, utilitarian concerns" and hence concludes that copyrightability "ultimately should depend on the extent to which the work reflects artistic expression uninhibited by functional considerations." Id. To state the Denicola test in the language of conceptual separability, if design elements reflect a merger of aesthetic and functional considerations, the artistic aspects of a work cannot be said to be conceptually separable from the utilitarian elements. Conversely, where design elements can be identified as reflecting the designer's artistic judgment exercised independently of functional influences, conceptual separability exists.

We believe that Professor Denicola's approach provides the best test for conceptual separability and, accordingly, adopt it here for several reasons. First, the approach is consistent with the holdings of our previous cases. In *Kieselstein–Cord,* for example, the artistic aspects of the belt buckles reflected purely aesthetic choices, independent of the buckles' function, while in *Carol Barnhart* the distinctive features of the torsos—the accurate anatomical design and the sculpted shirts and collars—showed clearly the influence of functional concerns. Though the torsos bore artistic features, it was evident that the designer incorporated those features to further the usefulness of the torsos as mannequins. Second, the test's emphasis on the influence of utilitarian concerns in the design process may help, as Denicola notes, to "alleviate the de facto discrimination against nonrepresentational art that has regrettably accompanied much of the current analysis." Id. at 745.[3] Finally, and perhaps most importantly, we think Denicola's test will not be too difficult to administer in practice. The work itself will continue to give "mute testimony" of its origins. In addition, the parties will be required to present evidence relating to the design process and the nature of the work, with the trier of fact making the determination whether the aesthetic design elements are significantly influenced by functional considerations.

Turning now to the facts of this case, we note first that Brandir contends, and its chief owner David Levine testified, that the original design of the RIBBON Rack stemmed from wire sculptures that Levine had created, each formed from one continuous undulating piece of wire. These sculptures were, he said, created and displayed in his home as a means of personal expression, but apparently were never sold or displayed elsewhere. He also created a wire sculpture in the shape of a bicycle and states that he did not give any thought to the utilitarian application of any of his sculptures until he accidentally juxtaposed the bicycle sculpture with one of the self-standing wire sculptures. It was not until November 1978 that Levine seriously began pursuing the utilitarian application of his sculptures, when a friend, G. Duff Bailey, a bicycle buff and author of numerous articles about urban cycling, was at Levine's home and informed him that the sculptures would make excellent bicycle racks, permitting bicycles to be parked under the overloops as well as on top of the underloops. Following this meeting, Levine met several times with Bailey and others, completing

---

3. We are reminded not only by Judge Gesell in the district court in *Esquire,* 414 F.Supp. 939, 941 (D.D.C.1976), but by Holmes in Bleistein v. Donaldson Lithographing Co., 188 U.S. 239, 251–52 (1903), by Mazer v. Stein, 347 U.S. at 214, and by numerous other opinions, that we judges should not let our own view of styles of art interfere with the decisionmaking process in this area. Denicola suggests that the shape of a Mickey Mouse telephone is copyrightable because its form is independent of function, and "[a] telephone shape owing more to Arp, Brancusi, or Moore than Disney may be equally divorced from utilitarian influence." 67 Minn.L.Rev. at 746. This is true, of course, of the artist Christo's "Running Fence," approved (following Professor Nimmer) as an example of conceptual separability in *Keiselstein–Cord,* 632 F.2d at 993.

the designs for the RIBBON Rack by the use of a vacuum cleaner hose, and submitting his drawings to a fabricator complete with dimensions. The Brandir RIBBON Rack began being nationally advertised and promoted for sale in September 1979.

In November 1982 Levine discovered that another company, Cascade Pacific Lumber Co., was selling a similar product. Thereafter, beginning in December 1982, a copyright notice was placed on all RIBBON Racks before shipment and on December 10, 1982, five copyright applications for registration were submitted to the Copyright Office. The Copyright Office refused registration by letter, stating that the RIBBON Rack did not contain any element that was "capable of independent existence as a copyrightable pictorial, graphic or sculptural work apart from the shape of the useful article." * * *

Applying Professor Denicola's test to the RIBBON Rack, we find that the rack is not copyrightable. It seems clear that the form of the rack is influenced in significant measure by utilitarian concerns and thus any aesthetic elements cannot be said to be conceptually separable from the utilitarian elements. This is true even though the sculptures which inspired the RIBBON Rack may well have been—the issue of originality aside—copyrightable. * * *

Had Brandir merely adopted one of the existing sculptures as a bicycle rack, neither the application to a utilitarian end nor commercialization of that use would have caused the object to forfeit its copyrighted status. Comparison of the RIBBON Rack with the earlier sculptures, however, reveals that while the rack may have been derived in part from one o[r] more "works of art," it is in its final form essentially a product of industrial design. In creating the RIBBON Rack, the designer has clearly adapted the original aesthetic elements to accommodate and further a utilitarian purpose. These altered design features of the RIBBON Rack, including the spacesaving, open design achieved by widening the upper loops to permit parking under as well as over the rack's curves, the straightened vertical elements that allow in- and above-ground installation of the rack, the ability to fit all types of bicycles and mopeds, and the heavy-gauged tubular construction of rustproof galvanized steel, are all features that combine to make for a safe, secure, and maintenance-free system of parking bicycles and mopeds. Its undulating shape is said in *Progressive Architecture,* January 1982, to permit double the storage of conventional bicycle racks. Moreover, the rack is manufactured from 2⅜–inch standard steam pipe that is bent into form, the six-inch radius of the bends evidently resulting from bending the pipe according to a standard formula that yields bends having a radius equal to three times the nominal internal diameter of the pipe. * * *

It is unnecessary to determine whether to the art world the RIBBON Rack properly would be considered an example of minimalist sculpture. The result under the copyright statute is not changed. Using the test we have adopted, it is not enough that, to paraphrase Judge Newman, the rack may stimulate in the mind of the reasonable observer a concept separate from the bicycle rack concept. While the RIBBON Rack may be worthy of admiration for its aesthetic qualities alone, it remains nonetheless the product of industrial design. Form and function are inextricably intertwined in the rack, its ultimate design being as much the result of utilitarian pressures as aesthetic choices. Indeed, the visually pleasing proportions and symmetricality of the rack represent design changes made in response to functional concerns. Judging from the awards the rack has received, it would seem in fact that Brandir has achieved with the RIBBON Rack the highest goal of modern industrial design, that is, the harmonious fusion of function and aesthetics. Thus there remains no artistic element of the RIBBON Rack that can be identified as separate and "capable of existing independently, of, the utilitarian aspects of the article." Accordingly, we must affirm on the copyright claim.

[The court ordered a remand for further consideration of the trademark infringement claim. See p. 651 infra.]

■ WINTER, CIRCUIT JUDGE, concurring in part and dissenting in part:

Although I concur in the reversal of the district court's grant of summary judgment on the trademark and unfair competition claims, I respectfully dissent from the majority's discussion and disposition of the copyright claim.

My colleagues, applying an adaptation of Professor Denicola's test, hold that the aesthetic elements of the design of a useful article are not conceptually separable from its utilitarian aspects if "[f]orm and function are inextricably intertwined" in the article, and "its ultimate design [is] as much the result of utilitarian pressures as aesthetic choices." Applying that test to the instant matter, they observe that the dispositive fact is that "in creating the Ribbon Rack, [Levine] has clearly adapted the *original* aesthetic elements to accommodate and further a utilitarian purpose." (emphasis added). The grounds of my disagreement are that: (1) my colleagues' adaptation of Professor Denicola's test diminishes the statutory concept of "conceptual separability" to the vanishing point; and (2) their focus on the process or sequence followed by the particular designer makes copyright protection depend upon largely fortuitous circumstances concerning the creation of the design in issue. * * *

My colleagues also allow too much to turn upon the process or sequence of design followed by the designer of the Ribbon Rack. They thus suggest that copyright protection would have been accorded "had Brandir merely adopted . . . as a bicycle rack" an enlarged version of one of David Levine's original sculptures rather than one that had wider upper loops and straightened vertical elements. I cannot agree that copyright protection for the Ribbon Rack turns on whether Levine serendipitously chose the final design of the Ribbon Rack during his initial sculptural musings or whether the original design had to be slightly modified to accommodate bicycles. Copyright protection, which is intended to generate incentives for designers by according property rights in their creations, should not turn on purely fortuitous events. For that reason, the Copyright Act expressly states that the legal test is how the final article is perceived, not how it was developed through various stages.   * * *

MORE NOTES AND QUESTIONS ON SEPARABILITY

(1) How do the uncopyrightable mannequins in *Barnhart* differ from the copyrightable dancing figure in *Mazer?*

(2) In Hart v. Dan Chase Taxidermy Supply Co., 86 F.3d 320 (2d Cir.1996), the Second Circuit distinguished *Barnhart* and agreed with the Fourth Circuit's conclusion in Superior Form Builders, Inc. v. Dan Chase Taxidermy Supply Co., 74 F.3d 488 (4th Cir.), cert. denied, 117 S.Ct. 53 (1996), that animal taxidermy mannequins are not useful articles and thus are not subject to the separability limitation; the function of animal mannequins is to portray their own form (see the definition of "useful article" in § 101), while the purpose of the torsos in *Barnhart* was to display clothing. (The Second Circuit also expressed a "strong preference" that the issue of merger of idea and expression be resolved as part of the infringement analysis and not in determining copyrightability; at the infringement stage the court will have the benefit of evidence offered on substantial similarity, which may help in determining whether all expressions of the idea are necessarily similar.) The Fourth Circuit's decision in *Superior Form Builders* alternatively concluded that even if taxidermy mannequins are useful articles, they would be copyrightable under the *Brandir* test for separability.

(3) The *Brandir* test was adopted with a qualification in National Theme Productions, Inc. v. Jerry B. Beck, Inc., 696 F.Supp. 1348 (S.D.Cal.1988). Plaintiff claimed copyright in a series of masquerade costumes; Judge Thompson said the costumes had an intrinsic utilitarian function and were therefore useful articles. He concurred with *Brandir* "to the extent it requires one to look to an artist or designer's creative process, and the decisions going into that process, in creating a useful article," but questioned the Second Circuit's emphasis on the sequence and chronology of creative decisions. The costumes were copyrightable since they embodied "aesthetic judgments exercised independently of functional considerations."

In Whimsicality, Inc. v. Rubie's Costume Co., 891 F.2d 452 (2d Cir. 1989), the Second Circuit held that an application for registration describing costumes as "soft sculpture" constituted a misrepresentation to the Copyright Office that invalidated the registration. But on remand, the district court accepted an affidavit from a Copyright Office examiner that "soft sculpture" was a term routinely allowed by the Copyright Office and that the costumes had been registered as containing separable artistic elements. See 836 F.Supp. 112 (E.D.N.Y.1993). Cf. Masquerade Novelty, Inc. v. Unique Industries, Inc., 912 F.2d 663 (3d Cir.1990) (plaintiff's animal nose masks are not useful articles and are copyrightable). A Copyright Office Policy Decision declares that, while masks are generally registrable, costumes are useful articles and unregistrable unless they contain separable pictorial, graphic, or sculptural features. 56 Fed.Reg. 56530 (Nov. 5, 1991).

(4) One of the editors of this casebook, commenting on the other's suggestions as described in *Brandir,* has said, "I have no quarrel with Denicola's aspirations for the criteria which should guide the Copyright Office and then the courts in making their judgments. I do have qualms about the practicality of the criteria. How are we to verify the impulses that guided a designer's hand? * * * It seems to leave too much room for self-serving declarations of aesthetic aims, even if such declarations could be deflated by cross-examination or simple skepticism." R. Brown, Design Protection: An Overview, 34 UCLA L.Rev. 1341, 1350–53 (1987). See also Lynch, Copyright in Utilitarian Objects: Beneath the Metaphysics, 16 U.Dayton L.Rev. 647 (1991), urging a shift in focus from the aesthetic aspects in which copyright is claimed to the utilitarian aspects that should remain unprotected.

(5) Could the plaintiff in *Brandir* have claimed that the defendant infringed the copyright in the original wire sculptures? Were those works copied by the defendant? Would § 113(b), discussed in Note (6), preclude such a claim?

(6) Consider the following ploy. An automobile manufacturer, intent on circumventing the limitations on copyright in useful articles, obtains a copyright registration for a photograph or clay model of next year's design. (Note that neither work is a "useful article.") It then argues that unauthorized production of the car portrayed in the work would infringe the copyright in the photo or model. If this stratagem works, the separability test becomes irrelevant.

It has long been the position of the Copyright Office that although others may not reproduce the photograph or model, the law is and should be that "copyright in a pictorial, graphic, or sculptural work, portraying a useful article as such, does not extend to the manufacture of the useful article itself." Report of the Register of Copyrights, General Revision of the U.S. Copyright Law, House Comm. on the Judiciary, 87th Cong., 1st Sess. 15 (1961). In the Register's Supplementary Report of 1965, p. 48, two lines of relevant cases are identified. One line includes Jack Adelman, Inc. v. Sonners & Gordon, Inc., 112 F.Supp. 187 (S.D.N.Y.1934), which held that copyright in a drawing of a dress "secured no exclusive monopoly of the dress shown in the drawing." It also includes Kashins v. Lightmakers, 155 F.Supp. 202 (S.D.N.Y.1956), holding that plaintiff's copyrighted catalogue containing photographs of its lamps was not infringed by the defendant's manufacture of similar lamps, or the subsequent publication of a catalogue containing photographs of the imitations.[j] The other line of

---

j. A more recent illustration is Russell v. Trimfit, Inc., 428 F.Supp. 91 (E.D.Pa. 1977), aff'd, 568 F.2d 770 (3d Cir.1978). Plaintiff registered drawings of socks with separate compartments for each toe. Her infringement action against a manufacturer of the socks was summarily dismissed. The court noted that there was no allegation that defendant had reproduced plaintiff's draw-cases identified in the Supplementary Report consists of two decisions holding that copyright in two-dimensional cartoon characters is infringed by three-dimensional dolls (see p. 244 infra), plus Jones Brothers Co. v. Underkoffler, 16 F.Supp. 729 (M.D.Pa.1936). The latter ruled that copyright in a drawing of a cemetery monument was infringed by construction of the depicted monument.

Can these two lines of cases be distinguished? Do the latter cases involve depictions of "useful articles" not themselves copyrightable? The Supplementary Report surprisingly concluded that it had not been possible "to find any statutory formulation that would express the distinction satisfactorily." The principle concern was "to make clear that there is no intention to change the present law." The result is the extraordinary cop-out in § 113(b).

What result in Kashins v. Lightmakers, supra, if the base of one of the lamps copied by defendant from plaintiff's copyrighted catalogue had consisted of a dancing figure?

(7) The relationship between copyright and industrial design seems equally awkward in other systems. There is an engrossing English case, George Hensher Ltd. v. Restawile Upholstery Ltd., [1974] 2 All Eng.Rep. 420 (H.L.), where no two of the seven judges who delivered opinions could agree on the meaning of the statutory phrase "works of artistic craftsmanship." See the acute comment by Bloom, Lost in the Bronx, 22 Bull.Copyr.Soc. 199 (1975). English law for some years has recognized full protection for utilitarian designs through copyright in technical drawings and plans. In 1986, however, the House of Lords created a "spare parts" exception to end the monopoly of automobile manufacturers over replacement parts. British Leyland Motor Corp. v. Armstrong Patents Co., [1986] 1 All Eng.Rep. 850 (H.L.). The British Copyright, Designs, & Patents Act, effective in 1989, continued protection for wholly functional designs, for a 15–year term, but with an allowance for copying "necessary for a spare part to fit or match." (In the United States, the insurance industry, fearful of monopoly pricing on automobile replacement parts, has been a conspicuous opponent of design protection legislation. See 43 Pat., Tm. & Copyr.J. (BNA) 304 (1992); 40 id. at 207 (1990).)

For a searching comparative view of design protection, see two articles by Reichman, Design Protection in Domestic and Foreign Copyright Law: From the Berne Revision of 1948 to the Copyright Act of 1976, 1983 Duke L.J. 1143, and Design Protection After the Copyright Act of 1976, 31 J.Copyr.Soc. 267 (1984).

(8) At this point, if not long before, one might well ask if the distinctions pursued in the 1976 Act are worth the effort. Would dire consequences follow if the whole of industrial design was brought within the subject matter of copyright? Would some alternative form of protection be preferable?

ings; it had only manufactured the article they depicted.

In 1988, a small electronics company redesigned its principal product, a compact radio antenna, in the form of a piece of modern sculpture. According to the company's founder, orders increased 400 to 500 percent "purely because of the design." New York Times, Feb. 12, 1989, p. F3. Does this argue for—or against—increased design protection?

PROPOSED DESIGN PROTECTION LEGISLATION

Several of the preceding decisions take note of proposals for separate design protection legislation. The limitations of both design patent and copyright have prompted a persistent search for alternatives. One such proposal was included as Title II, Protection of Ornamental Designs of Useful Articles, in the 1976 Copyright Revision Bill. It met the fate of its predecessors.[k]

Title II would have provided protection for "an original ornamental design of a useful article," § 201(a), "including its two-dimensional or three-dimensional features of shape and surface." § 201(b)(2). The standard of originality in the copyright sense, § 201(b)(4), was stiffened by the exclusion of "staple or commonplace" designs, § 202(b). Protection would extend for a maximum of ten years. § 205. There were notice provisions, § 206, and registration provisions. § 209. Unlike copyright, failure to register would divest protection. § 209(a).

The House Judiciary Committee deleted Title II in 1976, and the Senate conferees concurred. The House Report explains:

> Title II of S. 22 as passed by the Senate would create a new limited form of copyright protection for "original" designs which are clearly a part of a useful article, regardless of whether such designs could stand by themselves, separate from the article itself. Thus designs of useful articles which do not meet the design patent standard of "novelty" would for the first time be protected.
>
> S. 22 is a copyright revision bill. The Committee chose to delete Title II in part because the new form of design protection provided by Title II could not truly be considered copyright protection and therefore appropriately within the scope of copyright revision.

The House Report also made passing reference to the bill's failure to designate a specific agency to administer Title II (although the Copyright Office had by this time volunteered its services), and to the unresolved

---

k. Counting unsuccessful design protection bills is apparently a popular pastime. See, e.g., note 1 in *Nalbandian,* supra, and note 12 in *Esquire,* 591 F.2d at 800 n. 12 (counting 70 bills). The list continues to grow. See, e.g., H.R. 1790, 102nd Cong., 1st Sess. (1991), reprinted in 41 Pat., Tm. & Copyr.J. (BNA) 553 (1991).

Consult generally Ringer, Bibliography on Design Protection (Copyright Office 1955), Strauss, et al., 1959 Supplement, Mott, 1976 Supplement, compiling the very large literature and summarizing design protection bills from 1914 onward.

issue of protection for typeface designs (see p. 175 infra). The principal objection, however, was more fundamental:

> Finally, the Committee will have to examine further the assertion of the Department of Justice, which testified in opposition to the Title, that Title II would create a new monopoly which has not been justified by a showing that its benefits will outweigh the disadvantage of removing such designs from free public use. (H.R.Rep. p. 50.)

Proponents of specialized design protection were left with only an invitation to try again.

Beginning in 1985, proposed bills differed from their predecessors in dropping any reference to "ornamental designs"; instead, they referred to the "design of a useful article which makes the article attractive or distinctive." What difference would this make? Compare Fryer, Industrial Design Protection in the United States of America—Present Situation and Plans for Revision, 27 Industrial Property (WIPO) 115 (March 1988) (supporting the new version), with R. Brown, Copyright–Like Protection for Designs, 19 U.Balt.L.Rev. 308 (1989) (generally favoring Title II). See also Reichman, Design Protection and the Legislative Agenda, 55 L. & Contemp.Probs. (No. 2) 281 (1992) (critical of any expansion of protection beyond purely ornamental features).

Proponents of design legislation continue to argue that increased design protection is necessary to stimulate innovation and to protect American jobs from foreign knock-offs; opponents counter that design protection would stifle competition and injure consumers. The battle may be over, at least for now. Supporters of design protection, led by the automakers and the Industrial Designers Society, have conceded that the opposing coalition of consumer groups, insurance companies, and manufacturers of after-market repair parts have successfully blocked design legislation for the foreseeable future. Wall St.J., Mar. 22, 1993, p. 1.

NOTES ON DESIGN LEGISLATION, TYPEFACE, AND MASK WORKS

(1) Can you describe what the design protection bills would comprehend that now falls outside the subject matter of copyright and design patent?

(2) Title II would have done little for the fashion designer; § 202(e) excluded three-dimensional aspects of apparel. Subsequent bills have included a similar exclusion. (What groups might support such an exclusion?) In the world of fashion, copying of designs has long been stigmatized as "piracy," especially by the originators of high-priced lines who have seen their creations quickly duplicated for mass markets. The search for protection has a history—mostly of frustration—reaching back more than half a century. We already have seen that apart from the protection of fabric designs, copyright is of little use in the fashion industry. Design patents theoretically are available, but the standard of inventiveness and the protracted application process generally eliminates them as a practical alternative. Attempts to discourage imitators by self-help—"guild" undertakings enforced by penalties and boycotts—ran afoul of the antitrust laws. See Fashion Originators Guild of America, Inc. v. FTC, 114 F.2d 80 (2d Cir.1940), aff'd, 312 U.S. 457 (1941); Millinery Creators' Guild, Inc. v. FTC, 109 F.2d 175 (2d Cir.1940), aff'd, 312 U.S. 469 (1941). (As to the possibility of relief under common law unfair competition, see p. 638 infra.)[1]

(3) Technological changes introduced in the printing industry in the 1960s led to pressure for copyright or other protection for typeface designs. The House Report defines "typeface" as "a set of letters, numbers, or other symbolic characters, whose forms are related by repeating design elements consistently applied in a notational system and are intended to be embodied in articles whose intrinsic utilitarian function is for use in composing text or other cognizable combinations of characters." H.R.Rep. p. 55. The switch from metal fonts to photocomposition, which employed film strips rather than brass matrices, made the copying of typeface designs relatively inexpensive. Design patents were available, subject to the usual requirements, but the switch from metal to printed film fonts seemed to strengthen the claim to copyright. The Copyright Office had refused to accept registration of typeface designs as a "work of art" under the 1909 Act. See Eltra Corp. v. Ringer, 579 F.2d 294 (4th Cir.1978). Typeface manufacturers pressed their case during the revision process. For a time it appeared that Title II might afford a measure of relief. With the demise of Title II, the question of copyright became decisive.

The implications of extending copyright to typeface designs were unclear. Opponents feared that manufacturers would use their exclusive rights to enforce tying arrangements between their typeface designs and typesetting equipment. There was also general unease over potential liability for printed material composed with infringing type. See the Register's Second Supplementary Report on the General Revision 201–02 (Draft 1975). The House Report announced an intention to exclude typeface design from copyright, at least for the present:

> The Committee has considered, but chosen to defer, the possibility of protecting the design of typefaces. * * * The Committee does not regard the design of typeface, as thus defined, to be a copyrightable "pictorial, graphic, or sculptural work" within the meaning of this bill and the application of the dividing line in section 101. (H.R.Rep. p. 55.)

In the 1980s technological change again created pressure for copyright in typeface—this time in the programs and digital data used by computers to generate typefonts. The Copyright Office initially required registrants

---

1. Some of the rich history of fashion piracy is recounted in Agins, Fashion Knockoffs Hit Stores Before Originals as Designers Seethe, Wall St.J., Aug. 8, 1994, p. A1. As might be expected, French law is apparently more sympathetic to the fashion designer.

See Spindler, A Ruling by French Court Finds Copyright in a Design, New York Times, May 19, 1994, p. D4, reporting on a successful suit by Yves Saint Laurent against Ralph Lauren for copying a black tuxedo dress.

of computer programs that generate digitized typeface to disclaim copyright in the digitized representations themselves. 53 Fed.Reg. 38110 (1988). It eventually dropped the disclaimer and instead amended its regulation on Materials not Subject to Copyright, adding "(e) Typeface as typeface" to the list of exclusions. 37 C.F.R. § 202.1(e).

(4) Modern electronic technology relies on tiny components called semiconductor chips. They consist of layers of metallic and insulating materials on which patterns are etched or deposited. They are expensive to design, but cheap to reproduce. The patterns or "mask works" that are embodied in semiconductor chips are the subject of Chapter 9 of Title 17, added by the Semiconductor Chip Protection Act of 1984. (See §§ 901–14.) The amendment establishes sui generis protection tailored to the unique characteristics of "mask works."

The requirement of originality in mask works is strengthened by the exclusion of "staple, commonplace, or familiar" designs. § 902(b). The "owner" has the exclusive right to reproduce the mask work and to import or distribute chips in which the work is embodied, although a measure of protection is afforded to "innocent" infringers. §§ 905, 907. There is a registration system, § 908, and protection terminates if registration is not made within two years of first commercial use. There is also a notice provision, § 909, (this one with an M in a circle), but the presence of notice is not a condition of protection. Protection lasts for 10 years, commencing on registration or use. § 904. There are complex provisions protecting foreign mask works, designed to encourage protection of U.S. works abroad. §§ 902 and 914.

A major innovation appears in § 906 of the Act. That section permits reproduction of a protected mask work for purposes of analysis and evaluation; more significantly, it permits others to incorporate the results of such efforts in their own "original" mask work. It is an attempt to encourage the creation of improved derivative works through reverse engineering. In Brooktree Corp. v. Advanced Micro Devices, Inc., 977 F.2d 1555 (Fed.Cir.1992), after holding that the "substantial similarity" test applies to determine infringement under the Act, the court examined the defendant's "paper trail" of study and analysis to distinguish legitimate reverse engineering from actionable piracy. The court concluded that the "paper trail" indicated only that the defendant made an unsuccessful attempt to analyze the plaintiff's chip before resorting to copying. See Raskind, Reverse Engineering, Unfair Competition, and Fair Use, in the Symposium cited below.

"Equivalent" rights under state law in mask works are preempted, § 912, but the Act does not affect rights or remedies available under the remainder of the Copyright Act or under federal patent law. (Would the configurations and patterns embodied in semiconductor chips be protectable as "pictorial, graphic, and sculptural works" under § 101? Cf. § 113(b).)

The Act has spawned substantial commentary, including a treatise, R. Stern, Semiconductor Chip Protection, and a Symposium: The Semiconductor Chip Protection Act of 1984 and Its Lessons, 70 Minn.L.Rev. 263 (1985). See also McManis, International Protection for Semiconductor Chip Designs * * *, 22 Geo.Wash.J.Int'l L. 331 (1988).

(5) Does the Semiconductor Chip Protection Act signal a trend toward sui generis protection for other works? What subject matter would be appropriate for specialized treatment? Ornamental designs of useful articles? Computer programs? Compilations? What are the costs and benefits of the sui generis approach? See Kastenmeier and Remington, The Semiconductor Chip Protection Act of 1984: A Swamp or Firm Ground?, 70 Minn.L.Rev. 417 (1985). See also Reichman, Computer Programs as Applied Scientific Know–How: Implications of Copyright Protection for Commercialized University Research, 42 Vand.L.Rev. 639 (1989), advocating tailor-made protective regimes for all "intermediate technologies" that fall between the paradigms of patent and copyright. The implications of the sui generis approach for international protection are explored in Dreyfuss, Information Products: A Challenge to Intellectual Property Theory, 20 N.Y.U.J.Int'l L. & Pol. 897 (1988), suggesting a "generic" international treaty to subsume new technologies.

ARCHITECTURE

Robert R. Jones Associates, Inc. v. Nino Homes

United States Court of Appeals, Sixth Circuit, 1988.
858 F.2d 274.

■ Before MARTIN, JONES and MILBURN, CIRCUIT JUDGES.

■ BOYCE F. MARTIN, JR., CIRCUIT JUDGE.

Nino Homes and Michele Lochirco appeal the judgment entered by the district court in favor of Robert R. Jones Associates, Inc. The district court held that Nino Homes and Lochirco had violated the Copyright Act of 1976, 17 U.S.C. § 101 et seq., by copying Jones Associates' registered architectural drawings and by using those unauthorized copies to construct several houses, and the district court awarded Jones Associates actual damages, attorneys' fees, and prejudgment interest, 686 F.Supp. 160. This appeal presents a rather unusual question: whether the damages recoverable because of the infringement of copyrighted architectural drawings include, not only the losses attributable to the infringer's unauthorized reproduction of the copyrighted article, but also the losses suffered as a result of the infringer's subsequent use of the infringing copies. We affirm the finding of unlawful copying and subsequent use, but we reverse as to attorneys' fees and prejudgment interest.

Robert R. Jones Associates, Inc. designs, builds, and sells custom-made houses. Nino Homes also constructs and sells new houses. Michele Lochirco is the principal shareholder and president of Nino Homes, and he is also the company's chief executive and operating officer.

In 1980, Jones Associates hired an architect to prepare a complete set of architectural drawings, including floor plans and elevations, for a house which was eventually called the "Aspen". These plans were based on design concepts generated by Robert R. Jones, the sole shareholder of Jones Associates. After receiving the completed plans from the architect, Jones Associates constructed two model houses in accordance with the Aspen plans, one in the Grosse Pines subdivision in Rochester, Michigan, the other in the Maplewood North subdivision in West Bloomfield, Michigan. In order to promote sales of its houses in those two subdivisions, Jones Associates distributed to potential buyers brochures which contained abridged floor plans of the Aspen.

In June 1983, one of those potential customers informed Robert Jones that a competing developer was constructing houses that were very similar to the Aspen. Jones subsequently investigated this tip, and, while driving through Nino Homes' Clinton River Valley subdivision, a development less than three miles from Jones Associates' Grosse Pines subdivision, he recognized one of the houses as being nearly identical to his design. Jones then checked the building permit at the construction site, and from the information contained on the permit, Jones was able to locate the building plans filed by Nino Homes with the Rochester Hills Township. After examining these plans, Jones concluded that his Aspen plans had been copied, so he promptly registered the complete architectural drawings and the abridged floor plans. Immediately thereafter, Jones sent a letter to Nino Homes demanding that construction of the allegedly identical house cease. When Nino Homes denied that its house, which it called the "Riverside", was a copy of the Aspen, Jones Associates commenced this action.

During the trial which followed, Jones Associates offered evidence that Nino Homes had unlawfully copied its Aspen plans. The record shows that Nino Homes had hired an architectural firm called Diebele–Ginter to design a house. Before construction of the house initially designed by Diebele–Ginter had begun, however, Lochirco apparently gave Clifford Ginter, one of the two partners in the architectural firm, a photocopy of the Aspen abridged floor plans contained in the promotional brochure. According to the testimony of Richard J. Deibele, Ginter's partner, Lochirco instructed Ginter to copy these plans for use by Nino Homes. The photocopy allegedly given by Lochirco to Ginter, who died before the case went to trial, was subsequently discovered in Diebele–Ginter's files and introduced into evidence by Jones Associates.

On the basis of this evidence, and other documents which showed that the Riverside design was virtually identical to the Aspen design, the district court concluded that Nino Homes and Diebele–Ginter had infringed upon Jones Associates' copyright. The court then found that, had Nino Homes not sold seven houses which were built according to the infringing copies, Jones Associates would have sold seven additional houses. Therefore, the court awarded actual damages in the amount of $298,870: $212,550 for presumed profits not earned by Jones Associates because of Nino Homes' infringement, and $86,320 for the profits earned by Nino Homes from the sale of the houses built pursuant to the infringing plans. * * *

Nino Homes contends that the district court used an improper standard to compute the damages it awarded to Jones Associates. The court held that Jones Associates was entitled to recover the profits it would have earned on the sale of additional houses had Nino Homes not used infringing copies of the Aspen plans to build houses which it sold. Nino Homes maintains that this "lost profits" standard is not the appropriate measure of damages in an action for copyright infringement where the protected work is architectural plans. Rather, Nino Homes argues, the proper standard is the fair market value of the architectural plans at the time of the infringement. We disagree. But to appreciate fully the legal issue posed by this seemingly straightforward argument, one must understand the fundamental differences between copyright and patent laws. * * *

The protection of innovative ideas * * * is the province of patent law. In order to encourage technological advancement, patent law deems "new and useful" ideas as deserving of certain, specific protections. 35 U.S.C. § 101 (1982). Generally, patents are awarded to novel inventions and unique designs. But while a copyright merely confers on its owner an exclusive right to reproduce the original work, a patent gives its owner a far broader right: "the right to exclude others from making, using, or selling the invention" for a specific period of time. Id. at § 154. In order to be eligible for this right to exclusive use, though, the applicant for a patent must show that the idea is novel. In contrast, the applicant for a copyright need only establish that the creative work is original. See generally 1 Nimmer at § 2.01[A].

Because their work can rarely, if ever, satisfy the more rigorous novelty standard applied to patent applications, architects generally look to copyright law for protection of their creative works. * * *

Architectural plans, however, "are subject to certain qualifications peculiar to this form of work." 1 Nimmer § 2.08[D][2][a] at 2–105. The copyright statute "does not afford, to the owner of a copyright in a work that portrays a useful article as such, any greater or lesser rights with respect to the making, distribution, or display of the useful article so portrayed than those afforded to such works under the law ... in effect on December 31, 1977." 17 U.S.C. § 113(b). A "useful article" is one which has "an intrinsic utilitarian function." Id. at § 1.01. Because any building or house undoubtedly falls within this definition, architectural plans necessarily depict a useful article and are subject to this restriction. Therefore, the owner of a copyright in architectural plans has statutory copyright protection in the building depicted in those plans only to the extent that such protection was recognized by the law prior to January 1, 1978. The limitations of this protection were initially set by the Supreme Court in Baker v. Selden, 101 U.S. (11 Otto) 99 (1879).

* * * In essence, the plaintiff in *Baker* could prevent the unauthorized reproduction of the actual book, but, unless he had a patent, the plaintiff

could not prevent others from using the accounting forms, the useful article embodied in the book.

The doctrine enunciated in Baker v. Selden is particularly problematic where architectural plans are the copyrighted items because the principal value of such creative works lies in their use in constructing a building. If *Baker* is applied strictly, and the Copyright Act is interpreted as merely prohibiting others from selling copyrighted plans and not from using the plans to construct other buildings, then the statute may not afford the kind of protection necessary to give architects adequate incentive to create new architectural designs. Conversely, giving the owner of a copyright in architectural plans the right to prevent others from constructing buildings substantially similar to the one depicted in the copyrighted plans, without requiring the architect to show that the design is novel as opposed to merely original, would give architects unwarranted monopoly powers with the result that the costs of houses and other buildings would rise unnecessarily. Other courts have also struggled to balance these competing concerns—to remain faithful to *Baker,* yet afford architects the protection Congress clearly intended to provide them. * * *

In Imperial Homes Corp. v. Lamont, 458 F.2d 895 (5th Cir.1972), a builder advertised its houses by distributing brochures which contained a copy of the floor plan from the complete set of copyrighted architectural drawings. After visiting one of the builder's houses and obtaining one of the brochures, a potential customer proceeded to develop a set of drawings for a house which was to be substantially similar to the builder's design. The builder brought an action for copyright infringement and sought to enjoin the customer from using the allegedly infringing plans.

The court in *Imperial Homes* recognized that the *Baker* decision warned against extending a copyright into a patent. The court reasoned that "no copyrighted architectural plans ... may clothe their author with the exclusive right to reproduce the dwelling pictured." Id. at 899. The court, though, then stated that nothing in Baker v. Selden "prevents such a copyright from vesting the law's grant of an exclusive right to make copies of the copyrighted plans so as to instruct a would-be builder on how to proceed to construct the dwelling pictured." Id. Therefore, although the court expressly did "not hold that the [defendants] were in anywise restricted by the existence of Imperial's copyright from reproducing a substantially identical residential dwelling," the court held that, "if copyrighted architectural drawings of the originator of such plans are imitated or transcribed in whole or in part, infringement occurs." Id. * * *

Another federal district court recently addressed a similar issue. In Demetriades v. Kaufmann [680 F.Supp. 658 (S.D.N.Y.1988)], a real estate developer brought a copyright infringement action to enjoin another developer from completing construction of a house which the defendant conceded was being built pursuant to plans which were merely tracings of the plaintiff's copyrighted plans. The court recognized that, under Baker v. Selden, although the plaintiff may have a valid copyright in the architectural plans that served as the basis for its uniquely designed house, that copyright "protection simply does not extend to the design or the house itself absent a design patent." Demetriades v. Kaufmann, 680 F.Supp. at 665. The court held, however, "that the unauthorized reproduction of copyrighted architectural plans constitutes infringement." Id. Accordingly, although the court refused to enjoin construction of the defendant's substantially similar house, the court enjoined the defendants from further, unauthorized copying of plaintiff's architectural plans, and, of greater significance in the matter before us, the court "further enjoined [the defendants] from relying on any infringing copies of those plans." Id. at 666.[4]

The rule which emerges from these cases is that one may construct a house which is identical to a house depicted in copyrighted architectural plans, but one may not directly copy those plans and then use the infringing copy to construct the house. As a logical extension of this rule, we hold that, where someone makes infringing copies of another's copyrighted architectural plans, the damages recoverable by the copyright owner include the losses suffered as a result of the infringer's subsequent use of the infringing copies. Accordingly, the measure of damages in this case is the profits Jones Associates would have made on houses it would have sold but for Nino Homes' unauthorized duplication of the Aspen plans and Nino Homes' use of its infringing copies to build its Riverside houses. Therefore, the district court's decision to award Jones Associates $212,550 for profits it would have earned but for Nino Homes' sale of seven houses built pursuant to the infringing plans is correct.

In a copyright infringement action, the copyright owner is also entitled to recover "any profits of the infringer that are attributable to the infringement *and are not taken into account in computing the actual damages.*" 17 U.S.C. § 504(b) (emphasis added). Here, however, where the infringer's profit per house is less than the copyright owner's profit margin, and where all of the infringer's sales were counted as sales lost by the copyright owner, all of the infringer's profits attributable to the infringement were already taken into account in the actual damages awarded to the copyright owner. Therefore, the district court's decision to add Nino Homes' profits of $86,320 to the award of Jones Associates' lost profits constitutes the kind of double recovery clearly precluded by the statute. Accordingly, that aspect of the district court's decision is reversed.

[The court went on to conclude that the award of attorneys' fees was improper under § 412(2) because the infringement occurred before registration; the date the plans were copied controlled, not the dates of construction. The court also vacated the award of prejudgment interest,

---

4. In Muller v. Triborough Bridge Authority, 43 F.Supp. 298 (S.D.N.Y.1942), the court held that the copyright in a plan for the construction of an approach to a highway bridge did not give the copyright owner the power to prevent someone else from using the copyrighted plan to build the actual structure. The court in *Demetriades,* though, felt its decision was consistent with *Muller,* presumably because it was unclear in *Muller* whether the defendants had made infringing copies or had merely used the copyrighted original to construct the approach. See Demetriades v. Kaufmann, 680 F.Supp. at 664.

noting that the Copyright Act, unlike the Patent Act, contains no express authorization for prejudgment interest.]

NOTES ON COPYRIGHT IN ARCHITECTURAL PLANS

(1) *Jones Associates* restates the general rule that unauthorized construction is not in itself an infringement of copyright in architectural plans. A few courts, however, have indicated a willingness to enjoin construction as a remedy for infringement when copyrighted plans have been copied. See Herman Frankel Organization v. Wolfe, 184 U.S.P.Q. 819 (E.D.Mich.1974); see also Nucor Corp. v. Tennessee Forging Steel Service, Inc., 476 F.2d 386 (8th Cir.1973). On the measure of damages for infringement of copyright in architectural plans, see also Aitken, Hazen, Hoffman, Miller, P.C. v. Empire Construction Co., 542 F.Supp. 252 (D.Neb.1982); Rothschild v. Kisling, 417 So.2d 798 (Fla.App.1982).

Would the rule that construction alone does not infringe the copyright in the plans apply if some aspect of the structure depicted in the plans (a gargoyle, perhaps, or a design in wrought iron) is itself eligible for copyright? In Jones Brothers Co. v. Underkoffler, 16 F.Supp. 729 (M.D.Pa. 1936), it was held that copyright in a drawing of a cemetery monument was infringed by construction of the depicted monument. Can that case be distinguished from the construction in *Jones Associates?*

(2) The rules relating to common law copyright in architectural plans retain significance because the 1976 Act offers no protection to works that had previously entered the public domain through a general publication without copyright notice.

Common law protection for architectural plans was a fragile thing. Local building ordinances often require the filing of plans in a specified public office. One line of cases took the view that these filings amounted to a general publication; others cases disagreed. Construction also could threaten common law protection because a number of decisions saw construction as a publication of the underlying plans. Again, other cases disagreed, sometimes distinguishing design aspects easily observable in the structure from details shown only in the underlying plans. Much of the case law is reviewed in Edgar H. Wood Associates v. Skene, 347 Mass. 351, 197 N.E.2d 886 (1964).

NOTES ON COPYRIGHT IN ARCHITECTURAL WORKS

(1) The Berne Convention specifically lists "works * * * of architecture" among the subject matter to be protected by member nations. When the United States joined the Berne Convention in 1989, a reference to "architectural plans" was added to the § 101 definition of copyrightable "pictorial, graphic, and sculptural works" in an attempt to meet our treaty obligations. (The House Report accompanying the 1976 Act had already made it clear that "[a]n architect's plans and drawings would, of course, be protected by copyright." H.R.Rep. p. 55.) However, protection for architectural *works* (as distinguished from architectural *plans*) remained severely limited by the separability requirement applicable to copyright in useful articles: "[W]here the only elements of shape in an architectural design are conceptually inseparable from the utilitarian aspects of the structure, copyright protection for the design would not be available." Id. A 1989 report by the Copyright Office concluded that Berne demanded greater protection for architectural works. See 38 Pat., Tm. & Copyr. J. (BNA) 206, 230 (1989). Congress responded in 1990 with the Architectural Works Copyright Protection Act.

The 1990 amendments added "architectural works" to the list of protectable subject matter in § 102(a), with an accompanying definition in § 101. Protection extends to "the design of a building" (whether embodied in an actual building or in plans or drawings), subject to the limitations in § 120, which allows others to take photographs of the completed building and allows the owner of the building to alter or destroy it. (The legislation also added § 301(b)(4), which protects state and local preservation, zoning, and building codes from preemption.) The scope and effect of the architectural works amendments are described in the legislative history:

> [T]he term ["building"] encompassed habitable structures such as houses and office buildings. It also covers structures that are used, but not inhabited, by human beings, such as churches, pergolas, gazebos, and garden pavilions. * * *
>
> This provision amends section 102, title 17, United States Code, to create a new category of protected subject matter: "architectural works." By creating a new category of protectible subject matter in new section 102(a)(8), and, therefore, by deliberately not encompassing architectural works as pictorial, graphic, or sculptural works in existing section 102(a)(5), the copyrightability of architectural works shall not be evaluated under the separability test applicable to pictorial, graphic, or sculptural works embodied in useful articles. * * *
>
> The Committee does not suggest, though, that in evaluating the copyrightability or scope of protection for architectural works, the Copyright Office or the courts should ignore functionality. A two-step analysis is envisioned. First, an architectural work should be examined to determine whether there are original design elements present, including overall shape and interior architecture. If such design elements are present, a second step is reached to examine whether the design elements are functionally required. If the design elements are not functionally required, the work is protectible without regard to physical or conceptual separability. As a consequence, contrary to the Committee's report accompanying the 1976 Copyright Act with respect to industrial products, the aesthetically pleasing overall shape of an architectural work would be protected under this bill. H.R.Rep. No. 101–735, 101st Cong.2d Sess. 20–21 (1990).

(2) Separate registrations are required by the Copyright Office for claims in architectural plans as "pictorial, graphic and sculptural works" and for claims in the underlying "architectural works" as defined in the 1990 amendments. 37 C.F.R. § 202.11(c)(4). The regulations also state that a general distribution of the underlying plans is a publication of the architectural work, but construction of the building is not. § 202.11(c)(5).

The initial applications under the "architectural work" category have been characterized by a Copyright Office official as a "disappointing smattering of culturally insignificant claims" such as tract housing. Some applications have been rejected for lack of originality, such as a rectangular cinder block storage building. 45 Pat., Tm. & Copyr. J. (BNA) 115 (1992).

(3) Might other forms of protection serve the architect? Design patent theoretically is available. See In re Hadden, 20 F.2d 275 (D.C.Cir.1927) ("Modern Athletic Stadia"). According to an article on design patents in the New York Times, Jan. 6, 1964, "the most famous was awarded in 1879 to Auguste Bartholdi, the French sculptor, for the Statue of Liberty." Doubtless a handsome gesture—but a valid patent?

Patent and copyright aside, are there circumstances in which a defendant should be prohibited from duplicating the design of a building in which a competitor conducts business? Compare Fotomat Corp. v. Cochran, 437 F.Supp. 1231 (D.Kan.1977) with Fotomat Corp. v. Photo Drive– Thru, Inc., 425 F.Supp. 693 (D.N.J.1977). See Fletcher, Buildings as Trademarks, 69 Trademark Rep. 229 (1979). The design of a golf hole was protected on a trademark theory when a defendant built a replica of the hole on another course. Pebble Beach Co. v. Tour 18 I, Ltd., 942 F.Supp. 1513 (S.D.Tex.1996). The Rock and Roll Hall of Fame, however, was unsuccessful in an attempt to assert trademark rights in the design of its Cleveland museum against a defendant selling posters that depicted the unique structure created by celebrated architect I.M.Pei. Rock and Roll Hall of Fame and Museum, Inc. v. Gentile Prod., 134 F.3d 749 (6th Cir.1998).

CHOREOGRAPHY AND PANTOMIME

The movement of dancers in space can be described, although imprecisely, in words. By the use of Laban notation—a system of hieroglyphics that can be related to the musical score—a considerable degree of descriptive precision can be attained. Dance also can be recorded on film or videotape, or portrayed through computer graphics. That dance can be captured and reduced to a mechanical or written record, however, does not dispose of the question of copyrightability.

Case law is scanty. In Fuller v. Bemis, 50 Fed. 926 (S.D.N.Y.1892), Marie Louise Fuller copyrighted a word description of her "Serpentine Dance," which according to the petition had won her "great profit and credit." The infringement complained of was "the production by defendant of this 'dramatic composition' upon the public stage, with merely colorable alterations." The court stated that "[i]t is essential to [a dramatic] composition that it should tell some story," and spoke of Fuller's dance as "portraying no character, depicting no emotion." A preliminary injunction was denied.

Copyright Office regulations under the 1909 Act permitted registration under the category of "[d]ramatic or dramatico-musical compositions" for "[c]horeographic works of a dramatic character," but excluded "descriptions of dance steps and other physical gestures, including ballroom and social dances or choreographic works which do not tell a story, develop a character or emotion, or otherwise convey a dramatic concept or idea."

Pantomimes could be seen as a species of dramatic work, and therefore copyrightable. An early case extended protection to a "railroad scene" in a play, even though it was mostly in pantomime (it was the business of the villain tying the heroine to the tracks). Daly v. Palmer, 6 Fed.Cas. 1132 (C.C.S.D.N.Y.1868) (No. 3552). But copyright for dramatic compositions could not reach more abstract movement.

In the 1976 Act, Cinderella goes to the ball. "Pantomimes and choreographic works" are now one of the eight categories in § 102. The Act does not define these terms—the drafters believed them to "have fairly settled meanings." H.R.Rep. p. 53. The Report does say, however, that " 'choreographic works' do not include social dance steps and simple routines." Why not? Is this merely an application of the originality requirement? The requirement of creative authorship?

The Jan. 23, 1989 issue of *Sports Illustrated* reports on a claim by a San Antonio dermatologist and an Austin writer to copyright in a football formation. The formation, which the "authors" called the I–Bone, had been described by them in a 1984 article that appeared in a magazine for coaches. The claimants also created a playbook for the I–Bone. (The *Sports Illustrated* article states that a copyright registration was issued, although it does not say to what work the registration relates.) During the 1988 football season the "authors" claimed that they saw the University of Colorado using the formation in a game against Oklahoma. (Colorado lost, 17–14.) The two threatened legal action unless the university acknowledged them as the inventors. The Colorado coaching staff, which called its formation the Power–Bone, claimed independent creation. Assume instead that the coaching staff used the I–Bone playbook. Can the plays be seen as a form of copyrightable choreography? Would drawing the plays on a blackboard infringe the copyright? Would *running* the plays infringe?

Can copyright be obtained in aerobic exercise routines, or in the competitive routines of a gymnast or figure skater, or in the movements produced by a diver, or by a basketball player participating in a slam dunk contest?

———————

HORGAN v. MACMILLAN, 789 F.2d 157 (2d Cir.1986). In 1954 the renowned choreographer George Balanchine created his own version of the ballet "The Nutcracker." The ballet has become a classic. In 1981 Balanchine registered the work with the Copyright Office, depositing a videotape of a New York City Ballet Company dress rehearsal. The work also has been licensed to other ballet companies.

In 1985 the executrix of Balanchine's estate learned that the defendant was planning to publish a book about the New York City Ballet's performance of the work. Interspersed with the book's narration is a series of 60 color photographs of scenes from the Company's production. The estate sought an injunction, arguing that the book was both an infringing reproduction of the ballet and an unauthorized derivative work. Defendant Macmillan claimed that little if any of Balanchine's original choreography was shown in the photographs and noted that the plaintiff made no claim to copyright in the costumes or sets. The trial court found for Macmillan: "The still photographs in the Nutcracker book, numerous though they are, catch dancers in various attitudes at specific instances of time; they do not, nor do they intend to, take or use the underlying choreography. The staged performance could not be recreated from them."

The Second Circuit remanded the case, holding that the trial judge had applied an incorrect standard of liability. Judge Feinberg for the court said that "the standard for determining copyright infringement is not whether the original could be recreated from the allegedly infringing copy, but whether the latter is 'substantially similar' to the former." He also said that the district judge "took a far too limited view of the extent to which choreographic material may be conveyed in the medium of still photography." Among other issues to be determined on remand was "the degree to which the choreography would be distinguishable in the photographs without the costumes and sets."

NOTE

The number of copyright registrations for choreography and pantomimes is small. The fixation of choreographic works in tangible form is largely irrelevant to the day to day business of creating, teaching, and performing dance. Most dance remains unfixed, and the role of statutory copyright is thus a modest one. See Traylor, Choreography, Pantomime and the Copyright Revision Act of 1976, 16 N.Eng.L.Rev. 227 (1981); Singer, In Search of Adequate Protection for Choreographic Works: Legislative and Judicial Alternatives vs. The Custom of the Dance Community, 38 U.Miami L.Rev. 287 (1984).

As an unfixed work, dance remains eligible for protection under common law copyright, but there are few cases. See Dane v. M & H Co., 136 U.S.P.Q. 426 (N.Y.Sup.Ct.1963). See generally Roth, Common Law Protection of Choreographic Works, 5 Performing Arts Rev. 75 (1974).

WORKS OF THE UNITED STATES GOVERNMENT

Schnapper v. Foley

United States Court of Appeals, District of Columbia Circuit, 1981.
667 F.2d 102.
Certiorari denied 455 U.S. 948, 102 S.Ct. 1448 (1982).

■ Before ROBINSON, CHIEF JUDGE, McGOWAN, SENIOR CIRCUIT JUDGE, and PARKER, UNITED STATES DISTRICT JUDGE for the District of Columbia Circuit.

■ McGOWAN, SENIOR CIRCUIT JUDGE:

[The Administrative Office of the United States Courts commissioned Pittsburgh public broadcasting station WQED to produce a series of television films dramatizing famous cases arising in the early years of the Republic. The series, entitled "Equal Justice Under Law," was transmitted by the Public Broadcasting Service to its affiliates across the country.

[Plaintiff Schnapper and his Public Affairs Press alleged that the production contract required WQED to copyright the films and to assign the copyrights to the Government. (The Government denied that any such assignments had taken place.) Plaintiff asserted that the copyrights restricted public access to the films because permission for commercial broadcast had been refused. He also complained that the copyrights prevented him from publishing the text of the films. The complaint sought "both injunctive and declaratory relief not only to void the copyright subsisting in 'Equal Justice Under Law' but also to prevent the defendants from committing in the future acts that appellants contend are unlawful."

[The District Court dismissed the complaint. The Court of Appeals, proceeding on the assumption that the copyrights had been assigned to the Government, affirmed the dismissal.]

The most plausible point of departure for considering appellants' claims on the merits lies in their assertion that the copyright laws, both old and new, do not permit the registration of works commissioned by the Government, or the subsequent assignment of copyrights subsisting therein to the Government. As the series was copyrighted in 1976 under the old Copyright Act, and appellants seek a broad injunction of future applicability under the new Act, we will decide the fate of appellants' claims with respect to both the old and new Copyright Acts.

The status of works produced pursuant to a Government commission does not present any difficult problems under the new Copyright Act. Section 105 of the new Act, 17 U.S.C. § 105 (Supp. I 1977) states in its entirety:

> Copyright protection under this title is not available for any work of the United States Government, but the United States Government is not precluded from receiving and holding copyrights transferred to it by assignment, bequest, or otherwise.

The statute defines a "work of the United States" as one "prepared by . . . an employee of the United States Government as part of that person's official duties." 17 U.S.C. § 101 (Supp. I 1977). It is readily observable, therefore, that the language of the new Copyright Act does not prohibit copyright protection for federally commissioned works.

Whatever doubt there may be left after reading the statute is wholly dispelled by the legislative history, which states plainly that these commissioned works may be eligible for copyright protection:

> The bill deliberately avoids making any sort of outright, unqualified prohibition against copyright in works prepared under

> Government contract or grant. There may well be cases where it
> would be in the public interest to deny copyright. . . . However,
> there are almost certainly many other cases where the denial of
> copyright protection would be unfair or would hamper the produc-
> tion and publication of important works.

H.R.Rep. No. 1476, 94th Cong., 2d Sess. 59 (1976), U.S.Code Cong. &
Admin.News 1976, pp. 5659, 5672. That report also states that the
government agency may withhold copyright protection from the author if it
would be in the public interest to do so or if the commission is merely an
alternative to producing the work in-house. Id.; see also 1 Nimmer on
Copyright § 5.06[B][2] n. 19.2. In this case, however, the government did
not choose to withhold copyright protection from WQED.

Although section 105 explicitly allows the Government to obtain a
copyright by assignment, appellants argue that section 105 does not comprehend an assignment of a federally commissioned work. They assert
that this commission and assignment constitute an effort to avoid the
proscription of copyright subsisting in works produced by the Government,
and is therefore prohibited by the new law. In support of this analysis
they cite the following passage of Professor Nimmer's treatise:

> Could the U.S. Government thus claim a copyright in a work by
> this indirect method which it would be precluded from claiming if
> the work were in the first instance made in a for hire relationship?
> It seems unlikely that the courts would permit such a subterfuge.

1 Nimmer on Copyright § 5.06[B][3].

Without laying down a broad rule, we are reluctant to cabin the
discretion of government agencies to arrange ownership and publication
rights with private contractors absent some reasonable showing of a
congressional desire to do so. The legislative history noted above indicates
a desire to vest the government with some flexibility in making these
arrangements. The House Report provides no strong indicia of congressional intent that would lead this court to void the alleged assignment
provision. It states, "The effect of section 105 is intended to place all
works of the United States Government . . . in the public domain."
H.R.Rep. No. 1476, 94th Cong., 2d Sess. 59 (1976), U.S.Code Cong. &
Admin.News 1976, p. 5672. Works of the United States were defined by
section 101 to comprise works created by Government employees carrying
out their official duties. Section 105, therefore, is not necessarily subvert-
ed by assigning to the Government the copyright in a commissioned work
that is neither produced by current or former employees nor related to the
official duties of any Government employee, as here. Had the Government
employees been detailed as consultants or employees of WQED, we might
more readily find the purported assignment to be a "subterfuge," but
without any such allegation we simply lack the statutory warrant to void
the assignment.

The 1909 Act similarly provides no basis on which to deny copyright protection to a work commissioned by the Government or to void an alleged assignment of that work to the Government. * * *

We have come to the conclusion that neither the old nor the new copyright law proscribes, the registration of works commissioned by the Government for copyright, and that Congress possessed the power to enact these laws. In addition, when there is no allegation that the Government and the contractor have attempted to subvert the copyright laws through an assignment subsequent to registration of a commissioned work, we find that the copyright laws, in their present as well as former incarnation, will permit such an assignment. * * *

Appellants contend that the application of the copyright laws to works commissioned by the Government is, if authorized by Congress, violative of the First Amendment. * * *

Appellants' surviving First Amendment claims number but two: (1) that they have a constitutional right to reprint the screenplays for commercial gain, and (2) that the defendants acted unconstitutionally in failing to disclose the extent of government involvement in the series. Neither is meritorious. * * *

[The court here quoted Judge Fuld's comment in Estate of Hemingway v. Random House, p. 16 supra, that there is a "freedom *not* to speak publicly."] * * *

Chief Judge Fuld's statements explain why this court should not compel WQED to issue a license even if offered a royalty or other payment. The First Amendment interests to which he adverted are not based upon a desire for pecuniary gain, but upon the author's freedom to speak or remain silent as an end in itself. * * * We therefore conclude that the liberty of WQED to grant or deny a license to appellants, either gratuitously or for compensation, does not offend either the First Amendment or its underlying values.[6]

For similar reasons, we are not inclined to grant appellants' request that we require public broadcasters to, in the words of the complaint, "disclose[ ] the existence or extent of government control of the content of the films," Complaint ¶ 15, on First Amendment grounds. The First Amendment cannot be used to force the unwilling author to speak when he would rather remain silent, as we have just explained supra.

Underlying the appellants' First Amendment assault on the copyright obtained for "Equal Justice Under Law" is their professed concern that the Government may one day attempt to use the copyright law as an instrument of censorship. They seem to argue that if the Pentagon Papers [see New York Times Co. v. United States, 403 U.S. 713 (1971)] could have been copyrighted, their publication could have been enjoined. * * *

6. Nothing in the preceding discussion is intended to cast any doubt upon the constitutionality of the compulsory-licensing schemes in the new Copyright Act.

We are aware that there is at least a theoretical possibility that some copyright laws may be used by some nations as instruments of censorship. Fears had been expressed, for example, that the Soviet Union would, through use of a compulsory-assignment provision in its domestic copyright laws, attempt to prevent foreign publication of dissident works whose copyright it had assumed. See Newcity, The Universal Copyright Convention as an Instrument of Repression: The Soviet Experiment, in Copyright Law Symposium No. 24 (1980). The congressional response to this perceived threat was 17 U.S.C. § 201(e) (Supp. I 1977), protecting authors from involuntary transfers. * * *

We are unaware, however, of any effort on the part of the United States Government to throttle free expression through use of the copyright laws, and we are not inclined to hypothesize such an effort nor to hand down a decision invalidating an act of Congress on that hypothetical basis. It is important in this regard to recall that there is no tenable allegation in this case that any person interested in viewing "Equal Justice Under Law" has been denied the opportunity to do so, or that copies of the films and their scripts are other than freely available for public inspection.

We are confident that should the day come when the Government denies someone access to a work produced at its direction on the basis of a copyright, and if the doctrine of fair use and the distinction between an idea and its expression fail to vindicate adequately that person's interests—although we have no reason to believe that they would—the courts of the United States would on the basis of facts, not hypotheses, consider afresh the First Amendment interests implicated thereby. We are sure that they will comprehend the difference between that case and this one. * * *

The judgment of the District Court from which this appeal was taken is affirmed.

It is so ordered.

NOTES ON WORKS OF THE U.S. GOVERNMENT

(1) Section 105, in conjunction with the definition of a "work of the United States Government," prohibits both the United States and its employees from copyrighting works created in the course of official business. The House Report notes that the exclusion pertains to unpublished as well as published works, a point in some doubt under the 1909 Act.

Not every work produced by a government employee is a "work of the United States Government." The House Report tells us that an "official or employee would not be prevented from securing copyright in a work written at that person's own volition and outside his or her duties, even though the subject matter involves the Government work or professional field of the official or employee." H.R.Rep. p. 58. See Public Affairs Associates, Inc. v. Rickover, 268 F.Supp. 444 (D.D.C.1967), holding that speeches delivered to the Harvard Club and the American Public Power Association by nuclear power advocate Admiral Hyman Rickover were his "private property which he was entitled to copyright."[m]   See generally Tresansky, Copyright in Government Employee Authored Works, 30 Cath. U.L.Rev. 605 (1981).

(2) "Equal Justice Under Law" was not produced by an "official or employee of the United States Government." It was the work of private parties acting pursuant to a government contract. *Schnapper* holds that such works may be copyrighted by their creators. This aspect of the court's decision is supported by the House Report's discussion of § 105:

> * * * As the bill is written, the Government agency concerned could determine in each case whether to allow an independent contractor or grantee to secure copyright in works prepared in whole or in part with the use of Government funds. The argument that has been made against allowing copyright in this situation is that the public should not be required to pay a "double subsidy," and that it is inconsistent to prohibit copyright in works by Government employees while permitting private copyrights in a growing body of works created by persons who are paid with Government funds. Those arguing in favor of potential copyright protection have stressed the importance of copyright as an incentive to creation and dissemination in this situation and the basically different policy considerations applicable to works written by Government employees and those applicable to works prepared by private organizations with the use of Federal funds. * * *

> * * * Where, under the particular circumstances, Congress or the agency involved finds that the need to have a work freely available outweighs the need of the private author to secure copyright, the problem can be dealt with by specific legislation, agency regulations, or contractual restrictions. (H.R.Rep. p. 59.)

For an argument that this leaves too much to agency discretion, see Hartnick, Government and Copyright: Merely a Matter of Administrative Discretion, 4 Comm. & L. (No. 2) 3 (1982).

(3) Section 105 states that the federal government is not prohibited from holding copyrights "transferred to it by assignment, bequest, or otherwise." *Schnapper* says this language comprehends assignments of copyrights in works created at the instigation of the Government. Are you

---

m. Devotees of American history will enjoy United States v. First Trust Co., 251 F.2d 686 (8th Cir.1958). The action was one to quiet title to a "series of original writings on miscellaneous scraps of paper of various sizes" written by William Clark during the Lewis and Clark Expedition. The papers were found in an attic in 1952. The United States claimed "paramount title to the res as being a part of the work product of the Lewis and Clark Expedition." The court affirmed a finding that the documents were "the private and personal writings of Captain Clark" and not "the work product of a government representative engaged in the performance of his duties." It noted that Clark had assisted Lewis in the preparation of a separate official record of the Expedition. For a severe critique by a historian of the court's finding that the papers were "private," see Boyd, These Precious Monuments of * * * Our History, 22 Am.Archivist 147 (1959).

convinced by the court's analysis? Professor Nimmer was not. See Nimmer on Copyright § 5.06[B][3].

(4) Congress has considered bills that would permit the federal government to secure copyright in computer software developed by federal employees. Proponents argue that protection would enhance American competitiveness by encouraging private investment in the commercialization of the programs. See Chandler, Protection of U.S. Competitiveness in the International Software Markets: Reexamining the Question of Copyrighting Government–Created Software, 25 Geo.Wash.J.Int'l L. & Econ. 387 (1991). Opponents worry about a slippery slope toward evisceration of § 105. Is an exception to the prohibition against government copyright justified in the case of software? (Is it relevant that the federal government is not generally precluded from claiming patents for inventions?)

(5) Section 105 does not preclude *state* or *local* governmental entities from claiming copyright in the output of *their* officers and employees. See National Conference of Bar Examiners v. Multistate Legal Studies, Inc., 495 F.Supp. 34 (N.D.Ill.1980), aff'd, 692 F.2d 478 (7th Cir.1982), cert. denied, 464 U.S. 814 (1983) (state bar examinations held copyrightable). A long-standing exception, however, precludes copyright in state judicial opinions and statutes. See Banks v. Manchester, 128 U.S. 244 (1888); State of Georgia v. Harrison Co., 548 F.Supp. 110 (N.D.Ga.1982), vacated, 559 F.Supp. 37 (N.D.Ga.1983). (*Federal* decisions and statutes are in the public domain by virtue of § 105.) The exception does not extend to synopses or headnotes appended by private publishers. Callaghan v. Myers, 128 U.S. 617 (1888). Recall also the claim of copyright in the selection and arrangement of opinions upheld in West Publishing Co. v. Mead Data Central, Inc., 799 F.2d 1219 (8th Cir.1986), cert. denied, 479 U.S. 1070 (1987), p. 97 supra. One court, after an extensive review of the case law, concluded that privately drafted codes that are subsequently incorporated into state law might be ineligible for copyright. Building Officials & Code Administrators Int'l, Inc. v. Code Technology, Inc., 628 F.2d 730 (1st Cir.1980).[n] See generally Nodiff, Copyrightability of Works of the Federal and State Governments Under the 1976 Act, 29 St.L.U.L.J. 91 (1984).[o]

---

n. In CCC Information Services, Inc. v. Maclean Hunter Market Reports, Inc., 44 F.3d 61 (2d Cir.1994), cert. denied, 516 U.S. 817 (1995), the Second Circuit rejected an argument under *Building Officials and Code Administrators* that state adoption of a legal standard incorporating a copyrighted compilation of used car valuations resulted in a loss of copyright. The Ninth Circuit followed *CCC Information* in Practice Management Information Corp. v. American Medical Ass'n, 121 F.3d 516 (9th Cir.), cert. denied, 118 S.Ct. 339 (1997) (AMA's medical procedure coding system did not lose its copyright upon adop-

tion by a federal agency for use on Medicare forms).

o. See also Kidwell, Open Records Laws and Copyright, 1989 Wis.L.Rev. 1021, wondering whether state public records laws should preclude claims of copyright in compilations of data and other works produced by state and local governmental entities. The intersection of copyright and freedom of information statutes is also pursued in Perritt, Sources of Rights to Access Public Information, 4 Will. & Mary Bill of Rights J. 179 (1995).

(6) One consequence of § 105 should not be overlooked. In the words of the House Report, it "means that, as far as the copyright law is concerned, the Government could not restrain the employee or official from disseminating the work if he or she chooses to do so." H.R.Rep. p. 59.[p]

The plaintiff in *Schnapper* apparently argued that copyright in works produced under Government commission could become "an instrument of censorship." Professor Kaplan has reminded us that the development of copyright law owes much to the English Crown's fear of the newly-invented printing press. See B. Kaplan, An Unhurried View of Copyright 2–6 (1967). (The plaintiff's reference in *Schnapper* to the *Pentagon Papers* case was not entirely unfounded. The Government, attempting to stop publication in the *New York Times* of portions of a 47–volume report on the U.S. role in Southeast Asia, had argued to the Supreme Court that the documents leaked to the *Times* by Daniel Ellsberg were the "literary property" of the United States. See The Pentagon Papers as Published by the New York Times 689 (Quadrangle Books 1971).)

There are of course laws other than copyright that restrict access to Government works. See Nimmer, National Security Secrets v. Free Speech: The Issues Left Undecided in the Ellsberg Case, 26 Stan.L.Rev. 311 (1974).

COPYRIGHT AND MORALITY

May copyright be held and enforced in obscene publications? A 1958 opinion of the Attorney General cautiously concluded that the Register was not without power to withhold registration, but found that the law "imposes no duty upon him to deny registration of such claims." 41 Op.Att'y Gen. No. 73, 121 U.S.P.Q. 329 (1958).

The Copyright Office apparently makes no attempt to curb registration for obscenity. See Compendium II of Copyright Office Practices § 108.10. (How could it, in light of the Supreme Court's emphasis on "community standards"? See Miller v. California, 413 U.S. 15 (1973).) Despite some older cases to the contrary, recent judicial decisions have also rejected obscenity defenses in infringement actions. See Mitchell Brothers Film Group v. Cinema Adult Theater, 604 F.2d 852 (5th Cir.1979), cert. denied, 445 U.S. 917 (1980); Jartech, Inc. v. Clancy, 666 F.2d 403 (9th Cir.), cert. denied, 459 U.S. 826 (1982).

What of material published with intent to deceive or defraud? In Belcher v. Tarbox, 486 F.2d 1087 (9th Cir.1973), the court said it was no defense to an infringement action that the plaintiff's horse race handicapping system might be fraudulent: "There is nothing in the Copyright Act to suggest that the courts are to pass upon the truth or falsity, the soundness or unsoundness, of the views embodied in a copyrighted work."

p. Section 105 did not prevent the Government from seeking to regain physical possession of a document removed without permission by a former employee in Pfeiffer v. Central Intelligence Agency, 60 F.3d 861 (D.C.Cir.1995).

Finally, it might be noted that morality survives in § 2(a) of the federal Trademark Act, 15 U.S.C.A. § 1052(a), forbidding registration of a trademark that "comprises immoral, deceptive, or scandalous matter." The mark "Bubby Trap" for brassieres was denied registration, but "Badass" for musical instruments was not.[q]

q. See In re Runsdorf, 171 U.S.P.Q. 443 (Trademark Trial & App.Bd.1971); In re Leo Quan, Inc., 200 U.S.P.Q. 370 (T.T.A.B.1978).

See generally J. McCarthy, Trademarks and Unfair Competition § 19.27.

CHAPTER 3

SCOPE OF PROTECTION: INFRINGEMENT

SECTION 1. IDEAS AND EXPRESSION IN WORKS OF FICTION

Nichols v. Universal Pictures Corp.

United States Circuit Court of Appeals, Second Circuit, 1930.
45 F.2d 119.
Certiorari denied 282 U.S. 902, 51 S.Ct. 216 (1931).

■ Before L. HAND, SWAN, and AUGUSTUS N. HAND, CIRCUIT JUDGES.

■ L. HAND, CIRCUIT JUDGE. The plaintiff is the author of a play, "Abie's Irish Rose," which it may be assumed was properly copyrighted under section five, subdivision (d), of the Copyright Act, 17 U.S.C.A. § 5(d). The defendant produced publicly a motion picture play, "The Cohens and The Kellys," which the plaintiff alleges was taken from it. As we think the defendant's play too unlike the plaintiff's to be an infringement, we may assume, arguendo, that in some details the defendant used the plaintiff's play as will subsequently appear, though we do not so decide. It therefore becomes necessary to give an outline of the two plays.

"Abie's Irish Rose" presents a Jewish family living in prosperous circumstances in New York. The father, a widower, is in business as a merchant, in which his son and only child helps him. The boy has philandered with young women, who to his father's great disgust have always been Gentiles, for he is obsessed with a passion that his daughter-in-law shall be an orthodox Jewess. When the play opens the son, who has been courting a young Irish Catholic girl, has already married her secretly before a Protestant minister, and is concerned to soften the blow for his father, by securing a favorable impression of his bride, while concealing her faith and race. To accomplish this he introduces her to his father at his home as a Jewess, and lets it appear that he is interested in her, though he conceals the marriage. The girl somewhat reluctantly falls in with the plan; the father takes the bait, becomes infatuated with the girl, concludes that they must marry, and assumes that of course they will, if he so decides. He calls in a rabbi, and prepares for the wedding according to the Jewish rite.

Meanwhile the girl's father, also a widower, who lives in California, and is as intense in his own religious antagonism as the Jew, has been called to New York, supposing that his daughter is to marry an Irishman and a Catholic. Accompanied by a priest, he arrives at the house at the moment when the marriage is being celebrated, but too late to prevent it, and the two fathers, each infuriated by the proposed union of his child to a heretic, fall into unseemly and grotesque antics. The priest and the rabbi become friendly, exchange trite sentiments about religion, and agree that the match is good. Apparently out of abundant caution, the priest celebrates the marriage for a third time, while the girl's father is inveigled away. The second act closes with each father, still outraged, seeking to find some way by which the union, thus trebly insured, may be dissolved.

The last act takes place about a year later, the young couple having meanwhile been abjured by each father, and left to their own resources. They have had twins, a boy and a girl, but their fathers know no more than that a child has been born. At Christmas each, led by his craving to see his grandchild, goes separately to the young folks' home, where they encounter each other, each laden with gifts, one for a boy, the other for a girl. After some slapstick comedy, depending upon the insistence of each that he is right about the sex of the grandchild, they become reconciled when they learn the truth, and that each child is to bear the given name of a grandparent. The curtain falls as the fathers are exchanging amenities, and the Jew giving evidence of an abatement in the strictness of his orthodoxy.

"The Cohens and The Kellys" presents two families, Jewish and Irish, living side by side in the poorer quarters of New York in a state of perpetual enmity. The wives in both cases are still living, and share in the mutual animosity, as do two small sons, and even the respective dogs. The Jews have a daughter, the Irish a son; the Jewish father is in the clothing business; the Irishman is a policeman. The children are in love with each other, and secretly marry, apparently after the play opens. The Jew, being in great financial straits, learns from a lawyer that he has fallen heir to a large fortune from a great-aunt, and moves into a great house, fitted luxuriously. Here he and his family live in vulgar ostentation, and here the Irish boy seeks out his Jewish bride, and is chased away by the angry father. The Jew then abuses the Irishman over the telephone, and both become hysterically excited. The extremity of his feelings makes the Jew sick, so that he must go to Florida for a rest, just before which the daughter discloses her marriage to her mother.

On his return the Jew finds that his daughter has borne a child; at first he suspects the lawyer, but eventually learns the truth and is overcome with anger at such a low alliance. Meanwhile, the Irish family who have been forbidden to see the grandchild, go to the Jew's house, and after a violent scene between the two fathers in which the Jew disowns his daughter, who decides to go back with her husband, the Irishman takes her back with her baby to his own poor lodgings. The lawyer, who had hoped to marry the Jew's daughter, seeing his plan foiled, tells the Jew that his fortune really belongs to the Irishman, who was also related to the dead woman, but offers to conceal his knowledge, if the Jew will share the loot. This the Jew repudiates, and, leaving the astonished lawyer, walks through the rain to his enemy's house to surrender the property. He arrives in great dejection, tells the truth, and abjectly turns to leave. A reconciliation ensues, the Irishman agreeing to share with him equally. The Jew shows some interest in his grandchild, though this is at most a minor motive in the reconciliation, and the curtain falls while the two are in their cups, the Jew insisting that in the firm name for the business, which they are to carry on jointly, his name shall stand first.

It is of course essential to any protection of literary property, whether at common-law or under the statute, that the right cannot be limited literally to the text, else a plagiarist would escape by immaterial variations. That has never been the law, but, as soon as literal appropriation ceases to be the test, the whole matter is necessarily at large, so that, as was recently well said by a distinguished judge, the decisions cannot help much in a new case. Fendler v. Morosco, 253 N.Y. 281, 292, 171 N.E. 56. When plays are concerned, the plagiarist may excise a separate scene [Daly v. Webster, 56 F. 483 (C.C.A. 2); Chappel v. Fields, 210 F. 864 (C.C.A. 2); Chatterton v. Cave, L.R. 3 App.Cas. 483]; or he may appropriate part of the dialogue (Warne v. Seebohm, L.R. 39 Ch.D. 73). Then the question is whether the part so taken is "substantial," and therefore not a "fair use" of the copyrighted work; it is the same question as arises in the case of any other copyrighted work. Marks v. Feist, 290 F. 959 (C.C.A. 2); Emerson v. Davies, Fed.Cas. No. 4436, 3 Story, 768, 795–797. But when the plagiarist does not take out a block in situ, but an abstract of the whole, decision is more troublesome. Upon any work, and especially upon a play, a great number of patterns of increasing generality will fit equally well, as more and more of the incident is left out. The last may perhaps be no more than the most general statement of what the play is about, and at times might consist only of its title; but there is a point in this series of abstractions where they are no longer protected, since otherwise the playwright could prevent the use of his "ideas," to which, apart from their expression, his property is never extended. Holmes v. Hurst, 174 U.S. 82, 86; Guthrie v. Curlett, 36 F.2d 694 (C.C.A. 2). Nobody has ever been able to fix that boundary, and nobody ever can. In some cases the question has been treated as though it were analogous to lifting a portion out of the copyrighted work (Rees v. Melville, MacGillivray's Copyright Cases [1911–1916], 168); but the analogy is not a good one, because though the skeleton is a part of the body, it pervades and supports the whole. In such cases we are rather concerned with the line between expression and what is expressed. As respects plays, the controversy chiefly centers upon the characters and sequence of incident, these being the substance.

We did not in Dymow v. Bolton, 11 F.2d 690, hold that a plagiarist was never liable for stealing a plot; that would have been flatly against our rulings in Dam v. Kirk La Shelle Co., 175 F. 902 and Stodart v. Mutual Film Co., 249 F. 513, affirming my decision in (D.C.) 249 F. 507; neither of which we meant to overrule. We found the plot of the second play was too different to infringe, because the most detailed pattern, common to both, eliminated so much from each that its content went into the public domain; and for this reason we said, "this mere subsection of a plot was not susceptible of copyright." But we do not doubt that two plays may correspond in plot closely enough for infringement. How far that correspondence must go is another matter. Nor need we hold that the same may not be true as to the characters, quite independently of the "plot" proper, though, as far as we know, such a case has never arisen. If Twelfth Night were copyrighted, it is quite possible that a second comer might so closely imitate Sir Toby Belch or Malvolio as to infringe, but it would not be enough that for one of his characters he cast a riotous knight who kept wassail to the discomfort of the household, or a vain and foppish steward who became amorous of his mistress. These would be no more than Shakespeare's "ideas" in the play, as little capable of monopoly as Einstein's Doctrine of Relativity, or Darwin's theory of the Origin of Species. It follows that the less developed the characters, the less they can be copyrighted; that is the penalty an author must bear for marking them too indistinctly.

In the two plays at bar we think both as to incident and character, the defendant took no more—assuming that it took anything at all—than the law allowed. The stories are quite different. One is of a religious zealot who insists upon his child's marrying no one outside his faith; opposed by another who is in this respect just like him, and is his foil. Their difference in race is merely an obbligato to the main theme, religion. They sink their differences through grandparental pride and affection. In the other, zealotry is wholly absent; religion does not even appear. It is true that the parents are hostile to each other in part because they differ in race; but the marriage of their son to a Jew does not apparently offend the Irish family at all, and it exacerbates the existing animosity of the Jew, principally because he has become rich, when he learns it. They are reconciled through the honesty of the Jew and the generosity of the Irishman; the grandchild has nothing whatever to do with it. The only matter common to the two is a quarrel between a Jewish and an Irish father, the marriage of their children, the birth of grandchildren and a reconciliation.

If the defendant took so much from the plaintiff, it may well have been because her amazing success seemed to prove that this was a subject of enduring popularity. Even so, granting that the plaintiff's play was wholly original, and assuming that novelty is not essential to a copyright, there is no monopoly in such a background. Though the plaintiff discovered the vein, she could not keep it to herself; so defined, the theme was too generalized an abstraction from what she wrote. It was only a part of her "ideas."

Nor does she fare better as to her characters. It is indeed scarcely credible that she should not have been aware of those stock figures, the low comedy Jew and Irishman. The defendant has not taken from her more than their prototypes have contained for many decades. If so, obviously so to generalize her copyright, would allow her to cover what was not original with her. But we need not hold this as matter of fact, much as we might be justified. Even though we take it that she devised her figures out of her brain de novo, still the defendant was within its rights.

There are but four characters common to both plays, the lovers and the fathers. The lovers are so faintly indicated as to be no more than stage properties. They are loving and fertile; that is really all that can be said of them, and anyone else is quite within his rights if he puts loving and fertile lovers in a play of his own, wherever he gets the cue. The plaintiff's Jew is quite unlike the defendant's. His obsession is his religion, on which depends such racial animosity as he has. He is affectionate, warm and patriarchal. None of these fit the defendant's Jew, who shows affection for his daughter only once, and who has none but the most superficial interest in his grandchild. He is tricky, ostentatious and vulgar, only by misfortune redeemed into honesty. Both are grotesque, extravagant and quarrelsome; both are fond of display; but these common qualities make up only a small part of their simple pictures, no more than any one might lift if he chose. The Irish fathers are even more unlike; the plaintiff's a mere symbol for religious fanaticism and patriarchal pride, scarcely a character at all. Neither quality appears in the defendant's, for while he goes to get his grandchild, it is rather out of a truculent determination not to be forbidden, than from pride in his progeny. For the rest he is only a grotesque hobbledehoy, used for low comedy of the most conventional sort, which any one might borrow, if he chanced not to know the exemplar.

The defendant argues that the case is controlled by my decision in Fisher v. Dillingham (D.C.) 298 F. 145. Neither my brothers nor I wish to throw doubt upon the doctrine of that case, but it is not applicable here. We assume that the plaintiff's play is altogether original, even to an extent that in fact it is hard to believe. We assume further that, so far as it has been anticipated by earlier plays of which she knew nothing, that fact is immaterial. Still, as we have already said, her copyright did not cover everything that might be drawn from her play; its content went to some extent into the public domain. We have to decide how much, and while we are as aware as any one that the line, wherever it is drawn, will seem arbitrary, that is no excuse for not drawing it; it is a question such as courts must answer in nearly all cases. Whatever may be the difficulties a priori, we have no question on which side of the line this case falls. A comedy based upon conflicts between Irish and Jews, into which the marriage of their children enters, is no more susceptible of copyright than the outline of Romeo and Juliet.

The plaintiff has prepared an elaborate analysis of the two plays, showing a "quadrangle" of the common characters, in which each is represented by the emotions which he discovers. She presents the resulting parallelism as proof of infringement, but the adjectives employed are so general as to be quite useless. Take for example the attribute of "love" ascribed to both Jews. The plaintiff has depicted her father as deeply attached to his son, who is his hope and joy; not so, the defendant, whose father's conduct is throughout not actuated by any affection for his daughter, and who is merely once overcome for the moment by her distress when he has violently dismissed her lover. "Anger" covers emotions aroused by quite different occasions in each case; so do "anxiety," "despondency" and "disgust." It is unnecessary to go through the catalogue for emotions are too much colored by their causes to be a test when used so broadly. This is not the proper approach to a solution; it must be more ingenuous, more like that of a spectator, who would rely upon the complex of his impressions of each character.

We cannot approve the length of the record, which was due chiefly to the use of expert witnesses. Argument is argument whether in the box or at the bar, and its proper place is the last. The testimony of an expert upon such issues, especially his cross-examination, greatly extends the trial and contributes nothing which cannot be better heard after the evidence is all submitted. It ought not to be allowed at all; and while its admission is not a ground for reversal, it cumbers the case and tends to confusion, for the more the court is led into the intricacies of dramatic craftsmanship, the less likely it is to stand upon the firmer, if more naïve, ground of its considered impressions upon its own perusal. We hope that in this class of cases such evidence may in the future be entirely excluded, and the case confined to the actual issues; that is, whether the copyrighted work was original, and whether the defendant copied it, so far as the supposed infringement is identical. * * *

Decree affirmed.

REYHER V. CHILDREN'S TELEVISION WORKSHOP, 533 F.2d 87 (2d Cir.), cert. denied, 429 U.S. 980 (1976). Plaintiff's book for children, "My Mother is the Most Beautiful Woman in the World," retold a folktale of a lost Russian child who could describe his mother only in the words of the title. The search for the mother was hampered because objectively she was quite homely. Defendant's Sesame Street television playlet and two-page magazine recreation, called "The Most Beautiful Woman in the World," located the same story in Africa.

"The difficult task in an infringement action is to distill the nonprotected idea from protected expression. * * * While the line between idea and expression may not be susceptible to overly helpful generalization, it has been emphasized repeatedly that the essence of infringement lies in taking not a general theme but its particular expression through similarities of treatment, details, scenes, events, and characterizations."

Judge Meskill said the question was "whether defendants in the instant case utilized the idea in Reyher's book or instead descended so far into the concrete as to invade her expression." Finding the works "not similar in mood, details or characterization," the court affirmed a dismissal of the infringement claim.

Sheldon v. Metro–Goldwyn Pictures Corp.

United States Circuit Court of Appeals, Second Circuit, 1936.
81 F.2d 49.
Certiorari denied 298 U.S. 669, 56 S.Ct. 835.

■ Before L. HAND, SWAN, and CHASE, CIRCUIT JUDGES.

■ L. HAND, CIRCUIT JUDGE. The suit is to enjoin the performance of the picture play, "Letty Lynton," as an infringement of the plaintiffs' copyrighted play, "Dishonored Lady." The plaintiffs' title is conceded, so too the validity of the copyright; the only issue is infringement. The defendants say that they did not use the play in any way to produce the picture; the plaintiffs discredit this denial because of the negotiations between the parties for the purchase of rights in the play, and because the similarities between the two are too specific and detailed to have resulted from chance. The judge thought that, so far as the defendants had used the play, they had taken only what the law allowed, that is, those general themes, motives, or ideas in which there could be no copyright. Therefore he dismissed the bill.

An understanding of the issue involves some description of what was in the public demesne, as well as of the play and the picture. In 1857 a Scotch girl, named Madeleine Smith, living in Glasgow, was brought to trial upon an indictment in three counts; two for attempts to poison her lover, a third for poisoning him. The jury acquitted her on the first count, and brought in a verdict of "Not Proven" on the second and third. The circumstances of the prosecution aroused much interest at the time not only in Scotland but in England; so much indeed that it became a cause célèbre, and that as late as 1927 the whole proceedings were published in book form. An outline of the story so published, which became the original of the play here in suit, is as follows: The Smiths were a respectable middle-class family, able to send their daughter to a "young ladies' boarding school"; they supposed her protected not only from any waywardness of her own, but from the wiles of seducers. In both they were mistaken, for when at the age of twenty-one she met a young Jerseyman of French blood, Emile L'Angelier, ten years older, and already the hero of many amorous adventures, she quickly succumbed and poured out her feelings in letters of the utmost ardor and indiscretion, and at times of a candor beyond the standards then, and even yet, permissible for well-nurtured young women. They wrote each other as though already married, he assuming to dictate her conduct and even her feelings; both expected to marry, she on any terms, he with the approval of her family. Nevertheless she soon tired of him and engaged herself to a man some twenty years older who was a better match, but for whom she had no more than a friendly complaisance. L'Angelier was not, however, to be fobbed off so easily; he threatened to expose her to her father by showing her letters. She at first tried to dissuade him by appeals to their tender memories, but finding this useless and thinking herself otherwise undone, she affected a return of her former passion and invited him to visit her again. Whether he did, was the turning point of the trial; the evidence, though it really left

JUDGE LEARNED HAND

His opinions for more than half a century illuminated the law of copyright and
unfair competition. What George Wharton Pepper said of the *Sheldon* opinion
can be many times justly repeated about Judge Hand's writing: "The entire
opinion exhibits craftsmanship at its best and is entitled to be ranked as a model
of judicial style." 60 Harv.L.Rev. 333, 341 (1947).

the issue in no doubt, was too indirect to satisfy the jury, perhaps in part because of her advocate's argument that to kill him only insured the discovery of her letters.   It was shown that she had several times bought or tried to buy poison,—prussic acid and arsenic,—and that twice before his death L'Angelier became violently ill, the second time on the day after her purchase.   He died of arsenical poison, which the prosecution charged that she had given him in a cup of chocolate.   At her trial, Madeleine being incompetent as a witness, her advocate proved an alibi by the testimony of her younger sister that early on the night of the murder as laid in the indictment, she had gone to bed with Madeleine, who had slept with her throughout the night.   As to one of the attempts her betrothed swore that she had been with him at the theatre.

This was the story which the plaintiffs used to build their play.   As will appear they took from it but the merest skeleton, the acquittal of a wanton young woman, who to extricate herself from an amour that stood in the way of a respectable marriage, poisoned her lover.   The incidents, the characters, the mis en scène, the sequence of events, were all changed; nobody disputes that the plaintiffs were entitled to their copyright.   All that they took from the story they might probably have taken, had it even been copyrighted.   Their heroine is named Madeleine Cary; she lives in New York, brought up in affluence, if not in luxury; she is intelligent, voluptuous, ardent and corrupt; but, though she has had a succession of amours, she is capable of genuine affection.   Her lover and victim is an Argentinian, named Moreno, who makes his living as a dancer in night-clubs.   Madeleine has met him once in Europe before the play opens, has danced with him, has excited his concupiscence; he presses presents upon her.   The play opens in his rooms, he and his dancing partner who is also his mistress, are together; Madeleine on the telephone recalls herself to him and says she wishes to visit him, though it is already past midnight. He disposes of his mistress by a device which does not deceive her and receives Madeleine; at once he falls to wooing her, luring her among other devices by singing a Gaucho song.   He finds her facile and the curtain falls in season.

The second act is in her home, and introduces her father, a bibulous dotard, who has shot his wife's lover in the long past; Laurence Brennan, a self-made man in the fifties, untutored, self-reliant and reliable, who has had with Madeleine a relation, half paternal, half amorous since she grew up; and Denis Farnborough, a young British labor peer, a mannekin to delight the heart of well ordered young women.   Madeleine loves him; he loves Madeleine; she will give him no chance to declare himself, remembering her mottled past and his supposedly immaculate standards.   She confides to Brennan, who makes clear to her the imbecility of her self-denial; she accepts this enlightenment and engages herself to her high-minded paragon after confessing vaguely her evil life and being assured that to post-war generations all such lapses are peccadillo.

In the next act Moreno, who has got wind of the engagement, comes to her house. Disposing of Farnborough, who chances to be there, she admits Moreno, acknowledges that she is to marry Farnborough, and asks him to accept the situation as the normal outcome of their intrigue. He refuses to be cast off, high words pass, he threatens to expose their relations, she raves at him, until finally he knocks her down and commands her to go to his apartment that morning as before. After he leaves full of swagger, her eye lights on a bottle of strychnine which her father uses as a drug; her fingers slowly close upon it; the audience understands that she will kill Moreno. Farnborough is at the telephone; this apparently stiffens her resolve, showing her the heights she may reach by its execution.

The scene then shifts again to Moreno's apartment; his mistress must again be put out, most unwillingly for she is aware of the situation; Madeleine comes in; she pretends once more to feel warmly, she must wheedle him for he is out of sorts after the quarrel. Meanwhile she prepares to poison him by putting the strychnine in coffee, which she asks him to make ready. But in the course of these preparations during which he sings her again his Gaucho song, what with their proximity, and this and that, her animal ardors are once more aroused and drag her, unwillingly and protesting, from her purpose. The play must therefore wait for an hour or more until, relieved of her passion, she appears from his bedroom and while breakfasting puts the strychnine in his coffee. He soon discovers what has happened and tries to telephone for help. He does succeed in getting a few words through, but she tears away the wire and fills his dying ears with her hatred and disgust. She then carefully wipes away all traces of her fingerprints and manages to get away while the door is being pounded in by those who have come at his call.

The next act is again at her home on the following evening. Things are going well with her and Farnborough and her father, when a district attorney comes in, a familiar of the household, now in stern mood; Moreno's mistress and a waiter have incriminated Madeleine, and a cross has been found in Moreno's pocket, which he superstitiously took off her neck the night before. The district attorney cross-questions her, during which Farnborough several times fatuously intervenes; she is driven from point to point almost to an avowal when as a desperate plunge she says she spent the night with Brennan. Brennan is brought to the house and, catching the situation after a moment's delay, bears her out. This puts off the district attorney until seeing strychnine brought to relieve the father, his suspicions spring up again and he arrests Madeleine. The rest of the play is of no consequence here, except that it appears in the last scene that at the trial where she is acquitted, her father on the witness stand accounts for the absence of the bottle of strychnine which had been used to poison Moreno.

At about the time that this play was being written an English woman named Lowndes wrote a book called Letty Lynton, also founded on the story of Madeleine Smith. Letty Lynton lives in England; she is eighteen years old, beautiful, well-reared and intelligent, but wayward. She has had a more or less equivocal love affair with a young Scot, named McLean, who worked in her father's chemical factory, but has discarded him, apparently before their love-making had gone very far.   Then she chances upon a young Swede—half English—named Ekebon, and their acquaintance quickly becomes a standardized amour, kept secret from her parents, especially her mother, who is an uncompromising moralist, and somewhat estranged from Letty anyway.   She and her lover use an old barn as their place of assignation; it had been fitted up as a play house for Letty when she was a child.   Like Madeleine Smith she had written her lover a series of indiscreet letters which he has kept, for though he is on pleasure bent Ekebon has a frugal mind, and means to marry his sweetheart and set himself up for life.   They are betrothed and he keeps pressing her to declare it to her parents, which she means never to do.   While he is away in Sweden, Letty meets an unmarried peer considerably older than she, poor but intelligent and charming; he falls in love with her and she accepts him, more because it is a good match than for any other reason, though she likes him well enough, and will make him suppose that she loves him.

Thereupon Ekebon reappears, learns of Letty's new betrothal, and threatens to disclose his own to her father, backing up his story with her letters.   She must at once disown her peer and resume her engagement with him.   His motive, like L'Angelier's, is ambition rather than love, though conquest is a flattery and Letty a charming morsel.   His threats naturally throw Letty into dismay; she has come to loathe him and at any cost must get free, but she has no one to turn to.   In her plight she thinks of her old suitor, McLean, and goes to the factory only to find him gone. He has taught her how to get access to poisons in his office and has told of their effect on human beings.   At first she thinks of jumping out the window, and when she winces at that, of poisoning herself; that would be easier.   So she selects arsenic which is less painful and goes away with it; it is only when she gets home that she thinks of poisoning Ekebon.   Her mind is soon made up, however, and she makes an appointment with him at the barn; she has told her father, she writes, and Ekebon is to see him on Monday, but meanwhile on Sunday they will meet secretly once more. She has prepared to go on a week-end party and conceals her car near the barn.   He comes; she welcomes him with a pretence of her former ardors, and tries to get back her letters.   Unsuccessful in this she persuades him to drink a cup of chocolate into which she puts the arsenic.   After carefully washing the pans and cups, she leaves with him, dropping him from her car near his home; he being still unaffected.   On her way to her party she pretends to have broken down and by asking the help of a passing cyclist establishes an alibi.   Ekebon dies at his home attended by his mistress; the letters are discovered and Letty is brought before the coroner's inquest and acquitted chiefly through the alibi, for things look very bad for her until the cyclist appears.

The defendants, who are engaged in producing speaking films on a very large scale in Hollywood, California, had seen the play and wished to get the rights.   They found, however, an obstacle in an association of motion picture producers presided over by Mr. Will Hays, who thought the play obscene; not being able to overcome his objections, they returned the copy of the manuscript which they had had. That was in the spring of 1930, but in the autumn they induced the plaintiffs to get up a scenario, which they hoped might pass moral muster. Although this did not suit them after the plaintiffs prepared it, they must still have thought in the spring of 1931 that they could satisfy Mr. Hays, for they then procured an offer from the plaintiffs to sell their rights for $30,000. These negotiations also proved abortive because the play continued to be objectionable, and eventually they cried off on the bargain. Mrs. Lowndes' novel was suggested to Thalberg, one of the vice-presidents of the Metro–Goldwyn Company, in July, 1931, and again in the following November, and he bought the rights to it in December. At once he assigned the preparation of a play to Stromberg, who had read the novel in January, and thought it would make a suitable play for an actress named, Crawford, just then not employed. Stromberg chose Meehan, Tuchock and Brown to help him, the first two with the scenario, the third with the dramatic production. All these four were examined by deposition; all denied that they had used the play in any way whatever; all agreed that they had based the picture on the story of Madeleine Smith and on the novel, "Letty Lynton." All had seen the play, and Tuchock had read the manuscript, as had Thalberg, but Stromberg, Meehan and Brown swore that they had not; Stromberg's denial being however worthless, for he had originally sworn the contrary in an affidavit. They all say that work began late in November or early in December, 1931, and the picture was finished by the end of March. To meet these denials, the plaintiffs appeal to the substantial identity between passages in the picture and those parts of the play which are original with them.

The picture opens in Montevideo where Letty Lynton is recovering from her fondness for Emile Renaul. She is rich, luxurious and fatherless, her father having been killed by his mistress's husband; her mother is seared, hard, selfish, unmotherly; and Letty has left home to escape her, wandering about in search of excitement. Apparently for the good part of a year she has been carrying on a love affair with Renaul; twice before she has tried to shake loose, has gone once to Rio where she lit another flame, but each time she has weakened and been drawn back. Though not fully declared as an amour, there can be no real question as to the character of her attachment. She at length determines really to break loose, but once again her senses are too much for her and it is indicated, if not declared, that she spends the night with Renaul. Though he is left a vague figure only indistinctly associated with South America somewhere or other, the part was cast for an actor with a marked foreign accent, and it is plain that he was meant to be understood, in origin anyway, as South American, like Moreno in the play. He is violent, possessive and sensual; his power over Letty lies in his strong animal attractions. However, she escapes in the morning while he is asleep, whether from his bed or not is perhaps uncertain; and with a wax figure in the form of a loyal maid—Letty in the novel had one—boards a steamer for New York. On board she meets Darrow, a young American, the son of a rich rubber manufacturer, who is coming back from a trip to Africa. They fall in love upon the faintest provocation and become betrothed before the ship docks, three weeks after she left Montevideo. At the pier she finds Renaul who has flown up to reclaim her. She must in some way keep her two suitors apart, and she manages to dismiss Darrow and then to escape Renaul by asking him to pay her customs duties, which he does. Arrived home her mother gives her a cold welcome and refuses to concern herself with the girl's betrothal. Renaul is announced; he has read of the betrothal in the papers and is furious. He tries again to stir her sensuality by the familiar gambit, but this time he fails; she slaps his face and declares that she hates him. He commands her to come to his apartment that evening; she begs him to part with her and let her have her life; he insists on renewing their affair. She threatens to call the police; he rejoins that if so her letters will be published, and then he leaves. Desperate, she chances on a bottle of strychnine, which we are to suppose is an accoutrement of every affluent household, and seizes it; the implication is of intended suicide, not murder. Then she calls Darrow, tells him that she will not leave with him that night for his parents' place in the Adirondacks as they had planned; she renews to him the pledge of her love, without him she cannot live, an intimation to the audience of her purpose to kill herself.

That evening she goes to Renaul's apartment in a hotel armed with her strychnine bottle, for use on the spot; she finds him cooling champagne, but in bad temper. His caresses which he bestows plentifully enough, again stir her disgust not her passions, but he does not believe it and assumes that she will spend the night with him. Finding that he will not return the letters, she believes herself lost and empties the strychnine into a wine glass. Again he embraces her; she vilifies him; he knocks her down; she vilifies him again. Ignorant of the poison he grasps her glass, and she, perceiving it, lets him drink. He woos her again, this time with more apparent success, for she is terrified; he sings a Gaucho song to her, the same one that has been heard at Montevideo. The poison begins to work and, at length supposing that she has meant to murder him, he reaches for the telephone; she forestalls him, but she does not tear out the wire. As he slowly dies, she stands over him and vituperates him. A waiter enters; she steps behind a curtain; he leaves thinking Renaul drunk; she comes out, wipes off all traces of her fingerprints and goes out, leaving however her rubbers which Renaul had taken from her when she entered.

Next she and Darrow are found at his parents' in the Adirondacks; while there a detective appears, arrests Letty and takes her to New York; she is charged with the murder of Renaul; Darrow goes back to New York with her. The finish is at the district attorney's office; Letty and Darrow, Letty's mother, the wax serving maid are all there. The letters appear incriminating to an elderly rather benevolent district attorney; also the customs slip and the rubbers. Letty begins to break down; she admits that she went to Renaul's room, not to kill him but to get him to release her. Darrow sees that that story will not pass, and volunteers that she came to his room at a hotel and spent the night with him. Letty confirms this and mother, till then silent, backs up their story; she had traced them to the hotel and saw the lights go out, having ineffectually tried to dissuade them. The maid still further confirms them and the district attorney, not sorry to be discomfited, though unbelieving, discharges Letty.

We are to remember that it makes no difference how far the play was anticipated by works in the public demesne which the plaintiffs did not use. The defendants appear not to recognize this, for they have filled the record with earlier instances of the same dramatic incidents and devices, as though, like a patent, a copyrighted work must be not only original, but new. That is not however the law as is obvious in the case of maps or compendia, where later works will necessarily be anticipated. At times, in discussing how much of the substance of a play the copyright protects, courts have indeed used language which seems to give countenance to the notion that, if a plot were old, it could not be copyrighted. London v. Biograph Co. (C.C.A.) 231 F. 696; Eichel v. Marcin (D.C.) 241 F. 404. But we understand by this no more than that in its broader outline a plot is never copyrightable, for it is plain beyond peradventure that anticipation as such cannot invalidate a copyright. Borrowed the work must indeed not be, for a plagiarist is not himself pro tanto an "author"; but if by some magic a man who had never known it were to compose anew Keats's Ode on a Grecian Urn, he would be an "author," and, if he copyrighted it, others might not copy that poem, though they might of course copy Keats's. Bleistein v. Donaldson Lithographing Co., 188 U.S. 239, 249; Gerlach–Barklow Co. v. Morris & Bendien, Inc., 23 F.2d 159, 161 (C.C.A. 2); Weil, Copyright Law, p. 234. But though a copyright is for this reason less vulnerable than a patent, the owner's protection is more limited, for just as he is no less an "author" because others have preceded him, so another who follows him, is not a tort-feasor unless he pirates his work. Jewelers' Circular Publishing Co. v. Keystone Co., 281 F. 83, 92 (C.C.A. 2); General Drafting Co. v. Andrews, 37 F.2d 54, 56 (C.C.A. 2); Williams v. Smythe (C.C.) 110 F. 961; American, etc., Directory Co. v. Gehring Pub. Co. (D.C.) 4 F.2d 415; New Jersey, etc., Co. v. Barton Business Service (D.C.) 57 F.2d 353. If the copyrighted work is therefore original, the public demesne is important only on the issue of infringement; that is, so far as it may break the force of the inference to be drawn from likenesses between the work and the putative piracy. If the defendant has had access to other material which would have served him as well, his disclaimer becomes more plausible.

In the case at bar there are then two questions: First, whether the defendants actually used the play; second, if so, whether theirs was a "fair use." The judge did not make any finding upon the first question, as we said at the outset, because he thought the defendants were in any case justified; in this following our decision in Nichols v. Universal Pictures Corporation, 45 F.2d 119. The plaintiffs challenge that opinion because we said that "copying" might at times be a "fair use"; but it is convenient to define such a use by saying that others may "copy" the "theme," or "ideas," or the like, of a work, though not its "expression." At any rate so long as it is clear what is meant, no harm is done. In the case at bar the distinction is not so important as usual, because so much of the play was borrowed from the story of Madeleine Smith, and the plaintiffs' originality is necessarily limited to the variants they introduced.   Nevertheless, it is still true that their whole contribution may not be protected; for the defendants were entitled to use, not only all that had gone before, but even the plaintiffs' contribution itself, if they drew from it only the more general patterns; that is, if they kept clear of its "expression." We must therefore state in detail those similarities which seem to us to pass the limits of "fair use."   Finally, in concluding as we do that the defendants used the play pro tanto, we need not charge their witnesses with perjury.   With so many sources before them they might quite honestly forget what they took; nobody knows the origin of his inventions; memory and fancy merge even in adults.   Yet unconscious plagiarism is actionable quite as much as deliberate.   Buck v. Jewell–La Salle Realty Co., 283 U.S. 191, 198; Harold Lloyd Corporation v. Witwer, 65 F.2d 1, 16 (C.C.A. 9); Fred Fisher, Inc. v. Dillingham (D.C.) 298 F. 145.

The defendants took for their mis en scène the same city and the same social class; and they chose a South American villain.   The heroines had indeed to be wanton, but Letty Lynton "tracked" Madeleine Cary more closely than that.   She is overcome by passion in the first part of the picture and yields after announcing that she hates Renaul and has made up her mind to leave him.   This is the same weakness as in the murder scene of the play, though transposed.   Each heroine's waywardness is suggested as an inherited disposition; each has had an errant parent involved in scandal; one killed, the other becoming an outcast.   Each is redeemed by a higher love.   Madeleine Cary must not be misread; it is true that her lust overcomes her at the critical moment, but it does not extinguish her love for Farnborough; her body, not her soul, consents to her lapse.   Moreover, her later avowal, which she knew would finally lose her her lover, is meant to show the basic rectitude of her nature.   Though it does not need Darrow to cure Letty of her wanton ways, she too is redeemed by a nobler love.   Neither Madeleine Smith, nor the Letty of the novel, were at all like that; they wished to shake off a clandestine intrigue to set themselves up in the world; their love as distinct from their lust, was pallid.   So much for the similarity in character.

Coming to the parallelism of incident, the threat scene is carried out with almost exactly the same sequence of event and actuation; it has no prototype in either story or novel.   Neither Ekebon nor L'Angelier went to his fatal interview to break up the new betrothal; he was beguiled by the pretence of a renewed affection.   Moreno and Renaul each goes to his sweetheart's home to detach her from her new love; when he is there, she appeals to his better side, unsuccessfully; she abuses him, he returns the abuse and commands her to come to his rooms, she pretends to agree, expecting to finish with him one way or another.   True, the assault is deferred in the picture from this scene to the next, but it is the same dramatic trick.   Again, the poison in each case is found at home, and the girl talks with her betrothed just after the villain has left and again pledges him her faith.   Surely the sequence of these details is pro tanto the very web of the authors' dramatic expression; and copying them is not "fair use."

The death scene follows the play even more closely; the girl goes to the villain's room as he directs; from the outset he is plainly to be poisoned while they are together. (The defendants deny that this is apparent in the picture, but we cannot agree. It would have been an impossible dénoument on the screen for the heroine, just plighted to the hero, to kill herself in desperation, because the villain has successfully enmeshed her in their mutual past; yet the poison is surely to be used on some one.) Moreno and Renaul each tries to arouse the girl by the memory of their former love, using among other aphrodisiacs the Gaucho song; each dies while she is there, incidentally of strychnine not arsenic. In extremis each makes for the telephone and is thwarted by the girl; as he dies, she pours upon him her rage and loathing. When he is dead, she follows the same ritual to eradicate all traces of her presence, but forgets telltale bits of property. Again these details in the same sequence embody more than the "ideas" of the play; they are its very raiment.

Finally in both play and picture in place of a trial, as in the story and the novel, there is substituted an examination by a district attorney; and this examination is again in parallel almost step by step. A parent is present; so is the lover; the girl yields progressively as the evidence accumulates; in the picture, the customs slip, the rubbers and the letters; in the play, the cross and the witnesses, brought in to confront her. She is at the breaking point when she is saved by substantially the same most unexpected alibi; a man declares that she has spent the night with him. That alibi there introduced is the turning point in each drama and alone prevents its ending in accordance with the classic canon of tragedy; i.e., fate as an inevitable consequence of past conduct, itself not evil enough to quench pity. It is the essence of the authors' expression, the very voice with which they speak.

We have often decided that a play may be pirated without using the dialogue. Daly v. Palmer, Fed.Cas. No. 3,552, 6 Blatch. 256; Daly v. Webster, 56 F. 483, 486, 487; Dam v. Kirk La Shelle Co., 175 F. 902, 907; Chappell & Co. v. Fields, 210 F. 864. Dymow v. Bolton, 11 F.2d 690; and Nichols v. Universal Pictures Corporation, supra, 45 F.2d 119, do not suggest otherwise. Were it not so, there could be no piracy of a pantomine, where there cannot be any dialogue; yet nobody would deny to pantomine the name of drama. Speech is only a small part of a dramatist's means of expression; he draws on all the arts and compounds his play from words and gestures and scenery and costume and from the very looks of the actors themselves. Again and again a play may lapse into pantomime at its most poignant and significant moments; a nod, a movement of the hand, a pause, may tell the audience more than words could tell. To be sure, not all this is always copyrighted, though there is no reason why it may not be, for those decisions do not forbid which hold that mere scenic tricks will not be protected. Serrana v. Jefferson (C.C.) 33 F. 347; Barnes v. Miner (C.C.) 122 F. 480; Bloom et al. v. Nixon (C.C.) 125 F. 977. The play is the sequence of the confluents of all these means, bound together in an inseparable unity; it may often be most effectively pirated by leaving out the speech, for which a substitute can be found, which keeps the whole dramatic meaning.   That as it appears to us is exactly what the defendants have done here; the dramatic significance of the scenes we have recited is the same, almost to the letter.   True, much of the picture owes nothing to the play; some of it is plainly drawn from the novel; but that is entirely immaterial; it is enough that substantial parts were lifted; no plagiarist can excuse the wrong by showing how much of his work he did not pirate. We cannot avoid the conviction that, if the picture was not an infringement of the play, there can be none short of taking the dialogue.

The decree will be reversed and an injunction will go against the picture together with a decree for damages and an accounting.   The plaintiffs will be awarded an attorney's fee in this court and in the court below, both to be fixed by the District Court upon the final decree.

Decree reversed.

NOTES AND QUESTIONS ON IDEAS AND EXPRESSIONS

(1) In what respects did the similarities between "Abie's Irish Rose" and "The Cohens and The Kellys" differ from those shared by "Dishonored Lady" and "Letty Lynton"?   Can you describe the "expression" appropriated by the latter work?

(2) Judge Hand, in describing the defendants' infringement in *Sheldon*, states that "it is enough that substantial parts were lifted."   The standard of infringement is often said to be "substantial similarity."   See Nimmer on Copyright § 13.03.   When are similarities "substantial"?   Cases to follow offer various formulations.   For now, consider the comments of Judge Woolsey in the court below, responding to plaintiff's contention that the impression of the play and picture on the "average playgoer" was the appropriate criterion: "In a situation such as I have here, however, I must, as the trier of the facts, have a more Olympian viewpoint than the average playgoer.   I must look at the two opposing productions, the Play and the Picture, not only comparatively, but, as it were, genealogically," taking into account "the common origin of the plot of both the Play and Picture in a mid-nineteenth century trial."   What are the advantages—and disadvantages—of this approach?

Is Judge Hand's use of the term "fair use" in *Sheldon* consistent with its meaning in § 107 of the 1976 Act?

(3) Umbreit, A Consideration of Copyright, 87 U.Pa.L.Rev. 932 (1939), attacks the idea/expression distinction as not fairly descriptive of the cases, and relates the trend, as he sees it, toward broader protection to the decay of "classicism," with its intense preoccupation with form and corresponding lack of concern for novelty. Half a century later this thesis, which had influenced Kaplan, An Unhurried View of Copyright 24 (1967), flowered in the sudden attention devoted by literary scholars to copyright and the nature of authorship. See, e.g., The Construction of Authorship: Textual Appropriation in Law and Literature (Woodmansee and Jaszi ed.) (1993), a collection of essays first published in 10 Cardozo Arts & Ent.L.J. No. 2 (1992). The editors declare, "Taken as a whole these studies of writing practices from the Renaissance to the present suggest that the modern regime of authorship, far from being timeless and universal, is a relatively recent formation—the result of a quite radical reconceptualization of the creative process that culminated less than 200 years ago in the heroic self-presentation of Romantic poets. * * * Prior to this apotheosis of authorship words and texts circulated more freely * * * not because surveillance was lax, but because more corporate and collaborative norms of writing prevailed." See also M. Rose, Authors and Owners: The Invention of Copyright (1993), which explores 18th century conceptions.

(4) Several recent articles question the utility of the idea/expression dichotomy as a criterion for judging infringement. See Cohen, Copyright Law and the Myth of Objectivity: The Idea–Expression Dichotomy and the Inevitability of Artistic Value Judgments, 66 Ind.L.Rev. 175 (1990) (lacking a "philosophical or objective basis" for distinguishing ideas from expression, assessments of the artistic value of the appropriated elements predominate); Samuels, The Idea–Expression Dichotomy in Copyright Law, 56 Tenn.L.Rev. 321 (1989) (the dichotomy is used merely as an ex post facto characterization). Compare Wiley, Copyright at the School of Patent, 58 U.Chi.L.Rev. 119 (1991) (the question should be whether protection of the appropriated material is necessary to insure sufficient incentive to create), with Kurtz, Speaking to the Ghost: Idea and Expression in Copyright, 47 U.Miami L.Rev. 1221 (1993) (protection should not unduly interfere with the ability of later authors to create).

Should harm to the copyright owner be relevant in determining whether the similarity between two works is "substantial"? An affirmative argument is made in Lape, The Metaphysics of the Law: Bringing Substantial Similarity Down to Earth, 98 Dick.L.Rev. 181 (1994).

SOME REPRESENTATIVE LITERARY INFRINGEMENT CASES

The following cases illustrate the techniques of comparing allegedly infringed and infringing works, a matter that requires such lengthy descriptions as to preclude summaries here. The cases selected involve works of some past or present popularity.

Lewys v. O'Neill, 49 F.2d 603 (S.D.N.Y.1931) ("Strange Interlude"); Lowenfels v. Nathan, 2 F.Supp. 73 (S.D.N.Y.1932) ("Of Thee I Sing"); Kustoff v. Chaplin, 120 F.2d 551 (9th Cir.1941) ("Modern Times"); McConnor v. Kaufman, 49 F.Supp. 738 (S.D.N.Y.), aff'd, 139 F.2d 116 (2d Cir.1943) ("The Man Who Came to Dinner"); MacDonald v. Du Maurier, 75 F.Supp. 655 (S.D.N.Y.1948) (see also, on motion for judgment on the pleadings, 144 F.2d 696 (2d Cir.1944)) ("Rebecca"); Musto v. Meyer, 434 F.Supp. 32 (S.D.N.Y.1977), aff'd, 598 F.2d 609 (2d Cir.1979) (Sherlock Holmes and the "Seven Per Cent Solution"); Alexander v. Haley, 460

F.Supp. 40 (S.D.N.Y.1978) ("Roots") (This plaintiff lost, but another got a substantial settlement. See " 'Roots' Plagiarism Case is Settled," N.Y. Times, Dec. 15, 1978, p. 1.); Litchfield v. Spielberg, 736 F.2d 1352 (9th Cir.1984), cert. denied, 470 U.S. 1052, (1985) ("E.T.—The Extraterrestrial"); Zambito v. Paramount Pictures Corp., 613 F.Supp. 1107 (E.D.N.Y.) aff'd, 788 F.2d 2 (2d Cir.1985) ("Raiders of the Lost Ark"); Walker v. Time Life Films, Inc., 784 F.2d 44 (2d Cir.), cert. denied, 476 U.S. 1159 (1986) ("Fort Apache: The Bronx"); Denker v. Uhry, 820 F.Supp. 722 (S.D.N.Y. 1992), aff'd, 996 F.2d 301 (2d Cir.1993) ("Driving Miss Daisy"); Williams v. Crichton, 84 F.3d 581 (2d Cir.1996) ("Jurassic Park").

Interesting opinions arising out of television include: Bradbury v. CBS, 287 F.2d 478 (9th Cir.), cert. dism'd, 368 U.S. 801 (1961) ("Fahrenheit 451"); Davis v. E.I. DuPont de Nemours & Co., 240 F.Supp. 612 (S.D.N.Y. 1965) ("Ethan Frome"); Bevan v. CBS, 329 F.Supp. 601 (S.D.N.Y.1971) ("Hogan's Heroes"). See Goodson–Todman Enterprises, Ltd. v. Kellogg Co., 513 F.2d 913 (9th Cir.1975) ("To Tell the Truth") (see also Barris/Fraser Enterprises v. Goodson–Todman Enterprises, 5 U.S.P.Q.2d 1887 (S.D.N.Y.1988)); Twentieth Century–Fox Film Corp. v. MCA, Inc., 715 F.2d 1327 (9th Cir.1983) ("Star Wars" and "Battlestar Galactica").

SECTION 2.   MUSIC

This Section deals only with infringement of one musical composition by another. On infringement by public performance, see p. 311 infra; on infringement by unlicensed recordings, see p. 538 infra.

Fred Fisher, Inc. v. Dillingham

United States District Court, Southern District of New York, 1924.
298 Fed. 145.

Hearing upon bill and answer in a suit upon musical copyright. The composition in question was originally published as instrumental music, in which form it had small success. Later, when published as a song, it gained an enormous vogue, and was sung or played all over the country under the name "Dardanella," but, being of ephemeral quality, had subsided in popularity by the end of 1920. The supposed infringement was a vocal number in the light opera, "Good Morning, Dearie," composed by the defendant Jerome Kern. The number was called "Kalua," and also attained wide popularity, running into millions of mechanical records and published copies.

There is no similarity between the melodies of the two pieces in any part, but the supposed infringement is in the accompaniment of the chorus or refrain of "Kalua," which has in part an absolute identity with the accompaniment of the verse, though not the chorus, of "Dardanella." This accompaniment introduces the copyrighted song, and is known in music as an "ostinato," or constantly repeated figure, which produces the effect of a rolling underphrase for the melody, something like the beat of a drum or tom-tom, except that it has a very simply melodic character of its own. It consists of only eight notes, written in two measures and repeated again and again, with no changes, except the variation of a musical fifth in the scale to accommodate itself harmonically to the changes in the melody. Precisely the same eight notes are in the accompaniment to the chorus or refrain of "Kalua," used also as an "ostinato," precisely as they are used in "Dardanella," giving the same effect, and designed, as the composer says, to indicate the booming of a surf upon the beach.

The supposed infringement appeared shortly after the popularity of "Dardanella" had abated. The composer swears that he did not use the copyrighted song in any way, so far as he is conscious, but arrived at the accompaniment independently, as an appropriate foil or counterpoise to the sustained and somewhat languorous melody of the chorus, upon which "Kalua" depended for its popularity. Whether he was unconsciously using the copyrighted accompaniment, with which he was in fact familiar, he does not and cannot say.

The figure on which the plaintiff relies was by no means original with "Dardanella." It occurs with precisely or substantially the same intervals as a single phrase in Wagner's "Fliegende Holländer," in a toccata of Schumann, and in a cello number of one Kummer; but, although the figure in these compositions is repeated, it is always after an interval, and it is never used as an "ostinato." In a book of piano exercises by one Landon it does, however, appear as such, repeated a number of times in succession; the only substantial difference between this and "Dardanella" being that between each figure there is a pause, such as would in verse be a caesura, which interferes with the continued movement. The composition in Landon's book is stated to have been taken from the "Mermaid Song" in Weber's opera, "Oberon," to which it is used as an accompaniment. * * *

■ LEARNED HAND, DISTRICT JUDGE (after stating the facts as above). The copyright to the composition "Dardanella" covered the piece as a whole; there were not several copyrights for each part of it. Nevertheless the plagiarism of any substantial component part, either in melody or accompaniment, would be the proper subject of such a suit as this. To sustain it, however, more must appear than the mere similarity or even identity, of the supposed infringement with the part in question. In this lies one distinction between a patent and a copyright. One may infringe a patent by the innocent reproduction of the machine patented, but the law imposes no prohibition upon those who, without copying, independently arrive at the precise combination of words or notes which have been copyrighted. The plaintiff therefore concedes that it must show that Kern, the composer, used "Dardanella" as the source of his accompaniment.

The argument is a strong one. Not only is the figure in each piece exactly alike, but it is used in the same way; that is, as an "ostinato" accompaniment. Further, the defendants have been able to discover in earlier popular music neither this figure, nor even any "ostinato" accompaniment whatever. The fact that "Kalua" appeared shortly after "Dardanella" had faded out, and was written by one who had necessarily known it, as a musician knew it, makes it still more hard to assume any independent provenience for "Kalua." Can I suppose that such parallelism could be the result of coincidence only?

Mr. Kern swears that he was quite unconscious of any plagiarism, and on the whole I am disposed to give him the benefit of the doubt. * * *

Whether he unconsciously copied the figure, he cannot say, and does not try to. Everything registers somewhere in our memories, and no one can tell what may evoke it. On the whole, my belief is that, in composing the accompaniment to the refrain of "Kalua," Mr. Kern must have followed, probably unconsciously, what he had certainly often heard only a short time before. I cannot really see how else to account for a similarity, which amounts to identity. * * *

On the issue of infringement this conclusion is enough. The point is a new one, but I think it is plain. The author's copyright is an absolute right to prevent others from copying his original collocation of words or notes, and does not depend upon the infringer's good faith. Once it appears that another has in fact used the copyright as the source of his production, he has invaded the author's rights. It is no excuse that in so doing his memory has played him a trick. * * *

The most important point of law in the case is whether it is a defense that there was in the prior art substantially the same figure. First, I think there is a clear difference between its use at intervals, as in Wagner, Schumann, or Kummer, and its use by Bernard [in "Dardanella"] as an "ostinato." To the ear the two are toto coelo different, auditorially and emotionally, as different as eight notes when used alone and when used as part of a larger phrase. Musical melody is single, the sense of the earlier notes carrying over into those which succeed. Repetition is in substance the same in this respect, the effect upon the ear being entirely different when the figure is rolled over and over again. The only composition in the public domain which I should consider an anticipation, if this were a patent suit, is Landon's adaptation of Weber's "Mermaid Song."

The differences between Landon and the copyrighted "ostinato" are not enough to make the latter an "adaptation or arrangement" of the first, under section 6 (Comp.St. § 9522), had it been taken directly from Landon's work. There is a minimum of change which the law will disregard. Jollie v. Jaques, 1 Blatchf. 825, Fed.Cas.No. 7,437; Atwill v. Ferrett, 2 Fed.Cas. 195, No. 640; Cooper v. James, (D.C.) 213 F. 871. Yet there is no evidence to sustain the assertion that the Dardanella "ostinato" was in fact taken from Landon or from any other composition. For the purposes of this case it must be deemed to be original, if by original one means that it was the spontaneous, unsuggested result of the author's imagination. And so this case squarely raises the question whether it be a defense to a copyright that the precise work has independently appeared before it and is in the public domain. * * *

* * * It appears to me very obvious that the rule as to infringement has, and indeed must have, as its correlative, the rule that originality is alone the test of validity. Any subsequent person is, of course, free to use all works in the public domain as sources for his compositions. No later work, though original, can take that from him. But there is no reason in justice or law why he should not be compelled to resort to the earlier works themselves, or why he should be free to use the composition of another, who himself has not borrowed. If he claims the rights of the public, let him use them; he picks the brains of the copyright owner as much, whether his original composition be old or new. The defendant's concern lest the public should be shut off from the use of works in the public domain is therefore illusory; no one suggests it. That domain is open to all who tread it; not to those who invade the closes of others, however similar.

[Judge Hand then discusses the necessary recurrence of similar works in such fields as compilations, translations, directories, maps, and photographs, and their eligibility for copyright.]

I conclude, therefore, that the existence of Landon's "ostinato," though substantially the same as the "Dardanella" accompaniment, did not invalidate the copyright pro tanto, there being no evidence, or, indeed, any reasonable possibility, that it was the source of Bernard's conception. There remains only the question of relief.

The plaintiff may, of course, take the usual injunction, though under the circumstances it will apparently be of no service. As for damages, it seems to me absurd to suggest that it has suffered any injury. "Dardanella" had faded out before "Kalua" appeared; but, if it had been at the peak of its popularity, I do not believe that the accompaniment to the chorus of "Kalua" would have subtracted one copy or one record from its sales. The controversy is "a trivial pother" (Hough, J., dissentiente in Jewelers', etc., Co. v. Keystone Pub. Co. (C.C.A.) 281 F. 83, 95), a mere point of honor, of scarcely more than irritation, involving no substantial interest. Except that it raises an interesting point of law, it would be a waste of time for every one concerned. * * *

Settle decree on notice.

NOTES AND QUESTIONS ON "COPYING"

(1) According to Shafter, Musical Copyright (2d ed. 1939), before the "Dardanella" case it was common practice to establish a public domain equivalent to plaintiff's composition for the purpose of destroying the validity of the copyright. This case, by restating the rule that only originality and not novelty is necessary for copyright, effectively eliminated from consideration works such as the obscure examples adduced by the defendant, to which the plaintiff likely had no access. On the other hand, the decision also restates the rule that a defendant remains free to mine the public domain for herself, or to create independently even an exact duplicate of the plaintiff's work. These propositions, now familiar, had

been unsettled. (For a case in which the judge, entangling patent and copyright concepts, apparently did not recognize that access by the defendant to plaintiff's work must be established or inferred, see Hein v. Harris, 175 Fed. 875 (S.D.N.Y.) (Learned Hand's first reported copyright decision), aff'd, 183 Fed. 107 (2d Cir.1910).)

Do you agree with Judge Hand's determination of the appropriate remedy? Should the plaintiff have a claim to any of the profits earned by the infringing work? See p. 555 infra.

(2) On the necessity of establishing access to the copyrighted work, see Selle v. Gibb, 741 F.2d 896 (7th Cir.1984). A jury verdict for the plaintiff was set aside because no inference of access was plausible. Gibb, one of the Bee Gees, had composed "How Deep Is Your Love" at an isolated recording session; plaintiff's song, although registered, was unpublished, unrecorded, and unperformed, except on two or three occasions by his own band in Chicago. Copies of the music had been sent to several music publishing companies.

The Seventh Circuit recognized that when "the plaintiff does not have direct evidence of access, then an inference of access may still be established circumstantially by proof of similarity which is so striking that the possibilities of independent creation, coincidence and prior common source are, as a practical matter, precluded." (The two songs *were* remarkably similar. "The similarities between the Bee Gees' hit from *Saturday Night Fever* and the unpublished *Let It End* are amusing; it seems to defy chance that two composers could have hit upon the same ugly tune." Walsh, Has Somebody Stolen Their Song?, Time, Oct. 19, 1987, p. 86.) Judge Cudahy went on to explain, however, "that no matter how great the similarity between the two works, it is not their similarity *per se* which establishes access; rather, their similarity tends to prove access in light of the nature of the works, the particular musical genre involved and other circumstantial evidence of access. In other words, striking similarity is just one piece of circumstantial evidence tending to show access and must not be considered in isolation; it must be considered together with other types of circumstantial evidence relating to access. As a threshold matter, therefore, it would appear that there must be at least some other evidence which would establish a reasonable possibility that the complaining work was *available* to the alleged infringer."

The question of access also loomed large in another claim against the composer of a popular hit. In Gaste v. Kaiserman, 863 F.2d 1061 (2d Cir.1988), the plaintiff alleged that his song, "Pour Toi," written in 1956 as part of the score for a French movie, had been infringed in 1973 by the defendant Kaiserman (better known as Morris Albert) in composing the internationally successful "Feelings." The principal theory of access to plaintiff's virtually unknown song was strained: one of plaintiff's employees testified that in the 1950s he had sent copies of the sheet music to the owner of defendant's Brazilian publisher. Plaintiff's musical expert, in addition to pointing out general similarities between the two songs, identified "a unique musical 'fingerprint'"—he called it an "evaded resolution"—occurring at the same place in both works. He said that he had never seen this particular method of modulation. The trial judge instructed the jury that if works are "strikingly similar," then "access does not have to be proven." The Second Circuit, in an opinion by Judge Newman, upheld a verdict in favor of the plaintiff. Responding to the defendants' reliance on Selle v. Gibb, supra, Judge Newman said that in the Second Circuit, "the test for proof of access in cases of striking similarity is less rigorous. * * *"

"Appellants contend that undue reliance on striking similarity to show access precludes protection for the author who independently creates a similar work. However, the jury is only *permitted* to infer access from striking similarity; it need not do so. Though striking similarity alone can raise an inference of copying, that inference must be reasonable in light of all the evidence."

When evidence of access and similarity raise an inference of copying, the inference can be rebutted by evidence of independent creation or reliance on common sources. These are not affirmative defenses—the burden of persuasion remains on the copyright owner. Keeler Brass Co. v. Continental Brass Co., 862 F.2d 1063 (4th Cir.1988).

(3) A newspaper account of the trial of an infringement suit lodged by a reggae musician named Patrick Alley against Mick Jagger and his "Just Another Night" sets a colorful scene. "In the course of the seven-day trial, presided over by Judge Gerard L. Goettel, a Juilliard faculty member played piano; a top Jamaican studio musician, Sly Dunbar, played drums, and Mr. Jagger sang snatches of 'Jumpin' Jack Flash,' 'Brown Sugar,' and 'Miss You' from the witness stand." In addition to taped performances of the two works, Jagger, arguing independent creation, also played working tapes to show the genesis of his song, and "lawyers for both sides sang a few lines." The jury found no infringement. (The article also notes an out-of-court payment by Ray Parker Jr. in settlement of a claim relating to alleged similarities between his song "Ghostbusters" and "I Want a New Drug" by Huey Lewis and the News.) Pareles, U.S. Jury Says Jagger Did Not Steal Hit Song, New York Times, April 27, 1988, p. C.22.

Compare the plight of George Harrison, who in writing "My Sweet Lord" was found to have unconsciously copied "He's So Fine," which had topped the charts for a few weeks in 1963 in a version by the Chiffons. ABKCO Music, Inc. v. Harrisongs Music, Ltd., 722 F.2d 988 (2d Cir.1983). Damages would have been $1.6 million, but plaintiff Klein, who was the Beatles' former manager, was found guilty of a gross fiduciary breach in buying up the claim against Harrison, which limited his right to relief. (See also 944 F.2d 971 (2d Cir.1991), for further tortuous developments in the accounting phase of this twenty-year long case.)

Valuable articles on musical infringement include Jones, Music Copyright in Theory and Practice: An Improved Approach for Determining Substantial Similarity, 31 Duq.L.Rev. 277 (1993), and Metzger, Name That Tune: A Proposal for an Intrinsic Test of Musical Plagiarism, 5 Loy. Ent.L.J. 61 (1985) (by a conductor and musicologist).

(4) Are our modern ideas about authorship and originality too idealistic? In a review of a production of John Gay's *The Beggar's Opera*, music critic Richard Morrison, recounting how classical music has thrived on recycled melodies, points out how much poorer our musical heritage would be if current notions of copyright infringement had applied. He argues that Bach, for example, took melodies for a number of works from hymns in the Lutheran hymnbook (which in many cases the Lutherans had lifted from minstrel songs and ballads). When a friend remarked to Brahms that the finale of his *First Symphony* sounded a lot like the *Ode to Joy* from Beethoven's Ninth, Brahms responded that "any fool can hear that." Of the sixty-nine songs in the original version of *The Beggar's Opera* (described by Morrison as "the *magnum opus* of plagiarism"), apparently none had an original melody. Gay even took a tune from his popular contemporary George Frideric Handel, who could hardly complain since Handel himself was perhaps the biggest borrower of all. Handel, however, vastly improved whatever he took. "Handel took other men's pebbles and polished them into diamonds," according to composer William Boyce. Should that excuse the borrowing? The Times, April 7, 1993, p. 29.[a]

Arnstein v. Porter

United States Circuit Court of Appeals, Second Circuit, 1946.
154 F.2d 464.

Appeal from the District Court of the United States for the Southern District of New York.

Action by Ira B. Arnstein against Cole Porter for infringement of copyrights, infringement of right to uncopyrighted musical compositions and wrongful use of the titles of others. From a judgment dismissing action on defendant's motion for summary judgment, the plaintiff appeals.

Modified in part; otherwise reversed and remanded.

Plaintiff, a citizen and resident of New York, brought this suit, charging infringement by defendant, a citizen and resident of New York, of plaintiff's copyrights to several musical compositions, infringement of his rights to other uncopyrighted musical compositions, and wrongful use of the titles of others. Plaintiff, when filing his complaint, demanded a jury trial. Plaintiff took the deposition of defendant, and defendant, the deposition of plaintiff. Defendant then moved for an order striking out plaintiff's jury demand, and for summary judgment. Attached to defendant's motion papers were the depositions, phonograph records of piano renditions of the plaintiff's compositions and defendant's alleged infringing compositions, and the court records of five previous copyright infringement suits brought by plaintiff in the court below against other persons, in which judgments

a. Literature offers its own illustrations. Giants like Chaucer, Virgil, and Milton were all voracious appropriators. See A. Lindey, Plagiarism and Originality 65–77 (1952). According to one analysis, Shakespeare—described by Lindey as evincing "a marked propensity for avoiding unnecessary invention"—copied 1,771 lines and paraphrased another 2,373 in producing the 6,033 lines in *Henry VI, Pts. I, II, and III.* Id. at 73–75.

had been entered, after trials, against plaintiff. Defendant also moved for dismissal of the action on the ground of "vexatiousness."

Plaintiff alleged that defendant's "Begin the Beguine" is a plagiarism from plaintiff's "The Lord Is My Shepherd" and "A Mother's Prayer." Plaintiff testified, on deposition, that "The Lord Is My Shepherd" had been published and about 2,000 copies sold, that "A Mother's Prayer" had been published, over a million copies having been sold. In his depositions, he gave no direct evidence that defendant saw or heard these compositions. He also alleged that defendant's "My Heart Belongs to Daddy" had been plagiarized from plaintiff's "A Mother's Prayer."

Plaintiff also alleged that defendant's "I Love You" is a plagiarism from plaintiff's composition "La Priere," stating in his deposition that the latter composition had been sold. He gave no direct proof that plaintiff knew of this composition.

He also alleged that defendant's song "Night and Day" is a plagiarism of plaintiff's song "I Love You Madly," which he testified had not been published but had once been publicly performed over the radio, copies having been sent to divers radio stations but none to defendant; a copy of this song, plaintiff testified, had been stolen from his room. He also alleged that "I Love You Madly" ["Night and Day"?] was in part plagiarized from "La Priere." He further alleged that defendant's "You'd Be So Nice To Come Home To" is plagiarized from plaintiff's "Sadness Overwhelms My Soul." He testified that this song had never been published or publicly performed but that copies had been sent to a movie producer and to several publishers. He also alleged that defendant's "Don't Fence Me In" is a plagiarism of plaintiff's song "A Modern Messiah" which has not been published or publicly performed; in his deposition he said that about a hundred copies had been sent to divers radio stations and band leaders but that he sent no copy to defendant. Plaintiff said that defendant "had stooges right along to follow me, watch me, and live in the same apartment with me," and that plaintiff's room had been ransacked on several occasions. Asked how he knew that defendant had anything to do with any of these "burglaries," plaintiff said, "I don't know that he had to do with it, but I only know that he could have." He also said " * * * many of my compositions had been published. No one had to break in to steal them. They were sung publicly."

Defendant in his deposition categorically denied that he had ever seen or heard any of plaintiff's compositions or had had any acquaintance with any person said to have stolen any of them.

The prayer of plaintiff's original complaint asked "at least one million dollars out of the millions the defendant has earned and is earning out of all the plagiarism." In his amended complaint the prayer is "for judgment against the defendant in the sum of $1,000,000 as damages sustained by the plagiarism of all the compositions named in the complaint." Plaintiff, not a lawyer, appeared pro se below and on this appeal.

■ Before L. HAND, CLARK, and FRANK, CIRCUIT JUDGES.

■ FRANK, CIRCUIT JUDGE. 1. Plaintiff with his complaint filed a jury demand which defendant moved to strike out. Defendant urges that the relief prayed in the complaint renders a jury trial inappropriate. We do not agree. Plaintiff did not ask for an injunction but solely for damages. Such a suit is an action at "law." That it is founded solely on a statute does not deprive either party of a right to a trial by jury; an action for treble damages under the Sherman Act is likewise purely statutory, but it is triable at "law" and by a jury as of right.

2. The principal question on this appeal is whether the lower court, under Rule 56,[4a] properly deprived plaintiff of a trial of his copyright infringement action. The answer depends on whether "there is the slightest doubt as to the facts." Doehler Metal Furniture Co. v. United States, 2 Cir., 149 F.2d 130, 135 * * *. In applying that standard here, it is important to avoid confusing two separate elements essential to a plaintiff's case in such a suit: (a) that defendant copied from plaintiff's copyrighted work and (b) that the copying (assuming it to be proved) went so far as to constitute improper appropriation.

As to the first—copying—the evidence may consist (a) of defendant's admission that he copied or (b) of circumstantial evidence—usually evidence of access—from which the trier of the facts may reasonably infer copying. Of course, if there are no similarities, no amount of evidence of access will suffice to prove copying. If there is evidence of access and similarities exist, then the trier of the facts must determine whether the similarities are sufficient to prove copying. On this issue, analysis ("dissection") is relevant, and the testimony of experts may be received to aid the trier of the facts. If evidence of access is absent, the similarities must be so striking as to preclude the possibility that plaintiff and defendant independently arrived at the same result.

If copying is established, then only does there arise the second issue, that of illicit copying (unlawful appropriation). On that issue (as noted more in detail below) the test is the response of the ordinary lay hearer; accordingly, on that issue, "dissection" and expert testimony are irrelevant.

In some cases, the similarities between the plaintiff's and defendant's work are so extensive and striking as, without more, both to justify an inference of copying and to prove improper appropriation. But such double-purpose evidence is not required; that is, if copying is otherwise shown, proof of improper appropriation need not consist of similarities which, standing alone, would support an inference of copying.

Each of these two issues—copying and improper appropriation—is an issue of fact. If there is a trial, the conclusions on those issues of the trier of the facts—of the judge if he sat without a jury, or of the jury if there was a jury trial—bind this court on appeal, provided the evidence supports those findings, regardless of whether we would ourselves have reached the

---

4a. The Federal Rules of Civil Procedure, 28 U.S.C.A. following section 723c, are applicable to copyright actions; see amendment, adopted June 5, 1939 to Rule 1 of Rules of Practice under § 25 of the Copyright Act.

same conclusions. But a case could occur in which the similarities were so striking that we would reverse a finding of no access, despite weak evidence of access (or no evidence thereof other than the similarities); and similarly as to a finding of no illicit appropriation.

3. We turn first to the issue of copying. After listening to the compositions as played in the phonograph recordings submitted by defendant, we find similarities; but we hold that unquestionably, standing alone, they do not compel the conclusion, or permit the inference, that defendant copied. The similarities, however, are sufficient so that, if there is enough evidence of access to permit the case to go to the jury, the jury may properly infer that the similarities did not result from coincidence.

Summary judgment was, then, proper if indubitably defendant did not have access to plaintiff's compositions. Plainly that presents an issue of fact. On that issue, the district judge, who heard no oral testimony, had before him the depositions of plaintiff and defendant. The judge characterized plaintiff's story as "fantastic"; and, in the light of the references in his opinion to defendant's deposition, the judge obviously accepted defendant's denial of access and copying. Although part of plaintiff's testimony on deposition (as to "stooges" and the like) does seem "fantastic," yet plaintiff's credibility, even as to those improbabilities, should be left to the jury. If evidence is "of a kind that greatly taxes the credulity of the judge, he can say so, or, if he totally disbelieves it, he may announce that fact, leaving the jury free to believe it or not." * * * We should not overlook the shrewd proverbial admonition that sometimes truth is stranger than fiction.

But even if we were to disregard the improbable aspects of plaintiff's story, there remain parts by no means "fantastic." On the record now before us, more than a million copies of one of his compositions were sold; copies of others were sold in smaller quantities or distributed to radio stations or band leaders or publishers, or the pieces were publicly performed. If, after hearing both parties testify, the jury disbelieves defendant's denials, it can, from such facts, reasonably infer access. It follows that, as credibility is unavoidably involved, a genuine issue of material fact presents itself. * * *

We do not believe that, in a case in which the decision must turn on the reliability of witnesses, the Supreme Court, by authorizing summary judgments, intended to permit a "trial by affidavits," if either party objects. That procedure which, so the historians tell us, began to be outmoded at common law in the 16th century, would, if now revived, often favor unduly the party with the more ingenious and better paid lawyer. Grave injustice might easily result. * * *

4. Assuming that adequate proof is made of copying, that is not enough; for there can be "permissible copying," [18] copying which is not

---

18. Dymow v. Bolton, 2 Cir., 11 F.2d 690, 692; Oxford Book Co. v. College Entrance Book Co., 2 Cir., 98 F.2d 688, 692; Eggers v. Sun Sales Co., 2 Cir., 263 F. 373, 375; Mathews Conveyer Co. v. Palmer–Bee Co., 6 Cir., 135 F.2d 73, 84–85; cf. Folsom v.

illicit. Whether (if he copied) defendant unlawfully appropriated presents, too, an issue of fact. The proper criterion on that issue is not an analytic or other comparison of the respective musical compositions as they appear on paper or in the judgment of trained musicians.[19] The plaintiff's legally protected interest is not, as such, his reputation as a musician but his interest in the potential financial returns from his compositions which derive from the lay public's approbation of his efforts. The question, therefore, is whether defendant took from plaintiff's works so much of what is pleasing to the ears of lay listeners, who comprise the audience for whom such popular music is composed, that defendant wrongfully appropriated something which belongs to the plaintiff.

Surely, then, we have an issue of fact which a jury is peculiarly fitted to determine.[22] Indeed, even if there were to be a trial before a judge, it would be desirable (although not necessary) for him to summon an advisory jury on this question.

We should not be taken as saying that a plagiarism case can never arise in which absence of similarities is so patent that a summary judgment for defendant would be correct. Thus suppose that Ravel's "Bolero" or Shostakovitch's "Fifth Symphony" were alleged to infringe "When Irish Eyes Are Smiling."[23] But this is not such a case. For, after listening to the playing of the respective compositions, we are, at this time, unable to conclude that the likenesses are so trifling that, on the issue of misappropriation, a trial judge could legitimately direct a verdict for defendant.

At the trial, plaintiff may play, or cause to be played, the pieces in such manner that they may seem to a jury to be inexcusably alike, in terms of the way in which lay listeners of such music would be likely to react. The plaintiff may call witnesses whose testimony may aid the jury in reaching its conclusion as to the responses of such audiences. Expert testimony of musicians may also be received, but it will in no way be controlling on the issue of illicit copying, and should be utilized only to assist in determining the reactions of lay auditors. The impression made on the refined ears of musical experts or their views as to the musical excellence of plaintiff's or defendant's works are utterly immaterial on the issue of misappropriation; for the views of such persons are caviar to the general—and plaintiff's and defendant's compositions are not caviar. * * *

[After disposing of some minor points, Judge Frank considered defendant's motion for dismissal of the action as vexatious, pointing to five similar actions that Arnstein had brought against other defendants.]

Marsh, 9 Fed.Cas. No. 4901, at pages 344, 345; Chatterton v. Cave, 3 A.C. 483; Macmillan Co. v. King, D.C., 223 F. 862, 863; 13 C.J. 1127–1128, 1132; 18 C.J.S., Copyright and Literary Property, §§ 105, 109.

19. Where plaintiff relies on similarities to prove copying (as distinguished from improper appropriation) paper comparisons and the opinions of experts may aid the court.

22. It would, accordingly, be proper to exclude tone-deaf persons from the jury, cf. Chatterton v. Cave, 3 A.C. 483, 499–501, 502–504 [H.L.1878].

23. In such a case, the complete absence of similarity would negate both copying and improper appropriation.

* * * [W]e regard it as entirely improper to give any weight to other actions lost by plaintiff. * * * Absent the factors which make up res judicata (not present here), each case must stand on its own bottom, subject, of course, to the doctrine of stare decisis. Succumbing to the temptation to consider other defeats suffered by a party may lead a court astray; see, e.g., Southern Pacific Co. v. Bogert, 250 U.S. 483, 489, note 1. When a particular suit is vexatious, sometimes at its conclusion the court can give some redress to the victorious party. Perhaps the Legislature can and should meet this problem more effectively. But we surely must not do so, as defendant here would have us do, by prejudging the merits of the case before us.

Modified in part; otherwise reversed and remanded. * * *

■ CLARK, CIRCUIT JUDGE (dissenting). While the procedure followed below seems to me generally simple and appropriate, the defendant did make one fatal tactical error. In an endeavor to assist us, he caused to be prepared records of all the musical pieces here involved, and presented these transcriptions through the medium of the affidavit of his pianist. Though he himself did not stress these records and properly met plaintiff's claims as to the written music with his own analysis, yet the tinny tintinnabulations of the music thus canned resounded through the United States Courthouse to the exclusion of all else, including the real issues in the case. Of course, sound is important in a case of this kind, but it is not so important as to falsify what the eye reports and the mind teaches. Otherwise plagiarism would be suggested by the mere drumming of repetitious sound from our usual popular music, as it issues from a piano, orchestra, or hurdy-gurdy—particularly when ears may be dulled by long usage, possibly artistic repugnance or boredom, or mere distance which causes all sounds to merge. And the judicial eardrum may be peculiarly insensitive after long years of listening to the "beat, beat, beat" (I find myself plagiarizing from defendant and thus in danger of my brothers' doom) of sound upon it, though perhaps no more so than the ordinary citizen juror—even if tone deafness is made a disqualification for jury service, as advocated.

Pointing to the adscititious fortuity inherent in the stated standard is, it seems to me, the fact that after repeated hearings of the records, I could not find therein what my brothers found. The only thing definitely mentioned seemed to be the repetitive use of the note e^2 in certain places by both plaintiff and defendant, surely too simple and ordinary a device of composition to be significant. In our former musical plagiarism cases we have, naturally, relied on what seemed the total sound effect; but we have also analyzed the music enough to make sure of an intelligible and intellectual decision. Thus in Arnstein v. Edward B. Marks Music Corp., 2 Cir., 82 F.2d 275, 277, Judge L. Hand made quite an extended comparison of the songs, concluding, inter alia: " * * * the seven notes available do not admit of so many agreeable permutations that we need be amazed at the re-appearance of old themes, even though the identity extend through a sequence of twelve notes." See also the discussion in Marks v. Leo Feist,

Inc., 2 Cir., 290 F. 959, and Darrell v. Joe Morris Music Co., 2 Cir., 113 F.2d 80, where the use of six similar bars and of an eight-note sequence frequently repeated were respectively held not to constitute infringement, and Wilkie v. Santly Bros., 2 Cir., 91 F.2d 978, affirming, D.C.S.D.N.Y., 13 F.Supp. 136, certiorari denied Santly Bros. v. Wilkie, 302 U.S. 735, where use of eight bars with other similarities amounting to over three-quarters of the significant parts was held infringement.[1]

It is true that in Arnstein v. Broadcast Music, Inc., 2 Cir., 137 F.2d 410, 412, we considered "dissection" or "technical analysis" not the proper approach to support a finding of plagiarism, and said that it must be "more ingenuous, more like that of a spectator, who would rely upon the complex of his impressions." But in its context that seems to me clearly sound and in accord with what I have in mind. Thus one may look to the total impression to repulse the charge of plagiarism where a minute "dissection" might dredge up some points of similarity. Hence one cannot use a purely theoretical disquisition to supply a tonal resemblance which does not otherwise exist. Certainly, however, that does not suggest or compel the converse—that one must keep his brain in torpor for fear that otherwise it would make clear differences which do exist. Music is a matter of the intellect as well as the emotions; that is why eminent musical scholars insist upon the employment of the intellectual faculties for a just appreciation of music. * * *

Since the legal issue seems thus clear to me, I am loath to believe that my colleagues will uphold a final judgment of plagiarism on a record such as this. The present holding is therefore one of those procedural mountains which develop where it is thought that justice must be temporarily sacrificed, lest a mistaken precedent be set at large. The conclusion that the precedent would be mistaken appears to rest on two premises: a belief in the efficacy of the jury to settle issues of plagiarism, and a dislike of the rule established by the Supreme Court as to summary judgments. Now, as to the first, I am not one to condemn jury trials (cf. Keller v. Brooklyn Bus Corp., 2 Cir., 128 F.2d 510, 517; Frank, If Men Were Angels, 1942, 80–101;

---

1. In accord is Shafter, Musical Copyright, 2d Ed.1939, c. 6, particularly p. 205, where the author speaks of "the 'comparative method,' worked out by Judge Learned Hand with great success," and "his successful method of analysis," citing Hein v. Harris, C.C.S.D.N.Y., 175 F. 875, affirmed 2 Cir., 183 F. 107, and Haas v. Leo Feist, Inc., D.C.S.D.N.Y., 234 F. 105; and p. 194, where he approves of Judge Yankwich's course in attaching an exhibit of analysis to his opinion in Hirsch v. Paramount Pictures, Inc., D.C.S.D.Cal., 17 F.Supp. 816—"this sensible procedure," "a splendid model for future copyright decisions." I find nowhere any suggestion of two steps in adjudication of this issue, one of finding copying which may be approached with musical intelligence and assistance of experts, and another that of illicit copying which must be approached with complete ignorance; nor do I see how rationally there can be any such difference, even if a jury—the now chosen instrument of musical detection—could be expected to separate those issues and the evidence accordingly. If there is actual copying, it is actionable, and there are no degrees; what we are dealing with is the claim of similarities sufficient to justify the inference of copying. This is a single deduction to be made intelligently, not two with the dominating one to be made blindly.

Frank, Law and the Modern Mind, 1930, 170–185, 302–309, 344–348), since I think it has a place among other quite finite methods of fact-finding. But I should not have thought it pre-eminently fitted to decide questions of musical values, certainly not so much so that an advisory jury should be brought in if no other is available. And I should myself hesitate to utter so clear an invitation to exploitation of slight musical analogies by clever musical tricks in the hope of getting juries hereafter in this circuit to divide the wealth of Tin Pan Alley. * * *

[Judge Clark concludes his dissent with a spirited defense of federal summary judgment procedure, of which he was one of the chief architects.][b]

NOTES AND QUESTIONS

(1) Judges Frank and Clark continued their quarrel in Heim v. Universal Pictures Co., 154 F.2d 480 (2d Cir.1946). Some of the by-play accompanying their differences is recounted in Schuck, Judicial Relations in the Second Circuit, 1941–1951, 44 N.Y.U.L.Rev. 939, 943–46 (1969). Can you distinguish their views about summary judgment from their views about how infringement should be determined?

(2) Suppose plaintiff can establish that the defendant derived her song by playing plaintiff's song backward. A. Shafter, Musical Copyright 213 (2d ed. 1939), argues that this would be an infringement. Do you agree? Would Judge Frank or Judge Clark?

(3) Despite Arnstein v. Porter, summary judgments are often granted to defendants in infringement cases. Hartnick, Summary Judgment in Copyright: From Cole Porter to Superman, 3 Cardozo Arts & Ent.L.J. 53, 70 (1984), concludes that on the issue of summary judgment, "*Arnstein* is dead but not buried." In Walker v. Time Life Films, Inc., 784 F.2d 44 (2d Cir.), cert. denied, 476 U.S. 1159 (1986), for example, Judge Feinberg for the Second Circuit said that "a district court may determine noninfringement as a matter of law on a motion for summary judgment either when the similarity concerns only noncopyrightable elements of plaintiff's work, or when no reasonable trier of fact could find the works substantially similar," citing Warner Bros. v. American Broadcasting Co., p. 259 infra. The court affirmed a summary judgment in favor of the producers of the movie "Fort Apache: The Bronx" in the face of an infringement claim by the author of "Fort Apache," an anecdotal account of life in a South Bronx precinct of the New York City Police Department. The Ninth Circuit, although noting that "as a general rule, summary judgment is not highly favored on the substantial similarity issue in copyright cases," Berkic v. Crichton, 761 F.2d 1289 (9th Cir.), cert. denied, 474 U.S. 826 (1985), has said that "there is no special standard" for summary judgment on substan-

b. On Arnstein as a litigant, see Lindey, Plagiarism and Originality 193–95 (1952). In the instant case, a jury verdict for Porter was ultimately affirmed, 158 F.2d 795 (2d Cir.1946), cert. denied, 330 U.S. 851 (1947).

tial similarity. Frybarger v. International Business Machines Corp., 812 F.2d 525 (9th Cir.1987).

(4) In Hoehling v. Universal Cities Studios, Inc., p. 266 infra, the Second Circuit, quoting *Arnstein*, said that plaintiff "must demonstrate that defendants 'copied' his work and that they 'improperly appropriated' his 'expression.'" The court added that "[o]rdinarily, wrongful appropriation is shown by proving a 'substantial similarity' of *copyrightable* expression." In the "Fort Apache" case, supra, the court said that *Arnstein* and *Hoehling* required the plaintiff to "show that his book was 'copied,' by proving access and substantial similarity between the works, and also show that his expression was 'improperly appropriated,' by proving that the similarities relate to copyrightable material." In a later case, the Second Circuit noted that "the presence of a 'substantial similarity' requirement in both prongs of the analysis—actual copying and whether the copying constitutes an improper appropriation—creates the potential for unnecessary confusion." Laureyssens v. Idea Group, Inc., 964 F.2d 131 (2d Cir.1992). The court then proceeded to restate the required elements:

> A plaintiff must first show that his or her work was actually copied. Copying may be established either by direct evidence of copying or by indirect evidence, including access to the copyrighted work, similarities that are probative of copying between the works, and expert testimony. If actual copying is established, a plaintiff must then show that the copying amounts to an improper appropriation by demonstrating that substantial similarity to protected material exists between the two works.

Professor Latman, in the posthumously published "Probative Similarity" as Proof of Copying: Toward Dispelling Some Myths in Copyright Infringement, 90 Colum.L.Rev. 1187 (1990), is supportive of the two-step approach propounded in *Arnstein*. A variation of the two-step approach, introduced by the Ninth Circuit in Sid & Marty Krofft Television Productions v. McDonald's Corp., p. 248 infra, will be considered later.

EXPERT TESTIMONY IN INFRINGEMENT CASES

The use of expert witnesses in musical infringement cases apparently has been commonplace since the earliest American cases. In Reed v. Carusi, 20 Fed.Cas. 431 (C.C.D.Md.1845) (No. 11,642), defendant brought in experts to point out the dissimilarities between his ballad and the plaintiff's. However, a jury verdict following a charge by Chief Justice Taney went for the plaintiff. (Orth, The Use of Expert Witnesses in Musical Infringement Cases, 16 U.Pitt.L.Rev. 232, 247 (1955), found no other reported musical infringement case in which a plaintiff wanted a jury trial until Arnstein v. Porter, a century later.)

The majority in *Arnstein* is hostile to expert testimony on the issue of "improper appropriation." Judge Clark in dissent fears that the majority invites drowning the judgment of the trier of fact in an unanalyzed welter of seemingly similar sounds. But any expert testimony and close analysis offered on the issue of "copying" also will likely influence the determination of "improper appropriation."[c] And the majority does allow expert testimony even on "improper appropriation," limited to proving the probable reaction of "lay listeners of such music." In Baxter v. MCA, Inc., 812 F.2d 421 (9th Cir.), cert. denied, 484 U.S. 954 (1987), the Ninth Circuit, in a case in which the alleged infringing work was the musical theme from the motion picture "E.T.: The Extra–Terrestrial," took the similar position that " '[a]nalytic dissection' and expert testimony are not called for; the gauge of substantial similarity is the response of the ordinary lay hearer," citing *Arnstein*.

Why eschew the potential insights afforded by a detailed or expert comparison of the alleged infringed and infringing works in favor of the visceral reaction of an "ordinary lay hearer"? Does the choice reflect a decision about the underlying purpose of copyright law? Should the standard focus on the reaction of an ordinary person—or on the reaction of an ordinary member of the audience or market to which the work is directed? Which standard is adopted in Arnstein v. Porter? See Dawson v. Hinshaw Music Inc., 905 F.2d 731 (4th Cir.), cert. denied, 498 U.S. 981 (1990), adopting an "intended audience" interpretation of the ordinary observer test for works directed at consumers with specialized knowledge or expertise that might affect their purchasing decisions. See also Note, Copyright Infringement Actions: The Proper Role for Audience Reactions in Determining Substantial Similarity, 54 S.Cal.L.Rev. 385 (1981).

In the field of literary infringement, expert testimony also has been sharply criticized. See Judge Hand's strictures in the *Nichols* case, p. 195 supra, and Judge Yankwich's in Cain v. Universal Pictures Co., Inc., 47 F.Supp. 1013, 1015 (S.D.Cal.1942). It may be noted, however, that unduly elaborate dissections and unconvincing parallels are as likely to be the work of obsessed plaintiffs as of experts. For some ludicrous examples, see A. Lindey, Plagiarism and Originality, ch. 5 (1952).

Extensive dissection quite naturally will be undertaken in a crowded field like the fictionalized history of the Civil War to prove (or disprove) that the defendant borrowed from plaintiff's work rather than from source materials in the public domain. For two such cases where plaintiffs made plausible though unsuccessful demonstrations, see Eisenschiml v. Fawcett Publications, Inc., 246 F.2d 598 (7th Cir.1957), and Greenbie v. Noble, 151 F.Supp. 45 (S.D.N.Y.1957).

---

c. For an example of (conflicting) expert testimony on the "copying" issue, see Repp & K&R Music, Inc. v. Webber, 132 F.3d 882 (2d Cir.1997), involving Andrew Lloyd Webber and the "Phantom Song" from *The Phantom of the Opera*.

SECTION 3. SUBSTANTIAL SIMILARITY IN VISUAL WORKS

Steinberg v. Columbia Pictures Industries, Inc.

United States District Court, Southern District of New York, 1987.
663 F.Supp. 706.

■ STANTON, DISTRICT JUDGE.

In these actions for copyright infringement, plaintiff Saul Steinberg is suing the producers, promoters, distributors and advertisers of the movie "Moscow on the Hudson" ("Moscow"). Steinberg is an artist whose fame derives in part from cartoons and illustrations he has drawn for *The New Yorker* magazine. Defendant Columbia Pictures Industries, Inc. (Columbia) is in the business of producing, promoting and distributing motion pictures, including "Moscow." * * *

Plaintiff alleges that defendants' promotional poster for "Moscow" infringes his copyright on an illustration that he drew for *The New Yorker* and that appeared on the cover of the March 29, 1976 issue of the magazine, in violation of 17 U.S.C. §§ 101–810. Defendants deny this allegation and assert the affirmative defenses of fair use as a parody, estoppel and laches.

Defendants have moved, and plaintiff has cross-moved, for summary judgment. For the reasons set forth below, this court rejects defendants' asserted defenses and grants summary judgment on the issue of copying to plaintiff. * * *

The essential facts are not disputed by the parties despite their disagreements on nonessential matters. On March 29, 1976, *The New Yorker* published as a cover illustration the work at issue in this suit, widely known as a parochial New Yorker's view of the world. The magazine registered this illustration with the United States Copyright Office and subsequently assigned the copyright to Steinberg. Approximately three months later, plaintiff and *The New Yorker* entered into an agreement to print and sell a certain number of posters of the cover illustration.

It is undisputed that unauthorized duplications of the poster were made and distributed by unknown persons, although the parties disagree on the extent to which plaintiff attempted to prevent the distribution of those counterfeits. Plaintiff has also conceded that numerous posters have been created and published depicting other localities in the same manner that he depicted New York in his illustration. These facts, however, are irrelevant to the merits of this case, which concerns only the relationship between plaintiff's and defendants' illustrations.

Defendants' illustration was created to advertise the movie "Moscow on the Hudson," which recounts the adventures of a Muscovite who defects

Reproduced by permission of Columbia Pictures.

in New York. In designing this illustration, Columbia's executive art director, Kevin Nolan, has admitted that he specifically referred to Steinberg's poster, and indeed, that he purchased it and hung it, among others, in his office. Furthermore, Nolan explicitly directed the outside artist whom he retained to execute his design, Craig Nelson, to use Steinberg's poster to achieve a more recognizably New York look. Indeed, Nelson acknowledged having used the facade of one particular edifice, at Nolan's suggestion that it would render his drawing more "New York-ish." Curtis Affidavit ¶ 28(c). While the two buildings are not identical, they are so similar that it is impossible, especially in view of the artist's testimony, not to find that defendants' impermissibly copied plaintiff's.[1]

To decide the issue of infringement, it is necessary to consider the posters themselves. Steinberg's illustration presents a bird's eye view across a portion of the western edge of Manhattan, past the Hudson River and a telescoped version of the rest of the United States and the Pacific Ocean, to a red strip of horizon, beneath which are three flat land masses labeled China, Japan and Russia. The name of the magazine, in *The New Yorker's* usual typeface, occupies the top fifth of the poster, beneath a thin band of blue wash representing a stylized sky.

The parts of the poster beyond New York are minimalized, to symbolize a New Yorker's myopic view of the centrality of his city to the world. The entire United States west of the Hudson River, for example, is reduced to a brown strip labeled "Jersey," together with a light green trapezoid with a few rudimentary rock outcroppings and the names of only seven cities and two states scattered across it. The few blocks of Manhattan, by contrast, are depicted and colored in detail. The four square blocks of the city, which occupy the whole lower half of the poster, include numerous buildings, pedestrians and cars, as well as parking lots and lamp posts, with water towers atop a few of the buildings. The whimsical, sketchy style and spiky lettering are recognizable as Steinberg's.

The "Moscow" illustration depicts the three main characters of the film on the lower third of their poster, superimposed on a bird's eye view of New York City, and continues eastward across Manhattan and the Atlantic Ocean, past a rudimentary evocation of Europe, to a clump of recognizably Russian-styled buildings on the horizon, labeled "Moscow." The movie credits appear over the lower portion of the characters. The central part of the poster depicts approximately four New York city blocks, with fairly detailed buildings, pedestrians and vehicles, a parking lot, and some water towers and lamp posts. Columbia's artist added a few New York landmarks at apparently random places in his illustration, apparently to render the locale more easily recognizable. Beyond the blue strip labeled "Atlantic Ocean," Europe is represented by London, Paris and Rome, each

---

1. Nolan claimed also to have been inspired by some of the posters that were inspired by Steinberg's; such secondary inspiration, however, is irrelevant to whether or not the "Moscow" poster infringes plaintiff's copyright by having impermissibly copied it.

anchored by a single landmark (although the landmark used for Rome is the Leaning Tower of Pisa).

The horizon behind Moscow is delineated by a red crayoned strip, above which are the title of the movie and a brief textual introduction to the plot. The poster is crowned by a thin strip of blue wash, apparently a stylization of the sky. This poster is executed in a blend of styles: the three characters, whose likenesses were copied from a photograph, have realistic faces and somewhat sketchy clothing, and the city blocks are drawn in a fairly detailed but sketchy style. The lettering on the drawing is spiky, in block-printed handwritten capital letters substantially identical to plaintiff's, while the printed texts at the top and bottom of the poster are in the typeface commonly associated with *The New Yorker* magazine.[2]

To succeed in a copyright infringement action, a plaintiff must prove ownership of the copyright and copying by the defendant. Reyher v. Children's Television Workshop, 533 F.2d 87, 90 (2d Cir.1976); Durham Industries, [Inc. v. Tomy Corp., 630 F.2d 905, 911 (2d Cir.1980)]; Novelty Textile Mills, Inc. v. Joan Fabrics Corp., 558 F.2d 1090, 1092 (2d Cir.1977). There is no substantial dispute concerning plaintiff's ownership of a valid copyright in his illustration. Therefore, in order to prevail on liability, plaintiff need establish only the second element of the cause of action.

"Because of the inherent difficulty in obtaining direct evidence of copying, it is usually proved by circumstantial evidence of access to the copyrighted work and substantial similarities as to protectible material in the two works." *Reyher*, 533 F.2d at 90, citing Arnstein v. Porter, 154 F.2d 464, 468 (2d Cir.1946). See also *Novelty Textile Mills*, 558 F.2d at 1092. "Of course, if there are no similarities, no amount of evidence of access will suffice to prove copying." Arnstein v. Porter, 154 F.2d at 468. See also *Novelty Textile Mills*, 558 F.2d at 1092 n. 2. * * *

The definition of "substantial similarity" in this circuit is "whether an average lay observer would recognize the alleged copy as having been appropriated from the copyrighted work." Ideal Toy Corp. v. Fab–Lu Ltd., 360 F.2d 1021, 1022 (2d Cir.1966); Silverman v. CBS, Inc., [632 F.Supp. 1344, 1351–52 (S.D.N.Y.1986)]. A plaintiff need no longer meet the severe "ordinary observer" test established by Judge Learned Hand in Peter Pan Fabrics, Inc. v. Martin Weiner Corp., 274 F.2d 487 (2d Cir.1960). Uneeda Doll Co., Inc. v. Regent Baby Products Corp., 355 F.Supp. 438, 450 (E.D.N.Y.1972). Under Judge Hand's formulation, there would be substantial similarity only where "the ordinary observer, unless he set out to detect the disparities, would be disposed to overlook them, and regard their aesthetic appeal as the same." 274 F.2d at 489.

Moreover, it is now recognized that "[t]he copying need not be of every detail so long as the copy is substantially similar to the copyrighted work." Comptone Co. v. Rayex Corp., 251 F.2d 487, 488 (2d Cir.1958). See also

---

2. The typeface is not a subject of copyright, but the similarity reinforces the impression that defendants copied plaintiff's illustration.

Durham Industries, 630 F.2d at 911–12; *Novelty Textile Mills,* 558 F.2d at 1092–93.

In determining whether there is substantial similarity between two works, it is crucial to distinguish between an idea and its expression. * * *

There is no dispute that defendants cannot be held liable for using the *idea* of a map of the world from an egocentrically myopic perspective. No rigid principle has been developed, however, to ascertain when one has gone beyond the idea to the expression, and "[d]ecisions must therefore inevitably be ad hoc." Peter Pan Fabrics, Inc. v. Martin Weiner Corp., 274 F.2d 487, 489 (2d Cir.1960) (L. Hand, J.). As Judge Frankel once observed, "Good eyes and common sense may be as useful as deep study of reported and unreported cases, which themselves are tied to highly particularized facts." Couleur International Ltd. v. Opulent Fabrics, Inc., 330 F.Supp. 152, 153 (S.D.N.Y.1971).

Even at first glance, one can see the striking stylistic relationship between the posters, and since style is one ingredient of "expression," this relationship is significant. Defendants' illustration was executed in the sketchy, whimsical style that has become one of Steinberg's hallmarks. Both illustrations represent a bird's eye view across the edge of Manhattan and a river bordering New York City to the world beyond. Both depict approximately four city blocks in detail and become increasingly minimalist as the design recedes into the background. Both use the device of a narrow band of blue wash across the top of the poster to represent the sky, and both delineate the horizon with a band of primary red.[3]

The strongest similarity is evident in the rendering of the New York City blocks. Both artists chose a vantage point that looks directly down a wide two-way cross street that intersects two avenues before reaching a river. Despite defendants' protestations, this is not an inevitable way of depicting blocks in a city with a grid-like street system, particularly since most New York City cross streets are one-way. Since even a photograph may be copyrighted because "no photograph, however simple, can be unaffected by the personal influence of the author," Time Inc. v. Bernard Geis Assoc., 293 F.Supp. 130, 141 (S.D.N.Y.1968), quoting *Bleistein,* supra, one can hardly gainsay the right of an artist to protect his choice of perspective and layout in a drawing, especially in conjunction with the overall concept and individual details. Indeed, the fact that defendants changed the names of the streets while retaining the same graphic depiction weakens their case: had they intended their illustration realistically to depict the streets labeled on the poster, their four city blocks would not

---

3. Defendants claim that since this use of thin bands of primary colors is a traditional Japanese technique, their adoption of it cannot infringe Steinberg's copyright. This argument ignores the principle that while "[o]thers are free to copy the original ... [t]hey are not free to copy the copy." Bleistein v. Donaldson Lithographing Co., 188 U.S. 239, 250 (1903) (Holmes, J.). Cf. Dave Grossman Designs, Inc. v. Bortin, 347 F.Supp. 1150, 1156–57 (N.D.Ill.1972) (an artist may use the same subject and style as another "so long as the second artist does not *substantially copy* [the first artist's] specific expression of his idea.")

so closely resemble plaintiff's four city blocks. Moreover, their argument that they intended the jumble of streets and landmarks and buildings to symbolize their Muscovite protagonist's confusion in a new city does not detract from the strong similarity between their poster and Steinberg's.

While not all of the details are identical, many of them could be mistaken for one another; for example, the depiction of the water towers, and the cars, and the red sign above a parking lot, and even many of the individual buildings. The shapes, windows, and configurations of various edifices are substantially similar. The ornaments, facades and details of Steinberg's buildings appear in defendants', although occasionally at other locations. In this context, it is significant that Steinberg did not depict any buildings actually erected in New York; rather, he was inspired by the general appearance of the structures on the West Side of Manhattan to create his own New York-ish structures. Thus, the similarity between the buildings depicted in the "Moscow" and Steinberg posters cannot be explained by an assertion that the artists happened to choose the same buildings to draw. The close similarity can be explained only by the defendants' artist having copied the plaintiff's work. Similarly, the locations and size, the errors and anomalies of Steinberg's shadows and streetlight, are meticulously imitated.

In addition, the Columbia artist's use of the childlike, spiky block print that has become one of Steinberg's hallmarks to letter the names of the streets in the "Moscow" poster can be explained only as copying. There is no inherent justification for using this style of lettering to label New York City streets as it is associated with New York only through Steinberg's poster.

While defendants' poster shows the city of Moscow on the horizon in far greater detail than anything is depicted in the background of plaintiff's illustration, this fact alone cannot alter the conclusion. "Substantial similarity" does not require identity, and "duplication or near identity is not necessary to establish infringement." [Sid & Marty Krofft Television Productions, Inc. v. McDonald's Corp., 562 F.2d 1157, 1167 (9th Cir.1977)]. Neither the depiction of Moscow, nor the eastward perspective, nor the presence of randomly scattered New York City landmarks in defendants' poster suffices to eliminate the substantial similarity between the posters. As Judge Learned Hand wrote, "no plagiarist can excuse the wrong by showing how much of his work he did not pirate." Sheldon v. Metro–Goldwyn Pictures Corp., 81 F.2d 49, 56 (2d Cir.), cert. denied, 298 U.S. 669 (1936). * * *

I also reject defendants' argument that any similarities between the works are unprotectible *scenes a faire,* or "incidents, characters or settings which, as a practical matter, are indispensable or standard in the treatment of a given topic." [Walker v. Time Life Films, Inc., 615 F.Supp. 430, 434 (S.D.N.Y.1985), aff'd, 784 F.2d 44 (2d Cir.), cert. denied, 476 U.S. 1159 (1986)]. See also *Reyher,* 533 F.2d at 92. It is undeniable that a drawing of New York City blocks could be expected to include buildings, pedestrians, vehicles, lampposts and water towers. Plaintiff, however, does not complain of defendants' mere use of these elements in their poster; rather, his complaint is that defendants copied his *expression* of those elements of a street scene.   * * *

[The court next rejected defendants' "parody" defense under the fair use doctrine, finding that neither the movie nor the advertising poster was intended to parody the Steinberg illustration.   Judge Stanton then turned to the defendants' defenses of estoppel and laches.]

Defendants base their assertions of these equitable defenses on the following factual claims: (1) plaintiff's alleged "deliberate inaction" for eight years in the face of numerous counterfeits of his poster and adaptations of his idea to various other localities; * * *

The record, however, does not support defendants' claims.   First, Steinberg specifically requested that *The New Yorker* magazine attempt to identify the sources of the counterfeit posters and prevent their continued distribution.   As for the so-called adaptations of Steinberg's idea, there is no evidence that they infringed his copyright or that anyone ever believed that they did.   As plaintiff freely and necessarily admits, the law does not protect an idea, but only the specific expression of that idea.   The examples that defendants use to support their defense can at most be considered derivative of Steinberg's idea;   none is a close copy of the poster itself, as defendants' is.

[The court granted plaintiff's motion for summary judgment.]

NOTES AND QUESTIONS ON INFRINGEMENT OF VISUAL WORKS

(1) What happened to the two-step approach espoused in Arnstein v. Porter?   Judicial conflation of the "copying" and "improper appropriation" elements remains common, prompted in part by the relevance of "substantial similarity" to both elements of the plaintiff's case.

Did Columbia Pictures copy the "idea" of Steinberg's illustration?   Did Columbia Pictures copy Steinberg's "expression" of that idea?   Is Judge Stanton correct in viewing Steinberg's "style" and "choice of perspective" as aspects of copyrightable expression? (Do you find the two posters, which were not reproduced in the opinion, less similar than the court's descriptions suggest?)

(2) Judge Stanton's opinion declines to adopt the test for substantial similarity formulated by Learned Hand in Peter Pan Fabrics, Inc. v. Martin Weiner Corp., 274 F.2d 487 (2d Cir.1960).   That case involved infringement in the textile industry, a crowded and litigious field that has afforded numerous opportunities for judicial pronouncements on substantial similarity.   Judge Hand, upholding a preliminary injunction in favor of the owner of a design called "Byzantium," wrote:

"The test for infringement of a copyright is of necessity vague.   In the case of verbal 'works' it is well settled that although the 'proprietor's' monopoly extends beyond an exact reproduction of the words, there can be no copyright in the 'ideas' disclosed but only in their 'expression.'   Obviously, no principle can be stated as to when an imitator has gone beyond copying the 'idea,' and has borrowed its 'expression.' Decisions must therefore inevitably be *ad hoc*. In the case of designs, which are addressed to the aesthetic sensibilities of an observer, the test is, if possible, even more intangible. No one disputes that the copyright extends beyond a photographic reproduction of the design, but one cannot say how far an imitator must depart from an undeviating reproduction to escape infringement. In deciding that question one should consider the uses for which the design is intended, especially the scrutiny that observers will give to it as used. In the case at bar we must try to estimate how far its overall appearance will determine its aesthetic appeal when the cloth is made into a garment. Both designs have the same general color, and the arches, scrolls, rows of symbols, etc. on one resemble those on the other though they are not identical. Moreover, the patterns in which these figures are distributed to make up the design as a whole are not identical. However, the ordinary observer, unless he set out to detect the disparities, would be disposed to overlook them, and regard their aesthetic appeal as the same. That is enough; and indeed, it is all that can be said, unless protection against infringement is to be denied because of variants irrelevant to the purpose for which the design is intended."

How does Judge Hand's formulation differ from the one recited in *Steinberg,* which asks whether an observer "would recognize the alleged copy as having been appropriated from the copyrighted work"? In Ideal Toy Corp. v. Fab–Lu Ltd., 360 F.2d 1021 (2d Cir.1966), the doll infringement case from which the latter standard is taken, the test is followed by a citation to Hand's opinion in *Peter Pan Fabrics*. Judge Lumbard, in another textile design case, thought the two formulations interchangeable. See Dolori Fabrics, Inc. v. Limited, Inc., 662 F.Supp. 1347 (S.D.N.Y.1987).

In Loomskill, Inc. v. Stein & Fishman Fabrics, Inc., 332 F.Supp. 1288 (S.D.N.Y.1971), Judge Pollack found infringement clear, even though the defendant's fabric design "is built around figures of dogs whereas the copyrighted design is built around cats." Is that plausible? Judge Newman injected a note of caution in Beaudin v. Ben and Jerry's Homemade, Inc., 95 F.3d 1 (2d Cir.1996), holding that the ice cream maker's cow hats did not infringe plaintiff's black and white fabric design for cow jeans; when the quantum of originality is slight, only very close copying will infringe.

Another test for substantial similarity asks, again from the perspective of an ordinary observer, whether the defendant has captured "the total concept and feel" of the plaintiff's work. That phrase originated in Roth Greeting Cards v. United Card Co., 429 F.2d 1106 (9th Cir.1970), an interesting case about copyrightability and infringement of greeting cards. The standard has increasing currency, spurred especially by its recitation in Sid & Marty Krofft Television Productions, Inc. v. McDonald's Corp., another Ninth Circuit decision that appears at p. 248 infra. "Total concept and feel" now seems to be the principal test for substantial similarity of expression in the Ninth Circuit; it also has made appearances in other circuits.[a] Is the test a useful guide to decision? Does it stretch too far in defining infringement? None of the cases seem to pay any attention to the inclusion of "concept" in the catalog of subject matter barred from copyright in § 102(b).

(3) Video games now rival textile designs as a fertile ground for litigation. See, e.g., Data East USA, Inc. v. Epyx, Inc., 862 F.2d 204 (9th Cir.1988). See also Hemnes, The Adaptation of Copyright Law to Video Games, 131 U.Pa.L.Rev. 171 (1982) (valuable also for its general critique of infringement tests). Video games, dolls, and other modest works raise questions about when it is proper to find infringing substantial similarity in cases where there is an extensive public domain and a demand for naturalistic depictions. One approach is to be cautious about copyrightability. See, e.g., Kuddle Toy, Inc. v. Pussycat Toy Co., 183 U.S.P.Q. 642 (E.D.N.Y.1974) (insufficient originality in various versions of the classic teddy bear); Florabelle Flowers v. Joseph Markovits, Inc., 296 F.Supp. 304 (S.D.N.Y. 1968) (insufficient originality in plastic flowers). Another is to emphasize the limits of the plaintiff's exclusive rights. See, e.g., Data East USA, Inc., supra (similarities in video games follow from the idea of a martial arts game); Eden Toys, Inc. v. Marshall Field & Co., 675 F.2d 498 (2d Cir.1982) (no infringement because all snowmen dolls necessarily look alike).

(4) Can an ordinary observer test for substantial similarity deal adequately with the dichotomy between ideas and expressions? Consider McCulloch v. Albert E. Price, Inc., 823 F.2d 316 (9th Cir.1987). Plaintiff marketed a red dinner plate bearing a white floral design with the words "You Are Special Today" in white letters; defendant entered the market with a plate bearing the same phrase, although it was white with red letters and apparently had a different floral design. The court said that the question of infringement turned on "whether the 'ordinary reasonable person' would find the 'total concept and feel' of the works showed substantial similarity." Defendant argued that the uncopyrightable text should be discounted in evaluating substantial similarity; plaintiff responded that "proper analysis of this issue requires that all of the elements of the work, including the uncopyrightable text, be considered as a whole in determining copyright infringement." The court agreed with the plaintiff and affirmed a finding of infringement. Is this a sound result? See also Roulo v. Russ Berrie & Co., p. 642 infra, eschewing dissection and upholding a jury verdict that the defendant's greeting cards infringed the unique combination of otherwise common elements that characterized plaintiff's "sensitive verse" cards.

The Ninth Circuit refined its approach to substantial similarity in Aliotti v. R. Dakin & Co., 831 F.2d 898 (9th Cir.1987), a case about stuffed toy dinosaurs. Although adhering to the ordinary observer test, the court announced a qualification: "Although even unprotectable material should be considered when determining if there is substantial similarity of expres-

---

a. See, e.g., Knitwaves, Inc. v. Lollytogs, Ltd., 71 F.3d 996 (2d Cir.1995); Hartman v. Hallmark Cards, Inc., 833 F.2d 117, 120 (8th Cir.1987); Atari, Inc. v. North American Philips Consumer Electronics Corp., 672 F.2d 607, 614 (7th Cir.1982), cert. denied, 459 U.S. 880 (1982).

sion, see *McCulloch*, 823 F.2d at 320–21, no substantial similarity may be found under the intrinsic test where analytic dissection demonstrates that all similarities in expression arise from the use of common ideas." Because the similarities in the toys resulted either from the physiognomy of dinosaurs or the nature of stuffed animals, there was no infringement. A district court in California read *Aliotti* to mean that "[n]on-protectable matters in the works [one of which was the novel Gone With The Wind], such as ideas, facts and scenes-a-faire, must be excised before comparing the works as a whole to judge their total concept and feel." Trust Co. Bank v. The Putnam Pub. Group, Inc., 5 U.S.P.Q.2d 1874 (C.D.Cal.1988). Is *that* what the Ninth Circuit said in *Aliotti?* Is that what it *should have said?* Compare Concrete Machinery Co. v. Classic Lawn Ornaments, Inc., 843 F.2d 600 (1st Cir.1988), involving a menagerie of lawn statuary. Instructing the lower court on the standard for a preliminary injunction, the First Circuit said that "on rehearing, the court should 'dissect' the works to identify those aspects which [plaintiff] likely will be able to show are protected expression and were copied by [defendant]. Then, focusing on those aspects which are protected expression, the court should determine whether [plaintiff] is likely to prove, under the ordinary observer test, that [defendant's] works are substantially similar to its own."

Should the choice of approach turn on the nature of the works at issue? Abramson, How Much Copying Under Copyright? Contradictions, Paradoxes, Inconsistencies, 61 Temp.L.Rev. 133, 148 (1988), concludes that a "totalities" approach is suitable for musical and other nonverbal works, but less germane to literary works. *McCulloch,* supra, defending its "totalities" approach to the "You Are Special Today" plate, said that "factual" works would require a different approach. See, e.g., Cooling Systems and Flexibles, Inc. v. Stuart Radiator, Inc., 777 F.2d 485 (9th Cir.1985), rejecting "total concept and feel" in favor of a comparison of "the very small amount of protectible expression" in plaintiff's radiator catalog. (See also Hoehling v. Universal City Studios, Inc., p. 266 infra.) Cohen, Masking Copyright Decisionmaking: The Meaninglessness of Substantial Similarity, 20 U.C. Davis L.Rev. 719 (1987), expresses doubt about whether *any* version of the ordinary observer test can maintain an adequate distinction between idea and expression.

(5) Assuming access and a valid copyright, is plaintiff's toy ostrich "Popover" (see Figure 1) infringed by defendant's "Obee" (Figure 2)? See Gund, Inc. v. Russ Berrie & Co., 701 F.Supp. 1013 (S.N.D.Y.1988).

Is plaintiff Folio's fabric design "Pattern 1365" (Figure 3) infringed by defendant Lida's "Baroque Rose 7480" (Figure 4)? Does it matter that the plaintiff apparently took the background for its design from a source in the public domain? See Folio Impressions, Inc. v. Byer California, 937 F.2d 759 (2d Cir.1991).

(6) The issue of "substantial similarity" arose in a different context when Judge Newman considered a claim brought by the owner of a copyrighted work that had appeared without permission in the background of a scene in defendants' television series. "In cases involving visual works, like the

"Popover"
(Figure 1)

"Obee"
(Figure 2)

Folio's "Pattern 1365"
(Figure 3)

Lida's "Baroque Rose 7480"
(Figure 4)

pending one, the quantitative component of substantial similarity also concerns the observability of the copied work—the length of time the copied work is observable in the allegedly infringing work and such factors as focus, lighting, camera angles, and prominence." The court concluded that a four or five second segment in which most of the copyrighted work was visible (although not in perfect focus), reinforced by briefer segments in which smaller portions could be seen, was sufficient to establish actionable copying; it also reversed the lower court's summary judgment of fair use. Ringgold v. Black Entertainment Television, Inc., 126 F.3d 70 (2d Cir. 1997).

(7) The combination of laser and computer technologies raises new problems for the owners of copyrights in visual works, especially photographs. Photographs can be scanned by lasers and converted into digital data capable of being manipulated by a computer. The practical control over reproduction formerly maintained through physical possession of the negative has thus disappeared. The digital data can be altered to produce a new scene that never existed and parts of different works can be combined into a single image. *National Geographic* created a public controversy in 1982 when it "moved" two Egyptian pyramids closer together to fit a photograph onto its cover. Similarly, videotape can be scanned and altered frame by frame. This technology offers significant savings to producers—a handful of marching soldiers can be digitally cloned to create an infantry regiment or a photograph of Big Ben can be manipulated into the background of a movie or television scene shot in California.[b] The difficulty of distinguishing photographic fact from fiction is described in a cover story in *Scientific American*, February, 1994, illustrated with a "photograph" of Marilyn Monroe frolicking with Abraham Lincoln.

Is it infringement to take a cloud or a tree from a copyrighted photograph and use it as background in a new picture? And how can the owner even tell that a part of her work has been copied? Does unauthorized digital alteration by a licensee who has permission to reproduce the work infringe the copyright owner's derivative rights?

A NOTE ON COPYING THE COPY

Recall again Justice Holmes' remark in *Bleistein:* "Others are free to copy the original. They are not free to copy the copy." Consider the

b. An article in Discover, July, 1990, p. 53, reviews the technology and describes other examples: A cat that "for legal reasons" could no longer appear in a television commercial was digitally erased from each frame and the resulting hole closed by replicating additional background material. "Once the president of a major corporation gave a speech, which was videotaped, and part of his apparel wasn't zipped. That was fixed in the computer." In 1997 newspapers across the country ran an AP photograph of the National Spelling Bee winner leaping triumphantly with a large yellow placard identifying the New York Daily News as her sponsor hanging across her chest. When the rival New York Post ran the photo, the words "Daily News" had vanished from the picture. Herszenhorn, How Do You Spell E–R–A–S–E?, New York Times, June 1, 1997, Sec. 4, p. 2.

variation on the original subject—copy—second copy sequence that arises when an artist depicts something from nature, sells the copyright in that work, and then returns to the same subject. Two cases invite comparison:

(1) "One Rochlitz, an artist, posed a model in the nude, and therefrom produced a photograph, which he named the 'Grace of Youth.' A copyright was obtained therefor; all the artist's rights being sold and assigned to complainants. Two years later the same artist placed the same model in the identical pose, with the single exception that the young woman now wears a smile and holds a cherry stem between her teeth. He took a photograph of this pose, which he called 'Cherry Ripe'; this second photograph is published by defendants * * *." On this statement of facts, taken from Gross v. Seligman, 212 Fed. 930 (2d Cir.1914), is defendant an infringer? It was held that he was. But had Rochlitz copied the copy, or copied the original? Could he have claimed copyright in the second photograph?

(2) Gilbert, "a nationally recognized wildlife artist," made a painting in 1972 entitled "Cardinals on Apple Blossom." Copyright was assigned to National Wildlife Art Exchange, which sold prints of the painting. During 1975 and 1976, Gilbert made another painting called "The Cardinal" as part of a series for the Franklin Mint.

"In painting 'The Cardinal,' Gilbert used some of the same source material he had utilized for 'Cardinals on Apple Blossom,' including preliminary sketches from his collection, photographs, slides, and a working drawing. In addition, however, he used other slides of foliage taken after completion of the earlier painting and sketches specifically developed for 'The Cardinal,' as well as a series of cardinal photographs. He did not use the stuffed bird specimens which had served as models for 'Cardinals on Apple Blossom.' "

National sued for copyright infringement. In Franklin Mint Corp. v. National Wildlife Art Exchange, 575 F.2d 62 (3d Cir.), cert. denied, 439 U.S. 880 (1978), the Third Circuit agreed with the trial court that there was no infringement. After noting "that there are indeed obvious similarities," partly because "in ornithological art * * * minute attention to detail of plumage and other physical characteristics is required and the stance of the birds must be anatomically correct," the court said that "there are also readily apparent dissimilarities"—which it detailed. "[W]hile the ideas are similar, the expressions are not. A pattern of differences is sufficient to establish a diversity of expression rather than only an echo."

Are these cases distinguishable on the facts, or is there a difference in approach, in that the watercolorist is treated differently from the photographer. If the latter, which subsequent artist should be held to a greater variety of treatment? Judge Weis' elegant opinion in *Franklin Mint* raises other points, including "the tendency of some painters to return to certain basic themes time and time again." Cf. Schiller & Schmidt, Inc. v.

Nordisco Corp., 969 F.2d 410 (7th Cir.1992) (when the author of the two works is the same, similarities are less probative of copying).

Can similar issues arise in other art forms? An article in the New York Times, Bishop, A Victory for the Creative Process, Nov. 11, 1988, p. B.5, reports on an infringement suit brought by Fantasy Records, owners of the copyrights in songs composed by John Fogerty for Creedence Clearwater Revival from 1967 to 1972. Fantasy claimed that Fogerty had plagiarized himself by copying his 1970 hit "Run Through the Jungle" when he wrote "Old Man Down the Road" for his 1985 album "Centerfield." Fogerty's attorney argued that "[w]hat similarities there were between the two songs were the result of Mr. Fogerty having written both of them. Both of them came out of the same musical vocabulary." The jury found that the songs were not substantially similar. The article reports that a member of the jury, after first obtaining Fogerty's autograph, explained the decision this way: "Creative people have got to have rights to create without being harassed by too many business types." Attorneys for the plaintiff had a different view: "We got upstaged by a superstar." (The litigation ultimately produced an opinion by the Supreme Court on the standards governing awards of attorney's fees under the Copyright Act. See Fantasy, Inc. v. Fogerty, p. 565 infra.)

Consider another variation on the Holmes sequence, namely, the "recreation" of a copyrighted photograph by a different photographer. In Alt v. Morello, 227 U.S.P.Q. 49 (S.D.N.Y.1985), plaintiff, a young photographer, "created a photograph depicting a Cross pen and pencil positioned at an angle on a dark grid against a dark background, with the tips of the pen and pencil in a yellow toned circle lit from below." Defendant, an established advertising photographer who had seen plaintiff's work, created a photograph that the court found "virtually the same," although the pen and pencil were of a different brand, the angle between them was slightly different, and the circle was a different shade of yellow. (Defendant's photograph was published in a source book widely used by advertising directors, many of whom apparently assumed that it was the plaintiff who had copied.) The court found infringement; statutory damages were set at $20,000.[c] Compare Kisch v. Ammirati & Puris Inc., 657 F.Supp. 380 (S.D.N.Y.1987), where plaintiff's work was a black and white photograph of a seated woman holding a concertina, taken in a small corner of a nightclub with a mural as the background. Defendant created an advertisement for lime juice by taking a color photograph of musician John Lurie seated in front of the same mural, holding a saxophone. A table and a bottle of lime juice were included in defendant's photo, but the court said that the lighting and camera angles were similar. Defendant, conceding access, moved for summary judgment. What result?

c. See also Woods v. Universal City Studios, Inc., 920 F.Supp. 62 (S.D.N.Y.1996), finding plaintiff's pencil drawing infringed by a recreation of the scene in defendant's motion picture *12 Monkeys*.

SECTION 4.   COPYRIGHT IN CHARACTERS

King Features Syndicate v. Fleischer

United States Circuit Court of Appeals, Second Circuit, 1924.
299 Fed. 533.

■ Before ROGERS, HOUGH, and MANTON, CIRCUIT JUDGES.

■ MANTON, CIRCUIT JUDGE.   Appellant, the owner of the copyright of a book of cartoons known as "Barney Google and Spark Plug," sues the appellees, who are manufacturers of toys, and who manufacture a toy horse which they have fashioned after, labeled, and sold as "Spark Plug" and "Sparky." The appellant has been and is engaged, among other things, in selling, publishing, and syndicating to the publishers of newspapers, cartoons and comic strips, which are in turn published under a license from appellant. These newspapers have a wide and large reading public, and the cartoons and comic strips have great value to the publishers.   The appellant's employee prepared cartoons—that is, sketches and drawings—in series of representations of a male character known as "Barney Google," which depicts a character in a variety of ludicrous situations coupled with descriptive reading matter or dialogue.   From July, 1922, these cartoons appeared almost daily, and included a characteristic representation of a new grotesque and comic race horse called "Spark Plug," sometimes referred to as "Sparky."   Both figures, the man and the horse, are found to be the creation of the appellant's employee.   * * *

The appellees' infringement consisted of the reproduction of a substantial portion of the copyright, and also in publishing it as an advertisement in the trade paper entitled "Plaything" and in the newspaper called "Billboard."   The principal act of infringement, however, is the manufacturing and sale of a grotesque figure or toy, an exact reproduction of the horse "Spark Plug," or "Sparky," as copyrighted by the appellant.   * * *

The question presented to us is whether manufacturing and duplicating the horse as a figure doll is a copy of the copyrighted idea of the appellant's.   * * *

We do not think it avoids the infringement of the copyright to take the substance or idea, and produce it through a different medium, and picturing in shape and details in sufficient limitation to make it a true copy of the character thought of by the appellant's employee.   Doing this is omitting the work of the artisan, but appropriating the genius of the artist.   Falk v. Howell & Co. (C.C.) 37 F. 202.   * * *

* * * The Copyright Act protects the conception of humor which a cartoonist may produce, as well as the conception of genius which an artist or sculptor may use.   Hill v. Whalen (D.C.) 220 F. 359.

In the *Hill* Case, the complainant was the licensee of cartoon characters known as "Mutt and Jeff." The defendants produced a dramatic performance calling it "In Cartoonland." The characters were costumed exactly like the figures of "Mutt and Jeff," the cartoons, and their actions and speech were in harmony with the spirit of the cartoons. The court enjoined the defendants, upon the ground that representations of "Mutt and Jeff" dramatically was calculated to injuriously affect the copyright of the cartoons. A reproduction in materials of the copyrighted cartoon character, it would seem, is equally a violation of the copyright of the cartoon. Empire Amusement Co. v. Wilton (C.C.) 134 F. 132. * * *

The form of the horse, embodying the aspect of humor, was the essence of the cartoon; its end, within the artist's purpose, and its object, the production of amusement in contemplation. We think the copyright law was intended to give protection to the creation of that form, protection to its value in that form, to give amusement in contemplation. * * *

Here the book was copyrightable, and embodied the pictorial illustration of the horse "Sparky." The artist's concept of humor was embodied in the copyrightable form, was addressed to the contemplation of the observer and the reader; its essence was the concept of humor which that form embodied. We think it cannot be copied, by manufacturing a toy or doll as the appellees did, without taking the copyrightable form of that concept, and without at the same time taking the commercial value—the fruits of the cartoonist's genius which consisted in his capacity to entertain and amuse.

Decree reversed.

Detective Comics, Inc. v. Bruns Publications, Inc.

United States Circuit Court of Appeals, Second Circuit, 1940.
111 F.2d 432.

■ Before L. Hand, Augustus N. Hand, and Chase, Circuit Judges.

■ Augustus N. Hand, Circuit Judge. The complainant is the owner of eleven copyrights for a like number of monthly issues of a periodical known as "Action Comics". Judge Woolsey found that these copyrights were infringed by a magazine of the defendant Bruns Publications Inc., (hereinafter called Bruns) and known as "Wonderman" [28 F.Supp. 399]. He found infringement both by Bruns and by the defendants Kable News Company and Interborough News Co., who were the distributing agents of Bruns. The defendants all had access to complainant's periodicals, which had a wide sale.

We have compared the alleged infringing magazine of Bruns with the issues of "Action Comics" and are satisfied that the finding that Bruns copied the pictures in the complainant's periodical is amply substantiated. Each publication portrays a man of miraculous strength and speed called "Superman" in "Action Comics" and "Wonderman" in the magazine of Bruns. The attributes and antics of "Superman" and "Wonderman" are closely similar. Each at times conceals his strength beneath ordinary clothing but after removing his cloak stands revealed in full panoply in a skin-tight acrobatic costume. The only real difference between them is that "Superman" wears a blue uniform and "Wonderman" a red one. Each is termed the champion of the oppressed. Each is shown running toward a full moon "off into the night", and each is shown crushing a gun in his powerful hands. "Superman" is pictured as stopping a bullet with his person and "Wonderman" as arresting and throwing back shells. Each is depicted as shot at by three men, yet as wholly impervious to the missiles that strike him. "Superman" is shown as leaping over a twenty story building, and "Wonderman" as leaping from building to building. "Superman" and "Wonderman" are each endowed with sufficient strength to rip open a steel door. Each is described as being the strongest man in the world and each as battling against "evil and injustice."

Defendants attempt to avoid the copyright by the old argument that various attributes of "Superman" find prototypes or analogues among the heroes of literature and mythology. But if the author of "Superman" has portrayed a comic Hercules, yet if his production involves more than the presentation of a general type he may copyright it and say of it: "A poor thing but mine own". Perhaps the periodicals of the complainant are foolish rather than comic, but they embody an original arrangement of incidents and a pictorial and literary form which preclude the contention that Bruns was not copying the antics of "Superman" portrayed in "Action Comics". We think it plain that the defendants have used more than general types and ideas and have appropriated the pictorial and literary details embodied in the complainant's copyrights.

We have repeatedly held that irrespective of the sources from which the author of a work may derive the material which he uses, a picture or writing which is his own production cannot be copied. The prior art is only relevant as bearing on the question whether an alleged infringer has copied the author or has taken his material directly from the prior art. Sheldon v. Metro–Goldwyn Pictures Corporation, 2 Cir., 81 F.2d 49, 53.

So far as the pictorial representations and verbal descriptions of "Superman" are not a mere delineation of a benevolent Hercules, but embody an arrangement of incidents and literary expressions original with the author, they are proper subjects of copyright and susceptible of infringement because of the monopoly afforded by the act. Since the complainant is not entitled to a monopoly of the mere character of a "Superman" who is a blessing to mankind (Nichols v. Universal Pictures Corp., 2 Cir., 45 F.2d 119), we think the language of clause 4(c) of the decree somewhat too sweeping. It should be modified so as to read as follows: "(c) From printing, publishing, offering for sale or selling, or in any way distributing any cartoon or cartoons, or any periodical or book portraying any of the feats of strength or powers performed by 'Superman' or closely imitating his costume or appearance in any feat whatever." [a] * * *

---

[a] The paragraph before modification read as follows: "(c) From printing, publish-ing, offering for sale or selling, or in any way distributing any cartoon or cartoons, or any

The decree modified as provided in this opinion is affirmed, but without costs or any allowance for counsel fees upon this appeal.

NOTES AND QUESTIONS ON CARTOON CHARACTERS

(1) Is the language of the decree, as modified, consistent with the rest of the opinion? What difference, if any, was accomplished by the modification?

Were the visual similarities between "Superman" and "Wonderman" sufficient in themselves to constitute infringement under the rationale of the "Spark Plug" case? Was there an appropriation of other copyrighted "expression"?

(2) In a later "Superman" case, the adversary was "Captain Marvel." National Comics Pub., Inc. v. Fawcett Pub., Inc., 191 F.2d 594 (2d Cir. 1951). Judge L. Hand, in an opinion chiefly about problems of copyright notice, said that in the *Detective Comics* case "we limited the copyright to the specific exploits of 'Superman' as each picture portrayed them." In a per curiam response to a "Petition to Clarify Opinion," 198 F.2d 927 (1952), the court further stated:

> [W]e did not find which of the strips, which the plaintiff put in suit "Fawcett" had infringed: i.e., copied so closely as to be actionable under Detective Comics v. Bruns Publications, 2 Cir., 111 F.2d 432. That will demand a comparison of each strip put in suit by the plaintiff with "Fawcett's" strip, which the plaintiff asserts does so closely copy that particular strip. Each such comparison really involves the decision of a separate claim; there is no escape from it. The plaintiff may put in suit as many strips as it pleases, but it must prove infringement of each, or it will lose as to that strip.

Is the requirement of a "strip-by-strip" analysis consistent with the decision in *Detective Comics?* See also 191 F.2d at 603, on infringement by a "Captain Marvel" movie.

(3) In Atari v. North American Philips Consumer Electronics Corp., 672 F.2d 607 (7th Cir.), cert. denied, 459 U.S. 880 (1982), Judge Wood directed entry of a preliminary injunction against infringement of the audiovisual display of plaintiff's PAC–MAN video game, based on defendant's "substantial appropriation of the PAC–MAN characters * * *. The expression of the central figure as a 'gobbler' and the pursuit figures as 'ghost monsters' distinguishes PAC–MAN from conceptually similar video games. * * * Those characters are wholly fanciful creations, without reference to the real world."

periodical, book, magazine or other publication containing any cartoon or cartoons, portraying the figure of or embodiment of plaintiff's cartoon character Superman as set forth in plaintiff's copyrighted works (plaintiff's exhibits 12 to 22 inclusive in evidence herein) or any figure which is a copy or imitation thereof." Record on Appeal, p. 180.

Sid & Marty Krofft Television Productions, Inc. v. McDonald's Corp.

United States Court of Appeals, Ninth Circuit.
562 F.2d 1157 (1977).

■ Before CARTER, GOODWIN, and SNEED, CIRCUIT JUDGES.

■ JAMES M. CARTER, CIRCUIT JUDGE:

This is a copyright infringement action. Plaintiffs Sid and Marty Krofft Television Productions, Inc., and Sid and Marty Krofft Productions, Inc. were awarded $50,000.00 in their action against defendants McDonald's Corporation and Needham, Harper & Steers, Inc. Defendants were found to have infringed plaintiffs' "H.R. Pufnstuf" children's television show by the production of their "McDonaldland" television commercials. * * *

Facts

In 1968, Sid and Marty Krofft were approached by the NBC television network to create a children's television program for exhibition on Saturday morning. The Kroffts spent the next year creating the H.R. Pufnstuf television show, which was introduced on NBC in September 1969. The series included several fanciful costumed characters, as well as a boy named Jimmy, who lived in a fantasyland called "Living Island," which was inhabited by moving trees and talking books. The television series became extremely popular and generated a line of H.R. Pufnstuf products and endorsements.

In early 1970, Marty Krofft, the President of both Krofft Television and Krofft Productions and producer of the show, was contacted by an executive from Needham, Harper & Steers, Inc., an advertising agency. He was told that Needham was attempting to get the advertising account of McDonald's hamburger restaurant chain and wanted to base a proposed campaign to McDonald's on the H.R. Pufnstuf characters. The executive wanted to know whether the Kroffts would be interested in working with Needham on a project of this type.

Needham and the Kroffts were in contact by telephone six or seven more times. By a letter dated August 31, 1970, Needham stated it was going forward with the idea of a McDonaldland advertising campaign based on the H.R. Pufnstuf series. It acknowledged the need to pay the Kroffts a fee for preparing artistic designs and engineering plans. Shortly thereafter, Marty Krofft telephoned Needham only to be told that the advertising campaign had been cancelled.

In fact, Needham had already been awarded McDonald's advertising account and was proceeding with the McDonaldland project. Former employees of the Kroffts were hired to design and construct the costumes and sets for McDonaldland. Needham also hired the same voice expert who supplied all of the voices for the Pufnstuf characters to supply some of the voices for the McDonaldland characters. In January 1971, the first of the McDonaldland commercials was broadcast on network television. They continue to be broadcast.

Prior to the advent of the McDonaldland advertising campaign, plaintiffs had licensed the use of the H.R. Pufnstuf characters and elements to the manufacturers of toys, games, lunch boxes, and comic books. In addition, the H.R. Pufnstuf characters were featured in Kellogg's cereal commercials and used by the Ice Capades. After the McDonaldland campaign, which included the distribution of toys and games, plaintiffs were unable to obtain new licensing arrangements or extend existing ones.[3] In the case of the Ice Capades, the H.R. Pufnstuf characters were actually replaced by the McDonaldland characters. * * *

[A jury, after a three-week trial, returned a verdict in favor of the plaintiffs.]

Proof of Infringement

It has often been said that in order to establish copyright infringement a plaintiff must prove ownership of the copyright and "copying" by the defendant. See, e.g., Reyher v. Children's Television Workshop, 533 F.2d 87, 90 (2 Cir.1976); Universal Athletic Sales Co. v. Salkeld, 511 F.2d 904, 907 (3 Cir.1975); 2 M. Nimmer on Copyright § 141 at 610–11 (1976) (hereinafter "Nimmer"). "Copying," in turn, is said to be shown by circumstantial evidence of access to the copyrighted work and substantial similarity between the copyrighted work and defendant's work. Reyher v. Children's Television Workshop, supra, 533 F.2d at 90; 2 Nimmer § 141.2 at 613. But an analysis of the cases suggests that these statements frequently serve merely as boilerplate to copyright opinions.

Under such statements, infringement would be established upon proof of ownership, access, and substantial similarity. Application of this rule, however, would produce some untenable results. For example, a copyright could be obtained over a cheaply manufactured plaster statue of a nude. Since ownership of a copyright is established, subsequent manufacturers of statues of nudes would face the grave risk of being found to be infringers if their statues were substantially similar and access were shown. The burden of proof on the plaintiff would be minimal, since most statues of nudes would in all probability be substantially similar to the cheaply manufactured plaster one.

Clearly the scope of copyright protection does not go this far. A limiting principle is needed. This is provided by the classic distinction between an "idea" and the "expression" of that idea. It is an axiom of copyright law that the protection granted to a copyrighted work extends only to the particular expression of the idea and never to the idea itself. Mazer v. Stein, 347 U.S. 201, 217–18 (1954); Baker v. Selden, 101 U.S. 99,

---

3. The evidence reveals that certain persons with whom plaintiffs dealt for licensing believed that the H.R. Pufnstuf characters were being licensed to McDonald's for use in their McDonaldland campaign. Accordingly, they did not pursue licensing arrangements for the characters themselves.

102–03 (1879). This principle attempts to reconcile two competing social interests: rewarding an individual's creativity and effort while at the same time permitting the nation to enjoy the benefits and progress from use of the same subject matter.

The real task in a copyright infringement action, then, is to determine whether there has been copying of the expression of an idea rather than just the idea itself. "[N]o one infringes, unless he descends so far into what is concrete [in a work] as to invade . . . [its] expression." National Comics Publications v. Fawcett Publications, 191 F.2d 594, 600 (2 Cir. 1951). Only this expression may be protected and only it may be infringed.

The difficulty comes in attempting to distill the unprotected idea from the protected expression. No court or commentator in making this search has been able to improve upon Judge Learned Hand's famous "abstractions test" articulated in Nichols v. Universal Pictures Corporation, * * *. See also Chafee, Reflections on the Law of Copyright, 45 Colum.L.Rev. 503 (1945) * * *.

The test for infringement therefore has been given a new dimension. There must be ownership of the copyright and access to the copyrighted work. But there also must be substantial similarity not only of the general ideas but of the expressions of those ideas as well. Thus two steps in the analytic process are implied by the requirement of substantial similarity.

The determination of whether there is substantial similarity in ideas may often be a simple one. Returning to the example of the nude statue, the idea there embodied is a simple one—a plaster recreation of a nude human figure. A statue of a horse or a painting of a nude would not embody this idea and therefore could not infringe. The test for similarity of ideas is still a factual one, to be decided by the trier of fact. See International Luggage Registry v. Avery Products Corp., 541 F.2d 830, 831 (9 Cir.1976); Williams v. Kaag Manufacturers, Inc., 338 F.2d 949, 951 (9 Cir.1964).

We shall call this the "extrinsic test." It is extrinsic because it depends not on the responses of the trier of fact, but on specific criteria which can be listed and analyzed. Such criteria include the type of artwork involved, the materials used, the subject matter, and the setting for the subject. Since it is an extrinsic test, analytic dissection and expert testimony are appropriate. Moreover, this question may often be decided as a matter of law.

The determination of when there is substantial similarity between the forms of expression is necessarily more subtle and complex. As Judge Hand candidly observed, "Obviously, no principle can be stated as to when an imitator has gone beyond copying the 'idea,' and has borrowed its 'expression.' Decisions must therefore inevitably be ad hoc." Peter Pan Fabrics, Inc. v. Martin Weiner Corp., 274 F.2d 487, 489 (2 Cir.1960). If there is substantial similarity in ideas, then the trier of fact must decide whether there is substantial similarity in the expressions of the ideas so as to constitute infringement.

The test to be applied in determining whether there is substantial similarity in expressions shall be labeled an intrinsic one—depending on the response of the ordinary reasonable person. See International Luggage Registry v. Avery Products Corp., supra, 541 F.2d at 831; Harold Lloyd Corp. v. Witwer, 65 F.2d 1, 18–19 (9 Cir.1933). See generally Nimmer § 143.5. It is intrinsic because it does not depend on the type of external criteria and analysis which marks the extrinsic test. As this court stated in Twentieth Century–Fox Film Corp. v. Stonesifer, 140 F.2d 579, 582 (9 Cir.1944):

> "The two works involved in this appeal should be considered and tested, not hypercritically or with meticulous scrutiny, but by the observations and impressions of the average reasonable reader and spectator."

Because this is an intrinsic test, analytic dissection and expert testimony are not appropriate.

This same type of bifurcated test was announced in Arnstein v. Porter, [p. 219 supra]. * * *

We believe that the court in *Arnstein* was alluding to the idea-expression dichotomy which we make explicit today. When the court in *Arnstein* refers to "copying" which is not itself an infringement, it must be suggesting copying merely of the work's idea, which is not protected by the copyright. To constitute an infringement, the copying must reach the point of "unlawful appropriation," or the copying of the protected expression itself. We analyze this distinction in terms both of the elements involved—idea and expression—and of the tests to be used—extrinsic and intrinsic—in an effort to clarify the issues involved.

The Tests Applied

In the context of this case, the distinction between these tests is important. Defendants do not dispute the fact that they copied the idea of plaintiffs' Pufnstuf television series—basically a fantasyland filled with diverse and fanciful characters in action. They argue, however, that the expressions of this idea are too dissimilar for there to be an infringement. They come to this conclusion by dissecting the constituent parts of the Pufnstuf series—characters, setting, and plot—and pointing out the dissimilarities between these parts and those of the McDonaldland commercials.

This approach ignores the idea-expression dichotomy alluded to in *Arnstein* and analyzed today. Defendants attempt to apply an extrinsic test by the listing of dissimilarities in determining whether the expression they used was substantially similar to the expression used by plaintiffs. That extrinsic test is inappropriate; an intrinsic test must here be used. * * *

The present case demands an even more intrinsic determination because both plaintiffs' and defendants' works are directed to an audience of children. This raises the particular factual issue of the impact of the respective works upon the minds and imaginations of young people. * * *

Defendants would have this court ignore that intrinsic quality which they recognized to embark on an extrinsic analysis of the two works. For example, in discussing the principal characters—Pufnstuf and Mayor McCheese—defendants point out:

> " 'Pufnstuf' wears what can only be described as a yellow and green dragon suit with a blue cummerband from which hangs a medal which says 'mayor'. 'McCheese' wears a version of pink formal dress—'tails'—with knicker trousers. He has a typical diplomat's sash on which is written 'mayor', the 'M' consisting of the McDonald's trademark of an 'M' made of golden arches."

So not only do defendants remove the characters from the setting, but dissect further to analyze the clothing, colors, features, and mannerisms of each character. We do not believe that the ordinary reasonable person, let alone a child, viewing these works will even notice that Pufnstuf is wearing a cummerbund while Mayor McCheese is wearing a diplomat's sash. * * *

We have viewed representative samples of both the H.R. Pufnstuf show and McDonaldland commercials. It is clear to us that defendants' works are substantially similar to plaintiffs'.[9] They have captured the "total concept and feel" of the Pufnstuf show. Roth Greeting Cards v. United Card Co., 429 F.2d 1106, 1110 (9 Cir.1970). We would so conclude even if we were sitting as the triers of fact. There is no doubt that the findings of the jury in this case are not clearly erroneous.

Unity of Idea and Expression

[The court next rejected defendants' attempt to invoke the merger doctrine to justify a higher standard of infringement. "No standard more demanding than that of substantial similarity should be imposed here. This is not a case where the idea is indistinguishable as a matter of law from the expression of that idea." The court also found no merit in defendants' argument that the first amendment somehow limited the protection of plaintiffs' works. Some of its observations on this point are quoted at p. 414 infra.]

Access

In addition to substantial similarity, a plaintiff must show access in order to prove infringement. * * *

---

9. Even a dissection of the two works reveals their similarities. The "Living Island" locale of Pufnstuf and "McDonaldland" are both imaginary worlds inhabited by anthromorphic plants and animals and other fanciful creatures. The dominant topographical features of the locales are the same: trees, caves, a pond, a road, and a castle. Both works feature a forest with talking trees that have human faces and characteristics.

The characters are also similar. Both lands are governed by mayors who have disproportionately large round heads dominated by long wide mouths. They are assisted by "Keystone cop" characters. Both lands feature strikingly similar crazy scientists and a multi-armed evil creature.

It seems clear that such similarities go beyond merely that of the idea into the area of expression. The use of the basic idea of the works does not inevitably result in such similarities. Certainly a jury applying an intrinsic test could find such similarities of expression substantial.

In this case, representatives of Needham actually visited the Kroffts' headquarters in Los Angeles to discuss the engineering and design work necessary to produce the McDonaldland commercials. They did this *after* they had been awarded the contract by McDonald's and apparently with no intention to work with the Kroffts. We believe that this degree of access justifies a lower standard of proof to show substantial similarity. Since the subjective test applies, it is impossible to quantify this standard. But there is no question it is met here. * * *

Conclusion

The judgment of the district court finding infringement is affirmed. The McDonald commercials are based on the same ideas as the H.R. Pufnstuf series. The expression of that idea is sufficiently similar so that a jury applying an intrinsic test could find infringement. This is especially true here since there was strong evidence of access.

[There is also a discussion of "statutory damages" under the 1909 Act. The court concluded that such damages would be appropriate, and that their calculation was for the trial court. On remand, the court awarded $1,044,000. 221 U.S.P.Q. 114 (C.D.Cal.1983).]

NOTES AND QUESTIONS

Is the two-step, "extrinsic"/"intrinsic" approach announced in *Krofft* the same as the "copying"/"improper appropriation" distinction pursued in Arnstein v. Porter?[b] What is the purpose of determining similarity in ideas? Does it establish copying? Can a plaintiff who successfully establishes substantial similarity in *expression* under the "intrinsic" test ever *fail* to satisfy the "extrinsic" test for similarity in *ideas?* Or is the two-step process simply a way to keep clear cases of non-infringement from the jury? The Ninth Circuit's mode of analysis in *Krofft* is criticized in Cohen, Masking Copyright Decisionmaking: The Meaninglessness of Substantial Similarity, 20 U.C. Davis L.Rev. 719 (1987). But cf. Knowles and Palmieri, Dissecting *Krofft:* An Expression of New Ideas in Copyright, 8 San Fern. V.L.Rev. 109 (1980) (one of the authors was Judge Carter's law clerk).

WALT DISNEY PRODUCTIONS v. AIR PIRATES, 581 F.2d 751 (9th Cir.1978), cert. denied, 439 U.S. 1132 (1979). "This case involves the admitted copying of plaintiff Walt Disney Productions' ('Disney') cartoon characters in defendants' adult 'counter-culture' comic books. The present defendants are three individuals and two business entities operated by them.

---

b. In footnote 7 of his opinion in *Krofft,* Judge Carter wrote: " * * * We do not resurrect the *Arnstein* approach today. Rather, we formulate an extrinsic-intrinsic test for infringement based on the idea-expression dichotomy. We believe that the *Arnstein* court was doing nearly the same thing. But the fact that it may not have been does not subtract from our analysis."

The complaint alleges that they infringed Disney copyrights, a Disney trademark and engaged in unfair competition, trade disparagement and interference with Disney's business. Disney sought injunctive relief, destruction of infringing materials, damages, costs and attorney's fees. * * *

"The individual defendants have participated in preparing and publishing two magazines of cartoons entitled 'Air Pirates Funnies.' The characters in defendants' magazines bear a marked similarity to those of plaintiff. The names given to defendants' characters are the same names used in plaintiff's copyrighted work. However, the themes of defendants' publications differ markedly from those of Disney. While Disney sought only to foster 'an image of innocent delightfulness,' defendants supposedly sought to convey an allegorical message of significance. Put politely by one commentator, the 'Air Pirates' was 'an "underground" comic book which had placed several well-known Disney cartoon characters in incongruous settings where they engaged in activities clearly antithetical to the accepted Mickey Mouse world of scrubbed faces, bright smiles and happy endings.' It centered around 'a rather bawdy depiction of the Disney characters as active members of a free thinking, promiscuous, drug ingesting counterculture.' Note, Parody, Copyrights and the First Amendment, 10 U.S.F.L.Rev. 564, 571, 582 (1976)."

Defendants argued that "characters are never copyrightable and therefore cannot in any way constitute a copyrightable component part. That argument flies in the face of a series of cases dating back to 1914 that have held comic strip characters protectable under the old Copyright Act." * * *

"It is true that this Court's opinion in Warner Brothers Pictures v. Columbia Broadcasting System, 216 F.2d 945 (9th Cir.1954), certiorari denied, 348 U.S. 971, lends some support to the position that characters ordinarily are not copyrightable. There the mystery writer Dashiell Hammett and his publisher entered into a 1930 contract with Warner Brothers giving the movie production company copyright and various other rights to a 'certain story * * * entitled Maltese Falcon' involving the fictional detective Sam Spade. In 1946, Hammett and other defendants used the Maltese Falcon characters in other writings, causing Warner Brothers to sue for copyright infringement and 'unfair use and competition.' After pointing out the sophisticated nature of the plaintiff, we construed the contracts between the parties and held:

> 'We are of the opinion that since the use of characters and character names are nowhere specifically mentioned in the agreements [including the assignment of copyright instrument], but that other items, including the title, "The Maltese Falcon", and their use are specifically mentioned as being granted [to Warner Brothers], that the character rights with the names cannot be held to be within the grants, and that under the doctrine of *ejusdem generis,* general language cannot be held to include them.' (Footnote omitted.)

"After so holding, Judge Stephens' opinion considered 'whether it was ever intended by the copyright statute that characters with their names should be under its protection.' In that context he concluded that such a restriction on Hammett's future use of a character was unreasonable, at least when the characters were merely vehicles for the story and did not 'really constitute' the story being told. Judge Stephens' reasons for that conclusion provide an important indication of the applicability of that conclusion to comic book characters as opposed to literary characters. In reasoning that characters 'are always limited and always fall into limited patterns,' Judge Stephens recognized that it is difficult to delineate distinctively a literary character. Cf. Nichols v. Universal Pictures Corp., 45 F.2d 119 (2d Cir.1930), certiorari denied, 282 U.S. 902. When the author can add a visual image, however, the difficulty is reduced. See generally 1 Nimmer on Copyright § 30. Put another way, while many literary characters may embody little more than an unprotected idea (see Sid & Marty Krofft Television v. McDonald's Corp., 562 F.2d 1157 (9th Cir.1977)), a comic book character, which has physical as well as conceptual qualities, is more likely to contain some unique elements of expression. Because comic book characters therefore are distinguishable from literary characters, the *Warner Brothers* language does not preclude protection of Disney's characters."

The court rejected a defense of parody as fair use. "By copying the images in their entirety, the defendants took more than was necessary to place firmly in the reader's mind the parodied work and those specific attributes that are to be satirized." It also rejected a first amendment defense. Disney's summary judgment on its copyright claim was affirmed, but summary judgment on the trademark and unfair competition counts was reversed in the absence of an uncontested showing that purchasers were likely to be confused as to the source of the comics, which the court thought unlikely.

SHAW v. LINDHEIM, 919 F.2d 1353 (9th Cir.1990). Shaw, a well-known television writer and producer, developed a pilot script for a television series entitled "The Equalizer" under a contract with Lindheim, a programming executive at NBC. NBC declined to produce the show, and Lindheim subsequently took a position at Universal Television. Lindheim later wrote a series treatment, also called "The Equalizer," that became the pilot for the CBS series of that name. Shaw claimed that both the pilot and series infringed the copyright in his original script. The District Court, holding as a matter of law that there was no substantial similarity of expression, granted summary judgment to the defendants. The summary judgment was reversed on appeal in an opinion by Judge Alarcon that reinterpreted the Ninth Circuit's infringement analysis in *Krofft*.

"*Krofft* defined the extrinsic test as a 'test for similarity of ideas' under which 'analytic dissection and expert testimony are appropriate.' 562 F.2d at 1164. The intrinsic test, according to *Krofft,* should measure 'substantial similarity in expressions ... depending on the response of the ordinary reasonable person.... [I]t does not depend on the type of external criteria and analysis which marks the extrinsic test.' Id. In decisions under the intrinsic test, 'analytic dissection and expert testimony are not appropriate.' Id.

"Relying on this language, panels applying *Krofft* to literary works have included a lengthy list of concrete elements under the extrinsic test. Whereas *Krofft* listed 'the type of artwork involved, the materials used, the subject matter, and the setting for the subject' as criteria for consideration under the extrinsic test, id., a series of opinions beginning with the district court opinion in Jason v. Fonda, 526 F.Supp. 774 (C.D.Cal.1981), aff'd and incorporated by reference, 698 F.2d 966 (9th Cir.1982), have listed 'plot, themes, dialogue, mood, setting, pace, and sequence' as extrinsic test criteria. 526 F.Supp. at 777; see also Litchfield v. Spielberg, 736 F.2d 1352, 1356 (9th Cir.1984) (repeating this list), cert. denied, 470 U.S. 1052 (1985); Berkic v. Crichton, 761 F.2d 1289, 1293 (9th Cir.) (same), cert. denied, 474 U.S. 826 (1985); [Olson v. National Broadcasting Co., 855 F.2d 1446, 1450 (9th Cir.1988)] (same); [Narell v. Freeman, 872 F.2d 907, 912 (9th Cir.1989)] (adding 'characters' to the list and transforming 'sequence' into 'sequence of events').

"Now that it includes virtually every element that may be considered concrete in a literary work, the extrinsic test as applied to books, scripts, plays, and motion pictures can no longer be seen as a test for mere similarity of ideas. Because the criteria incorporated into the extrinsic test encompass all objective manifestations of creativity, the two tests are more sensibly described as objective and subjective analyses of *expression,* having strayed from *Krofft* 's division between expression and ideas. See *Narell,* 872 F.2d at 912 (referring to an *objective,* extrinsic test and a *subjective,* intrinsic test); *Berkic,* 761 F.2d at 1292 (same); *Litchfield,* 736 F.2d at 1356 (same). But see *Olson,* 855 F.2d at 1448–49 (adhering to *Krofft* 's idea/expression distinction). Indeed, a judicial determination under the intrinsic test is now virtually devoid of analysis, for the intrinsic test has become a mere subjective judgment as to whether two literary works are or are not similar. See *Berkic,* 761 F.2d at 1294 (reaching a result under the intrinsic test in one paragraph); *Olson,* 855 F.2d at 1453 (same). * * *

"We must determine in this matter whether a party that demonstrates a triable issue of fact under the extrinsic test has made a sufficient showing of substantial similarity to defeat a summary judgment motion. As noted above, the extrinsic test focuses on 'specific similarities between the plot, theme, dialogue, mood, setting, pace, characters, and sequence of events.... "the actual concrete elements that make up the total sequence of events and the relationships between the major characters." ' *Narell,* 872 F.2d at 912 (quoting *Berkic,* 761 F.2d at 1293). These are the measurable, objective elements that constitute a literary work's expression. Because these elements are embodied in the extrinsic test, we hold that it is improper for a court to find, as the district court did, that there is no substantial similarity as a matter of law after a writer has satisfied the extrinsic test. To conclude otherwise would allow a court to base a grant of summary judgment on a purely subjective determination of similarity. * * *

" * * * Once a court has established that a triable question of objective similarity of expression exists, by analysis of each element of the extrinsic test, its inquiry should proceed no further. What remains is a subjective assessment of the 'concept and feel' of two works of literature—a task no more suitable for a judge than for a jury."

Judge Alarcon, acknowledging that titles are not eligible for copyright (see p. 674 infra), held that the defendants' admitted copying of Shaw's title was nevertheless relevant in determining whether there was substantial similarity of protected expression. The court found similarities in the theme and plot of the works and concluded its comparison with an analysis of the respective characters.

"As the district court noted, both the dialogue and the characters in the respective works share some striking similarities. A particularly glaring example of similar personal traits is revealed by a comparison of the principal characters in both works. As the district court found, both scripts have 'similar lead characters.... Both leads are well dressed, wealthy and have expensive tastes. The most striking similarity is their self-assuredness, and unshakeable faith in the satisfactory outcome of any difficult situation.' Although James Bond may have the Equalizers' demeanor and the Ghostbusters may have their penchant for unpopular assignments, the totality of the similarities between the two characters goes beyond the necessities of the 'Equalizer' theme and belies any claim of literary accident. We find that defendants' copying of the Equalizer character and other characters extends to elements of protected expression. Because the similarities between the principals in each script and among the other common characters point to copying of more than a general theme or plot idea, they support the district court's finding that Shaw raised a triable issue of fact regarding substantial similarity under the extrinsic test. * * *

"We conclude that Shaw has satisfied the extrinsic test for literary works and thus has presented a triable issue of fact regarding substantial similarity of protected expression."

(In a later decision involving alleged similarities in "man-in-the-moon" masks, the Ninth Circuit refused to read *Shaw* as precluding summary judgment for defendants under the intrinsic test; the court said *Shaw*'s holding was limited to literary works, and *Shaw* itself had distinguished cases in which idea and expression are inseparable. Summary judgment is still appropriate where all the similarities necessarily result from the common idea. Pasillas v. McDonald's Corp., 927 F.2d 440 (9th Cir.1991).)

NOTES AND QUESTIONS ON LITERARY CHARACTERS

(1) Warner Brothers v. CBS—the "Sam Spade" case discussed in *Air Pirates*—had erected a virtually insurmountable obstacle to copyright in

literary characters. (Note the peculiar alignment of interests in the case). Compare Judge Hand's dictum on literary characters in *Nichols,* p. 198 supra. Even before *Air Pirates,* decisions in the First and Second Circuits had drawn away from the position taken by the Ninth Circuit in Warner Brothers v. CBS. In CBS Inc. v. DeCosta, p. 702 infra, Judge Coffin said that *Warner Brothers* held only "that the contract of assignment did not convey the exclusive right to use the characters in the novel." A footnote in Goodis v. United Artists Television, 425 F.2d 397, 406 n. 1 (2d Cir.1970), declared that if "Warner Brothers could have used the characters of the *Falcon* in a new series even without an exclusive copyright—by asserting, in effect, that now the *Falcon's* characters were in the public domain—we think such a conclusion would be clearly untenable from the standpoint of public policy, for it would effectively permit the unrestrained pilfering of characters."

The Ninth Circuit returned to literary characters, and to the "Sam Spade" case, in Olson v. NBC, Inc., 855 F.2d 1446 (9th Cir.1988). The court affirmed a j.n.o.v. in favor of defendant NBC against allegations that its television series "The A–Team" infringed the characters in plaintiff's screenplay. The court said that the standard in *Warner Brothers* was "arguably dicta," but found that plaintiff could not prevail even under a more lenient test of copyrightability. Referring to Judge Hand's formulation in *Nichols,* the court said that plaintiff's characters were neither Malvolio nor Sir Toby Belch (nor Mickey Mouse or Superman, distinguishing the graphic character cases). The Ninth Circuit's subsequent decision in Shaw v. Lindheim confirms its acceptance of literary characters as copyrightable subject matter.

(2) Protection for literary characters was recognized in Filmvideo Releasing Corp. v. Hastings, 509 F.Supp. 60 (S.D.N.Y.), aff'd on other grounds, 668 F.2d 91 (2d Cir.1981). Judge Werker enjoined the unauthorized performance of twenty-three motion pictures based on Clarence Mulford's "Hopalong Cassidy" books. (The films, made under license from the author, had entered the public domain because the copyrights had not been renewed; the books, however, were still under copyright.) "In my opinion, these characters [Hopalong, Windy, Johnny, and Lucky] and others were sufficiently delineated, developed and well known to the public to be copyrightable. The use of these characters for the purposes intended by Filmvideo therefore would constitute infringement * * * irrespective and independent of the similarity of the story line."

The character of "Tarzan" was found copyrightable in a district court decision dealing with termination of licenses, but in affirming, the Second Circuit thought it unnecessary to express a view on "the venerable question as to whether and in what circumstances an author's creation of a fictional character can be protected by copyright." Burroughs v. Metro–Goldwyn–Mayer, 519 F.Supp. 388 (S.D.N.Y.1981), aff'd, 683 F.2d 610 (2d Cir.1982) (see p. 488 infra). The Second Circuit eventually confirmed the copyrightability of literary characters when the issue again reached the court in Silverman v. CBS Inc., 870 F.2d 40 (2d Cir.), cert. denied, 492 U.S. 907 (1989).   Plaintiff sought a declaration that the characters from the "Amos 'n' Andy" radio programs broadcast between 1928 and 1948 were now in the public domain; he wanted to use the characters in a musical comedy.   Judge Newman said that the characters "were sufficiently delineated in the pre–1948 radio programs to have been placed in the public domain when the scripts entered the public domain."   (Is a finding of sufficient delineation necessary to this aspect of the holding?)   He also said, however, that plaintiff could not use "any further delineation of the characters contained in the post–1948 radio scripts and the television scripts and programs" if CBS could establish valid copyrights in the shows.

(3) In Silverman v. CBS, Judge Newman also held that CBS had abandoned any trademarks rights in the "Amos 'n' Andy" name. (See p. 702 infra.)   Names cannot be copyrighted. See 37 C.F.R. § 202.1(a), quoted at p. 60 supra.   Can the use of an identical name for a character in a subsequent work nevertheless contribute to a finding of substantial similarity?   Will it not conjure up the attributes of the named character as delineated in the original work?   Is that "copying"?

An argument against copyright protection for literary and other nonvisual characters is mounted in Nevins, Copyright + Character = Catastrophe, 39 J.Copyr.Soc. 303 (1992).

Warner Brothers, Inc. v. American Broadcasting Companies, Inc.

United States Court of Appeals, Second Circuit, 1983.
720 F.2d 231.

■ Before MANSFIELD, MESKILL, and NEWMAN, CIRCUIT JUDGES.

■ NEWMAN, CIRCUIT JUDGE:

The primary issue raised by this appeal is whether as a matter of law the fictional character Ralph Hinkley, the principal figure in a television series, "The Greatest American Hero," is not sufficiently similar to the fictional character Superman, the hero of comic books, television, and more recently films, so that claims of copyright infringement and unfair competition may be dismissed without consideration by a jury.   * * *

I.

Many of the significant facts are set out in our prior opinion affirming the denial of plaintiffs' motion for a preliminary injunction. Warner Bros. Inc. v. American Broadcasting Companies, Inc., 654 F.2d 204 (2d Cir.1981). Plaintiffs own the copyrights in various works embodying the character Superman and have thereby acquired copyright protection for the character itself.   See Detective Comics, Inc. v. Bruns Publications, Inc., 111 F.2d 432 (2d Cir.1940).   Since the creation of Superman in 1938, plaintiffs have exploited their rights with great success, portraying Superman in several media and licensing the character for a variety of merchandising purposes. Through plaintiffs' efforts, Superman has attained an extremely high degree of exposure and recognition.

In 1978, building on previous Superman works, plaintiff Warner Bros., Inc. released a motion picture entitled "Superman, The Movie" (*Superman I*) and more recently two sequels. * * *

The substantial commercial success of *Superman I* and the attendant publicity prompted many requests for licenses permitting use of the Superman character in connection with the merchandising of toys, greeting cards, apparel, and other products. It also led ABC to seek a license for production of a television series about "Superboy" based on the early adventures of Superman. Plaintiffs, who were planning to make their own sequels and derivative works, refused ABC permission to proceed with its proposed project.

Unable to obtain this license, ABC assigned to Cannell, the principal of the third-party defendant production company, the task of creating a "pilot" program for a TV series involving a superhero. Cannell produced a program, and subsequently a weekly series, entitled "The Greatest American Hero" (*Hero*), which he described as being about "what happens when you [the average person] become Superman." *Hero's* protagonist, Ralph Hinkley, was given attributes intended to identify him as an "ordinary guy." Hinkley is portrayed as a young high school teacher attempting to cope with a recent divorce, a dispute over the custody of his son, and the strain that his domestic problems place upon his work and his relationship with his girlfriend. Although Hinkley is attractive, his physical appearance is not imposing: he is of medium height with a slight build and curly, somewhat unkempt, blond hair. * * *

* * * Hinkley as a superhero is not an unqualified success. He uses his superpowers awkwardly and fearfully. When flying, Hinkley shouts with fright and makes crash-landings, sometimes crumpling in a heap or skidding nearly out of control to a stop. Though protected from bullets by his costume, Hinkley cringes and cowers when shot at by villains. * * *

The *Hero* series contains several visual effects and lines that inevitably call Superman to mind, sometimes by way of brief imitation, sometimes by mention of Superman or another character from the Superman works, and sometimes by humorous parodying or ironic twisting of well-known Superman phrases. Hinkley's suit invests him with most of Superman's powers, and the suit, like Superman's, is a tight-fitting leotard with a chest insignia and a cape. Their outfits differ in that Superman wears a blue leotard with red briefs, boots, and cape, while Hinkley's costume is a red leotard with a tunic top, no boots, and a black cape. In one scene, as Hinkley is running at super speed, smoke emerges from his footsteps, and the sound of a locomotive is heard. A similar scene occurs in *Superman I,* though even without seeing the movie it would be difficult not to be reminded by the *Hero* scene of Superman, who is regularly described as "more powerful than a locomotive." When Hinkley first views himself in a mirror holding his costume in front of him, he says, "It's a bird ... it's a plane ... it's Ralph Hinkley." The youngster, Jerry, watching Hinkley's unsuccessful first effort to fly, tells him, "Superman wouldn't do it that way." In a scene with his girlfriend, who is aware of the powers that come with the magic costume, Hinkley says, "Look at it this way ... you're already one

step up on Lois Lane. She never found out who Clark Kent really was."
* * *

The complaint alleged copyright infringement in violation of section 101 [501?] of the Copyright Act of 1976, 17 U.S.C. § 501 (Supp. V 1981), unfair competition in violation of the common law of New York, and impairment of the value of plaintiffs' trademarks and indicia associated with the Superman character in violation of New York's "anti-dilution" statute, N.Y.Gen.Bus.Law § 368–d (McKinney 1968). Chief Judge Motley denied a preliminary injunction that would have barred the showing of the *Hero* series, 523 F.Supp. 611, and this Court affirmed, 654 F.2d 204. The defendants then moved for summary judgment and dismissal of the complaint. Chief Judge Motley initially denied that motion, and prepared the case for bifurcated jury trials of the copyright infringement and unfair competition claims, Fed.R.Civ.P. 42(b). * * *

Prior to the start of the trial the District Judge, apparently harboring doubts as to the need for a trial, conducted an extended pretrial conference, lasting two weeks, to afford an opportunity to review the evidence to be offered by the plaintiffs. In the course of the pretrial conference, Chief Judge Motley ruled that the responses to an audience survey commissioned by the plaintiffs were inadmissible, "because they were too general to be of any benefit to the jury with respect to ... the copyright claim." [4] The District Judge also excluded all expert testimony on the copyright claim, including testimony, sought to be introduced by plaintiffs, offered to show the inability of young children to perceive the differences between Hinkley and Superman. * * *

* * * On December 16, 1981, the District Judge concluded that no reasonable jury could find that the parties' works were substantially similar and granted summary judgment to defendants on the entire copyright claim. * * * [S]he concluded that public confusion as to the origin of *Hero* was unlikely as a matter of law, and relied on this latter finding to preclude trial on the Lanham Act and common law unfair competition claims, and also on the New York "anti-dilution" claim. On January 20, 1982, the District Judge dismissed plaintiffs' complaint in a comprehensive opinion. 530 F.Supp. 1187. On September 27, 1982, the Court denied defendants' motion to amend the judgment to include an award of attorney's fees and additional costs.

II.

The basic issues concerning the copyright infringement claim are whether the *Hero* and *Superman* works are substantially similar so as to

---

4. The survey asked the following three questions:

> (1) Was there anything about the character Ralph Hinkley that reminded you of any other character you had seen before?

> (2) Did any scenes from that TV movie [*Hero*] remind you of scenes from any other TV programs or movies in theatres or on TV?

> (3) Aside from the actors, do you think that the people who wrote or made this movie were responsible for any other TV programs or movies in theatres or on TV?

support an inference of copying and whether the lack of substantial similarity is so clear as to fall outside the range of reasonably disputed fact questions requiring resolution by a jury. The similarity to be assessed must concern the expression of ideas, not the ideas themselves, Reyher v. Children's Television Workshop, 533 F.2d 87, 90–91 (2d Cir.), cert. denied, 429 U.S. 980 (1976); Nichols v. Universal Pictures Corp., 45 F.2d 119, 121 (2d Cir.1930), cert. denied, 282 U.S. 902 (1931), a distinction easier to assert than to apply, see Peter Pan Fabrics, Inc. v. Martin Weiner Corp., 274 F.2d 487, 489 (2d Cir.1960) (decisions "inevitably ... ad hoc"). Though the issue of substantial similarity is frequently a fact issue for jury resolution, see Twentieth Century–Fox Film Corp. v. MCA, Inc., 715 F.2d 1327 (9th Cir.1983); Hoehling v. Universal City Studios, Inc., 618 F.2d 972, 977 (2d Cir.), cert. denied, 449 U.S. 841 (1980), we have recognized that a court may determine non-infringement as a matter of law on a motion for summary judgment, either because the similarity between two works concerns only "*non*-copyrightable elements of the plaintiff's work," id., or because no reasonable jury, properly instructed, could find that the two works are substantially similar, Durham Industries, Inc. v. Tomy Corp., 630 F.2d 905, 918 (2d Cir.1980). See Twentieth Century–Fox Film Corp. v. MCA, Inc., supra, at 1330 & n. 6; 3 Nimmer on Copyright § 12.10 (1983) (hereafter "Nimmer"). Before assessing the District Court's determination that summary judgment was appropriate in this case, we consider the principles that guide decision in this area.

It is a fundamental objective of the copyright law to foster creativity. However, that law has the capacity both to augment and diminish the prospects for creativity. By assuring the author of an original work the exclusive benefits of whatever commercial success his or her work enjoys, the law obviously promotes creativity. At the same time, it can deter the creation of new works if authors are fearful that their creations will too readily be found to be substantially similar to preexisting works. The idea-expression dichotomy originated in the case law and is now codified in the statute, 17 U.S.C. § 102(b) (Supp. V 1981), in an effort to enable courts to adjust the tension between these competing effects of copyright protection. Though imprecise, it remains a useful analytic tool for separating infringing from non-infringing works, especially when the essence of the work sought to be protected is a story and the allegedly infringing work is accused of what Professor Nimmer calls "comprehensive nonliteral similarity," 3 Nimmer § 13.03 [A][1], duplicating the "fundamental essence or structure" of a work, id. Confronting a claim of that sort, courts have often invoked Learned Hand's "abstractions" test, or Professor Chafee's "pattern" test.[7]

When, as in this case, the claim concerns infringement of a character, rather than a story, the idea-expression distinction has proved to be especially elusive. In *Nichols*, Hand applied his "abstractions" test in determining that neither the plot nor the characters of "Abie's Irish Rose"

---

7. "No doubt, the line does lie some-where between the author's idea and the precise form in which he wrote it down. I like to say that the protection covers the 'pattern' of the work ... the sequence of events, and the development of the interplay were infringed by a similar play called "The Cohens and the Kellys."   He noted that no case then decided had found infringement of a character described only by written word, although he recognized the possibility that a literary character could be sufficiently delineated to support a claim of infringement by a second comer, 45 F.2d at 121.   Copyrightability of a literary character has on occasion been recognized, Burroughs v. Metro–Goldwyn–Mayer, Inc., 519 F.Supp. 388, 391 (S.D.N.Y.1981) (Tarzan), aff'd with issue expressly left open, 683 F.2d 610, 621 (2d Cir.1982).   However, there has been no doubt that copyright protection is available for characters portrayed in cartoons, even before *Nichols,* e.g., King Features Syndicate v. Fleischer, 299 Fed. 533 (2d Cir.1924) (Barney Google's horse, Spark Plug); Hill v. Whalen & Martell, Inc., 220 F.359 (S.D.N.Y.1914) (Mutt and Jeff); see also Empire City Amusement Co. v. Wilton, 134 F. 132 (C.C.D.Mass.1903) (Alphonse and Gaston) (claim sustained against demurrer), and after *Nichols,* e.g., Walt Disney Productions v. Air Pirates, 581 F.2d 751 (9th Cir.), cert. denied, 439 U.S. 1132 (1978) (Mickey Mouse and other Disney characters); Detective Comics, Inc. v. Bruns Publications, Inc., supra (Superman); see 1 Nimmer § 2.12.

In determining whether a character in a second work infringes a cartoon character, courts have generally considered not only the visual resemblance but also the totality of the characters' attributes and traits. * * * A pertinent consideration, formulated in a case concerning greeting cards in which characters were one element of the art work, Roth Greeting Cards v. United Card Co., 429 F.2d 1106, 1110 (9th Cir.1970), is the extent to which the allegedly infringing character captures the "total concept and feel" of the copyrighted character.   * * *

* * * A story has a linear dimension: it begins, continues, and ends. If a defendant copies substantial portions of a plaintiff's sequence of events, he does not escape infringement by adding original episodes somewhere along the line.   A graphic or three-dimensional work is created to be perceived as an entirety.   Significant dissimilarities between two works of this sort inevitably lessen the similarity that would otherwise exist between the total perceptions of the two works.   The graphic rendering of a character has aspects of both the linear, literary mode and the multidimensional total perception.   What the character thinks, feels, says, and does and the descriptions conveyed by the author through the comments of other characters in the work episodically fill out a viewer's understanding of the character.   At the same time, the visual perception of the character tends to create a dominant impression against which the similarity of a defendant's character may be readily compared, and significant differences readily noted.

Ultimately, care must be taken to draw the elusive distinction between a substantially similar character that infringes a copyrighted character despite slight differences in appearance, behavior, or traits, and a somewhat similar though non-infringing character whose appearance, behavior,

of characters."   Chafee, Reflections on the   14 (1945).
Law of Copyright, 45 Colum.L.Rev. 503, 513–

or traits, and especially their combination, significantly differ from those of a copyrighted character, even though the second character is reminiscent of the first one. Stirring one's memory of a copyrighted character is not the same as appearing to be substantially similar to that character, and only the latter is infringement. See Ideal Toy Corp. v. Kenner Products Division of General Mills Fun Group, Inc., 443 F.Supp. 291, 305 (S.D.N.Y. 1977). * * *

Applying these principles to this case, we conclude that Chief Judge Motley correctly entered summary judgment for the defendants on the claim of copyright infringement. Plaintiffs make no claim that the *Hero* pilot, subsequent episodes, or "promos" infringed the story of any Superman works. Their contention is that the *Hero* character, Ralph Hinkley, is substantially similar to Superman and that the *Hero* works impermissibly copied what plaintiffs call the "indicia" of Superman, a concept broad enough to include Superman's costume, his abilities, the well-known lines associated with him—in short, anything occurring in the *Hero* works that might remind a viewer of Superman.

The total perception of the Hinkley character is not substantially similar to that of Superman. On the contrary, it is profoundly different. Superman looks and acts like a brave, proud hero, who has dedicated his life to combating the forces of evil. Hinkley looks and acts like a timid, reluctant hero, who accepts his missions grudgingly and prefers to get on with his normal life. Superman performs his superhuman feats with skill, verve, and dash, clearly the master of his own destiny. Hinkley is perplexed by the superhuman powers his costume confers and uses them in a bumbling, comical fashion. In the genre of superheros, Hinkley follows Superman as, in the genre of detectives, Inspector Clouseau follows Sherlock Holmes.

However, we do not accept defendants' mode of analysis whereby every skill the two characters share is dismissed as an idea rather than a protected form of expression. That approach risks elimination of any copyright protection for a character, unless the allegedly infringing character looks and behaves exactly like the original. A character is an aggregation of the particular talents and traits his creator selected for him. That each one may be an idea does not diminish the expressive aspect of the combination. But just as similarity cannot be rejected by isolating as an idea each characteristic the characters have in common, it cannot be found when the total perception of all the ideas as expressed in each character is fundamentally different. * * *

* * * Appellants were prepared to offer expert testimony to show that some children would not perceive the negatives when the announcer says that Hinkley "may be unable to leap tall buildings in a single bound," "may be slower than a speeding bullet," and "may be less powerful than a locomotive." We do not doubt that some viewers may miss the point, but their misunderstanding does not establish infringement. Perhaps if *Hero* were a children's series, aired on Saturday mornings among the cartoon programs, we would have greater concern for the risk that lines intended to contrast Hinkley with Superman might be mistakenly understood to sug-

gest that *Hero* was a Superman program. Cf. Ideal Toy Corp. v. Fab–Lu, Ltd., 261 F.Supp. 238, 241–42 (S.D.N.Y.1966) (children's perception of television commercial for dolls). But when a work is presented to a general audience of evening television viewers, the possible misperception of some young viewers cannot prevent that audience from seeing a program that will readily be recognized by the "average lay observer," Ideal Toy Corp. v. Fab–Lu Ltd., 360 F.2d 1021, 1022 (2d Cir.1966), as poking fun at, rather than copying, a copyrighted work.

Our conclusion is not altered by plaintiffs' proffered evidence of a survey of persons who viewed the *Hero* pilot. The survey reported, among other things, that of the 45% of those interviewed who said Hinkley reminded them of some other character, 74% (33% of the entire sample) said they were reminded of Superman. We appreciate the problem plaintiffs confronted in designing the survey. If they asked too pointed a question, e.g., "Do you think Hinkley is substantially similar to Superman?", they would have been faulted for using a leading question. On the other hand, their open-ended questions caused Chief Judge Motley to rule the entire survey inadmissible because the responses were "too general." 530 F.Supp. at 1197 n. 3. That dilemma simply illustrates the problems that arise when surveys are sought to be used as an aid in determining issues of copyright infringement. See Ideal Toy Corp. v. Kenner Products Division of General Mills Fun Group, Inc., supra, 443 F.Supp. at 304 (cautioning against "the dangerous precedent of allowing trial by the court to be replaced by trial by public opinion poll"). The "substantial similarity" that supports an inference of copying sufficient to establish infringement of a copyright is not a concept familiar to the public at large. It is a term to be used in a courtroom to strike a delicate balance between the protection to which authors are entitled under an act of Congress and the freedom that exists for all others to create their works outside the area protected against infringement. We need not and do not decide whether survey evidence of the sort tendered in this case would be admissible to aid a jury in resolving a claim of substantial similarity that lies within the range of reasonable factual dispute. However, when a trial judge has correctly ruled that two works are not substantially similar as a matter of law, that conclusion is not to be altered by the availability of survey evidence indicating that some people applying some standard of their own were reminded by one work of the other. Courts have an important responsibility in copyright cases to monitor the outer limits within which juries may determine reasonably disputed issues of fact. If a case lies beyond those limits, the contrary view of a properly drawn sample of the population, or even of a particular jury, cannot be permitted to enlarge (or diminish) the scope of statutory protection enjoyed by a copyright proprietor. * * *

[Judge Motley's summary judgment had also disposed of plaintiff's unfair competition counts. The Court of Appeals affirmed in a crisp discussion that declared that "as with claims of copyright infringement, courts retain an important authority to monitor the outer limits of substantial similarity within which a jury is permitted to make the factual determination whether there is a likelihood of confusion as to source." An anti-dilution claim met a similar fate: "Even if Superman's trademarks are not as indestructible as the character that spawned them, no reasonable jury could find that the *Hero* series or 'promos' blurred or tarnished those marks."

The judgment of the District Court is affirmed.

NOTES AND QUESTIONS

(1) If Arnstein v. Porter's opposition to summary judgment is now discredited, does *Warner Brothers* stretch too far in the opposite direction?

(2) Does *Warner Brothers* introduce still another approach to adjudicating infringement? Is it significant that Judge Newman's comprehensive opinion makes no reference to the two-step techniques of *Arnstein* or *Krofft?*

(3) Superman, although born a cartoon character, became in maturity a star of television and motion pictures. Consider other characters created expressly for such media—Kramer of *Seinfeld,* for example, or Darth Vader of *Star Wars*. Are they more akin, for purposes of copyrightability and infringement, to cartoon characters or to literary characters?[c] See also Berman and Boxer, Copyright Infringement of Audiovisual Works and Characters, 52 S.Cal.L.Rev. 315 (1979). Is it relevant that the visual dimension of audiovisual characters often (but not always) consists chiefly of the physical appearance of a particular actor?

(4) Any appraisal of the total scope of protection available for characters must await exposure in Part Two of this casebook to the law of unfair competition. Both the copyright and unfair competition dimensions are comprehensively reviewed in Kurtz, The Independent Legal Lives of Fictional Characters, 1986 Wis.L.Rev. 429 (1986). See also D.J. Howell, Intellectual Properties and the Protection of Fictional Characters (1990).

SECTION 5.   NONFICTION WORKS

Hoehling v. Universal City Studios, Inc.
United States Court of Appeals, Second Circuit, 1980.
618 F.2d 972.
Certiorari denied 449 U.S. 841, 101 S.Ct. 121.

■ Before KAUFMAN, CHIEF JUDGE, TIMBERS, CIRCUIT JUDGE, and WERKER, DISTRICT JUDGE.

---

c. See Stallone v. Anderson, 11 U.S.P.Q.2d 1161 (C.D.Cal.1989), distinguishing the literary character cases and holding that "Rocky" as delineated in the movie series is a protectable character. In Metro–Goldwyn–Mayer, Inc. v. American Honda Motor Co., 900 F.Supp. 1287 (C.D.Cal.1995), the court granted the plaintiff motion picture studio a preliminary injunction protecting the "James Bond" character as expressed in sixteen movies against defendant Honda's television commercial in which a villain jumps from a helicopter onto the roof of a car occupied by a Bond-like character and female companion, who release the car's detachable roof to make their escape.

■ IRVING R. KAUFMAN, CHIEF JUDGE: * * *

This litigation arises from three separate accounts of the triumphant introduction, last voyage, and tragic destruction of the Hindenburg, the colossal dirigible constructed in Germany during Hitler's reign. The zeppelin, the last and most sophisticated in a fleet of luxury airships, which punctually floated its wealthy passengers from the Third Reich to the United States, exploded into flames and disintegrated in 35 seconds as it hovered above the Lakehurst, New Jersey Naval Air Station at 7:25 p.m. on May 6, 1937. * * *

Appellant A.A. Hoehling published *Who Destroyed the Hindenburg?*, a full-length book based on his exhaustive research in 1962. Mr. Hoehling studied the investigative reports, consulted previously published articles and books, and conducted interviews with survivors of the crash as well as others who possessed information about the Hindenburg. His book is presented as a factual account, written in an objective, reportorial style.

The first half recounts the final crossing of the Hindenburg, from Sunday, May 2, when it left Frankfurt, to Thursday, May 6, when it exploded at Lakehurst. Hoehling describes the airship, its role as an instrument of propaganda in Nazi Germany, its passengers and crew, the danger of hydrogen, and the ominous threats received by German officials, warning that the Hindenburg would be destroyed. The second portion, headed *The Quest,* sets forth the progress of the official investigations, followed by an account of Hoehling's own research. In the final chapter, spanning eleven pages, Hoehling suggests that all proffered explanations of the explosion, save deliberate destruction, are unconvincing. He concludes that the most likely saboteur is one Eric Spehl, a "rigger" on the Hindenburg crew who was killed at Lakehurst.

According to Hoehling, Spehl had motive, expertise, and opportunity to plant an explosive device, constructed of dry-cell batteries and a flashbulb, in "Gas Cell 4," the location of the initial explosion. An amateur photographer with access to flashbulbs, Spehl could have destroyed the Hindenburg to please his ladyfriend, a suspected communist dedicated to exploding the myth of Nazi invincibility.

Ten years later appellee Michael MacDonald Mooney published his book, *The Hindenburg.* Mooney's endeavor might be characterized as more literary than historical in its attempt to weave a number of symbolic themes through the actual events surrounding the tragedy. His dominant theme contrasts the natural beauty of the month of May, when the disaster occurred, with the cold, deliberate progress of "technology." The May theme is expressed not simply by the season, but also by the character of Spehl, portrayed as a sensitive artisan with needle and thread. The Hindenburg, in contrast, is the symbol of technology, as are its German creators and the Reich itself. The destruction is depicted as the ultimate triumph of nature over technology, as Spehl plants the bomb that ignites the hydrogen. Developing this theme from the outset, Mooney begins with an extended review of man's efforts to defy nature through flight, focusing on the evolution of the zeppelin. This story culminates in the construction of the Hindenburg, and the Nazis' claims of its indestructibility.   Mooney then traces the fateful voyage, advising the reader almost immediately of Spehl's scheme.   The book concludes with the airship's explosion.

Mooney acknowledges, in this case, that he consulted Hoehling's book, and that he relied on it for some details.   * * *

After Mooney prepared an outline of his anticipated book, his publisher succeeded in negotiations to sell the motion picture rights to appellee Universal City Studios.   * * *

The Gidding screenplay follows what is known in the motion picture industry as a "Grand Hotel" formula, developing a number of fictional characters and subplots involving them.   This formula has become standard fare in so-called "disaster" movies, which have enjoyed a certain popularity in recent years.   In the film, which was released in late 1975, a rigger named "Boerth," who has an anti-Nazi ladyfriend, plans to destroy the airship in an effort to embarrass the Reich.   Nazi officials, vaguely aware of sabotage threats, station a Luftwaffe intelligence officer on the zeppelin, loosely resembling a Colonel Erdmann who was aboard the Hindenburg.   This character is portrayed as a likable fellow who soon discovers that Boerth is the saboteur.   Boerth, however, convinces him that the Hindenburg should be destroyed and the two join forces, planning the explosion for several hours after the landing at Lakehurst, when no people would be on board.   In Gidding's version, the airship is delayed by a storm, frantic efforts to defuse the bomb fail, and the Hindenburg is destroyed. * * *

Upon learning of Universal's plans to release the film, Hoehling instituted this action against Universal for copyright infringement and common law unfair competition in the district court for the District of Columbia in October 1975.   Judge Smith declined to issue an order restraining release of the film in December, and it was distributed throughout the nation.

* * * After the completion of discovery, both Mooney and Universal moved for summary judgment, Fed.R.Civ.P. 56, which was granted on August 1, 1979.

It is undisputed that Hoehling has a valid copyright in his book.   To prove infringement, however, he must demonstrate that defendants "copied" his work and that they "improperly appropriated" his "expression." See Arnstein v. Porter, 154 F.2d 464, 468 (2d Cir.1946).   Ordinarily, wrongful appropriation is shown by proving a "substantial similarity" of *copyrightable* expression.   See Nichols v. Universal Pictures Corp., 45 F.2d 119, 121 (2d Cir.1930), cert. denied, 282 U.S. 902 (1931).   Because substantial similarity is customarily an extremely close question of fact, see *Arnstein,* supra, 154 F.2d at 468, summary judgment has traditionally been frowned upon in copyright litigation, id. at 474.   Nevertheless, while *Arnstein's* influence in other areas of the law has been diminished, see SEC v. Research Automation Corp., 585 F.2d 31 (2d Cir.1978); 6 Moore's Federal Practice ¶ 56.17[14] (2d ed. 1976), a series of copyright cases in the

Southern District of New York have granted defendants summary judgment when all alleged similarity related to *non*-copyrightable elements of the plaintiff's work, see, e.g., Alexander v. Haley, 460 F.Supp. 40 (S.D.N.Y. 1978); Musto v. Meyer, 434 F.Supp. 32 (S.D.N.Y.1977); Gardner v. Nizer, 391 F.Supp. 940 (S.D.N.Y.1975); Fuld v. National Broadcasting Co., 390 F.Supp. 877 (S.D.N.Y.1975). These cases signal an important development in the law of copyright, permitting courts to put "a swift end to meritless litigation" and to avoid lengthy and costly trials. Quinn v. Syracuse Model Neighborhood Corp., 613 F.2d 438, 445 (2d Cir.1980); accord, Donnelly v. Guion, 467 F.2d 290, 293 (2d Cir.1972); American Manufacturers Mutual Insurance Co. v. American Broadcasting–Paramount Theatres, Inc., 388 F.2d 272, 278 (2d Cir.1967). Drawing on these cases, Judge Metzner assumed both copying and substantial similarity, but concluded that all similarities pertained to various categories of non-copyrightable material. Accordingly, he granted appellees' motion for summary judgment. We affirm the judgment of the district court.

Hoehling's principal claim is that both Mooney and Universal copied the essential plot of his book—i.e., Eric Spehl, influenced by his girlfriend, sabotaged the Hindenburg by placing a crude bomb in Gas Cell 4. * * *

* * * [Mooney and Universal] argue that Hoehling's plot is an "idea," and ideas are not copyrightable as a matter of law. See Sheldon v. Metro–Goldwyn Pictures Corp., 81 F.2d 49, 54 (2d Cir.), cert. denied, 298 U.S. 669 (1936).

Hoehling, however, correctly rejoins that while ideas themselves are not subject to copyright, his "expression" of *his* idea is copyrightable. Id. at 54. He relies on Learned Hand's opinion in *Sheldon*, supra, at 50, holding that *Letty Lynton* infringed *Dishonored Lady* by copying its story of a woman who poisons her lover, and Augustus Hand's analysis in Detective Comics, Inc. v. Bruns Publications, Inc., 111 F.2d 432 (2d Cir.1940), concluding that the exploits of "Wonderman" infringed the copyright held by the creators of "Superman," the original indestructible man. Moreover, Hoehling asserts that, in both these cases, the line between "ideas" and "expression" is drawn, in the first instance, by the fact finder.

Sheldon and *Detective Comics*, however, dealt with works of fiction, where the distinction between an idea and its expression is especially elusive. But, where, as here, the idea at issue is an interpretation of an historical event, our cases hold that such interpretations are not copyrightable as a matter of law. In Rosemont Enterprises, Inc. v. Random House, Inc., 366 F.2d 303 (2d Cir.1966), cert. denied, 385 U.S. 1009 (1967), we held that the defendant's biography of Howard Hughes did not infringe an earlier biography of the reclusive alleged billionaire. Although the plots of the two works were necessarily similar, there could be no infringement because of the "public benefit in encouraging the development of historical and biographical works and their public distribution." Id. at 307; accord, Oxford Book Co. v. College Entrance Book Co., 98 F.2d 688 (2d Cir.1938). To avoid a chilling effect on authors who contemplate tackling an historical issue or event, broad latitude must be granted to subsequent authors who make use of historical subject matter, including theories or plots. Learned Hand counseled in Myers v. Mail & Express Co., 36 C.O.Bull. 478, 479 (S.D.N.Y.1919), "[t]here cannot be any such thing as copyright in the order of presentation of the facts, nor, indeed, in their selection."

In the instant case, the hypothesis that Eric Spehl destroyed the Hindenburg is based entirely on the interpretation of historical facts, including Spehl's life, his girlfriend's anti-Nazi connections, the explosion's origin in Gas Cell 4, Spehl's duty station, discovery of a dry-cell battery among the wreckage, and rumors about Spehl's involvement dating from a 1938 Gestapo investigation. Such an historical interpretation, whether or not it originated with Mr. Hoehling, is not protected by his copyright and can be freely used by subsequent authors.

The same reasoning governs Hoehling's claim that a number of specific facts, ascertained through his personal research, were copied by appellees.[6] The cases in this circuit, however, make clear that factual information is in the public domain. See, e.g., *Rosemont Enterprises, Inc.,* supra, 366 F.2d at 309; *Oxford Book Co.,* supra, 98 F.2d at 691. Each appellee had the right to "avail himself of the facts contained" in Hoehling's book and to "use such information, whether correct or incorrect, in his own literary work." Greenbie v. Noble, 151 F.Supp. 45, 67 (S.D.N.Y.1957). Accordingly, there is little consolation in relying on cases in other circuits holding that the fruits of original research are copyrightable. See, e.g., Toksvig v. Bruce Publications Corp., 181 F.2d 664, 667 (7th Cir.1950); Miller v. Universal City Studios, Inc., 460 F.Supp. 984 (S.D.Fla.1978). Indeed, this circuit has clearly repudiated *Toksvig* and its progeny. In *Rosemont Enterprises, Inc.,* supra, 366 F.2d at 310, we refused to "subscribe to the view that an author is absolutely precluded from saving time and effort by referring to and relying upon prior published material. ... It is just such wasted effort that the proscription against the copyright of ideas and facts ... are designed to prevent." Accord, 1 Nimmer on Copyright § 2.11 (1979).

The remainder of Hoehling's claimed similarities relate to random duplications of phrases and sequences of events. For example, all three works contain a scene in a German beer hall, in which the airship's crew engages in revelry prior to the voyage. Other claimed similarities concern common German greetings of the period, such as "Heil Hitler," or songs,

---

6. In detailed comparisons of his book with Mooney's work and Universal's motion picture, Hoehling isolates 266 and 75 alleged instances of copying, respectively. Judge Metzner correctly pointed out that many of these allegations are patently frivolous. The vast majority of the remainder deals with alleged copying of historical facts. It would serve no purpose to review Hoehling's specific allegations in detail in this opinion. The following ten examples, however, are illustrative: (1) Eric Spehl's age and birthplace; (2) Crew members had smuggled monkeys on board the Graf Zeppelin; (3) Germany's ambassador to the United States dismissed threats of sabotage; (4) A warning letter had been received from a Mrs. Rauch; (5) The Hindenburg's captain was constructing a new home in Zeppelinheim; (6) Eric Spehl was a photographer; (7) The airship flew over Boston; (8) The Hindenburg was "tail heavy" before landing; (9) A member of the ground crew had etched his name in the zeppelin's hull; and (10) The navigator set the Hindenburg's course by reference to various North Atlantic islands.

such as the German National anthem. These elements, however, are merely *scenes a faire,* that is "incidents, characters or settings which are as a practical matter indispensable, or at least standard, in the treatment of a given topic." [Alexander v. Haley, 460 F.Supp. 40, 45 (S.D.N.Y.1978)]; accord, Bevan v. Columbia Broadcasting System, Inc., 329 F.Supp. 601, 607 (S.D.N.Y.1971). Because it is virtually impossible to write about a particular historical era or fictional theme without employing certain "stock" or standard literary devices, we have held that *scenes a faire* are not copyrightable as a matter of law. See Reyher v. Children's Television Workshop, 533 F.2d 87, 91 (2d Cir.), cert. denied, 429 U.S. 980 (1976).

All of Hoehling's allegations of copying, therefore, encompass material that is non-copyrightable as a matter of law, rendering summary judgment entirely appropriate. We are aware, however, that in distinguishing between themes, facts, and *scenes a faire* on the one hand, and copyrightable expression on the other, courts may lose sight of the forest for the trees. By factoring out similarities based on non-copyrightable elements, a court runs the risk of overlooking wholesale usurpation of a prior author's expression. A verbatim reproduction of another work, of course, even in the realm of nonfiction, is actionable as copyright infringement. See Wainwright Securities, Inc. v. Wall Street Transcript Corp., 558 F.2d 91 (2d Cir.1977), cert. denied, 434 U.S. 1014 (1978). Thus, in granting or reviewing a grant of summary judgment for defendants, courts should assure themselves that the works before them are not virtually identical. In this case, it is clear that all three authors relate the story of the Hindenburg differently.

In works devoted to historical subjects, it is our view that a second author may make significant use of prior work, so long as he does not bodily appropriate the expression of another. *Rosemont Enterprises, Inc.,* supra, 366 F.2d at 310. This principle is justified by the fundamental policy undergirding the copyright laws—the encouragement of contributions to recorded knowledge. The "financial reward guaranteed to the copyright holder is but an incident of this general objective, rather than an end in itself." Berlin v. E.C. Publications, Inc., 329 F.2d 541, 543–44 (2d Cir.), cert. denied, 379 U.S. 822 (1964). Knowledge is expanded as well by granting new authors of historical works a relatively free hand to build upon the work of their predecessors.[7] * * *

The judgment of the district court is affirmed.

NASH v. CBS, INC., 899 F.2d 1537 (7th Cir.1990). "John Dillinger, Public Enemy No. 1, died on July 22, 1934, at the Biograph Theater in Chicago. He emerged from the air conditioned movie palace into a swelter-

7. We note that publication of Mooney's book and release of the motion picture revived long dormant interest in the Hindenburg. As a result, Hoehling's book, which had been out of print for some time, was actually re-released after the film was featured in theaters across the country.

ing evening accompanied by two women, one wearing a red dress. The 'lady in red', Anna Sage, had agreed to betray his presence for $10,000. Agents of the FBI were waiting. Alerted by Polly Hamilton, the other woman, Dillinger wheeled to fire, but it was too late. A hail of bullets cut him down, his .45 automatic unused."

Nash, an author with a fascination for crimes and criminals, believed that it was not Dillinger who died that night at the Biograph. In his book *The Dillinger Dossier,* published in 1983, Nash concludes that Dillinger had learned of the trap and had dispatched a small-time hoodlum who looked like him to take his place. Nash describes numerous discrepancies between Dillinger's physical appearance and the dead man, and notes that Dillinger's father had the corpse encased in concrete before burial. The FBI, Nash believed, mortified that it got the wrong man, went along with the cover-up, planting Dillinger's fingerprints in the morgue. After interviewing numerous people connected with Dillinger and the FBI, Nash claimed to have tracked Dillinger to the west coast, where he says Dillinger married and survived at least until 1979.

"Someone in Hollywood must have read *The Dillinger Dossier,* however, because in 1984 CBS broadcast an episode of its *Simon and Simon* series entitled *The Dillinger Print.*" The central premise of the episode is that Dillinger is alive and living in San Diego. There are references to the physical discrepancies between Dillinger and the corpse, and one of the characters plants a fake Dillinger fingerprint on a gun used in a bank robbery. Nash filed suit for copyright infringement. CBS, conceding access and the copying of factual material, moved for summary judgment. The trial court granted the motion, holding that the television episode did not appropriate any copyrightable material. Judge Easterbrook, writing for the Seventh Circuit, agreed.

" * * * Intellectual (and artistic) progress is possible only if each author builds on the work of others. No one invents even a tiny fraction of the ideas that make up our cultural heritage. Once a work has been written and published, any rule requiring people to compensate the author slows progress in literature and art, making useful expressions 'too expensive', forcing authors to re-invent the wheel, and so on. Every work uses scraps of thought from thousands of predecessors, far too many to compensate even if the legal system were frictionless, which it isn't. Because any new work depends on others even if unconsciously, broad protection of intellectual property also creates a distinct possibility that the cost of litigation—old authors trying to get a 'piece of the action' from current successes—will prevent or penalize the production of new works, even though the claims be rebuffed. Authors as a group therefore might prefer limited protection for their writings—they gain in the ability to use others' works more than they lose in potential royalties. See William M. Landes & Richard A. Posner, An Economic Analysis of Copyright Law, 18 J.Legal Studies 325, 332–33, 349–59 (1989).

"Yet to deny authors all reward for the value their labors contribute to the works of others *also* will lead to inefficiently little writing, just as surely as excessively broad rights will do. The prospect of reward is an important stimulus for thinking and writing, especially for persons such as Nash who are full-time authors. Before the first work is published, broad protection of intellectual property seems best; after it is published, narrow protection seems best. At each instant some new works are in progress, and every author is simultaneously a creator in part and a borrower in part. In these roles, the same person has different objectives. Yet only one rule can be in force. This single rule must achieve as much as possible of these inconsistent demands. Neither Congress nor the courts has the information that would allow it to determine which is best. Both institutions must muddle through, using not a fixed rule but a sense of the consequences of moving dramatically in either direction.

"If Nash had written a novel that another had translated into a screenplay, this would be a difficult case. Although *The Dillinger Print* is substantially original, it does not matter that almost all of the second author's expression is new. '[N]o plagiarist can excuse the wrong by showing how much of his work he did not pirate.' Sheldon v. Metro–Goldwyn Pictures Corp., 81 F.2d 49, 56 (2d Cir.1936) (L. Hand, J.). The TV drama took from Nash's works the idea that Dillinger survived and retired to the west coast, and employed many of the ingredients that Nash used to demonstrate that the man in the Cook County morgue was not Dillinger. CBS even used one of Nash's books as a prop: 'Twentieth Century Desperadoes' in *The Dillinger Print* is a ringer for Nash's *Blood-letters and Badmen.* To see that *The Dillinger Print* is in a sense a 'derivative work', we need only imagine how we would react if Nash had written a short story based on the premise that Dillinger was really a woman masquerading as a man, and CBS had used a switch in sex roles as the centerpiece of a drama. In such an event we would need to decide, as Hand did in *Sheldon,* whether the portions CBS took over were qualitatively so important that the original author's market would be diminished excessively by a rule allowing similar appropriations in the regular course.

"Nash does not portray *The Dillinger Dossier* and its companion works as fiction, however, which makes all the difference. The inventor of Sherlock Holmes controls that character's fate while the copyright lasts; the first person to conclude that Dillinger survived does not get dibs on history. If Dillinger survived, that fact is available to all. Nash's rights lie in his expression: in his words, in his arrangement of facts (his deployment of narration interspersed with interviews, for example), but not in the naked 'truth'. *The Dillinger Print* does not use any words from *The Dillinger Dossier* or Nash's other books; it does not take over any of Nash's presentation but instead employs a setting of its own invention with new exposition and development. Physical differences between Dillinger and the corpse, planted fingerprints, photographs of Dillinger and other gangsters in the 1930s, these and all the rest are facts as Nash depicts them. (Nash did not take the photographs and has no rights in them; *The Dillinger Print* used the photos but not Nash's arrangement of them.)" Judge Easterbrook then turned to the Second Circuit's decision in *Hoehling*, supra.

"*Hoehling* suggested that '[t]o avoid a chilling effect on authors who contemplate tackling an historical issue or event, broad latitude must be granted to subsequent authors who make use of historical subject matter, including theories or plots'. 618 F.2d at 978. As our opinion in [Toksvig v. Bruce Pub. Co., 181 F.2d 664 (7th Cir.1950)] shows, we are not willing to say that 'anything goes' as long as the first work is about history. *Toksvig* held that the author of a biography of Hans Christian Andersen infringed the copyright of the author of an earlier biography by using portions of Andersen's letters as well as some of the themes and structure. *Hoehling* rejected *Toksvig,* see 618 F.2d at 979, concluding that '[k]nowledge is expanded ... by granting new authors of historical works a relatively free hand to build upon the work of their predecessors.' Id. at 980 (footnote omitted). With respect for our colleagues of the east, we think this goes to the extreme of looking at incentives only *ex post*. The authors in *Hoehling* and *Toksvig* spent years tracking down leads. If all of their work, right down to their words, may be used without compensation, there will be too few original investigations, and facts will not be available on which to build.

"In *Toksvig* the first author, who knew Danish, spent three years learning about Andersen's life; the second author, who knew no Danish, wrote her biography in less than a year by copying out of the first book scenes and letters that the original author discovered or translated. Reducing the return on such effort, by allowing unhindered use, would make the initial legwork less attractive and so less frequent. Copyright law does not protect hard work (divorced from expression), and hard work is not an essential ingredient of copyrightable expression * * *; to the extent *Toksvig* confuses work or ideas with expression, it has been justly criticized. * * * We need not revisit *Toksvig* on its own facts to know that it is a mistake to hitch up at *either* pole of the continuum between granting the first author a right to forbid all similar treatments of history and granting the second author a right to use anything he pleases of the first's work."

Concluding that CBS had used Nash's "analysis of history but none of his expression," the court affirmed the summary judgment.

NOTES AND QUESTIONS ON COPYRIGHT IN "RESEARCH"

(1) Both *Hoehling* and *Nash* refer to Toksvig v. Bruce Pub. Co., 181 F.2d 664 (7th Cir.1950). Toksvig spent three years working with original Danish sources in writing a biography of Hans Christian Andersen. Defendant (who, as Judge Easterbrook notes in *Nash,* could not read Danish), wrote a novel based on Andersen's life, apparently quoting twenty-four passages from plaintiff's translations of letters written by Andersen. Not content to rest defendant's liability solely on that appropriation, the court noted that the defendant had also "obtained much value from the use in her work of many of the original concepts and ideas of plaintiff as to Andersen and his relationship with other persons * * *."

If the defendant had refrained from lifting specific language, *should* she be permitted to utilize the factual material in the biography as the basis for a novel? A second biography?

(2) The decision in Miller v. Universal City Studios, Inc., 460 F.Supp. 984 (S.D.Fla.1978), invoked along with *Toksvig* by plaintiff Hoehling, was later reversed by the Fifth Circuit, 650 F.2d 1365 (5th Cir.1981). The litigation had its origins in a bizarre Georgia kidnapping in 1971. The victim, rescued from an underground coffin in which she had been imprisoned for five days, collaborated with a reporter on a book detailing her ordeal. The reporter spent more than 2,500 hours on the work. Universal City Studios (after unsuccessfully attempting to purchase movie rights to the book) produced a television film portraying the crime. An internal memorandum indicated that the account depicted in the film had been constructed in large measure from the information in plaintiff's book. The issue on appeal was the propriety of a jury instruction that read in part: "Moreover, if an author, in writing a book concerning factual matters, engages in research on those matters, his research is copyrightable"; the jury found infringement. Rejecting *Toksvig* in favor of *Hoehling,* the Fifth Circuit ordered a new trial: "The valuable distinction in copyright law between facts and the expression of facts cannot be maintained if research is held to be copyrightable."

The Supreme Court, in a "fair use" case to be consider later, remarked on *Hoehling* and the problems posed by nonfiction works: "Especially in the realm of factual narrative, the law is currently unsettled regarding the ways in which uncopyrightable elements combine with the author's original contributions to form protected expression. Compare Wainwright Securities Inc. v. Wall Street Transcript Corp., [p. 366 infra] (protection accorded author's analysis, structuring of material and marshalling of facts), with [*Hoehling*] (limiting protection to ordering and choice of words)." Harper & Row, Publishers v. Nation Enterprises, p. 366 infra. Francione, Facing *The Nation:* The Standards for Copyright, Infringement, and Fair Use of Factual Works, 134 U.Pa.L.Rev. 519 (1986), uses *Harper & Row* to launch a full-scale attack on the notion that copyright can attach to a "totality" consisting in part of unprotectable facts and ideas.

On the *scenes a faire* doctrine described by Judge Kaufman in *Hoehling,* see Kurtz, Copyright: The Scenes A Faire Doctrine, 41 Fla.L.Rev. 79 (1989).

(3) The Ninth Circuit in Landsberg v. Scrabble Crossword Game Players, Inc., 736 F.2d 485 (9th Cir.), cert. denied, 469 U.S. 1037 (1984), relied on both *Hoehling* and *Miller* in a valiant effort to explicate the principles applicable to nonfiction works. Plaintiff complained that Selchow & Righter, producer of the Scrabble crossword game, had infringed the copyright in his manuscript entitled "Championship Scrabble Strategy." The defendant, after negotiating for rights in the manuscript (in bad faith, the district court found), produced a similar handbook. The lower court found infringement, but the Court of Appeals disagreed:

"One consequence of the policy in favor of free use of ideas is that the degree of substantial similarity required to show infringement varies according to the type of work and the ideas expressed in it [citing *Krofft,* p. 248 supra]. Some ideas can be expressed in myriad ways, while others allow only a narrow range of expression. Fictional works generally fall into the first category." The standard for "substantial similarity" as to these therefore may be relatively low.

"Factual works are different. Subsequent authors wishing to express the ideas contained in a factual work often can choose from only a narrow range of expression. For example, Landsberg's work states that '[t]he poor player simply attempts to make as many points as possible each turn.' The idea contained in that statement cannot be expressed in a wide variety of ways. Just about any subsequent expression of that idea is likely to appear to be a substantially similar paraphrase of the words with which Landsberg expressed the idea. Therefore, similarity of expression may have to amount to verbatim reproduction or very close paraphrasing before a factual work will be deemed infringed. * * *

"We have reviewed Landsberg's work, S & R's work, and Exhibit 45, a comparative table of similarities between the two works. While we find similarities between the two works, we think there is no more than the similarity that must unavoidably be produced by anyone who wishes to use and restate the unprotectable ideas contained in Landsberg's work.

"S & R's work does not duplicate the selection, coordination, and arrangement of the ideas in Landsberg's work, so we need not decide whether a work that rephrased in the same order as the original a substantial part of the ideas in another work might be held to infringe that work as a compilation, *see* 17 U.S.C.A. §§ 101, 103, even though none of the rephrasings of the individual ideas would constitute infringement when viewed in isolation."

The case was remanded to the district court to determine whether the plaintiff might have a claim for breach of an "implied-in-fact" contract to pay him for his ideas. That question brought the parties back before the Ninth Circuit two years later. See p. 796 infra.[a]

(4) The commitment to preserve unrestricted access to facts is evident in an odd series of cases denying protection to fictional material represented as fact. See, e.g., Mosley v. Follett, 209 U.S.P.Q. 1109 (S.D.N.Y.1980); Oliver v. Saint Germain Foundation, 41 F.Supp. 296 (S.D.Cal.1941). The facts of the *Oliver* case are particularly odd, even for California. The defendant was permitted to appropriate material from a copyrighted work because it had been represented by the plaintiff as the revelations of a

---

a. Cases claiming infringement of textbooks may be less interesting than the history or biography cases, but they too can require extensive comparisons. See McGraw–Hill, Inc. v. Worth Pub. Inc., 335 F.Supp. 415 (S.D.N.Y.1971); Meredith Corp. v. Harper & Row, Inc., 378 F.Supp. 686 (S.D.N.Y.), aff'd per curiam, 500 F.2d 1221 (2d Cir.1974) (preliminary injunction; on final judgment, see 413 F.Supp. 385 (S.D.N.Y.1975)); Morrison v. Solomons, 494 F.Supp. 218 (S.D.N.Y.1980) (similarities successfully explained during defendant's 22 days on the witness stand).

deceased entity from another world. (Would the interest in access to factual information be compromised if account were taken of the reasonable expectations of the copier? But see Arica Institute, Inc. v. Palmer, 970 F.2d 1067 (2d Cir.1992) (estoppel bars any claim of authorship in material represented as fact, even if a reasonable reader might disbelieve the representation).)[b]

(5) For an argument that *Hoehling* is too narrow in its view of copyrightable expression, see Ginsburg, Sabotaging and Reconstructing History: A Comment on the Scope of Copyright Protection in Works of History After *Hoehling v. Universal City Studios,* 29 J.Copyr.Soc. 647 (1982).

The nonfiction cases are discussed in Shipley and Hay, Protecting Research: Copyright, Common–Law Alternatives, and Federal Preemption, 63 N.C.L.Rev. 125 (1984); Gorman, Fact or Fancy? The Implications for Copyright, 29 J.Copyr.Soc. 560 (1982); and Denicola, Copyright in Collections of Facts: A Theory for the Protection of Nonfiction Literary Works, 81 Colum.L.Rev. 516 (1981).

SECTION 6.   COMPUTER PROGRAMS

Computer Associates International, Inc. v. Altai, Inc.

United States Court of Appeals, Second Circuit, 1992.
982 F.2d 693.

■ Before ALTIMARI, MAHONEY and WALKER, CIRCUIT JUDGES.

■ WALKER, CIRCUIT JUDGE.

* * *

Among other things, this case deals with the challenging question of whether and to what extent the "non-literal" aspects of a computer program, that is, those aspects that are not reduced to written code, are protected by copyright. While a few other courts have already grappled with this issue, this case is one of first impression in this circuit. As we shall discuss, we find the results reached by other courts to be less than satisfactory. Drawing upon long-standing doctrines of copyright law, we take an approach that we think better addresses the practical difficulties embedded in these types of cases. In so doing, we have kept in mind the necessary balance between creative incentive and industrial competition.

This appeal comes to us from the United States District Court for the Eastern District of New York, the Honorable George C. Pratt, Circuit Judge, sitting by designation. By Memorandum and Order entered August 12, 1991, Judge Pratt found that defendant Altai, Inc.'s ("Altai"), OSCAR

---

b. In Castle Rock Ent. v. Carol Pub. Group, Inc., 955 F.Supp. 260 (S.D.N.Y.1997), the author of a trivia book on the *Seinfeld* television show was not permitted to invoke the right to take facts from a copyrighted work, since here the "facts" taken from the television episodes were part of the fictional expression created by the copyright owner.

3.4 computer program had infringed plaintiff Computer Associates' ("CA"), copyrighted computer program entitled CA–SCHEDULER. Accordingly, the district court awarded CA $364,444 in actual damages and apportioned profits. Altai has abandoned its appeal from this award. With respect to CA's second claim for copyright infringement, Judge Pratt found that Altai's OSCAR 3.5 program was not substantially similar to a portion of CA–SCHEDULER called ADAPTER, and thus denied relief. Finally, the district court concluded that CA's state law trade secret misappropriation claim against Altai had been preempted by the federal copyright act. CA appealed from these findings.

Because we are in full agreement with Judge Pratt's decision and in substantial agreement with his careful reasoning regarding CA's copyright infringement claim, we affirm the district court's judgment on that issue. However, we vacate the district court's preemption ruling with respect to CA's trade secret claim, and remand the case to the district court for further proceedings.

BACKGROUND

We assume familiarity with the facts set forth in the district court's comprehensive and scholarly opinion. See Computer Assocs. Int'l, Inc. v. Altai, Inc., 775 F.Supp. 544, 549–55 (E.D.N.Y.1991). Thus, we summarize only those facts necessary to resolve this appeal.

I.   COMPUTER PROGRAM DESIGN

Certain elementary facts concerning the nature of computer programs are vital to the following discussion. The Copyright Act defines a computer program as "a set of statements or instructions to be used directly or indirectly in a computer in order to bring about a certain result." 17 U.S.C. § 101. In writing these directions, the programmer works "from the general to the specific." Whelan Assoc., Inc. v. Jaslow Dental Lab., Inc., 797 F.2d 1222, 1229 (3d Cir.1986), cert. denied, 479 U.S. 1031 (1987). See generally Steven R. Englund, Note, Idea, Process, or Protected Expression?: Determining the Scope of Copyright Protection of the Structure of Computer Programs, 88 Mich.L.Rev. 866, 867–73 (1990) (hereinafter "Englund"); Peter S. Menell, An Analysis of the Scope of Copyright Protection for Application Programs, 41 Stan.L.Rev. 1045, 1051–57 (1989) (hereinafter "Menell"); Mark T. Kretschmer, Note, Copyright Protection For Software Architecture: Just Say No!, 1988 Colum.Bus.L.Rev. 823, 824–27 (1988) (hereinafter "Kretschmer"); Peter G. Spivack, Comment, Does Form Follow Function? The Idea/Expression Dichotomy In Copyright Protection of Computer Software, 35 U.C.L.A.L.Rev. 723, 729–31 (1988) (hereinafter "Spivack").

The first step in this procedure is to identify a program's ultimate function or purpose. An example of such an ultimate purpose might be the creation and maintenance of a business ledger. Once this goal has been achieved, a programmer breaks down or "decomposes" the program's ultimate function into "simpler constituent problems or 'subtasks,' " Englund, at 870, which are also known as subroutines or modules. See Spivack, at 729. In the context of a business ledger program, a module or subroutine might be responsible for the task of updating a list of outstanding accounts receivable. Sometimes, depending upon the complexity of its task, a subroutine may be broken down further into sub-subroutines.

Having sufficiently decomposed the program's ultimate function into its component elements, a programmer will then arrange the subroutines or modules into what are known as organizational or flow charts. Flow charts map the interactions between modules that achieve the program's end goal. See Kretschmer, at 826.

In order to accomplish these intra-program interactions, a programmer must carefully design each module's parameter list. A parameter list, according to the expert appointed and fully credited by the district court, Dr. Randall Davis, is "the information sent to and received from a subroutine." See Report of Dr. Randall Davis, at 12. The term "parameter list" refers to the form in which information is passed between modules (e.g. for accounts receivable, the designated time frame and particular customer identifying number) and the information's actual content (e.g. 8/91–7/92; customer No. 3). Id. With respect to form, interacting modules must share similar parameter lists so that they are capable of exchanging information.

"The functions of the modules in a program together with each module's relationships to other modules constitute the 'structure' of the program." Englund, at 871. Additionally, the term structure may include the category of modules referred to as "macros." A macro is a single instruction that initiates a sequence of operations or module interactions within the program. * * *

In fashioning the structure, a programmer will normally attempt to maximize the program's speed, efficiency, as well as simplicity for user operation, while taking into consideration certain externalities such as the memory constraints of the computer upon which the program will be run. See id.; Kretschmer, at 826; Menell, at 1052. "This stage of program design often requires the most time and investment." Kretschmer, at 826.

Once each necessary module has been identified, designed, and its relationship to the other modules has been laid out conceptually, the resulting program structure must be embodied in a written language that the computer can read. This process is called "coding," and requires two steps. Whelan, 797 F.2d at 1230. First, the programmer must transpose the program's structural blueprint into a source code. This step has been described as "comparable to the novelist fleshing out the broad outline of his plot by crafting from words and sentences the paragraphs that convey the ideas." Kretschmer, at 826. The source code may be written in any one of several computer languages, such as COBAL, FORTRAN, BASIC, EDL, etc., depending upon the type of computer for which the program is intended. Whelan, 797 F.2d at 1230. Once the source code has been completed, the second step is to translate or "compile" it into object code. Object code is the binary language comprised of zeros and ones through which the computer directly receives its instructions. Id., at 1230–31; Englund, at 868 & n. 13.

After the coding is finished, the programmer will run the program on the computer in order to find and correct any logical and syntactical errors. This is known as "debugging" and, once done, the program is complete. See Kretschmer, at 826–27.

II. FACTS

* * *

The subject of this litigation originates with one of CA's marketed programs entitled CA–SCHEDULER. CA–SCHEDULER is a job scheduling program designed for IBM mainframe computers. Its primary functions are straightforward: to create a schedule specifying when the computer should run various tasks, and then to control the computer as it executes the schedule. CA–SCHEDULER contains a sub-program entitled ADAPTER, also developed by CA. ADAPTER is not an independently marketed product of CA; it is a wholly integrated component of CA–SCHEDULER and has no capacity for independent use.

Nevertheless, ADAPTER plays an extremely important role. It is an "operating system compatibility component," which means, roughly speaking, it serves as a translator. An "operating system" is itself a program that manages the resources of the computer, allocating those resources to other programs as needed. The IBM System 370 family of computers, for which CA–SCHEDULER was created, is, depending upon the computer's size, designed to contain one of three operating systems: DOS/VSE, MVS, or CMS. As the district court noted, the general rule is that "a program written for one operating system, e.g., DOS/VSE, will not, without modification, run under another operating system such as MVS." Computer Assocs., 775 F.Supp. at 550. ADAPTER's function is to translate the language of a given program into the particular language that the computer's own operating system can understand.

* * *

Starting in 1982, Altai began marketing its own job scheduling program entitled ZEKE. The original version of ZEKE was designed for use in conjunction with a VSE operating system. By late 1983, in response to customer demand, Altai decided to rewrite ZEKE so that it could be run in conjunction with an MVS operating system.

At that time, James P. Williams ("Williams"), then an employee of Altai and now its President, approached Claude F. Arney, III ("Arney"), a computer programmer who worked for CA. Williams and Arney were longstanding friends, and had in fact been co-workers at CA for some time before Williams left CA to work for Altai's predecessor. Williams wanted to recruit Arney to assist Altai in designing an MVS version of ZEKE.

At the time he first spoke with Arney, Williams was aware of both the CA–SCHEDULER and ADAPTER programs. However, Williams was not involved in their development and had never seen the codes of either program. When he asked Arney to come work for Altai, Williams did not know that ADAPTER was a component of CA–SCHEDULER.

Arney, on the other hand, was intimately familiar with various aspects of ADAPTER. While working for CA, he helped improve the VSE version of ADAPTER, and was permitted to take home a copy of ADAPTER's source code. This apparently developed into an irresistible habit, for when Arney left CA to work for Altai in January, 1984, he took with him copies of the source code for both the VSE and MVS versions of ADAPTER. He did this in knowing violation of the CA employee agreements that he had signed.

Once at Altai, Arney and Williams discussed design possibilities for adapting ZEKE to run on MVS operating systems. Williams, who had created the VSE version of ZEKE, thought that approximately 30% of his original program would have to be modified in order to accommodate MVS. Arney persuaded Williams that the best way to make the needed modifications was to introduce a "common system interface" component into ZEKE. He did not tell Williams that his idea stemmed from his familiarity with ADAPTER. They decided to name this new component-program OSCAR.

Arney went to work creating OSCAR at Altai's offices using the ADAPTER source code. The district court accepted Williams' testimony that no one at Altai, with the exception of Arney, affirmatively knew that Arney had the ADAPTER code, or that he was using it to create OS-CAR/VSE. * * * When the dust finally settled, Arney had copied approximately 30% of OSCAR's code from CA's ADAPTER program.

The first generation of OSCAR programs was known as OSCAR 3.4. From 1985 to August 1988, Altai used OSCAR 3.4 in its ZEKE product, as well as in programs entitled ZACK and ZEBB. In late July 1988, CA first learned that Altai may have appropriated parts of ADAPTER. After confirming its suspicions, CA secured copyrights on its 2.1 and 7.0 versions of CA–SCHEDULER. CA then brought this copyright and trade secret misappropriation action against Altai.

Apparently, it was upon receipt of the summons and complaint that Altai first learned that Arney had copied much of the OSCAR code from ADAPTER. After Arney confirmed to Williams that CA's accusations of copying were true, Williams immediately set out to survey the damage. Without ever looking at the ADAPTER code himself, Williams learned from Arney exactly which sections of code Arney had taken from ADAPTER.

Upon advice of counsel, Williams initiated OSCAR's rewrite. The project's goal was to save as much of OSCAR 3.4 as legitimately could be used, and to excise those portions which had been copied from ADAPTER. Arney was entirely excluded from the process, and his copy of the ADAPT-ER code was locked away. Williams put eight other programmers on the project, none of whom had been involved in any way in the development of OSCAR 3.4. Williams provided the programmers with a description of the

ZEKE operating system services so that they could rewrite the appropriate code. The rewrite project took about six months to complete and was finished in mid-November 1989. The resulting program was entitled OSCAR 3.5.

From that point on, Altai shipped only OSCAR 3.5 to its new customers. Altai also shipped OSCAR 3.5 as a "free upgrade" to all customers that had previously purchased OSCAR 3.4. While Altai and Williams acted responsibly to correct Arney's literal copying of the ADAPTER program, copyright infringement had occurred.

* * *

DISCUSSION

While both parties originally appealed from different aspects of the district court's judgment, Altai has now abandoned its appellate claims. In particular, Altai has conceded liability for the copying of ADAPTER into OSCAR 3.4 and raises no challenge to the award of $364,444 in damages on that score. Thus, we address only CA's appeal from the district court's rulings that: (1) Altai was not liable for copyright infringement in developing OSCAR 3.5; and (2) in developing both OSCAR 3.4 and 3.5, Altai was not liable for misappropriating CA's trade secrets. * * *

I.   COPYRIGHT INFRINGEMENT

* * * For the purpose of analysis, the district court assumed that Altai had access to the ADAPTER code when creating OSCAR 3.5. See *Computer Assocs.*, 775 F.Supp. at 558. Thus, in determining whether Altai had unlawfully copied protected aspects of CA's ADAPTER, the district court narrowed its focus of inquiry to ascertaining whether Altai's OSCAR 3.5 was substantially similar to ADAPTER. Because we approve Judge Pratt's conclusions regarding substantial similarity, our analysis will proceed along the same assumption.

As a general matter, and to varying degrees, copyright protection extends beyond a literary work's strictly textual form to its non-literal components. As we have said, "[i]t is of course essential to any protection of literary property . . . that the right cannot be limited literally to the text, else a plagiarist would escape by immaterial variations." Nichols v. Universal Pictures Co., 45 F.2d 119, 121 (2d Cir.1930) (L. Hand, J.), cert. denied, 282 U.S. 902 (1931). Thus, where "the fundamental essence or structure of one work is duplicated in another," 3 Nimmer, § 13.03[A][1], at 13–24, courts have found copyright infringement. * * *

A.   Copyright Protection for the Non-literal Elements of Computer Programs

It is now well settled that the literal elements of computer programs, i.e., their source and object codes, are the subject of copyright protection. See *Whelan*, 797 F.2d at 1233 (source and object code); * * * Here, as noted earlier, Altai admits having copied approximately 30% of the OSCAR

3.4 program from CA's ADAPTER source code, and does not challenge the district court's related finding of infringement.

In this case, the hotly contested issues surround OSCAR 3.5. As recounted above, OSCAR 3.5 is the product of Altai's carefully orchestrated rewrite of OSCAR 3.4. After the purge, none of the ADAPTER source code remained in the 3.5 version; thus, Altai made sure that the literal elements of its revamped OSCAR program were no longer substantially similar to the literal elements of CA's ADAPTER. * * *

CA argues that, despite Altai's rewrite of the OSCAR code, the resulting program remained substantially similar to the *structure* of its ADAPTER program. As discussed above, a program's structure includes its non-literal components such as general flow charts as well as the more specific organization of inter-modular relationships, parameter lists, and macros. In addition to these aspects, CA contends that OSCAR 3.5 is also substantially similar to ADAPTER with respect to the list of services that both ADAPTER and OSCAR obtain from their respective operating systems. We must decide whether and to what extent these elements of computer programs are protected by copyright law.

The statutory terrain in this area has been well explored. See Lotus Dev. Corp. v. Paperback Software Int'l, 740 F.Supp. 37, 47–51 (D.Mass. 1990); see also *Whelan,* 797 F.2d at 1240–42; Englund, at 885–90; Spivack, at 731–37. The Copyright Act affords protection to "original works of authorship fixed in any tangible medium of expression." 17 U.S.C. § 102(a). This broad category of protected "works" includes "literary works," id. at § 102(a)(1), which are defined by the Act as "works, other than audiovisual works, expressed in words, numbers, or other verbal or numerical symbols or indicia, regardless of the nature of the material objects, such as books, periodicals, manuscripts, phonorecords, film, tapes, disks, or cards, in which they are embodied." 17 U.S.C. § 101. While computer programs are not specifically listed as part of the above statutory definition, the legislative history leaves no doubt that Congress intended them to be considered literary works. See H.R.Rep. No. 1476, 94th Cong., 2d Sess. 54, reprinted in 1976 U.S.C.C.A.N. 5659, 5667 (hereinafter "House Report"); *Whelan,* 797 F.2d at 1234; *Apple Computer* [p. 120 supra].

The syllogism that follows from the foregoing premises is a powerful one: if the non-literal structures of literary works are protected by copyright; and if computer programs are literary works, as we are told by the legislature; then the non-literal structures of computer programs are protected by copyright. See *Whelan,* 797 F.2d at 1234 ("By analogy to other literary works, it would thus appear that the copyrights of computer programs can be infringed even absent copying of the literal elements of the program."). We have no reservation in joining the company of those courts that have already ascribed to this logic. * * * However, that conclusion does not end our analysis. We must determine the scope of copyright protection that extends to a computer program's non-literal structure.

As a caveat, we note that our decision here does not control infringement actions regarding categorically distinct works, such as certain types of screen displays. These items represent products of computer programs, rather than the programs themselves, and fall under the copyright rubric of audiovisual works. If a computer audiovisual display is copyrighted separately as an audiovisual work, apart from the literary work that generates it (i.e., the program), the display may be protectable regardless of the underlying program's copyright status. * * *

(1) Idea vs. Expression Dichotomy

* * *

The essentially utilitarian nature of a computer program further complicates the task of distilling its idea from its expression. See [SAS Inst., Inc. v. S & H Computer Sys., Inc., 605 F.Supp. 816, 829 (M.D.Tenn. 1985)]; cf. Englund, at 893. In order to describe both computational processes and abstract ideas, its content "combines creative and technical expression." See Spivack, at 755. The variations of expression found in purely creative compositions, as opposed to those contained in utilitarian works, are not directed towards practical application. For example, a narration of Humpty Dumpty's demise, which would clearly be a creative composition, does not serve the same ends as, say, a recipe for scrambled eggs—which is a more process oriented text. Thus, compared to aesthetic works, computer programs hover even more closely to the elusive boundary line described in § 102(b).

The doctrinal starting point in analyses of utilitarian works, is the seminal case of Baker v. Selden, 101 U.S. 99 (1879). * * *

To the extent that an accounting text and a computer program are both "a set of statements or instructions ... to bring about a certain result," 17 U.S.C. § 101, they are roughly analogous. In the former case, the processes are ultimately conducted by human agency; in the latter, by electronic means. In either case, as already stated, the processes themselves are not protectable. But the holding in *Baker* goes farther. The Court concluded that those aspects of a work, which "must necessarily be used as incident to" the idea, system or process that the work describes, are also not copyrightable. 101 U.S. at 104. Selden's ledger sheets, therefore, enjoyed no copyright protection because they were "necessary incidents to" the system of accounting that he described. Id. at 103. From this reasoning, we conclude that those elements of a computer program that are necessarily incidental to its function are similarly unprotectable.

While Baker v. Selden provides a sound analytical foundation, it offers scant guidance on how to separate idea or process from expression, and moreover, on how to further distinguish protectable expression from that expression which "must necessarily be used as incident to" the work's underlying concept. In the context of computer programs, the Third Circuit's noted decision in *Whelan* has, thus far, been the most thoughtful attempt to accomplish these ends.

The court in *Whelan* faced substantially the same problem as is presented by this case. There, the defendant was accused of making off with the non-literal structure of the plaintiff's copyrighted dental lab management program, and employing it to create its own competitive version. In assessing whether there had been an infringement, the court had to determine which aspects of the programs involved were ideas, and which were expression. In separating the two, the court settled upon the following conceptual approach: "[T]he line between idea and expression may be drawn with reference to the end sought to be achieved by the work in question. In other words, *the purpose or function of a utilitarian work would be the work's idea, and everything that is not necessary to that purpose or function would be part of the expression of the idea....* Where there are various means of achieving the desired purpose, then the particular means chosen is not necessary to the purpose; hence, there is expression, not idea." 797 F.2d at 1236 (citations omitted). The "idea" of the program at issue in *Whelan* was identified by the court as simply "the efficient management of a dental laboratory." Id. at n. 28.

So far, in the courts, the *Whelan* rule has received a mixed reception.
* * *

Whelan has fared even more poorly in the academic community, where its standard for distinguishing idea from expression has been widely criticized for being conceptually overbroad. * * * The leading commentator in the field has stated that, "[t]he crucial flaw in [*Whelan's*] reasoning is that it assumes that only one 'idea,' in copyright law terms, underlies any computer program, and that once a separable idea can be identified, everything else must be expression." 3 Nimmer § 13.03(F), at 13–62.34. This criticism focuses not upon the program's ultimate purpose but upon the reality of its structural design. As we have already noted, a computer program's ultimate function or purpose is the composite result of interacting subroutines. Since each subroutine is itself a program, and thus, may be said to have its own "idea," *Whelan's* general formulation that a program's overall purpose equates with the program's idea is descriptively inadequate.

Accordingly, we think that Judge Pratt wisely declined to follow *Whelan*. See *Computer Assocs.,* 775 F.Supp. at 558–60. * * *

(2) Substantial Similarity Test for Computer Program Structure: Abstraction—Filtration—Comparison

We think that *Whelan's* approach to separating idea from expression in computer programs relies too heavily on metaphysical distinctions and does not place enough emphasis on practical considerations. * * *

As discussed herein, we think that district courts would be well-advised to undertake a three-step procedure, based on the abstractions test utilized by the district court, in order to determine whether the non-literal elements of two or more computer programs are substantially similar. This approach breaks no new ground; rather, it draws on such familiar copyright doctrines as merger, *scenes a faire,* and public domain. In taking this approach, however, we are cognizant that computer technology is a dynamic field which can quickly outpace judicial decisionmaking. Thus, in cases where the technology in question does not allow for a literal application of the procedure we outline below, our opinion should not be read to foreclose the district courts of our circuit from utilizing a modified version.

In ascertaining substantial similarity under this approach, a court would first break down the allegedly infringed program into its constituent structural parts. Then, by examining each of these parts for such things as incorporated ideas, expression that is necessarily incidental to those ideas, and elements that are taken from the public domain, a court would then be able to sift out all non-protectable material. Left with a kernel, or possible kernels, of creative expression after following this process of elimination, the court's last step would be to compare this material with the structure of an allegedly infringing program. The result of this comparison will determine whether the protectable elements of the programs at issue are substantially similar so as to warrant a finding of infringement. It will be helpful to elaborate a bit further.

Step One: Abstraction

As the district court appreciated, see *Computer Assocs.,* 775 F.Supp. at 560, the theoretic framework for analyzing substantial similarity expounded by Learned Hand in the *Nichols* case is helpful in the present context. In *Nichols,* we enunciated what has now become known as the "abstractions" test for separating idea from expression * * *.

While the abstractions test was originally applied in relation to literary works such as novels and plays, it is adaptable to computer programs. In contrast to the *Whelan* approach, the abstractions test "implicitly recognizes that any given work may consist of a mixture of numerous ideas and expressions." 3 Nimmer § 13.03[F] at 13–62.34–63.

As applied to computer programs, the abstractions test will comprise the first step in the examination for substantial similarity. Initially, in a manner that resembles reverse engineering on a theoretical plane, a court should dissect the allegedly copied program's structure and isolate each level of abstraction contained within it. This process begins with the code and ends with an articulation of the program's ultimate function. Along the way, it is necessary essentially to retrace and map each of the designer's steps—in the opposite order in which they were taken during the program's creation. See Background: Computer Program Design, supra.

As an anatomical guide to this procedure, the following description is helpful: "At the lowest level of abstraction, a computer program may be thought of in its entirety as a set of individual instructions organized into a hierarchy of modules. At a higher level of abstraction, the instructions in the lowest-level modules may be replaced conceptually by the functions of those modules. At progressively higher levels of abstraction, the functions of higher-level modules conceptually replace the implementations of those modules in terms of lower-level modules and instructions, until finally, one is left with nothing but the ultimate function of the program. . . . A program has structure at every level of abstraction at which it is viewed. At low levels of abstraction, a program's structure may be quite complex; at the highest level it is trivial." Englund, at 897–98. Cf. Spivack, at 774.

Step Two: Filtration

Once the program's abstraction levels have been discovered, the substantial similarity inquiry moves from the conceptual to the concrete. Professor Nimmer suggests, and we endorse, a "successive filtering method" for separating protectable expression from non-protectable material. See generally 3 Nimmer § 13.03[F]. This process entails examining the structural components at each level of abstraction to determine whether their particular inclusion at that level was "idea" or was dictated by considerations of efficiency, so as to be necessarily incidental to that idea; required by factors external to the program itself; or taken from the public domain and hence is nonprotectable expression. See also Kretschmer, at 844–45 (arguing that program features dictated by market externalities or efficiency concerns are unprotectable). The structure of any given program may reflect some, all, or none of these considerations. Each case requires its own fact specific investigation.

Strictly speaking, this filtration serves "the purpose of defining the scope of plaintiff's copyright." Brown Bag Software v. Symantec Corp., 960 F.2d 1465, 1475 (9th Cir.) (endorsing "analytic dissection" of computer programs in order to isolate protectable expression), cert. denied, 506 U.S. 869 (1992). By applying well developed doctrines of copyright law, it may ultimately leave behind a "core of protectable material." 3 Nimmer § 13.03[F][5], at 13–72. Further explication of this second step may be helpful.

(a) Elements Dictated by Efficiency

The portion of Baker v. Selden, discussed earlier, which denies copyright protection to expression necessarily incidental to the idea being expressed, appears to be the cornerstone for what has developed into the doctrine of merger. * * *

CONTU recognized the applicability of the merger doctrine to computer programs. In its report to Congress it stated that: "[C]opyrighted language may be copied without infringing when there is but a limited number of ways to express a given idea.... In the computer context, this means that when specific instructions, even though previously copyrighted, are the only and essential means of accomplishing a given task, their later use by another will not amount to infringement." CONTU Report at 20. While this statement directly concerns only the application of merger to program code, that is, the textual aspect of the program, it reasonably suggests that the doctrine fits comfortably within the general context of computer programs.

Furthermore, when one considers the fact that programmers generally strive to create programs "that meet the user's needs in the most efficient manner," Menell, at 1052, the applicability of the merger doctrine to computer programs becomes compelling. In the context of computer program design, the concept of efficiency is akin to deriving the most concise logical proof or formulating the most succinct mathematical computation. Thus, the more efficient a set of modules are, the more closely they approximate the idea or process embodied in that particular aspect of the program's structure.

While, hypothetically, there might be a myriad of ways in which a programmer may effectuate certain functions within a program,—i.e., express the idea embodied in a given subroutine—efficiency concerns may so narrow the practical range of choice as to make only one or two forms of expression workable options. See 3 Nimmer § 13.03[F][2], at 13–63; see also *Whelan,* 797 F.2d at 1243 n. 43 ("It is true that for certain tasks there are only a very limited number of file structures available, and in such cases the structures might not be copyrightable. . . ."). Of course, not all program structure is informed by efficiency concerns. See Menell, at 1052 (besides efficiency, simplicity related to user accommodation has become a programming priority). It follows that in order to determine whether the merger doctrine precludes copyright protection to an aspect of a program's structure that is so oriented, a court must inquire "whether the use of *this particular set* of modules is necessary efficiently to implement that part of the program's process" being implemented. Englund, at 902. If the answer is yes, then the expression represented by the programmer's choice of a specific module or group of modules has merged with their underlying idea and is unprotected. Id. at 902–03. * * *

(b) Elements Dictated By External Factors

We have stated that where "it is virtually impossible to write about a particular historical era or fictional theme without employing certain 'stock' or standard literary devices," such expression is not copyrightable. Hoehling v. Universal City Studios, Inc., 618 F.2d 972, 979 (2d Cir.), cert. denied, 449 U.S. 841 (1980). * * * This is known as the *scenes a faire* doctrine, and like "merger," it has its analogous application to computer programs. Cf. [Data East USA, Inc. v. Epyx, Inc., 862 F.2d 204, 208 (9th Cir.1988)] (applying *scenes a faire* to a home computer video game).

Professor Nimmer points out that "in many instances it is virtually impossible to write a program to perform particular functions in a specific computing environment without employing standard techniques." 3 Nimmer § 13.03[F][3], at 13–65. This is a result of the fact that a programmer's freedom of design choice is often circumscribed by extrinsic considerations such as (1) the mechanical specifications of the computer on which a particular program is intended to run; (2) compatibility requirements of other programs with which a program is designed to operate in conjunction; (3) computer manufacturers' design standards; (4) demands of the industry being serviced; and (5) widely accepted programming practices within the computer industry. Id. at 13–65–71.

Courts have already considered some of these factors in denying copyright protection to various elements of computer programs. * * *

Building upon this existing case law, we conclude that a court must also examine the structural content of an allegedly infringed program for elements that might have been dictated by external factors.

(c) Elements Taken From the Public Domain

Closely related to the non-protectability of *scenes a faire,* is material found in the public domain. Such material is free for the taking and cannot be appropriated by a single author even though it is included in a copyrighted work. See E.F. Johnson Co. v. Uniden Corp. of America, 623 F.Supp. 1485, 1499 (D.Minn.1985); see also *Sheldon,* 81 F.2d at 54. We see no reason to make an exception to this rule for elements of a computer program that have entered the public domain by virtue of freely accessible program exchanges and the like. See 3 Nimmer § 13.03[F][4]; see also *Brown Bag Software,* 960 F.2d at 1473 (affirming the district court's finding that " '[p]laintiffs may not claim copyright protection of an ... expression that is, if not standard, then commonplace in the computer software industry.' "). Thus, a court must also filter out this material from the allegedly infringed program before it makes the final inquiry in its substantial similarity analysis.

Step Three: Comparison

The third and final step of the test for substantial similarity that we believe appropriate for non-literal program components entails a comparison. Once a court has sifted out all elements of the allegedly infringed program which are "ideas" or are dictated by efficiency or external factors, or taken from the public domain, there may remain a core of protectable expression. In terms of a work's copyright value, this is the golden nugget. See *Brown Bag Software,* 960 F.2d at 1475. At this point, the court's substantial similarity inquiry focuses on whether the defendant copied any aspect of this protected expression, as well as an assessment of the copied portion's relative importance with respect to the plaintiff's overall program.
* * *

(3) Policy Considerations

We are satisfied that the three step approach we have just outlined not only comports with, but advances the constitutional policies underlying the Copyright Act. Since any method that tries to distinguish idea from expression ultimately impacts on the scope of copyright protection afforded to a particular type of work, "the line [it draws] must be a pragmatic one, which also keeps in consideration 'the preservation of the balance between competition and protection....' " [Apple Computer, Inc. v. Franklin Computer Corp., 714 F.2d 1240, 1253 (3d Cir.1983), cert. dismissed, 464 U.S. 1033 (1984)].

CA and some *amici* argue against the type of approach that we have set forth on the grounds that it will be a disincentive for future computer program research and development. At bottom, they claim that if programmers are not guaranteed broad copyright protection for their work, they will not invest the extensive time, energy and funds required to design and improve program structures. While they have a point, their argument cannot carry the day. The interest of the copyright law is not in simply conferring a monopoly on industrious persons, but in advancing the public welfare through rewarding artistic creativity, in a manner that permits the free use and development of non-protectable ideas and processes. * * *

Recently, the Supreme Court has emphatically reiterated that "[t]he primary objective of copyright is not to reward the *labor* of authors...." Feist Publications, Inc. v. Rural Tel. Serv. Co., 499 U.S. 340, 349 (1991) (emphasis added). * * *

Feist teaches that substantial effort alone cannot confer copyright status on an otherwise uncopyrightable work. As we have discussed, despite the fact that significant labor and expense often goes into computer program flow-charting and debugging, that process does not always result in inherently protectable expression. Thus, *Feist* implicitly undercuts the *Whelan* rationale, "which allow[ed] copyright protection beyond the literal computer code ... [in order to] provide the proper incentive for programmers by protecting their most valuable efforts...." *Whelan*, 797 F.2d at 1237 (footnote omitted). We note that *Whelan* was decided prior to *Feist* when the "sweat of the brow" doctrine still had vitality. In view of the Supreme Court's recent holding, however, we must reject the legal basis of CA's disincentive argument.

Furthermore, we are unpersuaded that the test we approve today will lead to the dire consequences for the computer program industry that plaintiff and some *amici* predict. To the contrary, serious students of the industry have been highly critical of the sweeping scope of copyright protection engendered by the *Whelan* rule, in that it "enables first comers to 'lock up' basic programming techniques as implemented in programs to perform particular tasks." Menell, at 1087; see also Spivack, at 765 (*Whelan* "results in an inhibition of creation by virtue of the copyright owner's quasi-monopoly power"). * * *

Generally, we think that copyright registration—with its indiscriminating availability—is not ideally suited to deal with the highly dynamic technology of computer science. Thus far, many of the decisions in this area reflect the courts' attempt to fit the proverbial square peg in a round hole. The district court, see *Computer Assocs.*, 775 F.Supp. at 560, and at least one commentator have suggested that patent registration, with its exacting up-front novelty and non-obviousness requirements, might be the more appropriate rubric of protection for intellectual property of this kind. See Randell M. Whitmeyer, Comment, A Plea for Due Processes: Defining the Proper Scope of Patent Protection for Computer Software, 85 Nw. U.L.Rev. 1103, 1123–25 (1991); see also Lotus Dev. Corp. v. Borland Int'l, Inc., 788 F.Supp. 78, 91 (D.Mass.1992) (discussing the potentially supplemental relationship between patent and copyright protection in the context of computer programs). In any event, now that more than 12 years have passed since CONTU issued its final report, the resolution of this specific issue could benefit from further legislative investigation—perhaps a CONTU II. * * *

B.   The District Court Decision

We turn now to our review of the district court's decision in this particular case. At the outset, we must address CA's claim that the district court erred by relying too heavily on the court appointed expert's "personal opinions on the factual and legal issues before the court."

(1) Use of Expert Evidence in Determining Substantial Similarity Between Computer Programs

Pursuant to Fed.R.Evid. 706, and with the consent of both Altai and CA, Judge Pratt appointed and relied upon Dr. Randall Davis of the Massachusetts Institute of Technology as the court's own expert witness on the issue of substantial similarity. Dr. Davis submitted a comprehensive written report that analyzed the various aspects of the computer programs at issue and evaluated the parties' expert evidence. At trial, Dr. Davis was extensively cross-examined by both CA and Altai.

The well-established general rule in this circuit has been to limit the use of expert opinion in determining whether works at issue are substantially similar [citing Arnstein v. Porter, 154 F.2d 464 (2d Cir.1946)]. * * *

Historically, *Arnstein's* ordinary observer standard had its roots in "an attempt to apply the 'reasonable person' doctrine as found in other areas of the law to copyright." 3 Nimmer § 13.03[E][2], at 13–62.10–11. That approach may well have served its purpose when the material under scrutiny was limited to art forms readily comprehensible and generally familiar to the average lay person. However, in considering the extension of the rule to the present case, we are reminded of Holmes' admonition that, "[t]he life of the law has not been logic: it has been experience." O.W. Holmes, Jr., *The Common Law* 1 (1881).

Thus, in deciding the limits to which expert opinion may be employed in ascertaining the substantial similarity of computer programs, we cannot disregard the highly complicated and technical subject matter at the heart of these claims. Rather, we recognize the reality that computer programs are likely to be somewhat impenetrable by lay observers—whether they be judges or juries—and, thus, seem to fall outside the category of works contemplated by those who engineered the *Arnstein* test. * * *

In making its finding on substantial similarity with respect to computer programs, we believe that the trier of fact need not be limited by the strictures of its own lay perspective. * * * Rather, we leave it to the discretion of the district court to decide to what extent, if any, expert opinion, regarding the highly technical nature of computer programs, is warranted in a given case.

In so holding, we do not intend to disturb the traditional role of lay observers in judging substantial similarity in copyright cases that involve the aesthetic arts, such as music, visual works or literature. * * *

(2) Evidentiary Analysis

* * *

Since we accept Judge Pratt's factual conclusions and the results of his legal analysis, we affirm his dismissal of CA's copyright infringement claim based upon OSCAR 3.5. We emphasize that, like all copyright infringement cases, those that involve computer programs are highly fact specific. The amount of protection due structural elements, in any given case, will vary according to the protectable expression found to exist within the program at issue.

II.   TRADE SECRET PREEMPTION

[The court, after a rehearing, concluded that Computer Associates' trade secret claims against Altai were not preempted under § 301 of the Copyright Act.]

CONCLUSION

In adopting the above three step analysis for substantial similarity between the non-literal elements of computer programs, we seek to insure two things: (1) that programmers may receive appropriate copyright protection for innovative utilitarian works containing expression; and (2) that non-protectable technical expression remains in the public domain for others to use freely as building blocks in their own work. At first blush, it may seem counter-intuitive that someone who has benefitted to some degree from illicitly obtained material can emerge from an infringement suit relatively unscathed. However, so long as the appropriated material consists of non-protectable expression, "[t]his result is neither unfair nor unfortunate. It is the means by which copyright advances the progress of science and art." *Feist,* 499 U.S. at 350.

Furthermore, we underscore that so long as trade secret law is employed in a manner that does not encroach upon the exclusive domain of the Copyright Act, it is an appropriate means by which to secure compensation for software espionage.

Accordingly, we affirm the judgment of the district court in part; vacate in part; and remand for further proceedings. The parties shall bear their own costs of appeal, including the petition for rehearing.

■ [JUDGE ALTIMARI dissented from the court's preemption analysis.]

NOTES AND QUESTIONS ON INFRINGEMENT OF COMPUTER PROGRAMS

(1) In a subsequent decision, the Second Circuit refused to enjoin Computer Associates from pursuing the same infringement claim against Altai under French copyright law. Computer Associates Int'l, Inc. v. Altai, Inc., 126 F.3d 365 (2d Cir.1997).

Does Judge Walker's analogy to the scope of protection accorded other kinds of literary works provide a convincing justification for extending protection to the "non-literal" elements of computer programs? A case for protection limited to literal copying is made in Goldstein, Infringement of Copyright in Computer Programs, 47 Pitt.L.Rev. 1119 (1986). Karjala, A

Coherent Theory for the Copyright Protection of Computer Software and Recent Judicial Interpretations, 66 U.Cinn.L.Rev. 53 (1997), advocates narrow protection limited to aspects of programs subject to fast and cheap duplication that would prevent only literal copying and close derivatives.

(2) Is *Computer Associates* correct in rejecting the analysis in Whelan Associates v. Jaslow Dental Laboratories, which viewed a computer program's overall "purpose or function" as unprotected "idea" and any structural aspects not essential to the performance of that purpose or function as protectable "expression"? Did *Whelan* carry software protection into the forbidden realm of "idea, procedure, process, system, [or] method of operation"? The court in *Whelan* rejected the argument that progress in computer programming demands greater use of prior works than is necessary in other areas; the court's conclusion is itself rejected in Karjala, Copyright, Computer Software, and the New Protectionism, 28 Jurimetrics 33 (1987). Compare the full-blown defense of *Whelan* offered in Clapes, Lynch, & Steinberg, Silicon Epics and Binary Bards: Determining the Proper Scope of Protection for Computer Programs, 34 UCLA L.Rev. 1493 (1987), with Brinson, Copyrighted Software: Separating the Protected Expression from Unprotected Ideas: A Starting Point, 29 B.C.L.Rev. 803 (1988), concluding that *Whelan* overprotects and advocating application of the traditional "abstractions" test.

The "basic three-part analysis" in *Computer Associates* was adopted by the Tenth Circuit in Gates Rubber Co. v. Bando Chemical Indus., Ltd., 9 F.3d 823 (10th Cir.1993), which rejected the lower court's reliance on *Whelan*. "Filtration should eliminate from comparison the unprotectable elements of ideas, processes, facts, public domain information, merger material, *scenes a faire* material, and other unprotectable elements suggested by the particular facts of the program under examination." However, although emphasizing that copying of unprotectable elements cannot serve as the basis of liability, the court said that a comparison of the works as a whole may be useful in determining the fact of copying. The Eleventh Circuit in Bateman v. Mnemonics, Inc., 79 F.3d 1532 (11th Cir.1996), has said that although the technique pursued in *Computer Associates* was formulated for non-literal copying, a similar analysis is appropriate in cases of literal copying. Judge Baer in Harbor Software, Inc. v. Applied Systems, Inc., 925 F.Supp. 1042 (S.D.N.Y.1996), held that the abstraction and filtration necessary to determine the scope of copyright in a computer program is a matter for the court; the jury's role is limited to comparing protectable elements.

If *Computer Associates* is correct in its conclusion that the protection recognized in *Whelan* is excessive, does the filtration method move too far in the opposite direction? Is it possible that the sifting required by *Computer Associates* may be so fine as to ignore expressive selections and arrangements of programming elements? (See Judge Walker's warning in Apple Computer, Inc. v. Microsoft Corp., 779 F.Supp. 133 (N.D.Cal.1991).) In a subsequent non-literal copying case, the Second Circuit argued that the comparison of programs at successively higher levels of abstraction facilitates protection for original combinations and interrelationships of individually unprotected design elements. Softel, Inc. v. Dragon Medical and Scientific Communications, Inc., 118 F.3d 955 (2d Cir.1997), cert. denied, 118 S.Ct. 1300 (1998).

(3) Is *Computer Associates* correct in abandoning the ordinary observer test of substantial similarity? Is it relevant that the legislative history of the Semiconductor Chip Protection Act (p. 176 supra) says that expert testimony should be admissible on the issue of substantial similarity? See S.Rep. No. 98–425, 98th Cong., 2d Sess. 18 (1984). Some have argued that the substantial similarity standard should itself be abandoned for computer programs in favor of tests looking to the economic advantage gained by the copier through the use of the copyrighted program. See Conley & Bryan, A Unifying Theory for the Litigation of Computer Software Copyright Cases, 63 N.Car.L.Rev. 563 (1985). The argument stresses the § 106(2) exclusive right to prepare derivative works.

(4) The legitimacy of "reverse engineering" of computer programs was the central issue in Sega Enterprises Ltd. v. Accolade, Inc., 977 F.2d 1510 (9th Cir.1992). Sega markets video games that are played through its "Genesis" console. Accolade, desiring to develop games that would be compatible with the Genesis console, reconstructed the source code for the Sega games and console by "disassembling" the object code embedded in the game cartridges and console chip. It then produced games that were compatible with Genesis, but without any literal copying. The court, in a comprehensive opinion by Judge Reinhardt, concluded that although such "intermediate copying" would ordinarily constitute infringement, "where disassembly is the only way to gain access to the ideas and functional elements embodied in a copyrighted computer program and where there is a legitimate reason for seeking such access, disassembly is a fair use of the copyrighted work, as a matter of law." The court's discussion of the fair use factors in § 107 emphasized the public benefit in having more "independently designed video game programs offered for use with the Genesis console." This benefit was found to override the presumption that copying for commercial purposes is not a fair use, especially since the direct objective of the copying was analysis rather than resale. There is also a valuable discussion of the unprotected aspects of computer programs that is in harmony with *Computer Associates*. See also Atari Games Corp. v. Nintendo Inc., 975 F.2d 832 (Fed.Cir.1992), in which the Federal Circuit had jurisdiction (because a patent was involved) over another intermediate copying case, with Ninth Circuit law controlling. Atari was struggling to break the electronic "lock" for entry into the Nintendo console. The court said that Atari could have made fair use of the Nintendo program to derive unprotected ideas and processes; it also indicated that Atari could incorporate into its games aspects of the Nintendo program necessary to unlock the Nintendo console. Atari's copying, however, had gone further (and it had also gotten a copy of Nintendo's source code by perpetrating a fraud on the Copyright Office). The court affirmed a preliminary injunction.[a]

a. Karjala, Copyright Protection of Computer Documents, Reverse Engineering, and Professor Miller, 19 U. Dayton L.Rev. 975 (1994), and Rice, *Sega* and Beyond: A

(5) Consider again the question raised at p. 137 supra—should the protection of computer programs be achieved through some form of *sui generis* legislation analogous to that protecting semiconductor chips? Or is it best to heed the advice of Professor Kidwell, offered in Software and Semiconductors: Why Are We Confused?, 70 Minn.L.Rev. 533 (1985), that in the face of confusion and uncertainty, patience is a virtue.

Lotus Development Corp. v. Borland International, Inc.

United States Court of Appeals, First Circuit, 1995.
49 F.3d 807.
Affirmed per curiam, 516 U.S. 233, 116 S.Ct. 804 (1996).

■ Before TORRUELLA, CHIEF JUDGE, BOUDIN and STAHL, CIRCUIT JUDGES.

■ STAHL, CIRCUIT JUDGE:

This appeal requires us to decide whether a computer menu command hierarchy is copyrightable subject matter. In particular, we must decide whether, as the district court held, plaintiff-appellee Lotus Development Corporation's copyright in Lotus 1–2–3, a computer spreadsheet program, was infringed by defendant-appellant Borland International, Inc., when Borland copied the Lotus 1–2–3 menu command hierarchy into its Quattro and Quattro Pro computer spreadsheet programs. See Lotus Dev. Corp. v. Borland Int'l, Inc., 788 F.Supp. 78 (D.Mass.1992) (*"Borland I"*); Lotus Dev. Corp. v. Borland Int'l, Inc., 799 F.Supp. 203 (D.Mass.1992) (*"Borland II"*); Lotus Dev. Corp. v. Borland Int'l, Inc., 831 F.Supp. 202 (D.Mass. 1993) (*"Borland III"*); Lotus Dev. Corp. v. Borland Int'l, Inc., 831 F.Supp. 223 (D.Mass.1993) (*"Borland IV"*).

I.

Background

Lotus 1–2–3 is a spreadsheet program that enables users to perform accounting functions electronically on a computer. Users manipulate and control the program via a series of menu commands, such as "Copy," "Print," and "Quit." Users choose commands either by highlighting them on the screen or by typing their first letter. In all, Lotus 1–2–3 has 469 commands arranged into more than 50 menus and submenus.

Lotus 1–2–3, like many computer programs, allows users to write what are called "macros." By writing a macro, a user can designate a series of

Beacon for Fair Use Analysis ... At Least as Far as It Goes, id. at 1131, both argue for broad access to computer programs based on their essential functionality. For a comparative analysis, see McManis, Intellectual Property Protection and Reverse Engineering of Computer Programs in the U.S. and the European Community, 8 High Tech.L.J. 25 (1993). Cohen, Reverse Engineering and the Rise of Electronic Vigilantism: Intellectual Property Implications of "Lock Out" Programs, 68 S.Cal.L.Rev. 1091 (1995), presses for a sui generis approach to fair use of computer programs in order to promote competition and protect the public domain.

command choices with a single macro keystroke. Then, to execute that series of commands in multiple parts of the spreadsheet, rather than typing the whole series each time, the user only needs to type the single pre-programmed macro keystroke, causing the program to recall and perform the designated series of commands automatically. Thus, Lotus 1–2–3 macros shorten the time needed to set up and operate the program.

Borland released its first Quattro program to the public in 1987, after Borland's engineers had labored over its development for nearly three years. Borland's objective was to develop a spreadsheet program far superior to existing programs, including Lotus 1–2–3. In Borland's words, "[f]rom the time of its initial release ... Quattro included enormous innovations over competing spreadsheet products."

The district court found, and Borland does not now contest, that Borland included in its Quattro and Quattro Pro version 1.0 programs "a *virtually identical* copy of the entire 1–2–3 menu tree." *Borland III*, 831 F.Supp. at 212 (emphasis in original). In so doing, Borland did not copy any of Lotus's underlying computer code; it copied only the words and structure of Lotus's menu command hierarchy. Borland included the Lotus menu command hierarchy in its programs to make them compatible with Lotus 1–2–3 so that spreadsheet users who were already familiar with Lotus 1–2–3 would be able to switch to the Borland programs without having to learn new commands or rewrite their Lotus macros.

In its Quattro and Quattro Pro version 1.0 programs, Borland achieved compatibility with Lotus 1–2–3 by offering its users an alternate user interface, the "Lotus Emulation Interface." By activating the Emulation Interface, Borland users would see the Lotus menu commands on their screens and could interact with Quattro or Quattro Pro as if using Lotus 1–2–3, albeit with a slightly different looking screen and with many Borland options not available on Lotus 1–2–3. In effect, Borland allowed users to choose how they wanted to communicate with Borland's spreadsheet programs: either by using menu commands designed by Borland, or by using the commands and command structure used in Lotus 1–2–3 augmented by Borland-added commands.

Lotus filed this action against Borland in the District of Massachusetts on July 2, 1990, four days after a district court held that the Lotus 1–2–3 "menu structure, taken as a whole—including the choice of command terms [and] the structure and order of those terms," was protected expression covered by Lotus's copyrights. Lotus Dev. Corp. v. Paperback Software Int'l, 740 F.Supp. 37, 68, 70 (D.Mass.1990) ("*Paperback* ").[1]   * * *

[Both parties filed motions for summary judgment.] Because so many variations were possible, the district court concluded that the Lotus developers' choice and arrangement of command terms, reflected in the Lotus menu command hierarchy, constituted copyrightable expression.

---

1. Judge Keeton presided over both the *Paperback* litigation and this case.

In granting partial summary judgment to Lotus, the district court held that Borland had infringed Lotus's copyright in Lotus 1–2–3:

> [A]s a matter of law, Borland's Quattro products infringe the Lotus 1–2–3 copyright because of (1) the extent of copying of the "menu commands" and "menu structure" that is not *genuinely* disputed in this case, (2) the extent to which the copied elements of the "menu commands" and "menu structure" contain expressive aspects separable from the functions of the "menu commands" and "menu structure," and (3) the scope of those copied expressive aspects as an integral part of Lotus 1–2–3.

Borland II, 799 F.Supp. at 223 (emphasis in original). The court nevertheless concluded that while the Quattro and Quattro Pro programs infringed Lotus's copyright, Borland had not copied the entire Lotus 1–2–3 user interface, as Lotus had contended. Accordingly, the court concluded that a jury trial was necessary to determine the scope of Borland's infringement, including whether Borland copied the long prompts [2] of Lotus 1–2–3, whether the long prompts contained expressive elements, and to what extent, if any, functional constraints limited the number of possible ways that the Lotus menu command hierarchy could have been arranged at the time of its creation. * * *

Immediately following the district court's summary judgment decision, Borland removed the Lotus Emulation Interface from its products. Thereafter, Borland's spreadsheet programs no longer displayed the Lotus 1–2–3 menus to Borland users, and as a result Borland users could no longer communicate with Borland's programs as if they were using a more sophisticated version of Lotus 1–2–3. Nonetheless, Borland's programs continued to be partially compatible with Lotus 1–2–3, for Borland retained what it called the "Key Reader" in its Quattro Pro programs. Once turned on, the Key Reader allowed Borland's programs to understand and perform some Lotus 1–2–3 macros. * * * Accordingly, people who wrote or purchased macros to shorten the time needed to perform an operation in Lotus 1–2–3 could still use those macros in Borland's programs. The district court permitted Lotus to file a supplemental complaint alleging that the Key Reader infringed its copyright.

The parties agreed to try the remaining liability issues without a jury. The district court held two trials, the Phase I trial covering all remaining issues raised in the original complaint (relating to the Emulation Interface) and the Phase II trial covering all issues raised in the supplemental complaint (relating to the Key Reader). * * *

In its Phase I-trial decision, the district court found that "each of the Borland emulation interfaces contains a virtually identical copy of the 1–2–3 menu tree and that the 1–2–3 menu tree is capable of a wide variety of

---

2. Lotus 1–2–3 utilizes a two-line menu; the top line lists the commands from which the user may choose, and the bottom line displays what Lotus calls its "long prompts." The long prompts explain, as a sort of "help text," what the highlighted menu command will do if entered. * * *

expression." *Borland III,* 831 F.Supp. at 218. The district court also rejected Borland's affirmative defenses of laches and estoppel. Id. at 218–23.

In its Phase II-trial decision, the district court found that Borland's Key Reader file included "a virtually identical copy of the Lotus menu tree structure, but represented in a different form and with first letters of menu command names in place of the full menu command names." *Borland IV,* 831 F.Supp. at 228. In other words, Borland's programs no longer included the Lotus command terms, but only their first letters. The district court held that "the Lotus menu structure, organization, and first letters of the command names ... constitute part of the protectable expression found in [Lotus 1–2–3]." Id. at 233. Accordingly, the district court held that with its Key Reader, Borland had infringed Lotus's copyright. Id. at 245. The district court also rejected Borland's affirmative defenses of waiver, laches, estoppel, and fair use. Id. at 235–45. The district court then entered a permanent injunction against Borland, id. at 245, from which Borland appeals. * * *

II.

Discussion

On appeal, Borland does not dispute that it factually copied the words and arrangement of the Lotus menu command hierarchy. Rather, Borland argues that it "lawfully copied the unprotectable menus of Lotus 1–2–3." Borland contends that the Lotus menu command hierarchy is not copyrightable because it is a system, method of operation, process, or procedure foreclosed from protection by 17 U.S.C. § 102(b). Borland also raises a number of affirmative defenses.

A.   *Copyright Infringement Generally*

To establish copyright infringement, a plaintiff must prove "(1) ownership of a valid copyright, and (2) copying of constituent elements of the work that are original." Feist Publications, Inc. v. Rural Tel. Serv. Co., 499 U.S. 340, 361 (1991); * * *

In this appeal, we are faced only with whether the Lotus menu command hierarchy is copyrightable subject matter in the first instance, for Borland concedes that Lotus has a valid copyright in Lotus 1–2–3 as a whole and admits to factually copying the Lotus menu command hierarchy. * * *

B.   *Matter of First Impression*

Whether a computer menu command hierarchy constitutes copyrightable subject matter is a matter of first impression in this court. While some other courts appear to have touched on it briefly in dicta, see, e.g., Autoskill, Inc. v. National Educ. Support Sys., Inc., 994 F.2d 1476, 1495 n. 23 (10th Cir.), cert. denied, 510 U.S. 916 (1993), we know of no cases that deal with the copyrightability of a menu command hierarchy standing on its own (i.e., without other elements of the user interface, such as screen displays, in issue). Thus we are navigating in uncharted waters.

Borland vigorously argues, however, that the Supreme Court charted our course more than 100 years ago when it decided Baker v. Selden, 101 U.S. 99 (1879). * * * Borland argues:

> The facts of Baker v. Selden, and even the arguments advanced by the parties in that case, are identical to those in this case. The only difference is that the "user interface" of Selden's system was implemented by pen and paper rather than by computer.

To demonstrate that Baker v. Selden and this appeal both involve accounting systems, Borland even supplied this court with a video that, with special effects, shows Selden's paper forms "melting" into a computer screen and transforming into Lotus 1–2–3.

We do not think that Baker v. Selden is nearly as analogous to this appeal as Borland claims. Of course, Lotus 1–2–3 is a computer spreadsheet, and as such its grid of horizontal rows and vertical columns certainly resembles an accounting ledger or any other paper spreadsheet. Those grids, however, are not at issue in this appeal for, unlike Selden, Lotus does not claim to have a monopoly over its accounting system. Rather, this appeal involves Lotus's monopoly over the commands it uses to operate the computer. Accordingly, this appeal is not, as Borland contends, "identical" to Baker v. Selden.

C. Altai

Before we analyze whether the Lotus menu command hierarchy is a system, method of operation, process, or procedure, we first consider the applicability of the test the Second Circuit set forth in Computer Assoc. Int'l, Inc. v. Altai, Inc., 982 F.2d 693 (2d Cir.1992). The Second Circuit designed its *Altai* test to deal with the fact that computer programs, copyrighted as "literary works," can be infringed by what is known as "nonliteral" copying, which is copying that is paraphrased or loosely paraphrased rather than word for word. See id. at 701 (citing nonliteral-copying cases); * * *

In the instant appeal, we are not confronted with alleged nonliteral copying of computer code. Rather, we are faced with Borland's deliberate, literal copying of the Lotus menu command hierarchy. Thus, we must determine not whether nonliteral copying occurred in some amorphous sense, but rather whether the literal copying of the Lotus menu command hierarchy constitutes copyright infringement.

While the *Altai* test may provide a useful framework for assessing the alleged nonliteral copying of computer code, we find it to be of little help in assessing whether the literal copying of a menu command hierarchy constitutes copyright infringement. In fact, we think that the *Altai* test in this context may actually be misleading because, in instructing courts to abstract the various levels, it seems to encourage them to find a base level that includes copyrightable subject matter that, if literally copied, would make the copier liable for copyright infringement. While that base (or literal) level would not be at issue in a nonliteral-copying case like *Altai,* it is precisely what is at issue in this appeal. We think that abstracting menu command hierarchies down to their individual word and menu levels and then filtering idea from expression at that stage, as both the *Altai* and the district court tests require, obscures the more fundamental question of whether a menu command hierarchy can be copyrighted at all. The initial inquiry should not be whether individual components of a menu command hierarchy are expressive, but rather whether the menu command hierarchy as a whole can be copyrighted. * * *

D.   The Lotus Menu Command Hierarchy: A "Method of Operation"

Borland argues that the Lotus menu command hierarchy is uncopyrightable because it is a system, method of operation, process, or procedure foreclosed from copyright protection by 17 U.S.C. § 102(b). * * *

We think that "method of operation," as that term is used in § 102(b), refers to the means by which a person operates something, whether it be a car, a food processor, or a computer. Thus a text describing how to operate something would not extend copyright protection to the method of operation itself; other people would be free to employ that method and to describe it in their own words. Similarly, if a new method of operation is used rather than described, other people would still be free to employ or describe that method.

We hold that the Lotus menu command hierarchy is an uncopyrightable "method of operation." The Lotus menu command hierarchy provides the means by which users control and operate Lotus 1–2–3. If users wish to copy material, for example, they use the "Copy" command. If users wish to print material, they use the "Print" command. Users must use the command terms to tell the computer what to do. Without the menu command hierarchy, users would not be able to access and control, or indeed make use of, Lotus 1–2–3's functional capabilities.

The Lotus menu command hierarchy does not merely explain and present Lotus 1–2–3's functional capabilities to the user; it also serves as the method by which the program is operated and controlled. The Lotus menu command hierarchy is different from the Lotus long prompts, for the long prompts are not necessary to the operation of the program; users could operate Lotus 1–2–3 even if there were no long prompts.[9] The Lotus menu command hierarchy is also different from the Lotus screen displays, for users need not "use" any expressive aspects of the screen displays in order to operate Lotus 1–2–3; because the way the screens look has little

---

9. As the Lotus long prompts are not before us on appeal, we take no position on their copyrightability, although we do note that a strong argument could be made that the brief explanations they provide "merge" with the underlying idea of explaining such functions. See Morrissey v. Procter & Gamble Co., 379 F.2d 675, 678–79 (1st Cir.1967) (when the possible ways to express an idea are limited, the expression "merges" with the idea and is therefore uncopyrightable; when merger occurs, identical copying is permitted).

bearing on how users control the program, the screen displays are not part of Lotus 1–2–3's "method of operation"[10]   The Lotus menu command hierarchy is also different from the underlying computer code, because while code is necessary for the program to work, its precise formulation is not. In other words, to offer the same capabilities as Lotus 1–2–3, Borland did not have to copy Lotus's underlying code (and indeed it did not); to allow users to operate its programs in substantially the same way, however, Borland had to copy the Lotus menu command hierarchy. Thus the Lotus 1–2–3 code is not an uncopyrightable "method of operation."

The district court held that the Lotus menu command hierarchy, with its specific choice and arrangement of command terms, constituted an "expression" of the "idea" of operating a computer program with commands arranged hierarchically into menus and submenus. *Borland II,* 799 F.Supp. at 216. Under the district court's reasoning, Lotus's decision to employ hierarchically arranged command terms to operate its program could not foreclose its competitors from also employing hierarchically arranged command terms to operate their programs, but it did foreclose them from employing the specific command terms and arrangement that Lotus had used. In effect, the district court limited Lotus 1–2–3's "method of operation" to an abstraction.

Accepting the district court's finding that the Lotus developers made some expressive choices in choosing and arranging the Lotus command terms, we nonetheless hold that that expression is not copyrightable because it is part of Lotus 1–2–3's "method of operation." We do not think that "methods of operation" are limited to abstractions; rather, they are the means by which a user operates something. If specific words are essential to operating something, then they are part of a "method of operation" and, as such, are unprotectable. This is so whether they must be highlighted, typed in, or even spoken, as computer programs no doubt will soon be controlled by spoken words.

The fact that Lotus developers could have designed the Lotus menu command hierarchy differently is immaterial to the question of whether it is a "method of operation." In other words, our initial inquiry is not whether the Lotus menu command hierarchy incorporates any expression. Rather, our initial inquiry is whether the Lotus menu command hierarchy is a "method of operation." Concluding, as we do, that users operate Lotus 1–2–3 by using the Lotus menu command hierarchy, and that the entire Lotus menu command hierarchy is essential to operating Lotus 1–2–3, we do not inquire further whether that method of operation could have been designed differently. The "expressive" choices of what to name the command terms and how to arrange them do not magically change the uncopyrightable menu command hierarchy into copyrightable subject matter. * * *

_____

10. As they are not before us on appeal, we take no position on whether the Lotus 1– 2–3 screen displays constitute original expression capable of being copyrighted.

In many ways, the Lotus menu command hierarchy is like the buttons used to control, say, a video cassette recorder ("VCR"). A VCR is a machine that enables one to watch and record video tapes. Users operate VCRs by pressing a series of buttons that are typically labelled "Record, Play, Reverse, Fast Forward, Pause, Stop/Eject." That the buttons are arranged and labeled does not make them a "literary work," nor does it make them an "expression" of the abstract "method of operating" a VCR via a set of labeled buttons. Instead, the buttons are themselves the "method of operating" the VCR.

When a Lotus 1–2–3 user chooses a command, either by highlighting it on the screen or by typing its first letter, he or she effectively pushes a button. Highlighting the "Print" command on the screen, or typing the letter "P," is analogous to pressing a VCR button labeled "Play."

Just as one could not operate a buttonless VCR, it would be impossible to operate Lotus 1–2–3 without employing its menu command hierarchy. Thus the Lotus command terms are not equivalent to the labels on the VCR's buttons, but are instead equivalent to the buttons themselves. Unlike the labels on a VCR's buttons, which merely make operating a VCR easier by indicating the buttons' functions, the Lotus menu commands are essential to operating Lotus 1–2–3. Without the menu commands, there would be no way to "push" the Lotus buttons, as one could push unlabeled VCR buttons. While Lotus could probably have designed a user interface for which the command terms were mere labels, it did not do so here. Lotus 1–2–3 depends for its operation on use of the precise command terms that make up the Lotus menu command hierarchy.   * * *

That the Lotus menu command hierarchy is a "method of operation" becomes clearer when one considers program compatibility. Under Lotus's theory, if a user uses several different programs, he or she must learn how to perform the same operation in a different way for each program used. For example, if the user wanted the computer to print material, then the user would have to learn not just one method of operating the computer such that it prints, but many different methods. We find this absurd. The fact that there may be many different ways to operate a computer program, or even many different ways to operate a computer program using a set of hierarchically arranged command terms, does not make the actual method of operation chosen copyrightable; it still functions as a method for operating the computer and as such is uncopyrightable.

Consider also that users employ the Lotus menu command hierarchy in writing macros. Under the district court's holding, if the user wrote a macro to shorten the time needed to perform a certain operation in Lotus 1–2–3, the user would be unable to use that macro to shorten the time needed to perform that same operation in another program. Rather, the user would have to rewrite his or her macro using that other program's menu command hierarchy. This is despite the fact that the macro is clearly the user's own work product. We think that forcing the user to cause the computer to perform the same operation in a different way ignores Congress's direction in § 102(b) that "methods of operation" are not copyrightable. * * *

In holding that expression that is part of a "method of operation" cannot be copyrighted, we do not understand ourselves to go against the Supreme Court's holding in *Feist*. In *Feist*, the Court explained:

> The primary objective of copyright is not to reward the labor of authors, but to promote the Progress of Science and useful Arts. To this end, copyright assures authors the right to their original expression, but encourages others to build freely upon the ideas and information conveyed by a work.

Feist, 499 U.S. at 349–50 (quotations and citations omitted). We do not think that the Court's statement that "copyright assures authors the right to their original expression" indicates that all expression is necessarily copyrightable; while original expression is necessary for copyright protection, we do not think that it is alone sufficient. Courts must still inquire whether original expression falls within one of the categories foreclosed from copyright protection by § 102(b), such as being a "method of operation."

We also note that in most contexts, there is no need to "build" upon other people's expression, for the ideas conveyed by that expression can be conveyed by someone else without copying the first author's expression. In the context of methods of operation, however, "building" requires the use of the precise method of operation already employed; otherwise, "building" would require dismantling, too. Original developers are not the only people entitled to build on the methods of operation they create; anyone can. Thus, Borland may build on the method of operation that Lotus designed and may use the Lotus menu command hierarchy in doing so.
* * *

III.

Conclusion

Because we hold that the Lotus menu command hierarchy is uncopyrightable subject matter, we further hold that Borland did not infringe Lotus's copyright by copying it. Accordingly, we need not consider any of Borland's affirmative defenses. The judgment of the district court is

Reversed.

■ BOUDIN, CIRCUIT JUDGE, concurring.

* * * Most of the law of copyright and the "tools" of analysis have developed in the context of literary works such as novels, plays, and films. In this milieu, the principal problem—simply stated, if difficult to resolve—is to stimulate creative expression without unduly limiting access by others to the broader themes and concepts deployed by the author. The middle of the spectrum presents close cases; but a "mistake" in providing too much protection involves a small cost: subsequent authors treating the same themes must take a few more steps away from the original expression.

The problem presented by computer programs is fundamentally different in one respect. The computer program is a *means* for causing something to happen; it has a mechanical utility, an instrumental role, in accomplishing the world's work. Granting protection, in other words, can have some of the consequences of *patent* protection in limiting other people's ability to perform a task in the most efficient manner. Utility does not bar copyright (dictionaries may be copyrighted), but it alters the calculus.

Of course, the argument *for* protection is undiminished, perhaps even enhanced, by utility: if we want more of an intellectual product, a temporary monopoly for the creator provides incentives for others to create other, different items in this class. But the "cost" side of the equation may be different where one places a very high value on public access to a useful innovation that may be the most efficient means of performing a given task. Thus, the argument for extending protection may be the same; but the stakes on the other side are much higher.

It is no accident that patent protection has preconditions that copyright protection does not—notably, the requirements of novelty and non-obviousness—and that patents are granted for a shorter period than copyrights. * * *

Requests for the protection of computer menus present the concern with fencing off access to the commons in an acute form. A new menu may be a creative work, but over time its importance may come to reside more in the investment that has been made by users in learning the menu and in building their own mini-programs—macros—in reliance upon the menu. Better typewriter keyboard layouts may exist, but the familiar QWERTY keyboard dominates the market because that is what everyone has learned to use. See P. David, CLIO and the Economics of QWERTY, 75 Am.Econ. Rev. 332 (1985). The QWERTY keyboard is nothing other than a menu of letters. * * *

* * * [I]t is unlikely that users who value the Lotus menu for its own sake—independent of any investment they have made themselves in learning Lotus' commands or creating macros dependent upon them—would choose the Borland program in order to secure access to the Lotus menu. Borland's success is due primarily to other features. Its rationale for deploying the Lotus menu bears the ring of truth. * * *

Thus, for me the question is not whether Borland should prevail but on what basis. Various avenues might be traveled, but the main choices are between holding that the menu is not protectable by copyright and devising a new doctrine that Borland's use is privileged. No solution is perfect and no intermediate appellate court can make the final choice.

To call the menu a "method of operation" is, in the common use of those words, a defensible position. * * *

A different approach would be to say that Borland's use is privileged because, in the context already described, it is not seeking to appropriate the advances made by Lotus' menu; rather, having provided an arguably more attractive menu of its own, Borland is merely trying to give former Lotus users an option to exploit their own prior investment in learning or in macros. The difference is that such a privileged use approach would not automatically protect Borland if it had simply copied the Lotus menu (using different codes), contributed nothing of its own, and resold Lotus under the Borland label. * * *

But a privileged use doctrine would certainly involve problems of its own. It might more closely tailor the limits on copyright protection to the reasons for limiting that protection; but it would entail a host of administrative problems that would cause cost and delay, and would also reduce the ability of the industry to predict outcomes. Indeed, to the extent that Lotus' menu is an important standard in the industry, it might be argued that any use ought to be deemed privileged.

In sum, the majority's result persuades me and its formulation is as good, if not better, than any other that occurs to me now as within the reach of courts. Some solutions (e.g., a very short copyright period for menus) are not options at all for courts but might be for Congress. In all events, the choices are important ones of policy, not linguistics, and they should be made with the underlying considerations in view.

NOTE

The Supreme Court granted Lotus's petition for certiorari. Lotus argued that the First Circuit had misread § 102(b) to automatically bar copyright protection for any aspect of a computer program that embodies a "method of operation," regardless of the extent of its expressive elements. With Justice Stevens not participating, the decision was affirmed per curiam by an equally divided Court. 516 U.S. 233 (1996).

APPLE COMPUTER, INC. v. MICROSOFT CORP., 35 F.3d 1435 (9th Cir.1994), cert. denied, 513 U.S. 1184 (1995). Apple, maker of the MacIntosh computer, sued Microsoft, developer of the DOS and Windows operating systems, alleging that Microsoft had gone beyond the scope of its license from Apple in creating Windows 2.03 and 3.0 and in licensing NewWave to Hewlett–Packard. Microsoft in defense challenged the copyrightability of dozens of the elements of the MacIntosh user interface. Apple attempted to sweep aside the defense by arguing that the individual elements were all protected by its claim of copyright in the MacIntosh's overall "desktop" graphical interface. In a series of rulings the district court interpreted Microsoft's license to cover most of the similarities, and then dissected the works to conclude that most of the remaining similarities did not relate to protectable elements. "Some visual displays are or become so closely tied to the functional purpose of the article that they become standard. * * * Such standards in a graphical user interface would enlarge the market for computers by making it easier to learn how to use them." 799 F.Supp.

1006 (N.D.Cal.1992). The district court concluded that any infringement of Apple's works as a whole would require virtual identity. On Microsoft's subsequent motion for summary judgment under the virtual identity standard, the court ordered a judgment in favor of the defendants. 821 F.Supp. 616 (N.D.Cal.1993).

The Court of Appeals affirmed the summary judgment and remanded for further consideration of Microsoft's request for attorney's fees. Referring to Microsoft's license from Apple, Judge Rymer said that the district court "correctly decided first to identify which visual displays in Windows 2.03, 3.0 and NewWave are licensed and which are not."

"The district court then properly proceeded to distinguish ideas from expression, and to 'dissect' unlicensed elements in order to determine whether the remaining similarities lack originality, flow naturally from basic ideas, or are one of the few ways in which a particular idea can be expressed given the constraints of the computer environment. Dissection is not inappropriate even though GUIs [graphical user interfaces] are thought of as the 'look and feel' of a computer, because copyright protection extends only to protectable elements of expression.

"Having found that the similarities in Windows 2.03 and 3.0 consist only of unprotectable or licensed elements, and that the similarities between protectable elements in Apple's works and NewWave are de minimis, the district court did not err by concluding that, to the extent there is creative expression left in how the works are put together, as a whole they can receive only limited protection. When the range of protectable and unauthorized expression is narrow, the appropriate standard for illicit copying is virtual identity."

Reviewing the arguments made by Apple on appeal, the court remarked that "all of these contentions boil down to the same thing: Apple wants an overall comparison of its works to the accused works for substantial similarity rather than virtual identity." However, the court held that, "considering the license and the limited number of ways that the basic ideas of the Apple GUI can be expressed differently, we conclude that only 'thin' protection, against virtually identical copying, is appropriate."

"The district court's conclusion that the works as a whole are entitled only to limited protection and should be compared for virtual identity follows from its analytic dissection. By virtue of the licensing agreement, Microsoft and HP were entitled to use the vast majority of features that Apple claims were copied. Of those that remain, the district court found no unauthorized, protectable similarities of expression in Windows 2.03 and 3.0, and only a handful in NewWave. Thus, any claim of infringement that Apple may have against Microsoft must rest on the copying of Apple's unique selection and arrangement of all of these features. Under [Harper House, Inc. v. Thomas Nelson, Inc., 889 F.2d 197 (9th Cir.1989)] and [Frybarger v. International Business Machines Corp., 812 F.2d 525 (9th Cir.1987)], there can be no infringement unless the works are virtually identical."

NOTES AND QUESTIONS

(1) Is *Lotus* correct in rejecting District Judge Keeton's "abstraction" approach that separated the idea of operating a spreadsheet program through commands hierarchically arranged into menus from the expression of that idea through the choice of specific command terms and arrangements?

Under *Lotus*, would the graphical user interface of the MacIntosh computer that was before the Ninth Circuit in *Apple Computer* be classified as a "method of operation" and hence excluded from copyright? What about a computer's operating system program—is it too a "method of operation" according to the analysis in *Lotus?* Are you convinced by the court's policy argument in favor of compatibility? Recall the different response to similar arguments in Apple Computer v. Franklin Computer, p. 120 supra.

Weinreb, Copyright for Functional Expression, 111 Harv.L.Rev. 1149 (1998), viewing copyright law as a series of descriptive conventions rather than purposive rules, defends the outcome in *Lotus* as consistent with a traditional dichotomy between books and machines. Lunney, *Lotus v. Borland*: Copyright and Computer Programs, 70 Tulane L.Rev. 2397 (1996), also applauds the result (but not the rationale) of *Lotus*. Hamilton and Sabety, Computer Science Concepts in Copyright Cases: The Path to a Coherent Law, 10 Harv.J.L. & Tech. 239 (1997), urge the integration of computer science terminology into copyright discourse to define more precisely the protectable aspects of computer programs.

(2) Screen displays are often a dominant feature of the interface between a computer program and the user. Early cases were divided on whether copyright in a computer program extends to the screen displays that the program generates. Compare Broderbund Software, Inc. v. Unison World, Inc., 648 F.Supp. 1127 (N.D.Cal.1986), with Digital Communications Associates, Inc. v. Softklone Distributing Corp., 659 F.Supp. 449 (N.D.Ga.1987). Since 1988 the Copyright Office has taken the position that "all copyrightable expression owned by the same claimant and embodied in a computer program, or first published as a unit with a computer program, including computer screen displays, is considered a single work and should be registered on a single application form." 53 Fed.Reg. 21817 (1988).

When judging infringement of certain screen displays, notably video games, the courts have generally invoked the standards used for other audiovisuals works such as cartoons. Is a different analysis appropriate for screen displays that form part of a functional interface with the user of a computer program? Compare Atari, Inc. v. North American Philips Consumer Electronics Corp., 672 F.2d 607 (7th Cir.), cert. denied, 459 U.S. 880 (1982), with Manufacturers Technologies Inc. v. Cams, Inc., 706 F.Supp. 984 (D.Conn.1989). In MiTek Holdings, Inc. v. Arce Engineering Co., 89 F.3d 1548 (11th Cir.1996), the court followed the Ninth Circuit's approach in Apple v. Microsoft and required "bodily appropriation of expression" or "virtual identicality" to establish infringement of a compilation copyright in the elements of a user interface. What justifies this heightened standard for infringement? A limited range of available expression? An interest in standardization?

(3) Does the public interest in standardization and compatibility justify analytic dissection into constituent elements and the elimination of similarities that reflect attempts to respond to consumer preferences and expectations? Does the interest in standardized displays and command structures and compatible data formats and macros justify application of the merger doctrine? (Recall Franklin Computer's unsuccessful merger argument in Apple Computer, Inc. v. Franklin Computer Corp., p. 120 supra.) The Fifth Circuit in Engineering Dynamics, Inc. v. Structural Software, Inc., 26 F.3d 1335 (5th Cir.1994), endorsed the abstraction-filtration-comparison method for determining copyright in a user interface consisting primarily of input and output formats, but ordered a remand "to determine whether the existence of industry standards precludes copyright protection." See also Menell, Tailoring Legal Protection for Computer Software, 39 Stan. L.Rev. 1329 (1987).

(4) For useful commentary on the user interface issue, see Samuelson, Computer Programs, User Interfaces and Section 102(b) of the Copyright Act: A Critique of *Lotus v. Paperback,* 55 L. & Contemp.Prob. (No. 2) 311 (1992) (critical of broad protection); VerSteeg & Harrington, Nonobviousness as an Element of Copyrightability?, 25 U.C.Davis L.Rev. 331 (1992) (critical of any injection of a nonobviousness criterion into the test for copyright); Terry, GUI Wars: The Windows Litigation and the Continuing Decline of "Look and Feel," 47 Ark.L.Rev. 93 (1994) (analyzing Apple v. Microsoft).

SECTION 7. SOUND RECORDINGS

This Section deals with the infringement of sound recordings by unauthorized duplication. On infringement by unauthorized public performance, see p. 329 infra; on imitation of sound recordings, see p. 663 infra.

As the market for records and tapes became larger and more lucrative, so did the opportunities for sellers of unauthorized copies, commonly referred to as "pirates." Congress responded to the pleas of the record companies in 1971 with amendments to the 1909 Copyright Act creating a new, although limited, copyright in sound recordings "fixed, published and copyrighted" on or after February 15, 1972.[a] The Sound Recording Amendments of 1971 were eventually superseded by § 114 of the 1976 Act.

"Sound recordings" are defined in § 101; they are fixed in "phonorecords." (Note that sound tracks of motion pictures and other audiovisual works are excluded from the definition—those works are protected as components of the audiovisual work.) Sound recordings typically consist of

---

a. Pub.L. No. 92–140, 85 Stat. 391. On the protection of older sound recordings, see § 301(c) and p. 662 infra.

a recorded performance and should be distinguished from the musical, literary, or dramatic work being performed. Like other copyrightable works, sound recordings must satisfy the requirement of originality. What are the possible sources of creative authorship in a sound recording?

Rights in sound recordings, framed with an eye toward the record pirate, are carefully circumscribed in § 114. The exclusive right of reproduction is limited to physical duplication and excludes mere imitation of a sound recording.[b] There is also a special form of copyright notice—the letter P in a circle—applicable to sound recordings (§ 402). (In addition to civil liability for infringement, there are substantial criminal penalties for record piracy. See § 506 and 18 U.S.C.A. §§ 2318–19.)

DIGITAL SAMPLING

The limits of the reproduction right in sound recordings are being tested by the phenomenon of digital sampling. Digital recording of music makes it possible by computer to extract bits of sound and to manipulate the samples in endless ways. Sampled sounds can be electronically combined to make music without musicians. Backup musicians have already been replaced in some touring acts by digital samplers. Samplers now also produce some of the music used in motion pictures and commercials. Digital samplers also make it possible to extract sounds from one recorded performance and insert them into another recording. As an example, consider the handiwork of one New York sound engineer who "plugged into his sampler the sound of Madonna screaming 'hey!' on her song 'Like a Virgin,' raised it an octave and dropped the new sound into a few parts of a coming song by Jamie Bernstein. He took a horn blast from a James Brown song and turned it into a lush, mellow tone for a Japanese singer's love ballad. 'I didn't feel at all like I was ripping James Brown off,' he says." Miller, High–Tech Alteration of Sights and Sounds Divides Art World, Wall St.J., Sept. 1, 1987, p. 1. According to an article in *Time,* "Rap is rife with riffs sampled from other musicians without their consent, most notably James Brown." Garcia, Play It Again, Sampler, Time, June 3, 1991, p. 69.

What rights, if any, does sampling violate? Is it an infringement of the copyright in a sound recording to remove a sample of sound and put it into a new recording? How should one approach issues of substantial similarity and fair use? If the sample lasts, say, a few seconds, is it even a copyrightable entity? And at what point are rights in the underlying musical composition infringed? Few cases have been litigated, perhaps because record companies sample as much as they are sampled. In a rare reported opinion, one court, relying more on the Ten Commandments than on any principle of copyright law, enjoined the sale of rapper Biz Markie's

---

b. Protection under § 114 is not technically limited to record piracy. See Agee v. Paramount Communications, Inc., 59 F.3d 317 (2d Cir.1995) (unauthorized reproduction of a sound recording on the sound track of a television program infringed the owner's § 114 reproduction right).

album containing samples taken from Gilbert O'Sullivan's *Alone Again (Naturally)*, citing plaintiff's ownership of both the music and sound recording copyrights. Grand Upright Music Ltd. v. Warner Bros. Records, Inc., 780 F.Supp. 182 (S.D.N.Y.1991). Another court denied a sampler's motion for summary judgment because it had not established as a matter of law that the sampled portions of the copyrighted song were insubstantial; since plaintiff owned only the song and not the sound recording, the defendant did get summary judgment on the sound recording infringement claim. Jarvis v. A & M Records, 827 F.Supp. 282 (D.N.J.1993). Record companies have grown more cautious about using unlicensed samples and now routinely pay for a license. Some artists such as The Eagles, Led Zeppelin, and the Beatles rarely authorize sampling of their work. If enough music or lyrics are taken, the owner of the copyright in the musical work must also be paid. See Jones, Haven't I Heard that "Whoop" (or "Hoop") Somewhere Before?, New York Times, Dec. 22, 1996, Sec. 2, p. 44.

NOTES

(1) New technology that allows CD-quality digital audio files to be compressed ever smaller has made it increasingly easy to transmit and download sound recordings over the Internet. Some record companies are experimenting with electronic delivery of sound recordings—a market that may expand as downloaded recordings become more portable through technologies such as compact disc recorders. The ease of transmission has also opened the door for pirates. The Record Industry Association of America is now going after music websites that offer unauthorized recordings for downloading. Chervokas, Internet CD Copying Tests Music Industry, N.Y. Times, Apr. 6, 1998, p. D3.

(2) Ulmer, The Rome Convention for the Protection of Performers, Producers of Phonograms, and Broadcasting Organizations, 10 Bull.Copyr.Soc. 90, 165, 219 (1962), is a full description of a 1961 treaty aimed at establishing an international regime of protection for performers and record producers, including rights against unauthorized fixation, reproduction, and broadcast (but available only to performers and producers from contracting states). The United States declined to join the Rome Convention. In 1971, a conference in Geneva proposed a simple ban on the unauthorized duplication of sound recordings. The 1971 amendments to the 1909 Copyright Act met the requirements of this Convention for the Protection of Producers of Phonograms Against Unauthorized Duplication of Their Phonograms, and it entered into force with respect to the United States in 1974.

In foreign systems, performers' rights are often described as "neighboring rights"—*droit voisins*. "Neighboring rights derive their name from the fact that their origins are to be found in the neighborhood of copyright. However, neighboring rights not only differ from copyright in the extent of protection afforded them, but also with regard to the subjects to which they relate: the subjects of copyright are literary and artistic works; the subjects of neighboring rights are performances, phonograms and broadcasts."

Ulmer, supra, at 165. See generally S. Stewart and H. Sandison, International Copyright and Neighboring Rights (1989).

At a 1996 conference in Geneva sponsored by the World Intellectual Property Organization (WIPO), representatives adopted a treaty intended to secure copyright protection for sound recordings in the emerging digital environment. The Performances and Phonograms Treaty (reprinted in the Supplement) recognizes exclusive rights of reproduction and distribution. Performers are also given the exclusive right to authorize the broadcast or fixation of their unfixed performances (and paternity and integrity rights in both live and fixed performances—see p. 717 infra). With an eye toward the electronic delivery of sound recordings, Articles 10 and 14 of the treaty recognize on behalf of performers and producers "the exclusive right of authorizing the making available to the public of their performances fixed in phonorecords, by wire or wireless means, in such a way that members of the public may access them from a place and at a time individually chosen by them." The treaty also requires adequate legal protection against the circumvention of technological security measures used to prevent violations of the owner's rights and the removal or alteration of "rights management information"—information that identifies the work and specifies terms and conditions of use. Legislation to implement the treaty (limited to prohibitions against the circumvention of security measures and the protection of rights management information) is pending in Congress.

SECTION 8.   PERFORMANCE RIGHTS

Herbert v. The Shanley Co.

Supreme Court of the United States, 1917.
242 U.S. 591, 37 S.Ct. 232.

■ MR. JUSTICE HOLMES delivered the opinion of the court:

These two cases present the same question: whether the performance of a copyrighted musical composition in a restaurant or hotel without charge for admission to hear it infringes the exclusive right of the owner of the copyright to perform the work publicly for profit. Act of March 4, 1909, chap. 320, § 1(e), 35 Stat. 1075. The last numbered case was decided before the other and may be stated first. The plaintiff owns the copyright of a lyric comedy in which is a march called "From Maine to Oregon." It took out a separate copyright for the march and published it separately. The defendant hotel company caused this march to be performed in the dining room of the Vanderbilt Hotel for the entertainment of guests during meal times, in the way now common, by an orchestra employed and paid by the company. It was held by the Circuit Court of Appeals, reversing the decision of the District Court, that this was not a performance for profit within the meaning of the act. 221 F. 229.

The other case is similar so far as the present discussion is concerned. The plaintiffs were the composers and owners of a comic opera entitled "Sweethearts," containing a song of the same title as a leading feature in the performance. There is a copyright for the opera and also one for the song which is published and sold separately. This the Shanley Company caused to be sung by professional singers, upon a stage in its restaurant on Broadway, accompanied by an orchestra. The District Court after holding that by the separate publication the plaintiffs' rights were limited to those conferred by the separate copyright, a matter that it will not be necessary to discuss, followed the decision in 221 F. 229, as to public performance for profit. 222 F. 344. The decree was affirmed by the Circuit Court of Appeals. 229 F. 340.

If the rights under the copyright are infringed only by a performance where money is taken at the door they are very imperfectly protected. Performances not different in kind from those of the defendants could be given that might compete with and even destroy the success of the monopoly that the law intends the plaintiffs to have. It is enough to say that there is no need to construe the statute so narrowly. The defendants' performances are not eleemosynary. They are part of a total for which the public pays, and the fact that the price of the whole is attributed to a particular item which those present are expected to order, is not important. It is true that the music is not the sole object, but neither is the food, which probably could be got cheaper elsewhere. The object is a repast in surroundings that to people having limited powers of conversation, or disliking the rival noise give a luxurious pleasure not to be had from eating a silent meal. If music did not pay it would be given up. If it pays it pays out of the public's pocket. Whether it pays or not the purpose of employing it is profit and that is enough.

Decree reversed.

THE PUBLIC PERFORMANCE PROVISION

A right of public performance (now § 106(4)) was first granted to the copyright proprietor of musical works by an act of 1897 (29 Stat. 481). But it seems to have been of little practical importance,[a] even though it did not contain the "for profit" limitation of the 1909 Act.

Herbert v. The Shanley Co. was a great victory for the American Society of Composers, Authors and Publishers, formed in 1914 by Victor Herbert and other famous figures to license and monitor the public performance of music. Thereafter ASCAP and others continued in a series of cases to expand the boundaries of the public performance for profit right under the 1909 Act. They were uniformly successful in obtaining recognition that performances carrying any economic advantage were "for profit." The "for profit" requirement was eliminated from § 106(4), but the issue

---

a. "There is no record of a single cent being collected under that law." ASCAP, The Story of ASCAP 12 (1948).

survives in the form of an exemption in § 110(4). "Public" and "performance" were also generously interpreted under the 1909 Act until the Supreme Court took a sharp turn beginning with the *Fortnightly* case.

Fortnightly Corp. v. United Artists Television, Inc.

Supreme Court of the United States, 1968.
392 U.S. 390, 88 S.Ct. 2084.

■ MR. JUSTICE STEWART delivered the opinion of the Court.

The petitioner, Fortnightly Corporation, owns and operates community antenna television (CATV) systems in Clarksburg and Fairmont, West Virginia. There were no local television broadcasting stations in that immediate area until 1957. Now there are two, but, because of hilly terrain, most residents of the area cannot receive the broadcasts of any additional stations by ordinary rooftop antennas. Some of the residents have joined in erecting larger cooperative antennas in order to receive more distant stations, but a majority of the householders in both communities have solved the problem by becoming customers of the petitioner's CATV service. * * *

During 1960, when this proceeding began, the petitioner's systems provided customers with signals of five television broadcasting stations, three located in Pittsburgh, Pennsylvania; one in Steubenville, Ohio; and one in Wheeling, West Virginia. The distance between those cities and Clarksburg and Fairmont ranges from 52 to 82 miles. The systems carried all the programming of each of the five stations * * *.[6]

[Respondent United Artist Television licensed the television stations to broadcast motion pictures on which it held the copyrights, and these broadcasts were carried by petitioner to its customers. The licenses did not authorize CATV carriage. Respondent prevailed on infringement claims in the courts below.] * * *

At the outset it is clear that the petitioner's systems did not "perform" the respondent's copyrighted works in any conventional sense of that term, or in any manner envisaged by the Congress that enacted the law in 1909. But our inquiry cannot be limited to ordinary meaning and legislative history, for this is a statute that was drafted long before the development of the electronic phenomena with which we deal here. In 1909 radio itself was in its infancy, and television had not been invented. We must read the statutory language of 60 years ago in the light of drastic technological change.

The Court of Appeals thought that the controlling question in deciding whether the petitioner's CATV systems "performed" the copyrighted works was: "[H]ow much did the [petitioner] do to bring about the viewing and hearing of a copyrighted work?" 377 F.2d, at 877. Applying this test, the

---

6. Some CATV systems, about 10%, originate some of their own programs. We do not deal with such systems in this opinion.

court found that the petitioner did "perform" the programs carried by its systems.[18]   But mere quantitative contribution cannot be the proper test to determine copyright liability in the context of television broadcasting. * * *

The television broadcaster in one sense does less than the exhibitor of a motion picture or stage play; he supplies his audience not with visible images but only with electronic signals.   The viewer conversely does more than a member of a theater audience; he provides the equipment to convert electronic signals into audible sound and visible images.   Despite these deviations from the conventional situation contemplated by the framers of the Copyright Act, broadcasters have been judicially treated as exhibitors, and viewers as members of a theater audience.   Broadcasters perform.   Viewers do not perform.   Thus, while both broadcaster and viewer play crucial roles in the total television process, a line is drawn between them.   One is treated as active performer; the other, as passive beneficiary.

When CATV is considered in this framework, we conclude that it falls on the viewer's side of the line.[25]   Essentially, a CATV system no more than enhances the viewer's capacity to receive the broadcaster's signals; it provides a well-located antenna with an efficient connection to the viewer's television set.   It is true that a CATV system plays an "active" role in making reception possible in a given area, but so do ordinary television sets and antennas.   CATV equipment is powerful and sophisticated, but the basic function the equipment serves is little different from that served by the equipment generally furnished by a television viewer.   If an individual erected an antenna on a hill, strung a cable to his house, and installed the necessary amplifying equipment, he would not be "performing" the programs he received on his television set.   The result would be no different if several people combined to erect a cooperative antenna for the same purpose.   The only difference in the case of CATV is that the antenna system is erected and owned not by its users but by an entrepreneur. * * *

We have been invited by the Solicitor General in an *amicus curiae* brief to render a compromise decision in this case that would, it is said, accommodate various competing considerations of copyright, communications, and antitrust policy.   We decline the invitation.   That job is for Congress.   We take the Copyright Act of 1909 as we find it.   With due

---

18. The court formulated and applied this test in the light of this Court's decision in Buck v. Jewell–LaSalle Realty Co., 283 U.S. 191. See also Society of European Stage Authors & Composers v. New York Hotel Statler Co., D.C., 19 F.Supp. 1. But in *Jewell–LaSalle*, a hotel received on a master radio set an unauthorized broadcast of a copyrighted work and transmitted that broadcast to all the public and private rooms of the hotel by means of speakers installed by the

hotel in each room. The Court held the hotel liable for infringement but noted that the result might have differed if, as in this case, the original broadcast had been authorized by the copyright holder. 283 U.S., at 199, n. 5. The *Jewell–LaSalle* decision must be understood as limited to its own facts.

25. While we speak in this opinion generally of CATV, we necessarily do so with reference to the facts of this case.

regard to changing technology, we hold that the petitioner did not under that law "perform" the respondent's copyrighted works.

The judgment of the Court of Appeals is reversed.

■ MR. JUSTICE DOUGLAS and MR. JUSTICE MARSHALL took no part in the consideration or decision of this case.

MR. JUSTICE HARLAN took no part in the decision of this case.

MR. JUSTICE FORTAS, dissenting.

This case calls not for the judgment of Solomon but for the dexterity of Houdini. We are here asked to consider whether and how a technical, complex, and specific Act of Congress, the Copyright Act, which was enacted in 1909, applies to one of the recent products of scientific and promotional genius, CATV. * * * Applying the normal jurisprudential tools—the words of the Act, legislative history, and precedent—to the facts of the case is like trying to repair a television set with a mallet. * * *

* * * Our major object, I suggest, should be to do as little damage as possible to traditional copyright principles and to business relationships, until the Congress legislates and relieves the embarrassment which we and the interested parties face.

The opinion of the majority, in my judgment, does not heed this admonition. In an attempt to foster the development of CATV, the Court today abandons the teachings of precedent, including a precedent of this Court * * *.

* * * I believe [Buck v. Jewell–LaSalle, n. 18 supra] stands squarely in the path of the route which the majority today traverses. If a CATV system performs a function "little different from that served by the equipment generally furnished by a television viewer," and if that is to be the test, then it seems to me that a master radio set attached by wire to numerous other sets in various rooms of a hotel cannot be distinguished.[5] * * *

Buck v. Jewell–LaSalle may not be an altogether ideal gloss on the word "perform," but it has at least the merit of being settled law. I would not overrule that decision in order to take care of this case or the needs of CATV. This Court may be wrong. The task of caring for CATV is one for the Congress. Our ax, being a rule of law, must cut straight, sharp, and deep; and perhaps this is a situation that calls for the compromise of theory and for the architectural improvisation which only legislation can accomplish.

---

5. The majority attempts to diminish the compelling authority of Buck v. Jewell–LaSalle, by referring to a vague footnote in that opinion to the effect that the Court might not have found a "performance" if the original broadcast, which was picked up by the hotel and brought to its various rooms, had been authorized by the copyright hold- er—as it was not. I cannot understand the point. Whatever might be the case in a contributory infringement action (which this is not), the interpretation of the term "perform" cannot logically turn on the question whether the material that is used is licensed or not licensed.

I see no alternative to following *Buck* and to holding that a CATV system does "perform" the material it picks up and carries. I would, accordingly, affirm the decision below.

TELEPROMPTER CORP. V. COLUMBIA BROADCASTING SYSTEM, INC., 415 U.S. 394 (1974). This was a carefully presented test case. CBS charged infringement of representative copyrighted programs by five CATV installations belonging to defendant. Noting that *Fortnightly* was based on simpler technology that did nothing more than bring in telecasts that were blocked by mountainous terrain, CBS pointed out that CATV systems now import signals from distant markets and originate programming on non-broadcast channels, which makes them more akin to and competitive with regular broadcasters. The Court of Appeals held that "when a CATV system imports distant signals it is no longer within the ambit of the *Fortnightly* doctrine." 476 F.2d 338 (2d Cir.1973).

The Supreme Court, with Justice Stewart again writing, rejected the attempt to distinguish distant signals and found no significant difference from *Fortnightly*. "By importing signals that could not normally be received with current technology in the community it serves, a CATV system does not, for copyright purposes, alter the function it performs for its subscribers. * * * The reception and rechanneling of these signals for simultaneous viewing is essentially a viewer function, irrespective of the distance between the broadcasting station and the ultimate viewer."

Justice Douglas and Chief Justice Burger dissented, arguing that even if one accepted the analysis of *Fortnightly*, this extension of it was unnecessary and incorrect. Justice Blackmun, dissenting in part, considered the opinion in the Court of Appeals "an imaginative and well-reasoned solution."

Twentieth Century Music Corp. v. Aiken

United States Supreme Court, 1975.
422 U.S. 151, 95 S.Ct. 2040.

■ MR. JUSTICE STEWART delivered the opinion of the Court.

The question presented by this case is whether the reception of a radio broadcast of a copyrighted musical composition can constitute copyright infringement, when the copyright owner has licensed the broadcaster to perform the composition publicly for profit.

The respondent George Aiken owns and operates a small fast-service food shop in downtown Pittsburgh, Pa., known as "George Aiken's Chicken." Some customers carry out the food they purchase, while others remain and eat at counters or booths. Usually the "carry-out" customers are in the restaurant for less than five minutes, and those who eat there seldom remain longer than 10 or 15 minutes.

A radio with outlets to four speakers in the ceiling receives broadcasts of music and other normal radio programing at the restaurant. Aiken usually turns on the radio each morning at the start of business. Music, news, entertainment, and commercial advertising broadcast by radio stations are thus heard by Aiken, his employees, and his customers during the hours that the establishment is open for business.

[Petitioners' copyrighted songs were heard in Aiken's shop. The broadcaster had an ASCAP license, but Aiken did not. Aiken lost in the District Court, but won in the Court of Appeals, 500 F.2d 127 (3d Cir.1974), which relied on *Fortnightly* and *Teleprompter.*]

The limited scope of the copyright holder's statutory monopoly, like the limited copyright duration required by the Constitution, reflects a balance of competing claims upon the public interest: Creative work is to be encouraged and rewarded, but private motivation must ultimately serve the cause of promoting broad public availability of literature, music, and the other arts.[6] The immediate effect of our copyright law is to secure a fair return for an "author's" creative labor. But the ultimate aim is, by this incentive, to stimulate artistic creativity for the general public good. "The sole interest of the United States and the primary object in conferring the monopoly," this Court has said, "lie in the general benefits derived by the public from the labors of authors." Fox Film Corp. v. Doyal, 286 U.S. 123, 127. See Kendall v. Winsor, 62 U.S. 322, 327–328; Grant v. Raymond, 31 U.S. 218, 241–242. When technological change has rendered its literal terms ambiguous, the Copyright Act must be construed in light of this basic purpose.

The precise statutory issue in the present case is whether Aiken infringed upon the petitioners' exclusive right, under the Copyright Act of 1909, 17 U.S.C.A. § 1(e), "[t]o perform the copyrighted work publicly for profit." We may assume that the radio reception of the musical compositions in Aiken's restaurant occurred "publicly for profit." See Herbert v. Shanley, 242 U.S. 591. The dispositive question, therefore, is whether this radio reception constituted a "performance" of the copyrighted works.
* * *

* * * [In Buck v. Jewell–LaSalle Realty Co., 283 U.S. 191] the Court was called upon to answer the following question certified by the Eighth Circuit Court of Appeals: "Do the acts of a hotel proprietor in making available to his guests, through the instrumentality of a radio receiving set and loud speakers installed in his hotel and under the control and for the entertainment of his guests, the hearing of a copyrighted musical composition which has been broadcast from a radio transmitting station, constitute

---

6. Lord Mansfield's statement of the problem almost 200 years ago in Sayre v. Moore, quoted in a footnote to Cary v. Longman, 102 Eng.Rep. 138, 140n.(b) (1801), bears repeating:

"[W]e must take care to guard against two extremes equally prejudicial; the one, that men of ability, who have employed their time for the service of the community, may not be deprived of their just merits, and the reward of their ingenuity and labor; the other, that the world may not be deprived of improvements, nor the progress of the arts be retarded."

a performance of such composition within the meaning of 17 USC, Sec. 1(e)?'' The Court answered the certified question in the affirmative. In stating the facts of the case, however, the Court's opinion made clear that the broadcaster of the musical composition was not licensed to perform it, and at least twice in the course of its opinion the Court indicated that the answer to the certified question might have been different if the broadcast itself had been authorized by the copyright holder.[10]

We may assume for present purposes that the *Jewell–LaSalle* decision retains authoritative force in a factual situation like that in which it arose.[11] But, as the Court of Appeals in this case perceived, this Court has in two recent decisions explicitly disavowed the view that the reception of an electronic broadcast can constitute a performance, when the broadcaster himself is licensed to perform the copyrighted material that he broadcasts.
* * *

To hold in this case that the respondent Aiken ''performed'' the petitioners' copyrighted works would thus require us to overrule two very recent decisions of this Court. But such a holding would more than offend the principles of *stare decisis;* it would result in a regime of copyright law that would be both wholly unenforceable and highly inequitable.

The practical unenforceability of a ruling that all of those in Aiken's position are copyright infringers is self-evident. One has only to consider the countless business establishments in this country with radio or television sets on their premises—bars beauty shops, cafeterias, car washes, dentists' offices, and drive-ins—to realize the total futility of any evenhanded effort on the part of copyright holders to license even a substantial percentage of them.[12]

And a ruling that a radio listener ''performs'' every broadcast that he receives would be highly inequitable for two distinct reasons. First, a person in Aiken's position would have no sure way of protecting himself from liability for copyright infringement except by keeping his radio set turned off. For even if he secured a license from ASCAP, he would have no way of either foreseeing or controlling the broadcast of compositions whose copyright was held by someone else. Secondly, to hold that all in Aiken's position ''performed'' these musical compositions would be to authorize the

---

10. ''[W]e have no occasion to determine under what circumstances a broadcaster will be held to be a performer, *or the effect upon others of his paying a license fee.''* 283 U.S., at 198 (emphasis added). See also 283 U.S., at 199 n. 5.

11. The decision in *Jewell–LaSalle* might be supported by a concept akin to that of contributory infringement, even though there was no relationship between the broadcaster and the hotel company and, therefore, technically no question of actual contributory infringement in that case. 283 U.S., at 197 n. 4.

12. The Court of Appeals observed that ASCAP now has license agreements with some 5,150 business establishments in the whole country, 500 F.2d, at 129, noting that these include ''firms which employ on premises sources for music such as tape recorders and live entertainment.'' Id., at n. 4. As a matter of so-called ''policy'' or ''practice,'' we are told, ASCAP has not even tried to exact licensing agreements from commercial establishments whose radios have only a single speaker.

sale of an untold number of licenses for what is basically a single public rendition of a copyrighted work.   The exaction of such multiple tribute would go far beyond what is required for the economic protection of copyright owners,[14] * * *.

For the reasons stated in this opinion, the judgment of the Court of Appeals is affirmed.

It is so ordered.

■ MR. JUSTICE BLACKMUN, concurring in the result.

My discomfort, now decisionally outdated to be sure, with the Court's opinion and judgment is threefold:

1.   My first discomfort is factual.   Respondent Aiken hardly was an innocent "listener," as the Court seems to characterize him throughout its opinion * * *.

* * * Aiken installed four loudspeakers in his small shop.   This, obviously, was not done for his personal use and contentment so that he might hear the broadcast, in any corner he might be, above the noise of commercial transactions.   It was done for the entertainment and edification of his customers.   It was part of what Mr. Aiken offered his trade, and it added, in his estimation, to the atmosphere and attraction of his establishment.   Viewed in this light, respondent is something more than a mere listener and is not so simply to be categorized.

2.   My second discomfort is precedential.   [Justice Blackmun, discontented with *Fortnightly* and *Teleprompter*, thought that they, and not *Jewell–LaSalle*, should be limited to their facts.]

3.   My third discomfort is tactical.   I cannot understand why the Court is so reluctant to do directly what it obviously is doing indirectly, namely, to overrule *Jewell–LaSalle*.   * * * The Court dances around *Jewell–LaSalle*, as indeed it must, for it is potent opposing precedent for the present case and stands stalwart against respondent Aiken's position. I think we should be realistic and forthright and, if *Jewell–LaSalle* is in the way, overrule it.

Although I dissented in *Teleprompter,* that case and *Fortnightly,* before it, have been decided.   With the Court insisting on adhering to the rationale of those cases, the result the Court of Appeals and the Court reaches here is compelled.   Accepting the precedent of those cases, I concur in the result.

MR. CHIEF JUSTICE BURGER, with whom MR. JUSTICE DOUGLAS joins, dissenting.

---

14. The petitioners have not demonstrated that they cannot receive from a broadcaster adequate royalties based upon the total size of the broadcaster's audience. On the contrary, the respondent points out that generally copyright holders can and do receive royalties in proportion to advertising revenues of licensed broadcasters, and a broadcaster's advertising revenues reflect the total number of its listeners, including those who listen to the broadcasts in public business establishments.

* * * My primary purpose in writing is not merely to express disagreement with the Court but to underscore what has repeatedly been stated by others as to the need for legislative action.

[The Chief Justice gave some advice to Congress, in his footnote 3, as follows:]

3. Indeed, in its consideration of S. 1361, the Senate Committee on the Judiciary undertook to distinguish use of "ordinary radios" from situations "where broadcasts are transmitted to substantial audiences by means of loudspeakers covering a wide area." S.Rep. No. 93–983, 93d Cong., 2d Sess., 130 (1974). The value of this distinction, without drawing a line on the number of outlets that would be exempt is at best dubious; this version leaves the obvious gap in the statute to be filled in by the courts.

NOTES AND QUESTIONS ON PUBLIC PERFORMANCE

(1) The preceding opinions from the Supreme Court called upon Congress to act, and Congress responded in the 1976 Act. The response on cable television will be surveyed in a later chapter. The exclusive right of public performance appears now in § 106(4) (supported by definitions of "perform," "publicly," and "transmit" in § 101), but it is elaborately qualified in § 110.

Consider first the statutory definitions—do they overrule the Supreme Court's interpretation of the old law? They were clearly so intended:

Under the definitions of "perform," "display," "publicly," and "transmit" in section 101, the concepts of public performance and public display cover not only the initial rendition or showing, but also any further act by which that rendition or showing is transmitted or communicated to the public. Thus, for example: a singer is performing when he or she sings a song; a broadcasting network is performing when it transmits his or her performance (whether simultaneously or from records); a local broadcaster is performing when it transmits the network broadcast; a cable television system is performing when it retransmits the broadcast to its subscribers; and any individual is performing whenever he or she plays a phonorecord embodying the performance or communicates the performance by turning on a receiving set. (H.R.Rep. p. 63.)

The performance right encompasses only *public* performances—singing in the shower will not infringe, at least absent unusual circumstances. The § 101 definition of "publicly" was construed in Columbia Pictures Industries, Inc. v. Redd Horne, Inc., 749 F.2d 154 (3d Cir.1984), which held that "in-store rentals" of movie cassettes constituted public performance; the tapes were played in viewing rooms (complete with popcorn) that accommodated two to four people. "Simply because the cassettes can be viewed in private does not mitigate the essential fact that Maxwell's is unquestionably open to the public." In *Redd Horne,* store employees ran the cassettes from a central location. The customers in Columbia Pictures Industries, Inc. v. Aveco, Inc., 800 F.2d 59 (3d Cir.1986), took the cassettes into the viewing rooms. The court held that it was still a public performance.[b]

(2) Certain public performances are exempt under § 110. Note first that most of the exemptions apply only to specific types of works, although the main educational exemption in § 110(1) refers simply to "a work," as does § 110(5).

Would a school play performed in a high school auditorium be exempt under § 110(1)? The House Report says that it would not. H.R.Rep. p. 82. The ramifications of the classroom exemptions in § 110(1) and (2) are examined in Nevins, Copyright, Cassettes and Classrooms: The Performance Puzzle, 43 J.Copyr.Soc. 1 (1995).

(3) Could § 110(3) be challenged as an impermissible preference to religion? (What does the phrase "of a religious nature" modify? Apparently it was intended to modify only "a dramatico-musical work." See H.R.Rep. p. 84.)

(4) Section 110(4) is one consequence of dropping the general "for profit" limitation of the 1909 Act. When is a performance "without any purpose of direct or indirect commercial advantage"? According to the House Report, "This provision expressly adopts the principle established by the court decisions construing the 'for profit' limitation: that public performances given or sponsored in connection with any commercial or profit-making enterprises are subject to the exclusive rights of the copyright owner even though the public is not charged for seeing or hearing the performance." H.R.Rep. p. 85.[c]

Would the half-time performance of a high school or college band be exempt under § 110(4)? Does it matter if there is radio or television coverage of the game?

Would a performance by a school orchestra conducted by a music teacher who receives an annual salary be excluded from § 110(4) as involving "payment of any fee or other compensation for the performance"? The House Report indicates that it would not. Id.

b. Major motion pictures studios, operating through the Motion Picture Licensing Corporation, offer licenses to organizations and governmental institutions for public performances of movie videocassettes and videodiscs. See the MPLC website at http://www.mplc.com.

The Internet too is a vehicle for public performance, and ASCAP and other performing rights organizations are now offering licenses to computer bulletin boards and websites that include performances of musical works.

c. ASCAP suffered a public relations nightmare when it attempted to sign up the nation's camps to public performance licenses. News accounts, reporting that ASCAP was going after groups like the Girl Scouts, were full of stories about scouts afraid to sing *Puff the Magic Dragon* around the campfire. Would that be exempt under § 110(4)? Insisting that it had only meant to license performances by professional musicians at large resort camps, ASCAP returned the fees to 16 Girl Scout camps that had paid for licenses. Bumiller, ASCAP Asks Royalties from Girl Scouts, and Regrets It, New York Times, Dec. 17, 1996, p. B1.

Why, in the event of an admission charge, is the copyright owner allowed to prohibit use of the work? The House Report states that "otherwise, owners could be compelled to make involuntary donations to the fund-raising activities of causes to which they are opposed." H.R.Rep. p. 86. But how will the copyright owner know of the intended use? Users apparently are not required to provide notice; the Copyright Office regulations leave the initiative with the copyright owner. 37 C.F.R. § 201.13.

(5) Section 110(5) responds to the *Aiken* problem. If a tavern owner installs a television, the resulting public performances are exempt. (What of a "large screen" television—is it "a single receiving apparatus of a kind commonly used in private homes"?) What if the tavern uses a satellite dish receiver and entices customers with football games that are "blacked out" from local reception? That led to an injunction in National Football League v. McBee and Bruno's, Inc., 792 F.2d 726 (8th Cir.1986), primarily because the court did not consider the dish a "receiving apparatus of a kind commonly used in private homes." How many dishes (or big screens) must there be in private homes to qualify? Suppose the tavern owner, as enterprising ones have done, tapes the weekday installments of soap operas and then provides a saturnalia of soaps on Sunday afternoon. That is probably an infringement. Why? Or, on a standard stereo, the tavern owner plays tapes of copyrighted music. Is that within the safety of § 110(5)?

On all these problems, consult Shipley, Copyright Law and Your Neighborhood Bar and Grill: Recent Developments in Performance Rights and the § 110(5) Exemption. 29 Ariz.L.Rev. 475 (1987) (generally accepting the trend of the cases).[d]

As for George Aiken and his "radio with outlets to four speakers in the ceiling", the House Committee "considers this fact situation to represent the outer limit of the exemption." H.R.Rep. p. 87.

When chain stores with hundreds of fairly small retail outlets attempted to take advantage of § 110(5), they were at first briskly rebuffed. See Sailor Music v. Gap Stores, Inc., 668 F.2d 84 (2d Cir.1981), cert. denied, 456 U.S. 945 (1982); Broadcast Music, Inc. v. United States Shoe Corp., 678 F.2d 816 (9th Cir.1982). But as the following case illustrates, more recent decisions have gone in their favor.

(6) Section 110(10) was added in 1982. What is the justification for this exemption? Note the limited inclusion of college fraternities and sororities.

(7) *Jewell–LaSalle* and hotel and apartment house retransmissions were finally put to rest by § 111(a)(1). For what uses would a hotel now need a performing rights license? A hotel renting videodiscs that guests took to

d. In an attempt to head off possible legislation that would reduce their right to collect royalties for performances in commercial establishments, the performing rights organizations reached agreement with the trade association representing bars and taverns for discounted royalty rates and an exemption for many small operators. The National Restaurant Association has so far refused a similar deal and is pushing for expanded legislative exemptions. 52 Pat.,Tm. & Copyr.J. (BNA) 72 (1996).

their rooms (which were equipped with players and large-screen televisions) did not need a license; the guest rooms were not "public." Columbia Pictures Industries, Inc. v. Professional Real Estate Investors, 866 F.2d 278 (9th Cir.1989). But in On Command Video Corp. v. Columbia Pictures Industries, 777 F.Supp. 787 (N.D.Cal.1991), the court held that electronic delivery of videotaped movies from a central location to individual hotel rooms involved a transmission to the public and was not exempt. And another hotel needed a license when it used a satellite dish to bring in ESPN and HBO. ESPN, Inc. v. Edinburg Community Hotel, Inc., 735 F.Supp. 1334 (S.D.Tex.1985). Why?

Broadcast Music, Inc. v. Claire's Boutiques, Inc.

United States Court of Appeals, Seventh Circuit, 1991.
949 F.2d 1482,
Certiorari denied, 504 U.S. 911, 112 S.Ct. 1942 (1992).

■ Before CUMMINGS, WOOD, JR., and KANNE, CIRCUIT JUDGES.

■ CUMMINGS, CIRCUIT JUDGE.

When must the corporate owner of a chain of retail stores pay copyright license fees for playing radio broadcasts in its stores? Plaintiffs Broadcast Music, Incorporated ("BMI") and various named song publishers sued defendant Claire's Boutiques, Incorporated ("Claire's") for violating copyrights in certain musical compositions. The plaintiff publishers own the copyrights in the compositions at issue but grant to BMI the right to license public performances of these compositions. Claire's, which owns and operates a chain of over 700 retail stores, defended BMI's allegations in the district court by claiming shelter in § 110(5) of the Copyright Act. Section 110(5) exempts under certain circumstances persons who play their radio or television in a public place if received by a single receiving apparatus of a kind commonly used in private homes. Both parties moved for summary judgment. The district court granted Claire's motion, and BMI appealed.

I.   FACTS

Pursuant to the district court's request, the parties stipulated to the following facts for the purposes of their summary judgment motions.

A.   *The Parties*

BMI is a non-profit performing rights organization expressly recognized by the Copyright Act. See 17 U.S.C. § 116(e)(3). Individual publishers grant to BMI a nonexclusive right to license public performance rights in their musical compositions. Besides BMI, the plaintiffs in this case own the copyrights to 88 musical compositions that are the subject of this action.[2]

	Song	*Plaintiff Publisher*
2. The first five songs listed on a schedule to BMI's complaint are:	1) "Shout"	Virgin Songs, Inc.

Claire's owns and operates 719 stores under the name Claire's Boutiques and 30 stores under the name Arcadia. These retail establishments are located throughout the United States and are open to the public during normal business hours. Claire's stores range in size from 458 square feet to 2000 square feet. The average size of a Claire's Boutique store is 861 square feet, and 628 of the Boutique stores are less than 1055 square feet. The average size of each Arcadia store is 2022 square feet, and 27 out of the 30 Arcadia stores are greater than 1055 square feet.

During fiscal year 1990, Claire's had net sales of $168,674,000 and earned $13,402,000 in net income. The Claire's Boutiques stores accounted for the majority of these sales ($165,767,233).

B. *Claire's Sound System*

Claire's has a policy to provide the following stereo components to each of its stores: a Radio Shack Optimus STA-20 5-watt stereo receiver, two Realistic Minimus 7 speakers, an indoor antenna, and speaker wire. As a general rule, Claire's ships a radio receiver to each new Claire's store. * * *

The receivers are ordinarily kept in a small storage room at the back of Claire's stores. The door between this room and the selling area is typically closed during business hours. Two strands of speaker wire run from the speaker jacks in the back of the receiver to speakers in the store's selling area. Both strands run through a hole in the wall separating the storage room from the selling area. One strand is attached to a speaker that is hung from the ceiling in the rear corner of the selling area. The other strand of wire runs above the dropped ceiling and is connected to the second speaker which is also hung from the ceiling. The first speaker is an average of 5–15 feet from the receiver, and the second speaker is an average of 20–35 feet from the receiver. Both speakers are hidden by a decorative dropped ceiling.

C. *The Parties' Dispute*

BMI claims that Claire's violates the Copyright Act by playing radio broadcasts in its stores without first obtaining a license from BMI. BMI has offered to provide Claire's with a license at an annual cost of $240 for the first location and $45–$60 for each additional location. One license agreement would cover all of Claire's locations that use receivers to play radio broadcasts. For all the Claire's stores involved in this litigation, the annual BMI licensing fee would be $40,385, an average of $53.92 per store. * * *

Song	Plaintiff Publisher
2) "Sitting on the Dock of the Bay" a/k/a "Sittin' on the Dock of the Bay"	Irving Music, Inc.
3) "This Old Heart of Mine (Is Weak For You)" a/k/a "This Old Heart of Mine"	Steve Agate Music, Division of Jobete Music, Inc.
4) "Way You Make Me Feel" a/k/a "The Way You Make Me Feel" a/k/a "Hot Fever"	Michael Joe Jackson d/b/a Mijac Music
5) "You Keep Me Hangin' On"	Steve Agate Music, Division of Jobete Music, Inc.

* * * The district court agreed with Claire's that it was exempt under § 110(5), granted Claire's motion for summary judgment, and dismissed the complaint on December 28, 1990. Broadcast Music, Inc. v. Claire's Boutiques, Inc., 754 F.Supp. 1324 (N.D.Ill.1990). * * *

II. ANALYSIS

* * *

Even though Congress rejected the Supreme Court's conclusion that the defendant in *Aiken* had not performed, the legislative history reveals that Congress did not intend to make him liable for copyright infringement. See H.R.Rep. No. 94–1476, 94th Cong., 2d Sess. 86, 87 (1976), reprinted in 1976 U.S.C.C.A.N. 5659, 5701 [hereafter House Report] * * *. * * * Because it helps explain the exemption and because BMI and Claire's argue over its meaning and relevance, a significant portion of the legislative history is quoted below: * * *

> Under the particular fact situation in the *Aiken* case, assuming a small commercial establishment and the use of a home receiver with four ordinary loudspeakers grouped within a relatively narrow circumference from the set, it is intended that the performances would be exempt under clause (5). However, the Committee considers this fact situation to represent the outer limit of the exemption, and believes that the line should be drawn at this point. Thus, the clause would exempt small commercial establishments whose proprietors merely bring onto their premises standard radio or television equipment and turn it on for their customers' enjoyment * * *. Factors to consider in particular cases would include the size, physical arrangement, and noise level of the areas within the establishment where the transmissions are made audible or visible, and the extent to which the receiving apparatus is altered or augmented for the purpose of improving the aural or visual quality of the performance for individual members of the public using those areas.

House Report at 86–87, reprinted in 1976 U.S.C.C.A.N. 5659, 5700–5701. * * *

The legislative history reveals several reasons why Congress passed the § 110(5) exemption. Congress thought it unfair to impose liability on unsuspecting small business persons. Congress believed also that it was impractical to require small organizations to enter into licensing agreements with performing rights organizations. The secondary use of radio broadcasts in small establishments, Congress also recognized, would have only a minimal effect on authors' incentives to create new works.

On the face of the statute, the exemption is available only if (1) a single receiving apparatus is used, (2) the single receiving apparatus is of a kind commonly used in private homes, (3) the transmission is provided free of charge, and (4) the transmission is not "further transmitted" to the public. The parties agree that Claire's does not charge for the privilege of listening to the radio broadcasts in its stores. The parties contest, however, the applicability of the other three elements required by § 110(5). They also disagree on the proper meaning and relevance of the legislative history. * * *

A. *The "Single Receiving Apparatus" Issue*

Section 110(5) does not discuss how to treat chain stores such as Claire's. BMI contends that Claire's cannot claim that it uses a "single receiving apparatus" for the simple reason that, on a corporate-wide basis, it uses 669 receivers. Claire's counters that its activities must be viewed on a store-by-store basis and that it is stipulated that only one receiver is used in each store. * * *

In one sense, it seems more appropriate to consider Claire's as the infringer as opposed to its individual store managers. Claire's instituted and has carried out a policy of playing radio music without a license in its public stores. Its store managers, although they may have the discretion to choose which station to play, are merely following corporate policy when they switch on the receivers in their stores. The legal fiction of corporate personhood was developed precisely for this type of case.

That Claire's is the potential infringer does not mean, however, that all its receivers must be counted together for the purposes of § 110(5). The language of the statute speaks of one performance of one work, describes the type of receiving apparatus that may be used, and disallows an admission charge or further transmission. The statute asks: under what circumstances was the radio used to perform this one work? Was one receiving apparatus used, was a charge made, was the work further transmitted? The statute does not ask how many receiving apparatuses were used to receive a number of different works. The language of the statute thus strongly suggests that the proper analysis should be limited to the area where a single work is performed. * * *

B. *The "Small Business" and "Background Music Service" Tests*

BMI also relies on the legislative history and several reported cases for the proposition that § 110(5) cannot apply to a large profitable business such as Claire's. The legislative history refers to the exemption being for "a small commercial establishment * * * not of sufficient size to justify, as a practical matter, a subscription to a commercial background music service * * *." Conference Report at 75, 1976 U.S.C.C.A.N. at 5816. * * *

* * * As the district court stated, "Congress chose to effectuate [the intent to exempt small commercial establishments] by drawing a distinction based on the type of sound equipment utilized and the nature of the transmission." 754 F.Supp. at 1333. Any rule developed under § 110(5) based on the financial strength of the company seeking the exemption would be directly contrary to the terms of the statute. * * *

It is true that a holding that the financial strength of Claire's is irrelevant contradicts the language of several other cases. These cases, however, typically rely independently on an analysis of the stereo system that the infringer had installed in its store. * * *

In sum, BMI is not entitled to reversal just because Claire's is a large and profitable business. The district court properly held that these considerations, notwithstanding the conclusions of other courts, are not relevant under § 110(5).

C. *Commonly Used in Private Homes*

BMI also contends that, even when considered on a store-by-store basis, Claire's does not use a "receiving apparatus of a kind commonly used in private homes" (a "home-type system"). The district court, after a thorough analysis of a number of different factors, concluded that Claire's used a home-type system in its stores. * * *

Because we examine the entire stereo system, there are two ways a company can fall out of the § 110(5) exemption for failure to use a home-type system. If the company uses any non-home-type components in its stereo system, then the system is not home-type. Analysis does not end, however, if all the components are home-type. The company also may not claim the exemption if it configures and uses home-type components in a manner not commonly found in a home. See Hickory Grove Music v. Andrews, 749 F.Supp. 1031, 1037 (D.Mont.1990).

The components in this case are home-type. * * *

Legislative history is a proper guide in interpreting the somewhat ambiguous notion of a home-type system. In this case, the history reveals that Congress considered the stereo configuration in *Aiken* to represent the "outer limit" of the exemption. That stereo system consisted of a radio with outlets to four "loudspeakers" in the ceiling. The restaurant in *Aiken* was of the "fast-food" variety and only accommodated about 40 patrons. Although not mentioned in the legislative history or in the *Aiken* case at any level, the parties apparently agree that the restaurant in *Aiken* was 1055 square feet in size, with a serving area of 620 square feet.

Although the legislative history nowhere suggests a hard and fast rule, it is apparent that Congress intended the exemption to apply only to stereo systems that produce music over a limited area. * * *

Claire's stores are small. 631 out of 749 of Claire's stores are less than 1055 square feet. The smallest store is 458 square feet; the largest store is 3300 square feet. The parties stipulate that one speaker averages five to fifteen feet from the receiver, and the other speaker averages twenty to thirty-five feet from the receiver. The fact that the broadcast of music in this case covers these small areas strongly indicates that the stereo system is of a kind commonly used in private homes. We do note that Claire's larger stores (greater than 2000 square feet) are closer to exceeding the size of a typical home and thus present closer cases. Even the larger stores, however, are not of a sufficiently large size to deny automatically application of the exemption. * * *

D. *Further Transmission*

BMI's final argument is that Claire's further transmits the music broadcasts it receives in its stores and therefore fails to qualify for the § 110(5) exemption. The phrase "further transmitted" is not defined in the Copyright Act. To "transmit" is "to communicate [a performance] by any device or process whereby images or sounds are received beyond the place from which they are sent." 17 U.S.C. § 101. A radio station transmits its broadcasts, which are received by numerous radio sets. The question in this case is whether Claire's further transmits the broadcast it receives.

BMI argues that "it is undisputed that Claire's causes sounds to be received beyond the place where the performance is initially received" (Br. 39). This argument assumes that the performance is initially received at the receiver and then "further transmitted" via wire to other areas. Whatever its technical merits, this view of "further transmission" is contrary to the legislative history. The system in *Aiken* consisted of a radio set connected, presumably by wires, to four speakers. Congress intended such a system to be exempt under § 110(5). Yet BMI's proposed rule would deny the exemption to the store in *Aiken*. In addition, the statute uses the term "receiving apparatus," which, as discussed above, encompasses not just the receiver but all the components of an integrated music system. It is sensible to consider that the entire receiving apparatus, and not just the receiver, "receives" the performance.

* * *

To further transmit a performance must mean more than to run speaker wire through a wall. It must entail the use of some device or process that expands the normal limits of the receiver's capabilities. We recognize that this construction of "further transmission" means that most systems that further transmit also are not home-type. But since it is conceivable that even a home-type component could further transmit under this approach, the requirement of no "further transmission" is not mere surplusage.

III. CONCLUSION

A recurring theme in BMI's argument is that Congress never intended § 110(5) to apply to multimillion dollar corporations such as Claire's. This may be so, but the job of this Court is to apply the laws passed by Congress, and not to enforce a generalized and vague notion of intent. * * * The sound system used by Claire's passes the statutory tests for exemption, and therefore the judgment below for Claire's is affirmed.

NOTE

The Eighth Circuit promptly followed the Seventh in holding that the number of stores in a chain had nothing to do with eligibility for the exemption under § 110(5). Edison Brothers Stores, Inc. v. Broadcast

Music, Inc., 954 F.2d 1419 (8th Cir.), cert. denied, 504 U.S. 930 (1992). Edison had 2,500 stores; 220 with sophisticated audio and visual equipment had gotten licenses.

In 1998 the House passed a bill (H.R. 2589) that would expand the § 110(5) public reception exemption to all establishments of less than 3,500 square feet (and larger ones if they use no more than six speakers or two large-screen televisions).

PUBLIC PERFORMANCE OF SOUND RECORDINGS

Early attempts at common law to control the public performance of recordings (again, as distinguished from the musical works embodied in the recordings) produced famous cases and irreconcilable results.[e] Proposals to create an exclusive public performance right in sound recordings, which would be especially valuable against broadcasters, were coldly rebuffed in the early years of the copyright law revision process. In 1969, however, a performance right for sound recordings appeared in the revision bill then before Congress. It was part of § 114 and included a complex compulsory licensing scheme. Before the revision bill passed, the provision was dropped, replaced with a directive to the Register of Copyrights to report with recommendations on a performance right for sound recordings.

The Report of the Register of Copyrights on Performance Rights in Sound Recordings was duly submitted in 1978; it strongly supported an exclusive right of public performance for sound recordings. "Broadcasters and other commercial users of recordings have performed them without permission or payment for generations. Users today look upon any requirement that they pay royalties as an unfair imposition in the nature of a 'tax.' However, any economic burden on the users of recordings for public performance is heavily outweighed, not only by the commercial benefits accruing directly from the use of copyrighted sound recordings, but also by the direct and indirect damage done to performers whenever recordings are used as a substitute for live performances." The Report also responded to the broadcasters' argument that the benefits accruing to performers and record companies from the free airplay of their recordings is adequate compensation for the performance. "This is the strongest argument put forward by broadcasters and other users. There is no question that broadcasting and jukebox performances give some recordings the kind of exposure that benefits their producers and individual performers through increased sales and popularity. * * * The opportunity for benefit through increased sales, no matter how significant it may be temporarily for some 'hit records,' can hardly justify the outright denial of any performing rights to any sound recordings."[f]

---

e. Compare Waring v. WDAS Broadcasting Station, Inc., 327 Pa. 433, 194 A. 631 (1937), with RCA Manuf. Co. v. Whiteman, 114 F.2d 86 (2d Cir.), cert. denied, 311 U.S. 712 (1940).

f. On the performance right debate, compare Kim, The Performers' Plight in Sound Recordings, 10 Colum.-VLA J.L. & Arts 453 (1986) (supporting a performance

The Copyright Office had another opportunity to comment on performance rights in sound recordings when Congress requested a report on the implications of digital music transmissions, including digital broadcasting and cable delivery of digital audio programming. In a 1991 report entitled Copyright Implications of Digital Audio Transmission Services, the Copyright Office concluded that the development of digital transmission services increased the potential economic harm to the owners of sound recordings by providing recipients of the transmissions with the opportunity to make high quality copies; the Copyright Office took the occasion to renew its support for a public performance right.

In 1995, Congress passed the Digital Performance Right in Sound Recordings Act, Pub.L. No. 104–39. The Act creates a new—but sharply limited—public performance right for sound recordings. The amendments made by the Act begin with a deceptively simple addition to the list of exclusive rights—§ 106(6) now recognizes, for sound recordings, an exclusive right "to perform the copyrighted work publicly by means of a digital audio transmission," supported by a definition of "digital transmission" in § 101. However, the right is subject to the dizzying series of limitations imposed in § 114(d)-(j).

Note first that the performance right is limited to digital transmissions; it does not apply to analog transmissions such as traditional AM or FM broadcasts, or to public performances that do not involve a transmission, such as playing tapes or CDs as background music at a restaurant. Since the right covers only sound recordings, it does not apply to transmissions of audiovisual works (see § 114(j)(3)).

Transmissions potentially captured by the amendment include the delivery of digital signals by over-the-air broadcast, satellite, cable, or the Internet. However, many performances of sound recordings by digital transmission are exempt, including "nonsubscription transmissions"—essentially transmissions for which there is no charge. Other types of digital transmissions—"subscription transmissions"—can be eligible for a compulsory license (set by the Librarian of Congress at 6.5 per cent of gross revenues (63 Fed.Reg. 25394 (May 8, 1998)), rejecting a 5 per cent figure set by a copyright arbitration royalty panel—see p. 537 infra). "Subscription transmissions" are controlled transmissions to recipients who pay to receive them. They are eligible for the compulsory license if, among other conditions, they are not "interactive," meaning that they do not permit a recipient to receive on request a particular sound recording. There are also restrictions on publishing advance programming schedules and playing too many selections from a given recording or performer in a specified time period. All this is geared to preventing subscription services from cutting too heavily into sales of pre-recorded music. Half of the compulsory licensing fees are reserved for performers (45 per cent to the featured

right), with Bard and Kurlantzick, A Public Performance Right in Sound Recordings: How to Alter the Copyright System Without Improving It, 43 Geo.Wash.L.Rev. 152 (1974) (concluding, as the title suggests, that a performance right is not easily justified).

artists on the sound recording and 2 1/2 per cent each to funds for non-featured vocalists and musicians); the other half of the fees go to the record company that owns the copyright.

Subscription transmissions that do not qualify for a compulsory license—primarily interactive transmissions—must be authorized through voluntary licenses from the copyright owner (with statutory restrictions on the length of exclusive arrangements). The distribution of proceeds from these voluntary licenses is determined by the terms of the performers' contract with the record company.

A helpful summary of the 1995 amendment appears in Sobel, A New Music Law for the Age of Digital Technology, 17 Enter.L.Rep. (No. 6) 3 (1995). The performance right amendment has been touted as enabling American record companies and performers to claim their share of foreign performance royalties (estimated at over $150 million worldwide, with half attributable to the playing of American records). The United States remains one of the few nations that does not recognize a general performance right for sound recordings; Sobel doubts that the amendment's limited scope will be sufficient to coax foreign governments into "reciprocal" treatment for U.S. copyright owners.

PERFORMING RIGHTS ORGANIZATIONS

ASCAP

The organization and operation of ASCAP are described in the following excerpts from a paper by Herman Finkelstein, long the Society's general counsel until his retirement in 1973.[g]

"The performing right which will be discussed here is limited to musical compositions—particularly the non-dramatic, or so-called 'small' rights in such works.[h] In addition to the American Society of Composers, Authors and Publishers, which has been in existence since 1914, there are other licensing organizations such as Broadcast Music, Inc. (BMI) which is owned by and operated for the radio broadcast industry; and a third organization known as SESAC, Inc., originally called the Society of Europe-

---

g. Public Performance Rights in Music and Performance Rights Societies, originally in Seven Copyright Problems Analyzed 69 (1952), revised and separately published in 1956 and 1961 by the author; excerpts reproduced by permission from the 1961 publication. See also Korman and Koenigsberg, Performing Rights in Music and Performing Rights Societies, 33 J.Copyr.Soc. 332 (1986). For additional information, see the ASCAP website at http://www.ascap.com.

h. Rights to perform songs in a dramatic setting, or to perform integrated dramatic and musical works, are sometimes called "grand rights" and have their own problems

of definition, licensing, and protection. See especially Perrone, Small and Grand Performing Rights (Who Cared Before "Jesus Christ Superstar"), 20 Bull.Copyr.Soc. 19 (1972); S. Shemel and M. Krasilovsky, This Business of Music (1995); Kohn and Kohn, Kohn on Music Licensing (1995). On the often severe restrictions imposed on dramatic performances of well-known songs by the copyright successors to deceased composers and lyricists, see O'Toole, Ego, Paranoia and Power in the Land of Musical Rights, N.Y.Times, May 30, 1993, Sec. 2, p. 1.

an Stage Authors and Composers. This organization is privately owned.
* * *

"The American Society of Composers, Authors and Publishers unlike any of the other licensing organizations mentioned is made up entirely of composers, authors and publishers. It is a nonprofit organization. After payment of expenses, all of its receipts are divided equally between writers on the one hand and their publishers on the other. * * *

"The members, as I have said, grant only the non-dramatic rights. * * * Members license their works directly for the legitimate stage. Dramatic performances on television or radio are also reserved to and handled by the members independently of the Society.

"Users of music have the option of dealing individually with the members of the Society, or collectively with the Society. As a practical matter, of course, a radio station, or other large scale users of copyrighted musical works would find it wholly impractical to deal with individual copyright owners.

"The need for bulk licensing of performing rights is nowhere more evident than in the radio and television field where program directors require the greatest latitude in building their shows while protecting the station, its sponsors and artists from claims of infringement. The networks and most local stations have license agreements with ASCAP, BMI and SESAC, Inc. Network programs are cleared at the source by the Society, that is, if a network broadcasts a program using music in the Society's repertory, the network's license covers all the interconnected stations picking up that program. On purely local programs, the individual stations have their own agreement.

"Stations may have either a blanket or per program form of license. Both licenses are really on a blanket basis; that is, the license permits the station to play any composition in the licensor's repertory without separately negotiating therefor. The difference in the two types of license lies in the method of computing payments. Whereas, stations having a blanket license pay a percentage on all their receipts from the sale of 'time on the air', those stations having program licenses pay on only those programs in which music in the Society's repertory is performed. * * *

"Although radio and television together constitute the most extensive users of copyrighted musical compositions in the Society's repertory, a great variety of users obtain licenses to perform the vast repertory of compositions made available by the Society. These include restaurants, taverns, dance halls, hotels, department stores and such wired music concerns as Muzak, Seeburg and others. Of late, factories and similar industrial establishments have become important users of music. * * *

"The royalties collected by the Society are divided equally between the publishers and the writers. The publishers have their system of distribution and the writers have theirs. There are these overriding principles applicable both to writer and publisher-director: consideration must be given to the number of works that a member contributes, their nature, character, prestige, the length of time they have been a part of the catalogue of the Society, and their vogue and popularity; and primary consideration must be given to the performances of the members' works."

———————

The present structure of ASCAP is to a large extent regulated by a consent decree under the Sherman Act. The following statement by Victor R. Hansen, then Assistant Attorney General in charge of the Antitrust Division of the Department of Justice, describes the background and operation of this decree from the standpoint of the Department.[i]

"The Department's civil action against ASCAP in 1941 arose out of changes in the music business which began early in the 1930's. Prior to 1930, authors and publishers relied chiefly on the sale of sheet music for their incomes. With phonographs and radios replacing the pianos in American homes, and with a statutory limit on royalties for the sale of records, more writers and publishers turned to ASCAP to protect their source of income. The need for users of music to have access to ASCAP-controlled music also increased.

"As the radio industry expanded, ASCAP demanded larger royalty payments based on a percentage of gross revenues. Faced with virtually a single source of supply, the radio broadcasting industry refused to negotiate with ASCAP, and organized Broadcast Music, Inc., to secure copyrights and to obtain licenses from foreign societies. For nearly a year no ASCAP music was heard on the radio. This was the era when 'Jeanie With the Light Brown Hair' was burned in effigy on college campuses and the listening public was surfeited with Latin American rhythms.

"The Antitrust Division's civil complaint was filed February 25, 1941, and the various practices alleged reflect the types of complaints received by the Department and restraints felt to be objectionable. The complaint charged a violation of section 1 of the Sherman Act. It alleged that ASCAP controlled at least 75 percent of the music demanded and used by the people of the United States; and that absolute control of ASCAP affairs was vested in a self-perpetuating board of directors which had, and had exercised, the power to fix the price for and control of the public performance of a substantial part of the copyrighted music demanded in the United States. * * *

"The Government's complaint alleged that motion picture films included synchronized sound tracks containing much music controlled by ASCAP, which films could be shown in a theater only if the theater were licensed by ASCAP; and without such a license the films were worthless. Substantially the same allegations were made as to electrical transcriptions produced for the exclusive use of broadcasters. Charges were also made relating to

i. Statement of March 13, 1958, in House Select Comm. on Small Business, Subcomm. No. 5, Hearings, Policies of American Society of Composers, Authors, and Publishers 138–41 (March–April, 1958).

ASCAP's rule that it have the exclusive right to license songs in its repertory, thus eliminating competition among members in licensing their own works. Charges also related to the fact that, having a pool of copyrights, ASCAP issued only blanket licenses and refused to license on any other basis. * * *

"The charges were terminated by entry of a consent judgment on March 4, 1941. While this decree was revamped in 1950, it is in substance effective today. That early decree prohibited ASCAP from acquiring or asserting any exclusive licensing right, but with the proviso that, among other things, ASCAP might require its members to pay to ASCAP all revenues derived from licenses issued by them; and that such issuance be with prior notice to ASCAP. The decree prohibits discrimination among licensees similarly situated. ASCAP was required to offer per-program licenses to radio broadcasters and license radio networks on a basis which would not require affiliated stations to obtain an ASCAP license in order to use network programs. The same was required as to electrical transcriptions made for radio broadcast. The decree enjoined ASCAP from refusing to offer per-piece licenses to users other than broadcasters and from refusing to offer per-program licenses to broadcasters. * * *

"Then, on July 18, 1948, Judge Leibell, in the *Alden–Rochelle* case,[1] a suit instituted by certain theater operators, found ASCAP to be illegally restraining trade and an illegal monopoly. He found that ASCAP had the power to fix prices and eliminate competition; that many ASCAP publishers were affiliated with motion picture producers who received 37 percent of the publishers' share of ASCAP distributions; that there was an illegal conspiracy between such publishers and movie producers to extend their respective copyright monopolies; that producers refused to license movies to theaters not having an ASCAP license; and that ASCAP was an illegal copyright pool.

"Soon after the Leibell ruling, Judge Nordbye [2] in Minnesota endorsed the ruling. Both courts found that per-piece licensing was commercially impractical and Judge Nordbye suggested that to end ASCAP's power over exhibitors, members of ASCAP grant performance and synchronization rights simultaneously to movie producers.

"With the confusion in the entertainment industry resulting from these two decisions, coupled with mounting complaints of other users and ASCAP members, the Department undertook a revamping of the 1941 decree. * * *

"The changes contained in the amended judgment sought to add protection to users, including two new mediums, television and wired-music systems (such as Muzak). The new judgment took the approach that has been called open-door and open-window to ASCAP's internal operations. The major changes made in the 1941 decree were in substance as follows: ASCAP members were given the unrestricted right to license their own works. Membership requirements were eased so that a writer applicant

---

1. Alden–Rochelle, Inc. v. ASCAP, 80 F.Supp. 888 (S.D.N.Y.1948).

2. M. Witmark & Sons v. Jensen, 80 F.Supp. 843 (D.Minn.1948).

need have only one composition regularly published, and a publisher applicant need only have its publications distributed on a commercial scale for one year and bear the normal risk of the publishing business. Subject to contractual obligations of ASCAP, a member might withdraw and take his compositions with him. Thus the right of ingress and egress was adequately protected.

"The principle of licensing at the source was applied to television, wired-music service, and motion picture production; i.e., members were required to license performance rights when the synchronization rights were licensed. ASCAP was prohibited from licensing theater operators for performances of ASCAP music on film. The compulsory licensing provisions were extended to cover television broadcasting and ASCAP was required to use its best efforts to give its licensees a genuine economic choice among the various types of licenses.

"An important provision of the amended judgment protects users from any exorbitant demands by ASCAP for the use of an admittedly necessary collection of compositions. The amended judgment provides for compulsory licensing of performing rights and for court determination of what constitutes a reasonable royalty if the applicant and ASCAP are unable to agree in preliminary negotiations. * * *

"The 1950 amended judgment eliminated the subjective standards to be used to determine the basis of distribution of revenues to its members. It requires ASCAP to distribute its revenues primarily on the basis of objective surveys periodically made." [j]

In 1959 a further consent order was proposed by the Antitrust Division, with ASCAP's agreement, to sharpen and in some respects change the provisions of the 1950 decree affecting the ASCAP membership. Relations with licensees were not directly altered by these amendments. After hearing from some of the dissatisfied ASCAP members, and after a referendum of the membership had supported the order, it was approved on January 7, 1960.[k] The 1960 consent decree required elaborate surveys of public performances, particularly broadcasts, with account also taken of the varying economic significance of different kinds of performances. The formula for distribution of revenues to the writer members was changed to put greater emphasis on current performances over long-term averages and seniority. The consent decree also reformed ASCAP's voting and accounting procedures.

BMI

ASCAP members depend on the broadcasting industry for income and as an outlet for their compositions. In view of the great reservoir of

j. See the valuable discussion of the 1950 decree by Timberg, The Antitrust Aspects of Merchandising Modern Music: The ASCAP Consent Judgment of 1950, 19 L. & Contemp.Prob. 294 (1954). The author was chief of the Judgment and Enforcement Section of the Antitrust Division when the 1950 decree was negotiated.

k. The ASCAP consent decrees are in CCH 1940–43 Trade Cases ¶ 56,104; 1950–51 id. ¶ 62,595; 1960 id. ¶ 69,612.

popular and standard music licensed by ASCAP, the dependence is mutual. The likelihood of another impasse such as occurred in 1941 has been lessened by provisions of the consent decree that require ASCAP to issue licenses and permit a dissatisfied user to ask the district court to set a reasonable fee.

The broadcasters also created in 1941 an organization that has become a formidable rival to ASCAP. Broadcast Music, Inc., usually known as BMI, is not a performing rights society with a membership of writers and publishers. It is a corporation, and its stock is owned by broadcasters. It does not, however, pay any dividends, and considers itself a non-profit corporation. It deals with writers and publishers entirely on a contractual basis. Performances are measured through station logs and sampling, and are paid for entirely on a current basis, without the income-levelling formulas used by ASCAP. This has the result of providing larger initial payments for young writers than are available from ASCAP. Some of the tensions between BMI and ASCAP are discussed in United States v. ASCAP, 586 F.Supp. 727 (S.D.N.Y.1984).

BMI also operates under the terms of an antitrust consent decree (see CCH 1940–43 Trade Cases ¶ 56,096), but the restrictions of the decree are not comparable to the extensive control of ASCAP described earlier. The 1966 revisions to the consent decree provide that publishers and writers must be free to give non-exclusive licenses for specific works; the duration of BMI contracts is limited to five years. (CCH 1966 Trade Cases ¶ 71,-941.) In 1994, the Justice Department agreed to a proposed modification of the 1966 BMI decree that creates a mechanism for judicial resolution of licensing fee disputes. 59 Fed.Reg. 35752.[1]

A writer must decide whether to sign up with BMI or with ASCAP, though a writer may withdraw a work from BMI if an ASCAP publisher will publish it and a BMI publisher will not. Many publishers, operating through corporations, have both an ASCAP firm and a BMI firm.

BMI's gross income approaches that of ASCAP's. It has achieved this position, in the face of ASCAP's massive collection of popular works, by diligently seeking out new composers and publishers and exploiting the trends in popular music: Latin–American in the 1940s, then country and western, rhythm and blues, and rock and roll and its subdivisions.[m] BMI has been aggressive and, not being bound by distribution formulas, could offer advantageous deals when it spotted a trend.[n]

---

l. For additional information, see the BMI website at http://www.bmi.com.

m. With over 7 million performances, *You've Got that Lovin' Feeling*, written in 1964 by Phil Spector, Barry Mann, and Cynthia Weil, is now the most performed song in BMI's 3 million song repertoire, overtaking the prior champ, John Lennon and Paul McCartney's *Yesterday*. The 7 million performances, played back-to-back, would last 39.1 years. Rocky Mountain News, Mar. 16, 1997, p. 19D.

n. Affiliated Music Enterprises, Inc. v. SESAC, Inc., 160 F.Supp. 865 (S.D.N.Y.1958), aff'd on other grounds, 268 F.2d 13 (2d Cir. 1959), is revealing on the business practices of BMI and SESAC, a privately owned performing rights licensor, in wooing the publishers of "shaped-note gospel music."

A useful comparison of ASCAP and BMI relations with composers appears in S. Shemel and M. Krasilovsky, This Business of Music (1995). ASCAP and BMI writer agreements and licensing forms appear in Kohn and Kohn, Kohn on Music Licensing (1995).

PRIVATE ANTITRUST ACTIONS AGAINST ASCAP AND BMI: THE "BLANKET LICENSE"

In K–91, Inc. v. Gershwin Pub. Corp., 372 F.2d 1 (9th Cir.1967), cert. denied, 389 U.S. 1045 (1968), a radio station resisted an infringement action by claiming that ASCAP and its members were violating the antitrust laws.[o] Judge Barnes wrote:

"We agree with the trial court that the activities of ASCAP do not constitute a combination in restraint of trade or a monopoly within the meaning of the Sherman Act. ASCAP is certainly a combination, but not every combination is a combination in restraint of trade or a monopoly. ASCAP cannot be accused of fixing prices because every applicant to ASCAP has a right under the consent decree to invoke the authority of the United States District Court for the Southern District of New York to fix a reasonable fee whenever the applicant believes that the price proposed by ASCAP is unreasonable, and ASCAP has the burden of proving the price reasonable. In other words, so long as ASCAP complies with the decree, it is not the price fixing authority. We cannot agree with the contention that the danger of unreasonable activity that might arise from ASCAP's activities makes everything that it does a violation of the antitrust laws, when those of its potential activities that might have this effect are prohibited by the decree. No contention is here made that ASCAP's actual activities do not comply with the decree. In short, we think that as a potential combination in restraint of trade, ASCAP has been 'disinfected' by the decree."

Undismayed by these barriers, CBS in 1969 sued ASCAP and BMI, alleging that the customary "blanket" and "program" licenses violated the antitrust laws. CBS proposed that it be permitted to negotiate a "per use" license that would measure payments chiefly by the actual use of the repertory. ASCAP moved for summary judgment, relying on K–91 Inc. v. Gershwin Pub. Corp. After Judge Lasker denied the motion for summary judgment, CBS, Inc. v. ASCAP, 337 F.Supp. 394 (S.D.N.Y.1972), the case went to trial in 1973. In 1975 he decided against CBS. 400 F.Supp. 737. In July 1977, the Second Circuit reversed. 562 F.2d 130. Distinguishing (or rejecting) K–91 v. Gershwin, the court held blanket licensing to be price-fixing.

o. The defendant also attempted to rely on a Washington state statute aimed at curbing ASCAP. Such legislation, which had considerable impetus in the 1930s, has occasionally been invoked, but with no lasting results. See Watson v. Buck, 313 U.S. 387 (1941); Marsh v. Buck, 313 U.S. 406 (1941); Finkelstein, The Composer and the Public Interest—Regulation of Performing Right Societies, 19 L. & Contemp.Prob. 275, 289 (1954).

The Supreme Court in Broadcast Music, Inc. v. CBS, Inc., 441 U.S. 1 (1979), decided that the blanket license was not a *per se* violation of the Sherman Act. For one thing, it found that the convenience and flexibility of the blanket license made it a product distinct from the aggregation of songs. The Court concluded:

> * * * [T]he blanket license cannot be wholly equated with a simple horizontal arrangement among competitors. ASCAP does set the price for its blanket license, but that license is quite different from anything any individual owner could issue. The individual composers and authors have neither agreed not to sell individually in any other market nor use the blanket license to mask price fixing in such other markets. Moreover, the substantial restraints placed on ASCAP and its members by the consent decree must not be ignored. The District Court found that there was no legal, practical, or conspiratorial impediment to CBS obtaining individual licenses; CBS, in short, had a real choice.
>
> With this background in mind, which plainly enough indicates that over the years, and in the face of available alternatives, the blanket license has provided an acceptable mechanism for at least a large part of the market for the performing rights to copyrighted musical compositions, we cannot agree that it should automatically be declared illegal in all of its many manifestations. Rather, when attacked, it should be subjected to a more discriminating examination under the rule of reason. It may not ultimately survive that attack, but that is not the issue before us today.

On remand, the Second Circuit (through a panel that, because of two deaths, included only Judge Moore from the earlier panel) found close examination unnecessary. It agreed that CBS had the burden of proving that the blanket license had restrained competition, and that it had not carried that burden. CBS v. ASCAP, 620 F.2d 930 (2d Cir.1980), cert. denied, 450 U.S. 970 (1981). See Hartnick, The Network Blanket License Triumphant: The Fourth Round of the ASCAP–BMI–CBS Litigation, 2 Comm. & L. (No. 4) 49 (1980).

It was then the turn of the *local* television stations to take on ASCAP, BMI, and the blanket license. There are about 750 of them, of which 600 have network affiliations. All of them depend heavily on syndicated programs that they buy or lease. Complaining of the illegality and unfairness of blanket licenses, the local stations urged that the performing rights societies should be required to license performance rights through the syndicators ("source licensing"), who now buy (through the Harry Fox Agency, p. 541 infra) only synchronization rights—the right to record the music on the program.

The District Court found that the local stations had no viable alternative to blanket licenses (unlike CBS, which supposedly could manage direct licensing from composers if it wanted to), so there was a violation of § 1 of the Sherman Act. The Court of Appeals disagreed. Buffalo Broadcasting Co. v. ASCAP, 546 F.Supp. 274 (S.D.N.Y.1982), rev'd, 744 F.2d 917 (2d

Cir.1984), cert. denied, 469 U.S. 1211 (1985). It found that the impracticability of alternatives had not been established. As for the inability of the local broadcasters to induce syndicators to obtain performance licenses, that was not established either. There is competition in the syndication market, and that market might not be "unresponsive to aggregate demand from stations willing to pay a reasonable price for source licensing of music performing rights."

"The blanket license is not even amenable to scrutiny under section 1 unless it is a restraint of trade. * * * Since the blanket license restrains no one from bargaining over the purchase and sale of music performance rights, it is not a restraint unless it were proven that there are no realistically available alternatives." Judge Winter, concurring with Judge Newman's opinion for the court, went even further, declaring that a nonexclusive blanket license "cannot restrain competition."

Blocked in the courts, local television interests unsuccessfully sought relief from Congress in the form of "source licensing" legislation that would require the program producers to obtain performance licenses when they get permission to record copyrighted music in their programs. See Boucher, Blanket Licensing and Local Television: An Historical Accident in Need of Reform, 44 Wash. & Lee L.Rev. 1157 (1987) (written by a sponsor of the legislation).

Cable television operators and programmers also challenged the blanket license, but their antitrust claim against BMI was rejected in National Cable Television Ass'n, Inc. v. Broadcast Music, Inc., 772 F.Supp. 614 (D.D.C.1991). One programmer, trying a different strategy, invoked its rights under the ASCAP consent decree and requested a judicial determination of a reasonable licensing fee. The District Court reduced ASCAP's proposed price by 40%, and the new fee was affirmed in ASCAP v. Showtime/The Movie Channel, Inc., 912 F.2d 563 (2d Cir.1990).

Commentators have generally supported blanket licensing, preferably under a legislative exemption from the antitrust laws. See Sobel, The Music Business and the Sherman Act: An Analysis of the "Economic Realities" of Blanket Licensing, 3 Loy.Ent.L.J. 1 (1983); Developments, Blanket Licensing of Music Performing Rights: Possible Solutions to the Copyright–Antitrust Conflict, 37 Vand.L.Rev. 183 (1984).[p]

SECTION 9. DISTRIBUTION, DISPLAY, AND DERIVATIVE RIGHTS

Among the exclusive rights reserved to the copyright owner is the right "to distribute" copies of the work to the public. § 106(3). The right is

---

p. The economic benefits of collective rights organizations such as ASCAP and BMI are analyzed in Merges, Contracting Into Liability Rules: Intellectual Property Rights and Collective Rights Organizations, 84 Cal. L.Rev. 1293 (1996), concluding that the organizations are an efficient response to transaction costs.

described succinctly in the House Report: "Under this provision the copyright owner would have the right to control the first public distribution of an authorized copy or phonorecord of his work, whether by sale, gift, loan, or some rental or lease arrangement. Likewise, any unauthorized public distribution of copies or phonorecords that were unlawfully made would be an infringement." H.R.Rep. p. 62. An independent distribution right enables the copyright owner to secure relief against the vendors (even those with no knowledge of the infringement) as well as against the producers of infringing material.

The display right, § 106(5), is the first statutory recognition of an exclusive right to show the copyrighted work to the public. Both distribution and display rights, however, are limited by § 109, which incorporates what is commonly, although somewhat inaccurately, known as the "first sale" doctrine. The following case examines the first sale doctrine in the context of § 27 of the 1909 Act, the predecessor of § 109(a).

Independent News Co. v. Williams

United States Court of Appeals, Third Circuit, 1961.
293 F.2d 510.

■ Before GOODRICH, McLAUGHLIN and FORMAN, CIRCUIT JUDGES.

■ McLAUGHLIN, CIRCUIT JUDGE.

Can a second-hand periodical dealer who purchases cover-removed comics from waste paper dealers be enjoined under any one of six different legal theories, from marketing them as reading material? The district court refused to grant an injunction, holding that defendant's actions did not constitute conversion of the literary property in the comics, trademark infringement, copyright infringement, unfair competition, sales in violation of the legend appearing on each magazine or an invasion of the right of privacy.

Plaintiff, Independent News Co., Inc., is the distributor of the comics; plaintiff, National Comics Publications, Inc., is the publisher; plaintiff, Superman, Inc., owns the copyright and trademark. The defendant, Harry Williams, is a Philadelphia distributor of second-hand books and magazines.

The critical facts involve the distribution system used in marketing the comics. The distributor, Independent, pursuant to a written contract, sells the comics to the wholesaler. The comics are to be offered for sale during a period specified by the publisher. The wholesaler then sells them to the various retail outlets with the same restriction. At the end of the sales period, the wholesaler reacquires from the retail outlets all unsold comics and gives the retailer full credit. In turn the wholesaler is entitled to full credit from Independent. However, instead of returning the entire comic, the agreement provides that unless otherwise directed, the wholesaler need only return the covers. As to the remaining portion of the comic, the wholesaler is obligated to, " * * * destroy or mutilate the remaining portions thereof so as to render them unsalable as publications." He further agrees, " * * * that such destroyed or mutilated portions of return copies shall be disposed of or sold for no other purpose than waste paper, and *that he will obtain a written commitment from the purchasers of such destroyed or mutilated return copies that the same will be used only for waste and will not be resold.*" (Emphasis supplied.)

In the case at bar the district court found as a fact that the defendant had purchased cover-removed comics from waste paper dealers and then sold them on the open market; that although the contract between Independent and the wholesalers required that the wholesaler obtain a written commitment from the waste paper dealers, no such commitment was ever obtained; and that: "There is no evidence that the defendant had any knowledge that any of the wastepaper dealers from whom he purchased were obligated to sell their coverless comics as wastepaper only." [184 F.Supp. 879.] * * *

Plaintiffs' third theory is copyright infringement. They allege that under the Copyright Act, as amended 17 U.S.C.A. § 1 et seq., one of the rights granted a copyright holder is the exclusive right to "vend", the copyrighted work. Factually they contend that: "In the instant case defendant buys, not the literary work at the price specified by the owner of a copyright, but instead buys scrap paper at a small fraction of a cent per copy. He then turns around and makes the *first sale* of this periodical *as a literary work.*"

This argument is completely refuted by the holding in Harrison v. Maynard, Merrill & Co., 2 Cir., 1894, 61 F. 689. There the plaintiff-copyright holder entered into a contract with one Alexander to bind the books. During the course of their business, Alexander would bind additional copies of the book and store them in anticipation of plaintiff's orders. A fire occurred at Alexander's bindery and it was thought that these stored books were too damaged to be sold. Alexander, with the plaintiff's permission, sold the debris to one Fitzgerald, who in turn sold them to waste paper dealers, incorporating the following clause as part of the contract:

> *"It is understood that all paper taken out of the building is to be utilized as paper stock, and all books to be sold as paper stock only, and not placed on the market as anything else."* (Emphasis supplied.)

Subsequently copies of the copyrighted work appeared in the market offered for sale by the defendant, a secondhand book dealer. Plaintiff sought to restrain their sale by the defendant, asserting copyright infringement. The court held that since the plaintiff had parted with title to the copies, it was not a copyright infringement for the defendant to sell them as literature. Said the court at page 691:

> "But the right to restrain the sale of a particular copy of the book by virtue of the copyright statutes has gone when the owner of the copyright and of that copy has parted with all his title to it, and has conferred an absolute title to the copy upon a purchaser,

although with an agreement for a restricted use. The exclusive right to vend the particular copy no longer remains in the owner of the copyright by the copyright statutes. The new purchaser cannot reprint the copy. He cannot print or publish a new edition of the book; but, *the copy having been absolutely sold to him, the ordinary incidents of ownership in personal property, among which is the right of alienation, attach to it.* If he has agreed that he will not sell it for certain purposes or to certain persons and violates his agreement, and sells to an innocent purchaser, he can be punished for a violation of his agreement; but neither is guilty, under the copyright statutes, of an infringement. If the new purchaser participates in the fraud, he may also share in the punishment. Clemens v. Estes, C.C., 22 Fed. 899.'' (Emphasis supplied.)

And this the court stated was the pertinent principle irrespective of whether the defendant had notice of the original contractual restriction.

This appeal provides an even stronger basis for holding that the defendant has not infringed the plaintiffs' copyright. The waste paper dealers purchased full title to the coverless comics without any restriction on their use whatsoever.[3] Although the contract between the wholesaler and distributor provides that the wholesaler obtain a written commitment from the waste paper dealer, the district court's finding of fact number 8, which is sustained by the record, shows: "There is no evidence that any of the wastepaper dealers from whom the defendant purchased coverless comics had, in fact, any contractual obligation to use such comics as wastepaper only."

Apart from this, though the contract between the distributor and the wholesaler provided: "Wholesaler agrees that such destroyed or mutilated portions of return copies shall be disposed of or sold for no other purpose than waste paper, * * *'' under the rationale of the *Harrison* case, where the publisher has parted with the title to the copyrighted work and despite the fact that as between the immediate parties there is a contractual restriction on its use, this restriction does not bar subsequent purchasers from vending the periodical as a literary work free of the restriction. Harrison v. Maynard, Merrill & Co., supra. Cf. United States v. Wells, D.C.S.D.Tex.1959, 176 F.Supp. 630, 634.

Moreover, under the Copyright Act itself, it is provided that: '' * * * *nothing in this title shall be deemed to forbid, prevent, or restrict the transfer of any copy of a copyrighted work the possession of which has been*

---

3. Since we have decided under the conversion portion of the opinion that the waste paper dealer and in turn the defendant acquired full title to the coverless-comics, we need not discuss plaintiffs' assertion that under the contract documents the publisher retained title to the coverless comics and the wholesaler was his agent for a limited purpose. However, assuming this to be the proper characterization of the relation, the agent's lack of authority to sell the literary property in the comics cannot form the basis of a charge of copyright infringement. Cf. Kipling v. G.P. Putnam's Sons, 2 Cir., 1903, 120 F. 631 * * * *lawfully obtained.*" (Emphasis supplied.) 17 U.S.C.A. § 27 (1952). Under this provision, once there is lawful ownership transferred to a first purchaser, the copyright holder's power of control in the sale of the copy ceases. This aptly fits the present situation. * * * Having made this sale, the rights conferred by the Copyright Act are no longer operative. * * *

The judgment of the district court will be affirmed.

NOTES AND QUESTIONS ON THE "FIRST SALE" DOCTRINE

(1) Note that § 109(a) of the 1976 Act limits only the copyright owner's distribution right—the owner of a copy is not privileged to exercise other exclusive rights such as reproduction or public performance.

(2) Only the "owner" of a particular copy, or a person authorized by the "owner," is entitled under § 109(a) to sell or otherwise dispose of it. Ownership rights generally derive, as in the preceding case, from an initial sale authorized by the copyright owner—the "first sale." May ownership (and the concomitant § 109(a) immunity) be established in the absence of a "first sale"? A transfer by gift presumably would suffice. Suppose a manufacturer produces goods under license from the copyright owner. Would unauthorized sales be privileged under § 109(a)? Cf. Platt & Munk Co. v. Republic Graphics, Inc., 315 F.2d 847 (2d Cir.1963).

Recall, too, that § 109(a) pertains only to the disposition of "lawfully made" copies and phonorecords—sales of unauthorized copies infringe the copyright owner's distribution right.[a]

(3) A copyright owner who merely leases or lends copies or phonorecords retains exclusive distribution rights, § 109(d), but distinctions between sales and leases are not always easily drawn. See Rice, Digital Information as Property and Product: U.C.C. Article 2B, 22 U.Dayton L.Rev. 622 (1997), criticizing use of the "license" label on software transactions in an attempt to avoid the consequences of a first sale. It also may be difficult to determine whether the particular copies distributed by a remote vendor are ones originally sold by the copyright owner. In a suit alleging infringement of the distribution right, the burden of proof as to the fact of a "first sale" by the copyright owner can thus be decisive. See Nevins, The Film Collector, The FBI, and the Copyright Act, 26 Clev.St.L.Rev. 547 (1977). The House Report places the burden of proof on the defendant, at least

---

a. The distribution right was closely examined in Hotaling v. Church of Jesus Christ of Latter–Day Saints, 118 F.3d 199 (4th Cir. 1997). Plaintiff had copyrighted a collection of genealogical research materials; defendant purchased a copy for its main library and made several microfiche copies that it sent to branch libraries. The three-year statute of limitations prevented a suit for unauthorized reproduction, but plaintiff contended that the defendant had infringed by "distributing" the copies within the limitations period. The court reversed a summary judgment in favor of the defendant, holding that the library, by cataloging the copies and making them available for borrowing or browsing, "completed all the steps necessary for distribution to the public" in violation of § 106(3). A dissenter argued that § 106(3) is violated only by a defendant's sale or "rental, lease, or lending"; only "lending" could apply here, and with respect to the problem of tracing the origin of particular copies. Would such an allocation be permissible in a *criminal* infringement proceeding? (See § 506 and p. 566 infra.) The criminal cases have consistently placed the burden on the government (which usually has carried it with little difficulty). See, e.g., United States v. Moore, 604 F.2d 1228 (9th Cir.1979).

The first sale doctrine in the context of motion pictures is examined in Beard, The Sale, Rental, and Reproduction of Motion Picture Videocassettes: Piracy or Privilege, 15 N.Eng.L.Rev. 435 (1980).

(4) The popularity of VCRs has generated a lively market in pre-recorded films. Although sales to consumers have increased, purchases by video rental stores still account for a substantial portion of the market. The "first sale" doctrine prevents the motion picture studios from gaining direct control over the lucrative rental business. When the studios sell their cassettes, purchasers, both private and commercial, are free to rent or resell them as they choose, just as a library that has acquired ownership of a book is free to lend it without accounting to the copyright owner. (The latter principle is not universal. See Note (7) infra.)

Since a "first sale" does not impair the performance right,[b] a purchaser who subsequently rents the work for purposes of public performance may be liable as a contributory infringer. (See Kalem Co. v. Harper Brothers, 222 U.S. 55 (1911), discussed by the Supreme Court in its consideration of contributory liability in the *Sony* case, p. 453 infra.) Is it possible that the seriatim rental of a particular cassette for a series of private home viewings constitutes, in cumulative effect, a public performance? The argument is reviewed, and criticized, in Lewson, The Videocassette Rental Controversy, 30 J.Copyr.Soc. 1 (1982).

Could motion picture companies gain control over the rental market through contractual limitations attached to cassette sales? Would rentals in violation of a contractual restriction constitute an infringement of the distribution right? As the *Independent News Co.* case indicates, if there has been a "first sale," albeit with restrictions, they would not. The House Report confirms this point under the 1976 Act: "This does not mean that conditions on future disposition of copies or phonorecords, imposed by a contract between their buyer and seller, would be unenforceable between the parties as a breach of contract, but it does mean that they could not be enforced by an action for infringement of copyright." H.R.Rep. p. 79. The remedy in contract is itself problematic, however, in light of the general disinclination to enforce agreements restraining trade or alienation. See Lewson, supra. There is also, as *Independent News Co.* suggests, considerable difficulty in binding remote vendees; restrictive legends generally will not suffice. See Beard, Note (3) supra.

since the libraries did not allow the material to leave the premises, it had not been "lent".

b. There was an exception in § 109(e), which took effect on December 1, 1991. It allowed the owner of a coin-operated video game to publicly perform or display the game without the permission of the copyright owner, overruling Red Baron–Franklin Park, Inc. v. Taito Corp., 883 F.2d 275 (4th Cir.1989), cert. denied, 493 U.S. 1058, (1990). However, a "sunset" provision in the legislation states that the subsection does not apply to performances or displays occurring after October 1, 1995.

(5) The record industry also worried about the burgeoning rental market; the ease of home duplication magnified the threat posed by commercial rentals. In 1984, citing record rental advertisements bragging, "Never, ever buy another record"[c], the industry secured an amendment to the Copyright Act adding § 109(b). The Record Rental Amendment of 1984 excludes the commercial rental of phonorecords from the protection afforded by the first sale doctrine in § 109(a). The amendment as enacted included a five-year sunset provision, but the durational limit was later extended and eventually eliminated. The amendment does not affect rights in phonorecords acquired before Oct. 4, 1984. Why was Congress moved to intervene in record but not video cassette rentals? (As part of the intellectual property component of the Uruguay Round Trade Agreement (see p. 815 infra), member countries agree to recognize rights against the commercial rental of phonorecords, computer programs (see Note (6) infra), and "cinematographic works," but the obligation with respect to the latter works accrues only if rentals are "materially impairing" the exclusive right of reproduction.)

(6) Encouraged by the success of the music industry, software developers sought similar relief against the growing practice of commercial software rental. The ease of duplication here too presented a major threat to copyright owners. Armed with advertisements from rental firms boasting that customers could "save a bundle" by renting popular software "at a fraction of the cost," 40 Pat., Tm. & Copyr.J. (BNA) 290 (1990), the software industry won an amendment to § 109(b) prohibiting the commercial rental of computer programs.[d] There is an exception for video game cartridges and programs embodied in machines or products that preclude routine copying. There is also an exception for software lending by nonprofit libraries. (The required warning of copyright on library copies in § 109(b)(2)(A) is prescribed in 37 C.F.R. § 201.24.)

(7) Several nations, notably Great Britain, Germany, and the Scandinavian countries, have implemented schemes to compensate authors for library lending—a recognition of a public lending right. The various schemes are compared in Note, Closing the Book on the Public Lending Right, 63 N.Y.U.L.Rev. 878 (1988); see also Seemann, A Look at the Public Lending Right, 30 ASCAP Copyr.L.Symp. 71 (1983). Should a similar right be recognized here? Where would the money come from? From overburdened library budgets? From the federal treasury? From library patrons? In a panel discussion on the public lending right an editor of this casebook is quoted as arguing, "If you want people to read more, you don't make it more expensive." 34 Pat., Tm. & Copyr.J. (BNA) 41 (1987).

(8) The copyright owner's exclusive right of public display, § 106(5), is also subject to a "first sale" defense, § 109(c), which allows the owner of a lawful copy "to display that copy publicly, either directly or by the projection of no more than one image at a time, to viewers present at the place

---

c. See H.R.Rep. No. 98–987, 98th Cong., 2d Sess. (1984).

d. The prohibition in § 109(b) against commercial software rental was successfully invoked in Central Point Software, Inc. v. Global Software & Accessories, Inc., 880 F.Supp. 957 (E.D.N.Y.1995), to stop a "deferred billing plan" that allowed customers to return software after five days and pay only a "restocking fee."

where the copy is located." The exemption does not permit the transmission of an image beyond the place where the work is physically located; even when the object and the viewers are in the same place, the simultaneous projection of images on multiple television or computer screens would seem to violate the "one image at a time" restriction. "The committee's intention is to preserve the traditional privilege of the owner of a copy to display it directly, but to place reasonable restrictions on the ability to display it indirectly in such a way that the copyright owner's market for reproduction and distribution of copies would be affected." H.R.Rep. p. 80.

Goetzl and Sutton, Copyright and the Visual Artist's Display Right: A New Doctrinal Analysis, 9 Colum.-VLA Art. & L. 15 (1984), argue for a more robust display right undiminished by first sale. Also, note that several of the limitations in § 110 on a copyright owner's right of public performance also operate to limit the public display right.

Both distribution and display rights have taken on increased significance as a result of the growing dissemination of copyrighted works over the Internet. See p. 459 infra.

INFRINGING IMPORTATION

Section 602(a) of the 1976 Copyright Act states, "Importation into the United States, without the authority of the owner of copyright under this title, of copies or phonorecords of a work that have been acquired outside the United States is an infringement of the exclusive right to distribute copies or phonorecords under section 106, actionable under section 501." (The subsection also provides limited exceptions covering importation for governmental, private, and scholarly use.) Note that the restriction on importation is not limited to infringing copies. "Section 602 * * * deals with two separate situations: importation of 'piratical' articles (that is, copies or phonorecords made without any authorization of the copyright owner), and unauthorized importation of copies or phonorecords that were lawfully made." H.R.Rep. p. 169. By recording the copyright registration and paying the required fee, a copyright owner can enlist the aid of the U.S. Customs Service in preventing admission of infringing copies. 19 C.F.R. § 133.31 et seq.

The chief interpretive difficulty in § 602(a) comes from its reference to the exclusive right to distribute copies or phonorecords in § 106; does this incorporate into the scope of the importation restriction the first sale limitations on the distribution right in § 109?

Quality King Distributors, Inc., v. L'anza Research International, Inc.

Supreme Court of the United States, 1998.
___ U.S. ___, 118 S.Ct. 1125.

■ JUSTICE STEVENS delivered the opinion of the Court.

Section 106(3) of the Copyright Act of 1976 (Act), 17 U.S.C. § 106(3), gives the owner of a copyright the exclusive right to distribute copies of a copyrighted work. That exclusive right is expressly limited, however, by the provisions of §§ 107 through 120. Section 602(a) gives the copyright owner the right to prohibit the unauthorized importation of copies. The question presented by this case is whether the right granted by § 602(a) is also limited by §§ 107 through 120. More narrowly, the question is whether the "first sale" doctrine endorsed in § 109(a) is applicable to imported copies.

I

Respondent, L'anza Research International, Inc. (L'anza), is a California corporation engaged in the business of manufacturing and selling shampoos, conditioners, and other hair care products. L'anza has copyrighted the labels that are affixed to those products. In the United States, L'anza sells exclusively to domestic distributors who have agreed to resell within limited geographic areas and then only to authorized retailers such as barber shops, beauty salons, and professional hair care colleges. L'anza has found that the American "public is generally unwilling to pay the price charged for high quality products, such as L'anza's products, when they are sold along with the less expensive lower quality products that are generally carried by supermarkets and drug stores." App. 54 (declaration of Robert Hall). L'anza promotes the domestic sales of its products with extensive advertising in various trade magazines and at point of sale, and by providing special training to authorized retailers.

L'anza also sells its products in foreign markets. In those markets, however, it does not engage in comparable advertising or promotion; its prices to foreign distributors are 35% to 40% lower than the prices charged to domestic distributors. In 1992 and 1993, L'anza's distributor in the United Kingdom arranged the sale of three shipments to a distributor in Malta; each shipment contained several tons of L'anza products with copyrighted labels affixed. The record does not establish whether the initial purchaser was the distributor in the United Kingdom or the distributor in Malta, or whether title passed when the goods were delivered to the carrier or when they arrived at their destination, but it is undisputed that the goods were manufactured by L'anza and first sold by L'anza to a foreign purchaser.

It is also undisputed that the goods found their way back to the United States without the permission of L'anza and were sold in California by unauthorized retailers who had purchased them at discounted prices from Quality King Distributors, Inc. (petitioner). There is some uncertainty about the identity of the actual importer, but for the purpose of our decision we assume that petitioner bought all three shipments from the Malta distributor, imported them, and then resold them to retailers who were not in L'anza's authorized chain of distribution.

After determining the source of the unauthorized sales, L'anza brought suit against petitioner and several other defendants. The complaint alleged that the importation and subsequent distribution of those products bearing copyrighted labels violated L'anza's "exclusive rights under 17 U.S.C. §§ 106, 501 and 602 to reproduce and distribute the copyrighted material in the United States." App. 32. The District Court rejected petitioner's defense based on the "first sale" doctrine recognized by § 109 and entered summary judgment in favor of L'anza. Based largely on its conclusion that § 602 would be "meaningless" if § 109 provided a defense in a case of this kind, the Court of Appeals affirmed. 98 F.3d 1109, 1114 (C.A.9 1996). Because its decision created a conflict with the Third Circuit, see Sebastian Int'l, Inc. v. Consumer Contacts (PTY) Ltd., 847 F.2d 1093 (1988), we granted the petition for certiorari. 520 U.S. ___, 117 S.Ct. 2406 (1997).

II

This is an unusual copyright case because L'anza does not claim that anyone has made unauthorized copies of its copyrighted labels. Instead, L'anza is primarily interested in protecting the integrity of its method of marketing the products to which the labels are affixed. Although the labels themselves have only a limited creative component, our interpretation of the relevant statutory provisions would apply equally to a case involving more familiar copyrighted materials such as sound recordings or books. * * *

III

The most relevant portion of § 602(a) provides: "Importation into the United States, without the authority of the owner of copyright under this title, of copies or phonorecords of a work that have been acquired outside the United States is an infringement of the exclusive right to distribute copies or phonorecords under section 106, actionable under section 501...." It is significant that this provision does not categorically prohibit the unauthorized importation of copyrighted materials. Instead, it provides that such importation is an infringement of the exclusive right to distribute copies "under section 106." * * *

After the first sale of a copyrighted item "lawfully made under this title," any subsequent purchaser, whether from a domestic or from a foreign reseller, is obviously an "owner" of that item. Read literally, § 109(a) unambiguously states that such an owner "is entitled, without the authority of the copyright owner, to sell" that item. Moreover, since § 602(a) merely provides that unauthorized importation is an infringement of an exclusive right "under section 106," and since that limited right does not encompass resales by lawful owners, the literal text of § 602(a) is simply inapplicable to both domestic and foreign owners of L'anza's products who decide to import them and resell them in the United States.[14] * * *

---

14. Despite L'anza's contention to the contrary, see Brief for Respondent 26–27, the owner of goods lawfully made under the Act is entitled to the protection of the first sale

IV

L'anza advances two primary arguments based on the text of the Act: (1) that § 602(a), and particularly its three exceptions, are superfluous if limited by the first sale doctrine; and (2) that the text of § 501 defining an "infringer" refers separately to violations of § 106, on the one hand, and to imports in violation of § 602. The short answer to both of these arguments is that neither adequately explains why the words "under section 106" appear in § 602(a). * * *

The Coverage of § 602(a)

Prior to the enactment of § 602(a), the Act already prohibited the importation of "piratical," or unauthorized, copies.[16] Moreover, that earlier prohibition is retained in § 602(b) of the present act.[17] L'anza therefore argues (as do the Solicitor General and other *amici curiae*) that § 602(a) is superfluous unless it covers non-piratical ("lawfully made") copies sold by the copyright owner, because importation nearly always implies a first sale. There are several flaws in this argument.

First, even if § 602(a) did apply only to piratical copies, it at least would provide the copyright holder with a private remedy against the importer, whereas the enforcement of § 602(b) is vested in the Customs Service. Second, because the protection afforded by § 109(a) is available only to the "owner" of a lawfully made copy (or someone authorized by the owner), the first sale doctrine would not provide a defense to a § 602(a) action against any non-owner such as a bailee, a licensee, a consignee, or one whose possession of the copy was unlawful. Third, § 602(a) applies to a category of copies that are neither piratical nor "lawfully made under this title." That category encompasses copies that were "lawfully made" not under the United States Copyright Act, but instead, under the law of some other country.

The category of copies produced lawfully under a foreign copyright was expressly identified in the deliberations that led to the enactment of the 1976 Act. We mention one example of such a comment in 1961 simply to demonstrate that the category is not a merely hypothetical one. In a report to Congress, the Register of Copyrights stated, in part:

"When arrangements are made for both a U.S. edition and a foreign edition of the same work, the publishers frequently agree to divide the international markets. The foreign publisher agrees not to sell his edition in the United States, and the U.S. publisher agrees not to sell his edition in certain foreign countries. It has been suggested that the

doctrine in an action in a United States court even if the first sale occurred abroad. Such protection does not require the extraterritorial application of the Act any more than § 602(a)'s "acquired abroad" language does.

16. See 17 U.S.C. §§ 106, 107 (1970).

17. Section 602(b) provides in relevant part: "In a case where the making of the copies or phonorecords would have constituted an infringement of copyright if this title had been applicable, their importation is prohibited...." The first sale doctrine of § 109(a) does not protect owners of piratical copies, of course, because such copies were not "lawfully made."

import ban on piratical copies should be extended to bar the importation of the foreign edition in contravention of such an agreement." Copyright Law Revision: Report of the Register of Copyrights on the General Revision of the U.S. Copyright Law, 87th Cong., 1st Sess., 125–126 (H.R. Judiciary Comm. Print 1961).

Even in the absence of a market allocation agreement between, for example, a publisher of the U.S. edition and a publisher of the British edition of the same work, each such publisher could make lawful copies. If the author of the work gave the exclusive U.S. distribution rights—enforceable under the Act—to the publisher of the U.S. edition and the exclusive British distribution rights to the publisher of the British edition, however, presumably only those made by the publisher of the U.S. edition would be "lawfully made under this title" within the meaning of § 109(a). The first sale doctrine would not provide the publisher of the British edition who decided to sell in the American market with a defense to an action under § 602(a) (or, for that matter, to an action under § 106(3), if there was a distribution of the copies).

The argument that the statutory exceptions to § 602(a) are superfluous if the first sale doctrine is applicable rests on the assumption that the coverage of that section is co-extensive with the coverage of § 109(a). But since it is, in fact, broader because it encompasses copies that are not subject to the first sale doctrine—e.g., copies that are lawfully made under the law of another country—the exceptions do protect the traveler who may have made an isolated purchase of a copy of a work that could not be imported in bulk for purposes of resale. As we read the Act, although both the first sale doctrine embodied in § 109(a) and the exceptions in § 602(a) may be applicable in some situations, the former does not subsume the latter; those provisions retain significant independent meaning.

Section 501's Separate References to §§ 106 and 602

The text of § 501 does lend support to L'anza's submission. In relevant part, it provides:

> "(a) Anyone who violates any of the exclusive rights of the copyright owner as provided by sections 106 through 118 or of the author as provided in section 106A(a), or who imports copies or phonorecords into the United States in violation of section 602, is an infringer of the copyright or right of the author, as the case may be .... "

The use of the words "*or* who imports," rather than words such as "*including* one who imports," is more consistent with an interpretation that a violation of § 602 is distinct from a violation of § 106 (and thus not subject to the first sale doctrine set out in § 109(a)) than with the view that it is a species of such a violation. Nevertheless, the force of that inference is outweighed by other provisions in the statutory text.

Most directly relevant is the fact that the text of § 602(a) itself unambiguously states that the prohibited importation is an infringement of the exclusive distribution right "under section 106, actionable under section 501." Unlike that phrase, which identifies § 602 violations as a species of § 106 violations, the text of § 106A, which is also cross-referenced in

§ 501, uses starkly different language. It states that the author's right protected by § 106A is "independent of the exclusive rights provided in Section 106." The contrast between the relevant language in § 602 and that in § 106A strongly implies that only the latter describes an independent right.

Of even greater importance is the fact that the § 106 rights are subject not only to the first sale defense in § 109(a), but also to all of the other provisions of "sections 107 through 120." If § 602(a) functioned independently, none of those sections would limit its coverage. For example, the "fair use" defense embodied in § 107 would be unavailable to importers if § 602(a) created a separate right not subject to the limitations on the § 106(3) distribution right. Under L'anza's interpretation of the Act, it presumably would be unlawful for a distributor to import copies of a British newspaper that contained a book review quoting excerpts from an American novel protected by a United States copyright. Given the importance of the fair use defense to publishers of scholarly works, as well as to publishers of periodicals, it is difficult to believe that Congress intended to impose an absolute ban on the importation of all such works containing any copying of material protected by a United States copyright. * * *

V

The parties and their *amici* have debated at length the wisdom or unwisdom of governmental restraints on what is sometimes described as either the "gray market" or the practice of "parallel importation." In K Mart Corp. v. Cartier, Inc., 486 U.S. 281 (1988), we used those terms to refer to the importation of foreign-manufactured goods bearing a valid United States trademark without the consent of the trademark holder. Id., at 285–286. We are not at all sure that those terms appropriately describe the consequences of an American manufacturer's decision to limit its promotional efforts to the domestic market and to sell its products abroad at discounted prices that are so low that its foreign distributors can compete in the domestic market.[29] But even if they do, whether or not we think it would be wise policy to provide statutory protection for such price discrimination is not a matter that is relevant to our duty to interpret the text of the Copyright Act.

Equally irrelevant is the fact that the Executive Branch of the Government has entered into at least five international trade agreements that are apparently intended to protect domestic copyright owners from the unauthorized importation of copies of their works sold in those five countries.[30] The earliest of those agreements was made in 1991; none has been ratified by the Senate. Even though they are of course consistent with the position

---

29. Presumably L'anza, for example, could have avoided the consequences of that competition either (1) by providing advertising support abroad and charging higher prices, or (2) if it was satisfied to leave the promotion of the product in foreign markets to its foreign distributors, to sell its products abroad under a different name.

30. The Solicitor General advises us that such agreements have been made with Cambodia, Trinidad and Tobago, Jamaica, Ecuador, and Sri Lanka.

taken by the Solicitor General in this litigation, they shed no light on the proper interpretation of a statute that was enacted in 1976.

The judgment of the Court of Appeals is reversed.

It is so ordered.

■ JUSTICE GINSBURG, concurring.

This case involves a "round trip" journey, travel of the copies in question from the United States to places abroad, then back again. I join the Court's opinion recognizing that we do not today resolve cases in which the allegedly infringing imports were manufactured abroad. See W. Patry, Copyright Law and Practice 166–170 (1997 Supp.) (commenting that provisions of Title 17 do not apply extraterritorially unless expressly so stated, hence the words "lawfully made under this title" in the "first sale" provision, 17 U.S.C. § 109(a), must mean "lawfully made in the United States"); see generally P. Goldstein, Copyright § 16.0, pp. 16:1–16:2 (2d ed. 1998) ("Copyright protection is territorial. The rights granted by the United States Copyright Act extend no farther than the nation's borders.").

THE DERIVATIVE RIGHT—§ 106(2)

(1) The owner of a copyright enjoys the exclusive right "to prepare derivative works based upon the copyrighted work." The House Report offers this explanation: "The exclusive right to prepare derivative works, specified separately in clause (2) of section 106, overlaps the exclusive right of reproduction to some extent. It is broader than that right, however, in the sense that reproduction requires fixation in copies or phonorecords, whereas the preparation of a derivative work, such as a ballet, pantomime, or improvised performance, may be an infringement even though nothing is ever fixed in tangible form." After referring to the definition of "derivative work" in § 101, the Report continues: "Thus, to constitute a violation of section 106(2), the infringing work must incorporate a portion of the copyrighted work in some form; for example, a detailed commentary on a work or a programmatic musical composition inspired by a novel would not normally constitute infringement under this clause." H.R.Rep. p. 62.

Fixation aside, what, if anything, does the § 106(2) derivative right add to the protection afforded by the copyright owner's control over reproduction granted in § 106(1)? In Litchfield v. Spielberg, 736 F.2d 1352 (9th Cir.1984), cert. denied, 470 U.S. 1052 (1985), plaintiff Litchfield claimed that Steven Spielberg's motion picture "E.T.—The Extra Terrestrial" infringed her copyrighted musical "Lokey from Maldemar." Responding to her argument that *E.T.* was a derivative work based on *Lokey,* Judge Wright said: "Litchfield apparently believes that she does not have to show substantial similarity to show that *E.T.* is a derivative work." The court did not agree. "To prove infringement, one must show substantial similarity. * * * Litchfield's arguments that section 106(2) radically altered the protection afforded by the law of copyright are frivolous." See also Vault Corp. v. Quaid Software Ltd., 847 F.2d 255 (5th Cir.1988), using the absence of substantial similarity to reject a claim that defendant's "unlocking" program infringed plaintiff's derivative rights in its anti-copying software.

(2) Can the derivative right ensnare a defendant who has not reproduced even a portion of the copyrighted work? Suppose the defendant in Independent News Co. v. Williams, p. 340 supra, had cut out selected pages of the salvaged Superman comics, combining from different issues stories featuring particular villains. Would sales of the resulting anthologies infringe plaintiff's right to prepare derivative works? See National Geographic Society v. Classified Geographic, Inc., 27 F.Supp. 655 (D.Mass. 1939), which indicates that the answer might be yes. See also National Bank of Commerce v. Shaklee Corp., 503 F.Supp. 533 (W.D.Tex.1980), p. 732 infra, finding copyright infringement in defendant's insertion of advertising material into purchased copies of plaintiff's book distributed by the defendant to its customers as a promotion. Are these results consistent with the "rebinding" cases that protect defendants who recondition copyrighted books, including turning paperbacks into hardcover? See, e.g., Lantern Press, Inc. v. American Pub. Co., 419 F.Supp. 1267 (E.D.N.Y. 1976). In Paramount Pictures Corp. v. Video Broadcasting Systems, Inc., 724 F.Supp. 808 (D.Kan.1989), the court said that a video rental store's insertion of advertisements at the beginning of movie cassettes was not an infringement of the motion picture studios' right to create derivative works, since the defendant had not recast, transformed, or adapted the films.

Lee v. A.R.T. Company

United States Court of Appeals, Seventh Circuit, 1997.
125 F.3d 580.

■ Before BAUER, EASTERBROOK, and DIANE P. WOOD, CIRCUIT JUDGES.

■ EASTERBROOK, CIRCUIT JUDGE.

Annie Lee creates works of art, which she sells through her firm Annie Lee & Friends. Deck the Walls, a chain of outlets for modestly priced art, is among the buyers of her works, which have been registered with the Register of Copyrights. One Deck the Walls store sold some of Lee's notecards and small lithographs to A.R.T. Company, which mounted the works on ceramic tiles (covering the art with transparent epoxy resin in the process) and resold the tiles. Lee contends that these tiles are derivative works, which under 17 U.S.C. § 106(2) may not be prepared without the permission of the copyright proprietor. She seeks both monetary and injunctive relief. Her position has the support of two cases holding that A.R.T.'s business violates the copyright laws. Munoz v. Albuquerque A.R.T. Co., 38 F.3d 1218 (9th Cir.1994), affirming without published opinion, 829 F.Supp. 309 (D.Alaska 1993); Mirage Editions, Inc. v. Albuquerque A.R.T. Co., 856 F.2d 1341 (9th Cir.1988). *Mirage Editions,* the only full appellate discussion, dealt with pages cut from books and mounted on tiles; the court of appeals' brief order in *Munoz* concludes that the reasoning of *Mirage Editions* is equally applicable to works of art that were sold loose.   Our district court disagreed with these decisions and entered summary judgment for the defendant.   925 F.Supp. 576 (N.D.Ill.1996).

Now one might suppose that this is an open and shut case under the doctrine of first sale, codified at 17 U.S.C. § 109(a).   A.R.T. bought the work legitimately, mounted it on a tile, and resold what it had purchased. Because the artist could capture the value of her art's contribution to the finished product as part of the price for the original transaction, the economic rationale for protecting an adaptation as "derivative" is absent. See William M. Landes & Richard A. Posner, An Economic Analysis of Copyright Law, 17 J. Legal Studies 325, 353–57 (1989).   An alteration that includes (or consumes) a complete copy of the original lacks economic significance.   One work changes hands multiple times, exactly what § 109(a) permits, so it may lack legal significance too.   But § 106(2) creates a separate exclusive right, to "prepare derivative works", and Lee believes that affixing the art to the tile is "preparation," so that A.R.T. would have violated § 106(2) even if it had dumped the finished tiles into the Marianas Trench.   For the sake of argument we assume that this is so and ask whether card-on-a-tile is a "derivative work" in the first place.

"Derivative work" is a defined term:

> A "derivative work" is a work based upon one or more preexisting works, such as a translation, musical arrangement, dramatization, fictionalization, motion picture version, sound recording, art reproduction, abridgment, condensation, or any other form in which a work may be recast, transformed, or adapted.   A work consisting of editorial revisions, annotations, elaborations, or other modifications which, as a whole, represent an original work of authorship, is a "derivative work".

17 U.S.C. § 101.   The district court concluded that A.R.T.'s mounting of Lee's works on tile is not an "original work of authorship" because it is no different in form or function from displaying a painting in a frame or placing a medallion in a velvet case.   No one believes that a museum violates § 106(2) every time it changes the frame of a painting that is still under copyright, although the choice of frame or glazing affects the impression the art conveys, and many artists specify frames (or pedestals for sculptures) in detail.   *Munoz* and *Mirage Editions* acknowledge that framing and other traditional means of mounting and displaying art do not infringe authors' exclusive right to make derivative works.   Nonetheless, the Ninth Circuit held, what A.R.T. does creates a derivative work because the epoxy resin bonds the art to the tile.   Our district judge thought this a distinction without a difference, and we agree.   If changing the way in which a work of art will be displayed creates a derivative work, and if Lee is right about what "prepared" means, then the derivative work is "prepared" when the art is mounted; what happens later is not relevant, because the violation of the § 106(2) right has already occurred.   If the framing process does not create a derivative work, then mounting art on a

tile, which serves as a flush frame, does not create a derivative work.
* * *

Lee wages a vigorous attack on the district court's conclusion that A.R.T.'s mounting process cannot create a derivative work because the change to the work "as a whole" is not sufficiently original to support a copyright. Cases such as Gracen v. Bradford Exchange, Inc., 698 F.2d 300 (7th Cir.1983), show that neither A.R.T. nor Lee herself could have obtained a copyright in the card-on-a-tile, thereby not only extending the period of protection for the images but also eliminating competition in one medium of display. After the Ninth Circuit held that its mounting process created derivative works, A.R.T. tried to obtain a copyright in one of its products; the Register of Copyrights sensibly informed A.R.T. that the card-on-a-tile could not be copyrighted independently of the note card itself. But Lee says that this is irrelevant—that a change in a work's appearance may infringe the exclusive right under § 106(2) even if the alteration is too trivial to support an independent copyright. Pointing to the word "original" in the second sentence of the statutory definition, the district judge held that "originality" is essential to a derivative work. This understanding has the support of both cases and respected commentators. E.g., L. Batlin & Son, Inc. v. Snyder, 536 F.2d 486 (2d Cir.1976); Melville B. Nimmer & David Nimmer, 1 Nimmer on Copyrights § 3.03 (1997). Pointing to the fact that the first sentence in the statutory definition omits any reference to originality, Lee insists that a work may be derivative despite the mechanical nature of the transformation. This view, too, has the support of both cases and respected commentators. E.g., Lone Ranger Television, Inc. v. Program Radio Corp., 740 F.2d 718, 722 (9th Cir.1984); Paul Goldstein, Copyright: Principles, Law and Practice § 5.3.1 (2d ed. 1996) (suggesting that a transformation is covered by § 106(2) whenever it creates a "new work for a different market").

Fortunately, it is not necessary for us to choose sides. Assume for the moment that the first sentence recognizes a set of non-original derivative works. To prevail, then, Lee must show that A.R.T. altered her works in one of the ways mentioned in the first sentence. The tile is not an "art reproduction"; A.R.T. purchased and mounted Lee's original works. That leaves the residual clause: "any other form in which a work may be recast, transformed, or adapted." None of these words fits what A.R.T. did. Lee's works were not "recast" or "adapted". "Transformed" comes closer and gives the Ninth Circuit some purchase for its view that the permanence of the bond between art and base matters. Yet the copyrighted note cards and lithographs were not "transformed" in the slightest. The art was bonded to a slab of ceramic, but it was not changed in the process. It still depicts exactly what it depicted when it left Lee's studio. See William F. Patry, Copyright Law and Practice 823–24 (1994) (disapproving *Mirage Editions* on this ground).[1] If mounting works a "transformation," then

---

1. Scholarly disapproval of *Mirage Editions* has been widespread. Goldstein § 5.3 at 5:81–82; Nimmer & Nimmer § 3.03; Wendy J. Gordon, On Owning Information: Intellectual Property and the Restitutionary Impulse, 78 Va.L.Rev. 149, 255 n. 401 (1992).

changing a painting's frame or a photograph's mat equally produces a derivative work. Indeed, if Lee is right about the meaning of the definition's first sentence, then any alteration of a work, however slight, requires the author's permission. We asked at oral argument what would happen if a purchaser jotted a note on one of the note cards, or used it as a coaster for a drink, or cut it in half, or if a collector applied his seal (as is common in Japan); Lee's counsel replied that such changes prepare derivative works, but that as a practical matter artists would not file suit. A definition of derivative work that makes criminals out of art collectors and tourists is jarring despite Lee's gracious offer not to commence civil litigation.

If Lee (and the Ninth Circuit) are right about what counts as a derivative work, then the United States has established through the back door an extraordinarily broad version of authors' moral rights, under which artists may block any modification of their works of which they disapprove. No European version of *droit moral* goes this far. Until recently it was accepted wisdom that the United States did not enforce any claim of moral rights; even bowdlerization of a work was permitted unless the modifications produced a new work so different that it infringed the exclusive right under § 106(2). Compare WGN Continental Broadcasting Co. v. United Video, Inc., 693 F.2d 622 (7th Cir.1982), with Gilliam v. American Broadcasting Companies, Inc., 538 F.2d 14, 24 (2d Cir.1976). The Visual Artists Rights Act of 1990, Pub.L. 101–650, 104 Stat. 5089, 5123–33, moves federal law in the direction of moral rights, but the cornerstone of the new statute, 17 U.S.C. § 106A, does not assist Lee. Section 106A(a)(3)(A) gives an artist the right to "prevent any intentional distortion, mutilation, or other modification of that work which would be prejudicial to his or her honor or reputation". At oral argument Lee's lawyer disclaimed any contention that the sale of her works on tile has damaged her honor or reputation. What is more, § 106A applies only to a "work of visual art", a new term defined in § 101 to mean either a unique work or part of a limited edition (200 copies or fewer) that has been "signed and consecutively numbered by the author". Lee's note cards and lithographs are not works of visual art under this definition, so she could not invoke § 106A even if A.R.T.'s use of her works to produce kitsch had damaged her reputation. It would not be sound to use § 106(2) to provide artists with exclusive rights deliberately omitted from the Visual Artists Rights Act. We therefore decline to follow *Munoz* and *Mirage Editions*.

AFFIRMED.

NOTES

(1) Are cases such as the Ninth Circuit's decision in *Mirage Editions* that find infringement when a defendant modifies a purchased copy of a work consistent with the first sale doctrine? What rationales support recognition of a right in the copyright owner to prevent alterations to purchased copies?

(2) Does *Mirage Editions* restrict *use* of the copyrighted work? "The right to control the use of a work, although granted to inventors, has never been part of copyright except as performance may be considered 'use.' Indeed, the absence of a 'use right' helps justify the relatively casual approach to granting copyright as opposed to the more searching tests for patentability." R. Brown, Eligibility for Copyright Protection: A Search for Principled Standards, 70 Minn.L.Rev. 579, 588–89 (1985).

(3) Should infringement of the derivative right turn on whether the defendant has contributed original authorship—the question reserved by the court in *Lee*? Recall that the concept of a derivative work as defined in § 101 determines both infringement under § 106(2) and copyrightability under § 103.

Lewis Galoob Toys, Inc. v. Nintendo of America, Inc.

United States Court of Appeals, Ninth Circuit, 1992.
964 F.2d 965.
Certiorari denied, 507 U.S. 985, 113 S.Ct. 1582 (1993).

■ Before FARRIS and RYMER, CIRCUIT JUDGES, and KENYON, DISTRICT JUDGE.

■ FARRIS, CIRCUIT JUDGE:

Nintendo of America appeals the district court's judgment following a bench trial (1) declaring that Lewis Galoob Toys' Game Genie does not violate any Nintendo copyrights and dissolving a temporary injunction and (2) denying Nintendo's request for a permanent injunction enjoining Galoob from marketing the Game Genie. Lewis Galoob Toys, Inc. v. Nintendo of America, Inc., 780 F.Supp. 1283 (N.D.Cal.1991). We have appellate jurisdiction pursuant to 15 U.S.C. § 1121 and 28 U.S.C. §§ 1291 and 1292(a)(1). We affirm.

FACTS

The Nintendo Entertainment System is a home video game system marketed by Nintendo. To use the system, the player inserts a cartridge containing a video game that Nintendo produces or licenses others to produce. By pressing buttons and manipulating a control pad, the player controls one of the game's characters and progresses through the game. The games are protected as audiovisual works under 17 U.S.C. § 102(a)(6).

The Game Genie is a device manufactured by Galoob that allows the player to alter up to three features of a Nintendo game. For example, the Game Genie can increase the number of lives of the player's character, increase the speed at which the character moves, and allow the character to float above obstacles. The player controls the changes made by the Game Genie by entering codes provided by the Game Genie Programming Manual and Code Book. The player also can experiment with variations of these codes.

* * * The Game Genie is inserted between a game cartridge and the Nintendo Entertainment System. The Game Genie does not alter the data that is stored in the game cartridge. Its effects are temporary.

DISCUSSION

1. *Derivative work*

The Copyright Act of 1976 confers upon copyright holders the exclusive right to prepare and authorize others to prepare derivative works based on their copyrighted works. See 17 U.S.C. § 106(2). Nintendo argues that the district court erred in concluding that the audiovisual displays created by the Game Genie are not derivative works. * * *

A derivative work must incorporate a protected work in some concrete or permanent "form." The Copyright Act defines a derivative work as follows:

> A "derivative work" is a work based upon one or more preexisting works, such as a translation, musical arrangement, dramatization, fictionalization, motion picture version, sound recording, art reproduction, abridgment, condensation, *or any other form in which a work may be recast, transformed, or adapted.* A work consisting of editorial revisions, annotations, elaborations, or other modifications which, as a whole, represent an original work of authorship, is a "derivative work."

17 U.S.C. § 101 (emphasis added). The examples of derivative works provided by the Act all physically incorporate the underlying work or works. The Act's legislative history similarly indicates that "the infringing work must incorporate a portion of the copyrighted work in some form." 1976 U.S.Code Cong. & Admin.News 5659, 5675. See also Mirage Editions, Inc. v. Albuquerque A.R.T. Co., 856 F.2d 1341, 1343–44 (9th Cir.1988) (discussing same), cert. denied, 489 U.S. 1018 (1989). * * *

The district court's finding that no independent work is created, see *Galoob,* 780 F.Supp. at 1291, is supported by the record. The Game Genie merely enhances the audiovisual displays (or underlying data bytes) that originate in Nintendo game cartridges. The altered displays do not incorporate a portion of a copyrighted work in some concrete or permanent *form.* Nintendo argues that the Game Genie's displays are as fixed in the hardware and software used to create them as Nintendo's original displays. Nintendo's argument ignores the fact that the Game Genie cannot produce an audiovisual display; the underlying display must be produced by a Nintendo Entertainment System and game cartridge. Even if we were to rely on the Copyright Act's definition of "fixed," we would similarly conclude that the resulting display is not "embodied," *see* 17 U.S.C. § 101, in the Game Genie. It cannot be a derivative work.

Mirage Editions is illustrative. Albuquerque A.R.T. transferred artworks from a commemorative book to individual ceramic tiles. See *Mirage Editions,* 856 F.2d at 1342. We held that "[b]y borrowing and mounting the preexisting, copyrighted individual art images without the consent of the copyright proprietors . . . [Albuquerque A.R.T.] has prepared a derivative work and infringed the subject copyrights." *Id.* at 1343. The ceramic tiles *physically* incorporated the copyrighted works in a form that could be sold. Perhaps more importantly, sales of the tiles supplanted purchasers' demand for the underlying works. Our holding in *Mirage Editions* would have been much different if Albuquerque A.R.T. had distributed lenses that merely enabled users to view several artworks simultaneously.   * * *

Nintendo relies heavily on Midway Mfg. Co. v. Artic Int'l, Inc., 704 F.2d 1009 (7th Cir.), cert. denied, 464 U.S. 823 (1983). *Midway* can be distinguished. The defendant in *Midway,* Artic International, marketed a computer chip that could be inserted in Galaxian video games to speed up the rate of play. The Seventh Circuit held that the speeded-up version of Galaxian was a derivative work. *Id.* at 1013–14. Artic's chip substantially copied and *replaced* the chip that was originally distributed by Midway. Purchasers of Artic's chip also benefited economically by offering the altered game for use by the general public. The Game Genie does not physically incorporate a portion of a copyrighted work, nor does it supplant demand for a component of that work. The court in *Midway* acknowledged that the Copyright Act's definition of "derivative work" "must be stretched to accommodate speeded-up video games." *Id.* at 1014. Stretching that definition further would chill innovation and fail to protect "society's competing interest in the free flow of ideas, information, and commerce." Sony Corp. of America v. Universal Studios, Inc., 464 U.S. 417 (1984).

In holding that the audiovisual displays created by the Game Genie are not derivative works, we recognize that technology often advances by improvement rather than replacement.   * * * Some time ago, for example, computer companies began marketing spell-checkers that operate within existing word processors by signalling the writer when a word is misspelled. These applications, as well as countless others, could not be produced and marketed if courts were to conclude that the word processor and spell-checker combination is a derivative work based on the word processor alone. The Game Genie is useless by itself, it can only enhance, and cannot duplicate or recaste, a Nintendo game's output. It does not contain or produce a Nintendo game's output in some concrete or permanent form, nor does it supplant demand for Nintendo game cartridges. Such innovations rarely will constitute infringing derivative works under the Copyright Act.   * * *

2. *Fair use*

* * * The district court concluded that, even if the audiovisual displays created by the Game Genie are derivative works, Galoob is not liable under 17 U.S.C. § 107 because the displays are a fair use of Nintendo's copyrighted displays.   * * *

Much of the parties' dispute regarding the fair use defense concerns the proper focus of the court's inquiry: (1) Galoob or (2) consumers who purchase and use the Game Genie. Nintendo's complaint does not allege direct infringement, nor did it try the case on that theory. The complaint, for example, alleges only that "Galoob's marketing advertising [sic], promoting and selling of Game Genie has and will *contribute to* the creation of infringing derivatives of Nintendo's copyrighted . . . games." (emphasis added). Contributory infringement is a form of third party liability. *See* Melville B. Nimmer & David Nimmer, 3 Nimmer on Copyright § 12.04[A][2], at 12–68 (1991). The district court properly focused on whether consumers who purchase and use the Game Genie would be infringing Nintendo's copyrights by creating (what are now assumed to be) derivative works.

[The court agreed with plaintiff's fair use argument, relying on the conclusion of the lower court that use of the Game Genie by consumers was a noncommercial use that did not threaten Nintendo's actual or potential market; there was no reasonable likelihood that Nintendo would sell similarly altered versions of its games.]

NOTES

(1) Did Judge Farris adequately distinguish the Seventh Circuit's decision in *Midway*? That case offered this justification for its decision to treat the speeded-up game as an infringing derivative work: "A speeded-up video game is a substantially different product from the original game. As noted, it is more exciting to play and it requires some creative effort to produce. For that reason the owner of the copyright on the game should be entitled to monopolize it on the same theory that he is entitled to monopolize the derivative works specifically listed in § 101."

In emphasizing that the Game Genie did not incorporate or produce any portion of Nintendo's game in a permanent form, did the court in *Galoob* ignore the absence in § 106(2) of any requirement that the derivative work be embodied in a copy or phonorecord? Is the result nonetheless preferable to *Midway*?

(2) Cases such as *Midway* and *Galoob* are of special interest to software producers. Do users who modify copyrighted programs infringe the derivative right? Cf. § 117. See Samuelson, Modifying Copyrighted Software: Adjusting Copyright Doctrine to Accommodate a Technology, 28 Jurimetrics 179 (1988), arguing that the answer should be no. Are software companies that sell add-ons or enhancement programs designed to improve the performance of existing software liable as contributory infringers even if their products duplicate none of the copyright owner's expression? Who should profit from the added value of the enhanced software? For an argument that in the long run it is better to reward the subsequent entrepreneur than the original one, see Stern, Framing Prints, Giving the Mona Lisa a Moustache, Speeding Up Video Games, and Marketing Add-on Software: A Comment on the *Mirage* Case, 37 Pat., Tm. & Copyr.J. (BNA) 305 (1989).

CHAPTER 4

SCOPE OF PROTECTION: THE LIMITS OF LIABILITY

SECTION 1. FAIR USE

"The judicial doctrine of fair use, one of the most important and well-established limitations on the exclusive right of copyright owners, would be given express statutory recognition for the first time in section 107. * * *

General intention behind the provision

"The statement of the fair use doctrine in section 107 offers some guidance to users in determining when the principles of the doctrine apply. However, the endless variety of situations and combinations of circumstances that can rise in particular cases precludes the formulation of exact rules in the statute. The bill endorses the purpose and general scope of the judicial doctrine of fair use, but there is no disposition to freeze the doctrine in the statute, especially during a period of rapid technological change. Beyond a very broad statutory explanation of what fair use is and some of the criteria applicable to it, the courts must be free to adapt the doctrine to particular situations on a case-by-case basis. Section 107 is intended to restate the present judicial doctrine of fair use, not to change, narrow, or enlarge it in any way." H.R.Rep. pp. 65–66.

Two cases involving Boston worthies first gave the fair use doctrine definition and a name. The term "fair use" apparently appeared for the first time in Lawrence v. Dana, 15 Fed.Cas. 26 (C.C.D.Mass.1869) (No. 8,136), in which author-attorney Richard Henry Dana, Jr., was found to have infringed the work of an earlier editor in his preparation of a new edition of Wheaton's *Elements of International Law*. But Justice Story some twenty-eight years earlier in Folsom v. Marsh had already spoken of the "nice balance" that determines the question of infringement.

FOLSOM V. MARSH, 9 Fed.Cas. 342, No. 4901 (C.C.D.Mass.1841). Justice Story was confronted with what he described as "one of those intricate and embarrassing questions, arising in the administration of civil justice, in which it is not, from the peculiar nature and character of the controversy, easy to arrive at any satisfactory conclusion, or to lay down any general principles applicable to all cases. Patents and copyrights," he observed, "approach, nearer than any other class of cases belonging to forensic discussions, to what may be called the metaphysics of the law, where the distinctions are, or at least may be, very subtle and refined, and, sometimes, almost evanescent." The Rev. Charles W. Upham, in his *Life of Washington in the Form of an Autobiography,* derived 353 of its 866 pages from letters and other documents that had first appeared in Jared Sparks' monumental *Writings of President Washington,* a work of nearly 7,000 pages in twelve volumes, which had been published by plaintiffs. Justice Story decided that for all but a few of Washington's letters plaintiffs held the copyright. He further decided that defendants could not justify their work as an "abridgment" (considered lawful at the time of this decision); so defendants infringed unless their contention was accepted that they had a privilege to select and use plaintiffs' materials in a new work of their own. "The question, then, is, whether this is a justifiable use of the original materials, such as the law recognizes as no infringement of the copyright of the plaintiffs. * * * It is certainly not necessary, to constitute an invasion of copyright, that the whole of a work should be copied, or even a large portion of it, in form or in substance. If so much is taken, that the value of the original is sensibly diminished, or the labors of the original author are substantially to an injurious extent appropriated by another, that is sufficient, in point of law, to constitute a piracy pro tanto. * * * In short, we must often, in deciding questions of this sort, look to the nature and objects of the selections made, the quantity and value of the materials used, and the degree in which the use may prejudice the sale, or diminish the profits, or supersede the objects, of the original work." With the hope that "some means may be found, to produce an amicable settlement of this unhappy controversy," Justice Story enjoined defendants from any further distribution of Upham's book.

Time Inc. v. Bernard Geis Associates

United States District Court, Southern District of New York, 1968.
293 F.Supp. 130.

■ WYATT, DISTRICT JUDGE.

This is a motion by plaintiff for summary judgment "interlocutory in character" on the issue of liability alone, as authorized by Rule 56(c) of the Federal Rules of Civil Procedure. * * *

When President Kennedy was killed in Dallas on November 22, 1963, Abraham Zapruder, a Dallas dress manufacturer, was by sheer happenstance at the scene taking home movie pictures with his camera. His film—an historic document and undoubtedly the most important photographic evidence concerning the fatal shots—was bought a few days later by Life; parts of the film were printed in several issues of the magazine. As to these issues and their contents (including, of course, the Zapruder pictures) and as to the film itself, Life has complied with all provisions of the Copyright Act (17 U.S.C. § 1 and following; the Act).

Defendant Thompson has written a book, "Six Seconds in Dallas" (the Book), which is a study of the assassination. It is a serious, thoughtful and impressive analysis of the evidence. The Book contains a number of what are called "sketches" but which are in fact copies of parts of the Zapruder film. Defendant Bernard Geis Associates (Associates), a partnership, published the Book on November 18, 1967 and defendant Random House, Inc. has been distributing the Book to the public. Defendant Bernard Geis is the only general partner of Associates.

This action was commenced on December 1, 1967. The complaint in a single count charges that certain frames of the Zapruder film were "stolen surreptitiously" from Life by Thompson and that copies of these frames appear in the Book as published. The complaint avers that the conduct of defendants is an infringement of statutory copyrights, an unfair trade practice, and unfair competition. * * *

President Johnson on November 29, 1963 appointed a Commission with Chief Justice Warren as Chairman (the Commission) to investigate the killing of President Kennedy. This Commission on September 24, 1964 submitted its lengthy report (the Warren Report) and all the evidence before it.

The Commission made extensive use of the Zapruder film, and placed great reliance on it, as evidenced in the Report (for example, pp. 97, 98–115). Six of the Zapruder frames are shown in the body of the Report (at pp. 100–103, 108, 114) and some 160 Zapruder frames are included (in volume XVIII) in the Exhibits of the Commission printed and submitted with the Report. * * *

There gradually developed a substantial volume of criticism of the Report, centered on its findings (Report, pp. 18, 22) that all the shots were fired from one place and that the person firing those shots acted alone.

Thompson was among those particularly interested in the Report; he became convinced that the Report was incomplete and he doubted its principal conclusion. * * *

[Thompson became a consultant to Life and without authorization photographed frames from the Zapruder film. Life repeatedly denied Thompson permission to use the frames in his book, stating that it was corporate policy "not to allow anyone the use of any part of this film in the United States," that the film was "an invaluable asset of the corporation," and that "its use will be limited to our publications and enterprises." Thompson and the other defendants then hired an artist who made charcoal sketches of the frames for use in "Six Seconds in Dallas."]

There is thus an infringement by defendants unless the use of the copyrighted material in the Book is a "fair use" outside the limits of copyright protection. * * *

There is an initial reluctance to find any fair use by defendants because of the conduct of Thompson in making his copies and because of the deliberate appropriation in the Book, in defiance of the copyright owner. Fair use presupposes "good faith and fair dealing". Schulman, Fair Use and the Revision of the Copyright Act, 53 Iowa L.Rev. 832 (1968). On the other hand it was not the nighttime activities of Thompson which enabled defendants to reproduce copies of Zapruder frames in the Book. They could have secured such frames from the National Archives, or they could have used the reproductions in the Warren Report or in the issues of Life itself. Moreover, while hope by a defendant for commercial gain is not a significant factor in this Circuit, there is a strong point for defendants in their offer to surrender to Life all profits of Associates from the Book as royalty payment for a license to use the copyrighted Zapruder frames. It is also a fair inference from the facts that defendants acted with the advice of counsel.

In determining the issue of fair use, the balance seems to be in favor of defendants.

There is a public interest in having the fullest information available on the murder of President Kennedy. Thompson did serious work on the subject and has a theory entitled to public consideration. While doubtless the theory could be explained with sketches of the type used at page 87 of the Book and in The Saturday Evening Post, the explanation actually made in the Book with copies is easier to understand. The Book is not bought because it contained the Zapruder pictures; the Book is bought because of the theory of Thompson and its explanation, supported by Zapruder pictures.

There seems little, if any, injury to plaintiff, the copyright owner. There is no competition between plaintiff and defendants. Plaintiff does not sell the Zapruder pictures as such and no market for the copyrighted work appears to be affected. Defendants do not publish a magazine. There are projects for use by plaintiff of the film in the future as a motion picture or in books, but the effect of the use of certain frames in the Book on such projects is speculative. It seems more reasonable to speculate that the Book would, if anything, enhance the value of the copyrighted work; it is difficult to see any decrease in its value. * * *

The motion of plaintiff is denied.

The Clerk is directed to enter judgment in favor of defendants.

So ordered.

———————

Iowa State University Research Foundation, Inc. v. American Broadcasting Co., 621 F.2d 57 (2d Cir.1980). Plaintiff held the copyright in a film biography of Dan Gable, a student at Iowa State who won a gold medal in wrestling at the 1972 Munich Olympics. ABC, without authorization, used a 2½–minute segment of the film during its Olympic coverage. When sued for infringement, ABC raised a fair use defense. The court affirmed a judgment in favor of the plaintiff.

"The doctrine of fair use, originally created and articulated in case law, permits courts to avoid rigid application of the copyright statute when, on occasion, it would stifle the very creativity which that law is designed to foster. * * *

"The network relies most heavily on the first factor—the purpose and character of its use. It claims it was engaged in the laudable pursuit of disseminating the life history of an important public figure involved in an event of intense public interest. * * *

"This argument proves too much. * * * The public interest in the free flow of information is assured by the law's refusal to recognize a valid copyright in facts. * * * The fair use doctrine is not a license for corporate theft, empowering a court to ignore a copyright whenever it determines the underlying work contains material of possible public importance. Indeed, we do not suppose that appellants would embrace their own defense theory if another litigant sought to apply it to the ABC evening news."

On the issue of market effect, the court concluded that "ABC did foreclose a significant potential market to [plaintiff]—sale of its film for use on television in connection with the Olympics. In fact, because of its exclusive right to televise the games, ABC monopolized that market. When ABC telecast *Champion* without purchasing the film, it usurped an extremely significant market."

BROADWAY MUSIC CORP. v. F–R PUBLISHING CORP., 31 F.Supp. 817 (S.D.N.Y. 1940). The *New Yorker* magazine, commenting briefly in "The Talk of the Town" on the death of Pauline White, a film actress, quoted (supposedly from the editor's memory) twelve lines of the words of plaintiff's humorous song "Poor Pauline" published in 1914. The article concluded, "We forget the rest. As 1940 creeps on, it often seems to us that we have forgotten practically everything of any importance." No acknowledgement of source or authorship was made. Judge Conger, noting that "[t]here was no intent to commit an infringement," considered the publication of the song "only incidental" (though it made up most of the article), and a fair use. Karll v. Curtis Publishing Co., 39 F.Supp. 836 (E.D.Wis.1941), is in accord, where a four-page article in the *Saturday Evening Post* about the Green Bay Packers quoted, with a reference to plaintiff's authorship, the eight-line chorus of his "official Packer song." Contrast Sayers v. Spaeth, 20 Copyr.Dec. 625 (S.D.N.Y.1932). Defendant, in his book on American popular music, *Read 'Em and Weep*, reproduced the words and music of plaintiff's copyrighted version of "Ta–Ra–Ra–Boom–Der–E." He had permission from the assignee of the original copyright term, and credited plaintiff's authorship. However, plaintiff had obtained a renewal in 1919, so the permission was ineffective. A defense of fair use was rejected by Judge Patterson on the ground that defendant's use was "obviously more than quotation and comment." An injunction and minimum damages were awarded.

WAINWRIGHT SECURITIES, INC. V. WALL STREET TRANSCRIPT CORP., 558 F.2d 91 (2d Cir.1977), cert. denied, 434 U.S. 1014 (1978). This case rejected a fair use defense raised by the publisher of a weekly financial newspaper that promised its readers "a fast-reading, pinpointed account of heavy-weight reports from the top institutional research firms." Plaintiff, unhappy with defendant's practice of publishing abstracts of its copyrighted research reports, sought a preliminary injunction.

"It is, of course, axiomatic that 'news events' may not be copyrighted. * * * What is protected is the manner of expression, the author's analysis or interpretation of events [query], the way he structures his material and marshals facts, his choice of words, and the emphasis he gives to particular developments." The court noted that defendant contributed no independent research or analysis.

"The copying by the Transcript is easily distinguishable from the reporting of the Wainwright research reports by other publications. The Wall Street Journal articles referred to by appellants, for example, were published a year apart. There apparently was no attempt to provide readers regularly with summaries of the Wainwright reports and there is no indication that the Wall Street Journal launched an advertising campaign portraying itself as a publisher of the same financial analyses available to large investors, but at a lower price. By contrast, the appellants' use of the Wainwright reports was blatantly self-serving, with the obvious intent, if not the effect, of fulfilling the demand for the original work. * * * This was not legitimate coverage of a news event; instead it was, and there is no other way to describe it, chiseling for personal profit." The court affirmed a preliminary injunction.

Harper & Row, Publishers, Inc. v. Nation Enterprises

Supreme Court of the United States, 1985.
471 U.S. 539, 105 S.Ct. 2218.

■ JUSTICE O'CONNOR delivered the opinion of the Court.

This case requires us to consider to what extent the "fair use" provision of the Copyright Revision Act of 1976, 17 U.S.C. § 107 (hereinafter the Copyright Act), sanctions the unauthorized use of quotations from a public figure's unpublished manuscript. In March 1979, an undisclosed source provided The Nation magazine with the unpublished manuscript of "A Time to Heal: The Autobiography of Gerald R. Ford." Working directly from the purloined manuscript, an editor of The Nation produced a short piece entitled "The Ford Memoirs—Behind the Nixon Pardon." The piece was timed to "scoop" an article scheduled shortly to appear in Time Magazine. Time had agreed to purchase the exclusive right to print prepublication excerpts from the copyright holders, Harper & Row Publishers, Inc. (hereinafter Harper & Row) and Reader's Digest Association, Inc. (hereinafter Reader's Digest). As a result of The Nation article, Time canceled its agreement. Petitioners brought a successful copyright action against The Nation. On appeal, the Second Circuit reversed the lower court's finding of infringement, holding that The Nation's act was sanctioned as a "fair use" of the copyrighted material. We granted certiorari, 467 U.S. 1214 (1984), and we now reverse.

I

In February 1977, shortly after leaving the White House, former President Gerald R. Ford contracted with petitioners Harper & Row and Reader's Digest, to publish his as yet unwritten memoirs. The memoirs were to contain "significant hitherto unpublished material" concerning the Watergate crisis, Mr. Ford's pardon of former President Nixon and "Mr. Ford's reflections on this period of history, and the morality and personalities involved." App. to Pet. for Cert. C–14–C–15. In addition to the right to publish the Ford memoirs in book form, the agreement gave petitioners the exclusive right to license prepublication excerpts, known in the trade as "first serial rights." Two years later, as the memoirs were nearing completion, petitioners negotiated a prepublication licensing agreement with Time, a weekly news magazine. Time agreed to pay $25,000, $12,500 in advance and an additional $12,500 at publication, in exchange for the right to excerpt 7,500 words from Mr. Ford's account of the Nixon pardon. The issue featuring the excerpts was timed to appear approximately one week before shipment of the full length book version to bookstores. Exclusivity was an important consideration; Harper & Row instituted procedures designed to maintain the confidentiality of the manuscript, and Time retained the right to renegotiate the second payment should the material appear in print prior to its release of the excerpts.

Two to three weeks before the Time article's scheduled release, an unidentified person secretly brought a copy of the Ford manuscript to Victor Navasky, editor of The Nation, a political commentary magazine. Mr. Navasky knew that his possession of the manuscript was not authorized and that the manuscript must be returned quickly to his "source" to avoid discovery. 557 F.Supp. 1067, 1069 (SDNY 1983). He hastily put together what he believed was "a real hot news story" composed of quotes, paraphrases, and facts drawn exclusively from the manuscript. Ibid. Mr. Navasky attempted no independent commentary, research or criticism, in part because of the need for speed if he was to "make news" by "publish[ing] in advance of publication of the Ford book." App. 416–417. The 2,250 word article, reprinted in the Appendix to this opinion, appeared on April 3, 1979. As a result of The Nation's article, Time canceled its piece and refused to pay the remaining $12,500. * * *

II

We agree with the Court of Appeals that copyright is intended to increase and not to impede the harvest of knowledge. But we believe the

Second Circuit gave insufficient deference to the scheme established by the Copyright Act for fostering the original works that provide the seed and substance of this harvest. The rights conferred by copyright are designed to assure contributors to the store of knowledge a fair return for their labors. Twentieth Century Music Corp. v. Aiken, 422 U.S. 151 (1975).

Article I, § 8, of the Constitution provides that:

> "The Congress shall have Power ... to Promote the Progress of Science and useful Arts, by securing for limited Times to Authors and Inventors the exclusive Right to their respective Writings and Discoveries."

As we noted last Term, "[This] limited grant is a means by which an important public purpose may be achieved. It is intended to motivate the creative activity of authors and inventors by the provision of a special reward, and to allow the public access to the products of their genius after the limited period of exclusive control has expired." Sony Corp. v. Universal City Studios, Inc., 464 U.S. 417, 429 (1984). "The monopoly created by copyright thus rewards the individual author in order to benefit the public." Id., at 477 (dissenting opinion). This principle applies equally to works of fiction and nonfiction. The book at issue here, for example, was two years in the making, and began with a contract giving the author's copyright to the publishers in exchange for their services in producing and marketing the work. In preparing the book Mr. Ford drafted essays and word portraits of public figures and participated in hundreds of taped interviews that were later distilled to chronicle his personal viewpoint. It is evident that the monopoly granted by copyright actively served its intended purpose of inducing the creation of new material of potential historical value. * * *

Creation of a nonfiction work, even a compilation of pure fact, entails originality. See, e.g., Schroeder v. William Morrow & Co., 566 F.2d 3 (CA7 1977) (copyright in gardening directory); cf. Burrow–Giles Lithographic Co. v. Sarony, 111 U.S. 53, 58 (1884) (originator of a photograph may claim copyright in his work). The copyright holders of "A Time to Heal" complied with the relevant statutory notice and registration procedures. See §§ 106, 401, 408; App. to Pet. for Cert. C–20. Thus there is no dispute that the unpublished manuscript of "A Time to Heal," as a whole, was protected by § 106 from unauthorized reproduction. Nor do respondents dispute that verbatim copying of excerpts of the manuscript's original form of expression would constitute infringement unless excused as fair use. See 1 M. Nimmer, Nimmer on Copyright § 2.11[B], p. 2–159 (1984) (hereinafter Nimmer). Yet copyright does not prevent subsequent users from copying from a prior author's work those constituent elements that are not original—for example, quotations borrowed under the rubric of fair use from other copyrighted works, facts, or materials in the public domain—as long as such use does not unfairly appropriate the author's original contributions. Ibid.; A. Latman, Fair Use of Copyrighted Works (1958), reprinted as Study No. 14 in Copyright Law Revision Studies Nos. 14–16, Prepared for the Senate Committee on the Judiciary, 86th Cong., 2d

Sess., 7 (1960) (hereinafter Latman). Perhaps the controversy between the lower courts in this case over copyrightability is more aptly styled a dispute over whether The Nation's appropriation of unoriginal and uncopyrightable elements encroached on the originality embodied in the work as a whole. Especially in the realm of factual narrative, the law is currently unsettled regarding the ways in which uncopyrightable elements combine with the author's original contributions to form protected expression. Compare *Wainwright Securities Inc. v. Wall Street Transcript Corp.*, 558 F.2d 91 (CA2 1977) (protection accorded author's analysis, structuring of material and marshaling of facts), with *Hoehling v. Universal City Studios, Inc.*, 618 F.2d 972 (CA2 1980) (limiting protection to ordering and choice of words). See, e.g., 1 Nimmer § 2.11[D], at 2-164-2-165.

We need not reach these issues, however, as The Nation has admitted to lifting verbatim quotes of the author's original language totaling between 300 and 400 words and constituting some 13% of The Nation article. In using generous verbatim excerpts of Mr. Ford's unpublished manuscript to lend authenticity to its account of the forthcoming memoirs, The Nation effectively arrogated to itself the right of first publication, an important marketable subsidiary right. For the reasons set forth below, we find that this use of the copyrighted manuscript, even stripped to the verbatim quotes conceded by The Nation to be copyrightable expression, was not a fair use within the meaning of the Copyright Act.

III

A

Fair use was traditionally defined as "a privilege in others than the owner of the copyright to use the copyrighted material in a reasonable manner without his consent." H. Ball, Law of Copyright and Literary Property 260 (1944) (hereinafter Ball). The statutory formulation of the defense of fair use in the Copyright Act of 1976 reflects the intent of Congress to codify the common-law doctrine. 3 Nimmer § 13.05. Section 107 requires a case-by-case determination whether a particular use is fair, and the statute notes four nonexclusive factors to be considered. This approach was "intended to restate the [pre-existing] judicial doctrine of fair use, not to change, narrow, or enlarge it in any way." H.R.Rep. No. 94-1476, p. 66 (1976) (hereinafter House Report).

"[T]he author's consent to a reasonable use of his copyrighted works ha[d] always been implied by the courts as a necessary incident of the constitutional policy of promoting the progress of science and the useful arts, since a prohibition of such use would inhibit subsequent writers from attempting to improve upon prior works and thus ... frustrate the very ends sought to be attained." Ball 260. Professor Latman, in a study of the doctrine of fair use commissioned by Congress for the revision effort, see *Sony Corp. v. Universal City Studios, Inc.*, 464 U.S., at 462-463, n. 9 (dissenting opinion), summarized prior law as turning on the "importance of the material copied or performed from the point of view of the reasonable copyright owner. In other words, would the reasonable copyright owner have consented to the use?" Latman 15.[3] * * *

Perhaps because the fair use doctrine was predicated on the author's implied consent to "reasonable and customary" use when he released his work for public consumption, fair use traditionally was not recognized as a defense to charges of copying from an author's as yet unpublished works. Under common-law copyright, "the property of the author ... in his intellectual creation [was] absolute until he voluntarily part[ed] with the same." American Tobacco Co. v. Werckmeister, 207 U.S. 284, 299 (1907); 2 Nimmer § 8.23, at 8–273. This absolute rule, however, was tempered in practice by the equitable nature of the fair use doctrine. In a given case, factors such as implied consent through *de facto* publication on performance or dissemination of a work may tip the balance of equities in favor of prepublication use. See Copyright Law Revision—Part 2: Discussion and Comments on Report of the Registrar of Copyrights on General Revision of the U.S. Copyright Law, 88th Cong., 1st Sess., at 27 (H.R.Comm. Print, 1963) (discussion suggesting works disseminated to the public in a form not constituting a technical "publication" should nevertheless be subject to fair use); 3 Nimmer § 13.05, at 13–62, n. 2. But it has never been seriously disputed that "the fact that the plaintiff's work is unpublished ... is a factor tending to negate the defense of fair use." Ibid. Publication of an author's expression before he has authorized its dissemination seriously infringes the author's right to decide when and whether it will be made public, a factor not present in fair use of published works. Respondents contend, however, that Congress, in including first publication among the rights enumerated in § 106, which are expressly subject to fair use under § 107, intended that fair use would apply *in pari materia* to published and unpublished works. The Copyright Revision Act does not support this proposition.

* * * [The 1976 Act] recognized for the first time a distinct statutory right of first publication, which had previously been an element of the common-law protections afforded unpublished works. The Report of the House Committee on the Judiciary confirms that "Clause (3) of section 106, establishes the exclusive right of publications.... Under this provision the copyright owner would have the right to control the first public distribution of an authorized copy ... of his work." Id., at 62.

Though the right of first publication, like the other rights enumerated in § 106, is expressly made subject to the fair use provision of § 107, fair

---

3. Professor Nimmer notes, "[Perhaps] no more precise guide can be stated than Joseph McDonald's clever paraphrase of the Golden Rule: 'Take not from others to such an extent and in such a manner that you would be resentful if they so took from you.'" 3 Nimmer § 13.05[A], at 13–66, quoting McDonald, Non-infringing Uses, 9 Bull. Copyright Soc. 466, 467 (1962). This "equitable rule of reason," Sony Corp. v. Universal City Studios, Inc., 464 U.S., at 448, "permits courts to avoid rigid application of the copyright statute when, on occasion, it would stifle the very creativity which that law is designed to foster." Iowa State University Research Foundation, Inc. v. American Broadcasting Cos., 621 F.2d 57, 60 (CA2 1980). See generally, L. Seltzer, Exemptions and Fair Use in Copyright 18–48 (1978).

use analysis must always be tailored to the individual case. Id., at 65; 3 Nimmer § 13.05[A]. The nature of the interest at stake is highly relevant to whether a given use is fair. From the beginning, those entrusted with the task of revision recognized the "overbalancing reasons to preserve the common law protection of undisseminated works until the author or his successor chooses to disclose them." Copyright Law Revision, Report of the Register of Copyrights on the General Revision of the U.S. Copyright Law, 87th Cong., 1st Sess., 41 (Comm.Print 1961). The right of first publication implicates a threshold decision by the author whether and in what form to release his work. First publication is inherently different from other § 106 rights in that only one person can be the first publisher; as the contract with Time illustrates, the commercial value of the right lies primarily in exclusivity. Because the potential damage to the author from judicially enforced "sharing" of the first publication right with unauthorized users of his manuscript is substantial, the balance of equities in evaluating such a claim of fair use inevitably shifts. * * *

* * * We conclude that the unpublished nature of a work is "[a] key, though not necessarily determinative, factor" tending to negate a defense of fair use. Senate Report, at 64. See 3 Nimmer § 13.05, at 13–62, n. 2; W. Patry, The Fair Use Privilege in Copyright Law 125 (1985) (hereinafter Patry).

We also find unpersuasive respondents' argument that fair use may be made of a soon-to-be-published manuscript on the ground that the author has demonstrated he has no interest in nonpublication. This argument assumes that the unpublished nature of copyrighted material is only relevant to letters or other confidential writings not intended for dissemination. It is true that common-law copyright was often enlisted in the service of personal privacy. See Brandeis & Warren, The Right to Privacy, 4 Harv.L.Rev. 193, 198–199 (1890). In its commercial guise, however, an author's right to choose when he will publish is no less deserving of protection. The period encompassing the work's initiation, its preparation, and its grooming for public dissemination is a crucial one for any literary endeavor. The Copyright Act, which accords the copyright owner the "right to control the first public distribution" of his work, House Report, at 62, echos the common law's concern that the author or copyright owner retain control throughout this critical stage. See generally Comment, The Stage of Publication as a "Fair Use" Factor: Harper & Row, Publishers v. Nation Enterprises, 58 St. John's L.Rev. 597 (1984). The obvious benefit to author and public alike of assuring authors the leisure to develop their ideas free from fear of expropriation outweighs any short term "news value" to be gained from premature publication of the author's expression. * * *

B

Respondents, however, contend that First Amendment values require a different rule under the circumstances of this case. The thrust of the decision below is that "[t]he scope of [fair use] is undoubtedly wider when the information conveyed relates to matters of high public concern." Consumers Union of the United States, Inc. v. General Signal Corp., 724 F.2d 1044, 1050 (CA2 1983) (construing Harper & Row Publishers, Inc. v. Nation Enterprises, 723 F.2d 195 (1983) (case below), as allowing advertiser to quote Consumer Reports), cert. denied, 469 U.S. 823 (1984). Respondents advance the substantial public import of the subject matter of the Ford memoirs as grounds for excusing a use that would ordinarily not pass muster as a fair use—the piracy of verbatim quotations for the purpose of "scooping" the authorized first serialization. Respondents explain their copying of Mr. Ford's expression as essential to reporting the news story it claims the book itself represents. In respondents' view, not only the facts contained in Mr. Ford's memoirs, but "the precise manner in which [he] expressed himself [were] as newsworthy as what he had to say." Brief for Respondents 38–39. Respondents argue that the public's interest in learning this news as fast as possible outweighs the right of the author to control its first publication.

The Second Circuit noted, correctly, that copyright's idea/expression dichotomy "strike[s] a definitional balance between the First Amendment and the Copyright Act by permitting free communication of facts while still protecting an author's expression." 723 F.2d, at 203. No author may copyright his ideas or the facts he narrates. 17 U.S.C. § 102(b). See, e.g., New York Times Co. v. United States, 403 U.S. 713, 726, n. * (1971) (BRENNAN, J., concurring) (Copyright laws are not restrictions on freedom of speech as copyright protects only form of expression and not the ideas expressed); 1 Nimmer § 1.1[B][2]. As this Court long ago observed: "[T]he news element—the information respecting current events contained in the literary production—is not the creation of the writer, but is a report of matters that ordinarily are *publici juris;* it is the history of the day." International News Service v. Associated Press, 248 U.S. 215, 234 (1918). But copyright assures those who write and publish factual narratives such as "A Time to Heal" that they may at least enjoy the right to market the original expression contained therein as just compensation for their investment. Cf. Zacchini v. Scripps–Howard Broadcasting Co., 433 U.S. 562, 575 (1977).

Respondents' theory, however, would expand fair use to effectively destroy any expectation of copyright protection in the work of a public figure. Absent such protection, there would be little incentive to create or profit in financing such memoirs, and the public would be denied an important source of significant historical information. The promise of copyright would be an empty one if it could be avoided merely by dubbing the infringement a fair use "news report" of the book. See Wainwright Securities, Inc. v. Wall Street Transcript Corp., 558 F.2d 91 (CA2 1977), cert. denied, 434 U.S. 1014 (1978).

Nor do respondents assert any actual necessity for circumventing the copyright scheme with respect to the types of works and users at issue here.[6] Where an author and publisher have invested extensive resources in creating an original work and are poised to release it to the public, no legitimate aim is served by preempting the right of first publication. The fact that the words the author has chosen to clothe his narrative may of themselves be "newsworthy" is not an independent justification for unauthorized copying of the author's expression prior to publication. * * *

In our haste to disseminate news, it should not be forgotten that the Framers intended copyright itself to be the engine of free expression. By establishing a marketable right to the use of one's expression, copyright supplies the economic incentive to create and disseminate ideas. This Court stated in Mazer v. Stein:

> "The economic philosophy behind the clause empowering Congress to grant patents and copyrights is the conviction that encouragement of individual effort by personal gain is the best way to advance public welfare through the talents of authors and inventors in 'Science and useful Arts.' " 347 U.S. 201, 219 (1954).

And again in Twentieth Century Music Corp. v. Aiken:

> "The immediate effect of our copyright law is to secure a fair return for an 'author's' creative labor. But the ultimate aim is, by this incentive, to stimulate [the creation of useful works] for the general public good." 422 U.S., at 156.

It is fundamentally at odds with the scheme of copyright to accord lesser rights in those works that are of greatest importance to the public. Such a notion ignores the major premise of copyright and injures author and public alike. "[T]o propose that fair use be imposed whenever the 'social value [of dissemination] ... outweighs any detriment to the artist,' would be to propose depriving copyright owners of their right in the property precisely when they encounter those users who could afford to pay for it." Gordon, Fair Use as Market Failure: A Structural and Economic Analysis of the *Betamax* Case and its Predecessors, 82 Colum.L.Rev. 1600, 1615 (1982). And as one commentator has noted: "If every volume that was in the public interest could be pirated away by a competing publisher, ... the public [soon] would have nothing worth reading." Sobel, Copyright and the First Amendment: A Gathering Storm?, 19 ASCAP Copyright Law Symposium 43, 78 (1971). See generally Comment, Copyright and the First Amendment; Where Lies the Public Interest?, 59 Tulane L.Rev. 133 (1984).

Moreover, freedom of thought and expression "includes both the right to speak freely and the right to refrain from speaking at all." Wooley v. Maynard, 430 U.S. 705, 714 (1977) (Burger, C.J.). We do not suggest this right not to speak would sanction abuse of the copyright owner's monopoly

---

6. It bears noting that Congress in the Copyright Act recognized a public interest warranting specific exemptions in a number of areas not within traditional fair use, see, e.g., 17 U.S.C. § 115 (compulsory license for records); § 105 (no copyright in government works). No such exemption limits copyright in personal narratives written by public servants after they leave government service.

as an instrument to suppress facts.   But in the words of New York's Chief Judge Fuld:

> "The essential thrust of the First Amendment is to prohibit improper restraints on the *voluntary* public expression of ideas; it shields the man who wants to speak or publish when others wish him to be quiet. There is necessarily, and within suitably defined areas, a concomitant freedom *not* to speak publicly, one which serves the same ultimate end as freedom of speech in its affirmative aspect."   Estate of Hemingway v. Random House, 23 N.Y.2d 341, 348, 244 N.E.2d 250, 255 (1968).

Courts and commentators have recognized that copyright, and the right of first publication in particular, serve this countervailing First Amendment value.   See Schnapper v. Foley, 667 F.2d 102 (1981), cert. denied, 455 U.S. 948 (1982); 1 Nimmer § 1.10[B], at 1–70, n. 24; Patry 140–142.

In view of the First Amendment protections already embodied in the Copyright Act's distinction between copyrightable expression and uncopyrightable facts and ideas, and the latitude for scholarship and comment traditionally afforded by fair use, we see no warrant for expanding the doctrine of fair use to create what amounts to a public figure exception to copyright.   Whether verbatim copying from a public figure's manuscript in a given case is or is not fair must be judged according to the traditional equities of fair use.

IV

* * * The four factors identified by Congress as especially relevant in determining whether the use was fair are: (1) the purpose and character of the use; (2) the nature of the copyrighted work; (3) the substantiality of the portion used in relation to the copyrighted work as a whole; (4) the effect on the potential market for or value of the copyrighted work.   We address each one separately.

Purpose of the Use.   The Second Circuit correctly identified news reporting as the general purpose of The Nation's use.   News reporting is one of the examples enumerated in § 107 to "give some idea of the sort of activities the courts might regard as fair use under the circumstances." Senate Report, at 61.   This listing was not intended to be exhaustive, see id.; § 101 (definition of "including" and "such as"), or to single out any particular use as presumptively a "fair" use.   The drafters resisted pressures from special interest groups to create presumptive categories of fair use, but structured the provision as an affirmative defense requiring a case by case analysis.   See H.R.Rep. No. 83, 90th Cong., 1st Sess., 37 (1967); Patry 477, n. 4.   "[W]hether a use referred to in the first sentence of section 107 is a fair use in a particular case will depend upon the application of the determinative factors, including those mentioned in the second sentence."   Senate Report, at 62.   The fact that an article arguably is "news" and therefore a productive use is simply one factor in a fair use analysis.   * * *

The fact that a publication was commercial as opposed to nonprofit is a separate factor that tends to weigh against a finding of fair use. "[E]very commercial use of copyrighted material is presumptively an unfair exploitation of the monopoly privilege that belongs to the owner of the copyright." Sony Corp. v. Universal City Studios, Inc., 464 U.S., at 451. In arguing that the purpose of news reporting is not purely commercial, The Nation misses the point entirely. The crux of the profit/nonprofit distinction is not whether the sole motive of the use is monetary gain but whether the user stands to profit from exploitation of the copyrighted material without paying the customary price. See Roy Export Co. Establishment v. Columbia Broadcasting System, Inc., 503 F.Supp., at 1144; 3 Nimmer § 13.05[A][1], at 13–71, n. 25.3. * * *

Nature of the Copyrighted Work. Second, the Act directs attention to the nature of the copyrighted work. "A Time to Heal" may be characterized as an unpublished historical narrative or autobiography. The law generally recognizes a greater need to disseminate factual works than works of fiction or fantasy. * * * Some of the briefer quotes from the memoirs are arguably necessary adequately to convey the facts; for example, Mr. Ford's characterization of the White House tapes as the "smoking gun" is perhaps so integral to the idea expressed as to be inseparable from it. Cf. 1 Nimmer § 1.10[C]. But The Nation did not stop at isolated phrases and instead excerpted subjective descriptions and portraits of public figures whose power lies in the author's individualized expression. Such use, focusing on the most expressive elements of the work, exceeds that necessary to disseminate the facts.

The fact that a work is unpublished is a critical element of its "nature." 3 Nimmer § 13.05[A]; Comment, 58 St. John's L.Rev., at 613. Our prior discussion establishes that the scope of fair use is narrower with respect to unpublished works. While even substantial quotations might qualify as fair use in a review of a published work or a news account of a speech that had been delivered to the public or disseminated to the press, see House Report, at 65, the author's right to control the first public appearance of his expression weighs against such use of the work before its release. The right of first publication encompasses not only the choice whether to publish at all, but also the choices when, where, and in what form first to publish a work. * * *

Amount and Substantiality of the Portion Used. Next, the Act directs us to examine the amount and substantiality of the portion used in relation to the copyrighted work as a whole. In absolute terms, the words actually quoted were an insubstantial portion of "A Time to Heal." The District Court, however, found that "[T]he Nation took what was essentially the heart of the book." 557 F.Supp., at 1072. We believe the Court of Appeals erred in overruling the District Judge's evaluation of the qualitative nature of the taking. See, e.g., Roy Export Co. Establishment v. Columbia Broadcasting System, Inc., [503 F.Supp. 1137, 1145 (S.D.N.Y.1980)] (taking of 55 seconds out of one hour and twenty-nine minute film deemed qualitatively substantial). A Time editor described the chapters on the pardon as "the most interesting and moving parts of the entire manuscript." Reply Brief for Petitioners 16, n. 8. The portions actually quoted were selected by Mr. Navasky as among the most powerful passages in those chapters. He testified that he used verbatim excerpts because simply reciting the information could not adequately convey the "absolute certainty with which [Ford] expressed himself," App. 303; or show that "this comes from President Ford," id., at 305; or carry the "definitive quality" of the original, id., at 306. In short, he quoted these passages precisely because they qualitatively embodied Ford's distinctive expression.

As the statutory language indicates, a taking may not be excused merely because it is insubstantial with respect to the *infringing* work. As Judge Learned Hand cogently remarked, "no plagiarist can excuse the wrong by showing how much of his work he did not pirate." Sheldon v. Metro–Goldwyn Pictures Corp., 81 F.2d 49, 56 (CA2), cert. denied, 298 U.S. 669 (1936). Conversely, the fact that a substantial portion of the infringing work was copied verbatim is evidence of the qualitative value of the copied material, both to the originator and to the plagiarist who seeks to profit from marketing someone else's copyrighted expression.

Stripped to the verbatim quotes,[8] the direct takings from the unpublished manuscript constituted at least 13% of the infringing article. See Meeropol v. Nizer, 560 F.2d 1061, 1071 (CA2 1977) (copyrighted letters constituted less than 1% of infringing work but were prominently featured). The Nation article is structured around the quoted excerpts which serve as its dramatic focal points. See Appendix, infra. In view of the expressive value of the excerpts and their key role in the infringing work, we cannot agree with the Second Circuit that the "magazine took a meager, indeed an infinitesimal amount of Ford's original language." 723 F.2d, at 209.

Effect on the Market. Finally, the Act focuses on "the effect of the use upon the potential market for or value of the copyrighted work." This last factor is undoubtedly the single most important element of fair use.[9] See 3

---

8. See Appendix, infra, at 570. The Court of Appeals found that only "approximately 300 words" were copyrightable but did not specify which words. The court's discussion, however, indicates it excluded from consideration those portions of The Nation's piece that, although copied verbatim from Ford's manuscript, were quotes attributed by Ford to third persons and quotations from Government documents. At oral argument, counsel for The Nation did not dispute that verbatim quotes and very close paraphrase could constitute infringement. Tr. of Oral Arg. 24–25. Thus the Appendix identifies as potentially infringing only verbatim quotes or very close paraphrase and excludes from consideration Government documents and words attributed to third persons. The

Appendix is not intended to endorse any particular rule of copyrightability but is intended merely as an aid to facilitate our discussion.

9. Economists who have addressed the issue believe the fair use exception should come into play only in those situations in which the market fails or the price the copyright holder would ask is near zero. See, e.g., T. Brennan, Harper & Row v. The Nation, Copyrightability and Fair Use, Dept. of Justice Economic Policy Office Discussion Paper, 13–17 (1984); Gordon, Fair Use as Market Failure: A Structural and Economic Analysis of the *Betamax* Case and its Predecessors, 82 Colum.L.Rev. 1600, 1615 (1982). As the facts here demonstrate, there is a fully functioning market that encourages the creation and dissemination of memoirs of public

Nimmer § 13.05[A], at 13–76, and cases cited therein. "Fair use, when properly applied, is limited to copying by others which does not materially impair the marketability of the work which is copied." 1 Nimmer § 1.10[D], at 1–87. The trial court found not merely a potential but an actual effect on the market. Time's cancellation of its projected serialization and its refusal to pay the $12,500 were the direct effect of the infringement. The Court of Appeals rejected this fact finding as clearly erroneous, noting that the record did not establish a causal relation between Time's nonperformance and respondents' unauthorized publication of Mr. Ford's *expression* as opposed to the facts taken from the memoirs. We disagree. Rarely will a case of copyright infringement present such clear-cut evidence of actual damage. Petitioners assured Time that there would be no other authorized publication of *any* portion of the unpublished manuscript prior to April 23, 1979. *Any* publication of material from chapters 1 and 3 would permit Time to renegotiate its final payment. Time cited The Nation's article, which contained verbatim quotes from the unpublished manuscript, as a reason for its nonperformance. * * *

More important, to negate fair use one need only show that if the challenged use "should become widespread, it would adversely affect the *potential* market for the copyrighted work." Sony Corp. v. Universal City Studios, Inc., 464 U.S., at 451 (emphasis added); id., at 484, and n. 36 (collecting cases) (dissenting opinion). This inquiry must take account not only of harm to the original but also of harm to the market for derivative works. See Iowa State University Research Foundation, Inc. v. American Broadcasting Cos., 621 F.2d 57 (CA2 1980); Meeropol v. Nizer, supra, at 1070; Roy Export v. Columbia Broadcasting System, Inc., 503 F.Supp., at 1146. "If the defendant's work adversely affects the value of any of the rights in the copyrighted work (in this case the adaptation [and serialization] right) the use is not fair." 3 Nimmer § 13.05[B], at 13–77—13–78 (footnote omitted).

It is undisputed that the factual material in the balance of The Nation's article, besides the verbatim quotes at issue here, was drawn exclusively from the chapters on the pardon. The excerpts were employed as featured episodes in a story about the Nixon pardon—precisely the use petitioners had licensed to Time. The borrowing of these verbatim quotes from the unpublished manuscript lent The Nation's piece a special air of authenticity—as Navasky expressed it, the reader would know it was Ford speaking and not The Nation. App. 300c. Thus it directly competed for a share of the market for prepublication excerpts. The Senate Report states:

> "With certain special exceptions ... a use that supplants any part of the normal market for a copyrighted work would ordinarily be considered an infringement." Senate Report, at 65.

figures. In the economists' view, permitting "fair use" to displace normal copyright chan-nels disrupts the copyright market without a commensurate public benefit.

Placed in a broader perspective, a fair use doctrine that permits extensive prepublication quotations from an unreleased manuscript without the copyright owner's consent poses substantial potential for damage to the marketability of first serialization rights in general. "Isolated instances of minor infringements, when multiplied many times, become in the aggregate a major inroad on copyright that must be prevented." Ibid.

V

* * *

The Nation conceded that its verbatim copying of some 300 words of direct quotation from the Ford manuscript would constitute an infringement unless excused as a fair use. Because we find that The Nation's use of these verbatim excerpts from the unpublished manuscript was not a fair use, the judgment of the Court of Appeals is reversed and remanded for further proceedings consistent with this opinion.

It is so ordered.

APPENDIX TO OPINION OF THE COURT

The portions of The Nation article which were copied verbatim from "A Time to Heal," excepting quotes from Government documents and quotes attributed by Ford to third persons, are identified in boldface in the text. See n. 8, ante, at 565. The corresponding passages in the Ford manuscript are footnoted.

[The Appendix to the opinion of the Court contains the complete text of The Nation article, with parallel references to the Ford manuscript. Only a portion is reproduced below.]

THE FORD MEMOIRS
BEHIND THE NIXON PARDON

In his memoirs, *A Time To Heal,* which Harper & Row will publish in late May or early June, former President Gerald R. Ford says that the idea of giving a blanket pardon to Richard M. Nixon was raised before Nixon resigned from the Presidency by Gen. Alexander Haig, who was then the White House chief of staff.

Ford also writes that, but for a misunderstanding, he might have selected Ronald Reagan as his 1976 running mate, that Washington lawyer Edward Bennett Williams, a Democrat, was his choice for head of the Central Intelligence Agency, that Nixon was the one who first proposed Rockefeller for Vice President, and that he regretted his **"cowardice"** [1] in allowing Rockefeller to remove himself from Vice Presidential contention. Ford also describes his often prickly relations with Henry Kissinger.

The Nation obtained the 655–page typescript before publication. Advance excerpts from the book will appear in *Time* in mid-April and in *The*

---

1. I was angry at myself for showing cowardice in not saying to the ultra-conservatives, "It's going to be Ford and Rockefeller, whatever the consequences." p. 496.

Reader's Digest thereafter. Although the initial print order has not been decided, the figure is tentatively set at 50,000; it could change, depending upon the public reaction to the serialization.

Ford's account of the Nixon pardon contains significant new detail on the negotiations and considerations that surrounded it. According to Ford's version, the subject was first broached to him by General Haig on August 1, 1974, a week before Nixon resigned. General Haig revealed that the newly transcribed White House tapes were the equivalent of the **"smoking gun"** [2] and that Ford should prepare himself to become President.

Ford was deeply hurt by Haig's revelation: **"Over the past several months Nixon had repeatedly assured me that he was not involved in Watergate, that the evidence would prove his innocence, that the matter would fade from view."** [3] Ford had believed him, but he let Haig explain the President's alternatives.

He could **"ride it out"** [4] or he could resign, Haig said. He then listed the different ways Nixon might resign and concluded by pointing out that **Nixon could agree to leave in return for an agreement that the new President, Ford, would pardon him.** [5] Although Ford said it would be improper for him to make any recommendation, he basically agreed with Haig's assessment and adds, **"Because of his references to the pardon authority, I did ask Haig about the extent of a President's pardon power."** [6]

"It's my understanding from a White House lawyer," Haig replied, "that a President does have authority to grant a pardon even before criminal action has been taken against an individual."

But because Ford had neglected to tell Haig he thought the idea of a resignation conditioned on a pardon was improper, his press aide, Bob Hartmann, suggested that Haig might well have returned to the White House and told President Nixon that he had mentioned the idea and Ford seemed comfortable with it. "Silence implies assent."

Ford then consulted with White House special counsel James St. Clair, who had no advice one way or the other on the matter more than pointing out that he was not the lawyer who had given Haig the opinion on the pardon. Ford also discussed the matter with Jack Marsh, who felt that the mention of a pardon in this context was a "time bomb," and with Bryce

---

2. [I]t contained the so-called smoking gun. p. 3.

3. [O]ver the past several months Nixon had repeatedly assured me that he was not involved in Watergate, that the evidence would prove his innocence, that the matter would fade from view. p. 7.

4. The first [option] was that he could try to "ride it out" by letting impeachment take its natural course through the House

and the Senate trial, fighting against conviction all the way. p. 4.

5. Finally, Haig said that according to some on Nixon's White House staff, Nixon could agree to leave in return for an agreement that the new President Gerald Ford— would pardon him. p. 5.

6. Because of his references to pardon authority, I did ask Haig about the extent of a President's pardon power. pp. 5–6.

Harlow, who had served six Presidents and who agreed that **the mere mention of a pardon "could cause a lot of trouble." [7]**

As a result of these various conversations, Vice President Ford called Haig and read him a written statement: "I want you to understand that I have no intention of recommending what the President should do about resigning or not resigning and that nothing we talked about yesterday afternoon should be given any consideration in whatever decision the President may wish to make."

Despite what Haig had told him about the "smoking gun" tapes, Ford told a Jackson, Mich., luncheon audience later in the day that **the President was not guilty of an impeachable offense. "Had I said otherwise at that moment,"** he writes, **"the whole house of cards might have collapsed." [8]**

In justifying the pardon, Ford goes out of his way to assure the reader that **"compassion for Nixon as an individual hadn't prompted my decision at all." [9]** Rather, he did it because he had **"to get the monkey off my back one way or the other." [10]** * * *

Ultimately, Ford sums up the philosophy underlying his decision as one he picked up as a student at Yale Law School many years before. **"I learned that public policy often took precedence over a rule of law. Although I respected the tenet that no man should be above the law, public policy demanded that I put Nixon—and Watergate— behind us as quickly as possible." [17]**

Later, when Ford learned that Nixon's phlebitis had acted up and his health was seriously impaired, he debated whether to pay the ailing former President a visit. **"If I made the trip it would remind everybody of Watergate and the pardon. If I didn't, people would say I lacked compassion." [18]** Ford went:

He was stretched out flat on his back. There were tubes in his nose and mouth, and wires led from his arms, chest and legs to machines with orange lights that blinked on and off. His face was

7. Only after I had finished did [Bryce Harlow] let me know in no uncertain terms that he agreed with Bob and Jack, that the mere mention of the pardon option could cause a lot of trouble in the days ahead. p. 18.

8. During the luncheon I repeated my assertion that the President was not guilty of an impeachable offense. Had I said otherwise at that moment, the whole house of cards might have collapsed. p. 21.

9. But compassion for Nixon as an individual hadn't prompted my decision at all. p. 266.

10. I had to get the monkey off my back one way or another. p. 236.

17. Years before, at Yale Law School, I'd learned that public policy often took precedence over a rule of law. Although I respected the tenet that no man should be above the law, public policy demanded that I put Nixon—and Watergate—behind us as quickly as possible. p. 256.

18. My staff debated whether or not I ought to visit Nixon at the Long Beach hospital, only half an hour away. If I made the trip, it would remind everyone of Watergate and the pardon. If I didn't, people would say I lacked compassion. I ended their debate as soon as I found out it had begun. Of course I would go. p. 298.

ashen, and I thought I had never seen anyone closer to death.[19]
* * *

■ JUSTICE BRENNAN, with whom JUSTICE WHITE and JUSTICE MARSHALL join, dissenting.

The Court holds that The Nation's quotation of 300 words from the unpublished 200,000–word manuscript of President Gerald R. Ford infringed the copyright in that manuscript, even though the quotations related to a historical event of undoubted significance—the resignation and pardon of President Richard M. Nixon. Although the Court pursues the laudable goal of protecting "the economic incentive to create and disseminate ideas," ante, at 558, this zealous defense of the copyright owner's prerogative will, I fear, stifle the broad dissemination of ideas and information copyright is intended to nurture. Protection of the copyright owner's economic interest is achieved in this case through an exceedingly narrow definition of the scope of fair use. The progress of arts and sciences and the robust public debate essential to an enlightened citizenry are ill served by this constricted reading of the fair use doctrine. See 17 U.S.C. § 107. I therefore respectfully dissent.

I

A

This case presents two issues. First, did The Nation's use of material from the Ford manuscript in forms other than direct quotation from that manuscript infringe Harper & Row's copyright. Second, did the quotation of approximately 300 words from the manuscript infringe the copyright because this quotation did not constitute "fair use" within the meaning of § 107 of the Copyright Act. 17 U.S.C. § 107. The Court finds no need to resolve the threshold copyrightability issue. The use of 300 words of quotation was, the Court finds, beyond the scope of fair use and thus a copyright infringement. Because I disagree with the Court's fair use holding, it is necessary for me to decide the threshold copyrightability question.

B

* * * Not surprisingly, the test for infringement has defied precise formulation. In general, though, the inquiry proceeds along two axes: *how closely* has the second author tracked the first author's particular language and structure of presentation; and *how much* of the first author's language and structure has the second author appropriated.[6]

In the present case the infringement analysis must be applied to a historical biography in which the author has chronicled the events of his

---

19. He was stretched out flat on his back. There were tubes in his nose and mouth, and wires led from his arms, chest and legs to machines with orange lights that blinked on and off. His face was ashen, and I thought I had never seen anyone closer to death. p. 299.

6. The inquiry into the substantiality of appropriation has a quantitative and a qualitative aspect.

White House tenure and commented on those events from his unique perspective. Apart from the quotations, virtually all of the material in The Nation's article indirectly recounted Mr. Ford's factual narrative of the Nixon resignation and pardon, his latter-day reflections on some events of his Presidency, and his perceptions of the personalities at the center of those events. See ante, at 570–579. No copyright can be claimed in this information *qua* information. Infringement would thus have to be based on too close and substantial a tracking of Mr. Ford's expression of this information.[7]

The Language. Much of the information The Nation conveyed was not in the form of paraphrase at all, but took the form of synopsis of lengthy discussions in the Ford manuscript. In the course of this summary presentation, The Nation did use occasional sentences that closely resembled language in the original Ford manuscript. But these linguistic similarities are insufficient to constitute an infringement for three reasons. First, some leeway must be given to subsequent authors seeking to convey facts because those "wishing to express the ideas contained in a factual work often can choose from only a narrow range of expression." Landsberg v. Scrabble Crossword Game Players, Inc., 736 F.2d 485, 488 (CA9 1984). Second, much of what The Nation paraphrased was material in which Harper & Row could claim no copyright.[10] Third, The Nation paraphrased nothing approximating the totality of a single paragraph, much less a chapter or the work as a whole. At most The Nation paraphrased disparate isolated sentences from the original. A finding of

---

7. Neither the District Court nor the dissent in the Court of Appeals approached the question in this way. Despite recognizing that this material was not "per se copyrightable," the District Court held that the "totality of these facts and memoranda collected together with Mr. Ford's reflections . . . is protected by the copyright laws." 557 F.Supp. 1067, 1072–1073 (SDNY1983). The dissent in the Court of Appeals signaled approval of this approach. 723 F.2d 195, 213–214 (1983) (Meskill, J., dissenting). Such an approach must be rejected. Copyright protection cannot be extended to factual information whenever that information is interwoven with protected expression (purportedly in this case Mr. Ford's reflections) into an expressive "totality." Most works of history or biography blend factual narrative and reflective or speculative commentary in this way. Precluding subsequent use of facts so presented cannot be squared with the specific legislative intent, expressed in both House and Senate Reports, that "[c]opyright does not preclude others from using the . . . information revealed by the author's work." See S.Rep. No. 93–983, pp. 107–108 (1974).

H.R.Rep. No. 94–1476, pp. 56–57 (1976). The core purposes of copyright would be thwarted and serious First Amendment concerns would arise. An author could obtain a monopoly on narration of historical events simply by being the first to discuss them in a reflective or analytical manner.

10. Often the paraphrasing was of statements others had made to Mr. Ford. E.g., ante, at 571 ("He could 'ride it out' or he could resign, Haig said"). See generally ante, at 570–579. No copyright can be asserted in the verbatim representation of such statements of others. 17 U.S.C. § 102. See Suid v. Newsweek Magazine, 503 F.Supp., at 148; Rokeach v. Avco Embassy Pictures Corp., 197 USPQ, at 161. Other paraphrased material came from Government documents in which no copyright interest can be claimed. For example, the article quotes from a memorandum prepared by Henry S. Ruth, Jr., in his official capacity as assistant to Watergate Special Prosecutor Leon Jaworski. See ante, at 573. This document is a work of the United States Government. See 17 U.S.C. § 105.

infringement based on paraphrase generally requires far more close and substantial a tracking of the original language than occurred in this case. See, e.g., Wainwright Securities v. Wall Street Transcript Corp., 558 F.2d 91 (CA2 1977).

The Structure of Presentation. The article does not mimic Mr. Ford's structure. The information The Nation presents is drawn from scattered sections of the Ford work and does not appear in the sequence in which Mr. Ford presented it. Some of The Nation's discussion of the pardon does roughly track the order in which the Ford manuscript presents information about the pardon. With respect to this similarity, however, Mr. Ford has done no more than present the facts chronologically and cannot claim infringement when a subsequent author similarly presents the facts of history in a chronological manner. Also, it is difficult to suggest that a 2000–word article could bodily appropriate the structure of a 200,000–word book. Most of what Mr. Ford created, and most of the history he recounted, was simply not represented in The Nation's article.

When The Nation was not quoting Mr. Ford, therefore, its efforts to convey the historical information in the Ford manuscript did not so closely and substantially track Mr. Ford's language and structure as to constitute an appropriation of literary form.

II.

The Nation is thus liable in copyright only if the quotation of 300 words infringed any of Harper & Row's exclusive rights under § 106 of the Act. Section 106 explicitly makes the grant of exclusive rights "[s]ubject to section 107 through 118." 17 U.S.C. § 106. * * *

With respect to a work of history, particularly the memoirs of a public official, the statutorily prescribed analysis cannot properly be conducted without constant attention to copyright's crucial distinction between protected literary form and unprotected information or ideas. The question must always be: Was the subsequent author's use of *literary form* a fair use within the meaning of § 107, in light of the purpose for the use, the nature of the copyrighted work, the amount of literary form used, and the effect of this use of literary form on the value of or market for the original?

Limiting the inquiry to the propriety of a subsequent author's use of the copyright owner's literary form is not easy in the case of a work of history. Protection against only substantial appropriation of literary form does not ensure historians a return commensurate with the full value of their labors. The literary form contained in works like "A Time to Heal" reflects only a part of the labor that goes into the book. It is the labor of collecting, sifting, organizing, and reflecting that predominates in the creation of works of history such as this one. The value this labor produces lies primarily in the information and ideas revealed, and not in the particular collocation of words through which the information and ideas are expressed. Copyright thus does not protect that which is often of most value in a work of history, and courts must resist the tendency to reject the fair use defense on the basis of their feeling that an author of history has been deprived of the full value of his or her labor. A subsequent author's taking of information and ideas is in no sense piratical because copyright law simply does not create any property interest in information and ideas.

The urge to compensate for subsequent use of information and ideas is perhaps understandable. An inequity seems to lurk in the idea that much of the fruit of the historian's labor may be used without compensation. This, however, is not some unforeseen by-product of a statutory scheme intended primarily to ensure a return for works of the imagination. Congress made the affirmative choice that the copyright laws should apply in this way: "Copyright does not preclude others from using the ideas or information revealed by the author's work. It pertains to the literary . . . form in which the author expressed intellectual concepts." H.R.Rep. No. 94–1476, at 56–57. This distinction is at the essence of copyright. The copyright laws serve as the "engine of free expression," ante, at 558, only when the statutory monopoly does not choke off multifarious indirect uses and consequent broad dissemination of information and ideas. To ensure the progress of arts and sciences and the integrity of First Amendment values, ideas and information must not be freighted with claims of proprietary right.

In my judgment, the Court's fair use analysis has fallen to the temptation to find copyright violation based on a minimal use of literary form in order to provide compensation for the appropriation of information from a work of history. The failure to distinguish between information and literary form permeates every aspect of the Court's fair use analysis and leads the Court to the wrong result in this case. Application of the statutorily prescribed analysis with attention to the distinction between information and literary form leads to a straightforward finding of fair use within the meaning of § 107.

[Justice Brennan then proceeded to a consideration of the four fair use factors. With regard to purpose, he said The Nation's use was news reporting furthering the public interest in the dissemination of information; he also rejected the majority's reliance on the commercial nature of the use: "Many uses § 107 lists as paradigmatic examples of fair use, including criticism, comment, and *news reporting*, are generally conducted for profit in this country, a fact of which Congress was obviously aware when it enacted § 107."

[The nature of the work, Justice Brennan believed, also supported a finding of fair use. The scope of fair use for factual and historical works is broad, and a "categorical presumption against prepublication fair use" was unwarranted.

[On the amount and substantiality of the use, he emphasized that appropriations of information and ideas are irrelevant to the issue of substantiality, and that the borrowing of copyrightable material must be judged in light of the purpose of the use.

[Finally, with respect to market effect, Justice Brennan thought the majority had failed to distinguish between the use of information and the appropriation of literary form; only injury resulting from the latter was relevant to the fair use analysis. "Wholly apart from these quoted words, The Nation published significant information and ideas from the Ford manuscript. If it was this publication of information, and not the publication of the few quotations, that caused Time to abrogate its serialization agreement, then whatever the negative effect on the serialization market, that effect was the product of wholly legitimate activity."]

NOTES AND QUESTIONS

(1) Would the Court have reached a different conclusion if The Nation had published its article *after* publication of the Ford memoirs? The case for distinctive treatment of unpublished works is made in Kernochan, Protection of Unpublished Works in the United States Before and After the *Nation* Case, 33 J.Copyr.Soc. 322 (1986), with a hearty endorsement of the Supreme Court's decision.

Is it possible, as urged by Justice Brennan, to separate the consequences of The Nation's appropriation of facts and its appropriation of expression? If the defendant could establish that Time would have canceled its publication even if The Nation's article had included no quotations, would the use then be fair?[a]

Eight years after the decision in *Harper & Row,* the courts of England reached a somewhat different conclusion on remarkably parallel facts. *The Downing Street Years,* the memoirs of former British Prime Minister Margaret Thatcher, were soon to be published by HarperCollins; *The Sunday Times* had purchased serialization rights, with excerpts scheduled to appear just before publication of the book. The British newspaper *Daily Mirror* obtained a stolen copy of the manuscript and initiated a series of articles on the book, including excerpts, with particular emphasis on Lady Thatcher's disapproving remarks about her successor, John Major. (The *Daily Mirror* articles appeared during a Conservative Party conference at which Thatcher made a public display of support for Major.) HarperCollins and *The Sunday Times* sought an injunction against publication of additional excerpts, arguing copyright infringement and breach of confidence. The injunction was denied by the High Court in a decision affirmed by the Court of Appeal. The judges thought that the "extreme step" of enjoining publication was not warranted in light of the plaintiffs' ability to pursue a subsequent damage action against the defendant. But the judges also relied on the "public interest" in access to Thatcher's comments on Prime Minister Major, particularly in light of the image of unity being portrayed at the Conservative Party conference. The Sunday Times, Oct. 10, 1993, Sec. 3, p. 6. If Harper & Row had realized that a copy of the Ford manuscript had been given to *The Nation* in time to seek a prior

---

a. Time had prepublication rights scooped again in 1995 when Newsweek some- how got hold of a copy of Colin Powell's memoirs, *My American Journey.* Newsweek's injunction, would a restraint on publication have been upheld by the Supreme Court?

(2) Harper & Row v. Nation was invoked in Salinger v. Random House, Inc., 811 F.2d 90 (2d Cir.), cert. denied, 484 U.S. 890 (1987), which presented the issue of whether a biographer of author J.D. Salinger made fair use of his subject's unpublished letters. The letters had been donated to libraries by their recipients; they were made available to biographer Hamilton under agreements forbidding reproduction or publication. The biography quoted some 200 words, but Judge Newman also found numerous passages that "closely paraphrase" portions of the letters. (He gives as an example a quotation from Salinger describing Wendell Wilkie: "He looks to me like a guy who makes his wife keep a scrapbook for him"; the biography states that Salinger "had fingered [Wilkie] as the sort of fellow who makes his wife keep an album of his press clippings.") The Second Circuit rejected the claim of fair use, placing "special emphasis on the unpublished nature of Salinger's letters." Judge Leval in the district court, 650 F.Supp. 413 (S.D.N.Y.1986), had expressed sympathy with the biographer's argument that departure from Salinger's own words "distorts, sacrificing both accuracy and vividness of description." Judge Newman, remanding for a preliminary injunction, responded: "But the biographer has no inherent right to copy the 'accuracy' or the 'vividness' of the letter writer's expression. Indeed, 'vividness of description' is precisely an attribute of the author's expression that he is entitled to protect." Judge Newman emphasized that biographer Hamilton remained free to fashion a work that reported the facts found in the letters. (See also Newman, Copyright Law and the Protection of Privacy, 12 Colum.—VLA J.L. & Arts 459 (1988), in which Judge Newman goes beyond *Salinger,* proposing direct reliance on privacy interests in protecting works that are truly "unpublished.")

Craft v. Kobler, 667 F.Supp. 120 (S.D.N.Y.1987), involving a biographer's quotation and paraphrase of 3,500 words from the writings of composer Igor Stravinsky, afforded Judge Leval the opportunity for a rejoinder: "I agree with the defendants that the fair use doctrine gives latitude to the biographer of an author to quote limited excerpts of published copyrighted work to illustrate the descriptive skill, wit, power, vividness, and originality of the author's writing." *Salinger,* he said, "refers only to takings from *unpublished* copyrighted materials." Judge Leval concluded, however, that defendant's "appropriations of copyrighted materials are too extensive and important, and their justification too slight to support an overall claim of fair use." Distribution of the book was enjoined pending trial.

Judge Leval had another round with the Second Circuit over fair use of unpublished works in New Era Pub. Int'l, ApS v. Henry Holt & Co., 873 F.2d 576 (2d Cir.1989), cert. denied, 493 U.S. 1094 (1990). The work in question, *Bare–Faced Messiah,* was a hostile exposé of the life of the late L.

story, which beat publication of Time's excerpts and the book by a week, carefully avoided direct quotation, instead adopting the form of an analysis of the book's contents by senior Newsweek correspondents. Carmody, Time Questions Newsweek on Powell Memoirs Scoop, New York Times, Sept. 6, p. D6.

Ron Hubbard, the founder of Scientology. The plaintiff holds Hubbard's copyrights, including unpublished diaries and letters, from which defendant copied many excerpts. Judge Leval found 44 of them infringing, 695 F.Supp. 1493 (S.D.N.Y.1988). However, he declined to convert a temporary restraining order into an injunction, and left the plaintiff to monetary relief. He said that much of the author's use of Hubbard's expression was necessary to support critical judgments about Hubbard's life and character. The public interest in the material, even though it was unpublished, invoked first amendment concerns that weighed against the customary remedy of an injunction. Judge Miner for the Second Circuit repudiated almost every step of Judge Leval's analysis, reaffirming the strong protection that *Salinger* (and the *Nation* case) give to unpublished material. The court saw no copyright ground for withholding the injunction and also asserted the prevailing view that the fair use doctrine adequately protects free speech interests (see p. 414 infra). However, the appellate court affirmed the denial of an injunction because of laches while retaining the damages remedy, since New Era did not commence its action until the first printing of 12,000 copies had been shipped. (Plaintiff had lost on the same ground in Canada and England). Chief Judge Oakes concurred on the laches outcome only. His vigorous opinion repeatedly disagrees with the majority's fair use analysis. As to the availability of an injunction (absent laches), he wrote, "I totally disagree." The pointed debate continued in the denial of a rehearing en banc, this time in opinions by Judges Miner and Newman.[b] 884 F.2d 659 (2d Cir.1989).

A Hubbard biographer was again before the Second Circuit in New Era Pub. Int'l, ApS v. Carol Pub. Group, 904 F.2d 152 (2d Cir.), cert. denied, 498 U.S. 921 (1990), upholding the defendant's fair use defense in connection with quotations from Hubbard's *published* works; the quotations were used to convey Hubbard's "hypocrisy and pomposity, qualities that may best (or only) be revealed through direct quotation." See also Wright v. Warner Books, Inc., 953 F.2d 731 (2d Cir.1991) ("'sparing use" of unpublished writings in a biography of author Richard Wright held fair use).

(3) Authors complained to Congress that in reaction to cases such as Salinger v. Random House and New Era Pub. v. Henry Holt, their publishers were forbidding them from quoting unpublished sources. See 42 Pat., Tm. & Copyr.J. (BNA) 147 (1991). Congress responded in 1992 with an amendment adding the final sentence to § 107 emphasizing the applicability of the traditional fair use factors to unpublished works. Pub.L. 102–492, 106 Stat. 3145 (1992). Supporters in the Senate described the amendment as "designed to undo the harm caused by the overly restrictive standards adopted in *Salinger* and *New Era*, and to clearly and indisputably reject the

---

b. The disputes within the Second Circuit spilled over into extra-judicial pronouncements. See Leval, Toward a Fair Use Standard, 103 Harv.L.Rev. 1105 (1990); Miner, Exploiting Stolen Text: Fair Use or Fair Play?, 37 J.Copyr.Soc. 1 (1989); Newman, Not the End of History: The Second Circuit Struggles with Fair Use, *id.* at 12; Oakes, Copyrights and Copyremedies: Unfair Use and Injunctions, 18 Hofstra L.Rev. 983 (1990). See also Landes, Copyright Protection of Letters, Diaries, and Other Unpublished Works: An Economic Analysis, 21 J.Leg.Stud. 79 (1992).

view that the unpublished nature of the work triggers a virtual per se ruling against a finding of fair use." 44 Pat., Tm. & Copyr.J. (BNA) 633 (1992). The history of the amendment is recounted in Wanat, Fair Use and the 1992 Amendment to Section 107 of the 1976 Copyright Act, 1 Vill. Sports & Ent.L.F. 47 (1994).

(4) Cases analyzing the factors enumerated in § 107 are collected in W. Patry, The Fair Use Privilege in Copyright Law (1985). Dratler, Distilling the Witches' Brew of Fair Use in Copyright Law, 43 Miami L.Rev. 233 (1988), criticizes reliance on presumptions to avoid an explicit balancing of the fair use factors. Much of the scholarship on fair use is critically reviewed in Raskind, A Functional Interpretation of Fair Use, 31 J.Copyr.Soc. 601 (1984).

An imposing demonstration of the ambiguity and incoherence of the "factors" approach to fair use is mounted in Fisher, Reconstructing the Fair Use Doctrine, 101 Harv.L.Rev. 1659 (1988). A view of fair use as a regulatory limitation on the scope of the copyright monopoly is offered in Patterson, Understanding Fair Use, 55 L. & Contemp.Prob. (No. 2) 249 (1992). Weinreb, Fair's Fair: A Comment on the Fair Use Doctrine, 103 Harv.L.Rev. 1137 (1990), argues that the doctrine rests as much on established practices and expectations as on a refined calculus of incentive and dissemination.

(5) Book publishers sometimes insert notices like this: "No part of this book may be reproduced in any form without the permission of the publisher." What is the legal effect of such a notice? Is fair use premised on consent? Do such notices have extralegal effects? See Fischer, Reserving All Rights Beyond Copyright: Nonstatutory Restrictive Notices, 34 J.Copyr.Soc. 249 (1987).

PROBLEM: Plaintiff wrote a book consisting of interviews with 17 women discussing their experiences with abortion and unplanned pregnancies. The purpose of the work was "to further understanding of the Pro–Choice view." The women assigned their copyright interests in the interviews to the plaintiff. About 2,500 copies of the book were sold before it went out of print; plaintiff has indicated an intent to produce a "very small printing" of additional copies.

Defendant, a Catholic priest, decided to write a book that would state the case against abortion. He believed that, as a priest, conducting his own interviews would pose credibility problems. Defendant sought permission to quote from the interviews in plaintiff's book, offering to pay a fee. Plaintiff refused permission, explaining that the women had told their stories in support of their particular point of view, and "she promised to honor their wishes." Defendant, after consulting with legal counsel, published his book; it appeared soon after plaintiff's work went out of print. The book contains about 7,000 words quoted directly from the interviews. The quotations are arranged in a topical framework. Plaintiff believes that in many instances the quotations are taken out of context, distorting their actual meaning.

Plaintiff brings an action for infringement; defendant claims his use was fair. What result under § 107? See Maxtone–Graham v. Burtchaell, 803 F.2d 1253 (2d Cir.1986), cert. denied, 481 U.S. 1059 (1987).

TAPING

Sony Corp. of America v. Universal City Studios, Inc.

Supreme Court of the United States, 1984.
464 U.S. 417, 104 S.Ct. 774.

[Other portions of the Court's opinion appear at p. 1 supra and p. 453 infra.]

■ JUSTICE STEVENS. * * *

B. *Unauthorized Time–Shifting*

Even unauthorized uses of a copyrighted work are not necessarily infringing. An unlicensed use of the copyright is not an infringement unless it conflicts with one of the specific exclusive rights conferred by the copyright statute. Twentieth Century Music Corp. v. Aiken, 422 U.S. 151. Moreover, the definition of exclusive rights in § 106 of the present Act is prefaced by the words "subject to sections 107 through 118." Those sections describe a variety of uses of copyrighted material that "are not infringements of copyright notwithstanding the provisions of § 106." The most pertinent in this case is § 107, the legislative endorsement of the doctrine of "fair use."

That section identifies various factors that enable a court to apply an "equitable rule of reason" analysis to particular claims of infringement. Although not conclusive, the first factor requires that "the commercial or nonprofit character of an activity" be weighed in any fair use decision. If the Betamax were used to make copies for a commercial or profit-making purpose, such use would presumptively be unfair. The contrary presumption is appropriate here, however, because the District Court's findings plainly establish that time-shifting for private home use must be characterized as a noncommercial, nonprofit activity. Moreover, when one considers the nature of a televised copyrighted audiovisual work, see 17 U.S.C. § 107(2), and that time-shifting merely enables a viewer to see such a work which he had been invited to witness in its entirety free of charge, the fact that the entire work is reproduced, see id., at § 107(3), does not have its ordinary effect of militating against a finding of fair use.

This is not, however, the end of the inquiry because Congress has also directed us to consider "the effect of the use upon the potential market for or value of the copyrighted work." Id., at § 107(4). The purpose of copyright is to create incentives for creative effort. Even copying for noncommercial purposes may impair the copyright holder's ability to obtain the rewards that Congress intended him to have. But a use that has no demonstrable effect upon the potential market for, or the value of, the copyrighted work need not be prohibited in order to protect the author's incentive to create. The prohibition of such noncommercial uses would merely inhibit access to ideas without any countervailing benefit.

Thus, although every commercial use of copyrighted material is presumptively an unfair exploitation of the monopoly privilege that belongs to the owner of the copyright, noncommercial uses are a different matter. A challenge to a noncommercial use of a copyrighted work requires proof either that the particular use is harmful, or that if it should become widespread, it would adversely affect the potential market for the copyrighted work. Actual present harm need not be shown; such a requirement would leave the copyright holder with no defense against predictable damage. Nor is it necessary to show with certainty that future harm will result. What is necessary is a showing by a preponderance of the evidence that *some* meaningful likelihood of future harm exists. If the intended use is for commercial gain, that likelihood may be presumed. But if it is for a noncommercial purpose, the likelihood must be demonstrated.

In this case, respondents failed to carry their burden with regard to home time-shifting. The District Court described respondents' evidence as follows:

> "Plaintiffs' experts admitted at several points in the trial that the time-shifting without librarying would result in 'not a great deal of harm.' Plaintiffs' greatest concern about time-shifting is with 'a point of important philosophy that transcends even commercial judgment.' They fear that with any Betamax usage, 'invisible boundaries' are passed: 'the copyright owner has lost control over his program.' " 480 F.Supp., at 467.

Later in its opinion, the District Court observed:

> "Most of plaintiffs' predictions of harm hinge on speculation about audience viewing patterns and ratings, a measurement system which Sidney Sheinberg, MCA's president, calls a 'black art' because of the significant level of imprecision involved in the calculations." Id., at 469.

There was no need for the District Court to say much about past harm. "Plaintiffs have admitted that no actual harm to their copyrights has occurred to date." Id., at 451.

On the question of potential future harm from time-shifting, the District Court offered a more detailed analysis of the evidence. It rejected respondents' "fear that persons 'watching' the original telecast of a program will not be measured in the live audience and the ratings and revenues will decrease," by observing that current measurement technology allows the Betamax audience to be reflected. Id., at 466. It rejected respondents' prediction "that live television or movie audiences will decrease as more people watch Betamax tapes as an alternative," with the observation that "[t]here is no factual basis for [the underlying] assumption." Ibid. It rejected respondents' "fear that time-shifting will reduce audiences for telecast reruns," and concluded instead that "given current market practices, this should aid plaintiffs rather than harm them." Ibid. And it declared that respondents' suggestion "that theater or film rental exhibition of a program will suffer because of time-shift recording of that program" "lacks merit." 480 F.Supp., at 467.

After completing that review, the District Court restated its overall conclusion several times, in several different ways. "Harm from time-shifting is speculative and, at best, minimal." Ibid. "The audience benefits from the time-shifting capability have already been discussed. It is not implausible that benefits could also accrue to plaintiffs, broadcasters, and advertisers, as the Betamax makes it possible for more persons to view their broadcasts." Ibid. "No likelihood of harm was shown at trial, and plaintiffs admitted that there had been no actual harm to date." Id., at 468–469. "Testimony at trial suggested that Betamax may require adjustments in marketing strategy, but it did not establish even a likelihood of harm." Id., at 469. "Television production by plaintiffs today is more profitable than it has ever been, and, in five weeks of trial, there was no concrete evidence to suggest that the Betamax will change the studios' financial picture." Ibid.

The District Court's conclusions are buttressed by the fact that to the extent time-shifting expands public access to freely broadcast television programs, it yields societal benefits. Earlier this year, in Community Television of Southern California v. Gottfried, 459 U.S. 498, 508, n. 12 (1983), we acknowledged the public interest in making television broadcasting more available. Concededly, that interest is not unlimited. But it supports an interpretation of the concept of "fair use" that requires the copyright holder to demonstrate some likelihood of harm before he may condemn a private act of time-shifting as a violation of federal law.

When these factors are all weighed in the "equitable rule of reason" balance, we must conclude that this record amply supports the District Court's conclusion that home time-shifting is fair use. In light of the findings of the District Court regarding the state of the empirical data, it is clear that the Court of Appeals erred in holding that the statute as presently written bars such conduct.[40] * * *

---

40. The Court of Appeals chose not to engage in any "equitable rule of reason" analysis in this case. Instead, it assumed that the category of "fair use" is rigidly circumscribed by a requirement that every such use must be "productive." It therefore concluded that copying a television program merely to enable the viewer to receive information or entertainment that he would otherwise miss because of a personal scheduling conflict could never be fair use. That understanding of "fair use" was erroneous.

Congress has plainly instructed us that fair use analysis calls for a sensitive balancing of interests. The distinction between "productive" and "unproductive" uses may be helpful in calibrating the balance, but it cannot be wholly determinative. Although copying to promote a scholarly endeavor certainly has a stronger claim to fair use than copying to avoid interrupting a poker game, the question is not simply two-dimensional. For one thing, it is not true that all copyrights are fungible. Some copyrights govern material with broad potential secondary markets. Such material may well have a broader claim to protection because of the greater potential for commercial harm. Copying a news broadcast may have a stronger claim to fair use than copying a motion picture. And, of course, not all uses are fungible. Copying

JUSTICE BLACKMUN, with whom JUSTICE MARSHALL, JUSTICE POWELL, and JUSTICE REHNQUIST join, dissenting. * * *

There are situations, nevertheless, in which strict enforcement of this monopoly would inhibit the very "Progress of Science and useful Arts" that copyright is intended to promote. An obvious example is the researcher or scholar whose own work depends on the ability to refer to and to quote the work of prior scholars. * * * The scholar's work, in other words, produces external benefits from which everyone profits. In such a case, the fair use doctrine acts as a form of subsidy—albeit at the first author's expense—to permit the second author to make limited use of the first author's work for the public good. See Latman [Fair Use of Copyrighted Works, Copyr. Law Revision Study No. 14, 31 (1958)]; Gordon, Fair Use as Market Failure: A Structural Analysis of the *Betamax* Case and its Predecessors, 82 Colum.L.Rev. 1600, 1630 (1982).

A similar subsidy may be appropriate in a range of areas other than pure scholarship. The situations in which fair use is most commonly recognized are listed in § 107 itself; fair use may be found when a work is used "for purposes such as criticism, comment, news reporting, teaching, . . . scholarship, or research." The House and Senate Reports expand on this list somewhat, and other examples may be found in the case law. Each of these uses, however, reflects a common theme: each is a *productive* use, resulting in some added benefit to the public beyond that produced by the first author's work. The fair use doctrine, in other words, permits works to be used for "socially laudable purposes." See Copyright Office, Briefing Papers on Current Issues, reprinted in 1975 House Hearings 2051, 2055. I am aware of no case in which the reproduction of a copyrighted work for the sole benefit of the user has been held to be fair use. * * *

The making of a videotape recording for home viewing is an ordinary rather than a productive use of the Studios' copyrighted works. The District Court found that "Betamax owners use the copy for the same purpose as the original. They add nothing of their own." 480 F.Supp., at 453. Although applying the fair use doctrine to home VTR recording, as Sony argues, may increase public access to material broadcast free over the

for commercial gain has a much weaker claim to fair use than copying for personal enrichment. But the notion of social "productivity" cannot be a complete answer to this analysis. A teacher who copies to prepare lecture notes is clearly productive. But so is a teacher who copies for the sake of broadening his personal understanding of his specialty. Or a legislator who copies for the sake of broadening her understanding of what her constituents are watching; or a constituent who copies a news program to help make a decision on how to vote.

Making a copy of a copyrighted work for the convenience of a blind person is expressly identified by the House Committee Report as an example of fair use, with no suggestion that anything more than a purpose to entertain or to inform need motivate the copying. In a hospital setting, using a VTR to enable a patient to see programs he would otherwise miss has no productive purpose other than contributing to the psychological well-being of the patient. Virtually any time-shifting that increases viewer access to television programming may result in a comparable benefit. The statutory language does not identify any dichotomy between productive and nonproductive time-shifting, but does require consideration of the economic consequences of copying.

public airwaves, I think Sony's argument misconceives the nature of copyright. Copyright gives the author a right to limit or even to cut off access to his work. * * *

I recognize, nevertheless, that there are situations where permitting even an unproductive use would have no effect on the author's incentive to create, that is, where the use would not affect the value of, or the market for, the author's work. Photocopying an old newspaper clipping to send to a friend may be an example; pinning a quotation on one's bulletin board may be another. In each of these cases, the effect on the author is truly *de minimis*. Thus, even though these uses provide no benefit to the public at large, no purpose is served by preserving the author's monopoly, and the use may be regarded as fair. * * *

I therefore conclude that, at least when the proposed use is an unproductive one, a copyright owner need prove only a *potential* for harm to the market for or the value of the copyrighted work. * * *

The Studios have identified a number of ways in which VTR recording could damage their copyrights. VTR recording could reduce their ability to market their works in movie theaters and through the rental or sale of prerecorded videotapes or videodiscs; it also could reduce their rerun audience, and consequently the license fees available to them for repeated showings. Moreover, advertisers may be willing to pay for only "live" viewing audiences, if they believe VTR viewers will delete commercials or if rating services are unable to measure VTR use; if this is the case, VTR recording could reduce the license fees the Studios are able to charge even for first-run showings. Library-building may raise the potential for each of the types of harm identified by the Studios, and time-shifting may raise the potential for substantial harm as well. * * *

It is thus apparent from the record and from the findings of the District Court that time-shifting does have a substantial adverse effect upon the "potential market for" the Studios' copyrighted works. Accordingly, even under the formulation of the fair use doctrine advanced by Sony, time-shifting cannot be deemed a fair use. * * *

NOTES AND QUESTIONS ON "TAPING"

(1) The plaintiffs sought a rehearing in the Supreme Court, arguing that the issues should not be resolved "on the basis of facts that have demonstrably changed so radically in the five years since the district court made the findings on which this Court so heavily relies." They contended that technological innovations had increased the likelihood that commercials will be deleted from recordings or skipped during playback, thus reducing the licensing value of their works. Their petition was denied at 465 U.S. 1112 (1984). When the papers of Justice Marshall were opened to the public by the Library of Congress shortly after his death, they revealed that Justice Stevens' majority opinion in *Sony* was originally written as the dissent; Justice Blackmun had been assigned to write a majority opinion affirming defendants' liability, but it became the dissent when Justice

O'Connor was persuaded to join in Justice Stevens' opinion. Band and McLaughlin, The Marshall Papers: A Peek Behind the Scenes at the Making of *Sony v. Universal*, 17 Colum.-VLA J.L & Arts 427 (1993).

Sinclair, Fair Use Old and New: The *Betamax* Case and its Forebears, 33 Buff.L.Rev. 269 (1984), applauds the result in *Sony*, arguing that it is in step with the traditional understanding of fair use. Carter, Copyright Protection, The Right to Privacy and Signals that Enter the Home, 3 Cardozo Arts & Enter.L.J. 289 (1984), speculates on the implications for privacy, noting the traditional solicitude for conduct occurring within the home.

The distinction between productive and unproductive uses espoused by the dissenters in *Sony* is propounded at length in L. Seltzer, Exemptions and Fair Use in Copyright (1978). The Ninth Circuit in *Sony* had relied heavily on Seltzer in concluding that reproduction of a work in order to use it for its intrinsic purpose is not fair use—a proposition the court attempted to support by an analysis of the fair use factors: the copying did not further a traditionally accepted purpose of fair use; the nature of the works as entertainment counted against fair use; entire works had been reproduced; and the cumulative effect of mass reproduction serving the same purpose as the originals was sufficient to establish a tendency to diminish the plaintiffs' market. Was the Supreme Court correct in rejecting this analysis?

A different perspective on fair use is offered in Gordon, Fair Use as Market Failure: A Structural and Economic Analysis of the *Betamax* Case and its Predecessors, 82 Colum.L.Rev. 1600 (1982), which takes the view that "fair use is ordinarily granted when the market cannot be relied upon to allow socially desirable access to, and use of, copyrighted works," because of, say, high transaction costs, or the presence of externalities. See also Cirace, When Does Complete Copying * * * Constitute Fair Use? An Economic Analysis of the *Sony Betamax* and *Williams & Wilkins* Cases, 28 St. Louis U.L.J. 647 (1984). Lape, Transforming Fair Use: The Productive Use Factor in Fair Use Doctrine, 58 Alb.L.Rev. 677 (1995), worries that the emphasis on transformative uses displaces a more general analysis of the social utility of the defendant's use.

(2) The Board of Educational Services in Erie County, New York, was created under state law to provide educational services to local schools. It maintained a library of 4,500 videotapes, most of them obtained through off-the-air recording. A catalogue of its holdings was distributed to teachers, and upon request, a copy of the desired videotape would be furnished. In a suit brought by copyright owners, a fair use defense was unsuccessful. Encyclopedia Britannica Educational Corp. v. Crooks, 542 F.Supp. 1156 (W.D.N.Y.1982) (see also 558 F.Supp. 1247 (W.D.N.Y.1983)).

Representatives of various educational organizations, copyright proprietors, and creative guilds and unions, at the urging of the House Judiciary Committee, negotiated guidelines on the application of fair use to off-the-air recording by non-profit educational institutions. Since the guidelines were not completed until 1981, they cannot be considered part of the legislative history of the 1976 Act. They do, however, appear in the

Congressional Record with the endorsement of the Chair of the House Subcommittee with jurisdiction over intellectual property. The guidelines require that recordings be made only at the request of individual teachers. The tapes must be erased within 45 days. They may be used for instructional purposes (twice only) during the first 10 school days of the retention period, after which use is limited to "teacher evaluation." 127 Cong.Rec. 24048–49 (Oct. 14, 1981).

(3) A fair use defense raised by a defendant who copied plaintiff's videotape of the 1992 Los Angeles riots from an authorized network news broadcast and then transmitted the copy to other news organizations was rejected in Los Angeles News Service v. Reuters Television Int'l, Ltd., 942 F.Supp. 1265 (C.D.Cal.1996); the use was commercial and not transformative and it reduced the plaintiff's opportunity to market the work.[c]

A fair use defense also was unsuccessful in Pacific and Southern Co., Inc. v. Duncan, 744 F.2d 1490 (11th Cir.1984), cert. denied, 471 U.S. 1004 (1985), involving a commercial "news clipping" service that sold videotapes of television news broadcasts to the subjects of the news reports. The case is used to propound a constitutional theory of fair use and public access in Patterson, Free Speech, Copyright, and Fair Use, 40 Vand.L.Rev. 1 (1985). Another news clipping case involving the Cable News Network generated considerable controversy. A defendant preliminarily enjoined "from copying or selling any of [CNN's] programming" challenged the scope of the injunction before the Eleventh Circuit. Holding that the scope of relief for infringement was constrained by the requirement of copyright registration in § 411, the court concluded that an injunction could not extend to works not yet in existence or to existing works that had not been registered. Cable News Network, Inc. v. Video Monitoring Services, 940 F.2d 1471 (11th Cir.1991). However, the decision was vacated for rehearing *en banc,* 949 F.2d 378 (11th Cir.1991), and the appeal was ultimately dismissed. 959 F.2d 188 (11th Cir.1992). See also Olan Mills, Inc. v. Linn Photo Co., 23 F.3d 1345 (8th Cir.1994), holding that injunctions may issue "regardless of the registration status of the copyright."

(4) Suppose a consumer rents a videocassette of a favorite movie and makes a copy for personal use. A fair use? Soon after *Sony* the movie

---

c. The same plaintiff overcame a fair use defense to unauthorized performance when the Ninth Circuit reversed a summary judgement in favor of a local television station that obtained a copy of the plaintiff's tape from another station and without permission broadcast thirty seconds of the tape during several news programs; the appellate court was concerned that allowing such unlicensed use would undermine the investments made by independent news organizations like the plaintiff. Los Angeles News Service v. KCAL–TV Channel 9, 108 F.3d 1119 (9th Cir.1997), cert. denied, 118 S.Ct. 81 (1997). Compare Infinity Broadcasting Corp. v. Kirkwood, 965 F.Supp. 553 (S.D.N.Y.1997), involving an infringement claim by the operator of several radio stations against a defendant who set up receiving equipment connected to telephone lines in ten cities to allow subscribing advertisers to monitor by telephone the local radio programs that they sponsored. Despite the commercial nature of the use, the court held it was fair; the use had no apparent impact on the economic value of the broadcasts and any loss of potential licensing fees was irrelevant since the use was not a traditional or likely to be developed market for the plaintiff.

industry sought legislation requiring manufacturers of VCRs to equip their machines with a microchip that would interrupt recording when activated by a special signal incorporated into copyrighted tapes. See 32 Pat., Tm. & Copyr.J. (BNA) 605 (1986). Should the proposal have been enacted? A survey in 1996 estimated that there are more than 330 million unauthorized movie videocassettes in American households and that forty per cent of consumers admit to copying; industry losses are put at $370 million per year. Many videocassettes now incorporate copy protection aimed at foiling the making of useable copies. Video Week, Oct. 21, 1996, p. 2. The introduction of digital video discs that store full-length motion pictures with quality far superior to videocassettes was delayed by the movie studios' concerns over piracy. The studios agreed to release their products in the new format only after negotiating an agreement with the equipment manufacturers on a copy protection scheme that scrambles the video content on the discs. The studios also support legislation that would prohibit attempts to circumvent the anti-copying technology. Greenstein, Will DVD Live Up to All the Hype?, L.A. Times, Mar. 24, 1997, p. D1.

Movie makers are aggressively pursuing commercial copiers—chiefly street vendors selling cheap copies to consumers or video rental outlets that supplement their supply of popular titles with unauthorized copies. In some instances films have even been "borrowed" from editing facilities or advance screenings to produce copies of movies that have not yet been released in theaters. The Motion Picture Association of America has an investigatory staff to search out commercial pirates, backed by the substantial criminal penalties for piracy in 18 U.S.C.A. § 2319. See Lee, Video Bootleggers Cut Into Studio Profits, New York Times, July 7, 1997, p. D1.

(5) The issue of home taping looms even larger in the music industry. Does *Sony* compel the conclusion that off-the-air taping of musical works is a fair use? (Is such taping likely to be only for purposes of time-shifting?) Is it fair use to make a cassette copy of a newly-purchased compact disc for use in your car's cassette player? For use by a friend in her cassette player? Of what relevance are the results of a 1985 survey commissioned by the Office of Technology Assessment indicating that 7 out of 10 people believe copying "personal possessions" such as records and programing received on television is acceptable, and that a majority believe that copying and trading records or software with friends is also acceptable? See O.T.A., Intellectual Property Rights in an Age of Electronics and Information 209 (1987). At a Congressional hearing in 1985 economist Alan Greenspan estimated that home taping of musical works had resulted in about $1.5 billion in displaced sales during the preceding year.[d]

The stakes for the music industry were raised by the development of digital audio tape, or DAT, capable of recording in a digital format—the

---

d. Equipment manufacturers and record companies are now touting a new music format that would replace CDs with a disc called DVD audio that offers six-channel sound and higher fidelity. The record companies are demanding inclusion of anti-piracy technology into the new discs to prevent the production of unauthorized copies. Brinkley, Music CDs Face Upscale Competitor, New York Times, July 28, 1997, p. A1.

tape equivalent of a compact disc. With a DAT recorder, a consumer could make pristine copies of compact discs or other digital recordings or broadcasts. The record companies initially sought legislation barring the importation of DAT recorders (they are of course made in Japan) unless equipped with a scanning device that would disable the machine when activated by a signal that could be incorporated into a copyrighted recording. Testifying in support of the bill, singer Emmylou Harris said, "I can't think of any other business in America today where people would think they're entitled to a second item for free just because they paid for the first one." 34 Pat., Tm. & Copyr.J. (BNA) 51 (1987). The encoded signal was to consist of the removal of a "notch" of high frequency sound from the recorded music. The proposal lost momentum when the National Bureau of Standards confirmed that the notch audibly distorted the encoded recordings.

The issue of digital recording was ultimately resolved when representatives of the electronics industry, songwriters, and the record companies agreed on a new anti-copying device and a system of royalties on digital recording equipment and recording media. Appearing before Congress in favor of the royalty provisions in the proposed legislation, the president of Capitol–EMI Music claimed that eighty-five per cent of all pop recordings and ninety-five per cent of all classical recordings do not recover their costs. He argued that the industry is sustained by a small percentage of "hits," and uncompensated copying of those popular works means less money to develop new artists and to produce music in less popular areas such as jazz, gospel, folk, and classical. 43 Pat., Tm. & Copyr.J. (BNA) 344 (1992).

The agreement on digital recording was enacted as the Home Audio Recording Act, Pub.L. 102–563, 106 Stat. 4237 (1992). The Act is codified as Chapter 10 in Title 17. It applies to both current and future digital audio recording technologies.[e] Section 1002 prohibits the importation, manufacture, or distribution of digital audio recording devices unless the device is equipped with a "serial copy management system"—an electronic system that prevents "serial copying," defined in § 1001 essentially as the digital copying of a copy of a digital recording. (The system does not prevent users from making an unlimited number of copies of an *original* digital recording.) There is also a prohibition in § 1002 against importing, manufacturing, or distributing devices designed to circumvent the serial copy management system.

Importers and manufacturers who distribute digital audio recording devices are required to pay a royalty based on the price of the unit. There is also a royalty imposed on the distribution of digital audio recording media such as blank tapes. § 1003. The royalties are deposited with the

e. Although used by professionals, the digital audio tape recorders that spawned the 1992 amendment were a flop with consumers, primarily because the record companies, still fearful that the recorders would be used to duplicate CDs, generally refused to release their records in pre-recorded DAT format. However, the amendment applies to other digital audio recording formats such as recordable discs; it does not apply to equipment designed primarily for copying other digital works such as video or computer programs. See § 1001(3).

Copyright Office. Two-thirds of the money is to be distributed to the record companies and performers; the remaining one-third goes to the music publishers and composers. § 1006.

Finally, § 1008 puts to rest claims of contributory infringement against equipment manufacturers and direct infringement against consumers who make noncommercial use of either digital or analog recording equipment to copy musical recordings.

PARODY

BENNY v. LOEW'S INC., 239 F.2d 532 (9th Cir.1956). Loew's had made a successful movie (starring Charles Boyer, Ingrid Bergman, and Joseph Cotten) out of a successful play called "Gas Light." In 1945 Jack Benny with permission did a fifteen-minute burlesque on radio. In 1952 without permission CBS and Benny did a half-hour television show that was also a burlesque or parody of "Gas Light." Loew's sought to enjoin further telecasts of the show.

"The district court found, as a fact, that appellants' television play was copied by them, in substantial part, from appellees' motion picture photoplay, 'Gas Light,' and that the 'part so copied was and is a substantial part of [appellants' television] play, and of the copyrightable and copyrighted material in [appellees'] motion picture photoplay.' The district court found as facts '(1) that the locale and period of the works are the same; (2) the main setting is the same; (3) the characters are generally the same; (4) the story points are practically identical; (5) the development of the story, the treatment (except that defendants' treatment is burlesque), the incidents, the sequences of events, the points of suspense, the climax are almost identical and finally, (6) there has been a detailed borrowing of much of the dialogue with some variation in wording. There has been a substantial taking by defendants from the plaintiffs' copyrighted property.' 131 F.Supp. 171. Accordingly, the district court found that appellants were guilty of infringement of appellees' photoplay, 'Gas Light.' * * *

"Appellants' chief defense is that the use which they made of appellees' photoplay in their television play was a fair use, by reason of the fact that the material which they appropriated from the motion picture, 'Gas Light,' was used in the creation of a burlesque, and that by reason of such circumstance, they are not guilty of infringement.

" * * * But up to the time of the present controversy, no federal court, in any adjudication, has supposed that there was a doctrine of fair use applicable to copying the substance of a dramatic work, and presenting it, with few variations, as a burlesque. The fact that a serious dramatic work is copied practically verbatim, and then presented with actors walking on their hands or with other grotesqueries, does not avoid infringement of the copyright. * * *

"The finding of the district court that appellants had copied a substantial part of appellees' photoplay is clearly supported by the evidence. The judgment is affirmed upon the findings of fact and conclusions of law of the district court and for the reasons set forth in the opinion of Judge James M. Carter."

———————

COLUMBIA PICTURES CORP. V. NATIONAL BROADCASTING CO., 137 F.Supp. 348 (S.D.Cal.1955). This was a companion to the "Gas Light" case, decided by the same district judge. Sid Caesar and Imogene Coca presented over the defendant's television network a burlesque of the motion picture "From Here to Eternity," entitled "From Here to Obscurity." From the summaries it appears that the burlesque was clearly different in episode, spirit, and manner. For example, an important element in the novel and the film was the refusal of Prewitt, an army bugler, to engage in boxing because he had once blinded a friend. In the skit, "Montgomery Bugle" says he won't fight because he once "hit his brother in the eye and the eyeball was so hard it broke his hand so he couldn't hold the bugle." In holding for the defendant, Judge Carter expressed the hope that the two cases would "stride through the hazard of judicial review and still remain consistent companions." To "speed this case on its way" he disclaimed submitting a formal opinion, but in a "Comment" suggested these principles:

"(a) When the alleged infringing work is of the same character as the copyrighted work, viz., a serious work with a taking from another serious copyrighted work, then the line is drawn more strictly than when a farce or comedy or burlesque takes from a serious copyrighted work or vice versa.

"(b) In historical burlesque a part of the content is used to conjure up, at least the general image, of the original. Some limited taking should be permitted under the doctrine of fair use, in the case of burlesque, to bring about this recalling or conjuring up of the original.

"(c) Burlesque may ordinarily take the locale, the theme, the setting, situation and even bare basic plots without infringement, since such matters are ordinarily not protectible.

"(d) The doctrine of fair use permits burlesque to go somewhat farther so long as the taking is not substantial. It may take an incident of the copyrighted story, a developed character (subject to the limited right of an author in certain situations, * * *) a title (subject to right of protection under unfair competition, * * *) some small part of the development of the story, possibly some small amount of the dialogue.

"(e) When burlesque takes more than the matter ordinarily not protected, and referred to above, it runs a calculated risk, that on all the facts involved, a trier of fact may find the taking substantial.

"(f) The defense, 'I only burlesqued' the copyrighted material is not *per se* a defense. To hold otherwise would seriously jeopardize rights of property in copyrights and investments in such works, and would ultimately seriously damage the prices to be paid to authors for their literary works. * * *"

The "From Here to Eternity" case was not carried beyond the District Court.   The Supreme Court granted certiorari in the "Gas Light" case but then divided evenly and thus affirmed the decision of the Court of Appeals without opinion.   Columbia Broadcasting System, Inc. v. Loew's, Inc., 356 U.S. 43 (1958).

ELSMERE MUSIC, INC. v. NATIONAL BROADCASTING CO., 482 F.Supp. 741 (S.D.N.Y.), aff'd, 623 F.2d 252 (2d Cir.1980).   "In the dark days of 1977, when the City of New York teetered on the brink of bankruptcy and its name had become synonymous with sin, there came forth upon the land a message of hope.   On the television screens of America there appeared the image of a top-hatted Broadway showgirl, backed by an advancing phalanx of dancers, chanting:

'I–I–I–I–I–I Love New Y-o-o-o-o-o-o-rk!'

Repeated again and again (to musical accompaniment), with increasing intensity throughout the commercial, this slogan was to become the theme for an extensive series of advertisements that were to bring the nation assurances from the stars of Broadway, ranging from Dracula to the Cowardly Lion, that all was well, and that they too *loved* New York.   * * *

"The success of this campaign did not go unnoticed in the entertainment world.   On May 20, 1978, the popular weekly variety program 'Saturday Night Live' ('SNL') performed a comedy sketch over defendant National Broadcasting Company's network.   In this sketch the cast of SNL, portraying the mayor and the members of the Chamber of Commerce of the biblical city of Sodom, are seen discussing Sodom's poor public image with out of towners, and the effect this was having on the tourist trade.   In an attempt to recast the City's image in a more positive light, a new advertising campaign emphasizing the less sensational aspects of Sodom nightlife is unveiled.   As the highlight of this campaign the song 'I Love Sodom' is sung *a cappella* by a chorus line of three SNL regulars to the tune of 'I Love New York,' with the words 'I Love Sodom' repeated three times."

Judge Goettel held that the borrowing was a fair use.   In a per curiam affirmance consisting chiefly of a footnote, the Second Circuit took a broad view of the precedents:

"The District Court concluded, among other things, that the parody did not make more extensive use of appellant's song than was necessary to 'conjure up' the original.   482 F.Supp. at 747.   While we agree with this conclusion, we note that the concept of 'conjuring up' an original came into the copyright law not as a limitation on how much of an original may be used, but as a recognition that a parody frequently needs to be more than a fleeting evocation of an original in order to make its humorous point. Columbia Pictures Corp. v. National Broadcasting Co., 137 F.Supp. 348, 354 (S.D.Cal.1955).   A parody is entitled at least to 'conjure up' the original.   Even more extensive use would still be fair use, provided the parody builds upon the original, using the original as a known element of modern culture and contributing something new for humorous effect or commentary.''

Campbell v. Acuff–Rose Music, Inc.

Supreme Court of the United States, 1994.
510 U.S. 569, 114 S.Ct. 1164.

■ JUSTICE SOUTER delivered the opinion of the Court.

We are called upon to decide whether 2 Live Crew's commercial parody of Roy Orbison's song, ''Oh, Pretty Woman,'' may be a fair use within the meaning of the Copyright Act of 1976, 17 U.S.C. § 107 (1988 ed. and Supp. IV).   Although the District Court granted summary judgment for 2 Live Crew, the Court of Appeals reversed, holding the defense of fair use barred by the song's commercial character and excessive borrowing.   Because we hold that a parody's commercial character is only one element to be weighed in a fair use enquiry, and that insufficient consideration was given to the nature of parody in weighing the degree of copying, we reverse and remand.

I

In 1964, Roy Orbison and William Dees wrote a rock ballad called ''Oh, Pretty Woman'' and assigned their rights in it to respondent Acuff–Rose Music, Inc.   See Appendix A.   Acuff–Rose registered the song for copyright protection.

Petitioners Luther R. Campbell, Christopher Wongwon, Mark Ross, and David Hobbs, are collectively known as 2 Live Crew, a popular rap music group.   In 1989, Campbell wrote a song entitled ''Pretty Woman'' which he later described in an affidavit as intended, ''through comical lyrics, to satirize the original work....''   On July 5, 1989, 2 Live Crew's manager informed Acuff–Rose that 2 Live Crew had written a parody of ''Oh, Pretty Woman,'' that they would afford all credit for ownership and authorship of the original song to Acuff–Rose, Dees, and Orbison, and that they were willing to pay a fee for the use they wished to make of it. Enclosed with the letter were a copy of the lyrics and a recording of 2 Live Crew's song.   See Appendix B.   Acuff–Rose's agent refused permission, stating that ''I am aware of the success enjoyed by 'The 2 Live Crews', but I must inform you that we cannot permit the use of a parody of 'Oh, Pretty Woman'.''   Nonetheless, in June or July 1989, 2 Live Crew released records, cassette tapes, and compact discs of ''Pretty Woman'' in a collection of songs entitled ''As Clean As They Wanna Be.''   The albums and compact discs identify the authors of ''Pretty Woman'' as Orbison and Dees and its publisher as Acuff–Rose.   * * *

II

It is uncontested here that 2 Live Crew's song would be an infringement of Acuff–Rose's rights in ''Oh, Pretty Woman,'' under the Copyright

Act of 1976, 17 U.S.C. § 106, but for a finding of fair use through parody.[4]
* * *

In Folsom v. Marsh, 9 F. Cas. 342 (No. 4,901) (CCD Mass.1841), Justice Story distilled the essence of law and methodology from the earlier cases: "look to the nature and objects of the selections made, the quantity and value of the materials used, and the degree in which the use may prejudice the sale, or diminish the profits, or supersede the objects, of the original work." Id. at 348. Thus expressed, fair use remained exclusively judge-made doctrine until the passage of the 1976 Copyright Act * * *.

The task is not to be simplified with bright-line rules, for the statute, like the doctrine it recognizes, calls for case-by-case analysis. [Harper & Row, Publishers, Inc. v. Nation Enterprises, 471 U.S. 539, 560 (1985); Sony Corp. of America v. Universal City Studios, Inc., 464 U.S. 417, 448 and n. 31 (1984); H.R.Rep. No. 94–1476, pp. 65–66 (1976); S.Rep. No. 94–473, p. 62 (1975).] The text employs the terms "including" and "such as" in the preamble paragraph to indicate the "illustrative and not limitative" function of the examples given, § 101; see *Harper & Row,* supra, 471 U.S., at 561, which thus provide only general guidance about the sorts of copying that courts and Congress most commonly had found to be fair uses. Nor may the four statutory factors be treated in isolation, one from another. All are to be explored, and the results weighed together, in light of the purposes of copyright. See Leval [Toward a Fair Use Standard, 103 Harv.L.Rev. 1105, 1110–11 (1990).] [10] * * *

A

The first factor in a fair use enquiry is "the purpose and character of the use, including whether such use is of a commercial nature or is for nonprofit educational purposes." § 107(1). This factor draws on Justice Story's formulation, "the nature and objects of the selections made." Folsom v. Marsh, supra, at 348. The enquiry here may be guided by the examples given in the preamble to § 107, looking to whether the use is for

---

4. * * * 2 Live Crew concedes that it is not entitled to a compulsory license under § 115 because its arrangement changes "the basic melody or fundamental character" of the original. § 115(a)(2).

10. Because the fair use enquiry often requires close questions of judgment as to the extent of permissible borrowing in cases involving parodies (or other critical works), courts may also wish to bear in mind that the goals of the copyright law, "to stimulate the creation and publication of edifying matter," Leval 1134, are not always best served by automatically granting injunctive relief when parodists are found to have gone beyond the bounds of fair use. See 17 U.S.C. § 502(a) (court "*may* ... grant ... injunctions on such terms as it may deem reasonable to prevent or restrain infringement") (emphasis added); Leval 1132 (while in the "vast majority of cases, [an injunctive] remedy is justified because most infringements are simply piracy," such cases are "worlds apart from many of those raising reasonable contentions of fair use" where "there may be a strong public interest in the publication of the secondary work [and] the copyright owner's interest may be adequately protected by an award of damages for whatever infringement is found"); Abend v. MCA, Inc., 863 F.2d 1465, 1479 (CA9 1988) (finding "special circumstances" that would cause "great injustice" to defendants and "public injury" were injunction to issue), aff'd sub nom. Stewart v. Abend, 495 U.S. 207 (1990).

criticism, or comment, or news reporting, and the like, see § 107. The central purpose of this investigation is to see, in Justice Story's words, whether the new work merely "supersede[s] the objects" of the original creation, Folsom v. Marsh, supra, at 348; accord, *Harper & Row,* supra, at 562 ("supplanting" the original), or instead adds something new, with a further purpose or different character, altering the first with new expression, meaning, or message; it asks, in other words, whether and to what extent the new work is "transformative." Leval 1111. Although such transformative use is not absolutely necessary for a finding of fair use, *Sony,* supra, at 455, n. 40,[11] the goal of copyright, to promote science and the arts, is generally furthered by the creation of transformative works. Such works thus lie at the heart of the fair use doctrine's guarantee of breathing space within the confines of copyright, see, e.g., *Sony,* supra, at 478–480 (BLACKMUN, J., dissenting), and the more transformative the new work, the less will be the significance of other factors, like commercialism, that may weigh against a finding of fair use.

This Court has only once before even considered whether parody may be fair use, and that time issued no opinion because of the Court's equal division. Benny v. Loew's Inc., 239 F.2d 532 (CA9 1956), aff'd sub nom. Columbia Broadcasting System, Inc. v. Loew's Inc., 356 U.S. 43 (1958). Suffice it to say now that parody has an obvious claim to transformative value, as Acuff–Rose itself does not deny. Like less ostensibly humorous forms of criticism, it can provide social benefit, by shedding light on an earlier work, and, in the process, creating a new one. We thus line up with the courts that have held that parody, like other comment or criticism, may claim fair use under § 107. See, e.g., Fisher v. Dees, 794 F.2d 432 (CA9 1986) ("When Sonny Sniffs Glue," a parody of "When Sunny Gets Blue," is fair use); Elsmere Music, Inc. v. National Broadcasting Co., 482 F.Supp. 741 (SDNY), aff'd, 623 F.2d 252 (CA2 1980) ("I Love Sodom," a "Saturday Night Live" television parody of "I Love New York" is fair use); see also House Report, p. 65; Senate Report, p. 61, U.S.Code Cong. & Admin.News 1976, pp. 5659, 5678 ("[U]se in a parody of some of the content of the work parodied" may be fair use).

The germ of parody lies in the definition of the Greek *parodeia,* quoted in Judge Nelson's Court of Appeals dissent, as "a song sung alongside another." 972 F.2d, at 1440, quoting 7 Encyclopedia Britannica 768 (15th ed. 1975). Modern dictionaries accordingly describe a parody as a "literary or artistic work that imitates the characteristic style of an author or a work for comic effect or ridicule," [12] or as a "composition in prose or verse in which the characteristic turns of thought and phrase in an author or class of authors are imitated in such a way as to make them appear ridiculous." [13] For the purposes of copyright law, the nub of the definitions, and

---

11. The obvious statutory exception to this focus on transformative uses is the straight reproduction of multiple copies for classroom distribution.

12. The American Heritage Dictionary 1317 (3d ed. 1992).

13. 11 The Oxford English Dictionary 247 (2d ed. 1989).

the heart of any parodist's claim to quote from existing material, is the use of some elements of a prior author's composition to create a new one that, at least in part, comments on that author's works. See, e.g., Fisher v. Dees, supra, at 437; MCA, Inc. v. Wilson, 677 F.2d 180, 185 (CA2 1981). If, on the contrary, the commentary has no critical bearing on the substance or style of the original composition, which the alleged infringer merely uses to get attention or to avoid the drudgery in working up something fresh, the claim to fairness in borrowing from another's work diminishes accordingly (if it does not vanish), and other factors, like the extent of its commerciality, loom larger.[14] Parody needs to mimic an original to make its point, and so has some claim to use the creation of its victim's (or collective victims') imagination, whereas satire can stand on its own two feet and so requires justification for the very act of borrowing.[15] See Ibid.; Bisceglia, Parody and Copyright Protection: Turning the Balancing Act Into a Juggling Act, in ASCAP, Copyright Law Symposium, No. 34, p. 25 (1987).

The fact that parody can claim legitimacy for some appropriation does not, of course, tell either parodist or judge much about where to draw the line. Like a book review quoting the copyrighted material criticized, parody may or may not be fair use, and petitioner's suggestion that any parodic use is presumptively fair has no more justification in law or fact than the equally hopeful claim that any use for news reporting should be presumed fair, see *Harper & Row,* 471 U.S., at 561. The Act has no hint of an evidentiary preference for parodists over their victims, and no workable presumption for parody could take account of the fact that parody often shades into satire when society is lampooned through its creative artifacts, or that a work may contain both parodic and nonparodic elements. Accordingly, parody, like any other use, has to work its way through the relevant factors, and be judged case by case, in light of the ends of the copyright law.

Here, the District Court held, and the Court of Appeals assumed, that 2 Live Crew's "Pretty Woman" contains parody, commenting on and criticizing the original work, whatever it may have to say about society at large. As the District Court remarked, the words of 2 Live Crew's song

---

14. A parody that more loosely targets an original than the parody presented here may still be sufficiently aimed at an original work to come within our analysis of parody. If a parody whose wide dissemination in the market runs the risk of serving as a substitute for the original or licensed derivatives (see infra, discussing factor four), it is more incumbent on one claiming fair use to establish the extent of transformation and the parody's critical relationship to the original. By contrast, when there is little or no risk of market substitution, whether because of the large extent of transformation of the earlier work, the new work's minimal distribution in the market, the small extent to which it borrows from an original, or other factors, taking parodic aim at an original is a less critical factor in the analysis, and looser forms of parody may be found to be fair use, as may satire with lesser justification for the borrowing than would otherwise be required.

15. Satire has been defined as a work "in which prevalent follies or vices are assailed with ridicule," 14 The Oxford English Dictionary 500 (2d ed. 1989), or are "attacked through irony, derision, or wit," The American Heritage Dictionary 1604 (3d ed. 1992).

copy the original's first line, but then "quickly degenerat[e] into a play on words, substituting predictable lyrics with shocking ones ... [that] derisively demonstrat[e] how bland and banal the Orbison song seems to them." 754 F.Supp., at 1155 (footnote omitted). Judge Nelson, dissenting below, came to the same conclusion, that the 2 Live Crew song "was clearly intended to ridicule the white-bread original" and "reminds us that sexual congress with nameless streetwalkers is not necessarily the stuff of romance and is not necessarily without its consequences. The singers (there are several) have the same thing on their minds as did the lonely man with the nasal voice, but here there is no hint of wine and roses." 972 F.2d, at 1442. Although the majority below had difficulty discerning any criticism of the original in 2 Live Crew's song, it assumed for purposes of its opinion that there was some. Id., at 1435–1436, and n. 8.

We have less difficulty in finding that critical element in 2 Live Crew's song than the Court of Appeals did, although having found it we will not take the further step of evaluating its quality. The threshold question when fair use is raised in defense of parody is whether a parodic character may reasonably be perceived.[16] Whether, going beyond that, parody is in good taste or bad does not and should not matter to fair use. * * *

The Court of Appeals, however, immediately cut short the enquiry into 2 Live Crew's fair use claim by confining its treatment of the first factor essentially to one relevant fact, the commercial nature of the use. The court then inflated the significance of this fact by applying a presumption ostensibly culled from *Sony,* that "every commercial use of copyrighted material is presumptively ... unfair...." *Sony,* 464 U.S., at 451. In giving virtually dispositive weight to the commercial nature of the parody, the Court of Appeals erred.

The language of the statute makes clear that the commercial or nonprofit educational purpose of a work is only one element of the first factor enquiry into its purpose and character. * * * If, indeed, commerciality carried presumptive force against a finding of fairness, the presumption would swallow nearly all of the illustrative uses listed in the preamble paragraph of § 107, including news reporting, comment, criticism, teaching, scholarship, and research, since these activities "are generally conducted for profit in this country." *Harper & Row,* supra, at 592 (Brennan, J., dissenting). Congress could not have intended such a rule, which certainly is not inferable from the common-law cases, arising as they did from the world of letters in which Samuel Johnson could pronounce that "[n]o man but a blockhead ever wrote, except for money." 3 Boswell's Life of Johnson 19 (G. Hill ed. 1934). * * *

16. The only further judgment, indeed, that a court may pass on a work goes to an assessment of whether the parodic element is slight or great, and the copying small or extensive in relation to the parodic element, for a work with slight parodic element and extensive copying will be more likely to merely "supersede the objects" of the original. See infra, discussing factors three and four.

B

The second statutory factor, "the nature of the copyrighted work," § 107(2), draws on Justice Story's expression, the "value of the materials used." Folsom v. Marsh, 9 F.Cas., at 348. This factor calls for recognition that some works are closer to the core of intended copyright protection than others, with the consequence that fair use is more difficult to establish when the former works are copied.   * * *   We agree with both the District Court and the Court of Appeals that the Orbison original's creative expression for public dissemination falls within the core of the copyright's protective purposes. 754 F.Supp., at 1155–1156; 972 F.2d, at 1437. This fact, however, is not much help in this case, or ever likely to help much in separating the fair use sheep from the infringing goats in a parody case, since parodies almost invariably copy publicly known, expressive works.

C

The third factor asks whether "the amount and substantiality of the portion used in relation to the copyrighted work as a whole," § 107(3) (or, in Justice Story's words, "the quantity and value of the materials used," Folsom v. Marsh, supra, at 348) are reasonable in relation to the purpose of the copying. Here, attention turns to the persuasiveness of a parodist's justification for the particular copying done, and the enquiry will harken back to the first of the statutory factors, for, as in prior cases, we recognize that the extent of permissible copying varies with the purpose and character of the use.   * * *

The District Court considered the song's parodic purpose in finding that 2 Live Crew had not helped themselves overmuch. 754 F.Supp., at 1156–1157. The Court of Appeals disagreed, stating that "[w]hile it may not be inappropriate to find that no more was taken than necessary, the copying was qualitatively substantial.... We conclude that taking the heart of the original and making it the heart of a new work was to purloin a substantial portion of the essence of the original." 972 F.2d, at 1438.

The Court of Appeals is of course correct that this factor calls for thought not only about the quantity of the materials used, but about their quality and importance, too. In *Harper & Row,* for example, the Nation had taken only some 300 words out of President Ford's memoirs, but we signalled the significance of the quotations in finding them to amount to "the heart of the book," the part most likely to be newsworthy and important in licensing serialization. 471 U.S., at 564–566, 568 (internal quotation marks omitted). We also agree with the Court of Appeals that whether "a substantial portion of the infringing work was copied verbatim" from the copyrighted work is a relevant question, see id., at 565, for it may reveal a dearth of transformative character or purpose under the first factor, or a greater likelihood of market harm under the fourth; a work composed primarily of an original, particularly its heart, with little added or changed, is more likely to be a merely superseding use, fulfilling demand for the original.

Where we part company with the court below is in applying these guides to parody, and in particular to parody in the song before us. Parody presents a difficult case. Parody's humor, or in any event its comment, necessarily springs from recognizable allusion to its object through distorted imitation. Its art lies in the tension between a known original and its parodic twin. When parody takes aim at a particular original work, the parody must be able to "conjure up" at least enough of that original to make the object of its critical wit recognizable. See, e.g., *Elsmere Music*, 623 F.2d, at 253, n. 1; Fisher v. Dees, 794 F.2d, at 438–439. What makes for this recognition is quotation of the original's most distinctive or memorable features, which the parodist can be sure the audience will know. Once enough has been taken to assure identification, how much more is reasonable will depend, say, on the extent to which the song's overriding purpose and character is to parody the original or, in contrast, the likelihood that the parody may serve as a market substitute for the original. But using some characteristic features cannot be avoided.

We think the Court of Appeals was insufficiently appreciative of parody's need for the recognizable sight or sound when it ruled 2 Live Crew's use unreasonable as a matter of law. It is true, of course, that 2 Live Crew copied the characteristic opening bass riff (or musical phrase) of the original, and true that the words of the first line copy the Orbison lyrics. But if quotation of the opening riff and the first line may be said to go to the "heart" of the original, the heart is also what most readily conjures up the song for parody, and it is the heart at which parody takes aim. Copying does not become excessive in relation to parodic purpose merely because the portion taken was the original's heart. If 2 Live Crew had copied a significantly less memorable part of the original, it is difficult to see how its parodic character would have come through. See Fisher v. Dees, 794 F.2d, at 439.

This is not, of course, to say that anyone who calls himself a parodist can skim the cream and get away scot free. In parody, as in news reporting, see *Harper & Row,* supra, context is everything, and the question of fairness asks what else the parodist did besides go to the heart of the original. It is significant that 2 Live Crew not only copied the first line of the original, but thereafter departed markedly from the Orbison lyrics for its own ends. 2 Live Crew not only copied the bass riff and repeated it, but also produced otherwise distinctive sounds, interposing "scraper" noise, overlaying the music with solos in different keys, and altering the drum beat. See 754 F.Supp., at 1155. This is not a case, then, where "a substantial portion" of the parody itself is composed of a "verbatim" copying of the original. It is not, that is, a case where the parody is so insubstantial, as compared to the copying, that the third factor must be resolved as a matter of law against the parodists.

Suffice it to say here that, as to the lyrics, we think the Court of Appeals correctly suggested that "no more was taken than necessary," 972 F.2d, at 1438, but just for that reason, we fail to see how the copying can be excessive in relation to its parodic purpose, even if the portion taken is the original's "heart." As to the music, we express no opinion whether repetition of the bass riff is excessive copying, and we remand to permit evaluation of the amount taken, in light of the song's parodic purpose and character, its transformative elements, and considerations of the potential for market substitution sketched more fully below.

D

The fourth fair use factor is "the effect of the use upon the potential market for or value of the copyrighted work." § 107(4). It requires courts to consider not only the extent of market harm caused by the particular actions of the alleged infringer, but also "whether unrestricted and widespread conduct of the sort engaged in by the defendant . . . would result in a substantially adverse impact on the potential market" for the original. Nimmer § 13.05[A][4], p. 13–102.61 (footnote omitted); accord *Harper & Row,* 471 U.S., at 569; Senate Report, p. 65; *Folsom v. Marsh,* 9 F.Cas., at 349. The enquiry "must take account not only of harm to the original but also of harm to the market for derivative works." *Harper & Row,* supra, 471 U.S. at 568. * * *

* * * In assessing the likelihood of significant market harm, the Court of Appeals quoted from language in *Sony* that " '[i]f the intended use is for commercial gain, that likelihood may be presumed. But if it is for a noncommercial purpose, the likelihood must be demonstrated.' " 972 F.2d, at 1438, quoting *Sony,* 464 U.S., at 451. * * *

No "presumption" or inference of market harm that might find support in *Sony* is applicable to a case involving something beyond mere duplication for commercial purposes. *Sony's* discussion of a presumption contrasts a context of verbatim copying of the original in its entirety for commercial purposes, with the noncommercial context of *Sony* itself (home copying of television programming). In the former circumstances, what *Sony* said simply makes common sense: when a commercial use amounts to mere duplication of the entirety of an original, it clearly "supersede[s] the objects," *Folsom v. Marsh,* 9 F.Cas., at 348, of the original and serves as a market replacement for it, making it likely that cognizable market harm to the original will occur. *Sony,* 464 U.S., at 451. But when, on the contrary, the second use is transformative, market substitution is at least less certain, and market harm may not be so readily inferred. Indeed, as to parody pure and simple, it is more likely that the new work will not affect the market for the original in a way cognizable under this factor, that is, by acting as a substitute for it ("supersed[ing] [its] objects"). * * *

We do not, of course, suggest that a parody may not harm the market at all, but when a lethal parody, like a scathing theater review, kills demand for the original, it does not produce a harm cognizable under the Copyright Act. Because "parody may quite legitimately aim at garroting the original, destroying it commercially as well as artistically," B. Kaplan, An Unhurried View of Copyright 69 (1967), the role of the courts is to distinguish between "[b]iting criticism [that merely] suppresses demand

[and] copyright infringement[, which] usurps it." Fisher v. Dees, 794 F.2d, at 438.

This distinction between potentially remediable displacement and unremediable disparagement is reflected in the rule that there is no protectable derivative market for criticism. The market for potential derivative uses includes only those that creators of original works would in general develop or license others to develop. Yet the unlikelihood that creators of imaginative works will license critical reviews or lampoons of their own productions removes such uses from the very notion of a potential licensing market. "People ask ... for criticism, but they only want praise." S. Maugham, Of Human Bondage 241 (Penguin ed. 1992). Thus, to the extent that the opinion below may be read to have considered harm to the market for parodies of "Oh, Pretty Woman," see 972 F.2d, at 1439, the court erred. * * * [22]

In explaining why the law recognizes no derivative market for critical works, including parody, we have, of course, been speaking of the later work as if it had nothing but a critical aspect (i.e., "parody pure and simple," * * *). But the later work may have a more complex character, with effects not only in the arena of criticism but also in protectable markets for derivative works, too. In that sort of case, the law looks beyond the criticism to the other elements of the work, as it does here. 2 Live Crew's song comprises not only parody but also rap music, and the derivative market for rap music is a proper focus of enquiry, see *Harper & Row,* 471 U.S., at 568; Nimmer § 13.05[B]. Evidence of substantial harm to it would weigh against a finding of fair use, because the licensing of derivatives is an important economic incentive to the creation of originals. See 17 U.S.C. § 106(2) (copyright owner has rights to derivative works). Of course, the only harm to derivatives that need concern us, as discussed above, is the harm of market substitution. The fact that a parody may impair the market for derivative uses by the very effectiveness of its critical commentary is no more relevant under copyright than the like threat to the original market.[24]

Although 2 Live Crew submitted uncontroverted affidavits on the question of market harm to the original, neither they, nor Acuff–Rose, introduced evidence or affidavits addressing the likely effect of 2 Live Crew's parodic rap song on the market for a nonparody, rap version of "Oh, Pretty Woman." And while Acuff–Rose would have us find evidence of a rap market in the very facts that 2 Live Crew recorded a rap parody of "Oh, Pretty Woman" and another rap group sought a license to record a rap derivative, there was no evidence that a potential rap market was

---

22. We express no opinion as to the derivative markets for works using elements of an original as vehicles for satire or amusement, making no comment on the original or criticism of it.

24. In some cases it may be difficult to determine whence the harm flows. In such cases, the other fair use factors may provide some indicia of the likely source of the harm. A work whose overriding purpose and character is parodic and whose borrowing is slight in relation to its parody will be far less likely to cause cognizable harm than a work with little parodic content and much copying.

harmed in any way by 2 Live Crew's parody, rap version. The fact that 2 Live Crew's parody sold as part of a collection of rap songs says very little about the parody's effect on a market for a rap version of the original, either of the music alone or of the music with its lyrics. The District Court essentially passed on this issue, observing that Acuff–Rose is free to record "whatever version of the original it desires," 754 F.Supp., at 1158; the Court of Appeals went the other way by erroneous presumption. Contrary to each treatment, it is impossible to deal with the fourth factor except by recognizing that a silent record on an important factor bearing on fair use disentitled the proponent of the defense, 2 Live Crew, to summary judgment. The evidentiary hole will doubtless be plugged on remand.

III

It was error for the Court of Appeals to conclude that the commercial nature of 2 Live Crew's parody of "Oh, Pretty Woman" rendered it presumptively unfair. No such evidentiary presumption is available to address either the first factor, the character and purpose of the use, or the fourth, market harm, in determining whether a transformative use, such as parody, is a fair one. The court also erred in holding that 2 Live Crew had necessarily copied excessively from the Orbison original, considering the parodic purpose of the use. We therefore reverse the judgment of the Court of Appeals and remand for further proceedings consistent with this opinion.

It is so ordered.

APPENDIX A

"Oh, Pretty Woman" by Roy Orbison and William Dees

Pretty Woman, walking down the street,
Pretty Woman, the kind I like to meet,
Pretty Woman, I don't believe you, you're not the truth,
No one could look as good as you
Mercy
Pretty Woman, won't you pardon me,
Pretty Woman, I couldn't help but see,
Pretty Woman, that you look lovely as can be
Are you lonely just like me?
Pretty Woman, stop a while,
Pretty Woman, talk a while,
Pretty Woman give your smile to me
Pretty Woman, yeah, yeah, yeah
Pretty Woman, look my way,
Pretty Woman, say you'll stay with me
'Cause I need you, I'll treat you right
Come to me baby, Be mine tonight

Pretty Woman, don't walk on by,
Pretty Woman, don't make me cry,
Pretty Woman, don't walk away,
Hey, O.K.
If that's the way it must be, O.K.
I guess I'll go on home, it's late
There'll be tomorrow night, but wait!
What do I see
Is she walking back to me?
Yeah, she's walking back to me!
Oh, Pretty Woman.

APPENDIX B

"Pretty Woman" as Recorded by 2 Live Crew

Pretty Woman walkin' down the street
Pretty woman girl you look so sweet
Pretty woman you bring me down to that knee
Pretty woman you make me wanna beg please
Oh, pretty woman
Big hairy woman you need to shave that stuff
Big hairy woman you know I bet it's tough
Big hairy woman all that hair it ain't legit
'Cause you look like 'Cousin It'
Big hairy woman
Bald headed woman girl your hair won't grow
Bald headed woman you got a teeny weeny afro
Bald headed woman you know your hair could look nice
Bald headed woman first you got to roll it with rice
Bald headed woman here, let me get this hunk of biz for ya
Ya know what I'm saying you look better than rice a roni
Oh bald headed woman
Big hairy woman come on in
And don't forget your bald headed friend
Hey pretty woman let the boys
Jump in
Two timin' woman girl you know you ain't right
Two timin' woman you's out with my boy last night
Two timin' woman that takes a load off my mind
Two timin' woman now I know the baby ain't mine
Oh, two timin' woman
Oh pretty woman

■ JUSTICE KENNEDY, concurring.

I agree that remand is appropriate and join the opinion of the Court, with these further observations about the fair use analysis of parody. * * *

* * * It is not enough that the parody use the original in a humorous fashion, however creative that humor may be. The parody must target the original, and not just its general style, the genre of art to which it belongs, or society as a whole (although if it targets the original, it may target those features as well). See Rogers v. Koons, 960 F.2d 301, 310 (CA2 1992) ("[T]hough the satire need not be only of the copied work and may . . . also be a parody of modern society, the copied work must be, at least in part, an object of the parody"); Fisher v. Dees, 794 F.2d 432, 436 (CA9 1986) ("[A] humorous or satiric work deserves protection under the fair-use doctrine only if the copied work is at least partly the target of the work in question"). This prerequisite confines fair use protection to works whose very subject is the original composition and so necessitates some borrowing from it. See MCA, Inc. v. Wilson, 677 F.2d 180, 185 (CA2 1981) ("[I]f the copyrighted song is not at least in part an object of the parody, there is no need to conjure it up") * * *.

The fair use factors thus reinforce the importance of keeping the definition of parody within proper limits. More than arguable parodic content should be required to deem a would-be parody a fair use. Fair use is an affirmative defense, so doubts about whether a given use is fair should not be resolved in favor of the self-proclaimed parodist. We should not make it easy for musicians to exploit existing works and then later claim that their rendition was a valuable commentary on the original. * * *

The Court decides it is "fair to say that 2 Live Crew's song reasonably could be perceived as commenting on the original or criticizing it, to some degree." * * * While I am not so assured that 2 Live Crew's song is a legitimate parody, the Court's treatment of the remaining factors leaves room for the District Court to determine on remand that the song is not a fair use. As future courts apply our fair use analysis, they must take care to ensure that not just any commercial takeoff is rationalized *post hoc* as a parody.

With these observations, I join the opinion of the Court.

NOTES AND QUESTIONS ON PARODY

(1) Is 2 Live Crew's claim of fair use helped—or hurt—by the fact that they were refused a license to use *Oh, Pretty Woman*? In footnote 18 to its opinion the Supreme Court said, "[W]e reject Acuff–Rose's argument that 2 Live Crew's request for permission to use the original should be weighed against a finding of fair use. Even if good faith were central to fair use, 2 Live Crew's actions do not necessarily suggest that they believed their version was not fair use; the offer may simply have been made in a good

faith effort to avoid this litigation. If the use is otherwise fair, then no permission need be sought or granted. Thus, being denied permission to use a work does not weigh against a finding of fair use."

(2) In assessing the strength of the defendants' fair use defense, the Court distinguishes "parody" from "satire." In those terms, how would you characterize the Saturday Night Live sketch at issue in *Elsmere*? See also Rogers v. Koons, 960 F.2d 301 (2d Cir.), cert. denied, 506 U.S. 934 (1992), which rejected a "parody" claim by a flamboyant sculptor who closely copied plaintiff's postcard depicting a row of puppies (and got $367,000 for three duplicate originals); although the defendant's work may be "a satirical critique of our materialistic society," the court found that it was not a parody of the copyrighted work. The case elicited considerable commentary. See, e.g., McLean, All's Not Fair in Art and War: A Look at the Fair Use Defense After *Rogers v. Koons,* 59 Brooklyn L.Rev. 373 (1993). Quentel, "Bad Artists Copy. Good Artists Steal.": The Ugly Conflict Between Copyright Law and Appropriationism, 4 U.C.L.A. Ent.L.Rev. 39 (1996), uses Rogers v. Koons to urge leniency (via a compulsory license) for one-of-a-kind works of "appropriation art." Schaumann, An Artist's Privilege, 15 Cardozo Arts & Ent.L.J. 249 (1997), goes further, arguing that "artists should be free to copy whatever they like," at least absent a competitive threat to the original.

Campbell's emphasis on the extent of a defendant's parodic commentary on the original was pursued in Leibovitz v. Paramount Pictures Corp., 137 F.3d 109 (2d Cir.1998). Plaintiff owned the copyright in a photograph of a nude and pregnant Demi Moore that had appeared on the cover of *Vanity Fair*; defendant photographed a pregnant model in a similar pose and after superimposing the head of actor Leslie Nielsen, used the photo to advertise a new movie. Judge Newman said the defendant's advertisement could be perceived as commenting on the pretentiousness of the original and its interpretation of feminine beauty.

(3) In connection with the fourth fair use factor, Justice Souter says that "there is no protectable derivative market for criticism"; only harm to the market for the original or for other potential derivative uses that creators would develop or license counts against a fair use claim. On remand, what kinds of evidence would be relevant in measuring the potential harm to the derivative market for a non-parody rap version of the plaintiff's song?[f]

(4) A number of commentators have expressed concern about the potential chilling effect of the vague standards applicable to parodies. Burr, Artistic Parody: A Theoretical Construct, 14 Cardozo Arts & Enter.L.J. 65 (1996), argues for a compulsory license to alleviate the uncertainties, but that suggestion is rejected in Yonover, The Precarious Balance: Moral Rights,

---

f. Following the remand by the Supreme Court, the case was settled when the parties agreed to a license. Nashville Banner, June 5, 1996, p. B2. The oral arguments before the Supreme Court are recounted by defendant's counsel in Rogow, The Art of Making Law from Other People's Art, 14 Cardozo Arts & Enter.L.J. 127 (1996).

Parody, and Fair Use, id. at 79. Winslow, Rapping on a Revolving Door: An Economic Analysis of Parody and Campbell v. Acuff–Rose Music Co., 69 S.Cal.L.Rev. 767 (1996), urges increased focus on the nature and extent of the defendant's adaptations rather than on the quantum of use.

(5) Light, Parody, Burlesque, and the Economic Rationale for Copyright, 11 Conn.L.Rev. 615 (1979), advocates a broad license for the parodist, arguing that the economic effect on the parodied work is generally minimal. If so, why do copyright owners litigate such cases? To be able to collect for licenses to parody? (It was rumored that in the "Gas Light" case Jack Benny eventually paid Loew's $100,000 for a license. See Netterville, Copyright and Tort Aspects of Parody, Mimicry and Humorous Commentary, 35 S.Cal.L.Rev. 225, 233 (1962).) To protect the esteem of the plaintiff or the work? Is it relevant that many of the parodies in recent cases are decidedly off-color?[g]

A NOTE ON COPYRIGHT AND THE FIRST AMENDMENT

Professor Kaplan has expressed the "view that it was wrong—and possibly unconstitutional—to hold Jack Benny for his television parody of the movie *Gaslight*." B. Kaplan, An Unhurried View of Copyright 69 (1967). Is there an inherent conflict between freedom of speech and proprietary rights in forms of expression? The traditional response has been "no." The Ninth Circuit, for example, has said that the idea-expression dichotomy adequately accommodates the competing interests: "The 'marketplace of ideas' is not limited by copyright because copyright is limited to protection of expression." Sid & Marty Krofft Television Productions, Inc. v. McDonald's Corp., 562 F.2d 1157, 1170, p. 248 supra.

The accommodation achieved by the idea-expression dichotomy is not fortuitous—the concept of copyrightable expression is itself defined in part by reference to free speech interests. But are there situations in which the first amendment demands access, not merely to ideas, but also to copyrighted expression? Time, Inc. v. Bernard Geis Associates? Harper & Row Pub. v. Nation Enterprises? Benny v. Loew's Inc.? Another accommodation—fair use—often insures the necessary access. The Second Circuit, in *Wainwright Securities*, p. 366 supra, noted that "Conflicts between interests protected by the first amendment and the copyright laws thus far have been resolved by application of the fair use doctrine." See also, e.g., Los Angeles News Service v. Tullo, 973 F.2d 791 (9th Cir.1992) ("First Amendment considerations are relevant in determining whether the purpose of copying a work and the nature of the work copied militate in favor of finding a given use of a particular work to be a 'fair use' * * *").

---

g. For differing views on the utility of an economic analysis of the parody cases, compare Posner, When Is Parody Fair Use?, 21 J.Leg.Stud. 67 (1992), with Yen, When Authors Won't Sell: Parody, Fair Use, and Efficiency in Copyright Law, 62 U.Colo. L.Rev. 79 (1991). For a comprehensive survey emphasizing first amendment interests, see Dorsen, Satiric Appropriation and the Law of Libel, Trademark, and Copyright: Remedies Without Wrongs, 65 B.U.L.Rev. 923 (1985).

Shipley, Conflicts Between Copyright and the First Amendment After *Harper & Row, Publishers v. Nation Enterprises*, 1986 B.Y.U.L.Rev. 983, concludes that copyright law has the inherent capacity to accommodate free speech interests.   Abrams, First Amendment and Copyright, 35 J.Copyr.Soc. 1 (1987), in a critical comment on the *Salinger* case, reminds us that "the question is not whether these copyright doctrines are available to accommodate First Amendment values; it is whether they are, in fact, interpreted in a manner consistent with those values."   In answer to the latter question, another commentator concludes that copyright doctrines, especially the distinction between idea and expression, have not been interpreted in a manner that accommodates free speech interests.   Yen, A First Amendment Perspective on the Idea/Expression Dichotomy and Copyright in a Work's "Total Concept and Feel," 38 Emory L.J. 393 (1989).

Is the fair use doctrine sufficient to mediate copyright and free speech interests?   If Time, Inc. had suffered substantial economic injury as a result of Thompson's use of the Zapruder frames, for example, would the defendants nevertheless have prevailed on their fair use defense? Would it be constitutional to hold the defendants liable for their use?

In *Wainwright Securities* the Second Circuit indicated that in some cases (although not that one) courts might be required to recognize, apart from fair use, a first amendment limitation on copyright.   The Ninth Circuit in *Sid & Marty Krofft* made a similar concession, although it thought such instances "rare," and limited to "graphic expressions of newsworthy events."   (Is it true, as the court stated in a footnote, that "[b]ecause there are available alternatives in the form of expressing any verbal ideas, first amendment considerations should not limit copyright protection in this area"?   562 F.2d at 1171 n. 17.)

A district court did recognize a discrete first amendment defense to copyright infringement when it refused a request by the publisher of *TV Guide* to enjoin reproduction of the magazine's cover in comparative advertising promoting a television supplement in the *Miami Herald*. Triangle Pub., Inc. v. Knight–Ridder Newspapers, Inc., 445 F.Supp. 875 (S.D.Fla. 1978). However, when the case was appealed, the Fifth Circuit declined to endorse the district court's rationale, affirming instead on the basis of fair use. 626 F.2d 1171 (5th Cir.1080). Judge Tate, concurring, expressed the view that "under limited circumstances, a First Amendment privilege may, and *should* exist where utilization of the copyrighted expression is necessary for the purpose of conveying thoughts or expressions."   "[I]f fair use did *not* protect the defendant's use of the copyrighted cover, then I would agree completely with the district court, for the reasons expressed in its opinion, that the First Amendment prevented the plaintiff from enjoining reproduction of the cover."

See generally Denicola, Copyright and Free Speech: Constitutional Limitations on the Protection of Expression, 67 Calif.L.Rev. 283 (1979); Nimmer, Does Copyright Abridge the First Amendment Guarantees of Free Speech and Press?, 17 U.C.L.A.L.Rev. 1180 (1970); Goldstein, Copyright and the First Amendment, 70 Colum.L.Rev. 983 (1970).

Does the Supreme Court's rejection of the defendant's free speech argument in *Harper & Row* foreclose the possibility of a discrete first amendment defense to copyright infringement?

PHOTOCOPYING

Does the reader of a book infringe the copyright when she copies by hand passages for her own purposes? According to common understanding, she does not. May she not, then, use a photocopier to speed the process? But we quickly come to limiting cases: what if a large corporation makes hundreds of copies of technical articles for use by employees engaged in a profit-making enterprise?

American Geophysical Union v. Texaco Inc.

United States Court of Appeals, Second Circuit, 1994.
60 F.3d 913.
Certiorari dismissed, 116 S.Ct. 592 (1995).

■ Before NEWMAN, WINTER and JACOBS, CIRCUIT JUDGES.

■ NEWMAN, CHIEF JUDGE.

This interlocutory appeal presents the issue of whether, under the particular circumstances of this case, the fair use defense to copyright infringement applies to the photocopying of articles in a scientific journal. This issue arises on the appeal of defendant Texaco Inc. from the July 23, 1992, order of the United States District Court for the Southern District of New York (Pierre N. Leval, Judge) holding, after a limited-issue bench trial, that the photocopying of eight articles from the *Journal of Catalysis* for use by one of Texaco's researchers was not fair use. See American Geophysical Union v. Texaco Inc., 802 F.Supp. 1 (S.D.N.Y.1992). Though not for precisely the same reasons, we agree with the District Court's conclusion that this particular copying was not fair use and therefore affirm.

Background

The District Court Proceedings. Plaintiffs American Geophysical Union and 82 other publishers of scientific and technical journals (the "publishers") brought a class action claiming that Texaco's unauthorized photocopying of articles from their journals constituted copyright infringement. Among other defenses, Texaco claimed that its copying was fair use under section 107 of the Copyright Act, 17 U.S.C. § 107 (1988). Since it appeared likely that the litigation could be resolved once the fair use defense was adjudicated, the parties agreed that an initial trial should be limited to whether Texaco's copying was fair use, and further agreed that this issue would be submitted for decision on a written record.

Although Texaco employs 400 to 500 research scientists, of whom all or most presumably photocopy scientific journal articles to support their Texaco research, the parties stipulated—in order to spare the enormous expense of exploring the photocopying practices of each of them—that one scientist would be chosen at random as the representative of the entire group. The scientist chosen was Dr. Donald H. Chickering, II, a scientist at Texaco's research center in Beacon, New York. For consideration at trial, the publishers selected from Chickering's files photocopies of eight particular articles from the *Journal of Catalysis*.

In a comprehensive opinion, reported at 802 F.Supp. 1, the District Court considered the statutory fair use factors identified in section 107, weighed other equitable considerations, and held that Texaco's photocopying, as represented by Chickering's copying of these eight articles did not constitute fair use. The District Court certified its ruling for interlocutory appeal under 28 U.S.C. § 1292(b) (1988).

Essential Facts. Employing between 400 and 500 researchers nationwide, Texaco conducts considerable scientific research seeking to develop new products and technology primarily to improve its commercial performance in the petroleum industry. As part of its substantial expenditures in support of research activities at its Beacon facility, Texaco subscribes to many scientific and technical journals and maintains a sizable library with these materials. Among the periodicals that Texaco receives at its Beacon research facility is the *Journal of Catalysis* (*"Catalysis"*), a monthly publication produced by Academic Press, Inc., a major publisher of scholarly journals and one of the plaintiffs in this litigation. Texaco had initially purchased one subscription to *Catalysis* for its Beacon facility, and increased its total subscriptions to two in 1983. Since 1988, Texaco has maintained three subscriptions to *Catalysis*. * * *

The copies of the eight articles from *Catalysis* found in Chickering's files that the parties have made the exclusive focus of the fair use trial were photocopied in their entirety by Chickering or by other Texaco employees at Chickering's request. Chickering apparently believed that the material and data found within these articles would facilitate his current or future professional research. The evidence developed at trial indicated that Chickering did not generally use the *Catalysis* articles in his research immediately upon copying, but placed the photocopied articles in his files to have them available for later reference as needed. Chickering became aware of six of the photocopied articles when the original issues of *Catalysis* containing the articles were circulated to him. He learned of the other two articles upon seeing a reference to them in another published article. As it turned out, Chickering did not have occasion to make use of five of the articles that were copied.

Discussion

I. The Nature of the Dispute

The parties and many of the *amici curiae* have approached this case as if it concerns the broad issue of whether photocopying of scientific articles is fair use, or at least the only slightly more limited issue of whether photocopying of such articles is fair use when undertaken by a research scientist engaged in his own research. Such broad issues are not before us. Rather, we consider whether Texaco's photocopying by 400 or 500 scientists, as represented by Chickering's example, is a fair use. This includes the question whether such institutional, systematic copying increases the number of copies available to scientists while avoiding the necessity of paying for license fees or for additional subscriptions. We do not deal with the question of copying by an individual, for personal use in research or otherwise (not for resale), recognizing that under the fair use doctrine or the *de minimis* doctrine, such a practice by an individual might well not constitute an infringement. In other words, our opinion does not decide the case that would arise if Chickering were a professor or an independent scientist engaged in copying and creating files for independent research, as opposed to being employed by an institution in the pursuit of his research on the institution's behalf. * * *

A.   Fair Use and Photocopying

　　* * *

As with the development of other easy and accessible means of mechanical reproduction of documents, the invention and widespread availability of photocopying technology threatens to disrupt the delicate balances established by the Copyright Act. * * * As a leading commentator astutely notes, the advent of modern photocopying technology creates a pressing need for the law "to strike an appropriate balance between the authors' interest in preserving the integrity of copyright, and the public's right to enjoy the benefits that photocopying technology offers." 3 *Nimmer on Copyright* § 13.05[E][1], at 13–226.

Indeed, if the issue were open, we would seriously question whether the fair use analysis that has developed with respect to works of authorship alleged to use portions of copyrighted material is precisely applicable to copies produced by mechanical means. * * *

* * * However, we learn from the Supreme Court's consideration of copying achieved by use of a videotape recorder that mechanical copying is to be assessed for fair use purposes under the traditional mode of analysis, including the four statutory factors of section 107. See [Sony Corp. of America v. Universal Cities Studios, Inc., 464 U.S. 417, 447–56 (1984).] We therefore are obliged to apply that analysis to the photocopying that occurred in this case.

B.   The Precise Copyrights at Issue

We must first identify precisely the copyrighted works alleged to be infringed, since certain arguments made on appeal seem to focus on different works. The publishers typically hold two separate sets of copyrights in their journal publications. As a consequence of the publishers' requirement that authors transfer their copyrights when their articles are accepted for publication, the publishers usually possess the copyrights that subsist in each individual article appearing within their journals. Moreover, to the extent that the compilation of a journal issue involves an original work of authorship, the publishers possess a distinct copyright in each journal issue as a collective work, see 17 U.S.C. § 103; see also 17 U.S.C. § 101 (defining "compilation" and "collective work"). See generally Feist Publications, Inc. v. Rural Telephone Service Co., 499 U.S. 340, 356–61 (1991) (discussing extent of copyright protection in compilations and collective works).

From the outset, this lawsuit concerned alleged infringement of the copyrights in individual journal articles, copyrights assigned by the authors to the publishers. More specifically, by virtue of the parties' stipulation, this case now concerns the copyrights in the eight articles from *Catalysis* found in Chickering's files, copyrights now owned by Academic Press. There are no allegations that raise questions concerning Academic Press's potential copyrights in whole issues or annual volumes of *Catalysis* as collective works.

C. Burdens of Proof and Standard of Review

Fair use serves as an affirmative defense to a claim of copyright infringement, and thus the party claiming that its secondary use of the original copyrighted work constitutes a fair use typically carries the burden of proof as to all issues in the dispute. See [Campbell v. Acuff–Rose Music, Inc., 510 U.S. 569, 590 (1994)]. Moreover, since fair use is a "mixed question of law and fact," [Harper & Row, Pub., Inc. v. Nation Enterprises, 471 U.S. 539, 560 (1985)], we review the District Court's conclusions on this issue *de novo,* though we accept its subsidiary findings of fact unless clearly erroneous, see [Twin Peaks Prod., Inc. v. Publications Int'l, Ltd., 996 F.2d 1366, 1374 (2d Cir.1993)].

II. The Enumerated Fair Use Factors of Section 107

Section 107 of the Copyright Act identifies four non-exclusive factors that a court is to consider when making its fair use assessment, see 17 U.S.C. § 107(1)–(4). The District Court concluded that three of the four statutory factors favor the publishers. As detailed below, our analysis of certain statutory factors differs somewhat from that of the District Court, though we are in agreement on the ultimate determination. Our differences stem primarily from the fact that, unlike the District Court, we have had the benefit of the Supreme Court's important decision in *Campbell,* decided after Judge Leval issued his opinion.

A. First Factor: Purpose and Character of Use

* * * In Chickering's own words, the copies of the articles were made for "my personal convenience," since it is "far more convenient to have access in my office to a photocopy of an article than to have to go to the library each time I wanted to refer to it." Affidavit of Donald Chickering at 11 (submitted as direct trial testimony) [hereinafter Chickering testimony]. Significantly, Chickering did not even have occasion to use five of the photocopied articles at all, further revealing that the photocopies of the

eight *Catalysis* articles were primarily made just for "future retrieval and reference." Id.

It is true that photocopying these articles also served other purposes. The most favorable for Texaco is the purpose of enabling Chickering, if the need should arise, to go into the lab with pieces of paper that (a) were not as bulky as the entire issue or a bound volume of a year's issues, and (b) presented no risk of damaging the original by exposure to chemicals. And these purposes might suffice to tilt the first fair use factor in favor of Texaco if these purposes were dominant. * * *

The photocopying of these eight *Catalysis* articles may be characterized as "archival"—i.e., done for the primary purpose of providing numerous Texaco scientists (for whom Chickering served as an example) each with his or her own personal copy of each article without Texaco's having to purchase another original journal. The photocopying "merely 'supersede[s] the objects' of the original creation," *Campbell,* 510 U.S. at 579 (quoting Folsom v. Marsh, 9 F.Cas. 342, 348 (No. 4,901) (C.C.D.Mass. 1841)), and tilts the first fair use factor against Texaco. We do not mean to suggest that no instance of archival copying would be fair use, but the first factor tilts against Texaco in this case because the making of copies to be placed on the shelf in Chickering's office is part of a systematic process of encouraging employee researchers to copy articles so as to multiply available copies while avoiding payment.

Texaco criticizes three aspects of the District Court's analysis of the first factor. Relying largely on the Supreme Court's discussion of fair use in *Sony,* the District Court suggested that a secondary user will "win" this first factor by showing a "transformative (or productive) nonsuperseding use of the original, or [a] noncommercial use, generally for a socially beneficial or widely accepted purpose." 802 F.Supp. at 12. The District Court then concluded that Texaco's copying is "neither transformative nor noncommercial," id. at 13: not transformative because Texaco "simply makes mechanical photocopies of the entirety of relevant articles" and the "primary aspect" of Texaco's photocopying is to multiply copies, see id. at 13–15; and not noncommercial because, though it facilitates research, this research is conducted solely for commercial gain, see id. at 15–16.

Texaco asserts that the District Court mischaracterized the inquiry under the first factor and overlooked several relevant considerations. First, Texaco contends that the District Court inappropriately focussed on the character of the user rather than the nature of the use in labeling Texaco's copying as commercial. Texaco claims that its status as a for-profit corporation has no bearing on the fair use analysis, and that its use should be considered noncommercial since it photocopied articles in order to aid Chickering's research. Texaco emphasizes that "research" is explicitly listed in the preamble of section 107, a circumstance that Texaco contends should make its copying favored under the first factor and throughout the entire fair use analysis.

Second, Texaco contends that the District Court put undue emphasis on whether its use was "transformative," especially since the Supreme

Court appears to have rejected the view that a use must be transformative or productive to be a fair use. See *Sony,* 464 U.S. at 455 n. 40 ("The distinction between 'productive' and 'unproductive' uses may be helpful in calibrating the balance [of interests], but it cannot be wholly determinative."). * * *

Finally, Texaco claims that it should prevail on the first factor because, as the District Court acknowledged, the type of photocopying it conducted is widespread and has long been considered reasonable and customary. Texaco stresses that some courts and commentators regard custom and common usage as integral to the fair use analysis. See, e.g., Williams & Wilkins Co. v. United States, 487 F.2d 1345, 1353–56 (1973), aff'd by equally divided Court, 420 U.S. 376 (1975); Lloyd L. Weinreb, Fair's Fair: A Comment on the Fair Use Doctrine, 103 Harv.L.Rev. 1137, 1140 (1990) [hereinafter Weinreb, *Fair's Fair*]. We consider these three lines of attack separately.

1. *Commercial use.* We generally agree with Texaco's contention that the District Court placed undue emphasis on the fact that Texaco is a for-profit corporation conducting research primarily for commercial gain. Since many, if not most, secondary users seek at least some measure of commercial gain from their use, unduly emphasizing the commercial motivation of a copier will lead to an overly restrictive view of fair use. See *Campbell,* 510 U.S. at 584 * * *. Though the Supreme Court had stated in *Sony* that every commercial use was "presumptively" unfair, see 464 U.S. at 451, that Court and lower courts have come to explain that the commercial nature of a secondary use simply " 'tends to weigh against a finding of fair use.' " *Campbell,* 510 U.S. at 585 (quoting *Harper & Row,* 471 U.S. at 562) * * *.

Indeed, *Campbell* warns against "elevat[ing] ... to a *per se* rule" *Sony*'s language about a presumption against fair use arising from commercial use. 510 U.S. at 585. *Campbell* discards that language in favor of a more subtle, sophisticated approach, which recognizes that "the more transformative the new work, the less will be the significance of other factors, like commercialism, that may weigh against a finding of fair use." Id. at 579. * * *

We do not mean to suggest that the District Court overlooked these principles; in fact, the Court discussed them insightfully, see 802 F.Supp. at 12–13. Rather, our concern here is that the Court let the for-profit nature of Texaco's activity weigh against Texaco without differentiating between a direct commercial use and the more indirect relation to commercial activity that occurred here. Texaco was not gaining direct or immediate commercial advantage from the photocopying at issue in this case—i.e., Texaco's profits, revenues, and overall commercial performance were not tied to its making copies of eight *Catalysis* articles for Chickering. Cf. Basic Books, Inc. v. Kinko's Graphics Corp., 758 F.Supp. 1522 (S.D.N.Y. 1991) (revenues of reprographic business stemmed directly from selling unauthorized photocopies of copyrighted books). Rather, Texaco's photocopying served, at most, to facilitate Chickering's research, which in turn might have led to the development of new products and technology that could have improved Texaco's commercial performance. Texaco's photocopying is more appropriately labeled an "intermediate use." See [Sega Enterprises Ltd. v. Accolade, Inc., 977 F.2d 1510, 1522–23 (9th Cir.1992)] (labeling secondary use "intermediate" and finding first factor in favor of for-profit company, even though ultimate purpose of copying was to develop competing commercial product, because immediate purpose of copying computer code was to study idea contained within computer program).

We do not consider Texaco's status as a for-profit company irrelevant to the fair use analysis. Though Texaco properly contends that a court's focus should be on the *use* of the copyrighted material and not simply on the *user,* it is overly simplistic to suggest that the "purpose and character of the use" can be fully discerned without considering the nature and objectives of the user. * * *

As noted before, in this particular case the link between Texaco's commercial gain and its copying is somewhat attenuated: the copying, at most, merely facilitated Chickering's research that might have led to the production of commercially valuable products. Thus, it would not be accurate to conclude that Texaco's copying of eight particular *Catalysis* articles amounted to "commercial exploitation," especially since the immediate goal of Texaco's copying was to facilitate Chickering's research in the sciences, an objective that might well serve a broader public purpose. See *Twin Peaks,* 996 F.2d at 1375; *Sega Enterprises,* 977 F.2d at 1522. Still, we need not ignore the for-profit nature of Texaco's enterprise, especially since we can confidently conclude that Texaco reaps at least some indirect economic advantage from its photocopying. As the publishers emphasize, Texaco's photocopying for Chickering could be regarded simply as another "factor of production" utilized in Texaco's efforts to develop profitable products. Conceptualized in this way, it is not obvious why it is fair for Texaco to avoid having to pay at least some price to copyright holders for the right to photocopy the original articles.

2. *Transformative Use.* The District Court properly emphasized that Texaco's photocopying was not "transformative." After the District Court issued its opinion, the Supreme Court explicitly ruled that the concept of a "transformative use" is central to a proper analysis under the first factor, see *Campbell,* 510 U.S. at 578–583. The Court explained that though a "transformative use is not absolutely necessary for a finding of fair use, ... the more transformative the new work, the less will be the significance of other factors, like commercialism, that may weigh against a finding of fair use." Id. at 579. * * *

Texaco suggests that its conversion of the individual *Catalysis* articles through photocopying into a form more easily used in a laboratory might constitute a transformative use. However, Texaco's photocopying merely transforms *the material object* embodying the intangible article that is the copyrighted original work. * * *

Even though Texaco's photocopying is not technically a transformative use of the copyrighted material, we should not overlook the significant independent value that can stem from conversion of original journal articles into a format different from their normal appearance. See generally *Sony,* 464 U.S. at 454, 455 n. 40 (acknowledging possible benefits from copying that might otherwise seem to serve "no productive purpose"); Weinreb, *Fair's Fair,* at 1143 & n. 29 (discussing potential value from nontransformative copying). As previously explained, Texaco's photocopying converts the individual *Catalysis* articles into a useful format. Before modern photocopying, Chickering probably would have converted the original article into a more serviceable form by taking notes, whether cursory or extended;[10] today he can do so with a photocopying machine. Nevertheless, whatever independent value derives from the more usable format of the photocopy does not mean that every instance of photocopying wins on the first factor. In this case, the predominant archival purpose of the copying tips the first factor against the copier, despite the benefit of a more usable format.

3. *Reasonable and Customary Practice.* Texaco contends that Chickering's photocopying constitutes a use that has historically been considered "reasonable and customary." We agree with the District Court that whatever validity this argument might have had before the advent of the photocopying licensing arrangements discussed below in our consideration of the fourth fair use factor, the argument today is insubstantial. As the District Court observed, "To the extent the copying practice was 'reasonable' in 1973 [when *Williams & Wilkins* was decided], it has ceased to be 'reasonable' as the reasons that justified it before [photocopying licensing] have ceased to exist." 802 F.Supp. at 25. * * *

B. Second Factor: Nature of Copyrighted Work

    * * *

Though a significant measure of creativity was undoubtedly used in the creation of the eight articles copied from *Catalysis,* even a glance at their content immediately reveals the predominantly factual nature of these works. Moreover, though we have previously recognized the importance of strong copyright protection to provide sufficient incentives for the creation of scientific works, see [Weissmann v. Freeman, 868 F.2d 1313, 1325 (2d Cir.1989)], nearly every category of copyrightable works could plausibly assert that broad copyright protection was essential to the continued vitality of that category of works.

Ultimately, then, the manifestly factual character of the eight articles precludes us from considering the articles as "within the core of the

---

10. In stating that a handwritten copy would have been made, we do not mean to imply that such copying would necessarily have been a fair use. Despite the 1973 dictum in *Williams & Wilkins* asserting that "it is almost unanimously accepted that a scholar can make a handwritten copy of an entire copyrighted article for his own use ...," 487 F.2d at 1350, the current edition of the Nimmer treatise reports that "[t]here is no reported case on the question of whether a single handwritten copy of all or substantially all of a book or other protected work made for the copier's own private use is an infringement or fair use." 3 *Nimmer on Copyright* § 1305[E][4][a], at 13–229.

copyright's protective purposes," *Campbell,* 510 U.S. at 586; see also *Harper & Row,* 471 U.S. at 563 ("The law generally recognizes a greater need to disseminate factual works than works of fiction or fantasy."). Thus, in agreement with the District Court, we conclude that the second factor favors Texaco.

C.   Third Factor: Amount and Substantiality of Portion Used

The third statutory fair use factor is "the amount and substantiality of the portion used in relation to the copyrighted work as a whole." 17 U.S.C. § 107(3). The District Court concluded that this factor clearly favors the publishers because Texaco copied the eight articles from *Catalysis* in their entirety.

Texaco makes various responses to the District Court's straightforward conclusion. First, Texaco claims that this factor is significant only as a means to determine whether a copy unfairly supersedes demand for the original and should be considered "largely irrelevant" where, as here, a copy is not sold or distributed. Second, Texaco claims that, rather than focus on Texaco's copying of entire *articles,* it is more appropriate to consider that Texaco copied only a very small portion of any particular *issue or volume* of *Catalysis.* Finally, Texaco cites *Sony* and *Williams & Wilkins* for the proposition that the copying of entire copyrighted works can still constitute fair use. See *Sony,* 464 U.S. at 449–50; *Williams & Wilkins,* 487 F.2d at 1353.

Texaco's suggestion that we consider that it copied only a small percentage of the total compendium of works encompassed within *Catalysis* is superficially intriguing, especially since *Catalysis* is traditionally marketed only as a periodical by issue or volume. However, as the District Court recognized, each of the eight articles in *Catalysis* was separately authored and constitutes a discrete "original work[ ] of authorship," 17 U.S.C. § 102. As we emphasized at the outset, each article enjoys independent copyright protection, which the authors transferred to Academic Press, and what the publishers claim has been infringed is the copyright that subsists in each individual article—not the distinct copyright that may subsist in each journal issue or volume by virtue of the publishers' original compilation of these articles. The only other appellate court to consider the propriety of photocopying articles from journals also recognized that each article constituted an entire work in the fair use analysis. See *Williams & Wilkins,* 487 F.2d at 1353. * * *

Finally, though we are sensitive to Texaco's claim that the third factor serves merely as a proxy for determining whether a secondary use significantly interferes with demand for the original—a concern echoed by some commentators, see William W. Fisher III, Reconstructing the Fair Use Doctrine, 101 Harv.L.Rev. 1661, 1678 (1988) [hereinafter Fisher, *Reconstructing Fair Use*]—we think this factor serves a further end that advances the fair use analysis. Specifically, by focussing on the amount and substantiality of the original work used by the secondary user, we gain insight into the purpose and character of the use as we consider whether the quantity of the material used was "reasonable in relation to the purpose of the copying." See *Campbell,* 510 U.S. at 586. In this case, the fact that Texaco photocopied the eight *Catalysis* articles in their entirety weakens its assertion that the overriding purpose and character of its use was to enable the immediate use of the article in the laboratory and strengthens our view that the predominant purpose and character of the use was to establish a personal library of pertinent articles for Chickering. Cf. id. at 586–87 (intimating that extent of copying can provide insight into primary purpose of copying).

D. Fourth Factor: Effect Upon Potential Market or Value

The fourth statutory fair use factor is "the effect of the use upon the potential market for or value of the copyrighted work." 17 U.S.C. § 107(4). Assessing this factor, the District Court detailed the range of procedures Texaco could use to obtain authorized copies of the articles that it photocopied and found that "whatever combination of procedures Texaco used, the publishers' revenues would grow significantly." 802 F.Supp. at 19. The Court concluded that the publishers "powerfully demonstrated entitlement to prevail as to the fourth factor," since they had shown "a substantial harm to the value of their copyrights" as the consequence of Texaco's copying. See id. at 18–21. * * *

In analyzing the fourth factor, it is important (1) to bear in mind the precise copyrighted works, namely the eight journal articles, and (2) to recognize the distinctive nature and history of "the potential market for or value of" these particular works. Specifically, though there is a traditional market for, and hence a clearly defined value of, *journal issues and volumes,* in the form of per-issue purchases and journal subscriptions, there is neither a traditional market for, nor a clearly defined value of, *individual journal articles.* As a result, analysis of the fourth factor cannot proceed as simply as would have been the case if Texaco had copied a work that carries a stated or negotiated selling price in the market.

Like most authors, writers of journal articles do not directly seek to capture the potential financial rewards that stem from their copyrights by personally marketing copies of their writings. Rather, like other creators of literary works, the author of a journal article "commonly sells his rights to publishers who offer royalties in exchange for their services in producing and marketing the author's work." *Harper & Row,* 471 U.S. at 547. In the distinctive realm of academic and scientific articles, however, the only form of royalty paid by a publisher is often just the reward of being published, publication being a key to professional advancement and prestige for the author, see *Weissmann,* 868 F.2d at 1324 (noting that "in an academic setting, profit is ill-measured in dollars. Instead, what is valuable is recognition because it so often influences professional advancement and academic tenure."). The publishers in turn incur the costs and labor of producing and marketing authors' articles, driven by the prospect of capturing the economic value stemming from the copyrights in the original works, which the authors have transferred to them. Ultimately, the monopoly privileges conferred by copyright protection and the potential financial rewards therefrom are not directly serving to motivate authors to write individual articles; rather, they serve to motivate publishers to produce journals, which provide the conventional and often exclusive means for disseminating these individual articles. It is the prospect of such dissemination that contributes to the motivation of these authors. * * *

This marketing pattern has various consequences for our analysis of the fourth factor. First, evidence concerning the effect that photocopying individual journal articles has on the traditional market for journal subscriptions is of somewhat less significance than if a market existed for the sale of individual copies of articles. Second, this distinctive arrangement raises novel questions concerning the significance of the publishers' establishment of an innovative licensing scheme for the photocopying of individual journal articles.

1. *Sales of Additional Journal Subscriptions, Back Issues, and Back Volumes.* Since we are concerned with the claim of fair use in copying the eight individual articles from *Catalysis,* the analysis under the fourth factor must focus on the effect of Texaco's photocopying upon the potential market for or value of these individual articles. Yet, in their respective discussions of the fourth statutory factor, the parties initially focus on the impact of Texaco's photocopying of individual journal articles upon the market for *Catalysis* journals through sales of *Catalysis* subscriptions, back issues, or back volumes.

As a general matter, examining the effect on the marketability of the composite work containing a particular individual copyrighted work serves as a useful means to gauge the impact of a secondary use "upon the potential market for or value of" that individual work, since the effect on the marketability of the composite work will frequently be directly relevant to the effect on the market for or value of that individual work. Quite significantly, though, in the unique world of academic and scientific articles, the effect on the marketability of the composite work in which individual articles appear is not obviously related to the effect on the market for or value of the individual articles. Since (1) articles are submitted unsolicited to journals, (2) publishers do not make any payment to authors for the right to publish their articles or to acquire their copyrights, and (3) there is no evidence in the record suggesting that publishers seek to reprint particular articles in new composite works, we cannot readily conclude that evidence concerning the effect of Texaco's use on the marketability of *journals* provides an effective means to appraise the effect of Texaco's use on the market for or value of *individual journal articles*.

These considerations persuade us that evidence concerning the effect of Texaco's photocopying of individual articles within *Catalysis* on the traditional market for *Catalysis* subscriptions is of somewhat limited significance in determining and evaluating the effect of Texaco's photocopying "upon the potential market for or value of" the individual articles. We do not mean to suggest that we believe the effect on the marketability of journal subscriptions is completely irrelevant to gauging the effect on the market for and value of individual articles. Were the publishers able to demonstrate that Texaco's type of photocopying, if widespread, would impair the marketability of journals, then they might have a strong claim under the fourth factor. Likewise, were Texaco able to demonstrate that its type of photocopying, even if widespread, would have virtually no effect on the marketability of journals, then it might have a strong claim under this fourth factor.

On this record, however, the evidence is not resounding for either side. The District Court specifically found that, in the absence of photocopying, (1) "Texaco would not ordinarily fill the need now being supplied by photocopies through the purchase of back issues or back volumes . . . [or] by enormously enlarging the number of its subscriptions," but (2) Texaco still "would increase the number of subscriptions somewhat." 802 F.Supp. at 19. This moderate conclusion concerning the actual effect on the marketability of journals, combined with the uncertain relationship between the market for journals and the market for and value of individual articles, leads us to conclude that the evidence concerning sales of additional journal subscriptions, back issues, and back volumes does not strongly support either side with regard to the fourth factor. * * *

2. *Licensing Revenues and Fees.* The District Court, however, went beyond discussing the sales of additional journal subscriptions in holding that Texaco's photocopying affected the value of the publishers' copyrights. Specifically, the Court pointed out that, if Texaco's unauthorized photocopying was not permitted as fair use, the publishers' revenues would increase significantly since Texaco would (1) obtain articles from document delivery services (which pay royalties to publishers for the right to photocopy articles), (2) negotiate photocopying licenses directly with individual publishers, and/or (3) acquire some form of photocopying license from the Copyright Clearance Center Inc. ("CCC").[16] See 802 F.Supp. at 19. Texaco claims that the District Court's reasoning is faulty because, in determining that the value of the publishers' copyrights was affected, the Court assumed that the publishers were entitled to demand and receive licensing royalties and fees for photocopying. Yet, continues Texaco, whether the publishers can demand a fee for permission to make photocopies is the very question that the fair use trial is supposed to answer.

---

16. The CCC is a central clearing-house established in 1977 primarily by publishers to license photocopying. The CCC offers a variety of licensing schemes; fees can be paid on a per copy basis or through blanket license arrangements. Most publishers are registered with the CCC, but the participation of for-profit institutions that engage in photocopying has been limited, largely because of uncertainty concerning the legal questions at issue in this lawsuit. The CCC is fully described in the District Court's opinion. 802 F.Supp. at 7–9. A more extended discussion of the formation, development, and effectiveness of the CCC and its licensing schemes is contained in Stanley M. Besen & Sheila Nataraj Kirby, Compensating Creators of Intellectual Property: Collectives that Collect (1989).

It is indisputable that, as a general matter, a copyright holder is entitled to demand a royalty for licensing others to use its copyrighted work, see 17 U.S.C. § 106 (copyright owner has exclusive right "to authorize" certain uses), and that the impact on potential licensing revenues is a proper subject for consideration in assessing the fourth factor, see, e.g., *Campbell,* 510 U.S. at 592–93; *Harper & Row,* 471 U.S. at 568–69; * * *.

However, not every effect on potential licensing revenues enters the analysis under the fourth factor.[17] Specifically, courts have recognized limits on the concept of "potential licensing revenues" by considering only traditional, reasonable, or likely to be developed markets when examining and assessing a secondary use's "effect upon the potential market for or value of the copyrighted work." See *Campbell,* 510 U.S. at 592 ("The market for potential derivative uses includes only those that creators of original works would in general develop or license others to develop."); *Harper & Row,* 471 U.S. at 568 (fourth factor concerned with "use that supplants any part of the *normal* market for a copyrighted work") (emphasis added) (quoting S.Rep. No. 473, 94th Cong., 1st Sess. 65 (1975)); * * *.

Though the publishers still have not established a conventional market for the direct sale and distribution of individual articles, they have created, primarily through the CCC, a workable market for institutional users to obtain licenses for the right to produce their own copies of individual articles via photocopying. The District Court found that many major corporations now subscribe to the CCC systems for photocopying licenses. 802 F.Supp. at 25. Indeed, it appears from the pleadings, especially Texaco's counterclaim, that Texaco itself has been paying royalties to the CCC. See Complaint ¶ 38; First Counterclaim ¶ 71. Since the Copyright Act explicitly provides that copyright holders have the "exclusive rights" to "reproduce" and "distribute copies" of their works, see 17 U.S.C. § 106(1) & (3), and since there currently exists a viable market for licensing these rights for individual journal articles, it is appropriate that potential licensing revenues for photocopying be considered in a fair use analysis.

Despite Texaco's claims to the contrary, it is not unsound to conclude that the right to seek payment for a particular use tends to become legally

---

17. As Texaco notes and others have recognized, a copyright holder can *always* assert some degree of adverse affect on its potential licensing revenues as a consequence of the secondary use at issue simply because the copyright holder has not been paid a fee to permit that particular use. See Leval, *Toward a Fair Use Standard,* [103 Harv. L.Rev. 1105, 1124 (1990)] ("By definition every fair use involves some loss of royalty revenue because the secondary user has not paid royalties."); Fisher, *Reconstructing Fair Use,* at 1671 (noting that in almost every case "there will be *some* material adverse impact on a 'potential market'" since the secondary user has not paid for the use). Thus, were a court automatically to conclude in every case that potential licensing revenues were impermissibly impaired simply because the secondary user did not pay a fee for the right to engage in the use, the fourth fair use factor would *always* favor the copyright holder. See Leval, *Toward a Fair Use Standard,* at 1125; Fisher, *Reconstructing Fair Use,* at 1672.

For example, the Supreme Court recently explained that because of the "unlikelihood that creators of imaginative works will license critical reviews or lampoons" of their works, "the law recognizes no derivative market for critical works," *Campbell,* 510 U.S. at 592. * * *

cognizable under the fourth fair use factor when the means for paying for such a use is made easier. This notion is not inherently troubling: it is sensible that a particular unauthorized use should be considered "more fair" when there is no ready market or means to pay for the use, while such an unauthorized use should be considered "less fair" when there is a ready market or means to pay for the use. The vice of circular reasoning arises only if the availability of payment is conclusive against fair use. Whatever the situation may have been previously, before the development of a market for institutional users to obtain licenses to photocopy articles, see *Williams & Wilkins,* 487 F.2d at 1357–59, it is now appropriate to consider the loss of licensing revenues in evaluating "the effect of the use upon the potential market for or value of" journal articles. It is especially appropriate to do so with respect to copying of articles from *Catalysis,* a publication as to which a photocopying license is now available. We do not decide how the fair use balance would be resolved if a photocopying license for *Catalysis* articles were not currently available.

In two ways, Congress has impliedly suggested that the law should recognize licensing fees for photocopying as part of the "potential market for or value of" journal articles. First, section 108 of the Copyright Act narrowly circumscribes the conditions under which libraries are permitted to make copies of copyrighted works. See 17 U.S.C. § 108. Though this section states that it does not in any way affect the right of fair use, see id. § 108(f)(4), the very fact that Congress restricted the rights of libraries to make copies implicitly suggests that Congress views journal publishers as possessing the right to restrict photocopying, or at least the right to demand a licensing royalty from nonpublic institutions that engage in photocopying. Second, Congress apparently prompted the development of CCC by suggesting that an efficient mechanism be established to license photocopying, see S.Rep. No. 983, 93d Cong., 2d Sess. 122 (1974); S.Rep. No. 473, 94th Cong., 1st Sess. 70–71 (1975); H.R.Rep. No. 83, 90th Cong., 1st Sess. 33 (1968). It is difficult to understand why Congress would recommend establishing such a mechanism if it did not believe that fees for photocopying should be legally recognized as part of the potential market for journal articles.

Primarily because of lost licensing revenue, and to a minor extent because of lost subscription revenue, we agree with the District Court that "the publishers have demonstrated a substantial harm to the value of their copyrights through [Texaco's] copying," 802 F.Supp. at 21, and thus conclude that the fourth statutory factor favors the publishers.

E. Aggregate Assessment

We conclude that three of the four statutory factors, including the important first and the fourth factors, favor the publishers. We recognize that the statutory factors provide a nonexclusive guide to analysis, see *Harper & Row,* 471 U.S. at 560, but to whatever extent more generalized equitable considerations are relevant, we are in agreement with the District Court's analysis of them. See 802 F.Supp. at 21–27. We therefore agree with the District Court's conclusion that Texaco's photocopying of eight particular articles from the *Journal of Catalysis* was not fair use.

Though we recognize the force of many observations made in Judge Jacobs's dissenting opinion, we are not dissuaded by his dire predictions that our ruling in this case "has ended fair-use photocopying with respect to a large population of journals," 60 F.3d at 938–39, or, to the extent that the transactional licensing scheme is used, "would seem to require that an intellectual property lawyer be posted at each copy machine," id. at 937–38. Our ruling does not consider photocopying for personal use by an individual. Our ruling is confined to the institutional, systematic, archival multiplication of copies revealed by the record—the precise copying that the parties stipulated should be the basis for the District Court's decision now on appeal and for which licenses are in fact available. And the claim that lawyers need to be stationed at copy machines is belied by the ease with which music royalties have been collected and distributed for performances at thousands of cabarets, without the attendance of intellectual property lawyers in any capacity other than as customers. If Texaco wants to continue the precise copying we hold not to be a fair use, it can either use the licensing schemes now existing or some variant of them, or, if all else fails, purchase one more subscription for each of its researchers who wish to keep issues of *Catalysis* on the office shelf.

Conclusion

The order of the District Court is affirmed.[19]

■ JACOBS, CIRCUIT JUDGE, dissenting:

[Judge Jacobs took a different view of Dr. Chickering's copying, describing it as "integral to ongoing research by a scientist. In my view, all of the statutory factors organize themselves around this fact." Dr. Chickering's status as an employee of a major business corporation did not alter Judge Jacobs' perspective.]

The majority emphasizes *passim* that the photocopying condemned here is "systematic" and "institutional". These terms furnish a ground for distinguishing this case from the case that the majority expressly does not reach: the copying of journal articles by an individual researcher outside an institutional framework. For all the reasons adduced above, I conclude that the institutional environment in which Dr. Chickering works does not alter the character of the copying done by him or at his instance, and that the selection by an individual scientist of the articles useful to that scientist's own inquiries is not systematic copying, and does not become systematic because some number of other scientists in the same institution—four hundred or four—are doing the same thing.

---

19. Though neither the limited trial nor this appeal requires consideration of the publishers' remedy if infringement is ultimately found, we note that the context of this dispute appears to make ill-advised an injunction, which, in any event, has not been sought. If the dispute is not now settled, this appears to be an appropriate case for exploration of the possibility of a court-imposed compulsory license. See *Campbell,* 510 U.S. at 578 n. 10; 3 *Nimmer on Copyright* § 13.05[E][4][e], at 13–241 to 13–242.

[Judge Jacobs also disagreed that the development of licensing mechanisms such as the CCC should tip the balance against fair use.] I do not agree at all that a reasonable and customary use becomes unfair when the copyright holder develops a way to exact an additional price for the same product. * * *

In this case the only harm to a market is to the supposed market in photocopy licenses. The CCC scheme is neither traditional nor reasonable; and its development into a real market is subject to substantial impediments. There is a circularity to the problem: the market will not crystallize unless courts reject the fair use argument that Texaco presents; but, under the statutory test, we cannot declare a use to be an infringement unless (assuming other factors also weigh in favor of the secondary user) there is a market to be harmed. At present, only a fraction of journal publishers have sought to exact these fees. I would hold that this fourth factor decisively weighs in favor of Texaco, because there is no normal market in photocopy licenses, and no real consensus among publishers that there ought to be one.

NOTES AND QUESTIONS

(1) After its defeat in the Second Circuit, Texaco settled, agreeing to a "seven figure" payment as well as retroactive and prospective licensing fees payable through the Copyright Clearance Center. 51 Pat.,Tm. & Copyr.J. (BNA) 14 (1995).

Other victories by publishers against business copiers include Television Digest, Inc. v. United States Telephone Ass'n, 841 F.Supp. 5 (D.D.C. 1993), rejecting a fair use defense by a trade association that was making 12 to 26 extra copies of a $1250 per year subscription to plaintiff's *Communications Daily*, and Pasha Pub., Inc. v. Enmark Gas Corp., 22 U.S.P.Q.2d 1076 (N.D.Tex.1992), entering a consent judgment against a corporate subscriber that supplied its employees with copies of plaintiff's market newsletter by photocopying and fax.[h] The photocopying practices of businesses in the wake of the *Texaco* decision are surveyed in Crews, Copyright at a Turning Point: Corporate Responses to the Changing Environment, 3 J.Intell.Prop.L. 277 (1996).

Is the result in *Texaco* applicable to a school or college that furnishes similar photocopying services to its faculty? (Cf. Section I of the Guidelines for Classroom Copying, p. 434 infra.)

(2) Does the court make a convincing case for including potential photocopying fees in the analysis of the fourth fair use factor?

Judge Newman distinguished Williams & Wilkins Co. v. United States, 487 F.2d 1345 (Ct.Cl.1973)—for many years the principal precedent on photocopying. That case involved substantial copying of medical journals by

---

h. See also Washington Business Information v. Collier, Shannon & Scott, 42 Pat.,Tm. & Copyr.J. (BNA) 619 (E.D.Va. 1991), involving a settlement with a law firm for cover-to-cover photocopying of a legal newsletter.

two governmental libraries. The library at the National Institutes of Health, the Government's principal medical research organization, subscribed to about 3,000 medical journals. NIH researchers could obtain photocopies of articles from journals in the library's collection. In a typical year it photocopied over 93,000 articles. The National Medical Library, a repository of much of the world's medical literature, cooperated with other libraries in an interlibrary loan program. Upon request, it would provide a photocopy of the desired journal article; in a representative year, 120,000 photocopied articles were distributed. Reversing the trial court's finding of infringement, the Court of Claims decided, 4–3, that the photocopying was fair use. "Thus, the balance of risks is definitely on defendant's side—until Congress acts more specifically, the burden on medical science of a holding that the photocopying is an infringement would appear to be much greater than the present or foreseeable burden on plaintiff and other medical publishers of a ruling that these practices fall within 'fair use.'" (Has the subsequent development of licensing mechanisms such as the CCC now altered this balance?) The court rejected plaintiff's argument that its willingness to license the copying for a reasonable royalty undermined the claim of fair use. "Our difficulty with that response—in addition to the absence of proof that plaintiff has yet been hurt, and the twin doubts whether plaintiff has a viable license system and whether any satisfactory program can be created without legislation—is that the 1909 Act does not provide for compulsory licensing in this field."

The decision in the Court of Claims was affirmed without opinion by an equally-divided Supreme Court. 420 U.S. 376 (1975). Thus, of the sixteen judges who considered the case, eight thought the use fair and eight thought it infringing. For disapproving comments, see Perlman and Rhinelander, Williams & Wilkins Co. v. United States: Photocopying, Copyright, and the Judicial Process, 1975 Sup.Ct.Rev. 355 (1976); Goldstein, The Private Consumption of Public Goods, 21 Bull.Copyr.Soc. 204 (1974).

(3) The Copyright Clearance Center described in the *Texaco* case is a private, non-profit organization founded in 1977 that offers centralized photocopying authorization and collection services. Publishers who register works with the CCC grant users such as corporations advance permission to photocopy registered titles. Fees are set by the individual publishers and sometimes appear as part of a CCC code included on the publication. (See, e.g., the code appearing on BNA's *Patent, Trademark & Copyright Journal* ($1.00 per page)). Royalties paid to the CCC are distributed to the copyright owners; authors' shares depend on their individual publishing contracts. Cooperation between the CCC and other Reproduction Rights Organizations around the world provides a degree of international protection.

The success of any centralized collection system depends on the participation of a critical mass of publishers and users. The CCC claims about 9,200 publishers and 1.7 million registered titles. Participation by users is in some measure determined by the level of copying fees, the administrative costs of recordkeeping and reporting, and the strength of enforcement. Licenses from the CCC were initially available only on a transaction basis requiring detailed records of copying activity. To minimize administrative costs, the CCC later inaugurated an alternative blanket license available for an annual fee determined by factors such as the size of the user and data on the photocopying practices of the particular industry. More than 8,000 organizations are said to have licenses with the CCC (including 85 of the largest 100 corporations in the country).[i]

CLASSROOM COPYING

The ease with which teachers can produce multiple copies of material for classroom use has created strong pressure from educators to have such copying legitimized. Opposed to them are trade publishers and authors, especially publishers of textbooks and other teaching materials. Educators supporting extensive fair use or specific exemptions in favor of classroom photocopying weighed in late but vigorously in the copyright revision process. Such concessions as they attained were still in contention at the last stages of legislative action. The House Committee in 1976 added two phrases to § 107: in the first sentence, the phrase "(including multiple copies for classroom use)" was added to the list of examples of possible fair use; in the first of the four factors, the reference to "nonprofit educational purposes" was appended. The following excerpt from the House Report deals with the issue of classroom reproduction.

HOUSE REPORT (pp. 66–72)

Intention as to classroom reproduction

Although the works and uses to which the doctrine of fair use is applicable are as broad as the copyright law itself, most of the discussion of section 107 has centered around questions of classroom reproduction, particularly photocopying. The arguments on the question are summarized at pp. 30–31 of this Committee's 1967 report (H.R.Rep. No. 83, 90th Cong., 1st Sess.), and have not changed materially in the intervening years.

The Committee also adheres to its earlier conclusion, that "a specific exemption freeing certain reproductions of copyrighted works for educational and scholarly purposes from copyright control is not justified." At the same time the Committee recognizes, as it did in 1967, that there is a "need for greater certainty and protection for teachers." In an effort to meet this need the Committee has not only adopted further amendments to section 107, but has also amended section 504(c) to provide innocent teachers and other non-profit users of copyrighted material with broad insulation against unwarranted liability for infringement. The latter amendments are discussed below in connection with Chapter 5 of the bill.

In 1967 the Committee also sought to approach this problem by including, in its report, a very thorough discussion of "the considerations

---

i. Information on the Copyright Clearance Center is available at their website: http://www.copyright.com.

lying behind the four criteria listed in the amended section 107, in the context of typical classroom situations arising today." This discussion appeared on pp. 32–35 of the 1967 report, and with some changes has been retained in the Senate report on S. 22 (S.Rep. No. 94–473, pp. 63–65). The Committee has reviewed this discussion, and considers that it still has value as an analysis of various aspects of the problem.

At the Judiciary Subcommittee hearings in June 1975, Chairman Kastenmeier and other members urged the parties to meet together independently in an effort to achieve a meeting of the minds as to permissible educational uses of copyrighted material. The response to these suggestions was positive, and a number of meetings of three groups, dealing respectively with classroom reproduction of printed material, music, and audio-visual material, were held beginning in September 1975.

In a joint letter to Chairman Kastenmeier, dated March 19, 1976, the representatives of the Ad Hoc Committee of Educational Institutions and Organizations on Copyright Law Revision, and of the Authors League of America, Inc., and the Association of American Publishers, Inc., stated:

> You may remember that in our letter of March 8, 1976 we told you that the negotiating teams representing authors and publishers and the Ad Hoc Group had reached tentative agreement on guidelines to insert in the Committee Report covering educational copying from books and periodicals under Section 107 of H.R. 2223 and S. 22, and that as part of that tentative agreement each side would accept the amendments to Sections 107 and 504 which were adopted by your Subcommittee on March 3, 1976.

> We are now happy to tell you that the agreement has been approved by the principals and we enclose a copy herewith. We had originally intended to translate the agreement into language suitable for inclusion in the legislative report dealing with Section 107, but we have since been advised by committee staff that this will not be necessary.

> As stated above, the agreement refers only to copying from books and periodicals, and it is not intended to apply to musical or audiovisual works.

The full text of the agreement is as follows:

AGREEMENT ON GUIDELINES FOR CLASSROOM COPYING
IN NOT-FOR-PROFIT EDUCATIONAL INSTITUTIONS

WITH RESPECT TO BOOKS AND PERIODICALS

The purpose of the following guidelines is to state the minimum and not the maximum standards of educational fair use under Section 107 of H.R. 2223. The parties agree that the conditions determining the extent of permissible copying for educational purposes may change in the future; that certain types of copying permitted under these guidelines may not be permissible in the future; and conversely that in the future other types of copying not permitted under these guidelines may be permissible under revised guidelines.

Moreover, the following statement of guidelines is not intended to limit the types of copying permitted under the standards of fair use under judicial decision and which are stated in Section 107 of the Copyright Revision Bill.   There may be instances in which copying which does not fall within the guidelines stated below may nonetheless be permitted under the criteria of fair use.

GUIDELINES

I.   *Single Copying for Teachers*

A single copy may be made of any of the following by or for a teacher at his or her individual request for his or her scholarly research or use in teaching or preparation to teach a class:

A.   A chapter from a book;

B.   An article from a periodical or newspaper;

C.   A short story, short essay or short poem, whether or not from a collective work;

D.   A chart, graph, diagram, drawing, cartoon or picture from a book, periodical, or newspaper.

II.   *Multiple Copies for Classroom Use*

Multiple copies (not to exceed in any event more than one copy per pupil in a course) may be made by or for the teacher giving the course for classroom use or discussion; *provided that:*

A.   The copying meets the tests of brevity and spontaneity as defined below; *and,*

B.   Meets the cumulative effect test as defined below; *and,*

C.   Each copy includes a notice of copyright.

Definitions

Brevity

(*i*) Poetry: (a) A complete poem if less than 250 words and if printed on not more than two pages or (b) from a longer poem, an excerpt of not more than 250 words.

(*ii*) Prose: (a) Either a complete article, story or essay of less than 2,500 words, or (b) an excerpt from any prose work of not more than 1,000 words or 10% of the work, whichever is less, but in any event a minimum of 500 words.

[Each of the numerical limits stated in "i" and "ii" above may be expanded to permit the completion of an unfinished line of a poem or of an unfinished prose paragraph.]

(*iii*) Illustration: One chart, graph, diagram, drawing, cartoon or picture per book or per periodical issue.

(*iv*) "Special" works: Certain works in poetry, prose or in "poetic prose" which often combine language with illustrations and which are intended sometimes for children and at other times for a more general audience fall short of 2,500 words in their entirety. Paragraph "ii" above notwithstanding such "special works" may not be reproduced in their entirety; however, an excerpt comprising not more than two of the published pages of such special work and containing not more than 10% of the words found in the text thereof, may be reproduced.

Spontaneity

(*i*) The copying is at the instance and inspiration of the individual teacher, and

(*ii*) The inspiration and decision to use the work and the moment of its use for maximum teaching effectiveness are so close in time that it would be unreasonable to expect a timely reply to a request for permission.

Cumulative Effect

(*i*) The copying of the material is for only one course in the school in which the copies are made.

(*ii*) Not more than one short poem, article, story, essay or two excerpts may be copied from the same author, nor more than three from the same collective work or periodical volume during one class term.

(*iii*) There shall not be more than nine instances of such multiple copying for one course during one class term.

[The limitations stated in "ii" and "iii" above shall not apply to current news periodicals and newspapers and current news sections of other periodicals.]

III. *Prohibitions as to I and II Above*

Notwithstanding any of the above, the following shall be prohibited:

(A) Copying shall not be used to create or to replace or substitute for anthologies, compilations or collective works. Such replacement or substitution may occur whether copies of various works or excerpts therefrom are accumulated or reproduced and used separately.

(B) There shall be no copying of or from works intended to be "consumable" in the course of study or of teaching. These include workbooks, exercises, standardized tests and test booklets and answer sheets and like consumable material.

(C) Copying shall not:

(a) substitute for the purchase of books, publishers' reprints or periodicals;

(b) be directed by higher authority;

(c) be repeated with respect to the same item by the same teacher from term to term.

(D) No charge shall be made to the student beyond the actual cost of the photocopying.

Agreed MARCH 19, 1976.

Ad Hoc Committee on Copyright Law Revision:

> By SHELDON ELLIOTT STEINBACH.

Author–Publisher Group:

Authors League of America:

> By IRWIN KARP, *Counsel.*

Association of American Publishers, Inc.:

> By ALEXANDER C. HOFFMAN,
>
> *Chairman, Copyright Committee.*

* * *

The Committee appreciates and commends the efforts and the cooperative and reasonable spirit of the parties who achieved the agreed guidelines on books and periodicals and on music. Representatives of the American Association of University Professors and of the Association of American Law Schools have written to the Committee strongly criticizing the guidelines, particularly with respect to multiple copying, as being too restrictive with respect to classroom situations at the university and graduate level. However, the Committee notes that the Ad Hoc group did include representatives of higher education, that the stated "purpose of the . . . guidelines is to state the minimum and not the maximum standards of educational fair use" and that the agreement acknowledges "there may be instances in which copying which does not fall within the guidelines . . . may nonetheless be permitted under the criteria of fair use."

The Committee believes the guidelines are a reasonable interpretation of the minimum standards of fair use. Teachers will know that copying within the guidelines is fair use. Thus, the guidelines serve the purpose of fulfilling the need for greater certainty and protection for teachers. The Committee expresses the hope that if there are areas where standards other than these guidelines may be appropriate, the parties will continue their efforts to provide additional specific guidelines in the same spirit of good will and give and take that has marked the discussion of this subject in recent months.

NOTES ON CLASSROOM COPYING

(1) The House Report also contains "Guidelines for Educational Uses of Music," developed by representatives of music publishers, schools, and teachers. (H.R.Rep. pp. 70–71.)

In the next-to-last paragraph of the House statement, reference is made to the dissatisfaction of the American Association of University Professors and the Association of American Law Schools. Their concern that the Guidelines were too restrictive and might be misunderstood seemed warranted when after passage of the bill they were journalistically presented as "Do's and Don'ts," for example in the widely read *Chronicle of Higher Education*. This elicited a response, in which a signer of the Guidelines from the American Council of Education, an umbrella organization in higher education, joined:

The guidelines to which your article refers were signed by representatives of publishers and some education associations and were designed as an unofficial understanding of the *minimum* reach of the fair use doctrine in the context of copying for classroom teaching purposes. They are not part of the statute enacted by Congress, although they were inserted in the House and conference committee reports of the bill and referred to as a reasonable interpretation of fair use by both committees. * * *

Perhaps some of this confusion is engendered by your apparent assumption that whatever the guidelines do not expressly permit is therefore prohibited. The guidelines themselves, the committee reports, and the floor debates all emphasize that the guidelines are a statement of the minimum scope of the fair use doctrine. They are intended as a "safe harbor," assuring the teacher who stays within their scope that he or she will not be liable for infringement. * * *

It was fear of this type of misreading of the legislative history that caused the American Association of University Professors and the Association of American Law Schools to disassociate themselves from the promulgation of the guidelines. The American Council on Education is convinced that the guidelines were essential in obtaining a new statute from Congress but remains concerned that teachers not be restricted in their teaching, scholarly and research activities by a misreading and misapplication of the statute and its legislative history.

ROBERT A. GORMAN

Executive Committee, A.A.L.S. & A.A.U.P.

S.E. STEINBACH

Counsel, A.C.E.

LEO J. RASKIND

Copyright Comm., A.A.L.S.

JOHN STEDMAN

Copyright Comm., A.A.U.P.

(Chronicle of Higher Education, Nov. 15, 1976.)

(2) Reflect on the practices in your law school with respect to photocopying. Do they comport with the statute and its legislative history? Congressman Drinan (formerly Dean of the Boston College Law School), during the House debate on the revision bill, quoted a statement from the Association of American Law Schools:

> Requiring a law school teacher to meet all three tests of brevity, spontaneity and cumulative effect stifles the use of copyrighted material for classroom purposes. The realities of classroom teaching and the economics of our students are such that they cannot purchase or pay royalties on works other than the standard text and case books that are used as the major resources in classroom teaching. Thus the teacher's choice is not between purchasing and copying; it is between copying and not using. (122 Cong.Rec. 31986 (1976))[j]

Is there anything about copyright, unlike computers or photocopier supplies, that marks it for compulsory contributions, at one extreme to school districts in economically depressed communities, at the other to the education of professionals whose earnings prospects may be superior to those of many authors?

(3) The first major precedent on classroom photocopying was Basic Books, Inc. v. Kinko's Graphics Corp., 758 F.Supp. 1522 (S.D.N.Y.1991), resulting from an ambitious attack by a coalition of publishers against the "Professor Publishing" service offered by Kinko's, a nationwide chain with hundreds of photocopying centers. The suit challenged Kinko's production and sale of photocopied course packets. (Among the examples cited was a 388–page anthology for a social science course that contained material copied from 25 books, including excerpts ranging from 14 to 53 pages taken from six books published by the plaintiffs.) The court doubted whether Kinko's, as a for-profit copier, could claim protection under the Classroom Guidelines (cf. Section III(D) of the Guidelines), but found in any event that the Guidelines had been exceeded. The court rejected Kinko's fair use defense, finding the copying commercial, substantial, and damaging to the copyright owners' market. Plaintiffs got a $510,000 judgment and an injunction; a later settlement added $1.6 million in legal fees.

PRINCETON UNIV. PRESS v. MICHIGAN DOCUMENT SERVICE, 99 F.3d 1381 (6th Cir.1996), cert. denied, 117 S.Ct. 1336 (1997). Defendant MDS is a commercial photocopying shop that produced and sold "coursepacks" at the request of professors teaching classes at the University of Michigan. MDS president James Smith, after consulting an attorney and reading what he could find on the subject at the University of Michigan Law Library, concluded that the *Kinko's* decision was wrong; unlike most or all of its

---

j. See also Dratler, To Copy or Not To Copy: The Educator's Dilemma, 19 J.L. & Educ. 1 (1990), arguing that current law does not adequately serve the needs of educators.

competitors, MDS did not seek or pay for permission to copy. The course-packs at issue contained excerpts from plaintiffs' copyrighted books. The excerpts ranged from 17 to 95 pages in length, the latter comprising 30 per cent of Princeton Professor Nancy Weiss' *Farewell to the Party of Lincoln: Black Politics in the Age of FDR*. Plaintiffs got a summary judgment when the district court rejected defendant's fair use argument.

MDS won a surprising although temporary victory when the Sixth Circuit in a 2–1 decision reversed the district court and ordered summary judgment for the defendant. 74 F.3d 1512 (6th Cir.1996) (opinion withdrawn). Judge Ryan rejected the plaintiffs' attempt to invoke the classroom copying guidelines—the four statutory fair factors were "unambiguous," thus precluding resort to legislative history. Evaluating the "purpose and character of the use," the court refused to focus solely on defendant's reproduction; the ultimate educational use by the students was also relevant. On the substantiality of the copying, Judge Ryan argued that even with respect to the 95–page excerpt, there was no evidence that the copying "extracted the heart of the work." [How incompetent must a professor be to extract 95 pages and fail to get the "heart" of a book?] On the fourth factor, there was no evidence of damage to the market for the original works, according to the court, since the professors had signed declarations that they would not have assigned the entire books. As for lost permission fees, the court rejected the Second Circuit's position in *Texaco*, concluding "[i]t is circular to argue that a use is unfair, and a fee therefore required, on the basis that the publisher is otherwise deprived a fee."

The Sixth Circuit voted for a rehearing en banc, vacating the panel decision. After rehearing, the Sixth Circuit in an 8–5 decision affirmed the district court's summary judgment on liability (but remanded for reconsideration of statutory damages, finding that the defendant's infringement was not willful.) Judge Nelson, after stating the facts, began with a consideration of the fourth fair use factor.

"The burden of proof as to market effect rests with the copyright holder if the challenged use is of a 'noncommercial' nature. The alleged infringer has the burden, on the other hand, if the challenged use is 'commercial' in nature. Sony Corp. v. Universal City Studios, Inc., 464 U.S. 417, 451 (1984). In the case at bar the defendants argue that the burden of proof rests with the publishers because the use being challenged is 'noncommercial.' We disagree.

"It is true that the use to which the materials are put by the students who purchase the coursepacks is noncommercial in nature. But the use of the materials by the students is not the use that the publishers are challenging. What the publishers are challenging is the duplication of copyrighted materials for sale by a for-profit corporation that has decided to maximize its profits—and give itself a competitive edge over other copyshops—by declining to pay the royalties requested by the holders of the copyrights. * * *

"As noted above, most of the copyshops that compete with MDS in the sale of coursepacks pay permission fees for the privilege of duplicating and selling excerpts from copyrighted works. The three plaintiffs together have been collecting permission fees at a rate approaching $500,000 a year. If copyshops across the nation were to start doing what the defendants have been doing here, this revenue stream would shrivel and the potential value of the copyrighted works of scholarship published by the plaintiffs would be diminished accordingly.

"The defendants contend that it is circular to assume that a copyright holder is entitled to permission fees and then to measure market loss by reference to the lost fees. * * *

"Where * * * the copyright holder clearly does have an interest in exploiting a licensing market—and especially where the copyright holder has actually succeeded in doing so—'it is appropriate that potential licensing revenues for photocopying be considered in a fair use analysis.' American Geophysical, 60 F.3d at 930. * * *

"As to 'the purpose and character of the use, including whether such use is of a commercial nature or is for nonprofit educational purposes,' 17 U.S.C. § 107(1), we have already explained our reasons for concluding that the challenged use is of a commercial nature.

"The defendants argue that the copying at issue here would be considered 'nonprofit educational' if done by the students or professors themselves. The defendants also note that they can profitably produce multiple copies for less than it would cost the professors or the students to make the same number of copies. Most of the copyshops with which the defendants compete have been paying permission fees, however, and we assume that these shops too can perform the copying on a more cost-effective basis than the professors or students can. This strikes us as a more significant datum than the ability of a black market copyshop to beat the do-it-yourself cost.

"As to the proposition that it would be fair use for the students or professors to make their own copies, the issue is by no means free from doubt. We need not decide this question, however, for the fact is that the copying complained of here was performed on a profit-making basis by a commercial enterprise. And '[t]he courts have ... properly rejected attempts by for-profit users to stand in the shoes of their customers making nonprofit or noncommercial uses.' Patry, Fair Use in Copyright Law, at 420 n. 34. As the House Judiciary Committee stated in its report on the 1976 legislation,

> '[I]t would not be possible for a non-profit institution, by means of contractual arrangements with a commercial copying enterprise, to authorize the enterprise to carry out copying and distribution functions that would be exempt if conducted by the non-profit institution itself.' H.R.Rep. No. 1476, 94th Cong., 2d Sess. at 74 (1976), U.S.Code Cong. & Admin.News 5659, 5687–88."

After citing Litman, Copyright, Compromise, and Legislative History, 72 Cornell L.Rev. 857 (1987), for its description of the negotiating process that characterized the drafting of the 1976 Act, the court concluded that it was appropriate to consider the Guidelines for Classroom Copying.

"In its systematic and premeditated character, its magnitude, its anthological content, and its commercial motivation, the copying done by MDS goes well beyond anything envisioned by the Congress that chose to incorporate the guidelines in the legislative history. Although the guidelines do not purport to be a complete and definitive statement of fair use law for educational copying, and although they do not have the force of law, they do provide us general guidance. The fact that the MDS copying is light years away from the safe harbor of the guidelines weighs against a finding of fair use.

"Although the Congress that passed the Copyright Act in 1976 would pretty clearly have thought it unfair for a commercial copyshop to appropriate as much as 30 percent of a copyrighted work without paying the license fee demanded by the copyright holder, the changes in technology and teaching practices that have occurred over the last two decades might conceivably make Congress more sympathetic to the defendants' position today. If the law on this point is to be changed, however, we think the change should be made by Congress and not by the courts. * * *

"The defendants attach considerable weight to the assertions of numerous academic authors that they do not write primarily for money and that they want their published writings to be freely copyable. The defendants suggest that unlicensed copying will 'stimulate artistic creativity for the general public good.'

"This suggestion would be more persuasive if the record did not demonstrate that licensing income is significant to the publishers. It is the publishers who hold the copyrights, of course—and the publishers obviously need economic incentives to publish scholarly works, even if the scholars do not need direct economic incentives to write such works."

There were three dissenting opinions. Each argued that it was wrong to take account of potential licensing fees in judging the economic impact of the copying. Judge Martin raised another objection: "That the majority lends significance to the identity of the person operating the photocopier is a profound indication that its approach is misguided. Given the focus of the Copyright Act, the only practical difference between this case and that of a student making his or her own copies is that commercial photocopying is faster and more cost-effective." This theme was also pursued in a dissent by Judge Merritt. "There is nothing in the statute that distinguishes between copies made for students by a third person who charges a fee for their labor and copies made by students themselves who pay a fee only for use of the copy machines. Our political economy generally encourages the division and specialization of labor. There is no reason why in this instance the law should discourage high schools, colleges, students and professors from hiring the labor of others to make their copies any more than there is a reason to discourage lawyers from hiring paralegals to make copies for clients and courts. The Court's distinction in this case based on the division of labor—who does the copying—is short sighted and unsound economically." Judge Ryan dissented in an opinion that reiterated his argument in the vacated panel decision.

NOTES AND QUESTIONS

(1) Professor Jones announces in her American History 201 course that the assignment for the following week is pages 110 to 205 in *Farewell to the Party of Lincoln: Black Politics in the Age of FDR*. Professor Jones informs the students that the book is available at the University Bookstore for $14.95; she also tells them that several copies are on reserve at the library. Student A checks out a copy from the reserve desk, buys a $10 copycard for use in the library's photocopiers, and spends $4.75 making a photocopy of the required pages. Student B does the same, except he also makes a second copy for a classmate. Student C checks out the book, takes it across the street to a commercial copyshop, and has the pages copied for $2.85 plus tax. Is A, B, or C (or the library—see below) liable for copyright infringement? Should the answer, as the dissenters argue, determine the liability of the copyshop?

With respect to photocopying by students, is the fair use analysis altered if the copying consists, not of readings assigned for class, but of research materials collected by an individual student for a term paper?

(2) In response to the *Kinko's* case, the Copyright Clearance Center established an Academic Permissions Service offering teachers and copying centers centralized permission and fee collection services for photocopied course packets. It processes more than 100,000 requests per year.

(3) As part of the Clinton administration's Information Infrastructure Task Force, see p. 474 infra, a Conference on Fair Use (CONFU) was organized to bring together copyright owners and academic users in an effort to produce guidelines for the use of works in digital form by libraries and educators. CONFU released an interim report in December, 1996. The report contained three sets of proposed guidelines. The Guidelines for Digital Images applied to the creation of digital copies of collections of visual images such as artworks. The Guidelines on Distance Learning covered the use of copyrighted works in both live interactive and recorded distance learning transmissions. The Guidelines on Educational Multimedia covered the use of copyrighted works in multimedia projects by students and teachers. There was also a Statement on Use of Copyrighted Computer Programs (Software) in Libraries. The proposed guidelines are reproduced in Growing Pains: Adapting Copyright for Libraries, Education, and Society (L. Gasaway ed.) (1997). However, they failed to achieve sufficient support from users and copyright owners and have not secured final approval from CONFU.

LIBRARY COPYING—§ 108

According to Thomas Brennan, Chief Counsel to the Senate Subcommittee on Patents, Trademarks and Copyrights during the revision process, "Next to cable television, the most interesting legislative controversy focused on the library photocopying provisions of the bill." Some Observations on the Revision of the Copyright Law From the Legislative Point of View, 24 Bull.Copyr.Soc. 151, 156 (1977). The debate produced the intricate compromise embodied in § 108.

Initially, note that the § 108 exemptions for library copying do not extend to every entity that may style itself a "library or archives." Section 108(a) will eliminate many corporate and commercial collections, although the House Report notes that the "commercial advantage" referred to in subsection (a)(1) "must attach to the immediate commercial motivation behind the reproduction or distribution itself, rather than to the ultimate profit-making motivation behind the enterprise in which the library is located." H.R.Rep. p. 75.

Sections 108(b) and (c) govern copying for purposes such as preservation or replacement, with the exemption for published works subject to the requirement "that an unused replacement cannot be obtained at a fair price."

Copying at user request is subject to the limitations in subsections 108(d) and (e), the former for articles or small portions of copyrighted works, the latter for more extensive copying. (The warning notice required by both provisions is specified in 37 C.F.R. § 201.14.) Copying under these subsections is limited to certain materials, § 108(h), and the photocopies must become the property of the user. Note that the exemption in subsection (d) runs to the library, not to the user. § 108(f)(2). The library is also relieved of liability for the unsupervised use of copying equipment located on its premises. § 108(f)(1). Again, the statute requires a warning notice—the Copyright Office Regulations do not specify its form. (Under what theory could such liability be imposed, even in the absence of a warning notice? Contributory infringement? See p. 457 infra.) Section 108(f)(4) assures us that the library exemptions do not preclude reliance on the general right of fair use. (Is copying that exceeds the limits of § 108 likely to be characterized as "fair use" under § 107?)

The heart of § 108 is subsection (g). "Isolated and unrelated" reproduction of a single copy of the same material on separate occasions is permitted, but "related or concerted" reproduction of the same material is not. The latter extends to "related" requests by members of a group. The Senate Report[k] offers the example of students each requesting separate copies of an article assigned by a college professor. For materials described in § 108(d), chiefly articles from periodicals and journals, there is the further prohibition against "systematic" copying. § 108(g)(2). This provision, as it came from the Senate to the House in 1976, "provoked a storm of controversy, centering around the extent to which the restrictions on 'systematic' activities would prevent the continuation and development of interlibrary networks and other arrangements involving the exchange of photocopies." H.R.Rep. pp. 77–78.

     k. S.Rep. No. 94–473, 94th Cong., 1st Sess. 70 (1975).

When is copying "systematic"? Does the term imply some calculated plan or agreement, or will repeated copying suffice? Compare Nimmer on Copyright § 8.03[E][2], with Treece, Library Photocopying, 24 U.C.L.A. L.Rev. 1025 (1977).

The House softened the ban on "systematic" copying in § 108(g)(2) by adding the proviso authorizing "interlibrary arrangements" that do not "substitute for a subscription to or a purchase of such work." This proviso was the subject of guidelines proposed by CONTU, with the participation and substantial agreement of representatives of libraries, publishers and authors. The guidelines appear in the House–Senate Conference Report[1] and are reproduced below. The conference committee stated that the purpose of the guidelines "is to provide guidance in the most commonly-encountered interlibrary photocopying situations, that they are not intended to be limiting or determinative in themselves or with respect to other situations, and that they deal with an evolving situation that will undoubtedly require their continuous reevaluation and adjustment." Conference Rep. p. 71.

GUIDELINES FOR THE PROVISO OF SUBSECTION 108(G)(2)

1. As used in the proviso of subsection 108(g)(2), the words "... such aggregate quantities as to substitute for a subscription to or purchase of such work" shall mean:

(a) with respect to any given periodical (as opposed to any given issue of a periodical), filled requests of a library or archives (a "requesting entity") within any calendar year for a total of six or more copies of an article or articles published in such periodical within five years prior to the date of the request. These guidelines specifically shall not apply, directly or indirectly, to any request of a requesting entity for a copy or copies of an article or articles published in any issue of a periodical, the publication date of which is more than five years prior to the date when the request is made. These guidelines do not define the meaning, with respect to such a request, of "... such aggregate quantities as to substitute for a subscription to [such periodical]".

(b) With respect to any other material described in subsection 108(d), (including fiction and poetry), filled requests of a requesting entity within any calendar year for a total of six or more copies or phonorecords of or from any given work (including a collective work) during the entire period when such material shall be protected by copyright.

2. In the event that a requesting entity—

(a) shall have in force or shall have entered an order for a subscription to a periodical, or

---

1. H.R.Rep. No. 94–1733, 94th Cong., 2d Sess. 72 (1976).

> (b) has within its collection, or shall have entered an order for, a copy or phonorecord of any other copyrighted work,

material from either category of which it desires to obtain by copy from another library or archives (the "supplying entity"), because the material to be copied is not reasonably available for use by the requesting entity itself, then the fulfillment of such request shall be treated as though the requesting entity made such copy from its own collection. A library or archives may request a copy or phonorecord from a supplying entity only under those circumstances where the requesting entity would have been able, under the other provisions of section 108, to supply such copy from materials in its own collection.

3. No request for a copy or phonorecord of any material to which these guidelines apply may be fulfilled by the supplying entity unless such request is accompanied by a representation by the requesting entity that the request was made in conformity with these guidelines.

4. The requesting entity shall maintain records of all requests made by it for copies or phonorecords of any materials to which these guidelines apply and shall maintain records of the fulfillment of such requests, which records shall be retained until the end of the third complete calendar year after the end of the calendar year in which the respective request shall have been made.

5. As part of the review provided for in subsection 108(i), these guidelines shall be reviewed not later than five years from the effective date of this bill. (Conference Rep. pp. 72–73.)

NOTES AND QUESTIONS

(1) The guidelines are not applicable to interlibrary requests for copies of articles that are more than five years old. Should the approach to such copying be more or less generous than the guidelines? Can the interlibrary arrangements authorized under § 108(g)(2) be carried out by means of digital transmissions? (Note that the reproduction of articles under § 108(d) is not limited to copies in facsimile form.)

(2) The guidelines do not attempt to fix the reach of the subsection (g)(2) prohibition against "systematic reproduction" when the copying is done, not as part of an interlibrary arrangement, but rather from the library's own collection in response to a request from a user. How would the claim of the Williams & Wilkins Co. against the National Institutes of Health, p. 431 supra, have fared under § 108?

Suppose that a Texaco research facility happens to be located near a university library. After the decision in the *Texaco* case, researchers desiring copies of articles now walk across the street and request a photocopy from the library (or e-mail a request from the comfort of their desk). Can the library fill these requests under § 108—or would such copying be "related" or "systematic"?

(3) Former § 108(i) of the 1976 Act required the Register of Copyrights to submit to Congress five-year reports on the operation of § 108. The first Register's Report on Library Reproduction of Copyrighted Works, submitted in 1983, concluded that § 108 "provides a workable structural framework for obtaining a balance between creators' rights and users' needs, but that, in certain instances, the balance has not been achieved in practice." The Register's Report noted, for example, that although all copying permitted by § 108 involves the preparation of only one copy at any particular time, empirical evidence indicated that in one-quarter of library photocopying transactions multiple copies are produced. (It also describes the free license granted by many law reviews for classroom reproduction. See, e.g., the notices that appear at the beginning of the *Yale Law Journal* and the *Nebraska Law Review*.)

The Register's Second Report was issued in 1988. Like the first, it reported a consensus that the structure of § 108 is sound, although compliance remained a problem. The Report also contains information on photocopying practices abroad. Its primary focus, however, was on the emergence of "electrocopying"—the reproduction of works in digital form. The ease of electronic transfer encourages coordinated acquisitions by library consortia; it also can replace printed subscriptions with electronic copies. Rising storage and preservation costs also encourage reliance on the new technologies. When combined with the growing network of personal computers, the potential for dissemination is virtually unlimited. See p. 459 infra. (The requirement of five-year reports on library photocopying was repealed in 1992.)

Issues relating to library copying are reviewed in Coyne, Rights of Reproduction and the Provision of Library Services, 13 U.Ark. Little Rock L.J. 485 (1991); see also Heller, The Impact of Recent Litigation on Interlibrary Loan and Document Delivery, 88 L.Lib.J. 158 (1996). Copyright problems arising from the move by libraries to electronic media are examined in Jensen, Is the Library Without Walls on a Collision Course with the 1976 Copyright Act?, 85 L.Libr.J. 619 (1993). Cochran, Why Can't I Watch This Video Here?: Copyright Confusion and Performances of Videocassettes and Videodiscs in Libraries, 15 Comm/Ent 837 (1993), analyzes the application of the public performance right in the library environment.

SECTION 2.   INNOCENT, CONTRIBUTORY, AND VICARIOUS INFRINGERS

De Acosta v. Brown

United States Circuit Court of Appeals, Second Circuit, 1944.
146 F.2d 408.
Certiorari denied 325 U.S. 862, 65 S.Ct. 1197 (1945).

■ Before L. HAND, CHASE, and CLARK, CIRCUIT JUDGES.

■ CLARK, CIRCUIT JUDGE. Plaintiff has recovered a judgment below based on literary property in the "heart interest" which she has added to the life of a historical character with the avowed intent of making a biographical screen play palatable to the movie audiences of America. The historical character is that of Clara Barton, founder of the American Red Cross, who lived a long and very useful life from 1821 to 1912, in which, however, most of her biographers have found no love romance * * *. [Plaintiff established a channel of access to her unpublished manuscript by defendant Beth Brown, a prolific popular writer. Part of Brown's "biography" of Clara Barton was published by defendant Hearst in Cosmopolitan magazine. It contained so many detailed similarities both as to the love interest and other fictional flourishes that copying was clear. The court held that plaintiff's common law rights had been infringed.]

The injunction, therefore, and the judgment for an accounting of profits against both defendants and for damages against defendant Brown are clearly correct. There remains, therefore, only the question of damages against Hearst, in view of the court's finding that its copying was "innocent." In Barry v. Hughes, 2 Cir., 103 F.2d 427, certiorari denied 308 U.S. 604, in dealing with a copyrighted play, this court expressed a caveat on this issue, saying, "Laying aside a possible action for unjust enrichment, or for an injunction after discovery, we should hesitate a long while before holding that the use of material, apparently in the public demesne, subjected the user to damages, unless something put him actually on notice." But the court made it clear that it was leaving the point "for decision when it arises."

So far as copyrighted material is concerned, the authorities are too conclusive to allow of doubt. Indeed, the inference from the copyright law itself would seem to be most direct; for, while it makes significant distinctions in certain instances based on innocent or willful infringement, as the case may be, it does not do so in the general provision for award of profits and actual damages * * *. Hence we have the classic statement of Brandeis, J., in Buck v. Jewell–La Salle Realty Co., 283 U.S. 191, 198, "Intention to infringe is not essential under the Act," * * *.

Numerous lower court decisions are of the same tenor. Thus it appears usual to hold an innocent publisher of a copyrighted book liable, as in Gross v. Van Dyk Gravure Co., 2 Cir., 230 F. 412, 413, affirming the judgment of L. Hand, D.J., therein quoted, or in Sammons v. Larkin, D.C.Mass., 38 F.Supp. 649, which was affirmed on appeal as to the publisher, but reversed for inadequate allowance for the plaintiff, in Sammons v. Colonial Press, 1 Cir., 126 F.2d 341. In American Press Ass'n v. Daily Story Pub. Co., 7 Cir., 120 F. 766, 768, 769, appeal dismissed 193 U.S. 675, the court states that it is not material that the infringer in publishing the copyrighted story was not aware that the story was so protected, for "it published it at its peril, and ignorance will not avail," making use of the analogy of "title to a horse lost by the stealing of it, or by the unlawful sale of it to a stranger." And the dissenting opinion, which went on a different point—the scope of a granted license—specifically accepted the view that innocence was not a defense, and that title to copyright was not lost by theft or piracy of the manuscript. * * *

Should a different rule be applicable to uncopyrighted [unpublished] material? That would leave the issue very narrow, indeed, so narrow that nonliability would hardly make an appreciable difference to publishers in the conduct of their business, though it might occasionally rest heavily on a particular author. But generally speaking, damages will be difficult of proof and the amount of recovery is likely to be small. Nor does the rationale for such a distinction seem sound. It is suggested that recovery is contrary to the general doctrine of torts, apparently on the view that liability and damage should be limited to such as can be foreseen and avoided. But "torts" is a broad field of law; and while the doctrine may apply to negligence, it does not apply to conversion or appropriation. Cf. Restatement, Torts, 1934, §§ 222, 244, with § 289. Here the analogy of the cases has always been that of the conversion of literary property; and, as in the American Press case cited above, that analogy here is complete to justify recovery as against even an innocent copier. * * * This case well illustrates the dangers to authors if a different rule were to be established. For the finding of innocence of Hearst is based upon two factors only, namely, that Brown the infringer assured the Cosmopolitan editor of the research that she had done on the matter, and that the reputation of Brown was known to the editor—a reputation, however, distinctly other than in the field of historical research. And if it be suggested that other more effective means of inquiry are not conveniently available to publishers, then that seems an additional reason for not depriving authors so easily of the fruits of their labors.

Judgment affirmed.

■ [JUDGE L. HAND dissented.]

NOTES

"Innocent" infringement may take several forms. The copying may be unconscious. (See Judge Hand's charitable concessions in *Sheldon,* p. 201 supra, and Fred Fisher v. Dillingham, p. 213 supra.) Or the defendant may in good faith believe that the use does not infringe. Or, as in the preceding case, it may be unaware of the infringing activities of a related party. Such "innocence" does not excuse the infringement.

Are there means by which a publisher or broadcaster can protect itself against the sort of liability visited upon Hearst in *De Acosta*? On the use of indemnity agreements and insurance, see R. Brown, The Operation of the Damage Provisions of the Copyright Law: An Exploratory Study, Copyr. Law Revision Study No. 23 (1958), in 2 Studies on Copyr. 1067 (1963).

Shapiro, Bernstein & Co. v. H.L. Green Co.

United States Court of Appeals, Second Circuit, 1963.
316 F.2d 304.

■ Before WATERMAN and KAUFMAN, CIRCUIT JUDGES, and WEINFELD, DISTRICT JUDGE.

■ KAUFMAN, CIRCUIT JUDGE.

This action for copyright infringement presents us with a picture all too familiar in copyright litigation: a legal problem vexing in its difficulty, a dearth of squarely applicable precedents, a business setting so common that the dearth of precedents seems inexplicable, and an almost complete absence of guidance from the terms of the Copyright Act * * *. The plaintiffs in the court below, appellants here, are the copyright proprietors of several musical compositions, recordings of which have met with considerable popularity, especially amongst the younger set. The defendant Jalen Amusement Company, Inc. was charged in the complaint with having infringed the copyrights on these songs by manufacturing records, close copies of the "hit-type" authorized records of major record manufacturers in violation of 17 U.S.C. § 101(e): "in the absence of a license agreement" with the plaintiffs and without having served upon them a notice of intention "to use a copyrighted musical composition upon the parts of instruments serving to reproduce mechanically the musical work."

Jalen operated the phonograph record department as concessionaire in twenty-three stores of defendant H.L. Green Co., Inc., pursuant to written licenses from the Green Company. The complaint alleged that Green was liable for copyright infringement because it "sold, or contributed to and participated actively in the sale of" the so-called "bootleg" records manufactured by Jalen and sold by Jalen in the Green stores. * * *

At the time of suit, Jalen had been operating under license from Green the phonograph record department in twenty-three of its stores, in some for as long as thirteen years. The licensing agreements provided that Jalen and its employees were to "abide by, observe and obey all rules and regulations promulgated from time to time by H.L. Green Company, Inc. * * *" Green, in its "unreviewable discretion", had the authority to discharge any employee believed to be conducting himself improperly. Jalen, in turn, agreed to save Green harmless from any claims arising in connection with the conduct of the phonograph record concession. Significantly, the licenses provided that Green was to receive a percentage—in some cases 10%, in others 12%—of Jalen's gross receipts from the sale of records, as its full compensation as licensor.

In the actual day-to-day functioning of the record department, Jalen ordered and purchased all records, was billed for them, and paid for them. All sales were made by Jalen employees, who, as the District Court found, were under the effective control and supervision of Jalen. All of the daily proceeds from record sales went into Green's cash registers and were removed therefrom by the cashier of the store. At regular accounting periods, Green deducted its 10% or 12% commission and deducted the salaries of the Jalen employees, which salaries were handed over by the Green cashier to one of Jalen's employees to be distributed to the others. Social security and withholding taxes were withheld from the salaries of the employees by Green, and the withholdings then turned over to Jalen. Only then was the balance of the gross receipts of the record department given to Jalen. Customers purchasing records were given a receipt on a printed form marked "H.L. Green Company, Inc."; Jalen's name was wholly absent from the premises. The District Judge found that Green did not actively participate in the sale of the records and that it had no knowledge of the unauthorized manufacture of the records. * * *

* * * It is quite clear, for example, that the normal agency rule of *respondeat superior* applies to copyright infringement by a servant within the scope of his employment. See, e.g., M. Witmark & Sons v. Calloway, 22 F.2d 412, 414 (E.D.Tenn.1927). Realistically, the courts have not drawn a rigid line between the strict cases of agency, and those of independent contract, license, and lease. See Study No. 25, Latman & Tager, "Liability of Innocent Infringers of Copyrights", prepared for the Subcommittee on Patents, Trademarks, and Copyrights of the Senate Comm. on the Judiciary, 86th Cong., 2d Sess. 146. Many of the elements which have given rise to the doctrine of *respondeat superior*, see Seavey, Studies in Agency, 145–53 (1949), may also be evident in factual settings other than that of a technical employer-employee relationship. When the right and ability to supervise coalesce with an obvious and direct financial interest in the exploitation of copyrighted materials—even in the absence of actual knowledge that the copyright monopoly is being impaired, see De Acosta v. Brown, 146 F.2d 408 (2d Cir.1944), cert. denied, Hearst Magazines v. De Acosta, 325 U.S. 862 (1945)—the purposes of copyright law may be best effectuated by the imposition of liability upon the beneficiary of that exploitation.

The two lines of precedent most nearly relevant to the case before us are those which deal, on the one hand, with the landlord leasing his property at a fixed rental to a tenant who engages in copyright-infringing conduct on the leased premises and, on the other hand, the proprietor or manager of a dance hall or music hall leasing his premises to or hiring a dance band, which brings in customers and profits to the proprietor by performing copyrighted music but without complying with the terms of the Copyright Act. If the landlord lets his premises without knowledge of the impending infringement by his tenant, exercises no supervision over him, charges a fixed rental and receives no other benefit from the infringement, and contributes in no way to it, it has been held that the landlord is not liable for his tenant's wrongdoing. See Deutsch v. Arnold, 98 F.2d 686 (2d Cir.1938); cf. Fromont v. Aeolian Co., 254 F. 592 (S.D.N.Y.1918). But, the cases are legion which hold the dance hall proprietor liable for the infringement of copyright resulting from the performance of a musical composition by a band or orchestra whose activities provide the proprietor with a source of customers and enhanced income. He is liable whether the bandleader is considered, as a technical matter, an employee or an independent contractor, and whether or not the proprietor has knowledge of the compositions to be played or any control over their selection. * * *

We believe that the principle which can be extracted from the dance hall cases is a sound one and, under the facts of the cases before us, is here applicable. Those cases and this one lie closer on the spectrum to the employer-employee model than to the landlord-tenant model. * * * We therefore conclude, on the particular facts before us, that Green's relationship to its infringing licensee, as well as its strong concern for the financial success of the phonograph record concession, renders it liable for the unauthorized sales of the "bootleg" records.   * * *

Reversed and remanded.

NOTES ON VICARIOUS LIABILITY

(1) Vicarious liability in copyright law, as Judge Kaufman notes, extends beyond the traditional limits of *respondeat superior*.   The issue arises most frequently in connection with unauthorized performances.   The House Report offers the following summation:

> The committee has considered and rejected an amendment to this section intended to exempt the proprietors of an establishment, such as a ballroom or night club, from liability for copyright infringement committed by an independent contractor, such as an orchestra leader.   A well-established principle of copyright law is that a person who violates any of the exclusive rights of the copyright owner is an infringer, including persons who can be considered related or vicarious infringers.   To be held a related or vicarious infringer in the case of performing rights, a defendant must either actively operate or supervise the operation of the place wherein the performances occur, or control the content of the infringing program, and expect commercial gain from the operation and either direct or indirect benefit from the infringing performance.   The committee has decided that no justification exists for changing existing law, and causing a significant erosion of the public performance right.   (H.R.Rep. p. 159.)

The proprietor remains liable even if the infringing performance contravenes specific instructions. See, e.g., Warner Brothers, Inc. v. O'Keefe, 468 F.Supp. 16 (S.D.Iowa 1977). When vendors at a flea market were caught selling counterfeit sound recordings, the Ninth Circuit reversed the dismissal of the copyright owners' vicarious liability claim against the operator of the flea market based on allegations of the operator's ability to control the vendors and its financial benefit through admission fees and concession sales. (Dismissal of a claim for contributory liability, see infra, was also reversed because the operator had provided the physical site for known infringing sales.) Fonovisa, Inc. v. Cherry Auction, Inc., 76 F.3d 259 (9th Cir.1996).

(2) In Roy Export Co. Establishment v. Trustees of Columbia Univ., 344 F.Supp. 1350, 1352–53 (S.D.N.Y.1972), the owner of the copyright in Charlie Chaplin's film "Modern Times" sued a student organization and its president, as well as Columbia University, as a result of the former's unauthorized performances.   The court declined to include the University within the scope of its preliminary injunction:

"It is clear that before one may be held liable as a vicarious infringer, absent a special relationship, such as agency or partnership, he must have had the right and ability to supervise the infringing activities, as well as a direct financial interest in those activities.   * * *

"We do not think, however, that the University's policy of not interfering with its student organizations is synonymous with its not having the right or ability to have supervised the present infringing activities.   * * *

"However, in the present case, plaintiffs neither show benefit to the University, nor do they refute defendants Trustees' assertion that the University received no financial benefit from the two showings of the bootleg film.   * * *

"All of the cases plaintiffs cite in support of their contention that the University is a vicarious infringer are permeated with the profit motive."

(3) The vicarious liability of the sponsor of a television program was at issue in Davis v. E.I. DuPont De Nemours & Co., 240 F.Supp. 612 (S.D.N.Y.1965).   After finding the writers, producers, and broadcaster liable for infringing plaintiff's dramatization of Edith Wharton's novel "Ethan Frome," Judge Feinberg considered the vicarious liability of DuPont and its advertising agency.   Relying on *Shapiro,* he concluded "that DuPont had the ultimate power to determine content of the program and exercised that power through its [advertising agency]."   The program had been broadcast on the "DuPont Show of the Month."   "DuPont was not merely an advertiser buying time on a program produced by a station over whom it had no control."   Both were liable for the infringement.

For a contrary holding in the context of a "network-packaged as opposed to sponsor-packaged production," see Bevan v. CBS, Inc., 329 F.Supp. 601 (S.D.N.Y.1971) ("Hogan's Heroes").

Sony Corp. of America v. Universal City Studios, Inc.

Supreme Court of the United States, 1984.
464 U.S. 417, 104 S.Ct. 774.

[Other portions of the Court's opinion appear at pp. 1 and 389 supra.]

■ JUSTICE STEVENS * * *

III

The Copyright Act does not expressly render anyone liable for infringement committed by another.   In contrast, the Patent Act expressly brands anyone who "actively induces infringement of a patent" as an infringer, 35 U.S.C. § 271(b), and further imposes liability on certain individuals labeled "contributory" infringers, § 271(c).   The absence of such express language in the copyright statute does not preclude the imposition of liability for copyright infringements on certain parties who have not themselves engaged in the infringing activity.[17]　For vicarious liability is imposed in virtually all areas of the law, and the concept of contributory infringement is merely a species of the broader problem of identifying the circumstances in which it is just to hold one individual accountable for the actions of another.

Such circumstances were plainly present in Kalem Co. v. Harper Brothers, 222 U.S. 55 (1911), the copyright decision of this Court on which respondents place their principal reliance.　In *Kalem,* the Court held that the producer of an unauthorized film dramatization of the copyrighted book *Ben Hur* was liable for his sale of the motion picture to jobbers, who in turn arranged for the commercial exhibition of the film.　Justice Holmes, writing for the Court, explained:

> "The defendant not only expected but invoked by advertisement the use of its films for dramatic reproduction of the story.　That was the most conspicuous purpose for which they could be used, and the one for which especially they were made.　If the defendant did not contribute to the infringement it is impossible to do so except by taking part in the final act.　It is liable on principles recognized in every part of the law."　222 U.S., at 63.

* * *

Respondents argue that *Kalem* stands for the proposition that supplying the "means" to accomplish an infringing activity and encouraging that activity through advertisement are sufficient to establish liability for copyright infringement.　This argument rests on a gross generalization that cannot withstand scrutiny.　The producer in *Kalem* did not merely provide the "means" to accomplish an infringing activity; the producer supplied the work itself, albeit in a new medium of expression.　Sony in the instant case does not supply Betamax consumers with respondents' works; respondents do.　Sony supplies a piece of equipment that is generally capable of copying the entire range of programs that may be televised: those that are uncopyrighted, those that are copyrighted but may be copied without objection from the copyright holder, and those that the copyright holder would prefer not to have copied.　The Betamax can be used to make authorized or unauthorized uses of copyrighted works, but the range of its potential use is much broader than the particular infringing use of the film

---

17. As the District Court correctly observed, however, "the lines between direct infringement, contributory infringement, and vicarious liability are not clearly drawn.... " 480 F.Supp. 457–458.　The lack of clarity in this area may, in part, be attributable to the fact that an infringer is not merely one who uses a work without authorization by the copyright owner, but also one who authorizes the use of a copyrighted work without actual authority from the copyright owner.

We note the parties' statements that the questions of Sony's liability under the "doc-

trines" of "direct infringement" and "vicarious liability" are not nominally before this Court.　Compare Respondents' Brief, at 9, n. 22, 41, n. 90 with Petitioners' Reply Brief, at 1, n. 2.　We also observe, however, that reasoned analysis of respondents' unprecedented contributory infringement claim necessarily entails consideration of arguments and case law which may also be forwarded under the other labels, and indeed the parties to a large extent rely upon such arguments and authority in support of their respective positions on the issue of contributory infringement.

Ben Hur involved in *Kalem*. *Kalem* does not support respondents' novel theory of liability.

Justice Holmes stated that the producer had "contributed" to the infringement of the copyright, and the label "contributory infringement" has been applied in a number of lower court copyright cases involving an ongoing relationship between the direct infringer and the contributory infringer at the time the infringing conduct occurred. In such cases, as in other situations in which the imposition of vicarious liability is manifestly just, the "contributory" infringer was in a position to control the use of copyrighted works by others and had authorized the use without permission from the copyright owner.[18] This case, however, plainly does not fall in that category. The only contact between Sony and the users of the Betamax that is disclosed by this record occurred at the moment of sale. The District Court expressly found that "no employee of Sony, Sonam or DDBI had either direct involvement with the allegedly infringing activity or

---

18.   The so-called "dance hall cases," Famous Music Corp. v. Bay State Harness Horse Racing and Breeding Ass'n, 554 F.2d 1213 (CA1 1977) (racetrack retained infringer to supply music to paying customers); KECA Music, Inc. v. Dingus McGee's Co., 432 F.Supp. 72 (W.D.Mo.1977) (cocktail lounge hired musicians to supply music to paying customers); Dreamland Ball Room v. Shapiro, Bernstein & Co., 36 F.2d 354 (CA7 1929) (dance hall hired orchestra to supply music to paying customers) are often contrasted with the so-called landlord-tenant cases, in which landlords who leased premises to a direct infringer for a fixed rental and did not participate directly in any infringing activity were found not to be liable for contributory infringement. E.g., Deutsch v. Arnold, 98 F.2d 686 (CA2 1938).

In Shapiro, Bernstein & Co. v. H.L. Green Co., 316 F.2d 304 (CA2 1963), the owner of twenty-three chain stores retained the direct infringer to run its record departments. The relationship was structured as a licensing arrangement, so that the defendant bore none of the business risk of running the department. Instead, it received 10% or 12% of the direct infringer's gross receipts. The Court of Appeals concluded:

"[The dance-hall cases] and this one lie closer on the spectrum to the employer-employee model, than to the landlord-tenant model. . . . [O]n the particular facts before us, . . . Green's relationship to its infringing licensee, as well as its strong concern for the financial success of the phonograph record concession, renders it liable for the unauthorized sales of the 'bootleg' records.

". . . [T]he imposition of *vicarious* liability in the case before us cannot be deemed unduly harsh or unfair. Green has the power to police carefully the conduct of its concessionaire; our judgment will simply encourage it to do so, thus placing responsibility where it can and should be effectively exercised." Id., at 308 (emphasis in original).

In Gershwin Publishing Corp. v. Columbia Artists Management, Inc., 443 F.2d 1159 (CA2 1971), the direct infringers retained the contributory infringer to manage their performances. The contributory infringer would contact each direct infringer, obtain the titles of the musical compositions to be performed, print the programs, and then sell the programs to its own local organizations for distribution at the time of the direct infringement. Id., at 1161. The Court of Appeals emphasized that the contributory infringer had actual knowledge that the artists it was managing were performing copyrighted works, was in a position to police the infringing conduct of the artists, and derived substantial benefit from the actions of the primary infringers. Id., at 1163.

In Screen Gems–Columbia Music, Inc. v. Mark–Fi Records, Inc., 256 F.Supp. 399 (SDNY 1966), the direct infringer manufactured and sold bootleg records. In denying a motion for summary judgment, the District Court held that the infringer's advertising agency, the radio stations that advertised the infringer's works, and the service agency that boxed and mailed the infringing goods could all be held liable, if at trial it could be demonstrated that they knew or should have known that they were dealing in illegal goods.

direct contact with purchasers of Betamax who recorded copyrighted works off-the-air.'' 480 F.Supp., at 460. And it further found that ''there was no evidence that any of the copies made by Griffiths or the other individual witnesses in this suit were influenced or encouraged by [Sony's] advertisements.'' Ibid.

If vicarious liability is to be imposed on petitioners in this case, it must rest on the fact that they have sold equipment with constructive knowledge of the fact that their customers may use that equipment to make unauthorized copies of copyrighted material. There is no precedent in the law of copyright for the imposition of vicarious liability on such a theory. The closest analogy is provided by the patent law cases to which it is appropriate to refer because of the historic kinship between patent law and copyright law.[19]

In the Patent Act both the concept of infringement and the concept of contributory infringement are expressly defined by statute. The prohibition against contributory infringement is confined to the knowing sale of a component especially made for use in connection with a particular patent. There is no suggestion in the statute that one patentee may object to the sale of a product that might be used in connection with other patents. Moreover, the Act expressly provides that the sale of a ''staple article or commodity of commerce suitable for substantial noninfringing use'' is not contributory infringement. * * *

We recognize there are substantial differences between the patent and copyright laws. But in both areas the contributory infringement doctrine is grounded on the recognition that adequate protection of a monopoly may require the courts to look beyond actual duplication of a device or publication to the products or activities that make such duplication possible. The staple article of commerce doctrine must strike a balance between a copyright holder's legitimate demand for effective—not merely symbolic— protection of the statutory monopoly, and the rights of others freely to engage in substantially unrelated areas of commerce. Accordingly, the sale of copying equipment, like the sale of other articles of commerce, does not constitute contributory infringement if the product is widely used for

---

19. E.g., United States v. Paramount Pictures, 334 U.S. 131, 158 (1948); Fox Film Corp. v. Doyal, 286 U.S. 123, 131 (1932); Wheaton and Donaldson v. Peters and Grigg, 33 U.S. (8 Pet.) 591, 657–658 (1834). The two areas of the law, naturally, are not identical twins, and we exercise the caution which we have expressed in the past in applying doctrine formulated in one area to the other. See generally, Mazer v. Stein, 347 U.S. 201, 217–218 (1954); Bobbs–Merrill Co. v. Straus, 210 U.S. 339, 345 (1908).

We have consistently rejected the proposition that a similar kinship exists between copyright law and trademark law, and in the process of doing so have recognized the basic similarities between copyrights and patents. The Trade–Mark Cases, 100 U.S. 82, 91–92 (1879); see also, United Drug Co. v. Rectanus Co., 248 U.S. 90, 97 (1918) (trademark right ''has little or no analogy'' to copyright or patent); McLean v. Fleming, 96 U.S. 245, 254 (1877); Canal Co. v. Clark, 13 Wall. 311, 322 (1871). Given the fundamental differences between copyright law and trademark law, in this copyright case we do not look to the standard for contributory infringement set forth in Inwood Laboratories v. Ives Laboratories, 456 U.S. 844, 854–855 (1982), which was crafted for application in trademark cases. * * *

legitimate, unobjectionable purposes. Indeed, it need merely be capable of substantial noninfringing uses. * * *

In summary, the record and findings of the District Court lead us to two conclusions. First, Sony demonstrated a significant likelihood that substantial numbers of copyright holders who license their works for broadcast on free television would not object to having their broadcasts time-shifted by private viewers. And second, respondents failed to demonstrate that time-shifting would cause any likelihood of non-minimal harm to the potential market for, or the value of, their copyrighted works. The Betamax is, therefore, capable of substantial noninfringing uses. Sony's sale of such equipment to the general public does not constitute contributory infringement of respondent's copyrights. * * *

■ [JUSTICE BLACKMUN's dissenting opinion is omitted.]

NOTES AND QUESTIONS ON CONTRIBUTORY INFRINGEMENT

(1) In footnote 18 the Court makes reference to Gershwin Publishing Corp. v. Columbia Artists Management, Inc., 443 F.2d 1159 (2d Cir.1971). The defendant in *Gershwin,* in addition to managing concert artists, assisted in organizing and nurturing community associations that in turn sponsored annual concert series. It was sued in connection with an unlicensed performance that occurred during a community concert. The Second Circuit, reviewing its decision in *Shapiro,* noted that one may be a "vicarious" infringer if the person has the right and ability to supervise and a direct financial interest in the conduct. It then continued: "Similarly, one who, with knowledge of the infringing activity, induces, causes or materially contributes to the infringing conduct of another, may be held liable as a 'contributory' infringer. * * * The district court properly held [defendant] liable as a 'vicarious' and a 'contributory' infringer."

Is this distinction helpful?

(2) Suppose a record store installs a sophisticated self-service tape duplication system and, upon purchase of a blank cartridge, "lends" the customer tapes from its library of recordings. Is the store liable as a contributory infringer? See Elektra Records Co. v. Gem Electronic Distributors, Inc., 360 F.Supp. 821 (E.D.N.Y.1973); see also RCA Records v. All–Fast Systems, Inc., 594 F.Supp. 335 (S.D.N.Y.1984). Does a library that maintains an unsupervised photocopier risk liability if it does not display a warning notice in compliance with § 108(f)(1)? The court in *Elektra Records,* justifying a preliminary injunction, distinguished the record store's library analogy, emphasizing the store's financial stake in the copying. Is there nevertheless a negative implication in § 108(f)(1)?

In a post-*Sony* case, a tape copying machine that would accept only specially-notched blank tapes was said to be a staple article of commerce, precluding contributory liability. But the manufacturer and its principal shareholder were held to be vicarious infringers when the machines were used in retail stores to copy copyrighted recordings because of their "authority to control use of the machine" (it was lent rather than sold to retailers) and their "financial interest in the copying as the source for the notched blank tapes needed to use the machine." RCA/Ariola Int'l Inc. v. Thomas & Grayston Co., 845 F.2d 773 (8th Cir.1988); cf. A & M Records, Inc. v. General Audio Video Cassettes, Inc., 948 F.Supp. 1449 (C.D.Cal. 1996), imposing contributory liability on a supplier of blank tape cut specifically to match the duration of legitimate recordings pirated by the supplier's customer.

(3) The House Report notes that § 106 accords to the copyright owner the right "to authorize" the exercise of the specified rights. "Use of the phrase 'to authorize' is intended to avoid any questions as to the liability of contributory infringers. For example, a person who lawfully acquires an authorized copy of a motion picture would be an infringer if he or she engages in the business of renting it to others for purposes of unauthorized public performance." H.R.Rep. p. 61.

(4) In Original Appalachian Artworks, Inc. v. Cradle Creations, Inc., 223 U.S.P.Q. 80 (N.D.Ga.1983), the court, citing *Gershwin,* ordered judgment against the distributor of an instruction booklet for making "soft sculpture" dolls. "[B]ecause defendants were aware that their booklets would be used by others to make infringing copies of plaintiff's copyrighted dolls, and because defendants' booklet materially contributes to the infringing activities of others who use the instructions and patterns contained therein to produce such infringing copies, defendants' conduct constitutes contributory infringement."

The *Gershwin* formulation was also adopted in Atari, Inc. v. JS & A Group, Inc., 597 F.Supp. 5 (N.D.Ill.1983). The defendant was promoting an electronic device capable of duplicating video game cartridges. A manufacturer of video games sought a preliminary injunction, alleging contributory infringement. The court saw the issue as whether the device had a *"substantial* noninfringing use." It rejected the argument that the right to use the device to duplicate the few games marketed by defendant was itself a sufficient noninfringing use. It also rejected the contention that the duplication was within the "archival exception" for computer programs in § 117, since the games were not subject to the risk of loss for which the exemption was arguably intended. Sale of the device was enjoined. (An appeal led to an extended consideration of the appellate jurisdiction of the Court of Appeals for the Federal Circuit in cases involving a copyright or trademark claim joined with a claim for patent infringement (over which the C.A.F.C. has exclusive appellate jurisdiction). Atari, Inc. v. JS & A Groups, Inc., 747 F.2d 1422 (Fed.Cir.1984) (jurisdiction over copyright appeal upheld despite separation of the patent count).) But in Vault Corp. v. Quaid Software Ltd., 847 F.2d 255 (5th Cir.1988), the court rejected the "narrow construction of the archival exception" accepted in *Atari* and found that the defendant's Ramkey program, designed to facilitate the duplication of copy-protected diskettes, was capable of substantial noninfringing use, thus precluding contributory liability.

For an attempt to find the appropriate balance between the interests of the creators of copyrighted works and the interests of the creators of copying technology, see Oddi, Contributory Copyright Infringement: The Tort and Technological Tensions, 64 Notre Dame L.Rev. 47 (1989).

SECTION 3.   COPYRIGHT IN A DIGITAL AGE

"Throughout the time I've been groping around cyberspace, an immense, unresolved conundrum has remained at the root of nearly every legal, ethical, governmental, and social vexation to be found in the Virtual World. I refer to the problem of digitized property. The enigma is this: If our property can be infinitely reproduced and instantaneously distributed all over the planet without cost, without our knowledge, without its even leaving our possession, how can we protect it? How are we going to get paid for the work we do with our minds? And, if we can't get paid, what will assure the continued creation and distribution of such work?

"Since we don't have a solution to what is a profoundly new kind of challenge, and are apparently unable to delay the galloping digitization of everything not obstinately physical, we are sailing into the future on a sinking ship.

"This vessel, the accumulated canon of copyright and patent law, was developed to convey forms and methods of expression entirely different from the vaporous cargo it is now being asked to carry. It is leaking as much from within as from without.

"Legal efforts to keep the old boat floating are taking three forms: a frenzy of deck chair rearrangement, stern warnings to the passengers that if she goes down, they will face harsh criminal penalties, and serene, glassy-eyed denial.

"Intellectual property law cannot be patched, retrofitted, or expanded to contain digitized expression any more than real property law might be revised to cover the allocation of broadcasting spectrum (which, in fact, rather resembles what is being attempted here). We need to develop an entirely new set of methods as befits this entirely new set of circumstances. * * *

"In the absence of the old containers, almost everything we think we know about intellectual property is wrong." Barlow, The Economy of Ideas: A Framework for Rethinking Patents and Copyrights in the Digital Age, Wired, March 1994, p. 84.[a]

---

a. Reprinted with permission. The author is described as "a retired cattle rancher, a lyricist for the Grateful Dead, and co-founder and executive chair of the Electronic Frontier Foundation."

"With no more than minor clarification and limited amendment, the Copyright Act will provide the necessary balance of protection of rights— and limitations on those rights—to promote the progress of science and the useful arts. Existing copyright law needs only the fine tuning that techno- logical advances necessitate, in order to maintain the balance of the law in the face of onrushing technology." Information Infrastructure Task Force, Intellectual Property and the National Information Infrastructure 16–17 (1995).[b]

How should the law respond to the remarkable increase in our ability to disseminate and enjoy works of authorship made possible by modern computer technology? When the 1976 Copyright Act was drafted, comput- ers still occupied rooms rather than desktops and were fed by punch cards and reels of magnetic tape. Section 117 as originally enacted was a stand- still provision that tied a copyright owner's rights over computer use to the state of the law prior to the enactment of the 1976 Act. Presumably even then, the retrieval of a work from a computer in the form of a print-out would, absent fair use, constitute infringement. As for the creation of digital copies or their introduction into computer memory, however, the implications of White–Smith v. Apollo Co., p. 26 supra, with its emphasis on "intelligible" embodiments, left the issue in considerable doubt under the old law. The 1978 CONTU Report recommended repeal of § 117; it was replaced in 1980 by the current provision exempting certain reproductions of computer programs. As for the reproduction of other works in digital form, the CONTU Report offered this comment: "The introduction of a work into a computer memory would, consistent with the new law, be a reproduction of the work, one of the exclusive rights of the copyright proprietor. * * * Principles of fair use would be applicable in limited instances to excuse an unauthorized input of a work into computer memo- ry." Rep. p. 40.

The stakes for copyright owners rose in the 1980s when PCs with floppy disks and later hard drives appeared in so many homes and offices. Copyright owners, particularly sellers of software, scoured copyright, pat- ent, and trade secret law in an attempt to retain control over their products and markets. The issue of intellectual property rights in an increasingly digital age was pushed to center stage by the soaring popularity of the Internet and the development of the World Wide Web. The focus on copyright law and policy grows more intense with every technological innovation. "Streaming" technology, which eliminates the need for users to download bulky audio and video files, makes it practical to deliver live and recorded audio and video programming over the Internet. Improvements in the compression technology that shrinks the size of digital files creates ever-increasing opportunities for the digital delivery of a variety of works, including sound recordings. See p. 310 supra.

b.   The "White Paper".

The future of the digital revolution is sometimes captured by the metaphor of a celestial jukebox—a system of orbiting satellites that can instantaneously deliver any requested entertainment or information product to the user's all-purpose digital receiver. What role will copyright play in such a world? Is the bundle of rights in § 106 too broad, too narrow, or simply too antiquated to serve the needs of users and creators in a digital age?

Religious Technology Center v. Netcom On–Line Communication Services, Inc.

United States District Court, Northern District of California, 1995.
907 F.Supp. 1361.

◼ WHYTE, DISTRICT JUDGE.

This case concerns an issue of first impression regarding intellectual property rights in cyberspace.[1] Specifically, this order addresses whether the operator of a computer bulletin board service ("BBS"), and the large Internet[2] access provider that allows that BBS to reach the Internet, should be liable for copyright infringement committed by a subscriber of the BBS.

Plaintiffs Religious Technology Center ("RTC") and Bridge Publications, Inc. ("BPI") hold copyrights in the unpublished and published works of L. Ron Hubbard, the late founder of the Church of Scientology ("the Church"). Defendant Dennis Erlich ("Erlich")[3] is a former minister of

---

1. Cyberspace is a popular term for the world of electronic communications over computer networks. See Trotter Hardy, The Proper Legal Regime for "Cyberspace," 55 U.Pitt.L.Rev. 993, 994 (1994).

2. "The Internet today is a worldwide entity whose nature cannot be easily or simply defined. From a technical definition, the Internet is the 'set of all interconnected IP networks'—the collection of several thousand local, regional, and global computer networks interconnected in real time via the TCP/IP Internetworking Protocol suite...." Daniel P. Dern, *The Internet Guide for New Users* 16 (1994).

One article described the Internet as a collection of thousands of local, regional, and global Internet Protocol networks. What it means in practical terms is that millions of computers in schools, universities, corporations, and other organizations are tied together via telephone lines. The Internet enables users to share files, search for information, send electronic mail, and log onto remote computers. But it isn't a program or even a particular computer resource. It remains only a means to link computer users together.

Unlike on-line computer services such as CompuServe and America On Line, no one runs the Internet....

No one pays for the Internet because the network itself doesn't exist as a separate entity. Instead various universities and organizations pay for the dedicated lines linking their computers. Individual users may pay an Internet provider for access to the Internet via its server.

David Bruning, Along the InfoBahn, *Astronomy*, Vol. 23, No. 6, p. 76 (June 1995).

3. Issues of Erlich's liability were addressed in this court's order of September 22, 1995. That order concludes in part that a preliminary injunction against Erlich is warranted because plaintiffs have shown a likelihood of success on their copyright infringement claims against him. Plaintiffs likely own valid copyrights in Hubbard's published and unpublished works and Erlich's near-verbatim copying of substantial portions of plaintiffs' works was not likely a fair use. To the extent that Netcom and Klemesrud argue that plaintiffs' copyrights are invalid and that Netcom and Klemesrud are not liable

Scientology turned vocal critic of the Church, whose pulpit is now the Usenet newsgroup[4] alt.religion.scientology ("a.r.s."), an on-line forum for discussion and criticism of Scientology. Plaintiffs maintain that Erlich infringed their copyrights when he posted portions of their works on a.r.s. Erlich gained his access to the Internet through defendant Thomas Klemesrud's ("Klemesrud's") BBS "support.com." Klemesrud is the operator of the BBS, which is run out of his home and has approximately 500 paying users. Klemesrud's BBS is not directly linked to the Internet, but gains its connection through the facilities of defendant Netcom On–Line Communications, Inc. ("Netcom"), one of the largest providers of Internet access in the United States.

After failing to convince Erlich to stop his postings, plaintiffs contacted defendants Klemesrud and Netcom. Klemesrud responded to plaintiffs' demands that Erlich be kept off his system by asking plaintiffs to prove that they owned the copyrights to the works posted by Erlich. However, plaintiffs refused Klemesrud's request as unreasonable. Netcom similarly refused plaintiffs' request that Erlich not be allowed to gain access to the Internet through its system. Netcom contended that it would be impossible to prescreen Erlich's postings and that to kick Erlich off the Internet meant kicking off the hundreds of users of Klemesrud's BBS. Consequently, plaintiffs named Klemesrud and Netcom in their suit against Erlich, although only on the copyright infringement claims. * * *

1. Direct Infringement

Infringement consists of the unauthorized exercise of one of the exclusive rights of the copyright holder delineated in section 106. 17 U.S.C. § 501. Direct infringement does not require intent or any particular state of mind, although willfulness is relevant to the award of statutory damages. 17 U.S.C. § 504(c). * * *

a. *Undisputed Facts*

The parties do not dispute the basic processes that occur when Erlich posts his allegedly infringing messages to a.r.s. Erlich connects to Klemesrud's BBS using a telephone and a modem. Erlich then transmits his

---

because Erlich had a valid fair use defense, the court previously rejected these arguments and will not reconsider them here.

4. The Usenet has been described as

a worldwide community of electronic BBSs that is closely associated with the Internet and with the Internet community. ¶ The messages in Usenet are organized into thousands of topical groups, or "Newsgroups".... ¶ As a Usenet user, you read and contribute ("post") to your local Usenet site. Each Usenet site distributes its users' postings to other Usenet sites based on various implicit and explicit configuration settings, and in turn receives postings from other sites. Usenet traffic typically consists of as much as 30 to 50 Mbytes of messages per day. ¶ Usenet is read and contributed to on a daily basis by a total population of millions of people.... ¶ There is no specific network that is the Usenet. Usenet traffic flows over a wide range of networks, including the Internet and dial-up phone links.

Dern, *supra*, at 196–97.

messages to Klemesrud's computer, where they are automatically briefly stored. According to a prearranged pattern established by Netcom's software, Erlich's initial act of posting a message to the Usenet results in the automatic copying of Erlich's message from Klemesrud's computer onto Netcom's computer and onto other computers on the Usenet. In order to ease transmission and for the convenience of Usenet users, Usenet servers maintain postings from newsgroups for a short period of time—eleven days for Netcom's system and three days for Klemesrud's system. Once on Netcom's computers, messages are available to Netcom's customers and Usenet neighbors, who may then download the messages to their own computers. Netcom's local server makes available its postings to a group of Usenet servers, which do the same for other servers until all Usenet sites worldwide have obtained access to the postings, which takes a matter of hours. * * *

b. *Creation of Fixed Copies*

The Ninth Circuit addressed the question of what constitutes infringement in the context of storage of digital information in a computer's random access memory ("RAM"). MAI Systems Corp. v. Peak Computer, Inc., 991 F.2d 511, 518 (9th Cir.1993). In *MAI*, the Ninth Circuit upheld a finding of copyright infringement where a repair person, who was not authorized to use the computer owner's licensed operating system software, turned on the computer, thus loading the operating system into RAM for long enough to check an "error log." *Id.* at 518–19. Copyright protection subsists in original works of authorship *"fixed* in any tangible medium of expression, now known or later developed, from which they can be perceived, reproduced, or otherwise communicated, either directly or with the aid of a machine or device." 17 U.S.C. § 102 (emphasis added). A work is "fixed" when its "embodiment in a copy ... is sufficiently permanent or stable to permit it to be perceived, reproduced, or otherwise communicated for a period of more than transitory duration." *Id.* § 101. *MAI* established that the loading of data from a storage device into RAM constitutes copying because that data stays in RAM long enough for it to be perceived. *MAI Systems,* 991 F.2d at 518.

In the present case, there is no question after *MAI* that "copies" were created, as Erlich's act of sending a message to a.r.s. caused reproductions of portions of plaintiffs' works on both Klemesrud's and Netcom's storage devices. Even though the messages remained on their systems for at most eleven days, they were sufficiently "fixed" to constitute recognizable copies under the Copyright Act. *See* Information Infrastructure Task Force, Intellectual Property and the National Information Infrastructure: The Report of the Working Group on Intellectual Property Rights 66 (1995) ("IITF Report").

c. *Is Netcom Directly Liable for Making the Copies?*

Accepting that copies were made, Netcom argues that Erlich, and not Netcom, is directly liable for the copying. *MAI* did not address the question raised in this case: whether possessors of computers are liable for incidental copies automatically made on their computers using their software as part of a process initiated by a third party. Netcom correctly distinguishes *MAI* on the ground that Netcom did not take any affirmative action that directly resulted in copying plaintiffs' works other than by installing and maintaining a system whereby software automatically forwards messages received from subscribers onto the Usenet, and temporarily stores copies on its system. Netcom's actions, to the extent that they created a copy of plaintiffs' works, were necessary to having a working system for transmitting Usenet postings to and from the Internet. Unlike the defendants in *MAI,* neither Netcom nor Klemesrud initiated the copying. The defendants in *MAI* turned on their customers' computers thereby creating temporary copies of the operating system, whereas Netcom's and Klemesrud's systems can operate without any human intervention. Thus, unlike *MAI,* the mere fact that Netcom's system incidentally makes temporary copies of plaintiffs' works does not mean Netcom has caused the copying.[11] The court believes that Netcom's act of designing or implementing a system that automatically and uniformly creates temporary copies of all data sent through it is not unlike that of the owner of a copying machine who lets the public make copies with it.[12] Although some of the people using the machine may directly infringe copyrights, courts analyze the machine owner's liability under the rubric of contributory infringement, not direct infringement. * * * It is not difficult to conclude that Erlich infringes by copying a protected work onto his computer and by posting a message to a newsgroup. However, plaintiffs' theory further implicates a Usenet server that carries Erlich's message to other servers regardless of whether that server acts without any human intervention beyond the initial setting up of the system. It would also result in liability for every single Usenet server in the worldwide link of computers transmit-

---

11. One commentator addressed the difficulty in translating copyright concepts, including the public/private dichotomy, to the digitized environment. See Niva Elkin–Koren, Copyright Law and Social Dialogue on the Information Superhighway: The Case Against Copyright Liability of Bulletin Board Operators, 13 Cardozo Arts & Ent.L.J. 346, 390 (1993). This commentator noted that one way to characterize a BBS operation is that it "provides subscribers with access and services. As such, BBS operators do not create copies, and do not transfer them in any way. Users post the copies on the BBS, which other users can then read or download." Id. at 356.

12. Netcom compares itself to a common carrier that merely acts as a passive conduit for information. * * * However, the carrier must not have any direct or indirect control over the content or selection of the primary transmission. [17 U.S.C. § 111(a)(3)] * * *. In any event, common

carriers are granted statutory exemptions for liability that might otherwise exist. Here, Netcom does not fall under this statutory exemption, and thus faces the usual strict liability scheme that exists for copyright. Whether a new exemption should be carved out for online service providers is to be resolved by Congress, not the courts. *Compare* Comment, "Online Service Providers and Copyright Law: The Need for Change," 1 Syracuse J.Legis. & Pol'y, 197, 202 (1995) (citing recommendations of online service providers for amending the Copyright Act to create liability only where a "provider has 'actual knowledge that a work that is being or has been transmitted onto, or stored on, its system is infringing,' and has the 'ability and authority' to stop the transmission, and has, after a reasonable amount of time, allowed the infringing activity to continue'") *with* IITF Report at 122 (recommending that Congress not exempt service providers from strict liability for direct infringements).

ting Erlich's message to every other computer. These parties, who are liable under plaintiffs' theory, do no more than operate or implement a system that is essential if Usenet messages are to be widely distributed. There is no need to construe the Act to make all of these parties infringers. Although copyright is a strict liability statute, there should still be some element of volition or causation which is lacking where a defendant's system is merely used to create a copy by a third party. * * *

The court will now consider two district court opinions that have addressed the liability of BBS operators for infringing files uploaded by subscribers.

d. *Playboy Case*

Playboy Enterprises, Inc. v. Frena involved a suit against the operator of a small BBS whose system contained files of erotic pictures. 839 F.Supp. 1552, 1554 (M.D.Fla.1993). A subscriber of the defendant's BBS had uploaded files containing digitized pictures copied from the plaintiff's copyrighted magazine, which files remained on the BBS for other subscribers to download. *Id.* The court did not conclude, as plaintiffs suggest in this case, that the BBS is itself liable for the unauthorized *reproduction* of plaintiffs' work; instead, the court concluded that the BBS operator was liable for violating the plaintiff's right to publicly *distribute and display* copies of its work. *Id.* at 1556–57.

In support of their argument that Netcom is directly liable for copying plaintiffs' works, plaintiffs cite to the court's conclusion that "[t]here is no dispute that [the BBS operator] supplied a product containing unauthorized copies of a copyrighted work. It does not matter that [the BBS operator] claims he did not make the copies [him]self." *Id.* at 1556. It is clear from the context of this discussion[14] that the *Playboy* court was looking only at the exclusive right to distribute copies to the public, where liability exists regardless of whether the defendant makes copies. Here, however, plaintiffs do not argue that Netcom is liable for its public distribution of copies. Instead, they claim that Netcom is liable because its computers in fact made copies. Therefore, the above-quoted language has no bearing on the issue of direct liability for unauthorized reproductions. Notwithstanding *Playboy* 's holding that a BBS operator may be directly liable for *distributing or displaying* to the public copies of protected works, this court holds that the storage on a defendant's system of infringing copies and retransmission to other servers is not a direct infringement by the BBS operator of the exclusive right to *reproduce* the work where such copies are uploaded by an infringing user. *Playboy* does not hold otherwise.

---

14. The paragraph in *Playboy* containing the quotation begins with a description of the right of public distribution. Id. Further, the above quoted language is followed by a citation to a discussion of the right of public distribution in Jay Dratler, Jr., *Intellectual Property Law: Commercial, Creative and In-* *dustrial Property* § 6.01[3], at 6–15 (1991). This treatise states that "the distribution right may be decisive, if, for example, a distributor supplies products containing unauthorized copies of a copyrighted work but has not made the copies itself." Id. * * *

e. *Sega Case*

A court in this district addressed the issue of whether a BBS operator is liable for copyright infringement where it solicited subscribers to upload files containing copyrighted materials to the BBS that were available for others to download. Sega Enterprises Ltd. v. MAPHIA, 857 F.Supp. 679, 683 (N.D.Cal.1994). The defendant's "MAPHIA" BBS contained copies of plaintiff Sega's video game programs that were uploaded by users. *Id.* at 683. The defendant solicited the uploading of such programs and received consideration for the right to download files. *Id.* Access was given for a fee or to those purchasing the defendant's hardware device that allowed Sega video game cartridges to be copied. *Id.* at 683–84. The court granted a preliminary injunction against the defendant, finding that plaintiffs had shown a prima facie case of direct and contributory infringement. *Id.* at 687. The court found that copies were made by unknown users of the BBS when files were uploaded and downloaded. *Id.* Further, the court found that the defendant's knowledge of the infringing activities, encouragement, direction and provision of the facilities through his operation of the BBS constituted contributory infringement, even though the defendant did not know exactly when files were uploaded or downloaded. *Id.* at 686–87.

This court is not convinced that *Sega* provides support for a finding of direct infringement where copies are made on a defendant's BBS by users who upload files. Although there is some language in *Sega* regarding *direct* infringement, it is entirely conclusory:

> Sega has established a *prima facie* case of direct copyright infringement under 17 U.S.C. § 501. Sega has established that unauthorized copies of its games *are made* when such games are uploaded to the MAPHIA bulletin board, here with the knowledge of Defendant Scherman. These games are thereby placed on the storage media of the electronic bulletin board by unknown users.

Id. at 686 (emphasis added). The court's reference to the "knowledge of Defendant" indicates that the court was focusing on contributory infringement, as knowledge is not an element of direct infringement. Perhaps, *Sega*'s references to direct infringement and that "copies . . . are made" are to the direct liability of the "unknown users," as there can be no contributory infringement by a defendant without direct infringement by another. *See* 3 Nimmer on Copyright § 12.04[A][3][a], at 12–89. Thus, the court finds that neither *Playboy* nor *Sega* requires finding Netcom liable for direct infringement of plaintiffs' exclusive right to reproduce their works.[17]

---

17. To the extent that *Sega* holds that BBS operators are directly liable for copyright infringement when users upload infringing works to their systems, this court respectfully disagrees with the court's holding for the reasons discussed above. Further, such a holding was dicta, as there was evidence that the defendant knew of the infringing uploads by users and, in fact, actively encouraged such activity, thus supporting the contributory infringement theory. *Id.* at 683.

f. *Public Distribution and Display?*

Plaintiffs allege that Netcom is directly liable for making *copies* of their works. They also allege that Netcom violated their exclusive rights to publicly display copies of their works. There are no allegations that Netcom violated plaintiffs' exclusive right to publicly distribute their works. However, in their discussion of direct infringement, plaintiffs insist that Netcom is liable for "maintain[ing] copies of [Erlich's] messages on its server for eleven days for access by its subscribers and 'USENET neighbors'" and they compare this case to the *Playboy* case, which discussed the right of public distribution. Plaintiffs also argued this theory of infringement at oral argument. Because this could be an attempt to argue that Netcom has infringed plaintiffs' rights of public distribution and display, the court will address these arguments.

Playboy concluded that the defendant infringed the plaintiff's exclusive rights to publicly distribute and display copies of its works. 839 F.Supp. at 1556–57. The court is not entirely convinced that the mere possession of a digital copy on a BBS that is accessible to some members of the public constitutes direct infringement by the BBS operator. Such a holding suffers from the same problem of causation as the reproduction argument. Only the subscriber should be liable for causing the distribution of plaintiffs' work, as the contributing actions of the BBS provider are automatic and indiscriminate. * * * Where the BBS merely stores and passes along all messages sent by its subscribers and others, the BBS should not be seen as causing these works to be publicly distributed or displayed.

Even accepting the *Playboy* court's holding, the case is factually distinguishable. Unlike the BBS in that case, Netcom does not maintain an archive of files for its users. Thus, it cannot be said to be "suppl[ying] a product." In contrast to some of its larger competitors, Netcom does not create or control the content of the information available to its subscribers; it merely provides *access* to the Internet, whose content is controlled by no single entity. Although the Internet consists of many different computers networked together, some of which may contain infringing files, it does not make sense to hold the operator of each computer liable as an infringer merely because his or her computer is linked to a computer with an infringing file. It would be especially inappropriate to hold liable a service that acts more like a conduit, in other words, one that does not itself keep an archive of files for more than a short duration. Finding such a service liable would involve an unreasonably broad construction of public distribution and display rights. No purpose would be served by holding liable those who have no ability to control the information to which their subscribers have access, even though they might be in some sense helping to achieve the Internet's automatic "public distribution" and the users' "public" display of files.

g. *Conclusion*

The court is not persuaded by plaintiffs' argument that Netcom is directly liable for the copies that are made and stored on its computer.

Where the infringing subscriber is clearly directly liable for the same act, it does not make sense to adopt a rule that could lead to the liability of countless parties whose role in the infringement is nothing more than setting up and operating a system that is necessary for the functioning of the Internet. Such a result is unnecessary as there is already a party directly liable for causing the copies to be made. Plaintiffs occasionally claim that they only seek to hold liable a party that refuses to delete infringing files after they have been warned. However, such liability cannot be based on a theory of direct infringement, where knowledge is irrelevant. The court does not find workable a theory of infringement that would hold the entire Internet liable for activities that cannot reasonably be deterred. Billions of bits of data flow through the Internet and are necessarily stored on servers throughout the network and it is thus practically impossible to screen out infringing bits from noninfringing bits. Because the court cannot see any meaningful distinction (without regard to knowledge) between what Netcom did and what every other Usenet server does, the court finds that Netcom cannot be held liable for direct infringement. *Cf.* IITF Report at 69 (noting uncertainty regarding whether BBS operator should be directly liable for reproduction or distribution of files uploaded by a subscriber).[19]

2. Contributory Infringement

Netcom is not free from liability just because it did not directly infringe plaintiffs' works; it may still be liable as a contributory infringer. * * * Liability for participation in the infringement will be established where the defendant, "with knowledge of the infringing activity, induces, causes or materially contributes to the infringing conduct of another." Gershwin Publishing Corp. v. Columbia Artists Management, Inc., 443 F.2d 1159, 1162 (2d Cir.1971).

a. *Knowledge of Infringing Activity*

Plaintiffs insist that Netcom knew that Erlich was infringing their copyrights at least after receiving notice from plaintiffs' counsel indicating that Erlich had posted copies of their works onto a.r.s. through Netcom's system. Despite this knowledge, Netcom continued to allow Erlich to post messages to a.r.s. and left the allegedly infringing messages on its system so that Netcom's subscribers and other Usenet servers could access them. * * *

---

19. Despite that uncertainty, the IITF Report recommends a strict liability paradigm for BBS operators. *See* IITF Report at 122–24. It recommends that Congress not exempt on-line service providers from strict liability because this would prematurely deprive the system of an incentive to get providers to reduce the damage to copyright holders by reducing the chances that users will infringe by educating them, requiring indemnification, purchasing insurance, and, where efficient, developing technological solutions to screening out infringement. Denying strict liability in many cases would leave copyright owners without an adequate remedy since direct infringers may act anonymously or pseudonymously or may not have the resources to pay a judgment. * * *

* * * Netcom points out that the alleged instances of infringement occurring on Netcom's system all happened prior to December 29, 1994, the date on which Netcom first received notice of plaintiffs' infringement claim against Erlich.   * * * Thus, there is no question of fact as to whether Netcom knew or should have known of Erlich's infringing activities that occurred more than 11 days before receipt of the December 28, 1994 letter.

However, the evidence reveals a question of fact as to whether Netcom knew or should have known that Erlich had infringed plaintiffs' copyrights following receipt of plaintiffs' letter.   Because Netcom was arguably participating in Erlich's public distribution of plaintiffs' works, there is a genuine issue as to whether Netcom knew of any infringement by Erlich before it was too late to do anything about it.   If plaintiffs can prove the knowledge element, Netcom will be liable for contributory infringement since its failure to simply cancel Erlich's infringing message and thereby stop an infringing copy from being distributed worldwide constitutes substantial participation in Erlich's public distribution of the message. Cf. R.T. Nimmer, *The Law of Computer Technology* ¶ 15.11B, at S15–42 (2d ed. 1994) (opining the "where information service is less directly involved in the enterprise of creating unauthorized copies, a finding of contributory infringement is not likely"). * * *

b.   *Substantial Participation*

Where a defendant has knowledge of the primary infringer's infringing activities, it will be liable if it "induces, causes or materially contributes to the infringing conduct of" the primary infringer. *Gershwin Publishing,* 443 F.2d at 1162.   Such participation must be substantial. * * *

* * * Netcom allows Erlich's infringing messages to remain on its system and be further distributed to other Usenet servers worldwide.   It does not completely relinquish control over how its system is used, unlike a landlord.   Thus, it is fair, assuming Netcom is able to take simple measures to prevent further damage to plaintiffs' copyrighted works, to hold Netcom liable for contributory infringement where Netcom has knowledge of Erlich's infringing postings yet continues to aid in the accomplishment of Erlich's purpose of publicly distributing the postings.   Accordingly, plaintiffs do raise a genuine issue of material fact as to their theory of contributory infringement as to the postings made after Netcom was on notice of plaintiffs' infringement claim.

3. **Vicarious Liability**

Even if plaintiffs cannot prove that Netcom is contributorily liable for its participation in the infringing activity, it may still seek to prove vicarious infringement based on Netcom's relationship to Erlich.   A defendant is liable for vicarious liability for the actions of a primary infringer where the defendant (1) has the right and ability to control the infringer's acts and (2) receives a direct financial benefit from the infringement.   See Shapiro, Bernstein & Co. v. H.L. Green Co., 316 F.2d 304, 306 (2d Cir.1963).   Unlike contributory infringement, knowledge is not an element of vicarious liability.   3 Nimmer on Copyright § 12.04[A][1], at 12–70.

a. *Right and Ability To Control*

The first element of vicarious liability will be met if plaintiffs can show that Netcom has the right and ability to supervise the conduct of its subscribers. Netcom argues that it does not have the right to control its users' postings before they occur. Plaintiffs dispute this and argue that Netcom's terms and conditions, to which its subscribers must agree, specify that Netcom reserves the right to take remedial action against subscribers. * * * Further evidence of Netcom's right to restrict infringing activity is its prohibition of copyright infringement and its requirement that its subscribers indemnify it for any damage to third parties. Plaintiffs have thus raised a question of fact as to Netcom's right to control Erlich's use of its services.

Netcom argues that it could not possibly screen messages before they are posted given the speed and volume of the data that goes through its system. Netcom further argues that it has never exercised control over the content of its users' postings. * * * The court thus finds that plaintiffs have raised a genuine issue of fact as to whether Netcom has the right and ability to exercise control over the activities of its subscribers, and of Erlich in particular.

b. *Direct Financial Benefit*

Plaintiffs must further prove that Netcom receives a direct financial benefit from the infringing activities of its users. For example, a landlord who has the right and ability to supervise the tenant's activities is vicariously liable for the infringements of the tenant where the rental amount is proportional to the proceeds of the tenant's sales. *Shapiro, Bernstein,* 316 F.2d at 306. However, where a defendant rents space or services on a fixed rental fee that does not depend on the nature of the activity of the lessee, courts usually find no vicarious liability because there is no direct financial benefit from the infringement. * * *

* * * Plaintiffs cannot provide any evidence of a direct financial benefit received by Netcom from Erlich's infringing postings. Unlike *Shapiro, Bernstein,* * * * Netcom receives a fixed fee. There is no evidence that infringement by Erlich, or any other user of Netcom's services, in any way enhances the value of Netcom's services to subscribers or attracts new subscribers. * * * Because plaintiffs have failed to raise a question of fact on this vital element, their claim of vicarious liability fails.

[The court next concluded that Netcom was not entitled to a ruling that its use was fair as a matter of law.]

The court finds that plaintiffs have raised a genuine issue of fact regarding whether Netcom should have known that Erlich was infringing their copyrights after receiving a letter from plaintiffs, whether Netcom substantially participated in the infringement, and whether Netcom has a valid fair use defense. Accordingly, Netcom is not entitled to summary judgment on plaintiffs' claim of contributory copyright infringement. However, plaintiffs' claims of direct and vicarious infringement fail.

[As for Klemesrud, the bulletin board operator who dealt directly with Erlich, the court concluded that plaintiffs' allegations of direct and vicarious infringement failed for the same reasons applicable to Netcom. As with Netcom, however, summary judgment was denied with respect to the contributory infringement claim. The court nevertheless refused a request for a preliminary injunction against both defendants since plaintiffs had not established that they were likely to succeed in proving the knowledge and substantial participation necessary for contributory infringement.]

NOTES AND QUESTIONS

(1) The case against Netcom was ultimately settled when Netcom agreed to institute a protocol for removing material while investigating claims of infringement. It also agreed to post a warning to subscribers about copyright infringement. Los Angeles Times, Aug. 6, 1996, p. D2.

(2) Fair use aside, is there any doubt that Erlich infringed when he posted substantial portions of plaintiffs' copyrighted works on the Internet? The court had already issued a preliminary injunction against Erlich in an opinion at 923 F.Supp. 1231.[c] Which of the plaintiffs' § 106 rights did Erlich infringe? In its opinion on Erlich's liability, the court focused on "copying". The reproduction right was also successfully invoked by the publisher of *Playboy* against a defendant who copied its photographs onto a CD–ROM offered for public sale, Playboy Enter., Inc. v. Starware Pub. Corp., 900 F.Supp. 433 (S.D.Fla.1995), and against another defendant who placed plaintiff's photos on a commercial website, Playboy Enter., Inc. v. Webbworld, Inc., 991 F.Supp. 543 (N.D.Tex.1997).

The proposition that a reproduction of a copyrighted work in digital form is a "copy" for purposes of § 106(1) is ultimately limited by the statutory definitions of "copies" and "fixed", which require that the embodiment be sufficiently permanent to permit the work to be perceived, reproduced, or communicated for a period of more than transitory duration. The court in *Netcom* was bound by the Ninth Circuit's holding in MAI Systems Corp. v. Peak Computer, Inc., 991 F.2d 511 (9th Cir.1993), cert. dismissed, 510 U.S. 1033 (1994), that the embodiment of a work in a computer's random access memory (which is erased when the power is turned off) is still a "copy." Would it be appropriate to limit the concept of an infringing "copy" to more permanent reproductions on disks, tapes, or CD–ROMS? Even *MAI* does not purport to label all RAM embodiments "copies"—the embodiment there was sufficiently permanent to allow the user to read and make use of the output of the copyrighted program.[d]

c. A similar result was reached against another defendant who scanned and posted plaintiffs texts on the Internet, see Religious Technology Center v. Lerma, 40 U.S.P.Q.2d 1569 (E.D.Va.1996), but a third defendant whose use consisted primarily of scanning the texts into its own computer located in a private section of its library escaped a preliminary injunction on a fair use defense in Religious Technology Center v. F.A.C.T.NET, Inc., 901 F.Supp. 1519 (D.Colo.1995).

d. Cf. NLFC, Inc. v. Devcom Mid–America, Inc., 45 F.3d 231 (7th Cir.), cert. denied, 515 U.S. 1104 (1995) (proof that a

(3) Did Erlich's posting on the Usenet newsgroup implicate any other exclusive right under § 106? The court in *Netcom* implies that Erlich caused a public distribution of the copyrighted works. Did he, under § 106(3), distribute copies to the public "by sale or other transfer of ownership, or by rental, lease, or lending"? Technically, no copies changed hands—Usenet readers each viewed a new "copy." Was there nevertheless a "distribution"? In the Playboy v. Frena case discussed by Judge Whyte in *Netcom*, the court held that a computer bulletin board operator was liable for violating a copyright owner's public distribution right on the argument that it "supplied a product containing unauthorized copies of a copyrighted work." Citing *Playboy*, another court found a violation of the public distribution right when a defendant placed files containing copyrighted artwork on its web page. Marobie–FL, Inc. v. National Ass'n of Fire Equip. Distrib., 983 F.Supp. 1167 (N.D.Ill.1997). (If a work can be "distributed" over the Internet for purposes of § 106(3), does authorized access over the Internet constitute "publication" under the 1976 Act?)

Playboy v. Frena held that a bulletin board operator, by transmitting images to its subscribers, also infringed the copyright owner's public display right. Internet transmissions can also constitute a public performance. (Recall that under § 101 public performance or public display includes the transmission of a performance or display to the public.)

(4) Are computer users who access Erlich's Usenet posting in danger of being held liable as copyright infringers? Although users might display the work on their computer screens (and in other cases might perform the copyrighted work), in most instances these displays or performances will not be public and hence are not infringements. Also, unless the user further transmits the work, the user does not violate the public distribution right. But what of the exclusive right to reproduce the work in copies? If the user downloads the work onto a disk or into the computer's hard drive, or prints out a hard copy, reproduction has clearly occurred, although it may of course be a noninfringing fair use. See, e.g., Telerate Systems Inc. v. Caro, 689 F.Supp. 221 (S.D.N.Y.1988), which granted a preliminary injunction against the downloading of portions of plaintiff's copyrighted database.

What if the user merely "browses" the work—arguably the digital equivalent of reading a book or looking at a painting? Since a copy of at least a portion of the work must generally be created in the RAM memory of the user's computer in order to display the work on the screen, a potentially infringing reproduction has occurred, at least under the reasoning in *MAI Systems Corp.* Indeed, in the process of accessing the work, the user has probably created RAM copies in the server on which the work resides and in numerous intermediary computers located between the host computer and the user. Under an expansive reading of *MAI Systems Corp.*, all these copies are potentially infringing. The situation is further complicated by the phenomenon of caching. Caching is the temporary storage of

defendant remotely accessed copyrighted software stored on another computer did not establish that the defendant had made a "copy" of the software on its computer).

digital information "closer" to the user in order to speed access. Caching can occur on intermediary computers in the link between the host computer and the user and on the user's own computer. The user's browser software may automatically store retrieved data on the computer's hard drive for an extended period of time. Is caching, too, a potential infringement?[e]

Suppose that unlike the plaintiffs in *Netcom*, a copyright owner authorizes the uploading of a work onto a bulletin board or website. Is there then an implied license to make the temporary copies normally associated with accessing the work? An implied license to download the work?

Cate, The Technological Transformation of Copyright Law, 81 Iowa L.Rev. 1395 (1996), after reviewing the application of the various § 106 rights to digital works, urges either amendment or judicious application of fair use to preserve a sensible balance. Lemley, Dealing with Overlapping Copyrights on the Internet, 22 U.Dayton L.Rev. 547 (1997), points out that the multiple exclusive rights implicated by computer use make licensing more difficult and can frustrate statutory rules such as "first sale" that were formulated with only a single right in mind. Practical guidelines designed to reduce the risks faced by participants on the Internet are offered in Anawalt, Nine Guidelines and a Reflection on Internet Copyright Practice, id. at 393.

Would it be wiser to abandon the structure of § 106 and wholly rethink the appropriate scope of copyright in a digital environment? Litman, Revising Copyright Law for the Information Age, 75 Ore.L.Rev. 19 (1996), concludes that the touchstone for infringement should be commercial exploitation rather than reproduction.

(5) Is it an infringement of copyright to include on a web page a "hyperlink" that connects the user to another website containing copyrighted materials? The first major American case on linking was brought by The Washington Post Co. and five other media giants against Total News Inc. The defendant's website included a directory of links to other news and media sites. When a link was activated, the linked web page was displayed within a "frame" that continued to display the advertising located on the Total News site. Since the frame took up a portion of the screen, the linked page was partially obscured and users were required to scroll through it to see the entire contents, including the advertisements that appeared on the linked page. In addition, Total News' URL (Uniform Resource Locator—the electronic address of a web page) continued to be displayed at the top of the screen even after the user linked to another news source. Plaintiffs' complaint included counts of copyright infringement, trademark infringement, and unfair competition. The case was settled when Total News agreed to eliminate its "framing" and instead link directly to the plaintiffs' sites; the plaintiffs also purported to license the links to their websites.

e.   The legal implications of caching are analyzed in Hardy, Computer RAM "Copies": Hit or Myth? Historical Perspectives on Caching As a Microcosm of Current Copyright Concerns, 22 U.Dayton L.Rev. 423 (1997).

Richtel, Legal Situation is Confused on Web–Content Protection, New York Times, June 9, 1997, p. D5.

Is a license required for an ordinary link? Does a defendant who merely copies another's URL in programming a link to the other's website infringe any of the exclusive rights in § 106? Does the use of "framing" result in the creation of a derivative work? A different kind of link, sometimes called an "image" or "in-line" link, permits the creator of a web page to pull an image located on another site into the creator's own web page using only the address of the image. Is that an infringement? Are grounds other than copyright useful in challenging unwelcome links? See O'Rourke, Fencing Cyberspace: Drawing Borders in a Virtual World, 82 Minn.L.Rev. 609 (1998).

(6) The opinion in *Netcom* notes the differing views on the appropriate scope of liability for intermediaries such as bulletin board operators and Internet access providers.[f] The divergent results can be explained only partially by factual differences in the relative passivity of particular intermediaries. *Should* on-line service providers be strictly accountable, via findings of direct infringement, for copying by their customers? Should knowledge (which is an element only of contributory infringement) be a prerequisite to any liability?

On-line service providers have pushed hard for some form of legislative relief, urging, for example, that liability be limited to a "notice and take down" rule requiring only technologically feasible action to bar access following notification of an infringement. Their lobbying efforts contributed to the demise of bills drafted to implement the legislative recommendations of the "White Paper" and complicated the ratification process for the WIPO Copyright and Performances and Phonograms treaties. An agreement between copyright owners and on-line service providers ultimately formed the basis of proposed legislation generally exempting service providers from liability when they act as mere conduits for a transmission. Service providers would also be protected from liability for the storage of infringing material if they lack knowledge of the infringement, do not receive a direct financial benefit from the infringing activity, and act expeditiously to remove the material after notice.

THE "WHITE PAPER"

In 1993, President Clinton established the Information Infrastructure Task Force to articulate the administration's vision for a National Information Infrastructure (NII) intended to facilitate digital communication. A Working Group on Intellectual Property Rights was formed, chaired by

---

f. See also Marobie–FL, Inc. v. National Ass'n of Fire Equip. Distrib., 983 F.Supp. 1167 (N.D.Ill.1997) (no direct or vicarious liability on the operator of a computer that hosted an infringing website, but issues of fact concerning its knowledge of the infringement precluded summary judgment on a contributory liability count).

Bruce Lehman, Commissioner of Patents and Trademarks. The Working Group was charged with examining the intellectual property implications of the NII and recommending appropriate changes in U.S. intellectual property law and policy. The Working Group's report, entitled "Intellectual Property and the National Information Infrastructure", was released in 1995. It is commonly known as the "White Paper."

The White Paper advocates strong copyright protection for digitally-disseminated works. "Thus, the full potential of the NII will not be realized if the education, information and entertainment products protected by intellectual property laws are not protected effectively when disseminated via the NII." (p. 10.) It pursues this goal through broad interpretations of existing law and recommendations for congressional action.

Relying on cases like *MAI Systems Corp.*, the White Paper maintains that it is "clear under U.S. law" that the creation of a copy of any kind of work in a computer memory "for more than a very brief period" is a "reproduction" under the Copyright Act. (pp. 64–66.) This interpretation is used to support the report's contention that scanning or other digitizing, uploading, downloading, transferring files between computers, and accessing files located on another computer all generate potentially infringing copies. The report also emphasizes the applicability of the display right to "browsing" on the Internet.[g]

The White Paper maintains that the first sale doctrine in § 109 does not protect the transfer of copies by means of computer transmission (even if the sender deletes the original copy), arguing that the doctrine limits only the § 106(3) distribution right, while computer transmissions implicate the reproduction right by generating new copies rather than transferring existing ones. (pp. 90–95.)

The White Paper has little to say on the general issue of fair use, except to opine that it "may be overridden by contract" (p. 49) and that "technological means of tracking transactions and licensing will lead to reduced application and scope of the fair use doctrine." (p. 82). (Is the doctrine of fair use limited to curing market impediments?) The Task Force convened a Conference on Fair Use to prepare guidelines for digital use by libraries and educators, but the effort has been unsuccessful. See p. 443 supra.

g. The protectionist tone of the White Paper is illustrated by a section entitled "Education". The report advocates the development of model curricula on intellectual property that could be incorporated into all levels of education. Elementary school children would learn "that the taking of someone else's property, including copyrighted works, without their permission is not right." (pp. 205–06.) More advanced topics such as "the various forms of intellectual property, and why their protection is so important" would be introduced later. The economic and constitutional dimensions of intellectual property would become part of the high school curriculum. College students would not be exempt. "[B]asic patent and trade secret law could be taught in all science and engineering programs, while copyright law could be included in any instruction dealing with literature, art or computer science." (p. 207.) Unfortunately for your editors, the report stops just short of mandating a copyright course for every law student, although it does advocate the development of directories of attorneys with expertise in copyright issues.

The White Paper offered a number of legislative recommendations. To eliminate doubts concerning the scope of the § 106(3) distribution right, it advocated an amendment expressly covering distribution by transmission (which is already covered, the report said, under a "correct" interpretation of the distribution right). The report endorsed a full public performance right for sound recordings, at least with respect to all digital transmissions. Its recommendation to eliminate financial gain as an element of criminal liability for copyright infringement was implemented in 1997. See p. 566 infra. The report also recommended legislation to prohibit the manufacture or distribution of any device or the performance of any service whose primary purpose is to circumvent technological protection mechanisms employed by copyright owners. Another recommendation would prohibit the alteration or removal of "copyright management information" that identifies the copyright owner and specifies terms and conditions of use, helpful in electronic monitoring and tracking. (These latter two suggestions were eventually included in bills to implement the WIPO treaties, infra.)

Reaction to the White Paper was varied but intense. Education and library organizations (and many academics) have been strongly critical. See, e.g., Litman, The Exclusive Right to Read, 13 Card. A. & Ent.L.J. 29 (1994), concluding that the report lacked objectivity and balance and that its recommendations would amount to an exclusive right to read, view, and listen to copyrighted works; Samuelson, The Copyright Grab, Wired, Jan. 1996, p. 134, disagreeing with just about everything in the White Paper.[h] On the other hand, film, music, and software organizations loudly applauded both the White Paper and the bills introduced to implement its recommendations. Progress on the legislation was brought to a halt, however, by the lobbying efforts of on-line service providers intent on attaching provisions that would grant protection from infringement claims. The White Paper itself had concluded to the contrary that on-line service providers should be strictly liable as direct infringers, citing the *Playboy* and *Sega* cases discussed in *Netcom*. (Is the report's analogy to the strict liability of photo developers for infringement of the reproduction right and book sellers and record stores for infringement of the distribution right persuasive?)

---

h. See also Boyle, Intellectual Property Policy Online: A Young Person's Guide, 10 Harv.J.L. & Tech. 47 (1996), critical of the White Paper's failure to take account of the new marketing opportunities afforded to copyright owners by the Internet and also including Commissioner Lehman's response to objections raised by a group of law professors. For differing views on the appropriate role of intellectual property law in a digital environment, compare Hardy, Property (and Copyright) in Cyberspace, 1996 U.Chi.Leg. Forum 217 (1996), arguing that the practical ease of copying and low transaction costs on the Internet justify a regime of strong legal protection, with Perritt, Property and Innovation in the Global Information Infrastructure, id. at 261, concluding that the burden should rest primarily on the ingenuity of owners in developing protective technologies and marketing strategies.

THE WIPO COPYRIGHT TREATY

At a diplomatic conference in Geneva sponsored by the World Intellectual Property Organization in December, 1996, representatives from 160 countries adopted two treaties designed to insure copyright protection in the emerging digital environment—a Copyright Treaty and a Performances and Phonograms Treaty.[i] (On the latter, see p. 311 supra).

The Copyright Treaty requires contracting nations to treat computer programs as "literary works" within the meaning of the Berne Convention and requires protection for compilations of data that display creativity in selection or arrangement. The treaty also recognizes an exclusive distribution right for tangible copies and requires protection against the commercial rental of computer programs, phonograms, and cinematographic works (with an exception that protection for the latter works is not required absent widespread copying attributable to rentals).

The most significant provision in the treaty is Art. 8, which establishes that "authors of literary and artistic works shall enjoy the exclusive right of authorizing any communication to the public of their works, by wire or wireless means, including the making available to the public of their works in such a way that members of the public may access these works from a place and at a time individually chosen by them." In a bow to the telecommunications industry and other on-line service providers, an agreed statement interpreting Art. 8 specifies that "the mere provision of physical facilities for enabling or making a communication does not in itself amount to communication."

As originally proposed, the treaty included language stating that the reproduction right of authors "shall include direct and indirect reproduction of their works, whether permanent or temporary, in any manner or form." This provision, intended to capture RAM and other ephemeral electronic copies, was fiercely opposed by the telecommunications industry and other service providers, as well as by educational and library groups. The proposal was ultimately deleted. In the end, the delegates included only an agreed statement interpreting the reproduction right under Berne to include reproductions in digital form, with no mention of temporary copies. There are also treaty provisions requiring protection against the circumvention of technological measures taken by authors to protect their rights and against the removal or alteration of any "rights management information" that accompanies a work.

NOTES AND QUESTIONS

(1) The Clinton administration took a minimalist approach to the WIPO treaties, limiting implementing legislation to proposals relating to the circumvention of security measures and the protection of rights management information. Electronics and computer manufacturers complained

---

i. The WIPO treaties are reprinted in the Supplement. See also the WIPO website at http://www.wipo.org.

that, unlike WIPO, which focuses on acts of circumvention, the proposed legislation also bars the manufacture and sale of devices primarily designed for circumvention, thus undermining the relative immunity granted equipment makers by the Supreme Court in *Sony.*

(2) The technology of "rights management" is evolving rapidly. Digital "watermarks" with encoded ownership information already appear within some visual images to facilitate tracking. Publishers are experimenting with digital "branding" schemes to identify their literary works as a step toward regulating access. Technology firms are working to perfect digital "containers" that will guarantee their contents aren't revealed until the required payment has changed hands. The Copyright Clearance Center now offers electronic rights clearance.

Cohen, Some Reflections on Copyright Management Systems and Laws Designed to Protect Them, 12 Berkeley Tech.L.J. 161 (1997), pursues some of the legal and policy implications of rights management regimes. An earlier work, Cohen, A Right to Read Anonymously: A Closer Look at Copyright Management in Cyberspace, 28 Conn.L.Rev. 981 (1996), expresses alarm at the privacy implications of the monitoring and tracking associated with use restrictions and electronic licenses (pointing out that most states protect the identities of library patrons).[j]

(3) Bills have been proposed to deal with an assortment of other digital issues, including fair use, educational transmissions, first sale, and the enforceability of "click-on" licenses (which will also be affected by the proposed new Art. 2B of the Uniform Commercial Code). Will this uneasy alliance of law and technology ultimately serve to promote the progress of science and useful arts?

---

j. Compare Meurer, Price Discrimination, Personal Use and Piracy: Copyright Protection of Digital Works, 45 Buff.L.Rev. 845 (1997), concluding that the opportunities for price discrimination presented by technological protection and proposed restrictions on first sale and fair use will increase owners' compensation above current levels, with Bell, Fair Use vs. Fared Use: The Impact of Automated Rights Management on Copyright's Fair Use Doctrine, 76 N.C.L.Rev. 557 (1998), offering efficiency arguments in support of technological management systems.

CHAPTER 5

THE CALCULUS OF RIGHTS

SECTION 1. RENEWAL, DURATION, AND TERMINATION OF TRANSFERS

Fred Fisher Music Co. v. M. Witmark & Sons

Supreme Court of the United States, 1943.
318 U.S. 643, 63 S.Ct. 773.

■ MR. JUSTICE FRANKFURTER delivered the opinion of the Court.

This case presents a question never settled before, even though it concerns legislation having a history of more than two hundred years. The question itself can be stated very simply. Under § 23 of the Copyright Act of 1909, 35 Stat. 1075, as amended, [17 U.S.C.A. § 24] a copyright in a musical composition lasts for twenty-eight years from the date of its first publication, and the author can renew the copyright, if he is still living, for a further term of twenty-eight years by filing an application for renewal within a year before the expiration of the first twenty-eight year period. Section 42 of the Act [17 U.S.C.A. § 28] provides that a copyright "may be assigned ... by an instrument in writing signed by the proprietor of the copyright...." Concededly, the author can assign the original copyright and, after he has secured it, the renewal copyright as well. The question is—does the Act prevent the author from assigning his interest in the renewal copyright before he has secured it? ...

[This case was about rights in "When Irish Eyes are Smiling," written in 1912. One of its authors, Graff, had in 1917 assigned his renewal rights to the publisher, Witmark, along with an irrevocable power of attorney. Witmark exercised the power and renewed in its own interest on the first day of the twenty-eighth year. Graff soon after himself registered the renewal term and assigned it to Fisher. Witmark obtained a preliminary injunction denying rights in Fisher, which was affirmed by the Second Circuit. Justice Frankfurter ably reviewed the history of the renewal term, which finds its roots in the Statute of Anne and our statute of 1790, through various adaptations until its crystallization in the 1909 Act. Although there were intimations to the contrary in the 1909 committee proceedings, the Court found no legislative intent to bar assignments of renewal rights.]

By providing for two copyright terms, each of relatively short duration, Congress enabled the author to sell his "copyright" without losing his renewal interest. If the author's copyright extended over a single, longer term, his sale of the "copyright" would terminate his entire interest. * * *

* * * The policy of the copyright law, we are told, is to protect the author—if need be, from himself—and a construction under which the author is powerless to assign his renewal interest furthers this policy. We are asked to recognize that authors are congenitally irresponsible, that frequently they are so sorely pressed for funds that they are willing to sell their work for a mere pittance, and therefore assignments made by them should not be upheld. * * *

It is not for courts to judge whether the interests of authors clearly lie upon one side of this question rather than the other. If an author cannot make an effective assignment of his renewal, it may be worthless to him when he is most in need. Nobody would pay an author for something he cannot sell. We cannot draw a principle of law from the familiar stories of garret-poverty of some men of literary genius. Even if we could do so, we cannot say that such men would regard with favor a rule of law preventing them from realizing on their assets when they are most in need of funds. Nor can we be unmindful of the fact that authors have themselves devised means of safeguarding their interests. We do not have such assured knowledge about authorship, and particularly about song writing, or the psychology of gifted writers and composers, as to justify us as judges in importing into Congressional legislation a denial to authors of the freedom to dispose of their property possessed by others. While authors may have habits making for intermittent want, they may have no less a spirit of independence which would resent treatment of them as wards under guardianship of the law.

We conclude, therefore, that the Copyright Act of 1909 does not nullify agreements by authors to assign their renewal interests. We are fortified in this conclusion by reference to the actual practices of authors and publishers with respect to assignments of renewals, as disclosed by the records of the Copyright Office. * * *

In addition to all other books and pamphlets relevant to our problem, we have consulted all of the twenty treatises on the American law of copyright available at the Library of Congress. Eight of these state, without qualification, that an author can effectively agree to assign his renewal interest before it has been secured; two state the rule with some reservations; ten are either silent or ambiguous. And the forms of assignment of copyright in treatises and standard form-books generally contain a provision designed to transfer the renewal interest.

The available evidence indicates, therefore, that renewal interests of authors been regarded as assignable both before and after the Copyright Act of 1909. To hold at this late date that, as a matter of law, such interests are not assignable would be to reject all relevant aids to construction.

Affirmed.

■ MR. JUSTICE RUTLEDGE took no part in the consideration or decision of this case.

■ MR. JUSTICE BLACK, MR. JUSTICE DOUGLAS, and MR. JUSTICE MURPHY conclude that the analysis of the language and history of the copyright law in the dissenting opinion of Judge Frank in the court below, 125 F.2d 949, 954, demonstrates a Congressional purpose to reserve the renewal privilege for the personal benefit of authors and their families. They believe the judgment below should be reversed.

[Judge Frank's dissent in the Court of Appeals, which includes a long disquisition on laissez-faire and freedom of contract, dwelt on the necessitous and improvident traits of authors that would explain a Congressional policy of paternal restriction. He argued that the statutory history is uncertain, and that the text-writers were divided. The opinion emphasizes one element of great practical importance: the author's assignment of renewal rights was operative only if the author was living when the time came to effect the renewal (unless the statutory successors joined in the transfer). Such an expectancy is not worth much when it hangs on the author's survival for as long as twenty-seven years. Congress, Judge Frank believed, could reasonably have decided that it would be better for authors to have to wait for the renewal term to ripen, and that it was wrong for them to be in a position to put pressure on their spouse and children to sign away renewal rights under the statute.]

EXTENSION OF EXISTING COPYRIGHT TERMS

Works created after the effective date of the 1976 Act are entitled to the single term of copyright provided in § 302. The 1976 Act also makes elaborate arrangements for works already under copyright when it took effect on Jan. 1, 1978. §§ 303, 304. For copyrights already then in their renewal term, § 304(b) provides that the copyright endures for 75 years from the date it was originally secured. In the expectation that the slowly emerging revision bill would provide for a longer term than 56 years, Congress began extending the terms of renewal copyrights on Sept. 19, 1962, the effective date of P.L. 87–668, 76 Stat. 555, and continued this process until the 1976 Act was passed. Accordingly, all renewal copyrights that would have expired after Sept. 19, 1962 (i.e. those first registered after Sept. 18, 1906) were still subsisting on Jan. 1, 1978, and eligible for extension to a total term of 75 years under § 304(b), rounded to the end of the calendar year. § 305.[a]

---

a. An extraordinary special-interest extension of copyright was enacted in 1971, when the copyright in all editions of Mary Baker Eddy's *Science and Health with Key to the Scriptures* was extended for an *additional* period of 75 years. Priv.Law 92–60, 92d Cong. First published in 1875, and last revised by the author in 1906, copyright in the 1906 edition was subsisting as a result of the interim extensions described above. The extension was struck down under the establishment clause of the first amendment in United Christian Scientists v. Christian Science Board of Directors, First Church of Christ, Scientist, 829 F.2d 1152 (D.C.Cir.1987).

In Britain, special extension legislation proved more effective for J.M. Barrie's classic

For existing copyrights still in their first 28–year term on Jan. 1, 1978, § 304(a) initially required renewal in order to obtain a further term of 47 years, for a total duration of 75 years. Effective June 26, 1992, § 304(a) as amended by Pub.L. 102–307, 106 Stat. 264 (1992), automatically extends copyrights secured between Jan. 1, 1964 and Dec. 31, 1977 for an additional term of 47 years, thus doing away with the need for a renewal application. However, there are still incentives to file a renewal. A certificate of renewal obtained through a renewal application made during the year preceding expiration of the original term constitutes prima facie evidence of the validity of the copyright and of the facts stated in the certificate, which can be of particular value if the work had not been registered within five years of first publication. See § 410(c). If the copyright had not been registered during the original term, a renewal registration will also entitle the owner to the other benefits of copyright registration, including statutory damages and attorney's fees. (See the definition of "registration" in § 101.) There is also another incentive to file for renewal: failure to obtain a timely renewal registration deprives the renewal owner of the right to prevent continued exploitation of derivative works prepared during the original term. (See Stewart v. Abend, p. 512 infra.) Despite the incentives, reports from the Copyright Office indicate that renewal registrations are down since the advent of automatic renewal.

NOTES AND QUESTIONS ON RENEWAL—§ 304(a)

(1) The occasional advantage of a renewal term is illustrated by a popular tune of 1932, Bei Mir Bist du Schoen, which the prolific composer Sholom Secunda sold for $30, as he did hundreds of other songs. This one was a hit, chiefly through a swing version by the Andrews sisters with English lyrics by Sammy Cahn. But Secunda got back the renewal term, which continued to produce $5000 a year. (Obituary notice of Secunda, N.Y. Times, June 14, 1974, p. 36.)

(2) Suppose an author during the original term of copyright assigns his renewal interest to Publisher A. The author dies prior to the commencement of the twenty-eighth year of the original term. He has no widow or children. Under his will, the author's residuary estate, including any copyrights, passes to his nephews and nieces. The executor of the will renews the copyright, and the probate court orders distribution to the residuary legatees, who then assign their interests to Publisher B. In a contest between the two publishers, who prevails under § 304(a)? That was the issue in Miller Music Corp. v. Charles N. Daniel, Inc., 362 U.S. 373 (1960), a suit brought by the original assignee of the author's renewal interest in the song "Moonlight and Roses."

story *Peter Pan*. On his death in 1937, Barrie willed the remaining fifty years of the copyright to London's Great Ormond Street Hospital for Sick Children. When the copyright expired in 1988, Lady Callaghan, chair of a trustees group for the Hospital, asked her husband, former Prime Minister James Callaghan, to introduce special legislation to extend the copyright. The work is now under "perpetual" copyright, with all royalties going to the Hospital.

Douglas, J., for the majority, aided by concessions from plaintiff that if a widow, widower, or child was the claimant under the renewal provision, no prior assignment by the now-deceased author could bar them, said that the executor's statutory succession was similarly free of any obligations the author would have had by virtue of the assignment if he had survived. Harlan, J., writing for four dissenters, thought that an author should not be able to defeat an assignment of the renewal interest through a bequest. It was one thing to prefer the widow, widower, or children to the assignee of the deceased author, but since executors and next-of-kin were only later added to the list of statutory successors, symmetry of treatment was not required.   The majority's position, however, was followed by the Supreme Court in Stewart v. Abend, infra, which prompted severe criticism of *Miller Music* by Leval and Liman, Are Copyrights For Authors or Their Children?, 39 J.Copyr.Soc. 1 (1991), arguing that the author, not the statute, should control disposition of the renewal term.

(3) De Sylva v. Ballentine, 351 U.S. 570 (1956), was an action on behalf of composer De Sylva's illegitimate child against De Sylva's widow for a declaratory judgment and accounting.   "In this case, an author who secured original copyrights on numerous musical compositions died before the time to apply for renewals arose.   He was survived by his widow and one illegitimate child, who are both still living.   The question this case presents is whether that child is entitled to share in the copyrights which come up for renewal during the widow's lifetime.   * * * The controversy centers around the words 'or the widow, widower, or children of the author, if the author be not living.'   Two questions are involved: (1) do the widow and children take as a class, or in order of enumeration, and (2) if they take as a class, does 'children' include an illegitimate child."

The Court, per Harlan, J., after a review of the statutory development, concluded despite the statute's use of the disjunctive that the widow did not take to the exclusion of children, but rather that "the widow and children of the author succeed to the right of renewal as a class, and are each entitled to share in the renewal term of the copyright."

On the question whether an illegitimate child is included within the term "children", the Court said: "The scope of a federal right is, of course, a federal question, but that does not mean that its content is not to be determined by state, rather than federal law."   In the present case it was proper to consult state law.   De Sylva had acknowledged the child; this was thought enough to bring the child within the language of the copyright statute.

As to the respective rights of widow and child as members of the class, the Court refused to decide because the matter had not been passed on below or argued by the parties.

Douglas, J. (with whom Black, J. joined), filed a concurring opinion urging that the meaning of "children" should be settled without reference to state law; he would hold that illegitimate children are within the Act.[b]

---

b. A suit on equal protection grounds on behalf of an illegitimate child who would not inherit under the relevant state law was rebuffed in Jerry Vogel Music Co. v. Edward

The 1976 Act in § 101 has its own definition of "children", which includes both illegitimate and adopted children, but in Stone v. Williams, 970 F.2d 1043 (2d Cir.1992), cert. denied, 508 U.S. 906 (1993), the Second Circuit, upholding a claim to renewal rights by an illegitimate child of country and western star Hank Williams, said that state law continues to determine "children" for purposes of renewals under § 304(a).

How would you decide the unresolved question of how the widow and child should share in the renewal copyrights? What should be the answer if the renewals were held by the widow and more than one child? Cf. § 203(a)(2), which may influence the resolution of cases arising under § 304(a).

(4) As a practical matter, how can the assignee of an assignment of the renewal made during the original term of copyright obtain the best possible assurance against being displaced by a statutory taker under § 304(a)? See Kupferman, Renewal of Copyright, 44 Colum.L.Rev. 712, 725 (1944).

(5) Must the author, in order for an assignment of the renewal right to be effective, survive until (a) the first day of the twenty-eighth year, (b) the date on which the renewal application is filed during that year, or (c) through the end of the twenty-eighth year? As a result of the amendments made by Pub.L. 102–307 (1992), § 304(a) provides that if a renewal registration is made in the year preceding expiration of the original term, the renewal term vests in the person who is entitled to claim renewal at the time the application is filed; in the absence of a renewal registration, the renewal term vests in whoever is entitled to claim it at the end of the original term.

(6) The creators of Superman, Siegel and Shuster, were bound by contract to National Comics. In a state court action in 1948, facing a likely judgment that they had indeed in 1938 conveyed "all rights" in Superman to National (for $130), they agreed to a settlement including a consent judgment which recited that they had validly transferred "all of their rights in and to the comic strip Superman." Later, they claimed renewal rights. The Second Circuit held that the consent judgment was res judicata and that it included the renewal rights even though the words were not used. Siegel v. National Periodical Pub., 508 F.2d 909 (2d Cir.1974).[c] Absent the consent judgment, would this be the proper interpretation of "all rights"? Cf. Corcovado Music Corp. v. Hollis Music, Inc., 981 F.2d 679 (2d Cir.1993), invoking a presumption against inclusion of the renewal copyright if the contract does not expressly refer to future rights. A grant of rights "in

B. Marks Music Corp., 425 F.2d 834 (2d Cir.1969).

    c. After this defeat, Siegel and Shuster took to the media. Described as destitute, they won considerable attention in the press and eventually were given $30,000 per year annuities and had their byline restored by the comic book company that received $250 million of the $1 billion earned by the Superman character from movies, television, and commercial merchandise. Thomas, Jerry Siegel, Superman's Creator, Dies at 81, New York Times, Jan. 31, 1996, p. B6.

perpetuity", however, was found sufficient to include the renewal term in P.C. Films Corp. v. MGM/UA Home Video Inc., 138 F.3d 453 (2d Cir.1998).

(7) Section 304(a) confers the renewal term on the "proprietor" of a "posthumous work." When is a work posthumous? This problem was explored in Bartok v. Boosey & Hawkes, Inc., 523 F.2d 941 (2d Cir.1975). The Concerto for Orchestra, written under poignant circumstances in the composer's terminal illness, had not been published until after his death. But, Judge Oakes said, "Bartok had completed the Concerto, had heard it performed, had executed a contract for its copyright, and had corrected published proofs, all before his death." The work was held not posthumous, and thus followed the usual statutory scheme of succession. Which of the recited facts were or should be decisive? Judge Van Graafeiland, dissenting, believed that common understanding made posthumous publication alone decisive. He also considered these facts influential:

" * * * [T]he contest herein is not between the penurious family of a deceased composer and an 'unscrupulous' publisher; it is between a son and his mother. Bela Bartok, as a loving and thoughtful husband, executed a will in which he left the royalties from all copyrights and renewal copyrights in trust for his widow with the remainder, upon her death, to his son Peter, the appellant herein. Apparently, appellant is unwilling to wait for his remainder to accrue.

"He asks this Court to declare that appellee publisher has no right to renew the copyright of his father's works and to continue to pay all royalties following such renewal to his mother. Instead, he claims the right of renewal with his mother and brother, with the result that Bela Bartok's widow, to whom the composer left all the royalties during her lifetime, will end up getting only one-third of them, the remaining two-thirds going to appellant and his brother * * *."

The House Report states an intention to follow this decision. (H.R.Rep. p. 139)

(8) The inexorable working of the statutory scheme is further illustrated by Saroyan v. William Saroyan Foundation, 675 F.Supp. 843 (S.D.N.Y. 1987), aff'd, 862 F.2d 304 (2d Cir.1988). The author willed all his copyrights to the Foundation. He was survived by two estranged adult children. The childrens' rights were superior to the executor's under § 304; they were entitled to the renewals.

On this and other aspects of the operation of the renewal scheme, consult Nevins, The Magic Kingdom of Will Bumping: Where Estates Law and Copyright Law Collide, 35 J.Copyr.Soc. 77 (1988).

DURATION OF COPYRIGHT FOR POST–1977 WORKS

During the revision process leading to the 1976 Act, the Copyright Office abstracted basic issues on the duration of copyright as follows: Should copyright protection run for a single term or for original and renewal terms? Should the basic period of protection be a stated number of years (running from publication, public dissemination, creation of the work, or registration), or should the basic period (excluding works by corporations, etc.) be the author's life and a stated number of years after death? Should there be distinct measuring periods for particular classes of works?

In framing the revision proposals, strong support emerged for a single term measured by the life of the author plus 50 years. That term was adopted in § 302(a), with § 302(c) providing, for anonymous and pseudony-mous works and works made for hire, a term of 75 years from publication or 100 years from creation, whichever expires first. The House Report, supporting the life-plus–50 term, notes that "a very large majority of the world's countries have adopted" this term, which is the minimum required by the Berne Convention. (H.R.Rep. p. 135.)

Prompted by the European Union's 1993 Directive to extend the term of copyright in its member states to life-plus-seventy years, bills have been introduced in Congress to add twenty years to our own copyright term. Current proposals would change the basic term in § 302(a) to life-plus-seventy and add twenty years to the duration of copyright in anonymous, pseudonymous, and for hire works under § 302(c); the minimum protection under § 303 for unpublished works subsequently published before 2003 would also be extended by twenty years, as would the terms of still subsisting pre–1978 copyrights.

Proponents of extension argue that because of the Berne Convention's "rule of the shorter term" (art. 7(8)), U.S. copyright owners are unable to take advantage of longer protection abroad; extension of our term would thus allow domestic owners to receive foreign royalties for an additional twenty years. Not surprisingly, the music and motion picture industries are big supporters. Opponents point out that our 75 year term for works for hire already exceeds the corresponding term in most European countries— and it would go to 95 under the proposed legislation. More fundamentally, many critics argue that proponents of the legislation have not shown that the benefits of extension outweigh the harm from a diminished public domain. How likely is it that additional creative resources will be called forth by the prospect of an extra twenty years of protection commencing fifty years after the author's death?[d] The case for extension is critically reviewed in articles by Reichman, Hamilton, and Patry in 14 Cardozo Arts & Ent.L.J. 625, 655, and 661 (1996).

NOTES AND QUESTIONS

(1) How would you go about deciding the optimum duration for copyright? What values and expectations are to be maximized? See Chafee, Reflec-

---

d. Although he apparently favored perpetual copyright for authors, Samuel Clemens testified before Congress in 1906 in support of an unsuccessful proposal to extend the duration of copyright to life plus fifty years. "I think that will satisfy any reason-able author, because it will take care of his children," he said. "Let the grandchildren take care of themselves." Fox, Rights of Writers As a Mark Twain Obsession, N.Y. Times, Feb. 16, 1998, p. E1.

tions on the Law of Copyright: I, 45 Colum.L.Rev. 503, 506–11; II, id. 719–33 (1945); Finkelstein, The Copyright Law—A Reappraisal, 104 U.Pa. L.Rev. 1025, 1042–54 (1956); Cohen, Duration, 24 U.C.L.A. L.Rev. 1180 (1977). The limits range from zero to perpetuity, except that an unlimited term is banned by our Constitution. (Would a term of 999 years be constitutionally permissible?) [e]

(2) A patent for an invention lasts for 20 years from the date of application, 35 U.S.C. § 154.[f] There seems to be tacit acceptance of the great gap between the duration of patent and copyright. What is the justification for it?

(3) Have difficulties of administration and classification obscured possibilities of varying the length of the term with the nature of the work? There are some instances of this in foreign systems, e.g., short terms for photographs.

(4) How long will copyright in fact subsist under a life-plus–50 regime? Studies by the Copyright Office suggested an average span of around 75 years; this explains the extension of subsisting copyrights to 75 years, which almost triples the term available under the first Copyright Act of 1790: 14 years, renewable for 14 more by the author only. Among the arguments advanced for extending duration beyond the 56 years available under the 1909 Act was the increasing longevity of authors and their dependents. Another was thus stated by the House Committee:

> Under the preemption provisions of section 301 and the single Federal system they would establish, authors will be giving up perpetual, unlimited exclusive common law rights in their unpublished works, including works that have been widely disseminated by means other than publication. A statutory term of life–plus–50 years is no more than a fair recompense for the loss of these perpetual rights. (H.R.Rep. pp. 134–35.)

(5) While examining a box of manuscripts at the Mark Twain Papers, a major research collection at the University of California at Berkeley, a graduate student unearthed an unpublished manuscript on copyright law written by Samuel Clemens in 1898 while vacationing in Austria. The student would like to publish the manuscript in a book of Clemens' writings on copyright. What advice would you offer? (Clemens died in 1910.) See § 303, and Fox, Rights of Writers As a Mark Twain Obsession, N.Y. Times, Feb. 16, 1998, p. E1.

(6) The enjoyment of royalties for 50 years after the author's death leads to painful withdrawal pangs for heirs and publishers when the copyrights

---

e. The constitutional emanations from the "limited times" constraint in the patent and copyright clause are explored in Pollack, Unconstitutional Incontestability? The Intersection of the Intellectual Property and Commerce Clauses of the Constitution, 18 Seattle U.L.Rev. 259 (1995).

f. Except, *inter alia*, with respect to drugs; the pharmaceutical industry persuaded Congress that allowance should be made for the prolonged testing period that often precedes the permissible marketing of new drugs. See 35 U.S.C.A. § 155.

expire. In England, that time has come for the works of many giants of the first half of the century—for example, D.H. Lawrence, who died in 1930. According to Holroyd and Jobson, Copyrights and Wrongs: D.H. Lawrence, Times Literary Supplement, Sept. 3, 1982, p. 943, extraordinary claims were made that a new "corrected" edition of Lawrence, putatively entitled to copyright for whatever was new in it, was somehow entitled to a new copyright in the *un*altered text as well—because of the editors' work of collation with manuscripts and other editions. This is, of course, nonsense—isn't it? In the United States, the 75 year limit for pre–1978 works means that prominent publishers will soon lose the prestige and profits that came from exclusive rights to much of the classic literature of the 1920's, including major works by Fitzgerald, Hemingway, Eliot, and Joyce. Tabor, Publishers Wince as 1920's Classics Go Public, New York Times, May 29, 1995, p. 41.[g]

TERMINATIONS OF TRANSFERS

(1) One advantage of the renewal term—that it gives the author a second bite at the apple—dies hard. Part of the revision bargain between authors and publishers is § 203. It provides for an inalienable power, exercisable by the author, or the author's surviving spouse and issue, to terminate any transfer or license made by the author after Jan. 1, 1978 otherwise than by will. This power can be exercised during a five-year period that begins 35 years after the execution of the grant. With the experience under the renewal procedures of the 1909 Act to guide them, the drafters produced an intricate scheme that avoids most of the infelicities of those rules, while doubtless creating others. Compare the problems that have arisen in the interpretation of § 24 (and now § 304(a)), and see if you can find reactions to them in the drafting of § 203. In general, consult H.R.Rep. pp. 124–28.

(2) Consider also the operation of § 304(c), which creates a termination right parallel (but not identical) to that of § 203, applicable to grants that predate the 1976 Act; it can be invoked to recapture for the author or the author's statutory successors the 19 years that have been added to subsisting copyrights following their 56th year.

One of the first cases to arise under this termination provision stemmed from an attempt by the heirs of Edgar Rice Burroughs to terminate, under § 304(c), a 1931 grant to MGM that authorized it to use the character Tarzan, and other characters in his entourage, in an original Tarzan screenplay and remakes of that screenplay. Burroughs v. MGM, Inc., 683 F.2d 610 (2d Cir.1982). The action was aimed at stopping a 1981 version starring Bo Derek as Jane. A majority of the Second Circuit, per

g. A few old copyrights produce handsome returns all the way to expiration. *Happy Birthday to You,* written by the Hill sisters in 1935—and still under copyright—pulls in about $2 million a year. La Franco, Happy Birthday to Us, Forbes, March 11, 1996, p. 113. (What kinds of uses would you imagine are the primary contributors to this royalty stream?)

Judge Kearse, held that the notice of termination was ineffective because it failed to list five Tarzan books encompassed by the original grant. The bulk of the opinion is an engaging exploration of copying: had MGM, in view of changing times and mores (it maintained that the 1981 version appropriately subordinated violence in favor of nudity) stuck to its 1931 screenplay, or was it infringing the original Tarzan story? The court found no infringement, and similarly no breach of MGM's contractual obligation to stick to its original screenplay.

The first Tarzan copyright dates from 1912. Is the Tarzan character now in the public domain?

(3) In Mills Music, Inc. v. Snyder, 469 U.S. 153 (1985), the Supreme Court decided a § 304(c) case arising out of an important exception to the termination right:

> A derivative work prepared under authority of the grant before its termination may continue to be utilized under the terms of the grant after its termination, but this privilege does not extend to the preparation after the termination of other derivative works based on the copyrighted work covered by the terminated grant. (§ 304(c)(6)(A); see also § 203(b)(1))

This was overtly intended to respond to the complaints of moviemakers that, in view of their mammoth investment in making a film, the author of a story from which the film derived should not be in a position to block exhibition of the film by terminating the grant. Cf. Stewart v. Abend, p. 512 infra.

In the music-publishing industry composers routinely assign their copyrights to publishers who license a variety of uses, usually keeping 50% of the proceeds. *Mills Music* dealt specifically with mechanical reproductions, i.e. phonograph records, of a 1923 standard, "Who's Sorry Now." Its second term of copyright would have expired at the end of 1979 but for the 19–year extension, which was subject to termination under § 304(c). Snyder, one of the authors of the song, had transferred the renewal copyright to Mills Music in exchange for an advance payment and 50% of the royalties from mechanical reproduction. Mills Music, through the Harry Fox Agency, had issued more than 400 recording licenses for the song, including renditions by Judy Garland, Liza Minelli, and Nat King Cole. The recording rights were still pumping out $15,000 a year to the Harry Fox Agency, which brought this interpleader action to ascertain whether it should continue to pay 50% of the mechanical royalties to Mills Music now that Snyder had exercised his § 304(c) right to terminate his grant of the renewal term.

Mills Music maintained that the right to continue to utilize a derivative work under § 304(c)(6)(A), a right which the record-makers clearly enjoyed, also protected its own right to royalties. Surprisingly, the drafters did not address the status of an intermediate grantee (from the author) who is the grantor (to the record-makers) of the protected derivative right. The District Court decided, elaborately, in favor of Mills Music. Harry Fox

Agency v. Mills Music, 543 F.Supp. 844 (S.D.N.Y.1982). The Court of Appeals reversed, concluding that "it was authors, not publishers, who were the intended beneficiaries of the termination provisions." 720 F.2d 733 (2d Cir.1983).

The Supreme Court, in a 5–4 decision, held in favor of Mills Music. Justice Stevens found the "key" to the dispute in the statutory right to continue use of a derivative work "under the terms of the grant"—a phrase that he read "to encompass the original grant from Snyder to Mills."

" * * * If the Exception is narrowly read to exclude Mills from its coverage, thus protecting only the class of 'utilizers' as the Snyders wish, the crucial link between the record companies and the Snyders will be missing, and the record companies will have no contractual obligation to pay royalties to the Snyders. If the statute is read to preserve the total contractual relationship, which entitled Mills to make duly authorized derivative works, the record companies continue to be bound by the terms of their licenses, including any terms requiring them to continue to pay royalties to Mills. * * *

" * * * Rather than assuming that Congress was unaware of a common practice in one of the industries that the general revision of the copyright law, and the termination provisions, most significantly affected, we think it more probable that Congress saw no reason to draw a distinction between a direct grant by an author to a party that produces derivative works itself and a situation in which a middleman is given authority to make subsequent grants to such producers. * * *

"The obligation of an owner of a derivative work to pay royalties based on his use of the underlying copyright is not subject to renegotiation because the Exception protects it. The 'terms of the grant' as existing at the time of termination govern the author's right to receive royalties; those terms are therefore excluded from the bundle of rights that the author may seek to resell unimpeded by any ill-advised prior commitment. The statutory distinction between the rights that revert to the author and those that do not revert is based on the character of the right—not on the form or the number of written instruments that gave the owner of the derivative work the authority to prepare it. Nothing in the legislative history or the language of the statute indicates that Congress intended the Exception to distinguish between two-party transactions and those involving multiple parties. * * *

"Finally, respondents argue that the legislative history demonstrates that the Exception was designed to accomplish a well-identified purpose— to enable derivative works to continue to be accessible to the public after the exercise of an author's termination rights. Specifically, that history discloses a concern about the status of a number of motion-picture films that had been prepared pursuant to grants by book publishers. Without the Exception, the reversion that an author's termination effected would have given the author the power to prevent further utilization of the motion-picture films, or possibly to demand royalties that the film producers were unwilling to pay. Because the specific problem that the Exception addressed involved a potential confrontation between derivative-works utilizers and authors who had recaptured their copyrights, respondents argue that Congress must have intended its response to the problem to affect only those two interests.

"The argument is unpersuasive. It explains why the Exception protects the utilizer of a derivative work from being required to pay an increased royalty to the author. It provides no support, however, for the proposition that Congress expected the author to be able to collect an increased royalty for the use of a derivative work. On the contrary, this history is entirely consistent with the view that the terms of the grant that were applicable to the use of derivative works at the time of termination should remain in effect. The public interest in preserving the status quo with respect to derivative works is equally well served by either petitioner's or respondents' reading of the Exception. Respondents' argument thus sheds no light on the meaning of the phrase 'the terms of the grant.' Surely it does not justify the replacement of contractual terms that unambiguously require payment of royalties to a publisher with a new provision directing payment to an author instead."

Four dissenters, led by Justice White, remained unconvinced:

"The majority places great emphasis on indications that Congress was aware of multi-party arrangements in the movie and music-publishing industries, positing from this awareness an intention to extend the benefits of the Exception to middlemen such as Mills. But the majority cites not one word to indicate that Congress did in fact contemplate such a result when it enacted the Exception. On the contrary, when the Exception was being drafted by the Copyright Office, the hypotheticals offered to illustrate its operation were cast in terms of the motion picture industry and assumed that the creator of the underlying work, a story or novel, would deal directly with the creator of the derivative work, a film. If, as the majority asserts, Congress did consider the application of the Exception to the multiple-grant situation, it is indeed odd that it phrased the statutory language so ambiguously.

"That middlemen such as music publishers were to be excluded from the benefits conferred by the Exception is strongly supported by statements to that effect by music publishers themselves, made in the discussions that took place before the Copyright Office. When a version of the Exception first appeared in the 1964 preliminary draft bill, representatives of the music publishing industry protested. A representative of the Music Publishers Association of the United States stated that under the proposed exception, 'the royalties resulting from the license presumably rever[t] entirely to the author.'[5] A spokesman for the Music Publishers Protective

---

5. Preliminary Draft for Revised U.S. Copyright Law and Discussions and Comments on the Draft, 88th Cong., 2d Sess., Copyright Law Revision, Part 3, pp. 284–285 (H. Judiciary Comm. Print 1964) (statement of Phillip Wattenberg). See also id., at 296–297 (termination clause, including exception, would give author 100% of royalties) (statement of Mr. Kaminstein).

Association construed the exception as being 'for the benefit of everyone acquiring rights under a copyright other than the publisher.' [6]

"The legislative history thus lends no support for Mills' claimed right to share in the royalties from derivative works. Rather, it clearly evidences the underlying purpose of the Exception, which is, as the majority concedes, to protect the actual owners of derivative works, such as film producers, from having to renegotiate rights in underlying works, such as the novels or plays on which the films were based."

Mills Music is thoroughly analyzed in Abrams, Who's Sorry Now? Termination Rights and the Derivative Works Exception, 62 U.Det.L.Rev. 181 (1985). Abrams cautiously concludes that the intention, at least of the Copyright Office drafters, was to give all of the reversion to authors. In 1985 hearings on a bill to change the outcome in *Mills Music,* former Register of Copyrights Barbara Ringer declared, "It was my pen that drafted the section." *Mills Music,* she said, is "just dead wrong." 32 Pat., Tm. & Copyr.J. (BNA) 82 (1985).

(4) Woods v. Bourne Co., 60 F.3d 978 (2d Cir.1995), concerned a dispute over royalties for public performances of the song "When the Red, Red Robin Comes Bob, Bob, Bobbin Along," written in 1926 by Harry Woods. Woods' heirs exercised their right under § 304(c) to terminate the grant of rights to Bourne, Woods' publisher; Bourne argued that it was still entitled to its share of royalties for post-termination performances of pre-termination derivative works under the derivative works exception as interpreted in *Mills Music.*

As to performances of the song in movies and television programs, Judge Feinberg agreed with Bourne; like the mechanical royalties in *Mills Music*, performance royalties from derivative works still flowed according to the original grant. However, the court reached a different conclusion with respect to royalties from public performances of sound recordings embodying the song. Noting that, unlike audiovisual works, sound recordings do not enjoy an exclusive performance right, the court said that the performance of a sound recording was not "utilization" of a derivative work within the meaning of the exception. "[T]he Exception protects only authorized uses made by derivative work copyright owners, or their licensees." Royalties from performances of the song in sound recordings thus revert upon termination, unless the arrangement of the song as contained in the sound recording is itself a derivative work entitled to protection under the Exception. (Here, the court found that the arrangement was not sufficiently original to qualify as a derivative work.) In distinguishing audiovisual works and sound recordings, was the court correct in equating "utilization" of a derivative work with the exercise of an exclusive right in the derivative work?

(5) With Fred Fisher Music v. Witmark surely in mind, the drafters attempted to make certain that termination rights could not be lost before they became exercisable. See § 203(a)(5) and § 304(c)(5). "These limita-

---

6. Id., at 318–319 (written submission of Julian Abeles). * * *

tions," Nimmer observed, "undoubtedly will be subject to all of the challenges that the ingenuity of the bar representing so-called user groups can muster." Nimmer on Copyright § 11.07. Does your ingenuity suggest any?

(6) Motion picture contracts routinely transfer rights beyond the copyright in the story, for example, in its title, or in further use of the characters. Do such collateral rights also terminate? If not, may some kind of stalemate result? Compare Stein, Termination of Transfers and Licenses under the New Copyright Act: Thorny Problems for the Copyright Bar, 24 U.C.L.A. L.Rev. 1141, 1161 (1977), with Nimmer on Copyright § 11.02[B][1].

(7) Finally, we should note that termination rights do not exist in works made for hire. §§ 203(a), 304(c). What is the purpose of this exception? To protect employers from terminations by employees? (Does an employer own a work for hire by virtue of a "transfer or license" that could otherwise be terminated under § 203 or § 304(c)? See § 201(b).) To except grants made by employers, who are presumptively in less need of protection against unremunerative transfers? Compare Nimmer on Copyright § 11.02[A][2], with Goldstein, Copyright § 4.10.1.3.

On these and other problems consult Stein, supra; Curtis, Caveat Emptor in Copyright: A Practical Guide to the Termination-of-Transfer Provisions of the New Copyright Code, 25 Bull.Copyr.Soc. 19 (1977); Melniker & Melniker, Terminations of Transfers and Licenses Under the New Copyright Law, 22 N.Y.L.S.L.Rev. 589 (1977).[h]

SECTION 2. TRANSFERS OF INTERESTS: ASSIGNMENT AND LICENSE

Compare the rights comprised in a statutory copyright in 1790 with those making up today's copyright. The act of 1790 covered only maps, charts, and books, and conferred only "the sole right and liberty of printing, reprinting, publishing and vending." The 1909 Act eventually included fourteen "classes" of works in § 5, and the "exclusive right[s]" set forth in § 1 were extensive and varied. The 1976 Act restructures these and adds new classes and rights. It is unnecessary to dwell on the technical and industrial changes that lay behind the progressive expansion of the statute. Nor need we stress that the chief economic value of a work today often lies, not in its exploitation in the form originally conceived by the author, but rather in the exploitation of forms derived from it, such as a motion picture based on a novel or play. The author is often incapable of transforming the work into other artistic media and is usually incapable of managing the commercial exploitation of the work either in its original form or in any of its derivative forms. Hence the multitudinous transfers of interests, large and small, in copyrights.

h. For an entertaining account of problems attending termination rights in the works of Thomas "Fats" Waller, see Krasilowski and Meloni, Copyright Law as a Protection against Improvidence: Renewals, Reversions and Terminations, 5 Comm. & Law (No. 4) 3 (1983).

We can assume that in early days transfers of interests in copyrights tended to be transfers of all rights in solido. Even when the rights had obviously been divided, there was a certain convenience in locating "the copyright" in one person so that in the event of infringement there would be one person having the fundamental right to sue—a means of avoiding multiple recoveries. The holder of "the copyright" by transfer was denominated an assignee, and subtle disputes abound in the cases about whether particular transfers were such as to constitute the transferee an assignee or merely a licensee. In early cases it was stated or implied that only a transfer of all the rights comprised in the copyright could make the transferee an assignee; a transfer of less than all would constitute the transferee a licensee. This is an extreme version of the notion of "indivisibility" of copyright.

The 1976 Act goes pretty much all out in authorizing the separate ownership and transfer of rights, § 201(d)(2), and in accepting for recordation "[a]ny transfer of copyright ownership or other document pertaining to a copyright." § 205(a). Does the 1976 Act point to a classification that rests on distinctions between holders of "exclusive" and "non-exclusive" rights? See the § 101 definitions of "copyright owner" and "transfer of copyright ownership".

Section 204(a) of the 1976 Act says that a "transfer of copyright ownership" is not valid "unless an instrument of conveyance, or a note or memorandum of the transfer, is in writing and signed by the owner." What functions does the writing requirement serve? Should the rationales for the requirement exclude writings that are not contemporaneous with the purported transfer? Judge Kozinski was emphatic in Konigsberg Int'l, Inc. v. Rice, 16 F.3d 355, 357 (9th Cir.1994), that to comply with § 204(a), "the writing in question must, at the very least, be executed more or less contemporaneously with the agreement and must be a product of the parties' negotiations." But see, e.g., Arthur Rutenberg Homes, Inc. v. Drew Homes, Inc., 29 F.3d 1529 (11th Cir.1994) (oral assignment can be confirmed by a subsequent writing). Judge Kozinski had previously invoked § 204(a) to defeat a claimed assignment in Effects Associates, Inc. v. Cohen, 908 F.2d 555 (9th Cir.1990), cert. denied, 498 U.S. 1103 (1991) ("It doesn't have to be the Magna Charta; a one-line pro forma statement will do", rejecting defendant's "Moviemakers do lunch, not contracts" defense), although he concluded on the facts that an implied, nonexclusive license arose from a transfer to a movie studio of film footage (showing the destruction of "an alien life form that looks (and tastes) like frozen yogurt") for use in a motion picture. In Schiller & Schmidt, Inc. v. Nordisco Corp., 969 F.2d 410 (7th Cir.1992), Judge Posner held that the writing required under § 204 need not mention the word "copyright"; an agreement for the sale of a photography business, including negatives, carried with it the copyrights in the photographs.[a]

---

a. See Playboy Enter., Inc. v. Dumas, 53 F.3d 549 (2d Cir.), cert. denied, 516 U.S. 1010 (1995), deferring to the district court's determination that a legend on a check stat-

NOTE ON TRANSFERS AND RECORDATION

The materials in this Chapter furnish only an introduction to the question of how transferees of interests in published and unpublished works can assure themselves that they are getting what they think they have bargained for and that they will not be cut off by interests of whose existence they may be quite justifiably ignorant. The recordation machinery in § 205 gives some assurances, but surely does not eliminate the problem. It is hard to imagine a recordation system for this species of property that could approach the efficiency of a modern land recording system. The drafters had undertaken to give § 205 extra bite by providing in § 205(d) that a transferee could not maintain an infringement action unless the transfer was recorded. But the requirement was removed, presumably as an inappropriate formality, by the Berne Convention Implementation Act of 1988. On questions of "conveyancing" of copyright interests, see Latman, et al., Recordation of Copyright Assignments and Licenses, Copyr. Law Revision Study No. 19 (1958), in 1 Studies on Copyr. 761 (1963), addressing a variety of tangles, some of which § 205 attempts to unsnarl. See H.R.Rep. pp. 128–29. Consult also P. Alces and H. See, The Commercial Law of Intellectual Property (1994).[b] The creation, interpretation, and enforcement of licenses of copyrighted works may eventually be governed by proposed Uniform Commercial Code Article 2B—Licenses, now being considered by the American Law Institute and the National Conference of Commissioners on Uniform State Laws.

SECTION 3.   CONTRACT INTERPRETATION WITH RESPECT TO NEW USES

Harper Brothers v. Klaw

United States District Court, Southern District of New York, 1916.
232 Fed. 609.

■ HOUGH, DISTRICT JUDGE. Plaintiff Wallace owns the copyright of the well-known novel "Ben Hur," and Harper Bros. (a New York corporation) that of an authorized dramatization of the romance made in 1899 by one Young, who was employed for that purpose by the defendant partners, Klaw &

ing that endorsement acknowledges assignment "of all right, title and interest" in the described works was insufficient to evidence an intent to assign copyright as opposed to one-time publication rights.

b. Where should security interests in copyrights be recorded? See National Peregrine, Inc. v. Capitol Federal Savings and Loan Ass'n, 116 B.R. 194 (C.D.Cal.1990), which held that a bank that had taken 145 films as security for a loan should have recorded the transaction in the Copyright Office rather than by UCC filings in the relevant states. Accord, In re Avalon Software, Inc., 209 B.R. 517 (Bkrtcy.Ct.D.Ariz.1997) (for copyrighted works, whether registered or unregistered, the proper place to file is with the Copyright Office).

Erlanger (both New Yorkers), pursuant to a contract the true meaning of which is the ultimate problem presented by this case.

In 1899 Gen. Wallace's novel had long enjoyed popularity, and was known to be in many ways suitable for stage representation, with those spectacular accessories which the improved electrical and mechanical appliances of recent years have rendered possible. With the author's permission, therefore, Harper Bros. (the publishers of Ben Hur) agreed in writing with Klaw & Erlanger that (1) the latter should employ writers to produce "a dramatic version" of the novel; (2) such version should be approved by author and publishers of the novel, and copyrighted in the publishers' name; (3) after such approval the producers of the play should have no right to change the text or manner of performance in any material way; but (4) Klaw & Erlanger were granted the sole right (during the life of the copyright, if all conditions were duly complied with) of "producing on the stage," or "performing," the "dramatic version" provided for or created as above described.

In the preamble of the contract it is recited as the purpose thereof that the defendants are to obtain "the exclusive right of producing *such dramatic version* on the stage"; i.e., the dramatic version made by Young and paid for by Klaw & Erlanger. In pursuance of this written agreement the play was prepared, approved, and copyrighted. It follows the novel very closely, and it would (I think) be quite impossible to make another play that really told the story of Ben Hur without presenting substantially the same sequence of ideas as is presented by the copyrighted version of Young. That version in turn uses, far more frequently than is often the case, the exact words of the novel of which it is the derivative. When this contract was made the moving picture art was (in the trite phrase) in its infancy. There were moving pictures, but it was then completely beyond the known possibilities of the art to produce a series of pictures representing such and so spectacular and elaborate a play or performance as is the Ben Hur of Klaw & Erlanger.

For about 14 years Ben Hur has been produced in obedience to the contract of 1899, and apparently to the great pecuniary satisfaction both of the copyright owners and their licensees, Klaw & Erlanger. Lately, however, it is shown to have occurred to both parties to the contract that the public might be growing tired of the play as shown with actors speaking on the stage, and that (considering the enormous advances in recent years in the moving picture art) a photo-play of Ben Hur might reach, if not a new audience, at all events one that probably would not much longer pay ordinary theater prices to see so old a production. Thereupon both Harper Bros., as owners of the copyright, and Klaw & Erlanger, as licensees thereunder, assert that they and they alone possess the photo-play rights. The defendants have gone so far in the assertion of their position as to write a letter in which it is definitely said that they will produce Ben Hur as a photo-play when and as they choose. This bill is brought to restrain the defendants from carrying out that threat, on the ground that such a production would be an infringement of copyright.

* * * The sole question is whether Mr. Klaw's letter hereinabove referred to is or is not a threat of violating copyright; and it is such a threat unless it becomes, by reason of the contract of 1899, the mere assertion of a lawful right.   * * *

* * * It must be admitted (especially in this litigation) that the "exhibition of a series of photographs of persons and things arranged on films as moving pictures, and so depicting the principal scenes of an author's work as to tell the story, is a dramatization of such work," because all the parties to this litigation united in procuring such determination from the Supreme Court in Kalem Co. v. Harper Bros., 222 U.S. 55. If by the agreement of 1899 the defendants had been granted the exclusive right of dramatizing Ben Hur, or producing any play or plays that might be made out of Ben Hur, there would be no doubt at all as to their right to make a "movie play," as well as the kind of play that has heretofore been produced.

But the grant made by that agreement was far more limited. The right conferred was to produce one version only, and that in a particular manner, and in places limited to cities of a certain size. The contract prohibits any change in the manner of performance or text, and contains provisions as to royalties and their computation, confessedly incapable of application to any method of producing photo-plays in commercial use or known to witnesses or counsel. It is unnecessary to expand this thought. The whole arrangement made between the parties in 1899 is not only inconsistent with, but repugnant to, the thought of making "movies" out of Ben Hur.

This differentiates the case at bar from Frohman v. Fitch, 164 App.Div. 231, 149 N.Y.S. 633, with which I fully concur; but these defendants never got so ample a grant as did Mr. Frohman. It follows, since the copyright covers a photo-play, and Klaw & Erlanger got no license to make or produce one, they would infringe if their threat were carried out; therefore they must be enjoined.

Plaintiffs assert, and almost assume, that since defendants cannot make a "movie" out of Ben Hur, and such right must exist somewhere, it is in them, as being an unconveyed portion of the copyright estate wherefrom was carved defendants' limited license. In strictness of law I think this true; but it does not always follow that, because one owns a certain thing, he may use it to the detriment of another, especially if the owner is under contractual obligations to such other. The "movie" rights to Ben Hur undoubtedly existed in 1899, but in nubibus, or (what is frequently the same thing) in contemplation of law only. As matter of fact they are an accretion or unearned increment conferred of late years upon the copyright owners by the ingenuity of many inventors and mechanicians.

In my opinion there is implied a negative covenant on the part of the plaintiffs (the grantors of defendants' restricted license) not to use the ungranted portion of the copyright estate to the detriment, if not destruction, of the licensees' estate. Admittedly, if Harper Bros. (or Klaw & Erlanger, for the matter of that) permitted photo-plays of Ben Hur to infest the country, the market for the spoken play would be greatly impaired, if not destroyed. This being the fact, the law is analogous to that which implies, from a covenant to make a certain use of property, a covenant negative against doing anything else with it. High on Injunctions (4th Ed.) § 1151A, and cases cited.

The result is that plaintiffs may take the injunction prayed for against defendants, and the defendants may have the same relief against plaintiffs. The meaning of such double injunction is that, as long as the contract of 1899 exists, neither party thereto can produce a photo-play of Ben Hur except by bargain with the other.

There will be no costs.

———————

FROHMAN V. FITCH, 164 App.Div. 231, 149 N.Y.S. 633 (1914). Fitch in 1900 agreed to write a play and to "sell, assign, and transfer" to plaintiff Frohman "the exclusive right to produce the said play in the United States of America and in Canada." Fitch accordingly wrote "Captain Jinks of the Horse Marines." In 1914 his heir, a defendant in the action, conveyed motion picture production rights for the United States and Canada to defendant American Play Co. Plaintiff was held entitled to an injunction. "Even though it be conceded that neither party had in mind the production of the play in that manner," i.e., by means of a motion picture, the exclusive right conveyed to Frohman was "property" and defendants may not impair it.

———————

MANNERS V. MOROSCO, 252 U.S. 317 (1920). The plaintiff, author of "Peg O' My Heart," granted Morosco in 1912 an exclusive license to produce and perform it in the United States and Canada. Plaintiff seeks to enjoin Morosco from a motion picture production. "Every detail" of the contract, Justice Holmes wrote, "shows that a representation by spoken drama alone is provided for." The courts below had refused the injunction "upon the impossibility of supposing that the author reserved the right to destroy the value of the right granted * * * by retaining power to set up the same play in motion pictures a few doors off with a much smaller admission fee. We agree with the premise but not with the conclusion." The Supreme Court's conclusion, suggested by Harper Brothers v. Klaw, supra, was that "the plaintiff is entitled to an injunction against the representation of the play in motion pictures, but upon the terms that the plaintiff also shall abstain from presenting or authorizing the presentation of the play in that form in Canada or the United States."

NOTE ON SILENT TO SOUND MOTION PICTURES

The transition from silent to sound motion pictures created difficulty in interpreting contracts that made no explicit reference to sound. The leading case is L.C. Page & Co. Inc. v. Fox Film Corp., 83 F.2d 196 (2d Cir.1936). Plaintiff publisher in 1923 received from Laura Richards, author of "Captain January," the "exclusive moving picture rights"—she to receive 45% of the net proceeds. Plaintiff in 1923 granted all motion picture rights to Principal Pictures Corp., expressly reserving rights in any spoken words, and dramatic rights. Defendant Fox, wishing to make a talking picture, and with full knowledge of plaintiff's claim, in 1935 purchased silent rights from Principal and a "quitclaim conveyance" from Mrs. Richards. Plaintiff was awarded a preliminary injunction against the production of Fox's picture. The court said that though Mrs. Richards may not have contemplated sound motion pictures when she made the 1923 agreement with the plaintiff, the words used "were sufficient to embrace not only motion pictures of the sort then known but also such technical improvements in motion pictures as might be developed during the term of the license, namely, the term of the copyright. * * * As the plaintiff well says, 'talkies' are but a species of the genus motion pictures."

Cf. Kirke La Shelle Co. v. Paul Armstrong Co., 263 N.Y. 79, 188 N.E. 163 (1933). Plaintiff producer had a half-interest in the profits of any revivals of defendant's play "Alias Jimmy Valentine." [a] The agreement, made in 1921, prescribed that all contracts and licenses "affecting the title to the dramatic rights (exclusive of motion picture rights)" should be subject to plaintiff's approval. Defendant in 1928 sold the sound movie rights in "Alias Jimmy Valentine" to MGM for $15,000; the contract was not submitted to plaintiff. Since it was conceded that talking picture rights were not in the contemplation of the parties in 1921, these rights were, in effect, treated as excluded from the exclusion of "motion picture rights." The court thus found a breach of the defendant's obligation not to license dramatic rights without plaintiff's consent.

Bartsch v. Metro–Goldwyn–Mayer, Inc.

United States Court of Appeals, Second Circuit, 1968.
391 F.2d 150.
Certiorari denied 393 U.S. 826, 89 S.Ct. 86.

■ Before LUMBARD, CHIEF JUDGE, and WATERMAN and FRIENDLY, CIRCUIT JUDGES.

■ FRIENDLY, CIRCUIT JUDGE:

This appeal from a judgment of the District Court for the Southern District of New York raises the question whether, on the facts here appearing, an assignee of motion picture rights to a musical play is entitled to authorize the telecasting of its copyrighted film. Although the issue

---

a. This half-interest was an outgrowth of a once-important copyright infringement case, Dam v. Kirk La Shelle Co., 175 Fed. 902 (2d Cir.1910); see also Kirke La Shelle Co. v. Armstrong, 224 N.Y. 582, 120 N.E. 866 (1918).

seems considerably closer to us than it did to Judge Bryan, we affirm the judgment dismissing the complaint of the copyright owner.

In January 1930, the authors, composers, and publishers of and owners of certain other interests in a German musical play "Wie Einst in Mai," which had been produced in this country as "Maytime" with a changed libretto and score, assigned to Hans Bartsch

> the motion picture rights and all our right, title and interest in and in connection with such motion picture rights of the said operetta or musical play, throughout the world, together with the sole and exclusive rights to use, adapt, translate, add to and change the said operetta or musical play and the title thereof in the making of motion picture photoplays, and to project, transmit and otherwise reproduce the said work or any adaptation or version thereof, visually or audibly by the art of cinematography or any process analogous thereto, and to copyright, vend, license and exhibit such motion picture photoplays throughout the world; together with the further sole and exclusive rights by mechanical and/or electrical means to record, reproduce and transmit sound, including spoken words, dialogue, songs and music, and to change such dialogue, if extracted from said works, and to interpolate or use other dialogue, songs and music in or in connection with or as part of said motion picture photoplays, and the exhibition, reproduction and transmission thereof, and to make, use, license, import and vend any and all records or other devices required or desired for any such purposes.

In May of that year Bartsch assigned to Warner Bros. Pictures, Inc. [motion picture rights in language that was substantially identical to that just quoted]. * * *

A further clause recited

> The rights which the Purchaser obtains from the Owner in "Wie Einst in Mai" and/or "Maytime" are specifically limited to those granted herein. All other rights now in existence or which may hereafter come into existence shall always be reserved to the Owner and for his sole benefit, but nothing herein contained shall in any way limit or restrict the rights which Purchaser has acquired or shall hereafter acquire from any other person, firm or corporation in and to "Wie Einst in Mai" and/or "Maytime."

Warner Brothers transferred its rights to defendant Metro–Goldwyn–Mayer, Inc. early in 1935, which made, distributed and exhibited a highly successful motion picture "Maytime." The co-authors of the German libretto, one in 1935 and the other in 1938, transferred all their copyright interests and renewal rights to Bartsch, whose rights in turn have devolved to the plaintiff, his widow. The controversy stems from MGM's licensing its motion picture for television, beginning in 1958.

Although the district judge upheld MGM's contention that the 1930 assignment from Bartsch to Warner Brothers included the right to permit telecasting of the motion picture to be made from the musical play, he thought there was "a further reason why plaintiff cannot prevail in this action," namely, that Bartsch had granted all that he had. This does not do justice to plaintiff's argument. Her position is that in 1930 Bartsch not only did not but could not grant the right to televise the motion picture since, under the similar language of the assignment to him, it was not his to grant; her claim of infringement is based not on the 1930 assignment to Bartsch of the motion picture rights but on the authors' later assignments of the full copyright.

[The court did not accept the view of the District Court that the phrase "cinematography or any process analogous thereto" comprehended television.]

As we read the instruments, defendant's rights do not turn on the language we have been discussing but rather on the broad grant, in the assignments to and from Bartsch, of "the motion picture rights throughout the world," which were spelled out to include the right "to copyright, vend, license and exhibit such motion picture photoplays throughout the world." The "to project, transmit and otherwise reproduce" language appears rather to have been directed at how the musical play was to be made into a photoplay. This may well have seemed a more vexing problem in 1930, due to uncertainties as to the best method for linking visual and audible reproduction, cf. Paramount Publix Corp. v. American Tri–Ergon Corp., 294 U.S. 464 (1935), and whether a grant of motion picture rights to a play or novel included the right to sound reproduction, see L.C. Page & Co. v. Fox Film Corp., 83 F.2d 196 (2 Cir.1936), than today. Being unclear whether sound reproduction would require alterations in previous methods of converting a play into a photoplay, Warner Brothers sought and obtained a considerable degree of freedom in that regard. On this view the clause whose meaning has been so hotly debated is irrelevant to the point here at issue, and decision turns rather on whether a broad assignment of the right "to copyright, vend, license and exhibit such motion picture photoplays throughout the world" includes the right to "license" a broadcaster to "exhibit" the copyrighted motion picture by a telecast without a further grant by the copyright owner.

[Although plaintiff's copyright claim creates federal jurisdiction, New York state law, the court held, should govern the interpretation of the grant. But Judge Friendly found Manners v. Morosco, p. 498 supra, and Kirke La Shelle Co. v. Paul Armstrong Co., 499 supra, unhelpful.]

* * * While *Kirke La Shelle* teaches that New York will not charge a grantor with the duty of expressly saving television rights when he could not know of the invention's existence, we have found no case holding that an experienced businessman like Bartsch is not bound by the natural implications of the language he accepted when he had reason to know of the new medium's potential.[2]

---

2. In Ettore v. Philco Television Broadcasting Corp., 229 F.2d 481, cert. denied, 351   U.S. 926 (1956), the Third Circuit, applying Pennsylvania law, held that a 1935 contract

Plaintiff, naturally enough, would not frame the issue in precisely this way. Instead, she argues that even in 1930 Warner Brothers often attempted to obtain an express grant of television rights and that its failure to succeed in Bartsch's case should persuade us that, despite the broad language, only established forms of exhibition were contemplated. She buttresses this argument by producing a number of 1930 assignments to Warner Brothers, some of which specifically granted the right to televise motion pictures and others of which granted full television rights, and by adducing testimony of the Warner Brothers lawyer who had approved the assignment from Bartsch that on many occasions Warner Brothers attempted to secure an express grant of such rights but did not always succeed.

However, this is not enough to show that the Bartsch assignments were a case of that sort. For all that appears Warner Brothers may have decided that, in dealing with Bartsch, it would be better tactics to rely on general words that were sufficiently broad rather than seek an express inclusion and perhaps end up with the opposite, or may have used a form regular in the industry without thinking very precisely about television, or—perhaps most likely—may simply have parroted the language in the grant from Bartsch's assignors to him on the theory it would thus be getting all he had, whatever that might be. Indeed, it is really the assignment to Bartsch rather than the one from him that must control. While plaintiff suggests that Warner Brothers may have furnished Bartsch the forms to be used with his assignors, this is sheer speculation. There is no showing that the form was unique to Warner Brothers; indeed the contrary appears.

With Bartsch dead, his grantors apparently so, and the Warner Brothers lawyer understandably having no recollection of the negotiation, any effort to reconstruct what the parties actually intended nearly forty years ago is doomed to failure. In the end, decision must turn, as Professor Nimmer has suggested, The Law of Copyright § 125.3 (1964), on a choice between two basic approaches more than on an attempt to distill decisive meaning out of language that very likely had none. As between an approach that "a license of rights in a given medium (e.g., 'motion picture rights') includes only such uses as fall within the unambiguous core meaning of the term (e.g., exhibition of motion picture film in motion picture theaters) and exclude any uses which lie within the ambiguous penumbra (e.g., exhibition of motion picture film on television)" and another whereby "the licensee may properly pursue any uses which may reasonably be said to fall within the medium as described in the license," he prefers the latter. So do we. But see Warner, Radio and Television Rights § 52 (1953). If the words are broad enough to cover the new use, it seems fairer that the burden of framing and negotiating an exception

granting moving picture rights did not permit the grantee to televise the film. However, unlike Bartsch, the grantor, Ettore, was not an experienced businessman but a prize fighter, and the Court relied heavily on his lack of sophistication in determining whether it was fair to charge him with knowledge of the new medium. Id. at 491, n. 14.

should fall on the grantor; if Bartsch or his assignors had desired to limit "exhibition" of the motion picture to the conventional method where light is carried from a projector to a screen directly beheld by the viewer, they could have said so.   A further reason favoring the broader view in a case like this is that it provides a single person who can make the copyrighted work available to the public over the penumbral medium, whereas the narrower one involves the risk that a deadlock between the grantor and the grantee might prevent the work's being shown over the new medium at all. Quite apart from the probable impracticality, the assignments are broad enough even on plaintiff's view to prevent the copyright owners from licensing anyone else to make a photoplay for telecasting.   The risk that some May might find the nation's television screens bereft of the annual display of "Maytime," interlarded with the usual liberal diet of commercials, is not one a court can take lightly.

Affirmed.

NOTES AND QUESTIONS

(1) Is it not likely that the advent of television was foreseen long before it became economically significant, indeed too long before, so that producers or performers bargained away more than they were willing to concede when the rights became valuable?

On collective action by the American Federation of Musicians and the Screen Actors Guild to provide for payments to performers for television use, see Gilbert, "Residual Rights" Established by Collective Bargaining in Television and Radio, 23 L. & Contemp.Prob. 102, 117–18 (1958); see also the description of the Screen Actors Guild agreements in Rooney v. Columbia Pictures Industries, Inc., 538 F.Supp. 211, 221–22 (S.D.N.Y.), aff'd, 714 F.2d 117 (2d Cir.1982), cert. denied, 460 U.S. 1084 (1983).

(2) Does *Bartsch* justify the approach that it heralds in its final "further reason" for finding that television rights were conveyed? Is it relevant, in cutting off Bartsch's claim as assignee of rights in the German libretto from which "Maytime" was derived, that the dominant element in "Maytime's" success may be Sigmund Romberg's music, which was not part of the grant?

(3) Consider the following thesis advanced in Cohn, Old Licenses and New Uses: Motion Picture and Television Rights, 19 L. & Contemp.Prob. 184, 199–200 (1954): "The 'new use' problem is essentially not one of construction at all, and it should be so recognized and dealt with.   The problem is created, not by the cupidity or contrariness of the parties, nor by the ambiguity of language, but by the advent of an unforeseen circumstance freighted with important economic significance.   * * * The question is no longer one of express contract.   It is a question whether a court in the exercise of equitable discretion should exact new obligations and impose new duties."

Was the "negative covenant" of Harper Brothers v. Klaw perhaps a crude but effective device for forcing parties to renegotiate the disposition of a new use? See Cohn, supra, at pp. 196–98, for a comment on the application of the doctrine in other contexts. Is there any way a court can better adjust the interests of the various claimants in new markets that are created, as Judge Hough said in the "Ben Hur" case, "by the ingenuity of many inventors and mechanicians"?

(4) How, if at all, should the legislature attempt to tip the balance with respect to emerging technologies? The German Copyright Law, Art. 31(4), provides:

> The granting of licenses in respect of manners of exploitation which have hitherto not yet become known as well as covenants relating thereto shall not be effective.

Contrast a form contract provision in T. Selz, M. Simensky, and P. Acton, Entertainment Law F–34: a literary purchase agreement conveys to the motion picture studio rights with respect to "any and all media, methods, systems and processes now or hereafter known, invented, used or contemplated."

The current draft of Uniform Commercial Code § 2B–310(d) in proposed Article 2B—Licenses, provides that a grant of "all possible rights and media", or a grant in similar terms, includes "all rights then existing or created by law in the future and all uses, media, modes of transmission, and methods of distribution in all technologies or applications then existing or developed in the future."

VIDEOCASSETTES AND ELECTRONIC MEDIA

The burgeoning popularity of videocassettes in the 1980s raised the "new use" question with respect to movies made before this use was anticipated. Should standard contracts conveying motion picture rights extend to this market?

Rights in the videocassette medium were at issue in Platinum Record Co. v. Lucasfilm, Ltd., 566 F.Supp. 226 (D.N.J.1983). Plaintiff's predecessor in interest had granted Lucasfilm a "synchronization" right to use four songs on the soundtrack of the motion picture "American Graffiti." The grantee had the right "to exhibit, distribute, exploit, market and perform said motion picture * * * perpetually throughout the world by any means or methods now or hereafter known." Plaintiff made no objection to broadcasts of the film on over-the-air and cable television, but complained when the movie was released for sale and rental on videocassette.

Citing *Bartsch*, Judge Fisher granted defendants' motion for summary judgment. "A motion picture is exhibited when it is presented for viewing by an audience on a theater or television screen; the video cassette and video disc operate as a means of exhibition, not as something of an altogether different nature from exhibition." The court thought it "immaterial whether plaintiff anticipated all potential future developments in the manner of exhibiting motion pictures." [b]

But in Cohen v. Paramount Pictures Corp., 845 F.2d 851 (9th Cir. 1988), a different result emerged. Although the transaction involved another synchronization license to use a song in a movie, the 1969 contract was different. It granted "authority * * * to record in any manner, medium, form or language" (but it did not include "now or hereafter known"). It did include exhibition "by means of television * * * including 'pay television', 'subscription television' and 'closed circuit into homes' television." All rights except those granted were retained. "Perhaps the primary reason why the words 'exhibition by means of television' in the license cannot be construed as including videocassette reproduction is that, although in use by the networks, VCRs for home use were not invented or known in 1969, when the license was executed." To deprive the author of a reward for the "virtually unlimited access" that the public would now have to his song through videocassettes would "frustrate the purposes of the [Copyright] Act to reward authorship." *Platinum Record* was distinguished, as was Mickey Rooney's futile attempt to be paid for videocassettes of his many films. His grants were also comprehensive, referring for example to "means now known or unknown." Rooney v. Columbia Pictures Industries, Inc., Note (1) supra.

The *Cohen* case is severely criticized by an author who admires the approach of *Bartsch* in Nevins, Availability: The Hidden Value in Copyright Law, 15 Colum.–VLA J.L. & Arts 285 (1991).

Platinum Record and *Rooney* were again distinguished when the First Circuit interpreted a contract granting rights in the *Curious George* children's books "for television viewing"; unlike those cases, this contract "contained no general grant of rights in technologies yet to be developed, and no explicit reference to 'future methods' of exhibition." The court held that videocassette rights were not covered by the agreement. The contract had been drafted "by a professional investment firm accustomed to licensing agreements," while the copyright owner was "an elderly woman" not represented by counsel for much of the transaction; the ambiguities were construed against the drafter. Rey v. Lafferty, 990 F.2d 1379 (1st Cir.), cert. denied, 510 U.S. 828 (1993).

The "new use" issue has drawn fresh attention in connection with the distribution of works in digital form. Freelance writers are battling newspaper and magazine publishers over the right to reproduce the writers' contributions on CD–ROMs and on-line databases such as NEXIS. In the first major engagement, the publishers won a summary judgment. Tasini v. New York Times Co., 972 F.Supp. 804 (S.D.N.Y.), on reconsideration, 981

---

b. See also Boosey & Hawkes Music Pub., Ltd. v. Walt Disney Co., ____ F.3d ____, 1998 WL 210825 (2d Cir.1998), in which the Second Circuit, reaffirming *Bartsch*, held that Disney's license to use Stavinsky's "Rite of Spring" in it 1940 motion picture "Fantasia" included the right to release the film in home video formats, which earned Disney more than $360 million. (Stavinsky got $6000 for the 1938 license.) "[I]rrespective of the presence or absence of a clause expressly confirming a license over future technologies, the burden still falls on the party advancing a deviation from the most reasonable reading of the license to insure that the desired deviation is reflected in the final terms of the contract."

F.Supp. 841 (S.D.N.Y.1997). Although the court said that legends on payment checks referring to rights in "electronic library archives" were insufficient to transfer full electronic rights, the publishers prevailed on the basis of their rights under § 201(c) as the owners of copyright in collective works. That section allows collective work owners to reproduce individual contributions as part of "any revision" of the collective work. Over the writers insistence that the new technologies effectively distribute individual articles rather than collective works, the court held that the electronic versions preserved enough of the collective work to count as privileged "revisions." Meanwhile, some publishers are now insisting on freelance contracts that specifically cede rights in electronic media. The writers have countered by forming the Authors Registry, a clearinghouse for licensing electronic and photocopying rights in articles owned by authors.

SECTION 4.   DERIVATIVE WORKS AND UNDERLYING WORKS

G. Ricordi & Co. v. Paramount Pictures, Inc.

United States Court of Appeals, Second Circuit, 1951.
189 F.2d 469.

■ Before L. HAND, CHIEF JUDGE, and SWAN and FRANK, CIRCUIT JUDGES.

■ SWAN, CIRCUIT JUDGE.   This is a suit for a declaratory judgment with respect to motion picture rights in the copyrighted opera "Madame Butterfly," the renewal copyright of which is owned solely by the plaintiff. Federal jurisdiction is claimed on diversity of citizenship, the plaintiff being a partnership composed of Italian citizens and the defendant a New York corporation.   After answer, both parties moved for summary judgment upon the pleadings, affidavits and exhibits.   The district court granted the plaintiff's motion and awarded a judgment declaring the plaintiff to be the exclusive owner of motion picture rights in the renewal copyright of the opera and enjoining the defendant from interfering with the plaintiff's exercise of such rights.   The defendant has appealed.

There is no dispute as to the facts.   In 1897 John Luther Long wrote a novel entitled "Madame Butterfly," which was published in the Century Magazine and copyrighted by the Century Company.   In 1900 David Belasco, with the consent of the copyright owner, wrote a play based upon the novel and having the same title.   The play was not copyrighted until 1917.   In 1901 Long and Belasco made a contract with the plaintiff by which they gave it "the exclusive rights * * * to make a libretto for an Opera of his [Belasco's] dramatic version of Madame Butterfly, founded on the original theme, written by Mr. John Luther Long * * * the said Libretto and all rights therein, dramatic or otherwise, to be the exclusive property of Messrs. G. Ricordi & Company for all countries of the world." It is upon this agreement that the plaintiff grounds its claim to motion picture rights in the world-famous opera, with music and lyrics by Puccini in collaboration with Giacosa and Illica, which was copyrighted by the plaintiff in 1904, and of which the renewal copyright was acquired by the plaintiff from the son of Puccini.

The defendant does not deny that the plaintiff is the sole owner of the renewal copyright of the opera but it asserts that it owns the motion picture rights in the John Luther Long basic story and in the Belasco dramatic version thereof, and, consequently, if the plaintiff wishes to make a motion picture version of the opera, the defendant's consent must be obtained for the use of the Long novel and the Belasco play. Its primary contentions are two: (1) that the 1901 agreement of Long and Belasco with the plaintiff did not grant any motion picture rights; and (2) that in any event the expiration in 1925 of the copyright of Long's novel and the expiration in 1945 of the copyright of Belasco's play put an end to any exclusive license of the plaintiff to use the novel and the play for a motion picture version of the opera. Long had obtained in 1925 a renewal of the copyright on his novel and in 1932 his administrator granted to the defendant the motion picture rights therein. In the same year, 1932, the defendant obtained from the trustee under Belasco's will an assignment of the motion picture rights in Belasco's play. So far as appears there was no renewal of copyright in the play.

The district court was of opinion that the primary question for decision was whether the 1901 agreement granted to the plaintiff motion picture rights in the operatic version of the novel and of Belasco's dramatization of it. After an extensive review of the authorities, the court concluded that it did. The appellant argues strenuously that the court erred in so construing the agreement, but we do not find it necessary to decide this question. The right which Long had to make motion pictures of the story of his copyrighted novel did not extend beyond the term of the copyright; hence, if it be assumed that he assigned to the plaintiff any moving picture rights, they were necessarily similarly limited to the term of the copyright, unless the assignment included the right of renewal. It did not; the 1901 agreement made no allusion to renewal of copyright. In Fred Fisher Music Co. v. M. Witmark & Sons, 318 U.S. 643, which held that an author has power to assign his right of renewal during the term of the original copyright, no one suggested that rights assigned under the original copyright did not end with it, if nothing was said of renewal. We think they do. A copyright renewal creates a new estate, and the few cases which have dealt with the subject assert that the new estate is clear of all rights, interests or licenses granted under the original copyright.[1] It is true that the expiration of Long's copyright of the novel did not affect the plaintiff's copyright of so much of the opera as was a "new work" and entitled to be independently copyrighted as such. But the plaintiff has acquired no rights under Long's renewal of the copyright on his novel and the plaintiff's

---

1. See Fitch v. Shubert, D.C.N.Y., 20 F.Supp. 314, 315; Fox Film Corp. v. Knowles, D.C.N.Y., 274 F. 731, 732, reversed on other grounds, 261 U.S. 326; Ball, Law of Copyright and Literary Property, p. 535. Cf. In re Paper Bag Cases, 105 U.S. 766; Silverman v. Sunrise Pictures Corp., 2 Cir., 273 F. 909; White–Smith Music Pub. Co. v. Goff, 1 Cir., 187 F. 247.

renewal copyright of the opera gives it rights only in the new matter which it added to the novel and the play. It follows that the plaintiff is not entitled to make general use of the novel for a motion picture version of Long's copyrighted story; it must be restricted to what was copyrightable as new matter in its operatic version.[3]

The next question is whether the plaintiff's right to make use of Belasco's play for a motion picture version thereof is similarly restricted to what was copyrightable as new matter in its operatic version. After Long's novel was copyrighted, Belasco was given permission—a license—to make use of the story for a play. Apparently the license was oral and its precise terms are not disclosed by the record. If it be assumed that the license gave Belasco any motion picture rights, they were necessarily limited to the term of the copyright of the novel. However, Belasco as author of the play had the common law rights of an author, which include the right to copyright it. This was done in 1917. By so doing the play was dedicated to the public except for the rights reserved by the copyright, for that is the condition upon the grant of any copyright. When the copyright expired, the play was property in the public demesne, since the record discloses no renewal of the copyright. Consequently, the exclusive motion picture rights in the play, which the trustee under Belasco's will assigned to the defendant by the 1932 agreement, expired in 1945 with the expiration of the copyright of the play. Thereafter the plaintiff was as free to use the play as was the defendant in making a motion picture version of the play.

However, the defendant still has the motion picture rights in the renewal copyright of Long's novel. Therefore it may assert, as it did, that the plaintiff cannot make general use of the story of the novel for a motion picture version of its opera; and, as already stated, the plaintiff is restricted to using what was copyrightable as new matter in its operatic version of the novel but is not so restricted in using the play which is now in public demesne. It scarcely need be added that the defendant, while free to use the novel and the play in making a motion picture, may not make use of the plaintiff's opera without its consent.

The remaining contentions of the parties have been examined and found without merit. Discussion of them is deemed unnecessary.

So much of the judgment as declares that the plaintiff is "the rightful owner and sole proprietor of the valid renewal copyright in the Opera entitled Madame Butterfly and of all rights and interest therein including the sole and exclusive motion picture rights" is affirmed. The injunction granted the plaintiff is too broad unless it be construed to forbid only such assertions of claims by the defendant as exceed those which the defendant is entitled to make as shown by the foregoing opinion. Accordingly the injunction is modified to conform to our opinion. Each party shall bear its own appellate costs and no attorney's fees are awarded to either party.

---

3. See McCaleb v. Fox Film Corp., 5 Cir., 299 F. 48, 49; Glaser v. St. Elmo Co., Inc., C.C.S.D.N.Y., 175 F. 276, 277. The statute expressly provides that a copyright on a new work shall neither extend nor be construed to imply an exclusive right to use the original work from which the new work is derived. 17 U.S.C.A. § 7.

On Petition for Clarification

Paramount Pictures, Inc., asks for a clarification of that part of our opinion relating to the expiration and dedication of Belasco's copyright. We there said: "When the copyright expired, the play was property in the public demesne, since the record discloses no renewal of the copyright." What the petitioner desires is an express statement that only the new matter which Belasco's play added to Long's novel came into the public demesne upon the expiration of Belasco's copyright. It is implicit in the opinion as a whole that what is dedicated to the public as a condition of obtaining a copyright is only such matter as is copyrightable, but to avoid any possible cavil we will amend the above quoted sentence to read as follows: "When the copyright expired, the copyrightable new matter in the play was property in the public demesne, since the record discloses no renewal of the copyright".

QUESTIONS: **(1)** Under the decision of the court, what is the nature of the motion picture, if any, that Ricordi would be entitled to make without obtaining Paramount's consent?

(2) Does the decision have any bearing on Ricordi's right to publish the opera, if sued by the owner of the renewal term in the novel?

(3) Would you advise a client that she could freely produce the Belasco play?

ROHAUER v. KILLIAM SHOWS, INC., 551 F.2d 484 (2d Cir.), cert. denied, 431 U.S. 949 (1977). Edith Maude Hull, a British subject, owned a United States copyright after publication here in 1925 of her novel "The Sons of the Sheik." She sold all movie rights to defendant's assignor. She also agreed to renew the copyright and to assign the renewal motion picture rights. Mrs. Hull died in 1943. In 1952 her only daughter, Cecil Wynstanley Hull, renewed, and in 1965 assigned motion picture and television rights to plaintiff. The Rudolph Valentino film of 1926 was later revived on television, and this infringement action resulted.

Judge Friendly said, "The issue is this: When the author of a copyrighted story has assigned the motion picture rights and consented to the assignee's securing a copyright on motion picture versions, with the terms of the assignment demonstrating an intention that the rights of the purchaser shall extend through a renewal of the copyright on the story, does a purchaser which has made a film and obtained a derivative copyright and renewal copyright thereon infringe the copyright on the story if it authorizes the performance of the copyrighted film after the author has died and the copyright on the story has been renewed by a statutory successor under 17 U.S.C.A. § 24, who has made a new assignment of motion picture and television rights?"

Ricordi v. Paramount was distinguished on the ground that the contracts there made no reference to renewal rights, and that the holding of the case referred to Ricordi's disability to make a new film, a right which the defendants here were not claiming. "The equities," said the court, "lie preponderantly in favor of the proprietor of the derivative copyright" in a movie or an opera, who will "often have made contributions both literary, musical and economic as great as or greater than the original author." Judgment was ordered for the defendant.

Rohauer was subsequently distinguished in Russell v. Price and Filmvideo Releasing Corp. v. Hastings, infra; it was ultimately repudiated by the Supreme Court in Stewart v. Abend, infra.[a]

RUSSELL V. PRICE, 612 F.2d 1123 (9th Cir.1979), cert. denied, 446 U.S. 952 (1980).   George Bernard Shaw copyrighted his play "Pygmalion" in 1913.   The 1941 renewal, as extended, was good until 1988.   A licensed motion picture was made in 1938; its copyright was allowed to expire in 1966.   This action was brought under the 1909 Act to enjoin the unlicensed rental of the film following the expiration of copyright.

" * * * [W]e reaffirm, without finding it necessary to repeat the rationale, the well-established doctrine that a derivative copyright protects only the new material contained in the derivative work, not the matter derived from the underlying work.   1 Nimmer on Copyright § 3.04 (1979). Thus, although the derivative work may enter the public domain, the matter contained therein which derives from a work still covered by statutory copyright is not dedicated to the public.   * * * The established doctrine prevents unauthorized copying or other infringing use of the underlying work or any part of that work contained in the derivative product so long as the underlying work itself remains copyrighted.   Therefore, since exhibition of the film 'Pygmalion' necessarily involves exhibition of parts of Shaw's play, which is still copyrighted, plaintiffs here may prevent defendants from renting the film for exhibition without their authorization."

The court distinguished Classic Film Museum, Inc. v. Warner Bros., Inc., 597 F.2d 13 (1st Cir.1979), which gave a declaratory judgment that plaintiff could exhibit the 1937 motion picture "A Star is Born", on which copyright had expired, despite defendant's claim that the exhibition would infringe its common law copyright in the underlying story and screenplay. According to *Classic Film*, "Defendant's reliance upon the *Ricordi* line of cases is misplaced. Those cases solely concerned underlying works which were statutorily copyrighted; thus, any protection offered by the *Ricordi* doctrine was limited to the fixed life of the underlying copyright * * *. The *Ricordi* doctrine is not equally applicable where there is an underlying

a. For an astonishing behind-the-scenes account of *Rohauer,* see Jacoby, Examining   the "Rear Window" Decision, 39 J.Copyr.Soc. 49 (1991).

common-law copyright which might extend indefinitely." (Can this be explained by saying that publication of the derivative work also published the portions of the underlying work that it incorporated, thus destroying common law protection?[b])

FILMVIDEO RELEASING CORP. v. HASTINGS, 668 F.2d 91 (2d Cir.1981).   On the basis of a 1935 agreement with Clarence Mulford, author of the Hopalong Cassidy books, Paramount had made 23 movies exploiting the character.   Mulford or his estate had renewed copyright on all the novels; Paramount had let all the movie copyrights expire.   Plaintiff, in a declaratory judgment action, maintained that it could license prints of the films for television, although Mulford in the 1935 agreement had reserved television and radio rights.   Mulford's successors counterclaimed for infringement and prevailed.   After three reported opinions in the District Court,[c] the Court of Appeals was terse.

"The principal question on this appeal is whether a licensed, derivative, copyrighted work and the underlying copyrighted matter which it incorporates both fall into the public domain where the underlying copyright has been renewed but the derivative copyright has not.   We agree with the Ninth Circuit, Russell v. Price * * * that the answer is 'No'."

"Since 1909," Judge Van Graafeiland wrote, "the courts of this circuit have held almost without exception that a derivative copyright is a good copyright only with regard to the original embellishments and additions it has made to the underlying work.   * * * Since the proprietor of a derivative copyright cannot convey away that which he does not own * * * it follows that he cannot release that which he does not own into the public domain."

NOTES AND QUESTIONS

(1) Ricordi v. Paramount and its sequels spawned a formidable body of commentary.   See, e.g., R. Brown, The Widening Gyre: Are Derivative Works Getting Out of Hand?, 3 Cardozo Arts & Ent.L.J. 1 (1984); Goldstein, Derivative Rights and Derivative Works in Copyright, 30 J.Copyr.Soc. 209 (1983); Jaszi, When Works Collide: Derivative Motion Pictures, Underlying Rights, and the Public Interest, 28 U.C.L.A. L.Rev. 715 (1981); Nevins, The Doctrine of Copyright Ambush: Limitations on the Free Use of Public Domain Derivative Works, 25 St. Louis U.L.J. 58 (1981).

b. See Maljack Prod., Inc. v. UAV Corp., 964 F.Supp. 1416 (C.D.Cal.1997) (publication of derivative work publishes the underlying work). Cf. Harris Custom Builders, Inc. v. Hoffmeyer, 92 F.3d 517 (7th Cir.1996), cert. denied, 117 S.Ct. 956 (1997) (builder could not claim protection under the 1976 Act for architectural plans as unpublished works after portions were included in a brochure published without copyright notice in 1983).

c. The last of them, 509 F.Supp. 60 (S.D.N.Y.1981), is on copying, and paints very broadly in finding all the films infringing.

Why so much about so little? For one thing, there are significant doctrinal issues at stake. More pointedly, obstructed access to old movies stirs feelings, even passions. Movie-makers have been careless about preserving their past, as well as about renewing their copyrights; they are sometimes viewed as dogs in the manger, snapping at those who want to preserve and enjoy old movies. Emboldened by the (temporary) triumph in *Rohauer,* several writers propounded a "new property" in the film-maker. The film-maker was not simply an embellisher of the underlying work, but a creator who transformed a simple story into a larger art form. Such works should not be at the mercy of an underlying copyright owner, any more than Puccini's genius should be hobbled by John Luther Long, the Philadelphia lawyer in *Ricordi* with a flair for Japanese fantasies. That is the policy argument, oversimplified. It suffered a major setback in Stewart v. Abend, infra.

(2) Consider again Russell v. Price and Filmvideo Releasing Corp v. Hastings—both said that derivative works on which copyright had expired could not be exhibited because they embodied material from underlying works still under copyright. But consider this alternative solution: the derivative works are in the public domain and thus open to use as a necessary consequence of the expiration of copyright, but this consequence need not and does not divest copyright in the underlying work or in any other derivations; the movies can be exhibited, but no other use of the underlying work is permissible. Is that a sensible resolution?

Stewart v. Abend

Supreme Court of the United States, 1990.
495 U.S. 207, 110 S.Ct. 1750.

■ JUSTICE O'CONNOR delivered the opinion of the Court.

The author of a pre-existing work may assign to another the right to use it in a derivative work. In this case the author of a pre-existing work agreed to assign the rights in his renewal copyright term to the owner of a derivative work, but died before the commencement of the renewal period. The question presented is whether the owner of the derivative work infringed the rights of the successor owner of the pre-existing work by continued distribution and publication of the derivative work during the renewal term of the pre-existing work.

Cornell Woolrich authored the story "It Had to Be Murder," which was first published in February 1942 in Dime Detective Magazine. The magazine's publisher, Popular Publications, Inc., obtained the rights to magazine publication of the story and Woolrich retained all other rights. Popular Publications obtained a blanket copyright for the issue of Dime Detective Magazine in which "It Had to Be Murder" was published.

The Copyright Act of 1909, 17 U.S.C. § 1 et seq. (1976 ed.) (1909 Act), provided authors a 28–year initial term of copyright protection plus a 28–year renewal term. See 17 U.S.C. § 24 (1976 ed.). In 1945, Woolrich agreed to assign the rights to make motion picture versions of six of his stories, including "It Had to Be Murder," to B.G. De Sylva Productions for $9,250. He also agreed to renew the copyrights in the stories at the appropriate time and to assign the same motion picture rights to De Sylva Productions for the 28–year renewal term. In 1953, actor Jimmy Stewart and director Alfred Hitchcock formed a production company, Patron, Inc., which obtained the motion picture rights in "It Had to Be Murder" from De Sylva's successors in interest for $10,000.

In 1954, Patron, Inc., along with Paramount Pictures, produced and distributed, "Rear Window," the motion picture version of Woolrich's story "It Had to Be Murder." Woolrich died in 1968 before he could obtain the rights in the renewal term for petitioners as promised and without a surviving spouse or child. He left his property to a trust administered by his executor, Chase Manhattan Bank, for the benefit of Columbia University. On December 29, 1969, Chase Manhattan Bank renewed the copyright in the "It Had to Be Murder" story pursuant to 17 U.S.C. § 24 (1976 ed.). Chase Manhattan assigned the renewal rights to respondent Abend for $650 plus 10% of all proceeds from exploitation of the story.

"Rear Window" was broadcast on the ABC television network in 1971. Respondent then notified petitioners Hitchcock (now represented by co-trustees of his will), Stewart, and MCA Inc., the owners of the "Rear Window" motion picture and renewal rights in the motion picture, that he owned the renewal rights in the copyright and that their distribution of the motion picture without his permission infringed his copyright in the story. Hitchcock, Stewart, and MCA nonetheless entered into a second license with ABC to rebroadcast the motion picture. In 1974, respondent filed suit against these same petitioners, and others, in the United States District Court for the Southern District of New York, alleging copyright infringement. Respondent dismissed his complaint in return for $25,000.

Three years later, the United States Court of Appeals for the Second Circuit decided Rohauer v. Killiam Shows, Inc., 551 F.2d 484, cert. denied, 431 U.S. 949 (1977), in which it held that the owner of the copyright in a derivative work may continue to use the existing derivative work according to the original grant from the author of the pre-existing work even if the grant of rights in the pre-existing work lapsed. 551 F.2d, at 494. Several years later, apparently in reliance on *Rohauer,* petitioners re-released the motion picture in a variety of media, including new 35 and 16 millimeter prints for theatrical exhibition in the United States, videocassettes, and videodiscs. They also publicly exhibited the motion picture in theaters, over cable television, and through videodisc and videocassette rentals and sales.

Respondent then brought the instant suit in the United States District Court for the Central District of California against Hitchcock, Stewart, MCA, and Universal Film Exchanges, a subsidiary of MCA and the distributor of the motion picture. Respondent's complaint alleges that the re-release of the motion picture infringes his copyright in the story because petitioners' right to use the story during the renewal term lapsed when

Woolrich died before he could register for the renewal term and transfer his renewal rights to them.   * * *

* * * The District Court granted petitioners' motions for summary judgment based on *Rohauer* and the fair use defense and denied respondent's motion for summary judgment, as well as petitioners' motion for summary judgment alleging defects in the story's copyright. Respondent appealed to the United States Court of Appeals for the Ninth Circuit and petitioners cross-appealed.

The Court of Appeals reversed, holding that respondent's copyright in the renewal term of the story was not defective. 863 F.2d 1465, 1472 (1988). The issue before the court, therefore, was whether petitioners were entitled to distribute and exhibit the motion picture without respondent's permission despite respondent's valid copyright in the pre-existing story.   * * *

Petitioners also relied, as did the District Court, on the decision in Rohauer v. Killiam Shows, Inc., supra. In *Rohauer,* the Court of Appeals for the Second Circuit held that statutory successors to the renewal copyright in a pre-existing work under § 24 could not "depriv[e] the proprietor of the derivative copyright of a right ... to use so much of the underlying copyrighted work as already has been embodied in the copyrighted derivative work, as a matter of copyright law." Id., at 492. The Court of Appeals in the instant case rejected this reasoning, concluding that even if the pre-existing work had been incorporated into a derivative work, use of the pre-existing work was infringing unless the owner of the derivative work held a valid grant of rights in the renewal term.

The court relied on Miller Music Corp. v. Charles N. Daniels, Inc., 362 U.S. 373 (1960), in which we held that assignment of renewal rights by an author before the time for renewal arrives cannot defeat the right of the author's statutory successor to the renewal rights if the author dies before the right to renewal accrues.   * * *

In its debates leading up to the Copyright Act of 1909, Congress elaborated upon the policy underlying a system comprised of an original term and a completely separate renewal term. See G. Ricordi & Co. v. Paramount Pictures, Inc., 189 F.2d 469, 471 (CA2) (the renewal right "creates a new estate, and the ... cases which have dealt with the subject assert that the new estate is clear of all rights, interests or licenses granted under the original copyright"), cert. denied, 342 U.S. 849 (1951). "It not infrequently happens that the author sells his copyright outright to a publisher for a comparatively small sum." H.R.Rep. No. 2222, 60th Cong., 2d Sess., 14 (1909). The renewal term permits the author, originally in a poor bargaining position, to renegotiate the terms of the grant once the value of the work has been tested.   * * *

* * * Thus, the renewal provisions were intended to give the author a second chance to obtain fair remuneration for his creative efforts and to provide the author's family a "new estate" if the author died before the renewal period arrived.

* * * If the assignee of all of the renewal rights holds nothing upon the death of the assignor before arrival of the renewal period, then, *a*

fortiori, the assignee of a portion of the renewal rights, e.g., the right to produce a derivative work, must also hold nothing. See also Brief for Register of Copyrights as *Amicus Curiae* 22 ("*[A]ny* assignment of renewal rights made during the original term is void if the author dies before the renewal period"). Therefore, if the author dies before the renewal period, then the assignee may continue to use the original work only if the author's successor transfers the renewal rights to the assignee. This is the rule adopted by the Court of Appeals below and advocated by the Register of Copyrights. See 863 F.2d, at 1478; Brief for Register of Copyrights as *Amicus Curiae* 22. Application of this rule to this case should end the inquiry. Woolrich died before the commencement of the renewal period in the story, and, therefore, petitioners hold only an unfulfilled expectancy. Petitioners have been "deprived of nothing. Like all purchasers of contingent interests, [they took] subject to the possibility that the contingency may not occur." *Miller Music,* supra, 362 U.S., at 378.

The reason that our inquiry does not end here, and that we granted certiorari, is that the Court of Appeals for the Second Circuit reached a contrary result in Rohauer v. Killiam Shows, Inc., 551 F.2d 484 (1977). Petitioners' theory is drawn largely from *Rohauer.* The Court of Appeals in *Rohauer* attempted to craft a "proper reconciliation" between the owner of the pre-existing work, who held the right to the work pursuant to *Miller Music,* and the owner of the derivative work, who had a great deal to lose if the work could not be published or distributed. 551 F.2d, at 490. Addressing a case factually similar to this case, the court concluded that even if the death of the author caused the renewal rights in the pre-existing work to revert to the statutory successor, the owner of the derivative work could continue to exploit that work. * * *

Properly conceding there is no explicit support for their theory in the 1909 Act, its legislative history, or the case law, petitioners contend, as did the court in *Rohauer,* that the termination provisions of the 1976 Act, while not controlling, support their theory of the case. For works existing in their original or renewal terms as of January 1, 1978, the 1976 Act added 19 years to the 1909 Act's provision of 28 years of initial copyright protection and 28 years of renewal protection. See 17 U.S.C. §§ 304(a) and (b) (1988 ed.). For those works, the author has the power to terminate the grant of rights at the end of the renewal term and, therefore, to gain the benefit of that additional 19 years of protection. See 17 U.S.C. § 304(c). In effect, the 1976 Act provides a third opportunity for the author to benefit from a work in its original or renewal term as of January 1, 1978. Congress, however, created one exception to the author's right to terminate: the author may not, at the end of the renewal term, terminate the right to use a derivative work for which the owner of the derivative work has held valid rights in the original and renewal terms. See § 304(c)(6)(A). The author, however, may terminate the right to create new derivative works. Ibid. For example, if the petitioners held a valid copyright in the story throughout the original and renewal terms, and the renewal term in "Rear Window" were about to expire, petitioners could continue to distribute the motion picture even if respondent terminated the grant of rights, but could not create a new motion picture version of the story. Both the court in *Rohauer* and petitioners infer from this exception to the right to terminate an intent by Congress to prevent authors of pre-existing works from blocking distribution of derivative works. In other words, because Congress decided not to permit authors to exercise a third opportunity to benefit from a work incorporated into a derivative work, the Act expresses a general policy of undermining the author's second opportunity. We disagree. * * *

* * * Congress would not have stated explicitly in § 304(c)(6)(A) that, at the end of the renewal term, the owner of the rights in the pre-existing work may not terminate use rights in existing derivative works unless Congress had assumed that the owner continued to hold the right to sue for infringement even after incorporation of the pre-existing work into the derivative work. * * *

Accordingly, we conclude that neither the 1909 Act nor the 1976 Act provides support for the theory set forth in *Rohauer*. * * *

Finally, petitioners urge us to consider the policies underlying the Copyright Act. They argue that the rule announced by the Court of Appeals will undermine one of the policies of the Act—the dissemination of creative works—by leading to many fewer works reaching the public. *Amicus* Columbia Pictures asserts that "[s]ome owners of underlying work renewal copyrights may refuse to negotiate, preferring instead to retire their copyrighted works, and all derivative works based thereon, from public use. Others may make demands—like respondent's demand for 50% of petitioners' future gross proceeds in excess of advertising expenses ...— which are so exorbitant that a negotiated economic accommodation will be impossible." Brief for Columbia Pictures et al. as *Amicus Curiae* 21. These arguments are better addressed by Congress than the courts. * * *

[The Court also rejected petitioners' fair use defense.]

For the foregoing reasons, the judgment of the Court of Appeals is affirmed and the case is remanded for further proceedings consistent with this opinion.

It is so ordered.

■ JUSTICE WHITE, concurring in the judgment.

Although I am not convinced, as the Court seems to be, that the decision in Miller Music Corp. v. Charles N. Daniels, Inc., 362 U.S. 373 (1960), was required by the Copyright Act, neither am I convinced that it was an impermissible construction of the statute. And because *Miller Music,* in my view, requires the result reached by the Court in this case, I concur in the judgment of affirmance.

■ JUSTICE STEVENS, with whom THE CHIEF JUSTICE and JUSTICE SCALIA join, dissenting.

* * *

[Section 7 of the 1909 Act] deals with derivative works—works that include both old material and new material. The plain language of § 7 confers on the entire derivative work—not just the new material contained therein—the status of all other works of authorship, that of "new works subject to copyright under the provisions of this title." * * * Section 7, read together with § 3, plainly indicates that the copyright on a derivative work extends to both the new material and that "in which copyright is already subsisting." § 3. The author or proprietor of the derivative work therefore has the statutory right to publish and distribute the entire work. * * *

* * * In my opinion, § 7 was intended to do something more: to give the original author the power to sell the right to make a derivative work that upon creation and copyright would be completely independent of the original work. * * *

* * * By designating derivative works as "new works" that are subject to copyright and accorded the two terms applicable to original works, Congress evinced its intention that the derivative copyright not lapse upon termination of the original author's interest in the underlying copyright. The continued publication of the derivative work, after the expiration of the original term of the prior work, does not infringe any of the statutory successor's rights in the renewal copyright of the original work. The author's right to sell his derivative rights is exercised when consent is conveyed and completed when the derivative work is copyrighted. At that point, prior to the end of the first term, the right to prevent publication of the derivative work is no longer one of the bundle of rights attaching to the copyright. The further agreement to permit use of the underlying material during the renewal term does not violate § 24 because at the moment consent is given and the derivative work is created and copyrighted, a new right of property comes into existence independent of the original author's copyright estate.

* * * Ironically, by restricting the author's ability to consent to creation of a derivative work with independent existence, the Court may make it practically impossible for the original author to sell his derivative rights late in the original term and to reap the financial and artistic advantage that comes with the creation of a derivative work.[18]

NOTES AND QUESTIONS

(1) The Supreme Court's decision has generated critical commentary and inventive titles. See Allen and Swift, Shattering Copyright Law: Will James Stewart's *Rear Window* Become a Pain in the Glass, 22 Pac.L.J. 1 (1990); Hughes, Jurisprudential Vertigo: The Supreme Court's View of "Rear Window" is for The Birds, 60 Miss.L.J. 239 (1990). For guarded support of the decision, see D. Nimmer, Refracting the Window's Light: *Stewart v. Abend* in Myth and Fact, 39 J.Copyr.Soc. 18 (1991).

---

18. The creation of a derivative work often is in the best interests of both the original author and his statutory successors. As one commentator has noted: "The movie Rear Window became a selling point for anthologies containing the Woolrich story. The musical play Cats no doubt sent many people who dimly remembered the Love Song of J. Alfred Prufrock as the chief, if not the only oeuvre of T. S. Eliot to the bookstore for Old Possum's Book of Practical Cats." Weinreb, Fair's Fair: A Comment on the Fair Use Doctrine, 103 Harv. L. Rev. 1137, 1147 (1990).

After Stewart v. Abend, should creators of derivative works avoid making substantial investments in pre–1978 works that are still in their first term of copyright?

(2) One consequence of Stewart v. Abend is that Christmas is now celebrated without the continuous airing of Frank Capra's *It's A Wonderful Life,* in which despondent banker George Bailey (Jimmy Stewart again) is saved with the help of a whimsical angel named Clarence. Copyright in the 1946 film had expired in 1974 when Republic Pictures failed to renew. Everyone, including the film's owner, assumed that it was in the public domain and thus available for unlicensed use. But inspired by Stewart v. Abend, Republic looked more closely and found that it still owned the copyright in *The Greatest Gift,* an obscure short story on which the film was loosely based. (Republic also quietly bought up rights in the music used in the movie.) It has now asserted (so far successfully) that further unauthorized broadcasts are an infringement of its rights in the underlying works. One programming executive said sadly, "I used to work in an independent station and everyone was so happy when *It's A Wonderful Life* went into the public domain. It was like a gift, and now we hate to return it." Koseluk, Not a Wonderful Year, Chicago Tribune, Dec. 19, 1993, Arts, p. 22.

Is it possible after Stewart v. Abend to argue that a derivative work on which copyright has expired should be in the public domain as the ostensible consequence of the failure to renew, while all other rights in the underlying works remain intact? See Note (2), p. 512 supra.

(3) The 1976 Act's termination of grant provisions, with their exemption for continued use of derivative works, p. 489 supra, lighten for moviemakers the consequences of terminations. And for new works, they no longer have to attend to renewals. For movies made after 1978 as works for hire, i.e., made by the corporate employers of the many "authors," the copyright term is 75 years. §§ 201(b), 302(c). Is it possible that there could be underlying rights that might keep such works from entering the public domain even after 75 years? Consider this example:

An author born in 1965 publishes a novel in 1990. A movie based on the novel appears in 1995. The copyright in the movie will expire in 2070. But if the author dies in 2050 (aged 85), the copyright in the novel will last until 2100.

What will you advise a would-be distributor or exhibitor of the movie in 2071?

SECTION 5.   WORK MADE FOR HIRE AND JOINT WORK

COPYRIGHT IN "WORK MADE FOR HIRE"

The 1909 Act in its skimpy definition section, § 26, declared that "the word 'author' shall include an employer in the case of works made for hire." Under § 24, "an employer for whom such work is made for hire" held the renewal right. (See also § 304(a) of the 1976 Act.) As the statute came to be interpreted, persons who in other contexts would be considered "independent contractors," in that they created works on commission without having any continuing employment relationship with the commissioning party, were also brought within the reach of the "made for hire" doctrine. "Direction" and "supervision" by the supposed "employer" became the touchstone for finding work to be for hire. This trend in the decisions continued and indeed intensified [a] despite the prospect of statutory change.

In the revision process, authors and artists strove to avoid the presumption that work they did on commission was for hire.[b] The result was § 201(b), to be read in close conjunction with the definition of "work made for hire" in § 101. It is the definition that provides special treatment for commissioned works. Only nine kinds of commissioned works may be work for hire, and only "if the parties expressly agree in a written instrument signed by them that the work shall be considered a work made for hire." Note that photographs are not listed, nor architectural drawings, nor textile designs, nor computer programs. This formulation, including the portion of the definition that subsumes "a work prepared by an employee within the scope of his or her employment", was drafted by 1965. Between that date and the long-deferred 1976 passage of the revision statute, courts continued to employ the "supervision" test. Indeed, they did so with vigor even after the 1976 Act became effective.

For a time, the leading case under the 1976 Act was Aldon Accessories, Ltd. v. Spiegel, Inc., 738 F.2d 548 (2d Cir.), cert. denied, 469 U.S. 982 (1984). It relied almost entirely on cases decided between 1966 and 1975, and failed to find in the legislative history any intention to change the law.

The Fifth Circuit, in Easter Seal Society for Crippled Children and Adults of Louisiana, Inc. v. Playboy Enterprises, 815 F.2d 323 (5th Cir. 1987), cert. denied, 485 U.S. 981 (1988), departed significantly from *Aldon* in rejecting the "supervision" test: "Today we adopt a bright-line rule for determining whether a work was made 'for hire' under the 1976 Act. Only works by actual employees and independent contractors who fulfill the requirements of § 101(2) can be 'for hire' under the new statute. Copyright 'employees' are those persons called 'employees' or 'servants' for purposes of agency law."

The Ninth Circuit, in Dumas v. Gommerman, 865 F.2d 1093 (9th Cir.1989), went beyond *Easter Seal* to a literal reading of the statutory

a. Cf. Epoch Producing Corp. v. Killiam Shows, Inc., 522 F.2d 737 (2d Cir.1975), cert. denied, 424 U.S. 955 (1976), where renewal rights in "The Birth of a Nation" were at issue. The court delved into the making of the film in 1914 to establish that D.W. Griffith was not an employee working for hire.

b. See Angel and Tannenbaum, Works for Hire Under S.22, 22 N.Y.L.S. L.Rev. 209 (1976), for one account of the legislative tug-of-war.

reference to "employee." The court said that "only works produced by formal, salaried employees are covered by 17 U.S.C. § 101(1). Works by independent contractors are works for hire only when the requirements of 17 U.S.C. § 101(2) are satisfied." The invocation of "agency law principles" to find employee status, Judge Fletcher wrote, would reintroduce "the rejected 'supervision and control' test."

Each of these interpretations of "work made for hire" was urged upon the Supreme Court in the following case.

Community for Creative Non–Violence v. Reid

Supreme Court of the United States, 1989.
490 U.S. 730, 109 S.Ct. 2166.

■ JUSTICE MARSHALL delivered the opinion of the Court.

In this case, an artist and the organization that hired him to produce a sculpture contest the ownership of the copyright in that work. To resolve this dispute, we must construe the "work made for hire" provisions of the Copyright Act of 1976 (Act or 1976 Act), 17 U.S.C. §§ 101 and 201(b), and in particular, the provision in § 101, which defines as a "work made for hire" a "work prepared by an employee within the scope of his or her employment" (hereinafter § 101(1)).

I

Petitioners are the Community for Creative Non–Violence (CCNV), a nonprofit unincorporated association dedicated to eliminating homelessness in America, and Mitch Snyder, a member and trustee of CCNV. In the fall of 1985, CCNV decided to participate in the annual Christmas-time Pageant of Peace in Washington, D.C., by sponsoring a display to dramatize the plight of the homeless. As the District Court recounted:

"Snyder and fellow CCNV members conceived the idea for the nature of the display: a sculpture of a modern Nativity scene in which, in lieu of the traditional Holy Family, the two adult figures and the infant would appear as contemporary homeless people huddled on a streetside steam grate. The family was to be black (most of the homeless in Washington being black); the figures were to be life-sized, and the steam grate would be positioned atop a platform 'pedestal,' or base, within which special-effects equipment would be enclosed to emit stimulated 'steam' through the grid to swirl about the figures. They also settled upon a title for the work—'Third World America'—and a legend for the pedestal: 'and still there is no room at the inn.' " 652 F.Supp. 1453, 1454 (DC 1987).

Snyder made inquiries to locate an artist to produce the sculpture. He was referred to respondent James Earl Reid, a Baltimore, Maryland, sculptor. In the course of two telephone calls, Reid agreed to sculpt the three human figures. CCNV agreed to make the steam grate and pedestal for the statue. Reid proposed that the work be cast in bronze, at a total cost of approximately $100,000 and taking six to eight months to complete. Snyder rejected that proposal because CCNV did not have sufficient funds, and because the statute had to be completed by December 12 to be included in the pageant. Reid then suggested, and Snyder agreed, that the sculpture would be made of a material known as "Design Cast 62," a synthetic substance that could meet CCNV's monetary and time constraints, could be tinted to resemble bronze, and could withstand the elements. The parties agreed that the project would cost no more than $15,000, not including Reid's services, which he offered to donate. The parties did not sign a written agreement. Neither party mentioned copyright.

After Reid received an advance of $3,000, he made several sketches of figures in various poses. At Snyder's request, Reid sent CCNV a sketch of a proposed sculpture showing the family in a creche-like setting: the mother seated, cradling a baby in her lap; the father standing behind her, bending over her shoulder to touch the baby's foot. Reid testified that Snyder asked for the sketch to use in raising funds for the sculpture. Snyder testified that it was also for his approval. Reid sought a black family to serve as a model for the sculpture. Upon Snyder's suggestion, Reid visited a family living at CCNV's Washington shelter but decided that only their newly born child was a suitable model. While Reid was in Washington, Snyder took him to see homeless people living on the streets. Snyder pointed out that they tended to recline on steam grates, rather than sit or stand, in order to warm their bodies. From that time on, Reid's sketches contained only reclining figures.

Throughout November and the first two weeks of December 1985, Reid worked exclusively on the statue, assisted at various times by a dozen different people who were paid with funds provided in installments by CCNV. On a number of occasions, CCNV members visited Reid to check on his progress and to coordinate CCNV's construction of the base. CCNV rejected Reid's proposal to use suitcases or shopping bags to hold the family's personal belongings, insisting instead on a shopping cart. Reid and CCNV members did not discuss copyright ownership on any of these visits.

On December 24, 1985, 12 days after the agreed upon date, Reid delivered the completed statue to Washington. There it was joined to the steam grate and pedestal prepared by CCNV and placed on display near the site of the pageant. Snyder paid Reid the final installment of the $15,000. The statue remained on display for a month. In late January 1986, CCNV members returned it to Reid's studio in Baltimore for minor repairs. Several weeks later, Snyder began making plans to take the statue on a tour of several cities to raise money for the homeless. Reid objected, contending that the Design Cast 62 material was not strong enough to withstand the ambitious itinerary. He urged CCNV to cast the statue in bronze at a cost of $35,000, or to create a master mold at a cost of $5,000. Snyder declined to spend more of CCNV's money on the project.

In March 1986, Snyder asked Reid to return the sculpture. Reid refused. He then filed a certificate of copyright registration for "Third

World America" in his name and announced plans to take the sculpture on a more modest tour than the one CCNV had proposed. Snyder, acting in his capacity as CCNV's trustee, immediately filed a competing certificate of copyright registration.

Snyder and CCNV then commenced this action against Reid and his photographer, Ronald Purtee, seeking return of the sculpture and a determination of copyright ownership. The District Court granted a preliminary injunction, ordering the sculpture's return. After a 2–day bench trial, the District Court declared that "Third World America" was a "work made for hire" under § 101 of the Copyright Act and that Snyder, as trustee for CCNV, was the exclusive owner of the copyright in the sculpture. Id., at 1457. The court reasoned that Reid had been an "employee" of CCNV within the meaning of § 101(1) because CCNV was the motivating force in the statue's production. Snyder and other CCNV members, the court explained, "conceived the idea of a contemporary Nativity scene to contrast with the national celebration of the season," and "directed enough of [Reid's] effort to assure that, in the end, he had produced what they, not he, wanted." Id., at 1456.

The Court of Appeals for the District of Columbia reversed and remanded, holding that Reid owned the copyright because "Third World America" was not a work for hire. 846 F.2d 1485, 1494 (1988). Adopting what it termed the "literal interpretation" of the Act as articulated by the Fifth Circuit in Easter Seal Society for Crippled Children and Adults of Louisiana, Inc. v. Playboy Enterprises, 815 F.2d 323, 329 (1987), cert. denied, 485 U.S. 981 (1988), the court read § 101 as creating "a simple dichotomy in fact between employees and independent contractors." 846 F.2d, at 1492. Because, under agency law, Reid was an independent contractor, the court concluded that the work was not "prepared by an employee" under § 101(1). Id., 846 F.2d, at 1494. Nor was the sculpture a "work made for hire" under the second subsection of § 101 (hereinafter § 101(2)): sculpture is not one of the nine categories of works enumerated in that subsection, and the parties had not agreed in writing that the sculpture would be a work for hire. Ibid. The court suggested that the sculpture nevertheless may have been jointly authored by CCNV and Reid, id., 846 F.2d, at 1495, and remanded for a determination whether the sculpture is indeed a joint work under the Act. Id., 846 F.2d, at 1498–1499.

We granted certiorari to resolve a conflict among the Courts of Appeals over the proper construction of the "work made for hire" provisions of the Act. 488 U.S. 940 (1988). We now affirm.

II

A

The Copyright Act of 1976 provides that copyright ownership "vests initially in the author or authors of the work." 17 U.S.C. § 201(a). As a general rule, the author is the party who actually creates the work, that is, the person who translates an idea into a fixed, tangible expression entitled to copyright protection. § 102. The Act carves out an important exception, however, for "works made for hire." [3] If the work is for hire, "the employer or other person for whom the work was prepared is considered the author" and owns the copyright, unless there is a written agreement to the contrary. § 201(b). Classifying a work as "made for hire" determines not only the initial ownership of its copyright, but also the copyright's duration, § 302(c), and the owners' renewal rights, § 304(a), termination rights, § 203(a), and right to import certain goods bearing the copyright, § 601(b)(1). See 1 M. Nimmer & D. Nimmer, Nimmer on Copyright § 5.03[A], pp. 5–10 (1988). The contours of the work for hire doctrine therefore carry profound significance for freelance creators—including artists, writers, photographers, designers, composers, and computer programmers—and for the publishing, advertising, music, and other industries which commission their works. [4]

* * * The petitioners do not claim that the statue satisfies the terms of § 101(2). Quite clearly, it does not. Sculpture does not fit within any of the nine categories of "specially ordered or commissioned" works enumerated in that subsection, and no written agreement between the parties establishes "Third World America" as a work for hire.

The dispositive inquiry in this case therefore is whether "Third World America" is "a work prepared by an employee within the scope of his or her employment" under § 101(1). The Act does not define these terms. In the absence of such guidance, four interpretations have emerged. The first holds that a work is prepared by an employee whenever the hiring party [6] retains the right to control the product. See Peregrine v. Lauren Corp., 601 F.Supp. 828, 829 (Colo.1985); Clarkstown v. Reeder, 566 F.Supp. 137, 142 (SDNY 1983). Petitioners take this view. Brief for Petitioners 15; Tr. of Oral Arg. 12. A second, and closely related, view is that a work is prepared by an employee under § 101(1) when the hiring party has actually wielded control with respect to the creation of a particular work. This approach was formulated by the Court of Appeals for the Second Circuit, Aldon Accessories Ltd. v. Spiegel, Inc., 738 F.2d 548, cert. denied, 469 U.S. 982 (1984), and adopted by the Fourth Circuit, Brunswick Beacon, Inc. v. Schock–Hopchas Publishing Co., 810 F.2d 410 (1987), the Seventh Circuit, Evans Newton, Inc. v. Chicago Systems Software, 793 F.2d 889, cert. denied, 479 U.S. 949 (1986), and, at times, by petitioners, Brief for Petitioners 17. A third view is that the term "employee" within § 101(1) carries its common law agency meaning. This view was endorsed

---

3. We use the phrase "work for hire" interchangeably with the more cumbersome statutory phrase "works made for hire."

4. As of 1955, approximately 40 percent of all copyright registrations were for works for hire, according to a Copyright Office study. See Varmer, Works Made for Hire and On Commission, in Studies Prepared for the Subcommittee on Patents, Trademarks, and Copyrights of the Senate Committee on the Judiciary, Study No. 13, 86th Cong., 2d

Sess. 139, n. 49 (Comm.Print, 1960) (hereinafter Varmer, Works Made for Hire). The Copyright Office does not keep more recent statistics on the number of work for hire registrations.

6. By "hiring party," we mean to refer to the party who claims ownership of the copyright by virtue of the work for hire doctrine.

by the Fifth Circuit in Easter Seal Society for Crippled Children and Adults of Louisiana, Inc. v. Playboy Enterprises, 815 F.2d 323 (1987), and by the Court of Appeals below.   Finally, respondent and numerous *amici curiae* contend that the term "employee" only refers to "formal, salaried" employees.   See, e.g., Brief for Respondents 23–24; Brief for Register of Copyrights as *Amicus Curiae* 7.   The Court of Appeals for the Ninth Circuit recently adopted this view.   See Dumas v. Gommerman, 865 F.2d 1093 (1989).

The starting point for our interpretation of a statute is always its language.   Consumer Product Safety Comm'n v. GTE Sylvania, Inc., 447 U.S. 102, 108 (1980).   The Act nowhere defines the terms "employee" or "scope of employment."   It is, however, well established that "[w]here Congress uses terms that have accumulated settled meaning under . . . the common law, a court must infer, unless the statute otherwise dictates, that Congress means to incorporate the established meaning of these terms." NLRB v. Amax Coal Co., 453 U.S. 322, 329 (1981);   see also Perrin v. United States, 444 U.S. 37, 42 (1979).   In the past, when Congress has used the term "employee" without defining it, we have concluded that Congress intended to describe the conventional master-servant relationship as understood by common-law agency doctrine.   See, e.g., Kelley v. Southern Pacific Co., 419 U.S. 318, 322–323 (1974); Baker v. Texas & Pacific R. Co., 359 U.S. 227, 228 (1959) (*per curiam*); Robinson v. Baltimore & Ohio R. Co., 237 U.S. 84, 94 (1915).   Nothing in the text of the work for hire provisions indicates that Congress used the words "employee" and "employment" to describe anything other than " 'the conventional relation of employer and employe.' "   *Kelley,* supra, at 323, quoting *Robinson,* supra, at 94;   compare NLRB v. Hearst Publications, Inc., 322 U.S. 111, 124–132 (1944) (rejecting agency law conception of employee for purposes of the National Labor Relations Act where structure and context of statute indicated broader definition).   On the contrary, Congress' intent to incorporate the agency law definition is suggested by § 101(1)'s use of the term, "scope of employment," a widely used term of art in agency law.   See Restatement (Second) of Agency § 228 (1958) (hereinafter Restatement).

In past cases of statutory interpretation, when we have concluded that Congress intended terms such as "employee," "employer," and "scope of employment" to be understood in light of agency law, we have relied on the general common law of agency, rather than on the law of any particular State, to give meaning to these terms.   See, e.g., *Kelley,* 419 U.S., at 323–324, and n. 5; id., at 332 (Stewart, J., concurring in judgment); Ward v. Atlantic Coast Line R. Co., 362 U.S. 396, 400 (1960); *Baker,* supra, at 228. This practice reflects the fact that "federal statutes are generally intended to have uniform nationwide application."   Mississippi Choctaw Indian Band v. Holyfield, 490 U.S. 30, 43 (1989).   Establishment of a federal rule of agency, rather than reliance on state agency law, is particularly appropriate here given the Act's express objective of creating national, uniform copyright law by broadly pre-empting state statutory and common-law copyright regulation.   See 17 U.S.C. § 301(a).   We thus agree with the

Court of Appeals that the term "employee" should be understood in light of the general common law of agency.

In contrast, neither test proposed by petitioners is consistent with the text of the Act. The exclusive focus of the right to control the product test on the relationship between the hiring party and the product clashes with the language of § 101(1), which focuses on the relationship between the hired and hiring parties. The right to control the product test also would distort the meaning of the ensuing subsection, § 101(2). Section 101 plainly creates two distinct ways in which a work can be deemed for hire: one for works prepared by employees, the other for those specially ordered or commissioned works which fall within one of the nine enumerated categories and are the subject of a written agreement. The right to control the product test ignores this dichotomy by transforming into a work for hire under § 101(1) any "specially ordered or commissioned" work that is subject to the supervision and control of the hiring party. Because a party who hires a "specially ordered or commissioned" work by definition has a right to specify the characteristics of the product desired, at the time the commission is accepted, and frequently until it is completed, the right to control the product test would mean that many works that could satisfy § 101(2) would already have been deemed works for hire under § 101(1). Petitioners' interpretation is particularly hard to square with § 101(2)'s enumeration of the nine specific categories of specially ordered or commissioned works eligible to be works for hire, e.g., "a contribution to a collective work," "a part of a motion picture," and "answer material for a test." The unifying feature of these works is that they are usually prepared at the instance, direction, and risk of a publisher or producer.[7] By their very nature, therefore, these types of works would be works by an employee under petitioners' right to control the product test.

The actual control test, articulated by the Second Circuit in *Aldon Accessories,* fares only marginally better when measured against the language and structure of § 101. Under this test, independent contractors who are so controlled and supervised in the creation of a particular work are deemed "employees" under § 101(1). Thus work for hire status under § 101(1) depends on a hiring party's *actual* control, rather than *right to* control, the product. *Aldon Accessories,* 738 F.2d, at 552. Under the actual control test, a work for hire could arise under § 101(2), but not under § 101(1), where a party commissions, but does not actually control, a product which falls into one of the nine enumerated categories. Nonetheless, we agree with the Fifth Circuit Court of Appeals that "[t]here is simply no way to milk the 'actual control' test of *Aldon Accessories* from the language of the statute." *Easter Seal Society,* 815 F.2d, at 334. Section 101 clearly delineates between works prepared by an employee and

---

7. See Supplementary Report of the Register of Copyrights on the General Revision of the US Copyright Law: 1965 Revision Bill, 89th Cong., 1st Sess., Copyright Law Revision, pt. 6, pp. 66–67 (H. R. Judiciary Comm. Print 1965) (hereinafter Supplementary Report); Hardy, Copyright Law's Concept of Employment—What Congress Really Intended, 35 J. Copr. Soc. USA 210, 244–245 (1988).

commissioned works. Sound though other distinctions might be as a matter of copyright policy, there is no statutory support for an additional dichotomy between commissioned works that are actually controlled and supervised by the hiring party and those that are not.

We therefore conclude that the language and structure of § 101 of the Act do not support either the right to control the product or the actual control approaches.[8] The structure of § 101 indicates that a work for hire can arise through one of two mutually exclusive means, one for employees and one for independent contractors, and ordinary canons of statutory interpretation indicate that the classification of a particular hired party should be made with reference to agency law.

[The Court reviewed the legislative history and found an intent to preclude hiring parties from imposing "for hire" status on commissioned works that did not fall within the specifically enumerated categories.]

* * *

Finally, petitioners' construction of the work for hire provisions would impede Congress' paramount goal in revising the 1976 Act of enhancing predictability and certainty of copyright ownership. See H.R.Rep. No. 94–1476, supra, at 129. In a "copyright marketplace," the parties negotiate with an expectation that one of them will own the copyright in the completed work. *Dumas,* 865 F.2d, at 1104–1105, n. 18. With that expectation, the parties at the outset can settle on relevant contractual terms, such as the price for the work and the ownership of reproduction rights.

To the extent that petitioners endorse an actual control test, CCNV's construction of the work for hire provisions prevents such planning. Because that test turns on whether the hiring party has closely monitored the production process, the parties would not know until late in the process, if not until the work is completed, whether a work will ultimately fall within § 101(1). Under petitioners' approach, therefore, parties would have to predict in advance whether the hiring party will sufficiently control a given work to make it the author. "If they guess incorrectly, their reliance on 'work for hire' or on assignment may give them a copyright interest that they did not bargain for." *Easter Seal Society,* 815 F.2d, at

---

8. We also reject the suggestion of respondent and *amici* that the § 101(1) term "employee" refers only to formal, salaried employees. While there is some support for such a definition in the legislative history, see Varmer, Works Made for Hire 130; n. 11, infra, the language of § 101(1) cannot support it. The Act does not say "formal" or "salaried" employee, but simply "employee." Moreover, the respondent and those *amici* who endorse a formal, salaried employee test do not agree upon the content of this test. Compare, e.g., Brief for Respondent 37 (hired party who is on payroll is an employee within § 101(1)) with Tr. of Oral Arg. 31 (hired party who receives a salary or commissions regularly is an employee within § 101(1)); and Brief for Volunteer Lawyers for the Arts Inc. et al. as *Amici Curiae* 4 (hired party who receives a salary *and* is treated as an employee for Social Security and tax purposes is an employee within § 101(1)). Even the one Court of Appeals to adopt what it termed a formal, salaried employee test in fact embraced an approach incorporating numerous factors drawn from the agency law definition of employee which we endorse. See *Dumas,* 865 F.2d, at 1104.

333; accord *Dumas,* 865 F.2d, at 1103. This understanding of the work for hire provisions clearly thwarts Congress' goal of ensuring predictability through advance planning. Moreover, petitioners' interpretation "leaves the door open for hiring parties, who have failed to get a full assignment of copyright rights from independent contractors falling outside the subdivision (2) guidelines, to unilaterally obtain work-made-for-hire rights years after the work has been completed as long as they directed or supervised the work, a standard that is hard not to meet when one is a hiring party." Hamilton, Commissioned Works as Works Made for Hire Under the 1976 Copyright Act: Misinterpretation and Injustice, 135 U.Pa.L.Rev. 1281, 1304 (1987).

In sum, we must reject petitioners' argument. Transforming a commissioned work into a work by an employee on the basis of the hiring party's right to control, or actual control of, the work is inconsistent with the language, structure, and legislative history of the work for hire provisions. To determine whether a work is for hire under the Act, a court first should ascertain, using principles of general common law of agency, whether the work was prepared by an employee or an independent contractor. After making this determination, the court can apply the appropriate subsection of § 101.

B

We turn, finally, to an application of § 101 to Reid's production of "Third World America." In determining whether a hired party is an employee under the general common law of agency, we consider the hiring party's right to control the manner and means by which the product is accomplished. Among the other factors relevant to this inquiry are the skill required; the source of the instrumentalities and tools; location of the work; the duration of the relationship between the parties; whether the hiring party has the right to assign additional projects to the hired party; the extent of the hired party's discretion over when and how long to work; the method of payment; the hired party's role in hiring and paying assistants; whether the work is part of the regular business of the hiring party; whether the hiring party is in business; the provision of employee benefits; and the tax treatment of the hired party. See Restatement § 220(2) (setting forth a nonexhaustive list of factors relevant to determining whether a hired party is an employee). No one of these factors is determinative. See *Ward,* 362 U.S., at 400; Hilton Int'l Co. v. NLRB, 690 F.2d 318, 321 (CA2 (1982).

Examining the circumstances of this case in light of these factors, we agree with the Court of Appeals that Reid was not an employee of CCNV but an independent contractor. 846 F.2d, at 1494, n. 11. True, CCNV members directed enough of Reid's work to ensure that he produced a sculpture that met their specifications. 652 F.Supp., at 1456. But the extent of control the hiring party exercises over the details of the product is not dispositive. Indeed, all the other circumstances weigh heavily against finding an employment relationship. Reid is a sculptor, a skilled occupation. Reid supplied his own tools. He worked in his own studio in Baltimore, making daily supervision of his activities from Washington practicably impossible. Reid was retained for less than two months, a relatively short period of time. During and after this time, CCNV had no right to assign additional projects to Reid. Apart from the deadline for completing the sculpture, Reid had absolute freedom to decide when and how long to work. CCNV paid Reid $15,000, a sum dependent on "completion of a specific job, a method by which independent contractors are often compensated." Holt v. Winpisinger, 811 F.2d 1532, 1540 (1987). Reid had total discretion in hiring and paying assistants. "Creating sculptures was hardly 'regular business' for CCNV." 846 F.2d, at 1494, n. 11. Indeed, CCNV is not a business at all. Finally, CCNV did not pay payroll or social security taxes, provide any employee benefits, or contribute to unemployment insurance or workers' compensation funds.

Because Reid was an independent contractor, whether "Third World America" is a work for hire depends on whether it satisfies the terms of § 101(2). This petitioners concede it cannot do. Thus, CCNV is not the author of "Third World America" by virtue of the work for hire provisions of the Act. However, as the Court of Appeals made clear, CCNV nevertheless may be a joint author of the sculpture if, on remand, the District Court so determines that CCNV and Reid prepared the work "with the intention that their contributions be merged into inseparable or interdependent parts of a unitary whole." 17 U.S.C. § 101.[32] In that case, CCNV and Reid would be co-owners of the copyright in the work. See § 201(a).

For the aforestated reasons, we affirm the judgment of the Court of Appeals for the District of Columbia.

It is so ordered.

NOTES AND QUESTIONS

(1) The Second Circuit in Aymes v. Bonelli, 980 F.2d 857 (2d Cir.1992), concluding that software written for the plaintiff's business was not a work for hire, held that the weight accorded to the individual *CCNV* factors should vary with their significance in the particular case. For a comprehensive primer on the common law tests of "employee" and "scope of employment," see Kreiss, Scope of Employment and Being an Employee Under the Work–Made–For–Hire Provision of the Copyright Law: Applying the Common–Law Agency Tests, 40 Kan.L.Rev. 119 (1991).[c]

32. Neither CCNV nor Reid sought review of the Court of Appeals' remand order. We therefore have no occasion to pass judgment on applicability of the Act's joint authorship provisions to this case.

c. For another application of the *CCNV* test for "employee," see Saenger Organization, Inc. v. Nationwide Ins. Licensing Assoc., Inc., 119 F.3d 55 (1st Cir.1997). Schaumann,

Small Business and Copyright Ownership, 22 Wm. Mitchell L.Rev. 1469 (1996), emphasizes that even for an employee, a work is for hire only when created within the scope of the employment. See Avtec Systems, Inc. v. Peiffer, 21 F.3d 568 (4th Cir.1994), remanding for reconsideration of whether an employee's work on a computer program was within the scope of employment. In another computer

Should the 1976 Act as interpreted in *CCNV* be applied to settle ownership issues relating to works created when the 1909 Act was in effect? Roth v. Pritikin, 710 F.2d 934 (2d Cir.), cert. denied, 464 U.S. 961 (1983), held that for pre–1978 works, the old rules on work for hire still apply.

(2) Professor Hardy, in Copyright Law's Concept of Employment—What Congress Really Intended, 35 J.Copyr.Soc. 210 (1988), had argued for the position adopted in *Dumas,* limiting "employee" to formal, salaried employees. In An Economic Understanding of Copyright Law's Work-Made-for-Hire Doctrine, 12 Colum.–VLA J.L. & Arts 181 (1988), Hardy argues that what the courts have been trying to do (and as a policy matter should do?) is to allocate copyright in a commissioned work toward that participant in the deal who can most effectively exploit the work. How would one identify the efficient exploiter? Will the determination of copyright ownership indeed influence the efficiency of exploitation? Recall that copyrights are transferable. In an efficient market, the rights under copyright will move to the best exploiter regardless of initial ownership. Are there reasons why the market in copyrights might not operate efficiently?

(3) There is said to be acute dissatisfaction among freelancers who create commissioned works that can be considered "work made for hire" under part (2) of the definition in § 101 and who deal with buyers who know how to draft contracts that satisfy the statute.[d] There have been proposals to remove major categories of commissioned works from the § 101 definition, including contributions to collective works, parts of motion pictures, and instructional texts. See Colby, Copyright Revision Revisited: Commissioned Works as Works Made for Hire Under the U.S. Copyright Act, 5 Whittier L.Rev. 491 (1983) (producer's lawyer opposes changes); cf. Comment, Free Lance Artists, Works for Hire, and the Copyright Act of 1976, 15 U.C.Davis L.Rev. 703 (1982) (favoring deletion of "contributions to collective works" and "supplementary works"). What arguments can be made either for retaining or dropping any of the principal categories? An argument for eliminating all of them is made in Landau, "Works Made For Hire" After *Community for Creative Non–Violence v. Reid:* The Need for Statutory Reform and the Importance of Contract, 9 Cardozo Arts & Ent.L.J. 107 (1990).

For a wealth of information about work-for-hire practices in various industries, see Work Made for Hire—Practical Perspectives: A Roundtable Discussion (Karp. ed.), 14 Colum.–VLA J.L. & Arts 507 (1990).

software case, the development of litigation management software by a city attorney after hours with his own resources was found to fall outside the scope of his employment. Quinn v. City of Detroit, 988 F.Supp. 1044 (E.D.Mich.1997).

d. In Playboy Enter., Inc. v. Dumas, 53 F.3d 549 (2d Cir.), cert. denied, 516 U.S. 1010 (1995), Judge Oakes said that although the agreement necessary to turn listed commissioned works into works for hire must come before the work is created, the writing memorializing that agreement can come later.

(4) If a work is clearly produced "within the scope of * * * employment," a creator who wishes to retain the copyright must get an express written agreement. § 201(b). What does this do to the academic practice that lets professors copyright their scholarly work? For one view, see DuBoff, An Academic's Copyright: Publish and Perish, 32 J.Copyr.Soc. 17 (1984) (concluding that the traditional practice is inconsistent with the 1976 Act); see also Burr, A Critical Assessment of *Reid's* Work for Hire Framework and Its Potential Impact on the Marketplace for Scholarly Works, 24 J. Marshall L.Rev. 119 (1990) (illustrating the difficulty of applying the *Reid* criteria in an academic environment). Dreyfuss, The Creative Employee and the Copyright Act of 1976, 54 U.Chi.L.Rev. 590 (1987), musters a battery of arguments to preserve copyrights in professors and other "creative" employees. University copyright policies generally do so. See also Weinstein v. University of Illinois, 811 F.2d 1091, 1094 (7th Cir.1987) ("This has been the academic tradition since copyright law began") (dictum by Easterbrook, J., formerly of the University of Chicago law faculty). In Hays v. Sony Corp., 847 F.2d 412 (7th Cir.1988), Judge Posner, of identical background, discussed at some length the case for a "teacher exception" to work for hire and opined that, despite the seemingly literal grip of § 201(b), "we might, if forced to decide the issue, conclude that the exception had survived the enactment of the 1976 Act." See VerSteeg, Copyright and the Educational Process: The Right of Teacher Inception, 75 Iowa L.Rev. 381 (1990), finding the "teacher exception" desirable, but recommending reliance on contractual arrangements.

University copyright policies relating to the ownership of academic writings are reviewed in Lape, Ownership of Copyrightable Works of University Professors: The Interplay Between the Copyright Act and University Copyright Policies, 37 Vill.L.Rev. 223 (1992).

(5) You have your picture taken. For an agreed fee, the photographer delivers an agreed number of prints. There is no written contract. Who owns the copyright? Can you make copies of the prints? Can you prevent the photographer from selling a copy to your local newspaper? Who owns the negatives? See Marco v. Accent Pub. Co., 969 F.2d 1547 (3d Cir.1992), holding that photographs of jewelry were not works for hire despite some exercise of control by the commissioning party. There are remarkably few cases on rights in commissioned photographs.

(6) At this late date, is it still arguable that there are constitutional limits on declaring employers to be "authors"? See Judge Friendly's dissent in Scherr v. Universal Match Corp., 417 F.2d 497, 502 (2d Cir.1969), cert. denied, 397 U.S. 936 (1970).[e]

---

e. The patent statute, in contrast, requires the individual inventor to apply for the patent, 35 U.S.C.A. § 111, with special provisions for inventors who are dead or otherwise unavailable, 35 U.S.C.A. §§ 117, 118. Most inventors nowadays are employees who assign their patents to their employers. But unless the employee was hired to invent, the fact that he made the discovery using the employer's time and facilities does not give the employer ownership, only a non-exclusive license to practice the invention, known as a "shop right." U.S. v. Dubilier Condenser Corp., 289 U.S. 178 (1933). Consult Sted-

(7) No matter how the law defines works for hire, is there any way that buyers with sufficient economic power can be prevented from exacting "all rights" assignments or similar concessions from writers and artists?   In what ways will a copyright owner's rights differ if instead of taking under the work for hire rules, it relies on an assignment of copyright from the commissioned party?   See, e.g., §§ 203, 302(c), 304(c).   When are the differences likely to be important?

JOINT AUTHORSHIP

A possible way for a party to claim rights in a work is to characterize the work as "joint."   What does that mean?

"The authors of a joint work are coowners of copyright in the work." § 201(a).   The House Report summarizes the consequences of coownership: "Under the bill, as under the present law, coowners of a copyright would be treated generally as tenants in common, with each coowner having an independent right to use or license the use of a work, subject to a duty of accounting to the other coowners for any profits."   H.R. Rep. p. 121.

What is a "joint work"?   It is defined in § 101 as "a work prepared by two or more authors with the intention that their contributions be merged into inseparable or interdependent parts of a unitary whole."   This is amplified in the House Report: "The touchstone here is the intention, at the time the writing is done, that the parts be absorbed or combined into an integrated unit, although the parts themselves may be either 'inseparable' (as in the case of a novel or painting) or 'interdependent' (as in the case of a motion picture, opera, or the words and music of a song.)" H.Rep. p. 120.   Compare the definitions of "collective work" and "derivative work," also in § 101; how do they differ from a "joint work"?   See also § 302(b) on the duration of copyright in joint works.

The definition of joint work is tailored to correct the odd consequences of a series of cases mostly concerning the interests of composers and lyricists of popular music.   The Second Circuit consistently found a "joint" relationship between words and music created at different times without overt collaboration.   The high-water mark was the *Twelfth Street Rag* case, Shapiro, Bernstein & Co. v. Jerry Vogel Music Co., 115 F.Supp. 754 (S.D.N.Y.1953), rev'd, 221 F.2d 569 (2d Cir.), modified, 223 F.2d 252 (2d Cir.1955).   There the music was written and published without words. The composer assigned all rights to a publisher, who caused words to be written and published with the music without the composer's knowledge. The Court of Appeals held that the relevant intent was that of the assignee "to merge the two contributions into a single work."   This outcome was much criticised.   Cary, Joint Ownership of Copyright, Copyr. Law Revision Study No. 12 (1958), in 1 Studies on Copyr. 689 (1963), complains that

man, Rights and Responsibilities of the Employed Inventor, 45 Ind.L.J. 254 (1970), and The Employed Inventor, The Public Interest, and Horse and Buggy Law in the Space Age, 45 N.Y.U.L.Rev. 1 (1970).   See Restatement, Third, Unfair Competition § 42, Comment *e* (1995).

recognizing an undivided interest in a "joint" work in favor of one who has added new material long after the original work was created can have the effect of extending the term of protection for the initial work.   See also Ringer, Renewal of Copyright, Copyr. Law Revision Study No. 31 (1960), 1 Studies on Copyr. 503, 569–71 (1963) (a concise review of the cases), adding that disconnected joint works create confused interests on renewal. As interpreted in the House Report, the 1976 Act requires an intention by the authors at the time of creation to merge their contributions into a unitary whole.

Recognition of joint ownership has appeared as a solution in disputed work for hire cases.   We return to the homeless Holy Family case, this time to the decision below in the Court of Appeals.

Community for Creative Non–Violence v. Reid

United States Court of Appeals, District of Columbia Circuit, 1988.
846 F.2d 1485.
Aff'd, 490 U.S. 730, 109 S.Ct. 2166.

■ Before Mikva, Ruth Bader Ginsburg, and Silverman, Circuit Judges.

■ Ruth Bader Ginsburg, Circuit Judge:

* * *

III.

CCNV sought a declaration of copyright ownership. We have held that CCNV is not author of a work made for hire and see no other basis for a claim that CCNV is sole owner of copyright in "Third World America." But neither does the existing record bear out Reid's assertion that he is the exclusive owner of copyright in the work. The facts thus far found by the district court, however, indicate that "Third World America" may indeed qualify as a joint work. [The court set forth the relevant statutory provisions.]

Most prominently undercutting Reid's claim of sole ownership, the district court found that CCNV "was the motivating factor in the procreation of 'Third World America,'" "conceived the idea in starkly specific detail," and "directed enough of [Reid's] effort to assure that, in the end, he had produced what [CCNV] not he, wanted...."   652 F.Supp. at 1456. In making this point, we do not overlook the "idea/expression dichotomy"; as stated in the 1976 Act, "[i]n no case does copyright protection for an original work of authorship extend to any idea ... regardless of the form in which it is ... embodied in such work."   17 U.S.C. § 102(b). * * * "Third World America," however, was more than CCNV's abstract idea. Following CCNV's original conception of the sculpture, Snyder and other CCNV members, the district court found, monitored the progress of the work, not simply to approve Reid's embodiment of their idea, but to guide his expression and coordinate with his effort CCNV's construction of the steam grate pedestal.   See 652 F.Supp. at 1455–56.[17]

In sum, were it not for the prevailing confusion over the work for hire doctrine, this case—once more taking the record in its current state—might qualify as a textbook example of a jointly-authored work in which the joint authors co-own the copyright. We note in this regard Reid's original and creative contribution to the figures; CCNV's contribution to the steam grate pedestal added to its initial conceptualization and ongoing direction of the realization of "Third World America"; and the various indicia of the parties' intent, from the outset, to merge their contributions into a unitary whole, and not to construct and separately preserve discrete parts as independent works.   * * *

[The court took note of suggestions that other participants in the undertaking might also be joint authors, and not simply employees or agents of CCNV or Reid.] We therefore refer the matter to the district court with instructions to determine if there are any other parties who might qualify as "Third World America" authors and, on that account, should be joined in this action.   * * *

We address, finally, a peculiar feature of this case * * * on which the parties' presentations are cloudy. There is only one "copy" of the copyrighted work at issue, and that only existing copy is exclusively owned by CCNV. Joint authors co-owning copyright in a work "are deemed to be tenants in common," with "each having an independent right to use or license the copyright, subject only to a duty to account to the other co-owner for any profits earned thereby." W. Patry, [Latman's The Copyright Law (6th ed.1986)] at 116 (footnotes omitted). In the absence of an agreement specifying otherwise, any profits earned are to be divided equally, "even where it is clear that [the] respective contributions to the joint work are not equal." 1 M. Nimmer & D. Nimmer, supra note 8, § 6.08, at 6–20 (footnote omitted). But singular works of art, we recognize, do not fit comfortably into a scheme centrally concerned with reproduction of the underlying work. See Brenner, A Two–Phase Approach to Copyrighting the Fine Arts, 24 Bull. Copyright Soc'y 85, 85 (1976–77).

Reid, as we mentioned earlier, objected to CCNV's travel plans for "Third World America," and planned a more modest exhibition tour of his own. See 652 F.Supp. at 1456. Co-ownership (or even sole ownership) of the copyright does not appear to carry with it a right to stop or limit CCNV's tour or to gain possession of the unique work of art.   * * *

If CCNV reproduces "Third World America" in any medium and profits thereby, however, an accounting would be due to Reid as a copyright owner. Independent of Reid's ownership of the copyright, CCNV might be obliged to credit Reid as an author of the sculpture.   * * * Furthermore,

---

17. Case law concerning joint authorship in relation to the idea/expression dichotomy is sparse largely because the broad scope of the work for hire doctrine under the 1909 Act tended to draw disputes in which one party claimed to be the creative motivating force in the production of a copyrightable work into the ambit of that doctrine. With the substantial cutback of the work for hire doctrine under the 1976 Act, more cases of this genre can be expected to appear under the joint authorship rubric.

Reid, as an author, may have rights against CCNV should it publish an excessively mutilated or altered version of "Third World America." See Gilliam v. American Broadcasting Co., 538 F.2d 14 (2d Cir.1976) [p. 725 infra]; Kwall, Copyright and the Moral Right: Is an American Marriage Possible?, 38 Vand. L. Rev. 1, 17–34 (1985) (discussing various common law and statutory doctrines available to protect a creator against publication of excessively mutilated versions of his work but not against destruction); * * *

* * * [We] remand the case for further proceedings consistent with this opinion, particularly, for comprehensive consideration whether the sculpture called "Third World America" is a joint work and, if it is, for determination of the owners of copyright in the work.

[The Supreme Court likewise remanded on the "joint work" issue.]

NOTES

(1) The Court of Appeals decided, with no apparent difficulty, that the sole copy of the statue belongs to CCNV. Can you imagine a case where a unique copy would also be jointly owned?

The issue of joint authorship was subsequently settled by the parties. Reid was recognized as the sole author of the work, with control over 3–dimensional reproductions. The original copy will belong to CCNV, and the parties agreed to co-ownership of rights to 2–dimensional reproductions. Community for Creative Non–Violence v. Reid, Copyright L.Rep. (CCH) ¶ 26,753 (D.D.C.1991). Reid's access to the sculpture in exercise of his 3–dimensional reproduction rights, however, required further judicial intervention. See *id.* ¶ 26,860 (D.D.C.1991), recognizing an "implied easement of necessity" in favor of Reid.

(2) In Ashton–Tate Corp. v. Ross, 916 F.2d 516 (9th Cir.1990), the Ninth Circuit concluded that joint authorship requires each author to make a copyrightable contribution to the joint work. Cases in other circuits have reached similar results. See, e.g., Forward v. Thorogood, p. 14 supra (logistical support is insufficient for joint authorship); Erickson v. Trinity Theatre, Inc., 13 F.3d 1061 (7th Cir.1994) (noting that other contributors can protect their interests by contract). Cf. Andrien v. Southern Ocean County Chamber of Commerce, 927 F.2d 132 (3d Cir.1991) (one who acts as a mere amanuensis in fixing another's expression is not a joint author). VerSteeg, Defining "Author" for Purposes of Copyright, 45 Am.U.L.Rev. 1323 (1996), supports the case law requiring a contribution of copyrightable expression for joint authorship.

The Second Circuit in Childress v. Taylor, 945 F.2d 500 (1991), agreed that a joint author must make a copyrightable contribution and must intend, according to the statutory definition, that the contributions be merged into a unitary whole; but the court held this was not sufficient. "[A]n inquiry so limited would extend joint author status to many persons who are not likely to have been within the contemplation of Congress. For example, a writer frequently works with an editor who makes revisions to the first draft, some of which will consist of additions of copyrightable expression. Both intend their contributions to be merged into inseparable parts of a unitary whole, yet very few editors and even fewer writers would expect the editor to be accorded the status of a joint author, enjoying an undivided half interest in the copyright in the published work. * * * What distinguishes the writer-editor relationship * * * from the true joint author relationship is the lack of intent of both parties in the venture to regard themselves as joint authors. * * * Joint authorship entitles the co-authors to equal undivided interests in the work, see 17 U.S.C. § 201(a); Community for Creative Non–Violence v. Reid, 846 F.2d 1485, 1498 (D.C.Cir.1988), aff'd without consideration of this point, 490 U.S. 730 (1989). That equal sharing of rights should be reserved for relationships in which all participants fully intend to be joint authors." The court held that a defendant who contributed research, incidental suggestions, and minor bits of expression was not a joint author. Is this an appropriate gloss on the statutory definition?[f] For criticism of this and other judicial restrictions on joint work status, see Lape, A Narrow View of Creative Cooperation: The Current State of Joint Work Doctrine, 61 Alb.L.Rev. 43 (1997).

(3) Joint ownership of the copyright, although a seemingly Solomonic solution in difficult situations, creates its own problems of discordant use by co-owners who may be at odds, mitigated only somewhat by the obligation of each to account to the other. See Note, Accountability Among Co–Owners of Statutory Copyright, 72 Harv.L.Rev. 1550 (1959). Spyke, The Joint Work Dilemma: The Separately Copyrightable Contribution Requirement and Co–Ownership Principles, 40 J.Copyr.Soc. 463 (1993), argues in favor of a new understanding of co-ownership allowing for greater control by the individual authors when the work consists of interdependent rather than inseparable contributions. Chon, New Wine Bursting From Old Bottles: Collaborative Internet Art, Joint Works, and Entrepreneurship, 75 Ore.L.Rev. 257 (1996), uses the joint work doctrine to illustrate the misalignment of traditional principles with the fluidity of the networked computer environment.

(4) Authors of joint works, unlike creators of works for hire, do have the power to terminate grants. This has its problems too. Consider this situation:

In 1980 *A* and *B* collaborated on a novel; the work was registered as a joint work. *A* and *B* immediately granted exclusive movie rights to Paramount. In 2015, *A* is dead, survived by her

---

f. The *Childress* formulation proved decisive when a "dramaturg"—a "combination script doctor, editor, researcher, advice-giver and hand-holder"—sought joint authorship rights to the play "Rent", a smash hit taking in $500,000 per week on Broadway. Although her writing and suggestions (for which she had been paid about $12,000) were credited by many with radically transforming the original version into a polished hit, Judge Kaplan in Thompson v. Larson, No. 96–8876 (S.D.N.Y.1997), ruled that there was no evidence of an intent by Jonathan Larson, the play's author, to share ownership or authorship with the plaintiff. Evans, Court Evicts Lawsuit Over "Rent" Control, Variety, Aug. 3, 1997, p. 61.

husband and one child. *B* is living, and wishes to terminate the transfer to Paramount. Who must join *B* in exercising the termination right? See § 203(a).

On the problems of joint ownership and termination rights, see See, Copyright Ownership of Joint Works and Termination of Transfers, 30 Kan.L.Rev. 517 (1982).

SECTION 6.   INDUSTRIES AFFECTED BY COMPULSORY COPYRIGHT LICENSING

We now turn to situations where Congress has decided, for reasons that vary with each setting, that copyrights must be made available on terms that are outlined in the statute and administratively regulated. These are cable and satellite transmissions of television programs, §§ 111 and 119; the production of phonorecords, § 115; "coin-operated phonorecord players"—jukeboxes, former § 116, now superseded by the current § 116; and noncommercial broadcasting, § 118. The phonorecord recording license has its origin in § 1(e) of the 1909 Act; the jukebox license replaced an exemption conferred in the last paragraph of § 1(e). The others are creations of the 1976 Act.

THE COPYRIGHT ROYALTY TRIBUNAL

Another creation of the 1976 Act was an administrative body, the Copyright Royalty Tribunal, established in Chapter 8 of the Act. The Tribunal was charged with "periodically reviewing and adjusting statutory royalty rates for use of copyrighted materials pursuant to compulsory licenses provided in sections 111 (secondary transmissions by cable systems), 115 (mechanical royalties)[a] and 116 (jukebox) of the bill. In addition, the Commission will make determinations as to reasonable terms and rates of royalty payments as provided in section 118 (public broadcasting), and to resolve disputes over the distribution of royalties paid pursuant to the statutory licenses in sections 111 and 116." H.R.Rep. p. 173.

The Tribunal had a turbulent career. Only one of the five original commissioners had prior experience in copyright or communications law, and that trend continued. One chair, in 1981, proposed its abolition and resigned. Another chair resigned in 1985 amid charges of racism in writings unrelated to her position. In 1990 the number of commissioners was reduced from five to three. In 1993, the chair charged her two colleagues, both of whom favored dissolution of the Tribunal, with professional misconduct.

---

a. This label persists, although it profoundly misdescribes modern music recording techniques, as a remnant of old § 1(e), which spoke of "copyright controlling the parts of instruments serving to reproduce mechanically the musical work." The language in § 1(e) was adapted from the 1908 revision of Article 13 of the Berne Convention. See Peer, The Mechanical Right: A Pragmatic Perspective, 31 J.Copyr.Soc. 409, 411 (1984).

The Copyright Royalty Tribunal was abolished in December, 1993, by Pub.L. No. 103–198. The rate-setting and royalty distributing duties of the Tribunal were transferred to ad hoc arbitration panels convened by the Librarian of Congress. An appeal can be taken to the Librarian,[b] with judicial review by the D.C. Circuit Court of Appeals.

The rate-setting and royalty-allocating powers of the Tribunal and its successors, though circumscribed, diminish the autonomy of both authors and users. The then Register saw the growth of compulsory licensing as the most portentous aspect of the 1976 Act, and did not like what she saw. See Ringer, Copyright in the 1980s, 23 Bull.Copyr.Soc. 299 (1976). The experienced Chief Counsel of the Senate Subcommittee on Patents, Trademarks and Copyrights, Thomas C. Brennan, describing himself as "no fan of compulsory licensing," also had some tart observations. He noted that among other inconsistent postures, "Members of Congress who usually proclaim the virtues of the marketplace were promoting government intervention, while well-known civil libertarians were insisting that an author must not be allowed to prevent the public performance of his work." Some Observations on the Revision of the Copyright Law From the Legislative Point of View, 24 Bull.Copyr.Soc. 151, 152 (1976). He became the Tribunal's first chair. Consult his compact and occasionally biting appraisal, The Copyright Royalty Tribunal—An American Perspective, 34 J.Copyr.Soc. 148 (1987) (followed by articles on similar bodies abroad). A former general counsel of the Tribunal focuses on the positive aspects of its 16–year history in Cassler, Copyright Royalty Tribunal: Balancing the Record, 41 J.Copyr.Soc. 217 (1994).

PUBLIC BROADCASTING AND § 118

Both ASCAP and BMI at one time gave free licenses to educational broadcasting stations, with certain restrictions on popular songs. Public broadcasters, realizing that the tendency of the revision bill was toward expanded rights and that they might someday have to start paying, tried to get an amendment attached to the Senate bill in 1975. Section 118 in its narrow but intricate form was the outcome. See Korman, Performance Rights in Music under Sections 110 and 118 of the 1976 Copyright Act, 22 N.Y.L.S. L.Rev. 521 (1977).

Section 118 covers only published nondramatic musical works and published pictorial, graphic, and sculptural works. It explicitly encourages voluntary agreement. On the initial rate setting for musical works, see Korman and Koenigsberg, The First Proceeding Before the Copyright Royal Tribunal: ASCAP and the Public Broadcasters, 1 Comm. & L. (No. 1) 15 (1979) (the authors were ASCAP counsel).

---

b. The Copyright Office has concluded that review of arbitration royalty panel decisions by the Librarian of Congress is governed by the Administrative Procedure Act's arbitrary and capricious standard (5 U.S.C.A. § 706(2)(A)). 62 Fed.Reg. 6558 (Feb. 12, 1997).

The rates for musical works are generally negotiated. Rates for works not covered by a voluntary agreement are set by a copyright arbitration royalty panel.

THE RECORD INDUSTRY AND § 115

When recording rights were added to copyright in the 1909 Act to overcome the effect of the *White–Smith* case, p. 26 supra, fears were expressed that the granting of exclusive recording licenses by copyright owners would consolidate the monopoly of a "music trust," particularly in player-piano rolls; hence the compulsory license of § 1(e).[c] Although concern over the piano roll monopoly had subsided considerably by 1976, similar fears with respect to the record industry prompted continuation of the compulsory license in § 115. Its distinctive characteristic is that the license becomes available only after "phonorecords of a nondramatic musical work have been distributed to the public in the United States under the authority of the copyright owner." § 115(a)(1). The compulsory license is available only if the licensee's "primary purpose in making phonorecords is to distribute them to the public for private use"; it cannot be invoked to use music in movies or television programs—so-called synchronous use.

Does the structure of the modern recording industry support the earlier rationale of the compulsory license? There are still only a few dominant producers, but entrance to (and exit from) the industry are easy, and by some counts there are hundreds of smaller independent companies.[d]

What effect does the availability of a compulsory license for musical works have on the competitiveness of the record industry? Primarily, it makes possible the practice of "cover records." If a song becomes a hit, other performers can and will record it, and there is no way to preserve and exploit the monopoly of the first recording. In the pre-rock era, when to a considerable extent songs rather than performers were the key to success in popular music, cover records were ubiquitous. Then, with the dominance of performers, whether individuals or groups, multiple recordings were said to have declined, but they are still important.[e]

---

c. See Henn, The Compulsory License Provisions of the U.S. Copyright Law, Copyr.Law Revision Study No. 5 (1956), in 2 Studies on Copyr. 877 (1963); Blaisdell, The Economic Aspects of the Compulsory License, Copyr.Law Revision Study No. 6 (1958), id. p. 937.

d. For extensive information on practices in the recording industry, consult S. Shemel and M. Krasilovsky, This Business of Music (1995).

e. The New York Times, Sept. 7, 1973, p. 45, for example, reported that nearly 40 artists had recorded their own versions of Gilbert O'Sullivan's hit single, "Alone Again

(Naturally)." Aside from other melancholy balladeers, there was a jazz version by Hank Crawford, a country-music rendition by Brush Arbor, and a religious treatment by Anita Bryant.

What, exactly, does the compulsory license permit? When a defendant invoked the license in connection with a recording on a karaoke CD–ROM that included a video track that scrolled the lyrics across the screen, the court held that the use was beyond the scope of § 115. "[W]hile a compulsory license permits the recording of a 'cover' version of a song, it does not permit the inclusion of a copy of the lyrics. That requires the separate permission of the copyright holder." ABKCO

Of the thousands of records produced each year, most depend on Top 40 radio outlets for any hope of success, which only a few per cent will attain. Most new records never achieve any air play at all. In the desperate struggle of artists, their agents, and producers for money and recognition, copyrights and the compulsory license play a part.

"Every record company owns at least one publishing firm. * * * If a firm owned by the record company publishes a song composed and/or performed by one of the company's artists, the royalties paid to its publisher then go to one of its [own] subsidiaries. When an artist assigns the copyright to a song he has written to the publishing arm of the company for which he records, the company pays far less in (real) royalties and accrues greater profits in the event that the record becomes a 'hit.' One internal factor weighed by policymakers in deciding which records to release and promote is: who owns the copyright? * * *

"Unknown artists are generally contracted to record on a royalty basis of two to three percent of their records' sales. Established artists' contracts provide for higher royalties and a guaranteed minimum payment. Publishers' royalties from the record sales of a hit song generally exceed those from the sales of any one artist's rendition. A best-selling record on the Top 40 charts will appear in numerous other versions recorded by other performers, e.g., instrumental versions of vocal hits for the same market, 'softened' versions (for laundromats, restaurants, non-Top 40 radio music programming, jazz versions).

"When a record company owns the publishing firm which is assigned the copyright to a song, it receives royalties, as publisher, from all sales of other companies' recorded 'cover' versions of the hit song." R. Hirsch, The Structure of the Popular Music Industry 37–39 (1969).

And what does the songwriter get? If she is not a performer as well, customarily her contract with the publisher will divide evenly the mechanical right payments as well as other payments from third parties. If the music and lyrics have separate authors, another split occurs (these proportions can be altered by bargaining to favor a powerful writer). The initial recording contract is not legally constrained by the compulsory license rate, but the "cover" records of course need pay no more than the statutory royalty. Lesser amounts may be accepted, and for a long time the old two-cent per record statutory royalty was only a ceiling. Contracts were made at lower rates, like 1¾ cents. Then, with inflation, the old rate came to be viewed as inadequate, so the general revision in 1976 brought an increase in the compulsory license rate to 2¾ cents. § 115(c)(2). But inflation continued, and as soon as the law allowed, copyright owners resorted to the Copyright Royalty Tribunal, which after extensive hearings set a rate of 4 cents, or ¾ cents per minute. Both sides appealed.

In Recording Industry Ass'n of America v. Copyright Royalty Tribunal, 662 F.2d 1 (D.C.Cir.1981), the court found that the Tribunal had adequately justified the 4–cent rate.[f] The composers and publishers had argued

---

Music, Inc. v. Stellar Records, Inc., 96 F.3d 60 (2d Cir.1996).

f. Among the Tribunal's findings: "[F]rom 1955 to 1979 composers' royalties that the rate should be set high enough to leave "bargaining room," as had been the case in the pre-inflation past. The Tribunal and the court found no support for this position in the statutory objectives of § 801(b)(1).

The Tribunal had also proposed annual proceedings "to calculate appropriate interim adjustment figures." The court remanded this arrangement, finding it unauthorized in view of the precise and widely-separated adjustment intervals prescribed in the statute. But the court helpfully observed that "we see nothing in the statute precluding the Tribunal from adopting a reasonable mechanism for automatic rate changes in interim years." The Tribunal did just that. Succeeding increases have brought the rate to 7.1 cents per record effective January 1, 1998. By 2006, it will be 9.1 cents. See 37 C.F.R. § 255.

NOTES AND QUESTIONS

(1) The interim adjustments originally proposed by the Tribunal were to be related to increases in the average suggested retail prices of records (or representative wholesale prices if suggested retail prices were lacking). Can you think of any reason, aside from habit, why the basic statutory rate is a flat amount, rather than a percentage of revenues, as is the case in many other countries? See Peer, The Mechanical Right: A Pragmatic Perspective, 31 J.Copyr.Soc. 409, 418 (1984).

(2) For the composer-performer, the mechanical royalty is simply part of a package that also includes performers' royalties; the latter are limited only by bargaining strength, and for superstars can reach superfigures like 15% or more of retail prices. But on "cover" records made by other performers, the composer gets only mechanical royalties. The desire to share in those royalties is one incentive for record companies to have publishing affiliates.

(3) Could 2 Live Crew have invoked the compulsory license in § 115 to insulate its parody recording of *Oh, Pretty Woman*? See footnote 4 of the *Campbell* opinion, p. 401 supra.

(4) Section 115 was amended in 1995 as part of the legislation that created a digital performance right for sound recordings (see p. 330 supra). New subsection 115(c)(3) expanded the compulsory license to cover the distribution of sound recordings by digital transmission; the royalty rate for these distributions is set by voluntary negotiation or, on default, by a copyright arbitration royalty panel. Section 115(c)(3) endeavors to distinguish between a digital performance and the digital distribution of a sound recording through the definition of "digital phonorecord delivery" in § 115(d); a defining characteristic is the creation of "a specifically identifiable reproduction" of the recording by the recipient. Section 115(c) also preserves the

had declined from being slightly greater than performers' royalties to barely a quarter of the performers' share, * * * and that from 1964 to 1974 copyright owners' royalty payments declined from 11.2% of wholesale record price to 7.2%." 662 F.2d 11 n. 25.

immunity for copying granted to consumers under § 1008; no action may be brought against a consumer who receives a digital delivery. § 115(c)(3)(J).

(5) Is the compulsory mechanical license a continuing anachronism? Consider the various sources of income for a songwriter, none of them legally constricted except this one (and the constraints that the consent decrees impose on ASCAP's and BMI's rates for performance rights).

(6) One other important entity in the world of music is the Harry Fox Agency, Inc., named for its founder, and earlier affiliated with the National Music Publishers Association. It represents over 17,000 publishers in negotiating mechanical right licenses (with contracts that bypass some of the § 115 formalities) and synchronization right licenses for recording music on the soundtracks of motion pictures and other audiovisual works, whether made for theater or television (including the use of music on commercials).[g]

JUKEBOXES AND § 116

Performance of copyrighted music on "coin-operated machines" was exempted from the public performance for profit right of § 1(e) in the 1909 Act because the penny-arcade machines of that era were believed to be marginal and unprofitable. Then came the once ubiquitous jukebox, which in its heyday may have swallowed half a billion dollars a year in nickels and dimes. Attempts to repeal the exemption were frequent but unsuccessful. The operators who supply the machines and the taverns and other establishments who by custom get half the take constituted a broad political base, in contrast to the concentration of the popular music industry in a few urban centers. They also had the advantage of the status quo. Their only contention of any weight against paying was that they bought a lot of records. (See H.R.Rep. pp. 112–13 for a summary of the arguments for and against the exemption.)

The 1976 Act in § 116 initially replaced the jukebox exemption with a compulsory license at $8 a year for each machine, a modest amount that was concededly a compromise. The Copyright Royalty Tribunal was authorized to review the rate in 1980 and at decennial intervals thereafter.

The Tribunal, in a rule effective Feb. 4, 1981, increased the rate to $50, phased in through 1985 in order to minimize the shock. 46 Fed.Reg. 884 (1981). In the hearings, the Amusement and Music Operators Association (AMOA) could only estimate "that there are between 3,000 and 5,000 operators who operate between 251,000 and 388,000 jukeboxes." Id. at 886. It was accepted that the industry is declining, but the Association could not produce any acceptable data about costs and profits. The Tribunal found persuasive analogies in ASCAP's data on its license fees for

---

g. Information on the Harry Fox Agency is available on its website, http://www.nmpa.org/hfa.html.

establishments that make music by means other than jukeboxes, in fees paid for background music services (Muzak and others), and also in jukebox license fees in other countries. These easily justified the $50 fee. Indeed, Chairman James thought the fee should be higher and inquired why the operators give up half their take to the establishment owners. Why indeed? See an instructive Note, 3 Card. Arts & Ent.L.J. 343 (1984). The increase was upheld by the Seventh Circuit. Amusement and Music Operators Ass'n v. Copyright Royalty Tribunal, 676 F.2d 1144 (7th Cir.), cert. denied, 459 U.S. 907 (1982).

The Berne Convention, Art. 11, has been interpreted as prohibiting compulsory licensing of public performance rights in musical compositions, although its Art. 13(1) does permit such licenses for "mechanical rights" (like § 115). In 1985, in anticipation of our adherence to Berne, an agreement between the performing rights organizations and AMOA set up negotiated rates for the period 1985–90. The principle of negotiated rates supported by arbitration was embodied in a new § 116A of the Copyright Act, which conferred an antitrust exemption on participants in the arrangement. In 1993, the compulsory license in § 116 was eliminated; § 116A, amended and redesignated as § 116, now governs jukebox performances.

CABLE AND SATELLITE TELEVISION

1. *Introduction*

The last compulsory license to be considered is by all odds the most intricate. It can be understood, moreover, only in the context of an industry that has been on a roller coaster ride for three decades. Cable television has been alternately advanced and retarded by the Federal Communications Commission, the Congress, the courts, and the Copyright Royalty Tribunal. Meanwhile, technological advances, notably satellite transmission, have created both new opportunities and new forms of competition.

During the 1960s the Federal Communications Commission was urged to move against cable television by the broadcasters, who saw cable as a threat to "free" television. At first, cable was merely a convenience, providing wider and better reception of local stations. But then cable began to import signals from distant stations and to carry its own programming. (Recall the very different settings of the *Fortnightly* and *Teleprompter* cases, pp. 313 and 316 supra.)

The FCC in 1972 promulgated regulations based on the "consensus agreement," a compromise between broadcasters, program producers, and cable operators.[h] The regulations relaxed a "freeze" that the FCC had maintained for some years, but they severely restricted the ability of cable operators to import the most attractive distant signals. Another part of

----

h. The consensus agreement is set out at 37 Fed.Reg. 3341 (Feb. 12, 1972).

the consensus agreement insured protection for territorial exclusivity of syndicated programs.   Both for the makers of programs and for the networks and other broadcasters, syndicated exclusivity was thought to be the key to maximizing revenues and controlling entry.   But as long as cable was free of copyright liability under *Fortnightly* and *Teleprompter,* FCC action was necessary to protect the separation of first runs and reruns and control their timing and marketing.   The rules required imported cable signals to be blacked out whenever they carried programs covered under exclusive contracts in the local market.

Meanwhile, copyright revision was at a standstill, in part because of the lack of agreement about the obligation of cable operators to make some contribution to copyright owners.   A compromise was finally reached.   The House Report emphasized that the copyright law was not intended to change communications policy, which "should be left to the appropriate committees in the Congress for resolution"—a hint that the FCC patchwork was viewed as unstable.   H.R.Rep. p. 89.

2. *Section 111*

The copyright outcome, § 111, is surely the most indigestible segment of the 1976 Act.[i]   The House Report attempted this summary:

"In general, the Committee believes that cable systems are commercial enterprises whose basic retransmission operations are based on the carriage of copyrighted program material and that copyright royalties should be paid by cable operators to the creators of such programs.   The Committee recognizes, however, that it would be impractical and unduly burdensome to require every cable system to negotiate with every copyright owner whose work was retransmitted by a cable system.   Accordingly, the Committee has determined to maintain the basic principle of the Senate bill to establish a compulsory copyright license for the retransmission of those over-the-air broadcast signals that a cable system is authorized to carry pursuant to the rules and regulations of the FCC.

"The compulsory license is conditioned, however, on certain requirements and limitations.   These include compliance with reporting requirements, payment of the royalty fees established in the bill, a ban on the substitution or deletion of commercial advertising, and geographic limits on the compulsory license for copyrighted programs broadcast by Canadian or Mexican stations.   Failure to comply with these requirements and limitations subjects a cable system to a suit for copyright infringement and the remedies provided under the bill for such actions.

"In setting a royalty fee schedule for the compulsory license, the Committee determined that the initial schedule should be established in the bill.   It recognized, however, that adjustments to the schedule would be required from time to time.   Accordingly, the Copyright Royalty Commission, established in chapter 8, [after 1993, an arbitration royalty panel

i. Except perhaps for § 119, the 1988 amendment that created a related compulso-   ry license for satellite retransmission of television programming.   See p. 544 infra.

convened by the Librarian of Congress] is empowered to make the adjustments in the initial rates, at specified times, based on standards and conditions set forth in the bill.

" * * * The Committee determined, however, that there was no evidence that the retransmission of 'local' broadcast signals by a cable operator threatens the existing market for copyright program owners. Similarly, the retransmission of network programing, including network programing which is broadcast in 'distant' markets, does not injure the copyright owner. The copyright owner contracts with the network on the basis of his programing reaching all markets served by the network and is compensated accordingly.

"By contrast, their transmission of distant non-network programing by cable systems causes damage to the copyright owner by distributing the program in an area beyond which it has been licensed. Such retransmission adversely affects the ability of the copyright owner to exploit the work in the distant market. It is also of direct benefit to the cable system by enhancing its ability to attract subscribers and increase revenues. For these reasons, the Committee has concluded that the copyright liability of cable television systems under the compulsory license should be limited to the retransmission of distant non-network programing." [j]

Section 111 has survived for more than two decades despite dramatic changes in regulation, legislation, and technology. Among the major developments were these:

3. *An Interlude of Deregulation*

Heralded by two massive economic reports in 1979 [k] and encouraged by political pressure toward deregulation, the FCC in 1980 abolished both distant signal restrictions and the safeguards for syndicated exclusivity. The new dispensation was stayed pending an appeal, but in 1981 the Second Circuit upheld everything that the FCC had done, or rather undone. Malrite T.V. v. FCC, 652 F.2d 1140 (2d Cir.1981), cert. denied, 454 U.S. 1143 (1982).

The Copyright Royalty Tribunal responded to this unshackling of cable by setting higher royalty rates payable under § 111. Despite Congressional discomfort manifested by a legislated three-month stay of the new rates, the Tribunal's action was eventually upheld. National Cable Television Ass'n v. Copyright Royalty Tribunal, 724 F.2d 176 (D.C.Cir.1983).

4. *Satellite Retransmission*

Satellites, which can pick up broadcast transmissions and redirect them to satellite receiving dishes, were initially used by cable systems for bringing in programs beyond those of local broadcasters. They have now

---

j. H.R.Rep. pp. 89–90. Consult also Botein, The New Copyright Act and Cable Television—A Signal of Change, 24 Bull.Copyr.Soc. 1 (1976); Meyer, The Feat of Houdi-ni or How the New Act Disentangles the CATV—Copyright Knot, 22 N.Y.L.S. L.Rev. 545 (1977).

k. 71 F.C.C.2d 632 and 951 (1979).

largely superseded wire networks and microwave relay systems for delivering distant signals to cable companies.

Satellites, however, can also reach individual home viewers by way of the increasingly ubiquitous satellite dish, which can now be less than two feet in diameter. For a while dish owners got a free ride, until scrambling of signals by originators became prevalent. The obligations of satellite disseminators to copyright owners, and the attendant obligations of viewers who use home dishes, remained troublesome and unresolved until Congress in the Satellite Home Viewer Act, Pub.L. No. 100–667, added § 119 to the Copyright Act in 1988. This created a compulsory license in favor of satellite retransmission for private home viewing.[l] See generally White, Home Satellite Dish Industry: A Brief Study of Growth and Development, 34 Howard L.J. 243 (1991).

A further complication was added in 1991 when the Eleventh Circuit held that satellite retransmitters were cable systems entitled to the § 111 compulsory license. National Broadcasting Co. v. Satellite Broadcast Networks, Inc., 940 F.2d 1467 (11th Cir.1991). The Copyright Office, in regulations issued in 1992, took a contrary position on satellite carriers, and also concluded that "wireless" microwave delivery systems such as multipoint distribution service (MDS) (if it provides multichannel service it becomes MMDS) were also excluded from § 111.[m] The Eleventh Circuit eventually deferred in Satellite Broadcasting & Communications Ass'n v. Oman, 17 F.3d 344 (11th Cir.), cert. denied, 513 U.S. 823 (1994), but legislation in 1994 made microwave systems eligible for the compulsory license.[n]

5. *The Roller Coaster Rolls On*

Meanwhile, FCC and Congressional momentum favoring cable continued. The Cable Communications Policy Act of 1984, Pub.L. No. 98–549, 47

---

l. Section 119 is cast in terms of retransmission of signals of network stations and superstations. Superstations, in practice, are major non-network broadcasters such as WGN (Chicago) and WOR (New York), whose transmissions are extensively used by satellite retransmitters. The compulsory license permits satellite carriers to retransmit superstations to home dish owners anywhere in the United States, but network stations can be delivered only to "unserved" households that cannot receive an over-the-air signal of specified quality from one of the network's affiliate stations.

m. 57 Fed.Reg. 3290 (1992). The position is defended in a Report of the Register, The Cable and Satellite Carrier Compulsory License: An Overview and Analysis (1992). The Report also complained that judicial and FCC actions have made § 111 unmanageable.

n. In 1997 the Copyright Office concluded that satellite master antenna television (SMATV) systems, which use a dish to receive satellite transmissions and a master antenna for over-the-air signals and then distribute the programming to customers by cable are also eligible for the cable compulsory license. 62 Fed.Reg. 18705 (Apr. 17, 1997).

Satellite transmissions (as opposed to the programs being transmitted) are the subject of the Brussels Convention Relating to the Distribution of Programme–Carrying Signals Transmitted by Satellite (1974). The purpose of the Brussels Convention is to combat commercial piracy of satellite signals; it does not encompass reception for private use. The United States, viewing its existing copyright and communications laws as sufficient to satisfy the Convention, ratified it in 1984.

U.S.C.A. § 521 et seq., gave cable a tremendous boost when it drastically curtailed state and local authority over franchises and customer rates.

The courts also contributed to cable's emancipation. A substantial element in the 1976 compromise behind § 111 was cable's "must carry" obligation with respect to local channels imposed by the FCC. In 1985 the Court of Appeals for the District of Columbia surprised many observers by holding that the "must carry" rules violated the hitherto quiescent first amendment rights of cable operators. Quincy Cable TV, Inc. v. FCC, 768 F.2d 1434 (D.C.Cir.1985), cert. denied, 476 U.S. 1169 (1986). This alarmed independent broadcast stations of all types (VHF, UHF, low-power, and public). The FCC was quickly persuaded to restore "must carry" for five years. These interim regulations also fell before the first amendment. Century Communications Corp. v. FCC, 835 F.2d 292 (D.C.Cir.1987), cert. denied, 486 U.S. 1032 (1988). ("Must carry" was born again in the 1992 Cable Act, infra.)

About the only thing the FCC did in the 1980s that in any way curbed cable (in sharp contrast to the starvation diet the Commission had imposed in the pre–1976 era), was to reinstate exclusive programming contracts for broadcasters—syndicated exclusivity—that it had abolished in 1980. This meant that cable had to black out programs (typically reruns) if either local or superstations had exclusive rights in them. A challenge by the cable companies to the reinstatement of syndicated exclusivity was rejected in United Video, Inc. v. FCC, 890 F.2d 1173 (D.C.Cir.1989). (The Copyright Royalty Tribunal responded by reducing the extra fees it had imposed when syndicated exclusivity was abolished in 1980.) Meanwhile, to the dismay of many viewers, cable operators and programmers were themselves acquiring exclusive rights in programs such as sporting events that formerly had been on "free" television.

6.   *Putting the Brakes on Cable: The 1992 Cable Act*

The Cable Television Consumer Protection and Competition Act of 1992, Pub.L. No. 102–385 (which had the distinction of representing the only override of a veto by President Bush) refashioned the regulation of cable on several fronts.[o] In an effort to insure access to program material, cable operators with an interest in a programmer or vendor were generally prohibited from restricting access to the programming by competitors. The Act also imposed a complicated system of rate regulation that yielded only limited results.

In yet another attempt to give broadcasters the power to insist that cable systems carry their signals, the 1992 Act revives "must carry" obligations for cable operators (but also offers broadcasters the option to forgo their "must carry" rights and instead negotiate with cable operators for consent to retransmit their signal under the threat of withholding

---

o. See Allard, The 1992 Cable Act: Just the Beginning, 15 Hastings Comm/Ent L.J. 305 (1993). See also Allard & Lauerhass, Debalkanize the Telecommunications Marketplace, 28 Cal.West.L.Rev. 231 (1992).

permission). The "must carry" requirement, which had twice before been struck down as a burden on first amendment rights, was quickly challenged. When Turner Broadcasting System v. F.C.C. reached the Supreme Court, the Court initially temporized, remanding for further consideration of the governmental interests asserted, 512 U.S. 622 (1994), but when the case returned, the "must carry" obligation survived in a 5–4 decision. 117 S.Ct. 1174 (1997).

7.   *The Forces of Competition?*

After years of struggle, Congress rewrote the nation's communications laws in the Telecommunications Act of 1996, Pub.L. No. 104–104. Among other changes, the law encourages cable and telephone companies to enter each others' markets with a full range of services such as telephone, video, and high-speed data communications. In particular, the Telecommunications Act creates an "open video system" that allows telephone companies to retransmit broadcast television signals, subject to "must carry" obligations. So far at least, this attempt to unleash the forces of competition in the television and telephone markets has flopped as regional telephone companies scale back their once ambitious plans to enter the television market and cable companies retreat from similar designs on the telephone business.

Meanwhile, technology may blur the boundaries between cable and another potential competitor or partner—the computer. In some locales, customers can access the Internet through their cable connection. "Streaming" technology already permits Internet delivery of video programming and may soon be capable of delivering broadcast television signals to anyone with Internet access. The much-anticipated debut of digital television may further erode the distinction between computers and televisions.

8.   *The Future of the Compulsory License*

Amidst all this change, the compulsory licenses in § 111 and § 119 occupy an inconspicuous but not insignificant corner. Although the royalties generated by the licenses are relatively small (§ 111 produces roughly $200 million per year and § 119 only a fraction of that—but growing), the guaranteed access to programming that they provide is crucial, at least according to cable and satellite operators. However, there have been proposals to eliminate the compulsory licenses, backed by arguments that the industries are now more than capable of standing on their own in the marketplace.

At the request of the Chair of the Senate Judiciary Committee, the Copyright Office in 1997 conducted a review of the licensing regimes governing the retransmission of broadcast signals. At public hearings, content providers such as the Motion Picture Association argued that the compulsory licenses should be abolished. The cable companies argued in favor of some version of the current system; satellite operators also favored a compulsory license, but argued that the restrictions on retransmission in § 119 unfairly limit their ability to compete with cable. See 54 Pat.,Tm. &

Copyr.J. (BNA) 1 (1997). An Executive Summary of the Copyright Office's Report on Compulsory Licenses for Broadcast Signals appears id. at 311.

"[T]he Copyright Office finds that for licensing the copyrighted works retransmitted by cable systems and satellite carriers, the better solution is through negotiation between collectives representing the owner and user industries, rather than by a government administered compulsory license. However, the comments demonstrate that the cable and satellite licenses have become an integral part of the way broadcast signals are brought to the public, that business arrangements and investments have been made in reliance upon the compulsory licenses, and that the parties advocating elimination of the licenses at this time have not presented a clear path for such elimination at this time. For these reasons, the Copyright Office does not advocate the elimination of the compulsory licenses at the present time."

The Report does advocate simplification of the cable royalty rate structure, recommending a flat per subscriber per signal fee based on fair market value. Responding to advances in satellite transmission capabilities, the Report also recommends amending the satellite license to permit the retransmission of all local broadcasts within each station's local market, which would make satellite systems a more effective competitor of cable. Bills have been introduced to implement the recommendation on satellite retransmission into local markets; the bills would also subject satellite carriers to the same must-carry, syndicated exclusivity, and other FCC regulations applicable to cable.

As for the open video systems created for telephone companies in the 1996 Telecommunications Act, "Without deciding whether open video systems might qualify as a section 111 cable system under the current statute, the Copyright Office believes that open video systems should be eligible for a cable compulsory license, and that the statute should be amended to facilitate open video systems inclusion in section 111." The Report reached the opposite conclusion with respect to Internet retransmission of broadcast signals based on "the vast technological and regulatory differences between Internet retransmitters and the cable systems and satellite carriers that enjoy the compulsory licensing." "The instantaneous worldwide dissemination of broadcast signals via the Internet poses major issues regarding the national and international licensing of the signals that have not been fully addressed by federal and international policymakers, and it would be premature for Congress to legislate a copyright compulsory license to benefit Internet retransmitters."

The only certainty in all of this is that things will not remain as they are.

CHAPTER 6

JURISDICTION AND REMEDIES

SECTION 1. JURISDICTION OF FEDERAL AND STATE COURTS

28 U.S.C. § 1338

(a) The district courts shall have original jurisdiction of any civil action arising under any Act of Congress relating to patents, plant variety protection, copyrights and trade-marks. Such jurisdiction shall be exclusive of the courts of the states in patent, plant variety protection and copyright cases.

(b) The district courts shall have original jurisdiction of any civil action asserting a claim of unfair competition when joined with a substantial and related claim under the copyright, patent, plant variety protection or trade-mark laws.

(c) Subsections (a) and (b) apply to exclusive rights in mask works under chapter 9 of title 17 to the same extent as such subsections apply to copyrights.

NOTES AND QUESTIONS

(1) It is plain enough that if a copyright owner brings an infringement action against a stranger who has reproduced the copyrighted work, the federal courts have exclusive subject matter jurisdiction. What is it about copyright (and patent) that justifies the denial of concurrent jurisdiction in state courts?

(2) Not every action in which the word "copyright" is invoked will be treated as "arising under" the Copyright Act. An action to enforce a contract to pay royalties on a copyrighted work, for example, must be brought in state court, absent some other basis for federal jurisdiction. See, e.g., Danks v. Gordon, 272 Fed. 821 (2d Cir.1921); Golden West Melodies, Inc. v. Capitol Records, Inc., 274 Cal.App.2d 713, 79 Cal.Rptr. 442 (1969). Similarly, an action to foreclose a security interest in a copyright remains within the jurisdiction of the state courts. Republic Pictures Corp. v. Security–First National Bank of Los Angeles, 197 F.2d 767 (9th Cir. 1952).

(3) Allocating jurisdiction in disputes over copyright ownership has proved particularly troublesome. When the primary objective of the litigation is to determine the validity or effect of an assignment, federal jurisdiction is usually denied. See, e.g., T.B. Harms Co. v. Eliscu, 339 F.2d 823 (2d Cir.1964), cert. denied, 381 U.S. 915 (1965); Rotardier v. Entertainment

Co. Music Group, 518 F.Supp. 919 (S.D.N.Y.1981). Yet, if the complaint also raises a genuine issue of infringement, federal jurisdiction may be upheld. See Topolos v. Caldewey, 698 F.2d 991 (9th Cir.1983). As the latter case notes, "Courts have directed inquiry to what they have variously described as the 'primary and controlling purpose' of the suit, the 'principal issue,' the 'fundamental controversy,' and the 'gist' or 'essence' of the plaintiff's claim." If subsequently, "affidavits or other materials reveal the infringement claim to be spurious," the action should then be dismissed. Vestron, Inc. v. Home Box Office, 839 F.2d 1380 (9th Cir.1988).

How strong is the claim for exclusive federal jurisdiction in suits to establish joint authorship? See Goodman v. Lee, 815 F.2d 1030 (5th Cir.1987) (federal jurisdiction accepted); Merchant v. Levy, 92 F.3d 51(2d Cir.1996), cert. denied, 117 S.Ct. 943 (1997) ("Unlike a case where a dispute as to copyright ownership arises under an agreement between the parties, resolution of which depends on state contract law * * * copyright ownership by reason of one's status as a co-author of a joint work arises directly from the terms of the Copyright Act itself.").

In *T.B. Harms,* supra, Judge Friendly offered this oft-quoted analysis:

"Mindful of the hazards of formulation in this treacherous area, we think that an action 'arises under' the Copyright Act if and only if the complaint is for a remedy expressly granted by the Act, e.g., a suit for infringement or for the statutory royalties for record reproduction, * * * or asserts a claim requiring construction of the Act, * * * or, at the very least and perhaps more doubtfully, presents a case where a distinctive policy of the Act requires that federal principles control the disposition of the claim." 339 F.2d at 828.

(4) Suppose a licensee, in making use of a copyrighted work, exceeds the scope of its license. It is often advantageous, particularly with respect to remedies, for the copyright owner to pursue a claim for infringement in lieu of, or in addition to, one for breach of contract. Jurisdiction over such a claim will generally lie in federal court, see, e.g., Frankel v. Stein and Day, Inc., 470 F.Supp. 209 (S.D.N.Y.1979), aff'd, 646 F.2d 560 (2d Cir.1980); MGM Distrib. Corp. v. Bijou Theatre Co., Inc., 3 F.Supp. 66 (D.Mass.1933), even when the case requires interpretation of the agreement. See, e.g., Kamakazi Music Corp. v. Robbins Music Corp., 684 F.2d 228 (2d Cir.1982) (also upholding an arbitration clause construed to encompass infringement claims); Kanakos v. MX Trading Corp., 216 U.S.P.Q. 1030 (S.D.N.Y.1981).

In Schoenberg v. Shapolsky Pub., Inc., 971 F.2d 926 (2d Cir.1992), Judge Altimari attempted to sort out the jurisdictional issues in breach of contract/copyright infringement cases:

"In *T.B. Harms,* we held that the district court lacked subject matter jurisdiction because the claim did not arise under the Copyright Act, but rather was a dispute concerning ownership of the copyright. * * * By contrast, Schoenberg's complaint poses the much more difficult jurisdictional question anticipated but not decided by this Court in *T.B. Harms,* namely whether a claim asserting infringement as a result of a breach of a

contract licensing or assigning a copyright arises under the Copyright Act.
* * *

"* * * A district court must first ascertain whether the plaintiff's
infringement claim is only 'incidental' to the plaintiff's claim seeking a
determination of ownership or contractual rights under the copyright.
* * * If it is determined that the claim is not merely incidental, then a
district court must next determine whether the complaint alleges a breach
of a condition to, or a covenant of, the contract licensing or assigning the
copyright. See [Costello Pub. Co. v. Rotelle, 670 F.2d 1035, 1045 (D.C.Cir.
1981)]. As we noted above, if a breach of a condition is alleged, then the
district court has subject matter jurisdiction. Id. But if the complaint
merely alleges a breach of a contractual covenant in the agreement that
licenses or assigns the copyright, then the court must undertake a third
step and analyze whether the breach is so material as to create a right of
rescission in the grantor. If the breach would create a right of rescission,
then the asserted claim arises under the Copyright Act."

The jurisdictional issue is analyzed in Cohen, "Arising Under" Jurisdiction and the Copyright Laws, 44 Hastings L.J. 337 (1993).

(5) In Saturday Evening Post Co. v. Rumbleseat Press, Inc., 816 F.2d 1191
(7th Cir.1987), Judge Posner elaborately weaves a net of federal jurisdiction
to enmesh a recalcitrant licensee who was making porcelain figures from
Norman Rockwell illustrations in which plaintiff claimed copyright. Defendant resisted arbitration as called for in the license. The court held that
the validity of plaintiff's copyrights (turning on questions of ownership and
proper notice) was arbitrable in the context of the contract dispute. On its
own motion, the court also adjudicated in plaintiff's favor the enforceability
of a licensee's contractual obligation not to contest the licensor's copyrights. The scope of licensee estoppel is a vexed issue in patent law
because public policy favors allowing challenges to patentability. See Lear
v. Adkins, 395 U.S. 653 (1969). Should this policy apply with equal
strength to permit challenges by licensees to copyrightability? (Recall the
differences in the reach of the patent and copyright monopolies). The
opinion concluded with two alternative holdings:

"So we have a narrow and a broad holding on no-contest clauses: they
are valid in copyright licenses (broad); they are valid when no issue of
copyrightability is presented (narrow)."

(6) May a plaintiff who successfully invokes federal jurisdiction by alleging
copyright infringement join a claim for breach of contract? See § 1338(b).
The Ninth Circuit, noting § 1338(b)'s explicit reference to "unfair competition," said, "We do not read it to limit pendent jurisdiction in appropriate
cases over other types of claims." Lone Ranger Television, Inc. v. Program
Radio Corp., 740 F.2d 718, 724 (9th Cir.1984) (state law conversion claim).
See Frederick Fell Pub. v. Lorayne, 422 F.Supp. 808 (S.D.N.Y.1976) (pendent jurisdiction over contract claim accepted).

(7) There is also a special provision on venue in copyright actions—28 U.S.C.A. § 1400 (actions "may be instituted in the district in which the defendant or his agent resides or may be found"). See Milwaukee Concrete Studios, Ltd. v. Fjeld Mfg. Co., 8 F.3d 441 (7th Cir.1993) (venue is determined by contacts with the particular judicial district, not contacts with the state in which the district lies).

(8) Acts of infringement occurring wholly outside the territory of the United States are not actionable under the Copyright Act. See, e.g., Subafilms, Ltd. v. MGM–Pathe Communications Co., 24 F.3d 1088 (9th Cir.) (en banc), cert. denied, 513 U.S. 1001 (1994). *Subafilms* held that this principle applies even if a defendant has authorized the foreign conduct from within this country, interpreting the copyright owner's right under § 106 "to authorize" the exercise of its exclusive rights as establishing a kind of contributory liability, violated only if the acts authorized by the defendant are themselves cognizable under American law. But see Curb v. MCA Records, Inc., 898 F.Supp. 586 (M.D.Tenn.1995), rejecting *Subafilms* and holding that unlawful authorization can itself amount to a domestic infringement cognizable under the Copyright Act.

NOTE ON STATE LIABILITY FOR INFRINGEMENT

The eleventh amendment to the Constitution reads as follows: "The Judicial power of the United States shall not be construed to extend to any suit in law or equity, commenced or prosecuted against one of the United States by Citizens of another State, or by Citizens or Subjects of any Foreign State."

The eleventh amendment, as it has come to be understood, prohibits suit in federal court brought by an individual against a state without its consent. See, e.g., Hans v. Louisiana, 134 U.S. 1 (1890). This interpretation seemed to preclude the imposition of liability against a state for violations of federal copyright law. See, e.g., BV Engineering v. University of California, Los Angeles, 858 F.2d 1394 (9th Cir.1988), cert. denied, 489 U.S. 1090 (1989). However, in Pennsylvania v. Union Gas Co., 491 U.S. 1 (1989), the Supreme Court indicated that Congress had the power to abrogate a state's eleventh amendment immunity in the exercise of federal powers under art. I of the Constitution, in this case over interstate commerce. In 1990, Congress attempted to do precisely that through the addition to the Copyright Act of § 511. See Jones, Copyrights and State Liability, 76 Iowa L.Rev. 701 (1991). However, a subsequent decision by the Supreme Court has raised serious doubts about the liability of states under § 511.

Seminole Tribe v. Florida, 517 U.S. 44 (1996), involved a challenge to a federal statute granting Indian tribes the right to sue states in federal court on issues relating to the operation of gambling casinos on tribal land. Overruling Pennsylvania v. Union Gas, the Court in a 5–4 decision held that Congress could not abrogate a state's eleventh amendment immunity by invoking federal power under the Indian commerce clause. Justice

Rehnquist's rationale applies to all congressional powers under art. I, including the patent and copyright clause.

The decision in *Seminole Tribe* does not affect, and indeed reaffirms, congressional power over the states exercised pursuant to the fourteenth amendment. Could the power of Congress to enforce the fourteenth amendment's prohibition against deprivations of "property" without due process sustain the abrogation of state immunity for copyright infringement? Soon after its decision in *Seminole Tribe,* the Supreme Court granted a petition for certiorari in Chavez v. Arte Publico Press, 59 F.3d 539 (5th Cir.1995), which had upheld the congressional abrogation of state immunity under both § 511 of the Copyright Act and § 40 of the Trademark Act (15 U.S.C.A. § 1122). The Supreme Court remanded for reconsideration. 517 U.S. 1184 (1996). The Fifth Circuit on remand held that congressional power under the fourteenth amendment does not extend to the enforcement of federal copyright and trademark laws against the states. 139 F.3d 504 (5th Cir.1998). The court did note, however, that the decision in *Seminole Tribe* does not bar suits for prospective injunctive relief against state officials to force compliance with federal law.

Finally, note that the federal government has waived its own immunity for patent and copyright infringement in 28 U.S.C.A. § 1498. The remedy for copyright infringement, however, is limited to an action by the copyright owner to recover "his reasonable and entire compensation as damages for such infringement, including the minimum statutory damages as set forth in section 504(c) of title 17"; thus, a plaintiff cannot enjoin the infringement. For a comprehensive analysis of the use of copyrighted works by federal and state governments, see Kwall, Governmental Use of Copyrighted Property: The Sovereign's Prerogative, 67 Tex.L.Rev. 685 (1989), advocating an eminent domain analysis to compensate for "takings" of copyrighted works.

SECTION 2.   STANDING TO SUE

NOTES AND QUESTIONS

(1) Under the 1909 Act the various rights comprising copyright were considered an indivisible whole. A transfer of anything less than this whole was characterized as a mere license. Licensees did not have standing to sue for infringement, although an exclusive licensee could maintain an action by joining the copyright proprietor.

The 1976 Act in § 201(d) expressly abandons indivisibility. Exclusive rights, and subdivisions of exclusive rights, may be separately owned. Further, the definition of "transfer of copyright ownership" in § 101 includes not only an assignment of a copyright or exclusive right, but also an exclusive license. Thus, as the "owner" of an exclusive right, both an assignee and an exclusive licensee of any of the rights under copyright may, according to § 501(b), "institute an action for any infringement of that particular right committed while he or she is the owner of it." See, e.g., Kamakazi Music Corp. v. Robbins Music Corp., 534 F.Supp. 69 (S.D.N.Y. 1982). The exclusive right upon which the owner relies may be quite limited. The House Report states: "It is thus clear, for example, that a local broadcasting station holding an exclusive license to transmit a particular work within a particular geographic area and for a particular period of time, could sue, in its own name as copyright owner, someone who infringed that particular exclusive right." H.R.Rep. p. 123. See Eden Toys, Inc. v. Florelee Undergarment Co., Inc., 697 F.2d 27 (2d Cir.1982) (exclusive licensee for use of "Paddington Bear" on adult clothing has standing to sue for infringement); Gamma Audio & Video, Inc. v. Ean–Chea, 11 F.3d 1106 (1st Cir.1993) (exclusive licensee of distribution rights in particular states has standing).

(2) An action for infringement of an exclusive right may be instituted by the "legal or beneficial owner." § 501(b). The most significant example of the latter is "an author who had parted with legal title to the copyright in exchange for percentage royalties based on sales or license fees." H.R.Rep. p. 159. See, e.g., Cortner v. Israel, 732 F.2d 267 (2d Cir.1984) (brought by the composers of the theme music for ABC's Monday Night Football); Kamakazi Music Corp. v. Robbins Music Corp., supra. A work-for-hire employee has no beneficial interest according to Moran v. London Records, Ltd., 827 F.2d 180 (7th Cir.1987).

(3) Section 501(b) encourages a flexible response to the procedural problems inherent in divisibility. The court may order notice of the action served on all persons having an interest in the copyright; when the interest is "likely to be affected," notice is mandatory. Third parties claiming an interest in the copyright have a right to intervene, and the court, in its discretion, may order their joinder.

(4) Section 507(b) sets a three-year statute of limitations. "Fraudulent concealment" of the infringement may toll the statute, and one court has suggested that it might be sufficient for tolling if "a reasonable man would not have discovered the infringement." Taylor v. Meirick, 712 F.2d 1112 (7th Cir.1983). Although *Taylor* suggests that if some portion of the infringing acts occurred within the limitations period, the copyright owner may recover for the whole of the infringement, most cases hold that recovery is barred for any infringing acts occurring more than three years prior to suit. See, e.g., Stone v. Williams, 970 F.2d 1043 (2d Cir.1992), cert. denied, 508 U.S. 906 (1993); Roley v. New World Pictures, Ltd., 19 F.3d 479 (9th Cir.1994). Which approach best advances the rationale for statutes of limitations?[a]

a. Application of the statute of limitations to claims of joint authorship has proven particularly troublesome. The limitations period was fatal to a claim of joint authorship of the song *Why Do Fools Fall in Love* brought 32 years after the song was written, Merchant v. Levy, 92 F.3d 51 (2d Cir.1996), cert. denied, 117 S.Ct. 943 (1997), but when the plaintiff in Goodman v. Lee, 78 F.3d 1007 (5th Cir.), cert. denied, 117 S.Ct. 166 (1996),

(5) "Misuse" of the copyright monopoly may preclude an action for in-fringement.   See Lasercomb America, Inc. v. Reynolds, 911 F.2d 970 (4th Cir.1990) (restriction in plaintiff's licensing agreements against the cre-ation of competing works constitutes misuse of copyright that bars recovery for infringement, even against a defendant who was not a party to the license).   See also the Federal Circuit's discussion of the copyright misuse doctrine in Atari Games Corp. v. Nintendo of America, Inc., 975 F.2d 832 (Fed.Cir.1992). In DSC Comm. Corp. v. DGI Technologies, Inc., 81 F.3d 597 (5th Cir.1996), the possibility of a successful misuse defense prevented the owner of copyrighted operating system software from obtaining a prelimi-nary injunction. The plaintiff's licenses with its customers allowed the software to be used only with its own microprocessor cards; the Fifth Circuit affirmed the district court's refusal to enjoin a defendant from downloading the software into the RAM memory of a competing card in order to test its compatibility with the plaintiff's system. Citing *Lasercomb*, the court said that plaintiff might well be guilty of misuse in seeking to use its software copyright to obtain a monopoly over the unpatented micropro-cessor cards. *Lasercomb* was also invoked by the Ninth Circuit in holding that the American Medical Association had committed copyright misuse when it licensed a government agency to use its medical procedure code on condition that the agency not use any competing system. Practice Manage-ment Information Corp. v. American Medical Ass'n, 121 F.3d 516 (9th Cir.), cert. denied, 118 S.Ct. 339 (1997).

SECTION 3.   THE BATTERY OF REMEDIES

ACTUAL DAMAGES AND PROFITS

Section 504(b) authorizes the copyright owner to recover "the actual damages suffered by him or her as a result of the infringement."   In some instances damages may be measured by the decrease in market value of the copyrighted work.   See Universal Pictures Co. v. Harold Lloyd Corp., 162 F.2d 354 (9th Cir.1947).   In others, it may be useful to look to the consideration normally received by the copyright owner for similar uses. See Aitken, Hazen, Hoffman, Miller, P.C. v. Empire Construction Co., 542 F.Supp. 252 (D.Neb.1982).   Lost profits on lost sales are also a common measure of damage.   As in other contexts, however, it may be difficult to establish lost profits with the requisite certainty.   When should the court assume that every sale made by the infringer is a sale lost by the plaintiff? When are comparisons with the sales of other works relevant?   Should expert projections suffice?   See Stevens Linen Associates v. Mastercraft Corp., 656 F.2d 11 (2d Cir.1981).   And lost sales are not the same as lost profits.   If you sell less, you will ordinarily save some production costs, and

---

claimed joint authorship and an accounting in 1985 for the 1956 hit *Let the Good Times Roll*, the court said that the state ten-year limitations period for an accounting by a co-owner, running from when demand is made, was controlling.

these must be taken into account in computing damages. Taylor v. Meirick, 712 F.2d 1112 (7th Cir.1983).

Are there other losses, in addition to the economic injury occasioned by lost sales or diminished market value, that might be recovered by the victim of an infringement?

The copyright owner is not limited to an award of damages. Section 504(b) authorizes recovery of both actual damages "and any profits of the infringer that are attributable to the infringement and are not taken into account in computing the actual damages." Section 101 of the 1909 Act had generated considerable confusion with respect to the recovery of plaintiff's damages and defendant's profits. Some decisions read the prior law as presenting a choice, while others permitted recovery of both. Compare Universal Pictures Co. v. Harold Lloyd Corp., supra, with Thomas Wilson & Co. v. Irving Dorfman Co., 433 F.2d 409 (2d Cir.1970), cert. denied, 401 U.S. 977 (1971). Section 504(b) clearly authorizes a cumulative recovery, but the right to cumulate is not unlimited. The copyright owner may recover, in addition to damages, only defendant's profits "not taken into account in computing the actual damages." What is the effect of this latter limitation? The House Report offers this explanation:

> In allowing the plaintiff to recover "the actual damages suffered by him or her as a result of the infringement," plus any of the infringer's profits "that are attributable to the infringement and are not taken into account in computing the actual damages," section 504(b) recognizes the different purposes served by awards of damages and profits. Damages are awarded to compensate the copyright owner for losses from the infringement, and profits are awarded to prevent the infringer from unfairly benefiting from a wrongful act. Where the defendant's profits are nothing more than a measure of the damages suffered by the copyright owner, it would be inappropriate to award damages and profits cumulatively, since in effect they amount to the same thing. However, in cases where the copyright owner has suffered damages not reflected in the infringer's profits, or where there have been profits attributable to the copyrighted work but not used as a measure of damages, subsection (b) authorizes the award of both. (H.R.Rep. p. 161.)

When are the defendant's profits "nothing more than a measure of the damages"? When instead are damages "not reflected in the infringer's profits"? Suppose that a construction company, having contracted to use a set of architectural plans for one apartment building, uses them without permission for a second. Should the architect who retains copyright in the plans be permitted to recover, in addition to damages for re-use measured by the fair market value of the plans, the defendant's net profit on the construction contract? Compare Aitken, Etc. v. Empire Construction Co., supra, with Robert Jones Associates, Inc. v. Nino Homes, p. 177 supra. Taylor v. Meirick, supra, held that the owner of copyrighted maps that were reproduced and sold by an infringer could not recover both lost profits resulting from the diverted trade and defendant's profit on the infringing sales; plaintiff would be entitled to defendant's profits only to the extent they exceeded the plaintiff's own lost profits recovered as damages. The Second Circuit in Abeshouse v. Ultragraphics, Inc., 754 F.2d 467 (2d Cir.1985), acknowledged that "[d]ouble-counting may occur when an infringing seller has to disgorge profits on sales that a copyright holder might have made and for which he may therefore claim damages in the form of lost profits." But on the facts before it the court concluded that there was no double-counting in permitting the owner of a copyrighted poster to recover from a faithless exclusive distributor both its lost profits resulting from the defendant's purchases of infringing posters and the defendant's profits on subsequent sales of the infringing items to wholesalers. Plaintiffs "could not have sold their posters domestically to anyone but their exclusive distributor," and thus "could not properly have made the latter sales and therefore cannot claim any lost profits on them. Thus, requiring [defendant] to disgorge to appellees its profits on those sales contains no element of double-counting * * *."

Determining the "profits of the infringer that are attributable to the infringement" is itself a complex task. In many instances profits will reflect in part the value of defendant's own contributions. According to the House Report, "where some of the defendant's profits result from the infringement and other profits are caused by different factors, it will be necessary for the court to make an apportionment." H.R.Rep. p. 161.

SHELDON v. METRO–GOLDWYN PICTURES CORP., 309 U.S. 390, 60 S.Ct. 681 (1940). After the Second Circuit had found the defendant's motion picture "Letty Lynton" to be an infringement of the copyrighted play "Dishonored Lady" (p. 201 supra), the District Court awarded plaintiff the defendant's total profit from the movie, amounting to $587,604.34. 26 F.Supp. 134. The Second Circuit, on appeal, apportioned the profits, awarding 20%. 106 F.2d 45. Plaintiff sought reinstatement of the District Court's award. Chief Justice Hughes, after deciding that apportionment was proper under the 1909 Act, turned to the method of apportionment:

"Third. The controlling fact in the determination of the apportionment was that the profits had been derived, not from the mere performance of a copyrighted play, but from the exhibition of a motion picture which had its distinctive profit-making features, apart from the use of any infringing material, by reason of the expert and creative operations involved in its production and direction. In that aspect the case has a certain resemblance to that of a patent infringement, where the infringer has created profits by the addition of non-infringing and valuable improvements. And, in this instance, it plainly appeared that what respondents had contributed accounted for by far the larger part of their gains. * * *

"The testimony showed quite clearly that in the creation of profits from the exhibition of a motion picture, the talent and popularity of the 'motion picture stars' generally constitutes the main drawing power of the picture, and that this is especially true where the title of the picture is not identified with any well-known play or novel.   Here, it appeared that the picture did not bear the title of the copyrighted play and that it was not presented or advertised as having any connection whatever with the play. It was also shown that the picture had been 'sold,' that is, licensed to almost all the exhibitors as identified simply with the name of a popular motion picture actress before even the title 'Letty Lynton' was used.   In addition to the drawing power of the 'motion picture stars,' other factors in creating the profits were found in the artistic conceptions and in the expert supervision and direction of the various processes which made possible the composite result with its attractiveness to the public.

"Upon these various considerations, with elaboration of detail, respondents' expert witnesses gave their views as to the extent to which the use of the copyrighted material had contributed to the profits in question.   The underlying facts as to the factors in successful production and exhibition of motion pictures were abundantly proved, but, as the court below recognized, the ultimate estimates of the expert witnesses were only the expression 'of their very decided opinions.'   These witnesses were in complete agreement that the portion of the profits attributable to the use of the copyrighted play in the circumstances here disclosed was very small.   Their estimates given in percentages of receipts ran from five to twelve per cent; the estimate apparently most favored was ten per cent as the limit.   One finally expressed the view that the play contributed nothing.   There was no rebuttal.   But the court below was not willing to accept the experts' testimony 'at its face value.'   The court felt that it must make an award 'which by no possibility shall be too small.'   Desiring to give petitioners the benefit of every doubt, the court allowed for the contribution of the play twenty per cent of the net profits.

"Petitioners are not in a position to complain that the amount thus allowed by the court was greater than the expert evidence warranted.   Nor is there any basis for attack, and we do not understand that any attack is made, upon the qualifications of the experts.   By virtue of an extensive experience, they had an intimate knowledge of all pertinent facts relating to the production and exhibition of motion pictures.   Nor can we say that the testimony afforded no basis for a finding.   What we said in [Dowagiac Mfg. Co. v. Minnesota Moline Plow Co., 235 U.S. 641 (1915)] is equally true here,—that what is required is not mathematical exactness but only a reasonable approximation.   That, after all, is a matter of judgment; and the testimony of those who are informed by observation and experience may be not only helpful but, as we have said, may be indispensable. Equity is concerned with making a fair apportionment so that neither party will have what justly belongs to the other.   Confronted with the manifest injustice of giving to petitioners all the profits made by the motion picture, the court in making an apportionment was entitled to avail itself of the experience of those best qualified to form a judgment in the particular field of inquiry and come to its conclusion aided by their testimony.   We see no greater difficulty in the admission and use of expert testimony in such a case than in the countless cases involving values of property rights in which such testimony often forms the sole basis for decision.

"Petitioners also complain of deductions allowed in the computation of the net profits. These contentions involve questions of fact which have been determined below upon the evidence and we find no ground for disturbing the court's conclusions.

"The judgment of the Circuit Court of Appeals is Affirmed."

NOTES ON RECOVERY OF "PROFITS"

(1) In Sheldon v. Moredall Realty Corp., 29 F.Supp. 729 (S.D.N.Y.1939), the defendant was the operator of the Capitol Theatre in New York City, which had shown "Letty Lynton" for two weeks. Though "unquestionably an innocent infringer" it was required to give up 20% of its profits. Presumably, plaintiffs could have made like demands on other exhibitors.

(2) Problems of apportionment can become particularly intricate when the infringing work is sold as part of a larger unit—a song on a record album, for example. After George Harrison's "My Sweet Lord" was found to infringe the Chiffons' 1963 hit, "He's So Fine," the court was forced to apportion profits both with respect to relative contributions to the infringing work, as in *Sheldon* (75% due to the plagiarized tune), and the percentage of profits from the album and "single" (there *is* a "flip side") that were attributable to the presence of the infringing song. ABKCO Music, Inc. v. Harrisongs Music, Ltd., 508 F.Supp. 798 (S.D.N.Y.1981), modified, 722 F.2d 988 (2d Cir.1983). In Lottie Joplin Thomas Trust v. Crown Pub., Inc., 592 F.2d 651 (2d Cir.1978), an award of 50% of defendant's profits was upheld despite the fact that the infringing work occupied only 10% of defendant's five-record set of Scott Joplin music. The inclusion of the infringing work had made the defendant's collection the only "complete set."

How much did the unauthorized use of a photograph of Raquel Welch (unclad) on the cover of "Celebrity Skin" contribute to profits? In Sygma Photo News, Inc. v. High Society Magazine, Inc., 778 F.2d 89 (2d Cir.1985), the magistrate said 20%, but the District Court said 75%. The Court of Appeals settled for 50%. For a more prosaic illustration, see Orgel v. Clark Boardman Co., 301 F.2d 119 (2d Cir.1962), in which the court awarded 50% of the profits from defendant's legal treatise, although only 35% of the work made use of material from plaintiff's copyrighted text.

(3) It is defendant's profit, not gross revenue, to which a plaintiff may be entitled. Thus, aside from problems of apportionment, there are the inevitable disputes about expense deductions. The most obvious deductions are those related to the labor and materials expended in the production of the infringing work. See, e.g., Taylor v. Meirick, 712 F.2d 1112 (7th Cir.1983). Beyond that, questions quickly multiply. Should defendants be allowed a credit for income taxes paid on their profits? Should any deduction be permitted for "overhead"? If so, how should it be allocated? Judge Hand, in *Sheldon,* said that the "correct rule" as to overhead permits an allocated deduction for overhead that would "assist in the production of the infringement." 106 F.2d at 54. Judge Posner, no stranger to economic analysis, said in *Taylor,* "Costs that would be incurred anyway should not be subtracted, because by definition they cannot be avoided by curtailing the profit-making activity"—deductions are limited to "variable costs." Are these statements consistent? If not, which is more in keeping with the principle stated in the House Report, that "profits are awarded to prevent the infringer from unfairly benefiting from a wrongful act"? H.R.Rep. p. 161.

The difficulties of apportionment and deductions are lessened, at least for the copyright owner, by the burden of proof in § 504(b).

STATUTORY DAMAGES

(1) Section 504(c) offers the copyright owner an unusual election. In lieu of a recovery measured by plaintiff's losses and defendant's gains, the copyright owner may elect to recover "statutory damages," between $500 and $20,000,[a] "as the court considers just."

What is the purpose of such an award? As the preceding materials illustrate, proof of actual damages and profits is often difficult, sometimes impossible. Provision for statutory damages insures a remedy. It also insures a measure of deterrence. This may be particularly significant with respect to infringements such as unauthorized performances, where actual damages in individual cases may be trivial, yet aggregate effects substantial. Minimum statutory damages also provide the copyright owner with bargaining leverage. See R. Brown, The Operation of the Damage Provisions of the Copyright Law: An Exploratory Study, Copyr. Law Revision Study No. 23 (1958), in 2 Studies on Copyr. 1067 (1963).

The House Report emphasizes that recovery of damages and profits under § 504(b) and the award of statutory damages under § 504(c) are alternative, and the election is left to the copyright owner. An owner who delays registration of copyright, however, may forfeit the right to claim statutory damages as a result of the restrictions in § 412.

(2) What factors should influence the determination, within the statutory limits, of a "just" sum? Although a plaintiff who has elected to recover statutory damages is not obliged to submit proof of actual damages or defendant's profits, the House Report notes that nothing in § 504 prevents a court from taking into account evidence of actual damages and profits in fixing a statutory award. The nature of the defendant's conduct will also be weighed. The statute alters the minimum and maximum awards when the infringement is committed either innocently or willfully. § 504(c)(2). How should the latter term be interpreted? In Fitzgerald Pub. Co. v.

a. These amounts, double the previous levels, apply to infringements occurring after March 1, 1989. The maximum for willful infringement also doubled from $50,000 to $100,000. Berne Convention Implementation Act of 1988, P.L. 100–568, 102 Stat. 2853.

Baylor Pub. Co., Inc., 807 F.2d 1110 (2d Cir.1986), where a defendant printing company dealt with a scoundrel who it knew or should have known lacked authority, the "knowledge that its actions constitute an infringement establishes that the defendant acted willfully." See also Video Views, Inc. v. Studio 21, Ltd., 925 F.2d 1010 (7th Cir.), cert. denied, 502 U.S. 861 (1991) ("An infringement is 'willful' if the infringer knows that its conduct is an infringement or if the infringer has acted in reckless disregard of the copyright owner's right.") How much room does this leave for infringements that are neither "willful" nor innocent ("infringer was not aware and had no reason to believe that his or her acts constituted an infringement," § 504(c)(2))? Innocent infringement justified an award of reduced statutory damages against sellers of Batman T-shirts in D.C. Comics Inc. v. Mini Gift Shop, 912 F.2d 29 (2d Cir.1990).

In light of the ability to increase the statutory award in instances of willful infringement, separate punitive damages have been found "inappropriate." Kamakazi Music Corp. v. Robbins Music Corp., 534 F.Supp. 69, 78 (S.D.N.Y.1982). The opportunity to preclude a defendant from seeking refuge in innocent intent to mitigate statutory (or actual) damages is the sole surviving statutory incentive to the use of a copyright notice. See §§ 401(d) and 402(d). Note also, in § 504(c)(2), the small victory achieved by educators.

(3) A recovery within the prescribed limits is to be awarded for all infringements "with respect to any one work." The House Report explains that the statutory minimum and maximum are to be applied individually in the case of multiple works—if the defendant has publicly performed three of the plaintiff's songs, statutory damages of at least $1,500 must be awarded. For example, statutory damages of $9.1 million, representing the maximum $100,000 per work for the willful piracy of 91 sound recordings, was awarded in Sony Music Entertainment v. Cassette Prod., Inc., 41 U.S.P.Q.2d 1198 (D.N.J.1996). A licensor of syndicated television programs got $9 million in statutory damages from a licensee who continued to broadcast the programs after the license was terminated. The court said it was awarding $10,000 for each of 900 unauthorized broadcasts; defendant's failure to produce supporting evidence precluded its argument that many of the infringements involved multiple broadcasts of the same episode, and thus the number of infringed works was substantially less than 900 (see Note (4) infra). MCA Television Ltd. v. Feltner, 89 F.3d 766 (11th Cir. 1996), cert. denied, 117 S.Ct. 1248 (1997).

(4) What is the effect of multiple acts of infringement? Under prior law, courts sometimes treated a series of infringements as separate transactions, each supporting an award of at least minimum statutory damages. See, e.g., Robert Stigwood Group, Ltd. v. O'Reilly, 530 F.2d 1096 (2d Cir.), cert. denied, 429 U.S. 848 (1976), in which separate statutory damages were awarded for each of forty-eight unauthorized performances of "Jesus Christ Superstar." Section 504(c), however, provides for an award within the statutory limits "for all infringements involved in the action, with respect to any one work." The House Report is emphatic: "A single infringer of a single work is liable for a single amount between $250 and $10,000, no matter how many acts of infringement are involved in the action and regardless of whether the acts were separate, isolated, or occurred in a related series." H.R.Rep. p. 162. A comprehensive Note, Statutory Damages for the Multiple Infringement of a Copyrighted Work: A Doctrine Whose Time Has Come, Again, 6 Cardozo Arts & Ent.L.J. 463 (1988), argues that the statute is too restrictive and insufficiently sanctions massive infringements.

(5) Because copyright is divisible, a single infringing act may violate the exclusive rights of a number of "owners." The defendant, however, remains liable for only a single recovery of statutory damages. The House Report explains that "although the minimum and maximum amounts are to be multiplied where multiple 'works' are involved in the suit, the same is not true with respect to multiple copyrights, multiple owners, multiple exclusive rights, or multiple registrations." H.R.Rep. p. 162.

INJUNCTIVE RELIEF

(1) Injunctive relief, both preliminary and permanent, is authorized in § 502. In American Code Co. v. Bensinger, 282 Fed. 829, 835 (2d Cir. 1922), Judge Rogers said, "Where the plaintiff has made a prima facie case in regard to the existence of the copyright and its infringement, a temporary injunction will, as a general rule, be issued." Judge Clark said in Rushton v. Vitale, 218 F.2d 434, 436 (2d Cir.1955), "When a prima facie case for copyright infringement has been made, plaintiffs are entitled to a preliminary injunction without a detailed showing of danger of irreparable harm."

This relaxed attitude toward preliminary relief persists. See, e.g., Wainwright Securities Inc. v. Wall Street Transcript Corp., 558 F.2d 91, 94 (2d Cir.1977). When district judges do deny a preliminary injunction in copyright litigation, they risk reversal, despite the conventional position that the trial judge has considerable discretion with respect to preliminary relief. See Cadence Design Systems, Inc. v. Avant! Corp., 125 F.3d 824 (9th Cir.1997) ("A copyright infringement defendant cannot rebut the presumption of irreparable harm by showing that money damages are adequate," but noting other possible grounds for denying preliminary relief.); Concrete Machinery Co. v. Classic Law Ornaments, Inc., 843 F.2d 600 (1st Cir.1988). What accounts for this liberal approach to preliminary injunctions?

(2) Despite the customary reliance on injunctions, a permanent injunction need not always follow a decision for the plaintiff. See, e.g., Love v. Kwitney, 772 F.Supp. 1367 (S.D.N.Y.1991), aff'd, 963 F.2d 1521 (2d Cir.), cert. denied, 506 U.S. 862 (1992) (non-willful infringement comprised 2.6% of the defendant's book; the court withheld an injunction and awarded plaintiff 2.6% of the profits). In Abend v. MCA, Inc., 863 F.2d 1465 (9th Cir.1988), aff'd sub nom. Stewart v. Abend, 495 U.S. 207 (1990), p. 512 supra, the speculator who had bought the renewal term got only damages and apportioned profits. This resolution, not mentioned by the Supreme Court on appeal, was later endorsed by the Court in dictum in footnote 10 of its opinion in Campbell v. Acuff–Rose Music, Inc., p. 401 supra. Consult Oakes, Copyrights and Copyremedies: Unfair Use and Injunctions, 18 Hofstra L.Rev. 983 (1990).

The remedial provisions of the federal patent, copyright, and trademark statutes are compared in R. Brown, Civil Remedies for Intellectual Property Invasions: Themes and Variations, 55 L. & Contemp.Prob. (No. 2) 45 (1992). Hamilton, Appropriation Art and the Imminent Decline in Authorial Control Over Copyrighted Works, 42 J.Copyr.Soc. 93 (1994), argues broadly that the law may be gradually moving from a system of author control premised on property rights to a regime of remuneration based on compensation.

THE RIGHT TO TRIAL BY JURY

When the plaintiff in an infringement action seeks actual damages, either party is entitled, upon demand, to a jury; such an action is the heartland of "law." Conversely, if the plaintiff seeks only an injunction, the action is "equitable," and there is no right to a jury. But plaintiffs often demand both an injunction and damages. As a consequence of Beacon Theatres, Inc. v. Westover, 359 U.S. 500 (1959) and Dairy Queen, Inc. v. Wood, 369 U.S. 469 (1962), all damage claims in such actions are triable by a jury. Older cases sometimes distinguished between damages and an accounting of defendant's profits, treating the latter as a form of equitable relief. Following *Dairy Queen,* the right to a jury determination generally encompasses both.

When a plaintiff chose to forego both actual damages and an accounting of profits and sought instead only statutory damages, the right to a jury trial had been unsettled. Some courts, viewing the remedy of statutory damages as "legal," found a seventh amendment right to trial by jury. E.g., Cass County Music Co. v. C.H.L.R., Inc., 88 F.3d 635 (8th Cir.1996) (surveying the split among the circuits); cf. Video Views, Inc. v. Studio 21, Ltd., 925 F.2d 1010 (7th Cir.), cert. denied, 502 U.S. 861 (1991) (recognizing a right to a jury on issues of infringement and willfulness, but with the judge determining the amount of statutory damages). Others considered the remedy "equitable," raising no constitutional or statutory right to a jury. E.g., Twentieth Century Music Corp. v. Frith, 645 F.2d 6 (5th Cir.1981). (The plaintiffs in several of these cases were music publishers complaining of unauthorized public performances. Why would they want to avoid a jury?) In 1997, the Ninth Circuit in Columbia Pictures Television v. Krypton Broadcasting, Inc., 106 F.3d 284 (9th Cir.1997), aligned itself with the cases finding no statutory or constitutional right to a jury in a statutory damages case; the Supreme Court granted defendant's petition for certiorari.

In Feltner v. Columbia Pictures Television, Inc., 118 S.Ct. 1279 (1998), the Supreme Court found a right to a jury. Attempting to avoid the constitutional issue, the Court first considered whether the Copyright Act itself granted a jury trial in statutory damages cases, but concluded that "[t]he language of § 504(c) does not grant a right to have a jury assess statutory damages." Referring to § 504(c)'s requirement that damages be assessed in an amount that "the court considers just," Justice Thomas said that "[t]he word 'court' in this context appears to mean judge, not jury." Although the statute did not require a jury trial, the Court concluded that the Seventh Amendment did. "Before the adoption of the Seventh Amendment, the common law and statutes in England and this country granted copyright owners causes of action for infringement. More importantly, copyright suits for monetary damages were tried in courts of law, and thus before juries. * * * [W]e hold that the Seventh Amendment provides a right to a jury trial on all issues pertinent to an award of statutory damages under § 504(c) of the Copyright Act, including the amount itself."

IMPOUNDMENT AND DISPOSITION

The court in an infringement action has discretion to order the impoundment of infringing copies and related articles. § 503(a). The results can be dramatic. See Duchess Music Corp. v. Stern, 458 F.2d 1305 (9th Cir.1972) (25,000 tape recordings, blank cartridges, labels, machinery, and equipment seized). The impoundment procedures are specified in the Copyright Rules adopted by the United States Supreme Court.[b] Rule 1 provides that the Federal Rules of Civil Procedure are applicable in copyright proceedings. (Cf. Fed.R.Civ.P. 81(a)(1).) The remaining Copyright Rules detail the impoundment procedure. The House Report concludes that in light of the Copyright Rules, "there appears no need for including a special provision on the point in the bill." H.R.Rep. p. 160.

The Copyright Rules do not require a pre-seizure hearing; seizure may be ordered upon the posting of a bond by the plaintiff. The defendant may then make a post-seizure application for return of the articles. Does the lack of a pre-seizure hearing violate free speech or due process standards? Constitutional attacks have generally been unsuccessful. See Dealer Advertising Dev., Inc. v. Barbara Allan Financial Advertising, Inc., 197 U.S.P.Q. 611 (W.D.Mich.1977); Jondora Music Pub. Co. v. Melody Recordings, Inc., 362 F.Supp. 494 (D.N.J.1973), vacated, 506 F.2d 392 (3d Cir.), cert. denied, 421 U.S. 1012 (1975). But see Paramount Pictures Corp. v. Doe, 821 F.Supp. 82 (E.D.N.Y.1993) (arguing that the Copyright Rules have been superseded by the 1976 Act and that due process standards must be met). The issue is considered in Owens, Impoundment Proceedings under the Copyright Act: The Constitutional Infirmities, 14 Hofstra L.Rev. 211 (1985).

b.   214 U.S. 533 (1909), as amended, 307 U.S. 652 (1939), and 383 U.S. 1031 (1966).

Upon final judgment, destruction or other disposition of infringing copies may be ordered. § 503(b).

COSTS AND ATTORNEY'S FEES

The court, in its discretion, may award costs and attorney's fees. § 505. Although the former may apparently be assessed against either side, the latter is reserved for the "prevailing party." (It is not always easy to decide who has in fact prevailed. See Shapiro, Bernstein & Co. v. 4636 S. Vermont Ave., Inc., 367 F.2d 236 (9th Cir.1966).) Attorney's fees, like statutory damages, may be forfeited if the copyright owner delays registration. § 412.

Fee awards have been the subject of considerable judicial discussion in recent years, perhaps reflecting the mounting encroachments on the entrenched "American rule" that parties must pay their own legal expenses. Prevailing plaintiffs frequently received fees. The criteria for awards to prevailing defendants, however, varied among the circuits. The variations were surveyed in Lieb v. Topstone Industries, Inc., 788 F.2d 151 (3d Cir.1986), but were wiped out by the Supreme Court in Fogerty v. Fantasy, Inc., 510 U.S. 517 (1994), endorsing the "even-handed" approach exemplified by the Third Circuit in *Lieb*. "Prevailing plaintiffs and prevailing defendants," Chief Justice Rehnquist wrote, "are to be treated alike, but attorney's fees are to be awarded to prevailing parties only as a matter of the court's discretion." The Third Circuit's description in *Lieb* of the factors that may guide the exercise of that discretion was endorsed by the Supreme Court, 510 U.S. at 534, n. 19. "These factors include 'frivolousness, motivation, objective unreasonableness (both in the factual and in the legal components of the case) and the need in particular circumstances to advance considerations of compensation and deterrence.'"

The Third Circuit in *Lieb* had also discussed factors relevant to the amount of the award. As for "what amount is reasonable under the circumstances * * * the relative complexity of the litigation is relevant. Also, a sum greater than what the client has been charged may not be assessed, but the award need not be that large. * * * The relative financial strength of the parties is a valid consideration * * * as are the damages * * *. Where bad faith is present that, too, may affect the size of the award. * * * We emphasize that the aims of the statute are compensation and deterrence where appropriate, but not ruination."

The implications of *Fogerty* are debated in Marcus and Nimmer, Forum on Attorney's Fees in Copyright Cases: Are We Running Through the Jungle Now or is the Old Man Still Stuck Down the Road?, 39 Will. & Mary L.Rev. 65 (1997). The Trademark Act, § 35, authorizes attorney's fees in "exceptional cases." An interesting example with both copyright and trademark elements is Universal City Studios, Inc. v. Nintendo Co., 797 F.2d 70 (2d Cir.1986).

CRIMINAL INFRINGEMENT

Willful copyright infringement done for purposes of commercial advantage or private financial gain is a criminal offense. § 506(a)(1). Responding to United States v. LaMacchia, 871 F.Supp. 535 (D.Mass.1994), where a defendant who provided free access to copyrighted software through a computer bulletin board escaped criminal sanctions due to the absence of financial gain, Congress in 1997 extended criminal liability to the reproduction or distribution of infringing copies with a retail value of more than $1,000. § 506(a)(2). (It also added the liberal definition of "financial gain" in § 101.) Record and movie piracy account for most of the criminal prosecutions, although other infringers (including, alas, the Marx Brothers) are not immune. See Marx v. United States, 96 F.2d 204 (9th Cir.1938). The criminal penalties for infringement are specified in 18 U.S.C.A. § 2319. They can be severe.

On the relationship between civil and criminal infringement actions, consult Young, Criminal Copyright Infringement and a Step Beyond, 30 ASCAP Copyr.L.Symp. 157 (1980). See United States v. Cohen, 946 F.2d 430 (6th Cir.1991), allowing the introduction of evidence from a civil judgment in a criminal prosecution for duplicating videocassettes.

It is a violation of federal law, punishable by a $10,000 fine and ten years imprisonment, to transport "in interstate or foreign commerce any goods, wares, merchandise, securities or money, of the value of $5,000 or more, knowing the same to have been stolen, converted or taken by fraud." 18 U.S.C.A. § 2314. Does the interstate transportation of unauthorized copies of copyrighted works fall within the scope of this prohibition? The Supreme Court held it does not in Dowling v. United States, 473 U.S. 207 (1985).

Can the states apply their own criminal statutes to conduct that infringes federal copyright? See § 301; Crow v. Wainwright, 720 F.2d 1224 (11th Cir.1983), cert. denied, 469 U.S. 819 (1984) (criminal conviction under state record piracy statute overturned as preempted by federal copyright law). But cf. State v. Smith, 115 Wash.2d 434, 798 P.2d 1146 (1990) (defendant would buy a computer program, make copies for sale, and then return it; a state prosecution for theft was not preempted). Can these cases be distinguished? See p. 632 infra.

PART TWO

UNFAIR COMPETITION AND OTHER DOCTRINES BEYOND COPYRIGHT

CHAPTER 7

THE ROOTS OF UNFAIR COMPETITION

SECTION 1. PASSING OFF

Kellogg Co. v. National Biscuit Co.

Supreme Court of the United States, 1938.
305 U.S. 111, 59 S.Ct. 109.

■ MR. JUSTICE BRANDEIS delivered the opinion of the Court.

This suit was brought in the federal court for Delaware[1] by National Biscuit Company against Kellogg Company to enjoin alleged unfair competition by the manufacture and sale of the breakfast food commonly known as shredded wheat. The competition was alleged to be unfair mainly because Kellogg Company uses, like the plaintiff, the name shredded wheat and, like the plaintiff, produces its biscuit in pillow-shaped form.

Shredded wheat is a product composed of whole wheat which has been boiled, partially dried, then drawn or pressed out into thin shreds and baked. The shredded wheat biscuit generally known is pillow-shaped in form. It was introduced in 1893 by Henry D. Perky, of Colorado; and he was connected until his death in 1908 with companies formed to make and

---

1. The federal jurisdiction rests on diversity of citizenship—National Biscuit Company being a New Jersey corporation and Kellogg Company a Delaware corporation. Most of the issues in the case involve questions of common law and hence are within the scope of Erie R. Co. v. Tompkins, 1938, 304 U.S. 64. But no claim has been made that the local law is any different from the general law on the subject, and both parties have relied almost entirely on federal precedents.

market the article. Commercial success was not attained until the Natural Food Company built, in 1901, a large factory at Niagara Falls, New York. In 1908, its corporate name was changed to "The Shredded Wheat Company"; and in 1930 its business and goodwill were acquired by National Biscuit Company.

Kellogg Company has been in the business of manufacturing breakfast food cereals since its organization in 1905. For a period commencing in 1912 and ending in 1919 it made a product whose form was somewhat like the product in question, but whose manufacture was different, the wheat being reduced to a dough before being pressed into shreds. For a short period in 1922 it manufactured the article in question. In 1927, it resumed manufacturing the product. In 1928, the plaintiff sued for alleged unfair competition two dealers in Kellogg shredded wheat biscuits. That suit was discontinued by stipulation in 1930. On June 11, 1932, the present suit was brought. Much evidence was introduced; but the determinative facts are relatively few; and as to most of these there is no conflict.

In 1935, the District Court dismissed the bill. It found that the name "Shredded Wheat" is a term describing alike the product of the plaintiff and of the defendant; and that no passing off or deception had been shown. It held that upon the expiration of the Perky patent No. 548,086 issued October 15, 1895, the name of the patented article passed into the public domain. In 1936, the Circuit Court of Appeals affirmed that decree. Upon rehearing, it vacated, in 1937, its own decree and reversed that of the District Court, with direction "to enter a decree enjoining the defendant from the use of the name 'Shredded Wheat' as its trade-name and from advertising or offering for sale its product in the form and shape of plaintiff's biscuit in violation of its trade-mark; and with further directions to order an accounting for damages and profits." In its opinion the court described the trade-mark as "consisting of a dish, containing two biscuits submerged in milk". 3 Cir., 91 F.2d 150, 152, 155. We denied Kellogg Company's petition for a writ of certiorari, 302 U.S. 733, and denied rehearing 302 U.S. 777.

On January 5, 1938, the District Court entered its mandate in the exact language of the order of the Circuit Court of Appeals, and issued a permanent injunction. Shortly thereafter National Biscuit Company petitioned the Circuit Court of Appeals to recall its mandate "for purposes of clarification." It alleged that Kellogg Company was insisting, contrary to the court's intention, that the effect of the mandate and writ of injunction was to forbid it from selling its product only when the trade name "Shredded Wheat" is applied to a biscuit in the form and shape of the plaintiff's biscuit and is accompanied by a representation of a dish with biscuits in it; and that it was not enjoined from making its biscuit in the form and shape of the plaintiff's biscuit, nor from calling it "Shredded Wheat," unless at the same time it uses upon its cartons plaintiff's trade-mark consisting of a dish with two biscuits in it. On May 5, 1938, the Circuit Court of Appeals granted the petition for clarification and directed the District Court to enter a decree enjoining Kellogg Company (3 Cir., 96 F.2d 873):

"(1) from the use of the name 'Shredded Wheat' as its trade name, (2) from advertising or offering for sale its product in the form and shape of plaintiff's biscuit, and (3) from doing either." * * *

The plaintiff concedes that it does not possess the exclusive right to make shredded wheat. But it claims the exclusive right to the trade name "Shredded Wheat" and the exclusive right to make shredded wheat biscuits pillow-shaped. It charges that the defendant, by using the name and shape, and otherwise, is passing off, or enabling others to pass off, Kellogg goods for those of the plaintiff. Kellogg Company denies that the plaintiff is entitled to the exclusive use of the name or of the pillow-shape; denies any passing off; asserts that it has used every reasonable effort to distinguish its product from that of the plaintiff; and contends that in honestly competing for a part of the market for shredded wheat it is exercising the common right freely to manufacture and sell an article of commerce unprotected by patent.

First. The plaintiff has no exclusive right to the use of the term "Shredded Wheat" as a trade name. For that is the generic term of the article, which describes it with a fair degree of accuracy; and is the term by which the biscuit in pillow-shaped form is generally known by the public. Since the term is generic, the original maker of the product acquired no exclusive right to use it. As Kellogg Company had the right to make the article, it had, also, the right to use the term by which the public knows it. Compare Saxlehner v. Wagner, 216 U.S. 375; Holzapfel's Compositions Co. v. Rahtjen's American Composition Co., 183 U.S. 1. Ever since 1894 the article has been known to the public as shredded wheat.

It is contended that the plaintiff has the exclusive right to the name "Shredded Wheat," because those words acquired the "secondary meaning" of shredded wheat made at Niagara Falls by the plaintiff's predecessor. There is no basis here for applying the doctrine of secondary meaning. The evidence shows only that due to the long period in which the plaintiff or its predecessor was the only manufacturer of the product, many people have come to associate the product, and as a consequence the name by which the product is generally known, with the plaintiff's factory at Niagara Falls. But to establish a trade name in the term "shredded wheat" the plaintiff must show more than a subordinate meaning which applies to it. It must show that the primary significance of the term in the minds of the consuming public is not the product but the producer. This it has not done. The showing which it has made does not entitle it to the exclusive use of the term shredded wheat but merely entitles it to require that the defendant use reasonable care to inform the public of the source of its product. * * *

Second. The plaintiff has not the exclusive right to sell shredded wheat in the form of a pillow-shaped biscuit—the form in which the article became known to the public. That is the form in which shredded wheat was made under the basic patent. The patented machines used were designed to produce only the pillow-shaped biscuits. And a design patent was taken out to cover the pillow-shaped form.[4] Hence, upon expiration of the patents the form, as well as the name, was dedicated to the public. * * *

Where an article may be manufactured by all, a particular manufacturer can no more assert exclusive rights in a form in which the public has become accustomed to see the article and which, in the minds of the public, is primarily associated with the article rather than a particular producer, than it can in the case of a name with similar connections in the public mind. Kellogg Company was free to use the pillow-shaped form, subject only to the obligation to identify its product lest it be mistaken for that of the plaintiff.

Third. The question remains whether Kellogg Company in exercising its right to use the name "Shredded Wheat" and the pillow-shaped biscuit, is doing so fairly. Fairness requires that it be done in a manner which reasonably distinguishes its product from that of plaintiff.

Each company sells its biscuits only in cartons. The standard Kellogg carton contains fifteen biscuits; the plaintiff's twelve. The Kellogg cartons are distinctive. They do not resemble those used by the plaintiff either in size, form, or color. And the difference in the labels is striking. The Kellogg cartons bear in bold script the names "Kellogg's Whole Wheat Biscuit" or "Kellogg's Shredded Whole Wheat Biscuit" so sized and spaced as to strike the eye as being a Kellogg product. It is true that on some of its cartons it had a picture of two shredded wheat biscuits in a bowl of milk which was quite similar to one of the plaintiff's registered trade-marks. But the name Kellogg was so prominent on all of the defendant's cartons as to minimize the possibility of confusion.

* * * The obligation resting upon Kellogg Company is not to insure that every purchaser will know it to be the maker but to use every reasonable means to prevent confusion.

It is urged that all possibility of deception or confusion would be removed if Kellogg Company should refrain from using the name "Shredded Wheat" and adopt some form other than the pillow-shape. But the name and form are integral parts of the goodwill of the article. To share fully in the goodwill, it must use the name and the pillow-shape. And in the goodwill Kellogg Company is as free to share as the plaintiff. Compare William R. Warner & Co. v. Eli Lilly & Co., 265 U.S. 526, 528, 530. Moreover, the pillow-shape must be used for another reason. The evidence is persuasive that this form is functional—that the cost of the biscuit would be increased and its high quality lessened if some other form were substituted for the pillow-shape.

---

4. The design patent would have expired by limitations in 1909. In 1908 it was declared invalid by a district judge on the ground that the design had been in public use for more than two years prior to the application for the patent and theretofore had already been dedicated to the public. Natural Foods Co. v. Bulkley, No. 28,530, U.S.Dist. Ct., N.Dist.Ill., East Div. (1908).

Kellogg Company is undoubtedly sharing in the goodwill of the article known as "Shredded Wheat"; and thus is sharing in a market which was created by the skill and judgment of plaintiff's predecessor and has been widely extended by vast expenditures in advertising persistently made. But that is not unfair. Sharing in the goodwill of an article unprotected by patent or trade-mark is the exercise of a right possessed by all—and in the free exercise of which the consuming public is deeply interested. There is no evidence of passing off or deception on the part of the Kellogg Company; and it has taken every reasonable precaution to prevent confusion or the practice of deception in the sale of its product.

Fourth. By its "clarifying" decree, the Circuit Court of Appeals enjoined Kellogg Company from using the picture of the two shredded wheat biscuits in the bowl only in connection with an injunction against manufacturing the pillow-shaped biscuits and the use of the term shredded wheat, on the grounds of unfair competition. The use of this picture was not enjoined on the independent ground of trade-mark infringement. Since the National Biscuit Company did not petition for certiorari, the question whether use of the picture is a violation of that trade-mark although Kellogg Company is free to use the name and the pillow-shaped biscuit is not here for review.

Decrees reversed with direction to dismiss the bill.

MR. JUSTICE MCREYNOLDS and MR. JUSTICE BUTLER are of opinion that the decree of the Circuit Court of Appeals is correct and should be affirmed. To them it seems sufficiently clear that the Kellogg Company is fraudulently seeking to appropriate to itself the benefits of a goodwill built up at great cost by the respondent and its predecessors.

Boston Professional Hockey Association, Inc. v. Dallas Cap & Emblem Manufacturing, Inc.

United States Court of Appeals, Fifth Circuit, 1975.
510 F.2d 1004.
Certiorari denied 423 U.S. 868, 96 S.Ct. 132.

■ Before BROWN, CHIEF JUDGE, and GODBOLD and RONEY, CIRCUIT JUDGES.

■ RONEY, CIRCUIT JUDGE:

Nearly everyone is familiar with the artistic symbols which designate the individual teams in various professional sports. The question in this case of first impression is whether the unauthorized, intentional duplication of a professional hockey team's symbol on an embroidered emblem, to be sold to the public as a patch for attachment to clothing, violates any legal right of the team to the exclusive use of that symbol. Contrary to the decision of the district court, we hold that the team has an interest in its own individualized symbol entitled to legal protection against such unauthorized duplication.

The National Hockey League (NHL) and thirteen of its member hockey teams brought this action to enjoin Dallas Cap & Emblem Manufacturing,

Inc., from manufacturing and selling embroidered emblems depicting their trademarks. All plaintiffs assert a cause of action for common law unfair competition. The NHL and twelve of the plaintiff teams have secured federal registration of their team symbols as service marks for ice hockey entertainment services and seek relief under both provisions of the Lanham Act, 15 U.S.C.A. §§ 1114, 1125, which give statutory protection to such marks. The Toronto team has not secured federal registration of its symbol and, thus, has not alleged a cause of action against defendant for infringement of a registered mark under 15 U.S.C.A. § 1114, but is restricted to § 1125 which can encompass unregistered marks. The Vancouver team did not secure registration until after the alleged infringing act and has sued only for injunctive relief under § 1114, not for damages. None of the symbols of the various teams have been copyrighted.

The district court denied Lanham Act relief and granted only limited relief for unfair competition, requiring solely that defendant place on the emblems or the package a notice that the emblems are not authorized by or have not emanated from the plaintiffs. The claim for damages was denied.

The Facts

The controlling facts of the case at bar are relatively uncomplicated and uncontested. Plaintiffs play ice hockey professionally. In producing and promoting the sport of ice hockey, plaintiffs have each adopted and widely publicized individual team symbols. * * *

Plaintiffs have authorized National Hockey League Services, Inc. (NHLS) to act as their exclusive licensing agent. NHLS has licensed various manufacturers to use the team symbols on merchandise and has granted to one manufacturer, Lion Brothers Company, Inc., the exclusive license to manufacture embroidered emblems depicting the marks in question. In the spring of 1972, NHLS authorized the sale of NHL team emblems in connection with the sale of Kraft candies. That promotion alone was advertised on more than five million bags of candy.

Defendant Dallas Cap & Emblem Manufacturing, Inc., is in the business of making and selling embroidered cloth emblems. In August of 1968 and June of 1971, defendant sought to obtain from NHLS an exclusive license to make embroidered emblems representing the team motifs. Although these negotiations were unsuccessful, defendant went ahead and manufactured and sold without authorization emblems which were substantial duplications of the marks. During the month of April 1972, defendant sold approximately 24,603 of these emblems to sporting goods stores in various states. Defendant deliberately reproduced plaintiffs' marks on embroidered emblems and intended the consuming public to recognize the emblems as the symbols of the various hockey teams and to purchase them as such.

The Law

The complaint alleged that defendant's manufacture and sale of the team symbols constitutes (1) an infringement of the plaintiffs' registered marks in violation of 15 U.S.C.A. § 1114;[2] (2) false designation of origin in violation of 15 U.S.C.A. § 1125;[3] and (3) common law unfair competition.

The statutory cause of action emanates from what is commonly called the Lanham Act. 15 U.S.C.A. § 1051 et seq. The Lanham Act defines a service mark as "a mark used in the sale or advertising of services to identify the services of one person and distinguish them from the services of others" and a trademark as "any word, name, symbol, or device or any combination thereof adopted and used by a manufacturer or merchant to identify his goods and distinguish them from those manufactured or sold by others." 15 U.S.C.A. § 1127. Service mark infringement and trademark infringement are governed by identical standards. The terms can be used interchangeably when the marks are both service marks and trademarks. For convenience we use the word trademark in this opinion to designate both service mark and trademark use of the symbols involved.

A cause of action for the infringement of a registered mark in violation of 15 U.S.C.A. § 1114 exists where a person uses (1) any reproduction, counterfeit, copy or colorable imitation of a mark; (2) without the registrant's consent; (3) in commerce; (4) in connection with the sale, offering for sale, distribution or advertising of any goods; (5) where such use is likely to cause confusion, or to cause mistake or to deceive. A broadening of the protection afforded by the statute occurred by amendment in 1962 which deleted the previously existing requirement that the confusion or deception must relate to the "source of origin of such goods or service." Pub.L. 87–772, § 17, 76 Stat. 773 (1962). Continental Motors Corp. v. Continental Aviation Corp., 375 F.2d 857, 860 at n. 8 (5th Cir.1967).

* * * The use of an unregistered trademark can constitute a violation of § 1125 where

> ... the alleged unregistered trademarks used by the plaintiff are so associated with its goods that the use of the same or similar marks by another company constitutes a representation that its goods come from the same source.

2. 15 U.S.C.A. § 1114 reads in pertinent part:

(1) Any person who shall, without the consent of the registrant—

(a) use in commerce any reproduction, counterfeit, copy, or colorable imitation of a registered mark in connection with the sale, offering for sale, distribution, or advertising of any goods or services on or in connection with which such use is likely to cause confusion, or to cause mistake, or to deceive;

. . .

shall be liable in a civil action by the registrant for the remedies hereinafter provided.

3. 15 U.S.C.A. § 1125 reads in pertinent part:

(a) Any person who shall affix, apply, or annex, or use in connection with any goods or services, or any container or containers for goods, a false designation of origin, or any false description or representation, including words or other symbols tending falsely to describe or represent the same, and shall cause such goods or services to enter into commerce, ... shall be liable to a civil action by any person doing business in the locality falsely indicated as that of origin or in the region in which said locality is situated, or by any person who believes that he is or is likely to be damaged by the use of any such false description or representation.

[The text of § 1125(a) as subsequently amended in 1988 appears at p. 583 infra.]

Joshua Meier Co. v. Albany Novelty Mfg. Co., 236 F.2d 144, 147 (2nd Cir.1956).   * * *   Under § 1125, the registration of a mark is not a prerequisite of recovery as it is under § 1114.

Unfair competition is a broader area of the law than statutory trademark infringement.   B.H. Bunn Co. v. AAA Replacement Parts Co., 451 F.2d 1254 (5th Cir.1971).   Unfair competition is almost universally regarded as a question of whether the defendant is passing off his goods or services as those of the plaintiff by virtue of substantial similarity between the two, leading to confusion on the part of potential customers.   * * * As a general rule, therefore, the same facts which would support an action for trademark infringement would also support an action for unfair competition.

The Case

The difficulty with this case stems from the fact that a reproduction of the trademark itself is being sold, unattached to any other goods or services.   The statutory and case law of trademarks is oriented toward the use of such marks to sell something other than the mark itself.   The district court thought that to give plaintiffs protection in this case would be tantamount to the creation of a copyright monopoly for designs that were not copyrighted.   The copyright laws are based on an entirely different concept than the trademark laws, and contemplate that the copyrighted material, like patented ideas, will eventually pass into the public domain.   The trademark laws are based on the needed protection of the public and business interests and there is no reason why trademarks should ever pass into the public domain by the mere passage of time.

Although our decision here may slightly tilt the trademark laws from the purpose of protecting the public to the protection of the business interests of plaintiffs, we think that the two become so intermeshed when viewed against the backdrop of the common law of unfair competition that both the public and plaintiffs are better served by granting the relief sought by plaintiffs.   * * *

As to 15 U.S.C.A. § 1114.

Plaintiffs indisputably have established the first three elements of a § 1114 cause of action.   Plaintiffs' marks are validly registered and defendant manufactured and sold emblems which were (1) substantial duplications of the marks, (2) without plaintiffs' consent, and (3) in interstate commerce.   The issue is whether plaintiffs have proven elements four and five of an action for mark infringement under the Lanham Act, i.e., whether the symbols are used in connection with the sale of goods and whether such use is likely to cause confusion, mistake or deception.

The fourth requisite of a § 1114 cause of action is that the infringing use of the registered mark must be in connection with the sale, offering for sale, distribution or advertising of any goods.   Although the district court did not expressly find that plaintiffs had failed to establish element four, such a finding was implicit in the court's statement that "in the instant case, the registered trade mark is, in effect, the product itself."

Defendant is in the business of manufacturing and marketing emblems for wearing apparel. These emblems are the products, or goods, which defendant sells. When defendant causes plaintiffs' marks to be embroidered upon emblems which it later markets, defendant uses those marks in connection with the sale of goods as surely as if defendant had embroidered the marks upon knit caps. * * *

The fifth element of a cause of action for mark infringement under 15 U.S.C.A. § 1114 is that the infringing use is likely to cause confusion, or to cause mistake or to deceive. The district court decided that there was no likelihood of confusion because the usual purchaser, a sports fan in his local sporting goods store, would not be likely to think that defendant's emblems were manufactured by or had some connection with plaintiffs. Cf. Sun–Maid Raisin Growers of California v. Sunaid Food Products, Inc., 356 F.2d 467 (5th Cir.1966). This court has held that the findings of a district court as to likelihood of confusion are factual and not to be overturned unless clearly erroneous. Hang Ten International v. Sherry Manufacturing Co., 498 F.2d 326 (5th Cir.1974); American Foods, Inc. v. Golden Flake, Inc., 312 F.2d 619 (5th Cir.1963). In this case, however, the district court overlooked the fact that the act was amended to eliminate the source of origin as being the only focal point of confusion. The confusion question here is conceptually difficult. It can be said that the public buyer *knew* that the emblems portrayed the teams' symbols. Thus, it can be argued, the buyer is not confused or deceived. This argument misplaces the purpose of the confusion requirement. The confusion or deceit requirement is met by the fact that the defendant duplicated the protected trademarks and sold them to the public knowing that the public would identify them as being the teams' trademarks. The certain knowledge of the buyer that the source and origin of the trademark symbols were in plaintiffs satisfies the requirement of the act. The argument that confusion must be as to the source of the manufacture of the emblem itself is unpersuasive, where the trademark, originated by the team, is the triggering mechanism for the sale of the emblem.

The plaintiffs, with the exception of Toronto, have satisfied all elements of a cause of action for mark infringement in violation of 15 U.S.C.A. § 1114. Plaintiffs are entitled to an injunction permanently enjoining defendant from the manufacture and sale, in interstate commerce, of emblems embroidered with substantial duplications of plaintiffs' marks without plaintiffs' consent, and such other relief as might flow from the facts.

As to 15 U.S.C.A. § 1125.

The district court held that plaintiffs failed to prove a cause of action under 15 U.S.C.A. § 1125 for false designation of origin of the goods in question or for false description by means of symbols. Because all plaintiffs, with the exception of Toronto, have established a cause of action for registered mark infringement, the district court's decision in regard to a § 1125 cause of action only affects plaintiff Toronto. The district court based its denial of a § 1125 cause of action on two findings of fact: (1) there was no likelihood of confusion as to the source of the emblems and (2) defendant did not make any false representations concerning the origin of the emblems. Our decision that confusion is self-evident from the nature of defendant's use of plaintiffs' marks applies with equal force in plaintiff Toronto's case. We reverse. * * *

* * * In the language of § 1125, defendant used a symbol, Toronto's mark, which tended falsely to represent goods, the embroidered emblems, in commerce. Where the consuming public had the certain knowledge that the source and origin of the trademark symbol was in the Toronto team, the reproduction of that symbol by defendant constituted a violation of § 1125.

To warrant injunctive relief under § 1125, a plaintiff must demonstrate that the false representations have a tendency to deceive the consumer. Geisel v. Poynter Products, Inc., 283 F.Supp. 261 (S.D.N.Y.1968). Our decision that defendant's use of plaintiffs' marks entails a likelihood of confusion under § 1114 establishes that defendant's identical use of Toronto's mark constitutes a false representation under § 1125. See Girl Scouts v. Personality Posters Mfg. Co., 304 F.Supp. 1228 (S.D.N.Y.1969). Accordingly, we reverse the decision of the district court and hold that Toronto has established a cause of action under 15 U.S.C.A. § 1125.

As to Unfair Competition.

Although the district court denied plaintiffs relief under the applicable provisions of the Lanham Act, the court found that the actions of defendant constituted unfair competition. The court stated that defendant's use of plaintiffs' marks had ". . . the prospect of trading on the competitive advantage the mark originator has to the public which desires the 'official' product." Unfair competition is a question of fact, Volkswagenwerk Aktiengesellschaft v. Rickard, 492 F.2d 474 (5th Cir.1974). Our review is narrowly circumscribed by F.R.Civ.P. 52(a). We find that there is substantial evidence which reflects that defendant competed unfairly with plaintiffs and, accordingly, we affirm the decision of the district court in this regard.

The unfair competition cannot, however, be rendered fair by the disclaimer ordered by the district court. The exact duplication of the symbol and the sale as the team's emblem satisfying the confusion requirement of the law, words which indicate it was not authorized by the trademark owner are insufficient to remedy the illegal confusion. Only a prohibition of the unauthorized use will sufficiently remedy the wrong.

Additional Defenses to Relief

Defendant makes two arguments against an extension of Lanham Act protection to plaintiffs which need consideration. Adopting the district court's rationale, defendant asserts first, that plaintiffs' marks when embroidered on emblems for wearing apparel are functional and, thus, serve no trademark purpose and, second, that there is some overriding concept of free competition which, under the instant facts, would remove plaintiffs from the protective ambits of the Lanham Act.

The short answer to defendant's arguments is that the emblems sold because they bore the identifiable trademarks of plaintiffs. This fact clearly distinguishes the case from Pagliero v. Wallace China Co., 198 F.2d 339 (9th Cir.1952), relied upon by the district court. *Pagliero* involved designs on chinaware which were neither trademarked, patented nor copyrighted. The court found no unfair competition on the ground that the designs were functional, that is, they connoted other than a trademark purpose. "The attractiveness and eye-appeal of the design sells the china," 198 F.2d at pp. 343–344, not the trademark character of the designs. In the case at bar, the embroidered symbols are sold not because of any such aesthetic characteristic but because they are the trademarks of the hockey teams. * * *

The argument that the symbols could be protected only if copyrighted likewise misses the thrust of trademark protection. A trademark is a property right which is acquired by use. Trade–Mark Cases, 100 U.S. 82 (1879). It differs substantially from a copyright, in both its legal genesis and its scope of federal protection. The legal cornerstone for the protection of copyrights is Article I, section 8, clause 8 of the Constitution. In the case of a copyright, an individual creates a unique design and, because the Constitutional fathers saw fit to encourage creativity, he can secure a copyright for his creation for a period of 28 years, renewable once. After the expiration of the copyright, his creation becomes part of the public domain. In the case of a trademark, however, the process is reversed. An individual selects a word or design that might otherwise be in the public domain to represent his business or product. If that word or design comes to symbolize his product or business in the public mind, the individual acquires a property right in the mark. The acquisition of such a right through use represents the passage of a word or design out of the public domain into the protective ambits of trademark law. Under the provisions of the Lanham Act, the owner of a mark acquires a protectable property interest in his mark through registration and use. * * *

Reversed and remanded.

NOTES AND QUESTIONS

(1) Would copyright be a serviceable alternative to any of the trademark and unfair competition claims raised in *Kellogg* or *Boston Hockey?* Recall that the former concerned in part an illustration "consisting of a dish, containing two biscuits submerged in milk"; the latter, "artistic symbols" designating individual teams.

(2) Consider the various theories discussed in *Boston Hockey.* Each appears to require a finding that confusion is likely. The typical trademark case involves allegations that the defendant has used a trademark similar or identical to a mark associated with the plaintiff in a manner that is

likely to cause confusion as to the source or sponsorship of the defendant's goods. About what, exactly, were purchasers of defendant's patches confused? Confusion aside, do other interests support the result?

Boston Hockey has been distinguished and limited in later decisions for its loose interpretation of the confusion requirement. The issue is considered further at p. 689 infra.

NOTE ON "PRINTS OR LABELS"

The 1909 Copyright Act, in § 5(k), included among its classification of copyrightable works "prints or labels used for articles of merchandise." See Kitchens of Sara Lee, Inc. v. Nifty Foods Corp., 266 F.2d 541 (2d Cir.1959) (copyright in illustrations of bakery products held valid and infringed). In the 1976 Act prints and labels are absorbed into the category of "pictorial, graphic, and sculptural works," with no intention, it is said, to narrow the scope of copyright. H.R.Rep. p. 54. But copyright in labels and packaging is sharply limited by the requirement of authorship. The cases, echoing Copyright Office policy, demand "an appreciable amount of original text or pictorial material." *Kitchens of Sara Lee,* supra; Alberto–Culver Co. v. Andrea Dumon, Inc., 466 F.2d 705 (7th Cir.1972). Lists of ingredients or contents, serving directions, and brief descriptive texts are thus excluded from copyright, as are short phrases such as slogans, names, and titles. See 37 C.F.R. § 202.1(a).

A NOTE ON THE LAW OF TRADEMARKS AND UNFAIR COMPETITION

The two preceding cases bring into consideration a number of important elements of the law of trademarks and unfair competition. Both accept as axiomatic that attempts to pass off one's goods as those of another are actionable. This is the foundation of the expanding law of unfair competition. Unfair competition is a vigorous and sometimes unconfined companion of copyright. Application of its doctrines to literary and artistic works has become commonplace; Chapters 8 and 9 offer numerous illustrations. An understanding of the scope of contemporary unfair competition law calls for some knowledge of both common law trademark protection and the federal statutory regime that supplements (but does not supplant) it.

(1) *Common Law Protection.* The law of trademarks and unfair competition has its roots in the common law action of deceit. The gravamen of the original tort was the fraudulent marketing of goods through the imitation of another's trademark. Injury to the aggrieved trademark owner was direct—customers who by whim or design had chosen to patronize the plaintiff were diverted instead to an imposter. Consumer confusion was thus the touchstone.

The common law of trademarks, however, became entangled in an etymological thicket that sometimes obscured the dominant role of the confusion rationale. Trademarks that consisted of a coined word, such as KODAK on cameras, or an arbitrary word whose primary meaning was not relevant to the goods on which it appeared, such as SHELL on gasoline, were denominated "technical trademarks." These fanciful or arbitrary marks were protected upon adoption, and the owner's rights could be vindicated in an action for "trademark infringement." It was not uncommon to characterize the plaintiff's interest in such a mark as a property right. However, marks consisting of words whose primary meanings were descriptive of the goods to which they were affixed, such as RICH 'N CHIPS on chocolate chip cookies, were not accorded the status of technical trademarks. This distinction reflected a reluctance to permit the exclusive appropriation of terms in which competitors could claim some legitimate interest. Yet even the use of a descriptive term can cause confusion if the public has come to associate the term with a particular producer. This source significance for descriptive terms is what, in a triumph of obfuscation, came to be called "secondary meaning"—this despite the fact that in the relevant market the primary significance of the term is now one of identification rather than description. The word WHEATIES on a box of cereal, for example, will be understood as more than a description of the ingredients; use on a cereal sold by a competitor of General Mills will likely cause confusion as to source. The common law offered redress for appropriations of descriptive terms that had acquired "secondary meaning" through an action for "unfair competition." But plaintiff's rights extend only to the secondary meaning—a "fair use" of the term in its non-trademark, descriptive sense does not infringe. Cf. 15 U.S.C.A. § 1115(b)(4). The technical distinctions between actions for "trademark infringement" and "unfair competition" gradually fell into disuse; source significance, inherent or acquired, and the likelihood of consumer confusion, remain the dominant issues.

Protection against unfair competition can reach beyond words and symbols used on goods or services. The themes of identification and confusion extended easily to business and corporate names, and these too are protected at common law. The general appearance of labels and packaging, if duplicated by a competitor, also can create confusion, and the common law stood ready, upon a showing of source significance, to prohibit the infringement of a seller's "trade dress." Indeed, the appearance and design of the goods themselves nowadays often serve as an indication of origin; thus, product simulation that causes confusion of source can be actionable as "unfair competition."

The common law proscription against passing off was eventually supplemented at the state level by statutory trademark protection. Much of the modern legislation derives from the Model State Trademark Bill. With the exception of the anti-dilution provisions noted below, however, these state statutes merely reaffirm basic common law doctrines.

The development of the common law of unfair competition is traced in McClure, Trademarks and Unfair Competition: A Critical History of Legal Thought, 69 Trademark Rep. 305 (1979), supplemented by Trademarks and

Competition: The Recent History, 59 L. & Contemp.Prob. (No. 2) 13 (1996).

(2) *Registration Under the Lanham Act.* Federal trademark statutes until 1946 did little more than provide access to the federal courts through a system of trademark registration; a thoroughgoing revision of that year known as the Lanham Act, 15 U.S.C.A. § 1051 et seq., does much more, but it too remains in general congruence with common law doctrines. (Selected provisions of the Lanham Act are reproduced in the Statutory Supplement.)

The registration system established by the Lanham Act is administered by the Patent and Trademark Office of the Department of Commerce. Protection extends chiefly to "trademarks" and "service marks" that have been registered on the Principal Register. Business and corporate names, which the Lanham Act calls "trade names," are not registrable as such, but if the name is also employed as a trademark or service mark, it is in that capacity eligible for registration. Before the 1988 revision of the Lanham Act, actual use of the mark in interstate commerce was a prerequisite to registration. Section 1(b), 15 U.S.C.A. § 1051(b), now permits an application based on an intention to use the mark, thus providing a measure of security for pre-marketing expenditures. But intent must be followed in due course (generally six months) by actual use.

There are several important restrictions on the kinds of marks that will be received on the Principal Register. Section 2(d) of the Lanham Act, 15 U.S.C.A. § 1052(d), prohibits the registration of marks which so resemble marks or trade names used by another "as to be likely, when used on or in connection with the goods of the applicant, to cause confusion, or to cause mistake, or to deceive"; section 2(e) excludes "a mark which, (1) when used on or in connection with the goods of the applicant is merely descriptive or deceptively misdescriptive of them, (2) when used on or in connection with the goods of the applicant is primarily geographically descriptive of them * * *, or (4) is primarily merely a surname." These subsection (e) exclusions can be overcome, however, by meeting the requirements of § 2(f), which authorizes "the registration of a mark used by the applicant which has become distinctive of the applicant's goods in commerce"—that is, which has acquired secondary meaning. (A "Supplemental Register" is maintained for marks that are merely "capable of distinguishing" source, in aid of registration abroad where a domestic registration is often a prerequisite to foreign registration. §§ 23–28, 15 U.S.C.A. §§ 1091–96.)

A distinction is often drawn, both at common law and under the Lanham Act, between marks that are *descriptive* (and thus require a showing of secondary meaning) and those that are considered instead merely *suggestive* of the virtues or characteristics of the goods (and thus entitled to immediate registration and protection as inherently distinctive). Thus, "Tender Vittles" may be descriptive of a moist cat food, Ralston Purina Co. v. Thomas J. Lipton, Inc., 341 F.Supp. 129 (S.D.N.Y.1972); but "Mouse Seed" only suggestive of a rodent poison. W.G. Reardon Laboratories, Inc. v. B & B Exterminators, Inc., 71 F.2d 515 (4th Cir.1934). The distinction, at best, is a fragile one.

When a designation is said to be "generic," it means that it is used by consumers as the name of the product itself, regardless of source, and thus cannot be monopolized by a single producer. This was the holding with respect to "Shredded Wheat." Even a coined word that initially qualifies as a trademark can become generic. Famous examples include "aspirin" and "cellophane." Bayer Co., Inc. v. United Drug Co., 272 Fed. 505 (S.D.N.Y.1921); DuPont Cellophane Co. v. Waxed Products Co., 85 F.2d 75 (2d Cir.1936). Under § 14 of the Lanham Act, a registration may be canceled if the mark becomes the generic name for the goods or services. 15 U.S.C.A. § 1064(3). Such determinations can be delicate; a single word may function both as a product name and an indication of source. See Folsom & Teply, Trademarked Generic Words, 89 Yale L.J. 1323 (1980). (For a case that stirred considerable controversy as a result of its unusual formulation of the applicable standard, see Anti–Monopoly, Inc. v. General Mills Fun Group, Inc., 684 F.2d 1316 (9th Cir.1982), cert. denied, 459 U.S. 1227 (1983), holding generic the registered trademark "Monopoly" as used on the well-known board game. It prompted an amendment to § 14 emphasizing that a mark is not generic merely because it is also used as the name of a "unique" product; the "primary significance" of the word to the public is decisive.) Recall also that one of the questions before the Supreme Court in *Kellogg* was "whether Kellogg Company in exercising its right to use the name 'Shredded Wheat' * * * is doing so fairly."

Early decisions read the Lanham Act's definition of "trademark" to preclude registration on the Principal Register of product and container configurations; a more liberal view took root in 1958 with the registration by Haig & Haig of its "Pinch" bottle for scotch whiskey. Ex parte Haig & Haig, Ltd., 118 U.S.P.Q. 229 (Comm'r Pat.1958). Although occasionally a shape or feature will be considered inherently distinctive and thus entitled to immediate registration, applicants are usually required to demonstrate that the design has achieved secondary meaning as an indication of source.

Even though the appearance of an article may be distinctive of its source, neither the Lanham Act nor the common law will forbid others to imitate it if the design is "functional." Functional in this context means that the feature contributes to the efficient manufacture or performance of the product or otherwise yields a competitive advantage not easily duplicated by alternative designs. The Supreme Court, for example, found the shape of the shredded wheat biscuit functional and thus, absent a valid patent, not susceptible of exclusive appropriation. Plaintiffs proving source significance for functional features must be content with orders mandating labeling or other measures intended to minimize confusion. See, e.g., American Greetings Corp. v. Dan–Dee Imports, Inc., 807 F.2d 1136 (3d Cir.1986); Keene Corp. v. Paraflex Industries, Inc., 653 F.2d 822 (3d Cir.1981).

When goods are purchased in part for their aesthetic qualities, ornamental features unrelated to the physical operation of the product may be considered "functional" if a prohibition on imitation would substantially hinder competition. Thus, "aesthetic functionality" is not unknown in the case law. It was to these cases that the defendant in *Boston Hockey* unsuccessfully appealed.

(3) *The Test for Infringement.* Although registration under the Lanham Act provides a variety of procedural and remedial advantages, the standard of infringement remains, as at common law, the likelihood of confusion. Section 32(1), quoted by the court in *Boston Hockey,* bears repeating:

> Any person who shall, without the consent of the registrant—
>
> (a) use in commerce any reproduction, counterfeit, copy, or colorable imitation of a registered mark in connection with the sale, offering for sale, distribution, or advertising of any goods or services on or in connection with which such use is likely to cause confusion, or to cause mistake, or to deceive * * * shall be liable in a civil action by the registrant for the remedies hereinafter provided. * * * (15 U.S.C.A. § 1114(1))

One court set the stage for a determination of infringement by declaring:

> We begin with the oft-repeated observation that the essential question in any case of alleged trademark infringement brought under the Lanham Act or under the law of unfair competition is "whether a substantial number of ordinarily prudent purchasers are likely to be misled or confused as to the source of different products." [a]

Establishing a likelihood of confusion can be difficult. The impersonal nature of the marketplace may make proof of actual confusion impossible. The plaintiff's burden is sometimes lightened by the willingness of judges to project a likelihood of confusion on the basis of an examination of the goods and marks. Consumer surveys, properly conducted, can be decisive.

For a time the law of trademarks was concerned only with the use of confusingly similar marks on directly competing goods. Yet a trademark owner's reputation and goodwill may be endangered even when its mark is applied to types of products that the trademark owner does not sell. During the first half of this century the concept of unfair competition grew to include the unauthorized use of marks on non-competing goods, provided that the goods were sufficiently related to cause a likelihood of confusion. As usual, the classic formulation is Judge Hand's:

> There is indeed a limit; the goods on which the supposed infringer puts the mark may be too remote from any that the owner would be likely to make or sell. It would be hard, for example, for the

---

a. Information Clearing House, Inc. v. Find Magazine, 492 F.Supp. 147, 154 (S.D.N.Y.1980) (quoting Mushroom Makers, Inc. v. R.G. Barry Corp., 441 F.Supp. 1220, 1225 (S.D.N.Y.1977), aff'd, 580 F.2d 44 (2d Cir.1978), cert. denied, 439 U.S. 1116 (1979)).

seller of a steam shovel to find ground for complaint in the use of his trade-mark on a lipstick.

L.E. Waterman Co. v. Gordon, 72 F.2d 272, 273 (2d Cir.1934).

The likelihood of confusion can turn on a number of variables. Among the most important is the distinctiveness of the plaintiff's mark, often described in terms of "strong" versus "weak" marks. The archetype of strong marks is KODAK—fanciful, non-descriptive, prestigious, yet devoid of generic overtones. Probably no one else can use that word as a trademark on anything. Weak marks are typically descriptive or common—"Gold Medal" or "Acme." Their scope of protection is accordingly narrow.

In an extension of the non-competing goods cases, confusion of sponsorship has come to be an accepted basis for a finding of infringement. Unauthorized use of the name of a teenage fashion magazine in connection with the sale of girls clothing led to an early articulation of the principle. See Triangle Pub. v. Rohrlich, 167 F.2d 969 (2d Cir.1948). Confusion of sponsorship claims appear frequently in cases challenging the unauthorized use of symbols derived from the worlds of sport and entertainment. See, e.g., Dallas Cowboys Cheerleaders, Inc. v. Pussycat Cinema, Ltd., 604 F.2d 200 (2d Cir.1979); National Football League Properties, Inc. v. Wichita Falls Sportswear, Inc., 532 F.Supp. 651 (W.D.Wash.1982).

Neither the Lanham Act nor the common law, however, prohibits the *non-deceptive* use of another's trademark to communicate truthful information about a product, for example, in comparative advertising. See, e.g., Prestonettes, Inc. v. Coty, 264 U.S. 359 (1924); Smith v. Chanel, Inc., 402 F.2d 562 (9th Cir.1968).

(4) *Section 43(a) of the Lanham Act.* This section is an oddity among the provisions of the Lanham Act; unlike the remainder of the Act, § 43(a), 15 U.S.C.A. § 1125, is not about registered trademarks:

(a)(1) Any person who, on or in connection with any goods or services, or any container for goods, uses in commerce any word, term, name, symbol, or device, or any combination thereof, or any false designation of origin, false or misleading description of fact, or false or misleading representation of fact, which—

(A) is likely to cause confusion, or to cause mistake, or to deceive as to the affiliation, connection, or association of such person with another person, or as to the origin, sponsorship, or approval of his or her goods, services, or commercial activities by another person, or

(B) in commercial advertising or promotion, misrepresents the nature, characteristics, qualities, or geographic origin of his or her or another person's goods, services, or commercial activities,

shall be liable in a civil action by any person who believes that he or she is or is likely to be damaged by such act.

It is generally agreed that § 43(a) as originally enacted (see footnote 3 to *Boston Hockey*) was intended at least to overcome a much-criticized rule that false statements by a seller about itself or its products were not actionable by a competitor unless the plaintiff could show that the false-hoods were uniquely and directly damaging to it.   This was the rule of American Washboard Co. v. Saginaw Mfg. Co., 103 Fed. 281 (6th Cir.1900), as reinforced by Mosler Safe Co. v. Ely–Norris Safe Co., 273 U.S. 132 (1927).   Although § 43(a) may have been envisioned as a federal false advertising statute, it also evolved into something of a federal law of unfair competition, encompassing the infringement of unregistered marks, names, and trade dress.   It was for the latter purpose that the section was invoked in *Boston Hockey*.   The expansion of § 43(a) was sometimes criticized, see Germain, Unfair Trade Practices Under § 43(a) of the Lanham Act: You've Come a Long Way Baby—Too Far Maybe, 49 Ind.L.Rev. 84 (1973), but the 1988 revision confirms its application not only to false advertising, but also to infringement and passing off, which, apart from federally registered marks, had been the exclusive domain of the states since the demise of federal common law.

Section 43(a) is an important adjunct to copyright; it will be encountered often in the succeeding materials.   The breadth of § 43(a) is examined in McCarthy, Lanham Act § 43(a): The Sleeping Giant is Now Wide Awake, 59 L. & Contemp.Prob. (No. 2) 45 (1996); Bauer, A Federal Law of Unfair Competition: What Should be the Reach of § 43(a) of the Lanham Act?, 31 UCLA L.Rev. 671 (1984).

(5) *Dilution.*   The prevention of confusion is the primary aim of conventional trademark doctrine.   But there is also a persistent view that regards the identification function of trademarks as secondary, emphasizing instead the undoubted advertising and commercial values that inhere in successful symbols.   These symbols, it is argued, should be protected against dilution, that is, against any use that may drain off the potency of the mark, regardless of the likelihood of confusion.   This view was first propounded in this country in Schechter, The Rational Basis of Trademark Protection, 40 Harv.L.Rev. 813 (1927).   It has achieved statutory recognition in more than half of the states; the formulation in the Model State Trademark Bill § 12 (1964) is typical:

> Likelihood of injury to business reputation or of dilution of the distinctive quality of a mark registered under this Act, or a mark valid at common law, or a trade name valid at common law, shall be a ground for injunctive relief notwithstanding the absence of competition between the parties or the absence of confusion as to the source of goods or services.

(Compare the revised version in Model State Trademark Bill § 13 (1992)).

The wisdom of shielding marks against a dilution of their advertising and commercial value has been questioned.   See, e.g., R. Brown, Advertising and the Public Interest: Legal Protection of Trade Symbols, 57 Yale L.J. 1165 (1948), arguing that protection should be confined to the informational function of trademarks.   The dispute is part of a more general disagreement concerning the economic implications of extensive trademark protection.

Judicial hostility to the dilution statutes has been well documented. See, e.g., Pattishall, The Dilution Rationale for Trademark—Trade Identity Protection, Its Progress and Prospects, 71 Nw.L.Rev. 618 (1976). Some courts, for example, insisted upon some showing of confusion despite the plain dictates of the statutes. There is a trend, however, toward warmer acceptance of the dilution doctrine, at least when the plaintiff's mark is highly distinctive. See Deere & Co. v. MTD Prod., Inc., 41 F.3d 39 (2d Cir.1994); Hyatt Corp. v. Hyatt Legal Services, 736 F.2d 1153 (7th Cir.), cert. denied, 469 U.S. 1019 (1984); Allied Maintenance Corp. v. Allied Mechanical Trades, Inc., 42 N.Y.2d 538, 399 N.Y.S.2d 628, 369 N.E.2d 1162 (1977). Compare Pattishall, supra, with Pattishall, Dawning Acceptance of the Dilution Rationale for Trademark—Trade Identity Protection, 74 Trademark Rep. 289 (1984).

The dilution statutes have been invoked in two distinct situations. The distinctiveness of a mark as the identifying symbol of a particular company can be vitiated, even in the absence of confusion, if others use the same mark to identify themselves or their products. This was the theory relied upon by the owner of the LEXIS legal research service in its unsuccessful attempt to stop the use by Toyota of LEXUS on luxury cars. Mead Data Central, Inc. v. Toyota Motor Sales, U.S.A., Inc., 875 F.2d 1026 (2d Cir.1989). (Did the defendant's use in *Boston Hockey* pose a threat to the distinctiveness of the plaintiffs' marks?) In addition to this blurring of distinctiveness, courts sometimes have been induced to enjoin the "tarnishment" of trademarks. Confusion aside, the image of a prestigious mark can be damaged by its appearance on inferior products or on goods incompatible with those of the trademark owner, or by its use in other unflattering or unwholesome settings. Such injury frequently has been forestalled through manipulation of the confusion rationale;[b] the anti-dilution statutes offer more direct protection. When the defendant's use can be characterized as noncommercial speech, however, plaintiff's objection to the unwelcome reference may be met by an assertion of first amendment rights. Film-maker George Lucas, for example, was unsuccessful in his attempt to stop the media and public interest groups from using his STAR WARS trademark to characterize President Reagan's Strategic Defense Initiative, Lucasfilm Ltd. v. High Frontier, 622 F.Supp. 931 (D.D.C.1985), and L.L. Bean failed in an attempt to enjoin a prurient parody of its famous catalog. L.L. Bean, Inc. v. Drake Publishers, Inc., 811 F.2d 26 (1st Cir.), cert. denied, 483 U.S. 1013 (1987). In Cliffs Notes, Inc. v. Bantam Doubleday Dell Pub. Group, Inc., 886 F.2d 490 (2d Cir.1989),

---

b. See, e.g., Mutual of Omaha Ins. Co. v. Novak, 836 F.2d 397 (8th Cir.1987) (likelihood of confusion found in the use of an insurance company's Indian Head logo on T-shirts with the words "Mutant of Omaha" and "Nuclear Holocaust Insurance"); General Electric v. Alumpa Coal Co., 205 U.S.P.Q. 1036 (D.Mass.1979) ("Genital Electric" on T-shirts and briefs enjoined based on a likelihood of confusion); Coca–Cola Co. v. Gemini Rising, Inc., 346 F.Supp. 1183 (E.D.N.Y.1972) ("Enjoy Coca–Cola" design altered on posters to advocate "Enjoy Cocaine"; injunction issued on a confusion rationale).

Spy Notes, a parody by *Spy* magazine of the *Cliffs Notes* study guides, was protected on first amendment grounds against a § 43(a) claim of confusion. Should the trademark rights asserted in the poster and T-shirt cases cited in footnote b, supra, yield to a similar first amendment analysis? Some of the issues are discussed in Denicola, Trademarks as Speech: Constitutional Implications of the Emerging Rationales for the Protection of Trade Symbols, 1982 Wis.L.Rev. 158. Myers, Trademark Parody: Lessons from the Copyright Decision in *Campbell v. Acuff–Rose Music, Inc.,* 59 L. & Contemp.Prob. (No. 2) 181 (1996), applies learning from the copyright parody cases to trademark parodies. See also Dreyfuss, Expressive Genericity: Trademarks as Language in the Pepsi Generation, 65 Notre Dame L.Rev. 397 (1990), arguing that the courts have gone too far in providing protection against "expressive" uses of well-known trade symbols.

In 1995, protection against dilution became part of the Lanham Act through the addition of § 43(c) and the definition of "dilution" in § 45. "Famous" marks, both registered and unregistered, are protected from use that "causes dilution of the distinctive quality of the mark." Dilution, in turn, is defined as "the lessening of the capacity of a famous mark to identify and distinguish goods or services" without regard to competition or likelihood of confusion. (A separate prohibition against conduct likely to disparage or tarnish a mark that had appeared in an earlier version of the legislation was not included.) Can dilution, as defined in the Lanham Act, occur if a defendant does not use the symbol as a trademark to identify the defendant's own products? An argument that federal protection under § 43(c) reaches only uses that blur the distinctiveness of a trademark and does not extend to tarnishment is made in Denicola, Some Thoughts on the Dynamics of Federal Trademark Legislation and the Federal Dilution Act of 1995, 59 L. & Contemp.Prob. (No. 2) 75 (1996).

(6) *References.* A number of substantial areas of trademark law have not even been mentioned in this brief introduction, including such matters as registration procedures, the geographic limits of protection, assignment and licensing of marks, remedies, and antitrust problems. The most helpful treatise on the law of unfair competition is J. McCarthy, Trademarks and Unfair Competition (Clark Boardman Callaghan). See also Restatement (Third) of Unfair Competition (1995). On registration under the Lanham Act, see J. Gilson, Trademark Protection and Practice (Matthew Bender). Articles and other materials appear bimonthly in the Trademark Reporter.

For a concise orientation, see Treece and Stephenson, A Look at American Trademark Law, 29 Sw.L.Rev. 547 (1975). For an introduction to the economics of trademark doctrine, see Landes and Posner, Trademark Law: An Economic Perspective, 30 J.L. & Econ. 265 (1987).

There is also a complex system of international trademark protection, dominated by the 1883 Paris Union for the Protection of Industrial Property and its subsequent revisions. See generally S. Ladas, Patents, Trademarks, and Related Rights (1975).

SECTION 2. MISAPPROPRIATION

International News Service v. Associated Press

Supreme Court of the United States, 1918.
248 U.S. 215, 39 S.Ct. 68.

■ MR. JUSTICE PITNEY delivered the opinion of the Court.

The parties are competitors in the gathering and distribution of news and its publication for profit in newspapers throughout the United States. The Associated Press, which was complainant in the District Court, is a cooperative organization, incorporated under the Membership Corporations Law of the State of New York, its members being individuals who are either proprietors or representatives of about 950 daily newspapers published in all parts of the United States. * * * Complainant gathers in all parts of the world, by means of various instrumentalities of its own, by exchange with its members, and by other appropriate means, news and intelligence of current and recent events of interest to newspaper readers and distributes it daily to its members for publication in their newspapers. The cost of the service, amounting approximately to $3,500,000 per annum, is assessed upon the members and becomes a part of their costs of operation, to be recouped, presumably with profit, through the publication of their several newspapers. Under complainant's by-laws each member agrees upon assuming membership that news received through complainant's service is received exclusively for publication in a particular newspaper, language, and place specified in the certificate of membership, that no other use of it shall be permitted, and that no member shall furnish or permit anyone in his employ or connected with his newspaper to furnish any of complainant's news in advance of publication to any person not a member. And each member is required to gather the local news of his district and supply it to the Associated Press and to no one else.

Defendant is a corporation organized under the laws of the State of New Jersey, whose business is the gathering and selling of news to its customers and clients, consisting of newspapers published throughout the United States, under contracts by which they pay certain amounts at stated times for defendant's service. It has wide-spread news-gathering agencies; the cost of its operations amounts, it is said, to more than $2,000,000 per annum; and it serves about 400 newspapers located in the various cities of the United States and abroad, a few of which are represented, also, in the membership of the Associated Press.

The parties are in the keenest competition between themselves in the distribution of news throughout the United States; and so, as a rule, are the newspapers that they serve, in their several districts. * * *

The bill was filed to restrain the pirating of complainant's news by defendant in three ways: First, by bribing employees of newspapers published by complainant's members to furnish Associated Press news to defendant before publication, for transmission by telegraph and telephone to defendant's clients for publication by them; Second, by inducing Associated Press members to violate its by-laws and permit defendant to obtain news before publication; and, Third, by copying news from bulletin boards and from early editions of complainant's newspapers and selling this, either bodily or after rewriting it, to defendant's customers.

The District Court, upon consideration of the bill and answer, with voluminous affidavits on both sides, granted a preliminary injunction under the first and second heads; but refused at that stage to restrain the systematic practice admittedly pursued by defendant, of taking news bodily from the bulletin boards and early editions of complainant's newspapers and selling it as its own. The court expressed itself as satisfied that this practice amounted to unfair trade, but as the legal question was one of first impression it considered that the allowance of an injunction should await the outcome of an appeal. 240 Fed. 983, 996. Both parties having appealed, the Circuit Court of Appeals sustained the injunction order so far as it went, and upon complainant's appeal modified it and remanded the cause with directions to issue an injunction also against any bodily taking of the words or substance of complainant's news until its commercial value as news had passed away. 245 Fed. 244, 253. The present writ of certiorari was then allowed. 245 U.S. 644.

The only matter that has been argued before us is whether defendant may lawfully be restrained from appropriating news taken from bulletins issued by complainant or any of its members, or from newspapers published by them, for the purpose of selling it to defendant's clients. Complainant asserts that defendant's admitted course of conduct in this regard both violates complainant's property rights in the news and constitutes unfair competition in business. And notwithstanding the case has proceeded only to the stage of a preliminary injunction, we have deemed it proper to consider the underlying questions, since they go to the very merits of the action and are presented upon facts that are not in dispute. As presented in argument, these questions are: (1) Whether there is any property in news; (2) Whether, if there be property in news collected for the purpose of being published, it survives the instant of its publication in the first newspaper to which it is communicated by the news-gatherer; and (3) Whether defendant's admitted course of conduct in appropriating for commercial use matter taken from bulletins or early editions of Associated Press publications constitutes unfair competition in trade.

The federal jurisdiction was invoked because of diversity of citizenship, not upon the ground that the suit arose under the copyright or other laws of the United States. Complainant's news matter is not copyrighted. It is said that it could not, in practice, be copyrighted, because of the large number of dispatches that are sent daily; and, according to complainant's contention, news is not within the operation of the copyright act. Defendant, while apparently conceding this, nevertheless invokes the analogies of the law of literary property and copyright, insisting as its principal contention that, assuming complainant has a right of property in its news, it can be maintained (unless the copyright act be complied with) only by being kept secret and confidential, and that upon the publication with complainant's consent of uncopyrighted news by any of complainant's members in a newspaper or upon a bulletin board, the right of property is lost, and the subsequent use of the news by the public or by defendant for any purpose whatever becomes lawful.   * * *

In considering the general question of property in news matter, it is necessary to recognize its dual character, distinguishing between the substance of the information and the particular form or collocation of words in which the writer has communicated it.

No doubt news articles often possess a literary quality, and are the subject of literary property at the common law; nor do we question that such an article, as a literary production, is the subject of copyright by the terms of the act as it now stands.   * * *

But the news element—the information respecting current events contained in the literary production—is not the creation of the writer, but is a report of matters that ordinarily are *publici juris;* it is the history of the day.   It is not to be supposed that the framers of the Constitution, when they empowered Congress "to promote the progress of science and useful arts, by securing for limited times to authors and inventors the exclusive right to their respective writings and discoveries" (Const. art. 1, § 8, par. 8), intended to confer upon one who might happen to be the first to report a historic event the exclusive right for any period to spread the knowledge of it.

We need spend no time, however, upon the general question of property in news matter at common law, or the application of the copyright act, since it seems to us the case must turn upon the question of unfair competition in business.   And, in our opinion, this does not depend upon any general right of property analogous to the common-law right of the proprietor of an unpublished work to prevent its publication without his consent; nor is it foreclosed by showing that the benefits of the copyright act have been waived.   We are dealing here not with restrictions upon publication but with the very facilities and processes of publication.   The peculiar value of news is in the spreading of it while it is fresh; and it is evident that a valuable property interest in the news, as news, cannot be maintained by keeping it secret.   Besides, except for matters improperly disclosed, or published in breach of trust or confidence, or in violation of law, none of which is involved in this branch of the case, the news of current events may be regarded as common property.   What we are concerned with is the business of making it known to the world, in which both parties to the present suit are engaged.   * * * The parties are competitors in this field; and, on fundamental principles, applicable here as elsewhere, when the rights or privileges of the one are liable to conflict with those of the other, each party is under a duty so to conduct its own business as not unnecessarily or unfairly to injure that of the other.   * * *

* * * The question here is not so much the rights of either party as against the public but their rights as between themselves. See Morison v. Moat, 9 Hare, 241, 258. And, although we may and do assume that neither party has any remaining property interest as against the public in uncopyrighted news matter after the moment of its first publication, it by no means follows that there is no remaining property interest in it as between themselves. For, to both of them alike, news matter, however little susceptible of ownership or dominion in the absolute sense, is stock in trade, to be gathered at the cost of enterprise, organization, skill, labor, and money, and to be distributed and sold to those who will pay money for it, as for any other merchandise. Regarding the news, therefore, as but the material out of which both parties are seeking to make profits at the same time and in the same field, we hardly can fail to recognize that for this purpose, and as between them, it must be regarded as *quasi* property, irrespective of the rights of either as against the public. * * *

The question, whether one who has gathered general information or news at pains and expense for the purpose of subsequent publication through the press has such an interest in its publication as may be protected from interference, has been raised many times, although never, perhaps, in the precise form in which it is now presented.

Board of Trade v. Christie Grain & Stock Co., 198 U.S. 236, 250, related to the distribution of quotations of prices on dealings upon a board of trade, which were collected by plaintiff and communicated on confidential terms to numerous persons under a contract not to make them public. This court held that, apart from certain special objections that were overruled, plaintiff's collection of quotations was entitled to the protection of the law; that, like a trade secret, plaintiff might keep to itself the work done at its expense, and did not lose its right by communicating the result to persons, even if many, in confidential relations to itself, under a contract not to make it public; and that strangers should be restrained from getting at the knowledge by inducing a breach of trust. * * *

Not only do the acquisition and transmission of news require elaborate organization and a large expenditure of money, skill, and effort; not only has it an exchange value to the gatherer, dependent chiefly upon its novelty and freshness, the regularity of the service, its reputed reliability and thoroughness, and its adaptability to the public needs; but also, as is evident, the news has an exchange value to one who can misappropriate it.

The peculiar features of the case arise from the fact that, while novelty and freshness form so important an element in the success of the business, the very processes of distribution and publication necessarily occupy a good deal of time. Complainant's service, as well as defendant's, is a daily service to daily newspapers; most of the foreign news reaches this country at the Atlantic seaboard, principally at the city of New York, and because of this, and of time differentials due to the earth's rotation, the distribution of news matter throughout the country is principally from east to west; and, since in speed the telegraph and telephone easily outstrip the rotation of the earth, it is a simple matter for defendant to take complainant's news from bulletins or early editions of complainant's members in the eastern cities and at the mere cost of telegraphic transmission cause it to be published in western papers issued at least as early as those served by complainant. Besides this, and irrespective of time differentials, irregularities in telegraphic transmission on different lines, and the normal consumption of time in printing and distributing the newspaper, result in permitting pirated news to be placed in the hands of defendant's readers sometimes simultaneously with the service of competing Associated Press papers, occasionally even earlier. * * *

* * * The right of the purchaser of a single newspaper to spread knowledge of its contents gratuitously, for any legitimate purpose not unreasonably interfering with complainant's right to make merchandise of it, may be admitted; but to transmit that news for commercial use, in competition with complainant—which is what defendant has done and seeks to justify—is a very different matter. In doing this defendant, by its very act, admits that it is taking material that has been acquired by complainant as the result of organization and the expenditure of labor, skill, and money, and which is salable by complainant for money, and that defendant in appropriating it and selling it as its own is endeavoring to reap where it has not sown, and by disposing of it to newspapers that are competitors of complainant's members is appropriating to itself the harvest of those who have sown. Stripped of all disguises, the process amounts to an unauthorized interference with the normal operation of complainant's legitimate business precisely at the point where the profit is to be reaped, in order to divert a material portion of the profit from those who have earned it to those who have not; with special advantage to defendant in the competition because of the fact that it is not burdened with any part of the expense of gathering the news. The transaction speaks for itself and a court of equity ought not to hesitate long in characterizing it as unfair competition in business. * * *

The contention that the news is abandoned to the public for all purposes when published in the first newspaper is untenable. Abandonment is a question of intent, and the entire organization of the Associated Press negatives such a purpose. The cost of the service would be prohibitive if the reward were to be so limited. No single newspaper, no small group of newspapers, could sustain the expenditure. Indeed, it is one of the most obvious results of defendant's theory that, by permitting indiscriminate publication by anybody and everybody for purposes of profit in competition with the news-gatherer, it would render publication profitless, or so little profitable as in effect to cut off the service by rendering the cost prohibitive in comparison with the return. The practical needs and requirements of the business are reflected in complainant's by-laws which have been referred to. Their effect is that publication by each member must be deemed not by any means an abandonment of the news to the world for any and all purposes, but a publication for limited purposes; for the benefit of the readers of the bulletin or the newspaper as such; not for the purpose of making merchandise of it as news, with the result of depriving complainant's other members of their reasonable opportunity to obtain just returns for their expenditures.

It is to be observed that the view we adopt does not result in giving to complainant the right to monopolize either the gathering or the distribution of the news, or, without complying with the copyright act, to prevent the reproduction of its news articles, but only postpones participation by complainant's competitor in the processes of distribution and reproduction of news that it has not gathered, and only to the extent necessary to prevent that competitor from reaping the fruits of complainant's efforts and expenditure, to the partial exclusion of complainant, and in violation of the principle that underlies the maxim *sic utere tuo,* etc.

It is said that the elements of unfair competition are lacking because there is no attempt by defendant to palm off its goods as those of the complainant, characteristic of the most familiar, if not the most typical, cases of unfair competition. Howe Scale Co. v. Wyckoff, Seamans, etc., 198 U.S. 118, 140. But we cannot concede that the right to equitable relief is confined to that class of cases. In the present case the fraud upon complainant's rights is more direct and obvious. Regarding news matter as the mere material from which these two competing parties are endeavoring to make money, and treating it, therefore, as *quasi* property for the purposes of their business because they are both selling it as such, defendant's conduct differs from the ordinary case of unfair competition in trade principally in this that, instead of selling its own goods as those of complainant, it substitutes misappropriation in the place of misrepresentation, and sells complainant's goods as its own.

Besides the misappropriation, there are elements of imitation, of false pretense, in defendant's practices. The device of rewriting complainant's news articles, frequently resorted to, carries its own comment. The habitual failure to give credit to complainant for that which is taken is significant. Indeed, the entire system of appropriating complainant's news and transmitting it as a commercial product to defendant's clients and patrons amounts to a false representation to them and to their newspaper readers that the news transmitted is the result of defendant's own investigation in the field. But these elements, although accentuating the wrong, are not the essence of it. It is something more than the advantage of celebrity of which complainant is being deprived. * * *

As to securing "tips" from a competing news agency, the District Court (240 Fed. 991, 995), while not sanctioning the practice, found that both parties had adopted it in accordance with common business usage, in the belief that their conduct was technically lawful, and hence did not find in it any sufficient ground for attributing unclean hands to complainant. The Circuit Court of Appeals (245 F. 247) found that the tip habit, though discouraged by complainant, was "incurably journalistic," and that there was "no difficulty in discriminating between the utilization of tips and the bodily appropriation of another's labor in accumulating and stating information."

We are inclined to think a distinction may be drawn between the utilization of tips and the bodily appropriation of news matter, either in its original form or after rewriting and without independent investigation and verification; whatever may appear at the final hearing, the proofs as they now stand recognize such a distinction; both parties avowedly recognize the practice of taking tips, and neither party alleges it to be unlawful or to amount to unfair competition in business. * * *

There is some criticism of the injunction that was directed by the District Court upon the going down of the mandate from the Circuit Court of Appeals. In brief, it restrains any taking or gainfully using of the complainant's news, either bodily or in substance, from bulletins issued by the complainant or any of its members, or from editions of their newspapers, *"until its commercial value as news to the complainant and all of its members has passed away."* The part complained of is the clause we have italicized; but if this be indefinite, it is no more so than the criticism. Perhaps it would be better that the terms of the injunction be made specific, and so framed as to confine the restraint to an extent consistent with the reasonable protection of complainant's newspapers, each in its own area and for a specified time after its publication, against the competitive use of pirated news by defendant's customers. But the case presents practical difficulties; and we have not the materials, either in the way of a definite suggestion of amendment, or in the way of proofs, upon which to frame a specific injunction; hence, while not expressing approval of the form adopted by the District Court, we decline to modify it at this preliminary stage of the case, and will leave that court to deal with the matter upon appropriate application made to it for the purpose.

The decree of the Circuit Court of Appeals will be

Affirmed.[a]

■ MR. JUSTICE CLARKE took no part in the consideration or decision of this case.

■ MR. JUSTICE HOLMES:

When an uncopyrighted combination of words is published there is no general right to forbid other people repeating them—in other words there is no property in the combination or in the thoughts or facts that the words express. Property, a creation of law, does not arise from value, although exchangeable—a matter of fact. Many exchangeable values may be destroyed intentionally without compensation. Property depends upon exclusion by law from interference, and a person is not excluded from using any combination of words merely because some one has used it before, even if it took labor and genius to make it. If a given person is to be prohibited from making the use of words that his neighbors are free to make some other ground must be found. One such ground is vaguely expressed in the

---

a. The decree, entered by consent of the defendant on May 19, 1919, simply enjoined it from "gainfully using * * * complainant's news, either bodily or in substance, * * * until its commercial value as news to the complainant and all of its members has passed away." Complainant submitted to a like injunction.

phrase unfair trade. This means that the words are repeated by a competitor in business in such a way as to convey a misrepresentation that materially injures the person who first used them, by appropriating credit of some kind which the first user has earned. The ordinary case is a representation by device, appearance, or other indirection that the defendant's goods come from the plaintiff. But the only reason why it is actionable to make such a representation is that it tends to give the defendant an advantage in his competition with the plaintiff and that it is thought undesirable that an advantage should be gained in that way. Apart from that the defendant may use such unpatented devices and uncopyrighted combinations of words as he likes. The ordinary case, I say, is palming off the defendant's product as the plaintiff's but the same evil may follow from the opposite falsehood—from saying whether in words or by implication, that the plaintiff's product is the defendant's, and that, it seems to me, is what has happened here.

Fresh news is got only by enterprise and expense. To produce such news as it is produced by the defendant represents by implication that it has been acquired by the defendant's enterprise and at its expense. When it comes from one of the great news collecting agencies like the Associated Press, the source generally is indicated, plainly importing that credit; and that such a representation is implied may be inferred with some confidence from the unwillingness of the defendant to give the credit and tell the truth. If the plaintiff produces the news at the same time that the defendant does, the defendant's presentation impliedly denies to the plaintiff the credit of collecting the facts and assumes that credit to the defendant. If the plaintiff is later in western cities it naturally will be supposed to have obtained its information from the defendant. The falsehood is a little more subtle, the injury a little more indirect, than in ordinary cases of unfair trade, but I think that the principle that condemns the one condemns the other. It is a question of how strong an infusion of fraud is necessary to turn a flavor into a poison. The dose seems to me strong enough here to need a remedy from the law. But as, in my view, the only ground of complaint that can be recognized without legislation is the implied misstatement, it can be corrected by stating the truth; and a suitable acknowledgment of the source is all that the plaintiff can require. I think that within the limits recognized by the decision of the Court the defendant should be enjoined from publishing news obtained from the Associated Press for ___ hours after publication by the plaintiff unless it gives express credit to the Associated Press; the number of hours and the form of acknowledgment to be settled by the District Court.

■ MR. JUSTICE McKENNA concurs in this opinion.

■ MR. JUSTICE BRANDEIS dissenting. * * *

No question of statutory copyright is involved. The sole question for our consideration is this: Was the International News Service properly enjoined from using, or causing to be used gainfully, news of which it acquired knowledge by lawful means (namely, by reading publicly posted bulletins or papers purchased by it in the open market) merely because the news had been originally gathered by the Associated Press and continued to be of value to some of its members, or because it did not reveal the source from which it was acquired? * * *

News is a report of recent occurrences. The business of the news agency is to gather systematically knowledge of such occurrences of interest and to distribute reports thereof. The Associated Press contended that knowledge so acquired is property, because it costs money and labor to produce and because it has value for which those who have it not are ready to pay; that it remains property and is entitled to protection as long as it has commercial value as news; and that to protect it effectively the defendant must be enjoined from making, or causing to be made, any gainful use of it while it retains such value. An essential element of individual property is the legal right to exclude others from enjoying it. If the property is private, the right of exclusion may be absolute; if the property is affected with a public interest, the right of exclusion is qualified. But the fact that a product of the mind has cost its producer money and labor, and has a value for which others are willing to pay, is not sufficient to ensure to it this legal attribute of property. The general rule of law is, that the noblest of human productions—knowledge, truths ascertained, conceptions, and ideas—become, after voluntary communication to others, free as the air to common use. Upon these incorporeal productions the attribute of property is continued after such communication only in certain classes of cases where public policy has seemed to demand it. These exceptions are confined to productions which, in some degree, involve creation, invention, or discovery. But by no means all such are endowed with this attribute of property. The creations which are recognized as property by the common law are literary, dramatic, musical, and other artistic creations; and these have also protection under the copyright statutes. The inventions and discoveries upon which this attribute of property is conferred only by statute, are the few comprised within the patent law. There are also many other cases in which courts interfere to prevent curtailment of plaintiff's enjoyment of incorporeal productions; and in which the right to relief is often called a property right, but is such only in a special sense. In those cases, the plaintiff has no absolute right to the protection of his production; he has merely the qualified right to be protected as against the defendant's acts, because of the special relation in which the latter stands or the wrongful method or means employed in acquiring the knowledge or the manner in which it is used. Protection of this character is afforded where the suit is based upon breach of contract or of trust or upon unfair competition.

The knowledge for which protection is sought in the case at bar is not of a kind upon which the law has heretofore conferred the attributes of property; nor is the manner of its acquisition or use nor the purpose to which it is applied, such as has heretofore been recognized as entitling a plaintiff to relief.

First: Plaintiff's principal reliance was upon the "ticker" cases; but they do not support its contention. The leading cases on this subject rest the grant of relief, not upon the existence of a general property right in news, but upon the breach of a contract or trust concerning the use of news communicated; and that element is lacking here.   * * *

Second: Plaintiff also relied upon the cases which hold that the common law right of the producer to prohibit copying is not lost by the private circulation of a literary composition, the delivery of a lecture, the exhibition of a painting, or the performance of a dramatic or musical composition. These cases rest upon the ground that the common law recognizes such productions as property which, despite restricted communication, continues until there is a dedication to the public under the copyright statutes or otherwise. But they are inapplicable for two reasons: (1) At common law, as under the copyright acts, intellectual productions are entitled to such protection only if there is underneath something evincing the mind of a creator or originator, however modest the requirement. The mere record of isolated happenings, whether in words or by photographs not involving artistic skill, are denied such protection. (2) At common law, as under the copyright acts, the element in intellectual productions which secures such protection is not the knowledge, truths, ideas, or emotions which the composition expresses, but the form or sequence in which they are expressed; that is "some new collocation of visible, or audible points—of lines, colors, sounds, or words." See White–Smith Music Co. v. Apollo Co., 209 U.S. 1, 19; Kalem Co. v. Harper Bros., 222 U.S. 55, 63. An author's theories, suggestions, and speculations, or the systems, plans, methods, and arrangements of an originator, derive no such protection from the statutory copyright of the book in which they are set forth; and they are likewise denied such protection at common law. * * *

Third: If news be treated as possessing the characteristics not of a trade secret, but of literary property, then the earliest issue of a paper of general circulation or the earliest public posting of a bulletin which embodies such news would, under the established rules governing literary property, operate as a publication, and all property in the news would then cease. Resisting this conclusion, plaintiff relied upon the cases which hold that uncopyrighted intellectual and artistic property survives private circulation or a restricted publication; and it contended that in each issue of each paper, a restriction is to be implied, that the news shall not be used gainfully in competition with the Associated Press or any of its members. There is no basis for such an implication. But it is also well settled that where the publication is in fact a general one, even express words of restriction upon use are inoperative. * * *

Fourth: Plaintiff further contended that defendant's practice constitutes unfair competition, because there is "appropriation without cost to itself of values created by" the plaintiff; and it is upon this ground that the decision of this court appears to be based. To appropriate and use for profit, knowledge and ideas produced by other men, without making compensation or even acknowledgment, may be inconsistent with a finer sense of propriety; but, with the exceptions indicated above, the law has heretofore sanctioned the practice. Thus it was held that one may ordinarily make and sell anything in any form, may copy with exactness that which another has produced, or may otherwise use his ideas without his consent and without the payment of compensation, and yet not inflict a legal injury; and that ordinarily one is at perfect liberty to find out, if he can by lawful means, trade secrets of another, however valuable, and then use the knowledge so acquired gainfully, although it cost the original owner much in effort and in money to collect or produce.

Such taking and gainful use of a product of another which, for reasons of public policy, the law has refused to endow with the attributes of property, does not become unlawful because the product happens to have been taken from a rival and is used in competition with him. The unfairness in competition which hitherto has been recognized by the law as a basis for relief, lay in the manner or means of conducting the business; and the manner or means held legally unfair involves either fraud or force or the doing of acts otherwise prohibited by law. [Discussion of the categories of actionable unfair competition, and of the lawfulness, in Justice Brandeis' view, of the purpose of INS in taking news from AP, of its means of obtaining it, and its manner of using it, is omitted. INS, says Brandeis, was under no obligation to disclose the source of the news, and made no misrepresentation.]

Fifth: The great development of agencies now furnishing countrywide distribution of news, the vastness of our territory, and improvements in the means of transmitting intelligence, have made it possible for a news agency or newspapers to obtain, without paying compensation, the fruit of another's efforts and to use news so obtained gainfully in competition with the original collector. The injustice of such action is obvious. But to give relief against it would involve more than the application of existing rules of law to new facts. It would require the making of a new rule in analogy to existing ones. The unwritten law possesses capacity for growth; and has often satisfied new demands for justice by invoking analogies or by expanding a rule or principle. This process has been in the main wisely applied and should not be discontinued. Where the problem is relatively simple, as it is apt to be when private interests only are involved, it generally proves adequate. But with the increasing complexity of society, the public interest tends to become omnipresent; and the problems presented by new demands for justice cease to be simple. Then the creation or recognition by courts of a new private right may work serious injury to the general public, unless the boundaries of the right are definitely established and wisely guarded. In order to reconcile the new private right with the public interest, it may be necessary to prescribe limitations and rules for its enjoyment; and also to provide administrative machinery for enforcing the rules. It is largely for this reason that, in the effort to meet the many new demands for justice incident to a rapidly changing civilization, resort to legislation has latterly been had with increasing frequency.

The rule for which the plaintiff contends would effect an important extension of property rights and a corresponding curtailment of the free use of knowledge and of ideas; and the facts of this case admonish us of the danger involved in recognizing such a property right in news, without imposing upon news-gatherers corresponding obligations. A large majority of the newspapers and perhaps half the newspaper readers of the United States are dependent for their news of general interest upon agencies other than the Associated Press. The channel through which about 400 of these papers received, as the plaintiff alleges, "a large amount of news relating to the European war of the greatest importance and of intense interest to the newspaper reading public" was suddenly closed. The closing to the International News Service of these channels for foreign news (if they were closed) was due not to unwillingness on its part to pay the cost of collecting the news, but to the prohibitions imposed by foreign governments upon its securing news from their respective countries and from using cable or telegraph lines running therefrom.[b] [Brandeis speculates on the possibility that the newspapers subscribing to the INS service might have been glad to become members of AP if they could have done so. A legislature urged to enact a law to protect news from appropriation would have to consider what evils it might bring in its train, whether an injunction in addition to damages should be provided, whether a public utility concept should be adopted, etc.]

Courts are ill-equipped to make the investigations which should precede a determination of the limitations which should be set upon any property right in news or of the circumstances under which news gathered by a private agency should be deemed affected with a public interest. Courts would be powerless to prescribe the detailed regulations essential to full enjoyment of the rights conferred or to introduce the machinery required for enforcement of such regulations. Considerations such as these should lead us to decline to establish a new rule of law in the effort to redress a newly disclosed wrong, although the propriety of some remedy appears to be clear.

RECEPTION OF THE MISAPPROPRIATION RATIONALE

Despite the broad implications of the Court's opinion, it had for many years only sporadic influence. Judge Learned Hand, repeating the objections of Justice Brandeis, thought the decision a threat to the balance struck by Congress in the federal copyright and patent laws. In a series of opinions for the Second Circuit, he simply read *INS* out of existence.[c] Although his views eventually lost sway, see Capitol Records v. Mercury Records Corp., 221 F.2d 657 (2d Cir.1955), similar concerns would later reappear within the Supreme Court itself. The next section reviews the subsequent upheaval.

---

b. INS had been denied the use of cables controlled by the Allied powers in November 1916, for alleged violations of censorship and distortion of news. See Gramling, AP: The Story of News 285 (1940).

c. See Cheney Brothers v. Doris Silk Corp., p. 638 infra; RCA Mfg. Co. v. White-man, 114 F.2d 86 (2d Cir.), cert. denied, 311 U.S. 712 (1940); National Comics Pub. v. Fawcett Pub., 191 F.2d 594 (2d Cir.1951); G. Ricordi & Co. v. Haendler, 194 F.2d 914 (2d Cir.1952).

Typical of the cases rejecting a "misappropriation" claim is Germanow v. Standard Unbreakable Watch Crystals, 283 N.Y. 1, 27 N.E.2d 212 (1940). Plaintiff, with about 50% of the business in replacement watch crystals, supplied a special cabinet, together with a numbering system for locating the right crystal. Defendant offered, at a lower price, a line of crystals specifically adapted for plaintiff's cabinet and system. Plaintiff had no patent or other statutory protection, and dealers who were customers of both parties were not deceived. A decree for plaintiff was reversed.

A misappropriation claim raised by the National Football League against the use of its football scores in a state lottery was rejected in National Football League v. Governor of Delaware, 435 F.Supp. 1372, 1378 (D.Del.1977). "It is true that Delaware is thus making profits it would not make but for the existence of the NFL, but I find this difficult to distinguish from the multitude of charter bus companies who generate profit from servicing those of plaintiffs' fans who want to go to the stadium or, indeed, the sidewalk popcorn salesman who services the crowd as it surges towards the gate." Attempts to invoke the doctrine to prohibit the imitation of successful products have also been consistently rejected. See, e.g., Cheney Brothers v. Doris Silk Corp., p. 638 infra. Nevertheless, in a few areas, the doctrine flourished.

On the specific issue decided in *INS*—appropriation of news by a competitor—plaintiffs continued to prevail. Radio stations that relied on newspaper subscriptions rather than news bureaus, and trade journals guilty of appropriating information from competitors, were unable to escape the reach of *INS*.[d]

Another line of cases in which misappropriation arguments have sometimes succeeded involves the unauthorized broadcasting of sporting events. The leading case is Pittsburgh Athletic Co. v. KQV Broadcasting Co., 24 F.Supp. 490 (W.D.Pa.1938). Plaintiff granted a third party exclusive broadcasting rights to its baseball games; defendant was enjoined from broadcasting the games from vantage points outside the park. (But cf. WCVB–TV v. Boston Athletic Ass'n, 926 F.2d 42 (1st Cir.1991), refusing to enjoin an unauthorized telecast of the Boston Marathon, run on the public streets of Boston and neighboring towns.)

The *INS* rationale has occasionally triumphed in other contexts. It became an important tool in the battle against record piracy.[e] It also has been invoked to prevent the unauthorized sale of items as varied as photographs of a World's Fair,[f] recorded performances of the Metropolitan

d. See, e.g., Associated Press v. KVOS, 80 F.2d 575 (9th Cir.1935), reversed for want of jurisdiction, 299 U.S. 269 (1936); Pottstown Daily News Pub. Co. v. Pottstown Broadcasting, Co., 411 Pa. 383, 192 A.2d 657 (1963); McCord Co. v. Plotnick, 108 Cal. App.2d 392, 239 P.2d 32 (1951).

e. See, e.g., A & M Records, Inc. v. M.V.C. Distrib. Corp., 574 F.2d 312 (6th Cir. 1978); Mercury Record Prod., Inc. v. Economic Consultants, Inc., 64 Wis.2d 163, 218 N.W.2d 705 (1974), appeal dismissed, 420 U.S. 914 (1975). See p. 662 infra.

f. New York World's Fair 1964–1965 Corp. v. Colourpicture Pub., Inc., 141 U.S.P.Q. 939 (N.Y.Sup.Ct.), aff'd, 21 A.D.2d 896, 251 N.Y.S.2d 885 (1964).

Opera,[g] answers to problems in a college textbook,[h] and a photographic reproduction of another's typeset edition of a public domain book.[i] More recently it has been invoked to restrict the unauthorized use of well-known stock indices such as the Dow Jones Industrial Average in connection with the sale of stock market futures contracts.[j] Another decision, however, drew back from the stock indices cases in a suit involving use of the U.S. Golf Association's handicapping formula by a computerized handicapping service. After tracing the development of the misappropriation doctrine, the Third Circuit in United States Golf Ass'n v. St. Andrews Systems, Data–Max, Inc., 749 F.2d 1028 (3d Cir.1984), distinguished *INS* in that here the defendant's use was only indirectly competitive with the U.S.G.A. and thus "falls outside the misappropriation doctrine, since the public interest in free access outweighs the public interest in providing an additional incentive to the creator or gatherer of information." The court affirmed the defendant's summary judgment. "Where such a monopoly is unnecessary to protect the basic incentive for the production of the idea or information involved, we do not believe that the creator's interest in its ideas or information justifies such an extensive restraint on competition."

The cycles in the history of the misappropriation doctrine are traced in Sease, Misappropriation is Seventy–Five Years Old; Should We Bury or Revive It?, 70 N.Dak.L.Rev. 781 (1994).

NOTES AND QUESTIONS

(1) The opinion of the Supreme Court in *INS* invites analysis. Is the case best viewed as an assertion of natural law property rights? Why did the Court so intently examine the economics of news-gathering?

What is the cost of prohibiting the defendant's appropriation and from whom is it extracted?

Is it of any relevance that three decades after the decision the Associated Press was found to have violated the antitrust laws by unduly restricting both its membership and the disposition of its news by members? Associated Press v. United States, 326 U.S. 1 (1945).

(2) Does *INS* raise first amendment concerns? It was decided before the Supreme Court "discovered" the first amendment. If similar facts arose today, how would "freedom of the press" and "right to know" arguments influence the outcome or the remedy?

---

g. Metropolitan Opera Ass'n v. Wagner–Nichols Recorder Corp., 199 Misc. 786, 101 N.Y.S.2d 483 (Sup.Ct.1950), aff'd, 279 A.D. 632, 107 N.Y.S.2d 795 (1951).

h. Addison–Wesley Pub. Co. v. Brown, 207 F.Supp. 678 (E.D.N.Y.1962) (see also 223 F.Supp. 219 (E.D.N.Y.1963)).

i. Grove Press, Inc. v. Collectors Pub., Inc., 264 F.Supp. 603 (C.D.Cal.1967).

j. Standard & Poor's Corp. v. Commodity Exchange, Inc., 683 F.2d 704 (2d Cir. 1982) (but also finding a likelihood of confusion); Board of Trade of Chicago v. Dow Jones & Co., 98 Ill.2d 109, 456 N.E.2d 84 (1983). The cases are discussed in Baird, Note (3) infra.

(3) Among the numerous attempts to tame the misappropriation doctrine are Rahl, The Right to "Appropriate" Trade Values, 23 Ohio St.L.J. 56 (1962) and Baird, Common Law Intellectual Property and the Legacy of International News Service v. Associated Press, 50 U.Chi.L.Rev. 411 (1983). The attempt to curtail the misappropriation doctrine in § 38 of the Restatement (Third) of Unfair Competition (1995) is applauded in Myers, The Restatement's Rejection of the Misappropriation Tort: A Victory for the Public Domain, 47 S.Car.L.Rev. 673 (1996). See also Gordon, On Owning Information: Intellectual Property and the Restitutionary Impulse, 78 Va.L.Rev. 149 (1992), worrying that the impulse to grant relief results in overprotection at the expense of the community interest in access, and Raskind, The Misappropriation Doctrine as a Competitive Norm of Intellectual Property Law, 75 Minn.L.Rev. 875 (1991), also arguing that recognition of the misappropriation rationale should be limited. And in assessing the merits of any claim to intellectual property, we should not neglect the significance of the public domain "as a field of individual rights fully as important as any of the new property rights." Lange, Recognizing The Public Domain, 44 L. & Contemp.Prob. (No. 4) 147, 178 (1981).

In defining the formal precedential scope of *INS*, note that it was a diversity case presumably declaring federal common law. But may the states adopt the rationale as part of their own law of unfair competition? Only to the extent that it survives federal preemption, the topic of the following section.

SECTION 3. PREEMPTION

Sears, Roebuck & Co. v. Stiffel Co.

Supreme Court of the United States, 1964.
376 U.S. 225, 84 S.Ct. 784.

■ MR. JUSTICE BLACK delivered the opinion of the Court.

The question in this case is whether a State's unfair competition law can, consistently with the federal patent laws, impose liability for or prohibit the copying of an article which is protected by neither a federal patent nor a copyright. The respondent, Stiffel Company, secured design and mechanical patents on a "pole lamp"—a vertical tube having lamp fixtures along the outside, the tube being made so that it will stand upright between the floor and ceiling of a room. Pole lamps proved a decided commercial success, and soon after Stiffel brought them on the market Sears, Roebuck & Company put on the market a substantially identical lamp, which it sold more cheaply, Sears' retail price being about the same as Stiffel's wholesale price. Stiffel then brought this action against Sears in the United States District Court for the Northern District of Illinois, claiming in its first count that by copying its design Sears had infringed Stiffel's patents and in its second count that by selling copies of Stiffel's lamp Sears had caused confusion in the trade as to the source of the lamps and had thereby engaged in unfair competition under Illinois law. There was evidence that identifying tags were not attached to the Sears lamps although labels appeared on the cartons in which they were delivered to customers, that customers had asked Stiffel whether its lamps differed from Sears', and that in two cases customers who had bought Stiffel lamps had complained to Stiffel on learning that Sears was selling substantially identical lamps at a much lower price.

The District Court, after holding the patents invalid for want of invention, went on to find as a fact that Sears' lamp was "a substantially exact copy" of Stiffel's and that the two lamps were so much alike, both in appearance and in functional details, "that confusion between them is likely, and some confusion has already occurred." On these findings the court held Sears guilty of unfair competition, enjoined Sears "from unfairly competing with [Stiffel] by selling or attempting to sell pole lamps identical to or confusingly similar to" Stiffel's lamp, and ordered an accounting to fix profits and damages resulting from Sears' "unfair competition."

The Court of Appeals affirmed.[1] 313 F.2d 115. That court held that, to make out a case of unfair competition under Illinois law, there was no need to show that Sears had been "palming off" its lamps as Stiffel lamps; Stiffel had only to prove that there was a "likelihood of confusion as to the source of the products"—that the two articles were sufficiently identical that customers could not tell who had made a particular one. Impressed by the "remarkable sameness of appearance" of the lamps, the Court of Appeals upheld the trial court's findings of likelihood of confusion and some actual confusion, findings which the appellate court construed to mean confusion "as to the source of the lamps." The Court of Appeals thought this enough under Illinois law to sustain the trial court's holding of unfair competition, and thus held Sears liable under Illinois law for doing no more than copying and marketing an unpatented article.[2] We

---

1. No review is sought here of the ruling affirming the District Court's holding that the patent is invalid.

2. 313 F.2d, at 118 and nn. 6, 7. At least one Illinois case has held in an exhaustive opinion that unfair competition under the law of Illinois is not proved unless the defendant is shown to have "palmed off" the article which he sells as that of another seller; the court there said that "[t]he courts in this State do not treat the 'palming off' doctrine as merely the designation of a typical class of cases of unfair competition, but they announce it as the rule of law itself—the test by which it is determined whether a given state of facts constitutes unfair competition as a matter of law. ... The 'palming off' rule is expressed in a positive, concrete form which will not admit of 'broadening' or 'widening' by any proper judicial process." Stevens–Davis Co. v. Mather & Co., 230 Ill.App. 45, 65–66 (1923). In spite of this the Court of Appeals in its opinions both in this case and in Day–Brite Lighting, Inc. v. Compco Corp., 7 Cir., 311 F.2d 26, rev'd 375 U.S. 234, relied upon one of its previous decisions in a trade-name case, Independent Nail & Packing Co. v. Stronghold Screw Products, 205 F.2d 921 (C.A. 7th Cir.1953), which concluded that as to use of trade names the *Stevens–Davis* rule had been overruled by two subsequent Illinois decisions. Those two cases, however, discussed only misleading use of trade names, not copying of articles of trade. One prohibited the use of a name so similar to that of another seller as to deceive or confuse customers, even though the defendant company did not sell the same products as the plaintiff and so in one sense could not be said to have palmed off its goods as those of a competitor, since the plaintiff was not a competitor. Lady Esther, Ltd. v. Lady Esthgranted certiorari to consider whether this use of a State's law of unfair competition is compatible with the federal patent law.   374 U.S. 826.

Before the Constitution was adopted, some States had granted patents either by special act or by general statute,[3] but when the Constitution was adopted provision for a federal patent law was made one of the enumerated powers of Congress because, as Madison put it in *The Federalist* No. 43, the States "cannot separately make effectual provision" for either patents or copyrights.[4]   That constitutional provision is Art. I, § 8, cl. 8, which empowers Congress "To promote the Progress of Science and useful Arts, by securing for limited Times to Authors and Inventors the exclusive Right to their respective Writings and Discoveries."   Pursuant to this constitutional authority, Congress in 1790 enacted the first federal patent and copyright law, 1 Stat. 109, and ever since that time has fixed the conditions upon which patents and copyrights shall be granted, see 17 U.S.C.A. §§ 1–216; 35 U.S.C.A. §§ 1–293.   These laws, like other laws of the United States enacted pursuant to constitutional authority, are the supreme law of the land.   See Sperry v. Florida, 373 U.S. 379 (1963).   When state law touches upon the area of these federal statutes, it is "familiar doctrine" that the federal policy "may not be set at naught, or its benefits denied" by the state law.   Sola Elec. Co. v. Jefferson Elec. Co., 317 U.S. 173, 176 (1942).   This is true, of course, even if the state law is enacted in the exercise of otherwise undoubted state power.

The grant of a patent is the grant of a statutory monopoly;[5] indeed, the grant of patents in England was an explicit exception to the statute of James I prohibiting monopolies.[6]   Patents are not given as favors, as was the case of monopolies given by the Tudor monarchs, see The Case of Monopolies (Darcy v. Allein), 11 Co.Rep. 84 b., 77 Eng.Rep. 1260 (K.B. 1602), but are meant to encourage invention by rewarding the inventor with the right, limited to a term of years fixed by the patent, to exclude

---

er Corset Shoppe, Inc., 317 Ill.App. 451, 46 N.E.2d 165 (1943). The other Illinois case on which the Court of Appeals relied was a mandamus action which held that under an Illinois statute a corporation was properly denied registration in the State when its name was "deceptively similar" to that of a corporation already registered. Investors Syndicate of America, Inc. v. Hughes, 378 Ill. 413, 38 N.E.2d 754 (1941). The Court of Appeals, by holding that because Illinois forbids misleading use of trade names it also forbids as unfair competition the mere copying of an article of trade without any palming off, thus appears to have extended greatly the scope of the Illinois law of unfair competition beyond the limits indicated in the Illinois cases and beyond any previous decisions of the Seventh Circuit itself. Because of our disposition of these cases we need not decide whether it was correct in doing so.

3. See I Walker, Patents (Deller ed. 1937), § 7.

4. The Federalist (Cooke ed. 1961) 288.

5. Patent rights exist only by virtue of statute. Wheaton v. Peters, 8 Pet. 591, 658 (1834).

6. The Statute of Monopolies, 21 Jac. I, c. 3 (1623), declared all monopolies "contrary to the Laws of this Realm" and "utterly void and of none Effect." Section VI, however, excepted patents of 14 years to "the true and first Inventor and Inventors" of "new Manufactures" so long as they were "not contrary to the Law, nor mischievous to the State, by raising Prices of Commodities at home, or Hurt of Trade, or generally inconvenient...."   Much American patent law derives from English patent law. See Pennock v. Dialogue, 2 Pet. 1, 18 (1829).

others from the use of his invention. During that period of time no one may make, use, or sell the patented product without the patentee's authority. 35 U.S.C.A. § 271. But in rewarding useful invention, the "rights and welfare of the community must be fairly dealt with and effectually guarded." Kendall v. Winsor, 21 How. 322, 329 (1859). To that end the prerequisites to obtaining a patent are strictly observed, and when the patent has issued the limitations on its exercise are equally strictly enforced. To begin with, a genuine "invention" or "discovery" must be demonstrated "lest in the constant demand for new appliances the heavy hand of tribute be laid on each slight technological advance in an art." Cuno Engineering Corp. v. Automatic Devices Corp., 314 U.S. 84, 92 (1941); see Great Atlantic & Pacific Tea Co. v. Supermarket Equipment Corp., 340 U.S. 147, 152–153 (1950); Atlantic Works v. Brady, 107 U.S. 192, 199–200 (1883). Once the patent issues, it is strictly construed, United States v. Masonite Corp., 316 U.S. 265, 280 (1942), it cannot be used to secure any monopoly beyond that contained in the patent, Morton Salt Co. v. G.S. Suppiger Co., 314 U.S. 488, 492 (1942), the patentee's control over the product when it leaves his hands is sharply limited, see United States v. Univis Lens Co., 316 U.S. 241, 250–252 (1942), and the patent monopoly may not be used in disregard of the antitrust laws, see International Business Machines Corp. v. United States, 298 U.S. 131 (1936); United Shoe Machinery Corp. v. United States, 258 U.S. 451, 463–464 (1922). Finally, and especially relevant here, when the patent expires the monopoly created by it expires, too, and the right to make the article—including the right to make it in precisely the shape it carried when patented—passes to the public. Kellogg Co. v. National Biscuit Co., 305 U.S. 111, 120–122 (1938); Singer Mfg. Co. v. June Mfg. Co., 163 U.S. 169, 185 (1896).

Thus the patent system is one in which uniform federal standards are carefully used to promote invention while at the same time preserving free competition.[7] Obviously a State could not, consistently with the Supremacy Clause of the Constitution,[8] extend the life of a patent beyond its expiration date or give a patent on an article which lacked the level of invention required for federal patents. To do either would run counter to the policy of Congress of granting patents only to true inventions, and then only for a limited time. Just as a State cannot encroach upon the federal patent laws directly, it cannot, under some other law, such as that forbidding unfair competition, give protection of a kind that clashes with the objectives of the federal patent laws.

In the present case the "pole lamp" sold by Stiffel has been held not to be entitled to the protection of either a mechanical or a design patent. An

---

7. The purpose of Congress to have national uniformity in patent and copyright laws can be inferred from such statutes as that which vests exclusive jurisdiction to hear patent and copyright cases in federal courts, 28 U.S.C.A. § 1338(a), and that section of the Copyright Act which expressly saves state protection of unpublished writings but does not include published writings, 17 U.S.C.A. § 2.

8. U.S. Const., Art. VI.

unpatentable article, like an article on which the patent has expired, is in the public domain and may be made and sold by whoever chooses to do so. What Sears did was to copy Stiffel's design and to sell lamps almost identical to those sold by Stiffel. This it had every right to do under the federal patent laws. That Stiffel originated the pole lamp and made it popular is immaterial. "Sharing in the goodwill of an article unprotected by patent or trade-mark is the exercise of a right possessed by all—and in the free exercise of which the consuming public is deeply interested." Kellogg Co. v. National Biscuit Co., supra, 305 U.S. at 122. To allow a State by use of its law of unfair competition to prevent the copying of an article which represents too slight an advance to be patented would be to permit the State to block off from the public something which federal law has said belongs to the public. The result would be that while federal law grants only 14 or 17 years' protection to genuine inventions, see 35 U.S.C.A. §§ 154, 173, States could allow perpetual protection to articles too lacking in novelty to merit any patent at all under federal constitutional standards. This would be too great an encroachment on the federal patent system to be tolerated.

Sears has been held liable here for unfair competition because of a finding of likelihood of confusion based only on the fact that Sears' lamp was copied from Stiffel's unpatented lamp and that consequently the two looked exactly alike. Of course there could be "confusion" as to who had manufactured these nearly identical articles. But mere inability of the public to tell two identical articles apart is not enough to support an injunction against copying or an award of damages for copying that which the federal patent laws permit to be copied. Doubtless a State may, in appropriate circumstances, require that goods, whether patented or unpatented, be labeled or that other precautionary steps be taken to prevent customers from being misled as to the source, just as it may protect businesses in the use of their trademarks, labels, or distinctive dress in the packaging of goods so as to prevent others, by imitating such markings, from misleading purchasers as to the source of the goods.[9] But because of the federal patent laws a State may not, when the article is unpatented and uncopyrighted, prohibit the copying of the article itself or award damages for such copying. Cf. G. Ricordi & Co. v. Haendler, 194 F.2d 914, 916 (C.A.2d Cir.1952). The judgment below did both and in so doing gave Stiffel the equivalent of a patent monopoly on its unpatented lamp. That was error, and Sears is entitled to a judgment in its favor.

Reversed.

Compco Corp. v. Day–Brite Lighting, Inc.

Supreme Court of the United States, 1964.
376 U.S. 234, 84 S.Ct. 779.

■ MR. JUSTICE BLACK delivered the opinion of the Court.

As in Sears, Roebuck & Co. v. Stiffel Co., 376 U.S. 225, the question here is whether the use of a state unfair competition law to give relief

---

9. It seems apparent that Illinois has not seen fit to impose liability on sellers who do not label their goods. Neither the discus- sions in the opinions below nor the briefs before us cite any Illinois statute or decision requiring labeling.

against the copying of an unpatented industrial design conflicts with the federal patent laws. Both Compco and Day–Brite are manufacturers of fluorescent lighting fixtures of a kind widely used in offices and stores. Day–Brite in 1955 secured from the Patent Office a design patent on a reflector having cross-ribs claimed to give both strength and attractiveness to the fixture. Day–Brite also sought, but was refused, a mechanical patent on the same device. After Day–Brite had begun selling its fixture, Compco's predecessor began making and selling fixtures very similar to Day–Brite's. This action was then brought by Day–Brite. One count alleged that Compco had infringed Day–Brite's design patent; a second count charged that the public and the trade had come to associate this particular design with Day–Brite, that Compco had copied Day–Brite's distinctive design so as to confuse and deceive purchasers into thinking Compco's fixtures were actually Day–Brite's, and that by doing this Compco had unfairly competed with Day–Brite. The complaint prayed for both an accounting and an injunction.

The District Court held the design patent invalid; but as to the second count, while the court did not find that Compco had engaged in any deceptive or fraudulent practices, it did hold that Compco had been guilty of unfair competition under Illinois law. The court found that the overall appearance of Compco's fixture was "the same, to the eye of the ordinary observer, as the overall appearance" of Day–Brite's reflector, which embodied the design of the invalidated patent; that the appearance of Day–Brite's design had "the capacity to identify [Day–Brite] in the trade and does in fact so identify [it] to the trade"; that the concurrent sale of the two products was "likely to cause confusion in the trade"; and that "[a]ctual confusion has occurred." On these findings the court adjudged Compco guilty of unfair competition in the sale of its fixtures, ordered Compco to account to Day–Brite for damages, and enjoined Compco "from unfairly competing with plaintiff by the sale or attempted sale of reflectors identical to, or confusingly similar to" those made by Day–Brite. The Court of Appeals held there was substantial evidence in the record to support the District Court's finding of likely confusion and that this finding was sufficient to support a holding of unfair competition under Illinois law.[2] 311 F.2d 26. Although the District Court had not made such a finding, the appellate court observed that "several choices of ribbing were apparently available to meet the functional needs of the product," yet Compco "chose precisely the same design used by the plaintiff and followed it so closely as to make confusion likely." 311 F.2d, at 30. A design which identifies its maker to the trade, the Court of Appeals held, is a "protectable" right under Illinois law, even though the design is unpatentable.[3] We granted certiorari. 374 U.S. 825.

---

2. The Court of Appeals also affirmed the holding that the design patent was invalid. No review of this ruling is sought here.

3. As stated in Sears, Roebuck & Co. v. Stiffel Co., 376 U.S., at p. 228 n. 2, we do not here decide whether the Court of Appeals was correct in its statement of Illinois law.

To support its findings of likelihood of confusion and actual confusion, the trial court was able to refer to only one circumstance in the record. A plant manager who had installed some of Compco's fixtures later asked Day–Brite to service the fixtures, thinking they had been made by Day–Brite. There was no testimony given by a purchaser or by anyone else that any customer had ever been misled, deceived, or "confused," that is, that anyone had ever bought a Compco fixture thinking it was a Day–Brite fixture. All the record shows, as to the one instance cited by the trial court, is that both Compco and Day–Brite fixtures had been installed in the same plant, that three years later some repairs were needed, and that the manager viewing the Compco fixtures—hung at least 15 feet above the floor and arranged end to end in a continuous line so that identifying marks were hidden—thought they were Day–Brite fixtures and asked Day–Brite to service them. Not only is this incident suggestive only of confusion *after* a purchase had been made, but also there is considerable evidence of the care taken by Compco to prevent customer confusion, including clearly labeling both the fixtures and the containers in which they were shipped and not selling through manufacturers' representatives who handled competing lines.

Notwithstanding the thinness of the evidence to support findings of likely and actual confusion among purchasers, we do not find it necessary in this case to determine whether there is "clear error" in these findings. They, like those in Sears, Roebuck & Co. v. Stiffel Co., 376 U.S. 225, were based wholly on the fact that selling an article which is an exact copy of another unpatented article is likely to produce and did in this case produce confusion as to the source of the article. Even accepting the findings, we hold that the order for an accounting for damages and the injunction are in conflict with the federal patent laws. Today we have held in Sears, Roebuck & Co. v. Stiffel Co., 376 U.S. 225, that when an article is unprotected by a patent or a copyright, state law may not forbid others to copy that article. To forbid copying would interfere with the federal policy, found in Art. I, § 8, cl. 8, of the Constitution and in the implementing federal statutes, of allowing free access to copy whatever the federal patent and copyright laws leave in the public domain. Here Day–Brite's fixture has been held not to be entitled to a design or mechanical patent. Under the federal patent laws it is, therefore, in the public domain and can be copied in every detail by whoever pleases. It is true that the trial court found that the configuration of Day–Brite's fixture identified Day–Brite to the trade because the arrangement of the ribbing had, like a trademark, acquired a "secondary meaning" by which that particular design was associated with Day–Brite. But if the design is not entitled to a design patent or other federal statutory protection, then it can be copied at will.

As we have said in *Sears,* while the federal patent laws prevent a State from prohibiting the copying and selling of unpatented articles, they do not stand in the way of state law, statutory or decisional, which requires those who make and sell copies to take precautions to identify their products as their own. A State of course has power to impose liability upon those who, knowing that the public is relying upon an original manufacturer's reputation for quality and integrity, deceive the public by palming off their copies as the original. That an article copied from an unpatented article could be made in some other way, that the design is "nonfunctional" and not essential to the use of either article, that the configuration of the article copied may have a "secondary meaning" which identifies the maker to the trade, or that there may be "confusion" among purchasers as to which article is which or as to who is the maker, may be relevant evidence in applying a State's law requiring such precautions as labeling; however, and regardless of the copier's motives, neither these facts nor any others can furnish a basis for imposing liability for or prohibiting the actual acts of copying and selling. Cf. Kellogg Co. v. National Biscuit Co., 305 U.S. 111, 120 (1938). And of course a State cannot hold a copier accountable in damages for failure to label or otherwise to identify his goods unless his failure is in violation of valid state statutory or decisional law requiring the copier to label or take other precautions to prevent confusion of customers as to the source of the goods.[5]

Since the judgment below forbids the sale of a copy of an unpatented article and orders an accounting for damages for such copying, it cannot stand.

Reversed.

■ MR. JUSTICE HARLAN, concurring in the result.*

In one respect I would give the States more leeway in unfair competition "copying" cases than the Court's opinions would allow. If copying is found, other than by an inference arising from the mere act of copying, to have been undertaken with the dominant purpose and effect of palming off one's goods as those of another or of confusing customers as to the source of such goods, I see no reason why the State may not impose reasonable restrictions on the future "copying" itself. Vindication of the paramount federal interest at stake does not require a State to tolerate such specifically oriented predatory business practices. Apart from this, I am in accord with the opinions of the Court, and concur in both judgments since neither case presents the point on which I find myself in disagreement.

NOTE

The reaction to *Sears* and *Compco* was mixed, due in part to disagreement about what they meant. See, e.g., Symposium, Product Simulation: A Right or a Wrong?, 64 Colum.L.Rev. 1178 (1964). Does *Compco* go beyond *Sears* in limiting state authority? Do the cases hold that the patent and copyright clause of the Constitution itself precludes state interference with the right to copy objects within its scope? Or are the cases instead applications of the supremacy clause, holding that the state doctrines

---

5. As we pointed out in Sears, Roebuck & Co. v. Stiffel Co., 376 U.S., at p. 232 n. 9, there is no showing that Illinois has any such law.

* [This opinion applies also to Sears, Roebuck & Co. v. Stiffel Co., 376 U.S. 225.]

interfered with the policies implemented by Congress in the federal patent statute? The distinction is significant. It had implications, for example, in connection with attempts by the states to rein in the burgeoning trade in pirated records and tapes. See Kurlantzick, The Constitutionality of State Law Protection of Sound Recordings, 5 Conn.L.Rev. 204 (1972). If the patent and copyright clause was read to exclude all state regulation of "writings" and "discoveries," state protection of sound recordings would be void on its face. If the issue was instead the supremacy of federal law, the question became whether state protection interfered with the congressional policies embodied in the Copyright Act, which did not extend protection to sound recordings until 1972.

That issue, and others, were decided in the following case.

Goldstein v. California

Supreme Court of the United States, 1973.
412 U.S. 546, 93 S.Ct. 2303.

■ MR. CHIEF JUSTICE BURGER delivered the opinion of the Court.

We granted certiorari to review petitioners' conviction under a California statute making it a criminal offense to "pirate" recordings produced by others.

In 1971, an information was filed by the State of California, charging petitioners in 140 counts with violating § 653h of the California Penal Code. The information charged that, between April 1970 and March 1971, petitioners had copied several musical performances from commercially sold recordings without the permission of the owner of the master record or tape.[1] Petitioners moved to dismiss the complaint on the grounds that § 653h was in conflict with Art. I, § 8, cl. 8, of the Constitution, the "Copyright Clause," and the federal statutes enacted thereunder. Upon denial of their motion, petitioners entered pleas of *nolo contendere* to 10 of the 140 counts; the remaining counts were dismissed. On appeal, the Appellate Department of the Superior Court sustained the validity of the statute. After exhausting other state appellate remedies, petitioners sought review in this Court.

---

1. In pertinent part, the California statute provides:

"(a) Every person is guilty of a misdemeanor who:

"(1) Knowingly and willfully transfers or causes to be transferred any sounds recorded on a phonograph record, ... tape, ... or other article on which sounds are recorded, with intent to sell or cause to be sold, ... such article on which such sounds are so transferred, without the consent of the owner.

"(2) ...

"(b) As used in this section, 'person' means any individual, partnership, corporation or association; and 'owner' means the person who owns the master phonograph record, ... master tape, ... or other device used for reproducing recorded sounds on phonograph records, ... tapes, ... or other articles on which sound is recorded, and from which the transferred recorded sounds are directly or indirectly derived." * * *

I

Petitioners were engaged in what has commonly been called "record piracy" or "tape piracy"—the unauthorized duplication of recordings of performances by major musical artists. Petitioners would purchase from a retail distributor a single tape or phonograph recording of the popular performances they wished to duplicate. The original recordings were produced and marketed by recording companies with whom petitioners had no contractual relationship. At petitioners' plant, the recording was reproduced on blank tapes, which could in turn be used to replay the music on a tape player. The tape was then wound on a cartridge. A label was attached, stating the title of the recorded performance—the same title as had appeared on the original recording, and the name of the performing artists.[4] After final packaging, the tapes were distributed to retail outlets for sale to the public, in competition with those petitioners had copied.

Petitioners made no payments to the artists whose performances they reproduced and sold, nor to the various trust funds established for their benefit; no payments were made to the producers, technicians, or other staff personnel responsible for producing the original recording and paying the large expenses incurred in production.[5] No payments were made for the use of the artists' names or the album title. * * *

Petitioners' attack on the constitutionality of § 653h has many facets. First, they contend that the statute establishes a state copyright of unlimited duration, and thus conflicts with Art. I, § 8, cl. 8, of the Constitution. Second, petitioners claim that the state statute interferes with the implementation of federal policies inherent in the federal copyright statutes. 17 U.S.C.A. § 1 et seq. According to petitioners, it was the intention of Congress, as interpreted by this Court in Sears, Roebuck and Co. v. Stiffel Co., 376 U.S. 225 (1964), and Compco Corp. v. Day–Brite Lighting, 376 U.S. 234 (1964), to establish a uniform law throughout the United States to protect original writings. As part of the federal scheme, it is urged that Congress intended to allow individuals to copy any work which was not protected by a federal copyright. Since § 653h effectively prohibits the copying of works which are not entitled to federal protection, petitioners contend that it conflicts directly with congressional policy and must fall under the Supremacy Clause of the Constitution. Finally, petitioners argue that 17 U.S.C.A. § 2, which allows States to protect unpublished writings, does not authorize the challenged state provision; since the

4. An additional label was attached to each cartridge by petitioners, stating that no relationship existed between petitioners and the producer of the original recording or the individuals whose performances had been recorded. Consequently, no claim is made that petitioners misrepresented the source of the original recordings or the manufacturer of the tapes.

5. The costs of producing a single original longplaying record of a musical performance may exceed $50,000 or $100,000. Tape Industries Assn. of America v. Younger, 316 F.Supp., at 344 (1970); Hearings on S. 646 and H.R. 6927 before Subcommittee No. 3 of the Committee on the Judiciary, House of Representatives, 92d Cong., 1st Sess., at 27–28 (1971). For the performance recorded on this record, petitioners would pay only the retail cost of a single longplaying record or a single tape.

records which petitioners copied had previously been released to the public, petitioners contend that they had, under federal law, been published.

We note at the outset that the federal copyright statutes to which petitioners refer were amended by Congress while their case was pending in the state courts. In 1971, Pub.L. 92–140, 85 Stat. 391, was passed to allow federal copyright protection of recordings. However, § 3 of the amendment specifically provides that such protection is to be available only to sound recordings "fixed, published, and copyrighted" on and after February 15, 1972, and before January 1, 1975, and that nothing in Title 17, as amended is to "be applied retroactively or [to] be construed as affecting in any way any rights with respect to sound recordings fixed before" February 15, 1972. The recordings which petitioners copied were all "fixed" prior to February 15, 1972. Since, according to the language of § 3 of the amendment, Congress did not intend to alter the legal relationships which govern these recordings, the amendments have no application in petitioners' case.[7]

II

Petitioners' first argument rests on the premise that the state statute under which they were convicted lies beyond the powers which the States reserved in our federal system. If this is correct, petitioners must prevail, since the States cannot exercise a sovereign power which, under the Constitution, they have relinquished to the Federal Government for its exclusive exercise.

A

The principles which the Court has followed in construing state power were stated by Alexander Hamilton in Number 32 of The Federalist:

> "An entire consolidation of the States into one complete national sovereignty would imply an entire subordination of the parts; and whatever powers might remain in them, would be altogether dependent on the general will. But as the plan of the [Constitutional] convention aims only at a partial union or consolidation, the State governments would clearly retain all the rights of sovereignty which they before had, and which were not, by that act, *exclusively* delegated to the United States. This exclusive delegation, or rather this alienation, of State sovereignty, would only exist in three cases: where the Constitution in express terms granted an exclusive authority to the Union; where it granted in one instance an authority to the Union, and in another prohibited the States from exercising the like authority; and where it granted an authority to the Union, to which a similar authority in the

---

7. No question is raised in the present case as to the power of the States to protect recordings fixed after February 15, 1972.

States would be absolutely and totally *contradictory and repugnant*." [8]

The first two instances mentioned present no barrier to a State's enactment of copyright statutes. The clause of the Constitution granting to Congress the power to issue copyrights does not provide that such power shall vest exclusively in the Federal Government. Nor does the Constitution expressly provide that such power shall not be exercised by the States.

In applying the third phase of the test, we must examine the manner in which the power to grant copyrights may operate in our federal system. The objectives of our inquiry were recognized in Cooley v. Board of Wardens, 12 How. (53 U.S.) 299 (1851), when, in determining whether the power granted to Congress to regulate commerce was "compatible with the existence of a similar power in the States," the Court noted:

> "Whatever subjects of this power are in their nature national, or admit of only one uniform system, or plan of regulation, may justly be said to be of such a nature as to require exclusive legislation by Congress." Id., at 319.

* * * We must also be careful to distinguish those situations in which the concurrent exercise of a power by the Federal Government and the States or by the States alone *may possibly* lead to conflicts and those situations where conflicts *will necessarily* arise. "It is not ... a mere possibility of inconvenience in the exercise of powers, but an immediate constitutional repugnancy that can by implication alienate and extinguish a pre-existing right of [state] sovereignty." The Federalist, No. 32, at 243.
* * *

The objective of the Copyright Clause was clearly to facilitate the granting of rights national in scope. While the debates on the clause at the Constitutional Convention were extremely limited, its purpose was described by James Madison in No. 43 of the Federalist Papers:

> "The utility of this power will scarcely be questioned. The copyright of authors has been solemnly adjudged, in Great Britain, to be a right of common law. The right to useful inventions seems with equal reason to belong to the inventors. The public good fully coincides in both cases with the claims of individuals. The States cannot separately make effectual provision for either of the cases, and most of them have anticipated the decision of this point, by laws passed at the instance of Congress." [11]

The difficulty noted by Madison relates to the burden placed on an author or inventor who wishes to achieve protection in all States when no federal system of protection is available. To do so, a separate application is required to each state government; the right which in turn may be granted

---

8. The Federalist No. 32, p. 241 (B. Wright ed. 1961); see Cooley v. Board of Wardens, 12 How. 299, 318–319 (1851).

11. The Federalist, at 309.

has effect only within the granting State's borders.[12]   The national system which Madison supported eliminates the need for multiple applications and the expense and difficulty involved. In effect, it allows Congress to provide a reward greater in scope than any particular State may grant to promote progress in those fields which Congress determines are worthy of national action.

Although the Copyright Clause thus recognizes the potential benefits of a national system, it does not indicate that all writings are of national interest or that state legislation is, in all cases, unnecessary or precluded. The patents granted by the States in the 18th century show, to the contrary, a willingness on the part of the States to promote those portions of science and the arts which were of local importance. Whatever the diversity of people's backgrounds, origins, and interests, and whatever the variety of business and industry in the 13 colonies, the range of diversity is obviously far greater today in a country of 210 million people in 50 states. In view of that enormous diversity, it is unlikely that all citizens in all parts of the country place the same importance on works relating to all subjects.   Since the subject matter to which the Copyright Clause is addressed may thus be of purely local importance and not worthy of national attention or protection, we cannot discern such an unyielding national interest as to require an inference that state power to grant copyrights has been relinquished to *exclusive* federal control.

The question to which we next turn is whether, in actual operation, the exercise of the power to grant copyrights by some States will prejudice the interests of other States. As we have noted, a copyright granted by a particular State has effect only within its boundaries. If one State grants such protection, the interests of States which do not are not prejudiced since their citizens remain free to copy within their borders those works which may be protected elsewhere. The interests of a State which grants copyright protection may, however, be adversely affected by other States that do not; individuals who wish to purchase a copy of a work protected in their own State will be able to buy unauthorized copies in other States where no protection exists. However, this conflict is neither so inevitable nor so severe as to compel the conclusion, that state power has been relinquished to the exclusive jurisdiction of the Congress. * * *

Similarly, it is difficult to see how the concurrent exercise of the power to grant copyrights by Congress and the States will necessarily and inevitably lead to difficulty. At any time Congress determines that a particular category of "writing" is worthy of national protection and the incidental

---

12. Numerous examples may be found in our early history of the difficulties which the creators of items of national import had in securing protection of their creations in all States. For example, Noah Webster, in his effort to obtain protection for his book, A Grammatical Institute of the English Language, brought his claim before the legislatures of at least six States, and perhaps as many as 12. See B. Bugbee, The Genesis of American Patent and Copyright Law 108–110, 120–124 (Wash., D.C., 1967); H.R.Rep. No. 2222, 60th Cong., 2d Sess., at 2 (1909). Similar difficulties were experienced by John Fitch and other inventors who desired to protect their efforts to perfect a steamboat. See Federico, State Patents, 13 J.Pat.Off.Soc. 166, 170–176 (1931).

expenses of federal administration, federal copyright protection may be authorized.   Where the need for free and unrestricted distribution of a writing is thought to be required by the national interest, the Copyright Clause and the Commerce Clause would allow Congress to eschew all protection.   In such cases, a conflict would develop if a State attempted to protect that which Congress intended to be free from restraint or to free that which Congress had protected.   However, where Congress determines that neither federal protection nor freedom from restraint is required by the national interest, it is at liberty to stay its hand entirely.[16]   Since state protection would not then conflict with federal action, total relinquishment of the States' power to grant copyright protection cannot be inferred.

As we have seen, the language of the Constitution neither explicitly precludes the State from granting copyrights nor grants such authority exclusively to the Federal Government.   The subject matter to which the Copyright Clause is addressed may at times be of purely local concern.   No conflict will necessarily arise from a lack of uniform state regulation, nor will the interest of one State be significantly prejudiced by the actions of another.   No reason exists why Congress must take affirmative action either to authorize protection of all categories of writings or to free them from all restraint.   We therefore conclude that, under the Constitution, the States have not relinquished all power to grant to authors "the exclusive Right to their respective Writings."

B

Petitioners base an additional argument on the language of the Constitution.   The California statute forbids individuals from appropriating recordings at any time after release.   From this, petitioners argue that the State has created a copyright of *unlimited* duration, in violation of that portion of Art. I, § 8, cl. 8, which provides that copyrights may only be granted "for limited Times."   Read literally, the text of Art. I does not support petitioners' position.   Section 8 enumerates those powers which have been granted *to Congress;* whatever limitations have been appended to such powers can only be understood as a limit on congressional, and not state, action.   Moreover, it is not clear that the dangers to which this limitation was addressed apply with equal force to both the Federal Government and the States.   When Congress grants an exclusive right or monopoly, its effects are pervasive;   no citizen or State may escape its reach.   As we have noted, however, the exclusive right granted by a State is confined to its borders.   Consequently, even when the right is unlimited in duration, any tendency to inhibit further progress in science or the arts is narrowly circumscribed.   The challenged statute cannot be voided for lack of a durational limitation.

---

16. For example, Congress has allowed writings which may eventually be the subject of a federal copyright, to be protected under state law prior to publication.   17 U.S.C.A. § 2.

III

Our conclusion that California did not surrender its power to issue copyrights does not end the inquiry. We must proceed to determine whether the challenged state statute is void under the Supremacy Clause. No simple formula can capture the complexities of this determination; the conflicts which may develop between state and federal action are as varied as the fields to which congressional action may apply. "Our primary function is to determine whether, under the circumstances of this particular case, [the state] law stands as an obstacle to the accomplishment and execution of the full purposes and objectives of Congress." Hines v. Davidowitz, 312 U.S. 52, 67 (1941). We turn then to federal copyright law to determine what objectives Congress intended to fulfill.

By Art. I, § 8, cl. 8, of the Constitution, the States granted to Congress the power to protect the "Writings" of "Authors." These terms have not been construed in their narrow literal sense but, rather, with the reach necessary to reflect the broad scope of constitutional principles. While an "author" may be viewed as an individual who writes an original composition, the term, in its constitutional sense, has been construed to mean an "originator," "he to whom anything owes its origin." Burrow–Giles Lithographic Co. v. Sarony, 111 U.S. 53, 58 (1884). Similarly, although the word "writings" might be limited to script or printed material, it may be interpreted to include any physical rendering of the fruits of creative intellectual or aesthetic labor. Id.; Trade Mark Cases, 100 U.S. 82, 94 (1879). Thus, recordings of artistic performances may be within the reach of Clause 8.

While the area in which Congress *may* act is broad, the enabling provision of Clause 8 does not require that Congress act in regard to all categories of materials which meet the constitutional definitions. Rather, whether any specific category of "Writings" is to be brought within the purview of the federal statutory scheme is left to the discretion of the Congress. The history of federal copyright statutes indicates that the congressional determination to consider specific classes of writings is dependent not only on the character of the writing, but also on the commercial importance of the product to the national economy. As our technology has expanded the means available for creative activity and has provided economical means for reproducing manifestations of such activity, new areas of federal protection have been initiated.

Petitioners contend that the actions taken by Congress in establishing federal copyright protection preclude the States from granting similar protection to recordings of musical performances. According to petitioners, Congress addressed the question of whether recordings of performances should be granted protection in 1909; Congress determined that any individual who was entitled to a copyright on an original musical composition should have the right to control to a limited extent the use of that composition on recordings, but that the record itself, and the performance which it was capable of reproducing were not worthy of such protection.

In support of their claim, petitioners cite the House Report on the 1909 Act, which states:

> "It is not the intention of the committee to extend the right of copyright to the mechanical reproductions themselves, but only to give the composer or copyright proprietor the control, in accordance with the provisions of the bill, of the manufacture and use of such devices." H.R.Rep. No. 2222, 60th Cong., 2d Sess., 9 (1909).

* * * The section of the House Report cited by petitioners was intended only to establish the limits of *the composer's* right; composers were to have no control over the recordings themselves. Nowhere does the report indicate that Congress considered records as anything but a component part of a machine, capable of reproducing an original composition or that Congress intended records, as *renderings of original artistic performance,* to be free from state control.[23]

Petitioners' argument does not rest entirely on the belief that Congress intended specifically to exempt recordings of performances from state control. Assuming that no such intention may be found, they argue that Congress so occupied the field of copyright protection as to pre-empt all comparable state action. Rice v. Santa Fe Elevator Corporation, 331 U.S. 218 (1947). This assertion is based on the language of 17 U.S.C.A. §§ 4 and 5, and on this Court's opinions in Sears, Roebuck and Co. v. Stiffel Co., 376 U.S. 225 (1964), and Compco Corp. v. Day–Brite Lighting, 376 U.S. 234 (1964).

Section 4 of the federal copyright laws provides:

> "The works for which copyright may be secured under this title shall include all the writings of an author."

Section 5, which lists specific categories of protected works, adds:

> "The above specifications shall not be held to limit the subject-matter of copyright as defined in section 4 of this title. . . ."

---

23. Petitioners do not argue that § 653h conflicts with that portion of 17 U.S.C.A. § 1(e) which provides:

"[W]henever the owner of a musical copyright has used or permitted or knowingly acquiesced in the use of the copyrighted work upon the parts of instruments serving to reproduce mechanically the musical work, any other person may make similar use of the copyrighted work upon the payment to the copyright proprietor of a royalty of 2 cents on each such part manufactured. . . ."

Assuming, *arguendo*, that petitioners' use of the composition they duplicated constitutes a "similar use," the challenged state statute might be claimed to diminish the return which is due the composer by lessen-ing the number of copies produced, and thus to conflict with § 1(e). However, as we have noted above, the means presently available for reproducing recordings were not in existence in 1909 when 17 U.S.C.A. § 1(e) was passed. We see no indication that the challenged state statute detracts from royalties which Congress intended the composer to receive. Furthermore, many state statutes may diminish the number of copies produced. Taxing statutes, for example, may raise the cost of producing or selling records and thereby lessen the number of records which may be sold or inhibit new companies from entering this field of commerce. We do not see in these statutes the direct conflict necessary to render a state statute invalid.

Since § 4 employs the constitutional term "writings," it may be argued that Congress intended to exercise its authority over all works to which the constitutional provision might apply. However, in the more than 60 years which have transpired since enactment of this provision, neither the Copyright Office, the courts, nor the Congress has so interpreted it. The Register of Copyrights, who is charged with administration of the statute, has consistently ruled that "claims to exclusive rights in mechanical recordings ... or in the performances they reproduce" are not entitled to protection under § 4. 37 CFR § 202.8(b) (1972). With one early exception,[26] American courts have agreed with this interpretation;[27] and in 1971, prior to passage of the statute which extended federal protection to recordings fixed on or after Feb. 15, 1972, Congress acknowledged the validity of that interpretation. Both the House and Senate Reports on the proposed legislation recognized that recordings qualified as "writings" within the meaning of the Constitution, but had not previously been protected under the federal copyright statute. H.R.Rep. No. 92–487, 92d Cong., 1st Sess. (1971), at 2, 5; S.Rep. No. 92–72, 92d Cong., 1st Sess. (1971), at 4. In light of this consistent interpretation by the courts, the agency empowered to administer the copyright statutes, and Congress itself, we cannot agree that §§ 4 and 5 have the broad scope petitioners claim.

Sears and *Compco*, on which petitioners rely, do not support their position. In those cases, the question was whether a State could, under principles of state unfair competition law, preclude the copying of mechanical configurations which did not possess the qualities required for the granting of a federal design or mechanical patent. * * *

In regard to mechanical configurations, Congress had balanced the need to encourage innovation and originality of invention against the need to insure competition in the sale of identical or substantially identical products. The standards established for granting federal patent protection to machines thus indicated not only which articles in this particular category Congress wished to protect, but which configurations it wished to remain free. The application of state law in these cases to prevent the copying of articles which did not meet the requirements for federal protection disturbed the careful balance which Congress had drawn and thereby necessarily gave way under the Supremacy Clause of the Constitution. No comparable conflict between state law and federal law arises in the case of recordings of musical performances. In regard to this category of "Writings," Congress has drawn no balance; rather, it has left the area unattended, and no reason exists why the State should not be free to act.[28]

26. Fonotipia Limited v. Bradley, 171 F. 951, 963 (EDNY 1909).

27. Aeolian Co. v. Royal Music Roll Co., 196 F. 926, 927 (WDNY 1912); Waring v. WDAS Broadcasting Station, 327 Pa. 433, 437–438, 194 A. 631 (1937); Capitol Records v. Mercury Records Corp., 221 F.2d 657, 661– 662 (CA2 1955); Jerome v. Twentieth Century Fox–Film Corp., 67 F.Supp. 736, 742 (SDNY 1946).

28. Petitioners place great stress on their belief that the records or tapes which they copied had been "published." We have no need to determine whether, *under state*

IV

More than 50 years ago, Mr. Justice Brandeis observed in dissent in International News Service v. Associated Press:

"The general rule of law is, that the noblest of human productions—knowledge, truths ascertained, conceptions, and ideas—become, after voluntary communications to others, free as the air to common use." 248 U.S. 215, 250 (1918).

But there is no fixed, immutable line to tell us which "human productions" are private property and which are so general as to become "free as the air." In earlier times, a performing artist's work was largely restricted to the stage; once performed, it remained "recorded" only in the memory of those who had seen or heard it. Today, we can record that performance in precise detail and reproduce it again and again with utmost fidelity. The California statutory scheme evidences a legislative policy to prohibit "tape piracy" and "record piracy," conduct that may adversely affect the continued production of new recordings, a large industry in California. Accordingly, the State has, by statute, given to recordings the attributes of property. No restraint has been placed on the use of an idea or concept; rather, petitioners and other individuals remain free to record the same compositions in precisely the same manner and with the same personnel as appeared on the original recording.

In sum, we have shown that § 653h does not conflict with the federal copyright statute enacted by Congress in 1909. Similarly, no conflict exists between the federal copyright statute passed in 1971 and the present application of § 653h, since California charged petitioners only with copying recordings fixed prior to February 15, 1972. Finally, we have concluded that our decisions in *Sears* and *Compco,* which we reaffirm today, have no application in the present case, since Congress has indicated neither that it wishes to protect, nor to free from protection, recordings of musical performances fixed prior to February 15, 1972.

We conclude that the State of California has exercised a power which it retained under the Constitution, and that the challenged statute, as applied in this case, does not intrude into an area which Congress has, up to now, pre-empted. Until and unless Congress takes further action with respect to recordings fixed prior to February 15, 1972, the California statute may be enforced against acts of piracy such as those which occurred in the present case.

Affirmed.

■ MR. JUSTICE DOUGLAS, with whom MR. JUSTICE BRENNAN and MR. JUSTICE BLACKMUN concur, dissenting. * * *

law, these recordings had been published or what legal consequences such publication might have. *For purposes of federal law,* "publication" serves only as a term of the art which defines the legal relationships which Congress has adopted under the federal copyright statutes. As to categories of writings which Congress has not brought within the scope of the federal statute, the term has no application.

Prior to February 25, 1972, copyright protection was not extended to sound recordings. *Sears* and *Compco* make clear that the federal policy expressed in Art. I, § 8, cl. 8, is to have "national uniformity in patent and copyright laws," 376 U.S., at 231 n. 7, a policy bolstered by Acts of Congress which vest "exclusive jurisdiction to hear patent and copyright cases in federal courts ... and that section of the Copyright Act which expressly saves state protection of unpublished writings but does not include published writings." Ibid. * * *

California's law promotes monopoly; the federal policy promotes monopoly only when a copyright is issued, and it fosters competition in all other instances. Moreover, federal law limits its monopoly to 28 years plus a like renewal period, while California extends her monopoly into perpetuity.

Cases like *Sears* were surcharged with "unfair competition" and the present one with "pirated recordings." But free access to products on the market is the consumer interest protected by the failure of Congress to extend patents or copyrights into various areas. The drive for monopoly protection is strong as is evident from a reading of the committee reports on the 1971 Act.[5] Yet, Congress took but a short step, setting up a trial period to consider the new monopoly approach. It was told that state laws, such as we have in this case, were being challenged on the ground that the Federal Constitution had pre-empted the field, even in absence of a provision for making it possible to obtain a copyright for sound recordings. But the House Committee made only the following comment:

> "While the committee expresses no opinion concerning this legal question, it is clear that the extension of copyright protection to sound recordings would resolve many of the problems which have arisen in connection with the efforts to combat piracy in State courts."[6] * * *

I would reverse the judgment below.

■ MR. JUSTICE MARSHALL, with whom MR. JUSTICE BRENNAN and MR. JUSTICE BLACKMUN join, dissenting.

The argument of the Court, as I understand it, is this: Art. I, § 8, cl. 8, of the Constitution gives Congress the power "to promote the Progress of Science and useful Arts, by securing for limited Times to Authors and Inventors the exclusive Right to their respective Writings and Discoveries." The Framers recognized that individual States might have peculiarly local interests that Congress might not consider worthy of attention. Thus, the constitutional provision does not, of its own force, bar States from promoting those local interests. However, as the Court noted in Sears, Roebuck & Co. v. Stiffel Co., 376 U.S. 225 (1964), with respect to every particular item within general classes enumerated in the relevant statutes, Congress had balanced the need to promote invention against the desire to preserve free

5.   H.R.Rep. No. 92–487; S.Rep. No. 92–72.

6.   H.R.Rep., supra, n. 5, at 3.

competition, and had concluded that it was in the national interest to preserve competition as to every item that could not be patented. That is, the fact that some item could not be patented demonstrated that, in the judgment of Congress, it was best to let competition in the production of that item go unrestricted. The situation with regard to copyrights is said to be similar. There Congress enumerated certain classes of works for which a copyright may be secured. 17 U.S.C.A. § 5. Its silence as to other classes does not reflect a considered judgment about the relative importance of competition and promotion of "Science and useful Arts." Thus, the Court says, the States remain free to protect as they will "writings" not in the enumerated classes, until Congress acts. Since sound recordings fixed prior to February 15, 1972, were not enumerated by Congress as subject to copyrighting, the States may protect such recordings.

With respect, I cannot accept the final step of this argument. In my view, Congress has demonstrated its desire to exercise the full grant of constitutional power. Title 17, U.S.C.A. § 4, states: "The works for which copyright may be secured under this title shall include *all the writings of an author* " (emphasis added). The use of the constitutional terms "writings" and "author" rather strongly suggests that Congress intended to follow the constitutional grant. It could exercise the power given it by the Constitution in two ways: either by protecting all writings, or by protecting all writings within designated classes and leaving open to competition all writings in other classes. Section 5 shows that the latter course was chosen, for it enumerates various classes of works that may be registered. Ordinarily, the failure to enumerate "sound recordings" in § 5 would not be taken as an expression of Congress' desire to let free competition reign in the reproduction of such recordings, for, because of the realities of the legislative process, it is generally difficult to infer from a failure to act any affirmative conclusions. Cf. Cleveland v. United States, 329 U.S. 14, 22 (1946) (Rutledge, J., concurring). But in *Sears* and its companion case, Compco Corp. v. Day–Brite Lighting, Inc., 376 U.S. 234 (1964), the Court determined that with respect to patents and copyrights, the ordinary practice was not to prevail. In view of the importance of not imposing unnecessary restraints on competition, the Court adopted in those cases a rule of construction that, unless the failure to provide patent or copyright protection for some class of works could clearly be shown to reflect a judgment that state regulation was permitted, the silence of Congress would be taken to reflect a judgment that free competition should prevail. I do not find in *Sears* and *Compco* a limitation on that rule of construction to general classes that Congress has enumerated although, of course, on the facts of those cases only items in such classes were involved; rather, the broadest language was used in those cases.[3] Nor can I find in the course of legislation sufficient evidence to convince me that Congress determined to permit state regulation of the reproduction of sound recordings. For

3. It bears noting that in Sears, Roebuck & Co. v. Stiffel Co., 376 U.S. 225 (1964), the Court repeatedly referred to the patent and copyright statutes as if the same rules of interpretation applied to both. See, e.g., 396 U.S., at 228, 231 n. 7; Compco Corp. v. Day–Brite Lighting Inc., 376 U.S. 234, 237 (1964).

whenever technological advances made extension of copyright protection seem wise, Congress has acted promptly.   * * *   This seems to me to reflect the same judgment that the Court found in *Sears* and *Compco:* Congress has decided that free competition should be the general rule, until it is convinced that the failure to provide copyright or patent protection is hindering "the Progress of Science and useful Arts."

The business of record piracy is not an attractive one; persons in the business capitalize on the talents of others without needing to assess independently the prospect of public acceptance of a performance.   But the same might be said of persons who copy "mechanical configurations." Such people do provide low-cost reproductions that may well benefit the public.   In light of the presumption of *Sears* and *Compco* that congressional silence betokens a determination that the benefits of competition outweigh the impediments placed on creativity by the lack of copyright protection, and in the absence of a congressional determination that the opposite is true, we should not let our distaste for "pirates" interfere with our interpretation of the copyright laws.   I would therefore hold that, as to sound recordings fixed before February 15, 1972, the States may not enforce laws limiting reproduction.

———————

KEWANEE OIL CO. V. BICRON CORP., 416 U.S. 470 (1974).   Plaintiff Kewanee had a secret process for producing synthetic crystals.   Defendants, former employees of Kewanee, formed Bicron, a competitor.   The District Court enjoined defendants from using plaintiff's trade secrets, but the Court of Appeals held that Ohio trade secret law was in conflict with federal patent law in that plaintiff's techniques might have been patentable, but having been in commercial use for more than a year, they were no longer eligible for federal protection, 35 U.S.C.A. § 102(b).   (This possibility of preemption had been suggested in Lear v. Adkins, 395 U.S. 653 (1969).)   The Supreme Court, in an opinion by Chief Justice Burger, reinstated the judgment of the District Court:

"The first issue we deal with is whether the States are forbidden to act at all in the area of protection of the kinds of intellectual property which may make up the subject matter of trade secrets.   * * *

"Just as the States may exercise regulatory power over writings so may the States regulate with respect to discoveries.   States may hold diverse viewpoints in protecting intellectual property relating to invention as they do in protecting the intellectual property relating to the subject matter of copyright.   The only limitation on the States is that in regulating the area of patents and copyrights they do not conflict with the operation of the laws in this area passed by Congress, and it is to that more difficult question we now turn.

"The question of whether the trade secret law of Ohio is void under the Supremacy Clause involves a consideration of whether that law 'stands as an obstacle to the accomplishment and execution of the full purposes and objectives of Congress.' Hines v. Davidowitz, 312 U.S. 52, 67 (1941). * * *

"The laws which the Court of Appeals in this case held to be in conflict with the Ohio law of trade secrets were the patent laws passed by the Congress in the unchallenged exercise of its clear power under Art. I, § 8, cl. 8, of the Constitution. The patent law does not explicitly endorse or forbid the operation of trade secret law. However, as we have noted, if the scheme of protection developed by Ohio respecting trade secrets 'clashes with the objectives of the federal patent laws,' Sears, Roebuck & Co. v. Stiffel Co., supra, 376 U.S. at 231, then the state law must fall. To determine whether the Ohio law 'clashes' with the federal law it is helpful to examine the objectives of both the patent and trade secret laws.

"The stated objective of the Constitution in granting the power to Congress to legislate in the area of intellectual property is to 'promote the Progress of Science and useful Arts.' The patent laws promote this progress by offering a right of exclusion for a limited period as an incentive for inventors to risk the often enormous costs in terms of time, research, and development. The productive effort thereby fostered will have a positive effect on society through the introduction of new products and processes of manufacture into the economy, and the emanations by way of increased employment and better lives for our citizens. In return for the right of exclusion—this 'reward for inventions,' Universal Oil Co. v. Globe Co., 322 U.S. 471, 484 (1944)—the patent laws impose upon the inventor a requirement of disclosure. To insure adequate and full disclosure so that upon the expiration of the 17-year period 'the knowledge of the invention enures to the people, who are thus enabled without restriction to practice it and profit by its use,' United States v. Dubilier Condenser Corp., 289 U.S. 178, 187 (1933), the patent laws require that the patent application shall include a full and clear description of the invention and 'of the manner and process of making and using it' so that any person skilled in the art may make and use the invention. 35 U.S.C.A. § 112. When a patent is granted and the information contained in it is circulated to the general public and those especially skilled in the trade, such additions to the general store of knowledge are of such importance to the public weal that the Federal Government is willing to pay the high price of 17 years of exclusive use for its disclosure, which disclosure, it is assumed, will stimulate ideas and the eventual development of further significant advances in the art. The Court has also articulated another policy of the patent law: that which is in the public domain cannot be removed therefrom by action of the States.

'[F]ederal laws requires that all ideas in general circulation be dedicated to the common good unless they are protected by a valid patent.' Lear, Inc. v. Adkins, 395 U.S., at 668.

See also Goldstein v. California, 412 U.S., at 570–571; Sears, Roebuck & Co. v. Stiffel Co., supra; Compco Corp. v. Day–Brite Lighting, Inc., 376 U.S. 234, 237–238 (1964); International News Service v. Associated Press, 248 U.S. 215, 250 (1918) (Brandeis, J., dissenting.)"

Chief Justice Burger next examined the policies that underlie state trade secret law, and then turned to the question of whether state trade secret protection constituted "too great an encroachment on the federal patent system to be tolerated."

"As we noted earlier, trade secret law protects items which would not be proper subjects for consideration for patent protection under 35 U.S.C. § 101. As in the case of the recordings in Goldstein v. California, Congress, with respect to nonpatentable subject matter, 'has drawn no balance; rather, it has left the area unattended, and no reason exists why the State should not be free to act.' Goldstein v. California, supra, at 570. * * *

"Congress has spoken in the area of those discoveries which fall within one of the categories of patentable subject matter of 35 U.S.C. § 101 and which are, therefore, of a nature that would be subject to consideration for a patent. Processes, machines, manufactures, compositions of matter, and improvements thereof, which meet the tests of utility, novelty, and nonobviousness are entitled to be patented, but those which do not, are not. The question remains whether those items which are proper subjects for consideration for a patent may also have available the alternative protection accorded by trade secret law.

"Certainly the patent policy of encouraging invention is not disturbed by the existence of another form of incentive to invention. In this respect the two systems are not and never would be in conflict. Similarly, the policy that matter once in the public domain must remain in the public domain is not incompatible with the existence of trade secret protection. By definition a trade secret has not been placed in the public domain.

"The more difficult objective of the patent law to reconcile with trade secret law is that of disclosure, the *quid pro quo* of the right to exclude."

The Court concluded that "there is no real possibility that trade secret law will conflict with the federal policy favoring disclosure," chiefly because the scope of trade secret protection is limited; anyone not bound by confidence or contract may independently discover and exploit the secret. "The possibility that an inventor who believes his invention meets the standards of patentability will sit back, rely on trade secret law, and after one year of use forfeit any right to patent protection, 35 U.S.C. § 102(b), is remote indeed."

The Chief Justice also noted that "[t]rade secret law and patent law have co-existed in this country for over one hundred years," and concluded that "Congress, by its silence over these many years, has seen the wisdom of allowing the States to enforce trade secret protection. Until Congress takes affirmative action to the contrary, States should be free to grant protection to trade secrets."

Justice Marshall concurred in the result, accepting the co-existence argument. Justices Douglas and Brennan dissented, invoking *Sears* and *Compco* and the federal policy favoring disclosure in return for the patent monopoly.

BONITO BOATS, INC. v. THUNDER CRAFT BOATS, INC., 489 U.S. 141, 109 S.Ct. 971 (1989). Justice O'Connor wrote the opinion for a unanimous Court sustaining the defendant's challenge to a Florida statute that declared it "unlawful for any person to use the direct molding process to duplicate for the purpose of sale any manufactured vessel hull or component part of a vessel made by another without the written permission of that other person."

"We must decide today what limits the operation of the federal patent system places on the States' ability to offer substantial protection to utilitarian and design ideas which the patent laws leave otherwise unprotected. * * *

" * * * The federal patent system thus embodies a carefully crafted bargain for encouraging the creation and disclosure of new, useful, and nonobvious advances in technology and design in return for the exclusive right to practice the invention for a period of years. * * *

"The attractiveness of such a bargain, and its effectiveness in inducing creative effort and disclosure of the results of that effort, depend almost entirely on a backdrop of free competition in the exploitation of unpatented designs and innovations. The novelty and nonobviousness requirements of patentability embody a congressional understanding, implicit in the Patent Clause itself, that free exploitation of ideas will be the rule, to which the protection of a federal patent is the exception. Moreover, the ultimate goal of the patent system is to bring new designs and technologies into the public domain through disclosure. State law protection for techniques and designs whose disclosure has already been induced by market rewards may conflict with the very purpose of the patent laws by decreasing the range of ideas available as the building blocks of further innovation. The offer of federal protection from competitive exploitation of intellectual property would be rendered meaningless in a world where substantially similar state law protections were readily available. To a limited extent, the federal patent laws must determine not only what is protected, but also what is free for all to use. * * *

"The pre-emptive sweep of our decisions in *Sears* and *Compco* has been the subject of heated scholarly and judicial debate. See, e.g., Symposium, Product Simulation: A Right or a Wrong?, 64 Colum.L.Rev. 1178 (1964); Lear, Inc. v. Adkins, 395 U.S. 653, 676 (1969) (Black, J., concurring in part and dissenting in part). Read at their highest level of generality, the two decisions could be taken to stand for the proposition that the States are completely disabled from offering any form of protection to articles or processes which fall within the broad scope of patentable subject matter. See id., at 677. Since the potentially patentable includes 'anything under the sun that is made by man,' Diamond v. Chakrabarty, 447 U.S. 303, 309 (1980) (citation omitted), the broadest reading of *Sears* would prohibit the States from regulating the deceptive simulation of trade dress or the tortious appropriation of private information.

"That the extrapolation of such a broad pre-emptive principle from *Sears* is inappropriate is clear from the balance struck in *Sears* itself. The *Sears* Court made it plain that the States 'may protect businesses in the use of their trademarks, labels, or distinctive dress in the packaging of goods so as to prevent others, by imitating such markings, from misleading purchasers as to the source of the goods.' *Sears, supra,* 376 U.S., at 232 (footnote omitted). Trade dress is, of course, potentially the subject matter of design patents. See W.T. Rogers Co. v. Keene, 778 F.2d 334, 337 (CA7 1985). Yet our decision in *Sears* clearly indicates that the States may place limited regulations on the circumstances in which such designs are used in order to prevent consumer confusion as to source. Thus, while *Sears* speaks in absolutist terms, its conclusion that the States may place some conditions on the use of trade dress indicates an implicit recognition that all state regulation of potentially patentable but unpatented subject matter is not *ipso facto* pre-empted by the federal patent laws. * * *

"We believe that the Florida statute at issue in this case so substantially impedes the public use of the otherwise unprotected design and utilitarian ideas embodied in unpatented boat hulls as to run afoul of the teaching of our decisions in *Sears* and *Compco.* It is readily apparent that the Florida statute does not operate to prohibit 'unfair competition' in the usual sense that the term is understood. The law of unfair competition has its roots in the common-law tort of deceit: its general concern is with protecting *consumers* from confusion as to source. While that concern may result in the creation of 'quasi-property rights' in communicative symbols, the focus is on the protection of consumers, not the protection of producers as an incentive to product innovation. Judge Hand captured the distinction well in Crescent Tool Co. v. Kilborn & Bishop Co., 247 F. 299, 301 (CA2 1917), where he wrote:

'[T]he plaintiff has the right not to lose his customers through false representations that those are his wares which in fact are not, but he may not monopolize any design or pattern, however trifling. The defendant, on the other hand, may copy plaintiff's goods slavishly down to the minutest detail: but he may not represent himself as the plaintiff in their sale.'

"With some notable exceptions, including the interpretation of the Illinois law of unfair competition at issue in *Sears* and *Compco,* see *Sears, supra,* 376 U.S., at 227–228, n. 2, the common-law tort of unfair competition has been limited to protection against copying of nonfunctional aspects of consumer products which have acquired secondary meaning such that they operate as a designation of source. See generally P. Kaufmann, Passing Off and Misappropriation, in 9 IIC Studies in Industrial Property and Copyright Law 100–109 (1986). The 'protection' granted a particular design under the law of unfair competition is thus limited to one context where consumer confusion is likely to result; the design 'idea' itself may be freely exploited in all other contexts.

"In contrast to the operation of unfair competition law, the Florida statute is aimed directly at preventing the exploitation of the design and utilitarian conceptions embodied in the product itself. The sparse legislative history surrounding its enactment indicates that it was intended to create an inducement for the improvement of boat hull designs. * * *

"Our decisions since *Sears* and *Compco* have made it clear that the Patent and Copyright Clauses do not, by their own force or by negative implication, deprive the States of the power to adopt rules for the promotion of intellectual creation within their own jurisdictions.   * * *

"Nor does the fact that a particular item lies within the subject matter of the federal patent laws necessarily preclude the States from offering limited protection which does not impermissibly interfere with the federal patent scheme. As *Sears* itself makes clear, States may place limited regulations on the use of unpatented designs in order to prevent consumer confusion as to source. In *Kewanee*, we found that state protection of trade secrets, as applied to both patentable and unpatentable subject matter, did not conflict with the federal patent laws. In both situations, state protection was not aimed exclusively at the promotion of invention itself, and the state restrictions on the use of unpatented ideas were limited to those necessary to promote goals outside the contemplation of the federal patent scheme. Both the law of unfair competition and state trade secret law have coexisted harmoniously with federal patent protection for almost 200 years, and Congress has given no indication that their operation is inconsistent with the operation of the federal patent laws. See Florida Lime & Avocado Growers, Inc. v. Paul, 373 U.S. 132, 144 (1963); United States v. Bass, 404 U.S. 336, 349 (1971).

"Indeed, there are affirmative indications from Congress that both the law of unfair competition and trade secret protection are consistent with the balance struck by the patent laws.   Section 43(a) of the Lanham Act, 60 Stat. 441, 15 U.S.C. § 1125(a), creates a federal remedy for making 'a false designation of origin, or any false description or representation, including words or other symbols tending falsely to describe or represent the same....'   Congress has thus given federal recognition to many of the concerns which underlie the state tort of unfair competition, and the application of *Sears* and *Compco* to nonfunctional aspects of a product which have been shown to identify source must take account of competing federal policies in this regard.   * * *

"The Florida statute is aimed directly at the promotion of intellectual creation by substantially restricting the public's ability to exploit ideas which the patent system mandates shall be free for all to use.   Like the interpretation of Illinois unfair competition law in *Sears* and *Compco,* the Florida statute represents a break with the tradition of peaceful coexistence between state market regulation and federal patent policy.   * * *

"Congress has considered extending various forms of limited protection to industrial design either through the copyright laws or by relaxing the restrictions on the availability of design patents.   See generally Brown, Design Protection: An Overview, 34 U.C.L.A. L.Rev. 1341 (1987).   Congress explicitly refused to take this step in the copyright laws, see 17 U.S.C. § 101; H.R.Rep. No. 94–1476, p. 55 (1976), and despite sustained criticism for a number of years, it has declined to alter the patent protections presently available for industrial design. See Report of the President's Commission on the Patent System, S. Doc. No. 5, 90th Cong., 1st Sess., 20–

21 (1967); Lindgren, The Sanctity of the Design Patent: Illusion or Reality?, 10 Okla. City L. Rev. 195 (1985). * * * By offering patent-like protection for ideas deemed unprotected under the present federal scheme, the Florida statute conflicts with the 'strong federal policy favoring free competition in ideas which do not merit patent protection.' *Lear, Inc.,* 395 U.S., at 656. We therefore agree with the majority of the Florida Supreme Court that the Florida statute is preempted by the Supremacy Clause, and the judgment of that court is hereby affirmed."[a]

NOTES AND QUESTIONS ON THE PREEMPTION CASES

(1) In distinguishing *Sears* and *Compco,* the majority opinion in *Goldstein* concludes that in regard to mechanical configurations, Congress, through the patent laws, has determined not only what is to be protected, but also what is to be left in the public domain. In regard to writings, the Court concludes that, as to some, Congress had "left the area unattended." Is this distinction justified? Does Justice Marshall make a convincing case in dissent for interpreting the Congressional silence before 1971 as an indication of its intent to leave sound recordings in the public domain until it determined to bring them within the Copyright Act?

Congressional intent on the issue of pre–1972 sound recordings is considerably less ambiguous under the current Copyright Act. See § 301(c).

The recognition that the states have power to protect certain writings even after publication was foreshadowed in a study by Whicher, The Ghost of Donaldson v. Becket: An Inquiry into the Constitutional Distribution of Powers over the Law of Literary Property in the United States, 9 Bull.Copyr.Soc. 102 and 194 (1961–62), characterized as heresy in early editions of this casebook.

(2) Do *Goldstein* and *Kewanee* merely reflect the shift by the Burger court toward upholding state power against claims of federal preemption? See Note, The Preemption Doctrine: Shifting Perspectives on Federalism and the Burger Court, 75 Colum.L.Rev. 623 (1975). The Burger court considered the preemptive effect of federal patent law again in Aronson v. Quick Point Pencil Co., 440 U.S. 257 (1979), upholding a state contract law claim for royalties due on the sale of articles embodying an innovation for which a patent had been denied.

(3) Does *Bonito Boats* restore any erosion that *Sears* and *Compco* may have suffered from *Goldstein* or *Kewanee?*

(4) On the other hand, does Justice O'Connor's opinion—by its interpretation of the Illinois law at issue in *Sears* and *Compco* and its caution that "application of *Sears* and *Compco* to nonfunctional aspects of a product which have been shown to identify source must take account of the

---

a. In 1998, the House passed a bill (H.R. 2696) that would provide sui generis protection under federal law to vessel hulls, complete with its own registration system in the Copyright Office and a special design notice (a "D" in a circle).

competing federal policies" reflected in § 43(a)—rehabilitate state trademark protection for nonfunctional product features with secondary meaning? If so, the case represents a significant retreat from the sweeping language in *Compco*.

Compare the analysis of *Bonito Boats* in Shipley, Refusing to Rock the Boat: The *Sears–Compco* Preemption Doctrine Applied to *Bonito Boats v. Thunder Craft,* 25 Wake Forest L.Rev. 385 (1990), with Wiley, *Bonito Boats:* Uninformed But Mandatory Innovation Policy, 1989 Sup.Ct.Rev. 283. See also Heald, Federal Intellectual Property Law and the Economics of Preemption, 76 Iowa L.Rev. 959 (1991), applying the *Bonito Boats* rationale to other state doctrines including publicity rights, resale royalty rights, and trademark dilution.

STATUTORY PREEMPTION—§ 301

HOUSE REPORT (pp. 130–131)

Preemption of State law

The intention of section 301 is to preempt and abolish any rights under the common law or statutes of a State that are equivalent to copyright and that extend to works coming within the scope of the Federal copyright law. The declaration of this principle in section 301 is intended to be stated in the clearest and most unequivocal language possible, so as to foreclose any conceivable misinterpretation of its unqualified intention that Congress shall act preemptively, and to avoid the development of any vague borderline areas between State and Federal protection.

Under section 301(a) all "legal or equitable rights that are equivalent to any of the exclusive rights within the general scope of copyright as specified by section 106" are governed exclusively by the Federal copyright statute if the works involved are "works of authorship that are fixed in a tangible medium of expression and come within the subject matter of copyright as specified by sections 102 and 103." All corresponding State laws, whether common law or statutory, are preempted and abrogated. Regardless of when the work was created and whether it is published or unpublished, disseminated or undisseminated, in the public domain or copyrighted under the Federal statute, the States cannot offer it protection equivalent to copyright. Section 1338 of title 28, United States Code, also makes clear that any action involving rights under the Federal copyright law would come within the exclusive jurisdiction of the Federal courts. The preemptive effect of section 301 is limited to State laws; as stated expressly in subsection (d) of section 301, there is no intention to deal with the question of whether Congress can or should offer the equivalent of copyright protection under some constitutional provision other than the patent-copyright clause of article 1, section 8.

At the time the House Report was prepared, § 301(b) of the revision bill read as follows:

> (b) Nothing in this title annuls or limits any rights or remedies under the common law or statutes of any State with respect to
>
> * * *
>
> (3) activities violating legal or equitable rights that are not equivalent to any of the exclusive rights within the general scope of copyright as specified by section 106, including rights against misappropriation not equivalent to any of such exclusive rights, breaches of contract, breaches of trust, trespass, conversion, invasion of privacy, defamation, and deceptive trade practices such as passing off and false representation. (H.R.Rep. p. 24.)

The inclusion of "rights against misappropriation not equivalent to" copyright was a complete turnabout. An earlier House Report, commenting on a version of § 301(b) that did not include misappropriation in its list of non-equivalent rights, had said:

> In accordance with the Supreme Court's decision in Sears, Roebuck & Co. v. Stiffel Co., section 301 is not intended to preempt common law protection in cases involving activities such as false labeling, fraudulent representation, and passing off, even where the subject matter involved comes within the scope of the copyright statute. However, where the cause of action involves the form of unfair competition commonly referred to as "misappropriation," which is nothing more than copyright protection under another name, section 301 is intended to have preemptive effect.[b]

The Antitrust Division of the Department of Justice opposed the addition of misappropriation to the § 301(b)(3) list of preserved rights and pressed for its deletion when the bill was about to pass the Senate. See 122 Cong.Rec. 3836 (Feb. 19, 1976) (letter to Senator Scott). When this move was unsuccessful, a letter was written to the House Committee stressing the Department's position that remedies against misappropriation were anti-competitive and expressing concern that the list of allowable state rights might be misused "to nullify preemption." See Fetter, Copyright Revision and the Preemption of State "Misappropriation" Law, 25 Bull.Copyr.Soc. 367, 418–24 (1978). Nothing happened. But at the very last moment before passage of the bill in the House, Congressman Seiberling offered an amendment to strike the entire list of examples from subsection (b)(3). It evoked the following dialogue:

> Mr. SEIBERLING. Mr. Chairman, my amendment is intended to save the "Federal preemption" of State law section, which is section 301 of the bill, from being inadvertently nullified because of the inclusion of certain examples in the exemptions from preemption.

b. H.R.Rep. No. 2237, 89th Cong., 2d Sess. 129 (1966).

This amendment would simply strike the examples listed in section 301(b)(3).

The amendment is strongly supported by the Justice Department, which believes that it would be a serious mistake to cite as an exemption from preemption the doctrine of "misappropriation." The doctrine was created by the Supreme Court in 1922 [sic], and it has generally been ignored by the Supreme Court itself and by the lower courts ever since.

Inclusion of a reference to the misappropriation doctrine in this bill, however, could easily be construed by the courts as authorizing the States to pass misappropriation laws. We should not approve such enabling legislation, because a misappropriation law could be so broad as to render the preemption section meaningless.

Mr. RAILSBACK. Mr. Chairman, will the gentleman yield?

Mr. SEIBERLING. I yield to the gentleman from Illinois.

Mr. RAILSBACK. Mr. Chairman, may I ask the gentleman from Ohio, for the purpose of clarifying the amendment that by striking the word "misappropriation," the gentleman in no way is attempting to change the existing state of the law, that is as it may exist in certain States that have recognized the right of recovery relating to "misappropriation"; is that correct?

Mr. SEIBERLING. That is correct. All I am trying to do is prevent the citing of them as examples in a statute. We are, in effect, adopting a rather amorphous body of State law and codifying it, in effect. Rather I am trying to have this bill leave the State law alone and make it clear we are merely dealing with copyright laws, laws applicable to copyrights.

Mr. RAILSBACK. Mr. Chairman, I personally have no objection to the gentleman's amendment in view of that clarification and I know of no objections from this side.

Mr. SEIBERLING. I thank the gentleman.

(122 Cong.Rec. 32015 (Sept. 22, 1976))

The amendment was adopted and the revision bill passed. Of such is the legislative process.

NOTES AND QUESTIONS ON § 301

(1) Only state-created rights touching works "within the subject matter of copyright as specified by sections 102 and 103" are subject to preemption under § 301 of the 1976 Act. How should this criterion be interpreted? The House Report offers a partial explanation: "As long as a work fits within one of the general subject matter categories of sections 102 and 103, the bill prevents the State from protecting it even if it fails to achieve Federal statutory copyright because it is too minimal or lacking in originality to qualify, or because it has fallen into the public domain." H.R.Rep. p. 131. But what of works specifically excluded from copyright, such as the designs of useful articles that fail to satisfy the separability test of § 101? May state law, for instance, prohibit the copying of dress designs? They are not, literally, within the "subject matter of copyright." And what of ideas and facts, excluded from copyright by § 102(b)? Are these, by virtue of that exclusion, eligible for state protection?[c]

A few cases, equating "subject matter" with protected matter, have concluded that material which is excluded from copyright under the 1976 Act remains open to state protection. Thus, in Bromhall v. Rorvik, 478 F.Supp. 361 (E.D.Pa.1979), a state-law claim based on the appropriation of ideas from plaintiff's doctoral dissertation escaped preemption on the reasoning that "[c]opyright protection extends only to *expression* of an idea, not the idea itself." Similarly, in Vermont Castings, Inc. v. Evans Prod. Co., 215 U.S.P.Q. 758 (D.Vt.1981), the court concluded that because the inseparable design features of a stove could not command copyright protection, "there can be no preemption under § 301 of the Copyright Act of common law remedies for protection." See also H₂O Swimwear, Ltd. v. Lomas, 164 A.D.2d 804, 560 N.Y.S.2d 19 (1990) (because clothing designs are excluded from copyright, state protection is not preempted).

Should the subject-matter test in § 301 be seen instead as a codification of *Goldstein*, intended to distinguish "attended" from "unattended" areas? In Hoehling v. Univ. City Studios, p. 266 supra, the Second Circuit, operating under the 1909 Act, refused to permit a state unfair competition claim premised on the appropriation of plaintiff's facts and research: "Where, as here, historical facts, themes, and research have been deliberately exempted from the scope of copyright protection to vindicate the overriding goal of encouraging contributions to recorded knowledge, the states are pre-empted from removing such material from the public domain." The Second Circuit took the same position under the 1976 Act in National Basketball Ass'n v. Motorola, Inc., 105 F.3d 841 (2d Cir.1997) ("Section 301 preemption bars state law misappropriation claims with respect to uncopyrightable as well as copyrightable elements."). Other circuits agree. See, e.g., ProCD, Inc. v. Zeidenberg, 86 F.3d 1447 (7th Cir.1996), holding that data in an uncopyrightable compilation falls within the subject matter of the Copyright Act: "One function of § 301 is to prevent states from giving special protection to works of authorship that Congress has decided should be in the public domain, which it can accomplish only if 'subject matter of copyright' includes all works of a type covered by sections 102 and 103, even if federal law does not afford protection to them."; United States ex rel. Berge v. Board of Trustees of Univ. of Alabama, 104 F.3d 1453 (4th Cir.), cert. denied, 118 S.Ct. 301 (1997), holding that although the ideas in plaintiff' dissertation were

---

c. Compare R. Brown, Unification: A Cheerful Requiem for Common–Law Copyright, 24 U.C.L.A. L.Rev. 1070 (1977), with Goldstein, Preempted State Doctrines, Involuntary Transfers and Compulsory Licenses, id. at 1107.

excluded from copyright, they were still within the subject matter of the statute: "[S]cope and protection are not synonymous. Moreover, the shadow actually cast by the Act's preemption is notably broader than the wing of its protection."

(2) Section 301 preempts only rights "equivalent" to those specified in § 106. How is equivalency to be determined? The House Report, commenting on the penultimate version of § 301 (with its examples of nonequivalent rights), offers this analysis:

> The examples in clause (3), while not exhaustive, are intended to illustrate rights and remedies that are different in nature from the rights comprised in a copyright and that may continue to be protected under State common law or statute. The evolving common law rights of "privacy," "publicity," and trade secrets, and the general laws of defamation and fraud, would remain unaffected as long as the causes of action contain elements, such as an invasion of personal rights or a breach of trust or confidentiality, that are different in kind from copyright infringement. Nothing in the bill derogates from the rights of parties to contract with each other and to sue for breaches of contract; however, to the extent that the unfair competition concept known as "interference with contract relations" is merely the equivalent of copyright protection, it would be preempted.

> The last example listed in clause (3)—"deceptive trade practices such as passing off and false representation"—represents an effort to distinguish between those causes of action known as "unfair competition" that the copyright statute is not intended to preempt and those that it is. Section 301 is not intended to preempt common law protection in cases involving activities such as false labeling, fraudulent representation, and passing off even where the subject matter involved comes within the scope of the copyright statute. (H.R.Rep. p. 132.)

When does a state cause of action "contain elements * * * that are different in kind from copyright infringement"? Suppose the state doctrine demands a showing of wrongful intent? In Crow v. Wainwright, 720 F.2d 1224 (11th Cir.1983), cert. denied, 469 U.S. 819 (1984), a state criminal conviction for record piracy was overturned on the basis of federal preemption. "The additional element of scienter traditionally necessary to establish a criminal case merely narrows the applicability of the statute. The prohibited act—wrongfully distributing a copyrighted work—remains the same."[d] The Second Circuit in Harper & Row, Pub., Inc. v. Nation Enterprises, 723 F.2d 195 (2d Cir.1983), rev'd on other grounds, 471 U.S. 539 (1985) (p. 366 supra), determining equivalency by whether the "right defined by state law may be abridged by an act which, in and of itself,

---

d. Compare Hicks v. Maryland, 109 Md.App. 113 , 674 A.2d 55 (1996), upholding a conviction under a criminal statute forbidding the sale of records or videotapes that do not bear a label identifying the person who transferred the sounds or images; the labeling requirement was held not equivalent to the exclusive rights of copyright.

would infringe one of the exclusive rights," held that plaintiffs' claims for conversion and interference with contractual relations were preempted; the additional element of "intentional interference, not part of a copyright infringement claim, goes merely to the scope of the right; it does not establish qualitatively different conduct on the part of the infringing party, nor a fundamental nonequivalence between the state and federal rights implicated." In Rosciszewski v. Arete Associates, Inc., 1 F.3d 225 (4th Cir.1993), plaintiff brought a civil action under the Virginia Computer Crimes Act (Va.Code Ann. §§ 18.2–152.1 et seq.) against a former employee who made an unauthorized copy of plaintiff's software. The state statute required proof that the defendant "use[d] a computer," "without authority," "with the intent to * * * [c]onvert the property of another." As applied to the facts, the cause of action was preempted; the court said that the elements of the claim were not qualitatively different from copyright infringement.

The case law on "equivalent" rights continues to accumulate. Claims involving allegations of passing off or trademark infringement, with their required element of consumer confusion, generally escape preemption, even when the confusion results from the use of copyrightable material. See, e.g., Donald Frederick Evans & Associates, Inc. v. Continental Homes, Inc., 785 F.2d 897 (11th Cir.1986); John H. Harland Co. v. Clarke Checks, Inc., 207 U.S.P.Q. 664 (N.D.Ga.1980), aff'd, 711 F.2d 966 (11th Cir.1983); Warner Brothers v. ABC, Inc., p. 701 infra.[e] Similarly, protection under state trade secret law is not preempted, at least if there are allegations of a breach of confidence. Compare Gates Rubber Co. v. Bando Chemical Industries, Ltd., 9 F.3d 823 (10th Cir.1993) and Computer Associates Int'l, Inc. v. Altai, Inc., 982 F.2d 693 (2d Cir.1992), with Avco Corp. v. Precision Air Parts, Inc., 210 U.S.P.Q. 894 (M.D.Ala.1980), aff'd, 676 F.2d 494 (11th Cir.), cert. denied, 459 U.S. 1037 (1982). For conversion claims, courts have drawn a distinction between actions seeking redress for deprivations of physical property and those relating to exploitation through reproduction; the latter are preempted. See, e.g., Ehat v. Tanner, 780 F.2d 876 (10th Cir.1985), cert. denied, 479 U.S. 820 (1986); Mayer v. Josiah Wedgwood & Sons, Ltd., 601 F.Supp. 1523 (S.D.N.Y.1985).

What of claims for unjust enrichment? When the "enrichment" consists of the use of material within the subject matter of copyright, the cause of action generally has failed. See, e.g., Del Madera Properties v. Rhodes and Gardner, Inc., 820 F.2d 973 (9th Cir.1987); Selmon v. Hasbro

---

e. When the alleged deception is not, as in the usual case, passing off by a defendant of its own goods as those of the plaintiff, but instead, that the defendant by selling copies of the plaintiff's work is claiming the plaintiff's work as its own (so-called "reverse passing off"), the claim seems nearer to unauthorized reproduction and may not escape preemption. Compare Kregos v. Associated Press, 3 F.3d 656 (2d Cir. 1993), cert. denied, 510 U.S. 1112 (1994), and Fisher v. Dees, 794 F.2d 432 (9th Cir.1986), both holding that claims alleging false implications of authorship resulting from unauthorized reproduction are preempted, with Summit Machine Tool Manuf. Corp. v. Victor CNC Systems, Inc., 7 F.3d 1434 (9th Cir.1993) (dictum), and Tracy v. Skate Key, Inc., 697 F.Supp. 748 (S.D.N.Y.1988), both concluding that reverse passing off is not preempted.

Bradley, Inc., 669 F.Supp. 1267 (S.D.N.Y.1987). But see Schuchart & Associates, Professional Engineers, Inc. v. Solo Serve Corp., 540 F.Supp. 928 (W.D.Tex.1982).

Is the Supreme Court's preemption analysis in *Kewanee* useful in determining equivalent rights under § 301?

(3) Unwilling to rely solely on the protection afforded by intellectual property law, creators often seek to impose contractual limitations on the use of their creations. (The move to on-line dissemination of works has increased the opportunities for contractual relationships between producers and end users.) Do claims for breach of contract survive analysis under § 301? For the most part, the courts have said that they do. See, e.g., Acorn Structures, Inc. v. Swantz, 846 F.2d 923 (4th Cir.1988). In ProCD, Inc. v. Zeidenberg, 86 F.3d 1447 (7th Cir.1996), p. 133 supra, Judge Easterbrook stated broadly that contracts, since they affect only the parties, do not create "exclusive rights" and hence are not equivalent to copyright. (Equivalency aside, is there anything to the district court's argument that a contractual restriction on the reproduction of uncopyrightable data contained in a publicly distributed product should be preempted because it "erects a barrier on access to information that under copyright law should be accessible"? 908 F.Supp. 640, 658 (W.D.Wis.1996). See Note (5) infra.)

In National Car Rental Sys., Inc. v. Computer Associates Int'l, Inc., 991 F.2d 426 (8th Cir.), cert. denied, 510 U.S. 861 (1993), the Eighth Circuit held that a claim for breach of contract was not preempted under § 301, at least when, as here, the contract created rights that are not equivalent to any of the exclusive rights of copyright (in this case a restriction on certain uses of the work). Is this caveat necessary? Compare American Movie Classics Co. v. Turner Entertainment Co., 922 F.Supp. 926 (S.D.N.Y.1996), holding that a contract claim is preempted if the contract right is equivalent to a right under copyright, with Architectronics, Inc. v. Control Systems, Inc., 935 F.Supp. 425 (S.D.N.Y.1996), expressly rejecting *American Movie Classics* and holding that the defendant's promise is itself sufficient to make a contract claim different from copyright, even if the contract right is similar to one under § 106.

(4) The history of § 301 attests to the uncertain status of rights against misappropriation. Is a cause of action for "misappropriation" equivalent to the exclusive rights of reproduction, distribution, or performance?

The House Report, commenting on § 301 and its short-lived reference to "rights against misappropriation not equivalent" to copyright, states:

> "Misappropriation" is not necessarily synonymous with copyright infringement, and thus a cause of action labeled as "misappropriation" is not preempted if it is in fact based neither on a right within the general scope of copyright as specified by section 106 nor on a right equivalent thereto. For example, state law should have the flexibility to afford a remedy (under traditional principles of equity) against a consistent pattern of unauthorized appropriation by a competitor of the facts (i.e., not the literary

expression) constituting "hot" news, whether in the traditional mold of International News Service v. Associated Press, 248 U.S. 215 (1918), or in the newer form of data updates from scientific, business, or financial data bases. (H.R.Rep. p. 132.) **f**

Misappropriation claims seeking redress for the reproduction of works within the subject matter of copyright generally have failed to survive analysis under § 301, see, e.g., Warner Brothers, Inc. v. ABC, p. 700 infra, although when the taking relates to facts, the courts have been hard pressed to distinguish the House Report's favorable reference to *INS*. See, e.g., Financial Information, Inc. v. Moody's Investors Service, Inc., 808 F.2d 204 (2d Cir.1986), cert. denied, 484 U.S. 820 (1987) (misappropriation claim preempted, distinguishing *INS* on the basis of its "quantity of copying" and "immediacy of distribution"); Nash v. CBS, Inc., 704 F.Supp. 823 (N.D.Ill. 1989), aff'd, 899 F.2d 1537 (7th Cir.1990) (preempted claim did not involve "the 'systematic' appropriation of 'hot news' "). Misappropriation counts directed at unauthorized performances have also been unsuccessful. See Orth–O–Vision, Inc. v. Home Box Office, 474 F.Supp. 672 (S.D.N.Y.1979).

In a major statement on misappropriation and preemption, the Second Circuit in National Basketball Ass'n v. Motorola, Inc., 105 F.3d 841 (2d Cir.1997), vacated an injunction against the defendant's paging device that provided updated information on NBA basketball games. The defendant obtained the information from "reporters" who were assigned to monitor radio and television coverage of the games and relay specific data to the defendant by computer for transmission to the pagers. Judge Winter agreed with the district court's dismissal of the NBA's copyright claims; the games were not within the subject matter of copyright, and there was no infringement of the broadcasts since the defendant took only facts. The district court had based its injunction on common law misappropriation; the appeal turned on whether the claim was preempted under § 301.

Relying on the House Report's comment that state law could continue to provide relief against appropriations of "hot news" as in INS v. AP, the Second Circuit said that "[t]he crucial question, therefore, is the breadth of the 'hot-news' claim that survives preemption." The court concluded that the extra elements that allow a hot news claim to escape preemption are "(i) the time-sensitive value of factual information, (ii) the freeriding by a defendant, and (iii) the threat to the very existence of the product or service provided by the plaintiff." Although the information was time-sensitive, the court decided that the NBA had failed to satisfy the reminder of the test. The defendant's pagers did not threaten the NBA's primary business—conducting basketball games and licensing broadcasts. In re-

f. This passage of the House Report appears to have its origin in an American Bar Association Committee Report. Section of Patent, Trademark and Copyright Law, Reports to be Presented at [Aug. 1975] Meeting, Comm. No. 309, Copyright and New Technology 177, 180–82 (1975). This report raised alarms about "data updates," etc., and proposed the reinforcing addition of trespass and conversion to the catalog in § 301(b)(3). The ABA Report concludes with the suggested redraft of § 301(b), which was adopted by the Senate.

sponse to the NBA's argument that the misappropriation threatened its plans for a competing pager, Judge Winter argued that, in the context of the pager market, there was no freeriding since the defendant was bearing its own costs of collecting and transmitting the information. The misappropriation claim was therefore preempted.

If the NBA's claim could not squeeze under the "hot news" exception, is anything left of common law misappropriation under § 301? Judge Winter said in dictum that if a paging service appropriated facts from a competing pager, the claim might survive. Was the court justified in recognizing *any* exception for "hot news" based on comments in the House Report written before Congress struck all reference to misappropriation from § 301 of the copyright revision bill?

The preemption issue is analyzed in Abrams, Copyright, Misappropriation, and Preemption: Constitutional and Statutory Limits of State Law Protection, 1983 Sup.Ct.Rev. 509 (1984).

(5) Does the preemptive effect of the 1976 Copyright Act extend beyond § 301? What of state laws that are alleged to undermine rights granted by the Act to owners or users; if any such law "stands as an obstacle to the accomplishment and execution of the full purposes and objectives of Congress," Hines v. Davidowitz, 312 U.S. 52, 67 (1941) (quoted in *Goldstein*, p. 609 supra), would it not be preempted under the supremacy clause? For example, some states have tried to regulate the manner in which motion picture distributors license their films to exhibitors. Is this an impermissible interference with federal copyright policy? See Associated Film Distrib. Corp. v. Thornburgh, 683 F.2d 808 (3d Cir.1982), after remand, 800 F.2d 369 (3d Cir.1986), cert. denied, 480 U.S. 933 (1987); Allied Artists Pictures Corp. v. Rhodes, 496 F.Supp. 408 (S.D.Ohio 1980), aff'd, 679 F.2d 656 (6th Cir.1982). Enforcement of a New York statute requiring performance rights organizations like ASCAP to notify proprietors within 72 hours after commencing an investigation of unauthorized performances was enjoined in ASCAP v. Pataki, 930 F.Supp. 873 (S.D.N.Y.1996); the court said the statute was preempted under the supremacy clause as "an obstacle to the enforcement of the federal copyright statute." See also Rano v. Sipa Press, Inc., 987 F.2d 580 (9th Cir.1993), which reached the surprising conclusion that a California rule permitting termination at will of contracts that do not specify a particular duration is preempted when applied to copyright licenses; the court thought the rule would conflict with § 203 of the Copyright Act, which permits the termination of copyright licenses after 35 years. (See p. 488 supra.) Does it?

When New York passed a statute requiring the public filing of questions and answers on standardized tests within 30 days after release of the tests results, the law was challenged by the owner of the copyright in the MCAT test used in medical school admissions. Plaintiff argued that the statute was in conflict with its exclusive rights under § 106 to publish, copy, and distribute the test; it also argued that the statute facilitated infringement of its copyright. The District Court granted summary judgment against New York. On appeal, the Second Circuit in Association of

American Medical Colleges v. Cuomo, 928 F.2d 519 (2d Cir.), cert. denied, 502 U.S. 862 (1991), said that if the statute facilitated infringement, it would be preempted, but the court remanded the case for further consideration of New York's argument that the statute merely facilitated "fair uses." Kreiss, Copyright Fair Use of Standardized Tests, 48 Rutgers L.Rev. 1043 (1996), argues that disclosure of works that have been commercially exploited by their owner is fair use, and thus the New York statute does not conflict with federal copyright law, disagreeing with College Entrance Examination Bd. v. Pataki, 889 F.Supp. 554, modified, 893 F.Supp. 152 (N.D.N.Y.1995).

If contract rights survive § 301 as not equivalent to copyright, might some nevertheless interfere with federal copyright policy and thus fail under the supremacy clause? Does the buyer's promise in *ProCD* (p. 133 supra) not to make commercial use of the uncopyrightable data in plaintiff's directory interfere with the balance drawn in the Copyright Act? Would the court in *ProCD* uphold a shrink-wrap license accompanying a biography that required purchasers to promise that they would not use any of the facts in a subsequent book?

Karjala, Federal Preemption of Shrinkwrap and On–Line Licenses, 22 U.Dayton L.Rev. 511 (1997), argues that the contours of copyright protection are not mere default rules subject to variation by contract. In Vault Corp. v. Quaid Software Ltd., 847 F.2d 255 (5th Cir.1988), the court said that a Louisiana statute permitting software manufacturers to restrict copying and modifications by buyers through the use of "shrink wrap" licenses (see p. 133 supra) was in conflict with the rights granted under § 117 and hence preempted. However, two articles by O'Rourke, Drawing the Boundaries Between Copyright and Contract: Copyright Preemption of Computer License Terms, 45 Duke L.J. 479 (1995), and Copyright Preemption After the *ProCD* Case: A Market–Based Approach, 12 Berkeley Tech. L.J. 53 (1997), push toward a freedom of contract model, limited only by market factors raising antitrust or contract formation problems.

CHAPTER 8

APPLICATIONS OF UNFAIR COMPETITION

SECTION 1. IMITATION OF DESIGN AND APPEARANCE

To what extent can the state and federal law of unfair competition as described in the preceding sections be enlisted as a complement to copyright in the protection of artistic and literary works? The Second Circuit some 35 years before *Sears* and *Compco* had in a notable opinion by Judge Learned Hand declared a broad privilege to copy matter left unprotected by federal copyright.

CHENEY BROTHERS v. DORIS SILK CORP., 35 F.2d 279 (2d Cir.1929), cert. denied, 281 U.S. 728 (1930). Plaintiff manufactured silks; most of the designs had a short seasonal life. Design patents were not practically obtainable on the many patterns put out each year, and copyright was not then available for textile designs. A bill in equity was brought against a copier.

"The plaintiff asks for protection only during the season, and needs no more, for the designs are all ephemeral. It seeks in this way to disguise the extent of the proposed innovation, and to persuade us that, if we interfere only a little, the solecism, if there be one, may be pardonable. But the reasoning which would justify any interposition at all demands that it cover the whole extent of the injury. A man whose designs come to harvest in two years, or in five, has prima facie as good right to protection as one who deals only in annuals. Nor could we consistently stop at designs; processes, machines, and secrets have an equal claim. The upshot must be that, whenever any one has contrived any of these, others may be forbidden to copy it. This is not the law. In the absence of some recognized right at common law, or under the statutes—and the plaintiff claims neither—a man's property is limited to the chattels which embody his invention. * * *

"Of the cases on which the plaintiff relies, the chief is International News Service v. Associated Press, 248 U.S. 215. Although that concerned another subject-matter—printed news dispatches—we agree that, if it meant to lay down a general doctrine, it would cover this case; at least, the language of the majority opinion goes so far. We do not believe that it did. While it is of course true that law ordinarily speaks in general terms, there are cases where the occasion is at once the justification for, and the limit of, what is decided. This appears to us such an instance; we think that no more was covered than situations substantially similar to those then at bar. The difficulties of understanding it otherwise are insuperable. We are to suppose that the court meant to create a sort of common-law patent or copyright for reasons of justice. Either would flagrantly conflict with the scheme which Congress has for more than a century devised to cover the subject-matter.

"Qua patent, we should at least have to decide, as tabula rasa, whether the design or machine was new and required invention; further, we must ignore the Patent Office whose action has always been a condition upon the creation of this kind of property. Qua copyright, although it would be simpler to decide upon the merits, we should equally be obliged to dispense with the conditions imposed upon the creation of the right. Nor, if we went so far, should we know whether the property so recognized should be limited to the periods prescribed in the statutes, or should extend as long as the author's grievance. It appears to us incredible that the Supreme Court should have had in mind any such consequences. To exclude others from the enjoyment of a chattel is one thing; to prevent any imitation of it, to set up a monopoly in the plan of its structure, gives the author a power over his fellows vastly greater, a power which the Constitution allows only Congress to create. * * *

"True, it would seem as though the plaintiff had suffered a grievance for which there should be a remedy, perhaps by an amendment of the Copyright Law, assuming that this does not already cover the case, which is not urged here. It seems a lame answer in such a case to turn the injured party out of court, but there are larger issues at stake than his redress. Judges have only a limited power to amend the law; when the subject has been confided to a Legislature, they must stand aside, even though there be an hiatus in completed justice. An omission in such cases must be taken to have been as deliberate as though it were express, certainly after long-standing action on the subject-matter. Indeed, we are not in any position to pass upon the questions involved, as Brandeis, J., observed in International News Service v. Associated Press. We must judge upon records prepared by litigants, which do not contain all that may be relevant to the issues, for they cannot disclose the conditions of this industry, or of the others which may be involved. Congress might see its way to create some sort of temporary right, or it might not. Its decision would certainly be preceded by some examination of the result upon the other interests affected. Whether these would prove paramount we have no means of saying; it is not for us to decide. Our vision is inevitably contracted, and the whole horizon may contain much which will compose a very different picture.

"The order is affirmed, and, as the bill cannot in any event succeed, it may be dismissed, if the defendant so desires."

G. RICORDI & CO. V. HAENDLER, 194 F.2d 914 (2d Cir.1952).   The plaintiff had published the libretto and score of Verdi's opera "Falstaff."   Copyright having expired, the defendant photographically reproduced and sold copies of the work.   Plaintiff, conceding that the defendant was free to copy the book word for word, asserted that the photographic appropriation of its typography was unfair competition.

After examining the state law precedents urged by the plaintiff, Judge Learned Hand proceeded to higher ground:

"However, even if the law of New York were to that effect, we should feel obliged to disregard it, because the question before us is one of federal law: *i.e.* Did the plaintiff preserve any rights after publication in the book except those granted by the Copyright Act?   * * *

"We do not mean that the defendant could under no circumstances be guilty of 'unfair competition' in his use of the 'work'; but it would have to be by some conduct other than copying it.   Since he confined himself to that and gave notice that it was his product, the Copyright Act protected him.   This reasoning applies as well to any rights which may be supposed to flow from the doctrine of International News Service v. Associated Press, 248 U.S. 215, although, as we have several times declared, that decision is to be strictly confined to the facts then at bar."

The denial of plaintiff's motion for a preliminary injunction was affirmed.

NOTES AND QUESTIONS

(1) Textile designs came into copyright after Mazer v. Stein, p. 138 supra, but Judge Hand's views on the freedom to copy absent a copyright or patent still resonate in the wake of the Supreme Court's decision in *Bonito Boats,* p. 624 supra.   On the issues raised in this section, see generally R. Brown, Design Protection: An Overview, 34 U.C.L.A. L.Rev. 1341 (1987).

(2) As we have seen, an unfair competition claim based solely on the copying of an artistic or literary work is preempted under § 301.   For example, after finding insufficient originality to support a copyright in the wind-up versions of the Disney characters in Durham Industries, Inc. v. Tomy Corp., p. 73 supra, the Second Circuit went on to hold that "Tomy cannot achieve by an unfair competition claim what it failed to achieve under its copyright claim and therefore the copying of its Disney figures is legally irrelevant.   * * * To the extent that Tomy's unfair competition claim seeks protection against Durham's copying, it is a claim based on a right equivalent to 'exclusive rights within the . . . scope of copyright.'   As such, it is defeated by Section 301(a)."   See also, e.g., Financial Information, Inc. v. Moody's Investors Service, Inc., 808 F.2d 204 (2d Cir.1986), cert. denied, 484 U.S. 820 (1987).   As for the copying of products outside the scope of copyright, the preemption analysis in *Sears* and *Compco* has renewed vigor following the decision in *Bonito Boats*.   But *Sears* and *Compco,* and § 301, directly constrain only state law.   *Federal* unfair competition law, chiefly § 43(a) of the Lanham Act, has become a substantial adjunct to copyright, at least when some aspect of the plaintiff's creation serves as an indication of the source of the work.

PROTECTION OF DESIGN AND APPEARANCE AFTER *SEARS* AND *COMPCO*

It is customary to bracket *Sears* and *Compco,* but there is one passage in *Compco* that broke new ground. It is the last paragraph, and it bears repeating:

> That an article copied from an unpatented article could be made in some other way, that the design is "nonfunctional" and not essential to the use of either article, that the configuration of the article copied may have a "secondary meaning" which identifies the maker to the trade, or that there may be "confusion" among purchasers as to which article is which or as to who is the maker, may be relevant evidence in applying a State's law requiring such precautions as labeling; however, and regardless of the copier's motives, neither these facts nor any others can furnish a basis for imposing liability for or prohibiting the actual acts of copying and selling.

This was acclaimed by one commentator:

"Where, then, is the new ground in the Court's opinion? It lies in the repudiation of a familiar rule that prohibited the copying of aspects of a design that were found to be distinctive of the source of the goods, that is, to have a significance similar to that of a trademark. The recognition of trademark significance in design features is an application of the doctrine of 'secondary meaning'—a configuration, or an ornament, or a color combination, though primarily part of the design, may subsequently come to identify the source and thus be protected. But such protection was qualified by a recognition that it would be inappropriate to permit the 'functional' aspects of the design to serve in place of a trademark. A prohibition against 'functional' copying would effectively create a monopoly in the essence of the design even though it was ineligible for patent or copyright protection. Therefore the courts have generally restricted the recognition of this trademark-like interest to 'nonfunctional' parts of the design.

"[I]n *Compco* there was a finding—questionable on the record, but nevertheless a finding—that the appearance of Day–Brite's reflector did identify the product to the trade as coming from Day–Brite. This finding, and the conclusion by the court of appeals that it entitled Day–Brite to exclude others from using the design, created the occasion for the [above-quoted] declaration by the Supreme Court." R. Brown, Symposium, Product Simulation: A Right or a Wrong?, 64 Colum.L.Rev. 1216, 1220–21 (1964).

The passage quoted from *Compco* has sometimes been dismissed as dictum. In an opinion by the Eighth Circuit involving the imitation of a trailer truck design found to have acquired "secondary meaning" as an indication of source, the court rejected the defendant's argument that the copying was privileged under *Compco:* "The language relied upon is *dictum.* The law of trademark and the issues of functionality and secondary meaning were not before the Court. The issue before the Court was whether state law could extend the effective term of patent protection granted by the federal statutes." Truck Equip. Service Co. v. Fruehauf Corp., 536 F.2d 1210 (8th Cir.), cert. denied, 429 U.S. 861 (1976). Are the Court's concluding remarks in *Compco* indeed dictum? Was the Eighth Circuit's view effectively endorsed by the Supreme Court's own interpretation of *Compco* in *Bonito Boats*? The plaintiff in *Fruehauf* had relied, not upon state law, but on § 43(a) of the Lanham Act. Are *Sears* and *Compco* relevant to such a claim? [a]

Roulo v. Russ Berrie & Co.

United States Court of Appeals, Seventh Circuit, 1989.
886 F.2d 931.
Certiorari denied, 493 U.S. 1075, 110 S.Ct. 1124 (1990).

■ Before CUMMINGS, WOOD, JR., and RIPPLE, CIRCUIT JUDGES.

■ CUMMINGS, CIRCUIT JUDGE:

[Plaintiff Roulo designed a line of greeting cards known as "Feeling Sensitive" (FS). For two years Berrie had the exclusive right to manufacture and distribute Roulo's cards. When Roulo decided not to renew the arrangement, Berrie developed a similar line called "Touching You" (TY). Roulo claimed trademark infringement under the Lanham Act as well as copyright infringement. A jury found in favor of Roulo on both counts and awarded $4.3 million in damages. Berrie appealed.]

* * * Roulo's FS cards are beige, single-face (no fold) cards containing sentimental verses and frequently using ellipses written in Roulo's handwriting with brown ink. An example of a verse reads: "I want to shout and tell the world how much I love you ... but instead I'll just ...

---

a. In SK & F, Co. v. Premo Pharmaceutical Lab., Inc., 625 F.2d 1055 (3d Cir.1980), part of a huge battle between the manufacturers of prescription drugs and their generic equivalents, the Third Circuit held that even *state law* limitations on copying nonfunctional features possessing secondary meaning survive *Sears* and *Compco.* The Tenth Circuit agreed in Brunswick Corp. v. Spinit Reel Co., 832 F.2d 513, 526 n. 7 (10th Cir.1987), a case involving the design of a fishing reel. The shape of a parking meter was protected as a common law trademark in Time Mechanisms, Inc. v. Qonaar Corp., 422 F.Supp. 905 (D.N.J.1976), despite a *Sears–Compco* defense; a similar defense was rejected in Vermont Castings, Inc. v. Evans Productions Co., 510 F.Supp. 940 (D.Vt.1981), denying defendant's motion for summary judgment on a state unfair competition claim directed at the copying of a stove. But a blunt opinion by the Federal Circuit declared that any state law relief against the copying of a microwave oven was preempted. Litton Systems, Inc. v. Whirlpool Corp., 728 F.2d 1423 (Fed.Cir. 1984) (superseded as to choice of law in Cable Electric Products, Inc. v. Genmark, Inc., 770 F.2d 1015 (Fed.Cir.1985)).

whisper.'' Flanking the message on the left and right borders are a series of four stripes, two silver foil stripes enveloping one brown and one colored stripe in the middle. The FS cards are displayed in a four-sided freestanding rotating rack, each side containing eight cards of the same colored stripe displayed vertically. * * *

The TY cards are designed for occasions similar to the FS line, employing like, although not identical, sentimental verses. The TY cards are identically sized and priced, single-face cards on cream paper with cursive written messages in brown ink. The cards combine two stripes of color on the left side and one colored stripe on the right side, none of which are in foil. A colored foil butterfly is superimposed on the left stripes. The TY cards were also displayed in a four-sided, 32–card rack with each side displaying a single color scheme.

"Trade dress" refers to the total image of a product, including features such as "size, shape, color or color combinations, texture, graphics, or even particular sales techniques." John H. Harland Co. v. Clarke Checks, Inc., 711 F.2d 966, 980 (11th Cir.1983). An infringement of the trade dress is proven if: (1) the plaintiff's trade dress is inherently distinctive or has acquired secondary meaning, (2) the plaintiff's trade dress is primarily nonfunctional, and (3) the defendant's trade dress is confusingly similar, engendering a likelihood of confusion in the marketplace. * * *

Here Berrie asserts that Roulo has failed to demonstrate that the elements of her trade dress are distinctive or have acquired secondary meaning. Specifically, Berrie contends that Roulo's cards incorporated several common features such as stripes, dots, handwriting and other common design elements which are indigenous to all greeting cards and do not represent a trade-dress element capable of protection. To establish her claim of distinctiveness, Roulo introduced testimony of Sally Hopkins, a Hallmark cards curator, who testified that she was unable to find any cards in their collection from this century containing the same combination of elements as used in the FS line. In the alternative, Roulo introduced as evidence of secondary meaning the fact that her name and likeness appeared on the header to the rack displaying the cards, evidence of the success of her greeting cards as revealed by letters written to Berrie inquiring about Roulo's book of verse, an article in Greetings Magazine featuring her card line, and testimony by Berrie that her cards were as unusual as those of Boynton and Davis, other famous card designers. Roulo was also given 10% of sales, the highest percentage share of the sales receipts ever agreed to by Berrie for any card designer.

In order to undermine Roulo's evidence, Berrie simply asserts that Roulo failed to offer any evidence to demonstrate that her cards had acquired secondary meaning. Although Roulo did not offer any empirical evidence that consumers identified her trade dress with the Roulo name, there was certainly adequate evidence to allow the jury to conclude that Roulo's FS cards were distinctive. The adequacy of this evidence is augmented by Berrie's admission that the TY line was modeled after Roulo's FS cards once it was clear that Roulo would not renew her contract

I want to shout and tell the world how much I love you... but instead I'll just... whisper.

(Roulo card)

I don't want to wonder where my life would have gone without you... you are so important... to me

(Berrie card)

with Berrie. The fact that Berrie gave Roulo one of the highest commissions for her cards is also strong evidence that her line was unique. The fact that her cards incorporated common, indistinct elements such as lines and handwriting does not refute the fact that Roulo's combination of these elements was sufficiently unique to warrant trade-dress protection. Trade dress encompasses the overall appearance of a product, including its size, color or color combinations, texture, graphics, packaging or other visual features. Hartford House, Ltd. v. Hallmark Cards, Inc., 846 F.2d 1268, 1271 (10th Cir.1988), certiorari denied, 488 U.S. 908. Roulo did not offer as much evidence on the secondary meaning of her cards as on their distinctiveness, no doubt since it is easier to show the cards are unique than to poll greeting card consumers on whether they identify the FS cards with a single source. However, secondary meaning is not necessary where the trade dress is distinctive.

Once a trade dress is found to warrant protection, the plaintiff must establish that defendant's trade dress is sufficiently similar to create the likelihood of confusion between the two greeting card lines. In assessing the likelihood of marketplace confusion, the factors to be considered include the similarity of the trade dresses, the products to which the trade dresses are attached, the area and manner of concurrent use, the degree of care likely to be exercised by consumers, the strength of the plaintiff's trade dress, and the actual confusion and intent on the part of the alleged infringer to pass off the infringer's goods as those of the plaintiff.

[The court determined that there was adequate evidence to support the jury's conclusion that the public was likely to confuse the source of defendant's cards. The court also upheld a verdict of copyright infringement.]

TWO PESOS, INC. V. TACO CABANA, INC., 505 U.S. 763 (1992). Two Pesos copied the Mexican appearance and atmosphere of the Taco Cabana restaurants. In an action under § 43(a) of the Lanham Act: "The case was tried to a jury, which was instructed to return its verdict in the form of answers to five questions propounded by the trial judge. The jury's answers were: Taco Cabana has a trade dress; taken as a whole, the trade dress is nonfunctional; the trade dress is inherently distinctive; the trade dress has not acquired a secondary meaning in the Texas market; and the alleged infringement creates a likelihood of confusion on the part of ordinary customers as to the source or association of the restaurant's goods or services. Because, as the jury was told, Taco Cabana's trade dress is protected if it either was inherently distinctive or had acquired a secondary meaning, judgment was entered awarding damages to Taco Cabana." The judgment was affirmed by the Fifth Circuit. In the Second Circuit, a line of cases had required a showing of secondary meaning for the protection of trade dress. Certiorari was granted to resolve the conflict. The Supreme Court held that a finding of inherent distinctiveness would suffice. Justice

White for the Court saw no reason in § 43(a) "for treating inherently distinctive verbal or symbolic trademarks differently from inherently distinctive trade dress. * * *"

"On the other hand, adding a secondary meaning requirement would have anticompetitive effects, creating particular burdens on the start-up of small companies. It would present special difficulties for a business, such as respondent, that seeks to start a new product in a limited area and then expand into new markets. Denying protection for inherently distinctive nonfunctional trade dress until after secondary meaning has been established would allow a competitor, which has not adopted a distinctive trade dress of its own, to appropriate the originator's dress in other markets and to deter the originator from expanding into and competing in these areas."

Justice Stevens added a concurring opinion that traced the expansion of § 43(a). Justice Thomas, also concurring, said that trade dress "seems at common law to have been thought incapable ever of being inherently distinctive," but he saw no reason for maintaining that position under § 43(a).

NOTES AND QUESTIONS

(1) Were Roulo's cards sufficiently "distinctive" to justify the conclusion that their appearance signified to customers the source or origin of the product? Or should Roulo have been required to present evidence of secondary meaning such as consumer surveys or other evidence that customers actually think all similar cards come from the same source?

Distinguishing the "concrete expression" protected as trade dress in cases such as *Roulo*, Judge Newman in Jeffrey Milstein, Inc. v. Greger, Lawlor, Roth, Inc., 58 F.3d 27 (2d Cir.1995), held that a trade dress claim cannot be used to protect "an idea, a concept, or a generalized type of appearance." The court rejected plaintiff's attempt to protect vertically-folded greeting cards cut to the outline of the object depicted in the color photograph shown on the front panel; plaintiff "is effectively seeking protection for an idea or concept—die-cut photographic greeting cards."

(2) Trademark law was enlisted to prevent the imitation of an artistic style in Romm Art Creations Ltd. v. Simcha Int'l, Inc., 786 F.Supp. 1126 (E.D.N.Y.1992). Plaintiff was the exclusive distributor of limited edition prints and posters by Israeli artist Itzchak Tarkay. The litigation concerned a series of Tarkay's works known as "Women and Cafes"; plaintiff complained that the defendant was selling reproductions of similar paintings by another artist. The court, describing the case as involving "the application of trade dress protection to works of art," found that Tarkay's works were "inherently distinctive" and that the defendant's sales created a likelihood of confusion. A preliminary injunction was granted against the sale of a number of specifically identified works. Is this an appropriate application of "trade dress" protection? Does it cross the line propounded by Judge Newman in *Jeffrey Milstein*, supra? Cf. Galerie Furstenberg v. Coffaro, 697 F.Supp. 1282 (S.D.N.Y.1988), refusing to recognize trademark rights in images by Salvador Dali.

(3) *Roulo* and *Romm Art* invoke the concept of "trade dress" to prohibit imitation of a plaintiff's product. More typically, as in the next case, trade dress claims relate to packaging or labelling elements that contribute to the appearance of the product as presented to prospective purchasers. Recall, for example, the acknowledgement in *Sears* that "[d]oubtless a State may * * * protect businesses in the use of their trademarks, labels, or distinctive dress in the packaging of goods so as to prevent others, by imitating such markings, from misleading purchasers as to the source of the goods."

Should the plaintiff's burden of proving that the trade dress serves as an indication of source be higher when the claim relates, not merely to packaging, but to aspects of the product itself? Would differences in the remedy for imitation be appropriate? In judging inherent distinctiveness, some courts do distinguish product features from packaging. In Duraco Prod., Inc. v. Joy Plastic, 40 F.3d 1431 (3d Cir.1994), for example, the court concluded that a plastic Grecian urn planter was not inherently distinctive. The decision rejects the traditional generic to fanciful spectrum of distinctiveness used for other subject matter; to be inherently distinctive, the court said that a product configuration must be unusual or memorable, conceptually separable from the product, and likely to serve primarily as an indicator of source. Although hesitant to adopt a bright-line distinction, the Second Circuit in Landscape Forms, Inc. v. Columbia Cascade Co., 113 F.3d 373 (2d Cir.1997), said that while packaging can be judged under the traditional spectrum of distinctiveness developed for word marks, the inherent distinctiveness of product features turns more directly on whether the design is likely to be viewed as an indication of source.[b]

Dinwoodie, Reconceptualizing the Inherent Distinctiveness of Product Design, 75 N.C.L.Rev. 471 (1997), rejects any categorical distinctions by subject matter and urges instead direct focus on the fact-intensive issue of whether the trade dress is likely to identify the source of the product. What kinds of evidence could you present in an attempt to prove inherent distinctiveness? Remember, too, that even if the trade dress is not inherently distinctive, it may still be protected upon proof that consumers do in fact use it to distinguish the products of a particular producer—that is, upon proof of "secondary meaning." On the protection of packaging and product designs as trade dress, see generally J. McCarthy, Trademarks and Unfair Competition §§ 7:53–62 and §§ 8:1–21; Restatement, Third, Unfair Competition § 16 (1995).

Harlequin Enterprises Ltd. v. Gulf & Western Corp.

United States Court of Appeals, Second Circuit, 1981.
644 F.2d 946.

■ Before LUMBARD, MANSFIELD and MESKILL, CIRCUIT JUDGES.

■ LUMBARD, CIRCUIT JUDGE:

Defendant appeals from a preliminary injunction order entered by Judge Owen of the Southern District of New York. The order directs

---

b. See McLean, Opening Another Can of Worms: Protecting Product Configurations as Trade Dress, 66 U.Cinn.L.Rev. 119 (1997), assessing some of the peculiar problems of product features as trademarks.

Simon & Schuster, a division of the defendant, to cease using the cover format it had adopted for a new series of romance novels titled "Silhouette Romance." Judge Owen granted this relief on the ground that the "Silhouette Romance" cover design infringes upon that of the "Harlequin Presents" romance novel series sold by plaintiff Harlequin Enterprises Limited ("Harlequin") in violation of § 43(a) of the Lanham Act, 15 U.S.C. § 1125(a). He also decided that Harlequin's delay in seeking an injunction did not bar relief. We agree and, accordingly, affirm the order of the district court. * * *

For many years, Simon & Schuster was the exclusive United States distributor of the Harlequin Presents series and other books published by Harlequin. In early 1979, however, Harlequin notified Simon & Schuster that it planned to let the distributorship agreement expire by its terms and, beginning January 1, 1980, to conduct its own distribution in the United States.

Shortly thereafter, Simon & Schuster decided to launch its own line of romance fiction under the rubric "Silhouette Romance." In March, 1980, approximately one month before the Silhouette Romance series appeared on the market, Harlequin filed a trade dress infringement suit alleging that the Silhouette Romance cover design is virtually identical to that of the Harlequin Presents series. On July 3, 1980, Harlequin moved for preliminary relief against the use of the Silhouette Romance cover. * * *

On the undisputed facts in the record before us, we hold that the district court did not abuse its discretion in enjoining Simon & Schuster from further use of the Silhouette Romance cover.

The district court's conclusion that the Silhouette Romance cover is "substantially similar" to the Harlequin Presents cover is clearly supported by the evidence. Both books are bound with glossy white covers and are of identical dimensions in height, width and thickness. The series' number is set in black type in the upper left hand corner and the price is printed on the upper right hand corner of each book. Both books retail for $1.50. A collage of gold filigree, the publisher's colophon and the series' title appears in the top center of each cover. Harlequin's colophon, a black and white harlequin, is framed by a gold diamond; Simon & Schuster's colophon, black silhouettes of a man and woman, is cast in a gold oval. The series' titles are printed in similar black script with one word of the series' title appearing on each side of the colophon. Beneath the collage on each book, the author's name is printed in bold, colored capital letters. The book's title is printed below the author's name on both books in black lettering. The bottom half of each cover is devoted to an illustration of a man and a woman in a romantic setting suggesting the book's story line.

While there are also some differences, such as the series' names and the publishers' colophons, it is the "combination of features as a whole rather than a difference in some of the details which must determine whether the competing product is likely to cause confusion in the mind of the public." Perfect Fit Industries, Inc. v. Acme Quilting Co., 618 F.2d 950, 955 (2d Cir.1980). We, like the district court, are convinced that an ordinary buyer of romance fiction would not recognize the disparities without setting out to find them. A buyer who did notice the difference between the names and the colophons would be reasonably justified in believing both products come from the same publisher.

In addition to the startling similarities between the covers, the district judge determined that there was actual confusion between the two covers among romance readers and members of the trade. These findings are substantiated by the inquiries directed to Harlequin about the Silhouette Romance series and the extraordinary number of Silhouette Romance book returns sent to Harlequin by retailers. Finally, the district court received and credited substantial evidence that Simon & Schuster deliberately imitated the Harlequin Presents cover. Evidence of conscious imitation is pertinent because the law presumes that an intended similarity is likely to cause confusion. Perfect Fit Industries, Inc. v. Acme Quilting Co., 618 F.2d at 954; RJR Foods, Inc. v. White Rock Corp., 603 F.2d 1058, 1060 (2d Cir.1979); Harold Ritchie, Inc. v. Chesebrough–Pond's, Inc., 281 F.2d 755, 758–60 (2d Cir.1960).

Harlequin has also adduced sufficient evidence to support the district court's preliminary finding that the Harlequin Presents cover has a "secondary meaning" for romance readers. By secondary meaning, we mean that romance readers associate the Harlequin Presents cover with a particular series and publisher. See RJR Foods, Inc. v. White Rock Corp., 603 F.2d at 1059. Harlequin's extensive national advertising, its phenomenal sales success and the results of a consumer survey [2] indicate that romance readers correlate the Harlequin Presents cover with Harlequin and the Harlequin Presents series. See id. at 1060. The fact that the enthusiasm and loyalty of Harlequin's readers have been the subject of extensive, unsolicited media coverage further supports the district court's finding of secondary meaning. Scarves By Vera, Inc. v. Todo Imports, Ltd., 544 F.2d 1167, 1174 (2d Cir.1976). Perhaps the most significant evidence of secondary meaning in this case, however, was the attempt by Simon & Schuster to capitalize on the Harlequin Presents cover when it introduced its own romance series. RJR Foods, Inc. v. White Rock Corp., 603 F.2d at 1060.

Although secondary meaning usually is a prerequisite to trademark protection, New York law shields trade dress from deliberate copying even if it has not acquired a secondary meaning. Perfect Fit Industries, Inc. v.

---

2. Spencer Bruno Research Associates interviewed 500 romance readers in three cities. The readers were shown copies of unpublished Harlequin Presents titles with the Harlequin name and colophon deleted and asked to name the publisher. Fifty percent of the readers correctly identified Harle- quin as the publisher. While these results are not conclusive evidence of secondary meaning, particularly in light of Harlequin's market dominance, the district court properly found the results probative of secondary meaning. RJR Foods, Inc. v. White Rock Corp., 603 F.2d 1058, 1060 (2d Cir.1979).

Acme Quilting Co., 618 F.2d 950 (2d Cir.1980). Thus, even if romance readers did not associate the Harlequin Presents cover with a specific series and publisher, Harlequin would be entitled to an injunction against Simon & Schuster's deliberate imitation of its cover. * * *

The findings of the district court and terms of its preliminary injunction are amply supported by the record.

Affirmed.

NOTES AND QUESTIONS

(1) Why would New York law prohibit the imitation of trade dress "even if it has not acquired a secondary meaning"? Is this merely a recognition of "inherent distinctiveness" as discussed by the Supreme Court in the *Two Pesos* case? If "readers did not associate the Harlequin Presents cover with a specific series and publisher," how could a similar cover be "likely to create confusion"? The "New York rule" is criticized in J. McCarthy, Trademarks and Unfair Competition §§ 15:12–20.

(2) The publisher of *Reader's Digest* successfully invoked § 43(a) when the *Conservative Digest* adopted a cover format similar in size and graphic design to the cover used by the plaintiff. The similarities, according to the court, were likely to cause consumers to think that the two magazines came from the same publisher. As in *Harlequin Enterprises*, the court said that its finding of secondary meaning was bolstered by proof of intentional copying. In what way is that relevant? There was also a finding of copyright infringement. Reader's Digest Ass'n v. Conservative Digest, 821 F.2d 800 (D.C.Cir.1987).

Another publisher was less successful in fending off imitation by a competitor in Publications Int'l, Ltd. v. Landoll, Inc., 45 U.S.P.Q.2d 1277 (N.D.Ill.1997); its glossy, padded book covers and gold-colored gilded pages were not sufficiently unique or unusual to be automatically perceived as a trademark, and there was no evidence of secondary meaning.

(3) Beatrix Potter brought to life Peter Rabbit and other endearing characters in a series of books published by Frederick Warne & Co. beginning in 1902. In 1977 another publisher collected in a single volume seven of Miss Potter's stories that had entered the public domain. Included within the book were redrawings of the cover illustrations from the original Warne editions. Warne, claiming trademark rights in the illustrations, brought suit under § 43(a) and § 32 of the Lanham Act—three of the covers had been registered as trademarks for books. The defendant claimed a right to unrestricted use, insisting that the cover illustrations were now in the public domain. Summary judgment motions by both parties were denied: "[T]he proper factual inquiry in this case is not whether the cover illustrations were once copyrightable and have fallen into the public domain, but whether they have acquired secondary meaning, identifying Warne as the publisher or sponsor of goods bearing those illustrations, and if so, whether defendant's use of these illustrations in 'packaging' or 'dressing' its edi-

tions is likely to cause confusion." But plaintiff's burden was formidable—"it would not be enough that the illustrations in question have come to signify Beatrix Potter as author of the books; plaintiff must show that they have come to represent its goodwill and reputation as *publisher* of those books." And of course, plaintiff must also show a likelihood of confusion. Frederick Warne & Co. v. Book Sales Inc., 481 F.Supp. 1191 (S.D.N.Y. 1979).

(4) The plaintiff in Original Appalachian Artworks, Inc. v. Toy Loft, Inc., 684 F.2d 821 (11th Cir.1982), hit upon a novel technique for marketing dolls; the dolls were "adopted" rather than sold—a birth certificate and adoption papers accompanied the transaction, and a birthday card was sent to the buyer on the anniversary of the happy event. (These were the enormously successful "Cabbage Patch" dolls. Their extraordinary popularity is recounted in Original Appalachian Artworks, Inc. v. Blue Box Factory, Ltd., 577 F.Supp. 625 (S.D.N.Y.1983). They merited a cover story in *Newsweek,* What a Doll!: The Cabbage Patch Craze, Dec. 12, 1983, p. 78.) Defendant embarked on a similar marketing campaign. (He also copied plaintiff's dolls, prompting a finding of copyright infringement.) The trial court thought confusion likely. Declaring the adoption procedures protectable trade dress, the Eleventh Circuit affirmed an injunction under § 43(a). Should all this pandering to sentimentalism be protected as "trade dress"?

Brandir International, Inc. v. Cascade Pacific Lumber Co.

United States Court of Appeals, Second Circuit, 1987.
834 F.2d 1142.

[The portion of the court's opinion dealing with plaintiff's copyright infringement claim appears at p. 164 supra.]

As to whether the configuration of Brandir's bicycle rack can be protected under either section 43(a) of the Lanham Act, 15 U.S.C. § 1125(a), or New York State unfair competition law, we are reminded that the design of a product itself may function as its packaging or protectable trade dress. See LeSportsac, Inc. v. K mart Corp., 754 F.2d 71, 75 (2d Cir.1985). The district court dismissed Brandir's claims, saying that its analysis of the copyright issue was sufficient to dispose of the Lanham Act and common law claims. The court stated "the design feature of the Ribbon Racks is clearly dictated by the function to be performed, namely, holding up bicycles. If the steam pipes were not bent into the design, but instead remained flat, the bicycles would not stand up, they would fall down." But as Judge Newman noted in his dissent in *Carol Barnhart,* 773 F.2d at 420 n. 1, the principle of conceptual separability of functional design elements in copyright law is different from the somewhat similar principle of functionality as developed in trademark law. For trademark purposes, he pointed out, a design feature "has been said to be functional if it is 'essential to the use or purpose of the article' or 'affects the cost or quality of the article.'" Id. (quoting Inwood Laboratories, Inc. v. Ives

Laboratories, Inc., 456 U.S. 844, 850 n. 10 (1982)); see LeSportsac, Inc. v. K mart Corp., 754 F.2d at 75–76 (trade dress of a product is eligible for protection if it has acquired a secondary meaning and is nonfunctional).[4]

Here, the district court limited its inquiry to determining whether portions of the RIBBON Rack performed the function of a bicycle rack. But the fact that a design feature performs a function does not make it essential to the performance of that function; it is instead the absence of alternative constructions performing the same function that renders the feature functional. Thus, the true test of functionality is not whether the feature in question performs a function, but whether the feature "is dictated by the functions to be performed," Warner Bros. Inc. v. Gay Toys, Inc., 724 F.2d 327, 331 (2d Cir.1983) (quoted in LeSportsac, Inc. v. K mart Corp., 754 F.2d at 76), as evidenced by available alternative constructions. See Metro Kane Imports, Ltd. v. Rowoco, Inc., 618 F.Supp. 273, 275–76 (S.D.N.Y.1985), aff'd mem., 800 F.2d 1128 (2d Cir.1986) (finding high-tech design of orange juice squeezer not dictated by function to be performed as there was no evidence that design permitted juicer to be manufactured at lower price or with altered performance). There are numerous alternative bicycle rack constructions. The nature, price, and utility of these constructions are material issues of fact not suitable for determination by summary judgment.[5] For example, while it is true that the materials used by Brandir are standard-size pipes, we have no way of knowing whether the particular size and weight of the pipes used is the best, the most economical, or the only available size and weight pipe in the marketplace. We would rather think the opposite might be the case. So, too, with the dimension of the bends being dictated by a standard formula corresponding to the pipe size; it could be that there are many standard radii and that the particular radius of Brandir's RIBBON Rack actually required new tooling. This issue of functionality on remand should be viewed in terms of bicycle racks generally and not one-piece undulating bicycle racks specifically. See id. at 330–32; see also In re DC Comics, Inc., 689 F.2d 1042, 1045 (C.C.P.A.1982) (dolls generally and not Superman dolls are the class by which functionality is determined). We reverse and remand as to the trademark and unfair competition claims.

Wallace International Silversmiths, Inc. v. Godinger Silver Art Co.

United States Court of Appeals, Second Circuit, 1990.
916 F.2d 76.
Certiorari denied 499 U.S. 976, 111 S.Ct. 1622 (1991).

■ Before WINTER, MAHONEY and WALKER, CIRCUIT JUDGES.

■ WINTER, CIRCUIT JUDGE:

Wallace International Silversmiths ("Wallace") appeals from Judge Haight's denial of its motion for a preliminary injunction under Section

---

4. Because the district court viewed the rack as entirely functional, it therefore did not reach the next step of determining whether Brandir's RIBBON Rack had acquired secondary meaning by the time Cascade started to manufacture its bicycle rack.

5. Indeed, in addition to the numerous bicycle racks on the market, one may observe trees, awning supports, parking meters, signs, fire plugs, and many other objects used as bicycle racks.

43(a) of the Lanham Act, 15 U.S.C. § 1125(a) (1988), prohibiting Godinger Silver Art Co., Inc. ("Godinger") from marketing a line of silverware with ornamentation that is substantially similar to Wallace's GRANDE BAROQUE line. Judge Haight held that the GRANDE BAROQUE design is "a functional feature of 'Baroque' style silverware" and thus not subject to protection as a trademark. We affirm.

Wallace, a Delaware corporation, has sold sterling silver products for over one hundred years. Its GRANDE BAROQUE pattern was introduced in 1941 and is still one of the best-selling silverware lines in America. Made of fine sterling silver, a complete place setting costs several thousand dollars. Total sales of GRANDE BAROQUE silverware have exceeded fifty million dollars. The GRANDE BAROQUE pattern is fairly described as "ornate, massive and flowery [with] indented, flowery roots and scrolls and curls along the side of the shaft, and flower arrangements along the front of the shaft." Wallace owns a trademark registration for the GRANDE BAROQUE name as applied to sterling silver flatware and hollowware. The GRANDE BAROQUE design is not patented, but on December 11, 1989, Wallace filed an application for trademark registration for the GRANDE BAROQUE pattern. This application is still pending.

Godinger, a New York corporation, is a manufacturer of silver-plated products. The company has recently begun to market a line of baroque-style silver-plated serving pieces. The suggested retail price of the set of four serving pieces is approximately twenty dollars. Godinger advertised its new line under the name 20TH CENTURY BAROQUE and planned to introduce it at the Annual New York Tabletop and Accessories Show, the principal industry trade show at which orders for the coming year are taken. Like Wallace's silverware, Godinger's pattern contains typical baroque elements including an indented root, scrolls, curls, and flowers. The arrangement of these elements approximates Wallace's design in many ways, although their dimensions are noticeably different. The most obvious difference between the two designs is that the Godinger pattern extends further down the handle than the Wallace pattern does. The Wallace pattern also tapers from the top of the handle to the stem while the Godinger pattern appears bulkier overall and maintains its bulk throughout the decorated portion of the handle. Although the record does not disclose the exact circumstances under which Godinger's serving pieces were created, Godinger admits that its designers were "certainly inspired by and aware of [the Wallace] design when [they] created [the 20TH CENTURY BAROQUE] design." * * *

The core purpose of trademark law is to prevent competitors from copying those aspects of a product or its trade dress that identify the source of the product to prospective consumers. See Inwood Laboratories v. Ives Laboratories, 456 U.S. 844, 854 n. 14 (1982); Bose Corp. v. Linear Design Labs, Inc., 467 F.2d 304, 309–10 (2d Cir.1972). By giving the first user of a trademark exclusive rights in that mark, the law protects trademark owners' investments in creating goodwill and affords consumers a low-cost means of identifying the source of goods.   See *Inwood Laboratories,* supra; W.T. Rogers Co. Inc. v. Keene, 778 F.2d 334 (7th Cir.1985).   Although the paradigmatic trademark is a distinctive name, the "trade dress" of a product may also serve as a trademark.   A product's trade dress ordinarily consists of its packaging.   However, the design given a product by its manufacturer also may serve to distinguish it from the products of other manufacturers and hence be protectible trade dress.   See, e.g., Stormy Clime Ltd. v. Progroup, Inc., 809 F.2d 971, 974 (2d Cir.1987) ("The trade dress of a product 'involves the total image of a product and may include features such as size, shape, color or color combinations, texture, [or] graphics.' ") (quoting John H. Harland Co. v. Clarke Checks, Inc., 711 F.2d 966, 980 (11th Cir.1983)); [Warner Bros. v. Gay Toys, Inc., 658 F.2d 76 (2d Cir.1981)] (color and symbols on toy car);   Harlequin Enterprises Ltd. v. Gulf & Western Corp., 644 F.2d 946 (2d Cir.1981) (paperback book covers).

In order to maintain an action for trade dress infringement under Section 43(a) of the Lanham Act, the plaintiff must show that its trade dress has acquired secondary meaning—that is, the trade dress identifies the source of the product—and that there is a likelihood of confusion between the original trade dress and the trade dress of the allegedly infringing product.   LeSportsac, Inc. v. K Mart Corp., 754 F.2d 71, 75 (2d Cir.1985).   Even if the plaintiff establishes these elements, the defendant may still avoid liability on a variety of grounds, including the so-called functionality doctrine.   Our present view of that doctrine is derived from the Supreme Court's dictum in *Inwood Laboratories,* stating that "[i]n general terms, a product feature is functional if it is essential to the use or purpose of the article or if it affects the cost or quality of the article."   456 U.S. at 850 n. 10.   Our most recent elaboration of the doctrine was in *Stormy Clime,* where Judge Newman stated:

> the functionality inquiry ... should [focus] on whether bestowing trade dress protection upon [a particular] arrangement of features " 'will hinder competition or impinge upon the rights of others to compete effectively in the sale of goods.' "   Sicilia di R. Biebow & Co. v. Cox, 732 F.2d 417, 429 (5th Cir.1984) (quoting In re Morton–Norwich Products, Inc., 671 F.2d 1332, 1342 (Cust. & Pat.App.1982)).

Id. at 976–77.   * * *

Turning to the instant case, Judge Haight found that the similarities between the Godinger and Wallace designs involved elements common to all baroque-style designs used in the silverware market.   He noted that many manufacturers compete in that market with such designs and found that "[t]he 'Baroque' curls, roots and flowers are not 'mere indicia of source.'   Instead, they are requirements to compete in the silverware market."   Judge Haight concluded that "the 'Grande Baroque' design is a functional feature of 'Baroque' style silverware," relying on Pagliero v. Wallace China Co., 198 F.2d 339 (9th Cir.1952).

Although we agree with Judge Haight's decision, we do not endorse his reliance upon *Pagliero*. That decision allowed a competitor to sell exact copies of china bearing a particular pattern without finding that comparably attractive patterns were not available to the competitor. It based its holding solely on the ground that the particular pattern was an important ingredient in the commercial success of the china. Id. at 343–44. We rejected *Pagliero* in *LeSportsac*, supra at 77, and reiterate that rejection here. Under *Pagliero*, the commercial success of an aesthetic feature automatically destroys all of the originator's trademark interest in it, notwithstanding the feature's secondary meaning and the lack of any evidence that competitors cannot develop non-infringing, attractive patterns. By allowing the copying of an exact design without any evidence of market foreclosure, the *Pagliero* test discourages both originators and later competitors from developing pleasing designs. See Keene Corp. v. Paraflex Industries, Inc., 653 F.2d 822, 824–25 (3d Cir.1981).

Our rejection of *Pagliero*, however, does not call for reversal. Quite unlike *Pagliero*, Judge Haight found in the instant matter that there is a substantial market for baroque silverware and that effective competition in that market requires "use [of] essentially the same scrolls and flowers" as are found on Wallace's silverware. Based on the record at the hearing, that finding is not clearly erroneous and satisfies the requirement of *Stormy Clime* that a design feature not be given trade dress protection where use of that feature is necessary for effective competition. 809 F.2d at 976–77.

Stormy Clime is arguably distinguishable, however, because it involved a design that had both aesthetic and utilitarian features. If read narrowly, *Stormy Clime* might be limited to cases in which trademark protection of a design would foreclose competitors from incorporating utilitarian features necessary to compete in the market for the particular product. In the instant case, the features at issue are strictly ornamental because they neither affect the use of the silverware nor contribute to its efficient manufacture. The question, therefore, is whether the doctrine of functionality applies to features of a product that are purely ornamental but that are essential to effective competition.

Our only hesitation in holding that the functionality doctrine applies is based on nomenclature. "Functionality" seems to us to imply only utilitarian considerations and, as a legal doctrine, to be intended only to prevent competitors from obtaining trademark protection for design features that are necessary to the use or efficient production of the product. * * *

We put aside our quibble over doctrinal nomenclature, however, because we are confident that whatever secondary meaning Wallace's baroque silverware pattern may have acquired, Wallace may not exclude competitors from using those baroque design elements necessary to compete in the market for baroque silverware. It is a first principle of trademark law that an owner may not use the mark as a means of excluding competitors from a substantial market. * * *

In the instant matter, Wallace seeks trademark protection, not for a precise expression of a decorative style, but for basic elements of a style that is part of the public domain. As found by the district court, these elements are important to competition in the silverware market. We perceive no distinction between a claim to exclude all others from use on silverware of basic elements of a decorative style and claims to generic names, basic colors or designs important to a product's utility. In each case, trademark protection is sought, not just to protect an owner of a mark in informing the public of the source of its products, but also to exclude competitors from producing similar products. We therefore abandon our quibble with the aesthetic functionality doctrine's nomenclature and adopt the Draft Restatement's view that, where an ornamental feature is claimed as a trademark and trademark protection would significantly hinder competition by limiting the range of adequate alternative designs, the aesthetic functionality doctrine denies such protection. See Third Restatement of the Law, Unfair Competition (Preliminary Draft No. 3), Ch. 3, § 17(c) at 213–14. This rule avoids the overbreadth of *Pagliero* by requiring a finding of foreclosure of alternatives while still ensuring that trademark protection does not exclude competitors from substantial markets.

Of course, if Wallace were able to show secondary meaning in a precise expression of baroque style, competitors might be excluded from using an identical or virtually identical design. In such a case, numerous alternative baroque designs would still be available to competitors. Although the Godinger design at issue here was found by Judge Haight to be "substantially similar," it is not identical or virtually identical, and the similarity involves design elements necessary to compete in the market for baroque silverware. Because according trademark protection to those elements would significantly hinder competitors by limiting the range of adequate alternative designs, we agree with Judge Haight's denial of a preliminary injunction.

Affirmed.

———————————

W.T. ROGERS CO. v. KEENE, 778 F.2d 334 (7th Cir.1985). Rogers had designed a successful plastic stacking tray for letters and papers with a hexagonal profile instead of the conventional rectangle. Keene copied it. Rogers lost before a jury, but on appeal won a remand for better instructions. Judge Posner offers a wide-ranging discussion of the purpose of trademarks and canvasses all aspects of functionality. He offers many formulations, of which this is the most concise: "a functional feature is one which competitors would have to spend money not to copy but to design around."

In this case, "the hexagonal shape of the end panel does nothing to enhance the tray's utility in holding papers; the shape is as irrelevant to that function as the fluting in a column is irrelevant to the column's function of holding up the roof. And there is no suggestion that it makes a tray cheaper to produce; if anything, it probably makes it more expensive to produce, though probably trivially so."

"It is only when the term functional is expanded to embrace the aesthetic that it becomes possible to argue that the hexagonal shape is functional. A molded plastic stacking office tray is an inherently humble product, and the opportunities for adornment may be limited. But office workers are not indifferent to their surroundings, and if the hexagonal end panel imparts a degree of elegance that makes the tray worth more, the hexagonal design performs a genuine function. * * *

"But the fact that a design feature is attractive does not, to repeat, preclude its being trademarked. If effective competition is possible without copying that feature, then, by analogy to the distinction between arbitrary and generic brand names, it is not a functional feature. * * *

"* * * Though a producer does not lose a design trademark just because the public finds it pleasing, there may come a point where the design feature is so important to the value of the product to consumers that continued trademark protection would deprive them of competitive alternatives; and at that point the protection ceases. It is not a disaster for the owner of the trademark; should Rogers lose this case in the end and have to share its hexagonal design with competitors, it can (as it has begun to do) imprint a verbal or other trademark more emphatically, in order to identify its brand to consumers who can no longer look to the hexagon for identification of source. What Rogers may fear of course is not the loss of an identifying mark but the loss of a competitive advantage stemming from the exclusive possession of a popular design; but to protect the intellectual property that consists not of an identifying mark but of a pleasing design a manufacturer must seek the aid of the design-patent law, with its stringent requirements and its 14–year limitation, and not the aid of the trademark laws."

NOTES AND QUESTIONS

(1) Does the functionality limitation fully harmonize the respective spheres of patent and trademark law? To protect the integrity of the patent system, the Tenth Circuit in Vornado Air Circulation Systems, Inc. v. Duracraft Corp., 58 F.3d 1498 (10th Cir.1995), cert. denied, 116 S.Ct. 753 (1996), said that if a product configuration claimed in a utility patent is "a significant inventive aspect" of the patented invention, it is ineligible for trademark protection even if the configuration is nonfunctional in the trademark sense due to the existence of adequate alternative designs. (Cf. Thomas & Betts Corp. v. Panduit Corp., 138 F.3d 277 (7th Cir.1998), declining to apply the Vornado restriction when the product configuration is not specifically included within the patent claims.) A district court interpreting the decision in Vornado said that trademark protection for a product configuration that had been claimed in an expired utility patent should be denied even when the design is nonfunctional if the previously patented invention cannot be practiced competitively without the disputed configuration. Zip Dee, Inc. v. Dometic Corp., 931 F.Supp. 602 (N.D.Ill.1996).

(2) Would the aesthetic functionality doctrine as interpreted in *Wallace International* be potentially applicable to the greeting cards protected in Roulo v. Russ Berrie? To the artwork protected in Romm Art Creation v. Simcha Int'l, p. 646 supra? To the restaurant decor in *Two Pesos,* p. 645 supra? (The Supreme Court denied certiorari on the functionality issue.) And what of the "adoption" procedure protected as "trade dress" in Original Appalachian Artworks v. Toy Loft, p. 651 supra? See generally Restatement, Third, Unfair Competition § 17 (1995).

(3) Which party should have the burden of proof on the functionality issue? In LeSportsac, Inc. v. K Mart Corp., 754 F.2d 71 (2d Cir.1985), the Second Circuit, after observing some uncertainty in the case law, held that functionality is a defense, with the burden thus on the copier. But see Merchant & Evans, Inc. v. Roosevelt Building Products Co., 963 F.2d 628 (3d Cir.1992), also noting the split among the circuits, but concluding that the burden is on the party claiming trademark rights.

LANHAM ACT REGISTRATION OF CONFIGURATIONS

Kohler Co. v. Moen Inc.

United States Court of Appeals, Seventh Circuit, 1993.
12 F.3d 632.

■ Before CUDAHY and COFFEY, CIRCUIT JUDGES, and ESCHBACH, SENIOR CIRCUIT JUDGE.

■ COFFEY, CIRCUIT JUDGE.

This action began in 1987 when Moen, Incorporated ("Moen") filed two applications in the United States Patent and Trademark Office ("PTO") to register a faucet design and a faucet handle design as trademarks. Kohler Company ("Kohler") opposed the applications before the PTO's Trademark Trial and Appeal Board ("TTAB") on the ground that product shapes were not registrable as trademarks. The TTAB dismissed Kohler's oppositions. Kohler sought review of the TTAB's decision under 15 U.S.C. § 1071(b) in the district court. The parties filed cross summary judgment motions and stipulated first that they would rely on the record before the TTAB and further that no new evidence would be submitted. The district court entered summary judgment in favor of Moen and against Kohler. Kohler filed a timely appeal from the district court's judgment. We affirm.

Kohler and Moen are competitors in the business of manufacturing and selling plumbing products, including faucets and faucet handles. Moen sought and obtained trademark registration of its "LEGEND" kitchen faucet and the appearance of the handle used on the "LEGEND" and other Moen faucets. In support of registration of its product configurations as trademarks, Moen introduced voluminous evidence of sales and promotion-

al expenses with respect to each design, and also submitted substantial evidence that purchasers of its products recognized the source of the faucets by their distinctive shapes. The record included hundreds of declarations from persons in the plumbing business and from individual purchasers attesting to the distinctiveness of the shape of Moen's faucet and handle without reference to any markings. One of Moen's vice-presidents submitted a declaration stating that Moen's faucet design is not based upon utility or function, is not inexpensive to manufacture, and is only one of many competitive designs in the industry performing the same function. Moen also submitted a declaration from the chairman of one of its chief competitors, Price Pfister, that stated that Moen's faucet is distinctive, its design indicates a single point of origin, the design is neither functional nor utilitarian, and that trademark protection for the configuration would not hinder competition in the plumbing trade. Finally, a market research survey of 273 licensed plumbers in six cities revealed that eighty-two percent of those surveyed identified the faucet as a Moen product, and eighty-three percent identified the handle as a Moen product.
* * *

In dismissing Kohler's oppositions, the TTAB necessarily concluded that § 45 of the Act provides trademark protection for product configurations. Section 45 of the Act defines trademark to "*include*[ ] any word, name, symbol, or device or any combination thereof adopted and used by a manufacturer or merchant to identify his goods and distinguish them from those manufactured or sold by others." 15 U.S.C. § 1127 (1988). As Kohler notes, § 45 does not list "product configuration" among its examples of trademarks. Early decisions under the Act strictly construed the language of § 45 and held that a product or container shape was not entitled to trademark protection. See 1 McCarthy, McCarthy on Trademarks and Unfair Competition, § 7.31 (3d ed. 1992) [hereinafter McCarthy on Trademarks]; Ex Parte Minnesota Mining & Mfg. Co., 92 U.S.P.Q. 74 (1952). Subsequent TTAB decisions and the courts reviewing TTAB rulings, however, have interpreted § 45 to allow trademark protection for product configurations.

In Application of Kotzin, 276 F.2d 411, 414–15 (C.C.P.A.1960), the Court of Customs and Patent Appeals ("C.C.P.A.") held that the § 45 list ("word, name, symbol or device") did not restrict other items from receiving trademark protection if they satisfied the requirements for registration on the Principal Register. The court in *Kotzin* supported its interpretation of the statute by noting that the provision stated that trademarks "*include*" words, names, symbols or devices, not that "trademark" "*means*" words, names, symbols or devices. * * *

In Application of Mogen David, 328 F.2d 925 (C.C.P.A.1964), the C.C.P.A. held that the configuration of a container could be registered as a trademark for the product it contains. Id. at 929–30. The C.C.P.A. thereafter held that a product configuration itself could be registered as a trademark in Application of Honeywell, Inc., 497 F.2d 1344 (C.C.P.A.), cert. denied, 419 U.S. 1080 (1974). The C.C.P.A., the Federal Circuit, and the

TTAB have since interpreted § 45 to allow trademark protection for qualifying product configurations. * * *

* * * The persuasiveness of the TTAB and the Federal Circuit's interpretation of § 45 is reinforced by the legislative history accompanying the 1988 Lanham Act amendments. See Trademark Law Revision Act of 1988, Pub.L. 100–667, § 38, S.Rep. 515, 100th Cong., 2d Sess. 44 (1988), reprinted in, 1988 U.S.C.C.A.N. 5577, 5607. Although these amendments did not take effect until November 1989, approximately two years after the TTAB's decision in this case, as a codification of prior case law they validate the uniform preamendment interpretation of § 45 on the Act. The Senate Report accompanying the 1988 amendments specifically states "the words 'symbol or device,' " were retained in the Trademark Revision Act's revised definition of trademark "so as not to preclude the registration of colors, shapes, sounds *or configurations* where they function as trademarks." S.Rep. 100–515, 100th Cong., 2d Sess. at 44, reprinted in, 1988 U.S.C.C.A.N. at 5607 (emphasis added). Congress thus specifically approved the broad judicial interpretation of § 45's definition of "trademark" to include product configurations. * * *

Kohler asserts that granting trademark protection and allowing trademark registration for a product configuration directly conflicts with the rationale of the Constitution's Patent Clause and the Patent Act, 35 U.S.C. §§ 1–376 (1988). Kohler alleges that the Supreme Court's interpretation of the Patent Clause in Bonito Boats, Inc. v. Thunder Craft Boats, Inc., 489 U.S. 141, 146 (1989); Sears Roebuck & Co. v. Stiffel Co., 376 U.S. 225 (1964), and Compco Corp. v. Day–Brite Lighting, Inc., 376 U.S. 234 (1964), indicates that the TTAB and lower courts' interpretation of the Act to allow trademark protection for product configurations contravenes the Patent Clause's requirement that the exclusive right to "Writings and Discoveries" be for a "limited Time[ ]." To analyze the soundness of Kohler's claim that courts' interpretation of the Act runs afoul of the Patent Clause and implementing patent law, a brief discussion of the purpose of each is necessary.

To obtain patent protection, an applicant has to show that an invention or design is both novel and "not obvious at the time the invention was made to a person having ordinary skill in the art to which said art pertains." 35 U.S.C. § 103 (1988). Patent protection is limited in duration: utility patents last for seventeen years, 35 U.S.C. § 154 (1988), and design patents extend for fourteen years, 35 U.S.C. § 173 (1988). The innovation passes into the public domain after the patent expires.

Compared to patent protection, trademark protection is relatively weak because it precludes competitors only from using marks that are likely to confuse or deceive the public. Trademark protection is dependent only on public reaction to the trademark in the marketplace rather than solely on the similarity of the configurations. See Jay Dratler, Trademark Protection for Industrial Designs, 1988 U.Ill.L.Rev. 887, 896 (1988). * * * Significantly, while a patent creates a type of monopoly pricing power by giving the patentee the exclusive right to make and sell the innovation, a trademark gives the owner only the right to preclude others from using the mark when such use is likely to cause confusion or to deceive. See 1 McCarthy on Trademarks § 2.05[1]. * * *

In the *Sears/Compco* decisions, the Supreme Court reviewed two decisions from this court which held that Illinois unfair competition law prohibited unauthorized copying of unpatentable lighting fixture designs. The Supreme Court held in both cases that federal copyright and patent law preempted the state unfair competition law which prohibited the copying of a nonpatented product. *Sears,* 376 U.S. at 231–32; *Compco,* 376 U.S. at 237–38. Kohler argues that because state unfair competition and federal trademark law serve the same purpose, federal patent law also conflicts with federal trademark law. Kohler is mistaken. First, no Lanham Act issue was raised in either *Sears* or *Compco;* the decision in each case was based on the Supremacy Clause. Second, the Court in *Compco* noted that a defendant may copy at will if the design is "not entitled to a design patent *or other federal statutory protection . . . .*" *Compco,* 376 U.S. at 238. Of course, the Lanham Act falls under the rubric of "other federal statutory protection," and courts have expressly held that *Sears* and *Compco* do not preclude federal trademark protection of designs. * * *

As in *Sears,* however, the *Bonito Boats* Court recognized that states have the power to give unfair competition and trademark protection to trade dress. * * * The Court's holding in *Bonito Boats* is also inapplicable to federal trademark law because the Florida statute granted boat manufacturers patent-like rights far exceeding any right available under the Lanham Act. * * * As described earlier in this opinion, the underlying policies of federal trademark law, and the nature of the protection afforded, do not approximate the sweeping, perpetual patent-like state statutes that the Supreme Court found impermissible in *Sears, Compco,* and *Bonito Boats.* * * *

Kohler has conceded that under the facts of this case, Moen satisfied all of the requirements for trademark protection for product configurations. The Supreme Court's holdings and dicta in *Sears, Compco, Bonito Boats,* and *Two Pesos* offer no reason for this court to hold that every court that has allowed federal trademark protection for product configurations was mistaken. * * *

The district court's judgment is affirmed.

■ CUDAHY, CIRCUIT JUDGE, dissenting.

[Judge Cudahy, after extensive analysis, concluded that in view of the statutory provision for design patents, trademark protection for product configurations was fundamentally inconsistent with the Supreme Court's preemption cases.]

In my view, whatever new law has been developed in the lower courts to authorize the use of product configuration trademarks as a substitute for design patents is without sanction from the Supreme Court. The Court has spoken repeatedly to disfavor the use of unfair competition law to avoid the "limited times" provision of the Patent Clause. The Court has emphasized the importance of the right to copy as an aspect of the Patent Clause. The right to copy is constitutionally protected and is absolutely essential to the successful long-term operation of a free and competitive economy. I therefore respectfully dissent.

NOTES AND QUESTIONS ON REGISTRATION OF CONFIGURATIONS

(1) Section 45 of the Lanham Act states, "The term 'trademark' includes any word, name, symbol, or device, or any combination thereof * * *." "Device" was the gateway for registration of the pathbreaking Pinch bottle, Ex parte Haig & Haig, Ltd., 118 U.S.P.Q. 229 (Comm'r Pat.1958). The shape and packaging of a candy bar was approved for registration in In re World's Finest Chocolate, Inc., 474 F.2d 1012 (C.C.P.A.1973); In re Ovation Instruments, Inc., 201 U.S.P.Q. 116 (Trademark Trial & App.Bd. 1978), accepted the shape of a guitar for registration. Even building designs appear on the Principal Register. See, e.g., Fotomat Corp. v. Ace Corp., 208 U.S.P.Q. 92 (S.D.Cal.1980). If the configuration is sufficiently unique ("inherently distinctive"), it may be registered without a demonstration of secondary meaning on the theory that it will serve *per se* to identify to consumers the goods of the applicant. See, e.g., In re Days–Ease Home Products Corp., 197 U.S.P.Q. 566 (Trademark Trial & App.Bd.1977) (container for liquid drain opener shaped to resemble a pipe trap).

(2) The Court of Customs and Patent Appeals, and now the Court of Appeals for the Federal Circuit, has been alert to exclude functional elements from registration. See In re Deister Concentrator Co., 289 F.2d 496 (C.C.P.A.1961) (rhomboidal shape of ore concentrating table held functional). The exclusion is discussed at length in In re Morton–Norwick Products, Inc., 671 F.2d 1332 (C.C.P.A.1982), finding nonfunctional a container configuration used for spray starch and household cleaners.

SECTION 2. SOUND RECORDINGS

STATE PROTECTION AGAINST DUPLICATION

Both before and after the 1971 Sound Recording Amendments, state statutes such as the one applied in Goldstein v. California, p. 609 supra, also undertook to penalize duplication. *Goldstein* considered the duplication of sound recordings made before the effective date of the 1971 amendments; the Court said Congress had left these recordings subject to state control. There was some fumbling in the revision bill about these old recordings; the outcome was § 301(c). State anti-piracy laws remain effective until the year 2047 with respect to recordings fixed before Feb. 15, 1972, but the recordings continue to be excluded from federal copyright. (Why 2047? Because it is 75 years from 1972. Cf. § 302(c).)

Goldstein validated a state statute that, by creating a criminal offense, was found to have expressed a legislative decision to create a kind of state copyright. Some state statutes also offer civil remedies to victims of record piracy.[a] Note that § 301(c) also preserves rights and remedies under common law with respect to pre–1972 recordings. Relief against unauthorized duplication of records and tapes has sometimes been achieved under a common law misappropriation theory. In Capitol Records, Inc. v. Mercury Records Corp., 221 F.2d 657 (2d Cir.1955), the Second Circuit, over a strong dissent by Learned Hand, held that New York law would recognize in the originator an exclusive right to reproduce and sell its records.[b] Even after *Sears* and *Compco*, some courts, distinguishing "misappropriation" from mere "copying," took the position that the Supreme Court's decisions did not preclude relief against an "unauthorized appropriation, reproduction or duplication of the actual performances." Capitol Records, Inc. v. Greatest Records, Inc., 43 Misc.2d 878, 252 N.Y.S.2d 553 (Sup.Ct.1964); Capitol Records, Inc. v. Erickson, 2 Cal.App.3d 526, 82 Cal.Rptr. 798 (1969), cert. denied, 398 U.S. 960 (1970).

A misappropriation claim against a pirate was enthusiastically upheld in Mercury Records Prod., Inc. v. Economic Consultants, Inc., 64 Wis.2d 163, 218 N.W.2d 705 (1974). After reviewing the attacks on *INS*, which it associated chiefly with Learned Hand, the Wisconsin Supreme Court concluded that "*Goldstein* completely repudiates Judge Hand's rationale criticizing *I.N.S.* * * * *I.N.S.* stands." This view has been influential in subsequent piracy cases. See, e.g., A & M Records, Inc. v. M.V.C. Distrib. Corp., 574 F.2d 312 (6th Cir.1978); GAI Audio of New York, Inc. v. Columbia Broadcasting System, Inc., 27 Md.App. 172, 340 A.2d 736 (1975).

IMITATION OF SOUND RECORDINGS

Waits v. Frito–Lay, Inc.

United States Court of Appeals, Ninth Circuit, 1992.
978 F.2d 1093.
Certiorari denied, 506 U.S. 1080, 113 S.Ct. 1047 (1993).

■ Before BROWNING, BOOCHEVER, and REINHARDT, CIRCUIT JUDGES.

■ BOOCHEVER, CIRCUIT JUDGE:

Defendants Frito–Lay, Inc., and Tracy–Locke, Inc., appeal a jury verdict and award of $2.6 million in compensatory damages, punitive damages

---

a. State piracy statutes are examined in Pesserilo, State Anti–Sound Piracy Laws and A Proposed Model Statute, 8 Perf.Arts Rev. 1 (1978). Even post–1972 recordings are not entirely beyond the reach of the states. See Anderson v. Nidorf, 26 F.3d 100 (9th Cir. 1994), upholding a California criminal statute prohibiting the sale of recordings and audiovisual works that do not conspicuously disclose the identity of the manufacturer.

b. Judge Hand agreed with the majority that the renditions were "writings" with which Congress could deal if it wished; he

believed, however, that federal law would consider the recordings divestively published by public sale and that the states could not thereafter create rights in them. The definitive analysis in Kaplan, Performer's Right and Copyright: The Capitol Records Case, 69 Harv.L.Rev. 409 (1956), must now be viewed in the context of Goldstein v. California. This and others of the early record cases are considered from that perspective in R. Brown, Publication and Preemption in Copyright Law: Elegiac Reflections on Goldstein v. California, 22 U.C.L.A. L.Rev. 1022 (1975).

and attorney's fees, in favor of singer Tom Waits. Waits sued the snack food manufacturer and its advertising agency for voice misappropriation and false endorsement following the broadcast of a radio commercial for SalsaRio Doritos which featured a vocal performance imitating Waits' raspy singing voice. On appeal, the defendants mount attacks on nearly all aspects of the judgment. * * *

BACKGROUND

Tom Waits is a professional singer, songwriter, and actor of some renown. Waits has a raspy, gravelly singing voice, described by one fan as "like how you'd sound if you drank a quart of bourbon, smoked a pack of cigarettes and swallowed a pack of razor blades.... Late at night. After not sleeping for three days." Since the early 1970s, when his professional singing career began, Waits has recorded more than seventeen albums and has toured extensively, playing to sold-out audiences throughout the United States, Canada, Europe, Japan, and Australia. * * * Tom Waits does not, however, do commercials. He has maintained this policy consistently during the past ten years, rejecting numerous lucrative offers to endorse major products. Moreover, Waits' policy is a public one: in magazine, radio, and newspaper interviews he has expressed his philosophy that musical artists should not do commercials because it detracts from their artistic integrity.

Frito–Lay, Inc. is in the business of manufacturing, distributing, and selling prepared and packaged food products, including Doritos brand corn chips. Tracy–Locke, Inc. is an advertising agency which counts Frito–Lay among its clients. In developing an advertising campaign to introduce a new Frito–Lay product, SalsaRio Doritos, Tracy–Locke found inspiration in a 1976 Waits song, "Step Right Up." Ironically, this song is a jazzy parody of commercial hucksterism, and consists of a succession of humorous advertising pitches. * * *

The story of Tracy–Locke's search for a lead singer for the commercial suggests that no one would do but a singer who could not only capture the feeling of "Step Right Up" but also imitate Tom Waits' voice. The initial efforts of the ad agency's creative team, using a respected professional singer with a deep bluesy voice, met with disapproval from executives at both Tracy–Locke and Frito–Lay. Tracy–Locke then auditioned a number of other singers who could sing in a gravelly style.

Stephen Carter was among those who auditioned. A recording engineer who was acquainted with Carter's work had recommended him to Tracy–Locke as someone who did a good Tom Waits imitation. Carter was a professional musician from Dallas and a Tom Waits fan. Over ten years of performing Waits songs as part of his band's repertoire, he had consciously perfected an imitation of Waits' voice. When Carter auditioned, members of the Tracy–Locke creative team "did a double take" over

Carter's near-perfect imitation of Waits, and remarked to him how much he sounded like Waits. In fact, the commercial's musical director warned Carter that he probably wouldn't get the job because he sounded too much like Waits, which could pose legal problems. Carter, however, did get the job.

At the recording session for the commercial David Brenner, Tracy–Locke's executive producer, became concerned about the legal implications of Carter's skill in imitating Waits, and attempted to get Carter to "back off" his Waits imitation. Neither the client nor the members of the creative team, however, liked the result. After the session, Carter remarked to Brenner that Waits would be unhappy with the commercial because of his publicly avowed policy against doing commercial endorsements and his disapproval of artists who did. Brenner acknowledged he was aware of this, telling Carter that he had previously approached Waits to do a Diet Coke commercial and "you never heard anybody say no so fast in your life." Brenner conveyed to Robert Grossman, Tracy–Locke's managing vice president and the executive on the Frito–Lay account, his concerns that the commercial was too close to Waits' voice. As a precaution, Brenner made an alternate version of the commercial with another singer. * * *

The commercial was broadcast in September and October 1988 on over 250 radio stations located in 61 markets nationwide, including Los Angeles, San Francisco, and Chicago. Waits heard it during his appearance on a Los Angeles radio program, and was shocked. He realized "immediately that whoever was going to hear this and obviously identify the voice would also identify that [Tom Waits] in fact had agreed to do a commercial for Doritos."

In November 1988, Waits sued Tracy–Locke and Frito–Lay, alleging claims of misappropriation under California law and false endorsement under the Lanham Act. The case was tried before a jury in April and May 1990. The jury found in Waits' favor, awarding him $375,000 compensatory damages and $2 million punitive damages for voice misappropriation, and $100,000 damages for violation of the Lanham Act. The court awarded Waits attorneys' fees under the Lanham Act. This timely appeal followed.

DISCUSSION

I. *Voice Misappropriation*

In Midler v. Ford Motor Co., 849 F.2d 460, 463 (9th Cir.1988), cert. denied, 503 U.S. 951 (1992), we held that "when a distinctive voice of a professional singer is widely known and is deliberately imitated in order to sell a product, the sellers have appropriated what is not theirs and have committed a tort in California." The *Midler* tort is a species of violation of the "right of publicity," the right of a person whose identity has commercial value—most often a celebrity—to control the commercial use of that identity. See Motschenbacher v. R.J. Reynolds Tobacco Co., 498 F.2d 821, 824–25 (9th Cir.1974). See generally J.T. McCarthy, The Rights of Publicity and Privacy (1987) (hereafter Publicity and Privacy). We recognized in *Midler* that when voice is a sufficient indicia of a celebrity's identity, the right of publicity protects against its imitation for commercial purposes without the celebrity's consent. See *Midler,* 849 F.2d at 463. * * *

A. *Continuing Viability of Midler*

As a threshold matter, the defendants ask us to rethink *Midler,* and to reject it as an inaccurate statement of California law. *Midler,* according to the defendants, has been "impliedly overruled" by the Supreme Court's decision in Bonito Boats, Inc. v. Thunder Craft Boats, Inc., 489 U.S. 141 (1989). Additionally, they argue that the *Midler* tort is preempted by the federal Copyright Act. We review these questions of law de novo. See Kruso v. International Tel. & Tel. Corp., 872 F.2d 1416, 1421 (9th Cir. 1989), cert. denied, 496 U.S. 937 (1990).

Bonito Boats involved a Florida statute giving perpetual patent-like protection to boat hull designs already on the market, a class of manufactured articles expressly excluded from federal patent protection. The Court ruled that the Florida statute was preempted by federal patent law because it directly conflicted with the comprehensive federal patent scheme. In reaching this conclusion, the Court cited its earlier decisions in Sears Roebuck & Co. v. Stiffel Co., 376 U.S. 225 (1964), and Compco Corp. v. Day–Brite Lighting, 376 U.S. 234 (1964), for the proposition that "publicly known design and utilitarian ideas which were unprotected by patent occupied much the same position as the subject matter of an expired patent," i.e., they are expressly unprotected. *Bonito Boats,* 489 U.S. at 152.

The defendants seize upon this citation to *Sears* and *Compco* as a reaffirmation of the sweeping preemption principles for which these cases were once read to stand. They argue that *Midler* was wrongly decided because it ignores these two decisions, an omission that the defendants say indicates an erroneous assumption that *Sears* and *Compco* have been "relegated to the constitutional junkyard." Thus, the defendants go on to reason, earlier cases that rejected entertainers' challenges to imitations of their performances based on federal copyright preemption, were correctly decided because they relied on *Sears* and *Compco.* See Sinatra v. Goodyear Tire & Rubber Co., 435 F.2d 711, 716–18 (9th Cir.1970), cert. denied, 402 U.S. 906 (1971); Booth v. Colgate–Palmolive Co., 362 F.Supp. 343, 348 (S.D.N.Y.1973); Davis v. Trans World Airlines, 297 F.Supp. 1145, 1147 (C.D.Cal.1969). This reasoning suffers from a number of flaws.

Bonito Boats itself cautions against reading *Sears* and *Compco* for a "broad pre-emptive principle" and cites subsequent Supreme Court decisions retreating from such a sweeping interpretation. "[T]he Patent and Copyright Clauses do not, by their own force or by negative implication, deprive the States of the power to adopt rules for the promotion of intellectual creation." Bonito Boats, 489 U.S. at 165 (citing, *inter alia,* Goldstein v. California, 412 U.S. 546, 552–61, (1973) and Kewanee Oil Co. v. Bicron Corp., 416 U.S. 470, 478–79 (1974)). Instead, the Court reaffirmed the right of states to "place limited regulations on the use of unpatented designs in order to prevent consumer confusion as to source." Id. *Bonito Boats* thus cannot be read as endorsing or resurrecting the broad reading of *Compco* and *Sears* urged by the defendants, under which Waits' state tort claim arguably would be preempted.

Moreover, the Court itself recognized the authority of states to protect entertainers' "right of publicity" in Zacchini v. Scripps–Howard Broadcasting Co., 433 U.S. 562 (1977). In *Zacchini*, the Court endorsed a state right-of-publicity law as in harmony with federal patent and copyright law, holding that an unconsented-to television news broadcast of a commercial entertainer's performance was not protected by the First Amendment. Id. at 573, 576–78. The cases Frito asserts were "rightly decided" all predate *Zacchini* and other Supreme Court precedent narrowing *Sears'* and *Compco*'s sweeping preemption principles. In sum, our holding in *Midler,* upon which Waits' voice misappropriation claim rests, has not been eroded by subsequent authority.

The defendants ask that we rethink *Midler* anyway, arguing as the defendants did there that voice misappropriation is preempted by section 114 of the Copyright Act. Under this provision, a state cause of action escapes Copyright Act preemption if its subject matter "does not come within the subject matter of copyright ... including works or authorship not fixed in any tangible medium of expression." 17 U.S.C. § 301(b)(1). We rejected copyright preemption in *Midler* because voice is not a subject matter of copyright: "A voice is not copyrightable. The sounds are not 'fixed.'" *Midler,* 849 F.2d at 462. As a three-judge panel, we are not at liberty to reconsider this conclusion, and even if we were, we would decline to disturb it.

Waits' claim, like Bette Midler's, is for infringement of voice, not for infringement of a copyrightable subject such as sound recording or musical composition. Moreover, the legislative history of section 114 [301?] indicates the express intent of Congress that "[t]he evolving common law rights of 'privacy,' 'publicity,' and trade secrets ... remain unaffected [by the preemption provision] as long as the causes of action contain elements, such as an invasion of personal rights ... that are different in kind from copyright infringement." H.R.Rep. No. 1476, 94th Cong., 2d Sess. 132, reprinted in 1976 U.S.C.C.A.N. 5659, 5748. Waits' voice misappropriation claim is one for invasion of a personal property right: his right of publicity to control the use of his identity as embodied in his voice. See *Midler,* 849 F.2d at 462–63 ("What is put forward as protectable here is more personal than any work of authorship.... A voice is as distinctive and personal as a face.") The trial's focus was on the elements of voice misappropriation, as formulated in *Midler:* whether the defendants had deliberately imitated Waits' voice rather than simply his style and whether Waits' voice was sufficiently distinctive and widely known to give him a protectable right in its use. These elements are "different in kind" from those in a copyright infringement case challenging the unauthorized use of a song or recording. Waits' voice misappropriation claim, therefore, is not preempted by federal copyright law.

B. *Jury Instructions*

The defendants next contend that the district court committed prejudicial error by rejecting their proposed jury instructions on three elements of the *Midler* tort: the deliberate misappropriation for commercial purposes of (1) a voice, that is (2) distinctive and (3) widely known. * * *

(1) *"Voice" vs. "Style"*

The defendants argued at trial that although they had consciously copied Tom Waits' style in creating the Doritos commercial, they had not deliberately imitated his voice. * * *

* * * The court's voice misappropriation instructions limited the jury's consideration to voice, and in no way implied that it could consider style. Indeed, in addressing the jury in closing argument, Waits' attorney agreed with the defendants that style was not protected. Moreover, the court included an additional instruction that effectively narrowed the jury's focus to Waits' voice and indicated that style imitation alone was insufficient for tort liability. For the defendants to be liable for voice misappropriation, the court stated, the imitation had to be so good that "people who were familiar with plaintiff's voice who heard the commercial *believed plaintiff performed it*. In this connection it is not enough that they were reminded of plaintiff or thought the singer sounded like plaintiff...." [3] (Emphasis added.) Even if the jury were initially confused about whether the defendants could be liable simply for imitating Waits' style, this instruction would have disabused them of this notion.

(2) *Definition of "Distinctive"*

The defendants next argue that the court's instruction concerning the meaning of "distinctive" was an unfair and inaccurate statement of the law because it confuses the "distinctiveness" of a voice with its identifiability or recognizability. * * *

The defendants' technical argument that distinctiveness is a separate concept from identifiability, while supported by their experts' testimony, has no basis in law. Identifiability is properly considered in evaluating distinctiveness, for it is a central element of a right of publicity claim. See Publicity and Privacy § 3.4[A] & n. 1 (citing cases). Our *Midler* holding is premised on the fact that a person is as identifiable by voice as by any other indicia of identity previously recognized as protectable. Although we did not define "distinctiveness" in *Midler*, we stated: "A voice is as *distinctive* and personal as a face. The human voice is one of the most palpable ways *identity is manifested*. We are all aware that a friend is at once known by a few words on the phone.... [T]hese observations hold true of singing...." Midler v. Ford, 849 F.2d at 463 (emphasis added). See also *Motschenbacher*, 498 F.2d at 826–27 (rejecting trial court's ruling

---

3. This instruction effectively added an additional element to *Midler's* formulation of voice misappropriation: actual confusion. The validity of this instruction is not before us in this appeal and we express no opinion on this issue.

that because plaintiff's face was not recognizable in advertisement photograph, his identity had not been misappropriated, and finding that plaintiff was identifiable from distinctive decorations on race car).

The court's "distinctiveness" instruction informed the jury that it could consider the recordings of Waits' voice introduced into evidence and the testimony of expert and other witnesses. The court thus invited members of the jury to use their common sense in determining whether Waits has a distinctive enough voice to warrant protection, and to consider as well what the experts had to say. This was entirely appropriate. * * *

(3) *Definition of "Widely Known"*

The defendants next object to the district court's instruction concerning the element of "widely known" on the ground that it was too vague to guide the jury in making a factual determination of the issue. The court instructed the jury: "A professional singer's voice is widely known if it is known to a *large number* of people throughout a *relatively large* geographic area." (Emphasis added.) The court rejected an instruction proposed by the defendants, which reflected their contention at trial that Tom Waits is a singer known only to music insiders and to a small but loyal group of fans: "A singer is not widely known if he is only recognized by his own fans, or fans of a particular sort of music, or a small segment of the population."

The legal underpinnings of this proposed instruction are questionable. The defendants assert that because Waits has not achieved the level of celebrity Bette Midler has, he is not well known under the *Midler* standard. We reject this crabbed interpretation of *Midler*. The defendants' proposed instruction would have excluded from legal protection the voices of many popular singers who fall short of superstardom. "Well known" is a relative term, and differences in the extent of celebrity are adequately reflected in the amount of damages recoverable. * * *

C. *Compensatory Damage Award*

The jury awarded Waits the following compensatory damages for voice misappropriation: $100,000 for the fair market value of his services; $200,000 for injury to his peace, happiness and feelings; and $75,000 for injury to his goodwill, professional standing and future publicity value. The defendants contest the latter two awards, disputing both the availability of such damages in a voice misappropriation action and the sufficiency of the evidence supporting the awards. * * *

[The court upheld the award of damages for mental distress, relying in part on testimony from Waits that the commercial embarrassed him. "I had to call all my friends, that if they hear this thing, please be informed this is not me. I was on the phone for days. I also had people calling me saying, Gee Tom, I heard the new Doritos ad." The court also upheld the award for damage to Waits' goodwill and reputation.]

D. *Punitive Damage Award*

The jury awarded Waits a total of $2 million in punitive damages for voice misappropriation: $1.5 million against Tracy–Locke and $500,000 against Frito–Lay. The defendants ask that we vacate this award, arguing that punitive damages are unavailable as a matter of law, and alternatively, that the evidence was insufficient to support their award.

In California, exemplary or punitive damages are available "where it is proven by clear and convincing evidence that the defendant has been guilty of oppression, fraud, or malice." Cal.Civ.Code § 3294(a) (West Supp.1992). * * *

The defendants argue, however, that although they may have been aware that legal risks were involved, they had a good faith belief that Waits' rights would not be infringed because they read the legal precedents differently. This argument leaves us unpersuaded. Good faith cannot be manufactured by looking to the law of other jurisdictions to define the rights of California residents. *Midler* could not be more clear that, in California at least, a well-known singer with a distinctive voice has a property right in that voice. * * *

II. *Lanham Act Claim*

Section 43(a) of the Lanham Act, 15 U.S.C. § 1125(a), prohibits the use of false designations of origin, false descriptions, and false representations in the advertising and sale of goods and services. Smith v. Montoro, 648 F.2d 602, 603 (9th Cir.1981). Waits' claim under section 43(a) is premised on the theory that by using an imitation of his distinctive voice in an admitted parody of a Tom Waits song, the defendants misrepresented his association with and endorsement of SalsaRio Doritos. The jury found in Waits' favor and awarded him $100,000 in damages. The district court also awarded him attorneys' fees under section 35 of the Lanham Act. On appeal, the defendants argue that Waits lacks standing to bring a Lanham Act claim, that Waits' false endorsement claim fails on its merits, that the damage award is duplicative, and that attorneys' fees are improper. Before we address these contentions, however, we turn to the threshold issue of whether false endorsement claims are properly cognizable under section 43(a) of the Lanham Act, a question of first impression in this circuit.

A. *False Endorsement*

* * * Courts in other jurisdictions have interpreted [§ 43(a)] as authorizing claims for false endorsement. E.g., Better Business Bureau v. Medical Directors, Inc., 681 F.2d 397 (5th Cir.1982); Jackson v. MPI Home Video, 694 F.Supp. 483 (N.D.Ill.1988); Wildlife Internationale, Inc. v. Clements, 591 F.Supp. 1542 (S.D.Oh.1984); Geisel v. Poynter Prods., Inc., 283 F.Supp. 261, 267 (S.D.N.Y.1968). Moreover, courts have recognized false endorsement claims brought by plaintiffs, including celebrities, for the unauthorized imitation of their distinctive attributes, where those attributes amount to an unregistered commercial "trademark." See Dallas Cowboys Cheerleaders, Inc. v. Pussycat Cinema, Ltd., 604 F.2d 200, 205 (2d

Cir.1979) (recognizing claim under § 43(a) because uniform worn by star of X-rated movie was confusingly similar to plaintiffs' trademark uniforms, falsely creating impression that plaintiffs "sponsored or otherwise approved the use" of the uniform); Allen v. Men's World Outlet, Inc., 679 F.Supp. 360, 368 (S.D.N.Y.1988) (celebrity states a claim under § 43(a) by showing that advertisement featuring photograph of a look-alike falsely represented that advertised products were associated with him); Allen v. National Video, Inc., 610 F.Supp. 612, 625–26 (S.D.N.Y.1985) (recognizing celebrity's false endorsement claim under § 43(a) because celebrity has commercial investment in name and face tantamount to interests of a trademark holder in distinctive mark); see also Lahr v. Adell Chemical Co., 300 F.2d 256, 258 (1st Cir.1962) (imitation of unique voice actionable as common law unfair competition); cf. Sinatra v. Goodyear Tire & Rubber Co., 435 F.2d 711, 716 (9th Cir.1970) (rejecting common law unfair competition claim because plaintiff's voice not sufficiently unique to be protectable), cert. denied, 402 U.S. 906 (1971).

The persuasiveness of this case law as to the cognizability of Waits' Lanham Act claim is reinforced by the 1988 Lanham Act amendments. * * * Specifically, we read the amended language to codify case law interpreting section 43(a) to encompass false endorsement claims. In light of persuasive judicial authority and the subsequent congressional approval of that authority, we conclude that false endorsement claims, including those premised on the unauthorized imitation of an entertainer's distinctive voice, are cognizable under section 43(a).

B. *Standing*

According to the defendants, however, Waits lacks standing to sue for false endorsement. They assert that because he is not in competition with the defendants, he cannot sue under the Lanham Act. Common sense contradicts this argument, for the purported endorser who is commercially damaged by the false endorsement will rarely if ever be a competitor, and yet is the party best situated to enforce the Lanham Act's prohibition on such conduct. * * *

[Holding that the "dispositive question" on standing is whether plaintiff "has a reasonable interest to be protected against false advertising," the court concluded that § 43(a) "does not require 'actual competition' in the traditional sense; it extends to a purported endorser who has an economic interest akin to that of a trademark holder in controlling the commercial exploitation of his or her identity."]

C. *Merits*

The defendants next argue that Waits' false endorsement claim must fail on its merits because the Doritos commercial "did not represent that . . . [Waits] sponsored or endorsed their product." We disagree. The court correctly instructed the jury that in considering Waits' Lanham Act claim, it must determine whether "ordinary consumers . . . would be confused as to whether Tom Waits sang on the commercial . . . and whether he sponsors or endorses SalsaRio Doritos." The jury was told that in making this determination, it should consider the totality of the evidence, including the distinctiveness of Waits' voice and style, the evidence of actual confusion as to whether Waits actually sang on the commercial, and the defendants' intent to imitate Waits' voice.   * * *

At trial, the jury listened to numerous Tom Waits recordings, and to a recording of the Doritos commercial in which the Tom Waits impersonator delivered this "hip" endorsement of SalsaRio Doritos: "It's buffo, boffo, bravo, gung-ho, tally-ho, but never mellow .... try 'em, buy 'em, get 'em, got 'em." The jury also heard evidence, relevant to the likelihood of consumer confusion, that the Doritos commercial was targeted to an audience which overlapped with Waits' audience, males between the ages of 18 to 35 who listened to the radio. Finally, there was evidence of actual consumer confusion: the testimony of numerous witnesses that they actually believed it was Tom Waits singing the words of endorsement.

This evidence was sufficient to support the jury's finding that consumers were likely to be misled by the commercial into believing that Waits endorsed SalsaRio Doritos.

[The jury awarded $100,000 on the Lanham Act claim, representing the fair market value of Waits' services. The court vacated the award as duplicative of the damages awarded on the voice misappropriation claim. It did, however, uphold an award of attorneys' fees under the Lanham Act.]

Affirmed in part and vacated in part.

NOTES AND QUESTIONS

(1) In the Midler v. Ford Motor Co. case on which Judge Boochever so heavily relies, the Young and Rubicam advertising agency had prepared a series of television commercials for Ford designed to build an emotional connection with "yuppies" by stirring memories of their college days. The commercials used popular songs from the early seventies, in many instances sung by the original artist. When Bette Midler refused to participate, Young and Rubicam used one of Midler's former backup singers to imitate Midler's rendition of her 1973 hit *Do You Want to Dance.* In the opinion cited in *Waits,* the Ninth Circuit overturned a summary judgment for the defendants on Midler's appropriation of identity claim. She eventually won a $400,000 jury award, which was affirmed by the Ninth Circuit in an unpublished opinion. See 22 U.S.P.Q.2d 1478 (9th Cir.1991), cert. denied, 503 U.S. 951 (1992).[c]

---

c. The question of protection for a recognizable voice may arise in a new context with the development of computer systems capable of "speaking" in a specified "voice." Users may someday select "voice fonts" in computer applications in the way we now choose printer fonts—"[a] traveling businessman might have his electronic mail read to him over the phone in the sultry voice of Marlene Dietrich or the crisp English of Sir John Gielgud." Pollack, Future Computer Systems May Copy a Person's Voice, New York Times, Apr. 21, 1997, p. D1.

(2) The opinion in *Midler* distinguished the Ninth Circuit's earlier decision in Sinatra v. Goodyear Tire & Rubber Co., 435 F.2d 711 (9th Cir.1970), cert. denied, 402 U.S. 906 (1971), which at the time was the leading case on voice imitation. In *Sinatra,* an advertising agency (once again Young and Rubicam) had created a campaign for Goodyear to promote its "wide boots" tires. The commercials centered around the music and revised lyrics from *These Boots are Made for Walkin',* a song made popular by plaintiff Nancy Sinatra. She alleged that the singer used on the commercials imitated her voice and style. The Ninth Circuit affirmed a summary judgment in favor of the defendants. The court in *Midler* distinguished the *Sinatra* case with the following comments:

> The basis of Nancy Sinatra's complaint was unfair competition; she claimed that the song and the arrangement had acquired "a secondary meaning" which, under California law, was protectible. This court noted that the defendants "had paid a very substantial sum to the copyright proprietor to obtain the license for the use of the song and all of its arrangements." To give Sinatra damages for their use of the song would clash with federal copyright law. Summary judgment for the defendants was affirmed. * * * If Midler were claiming a secondary meaning to "Do You Want To Dance" or seeking to prevent the defendants from using that song, she would fail like Sinatra. But that is not this case. Midler does not seek damages for Ford's use of "Do You Want To Dance," and thus her count is not preempted by federal copyright law. Copyright protects "original works of authorship fixed in any tangible medium of expression." 17 U.S.C. § 102(a). A voice is not copyrightable. The sounds are not "fixed."

This distinction echoes one that the *Sinatra* court had itself drawn in response to plaintiff Sinatra's reliance on Lahr v. Adell Chemical Co., 300 F.2d 256 (1st Cir.1962). In that case actor and comedian Bert Lahr (the cowardly lion in *The Wizard of Oz*) brought an unfair competition claim in connection with a television commercial that used a cartoon duck speaking in a voice that imitated Lahr's unique vocal style. The First Circuit reversed an order dismissing the complaint. (It also upheld a count for defamation that alleged that the imitation would cause the public to believe that Lahr was reduced to making anonymous television commercials.) The court in *Sinatra* distinguished *Lahr:* "[I]n *Lahr* [and another case] the plaintiffs claimed a 'secondary meaning' in pure sound, their individual vocal characteristics. The protection sought was not for the combination of sound together with copyrighted lyrics, melody and arrangement, as here."

On imitation of performing "style," see also Shaw v. Time–Life Records, 38 N.Y.2d 201, 379 N.Y.S.2d 390, 341 N.E.2d 817 (1975), in which bandleader Artie Shaw objected to a re-creation of his arrangements and "sound" in a newly-recorded collection of "Swing Era" classics. The New York Court of Appeals affirmed that Shaw had no property interest in his "sound," but said that he was entitled to explore at trial whether the advertising and labeling of the records might cause purchasers to believe the recordings were actual Artie Shaw performances.

On the possibility of protecting elements of a performer's "style" as an aspect of the right of publicity (p. 743 infra), see Estate of Presley v. Russen, 513 F.Supp. 1339 (D.N.J.1981), in which the court, although declining to issue a preliminary injunction, found a likelihood of success on a right of publicity claim directed against a live stage production imitating an Elvis Presley performance.

(3) Is the decision in *Midler* imposing liability for an imitation of Bette Midler's recorded performance of *Do You Want to Dance* inconsistent with § 114 of the Copyright Act, which protects sound recording against duplication, but not against imitation? Is a distinction between imitation of "voice" and "style" sufficient to avoid potential conflict?

(4) The opinion in *Sinatra* worried that "[a]n added clash with the copyright laws is the potential restriction which recognition of performers' 'secondary meanings' places upon the potential market of the copyright proprietor. If a proposed licensee must pay each artist who had played or sung the composition and who might therefore claim unfair competition-performer's protection, the licensee may well be discouraged to the point of complete loss of interest." Does *Midler* or *Waits* place an inappropriate burden on the owner of the copyright in the underlying musical composition?

SECTION 3.   TITLES

Warner Brothers Pictures, Inc. v. Majestic Pictures Corp.

United States Circuit Court of Appeals, Second Circuit, 1934.
70 F.2d 310.

■ Before MANTON, AUGUSTUS N. HAND, and CHASE, CIRCUIT JUDGES.

■ AUGUSTUS N. HAND, CIRCUIT JUDGE. This is an appeal from an order denying a motion to enjoin the defendants pendente lite from producing a talking motion picture under the title "Gold Diggers of Paris." "The Gold Diggers" was the title of a play by Avery Hopwood which was produced by David Belasco at the Lyceum Theater in New York, and continued for 90 successive weeks after opening on September 30, 1919. Subsequently the play was taken on tour through the United States, and 528 performances were given between September 13, 1921, and April 21, 1923. There were gross receipts from the play of more than $1,900,000, and much money was expended in advertising. Even since April, 1923, there have been many performances by stock companies, some as late as 1932, under the title "The Gold Diggers."

In 1923 the complainant acquired the exclusive silent motion picture rights in "The Gold Diggers," and during that year produced a silent motion picture based on this play and distributed the picture under the same title. The gross receipts derived from licensing theater owners to exhibit it amounted to $470,000.

In 1929 complainant purchased the talking motion picture rights in "The Gold Diggers," and produced a talking motion picture based on the play at an expense of $725,000, which it opened at the Winter Garden in New York on August 30, 1929. This picture was exhibited in over 6,000 theaters in the United States and Canada under the title "Gold Diggers of Broadway." The total receipts from licensing it in the United States and Canada were $2,540,298.47. It was seen by millions of people, and complainant expended upwards of $74,000 in advertising it. Complainant received $1,395,344.54 upon licenses outside of the United States and Canada. Such was the success of this picture that complainant determined to produce a new talking motion picture version of the play under the title "Gold Diggers of 1933," for the production of which $199,983 had been expended at the time the motion for the preliminary injunction was made. In 1933 defendants produced a picture under the title "Gold Diggers of Paris," having certain characters similar to those in Hopwood's play.

The original play is said to have dealt with the lives and actions of two young women who had come to New York and there joined the chorus of a musical comedy. One of the young women who took the leading role was represented as having good moral instincts and as being somewhat dissatisfied with or uncomfortable in the life that she was leading. Her friend, who took the subordinate part and was responsible for the comedy element, was not so handicapped. She was decidedly the louder and more vulgar of the two, and was a low comedy character.

The complaint and the affidavits submitted in support of this motion for an injunction allege that the use of the title "Gold Diggers of Paris" was with intent to capitalize the good will and reputation of complainant and to deceive the public into associating defendants' motion picture with Avery Hopwood's play and complainant's motion pictures. * * *

Enough appears in the affidavits to show that the complainant would be an infringer of the copyright of the original play of Avery Hopwood if it had not purchased the right to make silent and talking picture versions thereof. Perhaps, if the play and the scenarios for the pictures were before us, we might not reach this conclusion, but when it appears that Warner Bros. Pictures, Inc., went to the expense of buying the silent and talking rights, and the affidavits state that all the pictures were based on the play, and no showing has been made to the contrary, we must assume that the moving pictures were thus founded. Complainant's asserted right to an injunction is not, however, based on infringement of a copyright of the play, but on an unfair use of the words "Gold Diggers." A copyright of a play does not carry with it the exclusive right to the use of the title. National Picture Theatres v. Foundation Film Corp. (C.C.A.) 266 F. 208; Atlas Mfg. Co. v. Street & Smith (C.C.A.) 204 F. 398; International F. Service Co. v.

Associated Producers (D.C.) 273 F. 585; Glaser v. St. Elmo Co. (C.C.) 175 F. 276; Corbett v. Purdy (C.C.) 80 F. 901; Harper v. Ranous (C.C.) 67 F. 904; Osgood v. Allen, Fed.Cas. No. 10,603. But complainant, by its purchase of the right to produce silent and talking motion pictures of Hopwood's play and by its investment of capital and labor in the pictures founded upon it, has built up a valuable good will in a business of pictures of this particular type. The cinematograph productions which it has advertised and distributed under the title "Gold Diggers" and "Gold Diggers of Broadway" have become associated in the public mind all over the United States with the Hopwood play and the productions of Warner Bros. Pictures, Inc., and the title "Gold Diggers" has thus acquired a distinctive meaning in the motion picture field as descriptive of film versions of the Hopwood play produced by complainant. The words have not before been used, either alone or in combination, to designate any other full-length motion pictures. It is true that they are words of general description and ordinarily would not be subject to preemption by any one, but they may not be used by a competitor to deceive a public which has long attributed them to complainant's moving pictures. National Picture Theatres, Inc. v. Foundation Film Corp. (C.C.A.) 266 F. 208; Underhill v. Schenck, 238 N.Y. 7, 20, 143 N.E. 773; Paramore v. Mack Sennett, Inc. (D.C.) 9 F.2d 66.

The trial judge denied an injunction on the ground that the public would not be misled by the title of defendants' motion picture. But the public, by the exhibition of complainant's pictures throughout the United States, has been educated to regard "Gold Diggers," when used in connection with a motion picture, as meaning one of complainant's pictures based on Hopwood's play. The wide publicity and success of complainant's pictures seem to us to lead to this inference inescapably unless it is rebutted by specific evidence, as it has not been. An intent to "gain the advantage" of complainant's "celebrity" (McLean v. Fleming, 96 U.S. at page 251) seems evident, and diversion of the latter's business and deception of the public are likely, if not inevitable, consequences of the acts complained of (National Picture Theatres v. Foundation Film Corp. [C.C.A.] 266 F. 208, 211; International F. Service Co. v. Associated Producers [D.C.] 273 F. 585, 587; Samson, etc., Works v. Puritan, etc., Mills, 211 F. at page 608; Miller, etc., Co. v. Behrend [C.C.A.] 242 F. at page 518). The defendants have produced a picture having some characters resembling those in Hopwood's play. But their picture apparently differs in many respects and is said to be based on another play, and it does not seem to be claimed by any of the parties that there is so great a similarity between defendants' picture and any of complainant's productions as to show an appropriation of the plot or literary content of the Hopwood play. Indeed, it may be assumed that defendants' picture is wholly different in origin and subject-matter. Nevertheless the use of the descriptive words "Gold Diggers" in the title of defendants' picture would be unfair and misleading, for they would represent to the public that the picture exhibited was produced by Warner Bros. Pictures, Inc., and based on Hopwood's play. The likelihood of confusion and proof of it are as strong as in National Picture Theatres v. Foundation Film Corp. (C.C.A.) 266 F. 208.

It is argued that the silent picture "Gold Diggers" and the talking picture "Gold Diggers of Broadway" have run their course and no longer need protection, and that defendants applied the name "Gold Diggers of Paris" to a new talking picture of their own before complainant put out "Gold Diggers of 1933." Even if this were so, it would seem to afford no excuse for defendants' acts. The words had become descriptive of any cinematograph productions of the complainant based upon the Hopwood play, and there is no more reason for depriving the complainant of their use in a new production based on the Hopwood play than there would be to limit a common law trade-mark of a clothing manufacturer to the styles of clothing he had previously sold and to deny protection where it was used in connection with new designs. * * *

Furthermore, even though "Gold Diggers of Broadway" and "Gold Diggers of 1933" should be found to have so little resemblance to the Hopwood play as not to be within the copyright, still it may be said that the title "Gold Diggers" through wide publicity and long use has come to mean a moving picture of the general type we have described produced by Warner Bros. Pictures, Inc., and that it is unfair for the defendants to use these words in connection with another motion picture play of the same general type. Irrespective of whether there is continuity of plot or composition in complainant's moving pictures and Hopwood's play, we think the defendants are precluded from using the title "Gold Diggers" for any motion picture play likely to compete with complainant's productions. The words signify origin and a certain standard of competence and achievement.

An injunction pendente lite should issue restraining the defendants from using the words "Gold Diggers" in connection with the motion picture "Gold Diggers of Paris" unless they place upon every piece of advertising used in connection with the picture and upon the motion picture film also, the words, in type as large as "Gold Diggers": "A production of Majestic Pictures Corporation, not based on Avery Hopwood's play or on the motion pictures of Warner Bros. Pictures, Inc.," or some equivalent words of differentiation which may be settled by the District Court after hearing the respective parties. In view of the fact that the words "Gold Diggers" are in themselves terms of general description, it is but to limit their use only so far as may be necessary to prevent unfair competition, and we think that may be done along the general lines which we have indicated. Ziegfeld Follies, Inc. v. Hill, 177 App.Div. 881, 163 N.Y.S. 1135.

Order reversed.

JACKSON v. UNIVERSAL INTERNATIONAL PICTURES, 36 Cal.2d 116, 222 P.2d 433 (1950). Plaintiff, a writer of long experience, wrote a play that he entitled "Slightly Scandalous." It rehearsed in Los Angeles, opened in

Philadelphia, and flopped in New York, closing after seven performances in 1944. About two years later, Universal, aware of the Jackson play, released a movie to which it gave the same name. There was no claim of any similarity in content. Jackson's action was based on the use of his title, for which he claimed secondary meaning. A jury awarded him $17,500. Judge Edmunds, writing for a unanimous court, affirmed:

"There is substantial evidence in the record to support the implied finding of the jury that 'Slightly Scandalous' had acquired a secondary meaning. Jackson's play was publicized in three of the largest cities in this country. The rehearsal and production of the play were announced in dramatic and motion picture journals in Hollywood and New York. Although only about 3,750 persons attended performances of the play, there is no basis for a holding, as a matter of law, that they and the undetermined number who saw the advertising are not sufficient in number to provide a basis for secondary meaning. * * *

"Universal claims that, in order to gain secondary meaning, the title must be associated specifically with the author of the play rather than with the play. The contention is unrealistic and contrary to authority. * * *

"In all probability only a very small percentage of persons who know something about plays can remember or identify the names of the authors. Usually, advertising and publicity are concentrated upon the title and the actors rather than the name of the playwright. There is no logical basis for holding that a public well acquainted with the title and the play could not confer secondary meaning upon that title merely because of unfamiliarity with the author's name."

NOTES ON THE PROTECTION OF LITERARY TITLES

(1) According to the regulations of the Copyright Office, "The following are examples of works not subject to copyright * * *: (a) Words and short phrases such as names, titles, and slogans * * *." 37 C.F.R. § 202.1. The "Gold Diggers" case reaffirms a collateral principle—copyright in a work is not infringed by an appropriation of its title. Why not?

(2) The protection of literary titles rests chiefly on the common law of unfair competition, supplemented by the federal codification in § 43(a) of the Lanham Act. Judge Learned Hand put it this way: "The plaintiff succeeds as soon as he shows an audience educated to understand that the title means his play * * *." International Film Service Co. v. Associated Producers, Inc., 273 Fed. 585 (S.D.N.Y.1921). But of course, the plaintiff must also show a likelihood of confusion.

Priority of use, absent secondary meaning, does not secure exclusive rights. To illustrate, in 1936 defendants published two issues of a magazine entitled "Information Please," printing a total of 18,000 copies. No further issues were published. A year and a half later, plaintiff initiated a stump-the-experts radio program also called "Information Please." (The court said that plaintiff adopted the name "in good faith," but it does not appear whether it was aware of the prior use.)   Within a year, plaintiff's program having achieved wide popularity, defendants made arrangements to resume publication under their old title.   Plaintiff successfully enjoined the defendants' use.   Golenpaul v. Rosett, 174 Misc. 114, 18 N.Y.S.2d 889 (Sup.Ct.1940).   See also Gordon v. Warner Brothers Pictures, Inc., 269 Cal.App.2d 31, 74 Cal.Rptr. 499 (1969) (prior use of "FBI Story" for a novel was not sufficient in itself to establish liability for defendant's later use of "The FBI Story" for a motion picture starring Jimmy Stewart).

Is it possible to acquire rights in a title prior to the release of the work?   That was the issue in Metro–Goldwyn Mayer, Inc. v. Lee, 212 Cal.App.2d 23, 27 Cal.Rptr. 833 (1963).   Plaintiffs were in the process of producing a motion picture based on the works of the Grimm Brothers, all in the public domain; the film was to be released under the title "The Wonderful World of The Brothers Grimm."   Defendant, distributing a German film entitled "Grimms Fairy Tales," adopted in its advertising the phrase "A wonderful world of the Grimm Brothers."   It was held that the pre-release publicity surrounding the MGM movie (which had been mentioned in gossip columns, trade journals, newspapers, and magazines) was sufficient to support a finding of secondary meaning; the defendant's ads were found to be misleading.   In Orion Pictures Co. v. Dell Pub. Co., 471 F.Supp. 392 (S.D.N.Y.1979), the court found that pre-release advertising had created secondary meaning in the movie title "A Little Romance"; a paperback publisher had changed the name of the book on which the movie was based to exploit the popularity of the film.   The court went on to say that even if secondary meaning had not yet been established, "secondary meaning 'in the making' " should be protected, at least against an intentional attempt to "capitalize on the efforts and goodwill of others."   The notion of "secondary meaning in the making," also known as "incipient secondary meaning," does not comport with the customary requirement of an established connection between the source and the claimed trade symbol; it was repudiated in Laureyssens v. Idea Group, Inc., 964 F.2d 131 (2d Cir.1992), and Black & Decker Mfg. Co. v. Ever–Ready Appliance Mfg. Co., 684 F.2d 546 (8th Cir.1982).

Secondary meaning, once established, may eventually be lost.   The plaintiff in Kirkland v. NBC, Inc., 425 F.Supp. 1111 (E.D.Pa.1976), aff'd, 565 F.2d 152 (3d Cir.1977), had in 1933 written a story entitled "Land of the Lost," which later became a radio program broadcast from 1943 to 1948.   In 1974, NBC adopted the same name for a Saturday morning children's program.   In response to plaintiff's claim of unfair competition, the court found that the public had ceased to associate the title with the plaintiff or her work.

(3) The likelihood of confusion depends on more than the similarity of the titles.   Comparisons of content, marketing techniques, and visual appearance often influence the result.   In Playboy Enterprises, Inc. v. Chuckleberry Pub., Inc., 687 F.2d 563 (2d Cir.1982), plaintiff was granted an injunction against the use of "Playmen" as the title for a magazine adopting a cover and format similar to "Playboy."   The court found it likely that some consumers would confuse the magazines themselves, while others might assume that the defendant's publication was sponsored by the plaintiff.[a]

Visual comparison proved fatal to a claim of unfair competition in Brown v. Lyle Stuart, Inc., 42 Misc.2d 909, 249 N.Y.S.2d 370 (Sup.Ct.1964). "Sex and the Single Girl" was a collection of advice by a magazine editor. She, her publisher, and Warner Brothers, which had bought the movie rights, sued the author and publisher of "Sex and the Single Man," a more explicit work by "an expert sexologist." Examination of the books and jackets revealed differences that made confusion unlikely. The court also made this observation: "Where titles of books are involved, as distinguished from those of plays, motion pictures and the like, the court will be much more reluctant to find unfair competition because book buyers generally place more importance upon the author than upon the title of a literary work." But it was more sympathetic to Warner Brothers' concern that defendants might sell their own movie rights and prejudice Warner's almost completed film. Because the defendants disclaimed any such intention, arguing that their work "is scarcely the kind of book that lends itself to motion picture treatment," the court saw no harm in granting the request for a limited injunction.

(4) It appears that Warner Brothers had paid $200,000 for "Sex and the Single Girl," essentially for its title, for that book too scarcely lent itself to movie treatment. See Angel, Legal Protection for Titles in the Entertainment Industry, 52 S.Cal.L.Rev. 279, 279–80 (1979). But if secondary meaning is the touchstone, what exactly did Warner Brothers buy? Or take the more extreme case where the seller has merely thought of an attractive title, but has not used it in connection with any work. If sales of titles are assimilated to sales of trademarks, they may be embarrassed by the orthodox rule that a trademark cannot be transferred in gross (i.e., without a transfer of the business or goodwill associated with the mark). Restatement, Third, Unfair Competition § 34 (1995); see also § 10 of the Lanham Act, 15 U.S.C.A. § 1060. Should titles be assimilated for this purpose to other commercial marks?

There is apparently a lively market in movie titles, supported by an unofficial title registry run by the Motion Picture Association of America. The MPAA issues daily registration reports, giving studios ten days to file a protest if they believe a new title is too similar to a registered title of their own. Among the hundreds of protests filed each year, only a few go to formal arbitration; most are settled through buy-outs or trades. See Goldstein, Hey, Let's Play the Movie Title Game!, Los Angeles Times, Aug. 20, 1997, p. F1.

---

a. One case has held that so-called "reverse confusion," wherein the infringer's use of the title causes confusion as to the source of the *plaintiff's* work, will also support a finding of unfair competition. Capital Films Corp. v. Charles Fries Prod., Inc., 628 F.2d 387 (5th Cir.1980) ("The Trial of Lee Harvey Oswald" used first as the title of plaintiff's film and later for an ABC television movie).

(5) Attempts to obtain federal trademark registration for titles of literary works have generally been unsuccessful. Application of Cooper, 254 F.2d 611 (C.C.P.A.1958), remains influential. Cooper, author of a children's book entitled "Teeny–Big," the story of "a little elf with magic powers of self-expansion," applied for registration of the title as a trademark for books. Registration was refused, the court likening the title to "a descriptive name like 'canned beans,' rather than a trademark like 'Sunkist.'" It concluded that since "Teeny–Big is no more than the name of a book, its only name, it is not a trademark under the statute, Section 2." (Is this exclusion consistent with § 14(3) of the Lanham Act, 15 U.S.C.A. § 1064(3), which says that a "mark shall not be deemed to be the generic name of goods or services solely because such mark is also used as a name of or to identify a unique product or service"?) The court conceded that series titles and the names of periodicals such as magazines and newspapers have been registered as trademarks. Is there a sound distinction?

(6) Periodical titles may sometimes receive protection without a demonstration of secondary meaning if they are arbitrary or suggestive rather than descriptive of the work's contents, and are thus considered "inherently distinctive." See C.L.A.S.S. Promotions, Inc. v. D.S. Magazines, Inc., 753 F.2d 14 (2d Cir.1985). However, titles of individual works have been subject to a different rule both in actions at common law and under § 43(a) of the Lanham Act. "Ordinarily a suggestive mark is entitled to protection without any showing of secondary meaning because it is inherently distinctive. However, we have applied a more stringent rule to literary titles in requiring the trademark proprietor to demonstrate secondary meaning notwithstanding the suggestive nature of the title." Twin Peaks Prod., Inc. v. Publications Int'l, Ltd., 996 F.2d 1366 (2d Cir.1993). On the protection of titles, see generally McCarthy, Trademarks and Unfair Competition §§ 10:1–40.

(7) Are the states free to offer protection against the confusing use of names or titles? Is a right to prevent the use of a confusingly similar title "equivalent to any of the exclusive rights" of copyright under the test for preemption in § 301?

The preemption issue is moot if § 43(a) of the Lanham Act is invoked in the protection of titles. (See § 301(d).) In National Lampoon, Inc. v. American Broadcasting Co., 376 F.Supp. 733 (S.D.N.Y.), aff'd, 497 F.2d 1343 (2d Cir.1974), plaintiff was the publisher of the magazine "National Lampoon" (having obtained a license for the name from the publishers of the "Harvard Lampoon," a century-old college humor magazine). It successfully invoked § 43(a) to enjoin the use of "Lampoon" as the title for a television show. Similarly, Simon & Schuster, publisher of William Bennett's "The Book of Virtues", offered sufficient proof of secondary meaning and likely confusion under § 43(a) to enjoin "The Children's Audiobook of Virtues." Simon & Schuster, Inc. v. Dove Audio, Inc., 970 F.Supp. 279 (S.D.N.Y.1997). Section 43(a) was invoked with like success in two cases involving movie titles, Orion Pictures Co. v. Dell Pub. Co., 471 F.Supp. 392 (S.D.N.Y.1979) ("A Little Romance") and Brandon v. Regents of the Univ.

of California, 441 F.Supp. 1086 (D.Mass.1977), the latter awarding, in addition to injunctive relief, an accounting of profits. But plaintiffs must still show secondary meaning and a likelihood of confusion. See Davis v. United Artists, Inc., 547 F.Supp. 722 (S.D.N.Y.1982) (denying relief under § 43(a) against the use of "Coming Home" as a movie title, despite plaintiff's prior use on a novel).

(8) Can the use of names or titles be challenged under the misappropriation doctrine? In Universal City Studios, Inc. v. Montgomery Ward & Co., 207 U.S.P.Q. 852 (N.D.Ill.1980), the owner of the movies "Jaws" and "Jaws 2" obtained a preliminary injunction against use of those terms in connection with a line of food waste disposers marketed by the defendant: "Likelihood of confusion is not required. Under the laws of Illinois, one may not use the mark of another to obtain a 'free ride' on his efforts to promote that mark." The court cited *INS,* but also found a likelihood of confusion as to approval, association, or sponsorship. For a similar result, see Universal City Studios, Inc. v. Kamar Industries, Inc., 217 U.S.P.Q. 1162 (S.D.Tex.1982) ("I Love E.T." on drinking mugs enjoined).

Can these results survive analysis under § 301? Is a right to prevent the misappropriation of titles "equivalent" to an exclusive right of reproduction? Is it a right in "the subject matter of copyright as specified by sections 102 and 103"?

TITLES OF WORKS OUT OF COPYRIGHT

Gotham Music Service, Inc. v. Denton & Haskins Music Publishing Co.

Court of Appeals of New York, 1932.
259 N.Y. 86, 181 N.E. 57.

Appeal from Supreme Court, Appellate Division, First Department.

Action by the Gotham Music Service, Inc., and another, against the Denton & Haskins Music Publishing Company, Inc. From a final judgment of the Appellate Division granting a permanent injunction and awarding damages, and an order of the Appellate Division reversing an order of the Special Term on reargument and directing resettlement of an interlocutory judgment (233 App.Div. 839, 250 N.Y.S. 929), defendant appeals.

Judgment reversed, and complaint dismissed.

■ POUND, C.J. Some years ago, as far back as 1925, a song called "Gambler's Blues" was sung and played throughout the country. It was a melancholy ballad purporting to have been sung by a gambler in a barroom after he had seen his sweetheart lying dead in the infirmary. It was not a copyrighted publication. Both song and melody became publici juris or of public right. Any one was free to produce them.

In March, 1929, the plaintiffs revived the old song under the title "St. James' Infirmary." The infirmary heretofore unidentified was given a name. They put forward an advertising and publicity campaign to sell the old composition under the new name. They made the song popular. On or about March, 1930, the defendant, a rival music publishing house, put on the market the same song and melody under the title "St. James' Infirmary or Gambler's Blues." Its nominal purpose was to link both titles under one name so that a customer who called for either might be supplied. The defendant has been restrained from using the title "St. James' Infirmary" or any simulation or imitation thereof as the title of a (i.e., any) musical composition, and judgment for damages has been entered against it.

Infringement of copyright is not involved. Respondents' brief so states, and the complaint contains no claim that copyright property has been misappropriated. If such were the grievance, the remedy would be in the federal courts. Underhill v. Schenck, 238 N.Y. 7, 143 N.E. 773. Plaintiffs have no property in the name "St. James' Infirmary." The name describes the song and, generally speaking, any one may use it to describe the same song. Black v. Ehrich (C.C.) 44 F. 793; Atlas Mfg. Co. v. Street & Smith (C.C.A.) 204 F. 398, 404; Merriam Co. v. Syndicate Pub. Co., 237 U.S. 618. The plaintiffs must establish that defendant's acts amount to an unlawful abuse of competition by creating a reasonable likelihood of deception; that persons who desire the song and melody because plaintiffs have made them popular may be misled by defendant into thinking that they are purchasing the plaintiffs' version of the song. This they have wholly failed to accomplish.

Defendant is not deceiving the public. The song is popular, not because plaintiffs publish it, but because they have advertised it and thus made it known to the public. Their names are not identified with the new name. The demand is for the song, and not for the publisher. * * *

* * * A name which is descriptive of one song may not be attached by a competitor to another when the duplication will mislead the public into the belief that the two songs are alike; but the name, so far as it is a symbol descriptive of the old song, is not protected unless it is identified with the source or origin of production. Underhill v. Schenck, supra. Here it is sought to protect the title because plaintiffs invented it, but no question of imitation or deception or mistake arises. No unlawful competition in trade is shown, nor breach of contract or trust. In the absence of the use of the name in such a way as to create a likelihood that people will be misled, the name is publici juris, and may be used by all.

The judgment of the Appellate Division should be reversed and the complaint dismissed, with costs in all courts.

CRANE, J. (dissenting). I view this case somewhat differently from the Chief Judge. True, the song, called "Gambler's Blues," became publici juris, and any one was free to use it, print copies of it, and sell it on the market. No one had or could have a restricted right to sell the song. Also, the name, the original name, "Gambler's Blues," followed the song, and any one could use this name in reproducing it. The plaintiffs, however, did more than this to make the song valuable. No one wanted it; it had passed out of use, had ceased to be popular; there was no demand for it. The plaintiffs made changes in tempo of the music, added a few verses, and gave it a new name, "St. James' Infirmary," and then started an advertising campaign, spending thousands of dollars in making the name, "St. James' Infirmary," known to the public. Under this name the plaintiffs advertised extensively throughout the country their rearrangement of this old song.

Now comes the defendant and seeks to reap the harvest of this advertising. It publishes the old song and gives it the name which the plaintiffs have made popular; namely, "St. James' Infirmary." If they had called it by its original name, "Gambler's Blues," no one could complain, and no rights would have been violated. This would not do; the defendant must reap the profits which legitimately should go to the plaintiffs as the result of their expenditures for advertising, and so the defendant takes "St. James' Infirmary" for no other reason than to gain the reward of others' work. * * *

"If a copyright does not exist, or, once existing, has been lost, the name is lost, too, in so far as it is merely a symbol descriptive of the copyrighted thing." Underhill v. Schenck, 238 N.Y. 7, 20, 143 N.E. 773, 778. Thus, the old name, "Gambler's Blues," is as free for use in connection with the old song as the song itself. This does not mean, however, that an established trade may not be built up for an arrangement under a new name which will prevent unfair competition by use of the same name and arrangement, even though no copyrights exist.

"The principles which interdict unfair competition in trade will protect a publisher who has imparted to his books peculiar characteristics, which enable the public to distinguish them from books published by others and containing the same literary matter, against the copying of the characteristics, though the copyright on the literary matter has expired." Merriam Co. v. Straus (C.C.) 136 F. 477, 478; Merriam Co. v. Saalfield Pub. Co. (C.C.A.) 238 F. 1, cited in Fisher v. Star Co., 231 N.Y. 414, 431, 132 N.E. 133.

Here the copyright on the song had expired; but this did not prevent the plaintiffs from having a right to their rearrangement and the new name which they had given it, especially when through much expenditure of money they had built up a demand for the song under that name.

The full and complete answer to the plea of the defendant is to go out and sell the original song under its old name and see how far it gets with it. When the defendant refuses to do this, it is evident that it wants the benefits coming from the plaintiffs' new arrangement and new name, which they have given the song. This is not fair.

The judgment should be affirmed.

■ LEHMAN, O'BRIEN, and CROUCH, JJ., concur with POUND, C.J.

■ CRANE, J., dissents in opinion in which HUBBS, J., concurs.

KELLOGG, J., not sitting.

Judgment reversed, etc.

G. & C. Merriam Co. v. Ogilvie

United States Circuit Court of Appeals, First Circuit, 1908.
159 Fed. 638.
Certiorari denied 209 U.S. 551, 28 S.Ct. 761 (1908).

Appeal from the Circuit Court of the United States for the District of Massachusetts.

■ Before PUTNAM and LOWELL, CIRCUIT JUDGES, and ALDRICH, DISTRICT JUDGE.

■ ALDRICH, DISTRICT JUDGE. This case involves a bill and a crossbill, each party claiming injunction relief against the other. There was an injunction below against each party. The Merriam Company appeal upon the ground that it should not be restrained, and also upon the ground that the injunction against Ogilvie was not broad enough. Ogilvie did not appeal.
* * *

The name "Webster" having been copyrighted by the Merriams, they were protected in its use under a statutory right during an expressed term of years. The protection, therefore, in that respect, came by virtue of the copyright rather than by virtue of its use in publication and trade.[b]

The statutory monopoly having expired under statutory limitation, the word "Webster," used in connection with a dictionary, became public property, and any relief granted upon the idea of title or proprietorship in the trade-name of "Webster" would necessarily involve an unwarrantable continuance of the statutory monopoly secured by the copyright.

The authorities and the discussion of this phase of the case by the learned judge in the Circuit Court (Ogilvie v. Merriam Co. [C.C.] 149 Fed. 858, where the facts sufficiently appear)[c] satisfy us in respect to the

b. Is this correct?

c. The lower court took the facts to be as follows: Having previously acquired all rights in Noah Webster's Dictionary from Webster's heirs, Merriam Co. published a number of editions under the title "Webster's". It published Webster's Unabridged Dictionary in 1847; the copyright on this edition expired in 1889. Until 1889 Merriam Co. was the sole publisher of dictionaries under the title "Webster's". After 1889 various editions of Webster's Dictionary were published by other publishers, "but, notwithstanding this circumstance, it is shown by a preponderance of evidence that the name 'Webster' still indicates to the public the dictionaries published and sold by the Merriam Company."

The last edition published by Merriam Co. prior to suit was Webster's International Dictionary. Plaintiff Ogilvie proceeded to put out a dictionary called Webster's Imperial Dictionary, "an enlarged and revised edition of Webster's Dictionary, based upon Webster's Unabridged Dictionary." On the cover of the Ogilvie book appeared the name "George W. Ogilvie," and on the title page, "George W. Ogilvie, Publisher." Ogilvie's circulars and advertisements conveyed the impression "that the Ogilvie book is a new edition of Webster's Dictionary published by the Merriam Company, and that it is the successor of Webster's International Dictionary"; Ogilvie had inserted in his circulars and advertisements matter taken from Merriam's promotional literature for the International.

Ogilvie in his bill sought to restrain Merriam Co. from sending letters to the trade stating that it had the exclusive right to the use of "Webster's" on dictionaries. By crossbill Merriam Co. sought to stop Ogilvie from using "Webster" on his dictionary and from sending out misleading literature.

(The facts as to Merriam Co.'s Webster's Dictionaries were not quite as the court soundness of the proposition that upon the expiration of the copyright the name "Webster" passed into the field of public right.

We perceive no difference in principle between patent rights and copyrights in this respect, and, as observed by Mr. Justice White in Singer Manufacturing Company v. June Manufacturing Company, 163 U.S. 169, "where, during the life of a monopoly created by a patent, a name, whether it be arbitrary or be that of the inventor, has become, by his consent, either express or tacit, the identifying and generic name of the thing patented, this name passes to the public with the cessation of the monopoly which the patent created." The Singer Case declares a general and undoubted principle which is quite decisive of the case under consideration so far as the name "Webster" is concerned, and though the name "Webster" as applied to the Merriam Company's dictionary had acquired a secondary meaning, indicating a particular book published and sold by them, it became public property when the copyright expired.

The right to use a copyrighted name, however, upon the expiration of the copyright, goes out to the public subject to a certain and well-understood limitation or condition, namely, that the public right to use shall be so exercised as not to deceive members of the public and lead them into the belief that they are buying the particular or identical thing which was produced under the copyright. That the right of public user of the name "Webster" was subject to such a condition was fully recognized by the learned judge who decided this case in the Circuit Court, and, indeed, the principle was forcibly stated by Mr. Justice White in the Singer case.

We think the conclusion reached by the Circuit Court, that the Merriam Company should be enjoined from sending out circulars to the effect that it has the exclusive right to use the name "Webster" in connection with dictionaries, was justified by the evidence and the authorities, and we are content to leave that branch of the case upon the reasoning contained in the opinion of the learned judge of the Circuit Court.

That court also points out, and we think the situation justifies it, that the Ogilvie circulars and advertisements are misleading and deceptive, and show an intention on the part of Ogilvie to trespass upon the reputation of the Merriam Company and to deceive purchasers into buying his dictionary for one of the series of Webster's dictionaries published by the Merriam Company, and it was held that Ogilvie should be enjoined from sending out circulars and advertisements in their present form. We agree that this should be so upon equitable principles, because it presents a situation in which a member of the public seeks to appropriate more than fairly and equitably belongs to him.

It is also our conclusion that the same purpose and the same reasoning hold good with respect to the title page of the Ogilvie publication.

---

thought. The story appears in greater detail in the opinions in other litigated cases. See especially Merriam v. Texas Siftings Pub. Co., 49 F. 944 (C.C.S.D.N.Y.1892); G. & C. Merriam Co. v. Saalfield, 190 F. 927 (6th Cir.1911); opinion of L. Hand, D.J., reproduced in G. & C. Merriam Co. v. Syndicate Pub. Co., 207 F. 515 (2d Cir.1913).)

It seems pretty evident from consideration of all the circumstances surrounding these publications, including the correspondence, the circulars, the advertisements, and the character of the litigation, that the purpose of Ogilvie was to put out such a publication and such circulars and advertisements as would lead the public into the supposition that they were buying the Webster Dictionary as improved and added to by the Merriam Publishing Company, and we think that the reasoning of the Circuit Court with respect to the circulars and advertisements applies with equal force to the title page of the Ogilvie publication.

We also think, in view of the ingenious arrangement of the prominent features of the Ogilvie title page, that its weight in the public eye is not fully and unmistakably overcome by printing the name "George W. Ogilvie" upon the back of the cover, or by printing the words "George W. Ogilvie, Publisher," as a part of the title page.

The reasoning of the Singer case, which we think applies here, is that the name must be accompanied by such indications as will unmistakably inform the public that the thing is something put out by the particular party who appropriates it and exercises the public right.

If the title page of the Ogilvie dictionaries had contained, for instance, the words "Webster's Dictionary, published by George W. Ogilvie," with other expressions correctly indicating the identity of the publication, the Merriam Company would have no just cause for complaint. But such is not this case. * * * [Judge Aldrich then describes a number of ways that Ogilvie subordinated his own name and suggested a connection with the Merriam dictionaries.]

It seems to us that Ogilvie was not content with using the word "Webster," which was at large as a word entitled to be used in connection with a dictionary, but purposely used words of description calculated to lead the ordinary purchaser to suppose that he was getting the publication which had been built up by the Merriams. This, we think, was an appropriation of something which he was not entitled to appropriate, and under the circumstances amounts to unfair competition. * * *

The decree of the Circuit Court with respect to the injunction against the Merriam Company is affirmed.

The decree of the Circuit Court for an injunction against Ogilvie in respect to circulars and advertisements is affirmed, and the case is remanded to that court with directions that the injunction against George W. Ogilvie, his agents, attorneys and servants, be so enlarged as to include the title pages and the backs of the dictionaries in the present form, or in any form calculated to deceive members of the public into purchasing his dictionary under the belief that it is a Merriam Webster's Dictionary, and for further proceedings not inconsistent with the opinion passed down this day. All questions of accounting, including the question whether or not the Merriam Company is entitled to an accounting, are open to the Circuit Court. Neither party recovers costs in this court.

NOTES AND QUESTIONS

(1) Upon remand, the lower court entered a decree unsatisfactory to Merriam Company, who again appealed. The Court of Appeals ordered the decree modified so as to require Ogilvie to print on the title page of his book: "This dictionary is not published by the original publishers of Webster's Dictionary, or by their successors." G. & C. Merriam Co. v. Ogilvie, 170 Fed. 167 (1st Cir.1909) (the final decree entered under direction of the Court of Appeals is reproduced in a connected case, G. & C. Merriam Co. v. Saalfield, 190 Fed. 927, 931 (6th Cir.1911)).

Merriam Company had also been unsuccessful in a number of previous attempts to deny others the use of the name "Webster's" after the older copyrights had expired. See the trial court's opinion in the principal case, 149 Fed. 858, 861–62, and particularly Merriam v. Holloway Pub. Co., 43 Fed. 450, 451–52 (C.C.E.D.Mo.1890), where Justice Miller said: "[I]t occurs to me that this proceeding is an attempt to establish the doctrine that a party who has had the copyright of a book until it has expired, may continue that monopoly indefinitely, under the pretense that it is protected by a trade-mark, or something of that sort. I do not believe in any such doctrine, nor do my associates. When a man takes out a copyright, for any of his writings or works, he impliedly agrees that, at the expiration of that copyright, such writings or works shall go to the public and become public property. I may be the first to announce that doctrine, but I announce it without any hesitation. * * * [T]he contention that complainants have any special property in 'Webster's Dictionary' is all nonsense, since the copyright has expired." Nevertheless, Justice Miller overruled a general demurrer to Merriam's bill on the ground that defendant's advertising, as alleged, might be shown to result in passing off.

Merriam Company, still seeking to prevent competitors from using the word "Webster's," advanced a different theory in litigation against Syndicate Publishing Co., namely, that the competitor's dictionaries had departed so far from the old Webster's that it would deceive the public if they were allowed to use that name on their altered versions. District Judge Learned Hand pointed out that Merriam had itself in its more recent editions come a long way from the original Webster's. Even its 1847 edition was markedly different from Noah Webster's 1828 original; it had not been edited by Noah, who had already died. "Webster's," Hand decided, must accordingly be taken to mean any work which could claim "literary descent" from the original Webster's, and defendant's dictionary had almost as much claim to this distinction as plaintiff's current works. G. & C. Merriam Co. v. Syndicate Pub. Co., 207 Fed. 515 (2d Cir.1913) (per curiam affirmance reproducing Judge Hand's opinion in the lower court), appeal dism'd, 237 U.S. 618 (1915).

Suppose, however, that defendant's dictionary could not claim such "literary descent," while plaintiff's could. Would use of the "Webster's" name by defendant, without more, constitute passing off? Might it instead be actionable as deceptive advertising? See § 43(a).

"Webster's" litigation rolls on. See Merriam–Webster, Inc. v. Random House, Inc., 35 F.3d 65 (2d Cir.1994), cert. denied, 513 U.S. 1190 (1995) (trade dress for the plaintiff's *Webster's Ninth New Collegiate Dictionary* was not infringed by the trade dress used for Random House's *Webster's College Dictionary.)*

(2) Can the theory posited in Judge Crane's dissent in *Gotham Music* that plaintiffs should be protected in their ability to reap the harvest of their efforts to popularize the old song escape preemption under § 301? Does the theory frustrate the policy of access to works in the public domain?

(3) In Walt Disney Prod., Inc. v. Souvaine Selective Pictures, 98 F.Supp. 774 (S.D.N.Y.), aff'd, 192 F.2d 856 (2d Cir.1951), plaintiff had at great expense produced an animated cartoon film based on Lewis Carroll's "Alice in Wonderland," carrying the same title. Advance ballyhoo was considerable and expensive. Meanwhile, a competitor also produced an "Alice in Wonderland" movie based on Carroll, using puppets with a live Alice; the production was less costly and had been given little advance publicity. The pictures were scheduled to open in New York at about the same time. Plaintiff sought an injunction, but its application was denied: "Anyone has a legal right to make a picture based on Louis [sic] Carroll's book and entitled 'Alice in Wonderland.'"

What additional facts might justify a measure of relief?

(4) On all these matters, consult Kurtz, Protection of Titles of Literary Works in the Public Domain, 37 Rutgers L.Rev. 53 (1984), advocating freedom to use public domain titles, even on derivative works, but with adequate protection against confusion, chiefly through explanatory disclaimers.

A NOTE ON MERCHANDISING RIGHTS

Several of the cases in this section find a likelihood of confusion even when the defendant's use of the name or title occurs in a different medium—a play and a film, a magazine and a radio program. But suppose a name or title is used in connection with an article of merchandise? If the source association is sufficiently strong, even this may cause confusion, if not of origin, at least of sponsorship. The "Playboy" name, for example, has been protected against unauthorized use on theaters and automobile parts in addition to competing publications,[d] and other magazine, television, and motion picture titles have received similar protection under the confusion rationale.[e] But does the unauthorized exploitation of famous

d. See HMH Pub. Co. v. Turbyfill, 330 F.Supp. 830 (M.D.Fla.1971); HMH Pub. Co. v. Brincat, 504 F.2d 713 (9th Cir.1974); Playboy Enterprises, Inc. v. Chuckleberry Pub., Inc., 687 F.2d 563 (2d Cir.1982). See also Turner v. HMH Pub. Co., 380 F.2d 224 (5th Cir.1967), cert. denied, 389 U.S. 1006 (1967) (restaurant).

e. See, e.g., Triangle Publications, Inc. v. Rohrlich, 167 F.2d 969 (2d Cir.1948) ("Seventeen" magazine title on girl's clothing); Penthouse Int'l Ltd. v. Penthouse Party & Travel Club, Ltd., 184 U.S.P.Q. 479 (E.D.Mich.1974) ("Penthouse" on travel agency); Esquire, Inc. v. Maira, 101 F.Supp.

names and titles inevitably beget a likelihood of confusion? The National Football League has produced surveys indicating that a majority of consumers who encounter emblems and sportswear bearing its team names and insignia do indeed believe them to be officially sponsored.[f] The decision in Boston Professional Hockey Ass'n v. Dallas Cap & Emblem Mfg., p. 571 supra, goes further, apparently equating mere recognition with confusion of sponsorship, and the court's approach is not unique. Widespread recognition of the Rolls–Royce hood ornament and grill was deemed sufficient to enjoin their use in automobile customizing kits. Rolls–Royce Motors, Ltd. v. A. & A. Fiberglass, Inc., 428 F.Supp. 689 (N.D.Ga.1977). On a smaller scale, a similar theory was employed to enjoin the sale of toy cars modeled on an automobile featured in a popular television program. Warner Brothers v. Gay Toys, Inc., 658 F.2d 76 (2d Cir.1981). But other cases decline to indulge in a presumption of confusion. When a fraternal organization sought an injunction against the sale of jewelry bearing its insignia, the Ninth Circuit in International Order of Job's Daughters v. Lindeburg & Co., 633 F.2d 912 (9th Cir.1980), cert. denied, 452 U.S. 941 (1981), ordered judgment for the defendant, specifically rejecting *Boston Hockey:*

> It is not uncommon for a name or emblem that serves in one context as a collective mark or trademark also to be merchandised for its own intrinsic utility to consumers. We commonly identify ourselves by displaying emblems expressing allegiances. Our jewelry, clothing, and cars are emblazoned with inscriptions showing the organizations we belong to, the schools we attend, the landmarks we have visited, the sports teams we support, the beverages we imbibe. Although these inscriptions frequently include names and emblems that are also used as collective marks or trademarks, it would be naive to conclude that the name or emblem is desired because consumers believe that the product somehow originated with or was sponsored by the organization the name or emblem signifies. * * *

398 (M.D.Pa.1951) ("Esquire" on men's clothing); Aurora Products Corp. v. Schisgall Enterprises, Inc., 176 U.S.P.Q. 184 (S.D.N.Y. 1972) ("Monday Night Football" on toy football game); Wyatt Earp Enterprises, Inc. v. Sackman, Inc., 157 F.Supp. 621 (S.D.N.Y. 1958) ("Wyatt Earp" on children's clothing).

    f. See National Football League Properties, Inc. v. Wichita Falls Sportswear, Inc., 532 F.Supp. 651 (W.D.Wash.1982); National Football League Properties, Inc. v. Dallas Cap & Emblem Mfg. Inc., 26 Ill.App.3d 820, 327 N.E.2d 247 (1975). Cf. Processed Plastic Co. v. Warner Communications, Inc., 675 F.2d 852 (7th Cir.1982) (survey indicating children believed toy car was sponsored by a television show).

    The National Football League apparently leads in the race to cash in on the estimated $14 *billion* market for licensed sports merchandise, with over $3 billion in sales; the National Basketball Association is said to be second with more than $2.5 billion in sales. New Orleans Times–Picayune, Jan. 24, 1997, p. S58.

    As for movies, *Jurassic Park* is king with over $1 billion in merchandising revenues generated by 500 licensees on 5,000 products. (Ticket sales by comparison were around $900 million.) The merchandising success was no accident. As part of a carefully orchestrated plan beginning well before release of the film, the budget for promotional marketing in the United States was three or four times higher than the advertising budget for the movie itself. Advertising Age, March 21, 1994, p. S1.

* * * Job's Daughters asserts that *Boston Hockey* supports its contention that even purely functional use of a trademark violates the Lanham Act. We reject the reasoning of *Boston Hockey*.

Interpreted expansively, *Boston Hockey* holds that a trademark's owner has a complete monopoly over its use, including its functional use, in commercial merchandising. But our reading of the Lanham Act and its legislative history reveals no congressional design to bestow such broad property rights on trademark owners. Its scope is much narrower: to protect consumers against deceptive designations of the origin of goods and, conversely, to enable producers to differentiate their products from those of others. * * *

Our holding does not mean that a name or emblem could not serve simultaneously as a functional component of a product and a trademark. * * * Accordingly, a court must closely examine the articles themselves, the defendant's merchandising practices, and any evidence that consumers have actually inferred a connection between the defendant's product and the trademark owner.

Reliance on *Boston Hockey* also proved futile when the University of Pittsburgh complained of the unauthorized use of its "Pitt" insignia on shirts, jackets, and other apparel made by Champion, the leading producer of "imprinted soft goods" on which it places the insignia of thousands of schools and colleges: "The notion that a university's name and insignia are its own property, to do with as it chooses, has a certain common-sense appeal. An examination of the law and the facts in this case has convinced us, however, that neither Congress, nor the Pennsylvania Legislature, nor the common law has created the property right that Pitt asserts here." The court found "as a matter of fact, that there is no likelihood of confusion, whether of source, origin, sponsorship, endorsement, or any other nature * * *." University of Pittsburgh v. Champion Products, Inc., 566 F.Supp. 711 (W.D.Pa.1983).[g]

In a case similar on its facts to *Job's Daughters,* the Fifth Circuit, narrowly construing its prior decision in *Boston Hockey,* also denied relief:

g. Although the colleges lost this legal battle, a headline on an AP story in the New Haven Register, March 12, 1989, p. F2, tells the final outcome—"Colleges Hit Pay Dirt Licensing Logos." How did they do it? First, the schools control entrée to the campus bookstores where much of the merchandise is sold. They also are major customers for athletic uniforms and other goods produced by manufacturers like Champion.

The Collegiate Licensing Co., which serves as the licensing agent for more than 160 universities, estimates the market for college merchandise at $2.5 billion annually. The top money-makers are said to include Notre Dame, Michigan, Nebraska, North Carolina, Florida State, and Alabama. Cantor, Revenue Bonanza Will Hail the Victors of NCAA Tourney, Detroit News, Mar. 30, 1997, p. B4. Since winning national football championships in 1994, 1995, and 1997, the University of Nebraska has taken in almost $3 million per year in licensing royalties. Athletic success is not a prerequisite; Harvard earns about $1 million annually in royalties. Both Harvard and Princeton license lines of upscale apparel and accessories including shoes, belts, slacks, and eyeglasses sold primarily in Japan and South Korea. Fiore, Ivy Institutions Find Their Names are Lucrative for Marketing Products Abroad, Chronicle of Higher Ed., Sept. 12, 1997, p. A44.

* * * Acknowledging, in reference to the *Boston Hockey* decision, that "[i]t is not unreasonable to conclude, given the degree to which sports emblems are used to advertise teams and endorse products, that a consumer seeing the emblem or name of a team on or associated with a good or service would assume some sort of sponsorship or association between the product's seller and the team," the district court in this case found that "[t]he practice with respect to fraternal emblems, and, in particular, fraternal jewelry is markedly different." That finding is supported by the evidence. In Kentucky Fried Chicken Corp. v. Diversified Packaging Corp., 549 F.2d 368 (5th Cir.1977), we explained that *Boston Hockey* does not always equate knowledge of a symbol's source with confusion sufficient to establish trademark infringement and we treated as a fact question the question whether in a given case knowledge of the source of the *symbol* supports the inference that many of the product's typical purchasers would believe that the *product itself* originated with or was somehow endorsed by the owner of the mark. 549 F.2d at 389.

Supreme Assembly, Order of Rainbow for Girls v. J.H. Ray Jewelry Co., 676 F.2d 1079 (5th Cir.1982). But *Boston Hockey* was endorsed, and *Job's Daughters* disapproved, in University of Georgia Athletic Ass'n v. Laite, 756 F.2d 1535 (11th Cir.1985) (defendant imitated the Georgia Bulldog on beer cans, although with a disclaimer). See also Boston Athletic Ass'n v. Sullivan, 867 F.2d 22 (1st Cir.1989) (rebuttable presumption of confusion arising from defendant's reference to plaintiff's Boston Marathon mark on T-shirts, also citing the *INS* case).

On the sports "patches" cases, compare Laff and Saret, Further Unraveling of *Sears–Compco:* Of Patches, Paladin and Laurel and Hardy, 66 Trademark Rep. 427 (1976) (by counsel for Dallas Cap & Emblem Mfg.), with Fletcher, Still More About Patches, 67 Trademark Rep. 76 (1977) (by counsel for Boston Professional Hockey Ass'n). See also Heald, Filling Two Gaps in the Restatement (Third) of Unfair Competition: Mixed Use Trademarks and the Problem with Vanna, 47 S.Car.L.Rev. 783 (1996), lamenting the absence of a clear privilege for ornamental use in the *Restatement*.

Should a trademark owner be permitted to enjoin even a non-deceptive appropriation of its mark? Could state misappropriation law prohibit the non-deceptive reproduction of the Boston Bruins insignia on caps or shirts? A few cases, citing the Supreme Court's decision in *INS,* have indeed enjoined the "misappropriation of merchandising properties." See Universal City Studios, Inc. v. Montgomery Ward & Co., 207 U.S.P.Q. 852 (N.D.Ill.1980); Universal City Studios, Inc. v. Kamar Industries, Inc., 217 U.S.P.Q. 1162 (S.D.Tex.1982). But others have reached a different conclusion. One court offered this analysis: "Although industry and investment are encouraged by protecting distinctive marks, they are also encouraged by a system that allows entrepreneurs to copy and exploit such marks in nonconfusing ways. Indeed, a system that permits nonconfusing copying may achieve greater social utility and wealth than a system that protects marks without a showing of confusion. The originator of a mark may in some circumstances lose far less in economic value because of copying by others than is gained by the copiers and the public.'' Bi–Rite Enterprises, Inc. v. Button Master, 555 F.Supp. 1188, 1194–95 (S.D.N.Y.1983) (but relief granted on right of publicity grounds). See also WCVB–TV v. Boston Athletic Ass'n, 926 F.2d 42 (1st Cir.1991) (interpreting its earlier reference to the *INS* case in Boston Athletic Ass'n v. Sullivan, supra, as not departing from the traditional requirement of a likelihood of confusion.)

Who would be the primary beneficiaries of an exclusive merchandising right? At whose expense? Some tentative conclusions are offered in Denicola, Institutional Publicity Rights: An Analysis of the Merchandising of Famous Trade Symbols, 62 N.C.L.Rev. 603 (1984). See generally G. Battersby and C. Grimes, The Law of Merchandise and Character Licensing.

SECTION 4.   CHARACTERS

CHAPLIN V. AMADOR, 93 Cal.App. 358, 269 P. 544 (1928). Commencing in 1913, Charlie Chaplin adopted a characteristic garb and behavior in motion pictures—he ''has generally worn a kind of attire peculiar and individual to himself, consisting of a particular kind or type of mustache, old and threadbare hat, clothes, and shoes, a decrepit derby, ill-fitting vest, tight-fitting coat, and trousers and shoes much too large for him, and with this attire, a flexible cane usually carried, swung, and bent as he performs his part. This character, and the manner of dress, has been used and portrayed by Charles Chaplin for so long and with such artistry, that he has become well known all over the world in this character to such an extent that a display of his picture with the word 'Charlie,' or even with no name at all, has come to mean the plaintiff.''

In the 1920s one Charles Amador and others produced a motion picture, ''The Race Track,'' in which Amador appeared under the stage name ''Charlie Aplin.'' Aplin's dress and antics were similar to Chaplin's. In advertising ''The Race Track'' to the trade as the first of a series of twelve two-reel comedies, the producers spoke of ''record breaking comedies featuring 'Charlie Aplin' in the well-known character, famous the world over.'' ''Our comedian is a world beater in this famous character.'' Along with views of Charlie Aplin in stage dress, the producers included a quotation from a newspaper stating, ''Aplin, whose name is like that of Charlie Chaplin, who looks like him and acts like him, and who is a regular fellow with it all * * *.''

Chaplin sought injunctive relief in a California court against Amador, et al. At the opening of trial, defendants stated their willingness to abandon the use of any name similar to Charlie Chaplin and to settle on those terms. This was evidently unsatisfactory to the plaintiff and the trial proceeded. The decree entered after trial was thus summarized by the appellate court: ''perpetually enjoining and restraining them, their servants, agents, and employees, and all persons acting in privity with them from, (a) disposing of, advertising, or dealing in a motion picture called 'The Race Track'; (b) from using the name 'Charles Aplin' or 'Charlie Aplin,' or any other name similar to that of plaintiff in connection with said motion picture, or any motion picture, in imitation of the motion pictures of plaintiff, which will be likely to deceive the public into believing that plaintiff is acting the role therein hereafter referred to; (c) from advertising, selling, or dealing in any motion pictures which are an imitation of the motion pictures of plaintiff, or style of dress, costume, or mannerisms constituting an imitation of the plaintiff in his name or in his playing or acting the part or character or role of Charlie Chaplin, and which are so like the motion pictures acted in and produced by the plaintiff, and in which the plaintiff plays the principal or leading or any part in such role, as to be likely to deceive the public in believing that said motion pictures are the motion pictures produced and acted by plaintiff, or which would have the likely effect of so deceiving." The judgment was affirmed.

QUESTIONS: **(1)** Should it make any difference whether Chaplin originated his garb and behavior or instead copied portions of his characterization from others?

(2) Is it relevant whether the Chaplin films were under copyright? Would the defendants' activities infringe the motion picture copyrights?

Lone Ranger, Inc. v. Cox

United States Circuit Court of Appeals, Fourth Circuit, 1942.
124 F.2d 650.

■ Before PARKER and DOBIE, CIRCUIT JUDGES, and CHESTNUT, DISTRICT JUDGE.

■ PARKER, CIRCUIT JUDGE. This is an action for damages and for injunction based upon alleged infringement of copyright and unfair competition. The plaintiff is the Lone Ranger, Inc., a Michigan corporation, which since the year 1933 has been broadcasting over the radio copyrighted dramatic serial stories featuring the heroic exploits of a mythical western cowboy, "The Lone Ranger", who rides about masked and on a white horse, called "Silver", championing the cause of the oppressed and redressing the wrongs of the community. Plaintiff has licensed a comic strip, entitled "The Lone Ranger", appearing in a number of newspapers and has licensed the use of the name, "The Lone Ranger", as a trademark to vendors of various articles. The radio programs of plaintiff are broadcast from one hundred or more radio stations, are very popular and appeal particularly to children. A "Lone Ranger" safety club, promoted in connection with the programs, has attained a membership of between three and four million young people.

The defendant Powell is a motion picture actor, who in 1937 played the part of Allan King as the "Lone Ranger" in a motion picture produced under license from plaintiff. He has been appearing, under contract with the defendant Cox, in a small circus in which he takes the part of the "Lone Ranger", riding masked on a white horse and giving the cry "Hi, yo Silver" or "Hi, yo, Silver, away!", which is the distinctive call of the "Lone Ranger" to his horse in each of plaintiff's radio programs. He is advertised by the circus as the original "Lone Ranger" or the "Lone Ranger" in person. The words "talking picture" or "of talking picture fame" are prefixed or added to the words "Lone Ranger" in the advertisements, but these qualifying words are in smaller lettering than "Lone Ranger", which is given great prominence. In some, the call to the horse, "Hi, yo, Silver" is prominently displayed. Newspaper advertisements are addressed particularly to children and stress that the "Lone Ranger" is appearing in person. In all, the effect of the advertisements is to create the impression that the original "Lone Ranger", made famous by the radio programs, is appearing with the circus—a result more easily achieved because the public interested is composed very largely of children.

The plaintiff did not produce its copyrights in evidence, relying upon the principles of unfair competition. Its contention is that the advertising and appearances of Powell are unfair in that they are an attempt on his part to appropriate to himself a portion of the good will which plaintiff has built up in connection with its radio programs, and in that the inevitable effect of this infringement upon its rights is to destroy the element of mystery surrounding the character of the "Lone Ranger" as presented by its programs and show him to be a very commonplace person in whom the young people have no further interest, once he has been seen. Plaintiff relies, also, upon a consent decree entered by the United States District Court for the Middle District of Pennsylvania, in which the same defendants were enjoined at the suit of plaintiff from using the name "Lone Ranger" except with reference to the fact that Powell had played the part of Allan King in the motion picture serial of that name, from using the phrases "Hi, yo, Silver" and "Hi, yo, Silver, away!", and from representing in any way, or doing anything that would lead the public to believe, that Powell was identified with the radio programs of plaintiff. * * *

Quite apart from any rights under the Pennsylvania decree or the copyrights relied on, we think that plaintiff, under the principles of unfair competition, was entitled to relief. Under the name or title of "The Lone Ranger", plaintiff had built up a radio feature of great value. The exploits of this mythical character, as portrayed in the radio programs, had become of great interest to countless young people throughout the country and were a source of large revenue to plaintiff. Defendants were attempting to avail themselves of the good will created by the broadcasting of the radio programs and the advertising connected therewith, including the "Lone Ranger" safety clubs. Their conduct in advertising Powell as the "Original Lone Ranger" was manifestly calculated and intended to lead the public to believe that he was the "Lone Ranger" of the radio programs and to attract to the circus those who were interested in the programs and particularly the young people who were members of the safety clubs. The fact that the advertisements contained a reference to the talking picture did little, if anything, to minimize the deception of the children to whom they were primarily addressed, and this deception was accentuated by use of the call "Hi, yo, Silver" in some of the advertisements and in Powell's act in the circus. The defendants were in the business of furnishing entertainment, just as was plaintiff, and there can be no doubt but that they were attempting to pass off their show as being identified with the radio programs of plaintiff, or at least as being connected in some manner therewith, and thus to benefit from the good will which had been built up by plaintiff through its broadcasts and advertising.

We entertain no doubts as to the power and duty of a court of equity to afford relief under such circumstances. While the case presented is not precisely similar to that kind of unfair competition involving the use of a corporate or business name or to the ordinary case involving the unfair use of trademarks and trade names, the principle involved is the same as that recognized in these cases, viz., that a court of equity should enjoin any form of "passing off" which involves fraudulent appropriation, through devices calculated to deceive or mislead the public, of the business or good will which another has built up. * * * We see no reason why the same principles are not applicable in the case of one who perpetrates a fraud both upon the public and upon the producer of radio programs by representing that his performance is connected in some way with such programs. * * *

"Obviously, the question of what is unfair competition in business must be determined with particular reference to the character and circumstances of the business." International News Service v. Associated Press, 248 U.S. 215, 236. * * * Here it is the use of the term "Lone Ranger" and his distinctive call to his horse in such way as to lead to the belief on the part of children interested in the programs of the radio broadcast that the entertainment of defendants is connected in some way with these programs. In all, there is involved the element of fraudulent attempt of some one to "reap where he has not sown" and to appropriate himself "the harvest of those who have sown". Cf. Chafee, Unfair Competition, 53 Harvard Law Review 1289, 1311. Even if relief under the principles of unfair competition were confined to cases of palming off of goods or services, we think that the case at bar would be one calling for relief; but we do not understand that relief in this class of cases is so limited. As said by the Supreme Court in International News Service v. Associated Press, supra: "It is said that the elements of unfair competition are lacking because there is no attempt by defendant to palm off its goods as those of the complainant, characteristic of the most familiar, if not the most typical, cases of unfair competition. Howe Scale Co. v. Wyckoff, Seamans [& Benedict], 198 U.S. 118. But we cannot concede that the right to equitable relief is confined to that class of cases." * * *

And we are not impressed by the argument that defendants are protected in what they have done because of Powell's connection with the motion pictures licensed by plaintiff. The contention that the advertisement is true is not correct. Powell is not the "Lone Ranger" at all.[a] He is merely a moving picture actor who took the part of the "Lone Ranger" in a motion picture play of that name produced long after the "Lone Ranger" of radio had become widely known. The only reason that defendant's desire to call him the "talking picture Lone Ranger" or the "Lone Ranger of talking picture fame", with "Lone Ranger" emphasized and the qualifying words in smaller lettering, is to attract the patronage of those who will confuse him in some way with the "Lone Ranger" of the radio programs; and the principle is applicable that, not only must one tell the truth, but he must tell it in a truthful way, i.e., so as not to deceive the public. 38 Cyc. 847. Thus, one may not use even his own name or the name of the town in which he does business as descriptive of his goods, if the effect will be to mislead the public to the prejudice of a competitor. See opinion of Holmes, J., in American Waltham Watch Co. v. United States Watch Co., 173 Mass. 85, 53 N.E. 141, and cases there cited; Nims, Unfair Competition, 3rd Ed. sec. 72; Chafee, Unfair Competition, 53 Harvard Law Review 1289, 1296. The use of the words "talking picture" or "of talking picture fame" in the advertisements was insufficient to protect defendants because the use of these words as they were used in the advertisements would not obviate the tendency of the use of "Lone Ranger" as emphasized therein to deceive and mislead the public. If it is desired to advertise Powell as the man who played the part of Allan King as the "Lone Ranger" in the motion picture of that name, this should be allowed; but any advertisement that he is the "Lone Ranger" must be avoided, as must any other language tending to imply connection with the "Lone Ranger" of plaintiff's radio programs or any form of advertising which will lead the public to believe that there is such connection. * * *

For the reasons stated, the judgment appealed from will be reversed and the cause will be remanded for further proceedings in accordance with this opinion.

Reversed.

NOTES ON THE "LONE RANGER"

(1) What relief could Lone Ranger, Inc. have secured on the basis of its copyrights? Cf. § 106.

On Judge Parker's reasoning, what should be the content of the decree? Does the opinion recognize in the plaintiff any interest beyond the prevention of confusion?

(2) In a later case, Lone Ranger, Inc. succeeded in enjoining appearances by another defendant under the name "Lone Star Ranger." Lone Ranger, Inc. v. Currey, 79 F.Supp. 190 (M.D.Pa.1948).

---

a. Who was the Lone Ranger? The New York Times, March 2, 1965, in an obituary of Brace Beemer, who played the part on radio from 1941 until the last live radio program in 1954, said that Beemer had had two predecessors on the program.

(3) The New York Times, Sept. 7, 1979, p. 12, reports on the unmasking of another Lone Ranger. Clayton Moore had portrayed the character in more than 200 half-hour television programs from 1949 to 1956. Since then he had made his living through personal appearances wearing a mask, white hat, and six-shooters. Lone Ranger Television, Inc., which had arranged for the production of a new motion picture based on the character, argued that at age sixty-four Moore was "no longer an appropriate physical representative of the trim 19th-century Western hero." "It's our mask. By wearing the mask, Moore is appearing as the Lone Ranger. But in spite of what Mr. Moore feels in his heart, he is not the Lone Ranger. We own the Lone Ranger." A judge ordered Moore to remove his mask. He replaced it with dark sunglasses. "They tried to shoot me down, but I stood up to them. I've lived by the Lone Ranger creed for 30 years and I'm fighting now for fair play, justice, law and order." These virtues triumphed. In 1985 the Wrather Corp., parent of Lone Ranger Television, lifted the restraint. (The 1981 movie it had sought to protect lost $11 million.) Moore claimed that one million signatures had been collected on his behalf. "Old Kemo Sabe plenty happy." Time, Feb. 4, 1985, p. 69.

Fisher v. Star Co.

Court of Appeals of New York, 1921.
231 N.Y. 414, 132 N.E. 133.
Certiorari denied 257 U.S. 654, 42 S.Ct. 94.

[Harry "Bud" Fisher originated the perennial comic strip figure "Mutt" in 1907 and his sidekick "Jeff" in 1908. Apparently the strips were not copyrighted as they appeared, although three annual collections were copyrighted by Fisher. In 1915 Fisher made an exclusive contract with a syndicator, Wheeler, and left Star Co. (publisher of the New York American). Star Co. kept publishing "Mutt and Jeff" strips drawn by its employees.]

■ CHASE, J. * * * This action is brought to enjoin the appellant from what the respondent asserts is unfair competition in making and publishing cartoons. The question on this appeal is whether the courts should use the equitable jurisdiction given to them to restrain a person or corporation from using in a cartoon, or in cartoons prepared for publication and sale as a business, certain grotesque figures, being imaginary and fictitious characters and the names applied to them, when such figures and names were originated and have been applied and used by a person in connection with his work as a cartoonist until they have become well known and have as such figures or characters, with their names, a definite place among cartoonists and the admirers of cartoons, and with the public at large, and as such are of substantial value. The plaintiff does not assert his right to injunctive relief by virtue of the copyright law, the enforcement of which is confined to the federal courts. * * * He does not assert his claim by virtue of the federal Trade–Mark Law * * * or the statutes relating to trademarks in this state * * *, or in other states.

* * * To sustain his claim the respondent relies entirely upon the authority of the courts in equity to prevent what is known as unfair competition. * * *

[Judge Chase, after citing and quoting *INS*, especially Justice Holmes' opinion, goes on to discuss cases involving the titles and the trade dress of newspapers, books, and other articles.]

It appears from the findings of fact that the grotesque figures in respondent's cartoons, as well as the names "Mutt" and "Jeff" applied to them have in consequence of the way in which they have been exploited by the respondent and the appearance and assumed characters of the imaginary figures have been maintained, acquired a meaning apart from their primary meaning, which is known as a secondary meaning. The secondary meaning that is applicable to the figures and the names is that respondent originated them and that his genius pervades all that they appear to do or say.

It also appears from the findings of fact that the respondent is the owner of the property right existing in the characters represented in such figures and names. They are of his creation. They were published and became well known as distinct characters before the contract was made with the appellant. * * *

As we have already stated, it is unnecessary to discuss the question of the rights of the public or of appellant to reproduce the particular cartoons that have been published because the plaintiff's claim in this action rests upon other facts and principles as stated herein. The figures and names have been so connected with the respondent as their originator or author that the use by another of new cartoons exploiting the characters "Mutt and Jeff" would be unfair to the public and to the plaintiff. No person should be permitted to pass off as his own the thoughts and works of another.

If appellant's employees can so imitate the work of the respondent that the admirers of "Mutt and Jeff" will purchase the papers containing the imitations of the respondent's work, it may result in the public tiring of the "Mutt and Jeff" cartoons by reason of inferior imitations or otherwise, and in any case in financial damage to the respondent and an unfair appropriation of his skill and the celebrity acquired by him in originating, producing and maintaining the characters and figures so as to continue the demand for further cartoons in which they appear.

The only purpose that another than respondent can have in using the figures or names of "Mutt" and "Jeff" is to appropriate the financial value that such figures and names have acquired by reason of the skill of the respondent. * * *

The judgment should be affirmed, with costs.

All concur, except CRANE, J., who dissents on the ground that plaintiff seeks to maintain rights which can only be had under the copyright law. The copyright law does not apply, and the plaintiff has no rights thereunder. This action in my judgment is in effect a substitute for the rights which the plaintiff might have had under the copyright law.

Judgment affirmed.

NOTES ON CHARACTERS AND UNFAIR COMPETITION

(1) Consider the closing paragraphs of Judge Chase's opinion. Does he recognize rights beyond the prevention of confusion? Would a claim for misappropriation of "the financial value that such figures and names have acquired by reason of the skill" of the plaintiff survive analysis under § 301? Judge Newman, in Warner Brothers, Inc. v. ABC, the "Greatest American Hero" case, p. 259 supra, thought a state law claim against ABC that relied "on the misappropriation branch of unfair competition" would be preempted. In Ideal Toy Corp. v. Kenner Products, Inc., 443 F.Supp. 291 (S.D.N.Y.1977), the producer of the movie "Star Wars" and one of its licensees failed to enjoin the sale of three toys "similar to the characters in the movie in that a tall, black-robed evil figure in a black helmet is an adversary to a medium-sized metallic humanoid robot and a smaller computer-type, round, metallic robot." The toys did not carry the characters' names from the film. The court thought confusion unlikely: "A finding of general 'association'—that the toys 'look like' the movie or remind someone of the movie—does not mean that the prospective purchaser thinks that the toys are derived from the movie or 'sponsored' by the movie." A copyright infringement claim was also rejected.

(2) Section 43(a) of the Lanham Act has become a popular vehicle for asserting trademark rights in characters. In DC Comics, Inc. v. Filmation Associates, 486 F.Supp. 1273 (S.D.N.Y.1980), the court, on defendant's motion to overturn a jury verdict, broadly construed the scope of protection for characters. Plaintiff had produced comic books and television shows featuring an extraordinary collection of characters including Aquaman and Plastic Man; defendant, who at one time produced a television series under contract with the plaintiff, began marketing its own animated television series with similar characters, including Manta and Superstretch. The court said that "where the product sold by plaintiff is 'entertainment' in one form or another * * * an ingredient of the product itself can amount to a trademark protectable under § 43(a) because the ingredient can come to symbolize the plaintiff or its product in the public mind." These "ingredients" include "names and nicknames of entertainment characters, as well as their physical appearances and costumes" (but not, the court thought, their personality traits or abilities, since these could not attain the "consistency of representation" necessary to constitute a symbol recognized by the public).

Judge Urbom in Midway Mfg. Co. v. Dirkschneider, 543 F.Supp. 466 (D.Neb.1981), held that the shapes and colors of the characters in plaintiff's Pac–Man video game were "non-functional design features" protectable under § 43(a) upon a showing of secondary meaning and likelihood of confusion. In another application of § 43(a), Theodor Seuss Geisel (Dr.

Seuss) sued a defendant who sold dolls based on characters in Geisel's cartoons (in which defendant held the copyright); defendant was enjoined from implying that the toys were designed or authorized by Dr. Seuss, Geisel v. Poynter Products, Inc., 283 F.Supp. 261 (S.D.N.Y.1968), but the defendant could truthfully represent that the dolls were "based on" Dr. Seuss characters.   295 F.Supp. 331 (S.D.N.Y.1968).

A claim under § 43(a) was rejected in the "Greatest American Hero" case, supra.   The lack of substantial similarity between Superman and the television character that had proved fatal to plaintiff's copyright infringement claim also precluded, as a matter of law, any likelihood of confusion. The court acknowledged that "the image of a cartoon character and some indicia of that character can function as a trademark to identify the source of a work," and conceded that "there may be some viewers among the television audience who think that the *Hero* series was produced or authorized by those responsible for the Superman movies," but it concluded that the issue of likelihood of confusion must be judged within an "outer limit" of reasonableness.   A state law unfair competition count was rejected on similar reasoning after Judge Newman held that the state "passing-off" claim was not preempted under § 301.   DC Comics, Inc. v. Filmation Associates, supra, reached the same conclusion on the preemption issue, and, as for the protection of characters under § 43(a), cited § 301(d) of the Copyright Act.

See the comprehensive treatment in Kurtz, The Independent Legal Lives of Fictional Characters, 1986 Wis.L.Rev. 429 (1986).   See also Brylawski, Protection of Characters—Sam Spade Revisited, 22 Bull.Copyr.Soc. 77 (1974) and Marks, The Legal Rights of Fictional Characters, 25 ASCAP Copyr.L.Symp. 35 (1975), both suggesting that protection under unfair competition should be limited to character names.

(3) A character may identify the source of goods or services and thus qualify for registration under the Lanham Act.   The Pillsbury character "Poppin' Fresh", for example, is apparently registered as a trademark, but the registration was of no help when *Screw* magazine published a picture depicting the character engaged in sexual intercourse with "Poppie Fresh," another Pillsbury trade character; the court found no likelihood of confusion as to sponsorship.   Pillsbury Co. v. Milky Way Productions, Inc., 215 U.S.P.Q. 124 (N.D.Ga.1981) (but relief granted under the Georgia antidilution statute).   In re DC Comics, Inc., 689 F.2d 1042 (C.C.P.A.1982), declared that a drawing of Superman (and also of Batman and Joker) could be registered as a trademark for toy versions of the characters.[b]

---

b.   The popularity of characters as trademarks is confirmed by the guest list at a reception given by the United States (now International) Trademark Association to celebrate the 1988 revisions to the Lanham Act, which in addition to amending § 43(a), p. 583 supra, eased the burden of "use" as a prerequisite to protection: "Coming to life to greet reception attendees were: Tony Tiger, the plain M & M's candy, Tweety Bird, the Tasmanian Devil, Porky Pig, Sylvester, Bugs Bunny, Daffy Duck, Wonder Woman, two Care Bears characters, Mr. Peanut, the Pink Panther, the Kool–Aid Pitcher, the computer-

Usually the owner of a comic strip attempts to obtain Lanham Act registration for the title of the strip; may the owner not also offer one of the characters for registration?

(4) If the name and appearance of a cartoon character become protectable as trademarks, will the protection be affected by the expiration of copyright in some or all of the cartoon strips?

In Harvey Cartoons v. Columbia Pictures Industries, 645 F.Supp. 1564 (S.D.N.Y.1986), the question was whether defendant's "Ghostbusters" logo infringed plaintiff's creation, "The Ghostly Trio," companions of "Casper, The Friendly Ghost." Copyrights on early representations of the "Trio" had not been renewed, but plaintiff had a registered trademark. The court, concluding that there was no confusing similarity, apparently assumed that the trademark remained enforceable despite the expiration of copyright.

The question of trademark life after copyright death was avoided in Silverman v. CBS, Inc., 870 F.2d 40 (2d Cir.), cert. denied, 492 U.S. 907 (1989), p. 259 supra, involving Amos 'n' Andy and related characters. Copyrights on the radio programs had expired because of non-renewal and the characters were therefore in the public domain. The court accepted that CBS had once had trademark rights in the characters, but found that the rights had been abandoned by more than 20 years of nonuse (caused, CBS and the District Court said, by a changed social climate that now made the comic black characters unacceptable to the public).

On trademark protection for characters no longer under copyright, see Kurtz, The Methuselah Factor: When Characters Outlive Their Copyrights, 11 Miami Ent. & Sports L.Rev. 437 (1994) (advocating disclaimers to avoid confusion); Adams, Superman, Mickey Mouse and Gerontology, 64 Trademark Rep. 183 (1974).

Columbia Broadcasting System, Inc. v. DeCosta

United States Court of Appeals, First Circuit, 1967.
377 F.2d 315.
Certiorari denied 389 U.S. 1007, 88 S.Ct. 565.

■ Before ALDRICH, CHIEF JUDGE, MCENTEE and COFFIN, CIRCUIT JUDGES.

■ COFFIN, CIRCUIT JUDGE.

This is an appeal by defendants from jury verdicts in the total amount of $150,000 awarded plaintiff on his claim that he created, and the defendants misappropriated, the character of Paladin, the protagonist of the CBS television series entitled "Have Gun Will Travel".

The story of this case—more bizarre than most television serial installments—is one of "coincidence" run riot. The plaintiff, of Portuguese parents, is a Rhode Island mechanic whose formal education ceased after

ized Heinz ketchup bottle, Mickey and Minnie Mouse, Chester Cheetah, the Campbell Soup Kids, and the Pillsbury Dough Boy." U.S.T.A. Bulletin, Apr. 3, 1989.

DeCOSTA AS PALADIN (1975)

the fourth grade.   During the Depression, having tired of factory work, he hopped a freight for the West, lived in hobo jungles, and eventually became a range hand on a Texas ranch.   After two years of riding and roping he returned to Rhode Island to work as a mechanic and later received training as a motor machinist in the Coast Guard.   But he retained his passion for all things western.   In 1947 he began to participate in rodeos, horse shows, horse auctions, and parades.

From the beginning plaintiff indulged a penchant for costume.   He was already equipped with a moustache.   He soon settled on a black shirt, black pants, and a flat-crowned black hat.   He had acquired a St. Mary's medal at a parade and affixed this to his hat.   He adopted the name Paladin after an onlooker of Italian descent had hurled an epithet at him containing the word "Paladino".   On looking up the word Paladin in a dictionary he found it meant "champion of Knights" and was content that people began so to call him.   One day when he had donned his costume in preparation for a horse show, and was about to mount his horse, one of a group waiting for him shouted "Have Gun Will Travel", a cry immediately picked up by the children present.

The finishing touches were a chess knight, bought for fifteen cents at an auction, which plaintiff thought was a good symbol, and which he used on a business card along with the words "Have", "Gun", "Will", "Travel", and "Wire Paladin, N. Court St., Cranston, R.I.", hand-printed with separate rubber stamps; a silver copy of the chess piece on his holster; and an antique derringer strapped under his arm.   So accoutered, he would appear in parades, the openings and finales of rodeos, auctions, horse shows, and a pony ring he once operated.   From time to time at rodeos he would stage a western gunfight, featuring his quick draw and the timely use of his hidden derringer.   He would pass out photographs of himself and cards—printed versions soon replacing the rubber-stamped ones.   Hospitals, drug stores, barber shops, sports shops, diners—all were the repositories of his cards, some 250,000 of them.   Children clamored for the cards, and clustered about him to the extent that he was likened to the Pied Piper and Gene Autry.   This was perhaps one of the purest promotions ever staged, for plaintiff did not seek anything but the entertainment of others. He sold no product, services, or institution, charged no fees, and exploited only himself.

Ten years after he had begun to live his avocational role of Paladin, he and his friends saw the first CBS television production of "Have Gun Will Travel", starring moustachioed Richard Boone, who played the part of an elegant knight errant of the Old West, always on the side of Good—for a fee.   The television Paladin also wore a black costume, a flat-crowned black hat bearing an oval silver decoration, and a silver chess knight on his holster, and announced himself with a card featuring a chess piece virtually—if not absolutely—identical with the plaintiff's and the words "HAVE GUN WILL TRAVEL, WIRE PALADIN, SAN FRANCISCO".   The series was notably successful; it appeared in 225 first-run episodes in the United

States, was licensed in foreign countries, and by the time of trial had grossed in excess of fourteen million dollars.

The writers and network executives responsible for the series testified in detail that the television Paladin was a spontaneous creation, developed in total ignorance of the attributes of his Rhode Island predecessor. The writers, Herb Meadow and Sam Rolfe, testified that the germ of the idea was the title, "Have Gun Will Travel", which Meadow had evolved from mulling over a familiar theatrical advertising phrase, "Have tux, will travel". The character was originally conceived as a denizen of contemporary New York, but was changed to a western hero because the network hoped to cast Randolph Scott in the role. The name "Paladin" resulted from a thesaurus search for words meaning "knight" or "hero" or "champion". The chess piece symbol was inspired by Meadow's observation, while teaching his son the game, that the knight's movements were uniquely erratic and unpredictable. In the pilot script for the series, Paladin used a hidden derringer because it was a convenient way to extricate him from the obligatory dangerous situation.

The show's original producer, Julian Claman, testified that after Randolph Scott and other "fairly well known" actors were found to be unavailable he selected Richard Boone to be tested for the role of Paladin. Boone appeared for the test with a moustache, for reasons unknown, and was outfitted in a black suit because it was the only available costume that fitted. The hat, bearing a silver "conche", was selected by Claman because it looked appropriate. The card, which had been described in Meadow and Rolfe's original prospectus, was realized by the CBS art department from a rough sketch by Claman. The "shocking similarity" to DeCosta's cards was pure coincidence. Boone's test was successful, and Claman, reluctant to change any element of a winning combination, decided to keep card, costume, and moustache intact for the pilot film. He also decided to add the silver chess knight to Paladin's holster because it produced a distinct article that would be marketable if the series succeeded.

Meadow, Rolfe, Claman, and the other witnesses for the defendants all testified that they had never seen DeCosta or any of his cards. The jury obviously disbelieved at least this much of their testimony, and we think it clear that they were amply justified. Thus, the plaintiff has had the satisfaction of proving the defendants pirates. But we are drawn to conclude that that proof alone is not enough to entitle him to a share of the plunder. Our Paladin is not the first creator to see the fruits of his creation harvested by another, without effective remedy; and although his case is undeniably hard, to affirm the judgments below would, we think, allow a hard case to make some intolerably bad law.

In the first place, it is by no means clear that such state law of intellectual property as we have found supports relief on these facts. Several cases have been cited around the general proposition that it is an actionable wrong to appropriate and exploit the product of another's creative effort; but all seem to involve distinguishable wrongs of at least equal or even superior significance. Most rest on the tort of "passing off":

appropriation not of the creation but of the value attached to it by public association (the so-called "secondary meaning"), by misleading the public into thinking that the defendant's offering is the product of the plaintiff's established skill. E.g., Lone Ranger, Inc. v. Cox, 4 Cir., 1942, 124 F.2d 650; Chaplin v. Amador, 1928, 93 Cal.App. 358, 269 P. 544.[4] Others add an element of injury to reputation caused by a poor imitation. E.g., Lahr v. Adell Chem. Co., 1 Cir., 1962, 300 F.2d 256. And at least one combined both of these with an element of injury to a valuable contract to assert "the broader principle that property rights of commercial value are to be and will be protected from any form of unfair invasion or infringement and from any form of commercial immorality * * *." Metropolitan Opera Ass'n v. Wagner–Nichols Recorder Corp., Sup.Ct. 1950, 199 Misc. 786, 793, 101 N.Y.S.2d 483, 492.

Plaintiff argues that he has established "secondary meaning" through testimony of some witnesses that they thought he was the Paladin on television and evidence that most people knew him only as Paladin, not as Victor DeCosta. Whether or not this assertion is true, it is here irrelevant, for the issue was not submitted to the jury. The complaint alleged three causes of action: misappropriation, trade and/or service mark infringement, and unfair competition by "passing off" the television Paladin as the plaintiff. Only the first was tried, the court reserving judgment on defendant's motions to dismiss the other two. The jury was instructed that the plaintiff would be entitled to the verdict if he established:

> "First. That he conceived and created said idea and character of 'Paladin, Have Gun Will Travel'; and that said idea and character was novel, original, and unique; and that he did not at any time abandon said idea and character by a publication thereof.

> "Second. That the defendants * * * did copy said idea and character without the permission of the plaintiff and used them in the television series, 'Have Gun Will Travel.'

And

> "Third. That the plaintiff sustained damages as a result of such copying and use of said idea and character. * * *"

Thus, the judgment can only be supported on a rule of law that would allow recovery upon proof of creation by the plaintiff and copying by the defendants, and nothing else. We do not find such a rule in the cases cited above.

Moreover, the leading case affording a remedy for mere copying, International News Serv. v. Associated Press, 1918, 248 U.S. 215, is no longer authoritative for at least two reasons: it was decided as a matter of general federal law before the decision in Erie R.R. v. Tompkins, 1938, 304

---

4. The plaintiff quotes the *Lone Ranger* case as involving "the element of fraudulent attempt of someone to 'reap where he has not sown' and to appropriate to himself 'the harvest of those who have sown'". 124 F.2d at 653. But the opinion makes it clear that the "harvest" is the goodwill generated by long establishment of the Lone Ranger in the public eye, and the element of fraud is quite as important as the element of appropriation.

U.S. 64; and, as it prohibited the copying of published written matter that had not been copyrighted (indeed, as news it could not be copyrighted, 248 U.S. at 234), it has clearly been overruled by the Supreme Court's recent decisions in Sears, Roebuck & Co. v. Stiffel Co., 1964, 376 U.S. 225, and Compco Corp. v. Day–Brite Lighting, Inc., 1964, 376 U.S. 234. While this normally would not prevent the state court from adopting the reasoning of *INS* in fashioning a rule of state law, we think it important to consider the scope of state power in this area in view of *Sears* and *Compco.*

It is true that *Sears* and *Compco* both deal with copying of articles covered by invalid design patents. But the opinions refer throughout to both copyright and patent; and in *Compco* the Court took pains to articulate the broad scope of its decisions:

> "Today we have held * * * that when an article is unprotected by a patent or a copyright, state law may not forbid others to copy that article. To forbid copying would interfere with the federal policy, found in Art. I, § 8, cl. 8, of the Constitution and in the implementing federal statutes, of allowing free access to copy whatever the federal patent and copyright laws leave in the public domain." 376 U.S. at 237.

More fully, that policy is to encourage intellectual creation by offering the creator a monopoly in return for the disclosure and eventual surrender of his creation to the public.

Does the language in *Compco,* "whatever the federal patent and copyright laws leave in the public domain", refer to creations that Congress has deliberately chosen not to protect or more broadly to those it has simply not protected, whether by choice or by chance? In the case of patents the two questions are coterminous, for Congress has deliberately chosen not to protect inventions lacking the element of originality, and an invention is thus either patentable or unprotectible. In the case of "writings" there is no such universal test of qualification. But Congress has established a procedural scheme of protection by notice and registration. The necessary implication of this approach, we conclude, is that, absent compliance with the scheme, the federal policy favoring free dissemination of intellectual creations prevails. Thus, if a "writing" is within the scope of the constitutional clause, and Congress has not protected it, whether deliberately or by unexplained omission, it can be freely copied. See Cheney Bros. v. Doris Silk Corp., 2 Cir., 1929, 35 F.2d 279. * * *

To this plaintiff gives two answers. He argues that a character is not copyrightable—by which we must understand that it is not within the scope of Congress's power under the copyright clause—and that in any event a creation in the form of a public performance is protectible as an unpublished work under 17 U.S.C.A. § 2. For the first proposition the authority cited is Warner Bros. Pictures, Inc. v. Columbia Broadcasting Sys., 9 Cir., 1954, 216 F.2d 945, which held that the assignee of the copyright of the novel *The Maltese Falcon* could not prevent the author from using the character Sam Spade in a sequel. But that case is inapposite, because it held only (a) that the contract of assignment did not convey the exclusive right to use the characters in the novel, and (b) that the sequel, *The Kandy Tooth* was not so similar as to infringe the copyright. That is far from saying that characters are inherently uncopyrightable.

A more substantial argument for this first proposition is that the plaintiff's creation is not a "writing" in the sense used in the copyright clause (or, what is the same thing, that it is not an "article" in the sense used in *Sears* and *Compco*). There is no question that the term is to be interpreted more broadly than its common meaning would indicate. See, e.g., Mazer v. Stein, 1954, 347 U.S. 201 (statuette used as a lamp base). But it has been argued that it should be limited to mean some identifiable, durable, material form. Nimmer, Copyright Publication, 56 Colum.L.Rev. 185, 196 n. 98 (1956). And it is argued here that the plaintiff's creation, being a personal characterization, was not reduced and could not be reduced to such a form.

To this argument there are several answers. First, while more precise limitations on "writings" might be convenient in connection with a statutory scheme of registration and notice, we see no reason why Congress's power is so limited. Second, we cannot say that it would be impracticable to incorporate into the copyright system a procedure for registering "characters" by filing pictorial and narrative description in an identifiable, durable, and material form. Finally, however, there comes a point where what is created is so slight a thing as not to warrant protection by any law. All human beings—and a good part of the animal kingdom—create characters every day of their lives. Individuals often go beyond the realm of unconscious creation and devise characterizations for their own and others' amusement. Many a starred performer has so begun, and continued to grow on the borrowings from others. At some point his innate talent and eclectic poaching may enable him to attract a following, and ultimately to secure the law's protection against imitators. At what point short of this there should be additional protection we do not say. But in view of the federal policy of encouraging intellectual creation by granting a limited monopoly at best, we think it sensible to say that the constitutional clause extends to any concrete, describable manifestation of intellectual creation; and to the extent that a creation may be ineffable, we think it ineligible for protection against copying *simpliciter* under either state or federal law.

For the second proposition, that the plaintiff's creation is an unpublished work protected under 17 U.S.C.A. § 2, the leading authority is Ferris v. Frohman, 1912, 223 U.S. 424, which held that the public performance of a play did not constitute publication in the sense of an abandonment to public use. But in that case the Court specifically noted that the play involved had not been "printed and published"; that is, no copies of the script had been distributed publicly.

Here, plaintiff's "performance" consisted of two components: appearing in public and passing out cards and photographs. No other "action" was involved, except an occasional "quick draw" demonstration at a rodeo. So far as his costume and menacing appearance were concerned, it was fully conveyed on the cards bearing his photograph—which also contained the chess piece, the slogan, and the name "Paladin". The cards were passed out in great quantities over the years to all who would have them. So far as any action accompanying his personal appearance is concerned, whether it be simply riding a horse, or staging a quick-draw gun fight, these are hallowed shelf items in the tradition of the early West. In any event, the theme and plots of defendants' television series could not be said to have derived from anything created by plaintiff which was not revealed by his cards.

The cards were unquestionably "writings" within the meaning of the copyright clause, and arguably were copyrightable under the statute. See 17 U.S.C. §§ 1, 5(g), 5(k); Burrow–Giles Lith. Co. v. Sarony, 1883, 111 U.S. 53. The consequence is that the plaintiff's character-creation was published, even under the doctrine of *Ferris,* and that this case falls squarely under the rule of *Sears* and *Compco.* Not having copyrighted the cards, the plaintiff cannot preclude others from copying them. We accordingly reverse.

DeCosta v. Columbia Broadcasting System, Inc.

United States Court of Appeals, First Circuit, 1975.
520 F.2d 499.
Certiorari denied 423 U.S. 1073, 96 S.Ct. 856 (1976).

■ Before COFFIN, CHIEF JUDGE, ALDRICH and McENTEE, CIRCUIT JUDGES.

■ COFFIN, CHIEF JUDGE. Plaintiff, a dozen years ago, began this suit against the Columbia Broadcasting System, Inc., and allied corporations (CBS) to seek compensation for their unauthorized use of a character concept he had developed, embodying a costume, slogan, name, and symbol. A mechanic living in Cranston, Rhode Island, his avocation had been to don an all black cowboy suit, with a St. Mary's medal affixed to his flat crowned black hat, a chess symbol to his holster, and an antique derringer secreted under his arm, and make public appearances at rodeos and other events, meeting innumerable children, and passing out his card, inscribed with a chess set knight, proclaiming "Have Gun Will Travel, Wire Paladin, N. Court St., Cranston, R.I." We described these events in greater detail when this case was before us on appeal from the first count in his complaint, Columbia Broadcasting System, Inc. v. DeCosta, (DeCosta I), 377 F.2d 315 (1967), cert. denied 389 U.S. 1007 (1968). As every well-versed television viewer of the late fifties and early sixties knows, the gestalt conveyed by plaintiff's costume and accessories found its way into defendants' television series, "Have Gun Will Travel", which enjoyed enormous popularity for over eight years in its initial run, grossing in excess of fourteen million dollars.

The claim below, in the remaining counts two and three of the complaint, asserted a wilful and intentional infringement of plaintiff's common law trademark and/or service mark and unfair competition. The plaintiff sought both injunctive and monetary relief, including an accounting for all profits made by defendants in broadcasting "Have Gun Will

Travel". The first count had been tried before a jury. When this court reversed the result obtained in that trial, the case was returned to the district court where the parties entered into a stipulation that counts two and three be determined by the district judge on the basis of the trial transcript, including all exhibits, together with a stipulation of additional testimony. 383 F.Supp. 326, 327.

[The case was then referred to a magistrate; his decision ordering an accounting of profits was affirmed by the district court.]

We proceed to review the magistrate's findings in the light of the pleadings, the evidence, and the law. In *DeCosta I* we considered only the first cause of action in the complaint—that for misappropriation of "the idea and character", seeking damages based on defendants' unjust enrichment. Before us now are plaintiff's second and third causes of action, for trademark and/or service mark infringement and for unfair competition. In the second cause of action, plaintiff alleges that the slogan "Have Gun Will Travel", together with a figure of a knight chess piece and the words "Wire Paladin", as used in his calling cards, constituted his distinctive common law service mark or marks, which defendants intentionally infringed, appropriating the goodwill created by plaintiff, causing him serious financial damage. In the third cause of action plaintiff alleges that defendants intentionally copied plaintiff's service marks and his manner of dress (black outfit, white tie, mustache, etc.), and passed off their television character of Paladin as the original Paladin portrayed by plaintiff, profiting and diluting plaintiff's established goodwill, thereby deriving unjust profits. Plaintiff sought injunctive relief, an accounting for all profits, a trebling of "profits lost and damages suffered by plaintiff", plus a separate item of $2,000,000 damages.   * * *

Picking our way through the cluster of issues in several related but different fields of the law, we start where we left off, at *DeCosta I*. We there gave what has since been characterized as an expansive reading to *Sears* and *Compco*. See, e.g., Comment, Copyright Preemption and Character Values; The Paladin Case as an Extension of Sears and Compco, 66 Mich.L.Rev. 1018 (1967–1968). We held that "if a 'writing' is within the scope of the constitutional clause, and Congress has not protected it, whether deliberately or by unexplained omission, it can be freely copied." 377 F.2d at 319. Since the cards—including the photograph—"were unquestionably 'writings' within the meaning of the copyright clause, and arguably were copyrightable under the statute", id. at 321, we concluded that plaintiff could prevent others from copying them.[22]

We now know, after Goldstein v. California, 412 U.S. 546, 560 (1973), that "under the Constitution, the States have not relinquished all power to grant to authors 'the exclusive Right to their respective Writings'." In

---

22. To the extent that a "character" was "ineffable", incapable of "concrete describable manifestation of intellectual creation", and therefore ineligible for copyright protection, we thought it also ineligible for any protection, state or federal. Pre–*Goldstein*, this supposition had respectable support. See Nimmer, The Law of Copyright, Vol. 1, § 30, p. 137, n. 595.

Kewanee Oil Co. v. Bicron Corp., 416 U.S. 470, 478–479 (1974), this holding was summarized: "at least in the case of writings, the States were not prohibited from encouraging and protecting the efforts of those within their borders by appropriate legislation." Were we to take this literally, we would see no reason to look on *Goldstein* as relevant to this case; plaintiff relies on a common law service mark as subsumed also by a federal statute, 15 U.S.C. § 1125 (part of the Lanham Act), but not state legislation. Nevertheless, since the countervailing state law found sufficient in *Kewanee* was common law, not statutory law, we do not read its capsule of *Goldstein* literally.

We face a dilemma. *Goldstein* tells us that we were, in our interpretation of the preemptive reach of the Copyright Clause, over-inclusive. And yet, what we decided in *DeCosta I* has settled, for this case, the issue of misappropriation. Had *Sears* and *Compco* remained unglossed, we might well rule that *DeCosta I* had predetermined our decision on the second and third causes of action. For if defendants could not be prohibited from copying the cards, which gave the defendants all that they took from plaintiff and incorporated in their series, would not any sanction, whether based on service mark infringement or unfair competition, denigrate their license? We do not, however, rest on any such implications of *DeCosta I*, realizing that we do not have a tabula rasa to write upon.

A starting point, of course, is the explicit domain left open in *Sears*, that a state "may protect businesses in the use of their trademarks, labels, or distinctive dress in the packaging of goods so as to prevent others, by imitating such markings, from misleading purchasers as to the source of such goods." 376 U.S. 225, 232. A second guideline is that in *DeCosta I* we dealt only with copying "simpliciter"; to the extent that other elements of other causes of action are relevant, we are free to consider them. In the context of the instant case, we are free to consider deception and passing off, secondary meaning and likelihood of confusion. * * *

What is not clear is whether plaintiff's activities in connection with his marks entitle him to the protection of trade and service mark law. As we said in *DeCosta I*, 377 F.2d at 316, "[t]his was perhaps one of the purest promotions ever staged, for plaintiff did not seek anything but the entertainment of others." * * *

Having exposed our misgivings, we do not rely on a holding that the absence of a profit-oriented enterprise disqualifies plaintiff from protection. We shall assume, therefore, that plaintiff's marks meet the requirements of common law service marks. We also shall assume that they are distinctive enough so that proof of secondary meaning is not essential. In the alternative, we shall accept the finding of the magistrate, adopted by the district court, that, at least among some people, plaintiff's name and card had come to be associated with him.

This brings us to the critical issue: whether there was a deceiving of the public as the result of defendants' actions. As we have noted, there was not and could not supportably have been a finding that defendants passed off or palmed off their "Paladin" and television program as the creations of plaintiff. Having already decided in *DeCosta I* that there was no culpable misappropriation, we are left with the issue of confusion, or its likelihood. * * *

There is another factor, we think, which should guide a judgment as to likelihood of confusion—the time when the evidence is submitted. There is ample reason, at the incipiency of an alleged infringement, in a suit seeking injunctive relief, for a plaintiff to argue and a court to rule that the similarity of marks is such that confusion is all too likely to ensue. Plaintiff should not be expected to stand by and await the dismal proof. Callman, Vol. 3, § 80.6, pp. 559–560. "[C]onversely", adds Callman, "after the lapse of substantial time if no one appears to have been actually deceived that fact is strongly probative of the defense that there is no likelihood of deception arising out of the use of the mark in question." Id. at 562. Defendants have urged that plaintiff, having delayed for almost the entire limitations period before bringing suit, should be barred by the doctrine of estoppel by laches from further prosecution of this litigation. Plaintiff's rejoinder is that he was, during this period, going from attorney to attorney, seeking assistance before he was able to make progress.[c] We do not find in the authorities sufficient support, where defendants' action was found by the jury to be deliberate and knowing, to invoke this doctrine. Nevertheless, we do say that the delay, for reasons stated, increases the quantum of proof of confusion which the plaintiff has the obligation to supply. * * *

The magistrate's findings being treated as final, they are here subject to the same standard of review as are district court findings under Fed.R.Civ.Pro. 52(a). They must be accepted unless clearly erroneous. On this issue, however, we see no alternative to saying the finding is not supported. * * * [T]he testimony of six witnesses that they thought, on first viewing the program, that the television character Paladin was plaintiff, seems to us either no evidence at all or such minimal evidence as not to support a finding of likelihood of confusion requiring an accounting of defendants' profits from a highly successful, 225 episode series grossing over fourteen million dollars. We do not blame plaintiff or counsel; we suspect that the most exacting search for proof would not have produced more.

We recognize that plaintiff has lost something of value to him. The very success of defendants' series saturated the public consciousness and in time diluted the attractiveness of plaintiff's creation, although he continued his appearances longer than defendants' first run. While he was not injured financially, there can be no doubt that he has felt deprived. As a commentator has observed, "[I]t could be argued that the most appropriate measure of damages would be the emotional harm that he suffered when CBS exploited his character and lured his audience away." 66 Mich.L.Rev. at 1034. But to give any relief, however tailored, we need a predicate of

---

c. According to the New York Times, April 17, 1974, p. 1, a report of DeCosta's success before the magistrate, "Mr. DeCosta went to eight law firms before he found Alan Dworkin, a Providence lawyer, who was willing to take the case."

liability.   Absent the ultimate fact of confusion, we cannot find a basis for liability for common law service mark infringement or unfair competition.

Judgment reversed.   Remanded with instructions to enter judgment for defendants.

■ ALDRICH, SENIOR JUDGE, (concurring).

I concur in the court's opinion, except in the possibilities it leaves open with respect to review of a magistrate's rulings of law.   * * *

DeCosta v. Viacom International, Inc.

United States Court of Appeals, First Circuit, 1992.
981 F.2d 602.
Certiorari denied 509 U.S. 923, 113 S.Ct. 3039 (1993).

■ Before BREYER, CHIEF JUDGE, COFFIN, SENIOR CIRCUIT JUDGE, and CYR, CIRCUIT JUDGE.

■ BREYER, CHIEF JUDGE.

* * *

DeCosta has now sued again.   He has sued Viacom, a company that CBS created, and to which it assigned re-run rights for the old Paladin programs.   He again complains that CBS copied his idea; and he says that Viacom, by broadcasting the old CBS programs, has violated federal and state trademark and unfair competition laws.   15 U.S.C. §§ 1114(1), 1125(a).   The district court permitted the suit to proceed.   DeCosta v. Viacom Int'l, Inc., 758 F.Supp. 807 (D.R.I.1991).   A jury found in DeCosta's favor.   And, Viacom appeals.   In our view, DeCosta's new suit depends for its success upon relitigating issues that this court already has decided against him.   And, for that reason, the doctrine of "collateral estoppel" bars his new claims.   We therefore reverse the district court and order judgment for the defendant.

I

DeCosta's Basic Legal Problems

* * *

Mr. DeCosta's present legal problem lies in the fact that he previously sued CBS and lost.   The traditional legal doctrine of "collateral estoppel" bars relitigation of any issue that, 1) a party had a "full and fair opportunity to litigate" in an earlier action, and that, 2) was finally decided in that action, 3) against that party, and that, 4) was essential to the earlier judgment.   * * *

Mr. DeCosta's argument on this appeal consists of an attempt to escape the bonds of "collateral estoppel" through a claim that legal and factual changes since 1975 (when we decided *DeCosta II*) make the "confusion" issue, in essence, a new one.   * * *

II

Trademark Registration

* * * DeCosta argues that the legal "confusion" issue in the case before us differs from the issue in his earlier 1975 case because, in 1976, he registered his mark. Columbia Broadcasting System, Inc. v. DeCosta, 192 U.S.P.Q. 453 (T.T.A.B.1976). The fact of registration, he says, changes the legal "burden of proof" rules, making it legally easier for a plaintiff to show "likelihood of confusion." [Judge Breyer concluded that the registration did not affect DeCosta's ultimate burden of proving likelihood of confusion.]

III

Reverse Confusion

DeCosta next argues that collateral estoppel does not bind him because, since 1975, there has occurred a "modification or growth in legal principles [that] effect a significant change" in the law. See Commissioner of Internal Revenue v. Sunnen, 333 U.S. 591 (1948); Restatement (Second) of Judgments § 28(2)(b). * * *

DeCosta finds these "new" legal principles in an area of trademark law called "reverse confusion," an area in which a plaintiff claims that the public will confusedly think that the plaintiff's product emanates in some way from the defendant, rather than the (more ordinary) contrary. * * *

The problem for DeCosta is that * * * "reverse confusion" is nothing particularly new. The principal trademark statute does not speak of "ordinary," or "reverse," confusion. It refers simply to copying that is "likely to cause confusion," without dividing confusion into types. 15 U.S.C. § 1114(1). It protects the holder from the harm that confusion might cause, without specifying whether that harm flows from a copier taking advantage of the holder's "good will," or from the copier potentially reducing the value of the mark, say by associating the holder with the copier's own "bad" name. * * * DeCosta cannot therefore claim that the *principle* (that trademark law protects against a buyer's being led to believe, wrongly and harmfully, that the copier is the source of the holder's product) was unavailable to him or that he was not aware of it in his initial case.

DeCosta's more plausible claim is that the law of "reverse confusion" has itself undergone significant expansion since 1975. Several dicta in the Second Circuit suggest that a plaintiff, claiming reverse confusion, can recover for harm suffered, not because the buying public may wrongly believe that the defendant makes or sponsors the plaintiff's product, but simply because the public wrongly believes that the plaintiff copied the defendant's name. See [Banff, Ltd. v. Federated Dep't Stores, Inc., 841 F.2d 486, 490 (2d Cir.1988).] * * *

We agree with DeCosta that one can find dicta, more recent than 1975, that seem to offer support for such a theory. And, we also agree that such a theory might have offered him a basis for success, had he known of its availability before 1975. The fatal problem for DeCosta in respect to this "change in the law," however, lies in our view that this change is not sound law. We find that it does not correctly state the law of trademarks.

Our reasons for this conclusion are several. First, to adopt this theory would undermine an important limitation central to the law of trademarks, the limitation of trademark protection to the protection of marks *as used* on particular goods to identify their source or sponsor. * * * Thus, at present the law often permits a person to take a pre-existing name or mark and use it on a different product in a different market. See, e.g., McGregor–Doniger, Inc. v. Drizzle, Inc., 599 F.2d 1126 (2d Cir.1979) (allowing manufacturer of expensive women's coats to use trademark "Drizzle," despite prior registration of "Drizzler" mark for plaintiff's cheaper golf jackets); King Research, Inc. v. Shulton, Inc., 454 F.2d 66 (2d Cir.1971) ("Ship Shape" on hairspray did not infringe registered "Ship Shape" trademark for comb and brush cleaners). If "falsely being thought a pirate" were an actionable harm, no one could safely use a mark ever previously used by another, no matter how different the product, place of sale, or class of buyer. * * *

Second, other, non-trademark law offers specifically tailored protection against the most obvious harms that may befall the falsely labeled "pirate." Copyright law, for example, protects the initial users of certain names and phrases against any copier. We have mentioned the possibility that DeCosta might have obtained such protection, at least for his calling card. See *DeCosta I*, 377 F.2d at 321. But, he did not do so.

A common law tort, the law against "commercial disparagement" (also known as "injurious falsehood"), may also protect a trademark holder against the false implication that he has "pirated" the work of another, where the defendant intends such harm. * * *

Both these areas of law, however, contain carefully crafted conditions and limitations, designed to prevent their becoming vehicles for unduly limiting the use of words, phrases, and other forms of speech where no serious harm, in fact, will likely occur. See, e.g., copyright law's "fair use" exemption, 17 U.S.C. § 107; see also [Big O Tire Dealers, Inc. v. Goodyear Tire & Rubber Co., 561 F.2d 1365, 1373 (10th Cir.1977)] (outlining the special requirements of "commercial disparagement," namely (1) false statement, (2) malice, and (3) special damages). The existence of these other carefully tailored types of protection also cautions strongly against introducing, into trademark law, a kind of overriding concept such as the actionable harm of "falsely being thought a pirate," which concept could well upset the balance between those interests favoring "protection" and those favoring free use and dissemination—a balance carefully developed by legislatures, and slowly by courts, over many years. * * *

For these reasons, insofar as the doctrine of "reverse confusion" may be thought significantly "new" (reverse confusion about "piracy"), we do not accept it. Insofar as we accept it (reverse confusion involving source or sponsorship), we do not believe it is significantly new. Hence, we do not believe that there are changes in the law here that can overcome the effects of "collateral estoppel."

IV

Factual Changes

DeCosta argues that facts have changed since 1975.   Hence, the issue of "confusion now" is significantly different than the issue of "confusion then."   * * *

DeCosta reminds us that, since findings as to likelihood of confusion can turn on the relation of the parties' uses, a prior finding of no likelihood of confusion will not always bar a subsequent action if circumstances of the parties' uses change.   See Sarah Coventry, Inc. v. T. Sardelli & Sons, Inc., 526 F.2d 20, 23 (1st Cir.1975), cert. denied, 426 U.S. 920 (1976).   The problem for DeCosta is that his evidence [of some actual confusion and of an expansion in his own activities] does not show a significant change.   And, in any event, that change would do a plaintiff no good where it consists of his expansion into a field where the record of litigation indicates that the defendant has priority in using the mark.

For these reasons, the judgment of the district court is

Reversed.

NOTES AND QUESTIONS

(1) Was DeCosta's creation, in the words of *DeCosta I,* too "slight a thing" to merit protection on one theory or another?

(2) Would the misappropriation claim pressed in *DeCosta I* survive § 301?   Was DeCosta's creation "within the subject matter of copyright"?   Was it "fixed in a tangible medium of expression"?   (What could be achieved by copyrighting the card and photograph—protection of the "character"?)   Is the case, in this regard, distinguishable from those involving cartoon characters?

(3) The court's opinion in *DeCosta III* wiped out a $3.5 million judgment and an injunction that had effectively prohibited further broadcasts of the television series, leaving DeCosta with nothing to show for thirty years of litigation except jury verdicts that CBS had stolen his creation.   DeCosta died at age 84 a month after the First Circuit's final decision.   His obituary by United Press International described him as the "former cowboy, rodeo star and construction worker who created the 'Have Gun, Will Travel' TV Western character known as Paladin."

CHAPTER 9

Moral Rights and Publicity Rights

Section 1. Protection of "Moral Rights"

Article 6*bis* of the Berne Convention for the Protection of Literary and Artistic Works (Paris Revision, 1971), reprinted in the Statutory Supplement, provides as follows:

> (1) Independently of the author's economic rights, and even after the transfer of the said rights, the author shall have the right to claim authorship of the work and to object to any distortion, mutilation or other modification of, or other derogatory action in relation to, the said work, which would be prejudicial to his honour or reputation.

> (2) The rights granted to the author in accordance with the preceding paragraph shall, after his death, be maintained, at least until the expiry of the economic rights, and shall be exercisable by the persons or institutions authorized by the legislation of the country where protection is claimed. However, those countries whose legislation, at the moment of their ratification of or accession to this Act, does not provide for the protection after the death of the author of all the rights set out in the preceding paragraph may provide that some of these rights may, after his death, cease to be maintained.

> (3) The means of redress for safeguarding the rights granted by this Article shall be governed by the legislation of the country where protection is claimed.

These rights are often called "moral rights." They recognize the author's right to claim "paternity" and to protect the "integrity" of a work. One of the copyright studies done in preparation for the drafting of the copyright revision bill describes the former as "the author's right to be made known to the public as the creator of his work, to prevent others from usurping his work by naming another person as the author, and to prevent others from wrongfully attributing to him a work he has not written." Strauss, The Moral Right of the Author, Copyr. Law Revision Study No. 4, 116 (1959), in 2 Studies on Copyr. 963, 966 (1963). The latter, the right to protect the integrity of the work, entitles the author to prevent unauthorized alterations. Moral rights are sometimes said to extend beyond paternity and integrity to encompass the right to publish or not to publish a work, to withdraw a work from sale, and to prevent other injuries to the author's personality as embodied in the work. The doctrine of moral rights finds its most complete expression in French law—hence the frequent reference, even in America, to *droit moral.*[a]

In the debates preceding our accession to the Berne Convention, the issue of moral rights provoked sharp disagreement. One group, composed mostly of magazine publishers and broadcasters, opposed adherence to Berne out of fears that writers and others would cripple the editing process by threatening to exert integrity rights. The motion picture studios, although anxious for Berne's increased protection abroad, expressed similar concerns about moral rights. These fears were nourished by the supposed position in French law that moral rights cannot be waived or transferred. At the other extreme were authors and film directors who argued that we could not join Berne in good faith without federal legislation that would recognize and strengthen moral rights. In the middle were "minimalists" who asserted that existing elements of federal and state law adequately recognized paternity and integrity rights, so that we could and should adhere to Berne.

The minimalist position triumphed,[b] and except for the Visual Artists Rights Act of 1990 described later in this section, it continues to reflect the American response to Berne. The Berne Convention Implementation Act of 1988 (Pub.L. 100–568) emphasized in § 2 that the Berne Convention was "not self-executing under the Constitution and laws of the United States" and that the obligations under Berne "may be performed only pursuant to appropriate domestic law." Section 3 of the Act reiterated that the provisions of the Convention "shall be given effect under title 17, as amended by this Act, and any other relevant provision of Federal or State law, including the common law," but "shall not be enforceable in any action brought pursuant to the provisions of the Berne Convention itself." See also § 104(c).

What is this body of existing law so solicitously enshrined?

Smith v. Montoro

United States Court of Appeals, Ninth Circuit, 1981.
648 F.2d 602.

■ Before PECK, ANDERSON, and PREGERSON, CIRCUIT JUDGES.

■ PREGERSON, CIRCUIT JUDGE:

This is an appeal from a judgment granting defendant's motion to dismiss under Fed.R.Civ.P. 12(b)(6) for failure to state a federal claim.

---

a. DaSilva, Droit Moral and the Amoral Copyright, 28 Bull.Copyr.Soc. 1 (1980), offers a summary of French law (and a comparison with that of the United States). See also Kwall, Copyright and the Moral Right: Is an American Marriage Possible?, 38 Vand.L.Rev. 1 (1985).

b. On this controversy as it appeared on the eve of adherence, see R. Brown, Adherence to the Berne Copyright Convention: The Moral Rights Issue, 35 J.Copyr.Soc. 196 (1988).

The district court held that the complaint did not allege facts sufficient to constitute a violation of section 43(a) of the Lanham Act, 15 U.S.C. § 1125(a).   Appellant argues that the district court erred since the acts alleged in the complaint are the economic equivalent of "palming off," or misuse of a trade name, thus meeting the district court's standard for stating a claim under section 43(a).   For the reasons stated below, we reverse.

Paul Smith contracted to star in a film to be produced by Producioni Atlas Cinematografica ("PAC"), an Italian film company.   The contract allegedly provided that Smith would receive star billing in the screen credits and advertising for the film and that PAC would so provide in any subsequent contracts with distributors of the film.   PAC then licensed defendants Edward Montoro and Film Venture International, Inc. ("FVI") to distribute the film in this country under the name "Convoy Buddies." Plaintiff complains, however, that Montoro and FVI removed Smith's name and substituted the name of another actor, "Bob Spencer," in place of Smith's name in both the film credits and advertising material.   Plaintiff alleges that, as a result of defendants' substitution, plaintiff has been damaged in his reputation as an actor, and has lost specific employment opportunities.

The complaint sought damages under several theories, including breach of contract, "false light publicity," violation of section 43(a) of the Lanham Act, and violation of Cal.Civ.Code § 3344 regarding commercial appropriation of a person's likeness.   There being no diversity of citizenship, federal subject matter jurisdiction was based solely on plaintiff's Lanham Act claim.   Plaintiff asserted that the district court had jurisdiction of the state law claims as a matter of pendent jurisdiction.   * * *

Appellant argues that defendants violated section 43(a) by affixing or using "a false designation or representation," i.e., another actor's name in place of appellant's, in connection with the movie's advertising and credits. Appellant claims standing under section 43(a) as a person "who believes that he is or is likely to be damaged" by the use of another actor's name in place of his.   Thus, appellant's claim, although one of first impression, appears to fall within the express language of section 43(a).

The district court appears to have rejected appellant's argument on the ground that, to state a claim under section 43(a), a complaint must allege merchandising practices "in the nature of, or economically equivalent to, palming off ... and/or misuse of trademarks and trade names."   * * *

To the extent that the district court's standard for section 43(a) claims could be read as limiting such claims to cases of palming off, such a narrow rule would be contrary to established case law.   * * *

The district court's ruling was entirely consistent with the vast majority of section 43(a) cases, however, to the extent that it indicated that a section 43(a) claim may be based on economic practices or conduct "economically equivalent" to palming off.   Such practices would include "reverse passing off," which occurs when a person removes or obliterates the original trademark, without authorization, before reselling goods produced by someone else. See Borchard, Reverse Passing Off—Commercial Robbery or Permissible Competition?, 67 Trademark Rep. 1 (1977). Reverse passing off is accomplished "expressly" when the wrongdoer removes the name or trademark on another party's product and sells that product under a name chosen by the wrongdoer. "Implied" reverse passing off occurs when the wrongdoer simply removes or otherwise obliterates the name of the manufacturer or source and sells the product in an unbranded state.

In the instant case, appellant argues that the defendants' alleged conduct constitutes *reverse* passing off and that appellant's complaint therefore stated a section 43(a) claim even under the district court's own standard. Appellees argue, however, that the protection afforded by the Lanham Act is limited to "sales of goods" and does not extend to claims that a motion picture shown to the public might contain false information as to origin.

The short answer to appellees' argument is that the Lanham Act explicitly condemns false designations or representations in connection with *"any* goods or *services."* The prohibitions of this section have been applied to motion picture representations. See, e.g., Dallas Cowboys Cheerleaders, Inc. v. Pussycat Cinema Ltd., 467 F.Supp. 366 (S.D.N.Y.), aff'd, 604 F.2d 200 (2d Cir.1979). Moreover, the names of movie actors and other performers may, under certain circumstances, be registered under the Lanham Act as service marks for entertainment services. See, e.g., Re Carson, 197 U.S.P.Q. (BNA) 554 (Trademark Trial & App.Bd.1977); Re Ames, 160 U.S.P.Q. (BNA) 214 (Trademark Trial & App.Bd.1966). Although appellant has not alleged that his name is registered as a service mark, registration of a trademark or service mark is not a prerequisite for recovery under section 43(a). * * *

According to appellant's complaint, defendants not only removed appellant's name from all credits and advertising, they also substituted a name of their own choosing. Appellees' alleged conduct therefore amounts to *express* reverse passing off. As a matter of policy, such conduct, like traditional palming off, is wrongful because it involves an attempt to misappropriate or profit from another's talents and workmanship. Moreover, in reverse palming off cases, the originator of the misidentified product is involuntarily deprived of the advertising value of its name and of the goodwill that otherwise would stem from public knowledge of the true source of the satisfactory product. * * * The ultimate purchaser (or viewer) is also deprived of knowing the true source of the product and may even be deceived into believing that it comes from a different source. Borchard, supra, at 4–5.

In the film industry, a particular actor's performance, which may have received an award or other critical acclaim, may be the primary attraction for movie-goers. Some actors are said to have such drawing power at the box office that the appearance of their names on the theater marquee can almost guarantee financial success. Such big box office names are built, in part, through being prominently featured in popular films and by receiving appropriate recognition in film credits and advertising. Since actors' fees for pictures, and indeed, their ability to get any work at all, is often based on the drawing power their name may be expected to have at the box office, being accurately credited for films in which they have played would seem to be of critical importance in enabling actors to sell their "services," i.e., their performances. We therefore find that appellant has stated a valid claim for relief under section 43(a) of the Lanham Act.[6] * * *

As the district court stated, a section 43(a) claim may be based on practices or conduct "economically equivalent" to palming off. We find that appellant did state such a claim by alleging that defendants engaged in conduct amounting to "express reverse palming off." Since appellant also has standing to sue under section 43(a), the district court's dismissal of the complaint for failure to state a federal claim is reversed. The dismissal of the pendent state law claims is also reversed.

Reversed and remanded.

NOTES AND QUESTIONS ON "PATERNITY"

(1) Identical analysis led to a like result when the authorship of two songs was falsely credited to others in Lamothe v. Atlantic Recording Corp., 847 F.2d 1403 (9th Cir.1988).

Suppose the defendants had merely deleted plaintiff's name; would that be a violation of § 43(a)—a "false designation of origin" or a "false or misleading representation of fact"? In Marling v. Ellison, 218 U.S.P.Q. 702 (S.D.Fla.1982), the court ruled "that in misappropriating plaintiffs' copyrighted material without acknowledgment of plaintiffs' ownership rights * * * defendant has violated § 43(a) of the Lanham Act," but there too defendant had substituted another name (his own) for the plaintiffs'. In Morita v. Omni Publications Int'l, Ltd., 741 F.Supp. 1107 (S.D.N.Y. 1990), vac'd on settlement, 760 F.Supp. 45 (S.D.N.Y.1991), the court said that § 43(a) did not create a duty of attribution, distinguishing misattributions from omissions. Declaring "[i]t makes no difference whether we label this claim for relief plagiarism, invasion of privacy, or *prima facie* tort," an Ohio court reversed a summary judgment entered against a medical researcher who alleged that the laboratory's director had taken a discovery made by the plaintiff and presented it to a national scientific

---

6. In a case involving very similar facts, the district court denied a motion to dismiss and ruled orally that a cause of action for unfair competition under section 43(a) had been stated. See Perin Film Enterprises v. TWG Productions, 400 P.T.C.Journ. (10–19–78) A–13 (S.D.N.Y.1978). The plaintiff had served as executive producer of the television series "For You ... Black Woman." During the second year of production, after having served as executive producer of the first 22 shows, plaintiff was dismissed and received no credit for his services. Instead, the name of an employee of the show's underwriter was substituted as the "executive in charge of production." The parties entered into settlement negotiations shortly after the court's ruling, and the ruling was never subsequently embodied in published opinion.

society as his own. "[I]s there a right in plaintiff to be recognized for his work product which was violated by defendant's claiming that work product as his own? We conclude that there is such a right. Although such right may not be invaded by a failure to give recognition to another upon an authorized publication, it is invaded when one claims the other's work product as his own." Bajpayee v. Rothermich, 53 Ohio App.2d 117, 123, 372 N.E.2d 817, 821 (1977).

The prevailing view has been that absent an express contractual obligation, a licensee or assignee is under no duty to credit authorship. Vargas v. Esquire, Inc., 164 F.2d 522 (7th Cir.1947), is a frequently cited example. For several years plaintiff Alberto Vargas had furnished drawings for publication in *Esquire* magazine under the title "Varga Girls," with plaintiff acknowledged as the artist. When the relationship terminated amid charges of fraud, the defendant began publishing the remaining pictures under the title "Esquire Girl", with no acknowledgment of authorship. Plaintiff failed to enjoin the publication; the court found that he had "divested himself of every vestige of title and ownership of the pictures." See also Harris v. Twentieth Century Fox Film Corp., 43 F.Supp. 119 (S.D.N.Y.1942).

Should an obligation to acknowledge authorship be implied in a license or assignment silent as to credit? The Seventh Circuit in *Vargas* thought not.

(2) American law has consistently afforded redress when another's work has been falsely attributed to the plaintiff. False or misleading attributions have been successfully contested under a variety of theories, most often unfair competition. When Time–Life Records began promoting "Artie Shaw versions" of "Swing Era" classics, Shaw was held entitled, under a claim of common law unfair competition, to explore whether consumers realized that the versions were not in fact Artie Shaw performances. Shaw v. Time–Life Records, 38 N.Y.2d 201, 379 N.Y.S.2d 390 (1975).

Novelist Ken Follett invoked § 43(a) of the Lanham Act to enjoin publication of a nonfiction work attributed to him as principal author; he had in fact merely edited the work. The court ordered an accurate credit line. Follett v. New American Library, Inc., 497 F.Supp. 304 (S.D.N.Y. 1980). Stephen King, prolific author of horror stories, successfully invoked § 43(a) against a motion picture advertised as "Stephen King's Lawnmower Man." Although King had assigned the movie rights to his short story of that name, the court found that the attribution used with the movie (which only loosely tracked the story) misrepresented King's involvement; he had no role in producing or approving the script or film. However, the defendant was allowed to describe the film as "based on" King's story. King v. Innovation Books, 976 F.2d 824 (2d Cir.1992). Jazz musician George Benson was also successful in a claim alleging misleading attribution. Distribution of a record album entitled "George Benson, Erotic Moods" was enjoined under § 43(a); the title was likely to mislead the public because the recordings, all several years old, involved a then unknown Benson playing merely as a group member. Benson v. Paul Winley

Record Sales Corp., 452 F.Supp. 516 (S.D.N.Y.1978). See also PPX Enterprises, Inc. v. Audiofidelity Enterprises, Inc., 818 F.2d 266 (2d Cir.1987) (Jimi Hendrix absent from some recordings and only a sideman on others). Another record case, in which the defendant had overdubbed words and music onto the unfinished performance of the named artists, was won on a passing off theory, this time under the Uniform Deceptive Trade Practices Act. Bonner v. Westbound Records, Inc., 49 Ill.App.3d 543, 364 N.E.2d 570 (1977).

A defamation claim involving an inaccurate attribution survived a motion to dismiss in Clevenger v. Baker Voorhis & Co., 8 N.Y.2d 187, 203 N.Y.S.2d 812 (1960). Plaintiff, author of "Clevenger's Annual Practice of New York," complained of a revised edition published under his name without permission. He alleged that the more than two hundred errors in the revision irreparably impaired his reputation as a lawyer and legal writer; a jury award of $50,000 in compensatory and punitive damages was reduced on appeal to $10,000. 14 N.Y.2d 536, 248 N.Y.S.2d 396 (1964). In another unauthorized revision case, continued use of the original author's name was held an invasion of privacy. Zim v. Western Publishing Co., 573 F.2d 1318 (5th Cir.1978).

For a detailed analysis of attribution practices in the entertainment industry, see T. Selz, M. Simensky, and P. Acton, Entertainment Law.

SHOSTAKOVICH v. TWENTIETH CENTURY-FOX FILM CORP., 196 Misc. 67, 80 N.Y.S.2d 575 (Sup.Ct.1948). "Plaintiffs are composers of international renown. They are citizens and residents of the Union of Soviet Socialist Republics. Defendant, a domestic corporation, has produced a picture known as 'The Iron Curtain' which is now being exhibited in theatres throughout this country. In the public mind, this title has come to indicate the boundary between that part of Europe which is under the sovereignty of, occupied by or under the influence of the U.S.S.R., as distinguished from the rest of the continent. The picture depicts recent disclosures of espionage in Canada attributed to representatives of the U.S.S.R. There is shown, preliminarily, but not as part of the picture proper, as is customary in the showing of motion pictures, the names of the players, the producer, the cameramen, and similar informative data. Included is this statement: 'Music—From The Selected Works of the Soviet Composers—Dmitry Shostakovich, Serge Prokofieff, Aram Khachaturian, Nicholai Miaskovsky— Conducted by Alfred Newman'. Such practice in the theatrical, advertising and kindred businesses is known as giving a 'credit line'. During the picture, music of the several plaintiffs is reproduced, from time to time, for a total period of approximately 45 minutes. The entire running time of the film is 87 minutes. The use of the music can best be described as incidental, background matter. Aside from the use of their music neither the plot nor the theme of the play, in any manner, concerns plaintiffs. In addition to the use of their names on the 'credit lines' the name of one plaintiff is used when one of the characters in the play is shown placing a recording of this particular plaintiff's music on a phonograph. Again this is incidental, the name is mentioned in an appreciative, familiar fashion, the impression given being that the character has come upon a record of a composition which he recognizes and appreciates hearing. All the music, it is conceded, for the purposes of this motion, is in the public domain and enjoys no copyright protection whatever.

"Plaintiffs seek to enjoin pendente lite and permanently the use of their names and music in the picture and in any advertising or publicity matter relating to it. * * *

" * * * The lack of copyright protection has long been held to permit others to use the names of authors in copying, publishing or compiling their works. Clemens v. Belford Clark & Co., C.C., 14 F. 728. * * *

" * * * The wrong which is alleged here is the use of plaintiffs' music in a moving picture whose theme is objectionable to them in that it is unsympathetic to their political ideology. The logical development of this theory leads inescapably to the Doctrine of Moral Right (53 Harvard Law Rev. 554). There is no charge of distortion of the compositions nor any claim that they have not been faithfully reproduced. Conceivably, under the doctrine of Moral Right the court could in a proper case, prevent the use of a composition or work, in the public domain, in such a manner as would be violative of the author's rights. The application of the doctrine presents much difficulty however. With reference to that which is in the public domain there arises a conflict between the moral right and the well established rights of others to use such works. Clemens v. Belford Clark & Co., supra. So, too, there arises the question of the norm by which the use of such work is to be tested to determine whether or not the author's moral right as an author has been violated. Is the standard to be good taste, artistic worth, political beliefs, moral concepts or what is it to be? In the present state of our law the very existence of the right is not clear, the relative position of the rights thereunder with reference to the rights of others is not defined nor has the nature of the proper remedy been determined. * * * The motion is accordingly denied in all respects."

NOTE

The Appellate Division affirmed with the following memorandum: "We assume that the film in question is not a news film. We do not pass upon the sufficiency of the alleged cause of action, but think that, under the circumstances of this case, the motion for a temporary injunction was properly denied." 275 A.D. 692, 87 N.Y.S.2d 430 (1949). Would a judgment for the plaintiffs be inconsistent with the concept of a public domain?

The *Shostakovich* case was later relitigated in France when an assignee of the Russian composers protested the use of their music in the film "Le Rideau de Fer." An appellate court, finding the composers entitled to copyright in France, justified seizure of the film on an infringement theory, but also found that there was "undoubtedly a moral damage." [c]

Gilliam v. American Broadcasting Companies

United States Court of Appeals, Second Circuit, 1976.
538 F.2d 14.

■ Before LUMBARD, HAYS and GURFEIN, CIRCUIT JUDGES.

■ LUMBARD, CIRCUIT JUDGE.   Plaintiffs, a group of British writers and performers known as "Monty Python," appeal from a denial by Judge Lasker in the Southern District of a preliminary injunction to restrain the American Broadcasting Company (ABC) from broadcasting edited versions of three separate programs originally written and performed by Monty Python for broadcast by the British Broadcasting Corporation (BBC). We agree with Judge Lasker that the appellants have demonstrated that the excising done for ABC impairs the integrity of the original work. We further find that the countervailing injuries that Judge Lasker found might have accrued to ABC as a result of an injunction at a prior date no longer exist. We therefore direct the issuance of a preliminary injunction by the district court.

Since its formation in 1969, the Monty Python group has gained popularity primarily through its thirty-minute television programs created for BBC as part of a comedy series entitled "Monty Python's Flying Circus." In accordance with an agreement between Monty Python and BBC, the group writes and delivers to BBC scripts for use in the television series. This scriptwriters' agreement recites in great detail the procedure to be followed when any alterations are to be made in the script prior to recording of the program. The essence of this section of the agreement is that, while BBC retains final authority to make changes, appellants or their representatives exercise optimum control over the scripts consistent with BBC's authority and only minor changes may be made without prior consultation with the writers. Nothing in the scriptwriters' agreement entitles BBC to alter a program once it has been recorded. The agreement further provides that, subject to the terms therein, the group retains all rights in the script.   * * *

In October 1973, Time–Life Films acquired the right to distribute in the United States certain BBC television programs, including the Monty Python series. Time–Life was permitted to edit the programs only "for insertion of commercials, applicable censorship or governmental ... rules and regulations, and National Association of Broadcasters and time segment requirements." No similar clause was included in the scriptwriters' agreement between appellants and BBC. Prior to this time, ABC had sought to acquire the right to broadcast excerpts from various Monty Python programs in the spring of 1975, but the group rejected the proposal

c. See Strauss, The Moral Right of the Author, Copyr.Law Revision Study No. 4, 139   n. 133 (1959), in 2 Studies on Copyr. 963, 989 n. 133 (1963).

for such a disjoined format. Thereafter, in July 1975, ABC agreed with Time–Life to broadcast two ninety-minute specials each comprising three thirty-minute Monty Python programs that had not previously been shown in this country. * * *

ABC broadcast the first of the specials on October 3, 1975. Appellants did not see a tape of the program until late November and were allegedly "appalled" at the discontinuity and "mutilation" that had resulted from the editing done by Time–Life for ABC. Twenty-four minutes of the original 90 minutes of recording had been omitted. Some of the editing had been done in order to make time for commercials; other material had been edited, according to ABC, because the original programs contained offensive or obscene matter.

In early December, Monty Python learned that ABC planned to broadcast the second special on December 26, 1975. The parties began negotiations concerning editing of that program and a delay of the broadcast until Monty Python could view it. These negotiations were futile, however, and on December 15 the group filed this action to enjoin the broadcast and for damages. Following an evidentiary hearing, Judge Lasker found that "the plaintiffs have established an impairment of the integrity of their work" which "caused the film or program . . . to lose its iconoclastic verve." According to Judge Lasker, "the damage that has been caused to the plaintiffs is irreparable by its nature." Nevertheless, the judge denied the motion for the preliminary injunction on the grounds that it was unclear who owned the copyright in the programs produced by BBC from the scripts written by Monty Python; that there was a question of whether Time–Life and BBC were indispensable parties to the litigation; that ABC would suffer significant financial loss if it were enjoined a week before the scheduled broadcast; and that Monty Python had displayed a "somewhat disturbing casualness" in their pursuance of the matter.

Judge Lasker granted Monty Python's request for more limited relief by requiring ABC to broadcast a disclaimer during the December 26 special to the effect that the group dissociated itself from the program because of the editing. A panel of this court, however, granted a stay of that order until this appeal could be heard and permitted ABC to broadcast, at the beginning of the special, only the legend that the program had been edited by ABC. We heard argument on April 13 and, at that time, enjoined ABC from any further broadcast of edited Monty Python programs pending the decision of the court.

I

* * *

Judge Lasker denied the preliminary injunction in part because he was unsure of the ownership of the copyright in the recorded program. Appellants first contend that the question of ownership is irrelevant because the recorded program was merely a derivative work taken from the script in which they hold the uncontested copyright. Thus, even if BBC owned the copyright in the recorded program, its use of that work would be limited by the license granted to BBC by Monty Python for use of the underlying script. We agree.

Section 7 of the Copyright Law, 17 U.S.C.A. § 7, provides in part that "adaptations, arrangements, dramatizations ... or other versions of ... copyrighted works when produced with the consent of the proprietor of the copyright in such works ... shall be regarded as new works subject to copyright...." Manifestly, the recorded program falls into this category as a dramatization of the script, and thus the program was itself entitled to copyright protection. However, section 7 limits the copyright protection of the derivative work, as works adapted from previously existing scripts have become known, to the novel additions made to the underlying work, Reyher v. Children's Television Workshop, 533 F.2d 87 (2d Cir.1976), and the derivative work does not affect the "force or validity" of the copyright in the matter from which it is derived. See Grove Press, Inc. v. Greenleaf Publishing Co., 247 F.Supp. 518 (S.D.N.Y.1965). Thus, any ownership by BBC of the copyright in the recorded program would not affect the scope or ownership of the copyright in the underlying script.

Since the copyright in the underlying script survives intact despite the incorporation of that work into a derivative work, one who uses the script, even with the permission of the proprietor of the derivative work, may infringe the underlying copyright. See Davis v. E.I. DuPont deNemours & Co., 240 F.Supp. 612 (S.D.N.Y.1965) (defendants held to have infringed when they obtained permission to use a screenplay in preparing a television script but did not obtain permission of the author of the play upon which the screenplay was based).

If the proprietor of the derivative work is licensed by the proprietor of the copyright in the underlying work to vend or distribute the derivative work to third parties, those parties will, of course, suffer no liability for their use of the underlying work consistent with the license to the proprietor of the derivative work. Obviously, it was just this type of arrangement that was contemplated in this instance. The scriptwriters' agreement between Monty Python and BBC specifically permitted the latter to license the transmission of the recordings made by BBC to distributors such as Time–Life for broadcast in overseas territories.

One who obtains permission to use a copyrighted script in the production of a derivative work, however, may not exceed the specific purpose for which permission was granted. Most of the decisions that have reached this conclusion have dealt with the improper extension of the underlying work into media or time, i.e., duration of the license, not covered by the grant of permission to the derivative work proprietor. See Bartsch v. Metro–Goldwyn–Mayer, Inc., 391 F.2d 150 (2d Cir.), cert. denied, 393 U.S. 826 (1968); G. Ricordi & Co. v. Paramount Pictures Inc., 189 F.2d 469 (2d Cir.), cert. denied, 342 U.S. 849 (1951). Cf. Rice v. American Program Bureau, 446 F.2d 685 (2d Cir.1971). Appellants herein do not claim that the broadcast by ABC violated media or time restrictions contained in the license of the script to BBC. Rather, they claim that revisions in the script, and ultimately in the program, could be made only after consultation with

Monty Python, and that ABC's broadcast of a program edited after recording and without consultation with Monty Python exceeded the scope of any license that BBC was entitled to grant.

The rationale for finding infringement when a licensee exceeds time or media restrictions on his license—the need to allow the proprietor of the underlying copyright to control the method in which his work is presented to the public—applies equally to the situation in which a licensee makes an unauthorized use of the underlying work by publishing it in a truncated version. Whether intended to allow greater economic exploitation of the work, as in the media and time cases, or to ensure that the copyright proprietor retains a veto power over revisions desired for the derivative work, the ability of the copyright holder to control his work remains paramount in our copyright law. We find, therefore, that unauthorized editing of the underlying work, if proven, would constitute an infringement of the copyright in that work similar to any other use of a work that exceeded the license granted by the proprietor of the copyright. * * *

Finally, ABC contends that appellants must have expected that deletions would be made in the recordings to conform them for use on commercial television in the United States. ABC argues that licensing in the United States implicitly grants a license to insert commercials in a program and to remove offensive or obscene material prior to broadcast. According to the network, appellants should have anticipated that most of the excised material contained scatological references inappropriate for American television and that these scenes would be replaced with commercials, which presumably are more palatable to the American public.

The proof adduced up to this point, however, provides no basis for finding any implied consent to edit. Prior to the ABC broadcasts, Monty Python programs had been broadcast on a regular basis by both commercial and public television stations in this country without interruption or deletion. Indeed, there is no evidence of any prior broadcast of edited Monty Python material in the United States. These facts, combined with the persistent requests for assurances by the group and its representatives that the programs would be shown intact belie the argument that the group knew or should have known that deletions and commercial interruptions were inevitable.

Several of the deletions made for ABC, such as elimination of the words "hell" and "damn," seem inexplicable given today's standard television fare. If, however, ABC honestly determined that the programs were obscene in substantial part, it could have decided not to broadcast the specials at all, or it could have attempted to reconcile its differences with appellants. The network could not, however, free from a claim of infringement, broadcast in a substantially altered form a program incorporating the script over which the group had retained control.

Our resolution of these technical arguments serves to reinforce our initial inclination that the copyright law should be used to recognize the important role of the artist in our society and the need to encourage production and dissemination of artistic works by providing adequate legal protection for one who submits his work to the public. See Mazer v. Stein, 347 U.S. 201 (1954). We therefore conclude that there is a substantial likelihood that, after a full trial, appellants will succeed in proving infringement of their copyright by ABC's broadcast of edited versions of Monty Python programs. In reaching this conclusion, however, we need not accept appellants' assertion that any editing whatsoever would constitute infringement. Courts have recognized that licensees are entitled to some small degree of latitude in arranging the licensed work for presentation to the public in a manner consistent with the licensee's style or standards. See Stratchborneo v. Arc. Music Corp., 357 F.Supp. 1393, 1405 (S.D.N.Y. 1973); Preminger v. Columbia Pictures Corp., 49 Misc.2d 363, 267 N.Y.S.2d 594 (Sup.Ct.), aff'd 25 A.D.2d 830, 269 N.Y.S.2d 913 (1st Dept.), aff'd 18 N.Y.2d 659, 273 N.Y.S.2d 80, 219 N.E.2d 431 (1966). That privilege, however, does not extend to the degree of editing that occurred here especially in light of contractual provisions that limited the right to edit Monty Python material.

II

It also seems likely that appellants will succeed on the theory that, regardless of the right ABC had to broadcast an edited program, the cuts made constituted an actionable mutilation of Monty Python's work. This cause of action, which seeks redress for deformation of an artist's work, finds its roots in the continental concept of droit moral, or moral right, which may generally be summarized as including the right of the artist to have his work attributed to him in the form in which he created it. See 1 M. Nimmer, supra, at § 110.1.

American copyright law, as presently written, does not recognize moral rights or provide a cause of action for their violation, since the law seeks to vindicate the economic, rather than the personal, rights of authors. Nevertheless, the economic incentive for artistic and intellectual creation that serves as the foundation for American copyright law, Goldstein v. California, 412 U.S. 546 (1973); Mazer v. Stein, 347 U.S. 201 (1954), cannot be reconciled with the inability of artists to obtain relief for mutilation or misrepresentation of their work to the public on which the artists are financially dependent. Thus courts have long granted relief for misrepresentation of an artist's work by relying on theories outside the statutory law of copyright, such as contract law, Granz v. Harris, 198 F.2d 585 (2d Cir.1952) (substantial cutting of original work constitutes misrepresentation), or the tort of unfair competition, Prouty v. National Broadcasting Co., 26 F.Supp. 265 (D.Mass.1939). See Strauss, The Moral Right of the Author 128–138, in Studies on Copyright (1963). Although such decisions are clothed in terms of proprietary right in one's creation, they also properly vindicate the author's personal right to prevent the presentation of his work to the public in a distorted form. See Gardella v. Log Cabin Products Co., 89 F.2d 891, 895–96 (2d Cir.1937); Roeder, The Doctrine of Moral Right, 53 Harv.L.Rev. 554, 568 (1940).

Here, the appellants claim that the editing done for ABC mutilated the original work and that consequently the broadcast of those programs as the creation of Monty Python violated the Lanham Act § 43(a), 15 U.S.C.A. § 1125(a). This statute, the federal counterpart to state unfair competition laws, has been invoked to prevent misrepresentations that may injure plaintiff's business or personal reputation, even where no registered trademark is concerned. See Mortellito v. Nina of California, 335 F.Supp. 1288, 1294 (S.D.N.Y.1972). It is sufficient to violate the Act that a representation of a product, although technically true, creates a false impression of the product's origin. See Rich v. RCA Corp., 390 F.Supp. 530 (S.D.N.Y. 1975) (recent picture of plaintiff on cover of album containing songs recorded in distant past held to be a false representation that the songs were new); Geisel v. Poynter Products, Inc., 283 F.Supp. 261, 267 (S.D.N.Y.1968).

These cases cannot be distinguished from the situation in which a television network broadcasts a program properly designated as having been written and performed by a group, but which has been edited, without the writer's consent, into a form that departs substantially from the original work. "To deform his work is to present him to the public as the creator of a work not his own, and thus makes him subject to criticism for work he has not done." Roeder, supra, at 569. In such a case, it is the writer or performer, rather than the network, who suffers the consequences of the mutilation, for the public will have only the final product by which to evaluate the work. Thus, an allegation that a defendant has presented to the public a "garbled," Granz v. Harris, supra (Frank, J., concurring), distorted version of plaintiff's work seeks to redress the very rights sought to be protected by the Lanham Act, 15 U.S.C.A. § 1125(a), and should be recognized as stating a cause of action under that statute. See Autry v. Republic Productions, Inc., 213 F.2d 667 (9th Cir.1954); Jaeger v. American Intn'l Pictures, Inc., 330 F.Supp. 274 (S.D.N.Y.1971), which suggest the violation of such a right if mutilation could be proven.

During the hearing on the preliminary injunction, Judge Lasker viewed the edited version of the Monty Python program broadcast on December 26 and the original, unedited version. After hearing argument of this appeal, this panel also viewed and compared the two versions. We find that the truncated version at times omitted the climax of the skits to which appellants' rare brand of humor was leading and at other times deleted essential elements in the schematic development of a story line.[12] We therefore agree with Judge Lasker's conclusion that the edited version broadcast by ABC impaired the integrity of appellants' work and represent-

---

12. A single example will illustrate the extent of distortion engendered by the editing. In one skit, an upper class English family is engaged in a discussion of the tonal quality of certain words as "woody" or "tinny." The father soon begins to suggest certain words with sexual connotations as either "woody" or "tinny," whereupon the mother fetches a bucket of water and pours it over his head. The skit continues from this point. The ABC edit eliminates this middle sequence so that the father is comfortably dressed at one moment and, in the next moment, is shown in a soaked condition without any explanation for the change in his appearance.

ed to the public as the product of appellants what was actually a mere caricature of their talents. We believe that a valid cause of action for such distortion exists and that therefore a preliminary injunction may issue to prevent repetition of the broadcast prior to final determination of the issues.[13] * * *

For these reasons we direct that the district court issue the preliminary injunction sought by the appellants.

■ GURFEIN, CIRCUIT JUDGE (concurring):

I concur in my brother Lumbard's scholarly opinion, but I wish to comment on the application of Section 43(a) of the Lanham Act, 15 U.S.C.A. § 1125(a). * * *

In the present case, we are holding that the deletion of portions of the recorded tape constitutes a breach of contract, as well as an infringement of a common-law copyright of the original work. There is literally no need to discuss whether plaintiffs also have a claim for relief under the Lanham Act or for unfair competition under New York law. I agree with Judge Lumbard, however, that it may be an exercise of judicial economy to express our view on the Lanham Act claim, and I do not dissent therefrom. I simply wish to leave it open for the District Court to fashion the remedy.

The Copyright Act provides no recognition of the so-called *droit moral,* or moral right of authors. Nor are such rights recognized in the field of copyright law in the United States. See 1 Nimmer on Copyright, § 110.2 (1975 ed.). If a distortion or truncation in connection with a use constitutes an infringement of copyright, there is no need for an additional cause of action beyond copyright infringement. Id. at § 110.3. An obligation to mention the name of the author carries the implied duty, however, as a matter of contract, not to make such changes in the work as would render the credit line a false attribution of authorship, Granz v. Harris, 198 F.2d 585 (2 Cir.1952).

So far as the Lanham Act is concerned, it is not a substitute for *droit moral* which authors in Europe enjoy. If the licensee may, by contract, distort the recorded work, the Lanham Act does not come into play. If the licensee has no such right by contract, there will be a violation in breach of contract. The Lanham Act can hardly apply literally when the credit line correctly states the work to be that of the plaintiffs which, indeed it is, so far as it goes. The vice complained of is that the truncated version is not what the plaintiffs wrote. But the Lanham Act does not deal with artistic

---

13. Judge Gurfein's concurring opinion suggests that since the gravamen of a complaint under the Lanham Act is that the origin of goods has been falsely described, a legend disclaiming Monty Python's approval of the edited version would preclude violation of that Act. We are doubtful that a few words could erase the indelible impression that is made by a television broadcast, especially since the viewer has no means of comparing the truncated version with the complete work in order to determine for himself the talents of plaintiffs. Furthermore, a disclaimer such as the one originally suggested by Judge Lasker in the exigencies of an impending broadcast last December would go unnoticed by viewers who tuned in to the broadcast a few minutes after it began. * * *

integrity. It only goes to misdescription of origin and the like. See Societe Comptoir De L'Industrie Cotonniere Etablissements Boussac v. Alexander's Dept. Stores, Inc., 299 F.2d 33, 36 (2 Cir.1962).

The misdescription of origin can be dealt with, as Judge Lasker did below, by devising an appropriate legend to indicate that the plaintiffs had not approved the editing of the ABC version.[1] With such a legend, there is no conceivable violation of the Lanham Act. If plaintiffs complain that their artistic integrity is still compromised by the distorted version, their claim does not lie under the Lanham Act, which does not protect the copyrighted work itself but protects only against the misdescription or mislabelling.

So long as it is made clear that the ABC version is not approved by the Monty Python group, there is no misdescription of origin. So far as the content of the broadcast itself is concerned, that is not within the proscription of the Lanham Act when there is no misdescription of the authorship.

I add this brief explanation because I do not believe that the Lanham Act claim necessarily requires the drastic remedy of permanent injunction. That form of ultimate relief must be found in some other fountainhead of equity jurisprudence.

NOTES AND QUESTIONS ON "INTEGRITY"

(1) The theory adopted in *Gilliam* had been presaged in Jaeger v. American Int'l Pictures, Inc., 330 F.Supp. 274 (S.D.N.Y.1971). Plaintiff, a film director, complained of alterations made by the American distributor of his work. The court, denying a motion to dismiss, found it "at least arguable" that the use of plaintiff's name on the altered work was actionable under § 43(a), but it declined to issue a preliminary injunction, noting that the scope of defendant's rights under the distribution contract would be determinative. A similar claim had prevailed under a contract theory in Granz v. Harris, 198 F.2d 585 (2d Cir.1952). The defendant had purchased master tapes of musical performances produced by the plaintiff and later sold records containing abbreviated versions. The harm, the court said, was not in the alterations themselves, but rather in the use of plaintiff's name on the altered versions; since the contract required attribution to the plaintiff, it carried "by implication" a "duty not to sell records which make the required legend a false representation."

Gilliam was cited with approval in National Bank of Commerce v. Shaklee Corp., 503 F.Supp. 533 (W.D.Tex.1980). The case was brought by Heloise Bowles, who wrote newspaper columns and books offering household hints. The defendant, a direct sales organization operating through independent distributors, purchased 100,000 copies of her book "All Around the House" as part of a promotional scheme. Prior to distribution, Shaklee placed advertisements for its products on the cover and at the

---

1. I do not imply that the appropriate legend be shown only at the beginning of the broadcast. That is a matter for the District Court.

conclusion of each chapter. Despite copyright in the name of her publisher, the court held that Heloise had standing as "equitable owner" to claim infringement since her publishing contract provided for royalties and for reassignment of the copyright at the conclusion of the agreement. The court held that the addition of the advertising material infringed the copyright. (On what theory?) It also found Shaklee guilty of unfair competition in causing consumers to believe that Heloise had endorsed its products.[d]

(2) Under the 1976 Act, statutory copyright could subsist in the Monty Python script. Which of the § 106 rights would be infringed by the ABC broadcasts? The performance right, despite the licenses? The right "to prepare derivative works"?

Note, An Author's Artistic Reputation Under the Copyright Act of 1976, 92 Harv.L.Rev. 1490, 1503 (1979), concludes that "[t]he clarifications and revisions of the 1976 Act improve its ability to protect an author against offensive adaptations of her work," chiefly because of the treatment of derivative works and the recognition of divisible copyright.[e] But an author's rights will ultimately be determined by the terms of the author's contracts. How likely is it that an author or artist will have sufficient bargaining power to reserve or restrict the right to modify or alter the work? And of course rights under copyright are of no use to an author who has assigned the whole of the copyright to another.

Damich, The Right of Personality: A Common–Law Basis for the Protection of the Moral Rights of Authors, 23 Ga.L.Rev. 1 (1988), advocates recognition of a right as described in the title, derived from the right of privacy and other sources, that would afford protection to the physical embodiments of artistic creativity as an aspect of the author's personality. But see Morris, Expanding Proprietary Entitlements and the Public Interest in Dissemination of Art, 7 Cardozo Art & Ent.L.J. 269 (1989), arguing that increased rights reduce public access. An economic analysis in support

---

d. A law student complaining of alleged mutilation of his Comment by the editors of a law review failed in an attempt to invoke the rationale of *Gilliam*. The court concluded that the student had not been presented as the author of a work not his own. (The student, in an affidavit criticizing typographical errors that appeared in the article, wrote that the typos were as much the "copy's [*sic*] editors'" fault as his own, "if not moreso [*sic*].") Choe v. Fordham Univ. School of Law, 920 F.Supp. 44 (S.D.N.Y.1995), aff'd, 81 F.3d 319 (2d Cir.1996).

e. Copyright ownership remains the most effective vehicle for protecting an author's artistic vision. When the licensor of the play *Steel Magnolias* learned that a Memphis theater intended to use a man in the role of Truvy (played by Dolly Parton in the movie

version), it ordered the producer to recast the role or lose the right to stage the play: "Robert Harling, the author of the play, does not want that. And considering it is his property, he has every right to disapprove and say no." Yellen, Man Seeks Female Role, But Playwright Says No, New York Times, Sept. 22, 1996, p. 20.

The National Cathedral in Washington and the sculptor who created its renowned entryway bas-relief *Ex Nihilo* depicting the Biblical creation scene invoked copyright to force Warner Brothers to agree to alter a scene in the video version of its film *Devil's Advocate*, in which figures in a substantially similar sculptural work come alive and engage in erotic groping. Clines, Creator of Religious Art Prevails on 'Devil' Film, N.Y. Times, Feb. 14, 1998, p. A5.

of the protection of moral rights, either directly or through copyright, is offered in Hansmann and Santilli, Authors' and Artists' Moral Rights: A Comparative Legal and Economic Analysis, 26 J.Leg.Stud. 95 (1997). Halpern, Of Moral Rights and Moral Righteousness, 1 Marq.Intell.Prop.L.Rev. 65 (1997), cautions that the issue of moral rights will remain unsettled until we reach a broader consensus on the role of the artist in American society.

(3) Suppose an artist sells a painting, assigning the copyright to the buyer. Does the artist have any right to prevent destruction of the work by the owner? Crimi v. Rutgers Presbyterian Church, 194 Misc. 570, 89 N.Y.S.2d 813 (Sup.Ct.1949), indicates that the artist does not. The work was a twenty-six by thirty-five foot fresco on the rear chancel wall of a church. The church had paid $6,800 for the work and taken an assignment of the copyright. Eight years later, without notice to the artist, the work was painted over. (There were indications that some parishioners objected that its portrayal of a bare-chested Christ emphasized physical at the expense of spiritual qualities.) The artist sought restoration of the work, removal from the church at defendant's expense, or damages. Judgment was entered for the defendant. "The time for the artist to have reserved any rights was when he and his attorney participated in the drawing of the contract with the church." [f]

Would the outcome differ if the artist had retained the copyright? Would the artist now prevail under the Visual Artists Rights Act of 1990, infra, which added § 106A? See § 106A(a)(3)(B). What is the purpose of the statutory requirement that the work be "of recognized stature"? To protect elementary school teachers who throw away student artwork? How can "stature" be appraised? See also the special rules in § 113(d) for visual art incorporated into buildings.

(4) Some years ago a furniture manufacturer reproduced in an advertisement Rembrandt's "Aristotle Contemplating the Bust of Homer"—it is of course in the public domain. The painting was altered in that the bust was shown resting on a mirrored dining table and the caption read, "Contemplating a Table." More recently, an insurance company reproduced van Gogh's "The Starry Night," put Snoopy and his doghouse in the fore-

---

f. An article by Schwartz, Ars Moriendi: The Mortality of Art, Art in America, Nov. 1996, p. 72, includes a curious account of the funeral plans made by Japanese industrialist Ryoei Saito, who in 1990 purchased van Gogh's *Portrait of Dr. Gachet* and Renoir's *Au Moulin de la Galette* for some $160 million. Saito later announced that he intended to have the two paintings incinerated with him on his funeral pyre. (He retracted the announcement in response to public outcries, and the two paintings survived his death in 1996.) Kernan, The Great Debate Over Artists' Rights, Washington Post, May 22, 1988, p. F1, recounts famous instances of art mutilation, including an incident in which two Australians purchased a Picasso linocut for $10,000 and cut it into 500 one-inch squares which they offered for $135 apiece. The problem is as old as art. The article reminds readers of the monks who cut a door right through the center of Leonardo da Vinci's *The Last Supper* and the owner of Rembrandt's *Polish Rider* who cut off the horse's legs to fit the painting into frame.

ground, and said, "We're the Old Masters of Financial Security." Would Rembrandt or van Gogh, if living, have any claim for relief?

THE VISUAL ARTISTS RIGHTS ACT

In 1990, moral rights received their first express recognition under federal law when the 1976 Act was amended by the Visual Artists Rights Act, Pub.L. 101–650. The rights created by the addition of § 106A extend only to a "work of visual art" as defined in § 101. What principles might explain the particular selection of subject matter encompassed by the definition? (Note the exclusion of work made for hire.) Authors of works of visual art have the right "to claim authorship" of their work. (Does this include a right to have their name appear on the work?) They can prevent the use of their name on works that they did not create or on a distorted, mutilated, or modified version of their work that would be prejudicial to their honor or reputation. They also have the right to prevent any such distortion, mutilation, or modification, as well as the right to prevent destruction of a work "of recognized stature." § 106A(a).

A substantial limitation on an artist's paternity and integrity rights is imposed in § 106A(c)(3)—use by another in connection with any of the items excluded from the § 101 definition, including posters, motion pictures, books, magazines, newspapers, periodicals, and advertising material is exempt. This point is emphasized in the legislative history. "For example, a newspaper, book, or magazine may include a photograph of a painting or a piece of sculpture. A motion picture may include a scene in an art gallery. The exclusion from the definition of a work of visual art would be of little or no value if these industries could be held liable under section 106A for the manner in which they depict, portray, reproduce, or otherwise make use of such a work. Moreover, because such actions do not affect the single or limited edition copy, imposing liability in these situations would not further the paramount goal of the legislation: to preserve and protect certain categories of original works of art." H.R.Rep. No. 101–514, 101st Cong., 2d Sess. 17–18 (1990). Section 106A would thus be of no help to the artists in Note (4) supra, or to Alberto Vargas in his dispute with *Esquire,* p. 722 supra. There is also the elaborate exception in § 113(d) for works incorporated into buildings, and an addition to § 301 that preempts equivalent rights in works of visual art under state law. § 301(f).

In the first major test of the Visual Artists Rights Act, three artists convinced a district judge to issue a permanent injunction against the removal of a large "walk-through sculpture" located in the lobby of a building; the new owner wanted to get rid of it. The Second Circuit reversed, holding that the sculpture was a work for hire and thus beyond the protection of § 106A. Carter v. Helmsley–Spear, Inc., 71 F.3d 77 (2d Cir.1995), cert. denied, 517 U.S. 1208 (1996).

The rights recognized under § 106A are exercisable only by the author, whether or not the author is the owner of the copyright in the work.

§ 106A(b). For works created after the effective date of the amendment (June 1, 1991), the rights endure for the life of the author. Preexisting works also qualify for protection if the author had not transferred title to the work prior to the amendment, but for these works the § 106A rights will terminate on the expiration of the copyright. § 106A(d).

Although the rights provided under § 106A cannot be transferred, they may be waived by the author in a signed writing that identifies the work and the uses to which the waiver applies. § 106A(e)(1). Concerned that artists might be forced to waive their rights without fair compensation, Congress directed the Copyright Office to undertake a study on the use and effect of the waiver provision. Although artists urged its repeal, a 1996 Copyright Office report entitled Waiver of Moral Rights in Visual Artworks cautioned that it was premature to assess the effect of the provision and concluded that no legislative action was warranted (except perhaps, in light of some broadly-worded waivers, for clarification of the requirement that the waiver specifically identify the use to which it applies). The report is analyzed in Kwall, How Fine Art Fares Post VARA, 1 Marq.Intell.Prop.L.Rev. 1 (1997), also reviewing the slowly accumulating case law under § 106A. See also Cotter, Pragmatism, Economics, and the *Droit Moral*, 76 N.C.L.Rev. 1 (1997), cautiously favoring a waivable right.

The Act is analyzed in Damich, The Visual Artists Rights Act of 1990: Toward a System of Moral Rights Protection for Visual Art, 39 Cath. U.L.Rev. 945 (1990). The effect of the Visual Artists Rights Act on the bargaining between producers and consumers of art is discussed in Ver-Steeg, Federal Moral Rights for Visual Artists: Contract Theory and Analysis, 67 Wash.L.Rev. 827 (1992). Yanover, The Precarious Balance: Moral Rights, Parody, and Fair Use, 14 Cardozo Arts & Ent.L.J. 79 (1996), considers the potential conflict between integrity rights under § 106A and parody as fair use under § 107.

MORAL RIGHTS AND THE COLORIZATION OF FILMS

The motion picture studios have long been a vocal opponent of moral rights. The studios argue that recognition of moral rights would disrupt the production of films and hamper their ability to adapt movies for the video and broadcast markets. Producers, directors, writers, and cinematographers all at various times urged Congress to legislate in favor of creators' rights in motion pictures, although the unanimity dissipated on the issue of who in the creative process should be entitled to such rights. See 39 Pat., Tm. & Copyr.J. (BNA) 206 (1990). Although artistic objections have also been aimed at editing techniques such as "panning and scanning," which selects portions of the original image to fit onto television screens, and "time compression," which speeds up movies to fit broadcast time constraints, the lightening rod for the debate has been the colorization of black and white films. The campaign to block colorization was waged on two fronts. The first attacked the acceptance of colorized films as copyrightable derivative works. The colorizers won. See p. 79 supra.

The second and more flamboyant front tried to advance the moral rights of film creators who did not want their classic works defaced (as they viewed it) by color. Such film greats as Woody Allen, Frank Capra, Walter Huston, and Jimmy Stewart were passionately engaged. There were two years of bills, hearings, and panels. The only legislative outcome was the creation of the National Film Preservation Board by Pub.L. No. 100–446 (1988). The Board can select up to 25 films each year for inclusion on the National Film Registry. Altered versions of films on the Registry were required to bear labels disclosing that the film had been altered. When the Board was reauthorized in 1992, Pub.L. No. 102–307, the labelling requirement for altered films was eliminated, but the seal of the Registry may be used only on pristine prints approved by the Librarian of Congress.

Meanwhile in France, director John Huston and later his children sought an injunction against the showing on French television of a colorized version of his 1950 film "The Asphalt Jungle." 37 Pat., Tm. & Copyr.J. (BNA) 165 (1988). The initial injunction was overturned on appeal in favor of a disclaimer; the opinion said that French law should not interfere with the contract between Huston and the American movie studio. 38 id. 295 (1989). In 1991 the Huston heirs finally prevailed in the highest civil court in France, winning an injunction against broadcast of the colorized version on the ground that it would violate Huston's moral rights. 42 id. 236 (1991).

In this country, the last word may be Ted Turner's, who paid $1.3 billion for the entire M–G–M collection: "The last time I checked I owned those films." See Kohs, Paint Your Wagon—Please! Colorization, Copyright, and the Search for Moral Rights, 40 Fed.Comm.L.J. 1, 2 (1988). But in a few cases, contract rights have prevailed. Woody Allen, for example, apparently retained the right to prevent "panning and scanning" of his films. See 38 Pat., Tm. & Copyr.J. (BNA) 680 (1989). And we have been spared a colorized version of *Citizen Kane* because of the total artistic control written into Orson Welles' 1939 contract with RKO Pictures. Masters, Turner Won't Colorize "Kane," Wash. Post, Feb. 15, 1989, p. C1.[g]

Colorization provides the springboard for a major skeptical inquiry into the validity of integrity rights in Beyer, Intentionalism, Art, and the Suppression of Innovation: Film Colorization and the Philosophy of Moral Rights, 82 Nw.U.L.Rev. 1011 (1988).

STATE "MORAL RIGHTS" STATUTES

(1) The California Art Preservation Act, Cal.Civil Code § 987, took effect on Jan. 1, 1980. It begins with the following declaration:

g. The rush to colorize movies may finally be over. Old movies, even colorized ones, are not much in demand by broadcast stations faced with competition from cable channels specializing in old films, and the latter won't touch a colorized version. Even Ted Turner's colorizing operation has apparently shut down. Carter, Colorized Films Losing Appeal, New York Times, Dec. 19, 1994, p. D10. Similar issues, however, are now surfacing in connection with the digital "restoration" of old films. See Pollack, Digital Film Restoration Raises Questions, N.Y. Times, Mar. 16, 1998, p. D1.

The Legislature hereby finds and declares that the physical alteration or destruction of fine art, which is an expression of the artist's personality, is detrimental to the artist's reputation, and artists therefore have an interest in protecting their works of fine art against any such alteration or destruction; and that there is also a public interest in preserving the integrity of cultural and artistic creations.

The substance of the Act is contained in subsections (c) and (d):

(c) *Mutilation, alteration, or destruction of a work.* (1) No person, except an artist who owns and possesses a work of fine art which the artist has created, shall intentionally commit, or authorize the intentional commission of, any physical defacement, mutilation, alteration, or destruction of a work of fine art.

(2) In addition to the prohibitions contained in paragraph (1), no person who frames, conserves, or restores a work of fine art shall commit, or authorize the commission of, any physical defacement, mutilation, alteration, or destruction of a work of fine art by any act constituting gross negligence. For purposes of this section, the term "gross negligence" shall mean the exercise of so slight a degree of care as to justify the belief that there was an indifference to the particular work of fine art.

(d) *Authorship.* The artist shall retain at all times the right to claim authorship, or, for a just and valid reason, to disclaim authorship of his or her work of fine art.

The Act protects only "fine art," defined in subsection (b) as "an original painting, sculpture, or drawing, or an original work of art in glass, of recognized quality, but shall not include work prepared under contract for commercial use by its purchaser." (In what sense is "original" to be taken?) "Commercial use" is defined as "fine art created under a work-for-hire arrangement for use in advertising, magazines, newspapers, or other print and electronic media." What is the justification for this exclusion? And what of the requirement that the work be "of recognized quality"—does it raise difficulties akin to those foreseen by Justice Holmes in *Bleistein*, p. 53 supra? The Act in subsection (f) states that "the trier of fact shall rely on the opinions of artists, art dealers, collectors of fine art, curators of art museums" and others in determining "recognized quality."

What is the effect of subsection (d)? Can the artist insist that her name appear on the work? And what "just and valid" reasons justify a disclaimer of authorship—would anything other than alteration suffice?

The Act offers injunctive relief, actual and punitive damages, and attorney's fees. (How might damages be measured in instances of alteration or destruction?) The statutory rights subsist in the artist or "his or her heir, beneficiary, devisee, or personal representative" until fifty years after the artist's death. But the rights and duties created by the Act may be waived by an instrument in writing signed by the artist. § 987(g)(3).

An article in the *Los Angeles Times* reports on some of the litigation under the California statute. The article was prompted by a suit initiated by an artist against a framer and others in connection with a dark and blotchy varnish that had been applied to his still lifes of fruits and vegetables done for a San Diego hotel. "The subtle color nuances were totally destroyed," according to artist Brian Ura. "I'm embarrassed to have people see my name on them." The article also reports on a small judgment won by an artist after his ex-girlfriend ripped up a painting he had given her and scribbled profanities on the pieces before mailing them back. In another case an artist won a settlement from a collector who removed $50 bills that were part of the artist's avant-garde work, apparently in order to spend them. It also describes the 18–year battle by Alexander Calder to restore a mobile entitled *Pittsburgh* that had been donated by a private collector to the city's airport. The city repainted the black and white mobile in the green and gold colors of the county and added a motor. It was finally restored after Calder's death. Lerner, Painter Going to the Mat Over Changes in Artwork for Hotel, L.A. Times, Mar. 5, 1990, p. B3.

Can the California Art Preservation Act survive a challenge under § 301? Is a right to claim or disclaim authorship, or a right to prevent mutilation or destruction, "equivalent" to copyright? What of a right to prevent "alteration"? And when invoked by living artists to protect works of "visual art," can any applications of the statute survive preemption under § 301(f) as not "equivalent" to the rights conferred by § 106A?

For comments on the California Act, see Petrovich, Artists' Statutory *Droit Moral* in California: A Critical Appraisal, 15 Loy.L.A.L.Rev. 29 (1981); Note, Artworks and American Law: The California Art Preservation Act, 61 B.U.L.Rev. 1201 (1981).

Massachusetts has a statute, Mass.Gen.Laws Ann. c. 231, § 85S, that is similar to California's but of wider reach. It encompasses "any original work of visual or graphic art of any media which shall include, but not limited to, any painting, print, drawing, sculpture, craft object, photograph, audio or video tape, film, hologram, or any combination thereof, of recognized quality." Other statutes on the California model include Connecticut, Gen.Stat.Ann. §§ 42–116s and 116t; New Mexico, Stat.Ann. §§ 13–4B–1 et seq.; and Pennsylvania, Stat.Ann. tit. 73, §§ 2101–2110.

(2) New York has also enacted a "moral rights" statute. Its Artists' Authorship Rights Act, N.Y.Arts. & Cult.Aff.L. § 14.03, took effect in 1984. Like the California Act, it grants to the artist "the right to claim authorship, or, for just and valid reason, to disclaim authorship," but it also expressly provides that this "shall include the right of the artist to have his or her name appear on or in connection with such work as the artist." § 14.03(2).

"Integrity" rights are protected only indirectly under the New York statute. Section 14.03(1) provides that no person "shall knowingly display in a place accessible to the public or publish a work of fine art * * * or a reproduction thereof in an altered, defaced, mutilated or modified form if the work is displayed, published or reproduced as being the work of the artist, or under circumstances under which it would reasonably be regarded as being the work of the artist, and damage to the artist's reputation is reasonably likely to result therefrom." Can liability be avoided by removing the artist's name from the altered work? But what of the statutory right to claim authorship? Would a disclaimer suffice? The Act excludes works "prepared under contract for advertising or trade use unless the contract so provides," and the right to redress, in an action for "legal and injunctive relief," runs only to the artist.

Statutes on the New York model include Louisiana, Rev.Stat.Ann. § 51:2151 et seq.; Maine, Rev.Stat.Ann. tit. 27, § 303; New Jersey, Stat. Ann. 2A:24A–1 et seq.; and Rhode Island, Gen.L. § 5–62–2 et seq.

See Taubman, New York Artists' Authorship Rights Act of 1983: Waiver and Fair Use, 3 Cardozo Arts & Ent.L.J. 113 (1984); Damich, The New York Artists' Authorship Rights Act: A Comparative Critique, 84 Colum.L.Rev. 1733 (1984).

(3) The New York statute was successfully invoked in Wojnarowicz v. American Family Ass'n, 745 F.Supp. 130 (S.D.N.Y.1990), by an artist whose works had been presented at an exhibition supported by the National Endowment for the Arts. The defendant, objecting to the sexually explicit images in plaintiff's works, published a pamphlet attacking the use of public funds for such purposes; the pamphlet included fragments from 14 of the plaintiff's works. The court upheld the statute against a claim of preemption under § 301. After concluding that attribution of the modified images to the plaintiff was a violation of the New York law, it enjoined further distribution of the pamphlet. In a footnote the court noted that Congress was then considering the Visual Artists Rights Act. Would § 106A afford any relief to the plaintiff? Would the Act, through § 301(f), preempt the plaintiff's claim for relief under the state statute?

Sculptor Richard Serra tried valiantly to fend off a proposal to dismantle his "Tilted Arc," a rusty slab 12 feet high and 120 feet long that traversed the plaza of the Javits Federal Office Building in lower Manhattan. It was unpopular with many of the local workers. He was unsuccessful in his contention that the work was "site-specific" and that its removal would infringe his first amendment rights. Serra v. United States General Services Admin., 847 F.2d 1045 (2d Cir.1988). The opinion does not mention moral rights or the New York statute. (Could they have any force against the United States Government, which owns the work?) See Serra, "Tilted Arc" Destroyed, 14 Nova L.Rev. 385 (1990). Would Serra now have a claim under § 106A?

DROIT DE SUITE

Article 14*ter* of the Berne Convention (Paris Revision, 1971) provides:

> 1. The author, or, after his death, the persons or institutions authorized by national legislation shall, with respect to original

works of art and original manuscripts of writers and composers, enjoy the inalienable right to an interest in any sale of the work subsequent to the first transfer by the author of the work.

2.   The protection provided by the preceding paragraph may be claimed in a country of the Union only if legislation in the country to which the author belongs so permits, and to the extent permitted by the country where this protection is claimed.

3.   The procedure for collection and the amounts shall be matters for determination by national legislation.

This article acknowledges the *droit de suite*—the right of an artist to share in the proceeds of subsequent resales of the work.   The *droit de suite* in one form or another is recognized in a number of foreign countries.[h]

In 1976 California adopted the *droit de suite*.   Cal.Civil Code § 986. Subsection (a) of the California Resale Royalties Act provides in part:

(a) Whenever a work of fine art is sold and the seller resides in California or the sale takes place in California, the seller or the seller's agent shall pay to the artist of such work of fine art or to such artist's agent 5 percent of the amount of such sale.   The right of the artist to receive an amount equal to 5 percent of the amount of such sale may be waived only by a contract in writing providing for an amount in excess of 5 percent of the amount of such sale.   An artist may assign the right to collect the royalty payment provided by this section to another individual or entity. However, the assignment shall not have the effect of creating a waiver prohibited by this subdivision.

The obligation to pay resale royalties does not apply if the resale price is less than $1,000, or less than the original price paid by the seller. § 986(b).   If the artist cannot be found, the royalty must be paid to the California Arts Council;   the artist then has seven years in which to file a claim with the Council.   Upon the death of the artist, the royalty right "shall inure to his or her heirs, legatees, or personal representative, until the 20th anniversary of the death of the artist."   § 986(a).

NOTES AND QUESTIONS

(1) What is the justification for the *droit de suite*?   Why do the creators of "fine art" require economic rights beyond those furnished by copyright?

(2) Consider the various factors that affect the resale price of art.   Which support a claim by the artist to a share of any appreciation?

---

h. The European Union is considering a directive that would require resale royalty rights for artists. Eleven EU members already have resale royalty legislation, but only eight are said to enforce the right. BNA Pat.,Tm. & Copyr.L. Daily (Apr. 29, 1997). Some of the European versions are examined in Note, The Applicability of the *Droit de Suite* in the United States, 3 B.C. Int'l & Comp.L.Rev. 433 (1980).

(3) Who are the chief beneficiaries of the *droit de suite*? Is there any reason to expect that resales will yield royalties that correlate with private equities or public policy? A study by Camp, Art Resale Rights and the Art Resale Market, 28 Bull.Copyr.Soc. 146 (1980), concludes, on the basis of an analysis of auctions at Sotheby Parke Bernet, that most of the benefits would go to a few important artists.

The justification for the *droit de suite* is examined in Price, Government Policy and Economic Security for Artists: The Case of the *Droit de Suite*, 77 Yale L.J. 1333, 1366 (1968), which concludes that "the *droit de suite* rewards the wrong painters with probably inconsequential amounts of money at the wrong time in their lives," and suggests legislative alternatives. The private alternative—contract—is discussed in Solomon and Gill, Federal and State Resale Royalty Legislation: "What Hath Art Wrought?," 26 U.C.L.A. L.Rev. 322 (1978).

(4) Is the California Resale Royalties Act preempted by federal copyright law? An art dealer challenged the constitutionality of the statute soon after it took effect. In Morseburg v. Balyon, 621 F.2d 972 (9th Cir.), cert. denied, 449 U.S. 983 (1980), the Ninth Circuit, in an opinion treating only the 1909 Act, found the Supreme Court's decision in Goldstein v. California controlling: "This is an additional right similar to the additional protection afforded by California's anti-pirating statute upheld in *Goldstein*." (*Goldstein* is in fact clearly inapposite, is it not?) The court rejected the dealer's contention that the Act contravened the first sale doctrine in § 27 of the 1909 Act (now § 109(a)): "The work can be transferred without restriction. The fact that a resale may create a liability to the creator artist or a state instrumentality and, at the same time, constitute an exercise of a right guaranteed by the Copyright Act does not make the former a legal restraint on the latter." The court also rejected constitutional challenges premised on the contracts and due process clauses.

Can the California Resale Royalties Act survive § 301 of the 1976 Act? Is the *droit de suite* "equivalent" to a distribution right? Compare the preemption analysis in Katz, Copyright Preemption Under the Copyright Act of 1976: The Case of *Droit de Suite*, 47 Geo.Wash.L.Rev. 200 (1978), with Note, The California Resale Royalties Act as a Test Case for Preemption, 81 Colum.L.Rev. 1315 (1981). The legislative history of the Visual Artists Rights Act says that resale royalty rights are not preempted under § 301(f). H.R.Rep. No. 101–514, 101st Cong., 2d Sess. 21 (1990).

As part of the Visual Artists Rights Act, the Copyright Office was directed to report on the feasibility of implementing a federal resale royalty system. In a report presented in December, 1992, the Copyright Office concluded that there was not sufficient justification for establishing a federal resale royalty right. The report noted that most artists do not have a resale market for their work, and a right to resale royalties might depress prices in the original market in anticipation of future royalty obligations. For comments on the report, see 40 J.Copyr.Soc. 241 et seq. (1992).

SECTION 2. PUBLICITY AND PRIVACY

Haelan Laboratories, Inc. v. Topps Chewing Gum, Inc.

United States Court of Appeals, Second Circuit, 1953.
202 F.2d 866.
Certiorari denied, 346 U.S. 816, 74 S.Ct. 26.

■ Before SWAN, CHIEF JUDGE, and CLARK and FRANK, CIRCUIT JUDGES.

■ FRANK, CIRCUIT JUDGE. After a trial without a jury, the trial judge dismissed the complaint on the merits. The plaintiff maintains that defendant invaded plaintiff's exclusive right to use the photographs of leading baseball-players. Probably because the trial judge ruled against plaintiff's legal contentions, some of the facts were not too clearly found.

1. So far as we can now tell, there were instances of the following kind:

(a). The plaintiff, engaged in selling chewing-gum, made a contract with a ball-player providing that plaintiff for a stated term should have the exclusive right to use the ball-player's photograph in connection with the sales of plaintiff's gum; the ball-player agreed not to grant any other gum manufacturer a similar right during such term; the contract gave plaintiff an option to extend the term for a designated period.

(b). Defendant, a rival chewing-gum manufacturer, knowing of plaintiff's contract, deliberately induced the ball-player to authorize defendant, by a contract with defendant, to use the player's photograph in connection with the sales of defendant's gum either during the original or extended term of plaintiff's contract, and defendant did so use the photograph.

Defendant argues that, even if such facts are proved, they show no actionable wrong, for this reason: The contract with plaintiff was no more than a release by the ball-player to plaintiff of the liability which, absent the release, plaintiff would have incurred in using the ball-player's photograph, because such a use, without his consent, would be an invasion of his right of privacy under Section 50 and Section 51 of the New York Civil Rights Law; this statutory right of privacy is personal, not assignable; therefore, plaintiff's contract vested in plaintiff no "property" right or other legal interest which defendant's conduct invaded.

Both parties agree, and so do we, that, on the facts here, New York "law" governs. And we shall assume, for the moment, that, under the New York decisions, defendant correctly asserts that any such contract between plaintiff and a ball-player, in so far as it merely authorized plaintiff to use the player's photograph, created nothing but a release of liability. On that basis, were there no more to the contract, plaintiff would have no actionable claim against defendant. But defendant's argument neglects the fact that, in the contract, the ball-player also promised not to give similar releases to others. If defendant, knowing of the contract, deliberately induced the ball-player to break that promise, defendant behaved tortiously. See, e.g., Hornstein v. Podwitz, 254 N.Y. 443, 173 N.E. 674; 6 Corbin, Contracts (1951) Sec. 1470.

Some of defendant's contracts were obtained by it through its agent, Players Enterprise, Inc.; others were obtained by Russell Publishing Co., acting independently, and were then assigned by Russell to defendant. Since Players acted as defendant's agent, defendant is liable for any breach of plaintiff's contracts thus induced by Players. However, as Russell did not act as defendant's agent when Russell, having knowledge of plaintiff's contract with a player, by subsequently contracting with that player, induced a breach of plaintiff's contract, defendant is not liable for any breach so induced; nor did there arise such a liability against defendant for such an induced breach when defendant became the assignee of one of those Russell contracts.

2. The foregoing covers the situations where defendant, by itself or through its agent, induced breaches. But in those instances where Russell induced the breach, we have a different problem; and that problem also confronts us in instances—alleged in one paragraph of the complaint and to which the trial judge in his opinion also (although not altogether clearly) refers—where defendant, "with knowledge of plaintiff's exclusive rights," used a photograph of a ball-player without his consent during the term of his contract with plaintiff.

With regard to such situations, we must consider defendant's contention that none of plaintiff's contracts created more than a release of liability, because a man has no legal interest in the publication of his picture other than his right of privacy, i.e., a personal and non-assignable right not to have his feelings hurt by such a publication.

A majority of this court rejects this contention. We think that, in addition to and independent of that right of privacy (which in New York derives from statute), a man has a right in the publicity value of his photograph, i.e., the right to grant the exclusive privilege of publishing his picture, and that such a grant may validly be made "in gross," i.e., without an accompanying transfer of a business or of anything else. Whether it be labelled a "property" right is immaterial; for here, as often elsewhere, the tag "property" simply symbolizes the fact that courts enforce a claim which has pecuniary worth.

This right might be called a "right of publicity." For it is common knowledge that many prominent persons (especially actors and ball-players), far from having their feelings bruised through public exposure of their likenesses, would feel sorely deprived if they no longer received money for authorizing advertisements, popularizing their countenances, displayed in newspapers, magazines, busses, trains and subways. This right of publicity would usually yield them no money unless it could be made the subject of an exclusive grant which barred any other advertiser from using their pictures. * * *

We said above that defendant was not liable for a breach of any of plaintiff's contracts induced by Russell, and did not become thus liable (for an induced breach) when there was assigned to defendant a contract between Russell and a ball-player, although Russell, in making that contract, knowingly induced a breach of contract with plaintiff. But plaintiff, in its capacity as exclusive grantee of a player's "right of publicity," has a valid claim against defendant if defendant used that player's photograph during the term of plaintiff's grant and with knowledge of it. It is no defense to such a claim that defendant is the assignee of a subsequent contract between that player and Russell, purporting to make a grant to Russell or its assignees. For the prior grant to plaintiff renders that subsequent grant invalid during the period of the grant (including an exercised option) to plaintiff, but not thereafter.[5] * * *

If, upon further exploration of the facts, the trial court, in the light of our opinion, concludes that defendant is liable, it will, of course, ascertain damages and decide what equitable relief is justified.

Reversed and remanded.

SWAN, CHIEF JUDGE (concurring in part). I agree that the cause should be reversed and remanded, and I concur in so much of the opinion as deals with the defendant's liability for intentionally inducing a ball-player to breach a contract which gave plaintiff the exclusive privilege of using his picture. * * *

NOTES AND QUESTIONS ON PUBLICITY AND PRIVACY RIGHTS

(1) In *Haelan*, Judge Frank gave a name to an emerging right and launched it on a lively course. Why did he think it necessary to move beyond the New York privacy statute, which offers monetary and injunctive relief to "[a]ny person whose name, portrait, picture or voice is used within this state for advertising purposes or for the purposes of trade * * *."? N.Y. Civ. Rights Law § 51. (See also § 50, which makes such conduct a misdemeanor!)

Our interest in privacy here is confined to the fourth of Dean Prosser's famous four-fold classification of this tort—a right against the commercial appropriation of one's identity, usually through use of a name or likeness. The other three are (1) a right against intrusion; (2) a right against unwarranted disclosure of private facts; and (3) a right against disclosure of information that puts one in a "false light." These have their own development and problems,[a] outlined in J. McCarthy, The Rights of Publici-

---

5. Since plaintiff asserts that, in all instances, defendant acted with knowledge of plaintiff's contracts, we need not consider whether and how far defendant would be liable to plaintiff, absent such knowledge, when, during the term of plaintiff's contract, defendant used a player's photograph without inducing a breach of that contract.

a. The right against intrusion refers largely to physical intrusions, or surveillance and harassment, and is the least problematic. Protection against the harmful disclosure of truthful private facts (e.g., a long-past criminal record) is readily overcome by a showing of newsworthiness. The classic case is Sidis ty and Privacy, ch. 1. McCarthy's overall emphasis is on the commercial appropriation tort, which is also the emphasis of this section.

The privacy tort is often thought of as protecting ordinary people who may have hurt feelings to be salved. For celebrities, publicity is something they may seek, yet at the same time wish to control. This is the essence of the "publicity right." See Felcher & Rubin, Privacy, Publicity and the Portrayal of Real People by the Media, 88 Yale L.J. 1577 (1979). But cf. McCarthy § 4.3 (non-celebrities can have publicity rights too). More than a dozen states, including New York and California, acknowledge the right by statute; in a number of other states it has been recognized as part of the common law. See generally Restatement, Third, Unfair Competition §§ 46–49 (1995).[b]

Typical of routine publicity cases are the many decisions enjoining the unauthorized use of a celebrity's name or likeness on merchandise such as posters, T–shirts, and buttons. See, e.g., Factors Etc., Inc. v. Pro Arts, Inc., 579 F.2d 215 (2d Cir.1978), cert. denied, 440 U.S. 908 (1979) (Elvis Presley poster); Bi–Rite Enterprises, Inc. v. Button Master, 555 F.Supp. 1188 (S.D.N.Y.1983) (likeness of rock musicians on buttons); Winterland Concessions Co. v. Sileo, 528 F.Supp. 1201 (N.D.Ill.1981), aff'd, 735 F.2d 257 (7th Cir.1984) (T–shirts). But cf. Allison v. Vintage Sports Plaques, 136 F.3d 1443 (11th Cir.1998), applying a "first sale" limitation on the common law right of publicity to protect a defendant who mounted and sold trading cards purchased from licensed manufacturers.

(2) The New York Court of Appeals has held (contrary to cases such as *Haelan*) that the New York privacy statute preempts recognition of any common law rights against commercial exploitation, notably in Arrington v. New York Times Co., 55 N.Y.2d 433, 449 N.Y.S.2d 941, 434 N.E.2d 1319 (1982), and Stephano v. News Group Pubs. Inc., 64 N.Y.2d 174, 485

---

v. F–R Pub. Corp., 113 F.2d 806 (2d Cir.), cert. denied, 311 U.S. 711 (1940). Its abolition has been proposed by Zimmerman, Requiem for a Heavyweight: A Farewell to Warren and Brandeis' Privacy Tort, 68 Corn. L.Rev. 291 (1983). The "false light" branch is so close to defamation that the Supreme Court in Time, Inc. v. Hill, 385 U.S. 374 (1967), held that its applicability is to be tested by the constitutional standards of New York Times Co. v. Sullivan, 376 U.S. 254 (1964). Zimmerman would also sharply confine the false light tort. See False Light Invasion of Privacy: The Light that Failed, 64 N.Y.U.L.Rev. 364 (1989).

Another related tort is the intentional infliction of emotional distress. Its invocation by public figures was severely curtailed by the Supreme Court in Hustler Magazine v. Falwell, 485 U.S. 46 (1988).

It is routine for plaintiffs who think they are injured by publicity, especially in scab-

rous publications like *Hustler*, to sue with counts in several or all of false light privacy, defamation, emotional distress, and right of publicity. Vivid examples are Lerman v. Flynt Distrib. Co., 745 F.2d 123 (2d Cir. 1984), cert. denied, 471 U.S. 1054 (1985) ($10 million verdict in favor of author Jackie Collins, negligently misidentified as the topless actress in a magazine photograph, reversed on first amendment grounds); Douglass v. Hustler Magazine, Inc., 769 F.2d 1128 (7th Cir.1985), cert. denied, 475 U.S. 1094 (1986) (false light privacy claim recognized when photographs of actress intended for *Playboy* appeared instead in *Hustler*).

b. The *Restatement*'s formulation of the publicity right is critically reviewed in Goodenough, Go Fish: Evaluating the Restatement's Formulation of the Law of Publicity, 47 S.Car.L.Rev. 709 (1996).

N.Y.S.2d 220, 474 N.E.2d 580 (1984), but with a footnote caveat on "whether the statute would also control assignment, transfer or descent of publicity rights." See Pirone v. MacMillan, Inc., 894 F.2d 579 (2d Cir. 1990) (there are no descendible rights under the New York statute). As for an assignee's standing, New York cases have consistently treated the statutory right as personal and non-assignable.

Rhode Island has a statute similar to New York's. *Life* magazine in 1945 published a photograph of a sailor kissing a nurse in Times Square in celebration of V–J day. The picture became famous. Forty years later (having learned the identity of the sailor) *Life* offered a limited-edition print at $1600! Is the use "for purposes of trade" and hence in violation of the statute? See Mendonsa v. Time, Inc., 678 F.Supp. 967 (D.R.I.1988).

(3) What policies support the recognition of an exclusive publicity right? An incentive rationale similar to that underlying copyright? Prevention of unjust enrichment? A regard for personal integrity and autonomy? Consider whether these or other interests justify protection in the following situations, some of which are discussed in the cases that follow:

(a) Johnny Carson, then host of "The Tonight Show," complains that the phrase "Here's Johnny" (which he employed nightly as an introduction) is being used by a defendant engaged in renting and selling "Here's Johnny" portable toilets. See Carson v. Here's Johnny Portable Toilets, Inc., 698 F.2d 831 (6th Cir.1983). Elroy "Crazylegs" Hirsch, an All–American football player at the University of Wisconsin, later a star with the Los Angeles Rams and eventually athletic director at Wisconsin, complains of the use of the name "Crazylegs" on a women's shaving gel. Hirsch v. S.C. Johnson & Son, Inc., 90 Wis.2d 379, 280 N.W.2d 129 (1979).

(b) Plaintiff, a well-known race car driver, has come to be associated with a distinctively decorated car. The R.J. Reynolds Tobacco Co. used a photograph of the car in a television commercial. Plaintiff's facial features were not visible in the photograph. After altering the photo by placing the word "Winston" on the car, defendant added a series of comic strip style "balloons"; one emanating from the plaintiff's car read, "Did you know that Winston tastes good, like a cigarette should?" See Motschenbacher v. R.J. Reynolds Tobacco Co., 498 F.2d 821 (9th Cir.1974).

(c) A group of professional athletes seek to enjoin the distribution of games that, while making no use of their names or likenesses in promotions, do include the names as part of the contents of the game, together with accurate data on the players' careers. See Uhlaender v. Henricksen, 316 F.Supp. 1277 (D.Minn.1970); Palmer v. Schonhorn Enterprises, Inc., 96 N.J.Super. 72, 232 A.2d 458 (1967).

(d) In a book entitled "Golf With the Masters," containing such headings as "Hitting Your Tee Shots With Sam Snead," various references are made to Ben Hogan. His name appears on the jacket. In a section on "Hogan's Secret?" the author gives his version of Hogan's secret to success in two pages of text. On five pages there are nine photographs of Hogan in various phases of his putting stroke. See Hogan v. A.S. Barnes & Co., 114 U.S.P.Q. 314 (Pa.Ct.C.P.1957).

(e) In Apple Corps Ltd. v. Leber, 229 U.S.P.Q. 1015 (Cal.Super.1986), Leber had created a production that featured Beatles imitators performing Beatles songs. It was a great success, grossing $45 million. Apple, for the Beatles, alleging invasion of publicity rights and unfair competition, prevailed on both theories. The following facts come from a helpful Note, Apple Corp. v. Leber: Did Beatlemania Infringe the Beatles' Right of Publicity?, 17 Sw.U.L.Rev. 755 (1988), and do not appear in the report of the decision: (1) Leber got a license to perform the songs from the copyright owner, the British conglomerate ATV; (2) the rights to exploit their names and likenesses had been assigned by the Beatles to plaintiff Apple Corps, the stock of which is owned by the Beatles and their heirs; (3) ATV told defendants this, and demanded and received an indemnity agreement lest it should be sued for a contributory violation of the Beatles' publicity rights. Damages with interest amounted to $12 million. As for unfair competition, the judge said that viewers might be confused into thinking that the Beatles had authorized or approved the production. See also Estate of Presley v. Russen, 513 F.Supp. 1339 (D.N.J.1981), p. 674 supra.

(f) What about the use of deceptive look-alikes in advertisements? A look-alike of Jackie Onassis was included with some consenting celebrities in an advertisement depicting a group of guests at a fictional wedding of the "Dior family." The resemblance was held close enough to constitute a "portrait or picture" within the New York statute. Onassis v. Christian Dior–New York, Inc., 122 Misc.2d 603, 472 N.Y.S.2d 254 (S.Ct.1984), aff'd, 110 A.D.2d 1095, 488 N.Y.S.2d 943 (1985). When Woody Allen had a similar grievance, Judge Motley had doubts about the applicability of the New York statute, but found enough likelihood of confusion to invoke § 43(a) of the Lanham Act. Allen v. National Video, Inc., 610 F.Supp. 612 (S.D.N.Y.1985). Another Woody Allen case was decided the same way by the same judge. A disclaimer was considered inadequate. Allen v. Men's World Outlet, Inc., 679 F.Supp. 360 (S.D.N.Y.1988). Is Judge Motley correct in hesitating to apply the language of the New York statute to look-alikes?

(4) On the scope and rationale of the publicity right see, in addition to McCarthy, supra, Ausness, The Right of Publicity: A "Haystack in a Hurricane," 55 Temple L.Q. 977 (1982); Halpern, The Right of Publicity: Commercial Exploitation of the Associative Value of Personality, 39 Vand. L.Rev. 1199 (1986). An attempt to define the scope of the right in terms of the purpose of the appropriation is made in Hetherington, Direct Commercial Exploitation of Identity: A New Age for the Right of Publicity, 17 Colum.–VLA J.L. & Arts 1 (1992). Consult also the critique of the publicity right in Lange, Recognizing the Public Domain, 44 Law & Contemp. Prob. (No. 4) 147 (1981).

(5) Would the rationale of the publicity cases extend to the unauthorized commercial exploitation of *corporate* names and symbols—to the *Boston*

Hockey case, for instance?   Compare Winner, Right of Identity: Right of Publicity and Protection for a Trademark's "Persona", 71 Trademark Rep. 193 (1981), with Denicola, Institutional Publicity Rights: An Analysis of the Merchandising of Famous Trade Symbols, 62 N.C.L. Rev. 603 (1984).

Martin Luther King, Jr., Center for Social Change, Inc. v. American Heritage Products, Inc.

United States Court of Appeals, Eleventh Circuit, 1983.
694 F.2d 674.

■ Before HENDERSON and CLARK, CIRCUIT JUDGES, and TUTTLE, SENIOR CIRCUIT JUDGE.

PER CURIAM:

In our previous consideration of this case, The Martin Luther King, Jr., Center for Social Change, Inc. v. American Heritage Products, Inc., No. 81–7264 (11th Cir., Apr. 1, 1982), we certified the following questions to the Supreme Court of Georgia pursuant to Georgia Code Annotated § 24–3902 permitting such procedure:

(1) Is the "right to publicity" recognized in Georgia as a right distinct from the right to privacy?

(2) If the answer to question (1) is affirmative, does the "right to publicity" survive the death of its owner? Specifically, is the right inheritable and devisable?

(3) If the answer to question (2) is also affirmative, must the owner have commercially exploited the right before it can survive his death?

(4) Assuming affirmative answers to questions (1), (2) and (3), what is the guideline to be followed in defining commercial exploitation and what are the evidentiary prerequisites to a showing of commercial exploitation?

The Supreme Court of Georgia, The Martin Luther King, Jr., Center for Social Change, Inc. v. American Heritage Products, Inc., 250 Ga. 135, 296 S.E.2d 697 (1982), has answered questions (1) and (2) affirmatively and question (3) in the negative in an opinion attached hereto as Exhibit A.

Pursuant to this opinion, the opinion of the Supreme Court of Georgia, and that court's answers to the first three certified questions, we reverse the judgment of the district court and remand for further proceedings.

Reversed and Remanded.

Exhibit A

In the Supreme Court of Georgia

Decided: Oct. 28, 1982

38748. The MARTIN LUTHER KING, JR., CENTER FOR SO-CIAL CHANGE, INC., et al. v. AMERICAN HERITAGE PRODUCTS, INC., et al.

■ HILL, PRESIDING JUSTICE.

These are certified questions regarding the "right of publicity". The certification comes from the United States Court of Appeals for the Eleventh Circuit. Code Ann. § 24–3902; see Miree v. United States of America, 242 Ga. 126, 131–133, 249 S.E.2d 573 (1978). The facts upon which the questions arise are as follows:

The plaintiffs are the Martin Luther King, Jr. Center for Social Change (the Center), Coretta Scott King, as administratrix of Dr. King's estate, and Motown Record Corporation, the assignee of the rights to several of Dr. King's copyrighted speeches. Defendant James F. Bolen is the sole proprietor of a business known as B & S Sales, which manufactures and sells various plastic products as funeral accessories. Defendant James E. Bolen, the son of James F. Bolen, developed the concept of marketing a plastic bust of Dr. Martin Luther King, Jr., and formed a company, B & S Enterprises, to sell the busts, which would be manufactured by B & S Sales. B & S Enterprises was later incorporated under the name of American Heritage Products, Inc.

Although Bolen sought the endorsement and participation of the Martin Luther King, Jr. Center for Social Change, Inc., in the marketing of the bust, the Center refused Bolen's offer. Bolen pursued the idea, nevertheless, hiring an artist to prepare a mold and an agent to handle the promotion of the product. Defendant took out two half-page advertisements in the November and December 1980 issues of Ebony magazine, which purported to offer the bust as "an exclusive memorial" and "an opportunity to support the Martin Luther King, Jr., Center for Social Change." The advertisement stated that "a contribution from your order goes to the King Center for Social Change." Out of the $29.95 purchase price, defendant Bolen testified he set aside 3% or $.90, as a contribution to the Center. The advertisement also offered "free" with the purchase of the bust a booklet about the life of Dr. King entitled "A Tribute to Dr. Martin Luther King, Jr."

In addition to the two advertisements in Ebony, defendant published a brochure or phamphlet which was inserted in 80,000 copies of newspapers across the country. The brochure reiterated what was stated in the magazine advertisements, and also contained photographs of Dr. King and excerpts from his copyrighted speeches. * * *

* * * Testimony in the district court disclosed that money had been tendered to the Center, but was not accepted by its governing board. * * *

On November 21, 1980, and December 19, 1980, the plaintiffs demanded that the Bolens cease and desist from further advertisements and sales of the bust, and on December 31, 1980, the plaintiffs filed a complaint in the United States District Court for the Northern District of Georgia. The district court held a hearing on the plaintiffs' motion for a preliminary injunction and the defendants' motion to dismiss the complaint. The motion to dismiss was denied and the motion for a preliminary injunction was granted in part and denied in part. The motion for an injunction sought (1) an end to the use of the Center's name in advertising and marketing the busts, (2) restraint of any further copyright infringement and (3) an end to the manufacture and sale of the plastic busts. The defendants agreed to discontinue the use of the Center's name in further promotion. Therefore, the court granted this part of the injunction. The district court found that the defendants had infringed the King copyrights and enjoined all further use of the copyrighted material.

In ruling on the third request for injunction, the court confronted the plaintiffs' claim that the manufacture and sale of the busts violated Dr. King's right of publicity which had passed to his heirs upon Dr. King's death. The defendants contended that no such right existed, and hence, an injunction should not issue. The district court concluded that it was not necessary to determine whether the "right of publicity" was devisable in Georgia because Dr. King did not commercially exploit this right during his lifetime. As found by the district court, the evidence of exploitation by Dr. King came from his sister's affidavit which stated that he had received "thousands of dollars in the form of honorariums from the use of his name, likeness, literary compositions, and speeches." The district court further found that "Dr. King apparently sold his copyrights in several speeches to Motown Records Corporation." Martin Luther King, Jr. Center for Social Change, Inc. v. American Heritage Products, Inc., 508 F.Supp. 854 (N.D.Ga.1981).

On plaintiffs' appeal of the partial denial of the preliminary injunction, the Eleventh Circuit Court of Appeals has certified the following questions: * * *

1.   Is the "right of publicity" recognized in Georgia as a right distinct from the right of privacy?

Georgia has long recognized the right of privacy. Following denial of the existence of the right of privacy in a controversial decision by the New York Court of Appeals in Roberson v. Rochester Folding–Box Co., 171 N.Y. 538, 64 N.E. 442 (1902), the Georgia Supreme Court became the first such court to recognize the right of privacy in Pavesich v. New England Life Ins. Co., 122 Ga. 190, 50 S.E. 68 (1905). See Prosser, Law of Torts, pp. 802–804 (1971).

In Pavesich v. New England Life Ins. Co., supra, the picture of an artist was used without his consent in a newspaper advertisement of the insurance company. Analyzing the right of privacy, this court held: "The publication of a picture of a person, without his consent, as a part of an advertisement, for the purpose of exploiting the publisher's business, is a violation of the right of privacy of the person whose picture is reproduced, and entitles him to recover without proof of special damage." 122 Ga. at 191(11), 50 S.E. at 68(11). * * *

Recognizing the possibility of a conflict between the right of privacy and the freedoms of speech and press, this court said: "There is in the publication of one's picture for advertising purposes not the slightest semblance of an expression of an idea, a thought, or an opinion, within the meaning of the constitutional provision which guarantees to a person the right to publish his sentiments on any subject." 122 Ga. at 219, 50 S.E. at 80. The defendants in the case now before us make no claim under these freedoms and we find no violation thereof. * * *

The "right of publicity" was first recognized in Haelan Laboratories, Inc. v. Topps Chewing Gum, Inc., 202 F.2d 866 (2d Cir.1953). * * *

The right to publicity is not absolute. In Hicks v. Casablanca Records, 464 F.Supp. 426 (S.D.N.Y.1978), the court held that a fictional novel and movie concerning an unexplained eleven day disappearance by Agatha Christie, author of numerous mystery novels, were permissible under the first amendment. On the other hand, in Zacchini v. Scripps–Howard Broadcasting Co., 433 U.S. 562 (1977), a television station broadcast on its news program plaintiff's 15 second "human cannonball" flight filmed at a local fair. The Supreme Court held that freedom of the press does not authorize the media to broadcast a performer's entire act without his consent, just as the media could not televise a stage play, prize fight or baseball game without consent. Quoting from Kalven, Privacy in Tort Law—Were Warren and Brandeis Wrong?, 31 Law & Contemp. Prob. 326, 332 (1966), the Court said (433 U.S. at 576): "The rationale for [protecting the right of publicity] is the straight-forward one of preventing unjust enrichment by the theft of good will. No social purpose is served by having the defendant get free some aspect of the plaintiff that would have market value and for which he would normally pay."

The right of publicity was first recognized in Georgia by the Court of Appeals in Cabaniss v. Hipsley, 114 Ga.App. 367, 151 S.E.2d 496 (1966). There the court held that the plaintiff, an exotic dancer, could recover from the owner of the Atlanta Playboy Club for the unauthorized use of the dancer's misnamed photograph in an entertainment magazine advertising the Playboy Club. Although plaintiff had had her picture taken to promote her performances, she was not performing at the Playboy Club. * * *

Thus, the courts in Georgia have recognized the rights of private citizens, *Pavesich,* supra, as well as entertainers, *Cabaniss* * * *, supra, not to have their names and photographs used for the financial gain of the user without their consent, where such use is not authorized as an exercise of freedom of the press. We know of no reason why a public figure prominent in religion and civil rights should be entitled to less protection than an exotic dancer or a movie actress. Therefore, we hold that the appropriation of another's name and likeness, whether such likeness be a photograph or sculpture, without consent and for the financial gain of the appropriator is a tort in Georgia, whether the person whose name and likeness is used is a private citizen, entertainer, or as here a public figure who is not a public official.

In *Pavesich,* supra, 122 Ga. 190, 50 S.E. 68, this right not to have another appropriate one's photograph was denominated the right of privacy; in Cabaniss v. Hipsley, supra, 114 Ga.App. 367, 151 S.E.2d 496, it was the right of publicity. Mr. Pavesich was not a public figure; Ms. Hipsley was. We conclude that while private citizens have the right of privacy, public figures have a similar right of publicity, and that the measure of damages to a public figure for violation of his or her right of publicity is the value of the appropriation to the user. Cabaniss v. Hipsley, supra; see also Uhlaender v. Henricksen, 316 F.Supp. 1277, 1279–1280 (Minn.1970). As thus understood the first certified question is answered in the affirmative.

2.   Does the "right of publicity" survive the death of its owner (i.e., is the right inheritable and devisable)?   * * *

The right of publicity is assignable during the life of the celebrity, for without this characteristic, full commercial exploitation of one's name and likeness is practically impossible. Haelan Laboratories v. Topps Chewing Gum, supra, 202 F.2d at 868. That is, without assignability the right of publicity could hardly be called a "right". Recognizing its assignability, most commentators have urged that the right of publicity must also be inheritable. Felcher and Rubin, The Descendibility of the Right of Publicity: Is there Commercial Life After Death?, 89 Yale L.J. 1125 (1980); Gordon, Right of Property in Name, Likeness, Personality and History, 55 Nw.U.L.Rev. 553 (1960); * * *.

The courts that have considered the problem are not as unanimous. In Price v. Hal Roach Studios, Inc., [400 F.Supp. 836 (S.D.N.Y.1975)], the court reasoned that since the right of publicity was assignable, it survived the deaths of Stanley Laurel and Oliver Hardy. Other decisions from the Southern District of New York recognize the descendibility of the right of publicity, which has also been recognized by the Second Circuit Court of Appeals (infra).

In Factors Etc., Inc. v. Pro Arts, Inc., 579 F.2d 215 (2d Cir.1978), Elvis Presley had assigned his right of publicity to Boxcar Enterprises, which assigned that right to Factors after Presley's death. Defendant Pro Arts published a poster of Presley entitled "In Memory". In affirming the grant of injunction against Pro Arts, the Second Circuit Court of Appeals said (579 F.2d at 221): "The identification of this exclusive right belonging to Boxcar as a transferable property right compels the conclusion that the right survives Presley's death. The death of Presley, who was merely the beneficiary of an income interest in Boxcar's exclusive right, should not in itself extinguish Boxcar's property right. Instead, the income interest, continually produced from Boxcar's exclusive right of commercial exploitation, should inure to Presley's estate at death like any other intangible property right. To hold that the right did not survive Presley's death, would be to grant competitors of Factors, such as Pro Arts, a windfall in the form of profits from the use of Presley's name and likeness. At the same time, the exclusive right purchased by Factors and the financial benefits accruing to the celebrity's heirs would be rendered virtually worthless."

In Lugosi v. Universal Pictures, 25 Cal.3d 813, 160 Cal.Rptr. 323, 603 P.2d 425 (1979), the Supreme Court of California, in a 4 to 3 decision, declared that the right of publicity expires upon the death of the celebrity and is not descendible. See Guglielmi v. Spelling–Goldberg Productions, 25 Cal.3d 860, 160 Cal.Rptr. 352, 603 P.2d 454 (1979), decided two days after *Lugosi,* supra. Bela Lugosi appeared as Dracula in Universal Picture's movie by that name. Universal had acquired the movie rights to the novel by Bram Stoker. Lugosi's contract with Universal gave it the right to exploit Lugosi's name and likeness in connection with the movie. The majority of the court held that Lugosi's heirs could not prevent Universal's continued exploitation of Lugosi's portrayal of Count Dracula after his death. The court did not decide whether Universal could prevent unauthorized third parties from exploitation of Lugosi's appearance as Dracula after Lugosi's death.

In Memphis Development Foundation v. Factors Etc., Inc., 616 F.2d 956 (6th Cir.1980), Factors, which had won its case against Pro Arts in New York (see above), lost against the Memphis Development Foundation under the Court of Appeals for the Sixth Circuit's interpretation of Tennessee law. There, the Foundation, a non-profit corporation, planned to erect a statue of Elvis Presley in Memphis and solicited contributions to do so. Donors of $25 or more received a small replica of the proposed statue. The Sixth Circuit reversed the grant of an injunction favoring Factors, holding that a celebrity's right of publicity was not inheritable even where that right had been exploited during the celebrity's life.[4] The court reasoned that although recognition of the right of publicity during life serves to encourage effort and inspire creative endeavors, making the right inheritable would not. The court also was concerned with unanswered legal questions which recognizing inheritability would create. We note, however, that the court was dealing with a non-profit foundation attempting to promote Presley's adopted homeplace, the City of Memphis. The court was not dealing, as we do here, with a profit making endeavor. * * *

For the reasons which follow we hold that the right of publicity survives the death of its owner and is inheritable and devisable. Recognition of the right of publicity rewards and thereby encourages effort and creativity. If the right of publicity dies with the celebrity, the economic value of the right of publicity during life would be diminished because the celebrity's untimely death would seriously impair, if not destroy, the value of the right of continued commercial use. Conversely, those who would profit from the fame of a celebrity after his or her death for their own benefit and without authorization have failed to establish their claim that they should be the beneficiaries of the celebrity's death. Finally, the trend since the early common law has been to recognize survivability, notwithstanding the legal problems which may thereby arise. We therefore answer question 2 in the affirmative.

4. The Second Circuit has now accepted the Sixth Circuit's interpretation of Tennessee law. Factors Etc., Inc. v. Pro Arts, Inc., 652 F.2d 278 (2d Cir.1981).

3. Must the owner of the right of publicity have commercially exploited that right before it can survive?

Exploitation is understood to mean commercial use by the celebrity other than the activity which made him or her famous, e.g., an inter vivos transfer of the right to the use of one's name and likeness.

The requirement that the right of publicity be exploited by the celebrity during his or her lifetime in order to render the right inheritable arises from the case involving Agatha Christie, Hicks v. Casablanca Records, supra, 464 F.Supp. at 429. * * * [T]he *Hicks* court held that the fictional account of Agatha Christie's 11 day disappearance was protected by the first amendment. Thus, the finding that exploitation during life was necessary to inheritability was actually unnecessary to that decision.

Nevertheless, the *Hicks* dicta has been relied upon. See Groucho Marx Productions, Inc. v. Day & Night Co., 523 F.Supp. 485, 490 (S.D.N.Y.1981).[5] However, in this case, involving the Marx brothers, it was found that, although Leo and Adolpho Marx ("Chico" and "Harpo") had not made inter vivos or specific testamentary dispositions of their rights, they had earned their livelihoods by exploiting the unique characters they created and thus had exploited their rights to publicity so as to make such rights descendible. Thus, even in the Southern District of New York where the requirement arose, exploitation beyond the "activity which made him or her famous" is not now required.

The cases which have considered this issue, see above, involved entertainers. The net result of following them would be to say that celebrities and public figures have the right of publicity during their lifetimes (as others have the right of privacy), but only those who contract for bubble gum cards, posters and tee shirts have a descendible right of publicity upon their deaths. See Groucho Marx Productions, Inc. v. Day & Night Co., supra, 523 F.Supp. at 490, 491–492. That we should single out for protection after death those entertainers and athletes who exploit their personae during life, and deny protection after death to those who enjoy public acclamation but did not exploit themselves during life, puts a premium on exploitation. Having found that there are valid reasons for recognizing the right of publicity during life, we find no reason to protect after death only those who took commercial advantage of their fame.

Perhaps this case more than others brings the point into focus. A well known minister may avoid exploiting his prominence during life because to do otherwise would impair his ministry. Should his election not to take commercial advantage of his position during life ipso facto result in permitting others to exploit his name and likeness after his death? In our view, a person who avoids exploitation during life is entitled to have his image protected against exploitation after death just as much if not more than a person who exploited his image during life.

5. On appeal of this case, the Second Circuit reversed, finding the law of California applicable, where, as noted above, the right of publicity is not inheritable. Groucho Marx Productions, Inc. v. Day & Night Co., 689 F.2d 317 (2d Cir.1982).

Without doubt, Dr. King could have exploited his name and likeness during his lifetime.   That this opportunity was not appealing to him does not mean that others have the right to use his name and likeness in ways he himself chose not to do.   Nor does it strip his family and estate of the right to control, preserve and extend his status and memory and to prevent unauthorized exploitation thereof by others.   Here, they seek to prevent the exploitation of his likeness in a manner they consider unflattering and unfitting.   We cannot deny them this right merely because Dr. King chose not to exploit or commercialize himself during his lifetime.

Question 3 is answered in the negative, and therefore we need not answer question 4.

Certified questions 1 and 2 answered in the affirmative, question 3 answered in the negative, and question 4 not answered.

All the Justices concur, except WELTNER, J., who concurs specially.

■ WELTNER, JUSTICE, concurring specially.

I concur specially because, although this matter is one of certified questions, I believe that the complaint states a claim upon which relief can be granted.   I disagree most decidedly with the substantive portion of the majority opinion, for reason that it generates more unsettling questions than it resolves.   * * *

[T]he majority says that the fabrication and commercial distribution of a likeness of Dr. King is not "speech," thereby removing the inquiry from the ambit of First Amendment or Free Speech inquiries.   * * *

Do not the statues of the Confederate soldiers which inhabit so many of our courthouse squares express the sentiments of those who raised them?

Are not the busts of former chief justices, stationed within the rotunda of this very courthouse, expressions of sentiments of gratitude and approval?

Is not the portrait of Dr. King which hangs in our Capitol an expression of sentiment?

Manifestly so.

If, then, a two-dimensional likeness in oil and canvas is an expression of sentiment, how can it be said that a three-dimensional likeness in plastic is *not*?

But, says the majority, our new right to publicity is violated only in cases involving financial gain.   * * *

Did the sculptors of our Confederate soldiers, and of our chief justices, labor without gain?   Was Dr. King's portraitist unpaid for his work?

If "financial gain" is to be the watershed of violation *vel non* of this new-found right, it cannot withstand scrutiny.   It is rare, indeed, that any expression of sentiment beyond casual conversation is not somehow connected, directly or indirectly, to "financial gain."   For example, a school child wins a $25 prize for the best essay on Dr. King's life. Is this "financial gain?" Must the child then account for the winnings?

The essay, because of its worth, is reprinted in a commercial publication. Must the publisher account?

The publication is sold on the newsstand. Must the vendor account?

The majority will say "free speech." Very well. The same child wins a $25 prize in the school art fair. His creation—a bust of Dr. King.

Must he account?

The local newspaper prints a photograph of the child and of his creation. Must it account?

The school commissions replicas of the bust to raise money for its library. Must it account?

UNICEF reproduces the bust on its Christmas cards. Must it account?

Finally, a purely commercial venture undertakes to market replicas of the bust under circumstances similar to those of this case. Must it account?

Obviously, the answers to the above questions will vary, and properly so, because the circumstances posited are vastly different. The dividing line, however, cannot be fixed upon the presence or absence of "financial gain." Rather, it must be grounded in the community's judgment of what, *ex aequo et bono,* is unconscionable. * * *

NOTES ON THE DESCENDIBILITY OF PUBLICITY RIGHTS

(1) Consider again the interests underlying the publicity right. Which, if any, support a post-mortem right?

Other cases finding a descendible right of publicity at common law include Nature's Way Products, Inc. v. Nature–Pharma, Inc., 736 F.Supp. 245 (D.Utah 1990) (Utah law) and Estate of Presley v. Russen, 513 F.Supp. 1339 (D.N.J.1981) (New Jersey law).

(2) In the *Memphis Development Foundation* case summarized by Justice Hill, the Sixth Circuit, after concluding "that making the right of publicity inheritable would not significantly inspire the creative endeavors of individuals," posed the following "practical problems" raised by a descendible publicity right: "How long would the 'property' interest last? In perpetuity? For a term of years? Is the right of publicity taxable? At what point does the right collide with the right of free expression guaranteed by the first amendment? Does the right apply to elected officials and military heroes whose fame was gained on the public payroll, as well as to movie stars, singers and athletes? Does the right cover posters or engraved likenesses of, for example, Farah Fawcett Majors or Mahatma Gandhi, kitchen utensils ('Revere Ware'), insurance ('John Hancock'), electric utilities ('Edison'), a football stadium ('RFK'), a pastry ('Napoleon'), or the innumerable urban subdivisions and apartment complexes named after famous people? Our legal system normally does not pass on to heirs other similar personal attributes even though the attributes may be shared during life by others or have some commercial value. Titles, offices and reputation are not inheritable. Neither are trust or distrust and friendship or enmity descendible. An employment contract during life does not create the right for heirs to take over the job. Fame falls in the same category as reputation; it is an attribute from which others may benefit but may not own." 616 F.2d at 959. (Did the majority in the *Martin Luther King* case neglect significant free speech interests of the kind alluded to in *Memphis Development*? That issue is pursued later in this section.)

The Tennessee legislature responded to the *Memphis Development* decision with the Personal Rights Protection Act of 1984, which declares that publicity rights survive (regardless of exploitation during life) for a period of ten years after death, and continue thereafter absent proof of non-use by the heirs or devisees for any two-year period subsequent to the initial ten-year term. (Tenn.Code Ann. § 47–25–1101 et seq.) [c]

(3) Hicks v. Casablanca Records, cited by Justice Hill for its holding that the right must be "exploited" during life in order to render it inheritable, involved an attempt by the heirs and assignees of Dame Agatha Christie to enjoin distribution of the motion picture "Agatha," which presented a fictionalized account of an incident in the author's life. On the question of inheritability the court said, "it would appear that a party claiming the right must establish that the decedent acted in such a way as to evidence his or her own recognition of the extrinsic commercial value of his or her name or likeness, and manifested that recognition in some overt manner, e.g., making an *inter vivos* transfer of the rights in the name (*Factors*), or posing for bubble gum cards (see *Haelan Laboratories, Inc.* * * *)." The court found sufficient exploitation in assignments by Dame Christie of rights to her literary works, including contracts for the use of her name in connection with movies and plays based on her books. (A motion for preliminary relief was nevertheless denied; citing first amendment concerns, the court held that the right of publicity could not be invoked to stop a motion picture.)

What is the function of an "exploitation" requirement?

(4) The reluctance of the California Supreme Court to recognize descendibility is discussed by the Second Circuit in Groucho Marx Productions, Inc. v. Day and Night Co., 689 F.2d 317 (2d Cir.1982), which also makes the point that if a name or likeness used in connection with a product or service acquires secondary meaning as an indication of source, post-mortem rights may be sustained on a trademark theory.

---

c. The Tennessee legislation, attributable to lobbying by the Presley estate, has nurtured a remarkable empire now run by Elvis Presley Enterprises, the estate's operating arm. It oversees everything from Elvis teddy bears, restaurants featuring Elvis' favorite deep-fried peanut butter and banana sandwiches, and the Graceland mansion. See Gywnne, Love Me Legal Tender, Time, Aug. 4, 1997, p. 63.

In 1984 the California legislature established the descendibility of publicity rights in an elaborate provision that includes a scheme of statutory succession, registration procedures, and minimum statutory damages. The Legislative Counsel's Digest summarized the legislation:

> This bill would enact a provision setting forth the statutory right to recover damages for the unauthorized commercial use of a deceased personality's name, voice, signature, photograph, or likeness, * * * and would specify that right is a property right which is transferable, and, if not transferred, exercisable after a person's death by the person's wife, children, or parents, as specified. The bill would require a person claiming the right to register the claim with the Secretary of State. It would provide that a successor-in-interest to the rights of a deceased personality may not recover damages for a use that occurs before registration. The bill would provide that no action could be brought to recover damages for a use occurring after 50 years from the death of the person. The bill would specifically exempt certain uses.

Among the exemptions are news and sports broadcasts and non-advertising uses in books, magazines, newspapers, films, and television programs, and use in single and original works of fine art. Cal.Civil Code § 990. A similar bill has failed of passage in New York. In addition to California and Tennessee, statutes in a half-dozen other states recognize descendible rights ranging from 20 years (Va.C.Ann. § 8.01–40) to 100 years! (Okla. Stat. tit. 12, § 1448(G)). Several other states, following New York, reserve statutory rights to living persons. And in many others, the very existence of the publicity right remains undecided.

On descendibility, in addition to the Felcher and Rubin article cited by Justice Hill and the other sources cited in this section, see Terrell and Smith, Publicity, Liberty, and Intellectual Property: A Conceptual and Economic Analysis of the Inheritability Issue, 34 Emory L.J. 1 (1985); Restatement, Third, Unfair Competition § 46, Comment *h* (1995).

(5) A different durational issue arose in Abdul–Jabbar v. General Motors Corp., 85 F.3d 407 (9th Cir.1996). Defendant, charged with making a false claim of endorsement under § 43(a) and infringement of the right of publicity, defended by arguing that basketball star Kareem Abdul–Jabbar had "abandoned" his former name, Lew Alcindor, which defendant used in its advertising. The court rejected defendant's analogy to trademark abandonment and reversed a summary judgment against the plaintiff.

(6) A *New York Times* story (inspired by a law review article!—Beard, Casting Call at Forest Lawn: The Digital Resurrection of Deceased Entertainers—A 21st Century Challenge for Intellectual Property Law, 8 High Technology L.J. 101 (1993)) speculates on the legal implications of emerging computer technology that may permit the digital reanimation of deceased film stars. Until now, to create a scene in which Fred Astaire dances with Whitney Houston, for example, the producer had to splice in footage from an old Astaire film, presumably with the permission of the owner of the copyright in the film. But computer technology may soon be able to extract digital images of performers from earlier works and manipulate them to create an entirely new performance—a western with Kevin Costner and John Wayne, for instance, or *Schindler's List* starring Clark Gable. Would such works violate anyone's legal rights? Recall the exclusion in California's descendible right of publicity for use in films and television programs. See Restatement, Third, Unfair Competition § 47, Comments *c–d* (1995). Would the extraction of the digital data necessary to recreate the performer infringe the copyright in the original film? Weber, Why Marilyn [d] and Bogie Still Need a Lawyer, New York Times, March 11, 1994, p. B18.[e]

White v. Samsung Electronics America, Inc.

United States Court of Appeals, Ninth Circuit, 1993.
971 F.2d 1395.
Petition for rehearing en banc denied, 989 F.2d 1512.
Certiorari denied, 508 U.S. 951, 113 S.Ct. 2443 (1993).

■ Before GOODWIN, PREGERSON, and ALARCON, CIRCUIT JUDGES.

■ GOODWIN, SENIOR CIRCUIT JUDGE:

This case involves a promotional "fame and fortune" dispute. In running a particular advertisement without Vanna White's permission, defendants Samsung Electronics America, Inc. (Samsung) and David Deutsch Associates, Inc. (Deutsch) attempted to capitalize on White's fame to enhance their fortune. White sued, alleging infringement of various intellectual property rights, but the district court granted summary judgment in favor of the defendants. We affirm in part, reverse in part, and remand.

Plaintiff Vanna White is the hostess of "Wheel of Fortune," one of the most popular game shows in television history. An estimated forty million people watch the program daily. Capitalizing on the fame which her participation in the show has bestowed on her, White markets her identity to various advertisers.

d. J. Gaines, Contested Culture: The Image, the Voice, and the Law 289–90 (1991), reports that, by way of a bequest to her psychiatrist, royalties from the exploitation of Marilyn Monroe's image go to the Hampstead Child Therapy Clinic in London, founded by Anna Freud, daughter of Sigmund Freud.

e. With the permission of his family, the Coors beer company digitally extracted the image of John Wayne playing a general in the 1965 film *To Cast a Giant Shadow* and used it in a commercial in which a drill sergeant grilling his platoon about beer in the barracks is interrupted by Wayne as the general looking for his Coors Light. Coors made a "seven-figure" donation to the John Wayne Cancer Institute. USA Today, May, 21 1996, p. 4B.

"Dead people have been turning up everywhere, from 'Forrest Gump' to television commercials to musical recordings. * * * Whether you are upset at seeing John Wayne turn up as an Army officer in a current Coors Light commercial may depend on whether you think Wayne's career was sacred or profane. But it seemed like the destruction of a beloved icon and a debasement of true art to watch Fred Astaire dance with that Dirt Devil [vacuum cleaner] when we want him to be with Ginger Rogers." James, Raising the Dead for TV Guest Appearances, N.Y. Times, May 14, 1998, p. E1.

The dispute in this case arose out of a series of advertisements prepared for Samsung by Deutsch. The series ran in at least half a dozen publications with widespread, and in some cases national, circulation. Each of the advertisements in the series followed the same theme. Each depicted a current item from popular culture and a Samsung electronic product. Each was set in the twenty-first century and conveyed the message that the Samsung product would still be in use by that time. By hypothesizing outrageous future outcomes for the cultural items, the ads created humorous effects. For example, one lampooned current popular notions of an unhealthy diet by depicting a raw steak with the caption: "Revealed to be health food. 2010 A.D." Another depicted irreverent "news"-show host Morton Downey Jr. in front of an American flag with the caption: "Presidential candidate. 2008 A.D."

The advertisement which prompted the current dispute was for Samsung video-cassette recorders (VCRs). The ad depicted a robot, dressed in a wig, gown, and jewelry which Deutsch consciously selected to resemble White's hair and dress. The robot was posed next to a game board which is instantly recognizable as the Wheel of Fortune game show set, in a stance for which White is famous. The caption of the ad read: "Longest-running game show. 2012 A.D." Defendants referred to the ad as the "Vanna White" ad. Unlike the other celebrities used in the campaign, White neither consented to the ads nor was she paid.

Following the circulation of the robot ad, White sued Samsung and Deutsch in federal district court under: (1) California Civil Code § 3344; (2) the California common law right of publicity; and (3) § 43(a) of the Lanham Act, 15 U.S.C. § 1125(a). The district court granted summary judgment against White on each of her claims. White now appeals.

I. Section 3344

White first argues that the district court erred in rejecting her claim under section 3344. Section 3344(a) provides, in pertinent part, that "[a]ny person who knowingly uses another's name, voice, signature, photograph, or likeness, in any manner, ... for purposes of advertising or selling, ... without such person's prior consent ... shall be liable for any damages sustained by the person or persons injured as a result thereof."

White argues that the Samsung advertisement used her "likeness" in contravention of section 3344. In Midler v. Ford Motor Co., 849 F.2d 460 (9th Cir.1988), this court rejected Bette Midler's section 3344 claim concerning a Ford television commercial in which a Midler "sound-alike" sang a song which Midler had made famous. In rejecting Midler's claim, this court noted that "[t]he defendants did not use Midler's name or anything else whose use is prohibited by the statute. The voice they used was [another person's], not hers. The term 'likeness' refers to a visual image not a vocal imitation." Id. at 463.

In this case, Samsung and Deutsch used a robot with mechanical features, and not, for example, a manikin molded to White's precise features. Without deciding for all purposes when a caricature or impressionistic resemblance might become a "likeness," we agree with the district court that the robot at issue here was not White's "likeness" within the meaning of section 3344. Accordingly, we affirm the court's dismissal of White's section 3344 claim.

II. Right of Publicity

White next argues that the district court erred in granting summary judgment to defendants on White's common law right of publicity claim. In Eastwood v. Superior Court, 149 Cal.App.3d 409, 198 Cal.Rptr. 342 (1983), the California court of appeal stated that the common law right of publicity cause of action "may be pleaded by alleging (1) the defendant's use of the plaintiff's identity; (2) the appropriation of plaintiff's name or likeness to defendant's advantage, commercially or otherwise; (3) lack of consent; and (4) resulting injury." Id. at 417, 198 Cal.Rptr. 342 (citing Prosser, Law of Torts (4th ed. 1971) § 117, pp. 804–807). The district court dismissed White's claim for failure to satisfy *Eastwood's* second prong, reasoning that defendants had not appropriated White's "name or likeness" with their robot ad. We agree that the robot ad did not make use of White's name or likeness. However, the common law right of publicity is not so confined. * * *

The "name or likeness" formulation referred to in *Eastwood* originated not as an element of the right of publicity cause of action, but as a description of the types of cases in which the cause of action had been recognized. The source of this formulation is Prosser, Privacy, 48 Cal. L.Rev. 383, 401–07 (1960), one of the earliest and most enduring articulations of the common law right of publicity cause of action. In looking at the case law to that point, Prosser recognized that right of publicity cases involved one of two basic factual scenarios: name appropriation, and picture or other likeness appropriation. Id. at 401–02, nn. 156–57.

Even though Prosser focused on appropriations of name or likeness in discussing the right of publicity, he noted that "[i]t is not impossible that there might be appropriation of the plaintiff's identity, as by impersonation, without the use of either his name or his likeness, and that this would be an invasion of his right of privacy." Id. at 401, n. 155. At the time Prosser wrote, he noted however, that "[n]o such case appears to have arisen." Id.

Since Prosser's early formulation, the case law has borne out his insight that the right of publicity is not limited to the appropriation of name or likeness. In Motschenbacher v. R.J. Reynolds Tobacco Co., 498 F.2d 821 (9th Cir.1974), the defendant had used a photograph of the plaintiff's race car in a television commercial. Although the plaintiff appeared driving the car in the photograph, his features were not visible. Even though the defendant had not appropriated the plaintiff's name or likeness, this court held that plaintiff's California right of publicity claim should reach the jury.

In *Midler,* this court held that, even though the defendants had not used Midler's name or likeness, Midler had stated a claim for violation of her California common law right of publicity because "the defendants . . .

for their own profit in selling their product did appropriate part of her identity" by using a Midler sound-alike.   Id. at 463–64.

In Carson v. Here's Johnny Portable Toilets, Inc., 698 F.2d 831 (6th Cir.1983), the defendant had marketed portable toilets under the brand name "Here's Johnny"—Johnny Carson's signature "Tonight Show" introduction—without Carson's permission.   The district court had dismissed Carson's Michigan common law right of publicity claim because the defendants had not used Carson's "name or likeness."   Id. at 835.   In reversing the district court, the sixth circuit found "the district court's conception of the right of publicity ... too narrow" and held that the right was implicated because the defendant had appropriated Carson's identity by using, inter alia, the phrase "Here's Johnny."   Id. at 835–37.

These cases teach not only that the common law right of publicity reaches means of appropriation other than name or likeness, but that the specific means of appropriation are relevant only for determining whether the defendant has in fact appropriated the plaintiff's identity.   The right of publicity does not require that appropriations of identity be accomplished through particular means to be actionable.   It is noteworthy that the *Midler* and *Carson* defendants not only avoided using the plaintiff's name or likeness, but they also avoided appropriating the celebrity's voice, signature, and photograph.   The photograph in *Motschenbacher* did include the plaintiff, but because the plaintiff was not visible the driver could have been an actor or dummy and the analysis in the case would have been the same.

Although the defendants in these cases avoided the most obvious means of appropriating the plaintiffs' identities, each of their actions directly implicated the commercial interests which the right of publicity is designed to protect.   As the *Carson* court explained:

> [t]he right of publicity has developed to protect the commercial interest of celebrities in their identities.   The theory of the right is that a celebrity's identity can be valuable in the promotion of products, and the celebrity has an interest that may be protected from the unauthorized commercial exploitation of that identity....   If the celebrity's identity is commercially exploited, there has been an invasion of his right whether or not his "name or likeness" is used.

Carson, 698 F.2d at 835.   It is not important *how* the defendant has appropriated the plaintiff's identity, but *whether* the defendant has done so. *Motschenbacher, Midler,* and *Carson* teach the impossibility of treating the right of publicity as guarding only against a laundry list of specific means of appropriating identity.   A rule which says that the right of publicity can be infringed only through the use of nine different methods of appropriating identity merely challenges the clever advertising strategist to come up with the tenth.   * * *

Viewed separately, the individual aspects of the advertisement in the present case say little.   Viewed together, they leave little doubt about the celebrity the ad is meant to depict.   The female-shaped robot is wearing a long gown, blond wig, and large jewelry. Vanna White dresses exactly like this at times, but so do many other women. The robot is in the process of turning a block letter on a game-board. Vanna White dresses like this while turning letters on a game-board but perhaps similarly attired Scrabble-playing women do this as well. The robot is standing on what looks to be the Wheel of Fortune game show set. Vanna White dresses like this, turns letters, and does this on the Wheel of Fortune game show. She is the only one. Indeed, defendants themselves referred to their ad as the "Vanna White" ad. We are not surprised.

Television and other media create marketable celebrity identity value. Considerable energy and ingenuity are expended by those who have achieved celebrity value to exploit it for profit. The law protects the celebrity's sole right to exploit this value whether the celebrity has achieved her fame out of rare ability, dumb luck, or a combination thereof. We decline Samsung and Deutch's invitation to permit the evisceration of the common law right of publicity through means as facile as those in this case. Because White has alleged facts showing that Samsung and Deutsch had appropriated her identity, the district court erred by rejecting, on summary judgment, White's common law right of publicity claim.

III.   The Lanham Act

[The court also reversed defendants' summary judgment on White's claim under § 43(a) of the Lanham Act. Judge Goodwin said that there was a genuine issue of material fact as to whether the advertisement created a likelihood of confusion concerning White's endorsement of the product.]

IV.   The Parody Defense

In defense, defendants cite a number of cases for the proposition that their robot ad constituted protected speech. The only cases they cite which are even remotely relevant to this case are Hustler Magazine v. Falwell, 485 U.S. 46 (1988) and L.L. Bean, Inc. v. Drake Publishers, Inc., 811 F.2d 26 (1st Cir.1987). Those cases involved parodies of advertisements run for the purpose of poking fun at Jerry Falwell and L.L. Bean, respectively. This case involves a true advertisement run for the purpose of selling Samsung VCRs. The ad's spoof of Vanna White and Wheel of Fortune is subservient and only tangentially related to the ad's primary message: "buy Samsung VCRs." Defendants' parody arguments are better addressed to non-commercial parodies.[3] The difference between a "parody"

---

3. In warning of a first amendment chill to expressive conduct, the dissent reads this decision too broadly. See Dissent at 1407. This case concerns only the market which exists in our society for the exploitation of celebrity to sell products, and an attempt to take a free ride on a celebrity's celebrity value. Commercial advertising which relies on celebrity fame is different from other forms of expressive activity in two crucial ways. First, for celebrity exploitation advertising to be effective, the advertisement must evoke the celebrity's identity. The more effective the evocation, the better the and a "knock-off" is the difference between fun and profit.

V.   Conclusion

In remanding this case, we hold only that White has pleaded claims which can go to the jury for its decision.

Affirmed in Part, Reversed in Part, and Remanded.

■ ALARCON, CIRCUIT JUDGE, concurring in part, dissenting in part:

Vanna White seeks recovery from Samsung based on three theories: the right to privacy, the right to publicity, and the Lanham Act. I concur in the majority's conclusions on the right to privacy. I respectfully dissent from its holdings on the right to publicity and the Lanham Act claims. * * *

I must dissent from the majority's holding on Vanna White's right to publicity claim. The district court found that, since the commercial advertisement did not show a "likeness" of Vanna White, Samsung did not improperly use the plaintiff's identity. The majority asserts that the use of a likeness is not required under California common law. According to the majority, recovery is authorized if there is an appropriation of one's "identity." I cannot find any holding of a California court that supports this conclusion. Furthermore, the record does not support the majority's finding that Vanna White's "identity" was appropriated. * * *

The interest of the California Legislature as expressed in California Civil Code section 3344 appears to preclude the result reached by the majority. The original section 3344 protected only name or likeness. In 1984, ten years after our decision in Motschenbacher v. R.J. Reynolds Tobacco Company, 498 F.2d 821 (9th Cir.1974) and 24 years after Prosser speculated about the future development of the law of the right of publicity, the California legislature amended the statute. California law now makes the use of someone's voice or signature, as well as name or likeness, actionable. Cal.Civ.Code sec. 2233(a) (Deering 1991 Supp.). Thus, California, after our decision in *Motschenbacher* specifically contemplated protec-

---

advertisement. If, as Samsung claims, its ad was based on a "generic" game-show hostess and not on Vanna White, the ad would not have violated anyone's right of publicity, but it would also not have been as humorous or as effective. Second, even if some forms of expressive activity, such as parody, do rely on identity evocation, the first amendment hurdle will bar most right of publicity actions against those activities. Cf. *Falwell*, 485 U.S. at 46. In the case of commercial advertising, however, the first amendment hurdle is not so high. Central Hudson Gas & Electric Corp. v. Public Service Comm'n of New York,

447 U.S. 557, 566 (1980). Realizing this, Samsung attempts to elevate its ad above the status of garden-variety commercial speech by pointing to the ad's parody of Vanna White. Samsung's argument is unavailing. See Board of Trustees, State Univ. of N.Y. v. Fox, 492 U.S. 469, 474–75 (1988); Bolger v. Youngs Drug Products Corp., 463 U.S. 60, 67–68 (1983). Unless the first amendment bars all right of publicity actions—and it does not, see Zachini v. Scripps–Howard Broadcasting Co., 433 U.S. 562 (1977)—then it does not bar this case.

tion for interests other than name or likeness, but did not include a cause of action for appropriation of another person's identity. The ancient maxim, *inclusio unius est exclusio alterius,* would appear to bar the majority's innovative extension of the right of publicity. The clear implication from the fact that the California Legislature chose to add only voice and signature to the previously protected interests is that it wished to limit the cause of action to enumerated attributes. * * *

The majority contends that "the individual aspects of the advertisement ... [v]iewed together leave little doubt about the celebrity the ad is meant to depict." Majority Opinion at p. 1399. It derives this conclusion from the fact that Vanna White is "the only one" who "dresses like this, turns letters, and does this on the Wheel of Fortune game show." Id. In reaching this conclusion, the majority confuses Vanna White, the person, with the role she has assumed as the current hostess on the "Wheel of Fortune" television game show. A recognition of the distinction between a performer and the part he or she plays is essential for a proper analysis of the facts of this case. As is discussed below, those things which Vanna White claims identify her are not unique to her. They are, instead, attributes of the *role* she plays. The representation of those attributes, therefore, does not constitute a representation of Vanna White. See Nurmi v. Peterson, 10 U.S.P.Q.2d 1775 (C.D.Cal.1989) (distinguishing between performer and role). * * *

The only characteristic in the commercial advertisement that is not common to many female performers or celebrities is the imitation of the "Wheel of Fortune" set. This set is the only thing which might possibly lead a viewer to think of Vanna White. The Wheel of Fortune set, however, is not an attribute of Vanna White's identity. It is an identifying characteristic of a television game show, a prop with which Vanna White interacts in her role as the current hostess. To say that Vanna White may bring an action when another blond female performer or robot appears on such a set as a hostess will, I am sure, be a surprise to the owners of the show. Cf. Baltimore Orioles, Inc. v. Major League Baseball Players Ass'n, 805 F.2d 663 (7th Cir.1986) (right to publicity in videotaped performances preempted by copyright of owner of telecast).

* * * The advertisement was intended to depict a robot, playing the role Vanna White currently plays on the Wheel of Fortune. I quite agree that anyone seeing the commercial advertisement would be reminded of Vanna White. *Any* performance by another female celebrity as a game-show hostess, however, will also remind the viewer of Vanna White because Vanna White's celebrity is so closely associated with the role. But the fact that an actor or actress became famous for playing a particular role has, until now, never been sufficient to give the performer a proprietary interest in it. I cannot agree with the majority that the California courts, which have consistently taken a narrow view of the right to publicity, would extend law to these unique facts.

[Judge Alarcon also disagreed with the majority's reversal of summary judgment on White's § 43(a) claim, concluding that the evidence would not permit a finding that confusion was likely. He also thought that the majority gave "short shrift" to the defendant's first amendment argument merely because the parody appeared in an advertisement. The latter issue was taken up by Judge Kozinski in a dissent from the rejection of defendant's request for rehearing en banc (989 F.2d 1512).]

■ KOZINSKI, CIRCUIT JUDGE, with whom CIRCUIT JUDGES O'SCANNLAIN and KLEINFELD join, dissenting from the order rejecting the suggestion for rehearing en banc.

Saddam Hussein wants to keep advertisers from using his picture in unflattering contexts.[1] Clint Eastwood doesn't want tabloids to write about him.[2] Rudolf Valentino's heirs want to control his film biography.[3] The Girl Scouts don't want their image soiled by association with certain activities.[4] George Lucas wants to keep Strategic Defense Initiative fans from calling it "Star Wars."[5] * * *

Something very dangerous is going on here. Private property, including intellectual property, is essential to our way of life. It provides an incentive for investment and innovation; it stimulates the flourishing of our culture; it protects the moral entitlements of people to the fruits of their labors. But reducing too much to private property can be bad medicine. Private land, for instance, is far more useful if separated from other private land by public streets, roads and highways. Public parks, utility rights-of-way and sewers reduce the amount of land in private hands, but vastly enhance the value of the property that remains.

So too it is with intellectual property. Overprotecting intellectual property is as harmful as underprotecting it. Creativity is impossible without a rich public domain. Nothing today, likely nothing since we tamed fire, is genuinely new: Culture, like science and technology, grows by accretion, each new creator building on the works of those who came before. Overprotection stifles the very creative forces it's supposed to nurture.[11]

The panel's opinion is a classic case of overprotection. Concerned about what it sees as a wrong done to Vanna White, the panel majority erects a property right of remarkable and dangerous breadth: Under the majority's opinion, it's now a tort for advertisers to *remind* the public of a celebrity. Not to use a celebrity's name, voice, signature or likeness; not to imply the celebrity endorses a product; but simply to evoke the celebrity's image in the public's mind. This Orwellian notion withdraws far more from the public domain than prudence and common sense allow. It conflicts with the Copyright Act and the Copyright Clause. It raises

---

1. See Eben Shapiro, Rising Caution on Using Celebrity Images, N.Y. Times, Nov. 4, 1992, at D20 (Iraqi diplomat objects on right of publicity grounds to ad containing Hussein's picture and caption "History has shown what happens when one source controls all the information").

2. Eastwood v. Superior Court, 149 Cal. App.3d 409, 198 Cal.Rptr. 342 (1983).

3. Guglielmi v. Spelling–Goldberg Prods., 25 Cal.3d 860, 160 Cal.Rptr. 352, 603 P.2d 454 (1979) (Rudolph Valentino); see also Maheu v. CBS, Inc., 201 Cal.App.3d 662,

668, 247 Cal.Rptr. 304 (1988) (aide to Howard Hughes). * * *

4. Girl Scouts v. Personality Posters Mfg., 304 F.Supp. 1228 (S.D.N.Y.1969) (poster of a pregnant girl in a Girl Scout uniform with the caption "Be Prepared").

5. Lucasfilm Ltd. v. High Frontier, 622 F.Supp. 931 (D.D.C.1985).

11. See Wendy J. Gordon, A Property Right in Self Expression: Equality and Individualism in the Natural Law of Intellectual Property, 102 Yale L.J. 1533, 1556–57 (1993).

Vanna White

Ms. C3PO?

serious First Amendment problems.   It's bad law, and it deserves a long, hard second look.   * * *

Consider how sweeping this new right is.   What is it about the ad that makes people think of White?   It's not the robot's wig, clothes or jewelry; there must be ten million blond women (many of them quasi-famous) who wear dresses and jewelry like White's.   It's that the robot is posed near the "Wheel of Fortune" game board.   Remove the game board from the ad, and no one would think of Vanna White.   See Appendix.   But once you include the game board, anybody standing beside it—a brunette woman, a man wearing women's clothes, a monkey in a wig and gown—would evoke White's image, precisely the way the robot did.   It's the "Wheel of Fortune" set, not the robot's face or dress or jewelry that evokes White's image.   The panel is giving White an exclusive right not in what she looks like or who she is, but in what she does for a living.[18]

This is entirely the wrong place to strike the balance.   Intellectual property rights aren't free: They're imposed at the expense of future creators and of the public at large.   Where would we be if Charles Lindbergh had an exclusive right in the concept of a heroic solo aviator?   If Arthur Conan Doyle had gotten a copyright in the idea of the detective story, or Albert Einstein had patented the theory of relativity?   If every author and celebrity had been given the right to keep people from mocking them or their work?   Surely this would have made the world poorer, not richer, culturally as well as economically.[19]   * * *

The panel, however, does more than misinterpret California law: By refusing to recognize a parody exception to the right of publicity, the panel directly contradicts the federal Copyright Act.   Samsung didn't merely parody Vanna White.   It parodied Vanna White appearing in "Wheel of Fortune," a copyrighted television show, and parodies of copyrighted works are governed by federal copyright law.   * * *

The majority's decision decimates this federal scheme.   It's impossible to parody a movie or a TV show without at the same time "evok[ing]" the "identit[ies]" of the actors.[26]   You can't have a mock *Star Wars* without a

---

18. Once the right of publicity is extended beyond specific physical characteristics, this will become a recurring problem: Outside name, likeness and voice, the things that most reliably remind the public of celebrities are the actions or roles they're famous for.   A commercial with an astronaut setting foot on the moon would evoke the image of Neil Armstrong.   Any masked man on horseback would remind people (over a certain age) of Clayton Moore.   And any number of songs—"My Way," "Yellow Submarine," "Like a Virgin," "Beat It," "Michael, Row the Boat Ashore," to name only a few—instantly evoke an image of the person or group who made them famous, regardless of who is singing.   * * *

19. See generally Gordon, supra note 11; see also Michael Madow, Private Ownership of Public Image: Popular Culture and Publicity Rights, 81 Cal.L.Rev. 125, 201–03 (1993) (an excellent discussion).

26. 17 U.S.C. § 301(b)(1) limits the Copyright Act's preemptive sweep to subject matter "fixed in any tangible medium of expression," but White's identity—her look as the hostess of Wheel of Fortune—is definitely fixed: It consists entirely of her appearances in a fixed, copyrighted TV show.   See Baltimore Orioles v. Major League Baseball Players Ass'n, 805 F.2d 663, 675 & n. 22 (7th Cir.1986).

mock Luke Skywalker, Han Solo and Princess Leia, which in turn means a mock Mark Hamill, Harrison Ford and Carrie Fisher. You can't have a mock *Batman* commercial without a mock Batman, which means someone emulating the mannerisms of Adam West or Michael Keaton. See Carlos V. Lozano, West Loses Lawsuit over Batman TV Commercial, L.A. Times, Jan. 18, 1990, at B3 (describing Adam West's right of publicity lawsuit over a commercial produced under license from DC Comics, owner of the Batman copyright). The public's right to make a fair use parody and the copyright owner's right to license a derivative work are useless if the parodist is held hostage by every actor whose "identity" he might need to "appropriate." * * *

Finally, I can't see how giving White the power to keep others from evoking her image in the public's mind can be squared with the First Amendment. Where does White get this right to control our thoughts? The majority's creation goes way beyond the protection given a trademark or a copyrighted work, or a person's name or likeness. All those things control one particular way of expressing an idea, one way of referring to an object or a person. But not allowing *any* means of reminding people of someone? That's a speech restriction unparalleled in First Amendment law.

What's more, I doubt even a name-and-likeness-only right of publicity can stand without a parody exception. The First Amendment isn't just about religion or politics—it's also about protecting the free development of our national culture. Parody, humor, irreverence are all vital components of the marketplace of ideas. The last thing we need, the last thing the First Amendment will tolerate, is a law that lets public figures keep people from mocking them, or from "evok[ing]" their images in the mind of the public. 971 F.2d at 1399.[29]

The majority dismisses the First Amendment issue out of hand because Samsung's ad was commercial speech. Id. at 1401 & n. 3. So what? Commercial speech may be less protected by the First Amendment than noncommercial speech, but less protected means protected nonetheless. Central Hudson Gas & Elec. Corp. v. Public Serv. Comm'n, 447 U.S. 557 (1980). * * *

In our pop culture, where salesmanship must be entertaining and entertainment must sell, the line between the commercial and noncommercial has not merely blurred; it has disappeared. Is the Samsung parody any different from a parody on Saturday Night Live or in Spy Magazine? Both are equally profit-motivated. Both use a celebrity's identity to sell things—one to sell VCRs, the other to sell advertising. Both mock their

---

29. The majority's failure to recognize a parody exception to the right of publicity would apply equally to parodies of politicians as of actresses. * * *

See also Samsung Has Seen the Future: Brace Yourself, Adweek, Oct. 3, 1988, at 26 (ER 72) (Samsung planned another ad that would show a dollar bill with Richard Nixon's face on it and the caption "Dollar bill, 2025 A.D.," but Nixon refused permission to use his likeness); Madow supra note 19, at 142–46 (discussing other politically and culturally charged parodies).

subjects. Both try to make people laugh. Both add something, perhaps something worthwhile and memorable, perhaps not, to our culture. Both are things that the people being portrayed might dearly want to suppress. See notes 1 & 29 supra.

Commercial speech is a significant, valuable part of our national discourse. The Supreme Court has recognized as much, and has insisted that lower courts carefully scrutinize commercial speech restrictions, but the panel totally fails to do this. The panel majority doesn't even purport to apply the *Central Hudson* test, which the Supreme Court devised specifically for determining whether a commercial speech restriction is valid. The majority doesn't ask, as *Central Hudson* requires, whether the speech restriction is justified by a substantial state interest. It doesn't ask whether the restriction directly advances the interest. It doesn't ask whether the restriction is narrowly tailored to the interest. See id. at 566. These are all things the Supreme Court told us—in no uncertain terms—we must consider; the majority opinion doesn't even mention them.

Process matters. The Supreme Court didn't set out the *Central Hudson* test for its health. It devised the test because it saw lower courts were giving the First Amendment short shrift when confronted with commercial speech. See *Central Hudson*, 447 U.S. at 561–62, 567–68. The *Central Hudson* test was an attempt to constrain lower courts' discretion, to focus judges' thinking on the important issues—how strong the state interest is, how broad the regulation is, whether a narrower regulation would work just as well. If the Court wanted to leave these matters to judges' gut feelings, to nifty lines about "the difference between fun and profit," 971 F.2d at 1401, it could have done so with much less effort.
* * *

For better or worse, we *are* the Court of Appeals for the Hollywood Circuit. Millions of people toil in the shadow of the law we make, and much of their livelihood is made possible by the existence of intellectual property rights. But much of their livelihood—and much of the vibrancy of our culture—also depends on the existence of other intangible rights: The right to draw ideas from a rich and varied public domain, and the right to mock, for profit as well as fun, the cultural icons of our time.

In the name of avoiding the "evisceration" of a celebrity's rights in her image, the majority diminishes the rights of copyright holders and the public at large. In the name of fostering creativity, the majority suppresses it. Vanna White and those like her have been given something they never had before, and they've been given it at our expense. I cannot agree.

———

CARDTOONS, L.C. V. MAJOR LEAGUE BASEBALL PLAYERS ASS'N, 95 F.3d 959 (10th Cir.1996). Cardtoons sought a declaratory judgment that its parody baseball cards did not infringe the publicity rights of the members of the Major League Baseball Players Association. Cardtoons' trading cards included caricatures of well-known players on the front of the cards and humorous commentary about their careers on the back, often focusing on the players' substantial salaries. The card for San Francisco Giants outfielder Barry Bonds, for example, calls him "Treasury Bonds" and shows a recognizable caricature of Bonds tipping a bat boy for a 24–carat gold bat. The district court, holding that the cards were protected by the first amendment, issued a declaratory judgment in favor of Cardtoons.

On appeal, Judge Tacha began by acknowledging that the trading cards violated the Oklahoma right of publicity statute that prohibits use of another's "name, voice, signature, photograph, or likeness, in any manner, on or in products, merchandise, or goods * * *."

"Because the parody trading cards infringe upon MLBPA's property rights, we must consider whether Cardtoons has a countervailing First Amendment right to publish the cards. * * *

"Cardtoons' parody trading cards receive full protection under the First Amendment. The cards provide social commentary on public figures, major league baseball players, who are involved in a significant commercial enterprise, major league baseball. While not core political speech (the cards do not, for example, adopt a position on the Ken Griffey, Jr., for President campaign), this type of commentary on an important social institution constitutes protected expression. * * *

"MLBPA also maintains that the parody trading cards are commercial merchandise rather than protected speech. However, we see no principled distinction between speech and merchandise that informs our First Amendment analysis. The fact that expressive materials are sold neither renders the speech unprotected, Virginia State Bd. of Pharmacy v. Virginia Citizens Consumer Council, Inc., 425 U.S. 748, 761 (1976), nor alters the level of protection under the First Amendment, Lakewood v. Plain Dealer Publishing Co., 486 U.S. 750, 756 n. 5 (1988). Cardtoons need not give away its trading cards in order to bring them within the ambit of the First Amendment. See *Lakewood,* 486 U.S. at 756 n. 5.

"MLBPA further argues that the parody cards are commercial speech and should therefore receive less protection under the First Amendment. The Supreme Court has defined commercial speech as 'expression related solely to the economic interests of the speaker and its audience.' Central Hudson Gas & Elec. Corp. v. Public Serv. Comm'n, 447 U.S. 557, 561 (1980). Speech that does no more than propose a commercial transaction, for example, is commercial speech. See *Virginia State Bd. of Pharmacy,* 425 U.S. at 762. Thus, commercial speech is best understood as speech that merely advertises a product or service for business purposes, see 44 Liquormart, Inc. v. Rhode Island, 517 U.S. 484, 495 (1996) (plurality opinion) (outlining a brief history of commercial speech that is, essentially, a history of advertising). As such, commercial speech may receive something less than the strict review afforded other types of speech. Id. at 501.

"Cardtoons' trading cards, however, are not commercial speech—they do not merely advertise another unrelated product. Although the cards are sold in the marketplace, they are not transformed into commercial speech merely because they are sold for profit. *Virginia State Bd. of Pharmacy,* 425 U.S. at 761. Contrary to MLBPA's argument, therefore, the cards are unlike the parody in the only other circuit court decision addressing the constitutional tensions inherent in a celebrity parody, White v. Samsung Electronics America, Inc., 971 F.2d 1395 (9th Cir.), cert. denied, 508 U.S. 951 (1992). * * * We disagree with the result in that case for reasons discussed in the two dissents that it engendered. Id. at 1407–08 (Alarcon, J., concurring in part and dissenting in part); White v. Samsung Elecs. Am., Inc., 989 F.2d 1512, 1512–23 (9th Cir.1993) (denial of rehearing en banc) (Kozinski, J., dissenting). Moreover, our case is distinguished by the fact that the speech involved is not commercial, but rather speech subject to full First Amendment protection. *White,* therefore, is inapposite, and we must directly confront the central problem in this case: whether Cardtoons' First Amendment right trumps MLBPA's property right. * * *

"This case instead requires us to directly balance the magnitude of the speech restriction against the asserted governmental interest in protecting the intellectual property right. We thus begin our analysis by examining the importance of Cardtoons' right to free expression and the consequences of limiting that right. We then weigh those consequences against the effect of infringing on MLBPA's right of publicity."

Judge Tacha argued that the plaintiff's interest in publishing its cards "implicates some of the core concerns of the First Amendment." "Parodies of celebrities are an especially valuable means of expression because of the role celebrities play in modern society." Noting that the Players Association had conceded that it would never license a parody that poked fun at the players, Judge Tacha concluded that enforcing the players' publicity rights "would not only allow MLBPA to censor criticism of its members, but would also have a chilling effect upon future celebrity parodies."

As to the magnitude of the governmental interest in protecting the players' property rights, the court concluded that the justifications for the publicity right are weak, particularly in the context of parody. "[T]he inducements generated by publicity rights are not nearly as important as those created by copyright and patent law, and the small incentive effect of publicity rights is reduced or eliminated in the context of celebrity parodies. In sum, it is unlikely that little leaguers will stop dreaming of the big leagues or major leaguers will start 'dogging it' to first base if MLBPA is denied the right to control the use of its members' identities in parody. * * * [T]he noneconomic justifications for the right of publicity are no more compelling than the economic arguments. Those justifications further break down in the context of parody, where the right to profit from one's persona is reduced to the power to suppress criticism."

" * * * The application of the Oklahoma publicity rights statute to Cardtoons' trading cards presents a classic case of overprotection. Little is to be gained, and much lost, by protecting MLBPA's right to control the use of its members' identities in parody trading cards. The justifications for the right of publicity are not nearly as compelling as those offered for other forms of intellectual property, and are particularly unpersuasive in the case of celebrity parodies. The cards, on the other hand, are an important form of entertainment and social commentary that deserve First Amendment protection. Accordingly, we Affirm.''

NOTES ON PUBLICITY RIGHTS AND FREE SPEECH

(1) The dissenting opinions written in *White* bring forward two points: first, that the use should not be considered an appropriation of White's "identity," and second, that the imposition of liability may contravene the first amendment. Are these issues related? On the former, do you agree with the dissenters' argument that the majority failed to distinguish the performer from the role she performed?[f] As to the first amendment, pursuing Judge Kozinski's view, how would White's claim fare under an explicit application of the Supreme Court's test in *Central Hudson*?[g]

(2) The court in *Cardtoons* leaned heavily on Madow, Private Ownership and Public Image: Popular Culture and Publicity Rights, 81 Calif.L.Rev. 127 (1993), a powerful critique of the right of publicity. (But see Kwall, Fame, 73 Ind.L.J. 1 (1997), a broad-based defense of the publicity right from a cultural and historical perspective.) Would the court have disagreed with Judge Frank's decision in *Haelan*?

---

f. Welkowitz, Catching Smoke, Nailing JELL–O to a Wall: The *Vanna White* Case and the Limits of Celebrity Rights, 3 J.Intell.Prop.L. 67 (1995), argues that the defendant's "metaphoric" use was not an appropriation of identity. The distinction between performer and role performed came before the Ninth Circuit again in Wendt v. Host Int'l, Inc., 125 F.3d 806 (9th Cir.1997), when actors George Wendt and John Ratzenberger objected to the use of "animatronic robotic figures" based on their characters Norm and Cliff in the television series *Cheers*; the figures were placed in airport bars modeled after the set used on the show. Judge Fletcher, finding issues of fact concerning the degree to which the figures resembled the plaintiffs, reversed a summary judgment that had dismissed their right of publicity claims; the defendants argued that the use appropriated only the identities of the characters. Is it possible for the copyright owner or its licensee to exploit the two characters in a commercially viable manner *without* appropriating the identity of the actors who portrayed them?

g. For more on Judge Kozinski's views, see his Trademarks Unplugged, 68 N.Y.U.L.Rev. 960 (1993), vividly describing the variety of roles, some protected and some not, played by trademarks in modern society. See also Dreyfuss, We Are Symbols and Inhabit Symbols, So Why Should We Be Paying Rent, 20 Colum.-VLA J.L. & Arts 123 (1993), decrying the trend she sees toward greater protection of images, both product and people. Barrett, First Amendment Limits on the Right of Publicity, 30 Tort & Ins.L.J. 635 (1995), argues that the constitutional principles governing commercial speech should limit publicity claims even for straightforward advertising use.

(3) When the appropriation of publicity rights involves no more than the merchandising of a famous name or likeness on goods such as clothing or posters, first amendment defenses are usually rejected. See, e.g., Factors Etc., Inc. v. Pro Arts, Inc., 579 F.2d 215 (2d Cir.1978), cert. denied, 440 U.S. 908 (1979) (posters); Winterland Concessions Co. v. Sileo, 528 F.Supp. 1201 (N.D.Ill.1981), aff'd, 735 F.2d 257 (7th Cir.1984) (distinguishing T-shirts from newspapers). Cf. Titan Sports, Inc. v. Comics World Corp., 870 F.2d 85 (2d Cir.1989), reversing a defendant publisher's summary judgment because of uncertainty as to whether posters stapled inside defendant's wrestling magazine were entitled to first amendment protection. Cases involving games have also rejected first amendment defenses. See Rosemont Enterprises, Inc. v. Urban Systems, Inc., 42 A.D.2d 544, 345 N.Y.S.2d 17 (1973). (Are the game cases such as those described on p. 747 supra, truly devoid of free speech implications?)

(4) The use of celebrity names and photographs in newspaper or magazine articles is generally shielded by the first amendment. See Cher v. Forum Int'l, Ltd., 692 F.2d 634 (9th Cir.1982), cert. denied, 462 U.S. 1120 (1983); Ann–Margret v. High Society Magazine, Inc., 498 F.Supp. 401 (S.D.N.Y. 1980). The former case also holds that a magazine may use a celebrity's name and likeness in advertising for the limited purpose of indicating content; see also Namath v. Sports Illustrated, 48 A.D.2d 487, 371 N.Y.S.2d 10 (1975), aff'd, 39 N.Y.2d 897, 386 N.Y.S.2d 397, 352 N.E.2d 584 (1976). The *Ann–Margret* case emphasizes that good taste is not a prerequisite to first amendment protection. See also New Kids on the Block v. News America Pub., Inc., 971 F.2d 302 (9th Cir.1992) (use of entertainers' names in a newspaper survey was "in connection with" a news account and not actionable under the California statute or common law). Books are also beyond the reach of the publicity right. Although Howard Hughes through Rosemont Enterprises successfully suppressed Howard Hughes games and tee shirts, he could not enjoin publication of an unauthorized biography: "The publication of a biography is clearly outside the ambit of the 'commercial use' contemplated by the 'right of publicity' * * *." Rosemont Enterprises, Inc. v. Random House, Inc., 58 Misc.2d 1, 294 N.Y.S.2d 122 (Sup.Ct.1968), aff'd, 32 A.D.2d 892, 301 N.Y.S.2d 948 (1969). The estate of Marilyn Monroe met a similar response when it objected to Norman Mailer's *Marilyn*: "We think it does not matter whether the book is properly described as a biography, a fictional biography, or any other kind of literary work. * * * It is enough that the book is a literary work and not simply a disguised commercial advertisement for the sale of goods or services." Frosch v. Grosset & Dunlap, Inc., 75 A.D.2d 768, 427 N.Y.S.2d 828 (1980). Hicks v. Casablanca Records, the Agatha Christie case, p. 758 supra, reached the same conclusion with respect to a fictional account in a motion picture.

For an impassioned defense of the fictionalization right in the face of right of publicity claims, see Justice Bird's concurring opinion in Guglielmi v. Spelling–Goldberg Productions, 25 Cal.3d 860, 160 Cal.Rptr. 352, 603

P.2d 454 (1979), involving a fictionalized television version of the life of Rudolph Valentino.[h]

When Ginger Rogers objected to a Fellini film, "Ginger and Fred," about a pair of "tattered, retired hoofers" who had adopted that sobriquet, Judge Newman for the Second Circuit concluded that the interest in free expression would defeat her right of publicity claim under Oregon law. (He also rejected claims of confusion of sponsorship and false advertising under § 43(a), finding the risk of deception outweighed by the danger of suppressing an "artistically relevant though ambiguous title.") Rogers v. Grimaldi, 875 F.2d 994 (2d Cir.1989).

(5) The Supreme Court considered the publicity right in Zacchini v. Scripps–Howard Broadcasting Co., 433 U.S. 562 (1977). Defendant, without permission, filmed plaintiff's "human cannonball" act at a county fair and showed the fifteen-second film on the eleven o'clock news, with commentary urging viewers to go see it. Zacchini claimed an "unlawful appropriation" of his property; the Ohio Supreme Court thought the claim implicated his right of publicity, but found the defendant's use privileged under the first amendment. The U.S. Supreme Court reversed, 5–4. Drawing an analogy to the goals of patent and copyright law, the Court determined that "Ohio's decision to protect petitioner's right of publicity here rests on more than a desire to compensate the performer for the time and effort invested in his act; the protection provides an economic incentive for him to make the investment required to produce a performance of interest to the public." As for the first amendment defense, the Court held: "It is evident, and there is no claim here to the contrary, that petitioner's state-law right of publicity would not serve to prevent respondent from reporting the newsworthy facts about petitioner's act. Wherever the line in particular situations is to be drawn between media reports that are protected and those that are not, we are quite sure that the First and Fourteenth Amendments do not immunize the media when they broadcast a performer's entire act without his consent." Does this adequately distinguish the magazine, book, and movie cases discussed in Note (4)?

The Court also noted that Zacchini's claim involved "not the appropriation of an entertainer's reputation to enhance the attractiveness of a commercial product, but the appropriation of the very activity by which the entertainer acquired his reputation in the first place." Is *INS* rather than *Haelan Laboratories* the more pertinent precedent?

The accommodation between the right of publicity and the first amendment is pursued in most of the articles already cited. See also Samuelson,

h. On the possibility of a "false light" privacy claim in the fictionalization—falsification context, see Lerman v. Flynt Distrib. Co., 745 F.2d 123 (2d Cir.1984), cert. denied, 471 U.S. 1054 (1985); Spahn v. Julian Messner, Inc., 21 N.Y.2d 124, 286 N.Y.S.2d 832, 233 N.E.2d 840 (1967), appeal dism'd, 393 U.S. 1046 (1969). On defamation claims, see Bindrim v. Mitchell, 92 Cal.App.3d 61, 155 Cal.Rptr. 29, cert. denied, 444 U.S. 984 (1979); Symposium, Defamation in Fiction, 51 Brooklyn L.Rev. 223 (1985).

Reviving *Zacchini:* Analyzing First Amendment Defenses in Right of Publicity and Copyright Cases, 57 Tul.L.Rev. 836 (1983); Kwall, The Right of Publicity vs. The First Amendment: A Property and Liability Rule Analysis, 70 Ind.L.J. 47 (1994), weighing various remedial responses.

(6) Are any of the manifestations of the publicity right preempted under § 301? Preemption arguments were unsuccessful in Waits v. Frito–Lay, Inc., p. 663 supra; Bi–Rite Enterprises v. Button Master, 555 F.Supp. 1188; Factors Etc., Inc. v. Pro Arts, Inc., 496 F.Supp. 1090 (S.D.N.Y.1980), rev'd on other grounds, 652 F.2d 278 (2d Cir.1981), cert. denied, 456 U.S. 927 (1982). But see Shipley, Publicity Never Dies; It Just Fades Away: The Right of Publicity and Federal Preemption, 66 Cornell L.Rev. 673 (1981), suggesting that the right of publicity might sometimes be equivalent to copyright in a fixed performance. In Baltimore Orioles, Inc. v. Major League Baseball Players Ass'n, 805 F.2d 663 (7th Cir.1986), cert. denied, 480 U.S. 941 (1987), where the players contended that publicity rights continued despite the authorized filming and broadcasting of their performances on the field, the court, after several citations to Shipley's article, found preemption. (The decision also is significant as an instance of work-for-hire.) But Shipley himself apparently disagrees. In Three Strikes and They're Out at the Old Ball Game: Preemption of Performers' Rights of Publicity Under the Copyright Act of 1976, 20 Ariz.St.L.J. 369 (1988), he argues energetically that the games as such are not within the subject matter of copyright and thus the publicity rights of the players are not preempted. See Restatement, Third, Unfair Competition § 46, Comment *i* (1995). Is "consent" a better rationale for denying the players' publicity claims?

CHAPTER 10

COMPENSATION FOR "IDEAS"

This Chapter concerns rights in ideas, especially ideas of supposed value in the entertainment industry. The cases are drawn from New York and California, the two centers of the entertainment business. The law in other jurisdictions, although generally less developed, favors one or another variation on these basic themes.

NEW YORK LAW

Bristol v. Equitable Life Assurance Society of the United States

Court of Appeals of New York, 1892.
132 N.Y. 264, 30 N.E. 506.

Appeal from judgment of the General Term of the Supreme Court in the first judicial department, entered upon an order made March 29, 1889, which affirmed a judgment in favor of defendant entered upon a decision of the court on trial at Special Term.

This action was brought to obtain an accounting and recover compensation for communicating to defendant a new system for soliciting life insurance, which plaintiff alleged, after a confidential disclosure thereof by him in a letter requesting employment, was adopted by defendant and used without his knowledge, and the use was continued, notwithstanding his protests, after discovery of its use, whereby defendant obtained a large amount of business.

Defendant demurred to the complaint on the ground that it did not state facts sufficient to constitute a cause of action, and the demurrer was sustained.

Further facts are stated in the opinion.

LANDON, J. Assuming, without deciding, that if the defendant has wrongfully appropriated, or converted to its own use, the plaintiff's property, or infringed upon his property rights or privileges, and has, without right, made use of them, it ought to respond to the plaintiff for such use, and should render an account to him respecting the same, the question arises upon this complaint whether the subject of the appropriation and use constituted property or property rights of the plaintiff.

The plaintiff does not allege that he was the exclusive possessor of the system. His letter to the defendant instances several companies which have used it to advantage, and states that "underlying the whole system is a common sense plan of advertising." Its use seems to be its disclosure. He does not complain of the use that the defendant has made of it, but seeks to recover for it as if defendant had used his property. His case is unlike those in which the injunctive process of the court is sought to restrain the disclosure of a secret, or the publication of a letter, which may prove injurious to business or character.

Nor is his case like that of one who writes a tale or treatise, or play, or composes a piece of music, or paints a picture, or makes an invention; in such case there is a production which can, by multiplying copies, be put to marketable use and its exclusive ownership be easily preserved and protected. Whoever infringes takes benefits or profits which otherwise would naturally come to the producer. Here the defendant has taken from the plaintiff no profits nor diverted them from him.

Without denying that there may be property in an idea, or trade secret or system, it is obvious that its originator or proprietor must himself protect it from escape or disclosure. If it cannot be sold or negotiated or used without a disclosure, it would seem proper that some contract should guard or regulate the disclosure, otherwise it must follow the law of ideas and become the acquisition of whoever receives it. (Peabody v. Norfolk, 98 Mass. 452.)

The allegation of the complaint that the defendant disclosed the system in confidence to the defendant is vague. It does not necessarily mean that the defendant agreed not to use it; it may mean something else. Defendant is at liberty to conduct its business in its own way; it obtained a valuable hint from the plaintiff and assumed no legal obligation to pay the plaintiff if it should conclude to act upon it.

Plaintiff communicated his system without marketing it. It was valuable to the defendant. But what has plaintiff lost thereby? He alleges nothing more than the loss of the sale to a single party who refused to buy. The system, we may assume, was valuable to those who had insurance to sell. Plaintiff does not allege that he had any to sell. He does not allege that his system was marketable or might have been made so but for the use made of it by defendant.

A. wishes to sell his house and lot. B. tells him in confidence that C. desires to buy it, and B. solicits employment to negotiate the sale. A. declines, but acting upon B.'s communication meets C., and himself negotiates and closes the contract of sale. B. has no cause of action against A. He had information which he hoped to market, but he parted with it without finding any market.

The plaintiff himself communicated his system to the defendant to induce it to employ him, and thus used it as an attractive adjunct to his own self commendation or in corroboration of it. He could not induce the defendant to "adopt this system and the writer with it." Yet as the defendant acted upon the hint the plaintiff gave to it and found it profitable to do so, the plaintiff asks the defendant to pay him a percentage of its profits.

We do not think the complaint states a cause of action.

Judgment should be affirmed.

All concur, except VANN, J., not sitting.

Judgment affirmed.

NOTE

Plaintiff's letter urging Equitable to "adopt this system and the writer with it," concluded: "In the meantime I need hardly to say that this letter must be considered of the most confidential nature." The "system" was evidently a method of soliciting insurance prospects by means of letters followed up by visits from agents. Plaintiff enclosed with his letter to Equitable a specimen "circular" of the kind he had in mind, which he said had already been used in large numbers, and he was not backward in claiming success in applying his system. See the opinion below, 52 Hun 161, 5 N.Y.S. 131 (Sup.Ct.1889).

SOULE v. BON AMI CO., 201 A.D. 794, 195 N.Y.S. 574 (1922), aff'd, 235 N.Y. 609, 139 N.E. 754 (1923). Plaintiff sued on an alleged contract whereby, in consideration of plaintiff's agreement to impart certain valuable information—(1) a method of increasing defendant's profits from a soap known as "Bon Ami," and (2) the reason why this method could be applied without injuring defendant's trade—the defendant promised to pay plaintiff one-half the profits produced by the suggested method. According to the proof, plaintiff's method was to increase defendant's price to grocers from $10 to $10.50 or $10.80 per gross, while holding the grocers' price to the public at 10 cents per package. Plaintiff told defendant that he had satisfied himself from actual experience with a similar but noncompeting product that this could be done without affecting the volume of sales. Defendant after receiving plaintiff's information increased the price to grocers by $1.00 per gross. On this proof the trial court directed a verdict for plaintiff for "one-half of the increased price upon the quantity of goods sold." (Plaintiff claimed that defendant's profits were increased in the amount of $131,364.)

On appeal to the Appellate Division, Judge Jaycox said the first question was whether consideration existed for the alleged contract. "[T]he very nature of the offer suggests that the information must be new." "This was not new, it was not original, and I am at a loss to understand how it could be deemed valuable. * * * No person can by contract monopolize an idea that is common and general to the whole world." Thus consideration was lacking. In the second place, the judgment could not stand unless plaintiff's plan was in fact adopted and put into operation. The trial court assumed that any increase in price must be in execution of plaintiff's plan; in other words, that after listening to plaintiff's plan defendant could not increase its price without incurring liability to plaintiff. Defendant should have been allowed to show that it was considering an increase before plaintiff's disclosure or that the increase in price was the result of commercial conditions unconnected with plaintiff's suggestion. The court reversed the judgment for the plaintiff and ordered the complaint dismissed. Two judges voted to grant a new trial on the issue of whether the plaintiffs' information was a "proximate cause" of the defendant's increased profits.

The Court of Appeals affirmed the dismissal without opinion, with four judges concurring "on ground plaintiff failed to prove profits resulting from change of plans."

Murray v. National Broadcasting Co.

United States Court of Appeals, Second Circuit, 1988.
844 F.2d 988.
Certiorari denied, 488 U.S. 955.

■ Before WINTER, PRATT and ALTIMARI, CIRCUIT JUDGES.

■ ALTIMARI, CIRCUIT JUDGE:

It was almost a generation ago that a young comedian named Bill Cosby became the first black entertainer to star in a dramatic network television series. That program, *I Spy*, earned Cosby national recognition as an actor, including three Emmy Awards (1966, 1967 and 1968) for best performance in a dramatic series, and critical acclaim for the portrayal of a character without regard to the actor's race. Although keenly aware of the significance of his achievement in breaking the color line on network television, Cosby set his sights then on "accomplish[ing] something more significant for the Negro on TV." [1] In an interview in 1965, he envisioned a different approach to the situation comedy genre made popular by *The Dick Van Dyke Show*. The *Daily News* described Cosby's "dream" series as not

> unlike other situation comedies. There'll be the usual humorous exchanges between husband and wife .... Warmth and domestic cheerfulness will pervade the entire program.
>
> Everything on the screen will be familiar to TV viewers. But this series will be radically different. Everyone in it will be a Negro.
>
> * * * * * * * * * * * * * * * * * * *
>
> ... "I'm interested in proving there's no difference between people," [explained Cosby]. "My series would take place in a middle-income Negro neighborhood. People who really don't know Negroes would find on this show that they're just like everyone else." [2]

1. Lardine, Looking to the Future: Bill Cosby Has Dreams of an All–Negro TV Series, New York Daily News, Sept. 19, 1965, Sunday Magazine, at 6.

2. Id.

Nearly twenty years later, on September 20, 1984, Cosby's dream for a "color-blind" family series materialized with the premier of *The Cosby Show*—a situation comedy about a family known as the Huxtables. Bill Cosby stars in the leading role as Heathcliff ("Cliff") Huxtable together with his TV wife Clair and their five children.

Plaintiff-appellant Hwesu Murray, an employee of defendant-appellee ("NBC"), claims in the instant case that in 1980, four years prior to the premier of *The Cosby Show* on NBC's television network, he proposed to NBC a "new" idea for a half-hour situation comedy starring Bill Cosby. * * *

* * * Because we agree with the district court's conclusion that, under New York law, lack of novelty in an idea precludes plaintiff from maintaining a cause of action to prevent its unauthorized use, we affirm the district court's order granting summary judgment and dismissing the complaint.

Plaintiff Hwesu S. Murray has been employed in the television industry for the past ten years. Murray holds a Bachelor of Arts degree in English and graduate degrees in broadcast journalism and law. In 1979, defendant-appellee NBC hired Murray as a Unit Manager and financial analyst in its sports division. A year later, plaintiff contacted an NBC official outside of NBC Sports about some "extracurricular" ideas he had for future television programs, and the official apparently instructed him to submit his proposals in writing. Soon thereafter, in June 1980, plaintiff submitted five written proposals, one of which was entitled "Father's Day." Murray allegedly informed NBC that if it were interested in any of the proposals, he expected to be named executive producer and to receive appropriate credit and compensation as the creator of the eventual program. Plaintiff also allegedly told NBC that his ideas were being submitted in confidence.

Murray's proposal for "Father's Day" is the subject matter of this action. The NBC official who originally had requested it encouraged Murray to "flesh out" his proposal and submit it to Josh Kane, then an NBC vice-president and a top official with NBC Entertainment, the division of NBC responsible for network television programming. Plaintiff thereupon submitted to Kane an expanded proposal for "Father's Day." In a two-page memorandum dated November 1, 1980, Murray first suggested that Bill Cosby play the part of the father. At that time, plaintiff also made several other casting suggestions, including roles for a working spouse and five children, and again indicated that the proposed series would "combine humor with serious situations in a manner similar to that of the old *Dick Van Dyke Show*" but "with a Black perspective." Murray's expanded proposal concluded with the observation that, "[l]ike *Roots,* the show will attempt to depict life in a [closely-knit] Black family, with the addition of a contemporary, urban setting."

NBC apparently decided not to pursue Murray's proposal. On November 21, 1980, Kane returned the "Father's Day" submission to plaintiff and informed him that "we are not interested in pursuing [its] development at this time."

Four years later, in the fall of 1984, *The Cosby Show* premiered on NBC. * * *

Less than a month after viewing the premier, plaintiff wrote to NBC to advise it that *The Cosby Show* had been derived from his idea for "Father's Day." In January 1985, NBC responded through its Law Department, stating its position that " 'Father's Day' played absolutely no role in the development of 'The Cosby Show' ... [since m]uch of the substance and style of 'The Cosby Show' is an outgrowth of the humor and style developed by Bill Cosby throughout his career." NBC further maintained that *The Cosby Show* was developed and produced by The Carsey–Werner Company ("Carsey–Werner"), an independent production company and the executive producers of the series.

In his complaint, plaintiff claimed that *The Cosby Show's* portrayal of a strong black family in a nonstereotypical manner is the essence of "Father's Day," and "[i]t is that portrayal of Black middle-class life that originated with plaintiff." Murray also alleged that Josh Kane showed plaintiff's "Father's Day" proposal to his superiors at NBC, including defendant-appellee Brandon Tartikoff, President of NBC Entertainment. Tartikoff, together with Cosby and Carsey–Werner, have been credited with the creation and development of *The Cosby Show*. Plaintiff maintains that NBC and Tartikoff deliberately deceived plaintiff into believing that NBC had no interest in "Father's Day" and then proceeded to develop and eventually produce plaintiff's idea as *The Cosby Show.*

Plaintiff's complaint stated a number of causes of action arising out of defendants' alleged appropriation of his idea. Among those relevant to this appeal are plaintiff's claims of race discrimination under 42 U.S.C. §§ 1981 and 1982, false designation of origin under the Lanham Act, 15 U.S.C. § 1125, and various state law claims, including misappropriation, conversion, breach of implied contract, unjust enrichment and fraud. Plaintiff sought, *inter alia,* damages and declaratory and injunctive relief as the "sole owner of all rights in and to the idea, proposal and property [known as] 'Father's Day.' "

In a decision dated July 15, 1987, 671 F.Supp. 236 (S.D.N.Y.), the district court considered whether plaintiff's idea was "property" that could be subject to legal protection. Since the parties agreed that New York law applied to plaintiff's claims, the district court proceeded to analyze defendants' motion for summary judgment in light of the New York Court of Appeals decision in Downey v. General Foods Corp., 31 N.Y.2d 56, 334 N.Y.S.2d 874, 286 N.E.2d 257 (1972). In *Downey,* the New York court established the general proposition that "[l]ack of novelty in an idea is fatal to *any* cause of action for its unlawful use." 334 N.Y.S.2d at 877, 286 N.E.2d at 259 (quoting Bram v. Dannon Milk Prods., Inc., 33 A.D.2d 1010, 307 N.Y.S.2d 571, 571 (1st Dep't 1970)) (emphasis added). The district court, therefore, determined that the "sole issue" before it was the novelty of plaintiff's "Father's Day" proposal, and accordingly assumed, for purposes of defendants' motion, that defendants in fact used plaintiff's idea in the development of *The Cosby Show*. See Ed Graham Productions, Inc. v.

National Broadcasting Co., 75 Misc.2d 334, 347 N.Y.S.2d 766, 769 (Sup.Ct. N.Y.Cty.1973) (even assuming defendant used plaintiff's idea, plaintiff may not recover if idea is "wholly lacking in novelty").   * * *

As the district court recognized, the dispositive issue in this case is whether plaintiff's idea is entitled to legal protection.   Plaintiff points to "unique"—"even revolutionary"—aspects of his "Father's Day" proposal that he claims demonstrate "genuine novelty and invention," see Educational Sales Programs, Inc. v. Dreyfus Corp., 65 Misc.2d 412, 317 N.Y.S.2d 840, 844 (Sup.Ct.N.Y.Cty.1970), which preclude the entry of summary judgment against him.   Specifically, plaintiff contends that his idea suggesting the nonstereotypical portrayal of black Americans on television is legally protectible because it represents a real breakthrough. * * *

We certainly do not dispute the fact that the portrayal of a nonstereotypical black family on television was indeed a breakthrough.   Nevertheless, that breakthrough represents the achievement of what many black Americans, including Bill Cosby and plaintiff himself, have recognized for many years—namely, the need for a more positive, fair and realistic portrayal of blacks on television.   While NBC's decision to broadcast *The Cosby Show* unquestionably was innovative in the sense that an intact, nonstereotypical black family had never been portrayed on television before, the mere fact that such a decision had not been made before does not necessarily mean that the idea for the program is itself novel.   See *Educational Sales Programs*, 317 N.Y.S.2d at 843 ("[n]ot every 'good idea' is a legally protectible idea").   * * *

Appellant would have us believe that by interpreting New York law as we do, we are in effect condoning the theft of ideas.   On the contrary, ideas that reflect "genuine novelty and invention" are fully protected against unauthorized use.   *Educational Sales Programs*, 317 N.Y.S.2d at 844.   But those ideas that are not novel "are in the public domain and may freely be used by anyone with impunity."   *Ed Graham Productions*, 347 N.Y.S.2d at 769.   Since such non-novel ideas are not protectible as property, they cannot be stolen.   * * *

Finally, as an alternative attack on the propriety of the district court's order granting summary judgment, plaintiff posits that even if his idea was not novel as a matter of law, summary judgment still was inappropriate because his proposal was solicited by defendants and submitted to them in confidence.   In this regard, Murray relies on Cole v. Phillips H. Lord, Inc., 262 A.D. 116, 28 N.Y.S.2d 404 (1st Dep't 1941).   Murray contends that *Cole* stands for the proposition that when an idea is protected by an agreement or a confidential relationship, a cause of action arises for unauthorized use of that idea irrespective of the novelty of the subject matter of the contract.   Plaintiff's reliance on *Cole* is misplaced in light of subsequent cases, particularly the New York Court of Appeals decision in Downey v. General Foods Corp., 31 N.Y.2d 56, 334 N.Y.S.2d 874, 286 N.E.2d 257 (1972).   See also Ferber v. Sterndent Corp., 51 N.Y.2d 782, 433 N.Y.S.2d 85, 86, 412 N.E.2d 1311 (1980) ("[a]bsent a showing of novelty, plaintiff's action to recover damages for illegal use of 'confidentially disclosed ideas' must fail as a matter of law"); *Educational Sales Programs,* 317 N.Y.S.2d at 844 ("[o]ne cannot be forever barred from using a worthwhile but unoriginal idea merely because it was once asked to be treated in confidence").

Consequently, we find that New York law requires that an idea be original or novel in order for it to be protected as property. See *Downey,* 334 N.Y.S.2d at 877, 286 N.E.2d at 259. Since, as has already been shown, plaintiff's proposal for "Father's Day" was lacking in novelty and originality, we conclude that the district court correctly granted defendants' motion for summary judgment.

Having determined that plaintiff's idea is not property under New York law, we turn now to a consideration of the district court's dismissal of the various claims in the complaint.

A. *State law claims*

"[W]hen one submits an idea to another, no promise to pay for its use may be implied, and no asserted agreement enforced, if the elements of novelty and originality are absent . . . ." *Downey,* 334 N.Y.S.2d at 877, 286 N.E.2d at 259. As the district court recognized, non-novel ideas do not constitute property. As a result, there can be no cause of action for unauthorized use of Murray's proposal since it was not unlawful for defendants to use a non-novel idea. We conclude therefore that the district court properly dismissed plaintiff's state law claims for breach of implied contract, misappropriation, conversion, and unjust enrichment. * * *

Similarly, plaintiff's fraud claim also fails since, as the district court recognized, plaintiff "cannot be defrauded of property that he does not own." Essential to a cause of action for fraud is a showing of injury as the proximate result of the alleged fraudulent conduct. See Dress Shirt Sales, Inc. v. Hotel Martinique Assocs., 12 N.Y.2d 339, 239 N.Y.S.2d 660, 663, 190 N.E.2d 10 (1963). Because plaintiff's idea for "Father's Day" was in the public domain when NBC allegedly used it in the creation of *The Cosby Show,* Murray suffered no injury. His cause of action for fraud thus was properly dismissed.

B. *Civil Rights claims*

[The court held that plaintiff's Civil Rights claims were also properly dismissed.]

C. *Lanham Act claim*

Lastly, we find that Judge Cedarbaum correctly determined that plaintiff's claim for false designation of origin, see Lanham Act § 43(a), 15 U.S.C. § 1125(a), regarding the credits to *The Cosby Show,* cannot survive in light of the court's granting of summary judgment against plaintiff on the issue of novelty. Even assuming defendants used plaintiff's idea, NBC's failure to designate Murray as the creator of *The Cosby Show* does not mean that the credits to the program are false since ideas in the public domain may be used with impunity and thus do not require attribution. * * *

Affirmed.

■ GEORGE C. PRATT, CIRCUIT JUDGE, dissenting:

Today this court holds that the idea underlying what may well be the most successful situation comedy in television history was, in 1980, so unoriginal and so entrenched in the public domain that, as a matter of law, it did not constitute intellectual property protected under New York law. Because I am convinced that the novelty issue in this case presents a factual question subject to further discovery and ultimate scrutiny by a trier of fact, I respectfully dissent. * * *

I agree with the majority that there is some evidence that Murray's idea was not novel. But clearly, there is also evidence indicating novelty. Initially, there is the admission by NBC, in its agreement with Carsey–Werner, that the television series is "unique, intellectual property." * * *

Nor is the agreement the only piece of evidence indicating an issue of fact as to novelty. In 1985, NBC admitted that Murray had "rights" in his idea, but determined it had no interest in acquiring those rights. At trial, both Cosby and Tartikoff stated that they believed *The Cosby Show* to be novel and unique. NBC admitted that the reason it normally returned rejected submissions, as it did in Murray's case, was that the "material belong[ed] to the submitter." In short, there is substantial evidence, both within and independent of the Carsey–Werner development agreement, which directly conflicts with the majority's holding that, as a matter of law, Murray's idea was not novel.

The fact that the basic idea had been expressed by Cosby some fifteen years before Murray submitted his proposal to NBC does not erase these factual issues. To say, as a matter of law, that an idea is not novel because it already exists in general form, would be to deny governmental protection to any idea previously mentioned anywhere, at anytime, by anyone. I do not believe New York law defines "novelty" so strictly, especially in the area of mass communications, an area long recognized by state courts as "a specialized field having customs and usages of its own" where "a property right exists" in "a combination of ideas evolved into a program." Cole v. Phillip H. Lord, Inc., 262 A.D. 116, 121, 28 N.Y.S.2d 404, 409 (1st Dep't 1941). Indeed, in a market the very existence of which depends on the generation and development of ideas, it may be impossible to formulate a concept that has not previously been expressed by someone, somewhere.

Novelty, by its very definition, is highly subjective. As fashion, advertising, and television and radio production can attest, what is novel today may not have been novel 15 years ago, and what is commonplace today may well be novel 15 years hence. In this instance, where Cosby expressed the concept almost a decade and a half before Murray submitted his proposal, where it was Murray's idea that NBC actually used, where there is no evidence indicating NBC knew anything of the program idea until Murray submitted it, compare Downey v. General Foods Corp., 31 N.Y.2d 56, 60,

334 N.Y.S.2d 874, 877–78, 286 N.E.2d 257 (1972) (no novelty because defendant had "envisaged" *and* "utilized" plaintiff's idea for "years before the plaintiff submitted it") with Werlin v. Readers Digest Ass'n Inc., 528 F.Supp. 451, 466 (S.D.N.Y.1981) (even though plaintiff's idea was in public domain, no evidence that defendant knew about or would have discovered the idea except through plaintiff's proposal; hence, the "idea was novel" as far as defendant was concerned), and where substantial conflicting evidence exists as to the "novelty" of the idea under New York law, there seems to be at least a triable issue.

The majority's decision prematurely denies Murray a fair opportunity to establish his right to participate in the enormous wealth generated by *The Cosby Show*. Accordingly, I would reverse the district court judgment and remand the case for further consideration.

NOTES AND QUESTIONS

(1) Does the Second Circuit mean to suggest that in the absence of novelty, even an *express* contract for the sale of an idea is unenforceable? Cf. High v. Trade Union Courier Pub. Corp., 31 Misc.2d 7, 69 N.Y.S.2d 526 (Sup.Ct. 1946), aff'd, 275 A.D. 803, 89 N.Y.S.2d 527 (1949). Plaintiff alleged an agreement to pay him 35% of the savings on telephone excise taxes. He then disclosed to defendant a relevant exemption in the Internal Revenue Code. Judge Hofstadter said:

> Defendant next assails the adequacy of the consideration upon the basis that disclosure of a public statute does not involve a secret or confidential information. It is clear, however, that an idea if valuable, may be the subject of contract. While the idea disclosed may be common or even open to public knowledge, yet such disclosure if protected by contract, is sufficient consideration for the promise to pay.

But see, in addition to the *Downey* case discussed in *Murray*, Granoff v. Merrill Lynch & Co., 775 F.Supp. 621 (S.D.N.Y.1991), aff'd, 962 F.2d 2 (2d Cir.1992), holding that under New York law, "to meet the requirement of minimal consideration, even actions on express contracts must involve the use of an idea which is novel."

The New York rule on express contracts was refined by the Court of Appeals in Apfel v. Prudential–Bache Securities, Inc., 81 N.Y.2d 470, 600 N.Y.S.2d 433, 616 N.E.2d 1095 (1993). Speaking of cases like *Murray* and *Soule*, where buyer and seller contract for disclosure of the idea, the court explained that the novelty requirement serves "to establish both the attributes of ownership necessary for a property-based claim and the value of the consideration—the disclosure—necessary for contract-based claims." But here, the contract to pay for use of the idea was made subsequent to plaintiff's disclosure. "In such a case, buyer knows what he or she is buying and has agreed that the idea has value, and the Court will not ordinarily go behind that determination. The lack of novelty, in and of itself, does not demonstrate a lack of value * * *."

(2) Mrs. Galanis wrote an unsolicited letter to Procter & Gamble stating that she had an idea for a new kind of soap, which she called "Blue." It was a soap with bluing added, to be used for washing laundry. The company replied thanking Mrs. Galanis for her interest and saying that it had considered such a soap many times in the past but had decided against it; it would be excellent for regular laundry, but was likely to be unpopular for colored fabrics and lingerie. The company later put out a soap called "Blue Cheer" that according to plaintiff combines soap with bluing as she suggested. She sued the company for $1,000,000. On defendant's motion for summary judgment, Judge Dawson said, "The general rule of law is that a mere idea is not property and that any right to its exclusive use is lost by its voluntary disclosure." Yet "courts have in certain cases recognized that even if plaintiff has no property right in an idea, and even though no contract for the sale or use of such idea has been established, nevertheless the defendant may be held liable in *quantum meruit* on the theory of unjust enrichment, where defendant utilized a concrete and novel idea submitted by plaintiff." For plaintiff to recover she would have to establish that her idea was novel and concrete and that it had been appropriated by defendant in developing its product. The court doubted that plaintiff could succeed in proving these propositions at trial, but felt constrained to deny summary judgment. Galanis v. Procter & Gamble Corp., 153 F.Supp. 34 (S.D.N.Y.1957).

See also Werlin v. Reader's Digest Ass'n, Inc., 528 F.Supp. 451 (S.D.N.Y.1981), reiterating the elements of novelty, concreteness, and appropriation. The court awarded damages on a quasi-contract theory to an author who, encouraged by Reader's Digest, submitted an article that inspired the magazine to prepare its own story based on plaintiff's idea. The court also held that the cause of action was not preempted by federal copyright law. Is that correct?

(3) When New York cases require an idea to be "concrete," what do they mean? Was Murray's idea "concrete"? What function is served by this requirement?

Consider also the meaning of "novelty". Is "novelty" viewed from the standpoint of the recipient only? See the *High* and *Werlin* cases, supra. Should one approach "business" ideas differently from "literary" ideas such as suggested formulas for television programs? The cases relied on in *Murray,* notably Educational Sales Programs, Inc. v. Dreyfus Corp. and Downey v. General Foods, were about marketing proposals. Should the courts take any account of the source of a submission—whether it is from an amateur, as in *Galanis,* supra, or from someone who makes it her business to work up proposals?

(4) How can "appropriation" be shown? Is it enough for the defendant to prove access to the idea from a different source? Suppose the defendant utilizes the idea in the sense of experimenting with it, but finishes with a product deviating materially from the submitted idea?

Switching to the West Coast for a moment, consider on the question of appropriation the express contract claim brought by columnist Art Buchwald against Paramount Pictures, which had purchased an option on his "treatment" for a movie tailored for Eddie Murphy. It was about an African ruler who is deposed while visiting the United States. Buchwald claimed that Paramount, after allowing the option to lapse, derived *Coming to America* (starring Eddie Murphy) from his synopsis. The contract required payment if Paramount made a movie "based upon Author's work." Should the test be "substantial similarity" in the copyright sense? The court in Buchwald v. Paramount Pictures Corp., 13 U.S.P.Q.2d 1497 (Cal.Super.1990), said that Paramount was liable if *Coming to America* was "based upon a material element of or was inspired by Buchwald's treatment"; the court held that it was.[a]

CALIFORNIA LAW

Whitfield v. Lear

United States Court of Appeals, Second Circuit, 1984.
751 F.2d 90.

■ Before OAKES and WINTER, CIRCUIT JUDGES, and CLAIRE, DISTRICT JUDGE.

■ WINTER, CIRCUIT JUDGE:

Thurman V. Whitfield, *pro se,* appeals from a grant of summary judgment. 582 F.Supp. 1186. His complaint invoked a variety of legal theories arising from defendants' alleged misappropriation of ideas contained in a television script he authored. Because we believe that the similarities between appellant's script and the appellees' television series can be appraised only by comparing the actual scripts, many of which are not in the record, we reverse and remand.

During the years 1975 through 1977, appellee Topper Carew worked on a proposed television series called "The Righteous Apples." On August 29, 1977, he filed a sixteen page registration with the Writers Guild[b] consisting of a brief description of the series, descriptions of the characters, and marketing and production information. The document describes "The Righteous Apples" as a situation comedy involving a multiracial rock band of six junior high school students aged 13 through 15. A seventh student is

a. Buchwald's contract called for a share of net profits, but Paramount rejoined that the film, which grossed over $300 million at the box office, produced no net profit to Paramount under the formula contained in the contract. The court later held the contract formula unconscionable. See Agnew, Profits of Doom: Net Profit Participation Contracts in the Motion Picture Industry, 15 Colum.–VLA J.L. & Arts 367 (1991). Buchwald got a judgment for $900,000; first Paramount appealed, but then it settled for more than $1 million. It may have been worried that an appeal might set a legal prece-

dent that would later haunt it; in another dispute it was claiming that *Forrest Gump*, which grossed $650 million, had yet to turn a profit. Abelson, The Shell Game of Hollywood "Net Profits," New York Times, Mar. 4, 1996, p. D1.

b. Idea submitters in the entertainment business sometimes attempt to protect their creations by registering them with the Writers Guild, which receives 30,000 submissions a year. See Craft, Hollywood's Storehouse of Scripts, Ideas, Movies, Los Angeles Times, Mar. 18, 1992, p. F3.

the group's business manager. A primary theme of the series is the interaction of youths in a multiracial setting.

Carew was president of defendant Rainbow Television Workshop. On February 3, 1978, Rainbow entered into an agreement with the Corporation for Public Broadcasting ("CPB") to determine the feasibility of producing a pilot film based on "The Righteous Apples." On December 19, 1978, CPB agreed to provide funding to produce a pilot, which was filmed but never aired. The shooting script for the pilot, entitled "The Righteous Apple Wrangle," is in the record. That script is a situation comedy involving the characters described supra, and the plot essentially traces the resolution of racial tensions between one of the band members and another student. Another pilot script, with similar characteristics, is in the record.

During this period, appellant Whitfield was also working on a format for a television series and eventually he copyrighted a script for a show entitled "Boomerang." This was a dramatic show about an interracial, crime-fighting rock band, called Boomerang. The band had five members, two white, one Spanish-surnamed, and two black. All five were recent graduates of the same high school where they had formed the band. In the "Boomerang" script, which is also in the record, the band members fight crime using their athletic talents and occasionally a boomerang as a weapon.

Following the copyrighting of "Boomerang," Whitfield added additional scenes to the script and circulated it to television producers. In March, 1979, he sent a mailgram to the defendant Norman Lear and his company, Tandem Productions, informing them that a script was forthcoming. Lear forwarded the mailgram to another company he controlled, defendant TAT Communications, and so informed Whitfield. In 1980–1981, a twenty-episode series entitled "The Righteous Apples," produced by Carew, was broadcast under CPB auspices. Whitfield contends that "The Righteous Apples" series differs from the original pilot script and that the series as actually broadcast bears a strong resemblance to "Boomerang," resulting from Carew's access to the latter script through Tandem Productions and his appropriation of the ideas contained therein.

On June 4, 1981, appellant commenced this action alleging federal and state claims and diversity of citizenship. His complaint alleged the following causes of action under California law:

(1) Breach of contract;

(2) Breach of confidential or fiduciary relationship;

(3) Breach of implied covenant of good faith and fair dealing;

(4) Fraud and misrepresentation;

(5) Misappropriation and commercial piracy;

(6) Unfair competition;

(7) False designation of origin and false advertising;

(8) Restitution based on quasi-contract and unjust enrichment.

He also alleged copyright infringement under 17 U.S.C. § 501 and a violation of the Lanham Act, 15 U.S.C. §§ 1051–1127. Appellees moved for summary judgment, and both parties submitted affidavits. Appellees conceded access to Whitfield's script, and, apparently, their group involvement for Carew's series, solely for purposes of the motion. Judge Glasser granted the motion. The appellant, who was represented in the district court by counsel, prosecuted this appeal *pro se*.

Appellant has never alleged that the appellees actually copied from his script, only that they misappropriated ideas contained therein. Such a claim does not implicate the federal copyright laws, and appellant withdrew his copyright and Lanham Act claims in the district court. He thus now relies solely on a variety of causes of action under California law.

Appellant claims an interest in the ideas contained in his script and seeks redress for misappropriation of the ideas, not their literary or artistic expression. This theory narrows the legal grounds available for recovery even further. Under California law, the fraud, misappropriation, unfair competition, and quasi-contract claims are actionable only to vindicate legally protected property interests, and an idea is not recognized as a property right. Weitzenkorn v. Lesser, 40 Cal.2d 778, 789, 256 P.2d 947, 956 (1953) (en banc). Recovery for the appropriation of an idea, therefore, may be had only on a contractual theory. See Donahue v. Ziv Television Programs, Inc., 245 Cal.App.2d 593, 601, 54 Cal.Rptr. 130, 137 (1966).

While an idea is not property and is not subject to copyright under California law, its disclosure may be valid consideration for a contract. There is no evidence of an express contract between Whitfield and any of the defendants. However, California law will imply a contract from the conduct of the parties in certain circumstances. Thus, if a producer accepts a submitted idea with full knowledge that the offeror expects payment in the event of use, California courts impose liability under a theory of implied-in-fact contract. Desny v. Wilder, 46 Cal.2d 715, 299 P.2d 257 (1956) (en banc). In that case, the plaintiff called Wilder, a writer/producer for Paramount Pictures Corp. and, when asked the purpose of his call by Wilder's secretary, told her of an idea he had for a motion picture. At the secretary's invitation, the plaintiff dictated a brief synopsis of his idea over the telephone. Following this disclosure, the plaintiff stated that he expected to be paid if the idea were used, and the secretary acknowledged that he would be. The California Supreme Court held these facts sufficient to survive defendant's motion for summary judgment in a suit alleging that the defendants had used the idea without payment. The court also set forth the circumstances in which a contract might be implied absent an express promise to pay:

> [T]he idea purveyor cannot prevail in an action to recover compensation for an abstract idea unless (a) before or after disclosure he has obtained an express promise to pay, or (b) the circumstances preceding and attending disclosure, together with the conduct of the offeree acting with knowledge of the circumstances, show a

promise of the type usually referred to as "implied" or "implied-in-fact."

Id. at 738, 299 P.2d at 270 (footnote and citations omitted). California courts still follow the *Wilder* test. See Klekas v. EMI Films, Inc., 150 Cal.App.3d 1102, 1114, 198 Cal.Rptr. 296, 304 (1984).

Appellees argue that, even accepting Whitfield's version of the facts surrounding submission of "Boomerang," there is insufficient evidence to support an implied contract. They rely upon the statement in *Wilder* that:

> The law will not imply a promise to pay for an idea from the mere facts that the idea has been conveyed, is valuable, and has been used for profit; this is true even though the conveyance has been made with the hope or expectation that some obligation will ensue.

46 Cal.2d at 739, 299 P.2d at 270.

In the instant case, Whitfield sent a mailgram to Lear and Tandem Productions informing them that a script was forthcoming and then sent the "Boomerang" script. An assistant to Lear wrote to Whitfield stating that, although Lear was not personally interested in "Boomerang," the mailgram had been forwarded to the Senior Vice President for Creative Affairs at TAT Communications. The parties had no further communications.

Whitfield contends that the custom in the television industry is that a studio or producer not desiring any outside submissions states so explicitly and, when a studio or producer is not interested in reviewing a particular script, the script is returned unopened. If, however, a studio or producer is notified that a script is forthcoming and opens and reviews it when it arrives, that studio or producer has by custom implicitly promised to pay for the ideas if used. See M. Nimmer, Nimmer on Copyright § 16.–05[c] (1984) (if recipient has advance warning of and opportunity to reject disclosure, and knows that person submitting expects payment, California law will infer promise to pay in the event of use).

We conclude that the communications in question and the allegation of custom in the industry are sufficient to withstand a motion for summary judgment on this point. In Minniear v. Tors, 266 Cal.App.2d 495, 72 Cal.Rptr. 287 (1968), the plaintiff produced a pilot film and permitted a television director to view it at the latter's request. The parties engaged in no negotiations. The director's company later produced an arguably similar television series. Based on the plaintiff's claim that "it is understood in the industry that when a showing is made, the offeror shall be paid for any ideas or materials used therein," id. at 500, 72 Cal.Rptr. at 291, the court held that a jury could infer that the defendant accepted the ideas with the knowledge that plaintiff expected payment.

The facts of the instant case are similar to *Minniear*. The correspondence between the parties, brief as it was, has some of the attributes of bargaining. Whitfield's mailgram described his experience as a radio broadcaster and his knowledge of the entertainment market. These statements were obviously designed to persuade the recipient to open the script and give it careful scrutiny. The letter from Lear's assistant stated that the Vice President for Creative Affairs at TAT Communications would contact him "should we be interested in accepting new material from writers outside of our organization." This is arguably an acknowledgment that Whitfield's ideas were not freely appropriable. If, as appellees argue, they were perfectly free to use Whitfield's ideas without compensation as soon as they received them, there was nothing to "accept," and no further communication with Whitfield was necessary. On the whole, the record raises a material issue of fact as to whether the appellees accepted Whitfield's submission on an understanding common in the industry that he expected payment if the ideas were used.

The appellant has a second hurdle to clear. To support recovery on an implied-in-fact contract, he must show not only access but also that the appellees actually used his ideas by demonstrating "some substantial similarity" between the ideas and themes of the two programs. Kurlan v. Columbia Broadcasting System, 40 Cal.2d 799, 809, 256 P.2d 962, 969 (1953). Access having been conceded for purposes of the motion for summary judgment, the district court concluded that "there are *no* similarities between the ideas contained in defendant's production and plaintiff's work." Mem. at 9 (emphasis in original).

We are unable to verify this conclusion. The scripts of the actual episodes of "The Righteous Apples" that appeared on television are not in the record and were not reviewed by the district court. The only "Righteous Apples" scripts in the record are pilots prepared *before* appellant's submission of "Boomerang" to Lear. However, the essence of Whitfield's claim is that "The Righteous Apples" as televised differed significantly from the appellees' original pilots.

Since no scripts of the actually televised series are in the record, the critical comparison can be made only on the basis of other materials submitted by the parties. However, these materials are in utter conflict over the existence of similarities between the televised series and the "Boomerang" script. Appellees thus describe the first ten televised episodes of "The Righteous Apples" in a manner wholly at odds with Whitfield's description of similarities between those episodes and his "Boomerang" script.

Assuming access by the defendants to the "Boomerang" script and accepting Whitfield's assertions regarding the content of the televised series as true, as we must on a motion for summary judgment, we conclude that the alleged similarities between the "Righteous Apples" series and "Boomerang," viewed in light of the earlier pilot scripts, are sufficient to allow a trier of fact to find that Whitfield's ideas were misappropriated under California law. There is thus dispute over material facts which can be resolved only by comparing the pilot scripts (in the record) prepared before the submission of "Boomerang," the Boomerang script (in the record), with "The Righteous Apples" scripts actually used in the televised series (not in the record). There were, therefore, insufficient grounds to grant summary judgment.

Reversed and remanded for further proceedings.

NOTES ON CONTRACT IMPLIED–IN–FACT

(1) It is easy enough to remit "idea" cases to the general canons of contract law, but it is apparent on reflection that interpretation of the varying situations in which "hot ideas" are submitted presents serious difficulties. The person with the idea is reluctant to disclose it without some contingent promise of compensation, but the potential "buyer" is reluctant to make any promises without more than an inkling of what the idea merchant has to sell. The transactions are therefore likely to be fuzzy ones in which express words of agreement will rarely be found. When it comes to "implications," the trier can make no headway in rational analysis without asking what, specifically, are the terms that the plaintiff seeks to imply, and what, specifically, are the features of the transaction from which these terms may fairly arise. On such analysis it may be hard to choose between conflicting interpretations of the facts.[c]

Plaintiffs' counsel have urged in effect, without a nice regard for contract theory, that a recipient is liable if after submission of an idea it comes out with a product embodying the idea or something reasonably close to it—unless perhaps it can show that it already had the idea in mind or was working on it. Cf. Teich v. General Mills, Inc., 170 Cal.App.2d 791, 339 P.2d 627 (1959). On the other side, defendants' counsel have urged that recovery should be barred unless the idea is submitted in response to a definite invitation. Meanwhile, corporations seek to invent routines for handling submissions that will avoid lawsuits and the perils of jury verdicts. These range from extreme measures such as routing letters from outsiders to independent readers so that the submitted idea never reaches decision-makers, to contract forms that seek to regulate the relationship expressly and thereby avoid claims based on inchoate and dubious facts.

(2) Is it significant that *Whitfield*'s description of the California rules on implied-in-fact contract makes no mention of "novelty" or "concreteness"? Under the California cases, neither is a prerequisite to recovery on a contract claim. California courts have continued almost routinely to uphold the triability of contract claims derived from idea and format submissions for movies and television programs. Examples, in addition to Minniear v. Tors, summarized in *Whitfield*, include Donahue v. Ziv Television Programs, 245 Cal.App.2d 593, 54 Cal.Rptr. 130 (1966), second appeal, Donahue v. United Artists Corp., 2 Cal.App.3d 794, 83 Cal.Rptr. 131 (1969), sustaining a $200,000 judgment; Blaustein v. Burton, 9 Cal.App.3d 161, 88 Cal.Rptr. 319 (1970), an account of a producer's promotion and demotion in the Burton–Taylor–Zeffirelli version of "The Taming of the Shrew"; Fink v. Goodson–Todman Enterprises, Ltd., 9 Cal.App.3d 996, 88 Cal.Rptr. 679

---

c. See Kaplan, Implied Contract and the Law of Literary Property, 42 Calif.L.Rev. 28 (1954); Kaplan, Further Remarks on Compensation for Ideas in California, 46 id. 699 (1958); Havighurst, The Right to Compensation for an Idea, 49 Nw.L.Rev. 295 (1954).

(1970). But see Faris v. Enberg, 97 Cal.App.3d 309, 158 Cal.Rptr. 704 (1979), affirming a summary judgment for defendant on plaintiff's implied-in-fact contract count in a suit involving the disclosure to sportscaster Dick Enberg of an idea for a sports quiz show.

Landsberg v. Scrabble Crossword Game Players, Inc., 802 F.2d 1193 (9th Cir.1986), invokes the implied-in-fact contract theory outside the television and film settings of the previous cases. Defendant plagiarized Landsberg's manuscript on Scrabble strategy, although not enough to constitute copyright infringement. See 736 F.2d 485 (9th Cir.1984), p. 275 supra. In this second appeal the court upheld a substantial recovery for breach of an implied contract stemming from the submission of the manuscript at defendant's request.

(3) In Reeves v. Alyeska Pipeline Serv. Co., 926 P.2d 1130 (Alaska 1996), the Supreme Court of Alaska examined the various theories available to the idea submitter, including contract implied-in-fact. After allegedly receiving assurances that his disclosure would be "between us", plaintiff Reeves revealed to a manager of the defendant (operator of the Trans–Alaska Pipeline) his idea for a visitor's center at a highway turnoff on defendant's property. Unknown at the time to either the manager or Reeves, the company had rejected a suggestion for a visitor's center at that location four years earlier. This time it went ahead with the center. Reeves brought suit on a variety of theories, but the trial court granted summary judgment against him on all counts because the idea lacked novelty.

Considering first Reeves' express contract claim, the appellate court said that since Reeves alleged additional consideration, it need not decide whether a non-novel idea could serve as consideration for an express contract in order to reverse the summary judgment. It turned next to the circumstances that might justify recognition of a contract implied-in-fact:

"There are three primary factual scenarios under which ideas may be submitted to another. See Nimmer, supra § 16.05. The first involves an unsolicited submission that is involuntarily received. Id. at 16–33. The idea is submitted without warning; it is transmitted before the recipient has taken any action which would indicate a promise to pay for the submission. Id. at 16–33 to 16–34. Under this scenario, a contract will not be implied. [Desny v. Wilder, 46 Cal.2d 715, 299 P.2d 257, 270 (1956)], Nimmer, supra, § 16.05[B], at 16–34.

"The second involves an unsolicited submission that is voluntarily received. Nimmer, supra, § 16.05[C], at 16–36. In this situation, the idea person typically gives the recipient advance warning that an idea is to be disclosed; the recipient has an opportunity to stop the disclosure, but through inaction allows the idea to be disclosed. Id. at 16–36 to 16–37. Under California law, if the recipient at the time of disclosure understands that the idea person expects to be paid for the disclosure of the idea, and does not attempt to stop the disclosure, inaction may be seen as consent to a contract. *Desny*, 299 P.2d at 267; Donahue v. Ziv Television Programs, Inc., 245 Cal.App.2d 593, 54 Cal.Rptr. 130, 139 (1966).

"This view has been criticized as unfairly placing a duty on the recipient to take active measures to stop the submission. Nimmer, supra § 16.05[C], at 16–38. The critics argue that inaction generally should not be considered an expression of consent to a contract. Id.

"We believe that a contract should not be implied under this scenario. An implied-in-fact contract is based on circumstances that demonstrate that the parties intended to form a contract but failed to articulate their promises. * * * Only under exceptional circumstances would inaction demonstrate an intent to enter a contract.

"The third scenario involves a solicited submission. Nimmer, supra § 16.05[D], at 16–40. Here, a request by the recipient for disclosure of the idea usually implies a promise to pay for the idea if the recipient uses it. *Desny*, 299 P.2d at 267; Nimmer, supra § 16.05[D] at 16–40."

Since the plaintiff alleged that defendant had requested the disclosure, summary judgment was improper. The court did agree, however, with the California rule that novelty is not a prerequisite for an implied-in-fact contract claim, rejecting the contrary rule in New York. "An idea may be valuable to the recipient merely because of its timing or the manner in which it is presented. * * * If the parties voluntarily choose to bargain for an individual's services in disclosing or developing a non-novel or unoriginal idea, they have the power to do so."

As for plaintiff's quasi-contact claim for unjust enrichment, that, the court said, was a property-based claim, sustainable only if the idea was novel. Summary judgment on that count was affirmed.

BREACH OF CONFIDENCE

If there is an existing confidential relationship between the parties, it is clear that they will be held to high standards in dealing with each other. See Carpenter Foundation v. Oakes, 26 Cal.App.3d 784, 103 Cal.Rptr. 368 (1972) (rights in unpublished papers by and about Mary Baker Eddy). But existing fiduciary-like relationships aside, courts sometimes speak of a "confidential relationship" merely to describe what happens when one person discloses information to another "in confidence." Is a "breach of confidence" in this sense actionable as such by the disclosing party? In Davies v. Krasna, 14 Cal.3d 502, 121 Cal.Rptr. 705, 535 P.2d 1161 (1975), a confused and protracted idea-submission case evoking references to Dickens' Jarndyce v. Jarndyce, plaintiff had lost in the jury on her contract claims. She had also pleaded a "breach of confidence" count. (The precise question was what statute of limitations should apply to such a count. The California Supreme Court held that it was a tort or quasi-contract, barred after two years, not constructive fraud with a three-year limit, which would be applicable to the breach of a true confidential relationship.) What is an actionable "breach of confidence"—aside from being something less than a breach of a formal confidential relationship? Justice Tobriner said "this court has never ruled that a cause of action for breach of confidence can rest upon a basis other than a contract that protects that confidence."

Here it was settled that there was no contract. But the court felt obliged to accept as the law of the case that "When defendant received Valentine Davies' idea, with the understanding that this idea was confidential, defendant incurred an obligation not to use or disclose that idea without the creator's consent." It proceeded to decide the limitations issue on that assumption; but it refused "to create a new genre of liability without full argumentation."

In Faris v. Enberg, described in Note 2, a California Court of Appeal did assert a willingness to recognize a cause of action for "breach of confidence." "An actionable breach of confidence will arise when an idea, whether or not protectable, is offered to another in confidence, and is voluntarily received by the offeree in confidence with the understanding that it is not to be disclosed to others, and is not to be used by the offeree for purposes beyond the limits of the confidence without the offeror's permission." But the court rejected the claim on the facts. "There must exist evidence of the communication of the confidentiality of the submission or evidence from which a confidential relationship can be inferred."

Faris v. Enberg was dissected in Tele–Count Engineers, Inc. v. Pacific Tel. & Tel. Co., 168 Cal.App.3d 455, 214 Cal.Rptr. 276 (1985), a business system case which held that plaintiff failed to achieve the necessary understanding that defendant was to treat the submitted forms in confidence. There are suggestions in the wide-ranging analysis that quasi-contract claims for unjust enrichment are supportable if the appropriate confidential relationship exists. Such a view trenches on the California position established in Weitzenkorn v. Lesser, 40 Cal.2d 778, 256 P.2d 947 (1953), that a quasi-contract claim in an idea case can be maintained only by showing plagiarism of expression—a showing nowadays preempted by copyright law.

Do these California decisions represent a doctrinal cast that is different from the New York cases? Judge Friendly, in Lehman v. Dow Jones & Co., 783 F.2d 285 (2d Cir.1986), remarked that "California law has gone quite far in finding implied-in-fact contracts," and noted that it "does not impose a requirement of novelty or originality where information is allegedly the subject of an implied-in-fact contract of confidentiality." Perhaps California simply reflects more emphatically the values of the entertainment business, where, as we have seen, titles, characters, personalities, and other intangible elements that the law outlines dimly if at all are worth large sums of money? [d]

d. See Libott, Round the Prickly Pear: The Idea–Expression Fallacy in a Mass Communications World, 14 U.C.L.A. L.Rev. 735 (1967); Sobel, The Law of Ideas, Revisited, 1 U.C.L.A. Ent.L.Rev. 9 (1994); Swarth, The Law of Ideas: New York and California Are More Than 3,000 Miles Apart, 13 COMM/ENT L.J. 115 (1990).

PART THREE

INTERNATIONAL ASPECTS OF COPYRIGHT

CHAPTER 11

U.S. INTERNATIONAL COPYRIGHT RELATIONS

SECTION 1. THE POSITION BEFORE 1891

The act of 1790 (1 Stat. 124) gave protection to "the author and authors * * * being a citizen or citizens of these United States, or resident therein," (§ 1), and emphasized in § 5 that "nothing in this act shall be construed to extend to prohibit the importation or vending, reprinting or publishing within the United States, of any map, chart, book or books, written, printed, or published by any person not a citizen of the United States, in foreign parts or places without the jurisdiction of the United States." It is perhaps not surprising that a have-not country should permit and even encourage poaching on foreign works, but the same policy continued as the nation grew. The act of 1831 (4 Stat. 436) accorded protection to "any person or persons, being a citizen or citizens of the United States, or resident therein, who shall be the author or authors," (§ 1), and stated in § 8 that "nothing in this act shall be construed to extend to prohibit the importation or vending, printing, or publishing, of any map, chart, book, musical composition, print or engraving, written, composed, or made, by any person not being a citizen of the United States, nor resident within the jurisdiction thereof." Again, the Revised Statutes, 1873, granted rights to "Any citizen of the United States or resident therein, who shall be the author," (§ 4952), and concluded in § 4971: "Nothing in this chapter shall be construed to prohibit the printing, publishing, importation, or sale of any book, map, chart, dramatic or musical composition, print, cut, engraving, or photograph, written, composed or made by any person not a citizen of the United States nor resident therein."

BRITISH–AMERICAN COPYRIGHT RELATIONS

ADDRESS OF BRITISH AUTHORS

(Presented to the Senate by Henry Clay, February 2, 1837) [a]

The humble address and petition of certain authors of Great Britain, to the Senate and House of Representatives of the United States, in Congress assembled, respectfully showeth—

1.   That your petitioners have long been exposed to injury in their reputation and property, from the want of a law by which the exclusive right to their respective writings may be secured to them in the United States of America.

2.   That, for want of such law, deep and extensive injuries have, of late, been inflicted on the reputation and property of certain of your petitioners; and on the interests of literature and science, which ought to constitute a bond of union and friendship between the United States and Great Britain.

3.   That, from the circumstance of the English language being common to both nations, the works of British authors are extensively read throughout the United States of America, while the profits arising from the sale of their works may be wholly appropriated by American booksellers, not only without the consent of the authors, but even contrary to their express desire—a grievance under which your petitioners have, at present, no redress.

4.   That the works thus appropriated by American booksellers are liable to be mutilated and altered, at the pleasure of the said booksellers, or of any other persons who may have an interest in reducing the price of the works, or in conciliating the supposed principles or prejudice of purchasers in the respective sections of your union: and that, the names of the authors being retained, they may be made responsible for works which they no longer recognize as their own.

5.   That such mutilation and alteration, with the retention of the authors' names, have been of late actually perpetrated by citizens of the United States: under which grievance, your petitioners have no redress.
* * *

8.   That American authors are injured by the non-existence of the desired law.   While American publishers can provide themselves with works for publication by unjust appropriation, instead of by equitable purchase, they are under no inducement to afford to American authors a fair remuneration for their labours: under which grievance American authors have no redress but in sending over their works to England to be

a.   S.Rep. No. 134, 24th Cong., 2d Sess.,   and Law 341 (1912).
reproduced in Bowker, Copyright, Its History

published, an expedient which has become an established practice with some of whom their country has most reason to be proud.

9.   That the American public is injured by the non-existence of the desired law.   The American public suffers, not only from the discouragement afforded to native authors, as above stated, but from the uncertainty now existing as to whether the books presented to them as the works of British authors, are the actual and complete productions of the writers whose names they bear.

10.   That your petitioners beg humbly to remind your Honours of the case of Walter Scott, as stated by an esteemed citizen of the United States, that while the works of this author, dear alike to your country and to ours, were read from Maine to Georgia, from the Atlantic to the Mississippi, he received no remuneration from the American public for his labours; that an equitable remuneration might have saved his life, and would, at least, have relieved its closing years from the burden of debts and destructive toils.

11.   That your petitioners, deeply impressed with the conviction that the only firm ground of friendship between nations, is a strict regard to simple justice, earnestly pray that your Honours, the representatives of the United States in Congress assembled, will speedily use, in behalf of the authors of Great Britain, your power "of securing to the authors the exclusive right to their respective writings."

NOTES AND QUESTIONS

(1) The Address of British Authors assumes that British writers could obtain no protection in the United States for their published books.   But the American statutes allowed copyright not only to citizens but to residents of the United States, and the question naturally arose whether a temporary sojourn by an alien author could be recognized as residence. Drone, writing in 1879, was of the opinion that resident "refers to a person who is residing in the United States with the intention of making this country his permanent place of abode."   Drone on Copyright 233.   Further, although the American statutes did not expressly provide where publication must be made in order to entitle the author to copyright, Drone thought that "an author forfeits his claim to copyright in this country by a first, but not by a contemporaneous, publication of his work abroad."   Id. at 296.[b]

Could American authors obtain protection for their works in Great Britain?   British law at that date appears to have given no copyright to an alien author who first published a book outside Great Britain.   Legislation commencing in 1838 (the so-called International Copyright Acts), together

b. Younger, Citizens Who Publish Abroad: A Study in the Pathology of American Copyright Law, 44 Corn.L.Q. 215, 216 (1959), takes the view, opposed to Drone's, that an American citizen could have obtained copyright here even though he first published abroad.   The article is an interesting survey of the odd gyrations of the law through the years on the copyright status here of works published by American citizens abroad.

with Orders in Council and a network of treaties, did have the effect of extending copyright to such cases, but on the condition (among others) that the alien's country granted reciprocal rights to British authors. The United States of course did not qualify. It appears to have been accepted, however, that an alien who first published a book in Great Britain could claim the benefit of the general British copyright statutes even though he had no other connection with that country. In the case of Jefferys v. Boosey, 4 H.L.Cas. 815, 10 Eng.Rep. 681 (1854), the House of Lords took the position that (apart from the International Copyright Acts) an alien author could obtain British copyright by first publication in Great Britain only if he was physically present within the British dominions at the time of the publication. By 1868 there was some opinion in the House of Lords that the visit to British dominions at the time of first publication could be dispensed with. See Routledge v. Low, 3 L.R.–E. & I.App. 100 (1868) (judgments of Lord Cairns and Lord Westbury). But for better assurance American authors still made the trip. The effect of all this was that a very cautious American author seeking British as well as American copyright would have to print in Great Britain and, while physically present somewhere in the British dominions, publish simultaneously in Great Britain and the United States.

(2) The piracy of British books by American publishers through most of the 19th century has been celebrated in song and story.[c] What is not so well known is the very considerable piracy of American works by British publishers during the same period—for it was a rare American author who could thread his way through the British law, which was in fact more complex and less certain than our short sketch suggests, and who could, besides, indulge in the luxury of complying with all its requirements.[d]

   In Matthews, American Authors and British Pirates, 4 New Princeton Rev. 201 (1887), 5 id. 47 (1888), there is an amusing exchange between lawyer-critic Brander Matthews and Samuel Clemens. Matthews deplores the British piracies. With customary gusto and ironic reflections on Matthews' lawyerly abilities, Clemens answers that he has been enjoying British copyright by following the British law; Matthews replies that the expedients Clemens has been using are not in practice available to less affluent authors.[e]

(3) Copyright relations among important European countries including Great Britain were simplified and improved upon the coming into effect of the Berne Convention in 1887, but there was no essential change in British–American copyright relations. In practice, however, piracy of British books in America had been brought under some unofficial restraint.

---

c. For Anthony Trollope's measured condemnation of American piracies, see Autobiography, ch. XVII (1883).

   d. See Gohdes, American Literature in 19th Century England (1944); Gohdes, Longfellow and His Authorized British Publishers, 55 Pub. of Mod.Lang.Ass'n 1165 (1940).

   e. Samuel Clemens was no admirer of copyright statutes. "Only one thing is impossible for God: to find any sense in any copyright law on the planet. Whenever a copyright law is to be made or altered, then the idiots assemble." Mark Twain's Notebook 381–82 (Harper & Bros. 1935).

According to a "trade understanding" of American publishers, when an American publisher bought sheets of a British work and republished the work in the United States, respectable competitors would ordinarily refrain from piracy.   There was in fact a lively market for early sheets of important British books, and British publishers and authors did in many cases profit from American publication.

SECTION 2.   FROM THE CHACE ACT TO THE UNIVERSAL COPYRIGHT CONVENTION

THE CHACE ACT OF 1891

On September 9, 1886, ten nations signed the Berne Convention, Additional Article and Final Protocol for the creation of an International Union for the Protection of Literary and Artistic Works—one of the great steps forward in securing international protection of copyright.[a]   Although the United States sent a delegation to the Berne meeting, it did not adhere to the Convention.   Within a short time, however, the United States adopted legislation granting a measure of copyright protection to nationals of foreign countries.   This was the Chace Act.   (Act of March 3, 1891, 26 Stat. 1106.)   Section 13 of the act provided:

"That this act shall apply to a citizen or subject of a foreign state or nation when such foreign state or nation permits to citizens of the United States of America the benefit of copyright on substantially the same basis as [to] its own citizens [so-called "national treatment"]; or when such foreign state or nation is a party to an international agreement which provides for reciprocity in the granting of copyright, by the terms of which agreement the United States of America may, at its pleasure, become a party to such agreement.   The existence of either of the conditions aforesaid shall be determined by the President of the United States by proclamation made from time to time as the purposes of this act may require." [b]

Fears that the American printing and publishing trades would be overwhelmed by foreign competition, however, were reflected in § 3 of the Act.   This provided that "in the case of a book, photograph, chromo or lithograph, the two copies" required to be deposited with the Library of Congress "shall be printed from type set within the limits of the United States, or from plates made therefrom, or from negatives, or drawings on stone made within the limits of the United States, or from transfers made therefrom"; and it provided that during the existence of copyright, the

a.   Texts in English of the international treaties on copyright and related subjects, together with information on adherences to each, are available at the World Intellectual Property Organization's website, http:// www.wipo.org.

b.   It appears that no Presidential proclamation ever issued on the latter basis of the existence of an "open" international agreement.

importation of books not complying with these requirements was prohibited. This was the first appearance of the so-called "manufacturing clause."

SUBSEQUENT LEGISLATION

The situation of foreign authors seeking copyright protection in the United States was somewhat improved by legislation enacted during the next several decades.

Section 8 of the original 1909 Act (corresponding to the text of what later was codified as § 9 up to the word "Provided" in subsection (b)) went beyond the Chace Act in allowing an alien author or proprietor domiciled in the United States at the time of first publication of the work to obtain copyright here even if his country had not been "proclaimed". A non-domiciled alien, however, still could obtain American copyright only if his country had been proclaimed, and the 1909 Act added to the two Chace Act bases for proclamation a third alternative, namely: "When the foreign state * * * grants * * * to citizens of the United States * * * copyright protection, substantially equal to the protection secured to such foreign author under this title or by treaty"—so-called "reciprocal treatment." But foreigners qualifying by American domicile or by reason of proclamations covering their countries also had to comply with the requirements for obtaining and preserving copyright in the United States, of which the most onerous was the manufacturing requirement. Under § 16 of the 1909 Act, copyright could be secured in books and periodicals only on condition of domestic manufacture—i.e., the type must be set, plates made, lithographic or photoengraving process performed, and printing and binding accomplished in the United States. Excepted was "the original text of a book or periodical of foreign origin in a language or languages other than English." Importation of copies of copyrighted works not complying with the manufacturing requirement was prohibited, subject to some exceptions. § 107. The 1909 Act introduced special "ad interim" protection for books published abroad in English before publication in this country; deposit of a copy of the foreign edition could secure a short-term copyright while the owner decided whether to publish an American edition in compliance with the manufacturing requirements. §§ 22–23.

The manufacturing clause, despite the ad interim arrangements, continued to hinder our international copyright relations. Its impact was lessened, however, by our adherence to the Universal Copyright Convention, infra, which eliminated the manufacturing requirement for foreign authors claiming protection through that Convention. § 9(c).

The manufacturing clause in attenuated form survived temporarily in § 601 of the 1976 Copyright Act. It was limited essentially to nondramatic literary works in English by American authors domiciled in the United States—that is, its effect was simply to prevent domestic authors from taking advantage of cheap foreign printing.

As enacted, the manufacturing requirements of § 601 were to expire on July 1, 1982. But when the time came, the usual protectionist arguments prevailed. (The arguments pro and con are rehashed in the House Report, pp. 165–66.) Congress voted an extension to July 1, 1986, overriding a veto by President Reagan. In 1986 there was no further extension. (Just before its expiration, an attempt to declare the manufacturing clause unconstitutional was rebuffed in Authors League of America v. Oman, 790 F.2d 220 (2d Cir.1986).)

FOREIGN AUTHORS AND THE 1976 ACT

In the 1976 Act, the status of foreign works is governed by § 104, amended in 1988 to subsume a "Berne Convention work" as defined in § 101. Note first that any unpublished work satisfying the standards of copyrightability in § 102 is protected "without regard to the nationality or domicile of the author."

For foreign authors seeking protection for published works under the 1976 Act, § 104(b) offers five overlapping categories of eligibility. Authors who at the time of first publication are nationals or domiciliaries of a treaty nation (including nations adhering to Berne or the UCC) can claim protection pursuant to § 104(b)(1); works first published in the United States or in a UCC country are protected under (b)(2). A "Berne Convention work" protected under § 104(b)(4) includes a work first published in a Berne country (and under the definition in § 101 also embraces works published in a Berne country within 30 days of first publication elsewhere). Can you describe a work that would *not* fall within any of the preceding categories?

Proclamations (see § 104(b)(5)) and bilateral treaties are now of diminished importance in view of the combined reach of the UCC and Berne. Two other multinational conventions, Mexico City of 1908 and Buenos Aires of 1911, are also now essentially obsolete; all of their participants are members of Berne or the UCC. Article 3 of Buenos Aires had a notice requirement: "[A] statement that indicates the reservation of the property right" had to appear on copies of the work. From this came the familiar legend "All Rights Reserved." [c]

SECTION 3. THE UNIVERSAL COPYRIGHT CONVENTION

THE ORIGINS OF THE UCC

Some Americans for a long time felt uneasy about our failure to enter wholeheartedly into international arrangements for copyright protection. (The position is well described by Judge Clark in Houghton Mifflin & Co. v. Stackpole Sons, 104 F.2d 306 (2d Cir.1939).) General revision bills introduced in Congress from 1924 to 1940 [a] sought—vainly, as it turned out—to

---

c. See Rinaldo, The Scope of Copyright Protection in the United States Under Existing Inter–American Relations, 22 Bull.Copyr.Soc. 417 (1975).

a. See Goldman, The History of U.S.A. Copyright Law Revision From 1901–1954, Copyr. Law Revision Study No. 1 (1955), in 2 Studies on Copyr. 1101 (1963).

create a pattern of law that would qualify this country for entrance into the Berne Union. These bills were not merely altruistic efforts to improve the position of foreign authors in this country. In the absence of an international modus vivendi comparable to Berne, American authors and producers seeking foreign markets were often obliged to inquire into and comply with the varying requirements of the laws of foreign countries in order to secure protection of their works, and the measure of protection actually secured was frequently in doubt.

It is true that Americans found a "back door" to Berne by which they could take the benefit of that compact even though the United States was not a member and had undertaken none of its burdens. Article 3(1) of the Convention [b] extends the protection of Berne to "authors who are not nationals of one of the countries of the Union, for their works first published in one of those countries, or simultaneously in a country outside the Union and in a country of the Union." Thus the practice sprang up of American authors making token publications of their works in Berne countries, say in Canada or Great Britain, simultaneously with publication in the United States. This tactic could not fail to arouse resentment abroad. As early as 1914 a section was added to art. 6 that created a possibility of retaliation: "Where any country outside the Union fails to protect in an adequate manner the works of authors who are nationals of one of the countries of the Union, the latter country may restrict the protection given to the works of authors who are, at the date of the first publication thereof, nationals of the other country and are not habitually resident in one of the countries of the Union." This provision was not in fact used against American authors, but it stood as a threat.

As the adherents to Berne were not disposed to alter the Convention to accommodate American law, and as efforts to change American law to accommodate to Berne had not succeeded, some new approach was needed. A solution satisfactory to the United States could be found by creating a new convention that could co-exist with Berne. A large intergovernmental project to formulate such a convention was launched shortly after World War II, with UNESCO serving as organizer and clearing agent for a series of meetings and written exchanges. This effort culminated on September 6, 1952, in the signing of the Universal Copyright Convention at Geneva. The UCC text with 1971 revisions is set out in the Statutory Supplement.

Domestic legislation needed to prepare this country for adherence to the UCC was approved in 1954 (68 Stat. 1030, amending §§ 9, 16, and 19 of the 1909 Act). On September 16, 1955, the Convention came into force.

---

b.   Quotations are from the 1971 Paris text.

The essentials of the Universal Copyright Convention are summarized by former Register of Copyrights Barbara Ringer as follows:

"1. *Adequate and effective protection.* Under article I, the contracting states are obliged to 'provide for the adequate and effective protection of the rights of authors and other copyright proprietors * * *.'

"2. *National treatment.* Article II provides that the 'published works of nationals of any Contracting State and works first published in that State shall enjoy in each other Contracting State the same protection as that other State accords to works of its nationals first published in its own territory.' There is a similar provision for unpublished works.

"3. *Formalities.* Article III, which represents the great compromise of the U.C.C., provides that the formal requirements, such as notice, registration, and manufacture, of a contracting state's copyright law are satisfied with respect to foreign U.C.C. works 'if from the time of first publication all of the copies of the work * * * bear the symbol © accompanied by the name of the copyright proprietor and the year of first publication placed in such manner and location as to give reasonable notice of claim of copyright.'

"4. *Duration of protection.* Another major compromise is embodied in article IV of the U.C.C. The minimum term, subject to various detailed qualifications and exceptions, is to be either 25 years from the death of the author or from the date of first publication.

"5. *Translation rights.* The U.C.C., in article V, requires contracting states to give exclusive translation rights to foreign U.C.C. authors for at least seven years; thereafter a rather cumbersome compulsory licensing system can be established. [This translation right was liberalized with respect to "developing countries" in article V*ter* of the 1971 Paris revision.]

"6. *Nonretroactivity.* Under article VII a contracting state is not obliged to protect works that are permanently in its public domain on the date the Convention becomes effective in that state.

"7. *Berne safeguard clause.* An enormously important provision of the U.C.C. is found in article XVII and the 'Appendix Declaration' attached to it. These provide, in effect, that no Berne country can denounce the Berne Convention and rely on the U.C.C. in its copyright relations with Berne Union members. [This was relaxed with respect to developing countries in the 1971 Paris revision.]

"Thus, at least in comparison with the 1948 Brussels revision of the Berne Convention, the Universal Copyright Convention represents a rather low-level copyright arrangement, resembling in many ways the original 1886 Berne text." c

c. Ringer, The Role of the United States in International Copyright—Past, Present, and Future, 56 Geo.L.J. 1050, 1061–62 (1968). The author was then Assistant Register of Copyrights. Reprinted by permission of the copyright holder, the Georgetown Law Journal.

STOCKHOLM (1967) TO PARIS (1971)

As the time approached for a conference at Stockholm in 1967 to consider revisions to the Berne Convention, hopes for the general revision of the United States copyright statute were high, and it was possible to give serious consideration to closing the gaps that still remained between Berne and American law. But at the same time, developing nations, many of them newly created, were organizing resistance to the trend of the multinational conventions toward ever-increasing protection of authors. The resulting collision led Ringer to observe that, "The 1967 Stockholm Conference on Intellectual Property was probably the worst experience in the history of international copyright conventions." [d]

The Stockholm Conference produced a "Protocol Regarding Developing Countries" allowing such nations to make certain reservations with respect to the provisions of Berne. These included a shorter term of protection and reduced broadcasting rights. Translation privileges and reproduction rights in connection with educational and instructional uses were also broadened for developing nations. [e]

The victory of the developing countries was an empty one. The developed countries could not be compelled to accede to the Protocol, and they did not.

Ringer, writing while the next steps were still in doubt, concluded, "The irony of the present American position in international copyright needs no elaboration. After a century as a virtual outlaw, a half century as an outsider, and 15 years as a stranger at the feast, the United States suddenly finds itself cast as a leading champion of literary property. Having refused to join the Berne Union because its standards were too high, the United States is now faced with the prospect of being unable to join it because the standards have become too low.

"In view of our dubious past performance we are hardly in a position to adopt a tone of moral indignation about the demands of the developing countries. Similarly, as a country that for years has accepted the benefits of the Berne Convention while assuming none of its obligations, we cannot blame other countries for what happened at Stockholm. But as the world's largest exporter of literary properties, we have an immediate stake in the future of international copyright. We can no longer afford to stand apart and content ourselves with sidelong glances." [f]

The Register of Copyrights, Abraham Kaminstein, and his colleagues (notably including Ringer) met this challenge. Taking the lead in three years of diligent negotiation, they helped fashion compromises that facilitated a concurrent revision of both the UCC and Berne. This feat was successfully performed at parallel conferences at Paris in 1971. Professor Ulmer succinctly characterized the "basic results" as follows:

> The UCC was extended by securing to authors the fundamental rights of reproduction, public performance and broadcasting as

----

d. Id. at 1070.   **f.** Id. at 1078.

e. Id. at 1070–74.

minimum rights. In both Conventions, essentially the same concessions were made to the developing countries. These concessions include limitations upon the rights of translation and reproduction for certain privileged purposes. As compared with the Stockholm provisions, the main difference here is the following: the Stockholm Protocol permitted any encroachment upon the copyright for the purposes of teaching, study, and research. The provisions in question would have made it possible to publish translations and reproductions without contacting the authors and publishers. The only right under the copyright that would have been preserved was the right to remuneration. In contrast to that, the compulsory licenses as provided for in the Revised Conventions do not only require the expiration of certain time limits starting with the first publication of the work, but they also require a request for authorization from the copyright owner and an administrative procedure within the developing country for granting the license and fixing the amount of compensation. Furthermore, the export of copies made under the licenses is prohibited in principle.[g]

Another maneuver was the modification of the "Berne safeguard" in the UCC. As explained by Kaminstein, "Article XVII and its Appendix Declaration constitute the 'Berne Safeguard Clause', one of the major compromises of the Geneva Conference establishing the UCC in 1952. The provision as it now exists makes the Berne Convention predominant over the UCC as between two countries, both of which belong to the two Conventions; and, equally important, it would preclude a Berne country from leaving the Berne Union and relying on the Universal Convention for protection of its works in Berne Union–UCC countries. The [Paris] text would remove the latter condition with respect to developing countries, leaving them free, without fear of retaliation or loss of protection, to be party to either or both Conventions." [h]

The United States in September, 1972, ratified the 1971 Paris revision of the UCC. It came into force on July 10, 1974, as did the revised Berne Convention. Approximately sixty countries have ratified the UCC 1971 Paris text. The earlier Geneva version remains in force for another thirty-five or so countries who have not ratified the Paris revision.

NOTES AND QUESTIONS ON THE UCC

(1) Even after the UCC, works of foreign authors could fall into the public domain in the United States if the author failed to find shelter from our

g. Ulmer, International Copyright After the Paris Revisions, 19 Bull.Copyr.Soc. 263, 264 (1972) (by the leading German authority).

h. Kaminstein, Report of the General Rapporteur of the Conference for Revision of the Universal Copyright Convention, 19 Bull.Copyr.Soc. 211, 259 (1972), a valuable guide to the revisions. Cf. Fernay, Paris 1971 ou les aventures d'un "package deal", 70 Revue Internationale du Droit d'Auteur 3 (1971) (with accompanying English translation).

copyright formalities through the use of the UCC notice specified in art. III. (Recall that until March 1, 1989, the 1976 Act required copyright notice on works whether "published in the United States or elsewhere.") Many of these copyrights have now been restored under § 104A. See p. 43 supra.

(2) In 1973 the former U.S.S.R. unexpectedly joined the UCC. It had not been a party to any multinational arrangements, nor was there any bilateral connection with the United States.

But gratification at the Soviet action soon curdled. Senator McClellan explained:

> Unfortunately, it now appears that the Soviet Government may contemplate using its adherence [to] the Universal Copyright Convention as a tool to tighten its control over the circulation of literature which does not meet with Communist approval. On February 21, the Supreme Soviet adopted a decree amending the Soviet copyright law in connection with that country's adherence to the Copyright Convention. According to an Associated Press dispatch from Moscow the law "could sharply restrict publication in the West of works by Russian authors considered anti-Soviet." The news reports indicate that the new Soviet law apparently is designed to permit that country to prevent publication abroad of anti-Soviet works by bringing suits for infringement of United States or other copyrights, against publishers in foreign countries who issue these works. Presumably the Soviet Union under its domestic statute would claim proprietary rights in the United States or other foreign copyrights in the works of these authors. (119 Cong.Rec. 9387 (March 26, 1973).)

A proposed anti-Soviet amendment metamorphosed into § 201(e) of the 1976 Act. It was a misguided attempt to generalize from a suspicion. See Goldstein, Preempted State Doctrines, Involuntary Transfers and Compulsory Licenses: Testing the Limits of Copyright, 24 U.C.L.A. L.Rev. 1107 (1977).

In 1995, the Russian Federation joined both the UCC and the Berne Convention.

(3) In 1990, the People's Republic of China enacted its first copyright law, which recognizes both economic and moral rights. See 41 Pat., Tm. & Copyr.J. (BNA) 37 (1990). In 1992, prompted by a trade agreement with the United States, China also joined both the UCC and Berne.

(4) Documentation and analysis on the UCC appear in A. Bogsch, The Law of Copyright Under the Universal Convention (1972); S. Stewart and H. Sandison, International Copyright and Neighboring Rights (1989).

SECTION 4.   THE BERNE CONVENTION

At several points in these materials we have addressed the changes in American law that have flowed from United States accession to the Berne

Convention for the Protection of Literary and Artistic Works. (The text of the Convention appears in the Statutory Supplement.) What follows is an overview of Berne, extracted from the House Judiciary Committee Report of May 6, 1988,[a] advocating adherence.

A. THE BERNE CONVENTION IN INTERNATIONAL COPYRIGHT

In order to appreciate the importance of U.S. adherence to the Berne Convention, it is useful to start with the Convention's history and successive revisions, its role in international copyright, administration of the Convention by the World Intellectual Property Organization, the relationship of Berne to the Universal Copyright Convention, and Berne and developing countries.

The Berne Convention is the oldest and most respected international copyright treaty.

In 1886, the Convention was concluded at Berne, Switzerland and the Berne Union came into being. Since then, the Convention has been successively completed and revised seven times: at Paris (1896), Berlin (1908), Berne (1914), Rome (1928), Brussels (1948), Stockholm (1967), and most recently, at Paris (1971). * * *

1. *History of the Convention*

The Berne Convention of 1886 culminated over 25 years of study and conferences which were undertaken by representatives of authors and artists, journalists, publishers, academics and governments, acting to replace the growing patchwork of European bilateral copyright arrangements with a simple, multilateral treaty respecting authors rights. These bilateral agreements often imposed a variety of conditions and restrictions upon rights as well as a variety of formalities which had to be complied with as conditions of protection. * * *

The original Convention was intended to promote five objectives: (1) the development of copyright laws in favor of authors in all civilized countries; (2) the elimination over time of basing rights upon reciprocity; (3) the end of discrimination in rights between domestic and foreign authors in all countries; (4) the abolition of formalities for the recognition and protection of copyright in foreign works; and, (5) ultimately, the promotion of uniform international legislation for the protection of literary and artistic works.

The first Berne Convention was a simple document in which two cardinal principles were established, both of continuing vitality today:

a. *The Union:* the states adhering to the Convention organized themselves into a Union for the protection of the rights of authors in their literary and artistic works. In forming the Union, the original members contemplated an essentially political as well as legal undertaking: that adherents to the Convention would function as a cooperative unit which

---

a. H.R.Rep. No. 100–609, 100th Cong., 2d Sess. 11–19 (1988).

would continue in existence regardless of future accessions or withdrawals from the Convention itself.

b.   *The Rule of National Treatment:* one of the cornerstones of international copyright is the rule, first recognized for copyright in the Berne Convention, that authors should enjoy in other countries the same protection for their works as those countries accord their own authors.

During the century of its existence, the Convention has been revised five times to meet changed conditions and technological development affecting authors' rights. Successive texts have generally improved and extended rights accorded authors and copyright proprietors; and, in 1967, the Berne Union confronted the special challenges to copyright policy posed by the emergence of numerous developing countries on the world scene.

2.   *Successive Revisions of the Berne Convention*

a.   *1908 Berlin Act.* The principal achievement of the Berlin Revision Conference was the prohibition of formalities as a condition of the enjoyment and exercise of rights under the Convention. The minimum duration of protection was set at the life of the author and fifty years post mortem, but made subject to exceptions for each country so as to make it less than a mandatory rule. The Convention further expanded the minimum subject matter of copyright under the Convention, including photographs. Moreover, the Berlin Revision recognized the exclusive rights of composers of musical works to authorize the adaptation of these works and gave explicit protection to the authors of cinematographic works.

b.   *1928 Rome Act.* This revision was the first to recognize expressly the "moral rights" of authors: the right to claim authorship of a work and the right to object to modifications of the work which prejudiced the honor or reputation of the author. The Rome revision specifically recognized the right to authorize broadcasting of works, leaving details to be elaborated by national legislation.

c.   *1948 Brussels Act.* This revision established the term of protection of life of the author and fifty years post mortem as mandatory. It added improvements in copyright protection including recognition of the right of public recitation; rules governing mutual recognition of optional "resale royalty" laws (so-called "droit de suite"); extension of the broadcasting article to secondary transmissions, including by wire; and, express recognition of cinematographic works and works produced by processes analogous to cinematography as distinct subjects of copyright protection.

d.   *1967 Stockholm Act.* For the first time, the implicit right of reproduction was expressly established in the Convention and special rules governing exceptions to that right were also included. Significant new rules relating to reconciling different national rules of authorship and ownership of motion pictures, defining the "nationality" of films for Convention purposes, were added at this revision. Protection was extended to include authors having habitual residence in a Union country, regardless of their citizenship. Finally, this revision established a "Protocol Regarding Developing Countries," which would have allowed developing countries broadly to limit rights of translation and reproduction. The 1967 Stockholm Act has not and will not come into force. It has effectively been superseded by the 1971 Paris Act.

e. *1971 Paris Act.* The 1971 Paris Act of Berne—the only Act now open to accession—is essentially the 1967 Stockholm Act with significant revisions made to the Protocol Regarding Developing Countries. The thrust of these revisions will be discussed in the context of relations with developing countries.

3.   *The Administration of the Convention*

The Berne Convention is administered by the World Intellectual Property Organization (W.I.P.O.), an intergovernmental organization with headquarters located in Geneva, Switzerland. The W.I.P.O. is a specialized agency within the United Nations system of organizations. It is responsible for the administration of various Unions, each rooted in a multilateral treaty and dealing with aspects of intellectual property. The twin objectives of the W.I.P.O. are to promote the protection of intellectual property throughout the world and to ensure administrative cooperation among Union states.

As regards copyright law, the W.I.P.O. plays a central role in promoting the vitality of the Berne Union.[13] The Convention itself establishes that the W.I.P.O. serves as the International Bureau of the Union. It is charged with special functions including publication of information concerning protection of copyright and providing expert services to countries of the Union on copyright matters. Its most important functions in respect of copyright, however, are twofold: first, to conduct studies and provide services "designed to facilitate the protection of copyright"; and second, the specific responsibilities of the Director General of the W.I.P.O. as the chief executive of the Berne Union and its representative.

Within this framework, the Berne Union through the W.I.P.O. conducts an ambitious program examining the relevance of the Convention to new media of creation, exploitation and consumption of copyrighted works. During the past decade, the W.I.P.O. has facilitated examination within the Union of the copyright aspects of cable television, satellite transmissions, including direct broadcast satellites, the rental of copies of protected works, private copying, and access to protected works by developing countries. * * *

4.   *The Relationship Between the Berne Convention and the Universal Copyright Convention*

* * *

---

13. The W.I.P.O. also administers The International Union for the Protection of Industrial Property. Patents for inventions and marks for goods and services are the most important subject matters of industrial property. * * *

A question concerns the future role of the Universal Copyright Convention in United States international copyright relations after adherence to Berne. Several observations are in order.

First, U.S. continued adherence to and vigorous participation in the work of the Universal Copyright Convention is obviously of undiminished importance. The United States would establish new or clarified copyright relations with a significant number of states now party only to Berne; however, it must not be forgotten that twenty-six states which belong to the UCC are not members of the Berne Union. * * * [T]hese states are principally developing countries of Africa and Latin America. A large number are neighbors of the United States from Central America and the Caribbean basin. * * *

5.   *The Berne Convention and Developing Countries*

[The Report here describes the Stockholm episode, p. 808 supra.]

In 1970, largely under the leadership of the United States through the Universal Copyright Convention, a compromise program was developed under which both Berne and the UCC would be revised to include less drastic concessions to developing countries, centered largely upon limited compulsory licensing options for translation and reprint rights in support of educational and developmental objectives. This program succeeded and in 1971 Berne and the UCC were jointly revised at Paris.

Since that time, relative stability in the Berne Convention has prevailed. Only two members of the Berne Convention and four members of the UCC have declared their intention, in accordance with the requirements of the two Conventions, to avail themselves of the compulsory licensing privileges of the Conventions. Indeed, as yet, no compulsory licenses have been issued in any of those countries. * * *

B.   THE BERNE CONVENTION AND INTERNATIONAL TRADE

Recently, protection of intellectual property, including copyrights, has become an international trade issue. Improved technology and communications greatly facilitate the global dissemination of ideas, cultural views, and creative activity. Technological changes also facilitate the unauthorized copying of the creative work-product.

The United States, as a leader in the creation and global exploitation of copyrighted works, has a great interest in a strong and viable international copyright system. Under the U.S. Constitution, the primary objective of copyright law is not to reward the author, but rather to secure for the public the benefits derived from the authors' labors. By giving authors an incentive to create, the public benefits in two ways: when the original expression is created and second when the limited term of protection expires and the creation is added to the public domain.

If framed properly, copyright protection fosters creative activity and innovation and encourages investment in commercialization of new ideas and technology. Trade in goods protected by American copyright law and the licensing of the rights to copyrighted works have expanded rapidly in the recent past. Domestic industries relying upon copyright protection to stimulate creative efforts represent a broad range of interests including all types of publishing, motion pictures, music and sound recordings and computer software. Goods and services produced by these industries consistently results in a trade surplus for the United States. A positive trade balance also sustains American jobs thereby stimulating the domestic economy. * * *

The United States successfully placed the topic of trade-related aspects of intellectual property on the agenda of the Uruguay Round Negotiations under the auspices of the General Agreement of Tariffs and Trade (GATT). The GATT meeting of Trade Ministers in Punte del Este recognized the relationship between trade and the protection and enforcement of intellectual property rights. Implicit in this recognition is the presumption that inadequate and ineffective protection of intellectual property rights can result in trade distortions. * * *

The Berne Convention represents an international consensus on copyright protection. The United States should be in a position to take advantage of that consensus, to encourage other countries to join the common ground, and to use it to encourage expansion of legitimate trade. As to the latter, the relationship of Berne adherence to promotion of U.S. trade is clear. American popular culture and information products have become precious export commodities of immense economic value. That value is badly eroded by low international copyright standards. Berne standards are both high, reasonable and widely accepted internationally. * * *

NOTES ON BERNE AND TRIPS

(1) The number of nations that have adhered to the Berne Convention is well over 100. Recall, however, that the Berne Convention is not self-executing under United States law; rights recognized under the Convention must be pursued through our domestic laws. Among other changes, the Berne Convention Implementation Act of 1988, Pub.L. No. 100–568, abolished the requirement of copyright notice, eliminated the necessity of recording transfers of copyright and (for foreign works) of registering the copyright prior to commencing suit, and weakened the jukebox compulsory license (later wholly repealed). Our treaty obligations under Berne also played a significant role in bringing architectural works within the subject matter of copyright and in extending moral rights to works of visual art.

For information on Berne, see Ricketson, The Berne Convention for the Protection of Literary and Artistic Works: 1886–1986 (1987); Papers Presented at a Conference to Celebrate the Centenary of the Berne Convention, 1886–1986, 11 Colum.-VLA J.L. & Arts 1 (1986).

(2) The United States in its bilateral relations has sometimes used the threat of trade sanctions in an effort to force increased protection of intellectual property abroad. In the 1980s the United States won inclusion

of intellectual property rights as a component in the GATT negotiations. The aim was to insure a high level of intellectual property protection throughout the world, backed by effective enforcement mechanisms that were lacking in the international conventions. The result was the Agreement on Trade–Related Aspects of Intellectual Property Rights (TRIPS), overseen by the World Trade Organization. (The Agreement is reproduced in the Statutory Supplement.)

With respect to copyright, TRIPS takes what has been described as a "Berne plus" approach. The Agreement incorporates by reference the minimum substantive standards contained in articles 1–21 of Berne (with the exception, at U.S. insistence, of article 6*bis* on moral rights).[b] TRIPS goes beyond Berne, however, in requiring protection for computer programs and creative compilations. Member countries must also provide rights against the commercial rental of computer programs, phonorecords, and cinematographic works, although protection for the latter is not required "unless such rental has led to widespread copying of such works which is materially impairing the exclusive right of reproduction."

The chief contribution of TRIPS, however, is in its provisions on enforcement. Member countries are required to implement adequate procedures and remedies for enforcement of the intellectual property rights guaranteed by TRIPS, and unlike Berne or the UCC, the World Trade Organization has substantial means available to spur compliance with the national obligations imposed by the Agreement.

Although generally supported by copyright owners, not everyone is enthusiastic about TRIPS. Some of its technical shortcomings, especially in high technology areas, are examined in McManis, Taking TRIPS on the Information Superhighway: International Intellectual Property Protection and Emerging Computer Technology, 41 Vill.L.Rev. 207 (1996). Hamilton, The TRIPS Agreement: Imperialistic, Outdated, and Overprotective, 29 Vand.J. Transnational L. 613 (1996), presents a more fundamental objection against the use of trade agreements to impose western cultural values on the rest of the world. Will enhanced copyright protection contribute to the development of democracy abroad? Netanel, Asserting Copyright's Democratic Principles in the Global Arena, 51 Vand.L.Rev. 271 (1998), argues that it may sometimes push in the opposite direction. Aoki, (Intellectual) Property and Sovereignty: Notes Toward a Cultural Geography of Authorship, 48 Stan.L.Rev. 1293 (1996), also laments the move to increased protection through supernational norms at the expense of national sovereignty.

(3) The monetary stakes in international copyright protection are huge. The International Intellectual Property Alliance estimated that foreign

b. The renewed pressure under TRIPS to comply with art. 18 of Berne relating to protection of works that have not yet fallen into the public domain in their country of origin led to the enactment of § 104A on restoration of copyright in foreign works. See p. 43 supra. The requirement under TRIPS to provide protection against the unauthorized recording of unfixed performances prompted the anti-bootleg provision in § 1101. See p. 21 supra.

piracy in 1995 resulted in losses of more than $14 billion to U.S. copyright owners. China remains the largest market for pirated goods. The Financial Times, Feb. 10, 1997, p. 6.

REFERENCES

Helpful works on foreign and international copyright include P. Geller, International Copyright Law and Practice (1995); W. Nordemann, K. Vinck, P. Hertin, and G. Meyer, International Copyright and Neighboring Rights Law (1990); S. Stewart and H. Sandison, International Copyright and Neighbouring Rights (1989); Symposium, The Impact of European Integration on Intellectual Property, 18 Brooklyn J. Int'l L. 665 (1992).

INDEX